ROCHDALE AFC
The Official History
1907 -2001

By Steven Phillipps

Published by:
Yore Publications
12 The Furrows, Harefield,
Middx. UB9 6AT.

British Library Cataloguing-in-Publication Data.
A catalogue record for this book
is available from the British Library.

ISBN 1 874427 09 7

Printed and bound by
Bookcraft, Midsomer Norton, Bath.

Acknowledgements:

The first word of thanks has to go to Mr. David Kilpatrick, Mr. Graham Morris and the other directors for (twice) saving the club in its darkest hours in the 1980's. Without their efforts an update of my earlier book would not have been needed.

As for this, the present book, I would like to thank all the numerous Dale followers and other statisticians who have contributed to the store of Dale related facts over the years, including Steve Birch, Andrew Wood, Garth Dykes and Mike Creasey. I would especially like to thank Ian Bailey for his recent efforts in delving into the Second World War team line-ups. I would also like to thank Tony Brown for the use of his data bases.

Finally a big thankyou to those at the football club for all their help, and for allowing this book to be the 'Official History of Rochdale AFC'.

Steven Phillipps
September 2001

Illustrations:

The best reproduction possible has been produced, but as original copies were not always available, the best source material to hand has been used. Consequently the reproductive quality is not always as good as would have been desired. However, in order to form a comprehensive historical record (both in writing and pictorially) such illustrations have been included.

The majority of illustrations are from the author's own collection (some of which came from Garth Dykes). These generally originated from either the club or the Rochdale Observer, and thanks are due for their allowing the use of same. A few illustrations have come from pre-War magazines and cigarette cards. Apologies are offered should copyright have otherwise been infringed.

CONTENTS:

A MEETING CONVENED BY MR HARVEY RIGG

The origins of organised football in Rochdale, as in the rest of Lancashire, date back to the latter part of the 19th century when the public school attending sons of the mill owners and other well to do citizens brought home both 'soccer' and 'rugger'. However, compared to neighbouring towns such as Bury, who had a prominent club by the early 1880's, Rochdale was slow to embrace the association game. Indeed, in the immediate locality it was Heywood which led the way, with several senior clubs, one of which, Heywood Central, was a leading member of the Lancashire Combination from its inception in 1889.

In Rochdale it was rugby that held sway among the workers in the cotton mills which dominated the town, with two major clubs, Rochdale Hornets and Rochdale St Clements vying for supremacy. Hornets in those days played at Dane Street, the long time home of Rochdale Cricket Club, while St Clements played on a pitch close to the church in Spotland which gave them their name, just opposite the Church Inn.

SEASON 1896/97							
	Pld	Won	Lost	Drn	For	Agst	Pts
Liverpool Reserve	28	23	4	1	78	30	47
Preston N.E. Res	28	18	4	6	82	34	42
Bury Reserve	28	15	8	5	70	36	35
Manchester City Res	28	17	10	1	75	40	35
Blackburn Rovers R	28	15	8	5	59	44	35
Rochdale	28	16	10	2	79	54	34
Burnley Reserve	28	12	10	6	64	44	30
Turton	28	10	9	9	58	64	29
Bolton Wanderers R	28	12	14	2	66	49	26
Padiham	28	9	11	8	55	56	26
Newton Heath Res	28	8	12	8	49	53	24
Darwen Reserve	28	9	14	5	65	89	23
Blackpool Reserve	28	7	18	3	41	88	17
Rawtenstall	28	3	22	3	33	113	
Oswaldtwistle Rovers	28	3	23	2	27	10	

The first Rochdale, the first final table (Lancs. Combination).

In 1895, the 'great schism' brought about by arguments over payments to players led to the formation of the breakaway Northern Union. Rochdale Hornets wholeheartedly supported the split with the southern amateurs, but St Clements' secretary Harvey Rigg (who had been at the meeting which formed the Northern Union) convinced the members of his club that they should stay within the Rugby Union.

This proved to be a major blunder - though key to our story. St Clements lost all their major opponents to the new league and played in front of minuscule crowds while Hornets prospered. In 1896, St.Clements moved to a field behind the Church Inn and voted to change codes. Rigg tried to get them elected to an expanded senior rugby league but failed and despite playing Leeds in the first ever Northern Union Cup, in March 1897, they went bankrupt in September that year. However, they reformed as a football club in 1905, which still exists.

Meanwhile the town's first senior association club had finally got off the ground. This was formed by members of Rochdale Athletic Club and the Rochdale Athletic Ground Company early in 1896 to play, as you might expect, at the Athletic Grounds. They recruited 16 experienced players from surrounding parts of South East Lancashire and entered the Lancashire Combination. (Local Rochdale and Heywood amateurs were recruited for the second team which was to play in the Central Lancashire League). The Lancashire Combination of the day was quite a powerful league, containing the reserve sides of the likes of Preston North End and Blackburn Rovers as well as old established clubs such as Turton and Padiham.

The new players warmed up with some practice games among themselves, such as "1st XI vs. XII of the Rest", which actually attracted 1300 spectators (probably because it was free). Then, on Wednesday 2nd September 1896, a Rochdale side appeared in a competitive game for the first time - and at Anfield at that. Liverpool Reserves scored virtually from the kick-off, but Rochdale equalised through Gibson and were far from disgraced in a 2-1 defeat by the eventual Combination champions. Rochdale went on to finish in a creditable 6th place, the highest of the non-reserve sides.

For the following season, though, they changed allegiance to the Lancashire League which boasted clubs like New Brighton Tower and Stockport County. Rochdale were much less successful this time round, collecting just 13 points from their 26 games and finishing third from the bottom (though not faring as badly as neighbours Bacup and Oldham County who both failed to finish the season). Even so, one of their forwards, the twenty year old Herbert Chapman, previously with Stalybridge Rovers, was transferred to Second Division Grimsby Town in May 1898. He would later become the greatest manager of his generation, winning hat-tricks of League championships with both Huddersfield and Arsenal.

Rochdale had also entered the FA Cup for the first time and met Moss Bay Exchange in Workington. A remarkable comeback saw Rochdale triumph 5-3 (with goals from Duerden, Crowther 2 and Powell 2) after trailing 3-0 at the break. The referee, incidentally, was Mr C.E. Sutcliffe, later the President of the Lancashire FA. Unfortunately in the next round Rochdale lost 6-2 to Horwich in a replay. In the next two seasons they went out in the first qualifying round to local rivals Middleton and also finished below them in the Lancashire League, 12th of 13, in 1898-99. The 1899-1900 season saw a slight improvement, with the side finishing 9th out of 15 clubs.

In 1900 there was a general reshuffle of the town's clubs, with Hornets moving to what would be their long term home at the Athletic Grounds and the football club taking over the area formerly used by St Clements at Spotland. However, despite playing a prestigious friendly against FA Cup holders Bury (at Dane Street), the club was in serious financial trouble, as it *"unfortunately did not secure the support it deserved from the public"*. The team proceeded through the first two qualifying rounds of the FA Cup, beating both Rossendale United and Freetown, but by the time the next game was due in November they were unable to raise a team to meet Workington and 'scratched'. The club officially folded on the first day of the new century, 1st January 1901.

Football generally was by now on a much stronger footing in Rochdale than it had been five years earlier, with the Rochdale and District Amateur Association Football League having formed in 1897 (the Rochdale Sunday Schools League followed in 1904). There was therefore little delay in the formation of a new club, Rochdale Town, which began life in the Lancashire League in September 1901, playing at Dane Street. They fared slightly better than their predecessors, ending their first season in 7th place, though a considerable way behind the champions, former Football League side Darwen. They also had some success in the FA Cup, walloping Black Lane Temperance Club 7-2 in the second qualifying round before losing 4-0 to Barrow in the third.

They were again placed 7th the following season and lost in the first round of the Lancashire Cup to Barrow, but undoubtedly had their finest moment in the FA Cup. After beating White Star Wanderers of Liverpool 5-1, they met Second Division Blackpool and sensationally won 1-0 away from home. In the third round they went out to Oswaldtwistle Rovers (who then lost narrowly to Manchester United in the next round).

For the 1903-04 season Rochdale Town, like the majority of the Lancashire League clubs, became members of the new second division of the Lancashire Combination.

The club also moved its matches up to Spotland, but like its predecessor, *"it proved rather a weakling and after a time died a natural death, due to the evergreen natural causes, short of cash and capital to carry on, which are the vital necessities of present day football"*. Their demise came in December 1903, and Atherton Church House took on their Lancashire Combination fixtures. Just prior to this date, their former Nelson forward Jimmy Hogan had moved to Burnley. After his playing career he was one of the most famous and progressive coaches on the continent, especially in his creation of the Austrian national 'wunderteam' of the 1930's.

Harvey Rigg, who held the lease on the fields at St Clements, thereby lost his main tenants for the third time. His next venture was to use the pitch they had vacated for local rugby competitions. However, when Hornets began their own tournament at the Athletic Grounds, he needed another way to pay the rent. Thus it was that the keen rugby man Rigg was at the forefront of the moves to revive interest in soccer in the town. Following *"strenuous efforts"* on his part, the Rochdale Observer of 15th May 1907 was able to report that *"At a meeting convened by Mr Harvey Rigg in the Central Council School, Fleece Street, last evening, with Mr Herbert Hopkinson in the chair, it was decided to form a club to be called Rochdale Association Football Club."*

Herbert Hopkinson was probably the leading figure in the association game in the town at the time as secretary of the Rochdale and District League and a well known referee. A committee comprising Hopkinson (as secretary), Rigg and Messrs Lindsay A. Anderson, Fred Stock, Thomas Alston, Alfred Wild, Tom Denham, Chas. E. Willis, Jno.Marshall and Granville Lingard was formed to carry out the decision of the meeting, *"and thus was born the Rochdale A.F.C."* The club, of course, would play on St Clements playing fields at Spotland.

Elsewhere in Edwardian footballing Britain, Newcastle had pipped Bristol City to the Football League championship, while at the other end of the League Burton United failed to gain re-election after finishing bottom of Division 2. As Burslem Port Vale resigned there were two vacancies and Rochdale's neighbours Oldham Athletic were elected along with Fulham, only the fifth southern club to join the Football League (Tottenham Hotspur, FA Cup winners six years earlier were still in the Southern League).

Interestingly, at the same Football League AGM, the representative of Rotherham Town proposed effectively a third division, with promotion to the League on merit, but this was rejected. Meanwhile in Scotland Celtic had just won the cup and league double, proving (as seen from the perspective of the year 2001) that some things never change.

A GRAND STRUGGLE   1907-1921

~ CHAPTER 1 ~

Two weeks after the inaugural meeting Rochdale were admitted into the Manchester League after securing sufficient votes to win one of the six vacant positions, and the committee set about acquiring suitable players for the new venture. The team's colours were to be *"black and white striped jerseys, white knickers and black stockings"*. The buying of the playing equipment was probably not a severe strain on the new club's finances, as a sports outfitter of the day was advertising *"Football Jerseys, vertical stripes"* for 39s. per dozen, or 12 complete sets of kit for 90 shillings (£4. 50).

The club had decided to adopt professionalism from the start and the committee quickly engaged their first professional player, one Zach Holden, an experienced performer in Lancashire junior soccer, lately with Haslingden, who was to captain the side. Holden, who had been brought up locally in Castleton, had in fact played for his new club's predecessors, Rochdale Town, at one time. Another well known local player was centre half Harker Morgan who had played in the Lancashire Junior Cup Final for Heywood in 1904.

A number of other players of varying pedigree were also obtained and they made their first public appearance on the 24th of August 1907, in a practice game between the prospective Manchester League team and the Rest. Somewhere between three and four hundred people turned up to watch, paying 1d. each for the privilege.

On September 3rd, Rochdale met Oldham Athletic, newly elected to the Second Division of the Football League, in a friendly at St. Clements playing fields, Spotland. The Rochdale team for this first ever encounter was - Hewitt; Alston, Ball; Earnshaw, Morgan, Holden; Pendlebury, Hepworth, Musgrave, Mills A. and Craven. The visitors won by four goals to one, but Craven (formerly of Oswaldtwistle) had the honour of scoring the first ever Rochdale goal, when he successfully converted a second-half penalty. A crowd of over 2,000 was attracted to this fixture and a similar number were present four days later, on September 7th 1907, when Rochdale A.F. C. played its first competitive match against Tonge. The opposition faced the following team - Hawkyard; Alston, Ball; Earnshaw, Morgan, Holden; Wynn, Naylor, Mills A. , Hepworth and Craven. The match was drawn , two goals apiece, with Craven and Wynn the Rochdale scorers.

Rochdale's first victory followed two weeks later when Ramsbottom came to Spotland, but not much joy was to be had away from home, the visit to league leaders Denton resulting in a 9-1 thrashing. Remarkably this was despite the fact that the club had pulled off something of a coup by persuading former Newcastle United and England custodian Matt Kingsley to join them. Noted for his huge fisted clearances, he was their regular goalkeeper for the rest of the season (though on two occasions when Kingsley was taken ill, the versatile Alston, who played variously at full-back, half-back and forward, deputised between the posts).

Some measure of recompense was gained the following week, though, when inside-right Tolley became the first player to score a hat-trick for Rochdale, doing so in the space of 15 minutes during a 4-1 defeat of Salford United. Another former Rochdale Town man, George Joy, made his debut in this game and became a regular in the defence along with Holden, Morgan and Martin Ball from Morris Green. The first and only away success of the season was achieved at Newton Heath in November thanks to two goals from outside right Meadowcroft (who later played in the Football League for Glossop and Bury), and the highest score of the season was gained at the expense of Stretford, who went down 7-1 at Spotland in the following match, Barlow netting three. Tolley got a second hat-trick when Rochdale ended Northwich Victoria's unbeaten record.

On January 11th 1908, Rochdale played in their first cup-tie, achieving a draw against Salford United in the Manchester Junior Cup despite the absence of Holden and Craven who had been selected to play for the Lancashire F.A. against Cheshire. (Lancashire won 6-3). Rochdale won the cup replay 4-0 and repeated that score against Denton in the next round, outside-left Joe Hardman scoring three of the goals. Another prominent player to turn out for them, albeit briefly, was George Ross, the long-serving skipper of the Bury side which won the F.A. Cup in 1900 and 1903.

The side enjoyed a quite successful run at this time, being unbeaten in 10 games, with the inside trio of Tolley, top scorer Barlow, and Aspinall all amongst the goals, but this sequence was ended in a replay of their cup semi-final, when they went down 1-0 to New Mills. They also suffered some reaction in the league, losing their next three encounters, but perked up to win their last two home fixtures.

In the match against Sale Holmfield victory was achieved despite being reduced to nine men by injuries to Meadowcroft and Joy. They thus ended the first campaign in 10th position out of 16, having won 10 and lost 12 of their 30 games.

On April 30th the committee met to discuss membership of the Lancashire Combination and entry into the F.A. Challenge Cup. It was decided to raise £250 to enable the club to approach the Lancashire Combination's representatives. At their annual meeting on May 21st, Harvey Rigg was allowed to present Rochdale's case in a three minute speech. Rochdale finished second to Stockport County Reserves in the subsequent poll and thus gained one of the four available places in the second division of the Combination.

The committee also secured the signatures of several new men during the close season of 1908, including former Black Lane Temperance Club goalkeeper John Taylor from Salford United to replace the retired Kingsley. New left full back William Openshaw had had experience with Grimsby Town in the Football League (after starting, appropriately, with Openshaw Clarence FC) while the all-rounder Patrick Galvin came from Second Division Glossop.

1908-09:
Rochdale started well in their new environment with a single goal victory over Earlestown, but lost the next four matches. These included the club's first ventures into both the Lancashire Junior Cup, a 3-2 defeat by Hindley Central, and the Football Association Cup, where they went down 5-3 at home to Accrington Stanley in the qualifying round. Plant scored in both these, but oddly, given that he was virtually the only regular member of the forward line through the season, he never managed a league goal.

Back in the league Rochdale were trounced 9-1 by Manchester City Reserves, but they then won three games in a row and steadily moved up the table, with Frank Pearson, the former Preston and Chelsea centre forward playing a number of games before moving on to Eccles Borough (and scoring twice for them on his debut, against Rochdale). Another notable player to appear briefly before emigrating to the USA was Charles Donaghy, who had played for Glasgow Rangers in the 1904 Scottish Cup Final. The "local Derby" against Heywood United attracted around 5,000 spectators, the biggest crowd to watch Rochdale up to this time.

Tommy Fleetwood was Rochdale's first major discovery. Signed in 1908 he was sold to Everton for £400 in 1911

Ernest Hawksworth who later played for Rochdale before and during World War I before moving to Blackburn Rovers.

Left back Openshaw scored both goals in the 2-2 draw with Pendlebury, a feat not repeated by a Rochdale full back for another 70 years. In November they defeated Brynn Central 7-0, Galvin (who played variously at right back, all along the half back line, at centre forward and in both inside forward positions) netting a hat-trick. This lifted the team into the top four and they maintained a similar position into the New Year.

The return game with Heywood set a new crowd record for Rochdale, when five and a half thousand paying customers saw Tommy Fleetwood score the only goal of the game. Fleetwood, who had been signed from Hindley Central after scoring twice against Rochdale in September, was another one who figured in half a dozen different positions during the season.

A more remarkable match was that against St. Helens Town, when the referee failed to turn up. The St. Helens reserve refereed the game and sent off Galvin, who had earlier scored two goals. Galvin was thus the first Rochdale player to be dismissed and there followed the first instance of crowd trouble at Spotland, when some of the home supporters became incensed. Despite this Rochdale managed to hold on to their 4-1 lead for the remainder of the game.

Another odd match was that at Hyde on Christmas Day, when Rochdale played most of the match with only nine men. Hardman failed to turn up at all, Ball arrived thirty minutes after the start, and Morgan missed the second half injured. Not surprisingly Hyde won 3-1. Three weeks later it was the spectators who failed to turn up, only 150 seeing Turton (one of the original powers in Lancashire football in the previous century) beat Rochdale 5-1 in deep snow.

Rochdale's form was not as good in the second half of the season and five defeats in six games dropped them back to mid-table. They were rather too good for Oswaldtwistle, however. The original game had been abandoned after 35 minutes with the score still at 0-0, but in the re-run Rochdale were amazingly three goals up within five minutes, had hit eight by half time and eventually eased up to win 9-0. Centre forward Barnes was the first Rochdalian to score four times, the other goals coming from Barlow, Mulrooney and three from youngster Bob Heap. Unfortunately setting a precedent for many later years, this was watched by Rochdale's lowest crowd since their formation, just 700.

Rochdale also won the next three home games to end the season in 10th place, again, with 16 wins and 17 defeats in their 38 games. Openshaw had the honour of being the first Rochdale player to go through a season as an everpresent and also scored six goals from full back, not far behind the ubiquitous Galvin who top scored with 10.

At the annual meeting at the end of May 1909, Herbert Hopkinson resigned as secretary, stating that the duties were too numerous to undertake on a part-time basis. Harvey Rigg, who became a vice-president along with Messrs. Heys, Irlam and Kenion, took over the financial affairs and it was decided to engage a manager to run the playing side. A new committee was elected, consisting of John Heap, James Carter, Tom Denham, J. H. Kenworthy jnr., A. Byrne, A. Ramsbottom, C. Wormwell, Harry Wood, W. Robinson, Albert Goodhew and C. Denham.

The meeting revealed that a profit of £32 10s 8d. had been made in the 1908-9 season, but as a loss of £177 5s 9d. had been incurred during the club's first year (despite a maximum wage of 7s 6d. - 37.5p - a week), they now had a deficit of £144 15 1d; £58 11s 8d. was owed to the bank and £86 3s 5d. to 'sundry tradesmen'. It is interesting to note in these days of million pound players that the total wage bill for first team men was £480 17s 6d., while travelling costs were £89 3s 11d., and hotels and meals cost £31 12s. Despite a wage bill of only £70 19s 6d. a serious loss of around £100 was made on the reserves and problems had been caused by players failing to turn up and committee members having to play. The reserves had hoped to join the Manchester League, but they would admit only first teams. Conversely the Rochdale League did not allow professional players, so it was decided to continue in the Manchester Federation, where they had finished 10th in the past season. They had also entered the Manchester Junior Cup, but lost in the first round to Hooley Hill.

The following month, June 1909, the committee appointed 33 year old Joe Blackett as player/manager and secretary. A right full-back, he had had a long career in top class football, most recently with Leicester Fosse. Former skipper Zach Holden was made the club's trainer. Other new players signed up included several ex-Football League players; experienced back Jimmy Freeborough from Bradford Park Avenue and forwards John Hall, formerly with Barnsley, Albert Worth of Stockport County and the manager's former Leicester club mate, Fred Bracey, the Derbyshire cricketer.

A player moving on to a higher level was Billy Hampson, who had been advised to move from Lancashire for his health and joined Norwich City in the Southern League. It must have worked as he subsequently had a remarkably lengthy career in the Football League, playing in the F.A. Cup Final for Newcastle when 41 years old, and not retiring until 1928.

1909-10:
The season started with a win over Bacup, but the next game was lost at Earlestown. In the F. A. Cup preliminary qualifying round Rochdale had their first success in this competition when they defeated Ramsbottom 4-0 in a replay, although only 500 supporters saw them do it. In the next round they went out to Haslingden. In the Lancs Junior Cup the side really went to town, running up double figures for the first time; the five forwards, Buckley (2), Fleetwood (2), Hall, Bracey(2) and Worth (2), and goalie Taylor (from the penalty spot) shared the goals in a 10-2 win over Padiham. Taylor remains the only Rochdale goalkeeper ever to score a senior goal and supporters would have been able to recognise the fact as this was the first season in which goalkeepers wore different coloured shirts to their colleagues (red, blue or white were allowed).

Back in the Combination, a number of games were drawn, including that against neighbours Heywood United which attracted 6,000 spectators. The crowd for the return game at Heywood was better still, 8,500 fans paying a total of £128 15s 7d. By contrast, the representative game between the Lancashire FA amateurs and their Birmingham FA counterparts at Spotland, *despite being freely advertised*", drew gross gate receipts of only £11 2s 9d.

By November the team was really in form and five league games in a row were won by an aggregate of 28 goals to 2. Well-travelled centre forward Frank Baker scored two hat-tricks in successive games, the first Rochdale player to do so, while the whole side joined in against Pendlebury, winning 11-0 with goals by Bracey (4), Hall (2), Fleetwood, Worth (2), Jones and Freeborough - five of them in the space of 11 minutes! Baker collected another hat-trick later in the season when Rochdale beat Walkden Central 8-0.

With only two defeats in a run of 16 games, Rochdale kept in touch with the league leaders and meantime reached the Final of the Lancashire Junior Cup, though not without difficulty; half back Greenhalgh had to play in goal against Darwen when Taylor failed to arrive. The game ended 3-3, Rochdale won the replay and went on to beat Rossendale and Earlestown. In the final, on Easter Saturday, March 26th, they met Eccles Borough at Burnden Park, Bolton and won thanks to two goals by Worth and one by Baker, after being two goals down. The Rochdale team which collected the club's first trophy after less than three years in existence was their strongest eleven, Taylor, Blackett, Openshaw, Morgan, Galvin, Freeborough, Hall, Fleetwood, Baker, Bracey and Worth, (the players did not collect their medals quite as quickly, though, as they had not been finished in time!). The league match two days later attracted Spotland's largest crowd to that date, around 7000, and they saw the 'homesters' beat Stockport County Reserves 4-1, Worth and Bracey getting two each.

Even so, two subsequent defeats left Rochdale in 5th place with only five games to go - four of them away from home. A tremendous final effort, including a 5-0 win at Clitheroe when Worth scored four times to take his tally to 25 for the season, gave them nine points out of 10. They thus finished in fourth place, a point ahead of Haslingden, thereby winning promotion to the first division of the Lancashire Combination. As it turned out, the crucial moment had been as far back as November 27th when Rochdale's match at Haslingden was abandoned after 82 minutes, due to bad light, with Rochdale at that point losing 3-1. When the match was replayed near the end of the season Rochdale won by two goals to nil.

Rochdale collected 54 points from their 38 games, with 23 victories. At home they won 15 and drew 4 and including cup-ties and friendlies were unbeaten in 29 games at Spotland, at one stage winning 17 in a row. Rochdale scored 120 goals in all competitive matches with all the regular forwards hitting double figures. Rochdale were awarded no less than 15 penalties during the season but missed seven of them. The skipper, Blackett, missed three but on two occasions netted rebounds after the goalkeeper had saved (the goalie not being required to stay on his line in those days). In a crucial game against Eccles near the end of the season both Openshaw and custodian Taylor failed from the spot but fortunately a third award gave Hall the chance to win the match 1-0.

Despite their sucess and the slightly better attendances, Rochdale made a loss of £79 18s 8½d due to the much larger wage bill (nearly £800) that was necessary to attract the better players. (The strength of the side was indicated by the several former League players, such as Andrew McShea of Barnsley, Joseph Thorp of Bolton, and Leeds and ex-Blackpool man Carthy, who were unable to gain regular places).

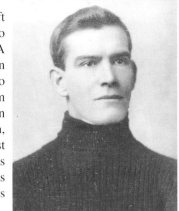

The reserves were disbanded in November for financial reasons. At the end of the season Albert Worth, having made a name with his *"lightening drives from the wing"*, was transferred to Grimsby Town, who then lost their place in Division 2 at the Football League AGM (they returned a year later). John Hall became player/manager of South Shields and Bob Heap, who had left to go to Cheltenham College, signed for First Division Bury, subsequently spending 12 years at Gigg Lane. Other regulars Taylor (who had been an everpresent), Openshaw, Galvin and Baker were also allowed to leave. Indeed only three of the successful squad, Blackett, Freeborough and Fleetwood, retained their first team places for the following year.

During the summer of 1910, which saw the accession of George V and a Liberal win in the General Election, the club thus set about signing a new set of players for their higher sphere of activity. The most notable of these was Albert Smith, who was signed from Bradford Park Avenue. Bradford had paid the tremendous fee of £1660 when they acquired him from Burnley in 1908. At 23 he had already represented the Football League and was destined for a long association with Rochdale.

Two other players with Football League experience were also obtained from Park Avenue, Bob Grierson and J. T. "Cracker" Manning, a powerhouse winger who had cost £450 when signed from Hull two years earlier (they were later joined by two others, former Paisley Abercorn full back Danny Crossan and forward Jimmy Kenyon). Half back Jimmy Henderson, *"a foot runner of some repute"*, had played in the First Division with Preston North End, while goalkeeper Billy Biggar, formerly understudy to the legendary 'Fatty' Foulke at Sheffield United, had had long experience in the Southern League, then almost as powerful as the Football League,

(Top) Billy Bigger: Rochdale's goalkeeper from 1910 to 1917. (Middle) Danny Crossan: Full-back from 1910 to 1918 when he tragically died from pneumonia. (Bottom) Albert Smith, pictured in 1912. Dale's record appearances holder until the 1970's. He played from 1910 to 1925.

playing over 200 times for Watford. William Cooper, said to be a half back *"of the impetuous school"*, had played in the Football League with Barnsley and in Scotland with Dundee. New centre half Edward Thomason had won his honours more locally, a Lancashire Junior Cup medal with Colne and a Manchester Junior Cup medal with Eccles.

Off the field, Harvey Rigg's original plan was completed at the end of July and Rochdale became a Limited Company with a capital of £2000 worth of five shilling shares. Robert Barlow was elected the first chairman of Rochdale A. F. C. Limited. Mr H. Morton was appointed as secretary in place of Joe Blackett, who remained as a player. George Coe, formerly of Bury, was appointed trainer.

1910-11:

Rochdale kicked off the 1910-11 season with a 3-0 win over Colne, but the next two games were lost before they launched into a splendid run of six consecutive victories, the best by 5-1 away to the reserves of First Division Blackburn Rovers. Though their first venture into the Lancashire Senior Cup was ended in round two - by Burnley - they were still in the 'English' (ie. F. A.) Cup and during another run of six successive wins they progressed to the fourth qualifying round (equivalent to the present first round proper), where they drew Stockport County of Division 2. (The 4-3 win at Heywood United in the 2nd qualifying round was actually recorded on the new-fangled cinematograph by a local enthusiast).

After two goalless draws - the first ending a run of 15 consecutive home wins and the second despite Henderson being sent off - Rochdale sensationally beat Stockport in a second replay at Boundary Park, Oldham, Blackett netting the only goal. In the next round Rochdale were paired with Southern League Luton Town and the match attracted a new record gate to Spotland, 9933 spectators paying £170 7s 7d. Although Fleetwood equalised an early goal by the visitors, Rochdale were unable to find a winning goal and later went down 3-2 in the replay, only their second defeat in 18 games.

Back in the league, they carried on where they had left off, notching up an eighth successive victory away to Manchester United Reserves, Kenyon netting twice. The next two games were rather eventful. The referee was attacked by the crowd at the end of the 2-2 draw at Southport and then against Preston North End Reserves Rochdale remarkably won 1-0 despite ending the game with eight men, Kenyon being injured and both Henderson and Manning having been sent off just before half-time. When leaders Everton Reserves visited Spotland in the middle of January, a best ever league attendance of 9,500 saw their men claim a 1-1 draw thanks to a debut goal by young Ernest Cutts, and they moved into second place in the table. Two weeks later Rochdale moved to the top after a dramatic match against Nelson.

Fleetwood scored what turned out to be the winner after 85 minutes, but there was still time for Smith to miss a penalty and Biggar to save one. Immediately knocked off their perch by Blackpool Reserves, they responded with four straight wins, the versatile Freeborough who played in seven different positions scoring key goals in two of them. They then consolidated their top position by picking up valuable points from the games in hand left by their cup run. Meantime, top scorer Fleetwood, with 21 goals to his credit already, had been sold to 1st Division giants Everton for the princely sum of £400, the equivalent of at least £400,000 by today's standards. The first major discovery by the club, he went on to win a First Division Championship medal and to represent England in Victory Internationals in a career lasting till 1924. Briefly coming into the side was a player who already had international appearances to his credit, one Eversley Mansfield, who had represented England as an amateur in 1907 while playing for Preston Winckley (playing alongside the likes of 'Spurs Vivian Woodward, he had scored twice in a 8-1 victory over Holland).

Five points from their three games in the first week of April - the everpresent Smith netting his second hat-trick of the season in the 4-0 defeat of Glossop Reserves - saw Rochdale within sight of the title. Against Liverpool Reserves on Good Friday they left it very late, though, Manning and Gregson, a recent signing from Bury Sunday Schools football, scoring in the last two minutes to earn a draw in front of 16,000 Anfield fans, by far the biggest crowd to watch Rochdale up to that time.

The following day the issue was settled. Two goals from Grierson against Preston Reserves left Rochdale 7 points clear of Everton Reserves with only three games to play. Though winning only once in those games, when Bracey in a rare outing hit a hat-trick against Blackburn Reserves, they ended the season well clear with 56 points from their 38 games. No less than 25 games had been won and at home only one point was dropped, that against runners-up Everton. Over the past two seasons Rochdale were now unbeaten in 56 home games. Unsurprisingly two of Rochdale's players, Smith and Grierson, were included in the Lancashire Combination Division One select team to play against Division Two.

Income was dramatically up during the season, to nearly £1,800 but with the better players recruited the wage bill had doubled and yet again a loss was incurred on the season, this time £102. During January Mr. Harry Marshall had taken over as secretary and this task was later undertaken by director Mr. C. Wormwell. Encouraged by their success in the Lancashire Combination, Rochdale applied for membership of the Football League for the 1911-12 season. At the AGM Barnsley were re-elected, gaining 28 votes, while Grimsby pipped Lincoln 18 votes to 17 to regain their place. Rochdale won one solitary vote as did fellow hopefuls Hartlepools.

Following this disappointment Rochdale's representative Herbert Hopkinson, along with members of the Lincoln, Hartlepools, Darlington and Chesterfield clubs, revived the call for the formation of a Third Division of the Football League. Advertisements were placed in the influential "Athletic News" and attracted 15 other applicants, mostly from the North and Midlands but also including the likes of Portsmouth, Cardiff and Croydon Common. The Southern League (which had wanted to combine with the Football League as a third division two years previously) felt this to be an "unfriendly act" which would undermine their status and the move was defeated at an Inter-League Board meeting later in the year.

At the end of May, Harvey Rigg and the representatives of Darwen and Chester addressed a meeting of northern League clubs who were planning to break away and form a Central League for their reserve sides, urging them to stay in the Lancashire Combination. Two weeks later Rigg was back again with Rochdale's application to join them in their new league! Rochdale were successfully voted in, but the Combination objected to this late defection and the FA vetoed the move, forcing Rochdale to stay in the now much weakened Combination for another season. Rochdale Reserves had reformed during the season, though playing only friendlies, but they now successfully applied to join the Manchester League, thus following in the footsteps of their senior side.

With several regulars having left to join better known clubs - both Cooper and Manning moved to Lincoln, Norman Riddell went to Second Division Clapton Orient and Jimmy Kenyon joined Millwall - a number of new players were signed during the summer. Perhaps surprisingly a number, like William Chick from Norwich, John Reynolds of New Brompton (Gillingham) and Thomas Meynell from Clapton Orient, were from well known southern clubs. Reynolds was a former Football League regular with Burton United and Grimsby who was said in his prime to be *"a rare handful"* for opposing full backs.

1911-12:
Rochdale set off the 1911-12 season in fine form, defeating Denton 5-0 at home - Frank Spriggs scored twice on his debut, as he had for Leicester in the Football League - and a week later they won 4-2 at Denton in the Manchester Senior Cup, the club's first venture into this tournament (though it must be said that the opposition only had eight men at the start).

A challenge match at Haslingden, the previous season's Lancashire Combination Division Two champions, was also won but then in the Lancashire Senior Cup a last minute penalty for Barrow ended Rochdale's unbeaten home run after 58 games. Coincidentally Rochdale's last home defeat had been to Barrow in April 1909.

In the Manchester Cup Rochdale progressed by beating Northern Nomads, Gregson scoring all three goals, and then recording a splendid 5-0 victory against Stockport County, two new men Tom Page and William Lovett getting among the goals. Lovett was a 17 year old inside forward from Fleetwood's old club Hindley Central while Page, who was soon joined at Spotland by his brother John, came from Liverpool junior football. Although Barrow had by this time also beaten them in the FA Cup (they had been exempted until the fourth qualifying round thanks to their excellent progress the previous year), Rochdale excelled in the Manchester Cup semi-final, winning 2-0 away to Manchester City.

In the league, Rochdale had dropped only three points in eight games and five consecutive victories followed, that by 7 goals to 1 at Bacup being Rochdale's best ever away win. Despite a couple of defeats, a 3-0 win over Chester on New Year's Day put Rochdale on top of the table and wins in the next five games as well gave them a healthy lead. Neighbours Heywood United ended their run of 19 consecutive home wins with a 2-2 draw, but the Rochdale side was unbeaten in 12 games when they met Manchester United in the final of the Manchester Senior Cup at Hyde Road, the game ending goalless *"after a grand struggle"*. Two further home wins and two away draws set the club up for the championship and they clinched it in great style by annihilating Bacup 9-0. Remarkably Tom Page scored four times, as he had in the earlier game at Bacup. Bogey side Barrow beat them in the next game but a 3-1 success against Walkden Central in the last match took Rochdale's points tally to 50 from 32 games, 23 matches being won. For the second year in succession only one point was dropped at home and Rochdale were now unbeaten for three years in league games at Spotland.

Three days after the last league game, Rochdale met a powerful Manchester United side in the replay of the Manchester Cup Final. Again a hard fought game ended all square, Alf Gregson netting Rochdale's goal, his 25th of the season, and the cup was shared by the two clubs. The Rochdale side that earned their share of the glory comprised Biggar; Blackett, Crossan; Chick, Meynell, Henderson; Reynolds, Gregson, T. Page, Lovett and Smith. In the first match Bracey had played in place of Page and reserve Tattum for Smith. Rochdale retained most of their successful side at the end of the season, but one departure was former skipper Blackett who joined Barrow. John Reynolds took up a coaching position in Switzerland. He later served the emerging Ajax club of Amsterdam for over 30 years and shared in their rise to European prominence.

The club made a loss of £600 during the season due to a decrease in receipts caused by the loss of most of the Lancashire Combination's better sides, but in the summer Rochdale again applied - successfully - to join the Central League and this time the move went through.

Incidentally, it is interesting to recall that it was during the summer the restriction was imposed that the goalkeeper could only handle the ball within his penalty area, one of the last major changes to the code. They were also given the opportunity to wear what became the traditional goalkeeping apparel for the next three quarters of a century, the green jersey.

1912-13:

New players for the 1912-13 season included ex-Football League men Jim Tully from Clapton Orient (a surprisingly common stopping off place for Rochdale players), *"right wing speed merchant"* Tommy Spink from Fulham and Ted Birnie, a cultured half back formerly of Newcastle, Chelsea and 'Spurs, who had been coaching Mulheim in Germany. New player/reserve team coach Dan Cunliffe had appeared for England against Ireland in 1900, when playing for Portsmouth, and had been one of New Brighton Tower's leading players during their brief Football League career.

The Rochdale half-back line for 1912-13, (left to right) William Chick, Ted Birnie and Jimmy Henderson. Inset is trainer George Coe.

Up in the North-East however, a second half penalty by Chick saw them home and into the draw for the first round proper (the same as the present third round). In fact, Rochdale nearly did not make it to Darlington at all. After missing a connection they had to hire a special train (for the grand sum of £11 12s 6d !) to get them there. In the league they overcame top of the table Manchester United Reserves but were thrashed 7-1 by Liverpool Reserves.

Against Blackpool Reserves, Chick became the first Rochdale half-back to score twice in one game, making his tally five goals in the last four games (he eventually netted the remarkable total of 12 during the season). Record receipts of £306 12s 6d were paid by the 8,801 supporters who attended the Cup-tie against Swindon (the club had made ground improvements in anticipation of a 15,000 crowd). However the Southern League side, Cup semi-finalists in 1910 and 1912, proved too strong and won 2-0 after Chick had hit the post. This match was again captured on film by the enterprising local cinematographer. A couple of weeks later the unbeaten home record was lost when Oldham Reserves won by the only goal after Chick missed a penalty. The run had lasted almost four years, since April 1909, and spanned 64 games, 57 of which had been won.

The Central League season started well, with a home win over Preston Reserves, but in a second replay of the previous season's Manchester Cup Final, Rochdale crashed 0-5 to Manchester United. Nevertheless, the earlier decision to share the trophy appears to have been adhered to. Four of the next five games were won and Rochdale surged to the top of the table at the beginning of October. In the F. A. Cup they safely dealt with Macclesfield and Newton Heath, but conceded six goals in two consecutive league games and slipped down to eighth. Further cup progress was made at the expense of Stalybridge Celtic and Accrington Stanley, with Tom Page netting four in the 6-1 win over the latter. His brother John had meantime been transferred to First Division Everton and a rearrangement of the defence had brought in Tom Broome, signed the previous year from Salford United. In the last qualifying round of the FA Cup, with 15 straight home wins behind them, Rochdale met Darlington at Spotland, but could manage only a one-all draw.

The team quickly recovered though, losing only once in ten games, moving back up the table to fourth place and escaping with a creditable draw at Bolton in the Manchester Cup with nine men when Goodwin was injured and Crossan was sent off. They thrashed Southport Central 8-0, with Gregson netting three, but failed to win any of their next six games. They did win their final match, however, Tom Page taking his tally for the season to 23 (the regular inside trio of Gregson, Page and Tully totalled 59 between them) and finally ended the season in seventh spot with 44 points from 38 games. Gates had been higher in the Central League and receipts passed the £2000 mark for the first time, but with an increased wage bill Rochdale still lost around £300 on the season.

The full back berths had proved to be problem positions, though Harker Morgan, a veteran of Rochdale's first ever game, became the first player to make 100 appearances for them. No fewer than eleven players were tried out, and at one stage the club sought Divine inspiration, the Reverend J. C. Jackson playing right back in a friendly against Heywood United. Strangely, though, one full back, Costelli, who had had the odd game the year before, never managed to get in the side but played several games for Glossop in Division Two the following term. In the end the right back spot fell to the 17 year old Jack Barton, though Rochdale were fined one guinea for signing him from junior club Southport Park Villa while he was still on Burnley's books.

At the end of the season Gregson was transferred to Grimsby and Lovett, who had lost his place to Tully, moved to Exeter. He later had the honour of playing in Brazil's first ever international game, when the Devon side toured South America. Tom Page followed his brother to Everton and both went on to enjoy long careers in the Football League, playing until the end of the 1920's. Younger brother Louis, later an England international, became famous for scoring six goals in his first game as a centre forward for Burnley, while a fourth brother, Willie, appeared briefly at Spotland after the war before joining Louis at Northampton. 'Ginger' Leigh, formerly of QPR and Fulham, moved on to play in South Wales and then for Goole Town before tragically committing suicide by jumping from his hospital window *"believing himself to be suffering from an incurable disease"*.

The board once again sought the assistance of a player/ manager to raise the side to an even higher level and Vince Hayes, well known former Manchester United full back, was appointed just before the start of the 1913-14 season. He had recently coached the Norwegian Olympic team and Wiener S. V. in Austria. Other new arrivals included half back Charlie Milne from Huddersfield and forwards Jack Allan of Leeds City and Bob Watson, formerly of Leeds and Arsenal. Bob Grierson returned after a spell with Hartlepool.

1913-14:
It was the centre forward Allan who had the most dramatic impact hitting five goals as Rochdale put seven past Bury Reserves on the opening day of the season. Subsequent progress was rather more subdued, the formerly impregnable home form being overcome in successive games by Port Vale - when Milne put through his own goal and Crossan was carried off - and Everton Reserves.

Good progress was made in the Lancashire Senior Cup, Nelson, Barrow the usual bogey side, and Bolton being dispatched en route to the semi-final. Played at Blackburn, this proved a disappointment as Blackpool soon took a 3-0 lead and ended winners by four goals to one.

In the league, form was patchy, though Rochdale did win away to Preston Reserves thanks to two debut goals by Ernest Hawksworth, and crowds were down on the previous term. Those who turned up to see Blackburn Reserves had their moneysworth however, as the home side three times took the lead but then fell 3-4 behind, before Albert Smith completed his hat-trick to win the match 5-4 (Smith was an everpresent on the left wing for the second time in three years and was also selected to represent the Central League against the North Eastern League).

Old enemies Barrow, with former Rochdale man Chick in their side, then removed Rochdale from the FA Cup, an injury to Biggar which forced Barton to go in goal not aiding their prospects. Centre half Broome was transferred to Preston North End in December but the side maintained a mid-table league position into the New Year. A run with only one defeat in eight games, including a 3-2 win at Anfield, gave rise to hopes of better things, but a subsequent poor spell saw the side slip back to tenth spot.

The Reserves' match against Macclesfield in February served as a benefit for the long-serving Harker Morgan, who had played in Rochdale's first ever game and was released at the end of the season. Top scorer Allan moved on to Southern League Coventry City and Tommy Spink was transferred to Grimsby. Charlie Milne, *"the worrying half"*, signed for Halifax but was soon back again.

Although wages were slightly lower than in the previous term, gate receipts were well down and a serious short fall of £856 resulted. Despite this, the club made an important investment for the future in February 1914, when they completed the purchase of the ground at Spotland for £1700, enabling them to develop it and make room for more spectators.

It was a relatively quiet close season at Spotland but unfortunately not so in the outside world. On June 26th, Rochdale signed former Scottish Junior International Robert Neave from Chesterfield, adding to the earlier signing of Archie Rawlings from Northampton, and former Newcastle and Manchester City forward, William Kelly. However two days later Archduke Ferdinand of Austria was assassinated in Sarajevo and even before the football season opened Great Britain was at war with Germany, with the British Expeditionary Force out in France. On the domestic scene however, life continued much as usual, with the frequently expressed assurance that *"it* (the war) *will all be over by Christmas"*.

1914-15:
Rochdale opened up the 1914-15 season with a 4-1 win over Liverpool Reserves and a number of other good home results were obtained, though away form was lacking in the league.

They did achieve a victory at Fleetwood in the Lancashire Senior Cup however, and this was followed by home wins over Nelson and South Liverpool, which earned a semi final clash with neighbours Oldham. Completely overturning the form book, Rochdale from the Central League (the same as Oldham's reserves) knocked out the Latics First Division side, thanks to two goals from the prolific William Brown, a close season signing from Brighton. The final was another matter however, and First Division Burnley ran out comfortable winners by four goals to one in the match at Hyde Road, former Burnley man Albert Smith getting the consolation goal for Rochdale. The following week Rochdale lost by the same score to Burnley's reserves in the league.

The side had also made progress in the FA Cup, though. A hat-trick by Kelly had seen off old rivals Stalybridge Celtic and further home draws in the next three rounds helped Rochdale overcome Hartlepool from the North East and two Southern League sides , Watford and Gillingham. In round two of the competition proper (today's fourth round, i.e., the last thirty-two) Rochdale again drew Oldham, then leading Division One and harbouring hopes of a cup and League double.

Almost inevitably, the Latics proved too strong this time, winning 3-0, but Rochdale were able to console themselves with their share of an 18,668 gate, the highest yet. This cup run was unequalled by a Rochdale side until the 1990's. (Oldham, incidentally, ended the season as League runners-up and were knocked out in the next round of the cup).

The league had taken something of a back seat throughout this excitement and despite two 6-1 wins, Brown netting a hat-trick in each, Rochdale found themselves rather too near the bottom for comfort. Against Barnsley Reserves fortune certainly seemed against Rochdale, as Biggar missed most of the first half through injury and his replacement Barton broke his leg later in the match. Unsurprisingly, Barnsley won 2-1. Thankfully, this proved the side's lowest ebb and only one defeat was sustained in the final eight games, which were highlighted by a 7-1 thrashing of bottom club Blackpool Reserves when Neave, usually a half back, netted four goals from inside left. Rochdale thus ended the season in ninth position, one higher than the previous campaign, though they gained two points fewer. The Reserves had an even more successful season, becoming champions of the Lancashire Combination Division Two, which they had joined only the year before.

To round off a season of cup exploits, Rochdale had also reached the final of the Manchester Senior Cup by beating Hurst 5-1, thanks to yet another Brown hat-trick, which gave him a club record 31 goals for the season. In a dramatic game, their 13th cup-tie of the season, Rochdale eventually went down 3-4 to Stockport County despite leading 3-2 after the first period of extra time. Kelly (2) and Hawksworth scored the Rochdale goals.

Needless to say, the war had not ended by Christmas 1914, and indeed showed no signs of ending in the near future. Earlier in the season, the powers that be had decided to continue with the first class fixture list as *it was the desire of the clubs to provide a healthy antidote to war........ preserving equable mind and counteracting any tendency to panic and monomania*. By now however the climate of public opinion had drastically changed; Lord Kitchener's "first hundred thousand" had been swallowed up by the mud of Flanders, his fierce countenance stared out from a similar number of recruiting posters and those at home deemed that football was no fit profession for young men who should be in the army. Many footballers had, in fact, already volunteered including Rochdale's Bob Lilley, who had joined the Royal Field Artillary in January, Brown, who went to serve in the Durham Light Infantry, and Kay, who enlisted in the Footballer's Battalion, or to give it its official title, the 17th (Service) Battalion, The Duke of Cambridgeshire's Own Middlesex Regiment, an infantry section comprised entirely of former and current players, officials and supporters. The Football League and other major professional leagues were thus suspended for the duration and all cup competitions were also discontinued, but despite hostility in some quarters, regional leagues were set up in their place.

1915-16:
Together with Southport Central, Rochdale were co-opted into the League - Lancashire Section. The top five sides in the Football League the previous season had been from Lancashire, so this was to all intents and purposes the First Division (though Blackburn Rovers did not compete in 1915-16). One notable acquisition before the start of the season was half back Jack Yarwood from Merthyr, who was to be associated with the club for several seasons, but Rochdale initially relied for the most part on the players who had been around the previous year.

The season started badly with a 6-1 hammering at Burnley, and though the next two games were won, the following ten games produced only three further points. Against Blackpool, three players arrived five minutes after the start, but, remarkably, their side was still on level terms and they celebrated their appearance by taking the lead, though Blackpool eventually took the measure of the eleven men and won 3-2.

Rochdale did manage to beat eventual runners-up Burnley, and then achieved a remarkable victory at Oldham, with Rawlings in goal in place of the absent 'keeper. Such successes were few however, and when the Principal Tournament was concluded Rochdale were thirteenth out of the fourteen teams, having won only seven games out of twenty-six. Subsequently, Rochdale were placed in the Midland Section - Northern Division (all the other teams being from Yorkshire) for the Subsidiary Tournament and though taking nine points from ten games, were fifth of six.

During Wartime football: (Left) Billy Halligan was Rochdale's main goal-scorer (Middle) Billy Hibbert, one of numerous guest players, and an England International before the War. (Right) Archie Rawlings played for Rochdale throughout, and went on to become an England International while with Preston.

Despite the obvious problems, Rochdale did field a fairly consistent side and 18 year old Fred Heap, brother of the earlier Rochdale player, led the scoring charts with ten goals before he was called up. Albert Smith completed 200 league appearances during the season, the first Rochdale player to do so. The previous year he had also been their first player to net 50 league goals.

Of the newcomers, goalkeeper Causer had been a Football League regular for Glossop until they had decided not to continue playing during the war, while George Kay had appeared for the Irish League pre-war, and after army service went on to be a well known figure for West Ham in the 1920's, captaining them in the first Wembley Cup Final. Other former Football League players who passed through included ex-Burnley centre-half Swift, who scored twice in the 2-2 draw with Manchester United; Bury and Birmingham forward Wally Smith, whose penalty settled a thrilling game against Bradford 4-3 in Rochdale's favour after both 'keepers had saved earlier spot kicks; and Joe Butler, the veteran goalie of Sunderland's League Championship side of 1913, and Causer's predecessor at Glossop.

A notable player who had a brief connection with Rochdale was the Scot Sandy Turnball, who had the unusual record of winning an FA Cup Winners medal with both Manchester City and Manchester United. After guesting for Rochdale against City, he subsequently joined the Footballers Battalion and was killed in action in 1917. Another player of note was the Glossop stalwart and captain, John Cuffe. Actually an Australian, Cuffe was also a prominent first class cricketer, appearing for New South Wales and Worcestershire. Rochdale and future Lancashire cricketer Billy Brown also figured briefly at full back. The players were paid, incidentally, by sharing out the gate money in odd pennies and sixpences after matches.

1916-17:
By the time the 1916-17 season came around, the Battle of the Somme had begun, conscription had been introduced and several Rochdale regulars had joined up.

Yarwood and Hawksworth were in the Cavalry Regiment, Barton in the Royal Engineers and Kay in the Royal Field Artillary, though many players were still available while on leave or stationed nearby. Billy Biggar was appointed the club's trainer, though he did return to playing later in the season. Manager Hayes was, meantime, working on Liverpool docks.

The most prominent new player to join the club was Irish international forward Bill Halligan, formerly of Leeds, Derby, Wolves, Hull and, most recently, Manchester United. Despite the presence of another ex-Wolves man, Fred Curtis, who had scored twenty-five goals in the last pre-war season, an away defeat at Stockport in the first match, led into a poor early season run, with only one victory in the first seven games. Indeed, Rochdale were literally hit for six at Blackburn, when Rovers' Chapman netted a double hat-trick. In the 2-2 draw against Manchester City, Tom Page, guesting for his old club, had a penalty saved but a retake was ordered due to encroachment by a dog! Guesting at right back in this game against his own club was Herbert Tyler, a regular for City during and after the war. Another man to appear for Rochdale against his own team was Stoke's Eli Turner, a stalwart at Crewe in the 'twenties, who actually did it again in 1918. Rochdale lent Preston one of their reserves, Litherland, when North End turned up a man short, and he helped them to a 2-1 win.

A rather more successful spell followed, despite a 6-0 home defeat by Bolton Wanderers. New signing Bob Thomas from Tranmere Rovers netted a hat-trick against Blackpool in a 4-1 win and the season's first away victory was secured at Preston. The best performances of the season - coinciding with the first appearances of centre half Pat O'Connell, another Irish international from Hull and Manchester United - were a 3-2 defeat of previously unbeaten Liverpool, after being two goals down, and a 4-0 scoreline against second placed Stockport County, on successive Saturdays. The latter was played 40 minutes each way because of a late start. By the turn of the year Rochdale had moved up to eighth position out of sixteen. They managed to maintain this level for the remainder of the Principal Tournament despite losing five of the last six games.

The subsidiary tournament was played over just six matches and with five wins and a draw Rochdale were able to secure the championship. The highlight was a 5-1 win against Bolton, when Walker grabbed four of the goals. Not noted as a prolific goalscorer, Walker had also netted a hat-trick against the same opponents in the Principal Tournament. The title was clinched by a 2-1 win at Oldham, despite Herbert Tierney being sent off, top scorer Halligan notching his 18th goal of the season. Goalkeeper Causer had joined up in February and his predecessor, Biggar, had finally retired after 232 senior appearances, so Rochdale had a new custodian for these games in Tom Kay of Bolton Wanderers. Another newcomer was trialist Jack Hebden from Castleford who became probably Rochdale's youngest ever first team player at just 16 years and 3 months.

During the season Rochdale twice fell foul of the authorities, first when they were fined £5 for playing Albert Smith without the consent of Bury or the League Management Committee (Smith had signed for Bury at the start of the season, but soon returned 'home'), and again later when Walkden Central reported them for 'poaching' inside forward Tom Meehan. At the end of the season Meehan joined Manchester United. He was to figure prominently for United and Chelsea after the war and won an England cap in 1923, shortly before his untimely death.

1917-18:
Despite the continued influx of men into the forces - Rawlings and Walker departed just after the start of the 1917-18 season - Rochdale had only one new player in the side which met Burnley on the opening day when they recorded a sensational 9-0 victory. The newcomer, Flaherty, netted four of the goals, as did Halligan, after O'Connell had opened the scoring; a great day for the Irish!

Southport - who arrived with only seven men and were loaned four Rochdale reserves to make up the numbers - were also soundly beaten 6-0, Flaherty taking his tally to seven goals in three games before moving to Oldham, and Rochdale went six games before suffering a reverse. An even higher scoring match, against Bury, saw the home side win 7-5, Halligan obtaining five of the goals, while six goals were also registered against Blackpool and Blackburn (Halligan netting another four). The then leaders, Liverpool, beat Rochdale 5-1, with Tom Bennett, later a Rochdale player, scoring all the goals. However, Rochdale gained revenge at Spotland and held a steady sixth spot in the league throughout the New Year with a run of 10 unbeaten games. Halligan grabbed yet another four goals at home to Bolton and went on to total 36 for the season, easily a club record, even if gained in somewhat strange circumstances. With most of the younger men in the forces, besides the two Irishmen, the other veterans like Crossan, Henderson, Tully and the manager Hayes were frequent performers.

Meanwhile, Tweedale Rigg, who had been on the fringes of the team for several seasons, finally secured a regular spot. A less likely addition to the team was Sam Lloyd who usually plied his trade in the Northern Union with Rochdale Hornets and Warrington. Fortunes were mixed in the Subsidiary Tournament which started in March, Rochdale taking six points from six games and finishing 10th out of 16. In the process, Tom Page, back from Everton again, took his overall tally to 54 goals in only 82 senior goals for Rochdale.

However, the Principal Tournament had not yet been concluded, as the match at Stoke - already confirmed as champions - had been postponed. Goals by Ernest Goodwin and Pat O'Connell ruined the Potters unbeaten home record and pushed Rochdale up to fourth place in the table. They won 15 of their 30 games and lost only six. The following week Goodwin guested for his former club Leeds City in their championship play-off against Stoke, Leeds' team also including another former Rochdale player Harry Millership.

During the season it had been reported that George Joy, one of the first Rochdale players back in 1907, had been killed in France. In June, Sgt. Norman Riddell of the Northumberland Fusiliers, who had been one of the first Rochdale players transferred to a Football League club, also died in action. Another aspect of the wartime conditions, the (partial) liberation of women, was reflected in the first ever ladies' match at Spotland, with the meeting of two teams of munitions workers, Westinghouse and Ironfounders. A couple of years later a crowd of 12,000 watched the then famous Dick Kerrs' Ladies play Fleetwood at Willbutts Lane.

1918-19:
Though more men were still being called up for the final Allied offensive on the Western Front, many of the previous season's side were still available when September 1918 came around, the main addition being Manchester City centre half Sam Spruce. Following a pre-season trial game in aid of the Prisoners of War Fund, the first two league games were both lost to Liverpool, manager Hayes having an equaliser - which would have been his first goal for over three years - disallowed in the home match. Ten points from the next six games quickly shot the side into the top six however. A victory away to Manchester United was followed by Rochdale taking three points off second placed Stoke.

By this time the Armistice had been signed and many former soldiers were beginning to return to this country, so that there was a new face or two in the side almost every week. Results deteriorated somewhat as a result, but attendances were now increasing, with 15,000 seeing the 1-1 draw at Hyde Road and 6,000 for the return which Manchester City won by the odd goal in nine.

The Rochdale centre forward in that match was the former England international Billy Hibbert of Newcastle United. In December 1918, stalwart full back Danny Crossan, who had been with the club since 1910, fell victim to the influenza epidemic which swept through Europe and died at the age of 31. A benefit match for his family was played on Christmas Day.

In view of Rochdale's quite successful time in the Lancashire Section during the war, the side having acquitted themselves well against some of the best sides from Division One, there was considerable optimism that the club's progress would be rewarded with a place in the expanded Division Two of the Football League when the professional game was resumed.

However, on March 10th 1919, Stoke were admitted and Leicester City re-elected without a vote (confirming the decision of the 1915 AGM). The remaining four places (Glossop having resigned) went to Coventry City (35 votes), West Ham (32), Rotherham County (28) and South Shields (28). Port Vale just failed with 27 votes, while Rochdale and Southport Vulcan gained only 7 votes apiece and Chesterfield none. Rochdale officials had travelled with high hopes given the relative status of the various applicants; Rotherham had finished a long way last in the Midland Section of the league, winning only two games all season; South Shield had not even engaged in any competitive matches between 1915 and January 1919; and Coventry had finished the last two pre-war seasons bottom of the first division and then mid-table in the second division of the Southern League. During the war Rochdale had also consistently finished higher than Port Vale who, as the highest placed of the unsuccessful teams, did gain a place a few months later when Leeds City were expelled.

After this disappointment, the next three matches in the Principal tournament were all lost, though the visit of champions Everton did attract 7,000 spectators to Spotland. On March 22nd, though, Rochdale players gained international recognition for the first time, when their two Irishmen O'Connell and Halligan were selected for the Victory international against Scotland at Ibrox Park. Halligan scored in a 2-1 defeat and was selected again the following month for the return match in Belfast.

Five of the six Subsidiary Tournament matches - which doubled as the qualifying competition for the revived Lancashire Cup - were also lost, but Rochdale did end on a successful note by defeating Oldham 5-0 in a postponed Principal Tournament game to finish in 10th place.

No less than 63 players appeared in the first team, including, near the end of the season, Leeds City players Jack Peart, who would make a much more substantial contribution to Rochdale football in later years, and Tom Hampson, goalkeeper brother of the much earlier Rochdale player, Bill.

Subsequent to the failure to gain Football League status, Vince Hayes took up an appointment as manager of First Division Preston North End and the basis of a top class side which he had been building up begun to disappear. War hero Stan Davies - he had won the Military Medal and the Belgian Croix de Guerre - followed his manager to Preston and during the next ten years made hundreds of First and Second Division appearances as well as playing 10 times for

Stan Davies followed Vince Hayes to Preston in 1919 and became a well-known Welsh International.

Wales. Indeed, he played in a Victory International within six months of leaving Rochdale. A second future Welsh international, Harry Millership, moved on to Rotherham County (who had just secured a League place, of course), as did another full back Fred Baines, only recently arrived from Leeds. The Irish international Bill Halligan, scorer of 68 goals in 94 games for the club, followed the trail to Deepdale (indeed, five former Rochdale men played for North End the following term, as Broome and Causer were already there and pre-war player John Marshall joined them from Southport).

The other Irish international Pat O'Connell signed for Dumbarton, and joining him in Scotland was Archie Rawlings at Dundee. Rawlings subsequently joined Preston too and played for England in 1921. Ernest Hawksworth, Tweedale Rigg and Jack Barton (for a reputed £1200 fee) were all transferred to Blackburn Rovers of Division One, Hawksworth being their leading scorer the following term. Jimmy Nuttall, a signing from Bolton, departed (temporarily) to Manchester United, Goodwin rejoined his old club Leeds and Tom Kay went back to Bolton before signing for Stoke. Fred Heap joined his brother Bob at Bury. Albert Smith, who had played 304 league games in his nine seasons at Rochdale and scored a total of 94 goals was transferred to Grimsby Town. Even local lad Harry Moody, a former RAF officer who had taken over from Kay in goal, went to Southern League Mid-Rhondda, as did his brother William. The long-serving Jack Yarwood also departed for Wales and Merthyr Town, while Bob Thomas joined another Southern League club, Luton Town (where he played under his real name of Tomlinson).

Indeed, affairs were at such a low ebb that there was even a proposal to disband the club in May 1919, but this was defeated and the club carried on, rejoining the Central League.

Councillor Goldsmith and Messrs Kershaw, Hamer, Arnold Rigg, Wormwell, Tomlinson, Shotton, Coates, A.Wilson and T. C. Wilson formed the new board of directors. To rub salt in the soccer men's wounds, Rochdale Hornets won the revived Northern Union, Lancashire Division and their Lancashire Cup Final against Oldham attracted a crowd of 19,000.

1919-20:
The first official peacetime game, on August 30th 1919, was won by two goals to one against Stalybridge Celtic with an almost completely new team. Just 1,000 spectators were on hand to see centre half Cooper score the winner, and Cooper also scored in the next two games as well, a remarkable start for a defender. Victories proved somewhat scarce however, despite a continual turnover of players. A welcome return was made by old half backs Charlie Milne and Jim Tully, and indeed a number of other former players turned out once more.

Home victories were recorded against Blackpool Reserves - the eventual champions - and Everton Reserves, but sandwiched between these was a 7-1 trouncing by Bolton's second string, though there was an excuse in as much as outside right Sheldon had to play in goal. Revenge for this was subsequently exacted to the tune of 6-0 at Willbutts Lane, Walker, just back from the forces, netting four times against his favourite opponents. The other goals came from two of the other fairly regular performers, *"left wing speed merchant"* Lingard and John Meehan, brother of Tom.

With the FA Cup now revived, Rochdale were drawn to play Monks Hall in Warrington in the fourth qualifying round, but the game was switched to Spotland where the home side were narrow winners. In the next round a single goal was again sufficient to dispose of Stalybridge Celtic, though in the Lancashire Junior Cup - Rochdale having been excluded from the senior one - Skelmersdale reversed that scoreline. Back in the FA Cup, South Liverpool were beaten 2-1 and the draw for the next round paired Rochdale with the Arsenal.

Although drawn at home, Rochdale agreed to switch the match to Highbury - crowds had continued to be around 1,000 at Willbutts Lane - and they were suitably rewarded financially by an attendance of just over 26,500, the highest ever at a Rochdale match. Amazingly, on a quagmire of a pitch, Rochdale led 2-1 at half time, both goals coming from inside left Harry Mallalieu, who had made his debut only the previous week after playing in local Sunday Schools league football for All Saints, Oakenrod. *"A few staunch supporters made the trip South and when the 'Dale took the lead, it sounded as if there were thousands there"*. The Gunners, with a strong wind and torrential rain behind them, came back after the interval to run out eventual winners by 4 goals to 2. But the minnows had had their moment and were duly complimented in the contemporary press. *"Rochdale put up a plucky fight and deserve great praise. Harry Mallalieu, their short light-haired player, was equal to any forward on the field and on yesterday's form would be an acquisition for many first division clubs, but the palm of best man on the pitch must go to Rochdale centre half Milne, for a superb display"*.

In fact, this game was the summit of Mallalieu's career. Though he did later make a couple of appearances for Rochdale in the Football League, he became more famous as a stage comedian, sometimes appearing with the town's most famous daughter, Gracie Fields.

In the league, the side continued a depressing run of eight games without a win - they even threw away a 4-0 interval lead against Bury Reserves - before winning 3-0 against Nelson thanks to goals from newcomers Tom Hesmondhalgh, James Mills, another ex-Sunday Schools player, who had survived the Galipoli landings during the war, and Jimmy Nuttall, now back from his spell at Manchester United. Rochdale's centre half in this game was Bury amateur George Horridge. In his ten games for the club he had also figured at centre forward, inside right and even in goal. In later years he became Bury's chairman no less than four times between 1937 and 1971.

Home form improved thereafter with 12 points from seven games, but the first away league win was still proving elusive. It was finally achieved against bottom side Stockport County Reserves on Easter Monday. A second was recorded at Bradford City Reserves but paradoxically the last four home games were all lost. Rochdale also conceded six to Bury and Aston Villa's reserves, though in the latter they had the excuse of losing experienced custodian Bould Hurst through injury. The season ended with a well earned point away to Liverpool Reserves, but Rochdale still finished 19th of 22 with only 34 points from 42 games. They used 57 different players during the season including the ubiquitous 'A. Newman', one of several men - presumably 'AWOL' or actually on some other club's books - to appear under assumed names.

In April, Mills was transferred to Bolton Wanderers and at the end of the season top scorer Hesmondhalgh moved to Exeter City. The long-serving Milne and Tully joined Pontypridd. Tully, who had made 204 league appearances, second only to Albert Smith, was awarded a benefit match, played between the current Rochdale team and a Rochdale Past side which included leading Football League players John and Tom Page, Tommy Fleetwood, Tom Broome, Tommy Spink, Bill Halligan and Albert Smith. Another long-serving player, Jimmy Henderson, in his tenth season, made his 192nd and last appearance at the age of 42.

Off the field, former Aston Villa and Bolton Wanderers player and Chorley secretary-manager, Mr Thomas Carter Wilson, the proprietor of the Wellington Hotel in the town centre, was elected chairman of the board of directors in October 1919 in succession to Mr J. R. Tomlinson. The following month, larger-than-life Rochdalian millionaire financier Mr Jimmy White became the club's president. Unfortunately for the football club, though, he spent much more of his fortune on his first love of cricket, for instance enabling Rochdale Cricket Club to pay their famous 'pro' England Test player Cec Parkin £10 a week, more than the maximum wage for even a First Division footballer.

He then turned them into perhaps the finest club side in the country before he committed suicide in 1927 after one of his deals went spectacularly wrong. Former Bury and Rochdale player George Ross also joined the board and his brother David, a pre-war player with Manchester City, made a couple of appearances in the first team. About this same time, Rochdale had applied to replace Leeds City when the latter were ejected from the Football League for financial irregularities. Probably fortunately given the low standing of the current side, they were overlooked in favour of Port Vale. Indeed, a contemporary report considered that *"the attendance at the Rochdale matches is like the play served up by the team - very poor"*. (Port Vale's reserves, taking over their seniors' Central League fixtures, were able to beat Rochdale 5-1 near the end of the season).

By 1920 the idea of a Third Division of the Football League, championed by Rochdale's Herbert Hopkinson back in pre-war days, had finally taken root. However, it was the old Southern League clubs, who had then blackballed the idea, who were now adopted en masse as the new division, as there were doubts in the upper echelons of the game over the financial viability of many of the northern clubs. The senior non-League sides in the North, continued to press for the acceptance of the idea of a Northern Section of the Third Division to come into existence a year later, but a decision on this was postponed until the following February. The coming season would therefore be vital to aspiring Football League clubs in the Midlands and North.

Efforts were therefore put in hand to strengthen the playing staff at Rochdale, and former England international Bill Bradshaw, who had won two League Championships in seventeen years with Blackburn Rovers, was appointed the club's player-manager. Four former Blackburn teammates of the new manager were also signed, forwards Harry Dennison (Rovers' youngest ever player before the war), and Thomas Byrom, veteran centre half Joe Wilson, who had represented the Southern League while at Millwall, and former England amateur international goalkeeper, army Captain and holder of the Military Cross, James J. Crabtree.

Rochdale further acquired the services of Sid Hoade, another former England amateur international (who had trained as a lawyer), from Manchester City, Tom Bamford, Burnley's Cup Final full back of 1914, two pre-war Bury regulars in veteran Scottish 'keeper Tom Macdonald and winger Ted Connor, plus another winger, William Clifton of Preston North End. War-time players Baines and Yarwood and one time guest John Broster also returned to Rochdale from Rotherham, Merthyr and Q.P.R. respectively.

1920-21:
The 1920-21 season started unpromisingly with a home defeat by Nelson, but this was quickly avenged in the next match.

This pattern was repeated against the next six opponents, the biggest turnaround coming when a 3-0 success against Southport was followed by a 5-0 away defeat. Between these matches Bradshaw, the player-manager, was given a free transfer as he had been unable to attend training sessions. The chairman T.C.Wilson - a former player and manager, himself, of course - took over responsibility for the playing side of the club, too (and keeping things in the family, his son Tom made his first team debut shortly afterwards).

When the FA Cup came around, Rochdale were thus in mid-table and they were able to overcome Fleetwood and Tranmere, each by a single goal. In the third round they faced a trip to Coventry City of Division 2, where 18,000 fans saw the visitors hold out for a 1-1 draw. Lowe, who had scored five in his first four games for the club got the Rochdale goal. The replay at Willbutts Lane three days later attracted a crowd of 9,000 paying £320, the second best gate ever, and they saw a penalty by Byrom just before half time give the tie to Rochdale by two goals to one. The following round saw Rochdale visiting Plymouth for the first time and in front of an even bigger crowd, of 24,287, they held out until the last 10 minutes before Argyle won through.

In the league, Rochdale continued to alternate victory - the best 5-1 against eventual runners-up Crewe Alexandra - with defeat, the first draw not coming until December 27th against Oldham Reserves. After the game the Latics signed Byrom for the substantial fee of £1150 (the Football League record was still only £4600). The Manchester Senior Cup also saw Rochdale paired with Oldham and they fought out a 4-4 draw at Boundary Park. Jimmy Crabtree saved a penalty at a crucial moment and debutant Robert Sandiford scored twice, another relative newcomer Arthur Collinge, from Rochdale Tradesmen's F.C., netting the others.

Rochdale achieved a notable double over champions-to-be Manchester United Reserves, Harry Dennison netting all the goals in 2-1 and 3-1 victories. He followed this with another hat-trick to see off Oldham 4-3 in the cup replay, and yet another against Liverpool Reserves soon afterwards.

Not surprisingly, he finished easily the top goalscorer with 23. In the semi-final of the Manchester Cup, the inside trio of Sandiford, Dennison and Collinge were all on target in a replay against Ashton National, but the final was something of a disappointment as Manchester United ran out comfortably 2-0 winners.

The league season ended with a couple of defeats by Port Vale Reserves, but nonetheless Rochdale ended in 10th place with 19 wins set against 18 defeats. In the close season Joe Wilson became player-coach at Fleetwood and Baines moved to Accrington Stanley. Lowe and Connor were also released but the remainder of the first team regulars were retained.

~ CHAPTER 2 ~

The most important event for Rochdale, and others, took place at the Football League meeting on March 16th, when the First and Second Division clubs agreed to the proposed further expansion of the League. They also unanimously accepted the Management Committee's recommendation that 14 clubs - Accrington Stanley, Ashington, Barrow, Chesterfield, Crewe Alexandra, Darlington, Durham City, Hartlepools United, Lincoln City, Nelson, Rochdale, Tranmere Rovers, Walsall and Wrexham - should be admitted to the new Division 3 (Northern Section) without a vote. (Wigan Borough, Halifax Town, Southport and Stalybridge Celtic also made it via the subsequent ballot). Rochdale could therefore look forward, at last, to playing in the Football League. Indeed, their representative at the meeting may have celebrated too well, as he was one of those who turned up late at a meeting the following day to sort out the fixture list and Rochdale began Football League life by being fined on the spot!

At the club's AGM in June 1921, the new chairman Mr J. G. Ramsbottom and secretary Mr J. Lomax were able to announce that the club was in the black to the tune of £726 19s 6d, and in view of their elevation to Football League status the club's share capital was raised from £2000 to £5000. T.C. Wilson, as a former professional player, was disbarred by the then League rules from serving on the board of directors, so responsibility for team affairs reverted to a selection committee, assisted by new trainer (and groundsman) George Vickers, the former Preston North End player.

On August 1st Rochdale's 24 professionals and 26 amateurs, 15 of whom had played the previous season, reported back for training. New men included Tommy Mort, a full back from Altrincham, and Peter Farrer, an Everton reserve half back. Two old faces returning were Jim Tully and Jack Barton, who signed from Pontypridd, the previous season's Welsh Cup finalists, along with their team-mates Reg Owens and Eugene Carney.

On August 27th, skipper Jimmy Nuttall led out his side for their first match in Division Three (North). A crowd of around 7000 saw the black and white stripes gain a 6-3 home win over Accrington Stanley, scoring five times in the last 20 minutes after going in a goal down at the interval.

The team for this historic encounter was Crabtree; Nuttall, Shehan; Hill, Farrer, Yarwood; Hoad, Sandiford, Dennison, Owens and Carney. Owens claimed a hat-trick on his debut (though the first may have been an own goal), while Dennison netted twice and Carney converted the first penalty ever awarded in the Third North after he had been fouled. Remarkably, this was the only game that local lad Shehan ever played in the first team.

In the return game the following Saturday, Stanley won by four goals to nil, unfortunately setting the pattern for much of the season. Rochdale beat Tranmere Rovers 2-1, but then went down 7-0 at Prenton Park. Against Stockport, Nuttall became the first Rochdale player to be sent off in the Football League, and in the return game right half Hugh Burns followed his captain's example and made history by being sent off on his League debut (there was no further instance of this until 1967).

One solitary win, 2-1 against Stalybridge Celtic, interrupted a bleak run of eight defeats including an FA Cup exit at the hands of Nelson. Numerous new players were tried out, most notably half back Fred Taylor who had won a cup winners medal with Chelsea, as well as Football League representative honours, in a long career starting with Gainsborough Trinity back in 1904. Other new men included trialist Tom Bennett, a record goalscorer with Liverpool in wartime soccer but who succumbed to consumption in 1923, and Wilson McGhee, the 23rd player used in just six games and the only doctor to play League football for Rochdale (another amateur on Rochdale's books at the time was one Captain Wyatt, a cavalry officer with the Bengal Lancers!).

Two more newcomers, George Daniels from Preston North End, and former Burnley reserve Hugh Cameron, were scorers in a remarkable game - Cameron's debut in fact - at Willbutts Lane on Christmas Eve. Only a goal to nil at half time, the final score of Rochdale 7 Walsall 0 remains one of the club's largest ever Football League victories. Owens again netted a hat-trick, while Dennison converted two penalties. This proved to be but a brief taste of success, however, as six of the next seven games were lost, as was the main stand roof, blown down in a gale on December 30th. The following day defeat at Hartlepool dropped Rochdale to bottom place in the table.

A dramatic game on February 11th gave Rochdale their first away League victory, thanks to an own goal, but at the cost of losing Owens with a broken leg in the last minute in an incident which lead to Lincoln's Fenwick being sent off. In their next match a disastrous first half saw Rochdale 6-0 down to Ashington, but a second half fight back salvaged some pride and made the final score 7-3. In the following six games not one goal was conceded in a first half!

Subsequently the side managed some better results, including three successive wins which took Rochdale off the foot of the table. This run coincided with the move of Jack Hill, a local player from John Bright's mill team, from half back to the forward line, where he scored six goals in four games. However, the last four games of the season were all lost, so Rochdale finished in 20th and last place, three points behind Tranmere and Halifax. The average home attendance during this first Football League season was 5200 but, confirming the doubts expressed the previous year, gate receipts at Northern Section clubs were only half that of their Southern Section counterparts.

Just before the season ended left back Tommy Mort was transferred to First Division giants Aston Villa for the sizeable fee of £1000 (1922 was the year of the first ever £5000 transfer). In a 13 year career at Villa Park he became the first Football League player for Rochdale to go on to win a full England cap, appearing three times for the national side between 1924 and 1926. Hoade had earlier moved on to Nelson where he won a Third North championship medal in 1923, and in the close season top scorer Dennison was transferred to Wigan Borough. Indeed, only six players were retained.

Rochdale successfully applied for re-election at the Football League AGM, gaining 31 votes compared to the nine of the closest aspirants, Doncaster Rovers. T. C. Wilson, now officially appointed manager, was therefore able to set about the task of signing players for a renewed attack on the Third North. The most important acquisition was without doubt David Parkes, a craggy experienced centre half from The Wednesday, who became club captain. Remarkably, six of the other new men had at one time played for Oldham Athletic. These were the full back pairing of veteran Bill Bradbury and upcoming Stan Charlton, half back Dick Jones and forwards Vince Foweather, Arthur Gee and the vastly experienced former Manchester United and England outside left George Wall. Wall had joined his first Football League club, Barnsley, back in 1902, five years before Rochdale A.F.C. was even formed!

1922-23:
Rochdale started 1922-23 brightly with away wins at Crewe in the League and Accrington in the Lancashire Cup. The centre half in the latter was old favourite Charlie Milne, back from Tranmere for his fifth spell at Willbutts Lane. George Guy from Bolton Wanderers, scored in each of these games and again in a 1-1 draw in the return match with Crewe. A further away victory at Lincoln helped to attract the first 10,000 gate to Willbutts Lane for the return which ended one-all.

Bill Bradbury..... Arthur Gee
Stan Charlton... George Wall

The side went on to trounce Wrexham 5-0 - Guy becoming the first Rochdale player to score four times in a Football League game - to go second in the table before suffering their first reverse of the season at Wrexham. A two-all draw with Darlington was a personal success for Davie Parkes as the Rochdale skipper, no doubt fortified by his regular pre-match training - a couple of pints in the Church Inn next to the ground - scored both goals, a feat no Rochdale centre half was to emulate until 1986 (the goal scoring, that is!).

An even more amazing goalscoring effort occurred in the 2-0 win at Hartlepools when regular custodian Jimmy Crabtree turned out at inside left and scored both goals.

Hartlepools must have been confused the following week when he was back in goal, leaving the goalscoring to former Fleetwood hot-shot William Sandham and Joe Walters, the ex-Aston Villa and Oldham veteran, who got two each.

In the FA Cup, Rochdale again made a rapid exit at the hands of Nelson, but gained revenge with a League victory over the leaders and eventual champions at Seedhill. On December 4th, Rochdale moved to the head of the table for the first time, ironically after a goalless draw at home to bottom club Tranmere Rovers. Though soon displaced, victories home and away against Southport, with Redditch Town's Billy Prouse (or to give him his full moniker, William Horatio Redvers Prouse) scoring twice on his debut, kept Rochdale in touch after only two defeats in 16 games. Despite some more variable results, a victory over Barrow saw Rochdale regain second place in mid January, but the reverse fixture was lost 4-1 and precipitated a disastrous run of 10 games which yielded only two points.

Early in March, Rochdale acquired the services of Norwich City's well travelled centre forward Jack Peart as player-manager. Rochdale were the 33 year old Peart's eleventh senior club, but even he could not halt a run of seven games without a single goal, a record not superseded until 1980. Finally, goals by Prouse and Hill against Stalybridge Celtic ended the drought, and Peart himself scored in victories over Durham City and Wigan Borough. The season ended, though, with an ignominious 6-0 defeat by the latter at Springfield Park.

Rochdale finished in 12th place. Stalybridge, who were one place higher, became the Third Division North's first casualty when they resigned due to financial difficulties, and an extension to the league saw both Doncaster Rovers and New Brighton voted in. Left back Stan Charlton had the honour of being Rochdale's first everpresent in the Football League, but was transferred to Exeter during the summer.

In a long career, Charlton went on to represent the FA on tour to Australia and the Professionals against the Amateurs in the Charity Shield. Near the end of the season, George Wall had played his 500th English and Scottish League match, only the seventh player to reach this milestone. His next stops were in the less exalted surroundings of the Ashton National Gas Company and Manchester Ship Canal F.C. teams.

Despite the successes earlier in the season, only four players were retained besides Peart; Harry Moody, who had returned from Grimsby to displace Crabtree as first choice goalkeeper, skipper David Parkes, and forwards Billy Prouse and Joe Campbell. Among those leaving was Jim Tully who had first appeared for Rochdale in 1912 and had accumulated a grand total of 283 senior games for the club. Nuttall was also released, but then re-signed at the start of the following term. Crabtree subsequently moved to Accrington Stanley, though he did appear at Spotland again in later years, when he was a Football League linesman. The veteran Joe Walters joined Crewe Alexandra, but the following winter - having survived service with the Royal Flying Corps during the Great War - tragically caught pneumonia and died.

Rochdale had a new chairman for the 1923-24 campaign, Mr George L. Foulds re-placing Mr Rams-bottom, who resigned due to business pressure. He had a somewhat alarming start, as in August Rochdale were expelled from the Football Association because a former player was still owed some wages. When it was explained to the Lancashire FA that the money had been sent, but the player had not received it due to being on holiday, the club were reinstated.

Of necessity, there were numerous new faces by the time the season started. Remarkably three of them, Bert Pearson from Llanelly, Billy Tompkinson from Aberdare and Frank Crowe, most recently of Chesterfield, had all represented the Welsh League.

Bert Pearson... Vince Foweather
Billy Tomkinson.... Frank Crowe

Three others, William Brown (from Llanelly), Jimmy Bissett from Southend and Bobby Willis had all played for Dundee. Willis came from quite a footballing family; his father David had played for Newcastle while his brother-in-law was Alex James, the future Arsenal legend. Arthur McGarry from Reading (and earlier of the splendidly named Colonel Blizzard's XI), Bert Whitehurst from Stoke and Joe Clarke of Southampton completed the major signings. Rochdale supporters also welcomed back former favourite Albert Smith, considered to have been the most popular of all early Rochdale players. Smith had, in fact, had a trial at Spotland the previous season, but a dispute with Grimsby had prevented him signing.

1923-24:

Of the other new men, only Pearson, who had been a regular for Liverpool immediately after the war, was by any means a well known figure, but the astuteness of Jack Peart's transfer dealings would soon become apparent. As a team, they took a little time to settle, a winning start against Durham being followed by a 3-0 defeat at Wigan which proved to be the worst result of the season. This game was watched by a 15,000 crowd, the largest yet to see Rochdale in the League. If the sides finished the goalless draw at Holiday Park, Durham, more than usually tired, it would not be surprising, as they had to forego the half time break so that Rochdale could catch their train home!

Rochdale also sustained a 4-2 defeat at Bradford, but home form was excellent with five successive victories without a goal conceded. Indeed it was not until December 15th that a visiting team managed to pass the home custodian Harry Moody, and even then it took a penalty award for Barrow to do so. But now, with the defence in miserly mood, Rochdale became equally hard to beat away from Spotland. Certainly no chances were taken early on in games for, amazingly, the Barrow penalty was the only goal conceded in the first half of 22 successive League matches. Rochdale did slip up in the FA Cup, though, losing by the only goal at Accrington after defeating amateurs Skelmersdale 4-0 thanks to a hat-trick on his debut by local boy Jack Hall.

By now in second spot, Dale beat Barrow away and did the double over both Lincoln and Crewe, thus taking their run to seven straight wins. Southport became only the second side to take a point from Willbutts Lane; two first half goals by Whitehurst looked to have put the home side in command, but in the end it was only Moody's penalty save, his second in successive home games, that preserved the long unbeaten run.

The following week, in front of just 4000 spectators, Billy Prouse's goal against Hartlepools took this run to 19 games and enabled Rochdale to take over from Wolverhampton Wanderers at the top of the table.

A penalty by full back Bissett was enough to see off Ashington, but the return at Portland Park was lost 1-0 allowing Wolves to retake the lead. Two further single goal victories over Walsall put Rochdale ahead in the race once more, but a midweek win by the Wolves gave them the advantage when the two sides met at Willbutts Lane on February 16th. A crowd of 16,161 assembled, far higher than any previous attendance at Spotland and paying record receipts of £796 16s 5d. Wolves had been beaten only twice all season, but they were glad to escape with a nil-nil draw after top scorer Prouse had the misfortune to miss two, much debated, open goals. New Brighton were not so lucky, losing their goalkeeper and going down 6-2. Whitehurst netted a hat-trick and Rochdale went top again but only 3000 spectators saw them do it. A mainly reserve side was thrashed 8-1 by Bury in the Manchester Senior Cup before the return at Rake Lane which was drawn one-all, Jack Peart scoring what turned out to be the last goal of his long career.

Defeat at Grimsby set Rochdale back in their race with Wolves - the chasing clubs were by now well adrift - but they fought back to win the return 4-2. Another big crowd, over 12,000, saw them face Wolves at Molineux, Parkes and his men holding out for another goalless draw. Halifax were beaten twice, then at Tranmere the match was abandoned due to bad light with the score standing at two-all. Meanwhile, Wolves had surprisingly been beaten at Walsall, and when they could only draw 1-1 at Lincoln while Rochdale were winning at Hartlepool, Rochdale again took over the leadership with 55 points to Wolves 54, though the latter had a game in hand.

Rochdale disappointingly dropped a home point in a goalless draw with Darlington to give Wolves the edge again, but single goal victories over Tranmere and Accrington pulled them back neck and neck with two games to play. The replayed game at Tranmere on the following Monday proved Rochdale's downfall however. Without right half Willis and regular goalie Moody, who had kept 28 clean sheets during the season, they went down 2-1. Wolverhampton's win a couple of days later effectively settled the issue, and although Rochdale made a valiant effort to salvage the situation with a 4-1 win over Accrington Stanley, Wolves gained the point they needed from a goalless draw at Tranmere.

Rochdale's tally of 62 points, which remains their highest ever (counting two points for a win), saw them eight points clear of Chesterfield in third place. They were unbeaten at home, dropping only four points and conceding just eight goals, with only five defeats in all, all club records which still stand. The defence, for the most part comprising Moody in goal and the two Scots Bissett and Brown at full back, was the best in the Division, and the 26 goals conceded set up a divisional record. Despite all this the average home attendance was still only 6,142.

Jack Peart, though still only 34 and the scorer of seven goals in 15 games, decided to retire at the end of the season to concentrate on the management. The decision may also have been influenced by the cumulative effects of a career which had earned him the tag of *"the most injured man in football"*. Former skipper Jimmy Nuttall also retired after a benefit game against his brother Harry's team, the FA Cup holders Bolton Wanderers, which raised £160. In the close season Jimmy Bissett was transferred to Middlesbrough and Billy Prouse was sold to Fulham for £1,200.

Elsewhere ex-Rochdale full back Tommy Mort played in the Aston Villa side beaten by Newcastle United in the FA Cup Final. Remarkably, his opposite number, at 41 years of age the oldest man to appear in a final, was Bill Hampson, who had turned out for Rochdale way back in 1908. This was the third season in a row in which former Rochdale players had appeared in the final, following Archie Rawlings for Preston in 1922 and George Kay for West Ham in the first Wembley final. It was, though, the last such occasion for 50 years.

Manager Peart made several signings before the start of 1924-25 to try to continue the progress of his first full season in charge. The best known was the former Burnley and Blackburn wing half, Levy Thorpe noted for his *"battling durability"*. Others included full backs Fred Mason from Cardiff City and 'Dai' Hopkins from Ebbw Vale (who played for a Welsh XI in Billy Meredith's testimonial) and, unusually, three forwards from London clubs, Harry Anstiss (Watford), Ted Roseboom (Clapton Orient) and Bobby Hughes (Brentford). Though considered a veteran, Hughes, a renowned goalscoring outside left, was still as tricky a winger as when he had represented the Southern League in his Northampton days before the Great War.

Despite early set backs away from home, when the side went down 5-0 at New Brighton and had Willis sent off in a goalless draw at Bradford, the tremendous home form of the previous season was kept up. A crowd of 11,000 saw Rochdale come from behind to defeat Wigan 3-2, thanks to two goals by Anstiss. He scored twice more to beat eventual runaway champions Darlington, whilst Wrexham, Chesterfield and Tranmere also went down at Willbutts Lane. When the away form was boosted by wins at Rotherham, Walsall and Lincoln, Rochdale climbed to second place in the table with 20 points and only one defeat in 13 games.

Levy Thorpe served several top Lancashire clubs either side of the Great War.

However, a quirk of the fixture list saw them with a run of seven consecutive away games and unsurprisingly they were unable to maintain their challenge. They did manage a 1-0 win at Halifax, thanks to an Alex Christie penalty, to record their first FA Cup victory over League opposition since their own election. In the next round they were eliminated by Norwich, Christie's former club. Christie, incidentally, had earlier become the first half back to score on his Football League debut for Rochdale.

When they did get back to Spotland, the side resumed their winning run with a 5-0 thrashing of Crewe on Christmas Day, and when they beat Durham 3-0 it gave them their tenth consecutive home win. The following week David Parkes became the first Rochdale player to make 100 Football League appearances, but team-mate Billy Tompkinson was sent off and Darlington won 2-0, effectively ending Rochdale's chance of catching the leaders. A minor highlight was a 10-0 win over Manchester University in the Manchester Cup, Rochdale's highest score in a first team game since 1909. Anstiss, Pearson and reserve centre forward Billy Oxley all netted hat-tricks. Anstiss hit 23 League and four cup goals during the season to set a new record for Rochdale as a Football League club.

The long unbeaten run at the Willbutts Ground finally ended after 34 games when lowly Accrington Stanley, who had picked up only five away points all season, won by the only goal with their debutant goalie playing a blinder. The run had lasted a month short of two years. Doncaster Rovers suffered the backlash a few days later, Rochdale winning by five goals to two, but only 1000 spectators turned up to see the game which was played on a Tuesday afternoon.

The pattern of good home results but poor away form was continued to the end of the season, with five consecutive home wins - the best by five goals against Barrow when Whitehurst netted a hat-trick - but seven successive away defeats. At Tranmere all three of the home side's goals were credited to an up an coming 17 year old by the name of Dixie Dean, though in later years Dean always described Davie Parkes as one of his toughest opponents. Parkes' most legendary battles, though, were with the equally robust Halifax centre forward Ernie Dixon. When Parkes missed the game against New Brighton in April it ended a run of 80 consecutive League matches for the rugged centre half, said by one contemporary scribe to be *"stronger than most horses"*.

Rochdale ended in a comfortable 6th position on 49 points, with 17 home wins to their credit. Roseboom was transferred to Chesterfield at the end of the season and Oxley, scorer of nine goals in only 13 games, moved to First Division Manchester City. The veteran campaigner Albert Smith, latterly the club's trainer, ended his association with Rochdale after a record 370 games and 95 goals. One of these records lasted for nearly 50 years but the other was to be surpassed in sensational style after only two seasons.

1925-26:

For the 1925-26 season, Rochdale had a new trainer and assistant trainer in former players Jimmy Henderson and Jack Hill respectively. Summer training was rather spectacularly interrupted one day when a Bristol Fighter from RAF Sealand crashed in a field at Greave and Henderson and Bobby Willis ran to rescue the pilot from the wreckage. Additions to the playing staff included William Fergusson from Reading, Billy Bertram from Durham City, John Hillhouse from non-League Workington and Nottingham Forest winger Harry Martin. The 33 year old England 'internationalist' Martin had come to prominence in the 1913 Sunderland side that won the League Championship and reached the FA Cup Final.

The most important change, however, was in the rule book, with the introduction of the new offside law which required only two defenders between a player and the opponents' goal, rather than three as previously. Rochdale quickly capitalised on this new found freedom that forwards were to enjoy, scoring six times without reply against Hartlepools, new signing Fergusson helping himself to two of them. Following three drawn games, the Rochdale attack again came into its own in a 5-3 win at Tranmere.

This was the first of four consecutive victories which set the side up for a *"grand encounter"* with League leaders Bradford on October 3rd. The newly finished covered stand at the Pearl Street end was filled to overflowing and a new record crowd of 16,295 saw goals by Pearson and Tompkinson give the home side victory and top place in the League.

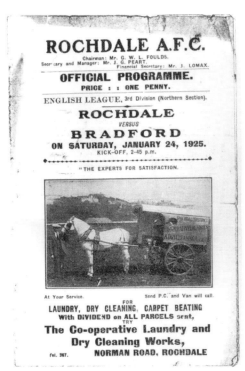

An early programme example from the Dale, 1924/25 season.

Billy Bertram spent six seasons with Rochdale (1925-1931)

The following week the roles were reversed as a record crowd at Blundell Park saw Grimsby displace Rochdale at the top. Despite a lapse at home to Ashington, three successive victories briefly regained the lead for Rochdale in what was already becoming a three horse race, but a surprising reverse at home to struggling Wrexham, allowed Bradford to move into a substantial lead.

A possible embarrassment in the FA Cup was forestalled when the home game against West Stanley was abandoned with the score 1-1. The West Stanley players refused to leave the pitch and their supporters demanded their money back, only being dispersed when police reinforcements arrived. Rochdale won the re-run 4-0 and, after becoming the first visiting side to win in the League at Lincoln, gained a one-all draw at Chilton Colliery in the next round. In the replay the miners from County Durham, semi-finalists in the FA Amateur Cup in each of the two previous seasons, were under almost constant pressure and had their centre half sent off, but broke away to grab the winning goal and provide one of the shocks the Cup is famous for.

The Christmas and New Year period, as so often, turned up some vital results. Despite beating Durham City 5-0 at home on Boxing Day, Rochdale found themselves down in third place, but must have been pleased enough to see Grimsby complete the double over Bradford. Rochdale also won at Durham and soon strung together three more home wins before travelling to Walsall and gaining a 5-1 victory thanks to two goals from Fergusson and one each from Whitehurst, Hughes and Martin. Fergusson had, at this point, scored in 12 in his last 14 league matches.

A disastrous first half, conceding four goals to fourth placed Chesterfield, saw another two vital home points lost before the crucial match at Bradford. Rochdale also lost the experienced Bertram, who was replaced by Cecil Halkyard, playing only his second League game. A massive crowd of 26,101, by far a record for a game in the Third Division (North), saw Park Avenue win 3-1 to go seven points clear at the top.

With Anstiss recalled to replace top scorer Fergusson, Rochdale bounced back to beat rivals Grimsby 5-2 at Spotland. Two further victories followed, but the chance of further progress was lost with a 3-2 defeat at Crewe, despite leading at half-time. However, with experienced half back Ernie Braidwood signed from Nelson to aid the cause, New Brighton and Braidwood's erstwhile teammates were both dispatched at Spotland to hoist Rochdale back into the fight, level with Grimsby and two points behind Bradford.

Another away defeat, 1-0, at the hands of lowly Wrexham, let things slip somewhat, but three victories over the Easter weekend, Bertram netting a hat-trick against Doncaster, gave Rochdale a one point lead at the top, though Bradford regained the lead the following day. In the next match, at Southport, Rochdale overran the Sandgrounders with both Anstiss and Whitehurst scoring hat-tricks and Bertram netting the other in a record 7-1 away win. Not to be outdone, Moody saved a penalty as he had in the other big away win at Walsall.

With just three games to go, Rochdale were thus still well in the running, but were then disastrously beaten by Lincoln. Meanwhile Grimsby cashed in on a game in hand, and despite a 3-1 win at Nelson, Rochdale's chance had gone when Grimsby gained a draw at Crewe in their penultimate game. Only 2000 spectators turned up at the Willbutts Ground to see the home side round off the season with a 4-1 win over Coventry. Bradford had also lost their grip with some costly lapses late in the season, and though they won 6-1 on the final day, a single goal victory was enough to give Grimsby the championship with 61 points to Bradford's 60 and Rochdale's 59. (Incidentally, the season's end, on May 1st, saved any agonising on the part of the Players' Union over whether to join the General Strike which began the following week).

Despite ultimately missing out on the real prize, Rochdale did set up a new goalscoring record for their division with 104 goals and cemented their position among the leading lights of the Northern Section. Their total of 49 away goals was surpassed only twice in the entire history of the Third North. Their 27 wins and 11 away wins were divisional records and still stand as the club records. In the final analysis though, it was the four home defeats that tipped the scales against them, Grimsby by contrast having dropped just one point in 21 home games.

At the end of the season, former regulars Willis and Pearson moved on to Halifax and Stockport, respectively, and despite his remarkable tally of 19 goals in 21 games, Fergusson was allowed to join Rotherham. In July Harry Anstiss, scorer of 39 goals in 72 games for Rochdale, was transferred to Sheffield Wednesday, and in due course his wanderings took him to nine Football League clubs, for whom he scored well over 100 goals.

1926-27:

The only major signings for the 1926-27 season were Southampton goalkeeper Len Hill, who had represented the Football League and the FA while at Q.P.R., and the Darlington inside forward Bill Hooper, nephew of the former Manchester United stalwart Charlie Roberts. Otherwise Peart was happy to rely on the players who had done so well the previous season.

Dale make it on a Magazine front cover!

The season kicked off with a 1-0 win at Accrington, followed by a home win over Crewe, but then Durham City became what transpired to be the only visiting side to triumph at Willbutts Lane. Rochdale's goal in the 3-1 defeat was scored by debutant centre forward Alex Ross from Dundee, but he was injured scoring the goal and, though soldiering on to the end of the match, had to have a cartilage operation and never played in the first team again. A long running problem at full back saw skipper Parkes deputise at left back in the next game, but Rochdale were demolished 4-0 by Crewe and the experiment was not repeated. Rochdale got back on track with a single goal victory at Tranmere and also won away at Barrow.

An important team change saw Brown switch to right back to accommodate former Lincoln City left back Fred "Yaffer" Ward, another in the Davie Parkes mould, his *"hefty kicking not always tempered with discretion"*. Two home wins took Rochdale into the top three but were followed by two defeats, at Burnley in the Lancashire Cup when Parkes was sent off, and at Stockport in the League, Rochdale failing to score in either. Manager Peart thus decided to make the tactical switch of moving Bert Whitehurst from inside left to lead the attack; up to this point Whitehurst had managed only three goals in 10 games.

The move immediately paid dividends, as Whitehurst scored in a 3-0 home win over Hartlepools and then got all the Rochdale goals in a 2-2 draw at Ashington and a 1-1 home draw with New Brighton. He scored again in a 3-0 win at Wigan and smashed in a hat-trick as Doncaster Rovers were annihilated 7-2. Rochdale were already 5-0 up at half time and Harry Martin also joined in the fun to become the first wingman to notch a Football League hat-trick for Rochdale. Rochdale's next trip was to Stoke, but Whitehurst's run came to a temporary halt against his former club, and the League leaders went six points clear of Rochdale with a 3-1 win. Rochdale bounced back to beat Rotherham but went out of the FA Cup by the odd goal in seven at Accrington. Another thriller the following week saw the home side fight back to a four-all draw with Walsall, and a further draw, at Rotherham, took Rochdale into second place in the table.

On December 18th came one of the club's most famous occasions, when they recorded their best ever Football League victory. Three up at half time, they went on to trounce Chesterfield - only one point behind them in the League - 8-1. Bert Whitehurst scored an individual record five goals and he was ably assisted by local amateur Bob Schofield who scored twice on his League debut. Harry Martin netted the other one. On Christmas Day, Rochdale ran in another seven against Lincoln's debutant goalkeeper, the season's best crowd of just over 10,000 being entertained by another Whitehurst hat-trick, two more goals from Schofield and a couple from Hughes, the Imps replying with three of their own. Rochdale also won the return game 3-2 on Boxing Day, Whitehurst taking his tally to 10 in three games. He had failed to score in only one of 13 games since he took over at centre forward and accumulated 23 goals in the process. Rochdale thus entered the New Year only three points adrift of Stoke.

Unfortunately, Rochdale were without winger Harry Martin for the next game (and indeed the rest of the season, with a knee injury), and fellow challengers Halifax Town halted Rochdale's run with a 1-0 win at the Shay. Bradford then inflicted Rochdale's worst defeat of the season by five goals to one.

Even struggling Accrington proved troublesome, before a penalty by Parkes settled the issue, but this win enabled Rochdale to recover some ground and a victory at Durham, thanks to another Whitehurst treble, took them back into second spot.

Rochdale continued to pile up the home wins (and goals), even when they fielded a totally reserve line-up in the Manchester Cup and beat Mossley 5-0. The strength of the Rochdale first team at this time is reflected in the scorers in this match. Reuben Butler was a well travelled centre forward, now 36 years old, for whom Oldham had once paid £1,850, while Jack Hall had played only three League games since his remarkable debut hat-trick three seasons earlier (he eventually gained a regular place as a half back in 1928), and Dick Duckworth was never able to break into the League side at all, though he went on to make nearly 300 Football League appearances with other clubs.

Eleven thousand fans saw Rochdale stretch their unbeaten run to six games by beating Stockport at Willbutts Lane, but without John Hillhouse, who had just been transferred to Notts County for an undisclosed fee, they went down 3-2 at Hartlepool. They immediately countered with a 5-0 win over Ashington, Whitehurst inevitably scoring three, and beat New Brighton and Wigan before defeat at Doncaster set them back again and cost 'keeper Hill his place in the side.

It was vital that Rochdale beat leaders Stoke City when they visited Willbutts Lane on April 2nd. The thirteen thousand supporters did not have long to wait before scorer-in-chief Bert Whitehurst put the home side ahead and Billy Bertram added a second. In the second half Bobby Hughes completed the rout, netting twice, and Harry Moody celebrating his recall with a clean sheet. Hughes finished the season with 16 goals, still (jointly) a record for a Rochdale winger. With Brown missing for the first time after a run of 85 games, Rochdale lost at Nelson but three home wins over the Easter period gave them an outside chance of the promotion spot, three points behind Stoke with three to play. A heavy defeat at Walsall ended that hope, but Rochdale gained two more victories to clinch second place. In the last game, at Chesterfield, Whitehurst netted twice more to give him a total of 44 League goals. He thus equalled Cookson's Northern Section record set the previous year, which had also been a Football League record at the time; George Camsell had just smashed that with 59 goals for Second Division champions Middlesbrough, though.

Rochdale were five points adrift of the champions, with 58, one fewer than the previous season, but they beat their own Division Three (North) record with 105 goals, the highest anywhere in the League that year. At home they scored in every game, totalling 72 goals (against 22) and won 18 times out of 21, including the last 12 in a row.

Home gates rose to an average of 7,095, the club's best ever. At the end of the season Hill joined Lincoln and Hooper, who had not hit his Darlington form, was released, whilst long-serving secretary Mr Lomax was succeeded by Mr M. Menzies.

The only major signings for the 1927-28 season were Halifax Town forward Jack Barber and 38 year old Joe Clennell, who had won League championship medals with both Blackburn and Everton before the Great War, as well as Football League representative honours. Both were prospective answers to the troublesome inside left spot. Otherwise, in the interests of strict economy, it was *intended to sign, in the early part of the season, men on monthly contracts".*

Joe Clennell

1927-28:
It was Barber who had the first opportunity - indeed he was the only new face in the side on the opening day - and scored in a 3-1 win at Barrow. Home victories over Stockport and Nelson made Rochdale the early pace-setters and a fourth successive win, 2-1 at Wigan, consolidated their first place. Although beaten at Rotherham, Rochdale put five past Southport, both Bertram and Whitehurst taking their tallies to five goals in six games. The side also went down at Durham but came back well with wins against Wrexham, their 16th in a row at Willbutts Lane, and at Chesterfield. The long unbeaten home run of 23 games fell decisively to Lincoln who won 3-0; Rochdale's failure to score for the first time in 33 League and cup games coincided with the end of Whitehurst's run of 80 consecutive Football League and FA Cup games in which he had scored 71 times. Rochdale also lost at New Brighton, leading to the long-serving Brown being left out of the side, but they made no mistake against amateurs Crook Town in the FA Cup, winning 8-2. Whitehurst hammered four goals and Joe Clennell revived memories of his famed dribbling and shooting with a hat-trick. (Barber, incidentally, was now at left half).

Although knocked out in the next round at Darlington, Rochdale scored four against both Crewe and Darlington at home in the League, to stay in fifth place. However, missing full back Ward, they suffered a disastrous Christmas, going down 5-2 at Doncaster and 4-1 at Bradford in front of a 22,000 crowd. With new signing John Stephenson from Durham City at right back, they beat Barrow on New Years Eve, but this proved a brief respite.

Stalwart custodian Harry Moody suffered a serious head injury, diving at a forward's feet, in the game at Stockport, which County went on to win 5-1. He subsequently spent three weeks in hospital and though he made a good recovery, he never played again.

His replacements fared just as badly; leaders Bradford won 4-0 at Willbutts Lane, bottom club Nelson piled in six, and in total four different goalkeepers conceded 24 goals in 5 games. Ironically, Wattie Shirlaw who had been signed from Bradford City as Moody's understudy had just returned to Valley Parade. The following year he was an everpresent when the Bantams won the Division 3 North championship. Finally, Jackie Mittell from Penrhiwceiber kept a clean sheet against Wigan Borough and earned himself the goalkeeper's jersey for the remainder of the season. Mittell had actually travelled through the night from South Wales to Ashington in Northumberland to play in the previous game, but arrived to find that the Dale had obtained another, local, goalie.

By now, Rochdale were down in mid-table and although suffering a run of away defeats, they did manage to regain their form at Spotland, winning four games in a row. Despite the defensive problems and the departure of Clennell to Ebbw Vale as player-manager, Whitehurst had continued to score prolifically, his two goals in the debacle at Nelson taking him past his century in League games for Rochdale. Against Chesterfield, clearly his favourite opponents, he almost repeated the previous season's devastation, scoring four times, and his goal at Lincoln was his 84th in his last 80 games.

When his goals did dry up temporarily, the side failed to score at all. Rather remarkably, considering a run of 11 consecutive away defeats, the game at Accrington was the first away match in which they had failed to score for well over a year. Amateur Allan Murray claimed his own small spot in club history when, in only his fifth game, he became the first Rochdale full back to score a Football League goal from open play. A depressing run without a victory extended to 12 games before a brace from Whitehurst - giving him 38 for the season - and one from Bertram sufficed to beat Accrington. Just 1768 spectators saw a victory over Doncaster on the final day of the season which lifted Rochdale back to 13th in the table.

The end of the 27-28 season, a bitter disappointment after the early hopes of continued success, was in many ways the end of an era. Besides the enforced retirement of Harry Moody, the last link with Rochdale's pre-League days, club captain and pivot David Parkes departed after 209 league games, a club record which he held for many years. The two of them were awarded a benefit by the club. Fred Ward also retired, though he soon reappeared at his old stamping ground of Lincoln.

Alex Christie, a regular for four seasons, and William Brown, 178 games in five seasons, were released along with long-serving reserves Hopkins and Halkyard and relative newcomer Stephenson, while wingers Billy Tompkinson and Bobby Hughes moved on to Stockport County and Wigan Borough, respectively, as it was impossible for Rochdale to pay their summer wages. Harry Martin was appointed assistant trainer, though he would also continue to play. Finally, in June, Bert Whitehurst, scorer of 117 league goals, a club record which stood for over 40 years, was sold to First Division Liverpool. Elsewhere, Durham City became the first Division Three (North) side to fail to be re-elected and were replaced by Carlisle United.

With the old team dismantled, manager Jack Peart brought in numerous new players for the 1928-29 season, though none came near to equalling the reputations of those who had left, only Andrew Martin from Halifax Town having made more than a handful of League appearances. In fact, the side which opened the campaign contained seven of the players who had been retained and Jack Barber, now installed at centre half, took over the captaincy. Peart had also introduced a more studied approach to tactics as pioneered by the likes of Herbert Chapman and used tea cups and lemonade bottles to represent the players. According to one story, his skipper Barber turned up late and, after enquiring what they were doing, replied *"Eh, I've gone and supped t' centre forward."*

1928-29:
The season got off to a bad start with a 3-1 home defeat by Doncaster Rovers and a wholly new inside trio of Reg Trotman, Jack Milsom and John Brierley appeared against Barrow, each of them scoring in a 3-3 draw. Trotman and Milsom had both been on the books of Bristol Rovers, but following a bad injury, the latter had more recently been playing for non-League Kettering. The first victory came in the home game against Barrow, the same three again scoring along with another newcomer, diminutive outside right George Stott from Barnsley, but after six games Rochdale were in 21st position. This was remedied by a 5-0 scoreline at home to Darlington and a six match unbeaten run also included four goals against New Brighton and five against Tranmere Rovers. A new face in the team was Tom Watson, a full back from Consett who soon became an automatic choice.

England international
Harry Martin,
Rochdale's player-trainer
in the late twenties.

Rochdale again made an early exit from the FA Cup, this time at Chesterfield, but two weeks later took part in a remarkable game at Willbutts Lane. Visitors Hartlepools were holding them two-all at the break.

But after a second half goal rush it ended 7-4, still the record aggregate for a League game at Spotland, with local lad Brierley netting four times. Home form, especially the goalscoring, remained no problem, with a 4-4 draw against Wrexham on Christmas Day and convincing 5-0 and 4-0 victories over Ashington and Carlisle early in the New Year. Milsom contributed seven of these goals including a hat-trick against Ashington. Away from Willbutts Lane, though, they struggled badly, conceding four or more goals in each of six consecutive League games. Mittell broke his nose at New Brighton and Rochdale also lost Eric Silverwood (better known in later years as a Rochdale cricketer) to end the 6-1 drubbing with nine men. This prompted the signing of the veteran former Portsmouth and Sunderland goalie Ed Robson from Grimsby. Two players moving on were Reg Trotman, scorer of 10 goals so far, and Walter Webster, a local product who had recently taken over at centre half, both of whom were transferred to Sheffield Wednesday to earn some much needed cash (though, oddly, 'Trotty' never played another Football League game anywhere).

A ten match run which yielded only four points dropped Rochdale down to 16th place again, though Milsom retained his form with a goal in each of seven consecutive games, eventually totalling 25 for the season. Two goals from Harry Lewis, a recent signing from Welsh club Dowlais United, earned full points against Chesterfield and a sterling defensive performance at Valley Parade, in front of a 22,000 crowd, saw them hold out for a goalless draw against promotion contenders Bradford City, Rochdale's first clean sheet in 38 away games. In their next away game, at Hartlepool, they went one better, gaining their first away win since October 1927, when they had also won at the Victoria Ground.

During the final week of the season, second in the table Bradford City and their new signing, one Bert Whitehurst, were the visitors to Spotland. Whitehurst had scored seven goals in a recent game against Tranmere Rovers to create a new Football League record. (At the time, he was said merely to have equalled the existing record of James Ross, who was credited with scoring all seven goals for Preston North End against Stoke in 1888, but modern research has determined that in fact Ross scored only four of them). By the end of the season, Whitehurst had surpassed even his Rochdale form, with 24 goals in 15 games. The match, played on a Tuesday evening, attracted Spotland's largest ever League crowd, 20,945 spectators paying record gate receipts of £1180-15s-4d.

Not only did many Rochdale supporters come along to see Whitehurst and a great horde cross the Pennines with City, but also large numbers of followers of then leaders Stockport County turned up to cheer on Rochdale in the hope of seeing the Yorkshiremen beaten, (some even paid to watch from neighbouring houses). Unfortunately for them, and Rochdale, the Bantams won 3-1 and marched on into Division Two. Rochdale meanwhile slumped 5-0 at Rotherham to finish in 17th position.

Full back George Lewins (freed by Reading the previous year) had already joined Manchester City and several more players were released in the close season, including Braidwood and Mittell. The latter joined Wigan Borough and later played a few First Division games for Birmingham as understudy to the England goalie Harry Hibbs.

1929-30:
Although some of his lesser know signings, such as Milsom, Trotman and Lewins, had proved successful, the overall decline of the side the previous year led Jack Peart to invest in some experience for the 1929-30 campaign. New players thus included Lawrie Baker from Barnsley, Evan Hooker from Stockport County, James Parton of Barrow (and previously the wonderfully named Barrow Submarine Engineers' Athletic) and Phil Hope, a full back *certainly not lacking in heftiness*" who had been with several League clubs prior to turning out for Washington Colliery. In the main, though, it was again the more unlikely signings who were to prosper, like Tommy Tippett, previously the scorer of just three League goals in 30 appearances for Doncaster, `Paddy' Lynch, a 6'-2", 19 year old, goalkeeper from Rhymney in South Wales, another Welsh trialist Idris Williams, 17 year old Dick Brown from Alnwick United, who had had a trial during the previous term and his Alnwick team-mate, full back Dougie Oliver.

A 0-0 draw at Lincoln on the opening day was followed by five straight victories - the goals against Chesterfield unusually coming from right back Hope and left half Barber - with the fifth, 4-1 against Darlington, taking Rochdale to second in the table. The run ended when Rotherham won at Willbutts Lane, then Wrexham annihilated Rochdale 8-0, their worst ever League defeat. They bounced back with a draw against South Shields at Horsley Hill and scored big home wins over Accrington, Barrow - Bertram netting four times - and New Brighton. These successes served to keep Rochdale in the top six despite further heavy away defeats. Jack Milsom scored in each of these games and in fact hit a brace in five consecutive League games. This form soon attracted other clubs and in December, with his tally of 15 goals in 16 games, he was sold to First Division Bolton Wanderers for £1,500. In a career lasting until the outbreak of World War Two, he scored over 200 League goals and was the First Division's top scorer in 1934-35 (though he never gained an England cap, he did play for England against The Rest in an international trial, when The Rest won 7-1!).

As it turned out, the departure of one goal scorer merely made room for another. Tommy Tippett, all 5'-7" of him, was chosen to lead the attack and responded with seven goals in the next seven games. The rest of the side was struggling, however, with a run of eight games without a win reaching its nadir in a 3-0 home defeat by next-to-bottom Halifax.

Rochdale did gain two remarkable victories, winning 4-0 at Rotherham and gaining some measure of revenge on Wrexham by beating the Welshmen 5-4, wee George Stott scoring a second half hat-trick. The defence was still none too secure, both Accrington Stanley and York City (in their first season since replacing Ashington) putting six past the overworked Lynch. However the good home form and the goalscoring of Tippett - who had the galling experience of scoring a hat-trick against Lincoln but still finishing on the losing side - edged Rochdale back up the table. In the midst of a hectic April, 13 games being played in the last five weeks of the season including four in five days over Easter, came the most remarkable goalscoring feat in the club's history. Visiting Hartlepool, often one of their more productive venues, Rochdale were 6-1 up after 45 minutes and finally romped home 8-2. Tommy Tippett scored six times, equalling the record individual tally by any Football League player in an away fixture (beaten since only by Ted Drake of Arsenal). Ironically, Hartlepool collected more points in 1929-30 than in any other inter-war season and conceded only 16 goals in all their other 20 home games. Tippett, meantime, easily topped the Dale's scoring charts with 35.

Closing the season with two further home wins, Rochdale finished in a comfortable 10th position. They also just missed out on reaching the Manchester Senior Cup Final, losing to Wigan Borough at the third attempt in the semi-final. Slightly surprisingly, the average attendance slumped to 3,714. At the end of the season outside right Brown was transferred to Sheffield Wednesday, while the long-serving Hall was released. Outside left Tom Lindsay was also on the move and became one of the game's great travellers, serving nine English and Scottish clubs in the space of six seasons. In July 1930 Jack Peart, who had managed the side through thick and thin since March 1923, left to take over as manager of Bradford City. Trainer-coach Jimmy Henderson also moved on, and Harry Martin was left in charge as acting manager.

Following the 'Wall Street Crash' of the previous October, the formerly booming world economy slumped dramatically, parallelling Rochdale's fall from grace. By the summer of 1930 the Depression had set-in in Britain, not least in the Lancashire cotton towns, and a depression of their own was about to descend upon the already financially straitened Rochdale A.F.C. (with typical irony, Rochdale had just signed up an amateur winger, Austin Trippier, who was a stock-broker).

ROCHDALE'S FINEST TALENT   1930-1938

~ CHAPTER 3 ~

Notwithstanding the success that had followed the appointment of a player-manager in Jack Peart, the board decided against promoting Harry Martin and appointed William Smith 'Kiltie' Cameron as manager. In a somewhat chequered career, Cameron had played for several top clubs, but when manager of Bury had been suspended sine die by the Football League for his part in "squaring" a match. In October, Martin was replaced as trainer by George Ward, also from Bury (though a former Rugby League player with Leigh) but did make one further League appearance, his 411th, when six months short of his 40th birthday. He later moved on to the staff at Mansfield Town.

Although 12 players had been retained, eight of whom figured in the League side on the opening day of the season, several new players were also signed. Of these, the Oldham forward Frank Hargreaves was probably the best known. Others who were to make regular appearances included centre forward or centre half Jack Everest from Stockport, back George Grierson from Preston and Claude W. Craddock, a well travelled inside man usually known as 'Joe'.

The season began in successful, if rather dramatic fashion, with a 5-4 home win against Nelson. Although the next two games were lost, a goalless draw at Barrow and home wins over Wrexham (4-3) and Barrow (4-2) gave no hint of what was to come. The next game did, though, as Tranmere crashed in seven at Prenton Park, Rochdale replying with three. There were two further League defeats before Rochdale crushed Rotherham 6-1. In the next game Wigan won 4-0 at Willbutts Lane, despite the debut of record signing David Cowan, a £300 buy from Scottish junior side Alva Albion Rangers. Indeed a home win against Lincoln and a rare away success at Gateshead (formerly South Shields) were the only high points in a run of 13 games during which Rochdale exited from both the Lancashire and FA Cups and slipped to 18th in the League. Even when Harry Lewis netted a hat-trick against Doncaster Rovers, the visitors still won 5-3.

Jack Milson, a Bolton star in the 30's, after being sold by Rochdale

Over the Christmas week three successive games were lost 4-0. William Blackburn from Black Lane Rovers had the misfortune to play in each of these, the only League games of his career. After the third defeat no less than six changes were made in the team, one of them the inclusion of the trainer's son George Ward junior, but they still managed only a goalless draw at bottom club Nelson. Things looked brighter in the New Year, Rochdale regaining a mid-table position with a win at Accrington, where Craddock scored twice, and two at home. The return match with Tranmere was again a turning point though. Rochdale went down 3-1 and were then thrashed 7-1 at Carlisle. They did win at Rotherham but lost six of the next seven games, crashing to a disastrous 6-1 home defeat at the hands of Accrington Stanley (the latter's only away win all season), thus slumping to the brink of the re-election zone.

They claimed a vital point at Stockport and beat New Brighton, so with three games left Rochdale still had every chance of avoiding the bottom two places, as only a handful of points covered the seven clubs immediately above doomed Nelson. However, two defeats left them just two points ahead of Hartlepools, who by chance were the final visitors to Willbutts Lane. Without regulars Oliver and Grierson in defence, Rochdale went down 2-1 and so slipped to 21st place on goal average. They thus had to apply for re-election for the first time since their debut season, finishing with only 30 points from their 42 games.

Nearly all the players were released at the end of the season. Apart from anything else, the club could not afford to way their wages over the summer. Among them was Billy Bertram after 198 games and 71 goals, tallies second only to Parkes and Whitehurst respectively in Football League games. Others to depart included Jack Barber, George Stott and Tom Watson, each with over 100 games to their credit, and Paddy Lynch. The latter, little daunted, went on to a long career, appearing at Spotland for Bangor as far on as 1947.

Expensive signing Davie Cowan was also freed, having failed to live up to the manager's expectations.

In February Harry Lewis had been transferred to Arsenal (to be Alex James' understudy) for a modest fee to raise some cash, and in the close season top scorer Tippett was sold to Port Vale. By chance, the pair teamed up again with Second Division West Ham in 1935. Despite a public appeal launched in February, it was announced at the AGM that Rochdale AFC had made a £2,500 loss over the year and was now £7,000 in the red. Home gates averaged only 3,078 and had slipped to around 1,000 by the end of the season. Indeed, the club were warned by the Football League that they would not be allowed to apply for re-election unless some of their debts were paid, and required them to raise £700 before the AGM. They were not alone, either, as Wigan Borough, Accrington Stanley, Port Vale, Halifax and New Brighton were all reported to be on the point of bankruptcy, along with some clubs in the Southern Section.

At the 1931 Football League AGM bottom club Nelson were voted out after a tie with Chester in the first ballot, but Rochdale - on the strength of their successes of the 1920's - gained easily enough votes to retain their status. Among the new signings made by Kiltie Cameron (several of them fellow Scots) were Harry Abbott, an experienced 'keeper formerly with Nelson and Luton, Ayr full back Jimmy Hamilton, and well travelled Swindon forwards David Murray (a South African international), George Guyan (once Hull City's most expensive signing) and Benny Jones. A number of former non-League and local players were also signed and the team for the opening game contained only three survivors from the previous season, George Ward junior, the versatile six-footer Jack Everest and Scottish full back Adam Plunkett (most noted for his red hair and bandy legs).

1931-32:
The first game was a 2-2 draw with Accrington in front of a near 7000 crowd; unbelievably today, this was twice the attendance at Manchester United's first home game. Presaging thing to come, the side was hammered 5-0 at Rotherham, but after two more defeats they appeared to regain some form, defeating Carlisle 4-3 with two goals from their new signing from Southampton, Bert Watson, holder of Oldham Athletic's career goalscoring record. Rochdale also beat Stockport, and although away form was non-existent, reasonable home results, helped by goals on his first two appearances by Joe McAleer from Arbroath, kept them in a relatively respectable position until the end of September. The next four games were lost though, before Rochdale played a seemingly ordinary match which, as the season unfolded, was to become firmly fixed in the history of the club and indeed (though mistakenly) of the Football League.

On November 7th New Brighton were the visitors, and as on many other occasions before and after (they never managed a victory at Spotland throughout their Football League career), they were beaten, by three goals to two, with Everest (2) and Jones scoring for Rochdale.

A week later, Rochdale were beaten 4-1 at Barrow then, despite the inclusion of two Sunderland reserves, Fred Brown and Ken Nisbet on loan, they went down 6-3 at home to Hull. The FA Cup was cause for further anguish as Rochdale visited Midland League Scunthorpe (Rochdale's reserves having played in this league until recently) and lost 2-1.

Defeat piled on defeat as Chester won 3-0 at Willbutts Lane and Hartlepools by the same score on their own ground. For the match at Tranmere on Christmas day, local 'keeper Bert Welch from Whitworth Parish was selected for his debut. By the end of the 90 minutes the unfortunate Welch must have had just about the unhappiest footballing Christmas on record, as he had to pick the ball out of the net nine times, Rovers' centre forward Watts leading the rout with five goals. The final score of 9-1 ranks along with a couple of 8-0 hidings as Rochdale's worst League results. Perhaps surprisingly only two changes were made for the return game on Boxing Day and Rovers rubbed it in by firing six more past the luckless Welch, Rochdale hitting three in reply this time.

On December 28th, Abbott returned in place of the shell-shocked Welch and conceded five to non-League Worcester City in a friendly. The following day it was announced that Cameron had resigned as manager and secretary Ernest Nixon assumed control of the club. By this point Rochdale were on the brink. Players wages were well in areas and, indeed, the club were threatened with expulsion from the League because of this. Response to a recent appeal had been abysmal, apparently because of antipathy towards the then manager and some of the directors.

Still no improvement was forthcoming on the field, Accrington and Lincoln both won comfortably on their own pitches and Wrexham and Carlisle each netted four. This led to the resignation of trainer George Ward, too, and in February, former incumbent Jimmy Henderson returned to take over the trainer's role again. Also leaving were Bert Watson, who was released (though he remained the top scorer at the season's end), and Jack Everest who escaped further punishment when he was sold to Blackpool for £500.

After a further defeat by Crewe, Rochdale finally dislodged the similarly struggling New Brighton from the foot of the table (actually 21st position, as Wigan Borough had earlier given up the financial struggle and resigned, apparently £20,000 in debt).

Despite numerous team changes and permutations (both Murray and Jones figured in six different positions), Darlington, Doncaster and Southport piled on the agony still further. For the home game against Southport four new signings made their debuts, three of them veterans recalled from non-League football. Jimmy Bimson was in his third spell in the Football League, having played for Southport and Wigan, while Frank Twine, formerly a sergeant in the Royal Welch Fusiliers, had been an outstanding amateur player, winning seven England caps. He had later played for Middlesbrough, but more recently had been sacked by Southern League Aldershot for a breach of club rules (reputedly being drunk at a club function). Arthur Hawes had an even longer pedigree. He had appeared for Norwich immediately after the Great War and later made a name at Sunderland where he played alongside the legendary Charlie Buchan, though lately he had been with Wombwell in the Midland League.

In the Manchester Cup, Manchester City won 6-0, with the hapless Eddie Plane, who had conceded 10 in his two previous appearances four years earlier, having his final outing in goal. Halifax, Walsall and Gateshead extended the run of League defeats to a massively depressing 17 before the visit to companions in distress New Brighton on March 19th resulted in a one-one draw thanks to Brown's second half equaliser. This also ended a run of 21 consecutive away defeats, 18 of them in the League. This was long considered to be the most prolonged run of consecutive defeats ever suffered in the Football League, but in fact there had been a worse case, when Darwen lost 18 Second Division games in a row in 1898-99. Also, Nelson lost all their last 24 away games as a League club.

With this success behind them, Rochdale managed to score twice at York, but conceded five in the process. A further drubbing, 6-0 at home to Barrow, then Rochdale's worst home defeat, led to the demise of Abbott and the return of Welch. Whether the latter appreciated the opportunity is rather debateable for the final six games all ended in heavy defeats as 28 goals flew past him. On April 11th, founding father and first secretary of the club in 1907, Herbert Hopkinson was appointed manager.

After leaving Rochdale, Hopkinson had become a top referee and had officiated in the Wales v. Ireland match of 1928. No respecter of persons, League newboys Chester beat his side 7-2 the following Saturday and an ignominious season ended with a 4-1 home defeat by Rotherham (McAleer's season having ended slightly earlier when he was sent off).

Rochdale collected just 11 points, only one of them away from home, with a paltry four wins. The total of 33 defeats was a Football League record, not equalled until 1985. They failed to win any of their last 26 games, 13 of them at home, collecting just one point in this period. Their last 26 away games had brought just two points. Not surprisingly, average crowds slipped below 3,000 for the first time since Rochdale entered the Football League.

As might be expected, only four players were retained, Hamilton (the one man to have played in all the long run of consecutive defeats), McAleer, reserve half back Bill Armstrong, one of the many ex-miners to try their luck, and the persistent Welch, who despite his traumatic beginning went on to make over 50 appearances and was still on the club's books in 1938. Indeed, all the players retained went on to lengthy League careers, as did the loan player Fred Brown and two of the local players who had been given a chance. Ernie Steele played for six Football League clubs and won a Third (South) championship medal with Millwall, while Ron Hornby made the grade with Burnley and played for them in the top flight as late as 1947-48. Two of the many players who, on the other hand, figured only briefly on the Spotland and Football League stages were Tom Flannigan and John Whitelaw, who unusually for their day spent part of their careers abroad, Flannigan in France and Whitelaw in Canada.

Money was desperately short and it was said that the club's continued existence depended more on the takings at chairman George Foulds' butchers shops than those at Willbutts Lane. It was not unusual for the Supporters Club officials to make a collection on the terraces in order to pay for the players' transport to the next away game. Rochdale lass made good, Gracie Fields, at the height of her stage and film career, lent her support from a distance. Indeed, 'Our Gracie' may have been responsible for the first ever recording of a football song, called *Pass, Shoot, Score*", in 1931. Nearer to home a public appeal in the town was augmented by money from a concert of *"Rochdale's finest talent"*, organised by former Dale hero, and now comedian, Harry Mallalieu. The long suffering fans, meanwhile, were left to hope for some finer talent out on the pitch.

At the Football League AGM, Mansfield Town were moved from the Third (South) to the Third (North) so that there was only one vacancy in the Northern Section. Rochdale with 47 votes were not seriously troubled by the challenge of Rhyl (5th in the Birmingham League) who got 2 votes, or the attempt by the newly formed Wigan Athletic (no votes).

F. TWINE.

No other senior non-League clubs in the North were prepared to gamble on a future in the full time game in the current financial climate, and Rochdale's efforts towards self-help over the past months found considerable favour with the football authorities.

New men for the 1932-33 season included full back Ben Wheelhouse, another former miner who had long experience in the Northern Section with Halifax Town (he had scored an own goal on Rochdale's behalf in 1929), and two vastly experienced half backs, Harry Nuttall and Billy Benton. Benton was a veteran of 350 League games for Blackpool, though he had spent the previous year at Fleetwood, while Nuttall, younger brother of former Dale skipper Jimmy, had three FA Cup winners medals and three full England caps from 12 years with Bolton Wanderers (after retiring from playing, he spent a further 29 years on the staff at Burnden Park, and he had actually been born there too, when his father was the Bolton trainer). Two Leeds United reserves, Jack Gordon and George Snow, the former Ashington and Carlisle stalwart William Watson and his Accrington namesake Tom Watson completed the major signings.

(Above) Ex-Blackpool skipper Billy Benton, a regular in 1932-33.
(Below) Bert Watson, Rochdale's top scorer in 1931-32

1932-33:

In the opening game 10 players made their Rochdale debuts but unfortunately the result was just the same as that of the previous season, as Carlisle travelled home happily with both points. The tide turned three days later with a 1-1 draw at Barrow and on September 3rd, Rochdale travelled to York and amazingly ended their run of 28 League games without a win (and 27 away games without a win over the past 18 months) by thrashing the home side 6-2. Nineteen year old Tom Watson, in only his third game for the club, scored four times and Snow got the other two. A goalless draw with Barrow then ended the Football League record run of 14 consecutive home defeats. It was also the first time that Rochdale had kept a clean sheet for 40 games.

Crewe spoilt the celebrations by winning 4-1 at Willbutts Lane, Rochdale employing the near 40 year old Bill Gardner at centre forward; Gardner was an England amateur international who had played in the 1915 FA Amateur Cup Final for Bishop Auckland. However, Rochdale then ended their run of 16 home games without a win by overcoming Mansfield 2-1. Both goals came from former Manchester United and Everton man David Bain on his debut. Despite this result, defeat at Rotherham left Rochdale 20th in the table.

But a good run when they collected seven points out of eight raised the spirits and the League position, another recent signing, the former Burnley centre forward and record goalscorer George Beel, making some valuable contributions.

Although knocked out of the FA Cup at the first attempt again, Rochdale strung together three successive home wins in the League. Over Christmas, not a productive period in preceding years, they achieved a draw with leaders Hull at Anlaby Road and recorded home and away victories over New Brighton which enabled them to reach the heady heights of 8th place. Bert Welch, restored to the goalkeeper's jersey for the Hull game, must have enjoyed this run even more than most, considering his baptism of fire the previous festive season.

Retribution for such effrontery was swift. Hartlepool secured a 3-0 home win and set Rochdale inexplicably on another disastrous slide. Six games were lost in succession and only two draws accrued from a run of 15 games which saw Rochdale crash to the foot of the table once more, scoring 11 goals and conceding 42 in the process (one of the draws was against mid-table Walsall who had just created a sensation by knocking the mighty Arsenal out of the FA Cup). Even so, young centre half Armstrong attracted the attention of Aston Villa and he was quickly sold on to keep Rochdale's bank manager happy. Ex-Burnley man Stan Bowsher, a Welsh international, was brought in to replace him.

Thoughts must already have been on a repeat of the previous season when Rochdale pulled out of the nose dive by beating Chester on Easter Monday and they proceeded, perversely, to put six past Hartlepool in the following game, Snow (2), Rigby (2), Benton and Williams netting. Welshman Ralph Williams was a "have boots, will travel" centre forward signed from Southport who played for no less than 17 Football League and senior non-League clubs between 1923 and 1938. Another player in the same mould was 'Tim' Williamson. Williamson (born William Gallagher) had survived fighting in the Battle of the Somme with the Black Watch when he was only 16 and was now well on his way to his total of 22 clubs in all four home countries.

Rochdale also won easily at Accrington, but were still in need of points when they met champions Hull City at Willbutts Lane on the final day.

36

In the event, Rochdale ended the season in style, winning 3-2 to finish in 18th place. Despite the erratic form displayed, and the Depression reaching its lowest ebb with over 3 million men on the dole, total attendances were up 50% on the previous term.

Despite the avoidance of the re-election positions, financial imperatives again dictated that most of the staff be freed, including the veterans Beel, Benton, Bowsher and Nuttall (though Benton did reappear for a few games), while three of the more successful younger members of the side, top scorer Snow, full back Hamilton and outside right Joe Shonakan all moved to Wrexham. William Watson signed for Accrington Stanley for whom he played his 400th Football League game, all of them, remarkably, in Division Three (North). Joe McAleer joined the travelling fraternity, appearing for a different Third Division club in each of the next five seasons. One player actually had worse luck elsewhere; in 1935 Lewis Caunce played in goal when Oldham lost 13-4 at Tranmere, the record Football League score.

With only five players retained for the 1933-34 season, Herbert Hopkinson again had to undertake a considerable amount of team building, and again went for a number of well known players now at the veteran stage. Foremost of these were the former Bolton Wanderers centre forward John Reid Smith, scorer of the winning goal in the first Wembley Cup Final, and Tony Weldon, who had starred alongside Dixie Dean in Everton's 1928 League championship winning side. Veteran full back Wally Webster had had experience with Sheffield United and left half Walter Buckley had played regularly for Lincoln when they won the Third North title two years earlier. Rochdale also had a new trainer in Frank Hudspeth, the Newcastle veteran who had created a record as the oldest man to make his England debut after winning League championship and FA Cup winners medals while at St. James' Park.

1933-34:
The season started for once with a win, 1-0 against Darlington, though not for the first time, away form was non-existent. Only Accrington returned home from Willbutts Lane with the points during the opening phase of the season. Indeed, when Rochdale won on their happy hunting ground of Sandheys Park, New Brighton, thanks to new 6'-1" goalie Cliff Warmsley keeping a clean sheet, they moved to 13th place. Rochdale had started the season with virtually no reserve strength, only the first choice eleven having appeared in the Football League before, and a number of extra players were soon drafted in. Trialists included the former Scottish international Daniel McRorie, who had had a meteoric rise to fame only three years earlier which had earned a transfer from Morton to Liverpool. A slightly longer lasting signing was Jimmy Collins who played regularly for the rest of the season.

A couple of years later he played a few games for Liverpool in Division One. Besides the large number of players used, a number found themselves playing in a variety of roles, David Bain, for instance figuring in all the outfield positions except right back and outside left.

Three more new men including Fred Fitton, one of the division's leading scorers the previous season when with Accrington, and well travelled winger Jack Robson appeared in the next match, which was abandoned because of bad light with York 2-1 ahead. There was no reprieve in the next match though, as Robson's previous club Chester ran in seven. Rochdale made the familiar quick exit from the FA Cup at the hands of amateurs Sutton, but the game did receive wide notice because of the referee's decision to blow for full time in the split second between J. R. Smith shooting for goal and what would have been the equaliser hitting the back of the net. Another Smith, Tom, made his debut in this game and subsequently became first choice centre half, nine players having been tried at pivot in the last twelve months.

Only one more win had been obtained by the turn of the year and Rochdale slumped to the foot of the table (as contrary as ever, the one win was against eventual champions Barnsley). In January Herbert Hopkinson resigned, leaving secretary Nixon in charge again. Though a couple of wins gave a temporary glimpse of better things, a home defeat by Chesterfield, with Buckley sent off, began a run of six defeats which left Rochdale anchored to the bottom. Spare a thought, too, for leading scorer Robson; the portly winger hit a first half hat-trick against York only for his defenders to concede six and only about 800 spectators were there to see it - this was the third season in a row that a left winger topped the scoring charts.

Rochdale had earlier been removed from the newly instituted Third Division (North) Cup by Stockport, and in the Manchester Cup they were well and truly annihilated by a Manchester United side which scored nine without reply, to post Rochdale's worst ever senior defeat (even though this was the season in which United only just escaped relegation to the Third North themselves). Local amateur Harry Longbottom made his debut at centre half in this game and somehow managed to impress sufficiently to play in the next two League games as well. Draws against New Brighton and Walsall, Weldon scoring all three goals in the latter, were the only successes in a run of 13 games before Rochdale amazingly trounced Chester 6-0 at Willbutts Lane thanks to another hat-trick, this time from J. R. Smith, which was quite a turn round from the 7-1 away defeat! Unfortunately this proved to be a flash in the pan, only one more point accruing from the final six games. The point, incidentally, was from a 1-1 draw with Stockport in a match which kicked off at 6.30 so as to avoid clashing with that afternoon's first ever live broadcast of the FA Cup Final on the wireless.

This left Rochdale bottom of the table with just 24 points, nine short of safety. Prompted by the club's financial state and uncertainty about the future with a re-election bid pending, not to mention the playing deficiencies, another complete clearout followed. Moves included Robson to Oldham, Gordon to Queen of the South and Weldon to Dundalk as player-coach. By the time the amateur Tom Smith moved to Luton Town, on obtaining a teaching post in Letchworth, only two players remained, Cliff Warmsley and Walter Buckley. Trainer Frank Hudspeth also departed.

Rochdale and Rotherham were unopposed in their bids for re-election, and during the summer of 1934 new chairman Mr William Whitehead appointed W. H. (Billy) Smith, the former Huddersfield and England international winger as player-manager. The 39 year England international was one of the most experienced players in the game, having spent 21 years at Huddersfield and winning three League championship medals with Herbert Chapman's great team.

Jack Robson.
Top scorer in 1933-34

Smith's signings included balding full back Arthur Worthy, an experienced campaigner in the Third North with Lincoln, whose shuddering tackles recalled another former Lincoln and Dale back, Yaffer Ward. Half back George Wyness was a former Southport regular while Ted Humpish had played for numerous clubs ranging from Wigan Borough to the Arsenal.

1934-35:
Rochdale turned out for their first match of the season at Lincoln in a new strip of blue shirts and white shorts. The change of colours did not bring a change of fortune as the Imps ran out 3-0 winners. A home defeat by Barrow, two draws and then two more defeats added up to Rochdale's worst ever start to a season. They achieved the first win of the season on September 29th against Walsall, thanks to a goal from new boy Les Sullivan from Lytham Town.

The next home game was also won, but Rochdale remained at the bottom of the League with a quarter of the season gone. The manager had by now added several more players to the staff, including his former Huddersfield colleagues Levi Redfern, from the 1928 cup final side, George Dobson and Gwyn Jones.

After a humiliating 5-0 home defeat by Stockport, Smith selected himself for the first time but was unable to prevent a 4-1 defeat at Crewe. The tide finally turned with a victory over Hartlepool, yet another newcomer Jim Nicol from Brechin scoring twice and the ever faithful Bert Welch returning in goal. Sam Skaife from Bradford Park Avenue, who made his debut in this match was the 24th player used in only 15 games, but no further new players appeared during the whole of the rest of the season. This ended a remarkable period in which no fewer than 118 players made their debuts in only four and a half seasons, an average of more than one every other game.

Wrexham were Rochdale's hosts in the FA Cup and duly won 4-1, but Dale escaped from Carlisle with a draw in the Third North Cup. A fortnight later a hat-trick from trialist Len Clarke secured victory over New Brighton, lifted Rochdale out of the bottom two and, not surprisingly, earned Clarke, also a scorer on his debut, a professional contract; he ended the season as top scorer. Rochdale followed up with their first away win of the season, at York, and when they beat promotion hopefuls Lincoln at the turn of the year they edged up to 18th.

Unfortunately, they then slipped back again, failing to win any of the next eight League games, though they did manage to win their cup replay with Carlisle. They came back to form with a 5-2 away win at Accrington and in the next match thrashed fellow strugglers Gateshead 6-1, the entire forward line of Harold Howe (with two), Redfern, Clarke, Nicol and Sullivan getting on the score sheet.

An equally valuable win was gained at the expense of Crewe, but the crowd at Willbutts Lane was less than 2000. A precious point was gained in a goalless draw at Hartlepool, but then three games were lost, including that against strugglers Southport, to leave Rochdale 21st again. Only a point was gained at Brunton Park against a doomed Carlisle, but the return on Easter Monday was won to edge Rochdale ahead of Southport.

New Brighton ended their own re-election worries, but increased Rochdale's when Worthy put through his own goal, so with one game to go it was between Gateshead, Southport and the Dale for the second re-election place. Gateshead secured the draw they needed on the final day, but Wrexham's 3-0 victory over Southport ensured that Rochdale's victory over York, thanks to goals from Redfern and Dobson, kept the men from Spotland safe from what would have been a fourth re-election bid in five years.

Despite the season's struggles, the Board and manager decided against the usual wholesale changes and eight of the regulars were kept on, Nicol and Dobson, though, moving to Crewe and Rotherham, respectively.

Indeed, despite one former director's statement during the season that Rochdale could not afford a football team, the new directors announced that they had now wiped off the overdraft and launched a team building fund. Plenty of people were certainly prepared to try their luck at Spotland; over 150 players applied for trials during the summer and the club had 70 applicants for the post of trainer.

Even with the lengthier than usual retained list, there was considerable close season activity in 1935. Experienced Northampton goalie Billy Baker, well travelled ex-Wolves inside man Harry Marshall (brother of Sunderland's Bob), and wingers George Emmerson, a former Cardiff regular, and Bert 'Smiler' Hales from Stockport were among the fairly well known names signed up, while on the eve of the season, Les Sullivan was transferred to Brentford in exchange for Matt Johnson. Two little known players were to make the biggest impression however, Joe Wiggins from Gillingham in the short term and Joe Duff, a 22 year old Newcastle reserve, over a considerably longer one, as he was with the club for most of the next 30 years.

1935-36:
A brighter start was made than in the previous season as Rochdale came from behind to beat Crewe 2-1 at Willbutts Lane. Although Stockport beat them 4-0 at Edgeley Park, Rochdale themselves hit four at Accrington, Johnson scoring twice on his debut and local amateur Fred Taylor once on his. Outside right Taylor (a draughtsman in Oldham) scored in each of the next two games as well but then faded from the scene.

Despite another heavy defeat, at Chester, Rochdale stood in 12th place after 7 games, but after losing 6-3 at Oldham in the Third North Cup, they slumped in the League as well, picking up only three points from nine games and conceding another six to Oldham back at Willbutts Lane. By odd coincidence, muscular right back Albert Worthy scored in each of the heavy defeats by Oldham, his only goals for the club. The only success came away from home, and at one of their least favourite grounds at that, when Duff's goal gave them their first ever victory at Wrexham.

On November 9th, with Rochdale two from the bottom, Billy Smith was sacked and secretary Ernest Dixon took over as caretaker-manager. This was the third occasion he had been in charge, though the first time he had been manager in name. He was unable to effect an immediate change in the side's fortunes, as four more defeats included an emphatic 4-0 FA Cup knockout at Halifax. However, one bright spot in the 5-2 defeat at Tranmere was the form of Joe Wiggins, the scorer of both goals. His only two previous League goals had been spread over 28 games for four different clubs in eight seasons. He scored twice more in the next game, against Gateshead, and Len Clarke in his first game of the season netted a hat-trick.

But this was a rare success and Rochdale had taken only 14 points when the season reached its half way point, though Southport and New Brighton were faring even less well.

Four successive draws in the New Year steadied the ship, the most impressive being at Chesterfield, the eventual champions. After a heavy defeat at Lincoln, Mr Nixon made the unusual move, given that 12 other players had been introduced in the interim, of returning to the same eleven who had appeared on the opening day. They repeated the success, too, even if it was an own goal by Halifax's Williams which settled the match. They lost at York, to return to the 20th spot they had occupied for most of the season, but further home wins were soon forthcoming. Wiggins' opening goal in the victory over Wrexham was Rochdale's 1000th in the Football League. The date of this game had been switched with the Mansfield fixture a fortnight before as a result of the bizarre "Pools war" between the Football League Management Committee and the Pools Promoters Association, the League keeping secret who would play who until the last minute to prevent the PPA printing their coupons. After two weeks of chaos and halved attendances the clubs unanimously voted down the Management Committee's plan.

At the end of March, Rochdale entertained Walsall, and the meagre crowd of under 2000 were rewarded when Wiggins netted his fifth brace of the season in a 6-4 thriller. Continued poor away form threatened to undo the good work, though, as all the last five away matches were lost without a single goal scored, even against bottom club New Brighton. Fortunately the return game was won and a draw against Darlington in the penultimate game ensured that Rochdale would not need to seek re-election. To wind up the season on an optimistic note, they held promoted Chesterfield one-all. This was their 10th home draw, and despite their lowly position, Rochdale were beaten only three times at home. For once, the team which started the season remained the most regular line up, all eleven playing in over half the matches.

Nevertheless, the players released included Walter Buckley, who with 111 League appearances had become the club's first centurion since the halcyon days of the 1920's, and George Wyness, who moved to Notts County. Sid Elliott, a centre forward with an excellent scoring record for several clubs, but who had proved an expensive disappointment with just one goal in eleven games following his £400 transfer from Bradford City, was also freed. Leading scorer Joe Wiggins, all of whose 14 goals came in an 18 match spell, was transferred to Oldham in the close season but never reproduced this form again.

Ten of the previous season's staff remained with the club, but as usual a number of new faces were in evidence by the start of the 1936-37 campaign.

Best known was goalkeeper (and former railway ticket collector) Des Fawcett, with over 250 League games and five League clubs behind him, while others included forwards Wally Hunt and Syd Protheroe (a Welsh junior international) from Torquay and former Bury full back Roy Clipson, whose varied career included a spell with Spanish club Espanol in between stints at the likes of Horwich RMI and Goole Town. Harold Wooten joined the club as trainer-coach.

1936-37:
A promising start was made with an away draw at Crewe despite having only 10 men in the second half, Hunt netting both Rochdale goals. This rapidly deteriorated with two home defeats and a 6-2 thrashing at Mansfield. Hartson scored five goals in this game to add to his hat-trick at Willbutts Lane the previous week. Rochdale also lost new centre half Charlie Robinson with a broken leg, sustained in a collision with a team-mate. Rochdale registered their first win by beating Southport and also overcame York, former Middlesbrough man Ted Marcroft, one of the few Rochdalians to play in the top flight (and a former cotton mill hand at that) making his debut.

However, away form remained poor and things came to a head when Wrexham, the next visitors to Spotland, won 6-0 to equal Rochdale's worst ever home defeat. A protest group was set up by supporters in an attempt to persuade the directors to appoint a full time manager, though it was not recognised by the official Supporters Club (nevertheless two of its members were later co-opted onto the Board). Despite the arrival of experienced Tranmere half back Hugh McLaren, a Scottish Cup winner in 1929 (remarkably, while on loan to Kilmarnock from Aberdeen), who took over the captaincy.

Further games were lost against fellow strugglers Darlington and Gateshead (the latter's first win of the season). After 17 games Rochdale were bottom of the table with only 9 points, a 4-0 win against New Brighton, thanks to a Wally Hunt hat-trick, was all they had to show from a dismal run of 14 games which included their exit from all three cup competitions. In the game at Lincoln, home centre forward Campbell emulated Hartson by getting a nap hand in their 5-3 win. Dale centre half Andrew Carr reputedly asked Campbell to ease up after the fifth, to save him from getting the sack!

With the nation talking of little else but the abdication of Edward VIII, now succeeded by his brother as King George VI, a goalless draw between Rochdale and Port Vale was hardly front page news. Nevertheless, this preceded an unusually festive Christmas, with two wins on successive days. Three further draws extended the run into the New Year, and although Rochdale were beaten 4-3 at Tranmere, the game was notable for two goals by Jimmy Wynn, a former schoolboy international signed from Rotherham earlier in the season. Wynn also scored in two more home wins, and though Rochdale lost 4-1 at both York, where Hunt was sent off, and Hartlepool, he scored in both of those games as well.

Earning his nickname of 'Lucky', Wynn then netted the only goal of the game at Wrexham, to end a run of 30 away games without a victory and avenge the disaster at Spotland earlier in the season. He scored the opener in a 4-0 defeat of Darlington, netted again in a defeat at Gateshead, and got on the score sheet for the ninth game in a row as Rochdale put four past Hull, one of the division's better sides (though it has to be said that the visitors were hampered by an injury to their goalkeeper).

During this spell Rochdale had risen to a relatively prosperous 15th place, but following the transfer of their strapping young left back Gwyn Jones to champions-to-be Stockport County, the defence went to pieces, conceding 19 goals in 5 games, all of which were lost (though Wynn still scored in four of them, meaning he had missed out only once in 14 games). New Brighton's Ainsworth scored a hat-trick in their 5-1 win and had a big part in a remarkable goal scored by his centre forward Hullett seconds after half time, only the two of them touching the ball before it ended up in the net.

Rochdale thus found themselves next to bottom again, with only four games to go. Fortunately they came back strongly over the final games, beating fourth placed Oldham 3-0, gaining a draw at Port Vale's Recreation Ground, and ending with home wins over Rotherham and Accrington, Hunt taking his season's tally to 27. Rochdale thus closed in 18th spot with 35 points, their best for seven years, and they collected a healthy 12 home wins, but were successful only once on their travels.

Players released included the experienced Albert Worthy and George Emmerson, while Matt Johnson signed for Crewe. Former Newton Heath Loco winger Cyril Crawshaw, who had played in two League games, made his next (and only other) League appearances for Hull City 10 years later. (This is not quite the record among Rochdale players, as there were 11 years between Jim Tully's last Football League game for Clapton Orient and his first for Rochdale after they were elected to the League in 1921).

Despite the outgoing transfers, Rochdale again made a loss over the season and prior to the start of the 1937-38 campaign, vice-chairman Mr F. Howarth, speaking at the club's AGM, reiterated the board's view that there was no need for a manager and that secretary Ernest Nixon would remain in charge of team affairs. He would be aided by new trainer Jimmy Mulrooney and his assistant Tweedale Rigg, the old Rochdale player.

Relatively few new signings were made during the summer, by far the most important being that of Ted Goodier, a powerfully built centre half now reaching the veteran stage (he had made his debut for Oldham back in 1925). Goodier's Crewe half back partner, Jimmy Eastwood, also crossed to Spotland. Full backs Tommy Baird from St. Mirren and Tommy Sneddon from Queen of the South were among six Scots to appear on the scene for various periods.

1937-38:
The start of the season was none too promising with two goalless draws at Willbutts Lane and two away defeats, but then successive home and away games were won against Southport and Halifax.

Rochdale were soundly beaten at Doncaster and for the next match, in the absence of McLaren, Goodier took over the captaincy. Unfortunately his former Alex team-mates proceeded to win 4-1, but the following week, the previous season's hero 'Lucky' Wynn returned for his first match of the season and scored in a 2-0 victory.

By this time the departure of Ernest Nixon had left the club without secretary, manager or coach, and the board was forced to appoint a manager after all. On October 6th, Sam Jennings, of Glentoran and formerly a player with no less than eight League clubs, not to mention Marseilles in France, was given the post of manager-coach.

His charges immediately won away at Barrow and then, despite going a goal down in the first minute, thrashed Wrexham 6-1, the Welsh side being hampered by an injury to their goalkeeper who went to play on the wing. Alex Graham, one of the close season signings, scored twice and was thereupon transferred to Second Division Bradford. Form overall was somewhat topsy-turvy, with home and away defeats interspersed between some good wins. Both Wynn and the widely travelled Jock Miller (who had played for Jennings at Glentoran during part of a seven year absence from the Football League and was said to be amongst the top five sprinters in Scotland) scored twice at Darlington.

Another signing from Ireland was Linfield winger Thomas McMurray who had the twin distinctions of being one of the very few Irishmen to play county cricket (for Surrey) and of being one of the shortest players, at just 5'-2", to play county cricket or League football (and along with 'Spurs Fanny Walden, almost certainly the smallest to do both).

A last minute penalty save enabled Lincoln to win at Spotland in the League and one of the best crowds for many years, 11,500, saw the FA Cup-tie against the same opponents which was drawn one-all. Lincoln won the replay to end hopes of a financial boost from a cup run, and with money as short as ever (despite wages of £4 a week for first team men), leading scorer Hunt with 10 goals to his name already, was sold to Stockport County who were struggling at the foot of Division Two.

Accrington won by the only goal at Rochdale on Christmas day but Jimmy Wynn's strike, reversed the scoreline the following day. On New Years Day he did even better, with a hat-trick in a remarkable 5-0 win at York. By January Rochdale were as high as ninth, but then four games were lost, promotion hopefuls Doncaster Rovers winning a thriller 5-4 at Willbutts Lane. Playing into a gale, Rochdale equalised three times only to immediately concede another each time.

Wynn successfully converted a rare Rochdale penalty (Hunt had missed three of the last four awarded), to launch his side on the way to a 4-0 win against Chester but the next four homes were only drawn and the intervening aways all lost, though there was some excuse for the defeat at New Brighton, as McLaren was forced to go in goal when Fawcett was injured.

Rochdale got back into the scoring habit with six in a friendly against the manager's old club Glentoran, Wynn scoring another hat-trick, and then defeated Carlisle home and away. On Easter Saturday, a massive 17,000 crowd turned up at Boundary Park to watch the clash of the near neighbours, which Oldham won 4-2 after former Rochdale 'keeper Caunce saved Wynn's penalty. Wynn finished with 20 goals in 28 games, but the season's last goal was an own goal by Halifax's Craig. Remarkably he was Rochdale's fifth opponent to put through his own net during the season.

At the end of this season of decidedly mixed fortunes, Rochdale finished in 17th place, though just one more win would have seen them in 12th. They won six away games, the best since the heady days of 1926-7, but only seven on their own ground, where ten games were drawn.

Despite the fact that he had been ill with pleurisy for some time, Sam Jennings was given a one-year managerial contract in April and he decided to build upon his current defence and the proven goalscoring abilities of Wynn. All the remaining first team players were released. These included the veteran Harry Marshall who went to Linfield, while Jimmy Eastwood became the latest of a number of players to move between Rochdale and Tunbridge Wells Rangers since George Beel went there as player/manager in 1933. One man who never got into the first team, but perhaps deserved to for effort, was an amateur named Stan McLaren; after he failed to make his mark in a trial match, it transpired that he had cycled all the way from Liverpool to get a game.

Syd Goodfellow signed in 1938

One of the Directors, Mr. T. Hall had taken over as secretary and at the club's general meeting, he was able to announce that in the previous year, a loss of only £254 had been sustained, a great improvement on the previous few years. Even so, the club was now in the red to the tune of £10,153-10s. A little money was made in the summer, though, by hosting the National Baseball Cup Final, in which local side Rochdale Greys beat Oldham Greyhounds.

Rochdale had few major signings for the 1938-39 season. They obtained Fred Reeve, a left half from Tottenham Hotspurs Reserves, plus two more Glentoran players, Syd Goodfellow and Arthur Griffiths. New reserve goalkeeper was Tommy Doyle from Celtic, while veteran winger George 'Shortie' Mee joined the club as reserve team trainer-coach. At the beginning of his career Mee had set up a record when, starting from his debut in 1920, he played 195 consecutive League games for Blackpool; his younger brother Bertie was the Arsenal manager of the 1970's.

1938-39:
Rochdale played two Football League Jubilee games against Halifax, before the season proper, both sides running up comfortable home wins in turn. Within 45 minutes of the start of the League campaign, Rochdale were four down at Rotherham and they eventually lost 7-1, their worst ever start to a season. Two home defeats followed and although Rochdale gained their first points with home draws against Doncaster and York, when manager Jennings stepped down through ill health in mid-September, his side was next to bottom, without a win in seven outings.

The board then made the bold decision to promote the side's extrovert skipper Ted Goodier to the post of acting player-manager. He quickly made changes, switching the roles of Syd Goodfellow and Joe Duff, bringing back Jimmy Wynn to lead the attack and selecting 'keeper Tommy Doyle and ex-Aldershot forwards Reg Kilsby and Tommy Prest for their debuts.

~ CHAPTER 4 ~

The transformation brought about by Ted Goodier was swift and impressive, at the Willbutts Ground at least. Gateshead were beaten 5-2, both Duff and Wynn responding with goals. (The relief in the Rochdale camp over this win was repeated on a national scale a few days later, when Prime Minister Neville Chamberlain returned from meeting Hitler with his famous piece of paper, proclaiming *"peace in our time"*). Warming to his task, Wynn then struck twice at Hartlepool, though Dale were defeated, then crashed in a hat-trick in a 6-1 win against Darlington.

Chester and Hull were also on the receiving end as Wynn and his co-attackers ran up big tallies. Having just signed former Accrington regular Wally Reynolds, the new manager now sold another wingman, Arthur Griffiths to Stoke, an early sign of the wheeler-dealing that became his trademark in later years.

Away from Spotland, Rochdale's miserable run continued unabated. Their eighth successive away defeat was spectacular by any standards, as they crashed out of the FA Cup on the wrong end of a 7-3 scoreline at Halifax. Former Rotherham full back Harry Roberts had the misfortune to make his debut in this match, and it proved to be his only first team game in Rochdale's colours. By coincidence his former Rotherham team-mate Harry Knowles made one cup appearance later in the season, but also failed to make a League appearance for Rochdale. Another one game man was the diminutive outside right John Latimer. Though he had made a number of Scottish League appearances, his previous Football League games had been for Portsmouth back in 1929-30.

After five straight home wins Rochdale missed out against Stockport but promptly made amends by ending their dismal away run in style, putting five past bottom club Accrington Stanley. Shortly afterwards, the 38 year old Mee, who had actually made three first team appearances, including his 500th Football League game, returned to Stanley, his previous club, as their player-coach, and masterminded their unexpected run to the final of the Third Division (North) Cup. Rochdale also secured an excellent victory against runaway League leaders Barnsley, the Tykes remaining undefeated away from home for the remainder of the season.

Although beaten twice over Christmas, Rochdale bounced back to defeat Southport 5-0, even though they were without their injured player-manager. On New Year's Day they obtained a highly prized victory, their first ever League win at Boundary Park over more prosperous neighbours Oldham Athletic. Wing half Reeve netted the winner in the second half, his third goal of the season. Two weeks later Dale achieved an astounding success by seven goals to nil at York. Peter Vause, a recent signing from Blackburn Rovers as a part-timer (he was a schoolmaster), scored a hat-trick on only his fifth appearance. Former Leeds man Joe Firth notched two and the old firm of Duff and Wynn completed the rout. This ranks alongside the 8-2 win at Hartlepool in 1930 as Rochdale's greatest ever away performance. Almost inevitably the next home game was a goalless draw.

After that, though, the goals continued to flow. A 2-2 draw at Gateshead, earned by Doyle's penalty save, edged Dale temporarily into the top half, but they then suffered reverses in two agonising games for the home supporters, going down 3-4 to Hartlepool and 4-5 to Halifax. This would have been particularly galling for Wynn, unlucky for once, as he scored five of the goals himself. He ended the season with an impressive 30, the third best in the division (the division's top scorer was Wynn's one time partner Wally Hunt who netted 33 times in 32 games, all bar one for Carlisle).

In January Ted Goodier had signed a two year contract as manager, to take effect when Jennings' ended. In fact Jennings decided to leave in March so Goodier now took up his appointment. Four consecutive draws followed before the home form was restored with 4-0, 5-0 and 4-1 wins to round off the season at Willbutts Lane. Further away wins had also been secured, and even though the last two games of the term were lost, Rochdale still finished in a respectable 15th spot with 39 points, their best since the departure of Jack Peart.

Despite the Munich Agreement of the previous September, international tensions were again worsening as a result of the increasingly aggressive stance of Hitler's Germany. War was again felt to be imminent and before the Crewe match near the end of the season, the secretary appealed to young men in the crowd to join up. Possibly by coincidence, the attendance for the next game was down by three and a half thousand.

Less response had been forthcoming the previous month when a shilling fund appeal had been launched to help pay the players' wages during the summer. After a week, it had raised the magnificent sum of - 1 shilling!

In the final week of the season Syd Goodfellow was transferred to Chesterfield who had just enjoyed their best ever season in Division Two, and Fred Reeve was transferred to Grimsby. These two were among the very few pre-war Rochdale players still plying their trade in the late 'forties, with Goodfellow figuring in the Accrington Stanley team as late as 1952-53. Tommy Doyle followed the well beaten path to Stockport's Edgeley Park and the man he had replaced in goal, Des Fawcett, was released after over 100 games for the club.

Carrying on regardless, despite the gathering war clouds, it was business as usual at Spotland in the summer of 1939. Indeed, the chairmen of the bigger clubs were more concerned by the *"sinister aspect"* of a questionnaire circulated by the Third Division clubs on the possibility of 4-up, 4-down (i.e. two clubs promoted from each section). Ted Goodier meantime indulged in some transfer dealings. Best known of his signings was Richard Rhodes, a wing half who had been 12th man for England in his Wolves days in the early 'thirties.

Three other experienced men were George Nevin from Lincoln, Tranmere's George Flowers, and Willie Harker of Stockport, who had served 13 Football League clubs between them; Flowers had also, when Doncaster's 12th man, run the line in a Football League game when the referee did not turn up. New goalkeeper was Peter Robertson of Arbroath who had first figured in top class Scottish football with Dundee back in 1927. The manager had decided to play less himself, so acquired the long-serving Bristol City pivot Jim Pearce, an ex-regular soldier and Welsh Amateur international. Alex Ferguson of Hearts, Tommy Dutton from Mansfield, Exeter's Harry Pollard, ex-Aldershot man Ernest Robson, Doug Redwood of Walsall, and Chesterfield's Arthur Richardson completed the squad. Joe Duff took over the captaincy.

The improvements under Goodier and the strong squad he had assembled had not gone unnoticed. The Topical Times Sporting Annual went so far as to suggest that they would be the season's surprise packet *"powerful and constructive at wing half and goalful in front"*. Unfortunately they were not to have the chance to show their potential, Mr Hitler would see to that.

1939-40:
Following a pre-season Jubilee game, again against Halifax, Goodier's side - sporting numbers on their jerseys for the first time - opened the League campaign with a defeat at Doncaster but snapped back to defeat Wrexham at Willbutts Lane.

Wynn netted the only goal, his 65th in just 88 League games for the club. On September 2nd, with the German invasion of Poland already underway and evacuation schemes being put in motion in Great Britain, Reynolds' goal gave Rochdale victory over York. At 11 o'clock the following morning the Prime Minister announced over the wireless that war was declared as from 5 p. m that afternoon.

Unlike in 1914, professional football was suspended at once. In any case, compulsory military service for all men between 18 and 41 not in reserved occupations had already come into operation. However, after a few weeks of the 'phony war', during which there was little sign of activity on the home front, the football authorities organised a number of regional leagues to fill the gap.

Rochdale's first match in the Regional League North West Division was against old rivals Barrow. Gwyn Jones, back from Tranmere, started the campaign by putting through his own goal and the visitors went home with a 3-1 win. Rochdale also lost at Southport but then thrashed Accrington 5-1 at Spotland to gain their first points in the new league. They only gained one further point in the first six games (against First Division Preston) but then won successive games against Carlisle and away to Oldham, where Arthur Richardson hit a hat-trick.

With matches only played on Saturdays and with a number of postponements, the season became rather disjointed, Rochdale playing only five times between early December and early March. Even when they did get back into regular action, they made little impression (they lost 4-1 at Accrington in front of just 300 spectators) and their first victory of 1940 did not materialise until April 6th when they won 2-1 at Carlisle with goals from former Swansea regular Tommy Olsen and skipper Joe Duff.

They were more successful in the War League Cup however, beating Accrington Stanley 3-0 in the preliminary round. A crowd of 7,500 turned up for the home leg of Rochdale's first round tie against Bury which they won by a single goal. Following a 7-2 thrashing by Blackpool in the League, Jock Dodds scoring one of his many wartime hat-tricks, Duff's goal earned the required draw in the second leg at Bury. In round two Everton won easily by five goals to one at Goodison, Tommy Lawton netting three. But back at Spotland Rochdale looked like they might pull off a miracle when they led 4-1, Duff scoring another couple in the eventual 7-5 aggregate defeat. Rochdale managed just one more success in the League before their season ended a month late on June 3rd, with just 353 spectators seeing a defeat at Blackburn, future Rochdale centre forward Tom Hargreaves netting a hat-trick. Despite taking only 15 points from 22 games, Rochdale finished ninth in the 12 team section. The Reserves, on the other hand, finished top of the Lancashire Combination.

Joe Duff and Jimmy Eastwood, who had returned from Tunbridge Wells, played in all the games, while QPR's Arthur Warburton was also a regular. Top scorer was Arthur Richardson with 14 goals in as many games.

As with teams everywhere, numerous guest players turned out for Rochdale. Many of these were from Bury - who won the division and finished a month before the Dale - including well known post-war player Reg Halton, former Newcastle United man Archie Livingstone, and their top scorer Tom Burdett. Other notables included QPR full back Bill Byrom, who served Rochdale on and off for nine years, veteran Bury and Bolton backs Tom Chester and Alick Robinson, Millwall's Syd Rawlings, the son of First World War Rochdale star Archie, who had already followed his father's footsteps to Preston (where Archie was trainer) and Northampton, and Jack Ellis, the Bristol Rovers goalkeeper the day Joe Payne scored 10 goals for Luton. Several former Rochdale players also guested back at Spotland, including Wally Hunt (Carlisle), Tom Smith (Burnley) and Ernie Steele (Millwall).

The wartime conditions meant that the players not in the forces had other jobs, indeed, Livingstone had a remarkable number of them. Besides playing for Bury and Dale he followed his real trade as a slater, but also worked in an aircraft factory, a stone quarry, a paper mill and as a clerk. Ellis was an RAF policeman, Robinson was serving as an auxiliary fireman and Halton was a postman before joining up. When Alfie Anderson, the former Bolton player, who was working as an upholsterer in Bury, agreed to guest for Rochdale, he insisted they insure him for £1000 against any injury which might prevent him carrying on his trade.

Even while Rochdale had been playing their last two games of the previous season, the dramatic evacuation of the British Army from Dunkirk had been underway and by the time they opened their next campaign, it was Churchill's 'Few' who were fighting it out with Goering's Luftwaffe in the Battle of Britain. The attitude of the public and the powers that be was rather different to that prevailing in the Great War, however, and during the 'Hitler War' diversions such as regular Saturday afternoon soccer were looked on as good for morale. (In true British fashion, a little later in the war when future Dale player Tommy Barkas was serving there, a message was sent from the beleaguered island of Malta asking that the BBC repeat the previous Saturday's football results *as a heavy bombing raid interfered with reception").

1940-41:
For the 1940-41 season, therefore, the regional competitions were extended and Rochdale found themselves in the North Regional League. The season began with a visit by Manchester United, who won 3-1, and further defeats followed.

Bury won 7-3 at Gigg Lane, before Rochdale managed to beat Preston North End (the eventual champions) in their sixth game. The next five games produced just one further success, at Southport, and included a 5-0 defeat in the return at Preston in front of just 300 supporters.

Rochdale then struck a run of excellent form, defeating Stockport County 5-3 (a young Harry Catterick scoring all three for the losers) and Burnley 1-0 before a remarkable 10-0 victory over Southport, Wally Sidebottom a pre-war Bolton Wanderers reserve netting five. He ended the season as top scorer but tragically did not live to fulfil this promise, as he was drowned later in the war when his ship was torpedoed.

Two more away wins, 4-2 at Bradford Park Avenue and 4-3 at Manchester United, just before Old Trafford was put out of action by a German bombing raid on the nearby industrial sites, were followed by a sixth successive victory, when they beat Crewe Alexandra by a single goal. Oldham Athletic ended the run by winning at Spotland on Christmas Day - it had originally been planned to play at Boundary Park in the morning and at Willbutts Lane in the afternoon, but the former was cancelled - and Bury did the same three days later. In the Lancashire Cup (the games also counting in the League), Rochdale were annihilated 9-1 at Maine Road, and Manchester City rubbed it in by winning the second leg 6-1. City's Jimmy Currie scored five times in each game against former Manchester United goalkeeper John Hall.

After a 5-0 win at home to Crewe in the League, Rochdale travelled to Newcastle for the first time and stunned the Geordies by winning 2-1 in the League War Cup, Dale's goals coming from local lad Percy Taylor and guest Arthur Bellis from Port Vale. In the second leg, Newcastle turned the tables, however, winning 3-1 thanks to a hat-trick from future Liverpool star Albert Stubbins (the only footballer on the famous Beatles' *Sergeant Pepper* album cover, incidentally), his fourth treble in five games. Rochdale then put another five past Crewe, newcomer Walter Horrabin claiming four of them, but saw their goals against column rapidly increased by their worst ever first team result, an 11-0 scoreline at Huddersfield (though fortunately only 356 fans saw it). The unfortunate 'keeper was Kenneth Heys, playing his only senior game. The final seven games produced just one further victory.

Due to the unequal numbers of games played by the various teams, the North Regional League was decided on goal average only. Given the Manchester City and Huddersfield results this was not Rochdale's strong suit and they finished 30th of 36 clubs. Jimmy Eastwood and Joe Duff were again consistent performers, along with Tommy Dutton and 'keeper Hall. A famous name to turn out regularly was Jim Cunliffe, the Everton and England man who was considered the classiest inside forward ever to have worn a Dale shirt.

Another was the splendidly named former Derby County and England wing half Errington Ridley Liddell Keen, Ike (or 'Snowy') for short. Two other England internationals made odd guest appearances, George Hunt of Bolton, one of the country's top goalscorers of the 1930's, and Middlesbrough's Mick Fenton, second highest scorer in the Football League in 1939. Long-serving Huddersfield full back Reg Mountford (an ARP warden) and Blackpool's George Farrow, who was rated by Stanley Matthews as the best uncapped player of his day, were also among the 48 players used by Rochdale, as was a player named Rothwell who happened to be in the ground one day when Rochdale were a man short. (This wasn't unusual, for a couple of years later Southport turned up with only nine men and their manager picked a couple of local amateurs out of the Willbutts Lane crowd). There were many famous names in opposition teams, too, of course, such as Bill Shankly and Tom Finney for Preston, Nat Lofthouse for Bolton and Bradford's Len Shackleton.

1941-42:
A further rearrangement for 1941-42 saw Rochdale in the Football League - Northern Section (or League North for short) in which a separate competition was to be played in each half of the season. They opened with a 3-2 win against Oldham but lost the return with the Latics at Boundary Park and did not gain another victory until the beginning of November, when they beat Southport 4-2. The worst results in the interim were heavy defeats by Preston, 5-1 at home and 6-0 away.

A better spell brought a double against Bury and three points off Bolton. Blackburn, though, won 8-2 at Ewood Park and Blackpool 5-0 at Spotland. In the return match on Christmas Day, which attracted 11,500 spectators, Rochdale *startled the football world by beating Blackpool on their merits*. With *Dodds completely subdued and Matthews under the influence of a brilliant Sneddon*, Jim Cunliffe scored the only goal after running through from the half way line, though this did not stop the home side finishing as champions. Rochdale ended up 22nd of 38 teams, with 16 points from 18 games in this first phase of the season.

The next set of matches was a qualifying competition for the League War Cup. Rochdale recorded two wins but were annihilated 8-2 at home by a strong Liverpool side and the Reds added another five at Anfield, Billy Liddell scoring a hat-trick to add to those scored by Balmer and Done in the first game.

In the Lancashire Cup, Rochdale beat Bury 7-5 on aggregate and then remarkably beat Blackpool, the top side in the North - they had recently won successive games 15-3 and 13-0 - for the second time in the season. Blackpool retrieved the deficit in the second leg and went on to take the trophy.

But the first leg defeat did cost the Tangerines the League championship for the second half of the season. Due to a number of postponements and the complicated fixture list, Rochdale only played 13 games after Christmas and were thus not eligible for the second championship, which required teams to have played at least 18 times.

Hull City player Jim Treanor actually made most appearances for Rochdale, missing just one game (Hull had temporarily pulled out of the League). Joe Duff, Tommy Sneddon, top scorer Jim Cunliffe and Bradford City's Duncan Colquhoun were also regular performers, but 57 players were used in all. Among the prominent guests were no less than seven internationals; Willie Gorman of Brentford, who played for both Northern Ireland and the Republic either side of the war, Newcastle goalkeeper Tom Swinburne who played for England in wartime internationals, his Newcastle colleague Bob Ancell of Scotland, Willie MacFadyen, one of Scottish football's all time greats and scorer of 53 goals for Motherwell in 1931-32, Swansea 'keeper Roy John, his Welsh team mate Les Boulter, another Brentford man, and the former Kingstonian centre half William Whittaker who had won an England Amateur cap at the age of 16 just before the war.

1942-43:
Rochdale again figured in the Football League North in 1942-43, though the competition was increased to 48 clubs. They started with a draw at Southport but lost the next three games before beating Oldham at home. They then lost six more games, conceding 25 goals in the last five. Recovering to beat Burnley and Stockport, Dale also took three points off Bolton, drawing 4-4 at Burnden Park. They ended the first tournament with two remarkable games against Bury, winning 6-3 at home but losing 7-3 at Gigg Lane on Christmas Day. Despite the late improvement Dale finished 41st out of 48.

They started well in the League Cup qualifying competition, winning two close games against Oldham and beating Blackburn 4-0. After a draw at Blackburn, Rochdale defeated Stockport twice, 4-3 away and 6-0 at home with a Jim Cunliffe hat-trick. They recorded a victory and a defeat against Bury and ended the qualifying section with a win and a draw against Burnley, George Murphy scoring a hat-trick in the home game. Murphy, of Bradford City, was one of wartime football's great travellers, at one time appearing for 8 different clubs in 9 weeks. At the end of the season he represented Wales against England.

Their excellent run had given Rochdale 16 points from 10 games and they finished second in the competition, behind Manchester City by a minute fraction on goal difference. However, in the first round proper Blackburn reversed the earlier form and won both legs.

Rochdale departed quickly from the Lancashire Cup, too, losing to Oldham on aggregate. They then played a couple of League matches in the second championship (as before, the cup-ties also counted in this competition), beating Burnley at home for the third time but losing at Turf Moor, on April 10th. Although the season went on for another month, Rochdale did not play any further fixtures and had to be content with 21st place out of 54 clubs, most of the others playing 20 games to Rochdale's 16.

Lewis Bradford, a former Preston North End player, appeared in all 34 games, while Jim Cunliffe missed only three and was again top scorer with 20 goals. The only other players to turn out regularly were Walsall 'keeper Jim Strong, who was Burnley's first choice for six seasons after the war, and a newcomer from Bolton, Eric Wood, who would render similar service to Rochdale. Notable guests included Scottish international centre half Tom Smith of Kilmarnock and Preston, long-serving Burnley full back Gilbert Richmond and two players with Football League careers going back to the 1920's - 'keeper Arthur Chesters from Crystal Palace and forward George Walton, recently of Cardiff City. Ron Hornby, now of Burnley, played his first game for Rochdale for 11 years. Guesting in the other direction, Dale's Wally Reynolds had the chance to play in a cup final when Sheffield Wednesday met Blackpool in the Football League North Cup Final.

In the summer manager Ted Goodier was tempted away to take over the managership of Birmingham, but fortunately for Rochdale soon decided against a change of scene and was back at his desk at Spotland after only three months. The lantern-jawed six footer, known to his players as 'The Cowboy' because of his habit of wearing a kind of stetson (and famous for his wonderful command of unprintable language!) became one of the Dale's most influential managers ever during his long spell in charge.

1943-44:
The size of the Football League North again changed slightly for 1943-44, a total of 50 clubs being involved. The first opposition was familiar enough, though, Blackpool (eventual champions again) scoring six home and away. The roles were reversed when Southport visited Spotland, ex-Bolton man Jack Harker scoring five times in a 6-1 win and then getting all the Rochdale goals in a 4-4 draw in the return.

Everton star Jim Cunliffe, who guested for Rochdale during the war.

Rochdale continued to win at home, but apart from a draw at Halifax did not have anything further to show from their travels until winning at Stockport in November. The home game the following week was Rochdale's shortest ever, the result standing at 2-0 even though the match was abandoned after 74 minutes due to the fog which also kept the crowd down to just 1100. Rochdale gained two excellent wins, 4-1 and 5-0 against Bury, despite only having 10 men in the away game, and ended the first championship in 13th place with 22 points from 18 games.

In the League Cup qualifying competition Rochdale got off to a flying start by beating Bolton 5-0, Harker getting another four against his old club as well as hitting the post three times. (He totalled 25 goals in only 22 appearances by the season's end). Rochdale also beat Blackburn and Burnley to extend their run to 11 straight wins at Willbutts Lane before being held to a goalless draw by Southport. Blackpool beat Rochdale twice (again), but the Dale still qualified for the competition proper in 25th place with 11 points from 10 games. In the first round they drew 3-3 at Burnley and a goal from Birmingham's Tom Sibley in extra time of the second leg settled the tie.

In the last sixteen Rochdale drew Blackpool and a crowd of 25,000 turned up at Bloomfield Road to see the Tangerines' star-studded side run in eight goals, including hat-tricks for past and future England centre forwards Ronnie Dix and Stan Mortensen. Stanley Matthews so mesmerised his marker, Bill Byrom, on one occasion, that the Dale full back literally fell to his knees as the maestro jinked past him. Two goals by Joe Duff in the second leg restored the balance a little, despite the 9-2 aggregate. Duff, incidentally, was working as a driver for the local Yelloways coach firm, transporting prisoners-of-war to northern camps, and frequently drove the bus taking him and his team mates to away games.

In the Lancashire Cup, Rochdale beat Oldham home and away, but were themselves beaten twice by Stockport. Rounding off the season with two points from two games with Tranmere (seeing fair play, the referee at Prenton Park was the local vicar!), Rochdale finished the second half of the season 24th of 56 clubs with 21 points from 20 games. Remarkably enough the champions were non-League Bath City who were in the six team Football League West in the first half of the season.

In the second championship this was merged with the Football League North, but Bath continued to play just their five western colleagues, meeting them 37 times in all!

Lewis Bradford again played in all the games and Eric Wood, Joe Duff, Bill Byrom and former Stockport man George Haigh played regularly, too. Most notable of the short term guests were post-war Blackburn regular John Wharton, veteran Palace half back Les Leivesley and Cardiff goalkeeper Bill Fielding, who won a wartime cup winners medal with Bolton the following year. Leivesley was killed in the tragic air crash in Italy in 1949 which wiped out the Torino team he was coaching.

1944-45:
D-Day had passed and the Allied invasion of Europe was well underway by the time friendlier battle was resumed on the football fields of England. Rochdale again met Blackpool in their first match of the 1944-45 season in the Football League North, and the visitors went one better than the previous year, winning 7-3 with another Mortensen hat-trick. Rochdale gained their first points at the fourth attempt, when they beat Blackburn to start an eight match unbeaten run which included a 5-2 victory over Preston. Against Oldham the usual trend was reversed, with each side winning the away fixture, but Rochdale wound up the first championship by losing at the Shay and then beating Halifax at Spotland. This gave them 19 points from 18 games and they finished exactly half way down the 54 teams competing.

Rochdale started the League North Cup qualifying fixtures well enough with a win at Accrington and three draws, but lost twice to Burnley, suffered the regulation demolition by Blackpool (6-3 and 4-0), and wound up losing 8-0 at home to Blackburn. Rovers also removed Dale from the Lancashire Cup, leaving them time for eight League matches in the second championship. They won the first two, then lost five in a row before ending the season with a 2-1 home win over Chester, thus finishing a fairly dismal 57th out of 60.

Joe Duff played in every match, but only five other players (of the 75 used) appeared in even half of them; George Haigh, Arthur Chesters, Ellis Cornwell, a full back signed from Chorley, Swansea's John Gallon, and John Neary who had played for Rochdale pre-war as a part-timer but had appeared infrequently up to now. The best known of the many guests were Hull City's former England winger Arthur Cunliffe, Jim's cousin, Alf Hanson - Chelsea's England wartime international (whose full name was, unfortunately for the time, Adolph), Bob Davies of Nottingham Forest, a wartime international for Wales, long serving Bury full back Jack Gemmell, veteran Doncaster man Albert Malam and New Brighton stalwart Alf (this time short for Alphonse) Ainsworth.

The latter had made quite a number of guest appearances over the years, as New Brighton did not play in several of the wartime seasons. Arthur Cunliffe had also guested for Aldershot while serving in the nearby army camp as a Physical training Instructor, and regularly appeared in a side containing half a dozen other internationals, such as Joe Mercer and Stan Culls who were also stationed there.

Four days after Rochdale's last match of the season, Britain celebrated V. E. day, the end of the war in Europe. On the same day Ted Goodier obtained the signature of a young forward who had been playing for Moss Grove, Billy Woods. He would, in due course, be one of Rochdale's new generation in the hopeful post-war world.

1945-46:
While Europe was now at peace, the war with Japan continued through the summer of 1945, but there too the end was in sight by August. Meanwhile the football authorities had begun to prepare for the return of normal football in 1946 and decided to operate a more regionalised version of the Third Division for the coming campaign, Rochdale being in the Third North West. Although guest players were still regularly in action, the clubs were preparing for peacetime soccer, too, signing more players on regular (though not necessarily full time professional) terms.

Rochdale's signings included Bolton wing half Joe McCormick, who became club captain, two full backs Edric (better known as Syd) Pomphrey of Notts County and Manchester City's Len Jackson, and youngster Don Partridge from Farnworth. Former guests, the veterans Arthur Chesters and Arthur Cunliffe also joined the playing staff, while the coaching staff under manager Goodier, comprised the 1920's Bury stalwart Dave Robbie and his assistant Billy Kelly.

Rochdale lost the opening match at Wrexham but gained revenge in the return. They also beat Oldham 4-2, thanks to a hat-trick from Jim Constantine. A couple of days later the centre forward, acquired from Ashton National the previous December, became Rochdale's first post-war transfer when he was sold to Manchester City for £1000. He later scored over 100 Football League goals for City, Bury and Millwall. Rochdale were thrashed 7-0 at Stockport but still managed to reverse the result at home, and did the double over Southport, Hanson hitting a hat-trick and their new centre forward from Rossendale, Joe Hargreaves, netting a brace in each of his first three games..

Rochdale met Stockport County in the first round of the FA Cup and Jack Brindle, a new signing from Burnley, scored his fifth goal in as many games in a 3-2 aggregate victory (for this season only, FA Cup ties were decided over two legs).

Rochdale warmed up for the second round with a 4-1 win at Crewe, but lost the first leg at Tranmere. Nevertheless, after Hargreaves had levelled the aggregate scores at Spotland, it was Sam Makin who came up with the goal to settle the tie in Rochdale's favour.

Although Dale beat Accrington on Christmas Day, Stanley's 4-2 victory in the return the following day consolidated their top spot in the section. Rochdale beat Crewe at Spotland a few days later but the first championship was then put into abeyance as cup-ties took over the scene. In the third round of the FA Cup, a crowd of 13,000 at Gigg Lane saw Rochdale earn a 3-3 draw, but despite two more goals by Hargreaves, Bury won the second leg 4-2. In the Third North West Cup qualifying competition, Rochdale started badly by losing at home to Southport, and despite beating Chester 6-1 thanks to an Eric Wood hat-trick, they failed to make the top eight with only six points from 10 games.

Nevertheless, young Rochdale 'keeper John Kirk, who had made just six first team appearances, was selected to play for Lancashire Amateurs and did so well that he was selected for the England side to play Wales in a Victory amateur international. Strangely enough after missing Rochdale's game to play for England he never regained his place in the team and was later transferred to non-League Peterborough. Around the same time, Jack Brindle was sold to Chelsea for £1000 and this helped to fund one of Ted Goodier's best ever buys, when he spent a club record £1500 on Huddersfield Town centre half Walter Birch, son of the former Sheffield Wednesday and Chesterfield goalie Arnold Birch.

In the Division Three North's second championship, Rochdale returned to form, beating Barrow twice and sharing the points with Lincoln, another new signing Joe Rodi from Grimsby scoring in each of his first three games. Rochdale then played their remaining game in the first championship and, fielding their sixth goalkeeper in seven games, Bill Roberts from Welsh junior football, the goalless draw with Tranmere was enough to secure them an excellent second place with 10 wins in their 18 games. Back in the second championship, they secured two victories over Oldham (winning 4-0 at Boundary Park), lost at Southport but then won the final match against the same opponents. This left Dale in second place again, just a point behind the season's top side in the Third North, Rotherham.

The most regular performers in the Third Division games were Arthur Cunliffe, Syd Pomphrey, skipper Joe McCormick and Eric Wood, but the top scorer was Joe Hargreaves with eight in League games and six in the FA Cup, even though, as a part-timer, he had to miss games through work commitments.

This had been Hargreaves' first taste of senior football at the ripe old age of 30, a fairly extreme case of a general phenomenon as players returned to top level action after a six year lay-off which had bitten deep into many careers.

Best known of the guests, many of them now at the veteran stage, were Ernie Toseland the former Manchester City star who had represented the Football League way back in 1929, Bradford City's Paddy Molloy (who represented the Irish League the following year), and goalkeeper Jack Breedon of Manchester United who had saved a penalty in the 1941 War Cup Final. A famous name, if not player, appearing on the team sheet near the end of the season was Harry Nuttall, nephew of the old England star and Dale player of the same name and son of the 1920's Dale skipper Jimmy. Unfortunately he was not destined to follow in their footsteps, a rather less than generous newspaper report of his single senior game stating that his presence was *"undoubtedly a handicap"*.

In March, Jimmy Wynn's had been a test case for the many footballers returning from the forces or war work, who sought reinstatement of their pre-war contracts. He lost the case in the courts but was in fact signed on for the rest of the season. A sadder case, showing that not everyone could carry on where they had left off, even though peace was restored, was that of Tom Jones. The former Accrington player had guested for the Dale early in the war, but had lost both feet when blown up by a land mine after the D-Day landings, and his former clubs played two benefit matches for him during the season.

In the close season, most of the remaining pre-war players, including Jim Pearce who had played regularly for the past season, were released along with many of the wartime acquisitions. To emphasise the break with the past, in June 1946 the long serving Joe Duff, who had been with the club since 1935 and made a tremendous 343 appearances and scored 65 goals, signed for Cheltenham. Nevertheless, some 28 players were still on the club's books, though only six were full time professionals. Of the others, Joe Hargreaves for instance was a clerk, Len Jackson was a machinist, Billy Woods was a mechanic and the former England star Arthur Cunliffe was working as a plumbers mate.

During the summer of 1946, several former guests were signed up, including Bill Byrom from QPR for £100 and Oldham's Charlie Hurst (whose then four year old son Geoff would be England's World Cup hero twenty years on). Amongst the other newcomers were Bill Hallard of Bradford Park Avenue and Queen of the South goalkeeper Bill Henderson, who had represented the Scottish FA in a representative game in India at the end of the war, plus Falkirk's Alec Carruthers, a one time reserve for Scotland.

The only pre-war player to return to the colours was Tommy Sneddon and even he soon left to coach in Czechoslovakia. Off the field the Rochdale board, with local business man Mr Fletcher Bolton as chairman and W. R. Commins as secretary, was joined by Mr F. S. Ratcliffe, at the age of 32, one of the youngest directors of a Football League club.

1946-47:

The campaign (whose fixtures followed those of the aborted 1939-40 season) started with a defeat at Doncaster, excusable in the light of subsequent events, as Rovers eventually amassed a phenomenal 72 points. Things went from bad to worse, though, when the first two home games were each lost by a single goal while Rochdale contrived to miss three penalties. The fifth game produced the first point, from New Brighton, but only two had accrued from the first eight games, despite the signing of the experienced Tommy Barkas, a member of a famous footballing family, from Halifax for £500 and full back Norman Kirkman from Burnley.

However when bottom of the table Rochdale entertained Carlisle United they annihilated them 6-0, with inside left Billy Woods on his Football League debut (the 22nd player used already) helping to lay on a hat-trick for Joe Hargreaves. Rochdale followed this up with a 3-2 win at Accrington and winger Carruthers scored twice on his debut in a win at Tranmere. After a convincing home victory over Darlington, a crowd of 22,712 - the highest for any Rochdale game since 1925 - saw them win 1-0 at Hull City's new ground at Boothferry Park. Rochdale gained a fourth consecutive away success at Hartlepool.

In the FA Cup Rochdale took on famous amateurs Bishop Auckland and slammed them 6-1. After an intervening goalless draw, they repeated this score in round two against Hartlepool, Billy Woods grabbing three of the goals. In the League, Rochdale had suffered just one defeat in 13 games, but went down home and away to Stockport over Christmas, conceding nine goals in the process.

Local 'all-rounder' Wally Jones, a star for both Rochdale Cricket Club and Rochdale Hornets, scored twice at Stockport on his second and last Football League appearance. In the next game runaway leaders Doncaster attracted a crowd of 13,555 paying the tidy sum of £922 (even with 'popular side' prices reduced from 1s 6d to 1s 3d), the best at Willbutts Lane for nearly 20 years, but it was the visiting contingent who went home happy after their side won 3-2.

In the third round of the FA Cup Rochdale visited Charlton Athletic of Division One and a still better crowd of 23,271 saw them go down, somewhat unluckily, by three goals to one to the eventual cup winners, many 'Addicks fans considering this to be their hardest tie of the whole cup run.

The Rochdale goal was a brilliant effort by Billy Woods and a few days later the red haired inside forward was on his way to Bradford Park Avenue for a club record £4,500, a considerable fee given that Park Avenue themselves had just received a post-war record £13,000 for the sale of the legendary `clown prince of soccer' Len Shackleton. Oddly enough, Woods had scored five goals in the cup but only one in the league.

Rochdale's eighth away win in nine games, at Carlisle, was their last match for a month due to the severe winter, the worst ever for postponements up to that time. Indeed only two games were possible between February 1st and the last week in March, one of them a heavy defeat at Darlington but the other an excellent 5-2 victory over Hull. Jackie Moss, a recent signing from Bury whose build belied his off field occupation of blacksmith, scored two of the goals (by coincidence Moss was from the same small village, Blackrod near Horwich, as both Arthur and Jim Cunliffe). This match also saw the debuts of wingers Tom Sibley, a former wartime guest who had also been signed by Ted Goodier for his previous club Birmingham, and Hugh O'Donnell of Blackpool, brother of Scottish international Frank and himself the possessor of both Scottish and English cup winners medals.

On the resumption, over 10,000 fans saw Rochdale beaten by Bradford City at Easter, one of only three defeats after the turn of the year, and nearly 12,000 turned up for the home game against second placed Rotherham, which the Dale would have won but for Eric Wood becoming their eighth different player to fail from the penalty spot during the season. Oddly enough, given Dale's appalling record, top scorer Hargreaves, who finished the season with 23 League and two cup goals, never took a penalty. This may have been because he was stone deaf and thus unable to hear the referee's signal to take the kick, though his disability did enable him to ignore abuse from the crowd if he missed a good chance!

The season should have ended on April 26th and the club had been keen to finish as early as possible in order to make ground improvements. However, a government ban prevented re-arranged games being played in mid-week so Rochdale still had five games to go. Meanwhile Rochdale Reserves had reached the final of the Lancashire Junior Cup. They had lost 4-1 in the first leg at South Liverpool, Alan Moorhouse, a railway fireman, scoring the Rochdale goal, but suitably strengthened by some current first-teamers who were eligible, they took the trophy for the first time since 1910 by winning 4-0 at home. The team was Roberts; Byrom, Kirkman; Partridge, Tom Hargreaves, Wood; Carruthers, Barkas, Joe Hargreaves, Moss and Cunliffe. Tommy Barkas (2), Joe Hargreaves and Jackie Moss netted the goals in what was Arthur Cunliffe's last game following his appointment as reserve team coach.

Rochdale drew 2-2 at Barrow despite Wood having to deputise in goal when Roberts was injured after only quarter of an hour, and gained convincing home wins over Accrington, thanks to a Barkas hat-trick, and Tranmere. For their final match, played as late as June 7th, Rochdale visited Rotherham, winners of all their previous 20 home games, and ended their longest ever season by claiming a 3-3 draw to spoil the Millers' perfect record.

Rochdale thus finished in 6th place with 48 points. Unusually more than half came in away games, the 10 away wins being the best since 1925-26. Along with most other clubs, Rochdale enjoyed the post-war boom in attendances, a grand total of 175,595 spectators passing through the turnstiles at Spotland at an average of 7,634, beating the previous best of 7,095 set 20 years earlier. Even crowds at reserve games reached 3,000 at times, more than at many first team games before the war. The Lancs Junior Cup Final attracted four and a half thousand. During the season, Rochdale were therefore able to make the sizeable profit of £3,712 17s 6d, another record. Nevertheless, at a meeting in February, Rochdale had supported a move to create national third and fourth divisions, but this was not the prevailing view among northern section clubs and their representatives voted against the idea at the Football League AGM. At the end of the season, there had been the threat of strike action from the players, which won some small concessions from the League on the maximum and minimum wage.

During the hot summer of 1947, Arthur Cunliffe was promoted to first team trainer in place of Dave Robbie, while Hilbert Barnes from Oldham became second team trainer and groundsman. The main transfer story was the reappearance of Jack Brindle from Chelsea for £500.

However towards the end of 1946-47 (in fact, in what should have been the close season), the manager had brought in a number of new players including Cyril Lawrence and Dick Withington from Blackpool, the massive 6'-2", 14 stone Clyde goalkeeper Charlie Briggs, and Chester outside right Jackie Arthur, nearly 30 but destined for a lengthy association with Rochdale (Lawrence had scored five for the Reserves against Bangor's ex-Rochdale goalie Paddy Lynch).

1947-48:
Thus for the first time ever, the side that opened the new campaign with a 2-2 draw against Barrow was composed entirely of players who had appeared the previous term. In the next game the Rochdale defence frustrated the Hull attack, and their 25,000 crowd - the second largest ever at a Rochdale League match - to gain a goalless draw. Not for the first time Rochdale lost heavily at Wrexham, but 11,200 fans saw them come from behind to beat Halifax before Accrington dented the home record.

Another seven points out of eight at home compensated for the poor away record which included defeats by the eventual top two, Lincoln and Rotherham. In the home game against Hartlepool, Rochdale fielded what was then a great rarity, an Australian goalkeeper, the Rochdale and Leicestershire cricketer Wally Cornock from Bondi, New South Wales. After the game full back Norman Kirkman was sold to Chesterfield for £4000.

In the FA Cup, Rochdale were drawn at York and won 1-0 thanks to Birch's penalty, their first away win in the cup since 1924 (apart from the 1945-46 season when two-legged matches were played). Non-League Gillingham were their next opponents and held the Dale to a 1-1 draw. The Rochdale players spent three days in Margate preparing for the replay, but that was the extent of their enjoyment as the ambitious Southern League outfit romped home 3-0 in front of a remarkable crowd of 17,078. No doubt manager Goodier's after match comments were even less printable than usual.

Rochdale continued to play well at home but not away, for instance losing 4-0 at Valley Parade on Christmas day but winning the return with Bradford City the day after. Perversely, the first away win, when it came, was achieved on New Year's Day against top of the table Accrington Stanley. Rochdale won five successive games at Willbutts Lane, the match against Oldham Athletic attracting a crowd of practically 13,000, but suffered heavy defeats at Tranmere and Gateshead. In the latter, new goalkeeper Les Bywater from Luton sustained a fractured skull in a collision. Remarkably enough, he was back in action before the end of the season.

Rochdale did record a win at Halifax, Ron Johnston netting twice, but they had a disastrous March, losing all six games. Seven changes were made for the Easter Saturday game at Carlisle which Rochdale lost 5-0. Reserve centre half Mike Skivington had the misfortune to put through his own goal in his only Football League match while the man he was marking, Jack Connor (later a Dale man himself) netted a hat-trick. The Rochdale goalkeeper in this game was Alex Anderson, who always, though illegally, wore a yellow jersey, the colour reserved for internationals; oddly enough both he and Skivington represented the League of Ireland while playing for Dundalk the following season.

Rochdale bounced back to beat leaders Rotherham with a goal from Arthur, held new table-toppers Lincoln one-all (the Imps eventually took the championship by a single point), and wound up the season with two wins and two draws. An extraordinary feature of the game against third placed Gateshead was the home debut of Dave Reid (signed from Glasgow Perthshire along with Ron Johnston) who became probably the only Third Division player to appear wearing glasses.

After he missed a couple of good chances the 'wags' in the crowd inevitably remarked that he should have worn stronger ones, but Reid had the last laugh when he netted the winning goal. Rochdale's other goal in the 2-1 win was scored by Jack 'Scoops' Livesey who had been signed from Doncaster a few days earlier and who, coincidentally, was one of the first players to use contact lenses. During his spell at Spotland, Livesey became a renowned foil to the volatile Ted Goodier. One story relates how *"Goodier stormed into the dressing room one day, " You're a **** shower of ****", says Ted. Up stands a belligerent Jack Livesey, "Are you talking to me boss?". "No not you Jack, you're alright, it's these other ****'s ."*

After a "funereal finish" against Tranmere, Rochdale ended in 12th position, thanks mainly to their excellent home record. In a complete reversal of the previous year's form they managed only three away wins. The major problem was lack of goals, just 16 in the 21 away games, and only 48 in total, their second lowest since entering the Football League. Leading scorer was Hugh O'Donnell who had managed nine before his move to Halifax in March. Previous top scorer Joe Hargreaves made only five appearances, scoring just once, and joined Stalybridge Celtic at the end of the season. Tommy Barkas had been transferred to Stockport in exchange for veteran centre forward 'Sam' Earle, and he in turn moved to New Brighton after only a few months, along with Jack Brindle who had been unable to recapture his wartime form. Several more players were released including former skipper McCormick who signed for Boston United. In June, Dick Withington was transferred to Chesterfield for £4000 leaving a nucleus of 12 players on which to build for the following season.

Harry Hubbick was still playing at the age of 40.

Despite the fairly average performances overall, the boom continued and attendances hit a new high, 182,467 fans seeing the 22 home games, an average of 8,294. Attendances at Rochdale's away fixtures were even better, averaging a shade over 10,000. Despite this the club still made a loss at the gate, though this was covered by the sale of Kirkman and Withington.

During the summer of 1948 Rochdale obtained the signatures of a number of players including veteran full back Bill Watson from Chesterfield, who was to prove to have a good few years left in him, and Scottish winger Tommy Dryburgh from Aldershot. Former England international George 'Diddler' Eastham who had first appeared for Bolton back in 1932 also signed on from Swansea. But Eastham made only a couple of appearances before moving to Lincoln, and thence to a long managerial career, during which he figured in the same Ards side as his son George junior (the latter also went on to play for England, the only instance of father and son both being England internationals).

1948-49:

The campaign opened with a 6-1 trouncing at Hartlepool but at Spotland the home side (with five changes) overcame Gateshead 3-0. Three goals were also obtained in the next home match, but Darlington struck four and Rochdale also lost goalie Bill Roberts through injury. A second half goal by Eric Wood settled the local derby at Oldham, which attracted a crowd of 17,741, while a goal in 20 seconds by Jack Livesey got Rochdale off to a flying start at New Brighton. Moss got the winner after playing a neat one-two off the referee.

Dale were less successful in subsequent away fixtures but continued to do well at home, regularly attracting crowds of over 10,000. On October 23rd Rochdale entertained League leaders Hull City, led by the legendary Raich Carter and the 14,967 fans who payed a total of £1,085, saw Rochdale earn a draw through a Birch penalty.

Following in the footsteps of his father, who had been famous as a penalty taking goalkeeper, Wally converted seven during the season. A fortnight later the tables were turned as lowly Bradford City visited Spotland and grabbed a point with a last minute spot kick. In the Lancashire Senior Cup Rochdale did well to win away ties at Bury and Everton, thereby gaining a place in the semi-final to be played near the end of the season.

During the season work had been underway to level the famous slope in the Willbutts Ground pitch and it was decided to complete the job in the week before the FA Cup tie with Barrow. Unfortunately, Barrow protested and though the job was done and the pitch relaid in time, the FA ordered the game to be played elsewhere. Oldham gave Rochdale the use of Boundary Park but Barrow escaped with a one-all draw, the Dale again conceding a late penalty after recent signing from Bradford City Alan Middlebrough had given them the lead with his third goal in successive games. Barrow went on to win the replay and Rochdale also lost at home to Hartlepool, but after signing George McGeachie, the ex-New Brighton centre half, and Jack Connor, the former Carlisle centre forward back from a spell in Ireland, they took three points off Stockport over Christmas.

Rochdale then crashed 6-1 at Darlington, prompting more transfer activity from Ted Goodier. Jackie Moss was transferred to Leeds United for a new club record of £7000 and the popular Billy Woods was re-signed from Bradford for a cut-price £1000 to replace him. In another shrewd move, Goodier obtained the signature of Leicester reserve 'keeper Trevor Churchill for £400, and this was quickly followed by the arrival of the 38 year old Port Vale full back Harry Hubbick, who took over the captaincy. Brown and Reid, meantime, were ruled out by long term injuries.

Rochdale's first away League win for four months came at Barrow and the goalless draw at Tranmere was well earned, too, as Churchill was injured after only 5 minutes. The crowd for the home game with Southport dipped to just over 4000 but a Jack Connor goal gave Rochdale the points and he then scored twice in a win at Crewe. Almost 10,000 turned up for the visit of leaders Rotherham and they saw a fine performance by the home side, who won 2-0. The following week Rochdale were watched by an incredible crowd of 36,509, by far the highest for any Rochdale game up to that time, when they visited the new leaders Hull City and led by a goal from Ron Hood until two minutes from time.

At the beginning of April, Rochdale were still in mid-table but despite a shortage of goals - they even lost 1-0 to bottom club Bradford City - they managed to win all their last five home games to move up to seventh place at the end of the season, with 45 points from 42 games despite only four away wins.

Meanwhile Rochdale had played Manchester City in the Lancs Cup semi-final and won 2-0 at Maine Road thanks to goals by Livesey and Connor. In the final they met Blackpool on neutral ground at Boundary Park and won a stirring contest 1-0. Jack Connor finally came out on top in his battle with the Tangerines' well known international goalkeeper George Farm, when he netted 10 seconds from time.

For the record, the team that won the Senior Cup for the first time was: Bywater; Watson, Hubbick; McGeachie, Birch, Wood; Lawrence, Livesey, Connor, Woods and Dryburgh.

Not surprisingly Ted Goodier retained all his regulars, though two former first team 'keepers, Bill Roberts and Les Bywater, left the club, the latter to join the police force. In later years he was again well known to Rochdale followers, when his coach firm supplied the team's transport to away games. His grandson Stephen followed him into the Dale side 50 years later. Tom Jones, who was one of Goodier's less successful forays into the transfer market, as he played just one senior game after his £750 move from Derby, was also released. Trialist Norman Case, who had figured in one friendly, moved on to Ards and made his name the following season when he appeared for the Irish League and commanded a £3,500 fee when he joined First Division Sunderland (though he never did become a Football League regular and reappeared at Spotland for a couple of games in 1952).

Although late season crowds were relatively low, the nationwide all-time high in attendances - Football League gates totalled over 41 million, 5 million of them in the Third North - was reflected at Spotland, where the average League crowd was a best ever 8,640. However the work on levelling the pitch and on the surrounding terracing cost the club nearly £7000, leading to an overall loss of £3,694.

1949-50:
Only one new face was in the side to face Gateshead on August 20th 1949, W. H. J. (Bill) Williams, a regular at inside forward in Bury's Central League side since the war. Unfortunately Gateshead won 3-1 and Williams promptly lost his place to Billy Woods for the game at Doncaster, which was drawn 0-0 in front of 21,500 supporters. Rovers won the return 1-0 and by a strange chance these three games so early in the season turned out to be crucial to Rochdale's prospects.

In between the Doncaster games, two goals by Lawrence had earned the season's first victory, at Hartlepool. Rochdale also defeated Darlington but suffered their third home defeat in four games at the hands of Chester. They maintained their excellent away form, though, by winning by four clear goals at New Brighton. Often a productive ground, it proved especially so for Jack Livesey who netted a first minute goal there for the second year in succession. Four changes had been made to the forward line for this game, and the other goals were scored by the recalled trio of Williams, Middlebrough and Dryburgh. Rochdale also managed to get their home form going with a single goal victory over struggling Halifax.

A massive crowd of 23,356 saw the local derby with Oldham at Boundary Park which ended in a goalless draw.

Churchill, who kept his fourth clean sheet in a row, had begun to be talked about as a possible future replacement for the England goalkeeper Frank Swift, and was said to have attracted a bid of over £4000 from a First Division club.

Two of the next three games were lost leaving Rochdale in mid-table, but aided by being able to field an unchanged side for a long spell, they then launched into a successful run beginning with a 2-1 win over one of the front runners, Crewe. They next won at Barrow, and after the game Billy Woods, currently out of the Dale side, was transferred to the Holker Street club for £1000, the second time that Goodier had sold him for a sizeable fee (though he only ever scored two League goals for Dale). The next match ended in a 2-0 home win over promotion contenders Lincoln City and had a much larger than usual audience as the second half was broadcast live on the wireless by the BBC. Despite losing 3-4 at Rotherham, after a frantic opening saw them 3-2 up in less than half an hour, three further victories saw Rochdale edge nearer the top positions and also into the second round of the FA Cup after a notably physical encounter with Rhyl.

Their next cup opponents were Notts County, leaders of the Southern Section of Division Three and with the famed England centre forward Tommy Lawton (the subject of the first ever £20,000 transfer) in their ranks. The crowd of 24,231 set an all-time record for Spotland which will surely never be beaten and brought in record receipts of £2285 9s 6d. Cyril Brown's early goal against his old team gave the home fans plenty to cheer about, but County fought back strongly in the second half and Lawton eventually came out on top in his stirring duel with Wally Birch (which had been 'built up' in the national papers' sports pages over the previous week), when he netted the winner 10 minutes from time.

Rochdale soon overcame their disappointment as they travelled to second placed Gateshead and won 3-1, thanks to a hat-trick from Jack Livesey. On Christmas Eve they trounced Hartlepool 4-0 and on Boxing Day a Spotland crowd of 13,406 saw goals by Livesey and Connor against Southport put Rochdale on top of the division for the first time in 20 years. Tragedy struck the following day, however, when with Rochdale leading the return 2-1, Walter Stanners the reserve goalkeeper, who had conceded only one goal in six appearances, broke his leg and Rochdale eventually went down 3-2. This, incidentally, was the day on which the all time aggregate record attendance at Football League matches was set, a staggering 1,272,185.

A fortnight later another 4-0 win against New Brighton, with both centre half Birch and left half McGeachie on the scoresheet, enabled Rochdale to take over at the top again, but it was another short stay as lowly Halifax beat them 3-2 at the Shay after Bill Watson put through his own goal.

This defeat coincided with the first change in the lineup (goalkeeper apart) for 14 games, 10 of which had been won. When Walter Birch missed the match at Mansfield it ended a run of 78 consecutive games for the centre half and a record sequence of 41 games for the entire half back line of Wood, Birch and McGeachie. (Eric Wood had a testimonial near the end of the season in which the great Tom Finney guested for Rochdale).

A tenth home League win in succession, against neighbours Oldham, kept Rochdale well in the hunt, over fourteen and a half thousand fans seeing Jack Connor net an 88th minute winner. Again it was the strugglers who set Rochdale back, Wrexham surprisingly beating them 3-0 at the Racecourse and Bradford City ending the home run with a 2-2 draw. But Rochdale came good again in amazing fashion. Two up at half time, they crashed five more past a bemused Mansfield in the space of 14 minutes. Livesey, again off to a flying start with a first minute goal, scored three, while Middlebrough netted twice and wingers Dryburgh and Arthur notched one apiece.

Rochdale also won the next two games to stay just a point adrift of leaders Doncaster, though having played two games more. Defeat at Lincoln was followed by five unbeaten games, including vital wins over fellow hopefuls Rotherham and Tranmere, which kept up the pressure as Doncaster stumbled at Mansfield. However Rovers cashed in on their remaining game in hand to go three points in front with two games left. In a mid-week game Rochdale were defeated in the semi-final of the Lancashire Cup by Burnley, and Accrington Stanley then ended the Dale's League hopes by winning 1-0 at Peel Park.

Rochdale's final match, a 1-1 draw with Wrexham, attracted only 3000 supporters, live television coverage of the FA Cup Final being blamed for poor attendances all over the country (despite the successes, average crowds at Willbutts Lane were down slightly on the previous year and another loss of £1000 was incurred). Rochdale finished in third place with 51 points, four behind Doncaster and trailing Gateshead by two, their two early season conquerors.

This was easily Rochdale's best since the heady days of Jack Peart in the mid-twenties. After the shaky start they had gone 17 home League wins without defeat, but conversely managed only one away win after Christmas. Doncaster, by contrast, had actually won more away games than home (in fact, only three sides won less often on their own grounds than did the champions). Rochdale conceded only 41 League goals, just 13 of them at home, their best since the change to the off-side rule in 1925. All told, Rochdale, mainly in the person of Trevor Churchill, kept 21 clean sheets.

The defence, with the two old timers Watson and the ever-present Hubbick at full back, kept it especially tight early in the games; in one run of 15 matches they conceded only one first half goal. However, a potential worry for the future was that eight of the regulars were now 30 or over and the backs' average age was 33.

In May Rochdale went on a brief tour to Scotland, their first such venture, during which they defeated 'B' division clubs Dunfermline and Arbroath. The main footballing interest in the summer of 1950, though, was England's first venture into the World Cup. Unfortunately it was an unknown Haitian by the named of Gaetjens who wrote his name into football history with the only goal of the game for a USA side *rated about average Third Division Northern Section standard"* (indeed, their skipper McIlvenny had made a few appearances for Wrexham in 1947), and the embarrassed England team was soon on its way back home from Brazil. Things looked quite bright at Rochdale, though, as they planned their campaign in the new 24 club Third North, the Football League having been extended to 92 clubs at its last AGM. (The Management Committee had also suggested the formation of an extra division and/or automatic relegation from Division Three but these were rejected).

Not surprisingly, all the main performers from the previous campaign had been retained, though during the close season Tommy Dryburgh was sold to Leicester City for £7000, equalling the club transfer record. An exchange deal saw Bill Williams join Aldershot, with Alan Steen making the opposite move to fill Dryburgh's outside left spot. Steen had been a pre-war 'boy wonder', making his League debut for First Division Wolves at the age of 16. During the war he was shot down in a bombing raid over Germany and became an inmate of the famous Stalag Luft IVB, who could have fielded a complete professional English soccer team. The other major new signings were inside forward Jim Whitehouse from Walsall and full back Harry Boyle from Southport. Off the field, Arthur Cunliffe left Spotland to take up the trainer's position at Bournemouth, where he remained for the next 25 years. Jimmy Pearce, the pre-war Rochdale centre half took his place, but did not stay long, and Harry Stafford took over in November. He was subsequently joined as second team trainer and groundsman by former Rochdale stalwart Joe Duff.

1950-51:
Rochdale started in excellent fashion with a 2-0 victory at Darlington and also won the next match, at Park Avenue, in front of a 19,000 crowd before Bradford won the return, to end Rochdale's long unbeaten home run. Despite this, a 5-0 thrashing of League newboys Shrewsbury, with Connor netting a hat trick, and an away win over the same opposition in which Connor took his tally to 8 goals in 5 games, saw Rochdale assume the leadership of the division.

Rochdale had a new goalkeeper for the Shrewsbury games in the shape of former Blackburn and Wales 'keeper 'Archie' Hughes, signed as cover for the injured Churchill. However he was not able to prevent Rochdale's stay at the top being as short as those of the previous season, Gateshead running four past him to go top themselves. This was also Dave Reid's last game in Rochdale colours as he was transferred to Bradford for £6000, a goodly sum for a 27 year old with only 36 Football League games to his credit.

Surprisingly vulnerable at Spotland, Rochdale did rather better away. At New Brighton Rochdale scored 5 goals in 14 minutes midway through the second half, two of them penalties given away by player-manager Galbraith and future Dale goalkeeper Jones, and converted by George McGeachie against his former club.

Barrow scored twice in the last five minutes to give themselves a 4-3 victory and by the time the FA Cup came around, Rochdale had slipped into mid-table. They were still too good for Amateur Cup holders Willington in the first round and part timers Ashington in the second, though. The winning goal in the latter game, which attracted the former League club's best ever crowd of 13,191, was scored by Alan Steen after he had been rushed to and from the local hospital for stitches in a gashed head.

In round three, Rochdale were drawn at home to First Division Chelsea and Ted Goodier decided to go for his most experienced men. Young reserve Middlebrough, who had scored five times in as many games, made way for the return of Connor, and the old half back line of Wood, Birch and McGeachie was selected together for what turned out to be the last time. Despite an icy pitch causing a postponement until the Tuesday afternoon, a crowd of 17,817 paid gate receipts of £1780 to make Rochdale's bank manager extremely happy. The team manager was less than ecstatic, though, when goalkeeper Bert Lomas fumbled a shot from Chelsea's England centre forward Roy Bentley into his own net to give the visitors a 3-2 victory. Indeed, Goodier kept to his after match statement that the unfortunate Lomas (who *"couldn't stop a pig in a ginnel"* according to his manager) would never play for Rochdale again. He did relent in later years and actually signed Lomas when he was boss of Wigan. The home crowd were also upset by what they saw as a clear penalty claim turned down when Connor was tumbled over. Connor and Arthur had earlier scored the Rochdale goals.

Back in the League, the first away win since September was achieved at Chester, while at home victory alternated with defeat. One of the home defeats, by Chester on a Tuesday afternoon in January, attracted the lowest post-war crowd yet of just 1435, while another one, by Oldham a month later, drew ten times that figure.

Following the arrival of wing half Alistair Buchan from Highland League side Huntley, Rochdale put together a good run, taking nine points out of 10 and scoring four times against both Bradford City and second placed Carlisle. Top scorer Jack Connor, who had been at odds with the management for some time, scored three in the Easter games against Bradford City, and shortly afterwards joined them for a fee of £2000. Without him, Rochdale netted goals in only three of the last nine games, though they did manage to win two of them. In fact they continued a run of 10 unbeaten home games to the end of the season. Support slumped however, none of the last six gates reaching even 4000. The last seven away games were all lost.

Rochdale finished 11th with 45 points from the extended programme of 46 games. They actually scored one more goal than in the previous successful season but conceded an additional 20 (though Churchill did kept 12 clean sheets in 28 games when he returned to the side). A couple of days after the end of the season, Rochdale Reserves met Morecambe in the Lancashire Junior Cup Final. In an era when even a club of Rochdale's status could field a full professional reserve eleven and probably a third string as well (the 92 League clubs employed around 3,500 professionals between them), this was a rare moment of glory for the 'Stiffs'. The unsung heroes who achieved a 1-0 victory and brought the cup back to Spotland for the third time were: Lomas; Rothwell, Webb; Iverson, Downes, Partridge; Blackshaw, Riley, Foulds (the goalscorer), Crowther and Heaton. Eric Downes was actually an England Amateur youth international before his move from Chester but had only just made his Football League debut at the age of 24, while the veteran Bill Heaton had been a Leeds regular just after the war, and Bill Blackshaw had topped Oldham's scoring charts in 1947 but never made it into the first team at Rochdale. One of the Morecambe side was Konrad Kapler, an expatriate Pole who had served in the Polish Grenadiers and played a few games for Rochdale the previous term after signing from Glasgow Celtic. A few days later, Rochdale entertained two Irish sides, Shamrock Rovers and Bohemians, in Festival of Britain games, drawing the first 0-0 and running out 5-0 winners in the second, thanks largely to a Whitehouse hat trick (though they attracted lower attendances than any other Festival games).

The end of the season signalled the break up of the side that Ted Goodier had built successfully since the end of the war. Eric Wood left the club after nine years, having made 148 peacetime League appearances, while Jack Connor's striking partner Jack Livesey was also transferred, moving to Southport for £1000, and McGeachie went to Crystal Palace for a similar fee. The indestructible Hubbick, now past 40, went into non-League football before starting an even longer career as a trainer and general factotum at a succession of League clubs. He was Preston's kit-man when in his late seventies.

The most remarkable move, though, was that of 18 year old Billy Webb. Arriving from Yorkshire side Wath and signing on professional terms after playing in the Festival games in May, he was sold to Second Division Leicester City for £1000 in June (and played for an FA XI in November).

Though not always appreciated by the supporters - the sale of Connor and Livesey, in particular, being much criticised - Ted Goodier's transfer acumen had been invaluable to a perpetually financially challenged Rochdale, and in his years with the club he made around £40,000 for them; a rumour, always denied, held that Goodier was paid a commission on outgoing transfers! During the past year this money had been put to good use, as the mortgage taken out in 1914 was finally paid off.

A dozen players were retained, but not many were experienced at League level and the manager brought in a number of new men to try and bolster the squad. These included a couple of players who had appeared pre-war, Fred Fisher the long serving Grimsby full back, and Bill Jennings, previously a regular scorer for Ipswich, though they figured but briefly in the first team. More productive were the signings of Harry Whitworth, a utility man from Bury who had guested for the Dale during the war when he was a Royal Navy petty officer, and Joe Lynn, a comparatively unknown half back from Exeter. In addition, trainer Harry Stafford left the club and was replaced by 1930's Rochdale player Ted Humpish.

1951-52:
The 1951-52 season got off to a terrible start with a 4-0 home defeat by Carlisle followed by two away defeats. However, in the second home game Middlebrough marked his recall with a hat trick in a 6-2 demolition of Darlington. Newly elected Workington fared no better at Willbutts Lane than the side they had replaced, New Brighton, losing their first visit 2-0. A 4-0 defeat at Barrow cost both Trevor Churchill and the veteran Wally Birch their regular first team places, former Bradford man Jimmy Nicholls becoming first choice between the posts, while Eric Downes took over at centre half. Nevertheless, during the season Birch surpassed David Parkes' record number of Football League appearances, his total reaching 221.

After a couple more home wins, Rochdale then crashed to six consecutive defeats, scoring only one goal in the process. During this spell, leading scorer Jim Whitehouse was sold to Carlisle for £3500. Then, after the acquisition of another outside left, Eric Betts, on whom West Ham had spent £5000 only a year earlier, Alan Steen also moved to Carlisle for £1250. This was one of Goodier's most legendary transfer deals; on hearing that the Carlisle outside left had suffered a broken leg, he placed Steen on the transfer list.

But Goodier somehow omitted to inform 90 of the other 91 clubs! Rochdale stopped the rot against Tranmere, two goals by Middlebrough on another temporary elevation to the first team helping them to a 3-2 win. They then picked up their first away win of the season, albeit at non-League Ilkeston in the FA Cup. This decidedly eventful game nearly had to be abandoned when the only remaining white ball - the first had been stolen - became stuck in a tree bordering the ground and, with their side losing, the local fans (and officials, according to the referee) tried to prevent it being retrieved. In an equally bad tempered game on the pitch, Betts scored twice, once from the penalty spot, but Middlebrough was sent off along with one of the home players. The attendance at the tiny Derbyshire ground was 9000, considerably more than at any of Rochdale's home games up to that point, and an FA enquiry resulted when some of the supporters tried to chase the referee and Dale trainer Humpish was assaulted by a woman fan.

In round two Rochdale travelled to Gillingham and gained revenge for the 1948 defeat by beating the Kent side, now back in the Third South, by three clear goals, another new signing, Frank Tomlinson from Oldham, getting two of them. Rochdale warmed up for the third round visit of Leeds United by gaining four draws - the two holiday games against Oldham attracting a total of over 35,000 fans - and then an excellent 4-1 victory over Barrow followed. Two of the goals this time came from Albert Foulds who had been released after a few games the previous season but quickly resigned after he started to score regularly for his new club Scarborough.

Thirty thousand tickets were printed for the Leeds game - the mind boggles at the thought of cramming 32,000 fans, the official limit at the time, into Spotland! Although the ground record was not in fact beaten, 21,526 fans turned up to see the game which Leeds (with a young John Charles in their squad) won comfortably enough by two goals to nil.

In the next match Rochdale beat Accrington in front of a Tuesday afternoon crowd of just 1792, but then suffered three heavy losses in a row, the most embarrassing a 5-1 home defeat by a Wrexham side who had not previously won away all season. Though the margin did not look as bad, Halifax's 2-0 win at Spotland was probably even more depressing as Halifax hadn't won away from the Shay since the '49-50 season.

Rochdale did manage four more draws, but then crashed to another awful home defeat, losing to fellow strugglers Chester by five clear goals. The next home game (on a Saturday) attracted the Dale's lowest attendance since the war, only 1226 turning out to see them lose again, this time to Scunthorpe. Indeed the run without a success grew to 13 games and dropped Rochdale to 21st in the table before they recorded a 1-0 win over Southport. Rochdale also gained two draws against Bradford over Easter, the goal in the home game coming from the extremely unlikely source of Don Partridge - it was his first goal in six seasons. They finally managed their first away win of the season, also against Southport, and thus ensured that they would avoid the two re-election places. In the end, the side won only two of the last 20 games, scored only 14 goals over the same period, and finished 21st.

Despite his goal every other game record throughout his four seasons at Spotland - he finished with 29 in 57 senior appearances - Alan Middlebrough was one of the players released at the end of the season, as was Alan Ball. Signed from the 'Latics in February, the latter went on to make a name as a well travelled manager, while his son Alan junior, then aged seven, would become one of England's World Cup heroes in 1966. Only five of the 17 new players tried during the season survived.

However, the most important news of the close season was the resignation of Ted Goodier on June 18th. He had been in charge for 14 years and was, and still is, easily Rochdale's longest serving manager.

Eric Betts, who was later sold to Crewe just before Harry Catterick moved in the opposite direction.

A CHANGE OF SCENE 1952-1960

~ CHAPTER 5 ~

July 1952 saw the appointment of Oldham player-coach Jack Warner as the club's new player-manager. Now 40 years of age, Warner had played for Wales as a wing half during his spell with Manchester United either side of the war. He inherited a staff of 18 including those Goodier had signed just before his departure, full backs Harry Potter from Shrewsbury and Harry Boyle who returned after a season with Bangor. The new manager's own pre-season signings included the experienced Bournemouth forward Dan Boxshall, holder of the Military Medal for his exploits in charge of a brengun crew in France after D-Day. Another addition to the staff was Eric Wood who made a return as third team player-coach.

For the fifth year running, the new campaign started with a defeat, Crewe winning by the only goal at Spotland. In fact all three games in the opening week were lost before an 88th minute goal by Foulds earned the first two points of the season against Bradford. Rochdale also won the next game, but these were the only successes in the first nine games.

Two further victories, including one away at Bradford City thanks to a Foulds hat trick, gave hope of better things. Seventeen year old Brian Sutton, lately of Norden Youth Club, kept three clean sheets in his first four outings. However five of the next six games ended in defeat, the exception being a surprising 4-1 victory over high-flying Wrexham, the veteran Jackie Arthur scoring twice on his recall to the side.

Ray Hoddington was signed by Jack Warner in November 1952.

Away games had been lost with monotonous regularity, and following a 3-0 home win over Tranmere, Rochdale, by some quirk of the fixture list, faced seven successive matches away from Spotland - and lost the lot. When they finally returned home they did manage a victory, beating Darlington with a hat trick from their recent capture from Bournemouth, Ray Haddington (yet another ex-'Latic). In the New Years' Day game at Gateshead, Foulds scored after only three minutes, but was later sent off and Rochdale lost 3-1. None of the next five games was won either, indeed Carlisle beat them 5-0 with former Dale man Whitehouse netting four times.

This left Rochdale in dire trouble at the foot of the table, still with only 18 points after 31 games. But then, perhaps inspired by easily the season's best crowd of 15,305, Rochdale defeated the eventual champions Oldham Athletic, Alistair Buchan setting the Dale on their way with a rare goal. The crowd at Boundary Park for the game earlier in the season had been nearly 23,000.

Rochdale appeared to have lost their chance in the next home game, when an early two goal lead was cancelled out by Barrow, but Dale then went to town with three goals in six minutes, the play-anywhere Whitworth filling in at centre forward and grabbing a hat trick in the eventual 6-2 win. Another bleak spell followed, though, leaving Rochdale lodged one off the bottom with six games to go. The one success had come against Bradford City when the manager, now aged 41½, and Rochdale's oldest Football League player, selected himself at inside left instead of his customary place among the half backs.

With the other veteran Bill Watson switched to centre half and Boxshall finally getting his chance at centre forward, Rochdale managed to beat Hartlepool. They then travelled to Workington with 17 successive away defeats behind them, but came from a goal down to take the two points and overtake their hosts on goal average. Draws in the midweek games kept the status quo, but then Rochdale beat bottom club Accrington Stanley thanks to a first minute strike by Haddington. However, Workington surprisingly beat Wrexham 4-0, ruining the latter's promotion hopes, and again levelling affairs in the re-election battle.

Both sides lost their penultimate game but Rochdale saved themselves at the last gasp by beating Mansfield thanks to a single second half goal from Bob Gilfillan, a former Cowdenbeath man who had become a regular in the attack. Rochdale thus finished one place and two points worse off than the previous year. They lost a record 21 of their 23 away games.

Ironically, while Rochdale were struggling, two of their ex-players Jim Whitehouse and Jack Connor became the Third North's two top scorers, notching 29 and 26, respectively, for their new clubs Carlisle and Stockport, Connor including a five against Workington in his haul. The day after the League campaign ended, Connor and Hornet's Wally Jones were among several former players to turn out in Walter Birch's testimonial game against an All Star XI which included the Manchester United quartet of John Aston (senior), Johnny Carey, Allenby Chilton and Roger Byrne, as well as Sheffield United's England 'B' goalkeeper Ted Burgin, who would be back between the sticks at Spotland again in later years. In true testimonial style, the final score was 8-7 to the All Stars!

The following week, Jack Warner resigned as manager. The Board, under Fred Ratcliffe who had become the youngest chairman of a Football League club when elected at the end of March, decided to offer the position to Crewe's player-manager Harry Catterick. The former Everton player took over in June 1953, though probably not many people elsewhere noticed, as they were too busy celebrating the coronation of Queen Elizabeth II.

Even though the majority of the previous season's players were still at Spotland (ironically, Betts had moved to Crewe for £2000 before Catterick left), the new manager was soon active in the transfer market. Top scorer Foulds moved to Crystal Palace in an exchange deal, while another swap brought Jimmy Anders to Spotland from Bradford City. Further recruits included Bill Morgan from Halifax, Neville Black from Exeter (who were now managed by former Dale player Norman Kirkman), and Sheffield United reserve goalkeeper Albert Morton, who at the age of 34 had made only 40 Football League appearances, yet had played in a wartime Cup Final. The other goalkeeper signed was John Cordell, who had arrived from Aston Villa just before Jack Warner's departure, Churchill having joined Swindon.

1953-54:
The new manager's first game in charge could hardly have been less auspicious. Carlisle ran amok at Brunton Park and slammed seven past the hapless Cordell on his debut in the Dale goal, Rochdale's worst ever start to a season. However, most of the Third North had kicked off their season the previous Wednesday with fixtures brought forward from Cup Final day. The second game realised the season's first points, when Haddington's second half goal accounted for Accrington Stanley, but things were looking decidedly bleak by the end of September when Dale were well adrift at the bottom of the League with just five points from 12 games.

Although goals flowed away from home, all too many of them against Rochdale, the first eight games at Spotland produced just eight, with only three of them to the home side.

To try and solve the chronic goal shortage, the manager had already tried nine inside/centre forwards including a South African, Bob Priday the former Liverpool man, and a Pole, Adam Wasilewski from local football. He then plunged into the transfer market, spending a club record £2000 to bring the former England international Jack Haines to Spotland from Park Avenue. This immediately paid off, as the Dale beat Mansfield at home and also won at Workington with a goal from another recent signing, Arnold Kendall, from the other half of Bradford. This form did not last, though, as six of the next seven League and cup games ended in defeat.

On November 25th a historic match saw the Mighty Magyars of Hungary become the first foreign team to beat England on their own soil when they won 6-3 at Wembley. Three days later Rochdale conceded six less unexpected goals to runaway leaders Port Vale, following a similar hammering at Hartlepool. The one respite was a 3-0 win over Darlington, with two goals from Haines and one on his debut from Des Frost, just acquired from Halifax in exchange for Haddington.

After 20 games Dale still had only 12 points, but the corner was turned in the next match. The 37 year old Bill Watson - three years older than his manager - was recalled to play at centre half, while Bill Morgan came in at right half and Neville Black was given another chance at inside left. The result was a 4-1 victory over Crewe, Jackie Haines scoring a hat trick.

Rochdale then gained further home wins over Carlisle and, on Christmas Day, Bradford City, to move out of the bottom two places. Unfortunately six changes had to be made for the return the following day and the Bantams won 4-0. For the next game most of the absentees were back, but a change was made at centre forward, 17 year old Frank Lord from Chadderton, who had had the misfortune to make his debut in the drubbing at Hartlepool, getting a second chance. He took it in style, scoring twice in a vital 4-0 win over fellow strugglers Chester. York City, another of the stragglers, took the two points at Spotland, but then Dale won five in a row, Lord going from strength to strength with another brace in the 4-1 victory over Grimsby and a hat trick when Wrexham were beaten 6-2. Winger Arnold Kendall, not usually a noted goalscorer, also chipped in with five in four games.

On February 16th, Rochdale witnessed an important and forward-looking innovation, with the first floodlit match at Spotland, a friendly against St. Mirren, which the Scots won 3-2 (it had originally been planned to turn on the new lights for a game against Bury the previous week, but this had not taken place). Spotland was in fact only the third ground in the North West to have lights, beating the likes of Old Trafford, Anfield and Goodison Park by three years.

However, as Harry Catterick ruefully recorded in a subsequent match programme, the crowd of just under 7000 was *"the lowest so far for the opening of any floodlight installation in the country"*. Rochdale later played further floodlit friendlies against Third Lanark (Lord hitting a nine minute hat trick) and Swindon. The Dale also visited the Wiltshire club for a return fixture under their lights. Rochdale Hornets made use of the Spotland lights, too, playing one of the first ever floodlit Rugby League games, against Keighley.

The Dale continued their winning ways at Spotland, a 4-2 victory over Workington making it nine wins in the last 10 games. Two of the scorers in this game were the brothers Eddie and George Lyons, a 33 year old former Crewe full back and an 18 year old winger respectively. They had earlier made their debuts in the same match, also a unique occurrence for Rochdale.

The side was unable to continue its excellent run, but they did remain unbeaten at Spotland until the final game of the season. The goalless draw with champions and FA Cup semi-finalists Port Vale drew one of Spotland's best ever League gates of nearly 15,000. With Walter Birch having been forced to retire with the injury sustained the previous year (he finished with the new record of 243 Football League appearances), an important signing towards the end of the season was that of the experienced Stockport County centre half Bev Glover for £1500.

Rochdale ended the season in 19th place with 40 points, which represented quite an improvement on their early season form, 28 points coming in the last 26 games. The majority of the players who had figured in the second half of the campaign were retained, though Bill Watson decided to call it a day. He had made exactly 200 Football League appearances for Rochdale, the third player to reach this landmark. With the departure of long serving reserve full back Ron Rothwell, this left Don Partridge as the only survivor from Rochdale's war-time sides. Jack Arthur also retired and was appointed 'A' team trainer-coach, subsequently becoming youth coach. Earlier in the season Ted Humpish had been replaced as trainer with Joe Duff promoted to his place, another pre-war Dale player Arthur Griffiths becoming assistant trainer.

The summer of 1954 saw the World Cup finals in Switzerland broadcast on BBC television for the first time. After England's quarter final defeat by Uruguay, intrigued viewers were able to watch the unfancied Germans beat the Hungarians in the final, despite the latter's new tactical ploy of dropping the centre forward back into midfield. It would be several years before such sophistication would filter down to the more parochial world of the Third Division North, so it was business as usual at Willbutts Lane.

Few new signings were forthcoming, though, and the only new faces on the opening day of the season were defender Bill McCulloch, who had over 300 League games for Stockport behind him, and the manager's former Crewe team mate, inside forward Frank Mitcheson.

1954-55:
A disastrous start to the campaign, not helped by a fire which had badly damaged the main stand the previous week, brought a 3-0 home defeat by Grimsby and cost Rochdale the services of their star centre forward discovery Frank Lord with a broken leg. The side then beaten by Bradford City included two more new signings, the former Sheffield United full back George Underwood and another ex-Crewe man Danny Murphy. Murphy had earlier had a long spell with Bolton Wanderers and had played in the 1945 War Cup Final as well as the tragic 'Bolton disaster' game against Stoke the following year.

The first victory was not forthcoming until the seventh game, when Tranmere Rovers were beaten by goals from Kendall and 19 year old debutant centre forward Brian Green. Green was a product of Haggate Lads in the Rochdale and District League, whose ranks had included future Bolton and England goalkeeper Eddie Hopkinson. Unfortunately Green was not able to consolidate his place in the side as he was called up for his National Service and spent most of the next two seasons playing for the Army.

However, the Dale began to improve dramatically and they gained an outstanding 4-1 success at Stockport, Des Frost scoring twice. A week later Frost was transferred to Crewe in exchange for the veteran centre forward Eric Gemmell, who had scored a record 110 goals in seven seasons at Oldham, including seven in the Latics 11-2 victory over Chester in 1952. Gemmell scored twice on his debut as Dale beat Hartlepool and netted two more the following week, while a single goal by Haines was enough to beat Gateshead at Redheugh. This was followed by a superb 3-0 defeat of eventual champions Barnsley in front of an eleven and a half thousand crowd at Spotland.

The crowds at further floodlit friendlies remained disappointing, only 3800 attending when Oldham were the visitors and 5500 when a team of former internationals provided the opposition. However, Rochdale did also play their first competitive game under lights in the Lancashire Cup, and made an incredible start against Blackburn with three goals in the first seven minutes, eventually winning 4-1. In the more serious business, Rochdale extended their unbeaten run to 13 games, putting them on the edge of the promotion hunt, and even when the run did come to an end, it was in a remarkable game which second placed Accrington Stanley won 5-4. The crowd of 12,000 certainly got its moneysworth, even at the recently increased price of 1s 9d (about 9p) which had attracted much adverse comment.

Rochdale immediately bounced back to beat Mansfield, but none of the next six games was won and Rochdale slipped steadily out of contention in the promotion race. On Christmas Day, Rochdale gave Carlisle the footballing Christmas present of all time when, after Anders had given Dale the lead, Murphy, Boyle and Underwood all put through their own goal. In all the home side ran in seven, Jim Whitehouse again enjoying himself at the expense of his old club. To end an unhappy holiday, George Underwood broke his leg in the return game at Spotland.

Meanwhile, Rochdale had won through to the third round of the FA Cup by beating Tranmere, in a replay, and then non-Leaguers Hinckley. Gemmell had made it 3-3 in the first game with a stunning 20 yard volley and proved to be an inspired signing, ending the season with 22 goals. In round three Rochdale met Charlton Athletic, and the Londoners repeated their success of 1947, winning 3-1, even if the Willbutts Lane fans did not appreciate the tactics of their more sophisticated opponents who *"used bodychecks like continental sides"*. The crowd of 16,938 was certainly a boost to Rochdale's finances, though; remarkably, for the second year running, a side from the Third North reached the cup semi-final, this time it was York City.

Form picked up again in the League, thanks to a run of games at Spotland where the Dale continued to enjoy considerable success. Indeed they played five home games in a row without conceding a goal, their best victory by four goals against Gateshead. Joe Lynn scored both goals against Workington from the penalty spot, a double only previously achieved by Harry Dennison and Jimmy Wynn, and ended with the best ever tally for a Dale half back of eight, seven of them from the spot. The Rochdale outside left in the 1-0 win against Stockport was local youngster George Johnson, but his next League game wasn't until 1963 when he had a spell at Southport.

Charlie Ferguson, who made 150 League appearances for Rochdale between 1955-1959.

The Dale also played a couple of unusual friendlies. They met continental opposition for the first time when they beat the touring Austrians of Columbia Wien 3-1, in front of a disappointing crowd of just over 3000. They then met the Army, who included two Rochdale men in their line-up, Brian Green and Kevin Barber, and beat them 5-2 thanks to four goals in the last 11 minutes.

Rochdale picked up a couple of away wins as well, but in the main it was the home form which kept them in the top half of the table.

The Boxing Day defeat by Carlisle was their only loss at Spotland after the first week of the season, a run of 21 games. Even a defeat by champions Barnsley in the last game left them in 12th spot with a very respectable 48 points, the same as the three sides immediately above them. With 25 players retained by Harry Catterick, including 17 first teamers, the only prominent departure at the end of the season was Jackie Haines who moved to Chester.

1955-56:
Two additions were made to the first team squad during the summer of 1955, Jim Storey from Bournemouth and John McClelland from Swindon. Neither had much League experience but they were both in the Dale side for the opening game of the season, McClelland netting in the 1-1 draw at Grimsby. An important absentee was centre half Glover, who was out with appendicitis, full back McCulloch filling the breach initially.

Rochdale were beaten 3-0 at Accrington but ran in four at home to Bradford. The Dale scored twice in the last 10 minutes to scrape a draw with Oldham after the Latics had put four past the former Leeds goalie Harry Fearnley in his only appearance for Rochdale. The game also saw the final appearance of the stalwart defender Don Partridge, the first and so far only player to appear in the Football League for Rochdale for 10 seasons, though he played only 101 games.

The goals continued to flow with a 5-1 win over Barrow, local lad Derek Andrews scoring on his debut and Bill McCulloch getting his first goal since 1948. This was followed by a 7-2 defeat at Chesterfield, both sides scoring twice in the last 10 minutes, a traumatic start for the Dale's then youngest Football League player, 17 year old centre half Ray Aspden. Not surprisingly, young Ray was left out for the next game and indeed made only one more appearance in the next three years, but he persevered to eventually become the club's Football League appearance record holder.

The tally of goals against led to the signing of experienced Accrington goalkeeper Jimmy Jones and his team mate Charlie Ferguson. Yet another new name was Calvin Symonds, a cricketer and taxi driver from Bermuda, the first West Indian to play for the Dale. Despite these changes, Rochdale won only once in seven games, a 4-2 victory over Chester thanks again to two Lynn penalties. The reappearance of Bev Glover coincided with victories at York, Rochdale's first away success since the previous Easter, and at home to Scunthorpe.

Eric Gemmell scored twice in each game. However these proved to be isolated successes and Rochdale did not win again for another six games, being knocked out of the FA Cup by York in the process.

Having failed to sign Blackpool's 1953 Cup Final hero Stan Mortensen, manager Catterick decided to invest in the experienced Southport inside forward Andy McLaren, a well known Scottish international and prolific goalscorer in his days with Preston during and after the war. McLaren inspired a run of eight games unbeaten, including a 2-0 win over runaway leaders Grimsby, Dale thus taking three points out of four from the eventual champions. Over Christmas, Rochdale did the double over old antagonists Carlisle, McLaren scoring twice in the 5-2 home win to gain some measure of recompense for the previous year's disasters. Debutant Harry Jackson scored in the away game, and had another effort disallowed, but was never given another senior chance.

Surprisingly, another poor run followed, with four successive defeats including a 5-0 home drubbing by Derby County and a 4-1 defeat at Gateshead (in front of only 1700 fans) when Jimmy Jones was knocked out in the first minute and Joe Lynn had to go in goal. Rochdale bounced back to beat York and Crewe, reserve full back Jim Storey and the diminutive Jimmy Anders (who had earlier scored in five consecutive games from his usual wing position) forming an unlikely but effective strike partnership. The Dale also won three of the next five games, though they were annihilated 6-0 by struggling Mansfield.

An Easter Monday victory at Workington saw a return to goal scoring action of the Dale's "forgotten man" Frank Lord, after almost two years in the wilderness. Lord went on to score four times in the last seven games which, despite a 5-1 home defeat by Chesterfield, earned enough points to enable Rochdale to creep into the top half of the table again. They had an almost identical record to the previous term, though the goals against column was decidedly worse with 84 conceded.

The long serving Partridge, Boyle and Lynn were released at the end of the season but were given a testimonial game - against Rochdale C.C., at cricket! Also departing for non-League football were Mitcheson, Black and top scorer Gemmell, while McClelland retired, leaving the squad rather short on experience. (Over at Stockport, former Dale man Jack Connor had just hit 30 goals for the third season in a row, having been the Third North's top scorer in two of those campaigns).

Off the field, trainer Joe Duff was injured in a coach crash and had to give up those duties, though he continued as the club's groundsman for many years. Former Manchester City player Joe Fagan moved from Bradford Park Avenue to take the trainer's job. Crowds at Spotland had sunk to the two and a half thousand mark by the end of the season and a yearly loss of over £10,000 was incurred for the first time.

Manager Catterick went back to his old club Everton for his main summer 'shopping' of 1956, obtaining the signatures of the experienced Jackie Grant and Eddie Wainwright, and youthful reserve Gwynfor Lewis for a combined fee of £6000. Grant, a *"pocket dynamo"*, had spent 15 years at Goodison Park, while Wainwright had been close to a full England cap earlier in his career, having represented the FA on tour to Canada and the Football League. Not to be outdone, Lewis was a Welsh youth international. Catterick's other former club, Crewe, supplied experienced wing half Jimmy McGuigan, while at the other end of his career was 17 year old Billy Duff who followed in his father Joe's footsteps by signing pro. forms for Dale. Although he never actually appeared in Dale's first team, he did later make Football League appearances for Grimsby and Accrington (and keeping to the family sporting tradition, his sister married Lancashire and England bowler Tommy Greenhough).

1956-57:

For the first time since the war, Rochdale opened their campaign with a win, Lewis' effort forcing Barrow's Cahil to put the ball past his own 'keeper for the only goal of the game. Unfortunately the match also attracted Rochdale's lowest opening day crowd, just 3500, compared to over 10,000 at many other Third North games that day.

Dave Pearson scored four goals against Halifax in September 1957.

Lewis scored twice in a 3-2 win at Mansfield (putting Dale temporarily in second place), before two away defeats and two nil-nil draws at Spotland dropped them back into mid-table. The match against Mansfield Town was notable though, for the use of the floodlights for part of a League match at Spotland for the first time.

To alleviate the everpresent money worries, the Dale's two former Bradford City wingers, Arnold Kendall and Jimmy Anders, were sold to City's neighbours Park Avenue. Accrington's Joe Devlin, a member of Stanley's all Scottish line-up of the previous term, was signed to take the outside left berth and scored on his debut in a 3-0 win over Scunthorpe.

This was the first of five successive victories, two goals from Gwyn Lewis helping to beat eventual champions Derby County, and another two contributing to a remarkable 6-1 away win at Crewe, Wainwright also netting a brace. At Tranmere it was the woodwork that suffered rather than the opposition, as 'keeper Jimmy Jones swung on the bar when a shot whistled over the top, and snapped it, the game having to be held up while repairs were effected.

On October 23rd Dale entertained leaders Hartlepool and a single goal by Wainwright sent the majority of the 12,262 crowd home happy and put Rochdale clearly in the promotion picture, five points behind the leaders and only one behind Derby. Unfortunately, despite the signing of another experienced ex-Evertonian, Cyril Lello, who had once scored seven goals in a match in wartime football, this was the high point of their challenge.

The turning point in Rochdale's season was a serious injury to their defensive kingpin Bev Glover. Without him, and another injury victim Joe Devlin, Rochdale went out of the cup at Scunthorpe and had Frank Lord sent off. A week later they lost a crucial home game to fellow contenders Accrington and a string of six defeats from mid-December plunged the Dale down the table. In fact Rochdale won only once during Glover's 14 match absence. His return in mid-February coincided with the debut of Eddie Moran, signed from Stockport, and the switch of Lord from the wing back to his proper position leading the attack. This move was in place of Gwyn Lewis, who had just been transferred to Chesterfield for £3500, despite not having scored since November; he netted 10 times for his new club, as he possibly did for Dale, depending on the interpretation of the opening day own goal.

The changes certainly worked as Rochdale romped to a 6-1 win over struggling Southport, Lord bagging a hat trick, and set off on another good run. His former team mates had a harder time getting to Chesterfield than did Lewis, as their coach broke down and they had to get out and push. Nevertheless, they still had the energy left to gain a two-all draw. Lord hit another treble in a 4-3 win against Hull while another newcomer, Dave Pearson from Oldham, scored on his debut as the Dale also put four past Bradford City. Home form was excellent until the end of the season with eight straight wins, but the last five aways brought just one point and Rochdale had to settle for 13th place, though only six points behind the side in fifth. When Glover had been available they had picked up 42 points from 33 games, compared to six from 13 when he was out.

Again a number of senior players departed for non-League football, including McLaren, Murphy and Lello, who became player-manager of Runcorn. Assistant trainer Arthur Griffiths also left and was replaced in the summer by the former Manchester City wing half Albert Emptage.

The most important development for Rochdale during the close season took place away from Spotland, though, when the Football League voted to create national Third and Fourth Divisions in place of the two regional leagues. This plan, imposed by the higher division clubs (who had most of the votes) in the face of falling attendances, had been long mooted but was not universally welcomed, especially in the Northern Section. Many club representatives feared that the effect of increased travelling expenses and the loss of many lucrative local 'derby' games would not be offset by the greater competition for places and the novelty of new opponents. On the other hand it did, at least, allow for more movement in the League.

With the top clubs having consistently voted against plans to allow more than the champions of each section to be promoted, many clubs like Rochdale had never been out of the Third North. In fact seven teams - Accrington Stanley, Barrow, Crewe Alexandra, Halifax Town, Hartlepools, Southport and Wrexham - had visited Spotland every year since 1921. Anyway, regardless of any arguments for or against, it was clear that the following season could be critical for lower division sides, as they fought to retain Third Division status by finishing in the top half of their section.

The club had decided to revert to their former colours of black and white striped shirts for the new season, though now with black shorts instead of the original white. Several new faces were in evidence when the Dale staged a pre-season practice match in which the 'Stripes' beat the 'Blues' 6-1. Harold Rudman, a full back who had been with Burnley since the war, though he had only recently established himself in their first team, Tom McGlennon from Blackpool's Central League side and Crighton (better known as Jock) Lockhart from Southend figured in the successful Stripes side. Colin Vizard, a former England Amateur youth international and Everton junior, and ex-Celtic reserve 'keeper (and chartered accountant) Bernard McCready, appeared for the second string. One man missing from either side was the unlucky Frank Lord. Demobbed from his National Service the previous week, he broke his leg for the second time just three days later in training, a terrible blow for the centre forward and his many fans.

1957-58:
Nevertheless, the Dale made a great start to 1957-58, travelling to Mansfield and comprehensively beating the Stags 4-2, Lockhart scoring two on his debut at outside right. This boosted the crowd for the game with old rivals Accrington past the 12,000 mark and the Dale recorded an excellent three goal win over the side which eventually finished second. A third straight win, against Workington at Spotland, put Rochdale in second spot, just behind Bury on goal average, but they lost their next two away games.

Pre-season training 1958, manager Harry Catterick (far right) addresses his troops. The following month he left to manage Sheffield Wednesday.

The match against Darlington on September 11th was one of the most remarkable even in the Dale's chequered history. Three-one in front at half time, the Quakers must have felt they had the match well and truly sewn up when they scored a fourth after the break. In a stirring fight-back Dale pulled it back to 3-4 despite having three efforts disallowed, then incredibly netted twice more in the last three minutes to gain an amazing victory. Even more remarkably the two last gasp heroes were the full backs, Harold Rudman and Charlie Ferguson, the first time that both Rochdale full backs had scored in the same game. And if that wasn't enough, it was the 32 year old Rudman's first ever League goal!

Rochdale recorded their fifth win in seven outings when Hull were the visitors, but Darlington gained revenge in another high scoring game, winning 4-2 at Feethams. Rochdale gained another good away victory, 3-0 at Stockport, before Scunthorpe visited Spotland and showed the style that took them to a clear win in the championship by beating the Dale 4-1. Even the Dale's goal was scored by a Scunthorpe player, Alan Bushby - who later moved to Rochdale - putting through his own goal. More 'high fying' the following day saw the start of the 'space age' with the launch of Sputnik 1.

The Dale recovered to thrash Halifax 5-1 with four goals from Dave Pearson, the first such feat for Rochdale since the war. However they then slipped right out of contention by gaining only one point from five games.

The solitary point was gained in a draw with neighbours Bury which attracted Spotland's best post-war League crowd of 18,896. Despite 30 goals in 14 games, Harry Catterick decided to add more firepower to the front line in the continued absence of Lord and surprisingly Workington allowed him to buy their record scorer Jim Dailey for a relatively modest fee. It quickly proved money well spent, as in his third game in Dale colours Dailey equalled Bert Whitehurst's record for a match at Spotland by bagging five goals in a 7-0 trouncing of Hartlepools (ten years earlier Dailey had scored a five for Sheffield Wednesday). Another transfer was that of Joe Devlin who followed the well trodden path to Bradford.

Though knocked out of the Cup by Darlington, the Dale's League form picked up again towards the end of the year, with only two defeats in 10 games - Crewe being beaten 3-0 even with only 10 men after Pearson was sent off. They also had, in Jim Dailey, the League's leading marksman with 20 goals. Even so the crowd for the Christmas Day fixture with Wrexham was a meagre 3342. The return fixture the following day attracted three times that figure.

After a slightly rocky spell there was even better to come as the Dale won five games out of seven to move up to fourth spot, seven points behind the leaders, by the middle of March. The home game with Tranmere was even honoured by the presence of the BBC who broadcast the second half on the wireless for a fee of 10 guineas (£10-50p).

Dailey continued to enjoy himself with a hat trick against Stockport and had now scored 18 goals in 19 games for Rochdale.

Unfortunately at this point his, and his colleagues', supply of goals ran out. In the remaining 11 games (a number of postponements having caused something of a backlog, and nine of these were played in the space of 25 days), the Dale scored just six goals. Nevertheless, Dailey's total of 25 goals for the Dale and Workington gave him joint fourth place in the division's scoring charts. In the end it was the defence who saved the day. Goalless draws in the away games at Crewe and Oldham in the last week of the season took the Dale's points tally to 46 and enabled them to finish 10th and thereby gain a place in the new Division Three, despite losing 4-1 at Halifax in the final game.

The top 12 places had been effectively decided the night before when Gateshead and Oldham both lost and had to settle for Division Four. In an amazingly tight finish there were only three points between Stockport in 9th and Hartlepools in 18th. York could count themselves the most unfortunate as they missed out on goal average, having the same points as Rochdale, Tranmere and Wrexham. Dale's reserves also had something to cheer about, having lost only twice all season on their way to winning the Lancashire League championship.

Despite double figure goal tallies Pearson and Lockhart were amongst the close season departures, Pearson being traded to Crewe in exchange for Don Whiston and Lockhart joining Gravesend & Northfleet. The veterans Bill McCulloch and Harold Rudman retired, the former to work as a commercial traveller. This again left about a dozen experienced men as the nucleus of the squad along with a number of local products who had been in the successful reserve team. Albert Emptage moved up to first team trainer in place of Joe Fagan who left to become assistant trainer at Anfield. He subsequently worked his way through the 'boot room' ranks under Bill Shankly and Bob Paisley to eventually manage Liverpool to the treble of League Championship, Football League Cup and European Cup in 1984; one of the numerous stories about his legendary boss Bill Shankly also concerned the Dale, `Shanks' denying that he took his wife to watch Rochdale as an anniversary present: *"It was her birthday - would I have got married during the football season? And anyway, it wasn't Rochdale, it was Rochdale Reserves."*

It was clear that Rochdale, who had not finished higher than 10th in the Northern Section since 1950, had an uphill struggle to hold their own among the best clubs from each region, especially as it was widely held that the general standard in the Third South had been higher than that in the Third North in recent seasons.

However, only a couple of significant additions were made to the squad over the summer, in Blackpool reserve full back Dai Powell and former Partick Thistle wing half Bert Thomson from Yeovil. Just after the campaign opened another exchange deal with Crewe saw the arrival of Bill Finney and the departure of Eddie Moran.

1958-59:
Then to add to the side's potential difficulties, on the eve of the season, Second Division Sheffield Wednesday offered Harry Catterick the boss's job at Hillsborough, and Rochdale's board allowed him to leave. The board also decided not to rush into signing a replacement so the manager's chair was vacant as the 1958-59 season got underway. It started with a trip to familiar territory and a rather familiar result, a single goal defeat at Stockport. A home defeat by Rochdale's first southern opponents Plymouth Argyle was followed by the season's first success, Dailey settling the match against Reading when Dale were awarded a penalty two minutes from the end.

A massive crowd of 26,691 saw an eventful return game with Plymouth, Dale going down 2-1, despite a first goal for local youngster Les Spencer. Tom McGlennon was sent off by referee Dennis Howell, later a well known politician and Minister for Sport, who accidentally played five minutes short in the first half. Although also beaten at Colchester, three points from the next two home games suggested that Rochdale might yet hold their own in their new company. Rochdale also led at Swindon until the 88th minute, but eventually lost to a goal scored four minutes into injury time. This was the signal for a catastrophic run of just two points from eight games which included a 6-1 hammering at Bury and tumbled the Dale to the bottom of the table.

At this point, Sheffield Wednesday and England trainer Jack Marshall took over as the club's new manager (having accepted the offer a couple of weeks earlier). To 'celebrate' his arrival the Dale lost at home to Notts County and young 'Jock' Wallace broke his leg in only his seventh senior game. Wallace had been signed near the end of the previous season from Scottish Junior side St. Roch's with a £500 donation made by the Supporters Club. Although on the staff for another couple of years he never regained his senior place.

Things did look marginally brighter over the next few weeks with a couple of draws and a home win over Accrington. In the FA Cup Rochdale met Hartlepool, drawing 1-1 in the North East and then 3-3 in a thrilling match at Spotland. Dale had been two down early on but then Charlie Ferguson missed the chance to win it from the penalty spot in extra time. The third game was scheduled for Old Trafford the following Monday but on the appointed evening thick fog blanketed the Manchester area and the match had to be put off until the Thursday.

Fog again descended, cutting the attendance to 6000 hardy souls, who would have looked lost in the expanse of Old Trafford, if anyone could have seen anything at all! Trainer Jackie Arthur had to walk the last two miles in front of the coach, otherwise the team wouldn't have found Old Trafford either. With the conditions getting worse, and the players at each end waiting for the ball to emerge from the murk, the game should have been abandoned while it was still tied in the second half, but amazingly the referee decided to play extra time. Hartlepool finally settled the issue in the 326th minute of the Dale's longest ever cup-tie. Rochdale goalie Jimmy Jones was making his comeback after a spell out with eye trouble, but wouldn't have seen much of the ball even with his new contact lenses!

Rochdale were then thrashed 7-1 at Bradford City, their ninth defeat in ten League games away from Spotland, Bev Glover subsequently losing his place at No.5 to Ray Aspden. Dale did manage three wins out of four at home around the turn of the year, scoring three goals in a League match for the first time that season, when they beat Wrexham. The men on target were Wainwright (with two) and Alan Moore, a well travelled winger signed from Swindon.

Making their debuts were former 'B' international Stan Milburn from Leicester and George Cooper from Crystal Palace. Milburn, already 32 and the recipient of benefits at each of his previous two clubs, came from the amazing Ashington family of four brothers who were all long-serving Football League full backs, while his cousin was the legendary 'Wor Jackie' of Newcastle and England, and his nephews Jack and Bobby Charlton were just starting their careers at Leeds and Manchester United, the latter having survived the tragic Munich air crash of the year before.

Rochdale were thrashed 6-1 at Southampton and two further defeats left them floundering with only 17 points from 31 games. They did beat Bury 1-0 and gained a creditable goalless draw against Chesterfield with Milburn in goal against his old club for 70 minutes, after Jones suffered a gashed head. The Dale centre forward that day was Bob Entwistle on his only outing for them. He later became a South African 'international', played for Bangor when they sensationally beat Napoli in the Cup Winners Cup, and completed the circle by becoming mine host at the Church Inn on Willbutts Lane.

It was obviously too little too late by now and the club was already clearing the decks for next year. Grant had already gone to Southport and Green followed him, at the start of a remarkable globe trotting career which saw him playing, coaching and managing at about 30 clubs worldwide in the next 25 years before he too came full circle and became the Rochdale manager.

In addition McCready was transferred to Oldham and youngsters like Jimmy Brown, Norman Bodell and 'keeper George Heyes were given their chance. Brown later overlooked Shankly's dictum and was the Dale's 12th man on his wedding day.

Fortunately the fans retained their sense of humour in adversity as illustrated by the inclusion of possibly the original of the 'pie joke' in the Supporters Club Handbook, i. e. *"Arriving late, one of our faithful supporters was paying his two bob at the turnstiles when a terrific roar came from within the ground. Rushing onto the terraces, he grabbed the first fellow he could and gaspingly asked "Have they scored?". "No", came the reply "the pies have just come".*

The next eight games brought two further wins but four defeats and relegation was a certainty with four games still to play, Hull - themselves on their way to Division Two - putting Dale out of their misery by beating them 2-1 at Boothferry Park. The four games yielded just one point (and no goals) so Rochdale finished on a meagre 28 points and with only 37 goals to their credit, less than half the number conceded. In fact, the defence had not done too badly, especially at home where Dale actually conceded fewer goals than the champions Plymouth. On the other hand, all the extra travelling round the country didn't seem to agree with them and they failed to win a single away game.

Not surprisingly, most of the former regulars were released, including Bev Glover who was awarded a testimonial game after 169 League appearances in six years. Jimmy McGuigan moved to Crewe as trainer-coach, thus starting on a long career as coach or manager to several League clubs, while Charlie Ferguson, who had been on the transfer list at his own request, moved to Oldham on a free transfer after appealing to an FA tribunal.

Half a dozen experienced men were added to the staff during the 1959 close season in an effort to strengthen the side enough to bounce straight back to Division Three. Full back Jack Edwards had spent ten years with Crystal Palace and half back Alan Bushby had seven with Scunthorpe. The forward recruits were Wrexham's Johnny Anderson, who had played for League clubs in Scotland, England and Wales, Tony Collins, another ex-Palace man now joining his eighth club, Ron Barnes, Stanley Matthews' understudy at Blackpool, who cost £1000, and Ron Cairns, their most expensive capture to date who joined them from Blackburn Rovers for £2500.

Even so the Dale squad was much smaller than in previous seasons. Former player Jack Connor and pre-war Manchester United manager Jimmy Porter joined Jack Marshall's staff as scouts.

A break from pre-season training, July 1959, for new signings (left to right)
Jack Edwards, Tony Collins, Ron Barnes, Ron Cairns, Alan Bushby and Johnny Anderson.

1959-60:

Rochdale kicked off their Fourth Division career with a draw at Southport after being two goals up, and a single goal by Cairns disposed of Gillingham. Thoughts that life might be easy in the lower division were soon dispelled as only one of the next seven games ended in victory. For the match against Barrow, full back Milburn (who had actually been figuring at centre half in recent games) was switched to centre forward.

Considering that in 13 seasons with his previous clubs Stan had just one goal to his credit, this might have seemed a rather unlikely move, but he came up trumps with a hat trick in a 4-1 win. After a couple more games he reverted to No.5 to shore up the defence, but even so netted in three successive games, each time from the penalty spot, a club record.

From the beginning of October Jimmy Jones kept clean sheets in seven consecutive League games at Spotland, six of them victories, and with a couple of away wins at Gateshead and Crewe, Dale moved into the top six. Almost 15,000 fans saw fellow promotion hopefuls Palace dent their prospects with a 4-0 win at Selhurst Park, but at Spotland attendances were only around the four to five thousand mark despite a 13 match unbeaten home run. Even the game against traditional rivals Oldham only attracted a crowd of 5298.

A more modern tactical approach surfaced at Spotland during this successful period, when the manager played Johnny Anderson in a withdrawn centre forward role, a tactic dubbed the 'Marshall plan', following the 'Revie plan' at Manchester City a few years earlier.

In the FA Cup Rochdale had been held at home by Carlisle but won the replay 3-1 after extra time. Remarkably this was the first time since joining the Football League that Rochdale had won a replay away from home. In the second round they were unable to pull off a repeat performance and went out at the second attempt to Third Division Bradford City.

Back in the League, Christmas brought home and away defeats at the hands of Notts County and from then on form was patchy, with some excellent results interspersed with too many defeats. Milburn, again at centre forward, scored twice in a 4-2 win over Torquay (who went on to be promoted), and converted a club record eighth penalty of the season when the Dale repeated that scoreline against Crewe, eventually top scoring with 15. Dale also netted four against Crystal Palace, with a rejuvenated Frank Lord back among the goals after almost three years out of the limelight. The crowd, though, was a meagre two and a half thousand. In the penultimate game, a crowd of nearly 18,000 at Vicarage Road saw Watford clinch promotion with a 2-1 win and Rochdale also lost their last game to Oldham who thus avoided finishing bottom.

....and player charicatures
from the period

Jimmy Jones

Alan Bushby

Stan Milburn

Ron Barnes

Even so, Dale ended in 12th spot, only seven points behind Millwall in 5th. Rochdale won 15 home games, equalling their best since the war, and their defensive record was the best for 10 years. Only 17 players appeared in the League side, the lowest ever at that time.

At the end of the season George Heyes, who had supplanted Jimmy Jones as the regular 'keeper, was transferred to First Division Leicester City for £7000, becoming understudy to England's Gordon Banks. Les Spencer joined him in the higher levels, moving to Second Division Luton Town, but unlike Heyes had a very short career, being forced to retire through injury after only seven games for the Hatters. All the other first teamers were retained except Anderson who joined Chester and Thomson who went to play for San Francisco Scots. The transfers had been forced on the club by the low gate receipts, the average attendance of just over 4000 being the worst since the 'thirties. Even then, only a massive donation of £10,000 from the Supporters Club kept them going.

The most amazing event of the summer, as far as supporters of lower division clubs were concerned, was the failure of Gateshead to secure re-election. They had finished third from bottom and were making their first application since 1937, but nevertheless failed to gain the support of the representatives of the clubs in the two top divisions who held the voting power.

~ CHAPTER 6 ~

Jack Marshall settled for just a couple of major signings, adding long standing Manchester City reserve wing half Ron Phoenix and Bury inside forward Stan Hepton to the ranks. Another local youngster, John Hardman from Bess's Boys, was also signed. The side lined up for the new season in a Real Madrid style all white strip (they had played in white shirts borrowed from Bolton in the previous season's two floodlit cup replays).

A familiar start was made with defeat at Stockport, but goals by Brown and Lord earned two away points at Mansfield. Two more Lord goals sealed a victory over Exeter in the first home game, but the crowd was a disappointing 2514, paying the increased entrance charge of 2s 6d (12.5p). Manager Marshall had meantime been offered the vacant manager's job at Blackburn, and on September 1st the Rochdale board agreed to release him.

Ronnie Phoenix

Jack Pollitt

Joffre Mackay

Stan Hepton

New signings for the 1960-61 season.

Two more goals by Lord completed the double over the Cumbrians and the Dale also took four points off Oldham, ex-Rochdale full back Ferguson helping them out with an own goal.

Although these successes were interleaved with defeats, home wins over Hartlepool and Chester at the beginning of October put the Dale on the fringe of the promotion pack. Frank Lord, hat trick hero against Hartlepool, had already notched 15 goals and had been linked with a move to Second Division Swansea. His sixteenth earned a draw against Second Division Scunthorpe in Rochdale's first match in the newly instigated Football League Cup (or "Hardacre's folly", as it was dubbed after the League secretary, according to the sceptics; since many of the top clubs did not bother to enter). Stan Hepton, scorer of the only goal, and former Ross County 'keeper Joffre McKay, who kept a clean sheet on his debut, were the heroes of the replay at the Old Showground, which gave Rochdale their first success against a higher division side since their non-League days (Lancashire Cup and wartime games apart). In the next round, three goals in the last 17 minutes, two of them from Barnes, saw off Third Division Southend 5-2. Rochdale were removed from the FA Cup by their fourth division rivals Crewe, under their new manager Jimmy McGuigan, the former Dale wing half.

An eventful match against League new boys Peterborough, in front of a crowd of 14,285, was eventually lost 4-3. Dale conceded two penalties, came from behind three times and then lost in the third minute of injury time. Winger Tony Collins, actually on the injured list following a cartilage operation, was appointed player-manager on the day of the next game, and his side celebrated with a win at Carlisle, Lord scoring for the fifth successive game.

In the League Cup third round, the Dale met First Division giants Blackburn Rovers, managed by their own former boss Jack Marshall. The Blackburn public showed little taste for the new competition, only six thousand fans attending the game including many who had travelled over from Rochdale. The Rovers team nearly paid for treating the game lightly, too, but eventually scraped through 2-1. The Dale scorer was 18 year old Joe Richardson, a £250 signing from Sheffield United who was making his senior debut.

Ron Barnes in action during the 1960-61 season.

The Dale's long unbeaten home run eventually fell after 17 games to a Bradford Park Avenue side on its way into Division Three, and the season petered out to leave Rochdale in 17th place. Though they were never in serious danger, they were only four points clear of the re-election zone at the end, though conversely they were only three behind the club in 10th place. Ron Cairns hit 20 League goals, the first player to do so since Joe Hargreaves in 1946-47. Frank Lord totalled 19 but after his spectacular start, his form had faded and he had been out of the side for a spell. Somewhat disillusioned after eight years with the club, in which he had made only 120 League appearances but scored 54 goals - a post-war record - he was put on the transfer list at his own request and was sold to Crewe for £2500 in July. He scored 60 goals in the next two seasons before further injuries took their toll and he became a long serving coach and manager.

The main footballing interest around Christmas was off the field rather than on it, with the PFA, led by Jimmy Hill of Fulham, threatening strike action after failing to reach agreement with the Football League over pay and conditions of contract. This was forestalled when the League finally agreed to scrap the maximum wage of £20 per week and usher in the so-called 'new deal' for professional footballers, the players (Frank Lord was Rochdale's representative) also gaining the right to negotiate more than the traditional one year contract.

In the New Year, the League form continued in a remarkably consistent fashion - with Cairns scoring regularly, the Dale were unbeatable at home, but they could not win away. Though lodged in mid-table they did play in some memorable games; the normally restrained Ray Aspden was sent off at Bradford, Dale led runaway leaders Peterborough 1-0, but then the match was abandoned due to fog, and they beat Millwall 4-0 with three goals coming in the 82nd, 83rd and 85th minutes.

Nearly 18,000 fans saw Palace beat Rochdale 4-1 at Selhurst Park. These were the first goals conceded by Dale's new goalkeeper, the 33 year old former England 'B' international Ted Burgin, in his fifth game since signing from Leeds. Known as one of the most injury prone 'keepers in the game, with a string of broken bones suffered in the course of his trade, Burgin was to have a new lease on life at Spotland. Two other signings before the transfer deadline in March were Exeter's Jim Thompson, bought for a new club record £4000, to take the left half spot, and the well travelled Brian Birch, an England youth international in his days at Manchester United. A rare Irishman in the Dale ranks was Ollie Norris, best known for his goal for Bournemouth which beat Spurs in the Cup.

Another major sale was Ron Barnes who went to Wrexham for £4000. Jimmy Jones retired after 175 League games for the Dale, becoming a licencee in Lincoln, and Dai Powell joined Rochdale Police. Near the end of the season Rochdale played a benefit game for their former player Bill McCulloch. In his playing days, he had been noted for his toughness, once scoring a cup-tie winning goal for Stockport despite being concussed and having to spend the next two weeks in hospital. Since retiring though, he had been struck down by multiple sclerosis and was unable to work. Four days after the game he died at the age of only 38.

1961-62:
There was a new look all round for the coming season. The playing kit was changed yet again, to white shirts and black shorts, and there were a number of new faces too. Full back Doug ('Jock') Winton, a former Scotland 'B' international arrived from Aston Villa for £1000, while Doug Wragg, a schoolboy international winger in his younger days, cost £2000 from Mansfield. Outside left Colin Whitaker had been a regular goalscorer in a long spell at Shrewsbury and new centre forward Lou Bimpson had played in the 1960 Cup Final for Blackburn.

The first serious game of the season also saw an innovation as the Dale met the Latics in a charity match for the Rose Bowl, donated by the respective local papers, the Rochdale Observer and the Oldham Chronicle.

Two goals by Douggie Wragg gave the Dale victory at Boundary Park and allowed them to bring home their first trophy since the Lancashire Junior Cup in 1951.

The League season too, started in cracking style with a 3-1 win over Hartlepool and an even better 4-1 success against Millwall, the eventual fourth division champions. The first set back was at Gresty Road, where the recently departed Frank Lord hit Crewe's winner. A draw at Millwall in front of over 11,000 fans and two more excellent home wins, Cairns taking his tally to six goals in as many games, put the Dale on top of the table. However, as so often before, they immediately came down to Earth with a bump, losing their next four League games. Nevertheless, they did set a club record when the same eleven players figured in each of the first eight games of the season.

Action from the opening day match of 1961-62.

Also, sandwiched in the run of League defeats was a remarkable success in the League Cup, when the Dale travelled to Second Division Southampton and came away with a goalless draw. This was largely due to Tony Collins' tactical ploy of utilising the 4-2-4 formation which the Brazilians had introduced in the previous World Cup. Stan Hepton was the man delegated to drop back alongside the regular centre half (a tactic not appreciated by the Saints' fans) in one of the first instances of a four man defensive line seen in domestic football. Back at Spotland, 'Big Lou' Bimpson, scored twice to upset the form book, though there were a few anxious moments after the Saints pulled one back two minutes from the end. This inspired another run of success, with a League win against York, and a League Cup victory over Doncaster by four clear goals; Rovers had earlier won at Spotland in the League. Bimpson scored twice in each of these games, as well.

A fourth win in a row, against Accrington, lifted the Dale's League position, but there was no joy in the next seven games, though a draw at Oldham was watched by a remarkable Fourth Division attendance of over 17,000. More cup success was forthcoming as Rochdale beat Third Division Halifax in the FA Cup. In the third round of the League Cup they met another Second Division side in Charlton Athletic, and gained revenge for the two post-war FA Cup defeats by beating the Londoners 1-0. Whitaker netted what proved to be the winner after Milburn had earlier missed a penalty, but the real hero was Jock Winton who cleared off the line in the last minute. Despite the level of the opposition, the attendance, as for the Southampton game, was only a shade over 5000, not much higher than for League games.

The crowd did reach 8741 for the second round FA Cup tie against Wrexham, but it was the Welsh contingent who went home happy. A goal by Cairns enabled Rochdale to gain a long awaited League victory, against Tranmere, but two away defeats left Dale rather too close to the bottom for comfort at Christmas. They finally managed their first away win on Boxing Day, beating Mansfield 1-0, and also won at Exeter, Joe Richardson who had just gained a regular place in the side scoring in each. It was just as well that Rochdale broke their away duck, as postponements due to the weather meant that they did not play at Spotland for seven weeks. They won their first two games on returning to home territory, but more remarkably won their next pair of away fixtures as well, thus ending a run of 20 matches on foreign soil without a win, by gaining four of them in succession.

Due to the strange arrangement of the competition, the Dale had been given a bye in the fourth round of the League Cup, and in the quarter final they met the other Fourth Division survivors York City. An early goal from Hepton and a pile driver of a shot from Thompson put Rochdale into the semis and also gave them a seventh straight win, the best run since 1923-24. Any chance of a serious promotion challenge faded though when the next two games ended in defeat. Nevertheless these games saw the side beat its own record run with no team changes, the same eleven playing in nine consecutive games; there were, however, two changes from the side who played in all the first eight games.

After losing a friendly to the British Police, who included Dai Powell in their ranks, Rochdale visited the sorely troubled Accrington Stanley and beat them 2-0, Cairns netting in the last minute. This turned out to be the last act at Peel Park, as a few days later Stanley resigned from the Football League because of their financial crisis.

The club folded, signalling a dire warning to other clubs in the lower divisions. It also, incidentally, cost Rochdale four points, as Stanley's record was expunged from the League table. To make up for it, Rochdale won three of their next four games as well, the match against Oldham attracting 9,200 fans to Spotland, the best League gate for five years.

In the League Cup semi-final Rochdale had again been paired with Blackburn Rovers of Division One, though the match had had to be put off for two weeks because of the weather (and ended up being played on manager Collins' birthday). Probably needing a good lead from the home leg to stand much chance, Rochdale were contained for an hour but then 'Little Joe' Richardson scored twice - a header from a Wragg cross and a 20 yard shot - to give them real hope. This appeared to have been dashed when England star Bryan Douglas pulled one back in the 88th minute, but the Dale weren't done yet and their ex-Blackburn men Bimpson and Cairns combined for the latter to bag their third in the dying seconds. The attendance at this, Rochdale's biggest match in their history - and against local First Division opposition at that - failed to reach 10,000.

ROCHDALE ASSOCIATION FOOTBALL CLUB

SEMI-FINAL FOOTBALL LEAGUE CUP

ROCHDALE
V.
BLACKBURN ROVERS

Kick-off 7.15 p.m.

MONDAY, 5th MARCH, 1962

•

Official Programme 4d

Big match, but a very mundane programme!

A fortnight later the teams met again at Ewood Park. Rovers scored from a Pickering penalty after only eight minutes, the ball just eluding Burgin's grasp as he almost pulled off a great stop in the mud. Nine minutes later though, Stan Hepton, just back from a spell out of the side, stormed through to restore the Dale's two goal advantage with a 25-yard shot which skidded past Else in the home goal. Although Douglas scored early in the second half, Blackburn could not find an equaliser against a valiant Dale defence, even centre forward Bimpson lending a hand with a crucial header off his own goal line, so Rochdale went through to a national cup final for the first time.

At this stage, at the beginning of April, Rochdale in mid-table still had a mathematical chance of making the top four, with nine games still to play. Indeed, they kept in the hunt a while longer with three wins out of the next five, including a remarkable comeback against Chester when they scored three times in the last 14 minutes to win 3-2. By the time the League Cup Final came around, two defeats suffered at the end of an impossibly exhausting six games in 10 days had ended their promotion hopes, and the Dale were unable to raise their game one last time when they met Second Division Norwich City in the first leg at Spotland.

With several key players appearing in their ninth game in the three weeks since the semi-final, Rochdale went down 3-0 in front of a crowd of 11,123. A week later they had much the better of the game at Norwich but failed to find the target, the Canaries pinching the only goal to win 4-0 on aggregate. This was almost certainly the only time that the reigning monarch has enquired about a Dale game, as the Queen - Norwich City's patron - was reputed to have asked about the score while at an official banquet! The Rochdale team, the only fourth division side ever to play in a League or FA Cup Final, was: Burgin; Milburn, Winton; Bodell, Aspden, Thompson; Wragg, Hepton, Bimpson, Cairns and Whitaker in the first leg. For the return Peter Whyke, who only ever played five League games for the Dale, and Richardson, replaced the injured Wragg and Hepton. Unluckiest man was Ron Phoenix who played in the semi-final and appeared in the League matches around the final, but did not make the team for either leg.

Even after ending the League season with a 4-2 defeat at Gillingham, the Dale had one last cup tie, their fourteenth of the season, when they lost their Lancashire Cup quarter-final replay to Liverpool. Rochdale finished 12th in Division Four but were a mere seven points behind promoted Carlisle and indeed only 11 behind the champions Millwall. Ron Cairns, top scorer with 21 goals, actually appeared in all 61 competitive games, as many as 10 players appeared at least 45 times in the various competitions, and uniquely six players reached double figures in goals. Not surprisingly Tony Collins, now officially retired from the playing side, retained all his regulars.

Whyke to Scarborough, Phoenix to Altrincham and Birch, at the start of a globe trotting career as a coach, were the only departures. Though Aspden had been on the transfer list for some time, fans started a testimonial fund for him to encourage him to stay.

1962-63:

Correspondingly few signings were therefore made in the summer of 1962, the best known being former Bury forward Don Watson who arrived from Barnsley. The season again kicked off with the Charity Rose Bowl match against Oldham, the Latics this time gaining a 3-2 success. This match, incidentally, saw the first use of substitutes in a competitive Rochdale match, three changes being made at half time.

Rochdale also lost their first League game, at Mansfield, but beat Workington at Spotland. The first away win was gained at Exeter where reserve defender John Hardman, playing his first game at centre forward, scored in the first minute. The only other success in the first ten games was a last gasp victory over Chesterfield, when Cairns scored in the 90th minute. Most disappointing was an extra time defeat by Southport in the first round of the League Cup after Milburn had missed a penalty, the Reserves, though, won all their first nine games of the season.

After beating York 1-0, Rochdale really came good, hammering Barrow 6-0 with five goals in the space of 20 minutes. Two of them were scored by teenager George Morton, a former Everton junior playing in only his second League game. Colin Whitaker also scored in what was his last game before his transfer to Oldham in exchange for Peter Phoenix plus cash. Another transfer shortly afterwards was that of youngster Tony Moulden. Signed from Bury in the summer, he was transferred to Peterborough for £6000 after just five League games for the Dale. The boot was on the other foot in the next game, when Dale crashed 4-0 at Hartlepool (who eventually finished bottom), but this was the only reverse in 11 League matches.

Although knocked out of the FA Cup by York, Rochdale beat League new boys Oxford United 2-1 and then won at Bradford City by the same score to move up to fourth place in mid-November. Two wins out of four in December - over the leaders Mansfield and fellow contenders Crewe - kept the Dale up there, though the gate for the top of the table clash with the Stags was a paltry 2735.

At this point, the worst winter in twenty years took a grip of the country and football ground to a halt. Rochdale played only one game in the next nine weeks - and must have wished that that one could have been abandoned too. Level one-all with second placed Oldham after an hour, they lost full back Milburn injured.

New signings, summer 1962, (from left) Tony Moulden, Don Watson, Jack Martin and Geoge Morton.

The team then crashed to a 5-1 defeat as their former player Whitaker, whom Milburn had been marking, scored twice. The attendance at Boundary Park was just short of 15,000 and there had been over 12,000 at the earlier drawn game between the sides at Spotland (more than at the previous season's League Cup Final).

Another casualty of the weather was the old 'hen-coop' wooden dressing room, which practically collapsed on an unsuspecting Doug Wragg, soaking in the bath, when his teammates tried to push a snowball through the window. Also on the subject of 'unsuspecting', Wragg and fellow winger Phoenix claimed that under Spotland's aging lights they could play 'one-twos' off the perimeter wall to beat full backs without the officials noticing!

When they did get back to serious action in March, the Dale started with five points from three home games to stay in the hunt. Against new leaders Brentford, Dale eventually went down 5-3 to surrender their unbeaten home record. They were still in touch in early April, but a disastrous spell of four games in which they failed to score effectively ended their promotion hopes. Nevertheless they won all their last four home games, though that against Exeter attracted only 1403 fans, the lowest attendance for 10 years. When the season eventually ended on May 23rd (with the Beatles at No.1 in the music charts for the first time, and ushering in the 'swinging sixties'), Rochdale were in 7th place.

Their 51 points saw them six short of promoted Mansfield in fourth spot. With only one home defeat, Rochdale collected 38 points at Spotland, equalling their best ever. The Reserves, meantime, won the Lancashire League Supplementary Cup.

Ted Burgin was an everpresent for the second year running and had now completed over 100 consecutive League games for the Dale. Norman Bodell had been granted a free transfer in April and in the close season he moved to Crewe, later becoming a well known coach and manager. The other notable departure was Lou Bimpson who joined non-League Wigan.

Tony Collins' 1963 close season signings included only one player with Football League experience, Dave Kerry from Chesterfield, a former England Youth International. More important in the long term were the signings of young Sheffield Wednesday winger Dave Storf and the gangling 6'-2" Brian Taylor, spotted playing in the Rusholme Sunday League.

1963-64:
For the third season in a row, the Rose Bowl was won by the away side, Dale triumphing 5-3. The team also started the League season in style, a goal by Cairns after only two minutes setting up a 3-0 win at York. The first home game was drawn one-all with Brighton but the good start in the League soon faded out. In the League Cup, a remarkable second half, in which all the goals were scored, saw Rochdale gain a 5-2 victory at Chester despite having Milburn in goal for a spell. In the next game Rochdale scored five more against Workington, ultimately one of the promoted sides, with Kerry continuing his run of scoring in each of his first four games for the club.

These successes appeared to be rather a flash in the pan when Rochdale gained just one more League win in the next eight games. However, a victory over struggling Hartlepool initiated another complete reversal of form, the Dale losing only once in eleven matches. These victories included a win at previously unbeaten Exeter, managed by former Dale full back Jack Edwards, and a hard earned goalless draw at Gillingham, the eventual champions. In the end, though, the most important result would turn out to be the 4-0 victory over struggling Southport. (Incidentally, if as is often said, everyone of that generation can remember what they were doing when President Kennedy was assassinated, the Dale players should recall that they were preparing for a home game against Lincoln the following day, which was drawn 2-2).

Another inexplicable turn about saw Dale fall apart completely in the New Year. Eight games passed without a win and the side managed just four goals in the process.

They arrested the slide with a couple of home successes following the introduction of the lanky Taylor into the defence, but then lost four on the trot to slip into serious re-election trouble.

Three draws in the next four games kept them teetering on the brink, but a 2-1 home defeat by Bradford City, after Watson had given Dale the lead in the first minute, left them with only three games in which to save themselves - two of them against the top pair, Gillingham and Carlisle. A draw at Aldershot allowed Southport to sneak a point ahead in the battle to avoid 21st place, while in the mid-week games both sides lost 1-0, eleven and a half thousand seeing Dale's match at Brunton Park.

On the final Saturday, amazingly the best defence in the whole Football League was breached after just one minute when winger Don McKenzie fired home for the Dale. In the second half Ron Cairns scored from the spot - Dale's only success from four penalties awarded during the season - to earn Dale a surprise 2-1 win. Southport could only manage a goalless draw at Oxford, so Rochdale escaped having to apply for re-election by the narrowest possible margin on goal average and Gillingham had to rely likewise to take the Fourth Division title. Rochdale totalled 39 points, having gained only 14 in the second half of the season. Reflecting this change of fortune, leading scorer Richardson netted only once after Christmas.

Milburn and Burgin each played their 500th League game during the season. Burgin also took his run of consecutive League games for Dale to 150, easily a club record, before missing a few matches near the end of the season, while Milburn, with 226 appearances, was now second only to Walter Birch in the Rochdale records. Among the players on the move was Ron Cairns, who joined Southport with a post-war record 68 goals in 197 League appearances to his credit. Stan Hepton also moved to Southport while Doug Wragg went to Chesterfield and Don Watson to Barrow.

Meantime, the Football League Management Committee, in an effort to think up a remedy to the continued decline in attendances, had in its wisdom decided that the best way to help the clubs was to throw many of them out and run just three smaller divisions. The Dale Supporters Club, along with many others, were quick to petition the League deploring the proposal. At a meeting of Third and Fourth division club chairmen, a resolution moved by Doncaster's chairman and seconded by Mr Ratcliffe, that the new arrangements were totally unacceptable, was sent to League headquarters. Fortunately the top clubs were in agreement and the proposals were thrown out. A cautionary and perceptive note was sounded, nonetheless, in the next Supporters Club Yearbook.

"Nevertheless, the Rochdale AFC and their poorer brethren must heed the potential danger to their future, and the possibility of other League Management proposals which could cause the sympathetic attitude of the bigger clubs to wane and bring about the 'order of the big boot'."

Over the summer of 1964, full back Roy Ridge arrived from Sheffield United where he had made only 11 appearances in 13 seasons as an understudy, and 19 year old Laurie Calloway came from Wolves. Two Bolton men, wing half Graham Cunliffe and winger Brian Birch, an England Youth International and FA Cup winner in 11 years at Burnden Park (though he was still only 26), plus Peterborough centre forward John Turley would also make their mark in the side. There is no doubt, though, that the £2250 that Tony Collins spent on Torquay inside forward Reg Jenkins represented the most inspired move of this or any other season, the Cornishman becoming over the years the greatest ever folk hero of his adopted town's football followers.

1964-65:

The opening to the season was the exact reverse of the previous year, with defeats in the Rose Bowl and at York in the first League fixture. Morton and Jenkins both scored twice when Stockport visited Spotland and Lincoln and Torquay were also beaten there, but it was not until the fourth attempt that Dale gained an away point. In the League Cup, Rochdale had won at Stockport, but in the second round, despite confounding Rotherham for 87 minutes by playing Brian Taylor, wearing number nine, as a second centre half (so repeating the earlier experiments with a four man defence in the League Cup run in 1961-62), the Second Division side eventually won 2-0.

Reverting to an all-out attacking policy, Rochdale won six of their next eight games and drew the other two, with Jenkins netting eight more goals, to storm into the top six. The only black spots were a sending off for Calloway at Crewe and an injury to Morton which put him out of action for a couple of months. In the victory over Hartlepool, Thompson and Storf both suffered slight electric shocks during a thunderstorm but neither was hurt. This came just a few weeks after the tragic death of Spurs' Scottish International forward John White, when he was struck by lightening while playing golf.

Dale's run ended with a disappointing 1-0 defeat at Southport, who managed only five home wins all season.

Nevertheless, another five points out of six took Dale into third place at the end of November. a home defeat by rivals York was a serious blow, and with a number of injuries hampering selection Christmas week brought two defeats by Tranmere, who actually 'won' the game at Spotland twice. The original match had been abandoned with them 1-0 ahead and they repeated that scoreline when the game was replayed.

The first goal, after 3 minutes from Jenkins in the seven goal thriller versus Bradford.

In the first game of 1965 the Dale were four up at half time but were made to sweat when Bradford pulled three back in the last 20 minutes. a valuable point at Oxford was followed by a 3-0 win against Barrow, the veteran Milburn, once more pressed into service at centre forward, opening the scoring.

Stan Milburn, deflects Reg Jenkins' shot past the Barrow 'keeper.

A couple of days later Rochdale went out and bought the Oldham centre forward Bert Lister for £2500 in an attempt to reinforce the side's scoring power. Lister had once scored six goals in a game when Oldham beat Southport 11-0. Although he scored only once himself, the next four games yielded six points to keep the Dale on the heels of the leaders, though they did lose stand-in defender John Hardman with a broken leg.

Joe Richardson also suffered a cracked jaw, and although not currently in the first team, Dave Storf was also put out of action for the season with a broken ankle suffered in training.

After a set-back at Darlington, Rochdale took another seven points out of eight, including a vital win away to fellow challengers Chester. In a remarkably tight race, seven clubs were still well in contention as mid-March came around, and just over 7000 fans were attracted to Spotland to see frontrunners Brighton in a match that had twice been postponed. A stormy game ended two-two after Bert Lister and the Albion centre half Norman Gall had been sent off for fighting.

After a surprise home defeat by Chesterfield, a 3-2 win at Newport kept the Dale in fifth place. They then took time off to play a testimonial game for the evergreen Stan Milburn (his third with different clubs in a 19 year career) against a side of former international stars including Tom Finney and Danny Blanchflower.

The Dale's draw at Doncaster and a home win against Aldershot, combined with results elsewhere, amazingly left the top six separated by just three points with four or five games to play. On Good Friday Rochdale travelled to fellow hopefuls Millwall, and a crowd of 15,359 saw a hard fought goalless draw. The Dale's lofty League position and the closeness of the promotion race was certainly good for attendances, their visits attracting five figure crowds at four grounds during the season. A similar goalless affair against another top six side, Bradford, left things equally tight.

The penultimate game was the return with Millwall which attracted a season's best crowd of 8011. Unfortunately the Dale's season long challenge petered out in the second half when the Lions were awarded a penalty and eventually ran out 2-0 winners. Although they beat Southport in their final game Rochdale remained in sixth place, three points behind Oxford, four behind Millwall and York and five short of the champions Brighton.

No fourth division side, before or after, ever gained more than the Dale's 58 points without gaining promotion (on the basis of two points for a win), apart, of course, from the equally luckless Tranmere, the longtime leaders, who finished 5th with 60 points. The Reserves also had a good season, winning the Lancashire League Supplementary Competition with a near perfect 22 points from 12 games.

Despite the successes, average gates - though up from just over 3000 to 4673 - were much less than those of the other contenders, who all averaged over 8000, with Brighton reaching almost 18,000. Even bottom club Stockport County, 30 points behind the Dale, averaged 5738.

Goalkeeper Ted Burgin, who had actually been freed the previous May before Tony Collins had a change of mind, was an everpresent for the third time in four years. Inside left Reg Jenkins also appeared in every game and was top scorer with 25 League goals, a new post-war record, bettered only by Bert Whitehurst, Tommy Tippett and Jimmy Wynn in more free-scoring pre-war days.

During the season Ray Aspden had passed the record 243 appearances of his predecessor in the No.5 shirt, Walter Birch, and his total now stood at 260. Stan Milburn, who retired at the end of the season, was third in the ranking with 238 appearances, good going for a player signed at the age of 32. 'Retired', here, is only a relative term, as Stan - known as the `India-rubber man' because he always bounced back - was still going strong in local football with Spotland Methodists in the 1980's, by which time he was in his mid-fifties. Oddly enough, all five players who had made 200 League appearances for Rochdale up to this time had been centre halves, Parkes, Birch and Aspden permanently, Watson and Milburn when not at right back, or, of course, centre forward in Stan's case.

Joe Richardson moved to Tranmere in the summer but tragically he was killed in a road accident the following year at the age of only 24. Just before the start of the following season, Graham Cunliffe decided to retire and concentrate on his newsagents business in Wigan.

There were few new names in the Dale squad for the 1965-66 season. Hartlepool's Neville Bannister, one of the quickest wingers in the division, and Barrie Ratcliffe from Scunthorpe would contest the wide positions with Dave Storf, now back in favour after a spell on the transfer list. Bobby Stephenson, son of pre-war Derby and England star George, was added to the forward strength and utility defender George Sievwright joined the club from Tranmere. Another change in the side was the inclusion of former Gainsborough Trinity goalkeeper Simon Jones, originally recommended to the club by his namesake and predecessor Jimmy Jones, who finally supplanted the veteran Burgin between the sticks. Bert Lister missed the opening of the season as he had been injured in training when he got in the way of one of his partner Reg Jenkins' piledrivers!

1965-66:
There was a shock in store for the fans on the opening day of the season, as Rochdale lined up in the 4-2-4 formation which had finally filtered down to Division Four - just in time for the top clubs to discard it in favour of 4-3-3 following England's success a year later. The initial two 'linkmen' in the new formation were Birch and Storf, and it was the latter who scored the only goal of the game against Aldershot. Another surprising decision was to play most of the subsequent home games on Friday nights.

The Dale also won at Bradford and followed this with a couple of draws for a thoroughly encouraging start. In the home game against Torquay, though, John Hardman in his first game back in the side, broke his leg again. Following the decision at the Football League AGM in the summer to allow substitutes for injured players, Neville Bannister thus became the first Rochdale No.12 to appear in a League game. (Hardman himself had worn the No.12 shirt first, on the opening day). Torquay, meanwhile won 3-2, the first of five successive defeats for Rochdale as the manager sought to find the correct pair of linkmen to make the new style function properly. Luton's winner came, bizarrely, from their reserve goalkeeper Tony Reid who (shades of Jimmy Crabtree) played at inside left.

Rochdale had managed to make progress in the League Cup, but in the second round, despite the recall of Burgin, they were no match for Southampton, whose future England centre forward Martin Chivers netted a hat trick.

The Dale then won three in a row, beating Bradford City 5-1, to regain a respectable mid-table position. A Reg Jenkins hat trick saw off Chester, and after Sievwright's diving header had dramatically saved his side from acute embarrassment in the FA Cup at Fleetwood, Jenkins did the trick again with three of Dale's five goals in the replay. The next four games were all lost, the Dale going down 4-0 at Southport and 6-2 at Tranmere. Even worse was a 3-1 home defeat by non-League Altrincham in the Cup. This proved to be former skipper Jim Thompson's 239th and last game for the club; he had asked for a transfer after being left out of the side the previous month and was soon transferred to Bradford City.

Rochdale came back to win their next two games, the entire forward line of Stephenson, Morton, McQueen (a local amateur in only his third game), Jenkins (who got two) and Bannister scoring in a 6-0 drubbing of Wrexham. The improvement did not last, as the first three games of the New Year all ended in defeat, though another goal for Ian McQueen earned him an elevation to the paid ranks. A win at Aldershot, with wing half Brian Taylor scoring two and full back turned centre forward Laurie Calloway getting the other, along with a seventh home win in nine games, held out hope of better things, but a catastrophic sequence of one draw and seven defeats plunged them to 22nd in the table by the middle of March.

All was clearly not well in the ranks, either, as besides the departure of Thompson, both Storf and Morton had put in transfer requests. Jenkins had been the subject of several bids by Port Vale and Notts County but (thankfully) these had been turned down by the board. Before the transfer deadline offers of £5000 for Taylor by Doncaster and for Morton by Torquay were also refused.

The side then suddenly revived with four wins, two of them by four goals to nil. Rather surprisingly in such a season, Rochdale had reached the semi-final of the Lancashire Cup but were easily beaten by a mostly reserve Burnley line-up. This was followed by three League defeats, the injured Lister being sorely missed.

Ted Burgin

Rochdale did rebuild their hopes by beating fellow strugglers Hartlepool, but were beaten in turn by Stockport, another side in trouble at the bottom. This in fact left an incredibly tight situation with only three points separating Hartlepool (22nd) from Crewe in 13th. Rochdale next played a testimonial match for Ted Burgin against his former club Leeds. Burgin had been forced to retire after 207 Football League appearances, a record for a Dale keeper, because of a finger injury suffered in the heavy defeat at Tranmere in December. The next League game, coincidentally, was the return with Rovers and they scored five more, Dale replying with three. Rochdale's No.7 in this game was the 17 year old Paul Crossley, who had been thrown in at the deep end for his League debut. Other results the following day dropped the Dale back to 22nd with only two games to play.

Due to the somewhat bizarre arrangement of this pre-World Cup season, Rochdale and the rest of the lower divisions then had a weekend off while Harry Catterick's Everton beat Sheffield Wednesday in the FA Cup Final. The top two divisions had already completed their fixtures but the Dale didn't finish until May 21st and some sides did not end their seasons until the week after that. A couple of days after the Cup Final Rochdale met Hartlepool again, knowing that only a win was good enough. The match ended goalless so Rochdale had to seek re-election for the first time since 1934. They also drew their last game to total 37 points, two fewer than Chesterfield in 20th but only 5 behind Stockport who had finished 13th. They won 12 home games, but lost 10, only one being drawn.

Regular Friday night football had proved a disaster from the financial as well as playing angle, average gates slumping to less than 3000.

The sudden fall from grace had the inevitable consequence of nine players being released. These included George Morton, scorer of exactly 50 goals in 148 League games, for whom Rochdale had reportedly turned down a sizeable offer earlier in the season, but who now went to non-League New Brighton. George Sievwright also went into non-League football with Macclesfield, but later figured in the first FA Trophy Final at Wembley when Macclesfield beat Telford in 1970.

At the Football League AGM, Rochdale were unsurprisingly re-elected, but must have been disappointed at polling less votes than the other sides seeking re-admittance. The summer of 1966 also saw, of course, the World Cup finals played in England. After a slow start Alf Ramsey's 'wingless wonders', with the whole country willing them on, fought their way through to the final where they famously overcame West Germany 4-2. Four of the triumphant England side in fact had Rochdale connections, hat-trick hero Geoff Hurst and midfield dynamo Alan Ball being the sons of former Dale players while Jack and Bobby Charlton were the nephews of Stan Milburn.

1966-67:
Rather more new men than of late were in the Dale side that opened the new campaign with a home defeat by the Latics in the Rose Bowl. Bob Williamson, one of the fairly rare breed of ex-Scottish League goalkeepers in England, arrived from Leeds, where he had been third choice behind Sprake and Harvey. Full back Graham Smith made the same move and would prove to be the second piece in a jigsaw that would take a couple more years to complete. Two men also arrived from Sheffield United, though by widely divergent routes, Brian Richardson who had made over 300 first team appearances in a dozen years with the Blades coming from Swindon, and former England Youth international cap Billy Russell joining Dale from Bolton.

However, the Oldham game was more notable for a player making his last appearance, than those making their debuts. An injury to Ray Aspden ruled him out of the opening League encounter, and though he was not initially expected to be out of action long, in fact he never played again. Despite more than one spell on the transfer list, disputes over contracts and occasional disciplinary action by the club, he had been with them for 12 seasons making 346 senior appearances, 297 of them in the League (299 if you count the expunged games against Accrington), though he did not break Don Partridge's record of playing League games in 10 seasons as he missed two while doing his National Service and this final one through injury.

New signing Barry Wheatley scored against his old club on the opening day of the League season, but Crewe still won 2-1. The next two games were also lost before the Dale gained a draw at York. The side finally hit form to beat Luton 3-0 at Spotland and also overcame Lincoln and Stockport before sliding quickly down the table again.

At this point Rochdale sold their 18 year old winger Paul Crossley to Preston for a record £8000, after just 18 senior appearances. Although he did not become a regular with North End, he went onto an extensive Football League career elsewhere and was still playing in the USA with Baltimore Blasts in the early 'eighties. Replacing him was veteran centre forward Bill Calder from Oxford. Calder scored on his debut in a 3-2 win over Hartlepool but Rochdale lost the influential Richardson through injury in the home game with Bradford City and were disastrously beaten in eight successive matches.

In one of these games there was a glimmer of hope for the future when the Dale fielded what was then their youngest ever side against Bury in the Lancashire Cup (always considered a first team fixture for Rochdale). Eleven of the twelve were 21 or younger, the exception being the 28 year old Wheatley, and of the seven youngsters given their senior debuts that day, six later appeared in the Football League and three of them would have a part to play in better times for the club.

It was the New Year before the Dale won again, recording the season's first away victory at Lincoln. The out of form Bert Lister, with just two goals all season, had perhaps surprisingly been signed by divisional leaders Stockport (where he scored 11 in 16 games), and replacing him at No.9 was Reg Jenkins, back in goalscoring form after a long injury layoff. Besides being a great marksman, Reg (the surname is superfluous to Dale fans of a certain vintage) was also a great character, with a typically Cornish sense of humour. One story, recounted by long time reporter on the Dale, Jack Hamil, concerns the return of our hero and his partner in crime Dave Storf to Rochdale late one night after a long away trip. The pair were walking back to their homes when a police car drove past. *"Always ready to pull someone's leg, Reg shouts 'Run', and he and Storf sprint off up the road. The police car turned around and the chase was on. Fifteen minutes and two miles later, the police caught up. 'Just a bit of training, m'dears', said Reg to the Law."*

Reg scored nine goals in ten games as the Dale picked up 14 valuable points, including one from a sterling two-all draw with top side Stockport at Edgeley Park, but Rochdale then crashed to five successive defeats, conceding 15 goals while scoring just three - and two of those were from defenders turned midfield men Brian Taylor and Kevin Connor.

Defenders were also to the fore when Dale beat Exeter 1-0 and drew 1-1 with Southport, full back Calloway and centre half Smith netting the precious goals.

A heavy defeat at Bradford City left Rochdale in 21st place, three points adrift of the sides immediately above them, but goals from two of the youngsters, Steve Melledew, an apprentice engineer at Whipp & Bourne's and member of their Sunday League side, and ex-Manchester City junior Joe Fletcher, gained them a victory over Halifax. They next travelled to Southport, winners of 19 of their 21 home games, and amazingly won 2-1, Jenkins from the penalty spot and Storf the scorers this time. Dale could also have done to beat next to bottom York, though one point did lift Rochdale temporarily out of the bottom four.

Defeat by Wrexham in the final home game allowed Notts County to overtake the Dale on goal average and for their final game, the Dale had to travel to Tranmere. Already all but promoted, Rovers ran out 3-1 winners in front of a twelve and a half thousand crowd. The Dale's only remaining hope was that County would lose heavily in their last two games. They did lose them both, but their goal average remained superior to Dale's by just 0. 03, so Rochdale had to apply for re-election for the second year running.

Among the numerous end of season departures was long serving reserve John Hardman. In the summer Dave Storf was transferred to Barrow for £7500 and Bob Stephenson left senior football to concentrate on his cricket career, joining Derbyshire's County staff. He later had a long spell as Hampshire's regular wicket keeper. In the end, only three players were left who had been with the club more than a year.

An oddly Rochdalian event had occurred during the course of the season, when the committee of the Supporters Club and the parent club's Board of Directors became so estranged in arguments over club affairs, that the board withdrew their official sanction of the Supporters Club, and the latter were forced to disband.

Rochdale again managed to secure re-election without too much trouble, though again getting less votes than the three sides who finished below them. (Bottom club Lincoln City, making their fourth application in five years, finished top of the poll). Manager Tony Collins had already signed the Hartlepool goalkeeper Les Green at the end of the previous term. Rather short for a 'keeper, he had played for Hull back in 1960 but still had to really make the grade. Dale soon added Northampton full back Vic Cockroft and a couple of well travelled veterans in the shape of utility man John Reid from Torquay and Halifax forward Barry Hutchinson, the scorer of well over a hundred Football League goals.

Brian Eastham, the former Bury defender, was given clearance to play for the Dale after appearing in a 'pirate' League in North America. Former Oldham manager Gordon Hurst, who had played in Charlton's 1947 FA Cup winning side, was appointed as the club's trainer-coach.

1967-68:

Although knocked out of the League Cup by Bury for the second year running, three points from the first two League games of 1967-68 was a reasonable return, young winger Hughie Riley netting twice in the 3-2 win over York. Despite constant shuffling of his pack by the manager, Rochdale then went 11 games without a win (though seven were drawn), the only noteworthy point coming in the home game with Lincoln when Steve Melledew became the first Rochdale substitute to come on and score. He later set the less enviable record of being sent off when making a substitute appearance (christened the 'Wild Bull' by the fans, he eventually scored eight goals, only two of them while playing as a forward).

After seven years in charge, Tony Collins resigned as manager at the end of September and was succeeded the following month by former Bury and Charlton boss Bob Stokoe. The barren spell was actually broken while the Dale were without a manager, when they beat ultimately promoted Barnsley 1-0. They celebrated the announcement of Stokoe's appointment over the tannoy at the ground by winning the next two games as well and - with Stokoe utilising the new 4-3-3 formation - even managed a draw with a strong Manchester United side in the Lancashire Cup. This proved to be the best spell of the season, defeats in four of the next five games, including a 5-1 cup knockout by Tranmere, undoing the good work. However, with Reg Jenkins at centre half - poacher turned gamekeeper, if ever there was one - Dale beat Newport 4-3 and ended 1967 by beating Wrexham 3-0 to go into the New Year with a respectable 22 points from 24 games.

A narrow defeat at Lincoln was followed by a humiliating 7-0 annihilation by Manchester United (Reserves) in the Lancs Cup, Smith giving away a penalty for a foul on Gowling (who got a hat-trick) after just 15 seconds. Eastham was subsequently sacked by the manager, apparently for 'lack of effort' (a foretaste of things to come in a later Stokoe era). Like the team, the stand roof also fell down on the job, collapsing under the weight of a heavy snowfall! A goalless draw at bottom club Bradford Park Avenue could hardly be rated a success, the Avenue managing only four wins all season, and a home defeat by next to bottom Workington was even more dire, only 1606 fans turning up, too. Centre forward Joe Fletcher scored his tenth goal of the season in a 2-0 win over Doncaster but the side then went another 11 games without a win, including defeat in the short-lived Northern Floodlit Cup by non-Leaguers Wigan Athletic.

Bob Stokoe had meantime made his first two signings. Bolton Wanderers winger Dennis Butler cost him £1000 and Grimsby's midfielder Billy Rudd, a veteran of nearly 300 senior games though he was still only 26, £1500, all of it soon to prove money well spent. Both men, coincidentally, had played for the same clubs as their uncles, Bolton's pre-war England star Billy Butler and York's Jimmy Rudd, respectively, while Rudd's father, Billy senior had actually played for the Dale during the war.

To balance the books Laurie Calloway was sold to Blackburn Rovers for £5500. Still only 22, he had made 161 Football League appearances for Dale and like former team mate Paul Crossley went on to a long career in the lower divisions before crossing the Atlantic to play and later coach in the USA, figuring prominently with San Jose Earthquakes. Stokoe also brought in the former Bury secretary Len Richley as assistant manager.

Four drawn games were the prelude to an unexpected win at promotion chasing Chesterfield, Kettlebrough being the Dale's fourth opponent to oblige by putting through his own goal during the season.

Dale also beat Bradford City, who ultimately missed promotion by one point, but then got themselves back into trouble and 21st spot by losing four times in a row. They had a game in hand on the side immediately above them, York City, and they made it count by beating Halifax. In the penultimate game, Rochdale visited Workington and gained a priceless two points with a goal by Butler. Although Rochdale ended their campaign with a Friday night defeat at Southend, Port Vale, York and Exeter all needed to win their last games to pass them on the final day. In the event only Vale did so, so Rochdale finished 19th and thus escaped a potentially dangerous third consecutive application for re-election.

The close season saw the departure of almost the entire staff. Only nine players were retained, and following his excellent season goalkeeper Les Green was bought by Brian Clough's Derby County for a new club record £8500. He was an everpresent in the Derby side which won the Second Division title the following year.

The long serving (by recent Rochdale standards) Brian Taylor was later transferred to Altrincham so this left just Jenkins, Smith, the three local lads Melledew, Fletcher and Riley, and Stokoe's recent signings Butler and Rudd

Joe Fletcher,
top scorer in 1967-68.

Recent signings....
(left) Billy Rudd, and
(right) Dennis Butler.

UP THE DALE 1968-1973

~ CHAPTER 7 ~

In the weeks immediately after the end of the season, Stokoe was hard at work behind the scenes and at the beginning of July 1968 he unveiled his new signings. Veteran 'keeper Chris Harker who had played with Stokoe at Newcastle back in the fifties, was signed from Grimsby, with Burnley's Scottish Junior international Matt Tyrie as his understudy. Full backs Vince Radcliffe and Derek Ryder, who arrived from Peterborough and Cardiff respectively, and right winger Norman Whitehead of Southport, had only a handful of League appearances to their credit, though Whitehead had played at Wembley, for Skelmersdale in the F.A.Amateur Cup Final. On the other hand, half backs Vinny Leech, who like Harker had played under Stokoe at Bury, Stockport's Colin Parry and Southend's Joe Ashworth all had many years' Football League experience. (Rochdale had offered Leech part-time terms - at £3 a week - before he played in the 1959 Youth Cup Final for Blackburn). All except Parry, who cost £1000, arrived on free transfers. Even including the two 'keepers this meant that the Dale had just 15 senior players. With their new team signed up, Rochdale also registered new colours, actually a return to a previous style, of blue shirts and white shorts.

The first seven names on the Dale team sheet on the opening day of the League campaign were making their debuts, but it was one of the old boys, centre forward Reg Jenkins who was the goalscoring hero, blasting two goals from the penalty spot in a 3-2 home win over Scunthorpe. The Dale lost at Workington in the League Cup despite a late goal by substitute Melledew who had missed the opening game through a suspension left over from the previous season.

Playing up front with Jenkins, Melledew really made his mark by scoring the Dale's goal in each of five successive one-one draws, a unique sequence in the Football League. The first defeat of the season was sustained against front runners Doncaster Rovers, but following the signing of Mansfield centre forward Terry Melling (a former Coldstream Guardsman) for £1000, Rochdale thrashed Bradford City 6-0 (Fletcher 2, Melledew 2, Rudd and Butler), the Dale's equal highest score since 1949. Unfortunately this used up the Dale's goal quota for some time as they played out four goalless draws before surrendering their unbeaten home record to Swansea who won 1-0.

Early in October Bob Stokoe left to take over Second Division Carlisle and his assistant Len Richley, who had been a successful non-League manager, stepped up to take his place. The staff was soon joined by former Aldershot trainer Dick Conner as Richley's assistant.

The Dale returned to form with a 3-1 win at Southend, and then amazingly repeated the drubbing of Bradford City by putting six past their neighbours Park Avenue as well. This time Billy Rudd got two and Melledew (his 12th in 17 games), Melling, Butler and full back Ratcliffe one each. Again the goal rush expended the Dale's efforts, with more blank score sheets following, even Graham Smith being tried at No. 9. Indeed, Rochdale scored in only three of a run of 15 League and cup games, but fortunately Dale's solid defence earned no less than seven goalless draws.

Nevertheless the side was hovering in an all too familiar position, in 15th place but only two points clear of the bottom four. The previous match had seen Reg Jenkins return to his old favourite No.10 shirt after a longish spell out of favour, and for the game at Workington on Boxing Day the other long-serving member of the side, Graham Smith, was handed his old No.2 spot.

Playing an all out attacking 4-2-4 formation (which had, of course, been considered excessively defensive only a few years earlier), the Dale won 2-1, inflicting the Reds first home defeat since the opening day of the season, and 'Big Reg' got both goals. Things went even better for the burly Cornishman the following week when he blasted a hat trick in a 6-1 win over Grimsby, and a second hat trick hero was Terry Melling when the Dale won 4-1 at Bradford to record their best away win for 12 years. The tough ex-soldier Melling had not expected to play in the game and appeared with his head bandaged, reputedly the result of falling off a bus the night before.

With their fans waking up to this rush of form - 3300 attended the next match as against 2000 for the Grimsby game - Rochdale crushed leaders Aldershot 3-0, totally outplaying them in one of their best displays of the season. After a drawn game at Newport, Butler scoring for Dale and Tony Buck for County, manager Richley stayed on in Newport and the following day was able to announce the capture of the blonde centre forward Buck for a new club record fee of £5000.

Chairman Fred Ratcliffe commented on the transfer *"We feel we are definite contenders for promotion and having met all the opposition have a great opportunity. That is why we decided to pay this record fee."* Fans of the financially pressed South Wales club, on the other hand, protested bitterly at the loss of their major asset - Buck's 13 goals kept him as Newport's leading scorer even though he was there only half the season, adding eight more for Dale, he finished only one behind the division's top scorer, Chester's Talbot.

Reg Jenkins (10) and Tony Buck (on right) in action during the season.

His successor at No.9 got a couple more in a draw at Exeter and the Dale then won three hard fought games in a row by the odd goal. Full back Smith got the winner against York, only his second goal in over a hundred games, but enough to stretch the Dale's unbeaten run to a post-war record 14 games.

The Dale were now in fourth spot and their clash with the League leaders Doncaster attracted their best crowd since 1955, 12,647 seeing a goalless draw between the sides with the best defences in the division. Rochdale's great run finally came to an end after 15 games with a defeat at Chester, despite Melledew coming on as substitute to score his first goal since November.

The next visitors to Spotland, after a spell of snowy weather, were the new leaders Darlington, but they fared no better than Aldershot and went down to two more Jenkins blasts. Third placed Colchester felt the full force of the rejuvenated Dale attack at Spotland, conceding goals to Butler twice, Jenkins and Buck. The gate for the home game against promotion rivals Lincoln was up to 5800 and Buck and Butler saw to it that the locals went home happy. After less than six months with the Dale, Terry Melling was sold to Darlington to recoup some of the money spent on Buck, reducing the squad to just 15 again.

Another invaluable away point, at a muddy Valley Parade against promotion rivals Bradford City (who had also come a long way since their 6-0 thrashing at Spotland in September), was followed by a revenge win over Chester, the Dale winning 4-1 to go third. This game also saw the first team change in 10 matches, Melledew changing places with Jenkins who moved to the bench. A dropped point in a goalless draw at home to Chesterfield and the loss of defender Joe Ashworth, through injury briefly threatened to halt Dale's progress, but a late penalty by Dennis Butler gave them a 2-1 win over Wrexham and lifted them to second place.

The Chesterfield game on April 19th should have been the season's final fixture, but in fact, due to postponements, the Dale still had five games to go.

Tony Buck again (No. 9) helps out defenders Graham Smith, Colin Parry and Joe Ashworth.

In the next match Dale were trailing Notts County 1-0 with six minutes left, when Len Richley sent on his substitute Reg Jenkins, and Reg saved the day, firing an 87th minute equaliser through a crowded goalmouth.

The other form team in the division, coming up fast with games in hand, was Halifax Town, and by a strange quirk both the Dale's fixtures against their Yorkshire rivals were amongst the postponements. Not surprisingly a massive crowd of 13,266, the best of the season, assembled on Wednesday 30th April to see the home 'leg' of the contest, a tense match settled by a goal from winger Dennis Butler.

An even more tense wait ensued as by the following week, the results of the other contenders' matches had presented a clear picture. Doncaster were the champions and the Dale would need just one point from their two remaining games to join them in Division Three. The Shay was packed out with over 17,000 fans who saw Halifax grab the only goal this time to guarantee their own promotion. Bradford City followed them up by beating Darlington.

Guarded optimism in the programme notes......

..... but it was well-founded. Reg gets the champagne treatment from chairman Fred Ratcliffe after promotion is secured.

Although needing just a point, Rochdale continued to press forward and were rewarded when Billy Rudd was flattened in the area. Reg Jenkins hammered the ball into the roof of the net to remove any lingering doubt that the Dale might slip up at the last hurdle. Still the Dale went forward, and Reg was in again to convert a centre from overlapping full back Graham Smith to confirm to the 9085 crowd that they really could celebrate Rochdale's first promotion since joining the Football League.

Unbeaten at home since November, they lost only twice in 24 games to take their final tally to 56 points and finish in third place. Indeed, they lost only eight matches all season, gaining as many as 13 away draws. They conceded 11 goals at Spotland and 35 all told, the least in the division, while their 68 goals for was bettered only by Southend and Chester. Goalkeeper Chris Harker was an everpresent and kept 20 clean sheets, the most since Harry Moody in 1924. In the second half of the season, occasional injuries apart, the same 12 players turned out in every match: Harker in goal, a back four of Smith, Parry, Ashworth and Ryder, the midfield duo of Leech and Rudd, Whitehead and Butler on the wings and two of Buck, Jenkins and Melledew up front, the other one being substitute.

Two days later, on Saturday May 10th 1969, came the match that the Dale and their fans had waited 48 years for. Appropriately the opposition was Southend, the one side who could pip Rochdale for promotion. Joe Ashworth, a former Southend man himself, was the Dale's only injury worry but he had his ribs strapped up and declared himself fit. Fifteen minutes into the match a Rochdale corner went from head to head in the box before Steve Melledew - no longer the 'Wild Bull', but 'Stevie Wonder' - nodded it into the net.

Earlier in the season Radcliffe had figured regularly at right back and Melling at centre forward, while Joe Fletcher and Hughie Riley also made a few appearances, but the use of only 16 players was a club record which will surely never be broken in these days of 16 man squads for each game. (The Dale staff had been extended slightly towards the end of the season when they signed their first ever apprentices, Andy Mandzuk and Brian Ashworth).

On May 23rd, the triumphant Dale players were guests of honour at a civic reception at the Town Hall, something that few people would have predicted nine months earlier when the club sold a grand total of 98 season tickets. Just five days later, as if to emphasise the passing nature of success, Len Richley gave free transfers to Vince Radcliffe, Joe Fletcher and reserve 'keeper Matt Tyrie. Tyrie later won a Scottish Junior Cup medal with Cambuslang Rangers.

July 1969 saw the epic first manned landing on the Moon, and two important signings for Rochdale's attack on Division Three. Midfield man Bobby Downes came from Peterborough, and 18 year old local lad Dave Cross, was signed on full-time terms.

The Dale warmed up for the season with four friendly games in a week and began in style by hammering neighbours Oldham, who for once had to look up at Dale from Division Four. Jenkins got quickly off the mark with a hat-trick. The most impressive and significant result came, though, when Rochdale beat a full-strength Everton side 4-3. Everton subsequently lost only five League games all season and ran away with the League Championship.

1969-70:
The Dale team for the opening League encounter showed only one change from the previous season, Downes replacing Vinny Leech who was out with an achilles tendon injury. However, Dale were brought down to earth with a bump as visitors Orient, the eventual champions, romped home 3-0. In the League Cup in midweek, Dale looked on their way to a shock win at Second Division Bolton but a 3-1 lead at half time disintegrated into a 6-3 defeat.

The first win came at Stockport and nearly 10,000 fans turned up at Spotland to see the battle with local rivals Bury which ended in a thrilling three-all draw. The trip to Brighton proved unproductive but the Dale then visited Walsall and hammered them 4-1, a brace by Jenkins giving him six goals in as many games. Steve Melledew netted the winner against Barrow and was then sensationally transferred to Everton, managed by the one-time Dale boss Harry Catterick, for a club record £15,000. Although he never made it to Everton's League side, he did go on to a long Football League career, eventually returning to Spotland.

His departure left the No.9 shirt for Tony Buck and he responded with both the Dale goals in a draw at Gillingham and a hat trick in another 3-3 thriller, at Bristol Rovers, while it was Downes' turn to get two in a 4-2 win over Rotherham A spot of luck at Bournemouth then gave the Dale the impetus for an amazing run of successes. To be more accurate it was bad luck for home 'keeper Roger Jones who let a header from Vinny Leech slip through his arms to give the midfield man his first goal in 150 matches, and then gave away the first of two penalties which the unflappable Jenkins blasted home in customary style. When placing the ball on the spot, Reg would usually bet his friends in the goalkeeping trade half-a-crown that he would score!. The Dale followed this by beating Shrewsbury 3-0 and Stockport 2-0 at home before journeying south again to meet Plymouth. A truly amazing start saw Argyle score within 20 seconds of the kick off, without a Dale player touching the ball, yet within three minutes Dale were ahead courtesy of two goals by Butler. They eventually won 3-2 with Jenkins celebrating the return to his first club with the winning goal.

Tranmere were slammed 4-0, Butler getting two more, and a sixth straight win, 3-0 at Southport, took the Dale into second spot. Two down at home to Reading, the Dale refused to give up and found an unlikely hero in full back Derek Ryder who scored his first ever goal to win the game 3-2. Another fightback gave them the points at Mansfield, sending them to the top of Division 3 for the first time since 1950. They had won all their last eight games and in the nine games since Leech's return to the side had rained in no less than 26 goals.

The run was ended by defeats at Halifax and new leaders Luton (and a shock FA Cup knockout by Fourth Division strugglers Workington), but the Dale bounced back against Mansfield. For the game at Bury on December 6th, manager Len Richley sent out the same 11 players for the 15th consecutive match, easily a record for the club. Nine of the side were still everpresents. Unfortunately fortune deserted them at this point, Vinny Leech limping out of the game against his former club (and on his birthday, at that) with a damaged knee which would eventually spell the end of his career.

The Dale lost 2-1, picking up just two points from seven games in which they scored only two goals. Dale's next win came at Bradford City, but by then they had a new manager. Len Richley resigned after a policy disagreement with his board and was replaced by his assistant Dick Conner. The new manager immediately changed the Dale's adventurous 4-2-4 formation, which had come unstuck of late, to a more restrained 4-3-3, with Whitehead dropping back into a midfield role, and was rewarded with a 3-0 win in his first game, Buck taking his tally for the season to 15. Rochdale also beat Plymouth at Spotland but lost Jenkins with an injury.

Before the game, Reg had been presented with the Gillette Sportsmanship award for Division Three. Pointers for the future, though, were goals from Hughie Riley, back in the side as Leech's replacement after 18 months in the shadows, and substitute Dave Cross.

The third and final blow to the Dale's prospects came when Tony Buck fell awkwardly on the frozen pitch at Reading and broke his leg. In this match Rochdale also lost their record as the only club not to have had a player cautioned all season, when the name of Hughie 'Tiger' Riley went into the referee's book. Without three of the mainsprings of the side, Dale struggled on to the end of the season, occasionally showing flashes of what might have been, as when they beat Halifax 5-0, the fit again Jenkins netting three of them.

In the last game Luton, already certain of promotion, denied the Dale a winning finale, but Reg Jenkins reached a personal landmark with his 20th League goal of the season and his 100th for Rochdale. The Dale ended in ninth place with 46 points and average home gates worked out at 6424, even better than during the promotion campaign.

Chris Harker, Derek Ryder and Billy Rudd were everpresent for a second season and were joined by Graham Smith and Colin Parry, emphasising the settled nature of the side. Tony Buck was voted the club's first 'Player of the Year' by the supporters. Uniquely Rochdale retained all of their 17 professionals.

A surprise move in the summer of 1970 saw club skipper Billy Rudd, who had appeared in 108 consecutive League games since his signing by Bob Stokoe, transferred to Bury in exchange for Alf Arrowsmith, winner of a League Championship medal with Liverpool in 1964. Rudd had already played in the League for 11 seasons but managed another seven at Gigg Lane. Chris Harker decided to take up a position as coach at Darlington under Len Richley, later becoming that rarity a goalkeeper player-manager with non-League Stockton.

Another veteran, the former Southampton 'keeper Tony Godfrey (who had played in the Saints side beaten at Spotland in the League Cup in 1961-62) was signed from Aldershot to replace him. Also following the trail from the Recreation Ground started by Dick Connor were experienced forward Peter Gowans, signed for £3000, and the former Rotherham centre half Peter Madden who became trainer-coach in succession to Gordon Hurst. Former Hartlepool boss Gus McLean became assistant manager.

1970-71:
The three new players were all in the side which drew with Bristol Rovers on the opening day and then beat Southport in the League Cup.

However, a severe injury sustained by the side's 'Iron Man', defensive king-pin Colin Parry, put him out of the side and the Dale took only three points from the next eight games to plummet to the bottom of the table.

Meanwhile, in the League Cup, Rochdale played at Crystal Palace, having their best ever season in Division One, and gained a remarkable 3-3 draw. Reg Jenkins had the 'honour' of scoring at both ends and Whitehead and Gowans netted the other Dale goals. Unfortunately Rochdale couldn't manage a repeat performance at home, Palace winning 3-1 despite a rare goal by Smith. The attendance was a rather disappointing 8911, less than at a couple of League games the previous term.

Fortunately, Parry passed himself fit to rejoin the fray for the big match against the aristocrats of Aston Villa who had temporarily fallen on hard times. A well fought draw with the top side in the division gave the Dale renewed confidence and they drew at Bristol Rovers and Brighton, too.

After three wins, the Dale looked to be well on the way to recovery, but with injuries striking key players they again lost five games in a row. Up until missing the game at Preston, left back Derek Ryder had completed a run of 124 consecutive games since signing for the Dale, partnering Graham Smith (who also missed the same match) in the last 96 of them, the most consistent run ever by any Rochdale full back pairing. By Christmas, the Dale were back down in 23rd place with just 14 points from 21 games.

In the FA Cup, though, two goals by Arrowsmith had seen them overcome Oldham in front of a huge crowd of 13,879, and a tricky trip to another Fourth Division side, Darlington, was also safely negotiated, Dick Conner coming out on top of the managerial battle with his former boss Len Richley. In the third round Rochdale were paired with First Division Coventry City and before that game came round, Dale also managed to rekindle their League form, Dennis Butler grabbing a hat trick in a 4-1 win at Halifax on Boxing Day; the Shaymen went on to finish 3rd in Division 3, their highest ever placing in the Football League.

The weather then intervened on the big day, so the Dale players had a little longer to ponder Coventry manager Noel Cantwell's pre-match comments: *"Rochdale, where's that? Seriously, this is a game we will win and then we shall just hope for a home draw in the 4th round."* The Coventry boss also objected to playing under the now rather ancient Spotland lights, so the match was re-arranged for the afternoon of Monday January 11th. The Dale fitted in a trip to Plymouth in the interim and did their confidence no harm with a 2-2 draw, Tony Buck on his return to first team action getting one of the goals and Graham Smith saving a point with a spectacular full length diving header off his own line.

For the Coventry tie just over 13,000 fans paying record gate receipts of £3996 packed into Spotland (a remarkable number of great aunts' funerals taking place that afternoon, according to local humorists). In the 39th minute Norman Whitehead got to the bye line and centred for Dave Cross to head the first goal. Coventry came back strongly after the interval and soon equalised, but with Dave Tennant performing heroics between the sticks and Hughie Riley and Colin Parry marking the Scottish internationals Willie Carr and Neil Martin out of the game the Dale held on.

Eleven minutes from time, Dennis Butler outpaced the Coventry defence to fire home the Dale's second, but the key moment was still to come. In a desperate last attack Coventry centre half Jeff Blockley headed against the crossbar, the ball ricochetting down onto the line before being cleared.

Dave Tennant and Joe Ashworth defend against Colchester.

Davis Cross scores the first goal against Coventry City

Despite Coventry protests, the referee ruled that the ball had not crossed the line and his final whistle signalled Rochdale's entry into the fourth round of the FA Cup for the first time (though they had reached the equivalent stage as a non-League side in 1915) and put Cantwell's *"Rochdale, where's that?"* into local folklore.

After a 3-3 draw with Brighton in the League, in which midfielder Hughie Riley became the only non-forward ever to hit a hat trick for Rochdale, Dale then met Fourth Division Colchester. With 10 minutes to go, a goal by Ashworth and two from Buck looked to have guaranteed them a place in round five, but Colchester scored twice in the dying minutes to grab a replay. Everything went wrong at Layer Road and Colchester won 5-0 to earn the fifth round tie against First Division leaders Leeds United in which the Essex side gained a sensational victory, one of the most famous giant-killing acts of all time.

Fortunately the Dale, now playing 4-4-2 to counter the flow of goals against, kept up their good run in the League, winning at Shrewsbury and gaining three home wins in a row. Indeed, in nine games with their new formation Dick Conner's side conceded only two goals. One of these was to Everton - actually a mostly reserve side containing the former Dale star Steve Melledew - in the third round of the Lancashire Cup, but Reg Jenkins on his return after a long lay-off scored twice. In the semi-final Rochdale struggled to beat Chorley, who included Melledew's old partner Joe Fletcher in their ranks, but eventually went through 2-1 after a replay.

Meanwhile the Dale's great post-Boxing Day run, reminiscent of the promotion season, reached 12 games before champions-to-be Preston won at Spotland in front of another excellent crowd of over 10,000. The Dale had by then risen to 14th in the table, earning Dick Conner a Third Division 'Manager of the Month' award. A temporary loss of form dropped them back into the bottom four, but the Dale then won their next three games. The one against Rotherham which finished 4-3 had its share of thrills and spills as both sides scored own goals and Jenkins both scored and missed from the penalty spot. Needing just one point from their last two games to be absolutely sure of staying up, Rochdale ended with a win at Doncaster and a draw at Reading which consigned both of these opponents to Division Four. Dale actually finished a fairly respectable 16th with 43 points, only three fewer than the previous season.

The season still had one game to go, though, the Lancashire Senior Cup Final, against neighbours Oldham Athletic who had just gained promotion from Division Four and also won the short-lived Ford Sporting League, based on goalscoring exploits and a good disciplinary record. The Dale's record not quite as good, Riley in particular running foul of referees several times, and he had just received a six week suspension. Playing in a remarkable 15th cup-tie of the season (they had not won a single one in the previous four years), the Dale collected the trophy for the first time since 1949 with a 3-2 win, thanks to two goals by Dave Cross and one from skipper Joe Ashworth. Dale's cup winning squad was: Godfrey, Smith, Ryder, Gowans, Blair, Ashworth, Whitehead, Jenkins, Cross, Downes and Butler. (Substitute Buck did not get on).

Norman Whitehead, voted the player of the year by the supporters, had been the subject of a *'name your own price'* bid by Malcolm Allison at Manchester City, but Dick Conner refused to part with him. Ronnie Blair, signed from Oldham near the end of the previous campaign, was recommended for a Northern Ireland under-23 cap during the season and provided cover in seven different positions (once figuring at full back, centre back, in midfield and on the wing in the space of five games).

Goalkeeper Dave Tennant, one of the heroes of the Coventry game, was given a free transfer and joined the police force, while Vinny Leech was forced to retire after an abortive comeback attempt and took a job as an insurance man. The only other player released was Dave Pearson, a former Wales under-23 cap who had made a couple of appearances after signing from Southport. (He later appeared at Wembley for Morecambe in the Challenge Trophy Final).

1971-72:
There was little activity on the transfer front during the summer of 1971. The one signing was Burnley reserve 'keeper Rod Jones who cost £4000, the most Rochdale had ever spent on a goalkeeper, but he had a disastrous debut when Notts County fired four past him in the first half hour of the League season. To compound the Dale's misery Joe Ashworth fell foul of the referees new 'get tough' campaign and was sent off.

The first home League game was more successful, with a 2-1 victory over Mansfield, despite an own goal by Ryder and a penalty miss by Jenkins. In the League Cup the Dale drew twice with Halifax before going out. In the home replay, Sir Matt Busby officially switched on Spotland's new £15,000 football Floodlights, one of the most modern systems at any League ground in the country. Subsequent games brought further home wins and away defeats until a goal by Cross, his third in consecutive games, earned a draw at Torquay.

David Cross, again,
scoring at Torquay

Hughie Riley made his first appearance after his long suspension in the home draw with Oldham which attracted a crowd of 10,926, but was then left out again to make room for new £6000 signing from Carlisle, Len Kinsella.

Dave Cross's two goals in the 5-0 victory over Torquay took his tally to 10 in 13 games. Not surprisingly this sort of form had been noted elsewhere and it was Second Division promotion hopefuls Norwich City who came in with the decisive bid, Cross moving to Carrow Road for £40,000 plus the signature of Norwich's Malcolm Darling.

Though they managed their first away win at Wrexham, the successes became fewer and the defeats more frequent. Joe Ashworth departed for Chester after a disagreement over club policy, Reg Jenkins taking over as club captain, while Hughie Riley

Tony Godfrey, Player of the Year: 1971-72.

signed for Crewe and went on to make well over 300 League appearances for various League clubs. Another incoming player was Bolton centre half Arthur Marsh for whom Rochdale paid £7000. Injuries and illness also played havoc with the Dale squad. In the New Year game at Oldham, Ronnie Blair turned out at centre forward, one of only two outfield positions he had not previously occupied for Rochdale, but was himself carried off with a broken rib.

Rochdale did pull off a surprise 1-0 win over Aston Villa, the eventual champions, thanks to a Norman Whitehead penalty (Butler, Jenkins and Gowans had previously missed five between them), and they also beat Halifax at Spotland thanks to two goals by Jack Howarth, the third record signing of the season when he arrived from Aldershot for £8000. Howarth, scorer of 118 goals in six years with the 'Shots, was making his home debut, but the other scorer had taken a little longer to find the net, centre half Colin Parry having made 164 previous appearances without a goal.

Nevertheless, the Dale's League position was looking none too healthy when they suddenly came up with three straight wins. These coincided with the appearance of yet another new man and the disappearance of another of the promotion team, Lee Brogden having been signed from Rotherham in part exchange for Norman Whitehead who had been on the transfer list at his own request for some time.

Unfortunately this burst of form was shortlived, another succession of draws and defeats pushing Dale ever nearer to the relegation zone.

A disastrous 5-1 defeat at Rotherham, a repeat of the previous year's scoreline, left the Dale in 20th spot with four games to go. A point was salvaged against Bolton with two second half goals, but then Brighton netted a disputed last minute winner at Spotland. Although other results dropped the Dale into the bottom four, it was clear that barring a major disaster one point from the last two games would keep Rochdale up.

The penultimate game was at Brighton, a game which should have been played earlier in the season but had been postponed due to the football floodlight ban imposed during the power crisis that had been brought on by the miners' strike. Brighton themselves were on the verge of promotion and a massive crowd of 34,766 assembled to cheer them on into Division Two. After the Albion scored an early goal, the Dale gradually worked their way back into the game and when Peter Gowans fired home a terrific equaliser from 35 yards, both sides were happy to settle for the point they needed for their different objectives.

Rochdale also drew their last game (anything less drastic than a five goal defeat would have done) to finish in 18th place despite not winning any of their last 14 games. Tony Godfrey was voted the player of the year but during the summer he rejoined his old club Aldershot, playing for them until he retired at the age of 37. Dave Cross, though transferred back in early October, remained the only player to reach double figures in goals.

At the start of a lengthy and widely travelled career in the top divisions, Dave Cross scored eight more for Norwich as they claimed the Second Division title. Derek Ryder, who had been in dispute with the club for some time, moved to Southport at the end of the season, while Colin Parry was among the players released, marking the final break up of the promotion winning squad.

With a shorter retained list than of late, Dick Conner was again active in the transfer market. The powerful Portsmouth centre half Colin Blant was signed for £7000 to take over from Parry, while experienced left back Dick Renwick, another of the ex-Aldershot contingent, arrived from Stockport on a free to replace Ryder. The massive 6'-4" York goalkeeper, and sometime professional boxer, Gordon Morritt, came on trial and Oldham midfielder Keith Bebbington was signed in exchange for Ronnie Blair (who later gained several Northern Ireland caps while at Boundary Park).

1972-73:
After a trip to Scotland to play Clydebank and East Stirling then a return visit by the 'Bankies, the 1972-73 season started as the previous one had ended with a draw against Port Vale. In the League Cup, Rochdale made progress with a win at Blackburn, Malcolm Darling netting the only goal against

Joe Ashworth who departed during the 1971-72 season.

one of his former clubs. Renwick had missed the earlier games through injury but his belated debut saw a 2-1 win at Southend, the first League success for 17 games. The Dale followed up with a first ever win at the Vetch Field, Swansea, but suffered a serious blow when Bobby Downes broke his leg in a tackle with Rodney Marsh in a 4-0 League Cup defeat by Manchester City. Fortunately Downes made an excellent recovery and was back within three months.

At Scunthorpe, Rochdale recorded their third away win in five games - they had managed only one win and eight points away from home in the whole of the previous season - so although the 1-0 victory over Wrexham was the side's first home win since March it lifted the Dale to fourth in the table. Two days later they met leaders Walsall and Gordon Morritt earned the hero's laurels with a brilliant penalty save five minutes from the end which enabled the Dale to win 2-1 and take over at the top of the table.

In the very next match ecstasy turned to agony for Morritt as he was stretchered off with a broken leg and a ten man Dale side with Peter Gowans in goal finally succumbed to a disputed Grimsby goal.

With Grimsby's reserve 'keeper Harry Wainman successfully deputising for Morritt, Dale took three points from the next two home games to stay in second place. However, fielding a more adventurous line-up they then crashed to three defeats in four games, leading Dick Conner to re-introduce a five man back line, with Marsh, Blant and Kinsella as the central barrier. Another player to make brief appearance was the former Latics stalwart Jim Bowie who was signed up from the Labour Exchange in Oldham. He was offered a longer trial but preferred to go back on the dole.

The Dale did repeat their victory over Walsall, recording their first clean sheet away from Spotland for 74 games, but hindered by numerous injuries lost three more home games in a row. The middle one was one of their most embarrassing defeats for some time, as they went down 2-1 to non-Leaguers Bangor in the FA Cup. The game against Chesterfield saw ITV cameras at Spotland to record the match for Grenada's Sunday afternoon programme for the first time. Unfortunately the Dale went down 2-1 but the large TV audience (there were less than 2000 present in the flesh) did see a bit of Dale history when apprentice Paul Fielding came on as substitute, replacing another young debutant Barry Bradbury. A week short of his 17th birthday, Fielding became the youngest player to appear in the Football League for Rochdale.

Jack Howarth had meanwhile been transferred back to his old stomping ground of Aldershot (he eventually totalled a massive 171 goals in 422 games for them), while Wainman returned to Grimsby at the end of his loan spell (and went on to make over 400 appearances for his club, too). Another departure was old favourite Tony Buck who moved to Northampton for £2000. Moving in to take the No.9 shirt was the well travelled veteran Bill Atkins who was bought from Halifax for a similar amount.

After three goalless draws came a more remarkable draw at Wrexham, with Rochdale hitting three in the first half and the home side a trio in the second. This was definitely the odd game out as the next five games brought just two goals for and two against, Morritt making a successful return in goal. In the Lancashire Cup the Dale went down 5-1 to Bury and their annoyed manager fielded the same side in the reserves' next match. They beat Wigan Reserves 4-0 and this obviously rekindled their goal scoring form as they then proceeded to beat promotion contenders Notts County 4-1.

Reg Jenkins' two goals in this game took his tally to 119 Football League goals for the Dale, thus beating Bert Whitehurst's 45 year old club record. Inexplicably Rochdale lost their next home game 6-0 to Plymouth to equal their worst home defeat that had been sustained in the grim days of 1932.

The following game was back to normal, a nil-nil draw at Watford, but it did see Reg Jenkins break another record as the popular striker turned out in his 300th Football League game for the Dale, the first player to do so. Dale stayed around the middle of the table until three defeats slipped them right down a packed League table to 20th at the beginning of April. At Chesterfield, apprentice Charlie Simpson scored in what turned out to be his only League appearance, the first time this had happened for some years.

The 1-0 home defeat by Rotherham was watched by a meagre crowd of 1588, and indeed crowds much over 2500 had been the exception rather than the rule at Spotland all season; by contrast nine of their away games had attendances over 8000, the highest 18,154 at Bolton. However, a win at York and a couple more goalless draws took the Dale to 41 points and for the last three games the League allowed the Dale to field their post-deadline signing Leo Skeete who had cost £1500 from Ellesmere Port. The lanky West Indian Liverpudlian promptly scored a brilliant winning goal against Grimsby and also netted in the two remaining games.

Rochdale thus finished in 13th place with 45 points, 12 behind promoted Notts County. As it turned out 41 points were not, as they would have been in any other season, enough to guarantee survival, as an amazing late run by apparently doomed Halifax consigned Rotherham to relegation despite reaching that tally.

One of Dale's expensive buys in 1971-72, Jack Howarth, centre, during the next season.

The Dale skipper Blant, nicknamed 'Garth' after the comic strip hero, missed matches only through two periods of suspension. During the season he had been a close second to Leeds hard man Norman 'Bites yer Legs' Hunter in the number of bookings collected, reaching nine even with the relatively generous refereeing of the 1970's.

Although the past season had been slightly disappointing in the final analysis, and some of the fans were not happy with the modern, increasingly defensive disposition of the team under Dick Conner, Dale fans could now look back on a dozen pretty successful years by Rochdale standards.

There had been the remarkable run to the final of the League Cup in 1962, their best ever Fourth Division points tally in 1964-65, the long awaited success of the promotion season, the cup exploits in beating Coventry and winning the Lancashire Cup in 1970-71, and the honour of topping the Third Division for a time in both 1969-70 and the season just ended. With the defensive strength of the current side and the addition of two exciting up and coming strikers in Skeete and Alan Taylor, signed at the end of the season from Morecambe, there seemed no reason to doubt the chairman's earlier pronouncement that there would be *no going back* to the dark days of Division 4.

However, impatient for even greater successes and mindful of supporters' disquiet, the board decided not to renew Dick Conner's contract at the end of the season and to seek a new manager. After some delay the board also decided to release their longest serving player Reg Jenkins. Reg, a stalwart of nine seasons, had compiled a total of 119 League goals in 305 games, and in all senior games had netted 141, all these figures representing all-time records. Despite offers from other League clubs Reg immediately retired to his native Cornwall to play for his home town club Millbrook, and eventually hoisted them to the undreamt of heights of the South Western League. Clearly the new season would see the start of a new era for Rochdale.

WINTERS OF DISCONTENT 1973 - 1980

~ CHAPTER 8 ~

At the beginning of June, Rochdale appointed Oldham's youth team coach Walter Joyce as their new manager, despite a late counter-offer from Manchester United who wanted him to take over their youth scheme. With Peter Madden following his boss Dick Conner to Darlington, Dennis Butler (who had been forced to retire due to knee and back injuries) was appointed trainer-coach, with Oldham's assistant coach Frank Campbell moving to Spotland to look after the youth team. The Dale registered a 'trendy' new strip of all white with a yellow and blue Crystal Palace style diagonal stripe.

Acting manager Gus McLean had already added Liverpool reserve midfield man Steve Arnold to the staff and the new boss signed former Manchester City reserve defender Keith Hanvey and a number of youngsters such as the England Grammar Schools centre forward Gary Cooper from Hor-wich RMI and Ever-ton apprentice Don Tobin, who had partnered future Eng-land star Peter Reid in the Huyton side which won the England Schools Trophy.

Graham Smith and Stan Horne (on the ground) do battle against Cambridge in February 1974, in front of the lowest FL crowd for 20 years, just 588.

A busy programme of pre-season friendlies, including an impressive 4-2 defeat of a Leeds side, led up to the opening day fixture against Brighton, in which Malcolm Darling was both hero and villain, missing a penalty but scoring a second half equaliser. Former Oldham youth team player Paul Brears had a very short Football League baptism, being carried off with damaged knee ligaments after only 25 minutes and not playing again until the following season. Skipper Colin Blant who had not been included in the squad for the game immediately put in a transfer request. In addition Gordon Morritt followed the trail to Darlington when Rod Jones, given a free at the end of the previous term, was re-signed and made first choice 'keeper.

The next game gave no sign of trouble ahead as the Dale powered through their League Cup-tie against Hartlepool 5-3 with Atkins, Darling, Taylor and Skeete all finding the net. A goalless draw at Walsall was followed by the season's first defeat, at home to Tranmere, and a 5-0 drubbing at Plymouth, whose debutant centre forward Peter Mariner, later of Ipswich and England fame, scored twice. Another away defeat dumped them to the bottom of the table, but Rochdale did manage to salvage a point at Spotland when they came back from three down to Bournemouth thanks to late goals from defenders Kinsella and Hanvey.

The next match saw a change in goal when former Coventry youngster Mick Poole made his League debut in a 2-2 draw. The Dale gained their first League success of the season at Southend thanks to a storming solo effort by Arnold and a first Football League goal, from the penalty spot, for Alan Taylor. Before this game manager Joyce had sold the two experienced strikers, Mal Darling (to Bolton for £12,000) and Bill Atkins (Darlington, £2000) and used some of the money on Manchester City reserve striker Mick Brennan. Darling subsequently became one of the game's great travellers and arguably the least successful manager of all time when Darwen lost every match under his management. (To be fair, it should be pointed out that at the time Darwen got through five managers in half a season).

Rochdale managed another home draw, against Huddersfield, but still had only seven points from 10 games. And that was the high spot of the season! The next eight games contributed one League point while Bolton won 4-0 in both the League and Lancashire Cups.

In the draw with Grimsby, another Manchester City junior - Eamon Kavanagh - became the 23rd player used in only 14 games. (He went on to be a regular for both Workington and Scunthorpe).

Walter Joyce had by now decided that he had no further use for his experienced defenders Blant, Kinsella and Renwick, either, so that six of the previous season's regulars had disappeared to be replaced by untried youngsters. Both Blant and Renwick joined the exodus to Darlington.

In the FA Cup, Arthur Marsh scored his first ever senior goal to help Dale overcome South Shields. They then drew at Southern League Grantham, Skeete being denied a last minute winner when his shot came back off a post. In the replay Rochdale were two up in eight minutes and led 3-1 at half time, but slipped up physically and metaphorically on the icy surface to allow the non-Leaguers to force extra time and eventually run out 5-3 winners.

In a last effort to revive the side, the manager signed the experienced Chester pair Stan Horne and Jim Grummett for a joint fee of £10,000. Horne had played a few games for Manchester City when they won the League Championship in 1968, but had started the current campaign by being sent off on the opening day. Grummett, a former England youth international had played 250 times for Lincoln, following in the footsteps of his father Jim senior.

This did engender a slight improvement, Lee Brogden's fifth goal in seven games earned a draw against Southend and on January 12th Rochdale finally won their first home League game of the season when they beat struggling Shrewsbury 3-2 in front of just 957 spectators, the lowest gate at Spotland since the war. The following Sunday, at Brighton, Graham Smith set a new record with his 306th Football League appearance for the Dale. The crowd for Rochdale's first ever Sunday game was almost 19,000 even though Brighton themselves only finished six off the bottom. The first Sunday fixture at Rochdale, which the Dale lost to York, attracted a reasonable gate of 2205.

Stan Horne, who had never scored for any of his previous clubs netted in the York game and, oddly enough, in the return at York a few weeks later.

The Sunday games had been arranged because of staggered three day working due to the power workers strike during the 'winter of discontent'. For the same reason a ban on floodlights meant that the Dale's home game with Cambridge was played on a Tuesday afternoon. The attendance reported in the press was 450 and even the later official figure given by the club, 588, was the worst for any Football League game since Gateshead against Accrington Stanley in 1952 (usually given as 484, but recorded as 622 in the Accrington 'Complete Record', in which case the only lower crowd was the 469 for Thames v. Luton in 1930). Although Cambridge were ultimately relegated, too, they won 2-0, one of six consecutive defeats for the Dale, both Grimsby and Huddersfield obtaining nap hands.

Five of the players from the 1974-75 season. (top) Keith Hanvey Paul Hallows Gary Cooper (bottom) Mike Poole Mike Ferguson

Despite the odd decent result, such as a draw at leaders Bristol Rovers, it was mathematically impossible for Rochdale to avoid relegation as early as April 1st. The only noteworthy game of the season's final month was the 3-3 draw at Cambridge in which their new signing from Preston Dave Carrick scored twice, the only player to do so all season. Earlier, Carrick had had possibly the unique experience of earning his club a negative number of points when he played his only two games for North End before his transfer became official, causing them to be docked two points. With nothing left to play for, Jim Grummett was allowed to fly off for a summer with Denver Dynamos in the USA where he was soon joined by Stan Horne and Mick Poole. The Dynamo's manager was Ken Bracewell who had spent a brief period at Spotland in the 'sixties.

Rochdale managed a miserable 21 points, exactly half as many as Port Vale just above the drop zone. This added the record low points total for Division Three to their corresponding record for the Third North from 1931-32. They only won two games, just one at home, which were also Football League records.

Dale managed a meagre 38 League goals, 9 of them credited to Leo Skeete, though he was picked for barely half the games. Skeete's most sensational goal was against Blackburn early in the season when the referee mistakenly disallowed it, thinking it had not actually gone in the net. He booked Skeete and appeared to send off Bebbington for dissent before changing his mind after consulting his linesman. At the other end Dale conceded an appalling 111 goals, 94 of them in the League, and most of them flying past young Poole who nonetheless was voted the supporters' player of the year; Bert Welch, the sufferer in 1932, would surely have approved. Not surprisingly average attendances slumped to around 1500, with five games not even attracting 1000 fans.

Essentially all the remaining experienced players were released at the end of the season. Graham Smith departed after a record 317 Football League appearances (coincidentally matching the mostly pre-Football League record of his namesake Albert Smith), and 373 in all competitions, the most ever for the club. At the end of the season Rochdale played a joint benefit game for Smith, Jenkins and Butler against Oldham. Making up the team alongside the beneficiaries and their guests was 18 year old Paul Fielding, who was just 2 years of age when Reg made his League debut, but who became the club's longest serving player when Bobby Downes was transferred to Watford for £10,000. Only 24 himself, Downes had made 174 Football League appearances for the Dale and over the next 10 years took his tally to around 500 before concentrating on the coaching side of the game.

The close season of 1974 saw the signing of two very experienced men in former Manchester City star Neil Young, the winner of League Championship and European medals (best remembered for his winning goal in the 1969 FA Cup Final), and the well travelled veteran Mike Ferguson, who had played in Accrington Stanley's last match, against Dale, in 1962. Two less known players were Bolton full back Paul Hallows, who had recovered from fracturing his skull in a match a couple of years earlier, and Manchester City reserve Tony Whelan. Again Walter Joyce signed up a number of youngster as well as 22 year old schoolteacher Dave Seddon who had first figured in the Dale's junior sides when he was 14 and had since played for British Colleges while studying for his degree. Hallows, who cost £2000, was the only one not to arrive on a free transfer.

1974-75:

The Dale's return to Division 4 (and to their old colours of blue and white) began with a draw at Shrewsbury courtesy of a penalty miss by the home side, but they were quickly knocked out of the League Cup by Young's former club Preston. The first victory came in the fourth game, a 3-1 defeat of Barnsley, helped by a freak goal by skipper Stan Horne from the halfway line. This ended a run of 26 games without success. The first away win for a year soon followed when Dale won 2-0 at Darlington thanks to two tap-ins by Alan Taylor. But the next eight games showed that the Fourth Division wasn't going to be that easy, as they produced just four points. Particularly unfortunate was on loan goalkeeper John Taylor who twice saved a penalty on his debut only for the referee to order retakes each time. In the same match, a 3-3 draw at Swansea, substitute Gary Hulmes, a 17 year old amateur who had scored five for the youth team the previous week, netted just three minutes after coming on for his debut. Strangely he was not selected for another game for several months and never scored another Football League goal (though he did later make a name in the League of Ireland, playing European football for Sligo and representing the League against the Argentinian 1978 World Cup winning side).

Long serving full-back Paul Hallows (1974-1980).

A longer lasting signing was 32 year old Oldham centre half Dick Mulvaney, a former team-mate of Joyce at Blackburn. This was also the cause of a more peculiar transfer when a large number of 'Dick Mulvaney badges' moved from the Latics' club shop to Dale's! After a heavy defeat at Chester a number of changes were made, Mulvaney linking up with Keith Hanvey in the middle of the back four (Horne and Grummett, though signed as midfield men, had been playing there), and Tony Whelan (who had started out at left back) moving from midfield to centre forward. This inspired a more successful run which saw Rochdale unbeaten in five League games and progress to the second round of the FA Cup.

Meantime Alan Taylor, scorer of seven goals thus far, and who had missed the cup-tie at Marine due to a providential bout of 'flu, was transferred to First Division West Ham for £40,000. Leo Skeete also moved on, to Mossley, becoming one of the most feared goalscorers in the country at non-League level, and representing the England semi-professional side. Off the field Dennis Butler left the club, later becoming one of the few ex-Dale players to manage a Football League side when he took over at Port Vale.

Butler was replaced as coach by Harold Holbert. Tom Nichol, a Rochdale scout for over 20 years and the discoverer of the likes of Steve Melledew and Dave Cross, was appointed Youth Organiser, emphasising the manager's dedication to a youth policy.

Dale went down 1-0 at Tranmere in a cup replay (old boy Paul Crossley getting the goal) and they also lost skipper Stan Horne to an injury which subsequently forced his retirement. In the next game the Dale suffered their worst defeat of the year, 5-0 at Hartlepool. Apprentice left back George Townsend, who had had a trial with the England Youth squad at Lilleshall, made his debut and despite the scoreline kept his place for the rest of the season.

Three other youngsters, Fielding, Brears and Tobin, had gained regular places in midfield, but it was a more seasoned pro who made the biggest impact. This was Bob Mountford, from the hard school of Gordon Lee's Port Vale, who scored twice on his debut against Darlington despite the attentions of former Dale defenders Marsh and Blant.

Unfortunately this was the height of their season's endeavours, and they then won only once in twelve games. The victory, 4-2 at home to bottom club Scunthorpe, owed much to Mountford's brace of goals, but on the other side of the coin he was sent off in the reverse fixture after a scuffle. On his return after suspension, he was immediately sent off again along with Workington's Dave Helliwell, later a Dale man himself.

The next victory gave Rochdale revenge on Hartlepool and they also beat fellow strugglers Stockport, player-of-the-year Whelan netting twice, but two further defeats left them on the brink of the re-election zone with one game to play - a crunch one against Swansea who were one point worse off than Dale. With Mountford back from his second suspension and Young and Seddon recalled after long absences, the Dale won 1-0, Mountford grabbing the all important goal which meant safety for Dale and a first ever re-election application for the Swans.

Dale collected only one point from their last 11 away games but fortunately lost only two of their last 15 at Spotland. Even so, average attendances fell further to about 1400. Despite their successful recall for the final game, Seddon and Young were among those released a few days later.

Meanwhile, Alan Taylor had made a surprise appearance for West Ham in the FA Cup quarter final at Arsenal and scored twice. Remarkably he repeated this in the semi-final, and to end a fairytale season (only his second as a Football League player) he scored two opportunist goals at Wembley as the Hammers beat Fulham. The following season he played in the European Cup Winners Cup Final against Anderlecht.

With the Dale not yet looking like living up to their manager's prediction that, following Burnley's example, the youth policy would make them the 'team of the eighties', he brought in a couple of seasoned pros in the form of Port Vale defenders Bill Summerscales and Tony Lacey to help things along. A revival off the field was that of the Supporters Club, a new official Rochdale AFC Supporters Club (1975) being formed through the efforts of a number of young fans led by Steve Birch, their first chairman.

1975-76:
Luck deserted the Dale right from the off, as the first goal of 1975-76 was credited to Reading when a shot actually hit a stanchion outside the net. Mountford's two goals gave the Dale the advantage over Swansea in the first match at Spotland, but Bury won easily in the League Cup, the first round ties being played over two legs for the first time. Dale nearly gave away a four goal lead against Newport, finally triumphing 4-3 and this also expended most of the Dale's goal supply for a while, though they did win at Stockport. Two more goals in another away win, at Scunthorpe, gave Mountford seven in 10 games, but the rest of the side had managed only three between them.

A resounding 4-1 defeat of leaders Tranmere at the beginning of November took the Dale to 8th place in the table. Midfield man Don Tobin, who had never scored a senior goal previously, scored in four successive games. As in previous years though, Dale only flattered to deceive as they failed to win any of their next seven League encounters. Against bogey team Brentford (whom they had never beaten in 15 attempts) Dale 'keeper Mick Poole was sent off along with two Brentford players, the Bees winning 3-0. On the other hand, the Dale did win through to the third round of the FA Cup for the first time in five years by beating both Workington and non-League Gateshead in replays, the latter contributing to their own downfall with an own goal in each match. The Dale goalkeeper at Gateshead was ex-Bury apprentice Brian Oliver who had actually been released by the Dale the previous month, but was urgently recalled to make his senior debut in place of the suspended Poole, as any new signing would have been ineligible for a cup-tie at such short notice.

The Dale warmed up for round three by beating Darlington 1-0 with a goal from Joe Murty. Murty, another former Oldham junior, had had trials with the Scottish youth squad and earlier in the season had been the scorer of one of four separate hat-tricks (even the substitute Sante Fracassi got one), when Rochdale's youth team beat Skelmersdale by the staggering margin of 16-1 in the FA Youth Cup.

The FA Cup-tie with First Division Norwich City in the New Year produced an unlikely result and an even more unlikely hero. Norwich scored from the penalty spot after only four minutes, but the Dale came back to force a replay.

The second chance was thanks to a goal from non-contract player Phil Mullington, yet another former Oldham reserve, who was making only his third senior appearance. Over 8000 fans attended the replay at Spotland which the Dale almost clinched in the last minute of extra time, when Mountford had a shot kicked off the line. With Norwich declining to toss for the venue of the second replay, the Dale had little alternative but to opt for the more financially rewarding trip to Norwich, rather than a game on a neutral ground. Helped by another penalty, Norwich finally managed to dispose of their Fourth Division opponents 2-1, but the Dale did have the consolation of their share of a 19,000 gate.

Dale then embarked on an excellent run, going unbeaten for nine games. This included five successive draws, one of them at second placed Northampton when Poole made a last minute penalty save, and an excellent away win at Tranmere who lost only one other home game all season. The one home win in this spell was against Southport, who were struggling desperately both financially and on the playing side and had to field an outfield player in goal.

Unfortunately, the Dale then fell back again, failing to win any of their next ten games. A victory over Doncaster ended the spell and prevented the Dale getting into re-election trouble at the last minute. Two of the last three games were drawn, making the total of draws for the season up to a record 18, with 11 of them at home. They ended 15th in the table yet scored only 40 goals. Rather more numerous were disciplinary points, the Football League at one point ordering the club to clean up its act after accumulating 100 points from cautions (and Poole's sending off). Despite the early season promise and the mid-table finish, crowds rarely rose much above the 1400 mark and two failed to reach four figures.

Right back Paul Hallows was the supporters' player of the year, while Bob Mountford was easily top scorer with a total of 17 and had been the subject of a £15,000 bid by Colchester. But it was Tony Whelan who impressed his fellow pros and was included in the Fourth Division 'team of the year' at the PFA awards.

Mike Ferguson had already left to manage the Icelandic champions IA Akranes and at the end of the season most of the manager's young hopefuls were freed. Youthful veteran Paul Fielding joined Irish club Sligo and subsequently became the youngest player-manager in senior football in the British Isles at the age of 26, and steered his team to qualification for Europe. A week later manager Walter Joyce and reserve coach Harold Holbert left Rochdale 'by mutual agreement'. Applicants for the job were said to include former Arsenal player George Graham (later the Arsenal and 'Spurs boss) and Sunderland coach Arthur Cox (subsequently in charge at Newcastle and Derby).

But the favourite for the job was ex-Dale player Brian Green, who had recently returned to England after a successful stint as manager of the Australian national side. As expected, Green took over at the beginning of June 1976 and maintaining the antipodean connection, New Zealand coach Alan Vest became his assistant. Green's first move was to re-sign another ex-Dale centre forward of a later vintage, Steve Melledew, and make him club captain. The previous year Melledew had played in the NASL for Boston Minutemen alongside Eusebio. Other signings were Workington's Dave Helliwell and the Shrewsbury pair Alan Tarbuck and Nigel O'Loughlin. Though born in Rochdale, O'Loughlin had been brought up in Denbigh and represented Wales Schoolboys. With no further signings, the Dale were left to start the season with a minute first team squad of 14.

1976-77:
Before the season even started injuries cut the numbers to a bare 11 and amateur central defender Billy Boslem made up the squad on the opening day. An innovation this season was the playing of both legs of the first round League Cup-ties before the first League match and the Dale duly disappeared from the competition at the hands of Blackburn, before opening their League campaign with a 1-0 win at Scunthorpe. This was the first time the Dale had kicked off their League season with an away win since 1963. Another single goal victory against Colchester maintained the excellent start and a defeat at Exeter was the only early set-back. When Rochdale won at Workington in early October they moved to third in the table. Their leading scorer at this juncture was centre back Keith Hanvey who had netted four times.

They lost disappointingly to lowly Hartlepool but won the next two games to stay in the top four. Three further draws meant that the Dale had lost only two of their first 16 Football League games under Green. Dick Mulvaney, though, had decided to retire to take up a more lucrative job on the docks in his native North East, and though Boslem was signed on professional terms to keep the numbers up, the Dale had no experienced cover when Keith Hanvey and Bob Mountford were injured against Darlington.

In the FA Cup, Rochdale drew twice with Northwich Victoria but in a second replay at Maine Road, the Dale suffered their third embarrassing defeat by a non-League side in five years. A defeat by Bradford City cost the Dale their unbeaten home record and pushed them into the bottom half of the table for the first time, but two more 1-0 victories around the turn of the year gave renewed hope. With the shortage of first team players, apprentice Ian Bannon was thrown in at the deep end, but he adapted remarkably quickly and in the first six games in which he partnered the experienced Summerscales in the middle of the back four, the Dale conceded only three goals.

Indeed he did so well that when Hanvey returned to the side it was in midfield rather than defence.

When the Dale thrashed Scunthorpe 5-0, Gary Cooper being the first Rochdale substitute to score twice, they got back to 8th spot, only six points behind the leaders. However, the week

Die hard support - 1976-77 season.

before Alan Tarbuck had broken his leg in the goalless draw with leaders Cambridge and further set-backs followed. Barnsley were gifted the points at Spotland when both Bannon and Mountford put through their own goal and with Lacey suspended Rochdale also lost their next two games.

Although gates had been much better up to this point, averaging around 2000, the Dale were as short of money as ever and a £12,000 fee was sufficient to persuade them to part with Keith Hanvey who moved to Grimsby Town of Division 3. A desperately thin squad was depleted even further, in fact to just 12 players, when Tony Whelan joined Fort Lauderdale Strikers in the NASL. He had been in conflict with the club ever since his mentor Walter Joyce had left, over his desire to emigrate to the USA, and a special tribunal had recently ruled in his favour, so that he was allowed to move without Rochdale receiving the £14,000 fee they had wanted.

Dale did beat Halifax 4-1 and Southport 3-0, with a brace from Melledew, but a seven match run without a win included an abysmal 3-0 home defeat by bottom club Workington who managed only 19 points all season. Indeed it proved the Reds last victory in the Football League as they were voted out at the AGM in the summer. Rochdale's bad run ended with a victory at Darlington, on loan Oldham striker John Dungworth netting one of the goals, but the Dale lost five of the last six games to slump to 18th, only two points ahead of re-elected Halifax. They had picked up just 11 points in the second half of the season, losing 16 of the 23 games. Unsurprisingly, after signs of improvement, crowds dropped below the 1000 mark for three games. Mick Poole, who had already left for his summer in America, was voted player of the year, becoming the first to win it twice.

His replacement in the Dale goal was Chris Shyne, coming late to the professional game from local football with Dyers Arms at the age of 26 (and still going strong in Sunday football 20 years later). Paul Hallows was an everpresent, having now missed only one game in three seasons. Summerscales and Lacey were somewhat surprisingly among those released, along with Cooper, Mullington and Helliwell.

Helliwell had spent most of the season on the bench, being substitute 19 times, but towards the end of the campaign had become something of a crowd favourite, nicknamed Smokin' Joe. Alan Vest returned 'Down Under' to another coaching job and Tony Lacey also moved into coaching with his old club Stoke, later serving as acting manager there for a while.

Summer signings in 1977 comprised just four players, the massive 6-'3", 13½ stone centre half Bob Scott from Hartlepool, midfielders Ian Seddon from Cambridge and Tony Morrin of Stockport, plus Everton reserve striker Dave Esser. Brian Green's efforts to sign further players foundered - John Dungworth, for instance, choosing to go to Aldershot where he scored 23 times in the coming season - and the Dale were forced to start the season with just 13 men including their two goalkeepers. In particular they had failed to replace Lacey at left back and O'Loughlin had to drop back from midfield to cover that position.

1977-78:
The season started successfully, at least in terms of the result, when the Dale drew at home to Halifax (Tarbuck scoring in the last minute on his comeback) and then won the away leg of their League cup-tie, Mountford and Esser netting.

However in the first game Esser had become one of the very few players sent off on their senior debut, the visitors Lawson also going for an 'early bath'. With Mountford still serving a suspension carried over from the previous year, this left the Dale with only 10 available professionals for the opening League match (in fact, strictly speaking only 9 as Bannon was still an apprentice). Another apprentice, Ted Oliver, was selected at full back (O'Loughlin going up front), and 18 year old amateur Paul Cuddy got the No.12 shirt, his only taste of League action (though he was later a regular with top non-Leaguers Altrincham). Oliver, at 16 years 5 months, was easily the youngest ever Dale first-teamer, and one of the youngest League players over the previous few years. Unsurprisingly Barnsley won 4-0.

Dale beat Darlington 2-0 in the next match but had Hallows sent off in the last minute. His automatic suspension meant that Oliver had to be selected for the League Cup second round match against First Division giants Leeds. The Dale made Leeds (whose squad contained more internationals than there were professionals at Rochdale) fight all the way and were far from disgraced by a 3-0 final score. However, the gate money was not as big a consolation as might have been expected - the club had hoped for a crowd of 16,000 but got only half that number.

Dale held the lead against Grimsby until giving away an 88th minute penalty, and lost 2-1. Despite signing striker Terry Owen from Chester, even more trouble befell the Dale at Swansea, where they went a goal down in 28 seconds and a bad tempered match of many bookings ended with Mountford being sent off, the third Dale player to receive his marching orders in less than a month. The defeat left Dale bottom of the table and after the game Brian Green announced his resignation to take up a coaching position at Leeds.

Former Dale skipper Mike Ferguson was given the job of caretaker manager.

He had been away from Spotland only 18 months but just four of his former team-mates remained. One of those did not stay much longer either, as Mountford was sold to Huddersfield for £10,000. The change at the top made little difference to the team's performances as they lost eight games in a row. Indeed when Ferguson was officially appointed manager he must have set a record of sorts when his side conceded a goal 33 seconds into his first match.

Skipper Steve Melledew ended the slump with a couple of goals which beat Halifax, and in fact after switching from midfield to his old centre forward role managed six goals in seven games. A home win against Doncaster and three draws, including the season's first away point at York, held out a certain amount of hope but with Seddon suffering a long term injury and Tarbuck breaking his leg again, the Dale were once more struggling desperately just to find a team. Apprentices Ted Oliver and Steve Shaw were included in the side together on several occasions, while the still teenage Bannon and Boslem had by now to be considered senior players.

Five more defeats included a no longer surprising cup knockout by non-League opponents, Scarborough winning 4-2. Against Halifax, Dale's scorer Bob Scott was sent off and actually incurred two suspensions, one for the dismissal and one for bringing the game into disrepute by swearing at the referee on his way off. A couple of goals by Bobby Scaife, who had arrived on a free from Hartlepool saw the Dale to a surprisingly easy victory over League new boys Wimbledon, and top scorer (and eventual player of the year) Owen got a brace at Reading, though the home side won 4-3 thanks to an own goal by Scott, whose month it certainly was not.

Three long-serving players of the period:
(Top) Nigel O'Loughlin (1976 - 1982)
Dave Esser (sent off on his debut), and (Bottom) left back Eric Snookes.

The New Year came in with the Dale anchored at the bottom of the table. Mick Poole had by now been transferred permanently to Portland Timbers and replaced by 18 year old Andy Slack, a sorter at a Heywood tannery. Slack made a promising start to his career, but was injured early the next term and despite several attempted comebacks was forced to retire. Steve Melledew had also put in a transfer request as he considered his wages were too low (he subsequently joined Hillingdon Borough and then went into non-League management), and O'Loughlin assumed the captaincy. A more unusual departure was of the ex-Huddersfield winger Bobby Hoy who decided to leave to concentrate on his folk singing career. Coach Frank Campbell also left, joining Alan Vest in Australia, and was replaced by the former Burnley player Jimmy Robson.

It was the end of February before the Dale gained their first win of 1978, beating Swansea, one of the sides to be promoted, and then Stockport, who had their player-coach Mike Summerbee sent off. A 4-0 drubbing at Brentford ended any hope of a significant revival and before March was out it was already impossible for the Dale to escape the bottom four. The last few games produced one victory, when a debut goal by yet another local amateur Mark Hilditch beat Reading.

Rochdale thus ended their 50th League season the way they ended their first - bottom. They garnered a meagre 24 points, losing no less than 30 of their 46 games, even more than in 1973-74 (this did not give Dale yet another unwanted Fourth Division record, though, as Workington had lost 32 games two years earlier). Rochdale had been bottom continuously since September 17th and finished seven points adrift of next club Southport.

Perhaps surprisingly, 14 players were retained, though this did include several former amateurs and apprentices signed on professional terms. One of them, Ian Bannon, had already made 66 appearances for the senior side, more than anyone on the staff bar Hallows and O'Loughlin, and was still only 18. Attendances late in the season were very consistent, the last eight home gates all being reported as apparently somewhere between 1002 and 1046. In fact, the last seven were entirely fictitious, the chairman having ordered - with a view to minimising adverse publicity before the re-election voting - that the club should not admit to any gates below 1000. In reality they dipped as low as 734 for the Reading game (the previous match, at Southend, having attracted 11,565).

Though the Dale had not had to seek re-election for over 10 years, many a supporters' heart missed a beat when the news was announced that at the Football League AGM, Wigan Athletic had gained admission. In fact it was the Dale's long standing Lancashire rivals Southport, next to bottom in each of the last three seasons, who failed in their re-election bid.

They became the fourth side in nine years to lose their League place, following Bradford Park Avenue, Barrow and Workington. Even with Mr Ratcliffe to canvas on their behalf, clearly the Dale could not risk another disastrous season like the one just ended.

Mike Ferguson had been with Accrington when they departed the League scene and he moved quickly to sign two of Southport's players whose registrations had reverted to the Football League. They were full back Eric Snookes and striker Phil Ashworth. Ashworth had the unfortunate record of being top scorer with both Workington and Southport when they lost their League status in consecutive seasons. Ferguson also optimistically attempted to sign Icelandic international Peter Peterson from his old club IA Akrannes. For some reason the Icelandic star preferred to join Feyenoord instead!

1978-79:
The Dale lost both legs of their League Cup-tie with Crewe, the home match in acrimonious circumstances which led to an official complaint about the refereeing, and the first League game of 1978-79 ended in a home defeat by York. Draws against Aldershot and Port Vale, with Terry Owen getting late equalisers each time, provided the only points from the first eight games. League new boys Wigan gained their first victory at Dale's expense and Rochdale also had Scott sent off. Against leaders Wimbledon, on the other hand, Rochdale surprisingly held the upper hand and would have won but for a last minute penalty miss by O'Loughlin. The goalless affair at Newport provided the Dale's first clean sheet in 32 away games. The 'keeper who managed it was Bolton's Dave Felgate who had joined Dale on loan for the rest of the season. He returned again the following year and in all made the rather remarkable total of 47 loan appearances. Indeed, despite becoming a Welsh international and spending long periods with a couple of clubs, he also made quite a career of being a loan player.

Behind the scenes a number of businessmen had been rumoured to be interested in taking over the club, now heavily in debt, and eventually the so-called 'gang of six' were all voted on to the existing board. Later in the season one of them, Mr. B.A. Hindle, became joint Chairman with Mr Ratcliffe. One quite successful money-spinner was a friendly against Derby County, with a guest appearance for the Dale by former Manchester United legend Bobby Charlton - who scored one of their goals in a 3-2 defeat - and attracted a crowd of 3597.

Rochdale finally managed a victory in their 14th League game, when they beat Darlington 2-1, and they repeated the scoreline against Crewe with Bobby Hoy, back from his singing, scoring both goals. With Hallows out due to a long term injury, Dale then slumped back to their worst form, losing six games in a row and not scoring a single goal.

Worst of all was a humiliating home defeat by Cheshire League Droylsden, probably the lowest in status of the many non-League sides to beat the Dale in the cup over the years. This was their fifth defeat by non-League opposition in seven years and to rub it in they had Snookes sent off for a wild challenge. The week after the cup defeat Mike Ferguson was sacked. Trainer Jimmy Robson had already left and former Dale coach Peter Madden, lately manager of Darlington, was appointed caretaker manager, coach and trainer. Jack Butterfield, formerly of Burnley and Yorkshire County Cricket Club, became the club's commercial and general manager.

In the week before Christmas, Madden signed Doncaster's Brian Taylor and Chris Jones, the latter a well travelled centre forward now joining his ninth League club, as well as former Doncaster man Peter Creamer. Although unluckily defeated in their first match, the reshaped Dale side then travelled to Scunthorpe and amazingly came away with a 4-0 victory, goals from Terry Owen, Bobby Hoy (2) and Chris Jones giving the Dale their biggest away win for over 20 years.

In January, former Burnley midfielder Doug Collins, who had been on Derby's coaching staff for the past year, was appointed the Dale's player-manager, with Peter Madden becoming assistant manager and coach. It was some time before the new boss saw much of his team, though, as they played only twice in the next two months. Both games were against leading sides and the Dale impressed in a draw at Portsmouth and a narrow defeat at Wimbledon. They didn't manage a game at Spotland between December 9th and March 10th.

As March came in, the Dale still had only 13 points, but had 22 games to play. Remarkably enough Rochdale were not bottom of the League as Halifax had only mustered nine points at this juncture. Doug Collins' playing debut (as substitute) coincided with a win at Darlington but only four points accrued from the next seven games. Grimsby scored five at Spotland, a young Tony Ford getting the first, after Dale had taken an early two goal lead, and the lone victory was a surprise 1-0 defeat of title-chasing Reading (who did not concede another goal for the rest of the season). This left the Dale with just 19 points from 32 games, but they then recorded three home victories in four games, centre half Bob Scott twice netting winning goals. Even so, defeats in the next two away games made it appear to be out of the question that the Dale could escape the clutches of the re-election places with only eight games to go.

A goal by defender Brian Taylor saw off Scunthorpe to edge Dale into 22nd spot, their highest since the fourth game of the campaign and another single goal, by Dave Esser, dealt likewise with Newport.

Alan Clarke's Barnsley were red hot promotion favourites, but it was the travelling Dale fans who were celebrating at the end of their match at Oakwell after a stunning 3-0 victory thanks to two goals by top scorer Terry Owen and one by player of the year Bobby Hoy. Over 12,000 supporters were there to see it, too, not to mention the TV audience the following day when the highlights were broadcast on ITV.

Back at Spotland the amazing run continued with a 2-0 victory over Stockport, and a superb last half hour against Northampton saw the Dale come from behind to win 4-1. Teddy Oliver, who along with Ian Bannon had regained his place in the side during the final run in, opened the Dale's account with his first ever senior goal. Fellow strugglers Halifax put a stop to the Dale's run but a goal from Mark Hilditch against Torquay gave them their ninth home win in ten games. This was enough to take the Dale out of the bottom four with one game to go and gave rise to wild celebrations on the terraces more usually associated with winning promotion.

Prolonging the agony, the Dale's final match was postponed when six of their side were taken ill, but Darlington losing their last match meant that one point from the game at Crewe would be enough to complete the 'Great Escape'. In fact, despite being without young defender Brian Hart who was serving the second suspension of his first full season, Dale gave their fans a winning end to the season and the large travelling contingent celebrated with chants of "We are staying in the Football League". Seven wins in the last eight games had taken the Dale's points tally to 39 and ensured their 20th place in the table. In the final week Dale overtook Doncaster who as late as mid-March had been 13 points ahead of them.

Bob Scott was released at the end of the season and spent the next six years as a regular at Crewe, eventually becoming their coach. Terry Owen, who had been given a free transfer because he did not want to move his home nearer to Rochdale (he had missed the Northampton game when his car broke down en route to the ground), joined Port Vale (and shortly afterwards became a father, son Michael in due course becoming a star striker for Liverpool and England). A rarer move for a Dale player took former Sunderland apprentice Mike Milne to Scottish League Montrose.

The euphoria of the end of season rush continued into the 1979 close season and it was confidently predicted that the Dale would be among the Fourth Division pacemakers in the coming season. One local bookmaker reportedly refused to take any bets on the Dale gaining promotion in case there were too many takers. The manager, with the board's backing, added to these hopes by spending a club record £12,000 on Sunderland's England Youth Team captain Alan Weir and £8000 on Darlington midfielder Dennis Wann.

Brian Taylor took over as club captain and Jack Corless joined the staff as trainer. One effort to recoup some money fell through when the Football League Management Committee refused to sanction the use of Spotland for a floodlit cricket match as part of Lancashire and England all-rounder Barry Wood's testimonial season.

1979-80:
Immediately before the season started, Dale entertained Dutch second division outfit Den Bosch and trounced their (relatively) illustrious visitors 7-2 to add to the optimism around the club. In the opening League Cup game the Dale drew away to Third Division Blackpool, managed by Rochdale's former boss Bob Stokoe, despite having Wann sent off on his debut (echoing Dave Esser's debut two years earlier).

The second leg was lost 1-0 and the first League game ended in a home defeat by Bournemouth. A point at Stockport and a home win over Hartlepool looked more promising - all of these early home games attracting gates of well over 2000 - but the promise soon faded. Eventually a run of 12 games without a win ended when Chris Jones' hat-trick beat Northampton 3-2. This was the first hat-trick by a Dale player since 1971 when Hughie Riley notched his against Brighton. Even then, after 19 games the Dale had only a miserable 10 points.

There was certainly no shortage of off-field activity by the manager. Phil Ashworth, who had not appeared in the first team for a year, following a hernia operation, moved to front runners Portsmouth (where he scored four goals in his first two games), two of the manager's former Burnley team-mates Eddie Cliff and Colin Waldron came in, Bobby Hoy, Brian Hart and Paul Hallows were placed on the transfer list, and Chris Jones' old striking partner Jimmy Seal was signed from Darlington for £5000 (leading to the memorable but less than complimentary descriptions of the side as *like a circus - ten clowns and a performing Seal*).

It was on the field that the fans thought Collins should be, though (he had not played since the previous April). The board - with a new chairman for the first time in 27 years, Andrew Hindle having replaced Fred Ratcliffe who became club president - came to the same conclusion and in the week of the FA Cup first round, Doug Collins was sacked.

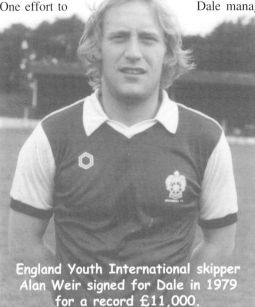

England Youth International skipper Alan Weir signed for Dale in 1979 for a record £11,000.

The following day Bob Stokoe was appointed to the Dale managership for the second time. Since leaving Spotland in 1968, his finest moment had undoubtedly been in guiding Second Division Sunderland to their FA Cup Final victory over Leeds United in 1973.

The new manager's first game ended in a 2-1 cup victory over Scunthorpe, but the Iron immediately gained revenge in a League game in which Paul Hallows, whom Stokoe had just made captain, suffered an injury which put him out for the season. This ultimately ended his career after 197 Football League games for the Dale. In the previous couple of weeks both Cliff and Hoy had suffered similar long term injuries. Nevertheless Rochdale beat Aldershot at home and managed their first away success when they won at Bradford City (who ultimately missed promotion on goal difference). In the cup, the Dale had further success, disposing of Tranmere after a replay. Hilditch, who had managed only one League goal to date, scored three times in the two games, while Brian Hart, who never scored a League goal, followed his first round effort against Scunthorpe with the winner in the second.

In the third round, the Dale met Third Division Bury, whom Stokoe had previously managed, and with whose players there was apparently no love lost. Another connection was former Dale skipper Billy Rudd (one of Stokoe's first signings at Spotland in 1968), who had just moved from a coaching job at Gigg Lane to rejoin the Dale as reserve team coach. The game at Spotland attracted the first 10,000 crowd since 1971 and ended one-all. In the replay Bobby Scaife twice gave Rochdale the lead but Bury came back to win 3-2, the Dale having reason to curse the postponements which had led to their regular centre backs Waldron and Taylor having to miss this particular match through suspensions.

A couple of days later the Dale met Tranmere again and were trounced 5-1. Bob Stokoe fined the whole first team for *lack of effort*, bringing a rapid response from the players, who strongly rejected the accusation that they had not been trying. The players' union was soon brought into the dispute, claiming that the manager had no right to levy such a fine, and within a few days the affair had reached such a pitch that the Football League itself convened a tribunal which ruled that the manager's action was legal.

The PFA, whose case was put by their secretary Cliff Lloyd and the Rochdale players' representative Bobby Scaife, immediately announced that they would appeal to an independent tribunal. Finally, a month after the game which had caused the furore, Bob Stokoe withdrew the fines on the eve of the appeal being heard.

In the meantime, because of postponements the Dale had played only three games, winning the one against Doncaster 3-2, but further defeats led to them finally being passed by Crewe to drop to the bottom of the table. After Esser's goal earned a draw at Lincoln, Rochdale unbelievably went nine games without scoring a single goal (unless you count Bannon's perfect lob over his own 'keeper's head at Doncaster), so they had but one goal to their credit in over 1400 minutes of football. These 15 games had, of course, contributed only a handful of points, so it was already impossible for the Dale to escape the dreaded bottom four.

They did manage to win two of their last three home games, beating promoted Newport in one of them, to reach just 27 points. In the last game they lost to another of the re-election sides, Hereford, Weir ending a dismal season on a suitably woeful note by blasting a late penalty high, wide and not very handsome.

Even before the final match, Stokoe had given free transfers to eleven players and put four others on the transfer list. An odd note was the selection of local lad John Cohen as substitute for the first time the day after he had been freed. Another was the supporters voting top scorer Chris Jones as the player of the year after he too had been released.

The Dale managed 33 League goals in all, their worst ever. At Wembley, though, one of their more successful centre forwards, Dave Cross, won a Cup winners medal with West Ham. This had been Cross's second trip to Wembley, having gained a losers medal in the League Cup while with Norwich.

Before the Football League AGM (indeed for the last couple of months of the season), Rochdale suffered what many felt was an unfair campaign of adverse publicity in the media. Despite comments about Rochdale applying for re-election "yet again" and "always" being at the bottom, it was, after all, only the second time they had finished in the bottom four in the last 13 years (and their fourth re-election bid in nearly fifty). With top non-Leaguers Altrincham mounting a concerted effort to gain the necessary votes, there was considerable pressure on the Dale before the meeting. There had been rumours earlier in the season - denied by the board - that the club would close down, and many fans feared that this would happen if they were voted out of the League. Indeed some felt that the board had not done enough to try and ensure the Dale's survival. On the day, the voting ended Rochdale 26, Altrincham 25, with two votes not cast, the Grimsby representative being in the wrong part of the meeting room (which prevented him from voting), and the Luton man, who had mixed up the time of the meeting, arriving late; it was believed that the two vote absentees had promised their support for the non-Leaguers. The Dale had survived again, this time by the skin of their teeth.

Even so, there was more turmoil ahead at Spotland. Commercial manager Jack Butterfield had already left and shortly after the Football League meeting, chairman Hindle resigned and was replaced by Messrs Wrigley and Faulks as co-chairmen. Back in April, with financial troubles mounting, it had been announced that negotiations were underway to sell the Spotland ground, and it was now admitted that the sale had actually taken place, an anonymous buyer having acquired the ground for £175,000 and loaned it back to the club. It later transpired that the anonymous buyer was in fact Euroway Cars, owned by the then Rochdale chairman Andrew Hindle. Accounts published later showed that a massive loss of £91,956 had been incurred during the 79-80 season. As 15 years earlier, regular Friday night soccer at Spotland proved a flop. Finally, at the end of June 1980 Bob Stokoe resigned, saying that the job was too big for him.

Mark Hilditch (right) had two spells at Spotland between 1977 and 1991.
Barry Wellings (Left) was Dale's top scorer 1980-81.

ONE STEP FORWARD, TWO STEPS BACK 1980-1988

~ CHAPTER 9 ~

The day after Stokoe's departure, his assistant Peter Madden stepped up to the manager's job with his predecessor's comment ringing in his ears, that if he kept the Dale out of the bottom four he would have performed a miracle. Madden started his campaign by giving the players a fresh start, persuading those who had been retained to sign new contracts, taking four players off the transfer list and re-signing former skipper O'Loughlin who had been released. He then raided his native county of Yorkshire for newcomers Eugene Martinez and Alan Jones from Bradford City, Peter Burke from Halifax and Barry Wellings from York.

The new team warmed up for the 1980-81 season by beating Irish League champions Cliftonville, and although beaten over two legs in the League Cup by Third Division Carlisle (and in particular a young forward by the name of Peter Beardsley), the Dale gained a 2-2 draw at Stockport in the first League game. The two centre backs Burke and Taylor then got on the scoresheet as the Dale trounced Scunthorpe 4-0, remarkably enough their best start to a campaign at Spotland since 1925. Amazingly the Dale were actually in the top four, not the bottom four.

Nearly 3000 fans saw the next game, a 1-1 draw with Hartlepool in which Hilditch scored his fourth League goal of the season to beat his output for the whole of the previous term. On the debit side, Snookes was sent off again. Tranmere inflicted the Dale's first League defeat after Peter Burke got stuck in a traffic jam and missed the match, but Rochdale immediately bounced back to beat Torquay, despite a crazy own goal when on-loan goalkeeper Chris Pearce's goalkick hit Taylor on the back of the head.

For the next game, the Dale had another new 'keeper in Graeme Crawford, best known for once keeping 11 clean sheets in a row for York. After a loan spell he became the Dale's first professional goalkeeper of their own for two years when he was signed for £2000. The next five matches brought only two draws, though the goalless affair against Hereford was fairly eventful, with future Dale player Keith Hicks being sent off and Dennis Wann missing a penalty.

At Darlington, the Dale took a two goal lead early on, but after the home side were given two penalties it took a last gasp equaliser by Wellings to give the Dale their first ever 4-4 draw away from home in their long Football League career. In the next game the Dale let in four more, surprisingly suffering their worst home defeat for a couple of years, and their conquerors Mansfield also put them out of the FA Cup, winning 3-1 in a game of three penalties.

A 1-0 win over Lincoln, who went on to finish second, set up Dale's best run of the season, with only 2 defeats in 13 games. The first away win of the campaign was gained at Doncaster, another side eventually promoted, and Alan Jones became the first Rochdale full back to score twice in a Football League game when they beat Crewe. This put the side - nicknamed 'Madden's Mercenaries' by the press - in 8th spot, just two points short of a promotion place, at the turn of the year. Barry Wellings was the man in goalscoring form with nine in 10 games, but the real crowd favourite was winger 'Eui' Martinez.

The Dale twice fought back from two goal deficits to gain valuable points, but then squandered a similar advantage when they lost 3-2 to Peterborough at the beginning of February. Although they gained an excellent win at Wigan in Larry Lloyd's first game in charge at Springfield Park, as part of a unique 'double header' - they played at Wigan on the Saturday and Bradford on the Sunday - they were unable to make up the ground lost. In April Rochdale played their first Sunday games at Spotland (discounting those during the power crisis a few years earlier), beating Port Vale and York. Centre back Brian Taylor hit his sixth goal of the campaign against York and was quickly followed by Alan Jones who scored his sixth from full back when the Dale drew away to champions Southend (who conceded only six goals at Roots Hall all season). These were the highest ever tallies for any Dale defenders apart from penalty kings Birch and Milburn.

Although the season ended with a home defeat, the Dale still finished in 15th place with 43 points. Peter Madden, who had earlier described it as *"not a job but a cause"* had accomplished his 'miracle' in style. Only 17 players were used all season, and four of those made only a handful of appearances. Nigel O'Loughlin, who became the tenth player to appear in 200 Football League games for the Dale, and the first for ten years, was voted player of the year. Alan Jones and Jimmy Seal were the only regulars released.

It was a busy summer behind the scenes in 1981 as a wrangle developed over the ownership of the ground at Spotland, the former chairman's company Euroway having been placed in the hands of the Official Receiver. In addition the club's AGM approved a plan to issue a further £50,000 of shares. On the playing side, former manager Dick Conner, who had been helping out with the coaching, was appointed assistant manager to his long time number two Peter Madden. The latter completed the signings of the experienced Terry Cooper and Terry Dolan from Bradford City, Bury forward Dave Goodwin, and Mansfield midfield man Neville Hamilton.

Also signed was Newport's Steve Warriner, reputedly after the respective assistant managers got at cross purposes about who the Dale actually wanted. With the players' new found freedom of contract, Dennis Wann decided to leave Rochdale and sign for his home town club Blackpool, where he ran a hotel. Coming back to the fold was Mick Poole after a long spell in the USA where he had been rated one of the top 'stoppers' in the NASL. Local lad Stuart Thompson, the first Rochdale schoolboy to play for England Schools was signed as an apprentice. Club colours changed slightly to blue shirts with white sleeves.

1981-82:

The side warmed up for the season by beating Second Division Oldham in the revived Rose Bowl match, last played in 1972, with Hilditch scoring the only goal. The season proper started with a decisive 3-0 defeat at Bury and a 2-1 victory over Hartlepool in the first home game (which earned the Dale their first three points for a win instead of the traditional two) turned out to be the only success in the first 12 games.

They won at bottom club Crewe and finally recorded the big score they had been threatening at Spotland when they beat Stockport 4-1. The victory was inspired by two goals from Eui Martinez in the first four minutes. The previous week he had been the subject of a £20,000 bid by Bournemouth which had been turned down. In the wake of the Falklands conflict Martinez was frequently abused by opposition supporters who thought he must be an Argentinian - he was actually brought up in Harrogate. The Dale also beat Torquay at Spotland but lost a thriller at Mansfield 4-3, each side scoring twice in the space of 10 minutes midway through the second half.

In the FA Cup Dale twice held frontrunners Hull City to draws before going out 1-0 after extra time in a second replay at Leeds, but then ran into a string of postponements. On one occasion the Dale team trekked off through arctic conditions to Hartlepool, only to arrive at a deserted ground. The referee had called off the game and everyone had gone home - according to some sources, because they thought the Dale's coach was stuck somewhere on the Pennines. The delays meant that Eric Snookes, who had been sent off at Wigan in November, did not serve his automatic one match ban until the middle of January.

The Dale also played a succession of draws - nine in 12 games before three defeats put them back in re-election trouble, and also led to the return of Graeme Crawford in goal. He had lost his place at the start of the season after a nightmare match against Huddersfield in which he let in a hopeful punt from the halfway line. Despite the Dale's problems, apart from the odd game, they had used the same 13 players throughout the season so far. After a 3-3 draw in a friendly against Leeds United, Rochdale repeated their earlier revival by again beating Crewe and hammering Stockport, this time 4-0 at Edgeley Park.

When the match against Crewe on a mudbath of a pitch ended, most of the supporters thought that the Dale's ill luck had continued and that the referee had abandoned the game, but it transpired that he had mistakenly blown for time five minutes early. After beating Darlington, Dale picked up only one win and four draws in nine games, and even one of the draws, against fellow strugglers Mansfield, in which Cooper - skipper in the absence of the suspended Taylor - was sent off, would prove to be a costly two points dropped rather than one gained.

Dale did beat York twice, Wellings scoring a penalty against his former club in the first, and Rochdale's other former York player Graeme Crawford saving one in the second. Wellings also scored a penalty when coming on as substitute against Scunthorpe, the first time he had not been in the starting line-up since signing two years before. He then missed one against promotion contenders Bradford City but Terry Dolan equalised from the spot when a second opportunity arose. This kept the Dale in 20th spot with three games to go, but having just drawn with the sides who finished second and third, they had next to visit champions-to-be Sheffield United. A massive crowd of 21,000 saw the Blades clinch promotion with a 3-1 win. United had also attracted the best crowd of the season to Spotland, almost 4000.

Other results now appeared to mean that the Dale would have to win both of their remaining games to escape the bottom four by passing Mansfield, and in a bid to force a winner at Hull, the Dale gave away a late breakaway goal. The Football League then announced that Mansfield had been fined two points for fielding an ineligible player in their win against Crewe (the relevant committee having omitted to change the penalty in line with the new three points for a win), so that one point from the Hull game would have given Dale a chance after all!

As it turned out, the Dale did indeed win their last game, and in impressive style too, beating Northampton 5-3, despite trailing three times and losing Brian Taylor with a broken leg. This left them just that one tantalising point behind Mansfield and with a greatly superior goal difference. To rub it in, Dale would have been 19th, rather than 21st, if the old two points for a win had still applied. Mark Hilditch was top scorer for the first time but player of the year was utility defender Alan Weir. Only 18 players were used in all, including two local lads who appeared late in the season; Bill Williams from Sunday League side Ashe Labs and university student Dave Thompson who had turned out for Dale's reserves for some time.

A number of the experienced players were released, Terry Dolan coming up with the classic quote *"When a club like Rochdale gives you a free transfer you have to seriously question your future in the game"*. Nigel O'Loughlin, now a veteran of 245 games for the Dale (which put him fourth in their all time list), turned down part-time terms for the following season and went into local football.

Off the field O'Loughlin was also a trained mechanic and in addition drove coaches for former Dale player Les Bywater. On one occasion when not selected, he had driven the team coach to Torquay, only to find that one of the other players could not turn out and he would have to play!

Financially the club had been as hard pressed as ever and in March the new chairman Mr David Kilpatrick, a funeral director, had appealed for £30,000 to help keep the club going beyond the end of the season. Even with a relatively modest wage bill of £3,000 per week, the Dale were losing money steadily. For instance, after expenses and the visitors minimum share of the gate, the Darlington match at Spotland had brought in just £208, while that against Crewe (when the attendance was 1060) actually made a loss of £9. 73. Discussions were reported to have taken place with Rochdale Hornets on the possibility of groundsharing, but this idea was shelved at the club's meeting in June.

Despite a last minute switch from Alliance League champions Runcorn to the better known Telford as the non-League challengers, Rochdale and the other teams up for re-election all comfortably retained their places at the 1982 Football League AGM. After a number of other prospective deals fell through, signings for the new season included Blackburn 'keeper Chris Pearce, who had been on loan at Spotland in 1980, Aldershot centre forward Micky French, an England amateur youth international when playing for his native Eastbourne, midfield man Peter Farrell from Port Vale and former Dale player of the early 'seventies Ronnie Blair, back again from Oldham. Blair soon decided that he couldn't devote enough time to the game as a part-timer and quit. Having failed in his other attempts to sign a centre half, Peter Madden gave a trial to the well travelled Jack Trainer, a Scot who had played in Ireland and Hong Kong. Another change of colours saw the team turning out in white with red and blue trim.

1982-83:
The season started with three games in the revived Lancashire Cup, now sponsored by the Manx Tourist Board, and played in two qualifying groups. The points gained were not enough for them to qualify for the final, but the draw at Second Division Oldham did enable them to retain the Rose Bowl. The defeat at Bury was more contentious as a dispute over the home side's late winner led to Steve Warriner being sent off for dissent after the final whistle.

The Dale also lost all the first three games of the season proper without managing a single goal. Graeme Crawford, playing for the reserves, did not fare any better, being sent off for the first time in an 18 year career following the refereeing clampdown on 'professional fouls'. Goals by Barry Wellings and trialist Andy Stafford from Stockport (in his only match) gave the Dale victory over Hartlepool and two more from Wellings gave them an aggregate win against Port Vale in the Milk (formerly League) Cup. However, even at this stage, injuries had struck and Peter Madden quickly signed the former Port Vale full back Gerry

Keenan (who had been sent off on Vale's visit to Spotland the year before), though when Trainer was released, the Dale were back to just 13 effective players including their two goalkeepers.

Blackburn's Paul Comstive managed to score on his debut, on loan, playing at full back, but the Dale still lost. Former Aberdeen centre half Willie Garner came on loan from Celtic and had a more rewarding debut in a goalless draw with Bury, Pearce saving a penalty from future Dale striker Steve Johnson. Garner looked to be the answer to the Dale's prayers for a top class central defender but after only four games, from which Dale picked up six points, he was tempted back to Scotland as player-manager of Alloa Athletic.

Even so, the Dale were hovering on the edge of the re-election zone and they also went out to Bradford City in the Milk Cup, the patently unfit Brian Taylor having to make a premature comeback to make up the numbers. They also suffered an all too familiar FA Cup knockout by non-League opponents, this time arch rivals Altrincham. The match was more remarkable, though, for the performance of referee Callow who sent off two players from each side, Dale forwards Martinez and French and their markers Anderson and Kenyon, the former Everton centre half. A couple of weeks earlier Bill Williams had been sent off along with a Northampton forward, so the Dale's games certainly contributed to the season's then record number of dismissals.

The Rochdale board announced that Peter Madden's position was under review following the run of poor results, but in fact the Dale did rather better over the next month, winning three times at home and gaining a rare away point at promotion chasing Scunthorpe. Just before Christmas the team played a match in tribute to president Fred Ratcliffe ('Mr. Rochdale') against an All Star XI containing famous names like Bobby Charlton and Roy McFarland. With many old faces such as Stan Milburn, Wally Birch and Tony Collins in attendance, the evening saw the renaming of the refurbished Willbutts Lane side of the ground as the F.S. Ratcliffe Stand.

Bobby Charlton at Spotland

The Dale won the match 4-1 thanks to a hat-trick from substitute Barry Wellings, who had been left out of the side the previous week, ending a run of 127 consecutive League and cup appearances.

Wellings was released in February and moved to Tranmere, but the influx of new players continued, notably the ex-Bolton contingent of Gerry McElhinney (on loan), Peter Nicholson, and Roy Greaves, who became player-coach. Greaves, who had just returned from a spell in the USA, and Nicholson, had well over 900 games for Bolton to their credit. After he returned to Bolton, former Gaelic footballer McElhinney had a meteoric rise in fortune, gaining a regular first team place and playing for Northern Ireland when they sensationally won 1-0 in West Germany six months later.

The Greenhoff brothers arrive at Rochdale.

In their penultimate game the team met Hull, the Tigers clinching promotion with a 3-1 win. This meant that both Rochdale and Tranmere needed one point to escape the bottom four and consign Blackpool to the indignity of a re-election application for the first time in their history - and they had to play each other in the last match. Fielding their most experienced possible line-up, given the injury problems which had plagued them all season, Dale played out the requisite goalless draw at Prenton Park to finish 20th with 49 points, heading Blackpool by the narrowest possible margin. Each had the same number of points and had scored 55 goals, but the Dale had conceded 73 to Blackpool's 74.

In the New Year, the Dale lost at Hull when the home side were given two bites at a late penalty, but then defeated Tranmere 4-2 to move up to 14th place, their highest for two years. However, a 5-2 defeat at Chester (notable for the first player with a name starting with 'Z' to get on the score sheet for Rochdale, when Peter Zelem put through his own goal!) precipitated a slide back to 22nd. The final straw was a goalless draw at struggling Halifax who had appealed to the Football League for a postponement as they only had five fit players. A couple of days later Peter Madden was sacked and replaced by Jimmy Greenhoff, the former Manchester United star often referred to as the finest uncapped English player of his generation. His first move as the Dale boss was to sign his younger brother Brian of Manchester United, Leeds, England and most recently Hong Kong (who already lived in the Rochdale area anyway), both Greenhoffs boasting a string of domestic and European club honours.

The new manager had a great start to his reign as the Dale trounced Hereford 4-1, Micky French grabbing only the Dale's second hat-trick in 12 seasons and apprentice Stuart Thompson scoring on his second full appearance. The Dale also beat Crewe but were hammered by Jimmy Greenhoff's former Port Vale team-mates.

They still could not break their away duck, but the jinx was stretched to its limit at Northampton, where the home side did not equalise until the fifth minute of injury time. One of the highest scoring Rochdale games of all time ended 6-4 to Aldershot with both the 'Shots' strikers, Dale(!) Banton and Trevor Senior hitting hat-tricks. Farrell with two (he got eight from midfield during the season), Hilditch and Dave Thompson replied for the visitors. The Dale hoisted themselves out of the bottom four by beating Colchester with goals by French and the eighth centre half of the season, Andy Higgins (a former Port Vale man whose brother Bob had figured briefly for the Dale a couple of years earlier).

Winger Dave Thompson, in his first full season, played in every game, was voted the player of the year and won a national 'young player of the month' award. Just seven players were kept on, including the manager himself and the three youngsters Bill Williams plus the non-related Dave and Stuart Thompson. A notable departure was Mark Hilditch who followed his striking partner Wellings to Tranmere after 197 Football League games for the Dale in which he scored 40 goals. Eric Snookes, veteran of 183 Dale games, moved up a division to join Bolton. Weir moved to Hartlepool, Martinez to Newport and Pearce to Port Vale.

Even allowing for the arrival of the Greenhoff brothers and the re-election escape, the most important progress of the season had undoubtedly been made by the board of directors. In March they had bought Spotland back from the Official Receiver for a giveaway £60,000 using a Council loan. Since the ground sale in 1980 debts of £250,000 had been cleared, the operation being masterminded by director and accountant Mr. Graham Morris. Elsewhere the season had been notable for the many clubs who suffered drastic money troubles, Bristol City, Hull, Tranmere and Stockport all having been threatened with extinction in the previous year or so.

Easily the best known of the 1983 summer signings was the former Manchester City stalwart and England international Mike Doyle. He had spent 14 years at Maine Road winning all possible domestic honours as well as European trophies in the course of some 600 senior games. Nevertheless he was challenged in the experience stakes by Bradford City's Les Chapman who had played for Oldham against Rochdale way back in 1967. The Dale spent a record £13,500 on Bury striker Steve Johnson (the fee being set by a tribunal after Bury asked for £60,000) and another £2000 on Halifax's Vernon Allatt.

They also signed their first youngsters on the Government's Youth Training Scheme, one of them being Shaun Reid, younger brother of the Everton and England midfielder Peter. Later, Brian Greenhoff returned from a season abroad to become player-coach.

On the financial side, Rochdale's commercial manager Brian Johnson finalised a sponsorship deal with Sheridan Electricals of Milnrow who, following the Leagues's decision to allow such advertising, would have their name on the Dale shirts (which reverted to the former blue).

1983-84:
In a warm up friendly, a hat-trick from centre half turned centre forward Andy Higgins inspired a 6-0 Dale win against Yorkshire side Thackley, who were coached by former Dale stalwart Graham Smith and had more recent Dale player Terry Dolan in their ranks. The first League game ended successfully when Peter Farrell converted a late penalty against Crewe, but in the Milk Cup the Dale went out to Stockport. Wrexham thrashed Rochdale 5-1 after Higgins was sent off, but Dale gained an excellent 4-1 win over Reading (who went on to gain promotion). Despite variable results, three wins in five outings carried the team to within four points of the side in second position. They failed to cash in at Swindon when the home side lost their goalkeeper through injury, but finally ended a run of 30 away games without a win by beating Blackpool.

Unfortunately this proved to be the season's high point, though in the FA Cup, lightning did strike twice as far as Crewe were concerned, a single Peter Farrell goal again settling things. In round two Rochdale gained a surprise 2-0 victory at runaway leaders York thanks to one of the season's quickest goals, Steve Johnson netting after 14 seconds.

Rochdale went 12 games without a League win, even though both Johnson and Farrell had taken their tallies to 10 goals by the half way point of the season. (At the other end Higgins had the unfortunate experience of diverting the ball past his own 'keeper for own goals in successive games). Given the Dale's propensity for FA Cup disasters, it was no surprise that, rather than some money-spinning tie, they pulled out the one remaining non-League side, Telford, in round three, and lost 4-1.

Manager Greenhoff, who had been unable to play for most of the season through injury, immediately made the whole first team squad, apart from Johnson, available for transfer. However, it was Johnson for whom Wigan came in with a bid and he eventually moved to Springfield Park - against the wishes of the manager - for £25,000 (though some of the profit went to Bury, anyway, under the terms of the tribunals's decision the previous summer). Meantime Dale had beaten Crewe 1-0 for a third time. They had two debutants in their ranks, with Ian McMahon on loan from Oldham and YTS lad Shaun Reid.

The goalscorer was another youngster Geoff Thomas who had played in local football for Ashe Labs with Bill Williams (and had represented the England amateur youth team along with two other Dale juniors, Andy Lamb and the former manager's son Carl Madden). Later in the season his victims, Crewe, offered Thomas professional terms and he soon became a regular at Gresty Road, going on to be transferred to Crystal Palace and, in due course, play for England, the first former Rochdale player to do so since Archie Rawlings in 1920.

Dale managed a 0-0 draw against high flying Reading, who scored in all their other home games, despite McMahon being sent off. McMahon thus had the odd experience of being suspended when he signed permanently for the Dale the following week. Dale lost abysmally at Chester who had won only two previous games all season and were quickly knocked out of the new (but long mooted) Associate Members Cup. They finally won their first home game since October when they defeated Darlington, but lost the next three. Exactly one year to the day after taking the job, Jimmy Greenhoff resigned as manager, quoting *"lack of communication with the Board"*. Brian Greenhoff also resigned as assistant manager, and senior pro Les Chapman was appointed caretaker manager until the end of the season.

Chapman started well with a draw at promotion chasing Bristol City and a 1-0 win over Blackpool (which was followed by some of the worst football violence seen in the town, when visiting hooligans went on the rampage). With injuries continuing to decimate the side, four of the next five games were lost. The Dale did manage a goalless draw against Colchester, but the game was only memorable for Allatt's sending off and bookings for 'keeper Steve Conroy (later voted player of the year) and young Shaun Reid, his sixth caution in a career spanning 13 games. Earlier in the season Conroy had been 'booked' by the police following an altercation with an abusive visiting fan behind his goal. A Dale side easily beat Finnish first division club Pallo Iriot 4-0, but in the serious business they were soundly thrashed 5-0 by fellow strugglers Halifax.

Unpredictable as ever, Dale bounced back to beat fifth placed Aldershot, but had only two games left in which to save themselves. With Allatt, who had made quite an impression as an emergency centre back, suspended for his sending off, the manager serving the first suspension of his 18 year career and Shaun Reid his first after less than 18 games, it was a very inexperienced side which travelled to second placed Doncaster, and not surprisingly Rovers won 3-0. A rare goal by Williams was enough to beat Torquay in the last match and edge Dale up to 20th, but both Halifax and Wrexham below them still had games to play.

Although the side had recovered somewhat under caretaker manager Chapman, the board decided to offer the manager's job to Vic Halom, the 35 year old former Sunderland player who was currently manager of Northern Premier League champions Barrow (Chapman becoming his assistant).

Halom had the somewhat strange start to his career as Rochdale boss of seeing his new side sink into the bottom four the following day without playing, when Halifax won their game in hand, and Wrexham later won theirs, too.

Vic Halom greets the players.

Not surprisingly few of the senior players were retained and among the departures was Neville Hamilton, the side's longest serving player after three seasons, though the first two had been badly interrupted by injuries. He looked set for a remarkable turn round in his fortunes when Tommy Docherty signed him for Second Division Wolverhampton Wanderers, but sadly he had a heart attack on the eve of the season and was forced to retire from the game, the Dale later helping with his benefit fund.

As widely expected it was Hartlepool, not the Dale, who were most under threat at the 1984 Football League AGM, Rochdale in fact polling 50 votes to 'Pool's 32, with Alliance League champions Maidstone gaining 22 votes. As in the previous summer, the major spending was on a new strike force. Allatt had been transferred to Crewe for £3000 and moving in were Les Lawrence, a £15,000 buy from Aldershot where he had hit 22 goals the previous term, and Barry Diamond, scorer of 37 goals for the manager's former side Barrow, who cost £3000. The best known, nationally, of the new players was former Manchester City and England under-23 star Ged Keegan who had played for Oldham alongside Halom and Chapman in the late seventies. Dale old boy Keith Hanvey returned from Huddersfield and the Dominican Republic born Yorkshireman Joe Cooke arrived from Bradford City. A centre forward turned centre half, familiar to all followers of clubs in the lower divisions, Cooke was a veteran of nearly 400 Football League games though; having started when he was 16, he was still only 29. The side had yet another new playing strip, appearing in white shirts carrying the watering can emblem of their new sponsors the All-in-One Garden Centre, and blue shorts.

1984-85:
In its third season of existence, the Dale finally won a game in the Manx Tourist Board's Lancashire Cup, beating Burnley 1-0, but they lost the other two, Steve Johnson netting a hat-trick for Wigan. This was the prelude to a catastrophic start to the real campaign, as the Dale lost all their first five games before Durham City goalkeeper Paul Malcolm kept a clean sheet in his first three games, and goals by Lawrence and trialist Tom English, the former Coventry and Leicester striker, gave Dale their first points of the season against Hartlepool.

John Cavanagh, who had played in the previous season's Trophy Final for Bangor, was sent off in the draw at Stockport, and though Dale beat high-flying Peterborough with two goals from Diamond, further defeats left them bottom of the League. The FA Cup defeat by Doncaster proved to be Keith Hanvey's last senior game, as an injury he sustained forced him to retire. Later in the season an All Star XI including the likes of Manchester United's Arnie Muhren and Gordon McQueen played a testimonial game for him at Spotland against his previous club Huddersfield.

At this point Les Lawrence was sold to Third Division Burnley for £20,000. In his place Vic Halom signed Stockport striker Steve Taylor, who was now joining his ninth League club. A number of other players had already moved on, some like Keegan and English after very brief stays. The longer serving Farrell and Griffiths were transferred to Crewe and Port Vale respectively. A well known player who also had an extremely brief stay was former Fulham stalwart Les Strong, who managed just one game, while later in the term former Manchester City and England man Tony Towers played two half games. The shortest stay of all was by another ex-Oldham player Nick Sinclair, who signed non-contract forms for the Dale on a Tuesday and then did likewise for Tranmere in time to play for them on the Saturday.

The side gained only its second home win of the season by beating League leaders and eventual champions Chesterfield 3-1 with goals from Diamond, McMahon and Taylor, even though Diamond was later sent off, and Dale the won the next two home games as well.

Two more new faces in the Dale ranks after Christmas were Frank Gamble, another of Vic Halom's Barrow side, and former 'Spurs regular Don McAllister, who had a very long-awaited but brief debut.

On his return from playing in Portugal he had a trial at Spotland but then went off to Luton before reappearing at Rochdale. He then had to wait a month for a game, only to limp off with a pulled muscle after 10 minutes.

Eight League games brought six defeats, but even so the Dale in 21st spot were still well in touch with the sides above them and had games in hand. One player taking no further part in the proceedings was Shaun Reid. Having already served two suspensions in his brief career and been sent off in a reserve game, he was simultaneously dismissed and carried off in a 4-2 defeat at Scunthorpe when his crunching tackle did more damage to himself than to his opponent. In the Freight Rover Trophy (formerly Associate Members Cup), Preston's Kelly was sent off after only five minutes, possibly the quickest ever dismissal at Spotland.

Halom had already brought in Sheffield Wednesday goalkeeper Dave Redfern on loan and he next acquired two highly experienced defenders in the shape of Cardiff's Dave Grant and Phil Dwyer. 'Joe' Dwyer, the hero of the Cardiff fans, had compiled a record 471 Football League appearances for the South Wales club as well as winning 10 Welsh caps. Built like a prop forward, he elicited the comment *"I thought players like him were extinct"* from his new boss. Yet another new man was the ex-Burnley and Sparta Rotterdam defender Peter Robinson who signed up from Blyth Spartans immediately after representing England at semi-pro level.

A 2-2 draw at high-flying Bury was followed by a first ever win at Hereford thanks to goals from right back Paul Heaton and a home defender. This was Dale's first win south of Birmingham for nearly nine years. Dale extended their unbeaten run to six games before a couple of disappointing defeats dropped them back to fourth from the bottom. This was to be the last real scare though, as the Dale beat Hartlepool 4-3 at Spotland (being 4-0 up at one stage) and then won at Southend. Diamond scored a brace of penalties against Scunthorpe and, remarkably, the Iron's Cammack did likewise.

A goalless draw against champions Chesterfield at Saltergate guaranteed Dale's safety, but the excellent result was tempered by the tragic news of the disastrous Bradford City fire which was to have huge implications for all the smaller clubs. Indeed, Rochdale's final home game saw both the 'B' Stand and the Pearl Street End closed as a precaution. Skipper and player of the year Joe Cooke fittingly scored the injury time winner against Mansfield, and despite a 5-0 hammering at Aldershot, Rochdale finished 17th. After the disastrous start, they had picked up to such an extent that they gained 24 points in 14 games after the advent of Dwyer, Grant and Robinson.

The new manager got through a total of 38 players in all games to set a new peacetime record. Injuries certainly kept physio Steve Wandless busy; at one stage the manager held a training session with just three players.

Among several newcomers to League football were Ian Johnson from Curzon Ashton, who signed professional terms at the relatively advanced age of 24 (and quoted his boyhood hero as Les Chapman!), and John Pemberton from Chadderton who played just one game and subsequently signed professional for Crewe. The Cheshire club later sold him to Crystal Palace for £200,000 and he played for them in the FA Cup Final, later appearing in the Premier League for Leeds. At the other end of the scale of good fortune, Neil Ashworth, son of former Dale skipper Joe, made his debut in the 5-0 defeat at Aldershot at the end of the season and in his only two games the following term Dale lost 7-0 and 4-0.

Les Chapman, who played his 700th senior game during the season, was one of the players released, going to Stockport along with Bill Williams and subsequently becoming County's player-manager. Phil Dwyer retired and joined South Wales Police, while Peter Robinson, though only a non-contract player, cost Darlington £3000 when they signed him during the summer.

Dave Thompson had won the Sunday People award as the Fourth Division Player of the Season, but before the start of 1985-86 'Tommo' had gone on trial to Brighton and then on loan to Manchester United. On the other hand, Dave Redfern was re-signed and eventually joined the Dale permanently for £11,000, easily a record for a Rochdale goalkeeper. The well travelled John Seasman, who had also been on loan at Spotland, was signed from Chesterfield. The only completely new faces were former Oldham and Hereford stalwart Keith Hicks (who had been sent off when opposing Rochdale on more than one occasion and rejoiced in the nickname of 'Animal', after the Muppett character) plus Charlton's Ronnie Moore, who had twice been transferred for six figure fees during a long career. Coincidently Seasman and Moore had both started out with Tranmere in the early 'seventies and then played for Rotherham and Cardiff.

Former Dale skipper Brian Taylor, who had been playing for Cock & Magpie in the Rochdale Sunday League, was appointed reserve team player-coach. Shortly after the start of the season the club, for financial reasons, dispensed with the services of John King, the former (and future) Tranmere boss, who had been working as Halom's assistant. A new but well known face in the boardroom was that of comedian Tommy Cannon of 'Cannon and Ball' fame. (Partner Bobby Ball joined the board at Rochdale Hornets).

1985-86:
The pre-season Lancs Cup tournament was a shambles by any standards as Rochdale lost all three games, did not score a goal, and went down to their heaviest ever home defeat in a senior game, losing 7-0 to Burnley. Nevertheless they won their first League game 2-0 against Aldershot, though losing Hicks through injury. The Dale had already accumulated a long list of injuries and Hicks was replaced by their first ever 'hyphenated' player, Philip Martin-Chambers, a veteran of well over 400 Football League games for Barnsley.

The Dale went down 4-0 in the League Cup at Wrexham and lost another of their squad when Shaun Reid broke his leg.

Undaunted, they won at Torquay for the first time ever and thrashed Stockport 4-1, with goals from Moore, Seasman, Taylor and Heaton, to go to the top of Division 4 for the first time for many years. Sadly, the Dale's president and long time chairman Fred Ratcliffe died at the end of that week,

New Director Tommy Cannon watched by skipper Joe Cooke and other players.

but 'Mr Rochdale' did see his beloved club on top of the table again. Later in the season, Mrs Lillian Stoney, widow of Joe Stoney, for many years vice-chairman under Mr Ratcliffe, became the new club president.

After a draw at Port Vale, a victory over the other leading side Peterborough, Frank Gamble scoring twice, gave Dale their best ever start to a season and the top spot again. Hartlepool inflicted the Dale's first defeat and the bubble looked to have burst after four defeats in five games, Orient hammering the Dale 5-0 when Moore was sent off.

However a goal by Steve Taylor which beat Crewe, and gave the Dale six home wins in a row, set the No.8 on a remarkable run. He got two penalties in a victory over Wrexham but Dave Thompson broke his ankle in his first full game back, and the unfortunate Reid was still out, too, having broken his leg again after only five minutes of his comeback in the reserves.

Taylor then hit two late goals to beat Third Division Darlington in the FA Cup, his single strike beat Scunthorpe in the League, and he scored again at Mansfield, though hardly anyone saw it as the game was played in farcical conditions of thick fog. Visibility was so bad that the manager took off left winger Gamble by mistake: it was left back Grant who was injured but they couldn't see that far from the bench! In the cup again, Taylor's two goals at Scunthorpe earned Dale a replay and amid wild excitement among the Spotland faithful, Taylor and partner Moore won Dale a glamourous and lucrative third round tie against Manchester United, the leaders of Division 1.

The twin strikers got two apiece as Dale celebrated by thrashing Torquay 5-0 and the team stayed in contention in the promotion race with a draw at Halifax on Boxing Day, that man Taylor scoring again.

Though only 9th in the table, the Dale had two games in hand on most of their rivals and were only four points behind 4th placed Port Vale. Taylor had scored in the last seven games, the best run by a Dale player since Jimmy Wynn in the 'thirties, and had failed to score in only two of the last 14, totalling 21 for the season thus far.

Sadly, when the run came to an end, the wound was partly self inflicted. With his strikers functioning so well together, Vic Halom allowed Barry Diamond to go on loan to Les Chapman's Stockport County and somewhat over-confidently Rochdale allowed them to play him in the match between the sides. In a game destined to enter Rochdale folklore for all the wrong reasons, Diamond was instrumental in gaining two disputed penalties and was involved in an incident with his erstwhile colleague Joe Cooke which led to the Dale skipper being sent off. Diamond subsequently signed for Halifax (and according to a book by journalist and subsequent Dale director Richard Bott only reached the heights after giving up football, when he became a roofer!)

The Dale did beat Cambridge before the big cup game, but with all the preparations made, unbelievably the undersoil heating system at Old Trafford failed and the match had to be postponed twice. Even this delay could not dampen the enthusiasm of the Dale fans who helped boost the gate to a reported 38,500, the highest ever at a Rochdale game. Goals by Frank Stapleton in the first half and Mark Hughes late on gave United victory, but they had to work hard for it against 'Halom's Heroes'. The exact gate was later given as 40,223, the undercount being larger than many gates at Spotland. The Dale's share of the receipts was £34,592, almost exactly half those for a typical whole season at Spotland. Even though the club had run at a small profit in each of the three previous seasons - certainly making them one of the few clubs who could boast that - the cost of improvements to the ground in line with the new safety standards, and the loss of revenue from televised football (there had been none in the first half of the season as the League and the TV companies had not been able to agree a fee), meant that this windfall was quickly swallowed up by running costs.

The end of Dale's magnificent unbeaten home run after 19 games, at the hands of Hartlepool (McMahon being sent off into the bargain), spelled the end of Rochdale as realistic promotion challengers. Sheffield Wednesday's David Mossman was signed for £10,000 at the end of Jannuary.

The newcomer took the left wing slot from Gamble who soon moved on to Morecambe. However, Mossman himself was sold to Stockport after a mere 10 games. Other players to appear briefly on the Spotland stage included Newcastle defender Steve Carney, a hero of Blyth Spartans' amazing 1978 cup run, long-serving Brighton winger Tony Towner and Cardiff's Dave Tong, who played for four clubs during the season.

Cooke and Seasman had already been out for some time and the Dale's troubles were compounded when McMahon was put out of action with a knee injury. After taking an excellent away point off leaders Chester the Dale also suffered a spell of four successive defeats. (The home game against Chester earlier in the season had been postponed because of an outbreak of 'flu but, underlining the old adage of not believing everything you read in the press, several national papers the following morning reported a scoreline of Rochdale 1 Chester 0!).

Fortunately Dale's home form revived as they overcame Burnley 1-0 despite being down to 10 fit professionals. YTS lad Jason Smart came into the side and distinguished himself on his debut alongside Joe Cooke in the back four. However, Dale old boy Steve Johnson scored a last minute winner for Chester when the game really was played. Rochdale were thrashed 5-0 at struggling Southend and went down 4-1 at home to Orient, Steve Castle, who scored just one other goal that season, netting all four for the O's. This suddenly dropped Dale to 22nd and left them needing a point from the last game to escape the re-election zone. They managed it, not without some effort, with a 1-1 draw at Peterborough, full back Heaton netting the all important second half equaliser. Rochdale totalled 55 points but the second half of the season had brought in just 17 of them.

Despite this slump, Steve Taylor hit a post-war record 31 goals, 25 of them in the League to equal Reg Jenkins 1964-65 tally. This made Taylor easily the top scorer overall in Division 4 (though Southend's Cadette matched his 25 in the League) to win him the Adidas Golden Boot award for the division. He was joint third, behind Gary Lineker of Everton and Ian Rush of Liverpool in the whole Football League . Taylor's tally included eight penalties. Indeed, there was no shortage of spot kicks in Dale games, Rochdale being awarded 15 and conceding 18. Unsurprisingly, Taylor was named the player of the year, while a new award, the young player of the year, went to Ian McMahon.

Tragically, though, an apparently routine cartilage operation had given rise to complications and despite months at a rehabilitation centre McMahon had to retire at the age of 21. Moving into sports administration, he later reappeared at Spotland on Rochdale Hornets staff and was executive director at Doncaster Rovers during their bleak days in the late 1990's.

Besides being busy juggling his playing resources through a string of injury crises, manager Vic Halom had a busy season in other ways too. He made a return to playing in the reserves (including one match that they won 9-0, though he did have the help of most of the first team, who were getting some match practice), had his boots stolen and 'held to ransom', and even ended up washing the players' kit in his local launderette.

Twin strikers Ronnie Moore (left) and Steve Taylor.

Last gasp hero Paul Heaton was given a free transfer along with some of the younger members of the squad. In addition several of the more senior players, on relatively high wages, were placed on the transfer list in an attempt to save money. During the season there had been great debate on the future of the game and threats of a break-away 'super-league' by the big clubs if the League was not 'restructured'. *"On only one thing did they* [the factions] *agree; the Third and Fourth Division clubs should be cast adrift".*

The leading clubs instead voted themselves a bigger share of the cake at the expense of their lesser brethren. This would cost the Dale and their ilk £55,000 apiece in the coming season, roughly a quarter of their total income, but just what good their extra £55,000 would do to the leading clubs with annual turnovers - and debts - running into millions of pounds was never explained. Average attendances in the fourth division had actually risen in the past season, the Dale's by 40%. In addition, the League decided to 'update' the traditional promotion and relegation, by introducing play-offs (essentially a return to the long forgotten `test matches' of the 1890's) for some of the promotion places. Given their recent history, probably of more immediate import to Rochdale was the introduction of automatic dismissal to non-League obscurity for the side finishing bottom of Division 4 in future.

In what might be seen as a suitably Rochdalian move, funeral director David Kilpatrick stepped down as chairman and was replaced by comedian Tommy Cannon.

In the run up to the Manchester United game the previous Christmas, their famous director had enabled the Dale to reach a new audience when Cannon and Ball included 'patter' about the upcoming match in their pantomime routines! The Dale also gained some worldwide publicity during the summer when a large Rochdale flag was to be seen at many of the 1986 World Cup matches in Mexico.

The accent was more on departures than arrivals during the close season. Ronnie Moore rejoined his first club Tranmere Rovers before launching into a managerial career. Dave Thompson, easily the Dale's longest serving player, was transferred to Notts County for £10,000 plus former quarter of a million pound striker Alan Young. Skipper and crowd favourite Joe Cooke was sold to Wrexham for £11,000, but two new central defenders were signed up in the shape of the experienced John Bramhall from Bury and Simon Gibson, a £5000 buy from Preston. Also added to the squad were Neil Mills, a well known player in local soccer with Tim Bobbin, one of the best Sunday sides in the North West, and Peter Conning, a Liverpool University student who had recently played at Wembley with Altrincham.

1986-87:
The Dale kicked off with a draw at Blackburn in the Lancs Cup, their goalscorer being the former Liverpool 'super sub' David Fairclough, who had the odd game before signing for Belgian club Beveran. The League campaign opened with a draw against Crewe, the visitors equalising Young's early strike in the last minute. The unfortunate Keith Hicks was carried off in the first game of the season for the second year running, and this time the injury brought about his retirement. Jason Smart had played on the opening day as Gibson was suspended, Dale operating with three centre backs, and the youngster kept his place as Hicks' replacement.

The season's first victory came in the second leg of their Littlewoods Cup-tie against Burnley, when they won 3-1 with goals from Neil Mills and debutant Peter Shearer, who got two. Despite this, centre forward Shearer, an ex-Birmingham apprentice defender, played only one League game before being sold to Nuneaton for a small fee. Several years later he reappeared in the Football League with Bournemouth who sold him back to Birmingham for £250,000.

Northampton, at the start of an amazing run at the top of the table, inflicted the Dale's first defeat, while their first League win came at the sixth attempt against Colchester. In the Littlewoods Cup, a goal by Conning gave the Dale a shock draw away to First Division Watford, and Rochdale gave their more illustrious opponents a tough time at Spotland, too, before going down 2-1. Taylor's seventh goal of the season gained Dale a draw at Peterborough, despite them finishing with nine men and the home side 10, in a match likened by one spectator to a sponsored walk. Following a string of bids which had been turned down, Taylor was then sold to promotion hopefuls Preston for £20,000.

Taylor had scored 42 goals in 84 League games for the Dale, a phenomenal strike rate unmatched by any recent Rochdale player. While £20,000 profit on a 31 year old was obviously good financial business, it remained to be seen whether the side could survive the loss of a striker who had single-handedly scored half of their total goals over the last two years. The sale of such a crowd favourite caused the greatest furore among the Dale supporters for many years.

A prospective replacement had already arrived in the shape of £2000 signing from Carlisle Robbie Wakenshaw, who had played for England at youth level only the previous year. He and Young both scored when Dale beat Hereford, but the partnership was immediately disrupted by the suspension of both strikers as a result of their sendings off at Peterborough. Full back Ian Johnson scored at Nuneaton in the cup to become - the departed Taylor apart - the joint top scorer, with two. Winston White, on loan from Bury, figured in the Dale side and was opposed by his cousin Everton Carr who had played for the Dale under Jimmy Greenhoff. Officially, one of the Dale substitutes was John Seasman, though he was actually sitting in the stand with his leg in plaster; the club had forgotten that two substitutes were now required in the FA Cup.

The Dale lost at Aldershot to drop to 22nd in the table, and by the time Rochdale were 0-3 down at home to next-to-bottom Torquay, the crowd were chanting for the manager's head. Even though two goals from centre half John Bramhall and one from full back Dave Grant salvaged a point, the directors felt it necessary to request police protection for their own manager. Following a draw at Darlington in the Freight Rover, the Dale's 13th of the season in 25 games, of which only four had been won, the board decided to dispense with the services of Vic Halom. Reserve coach Brian Taylor, who also had the title of Stadium Manager, was given the job of temporary caretaker manager. He did not have much luck in his new role as Wrexham won easily at Spotland in the FA Cup.

An interesting name on the team sheet was the substitute, Simon Holden. A former associate schoolboy, he had played in a Lancashire Cup-tie a couple of years earlier at the age of 16 years 5 months, just 6 days older than Ted Oliver had been when becoming the youngest Dale first teamer. Holden had then drifted back into local football with Wheatsheaf. One humorous note on an otherwise depressing day for the Dale was the presentation to Tommy Cannon of a bucket, engraved 'Sorry', by Wrexham manager Dixie McNeil. The previous season McNeil had kicked the Dale trainer's bucket and smashed it, when a highly dubious goal had been given the Dale's way!

The following week the former Scottish international Eddie Gray M.B.E., who had spent two decades at Leeds as player and manager, was appointed the new Dale boss. His former assistant at Leeds, Jimmy Lumsden, took up the same position at Spotland.

A goal from non-contract player Micky Woods from Guiseley gave Gray a point from his first match, and Woods in fact managed three goals in only five games (to become the side's top scorer!) before departing for Colne Dynamos (playing for them in the FA Vase final the following year along with another ex-Dale striker Barry Diamond).

Lyndon Simmonds on his debut v Southend, February 1987 (notice the size of the 'crowd').

The Lincoln match in mid-March appeared to be a case of two points lost, rather than one gained when the visitors, then 13 points ahead of the Dale, equalised in the dying seconds after Simmonds had missed a penalty.

The Dale put themselves back in the hunt by winning at Hereford and then beat Peterborough 3-2, Simmonds with two and skipper Bramhall netting. Two draws took the Dale's unbeaten run to eight games, and their position to 22nd, but a crushing defeat at Crewe undid some of the good work and after both Preston and Wolves won at Spotland, the Dale descended once more to bottom spot. Next Dale had to visit high-flying Preston and their new plastic pitch (despite which, the game had had to be postponed earlier in the season). After defender Johnson gave them the lead, two strikes by substitute Wakenshaw - nicknamed 'Teddy Tint' by his teammates on account of his blond hair - sealed a remarkable 4-2 win in front of a crowd of over 10,000.

With the five man back line dispensed with, but no immediate improvement up front, the Dale sank to the foot of the table. However, on New Year's Day Rochdale travelled to Burnley and amazingly triumphed 3-0, Derek Parlane netting on his debut. Parlane, a team-mate of Eddie Gray's for Scotland, and later at Leeds, had won a dozen Scottish caps and almost as many Scottish League championship and cup winners medals during ten years at the top with Rangers.

Regular 'keeper Dave Redfern injured a hand in a 5-0 drubbing by runaway leaders Northampton, so YTS recruit Keith Welch was thrown in at the deep end for the Freight Rover game against Third Division Chesterfield, and the youngster proved his worth in an excellent 3-0 win. In the Northern Quarter Final, the Dale held Third Division leaders Middlesbrough to no score after extra time. For the first time, a Dale match had to be settled on penalties, and though Welch saved one, 'Boro won 4-3.

The next two League games were lost, again leaving Dale stranded at the bottom, as the struggle to avoid relegation to the G.M. Vauxhall Conference really started to hot up. Indeed, with Rochdale five points behind Torquay and nine adrift of Stockport in 22nd place, doom and gloom were prevalent. A certain amount of 'clutching at straws' was also evident, as the possibility of a merger forming Fulham Park Rangers or the bankruptcy of Halifax Town leaving the League a club short were discussed. The club shop reported record sales as 'ghouls' bought up souvenirs before the Dale went out of business, although a representative optimistically added *"but they are bound to catch on sometime that it's all a ploy to sell more things"*. With goalscoring at a premium, manager Gray went back to his old club Leeds to acquire reserve striker Lyndon Simmonds. A Wales under-21 international, "Taffy" had earlier been on loan to Swansea and scored a late winner when Dale visited the Vetch.

The next match had every appearance of being the make-or-break encounter, once mighty Burnley, League champions 25 years earlier but now sinking fast towards the foot of the table, visited Spotland in an attempt to stave off relegation to 'division five'. Rochdale never got going and the Burnley fans in the crowd of 5739 (which beat that for the cup-tie against First Division Watford) went home happy after a 2-0 win which looked to have saved them whilst, according to at least one newspaper, leaving the Dale *"needing a miracle"*. However, the Dale had been written off too many times in the past to take much notice of such pronouncements.

Rochdale had six games to play in the last two weeks, as the League insisted that all teams should finish their programmes on the appointed day, so that the play-offs could start on time; they actually played 12 games in the last month of the season. It looked as if vital points might elude the Dale when Cambridge visited Spotland, until Simmonds was unnecessarily held down in the box and the little striker converted the penalty. Another Simmonds penalty clinched a 2-0 win against Swansea, who had refused to fulfil the fixture earlier in the season, despite the League ordering them to play, as illness and injury had left them only nine or 10 fit players (hardly an unusual occurrence for the Dale and some of their ilk).

Rochdale then visited Torquay, who headed them only on goal difference, but blew their chance of getting clear by losing 2-1. Two days later Halifax visited Spotland and the trap door looked to be opening when Halifax went into a 2-1 lead in the second half. However, in a dramatic finale, big John Bramhall powered in his second brace of the season to lead a rejuvenated Dale to a sensational 5-3 victory. Another two days on and it was Stockport's turn to visit Spotland. With a massive home crowd of almost 5000 rallying behind them, the Dale made heavy weather of it, even to the extent of Simmonds having a penalty saved, before two priceless strikes by Parlane and Simmonds in the space of three minutes. Even then, nerves nearly undid them and County pulled one back with 13 minutes left, but Dale hung on to take the three points that guaranteed survival. The tension had got to the supporters just as much as the team, but at the end the players were chaired off the pitch to chants of *"staying up, staying up"* in scenes the like of which had not been seen at Spotland since promotion was gained 18 years before.

The final weekend of the season was dominated by the battle to avoid the catastrophe that the Dale had just averted. Burnley - who had not endeared themselves to their fellow strugglers by asking the Football League to make an exception on their behalf should they finish bottom, on the grounds that they had been founder-members of the League - managed a desperate final victory in front of 15,000 fans, while Torquay grabbed a last gasp equaliser in the time added on for a dog biting one of their players, so it was Lincoln who occupied bottom spot when the curtain came down on the Fourth Division campaign. The Dale were beaten by Scunthorpe in a now unimportant fixture (most of the fans spending more time listening to the other games on their radios than watching this one) and ended the season in 21st place but with a fairly respectable 50 points, only five fewer than the previous term when they had topped the table for a while.

The massively dependable John Bramhall was an everpresent at centre half and was amazingly also the side's joint top scorer with 10 goals, nine of them in the League. At one point he netted eight in 24 games, a rate that most strikers would settle for. He twice scored two goals in a game, the first time that a Dale centre half had bagged even one brace since that stalwart of earlier times David Parkes back in 1924. Not surprisingly Bramhall was the supporters' player of the year, while Jason Smart, who had celebrated his 18th birthday by winning the 'young player of the month' award for the North West in February, also won the Dale's young player of the year. The on-loan Lyndon Simmonds, the inspiration behind the late run, was the other top scorer with 10 goals in only 22 Football League games.

Grant, Conning and Johnson were freed, leaving Shaun Reid as by far the longest serving member of the staff, only four of whom had been at Spotland more than a year. Wakenshaw was sold to Crewe for £3000.

Eddie Gray and Jimmy Lumsden signed two year contracts with the club during the summer of 1987 and the Dale board, under Tommy Cannon, allowed Gray to speculate in the transfer market to an extent unheard of in recent years. (Cannon had also offered to put £50,000 into a school of excellence for young players). In addition to signing Simmonds permanently, Gray bought Middlesbrough reserve midfielder Ronnie Coyle and signed Bolton (and ex-Leeds) winger Mark Gavin for a new club record £20,000.

1987-88:
The new season saw the allowance of two substitutes in League games for the first time. Finding 12 players had often been hard enough for Dale, now they needed 13! With Alan Young ruled out with a further recurrence of his knee injury, which this time ended his career (he became manager of Shepshed Charterhouse), Rochdale's whole first team squad amounted to only 15 players.

Rochdale managed a goalless draw at Hereford to open the campaign, and came back from a goal down to beat Tranmere in the Littlewoods Cup, despite Simmonds being sent off. A 2-1 win at Halifax moved them into the top six but they lost to a goal scored after only 45 seconds at Scunthorpe. After a 5-0 thrashing by the season's surprise packet, Torquay, the Dale plunged back to more familiar territory, with only Newport below them. At least none of the Dale's long suffering fans had to watch the drubbing at Plainmoor, as Torquay had joined the ranks of those clubs who had banned all away supporters. Elsewhere, the Government, via the Football League, had imposed a 50% membership scheme at all grounds in an attempt to combat hooliganism, much to the disgust of many Spotland regulars.

Rochdale were without the experienced Bramhall and Parlane at Exeter and replaced them with Zac Hughes, their youngest ever first team player at 16 years and three months, and Mark Hunt, who netted the equaliser in what turned out to be his only full game in the League. An odd note was the booking of Dale trainer Trevor Jones -'Jones the sponge' - for 'illegally' treating the injured Welch. In the Littlewoods Cup, Rochdale surprised their First Division visitors Wimbledon - themselves used to putting one over their supposed betters in the top flight - by gaining a 1-1 draw. Depressingly, though, the visit of a high flying, if reputedly unglamourous, First Division side could attract only 2801 fans to Spotland.

As if to emphasise the Dale's struggle for support, local rivals Burnley brought enough followers to boost the next Spotland gate for an ordinary League match to almost 4500. Goals from old hands Bramhall and Parlane gave the Dale the points, but they lost star winger Gavin to a cynical foul. Struggling Carlisle were the next visitors but the Dale sank to new depths of ineptitude by losing at home to nine men after the Cumbrians had two men sent off and seven booked in a serious of unsavoury incidents.

Rochdale put up a far better show in the second leg against Wimbledon, only going down 2-1 after debutant ex-Burnley striker Derrick Parker had given them the lead. Dale were annihilated 6-1 by Tranmere, one of the two sides below them in the League and scorers of just five goals in their previous 10 games, but even this paled into insignificance when Leyton Orient, always a thorn in the Dale's flesh, totally overran them to record a horrific 8-0 scoreline - and it could easily have been worse but for the intervention of the woodwork and the referee. This matched Rochdale's worst ever League defeats from the 1930's.

John Bramhall in action versus Burnley, Dean Walling against Rotherham.

With just one point from nine League games, the Dale might have been dead and buried but for the failings of others, primarily Newport and Tranmere, which meant they were still only one point behind at the foot of the table. Not surprisingly there were rumblings of discontent among the fans and in the local press, with supporters calling for the resignation of the manager and some action from the board. The playing situation was, indeed, far worse, with 12 defeats in 18 League games, than at the same stage the previous season when Vic Halom was sacked after six defeats in 16 games. However, it was an apparently trivial turn of events in the background which was to cause the shake-up.

Earlier in the season two shareholders, including local solicitor Peter Riley, had requested an Extraordinary General Meeting of Rochdale A.F.C. Ltd, to propose that a clause be inserted into the club's Articles of Association to the effect that the board could not sell, lease or charge (i.e. put forward as security for a loan) the ground at Spotland without the consent of a full shareholders meeting. As for the board itself, all of the earlier members had resigned at the start of the season for various reasons, and the numbers had been made up by, amongst others, the chairman's wife and the club secretary. The board said that they wished the word *"charge"* to be removed but otherwise had no objection to the proposal.

However, at the E.G.M. the proposal was carried as it stood and out of the blue, chairman Tommy Cannon and the board announced that they took this as a vote of no confidence, and all bar two of them resigned. Mr Graham Morris, the club's former financial director, took over the meeting and stated that, contrary to earlier assurances from the board, in his professional opinion the company was insolvent.

The value of the ground, their major asset, did not cover their debts. An emergency committee was formed from other former directors from various eras, plus the Supporters Club vice-chairman Brian Clough, and the two remaining members of the previous board. Former Bury chairman Mr Ron Clarke took over as chairman but both he and the other remaining director resigned shortly afterwards. It later transpired that Clarke and four of the other directors had not owned a single share in the club at the time of the 'coup'. Turning back the clock, Messrs. Lord, Brierley, Hilton, Walkden, Dronsfield, Kilpatrick and Morris were voted back on to the board under the chairmanship of Mr Jim Marsh. Coincidentally, in the week which saw some of his old boardroom colleagues back in charge at Spotland, the former social club was renamed the Ratcliffe Arms after the late Fred Ratcliffe.

Accountants were called in to ascertain the extent of the financial crisis and supporters were warned that unless drastic action was taken the club could fold in a matter of weeks. Accumulated debts were found to total £245,000, over £150,000 having been lost in the last 18 months. The new board reported that various rescue packages were being perused, one possibility being that Rochdale Hornets might buy and share Spotland on completion of the planned multi-million pound sale of the Athletic Grounds.

On a lighter note, man of the moment (and many clubs) Robert Maxwell was rumoured to have been seen around the ground. The board itself demonstrated the sense of humour required for the situation (no doubt also useful in his previous career as a funeral director), when Mr. Kilpatrick was quoted as saying that they were looking for a *"knight in shining armour, two days away from going into a mental hospital, but with £2 million in his back pocket"*.

Remarkably, amidst this mayhem, the players came up trumps with a 2-1 win at Cambridge thanks to goals from Simmonds and full back Peter Hampton, but the financial constraints imposed by the new board in the cause of survival meant that Hampton and Derek Parlane, who were on monthly contracts, had to be released. Assistant manager Jimmy Lumsden and physio Steve Wanless were made redundant, and expensive buy Mark Gavin was placed on offer to the highest bidder.

Simon Holden and former Leeds junior Dean Walling were brought in for their first full League games of the season and another YTS lad, David Mycock, for his second (his debut had been the debacle at Orient), to join another recent signing from Leeds, Lee Warren, in a hugely inexperienced side. Eight of the thirteen man squad were teenagers, but they put up Dale's best League perf-

At this point Rochdale had picked up 34 points from the last 23 games, virtually promotion form (indeed Swansea eventually went up with 70 points from 46 games).

The Dale did not in fact maintain this form, being narrowly beaten in four of the last five games. The one exception was at Newport when a goal from substitute Walling was enough

ormance of the season to win 2-1 at Wrexham. The next game was a dog-eat-dog affair against bottom placed Newport which the Dale youngsters comfortably won 3-0, to suddenly stretch the gap between themselves and the South Wales side to 10 points.

Five draws kept the Dale clear of trouble while Coyle was sold to Raith Rovers for £10,000 and Gavin to Hearts for £30,000. Remarkably enough, only one Dale player had moved to a Scottish League club since the 'fifties, but now three had done so in a couple of months, following Parlane's move to Airdrie. Added to the squad was non-contract player Carl Harris, a Welsh international in his days at Leeds.

The enforced changes certainly did no harm, with three wins in the next four games, that against Scunthorpe courtesy of two own goals, and with Newport having hit their own financial crisis and put all their senior players up for sale, barring disasters/miracles (depending on your point of view), this ended any worries of the Dale dropping into the Conference. The pies were still going strong, too, an article in the Independent noting that Spotland *"is deservedly renowned as the Maxim's of al fresco pie consumption"*.

With four of the remaining seniors injured or suspended, the Dale had to field their youngest ever side at Carlisle. With seven past or present YTS's in the squad, including debutant Stewart Mellish (who was later voted young player of the year), the average age of the side - which contained nine teenagers - was just pushed past 20 by the presence of 'grandad' Brian Stanton, aged 32 (the next oldest was skipper, and senior player of the year, Geoff Lomax at 23). The Dale stunned promotion hopefuls Swansea by winning 3-0 at the Vetch, two goals coming from former Swan Lyndon Simmons and the third from veteran centre forward Ernie Moss, on loan from Scarborough. The 39 year old Moss had been a pro before most of his teammates were born, having scored nearly 250 goals over the past 20 seasons.

to drive the final nail into County's coffin on their way out of the League. Remarkably this was the 37th time that Walling had started a match on the bench. Rochdale won more games away than at home, and in fact gained their most away wins for 15 years. They were especially successful in Wales; for the first (and last) time all four of the Principality's major sides were in Division 4 and the Dale beat three of them.

Off the field, the appointment of former United goalkeeper Alex Stepney as commercial manager had been shortlived, but a remarkable number of money-making schemes were thought up to help keep the Dale afloat. These included a sponsored 'paint-in' by local soccer journalist and painter Jack Hamil, the auctioning of some of his works by Rochdale MP Cyril Smith, collections round the ground on matchdays and an inventive sponsorship scheme for square yards of the Spotland pitch (though what the pitch had to do to earn its money was not clear!). Spotland was also used for the Lancashire Sunday Cup Final (on a Tuesday), which was won by local side Tim Bobbin with four ex-Dale men, Chris Shyne, Neil Mills, Bobby Finc and Charlie Simpson in their team.

The most surprising name on the list of players not retained at the end of the season was John Bramhall (who had also had the misfortune to break his ankle in the season's final game). The board also announced that John Seasman, whom Gray had lined up as player-coach, would have to be released as an economy measure. This left just eight professionals, added to when Gray persuaded Carl Harris to sign a full contract and arranged the transfers of two more of his former Leeds juniors, Steve O'Shaughnessy (from Bradford City) and Andy Armitage. However in June Eddie Gray accepted an offer of the manager's job at Hull City and Dale started the familiar process of looking for a new occupant for the 'hot seat'. Another - prospectively even more far reaching - move for the future came with the announcement that the Hornets would share Spotland with the Dale the following year.

ONE WORD OF ENCOURAGEMENT 1988 - 1999

~ CHAPTER 10 ~

After the usual variety of names had been bandied about, the Club managed to upstage their supporters, who thought they had seen all possible breeds of manager in recent years, by appointing a former Uruguayan youth international who had played professionally in Spain before coaching in the UK - Danny Bergara. The new boss quipped that he knew lots of people in football but Ruud Gullit (Holland's star in the recent European Championships) had declined an offer to come to Rochdale!

Two who did arrive, just a couple of days later, were Chris Beaumont and Simon Copeland who had been juniors at Sheffield United under Bergara. They were soon joined by David Frain and Mark Smith, both of whom also had Bramhall Lane connections, and experienced Bolton centre half Dave Sutton.

Though the Dale were without Simmonds through an injury which turned out to be much more serious than originally thought, pre-season games went well for once, with two wins and a draw (all against Third Division opponents) in the Lancashire Cup. Unfortunately, though, Dale - playing once more in their old blue and white colours - were pipped for a place in the final by Bolton after a penalty shoot out.

This promising beginning was followed, almost inevitably, by a failure to win any of the first five 'serious' games, while Dale also lost the services of Lee Warren, who followed Gray to Hull for £20,000 and jinxed youngster Zac Hughes, carried off in his first game of the season. Victory finally came in the home League game against Exeter, Frain netting the winner in a game watched by just 1216 fans, and to completely reverse the form book Dale won five in a row to move from 21st to 3rd place in the table.

Dale's gallop was halted at the Shay when Halifax won 4-1, but victory over Scunthorpe and a breathtaking 4-4 draw at Hereford might have signalled a continuation of the good form, had not Dale then let bottom side Darlington grab an injury time equaliser at Spotland. In the Cup, Dale had drawn at Huddersfield, but lost the replay 4-3. This, on top of the 4-4 and no less than three 3-3 draws led Bergara to reconsider his side's all out attacking "South American" style.

Dale's defence did indeed improve for a while, but the attack fizzled out completely. O'Shaughnessy's goal against bottom club Colchester was the only one in seven games and Dale managed just two draws in 10 games as Bergara rang the changes.

Two permanent changes were the departures of Shaun Reid to York for £32,500 and Mark Smith to Huddersfield for £50,000. Over 10,000 fans saw Dale's defeat at struggling Carlisle, though it should be said that the sale of tickets for a forthcoming cup-tie against Liverpool may have been the major attraction!

Even a Frain inspired victory over Burnley in front of the best League gate at Spotland since 1973-74, of 5799, could not stop the rot, though the side did show its mettle in a draw against the odds at Doncaster; Frain was sent off for disputing the penalty that gave Rovers the lead and new man Neil Edmunds followed him for a comment to the referee while celebrating the equaliser.

Apparently at the Board's insistence, new players were drafted in, ranging from the 16 year old Carl Alford, later a top non-League striker, to former Dale hero Steve Taylor, who was re-signed from Burnley. With Dave Sutton forced to quit through injury, Bergara also signed the experienced Malcolm Brown from Huddersfield and former Bolton stalwart Paul Jones from Galway. Coincidentally both had at one time been defensive partners of Sutton. One who didn't arrive was former Argentinian 'golden boy' Alex Sabella who had been with Bergara at Sheffield United. Off the field, former Celtic and Barnsley star Ronnie Glavin, who had arrived as reserve team player-coach, left again in March and was replaced by Jimmy Robson who returned to Spotland from Huddersfield.

It was March 11th before Dale registered their second win in 18 attempts since November, and gave the fans the chance to wave their new inflatable penguins - these were unkindly said to be ideal for the Dale as they were weak on the wings and useless in the air! However, a victory over promotion contenders Tranmere was followed by a priceless victory over next to bottom Darlington who were eventually relegated. Paul Jones scored both goals versus Scarborough to make it three wins in a row since his arrival.

The following week Stockport County sacked their manager Asa Hartford, and Danny Bergara, a friend of the County chairman, was immediately linked with the job. A few days later Bergara quit to take over at Edgeley Park and Dave Sutton was given the caretaker's job at Spotland until the arrival of the next incumbent, former Dale player and Bradford City manager Terry Dolan. Dolan's stewardship started on the right note with a 2-1 win over Cambridge, and in the last eight games of the season Dale at least broke even with two wins, four draws and two defeats.

A roller coaster season saw them end in 18th place with 53 points. Steve Taylor scored his 157th, and unfortunately last, League goal in the end of season game at Wrexham, while Paul Jones passed 600 League appearances. Dave Frain, alias "Roy of the Rovers", was the Player of the Year. He had also won three of the monthly awards, one of which had brought the wry comment from director David Walkden that February had been a bad month, but Dale did win two corners and Frain took them both, so he must get the award.

Terry Dolan takes charge in April 1989.

One time Leeds player Tony Brown, whose career had been threatened by injury, signed on a weekly contract.

1989-90:
Dale started the 1989-90 Football League season in good heart with a 2-1 win over now regular opponents Burnley in front of a 5,500 crowd. With 10 new men in the side, they also beat Third Division neighbours Bolton in the first leg of their League cup-tie and went second in the League by winning at Scunthorpe. They then fell apart in a big way, losing 5-1 in the second leg at Bolton and 3-0 at home to Wrexham, their first defeat at Spotland for seven months.

Only two players, Edmunds and Taylor were contracted for the following term. Seven others were offered terms but everyone else was released, so a busy close season was in prospect. Indeed, as it turned out only four of the seniors would appear in Dale colours again. Dave Sutton became the club physio and first team trainer, while Terry Dolan's former Bradford assistants Jeff Lee and Bernard Ellison joined him at Spotland. Chairman Jim Marsh stepped down and was replaced by David Kilpatrick for his second spell in charge. The club was able to report that the crippling debts of a couple of years ago had been whittled down to £100,000. A profit of £124,871 had been made in the year to May 1989.

Despite a rumoured agreement that Danny Bergara would not 'poach' any of his former Dale squad, it was no real surprise when Dave Frain, Chris Beaumont and Malcolm Brown turned down the terms offered by Rochdale and signed for Stockport (as did Paul Jones). Jason Smart also decided on a move, and signed for Crewe. Tribunal set fees for Frain, Smart and Beaumont brought in over £100,000 for players who had cost the Dale nothing. On the debit side former top scorer Lyndon Simmonds who had not played for a year was forced to retire through injury, and Steve Taylor soon had to give up too.

Best known of the 14 incoming (free) transfers were veteran ex-Everton midfielder Alan Ainscow and Darlington forward Kevin Stonehouse who, like Ainscow, numbered Blackpool and Blackburn among his previous clubs. Others with a fair amount of experience, mainly in the lower leagues, included Crewe full back Wayne Goodison, Torquay centre half Dave Cole, and ex-Wolves midfielder Micky Holmes. Two lesser known players who would earn regular first team places were Huddersfield midfield man Peter Ward and Manchester City reserve defender Wilie Burns, a Scottish Youth International and nephew of former Manchester United and Scotland star Francis Burns.

The injury jinx also struck new left back Vinnie Chapman who was injured in each of his first three games - and put through his own goal on his fourth (Chapman won Dale's young player of the year award in 1991 before being forced to retire injured). Dale's second home win did not come until mid-October when they defeated Exeter (who went on to win the championship). The Liverpool and Rangers managers Dalgleish and Souness were among the meagre crowd of 1337. Dale's inexperienced attack had by now been pepped up by the signing of Steve Elliott from Bury for £10,000 and he was soon joined by the old Dale favourite Steve Johnson, back from a spell in Sweden. The manager also borrowed two of his former Bradford City players, Jimmy Graham (brother of Scottish international Arthur) and Lee Duxbury.

Dale enjoyed, if that is the right word, an incredible switchback of results, alternating winning and losing games regardless of the level of the opposition. Fortunately the first round of the FA Cup came up on a winning week and Dale were able to record a victory at Anfield, though it was local non-Leaguers Marine not the mighty Liverpool who were dispatched 1-0. Remarkably, one of the Marine side, Peter Smith, had played for them in the previous meeting between the sides 15 years earlier.

Dale also won away League games at Hereford and Cambridge, youngster Jason Dawson coming off the bench to score a debut goal at the Abbey Stadium. Dale managed to get off the roller coaster and win the next home game too, "master-blaster" O'Shaughnessy thundering in the last of three goals which saw off Lincoln in the second round of the cup. Dale then drew one of the remaining non-League sides, Whitley Bay, whose manager Bobby Graham was unwise enough to be quoted as saying that getting Dale was a "Micky Mouse draw".

Though he quickly retracted his remark, Dale's supporters were quick to latch on to it, hoping it would act as a similar spur to Noel Cantwell's infamous *"Rochdale, where's that?"* They also entered in to the spirit of the thing on matchday, several fans turning up dressed as Micky or Minnie. The mice went home happy, too, thanks to a strike by Steve Johnson - described on the radio by the ever picturesque Stuart Hall as a *"brick outhouse of a centre forward"*. The normally dour Terry Dolan also joined in the merriment, remarking that his opposite number *"must be feeling a bit cheesed off"*.

Dale also beat Lincoln in the League (Dolan keeping quiet about Ward's suspension and Elliott's broken toe to confuse the self proclaimed master strategist Colin Murphy), but defeat by the Dale 'old boys' at Stockport was no surprise, even if the winning goal did come from the unlikeliest of them, full back Malcolm Brown netting from 40 yards.

In January Dale claimed a victory still recalled with great relish by their supporters, when they overcame now deadly rivals Burnley 1-0, despite the sending off of O'Shaughnessy and Burns. When 'Shosh' was dismissed, a local radio commentator, perhaps understandably getting his sports mixed, reported that Dale were down to 12 men, while Dolan was apparently congratulated by the police for showing commendable calm. One of the directors later commented that *"we went into one of the lounges at Turf Moor after the match to see our goal on TV, but the Burnley people switched channels and watched Daffy Duck. I think they were a bit upset"*. (Burnley supporters, on the other hand, claimed never to see the Dale as real rivals, as traditionally they were used to being two or three divisions higher).

The best crowd for over 10 years, 9048, saw Dale record a fourth straight win by demolishing Third Division Northampton 3-0, with goals from O'Shaughnessy, Dawson and a Goodison penalty. This put them in the last 16 of the Cup for the first time in their history. The fifth round saw Dale visit First Division Crystal Palace, and the squad toned up for the game by spending a couple of days at the hotel used by England when preparing for games at Wembley. The game ended 1-0 to Palace, but only after a stunning performance by 'keeper Keith Welch which earned him star billing on Match of the Day, and a last gasp save by actual £1m goalkeeper Nigel Martyn to deny Peter Ward an equaliser.

League form had been somewhat mixed again, though Welch equalled a club record by keeping five consecutive clean sheets, but after the Palace game Dale strung together three more wins, making it six in the last nine games. The best was a victory at leaders Carlisle when substitute Dean Walling netted with his first touch to win Dale the Barclays 'performance of the week' award. This meant that Dale were now only five points behind the side in third spot, and with games in hand, but they found it hard to make up any further ground.

Dale supporters on their way to Crystal Palace for the Cup-tie.

For instance they ran into leaders Exeter in rampant mood and lost 5-0, Exeter's centre back McNichol scoring three. A win at Cambridge - in what would have been a rehearsal for a unique all Fourth Division FA Cup quarter final if only Dale could have overcome Palace - was then followed, as for most of the season, by a defeat to struggling Halifax.

As the season reached its close, they did win three games out of five - and it would have been four, but for an injury time equaliser by Frain in the fans' 'grudge match' against Stockport. The FA later investigated an alleged 'incident' between Peter Ward and former Dale man Bill Williams in the players' tunnel after the game. This kept their outside play-off hopes alive until the penultimate game when Doncaster trounced them 4-0. They did at least end on a high note with a 5-2 victory over Hereford. Andy Milner, a mid-season £20,000 buy from Manchester City, netted three, the Dale's first hat-trick for eight years, and midfielder come defender O'Shaughnessy got two. Remarkably 'Shosh' ended as top scorer with 10.

Despite missing out on any tangible reward - they missed the play-offs by five points - Dale managed a top half finish (12th) for the first time for 20 years. A local joke ran: *"I was 10 years old before I realised the club's name wasn't Lowly Rochdale"*. The team won nine away games, the most in the division, and their own best since 1946-47, and of course they had their best FA Cup run ever. Player of the year Keith Welch was an everpresent for the third year running and had now appeared in a remarkable run of 198 straight games since his debut. Most of the squad were retained, only Ainscow, Stonehouse and Walling - a substitute no less than 68 times in his three seasons with the club - plus some young reserves being released (though Steve Johnson left for Limerick at the start of the next campaign). After spells in Canada and in non-League football, Walling came good - as a central defender - with Carlisle when they won the Third Division championship and won international caps for St. Kitts. One of the reserves, Chris Lucketti, who had managed one League game the previous year but had been troubled by injury since, later made a big impression playing for Bury and Huddersfield.

Another promising youngster, Steve Milligan, unfortunately broke a leg while on holiday over the summer and didn't play again in the Football League. Dale's Reserves had had one of their most successful seasons for years, finishing 5th in the Lancashire League, despite sometimes running up against the likes of England skipper Bryan Robson having a run out after injury for Manchester United 'A'. For the following term they moved up to the higher class of the Midland League.

Apart from the cup-ties and Lancashire derby matches, crowds had remained low, the majority failing to reach 2000. Only 787 turned up for a Leyland-Daf Trophy game against Chester the week before Rochdale Hornets attracted 8150 to Spotland to watch the Boxing Day game against Oldham. Nevertheless a profit of £894 accrued for the year to May 1990, the cup-tie income and outgoing transfers just outweighing the increasing wage bills. During the season it was finally agreed that a Stadium Company would be formed, Dale receiving £400,000 from Hornets who would, like Dale, have a 45% stake in the stadium, the local council holding the other 10%. Grounds were also in the news following the Taylor report on the Hillsborough disaster; after the good news that the Government would not enforce 100% membership schemes and ID cards at all League grounds came the bad news for small clubs that all stadia would have to become all seated by 1999.

Terry Dolan's 1990 summer shopping was mainly restricted to a raid on his former club, as he acquired Jimmy Graham for £15,000 (Bradford had asked £150,000), Peter Costello for £10,000, Chris Lee (son of assistant manager Jeff) and junior Paul Butler. A familiar face back in the ranks was

Peter Ward

Mark Hilditch after seven years away. New reserve goalkeeper was Gareth Gray whose penalty save in his only senior game for Bolton had cost Dale a place in the Lancashire Cup Final two years earlier. Another change was in the club's sponsors, the side now appearing wearing the name of 'A. & M. Smith Metals' on their shirts.

1990-91:
The first League game provided one of Rochdale's best ever openings to a season when they demolished Aldershot 4-0. The Shots, threatened by a winding-up order throughout the summer, were just glad to have survived to play the match. Dale's previous 4-0 win had been in 1981-82 when Dolan was playing and Hilditch scored, as he did now. Despite this start only 1400 fans turned up for the next game when Dale repeated the same scoreline in the Rumbelows League Cup-tie against Scarborough.

O'Shaughnessy netted one goal with a 45 yard free-kick; well worthy of his sponsors "The Exocet Boot Company". A 3-3 draw in the second leg meant that after 10 days of the season nine different players had already got on the scoresheet.

A goalless draw at Blackpool and a rather fortunate 1-0 victory over Stockport left Dale as the only League side in England or Scotland yet to concede a goal, but they were brought down to earth by early leaders Doncaster. Dale even missed the same penalty three times, Rovers' Crighton saving twice from O'Shaughnessy, and after each had been ordered to be retaken, he kept out the third attempt by Goodison.

In the Rumbelows Cup, Dale held First Division Southampton to one goal until the last 15 minutes, before future superstars Shearer and Le Tissier finally escaped the shackles and ran in four more. A hat-trick from debutant Banger in the second leg resulted in an undeservedly embarrassing 8-0 aggregate).

Saints had fielded their Soviet international Gotsmanov, and Dale's game against Walsall continued the cosmopolitan theme with the first appearance of a Cameroonian international at Spotland - Charlie Ntamark, well known for his TV appearances with "Saint and Greavsie" during the World Cup. This game also saw a remarkably short, but eventful, contribution from the 16 year old substitute Paul Butler. He was on the field just 30 seconds before giving away a penalty and being concussed at the same time - without ever having touched the ball! Walsall later had a man sent off and Dale eventually won 3-2 thanks to a late penalty converted by Micky Holmes.

An excellent run of away results pushed Dale up to second in the table, but a chance for even greater glory went begging when Holmes this time had his last minute penalty saved, to leave the top of the table battle with Torquay locked at 0-0. Injuries had continued to bite deeply into the squad and despite two loan signings Dolan had only six fit players in training at the end of October.

An own goal and another missed penalty in successive League games cost Dale vital points and in the FA Cup, Dale led Scunthorpe by Costello goals in both games before going out in extra time of the replay. In fact Dale went eight games without a win before beating Wrexham in the League and Carlisle in the Leyland Daf Trophy. The latter was the first match missed by Keith Welch since his debut, a run of 214 League and cup games.

Despite the signing of the vastly experienced midfield man Steve Doyle from Hull for £10,000, the patchy form continued into the New Year. Even so, a victory over Blackpool in mid-January edged Rochdale back into a play-off position. Coincidentally, Blackpool's commercial manager Stephen Walmsley had taken over Dale's commercial office three days earlier. Jason Dawson then bagged both goals in a draw at Aldershot, though the game was mostly notable for the Shots ending with only nine men.

By now, though, the fans had become increasingly antagonistic to Terry Dolan's team selections and tactics, particularly the continued inclusion of Chris Lee at the expense of Micky Holmes, who was eventually sold to Torquay for £10,000. Poor Lee was subjected to probably a greater barrage of criticism than any other Dale player of around that period, much of it the result of accusations of nepotism on the part of his father, the assistant manager. Hull had just sacked their manager, but were refused permission to approach Dolan by the Rochdale board. Nevertheless, Dolan, Lee and youth organiser Bernard Ellison all resigned from their posts at Spotland and were quickly installed at Boothferry Park. The board responded by appointing physio Dave Sutton as caretaker manager and reporting Hull for 'poaching'.

Sutton's reign started in sensational fashion when, with the Dale looking the more likely winners, the referee adjudged Keith Welch's challenge on a Hereford player to be a professional foul and sent him off, the home side taking the lead from the resulting spot kick despite stand-in Goodison's brave effort. Chris Lee, incidentally, was dropped to sub for Sutton's first game and was soon transferred to Scarborough where he continued as a Fourth Division regular.

It was Peter Costello who earned Sutton his first win as a manager, and the Dale their only victory in 10 games, with both goals against Scunthorpe. The new boss nearly gave his players and the crowd heart failure, though, when he accidentally held up the board with No.1 on it, rather than 7, when he wanted to make a substitution. Costello also netted an extraordinarily late equaliser against Northampton in a game which did not end until nearly 5 o'clock. The club later refused to give the referee a mark at all for his performance. Manager Sutton was prone to comments about officials, such as *"if we laid all the good referees we've had this season end to end, starting at the bottom of Spotland Road, nobody would have noticed him."*

On transfer deadline day Costello was sold to Peterborough for £30,000, though eccentric Posh boss, Barry Fry then hardly used him or the four other players he signed the same day.

A determined Andy Milner.

Andy Milner, meanwhile, turned down a £50,000 move to West Brom. Coming in was Oldham's Steve Morgan who scored both goals in the 2-0 win at York on his debut. Dale also won their next away game at Maidstone (or more exactly Dartford, where the 'Stones groundshared'), thanks to a late goal set up by one substitute, Jon Hill, and scored by the other, Andy Milner

Indeed, by the time Hill came on to get the first goal of his senior career to secure the double over York, Rochdale had actually resurrected an outside chance of a play-off place, but then they lost their way again, scoring in only two of the last six games of the season to finish 12th again. Most of the action was actually on the terraces - after Burnley had insisted that their allocation of tickets for the end of season derby was far too small, three sides of Spotland were assigned to visiting fans, and Daleites staged a protest sit-in about the decision to give Burnley fans the Sandy Lane End. Further discussions returned 'their' end to Dale fans and allowed for an 11,000 capacity. In the end the crowd was 7344, twice the previous best of the season (for the cup-tie with First Division Southampton).

Welch and Ward won player of the year awards, the former the 'official' J. W. Lees one and Ward the supporters club version. In addition Welch, together with old boys Brown and Frain over at Stockport, was voted into the PFA Division 4 team of the year. At a more elevated level, Crystal Palace's Geoff Thomas, to whom Rochdale had been unable to offer a full time contract due to lack of money, back in Les Chapman's time, became the first Dale product to win an England cap for nearly 70 years.

Besides the release of eight of the senior squad, Peter Ward was transferred to Stockport County for £30,000 plus Mark Payne and Steve O'Shaughnessy went to Exeter for £10,000. The deal that had long been expected finally went through when Keith Welch, a target for scouts from the top clubs for the past couple of seasons signed for Bristol City, a tribunal eventually setting a fee of £200,000, easily the Dale record. The same day, the incoming transfer record was also smashed, with Scunthorpe's top scorer Andy Flounders costing Dale £80,000. Other major signings were Alex Jones from Carlisle for £17,500, his teammate John Halpin, John Ryan from Chesterfield, Alan Reeves from Chester, and non-League Southport's Steve Whitehall (for £10,000 plus another £10,000 if he scored 20 goals for the Dale). Off the field Mick Docherty, son of the legendary Tom, and himself a former Sunderland manager, was confirmed as Sutton's assistant, with former coach Jimmy Robson returning to the club as Youth Development Officer.

1991-92:

With Welch's deputy Gareth Gray injured, the Dale started the season proper with 'Spurs' third choice 'keeper Kevin Dearden as their No.1 (in one of a dozen or more loan spells that Dearden experienced in his Tottenham days), but the rest of the numbering would have confounded any purist. Full backs Reeves and Graham wore 5 and 7, while striker Whitehall was 2 and midfielder Ryan at 3. The first game was drawn, courtesy of a last minute own goal by York's Tuthill, but in the League Cup Rochdale trounced Carlisle 5-1, 'full backs' Whitehall and Ryan both getting on the scoresheet. The second leg saw the return to Rochdale of Malcolm Brown to fill the right back slot (wearing No. 10!), thus freeing Reeves to play in his natural position of centre half. Dale then ran up four straight League wins, Reeves heading the winner at Cardiff in the 90th minute.

A hard earned draw with leaders Rotherham was followed by the result all the fans now most wanted, a win at Burnley, loan 'keeper David Williams helping to keep at bay his erstwhile team-mates and put Dale equal on points with Blackpool and Barnet at the top. The second round of the League Cup saw Dale go out on aggregate to Coventry, but they did have the pleasure of beating their favourite First Division victims again at Spotland. Dale never got going against bottom club Doncaster and manager Sutton substituted two of his players after just 20 minutes. Even after Rovers were reduced to 10 men, Dale still gifted them an equaliser when Milner sliced a clearance into his own net.

Dale equalled their 1925 longest unbeaten run at the start of a season, before losing to Mansfield in the 10th match. The season's worst defeat, 6-2, came at Scunthorpe despite a show of defiance by substitute Jon Bowden, a recent signing from Wrexham, who got both the Dale goals. He also netted when Dale toppled leaders Barnet, the League's new boys.

The Reserves had gained their first Midland League win of the season thanks to a hat-trick from Mark Hilditch, but this proved to be the striker's swansong. Persistent back trouble had restricted him to just three substitute appearances for the first team in the current campaign, but these did at least allow him to claim the record for the longest span of Football League appearances for Dale, covering 15 seasons (though he was only at Spotland for 8 of them).

The first round of the FA Cup paired Rochdale with Northern League Gretna, the first Scottish side to appear in the competition proper since 1890-91. Dale had an uneasy (televised) afternoon as the representatives of the "auld enemy" and were thankful to escape with a goalless draw. Goalkeeper Gray was fortunate to stay on the field after bringing down a Gretna forward outside the area. Dale won the replay but went out in the next round to Huddersfield. Dave Sutton meantime had signed a three year contract as manager and had added Bolton's Kevin Rose to the staff. The goalkeeper immediately won the Match magazine 'matchman of the month' for Division 4 as Dale came good again with three straight wins to end the year.

The highlight was a 4-2 victory over Blackpool thanks to two goals from Steve Whitehall who only came on for the last 10 minutes. With Flounders scoring in eight games out of nine, a string of draws stretched Dale's unbeaten run into the New Year, yet left them no higher in the table (8th) than when they started (despite only three defeats in 25 games). Youngster Paul Butler had established himself so well in the back four that Alex Jones was sold to Scottish Premier League side Motherwell for £40,000. When both regular full backs were put out of action, Sutton had to move quickly to shore up the side, signing experienced former West Brom man Barry Cowdrill and non-contract player Carl Parker from Rossendale.

After losing at Blackpool, Dale won another three games on the trot in early March. When Dale beat Hereford 3-1 on March 21st they reached 61 points from 34 games, but this was reduced to 60 when bankrupt Aldershot were forced to resign from the League. Many of the other promotion hopefuls lost more, however, as Dale had been one of the few sides not to beat the unfortunate Shots. The recalculated League table saw Dale in 5th place with a seven point cushion between themselves and Scunthorpe in 8th. On the other hand, they still had five of their rivals to play in the last nine games.

Transfer deadline day saw the arrival of a player Dave Sutton had been chasing for some time, Bradford City striker Mark Leonard, who cost £40,000, as well as John Stiles (son of the legendary Nobby), on loan from Doncaster. With Steve Doyle injured against Hereford and unable to play for the remainder of the season, plus three other regulars also missing, a patched up side lost 3-0 at Barnet. However, a draw at Northampton and a 2-0 win over Cardiff brought Dale to within three points of 3rd placed Mansfield with two games in hand. Four or five wins in the last six games would now secure automatic promotion, while a mere point a game would surely be enough for a play-off place.

Three of the points looked to be in the bag when Flounders gave Dale (just one home defeat all season) a half time lead against struggling Maidstone (one away win all season), but in atrocious conditions Dale let the Stones gain what turned out to be their last ever victory. Maidstone brought 11 supporters with them, but the authorities insisted that the Pearl Street End be given over to them, and policed as normal   Two days later, the General Election saw a comparable disaster for the Labour party.

With defenders Tony Brown and Paul Butler now injured as well, Dale were beaten by rivals Rotherham who went on to finish second. The matches against Wrexham and champions-elect Burnley were then postponed because Spotland was waterlogged, some of the football followers blaming the joint use by Rochdale Hornets for the poor state of the pitch. The next game was thus at bottom club Doncaster and yet again they dented Dale's hopes, winning 2-0.

Dale did manage to beat Wrexham to stay in the frame, though the fans had apparently already given up, only 1945 bothering to attend. The penultimate Saturday was a free one for Dale due to Aldershot's demise, though a lack of detective work led to a special constable putting 200 parking cones all along Willbutts Lane before someone told him there wasn't a match. But elsewhere Burnley clinched the title, giving Rochdale a great chance to catch them still celebrating. Unfortunately, Spotland was again waterlogged and the match had to be put off to beyond the scheduled end of the season, drawing protests from Barnet, the side most likely to be effected by the result, though Dale would much sooner have played the match than see it postponed again.

Holding third placed Mansfield 0-0 at halftime on the final Saturday, Dale were within 45 minutes of the play-offs, as Barnet were also scoreless, but everything went adrift in the second period, Rochdale going down 2-1 and Barnet blasting York 4-1. Still there was the Burnley game to come and over 8000 fans turned up to see the match which would decide Dale's fate (though apparently more in hope than expectation, one report noting that the home 'support' appeared to consist of a "concerted moan". In fact, John 'Rhino' Ryan gave Dale the lead early on, but Ian Measham of all people, an ex-Dale full back who hadn't scored for two years, netted an equaliser and the Clarets went on to score twice more. Dale's last desperate hope evaporated when David Williams, now on the other side, saved top scorer Flounders' spot kick.

Dale thus finished 8th with 67 points, having lost five of the last six games after losing only six of the previous 36 (or 37 counting Aldershot). Despite the sad ending this was Dale's best points tally since the introduction of three points for a win. Indeed, in any other (42 match) season it would have been easily enough to earn a play-off place. Defender Alan Reeves was voted player of the year.

The most notable 'departures' were probably the famous Hilton's meat pies, sold on the ground for many a year and the club's main claim to fame in darker days. These had to be 'substituted' when director Len Hilton retired from his bakery business. Considering the excellent form of the team until the final run in, maybe the loss of the pies accounted for the relatively modest attendances. Throughout the season home gates hovered just over the 2000 mark, with the exception of a few local derbies. This made proposed increases in policing charges, from £893 to £4259 per match, all the more unpalatable as they would amount to £2 for each spectator! The club actually made a trading loss of £181,000 over the year, with a wage bill of £520,000 compared to gate income of £250,000.

The summer of 1992 was dominated by the formation of the long threatened breakaway superleague, now officially the F.A. Premier League. The remaining three divisions of the Football League adopted a democratic 1 club 1 vote system, so Len Hilton was able to be the first Rochdale director to vote at a Football League AGM.

Not long after the season started, though, Mr Hilton resigned from the board, stating that he was disillusioned with other people having the final say in what happened at Spotland, the last straw coming when the authorities demanded the Sandy Lane End be closed and the police charged £1270 to cover a match for which Dale's share of the gate was £905. Another director later got into trouble with the licensing authority for giving a "flippant response" when asked what contingency plans there were in case a Jumbo Jet crashed on Spotland during a game, viz. "At the worst we would abandon the game, but if we were winning we might play round it".

Dale, of course, were now in the renamed Division 3, but with less money expected from the League, television etc., their financial position was less secure than previously. Indeed, even before the season proper got under way, star goalscorer Andy Flounders and several other unnamed players were put up for sale to the highest bidder. In the event it was recent signing Mark Leonard who moved on to Preston, Dale recouping their £40,000.

The only incoming transfers had seen Andy Thackeray arrive from Wrexham for £15,000 and the reappearance of old boy Shaun Reid from York. At the same time, Rochdale's financial worries paled into insignificance when Maidstone United, once the flagship of non-League football, admitted that they would not be able to fulfill their fixture against Scunthorpe and went out of business after just three seasons in the Football League.

1992-93:
Halifax won the opener 3-2, diminutive ex-Dale man Ronnie Hildersley scoring two goals for the only time in his career. Dale also lost both legs of their Coca Cola Cup-tie against Crewe and the next League game, thus making it nine defeats in the last 10 major games.

Dale's cause was not helped by them having only 12 fit senior players (Doyle and Butler were long term casualties). When even trialist Jackie Ashurst, the veteran former Sunderland centre half, was injured and Tony Brown was taken seriously ill, an SOS was sent north of the border and Alex Jones rejoined the fray on loan from Motherwell.

Dale had finally cracked it at the fifth attempt, convincingly beating Scarborough, and with Whitehall amongst the goals embarked on a seven match unbeaten run - eight if you count a nine run victory over Central Lancashire League side Littleborough in a cricket match played as part of the testimonial year for long-serving backroom boy and scout Tom Nichol! A more normal footballing testimonial was played at the end of the season, between the Chairman's XI and Dave Cross's All Star XI with various guests such as Tommy Booth (ex-Manchester City) and Martin Buchan (ex-Manchester United), Cross himself (one of Tom Nichol's discoveries) turning back the years with a spectacular goal.

Dale were soon in centre back trouble again though, as Motherwell, who had sunk to the foot of the Scottish Premier League table, decided to recall Jones, Butler suffered a recurrence of his toe injury and Tony Brown was forced to quit. The job of partnering Alan Reeves finally fell to the versatile Jon Bowden who held the fort until Dave Sutton was able to re-sign Jones on a permanent basis for £30,000 (to be paid in instalments when Dale found the money).

There was no shortage of incident on the field, either, with 11 goals for and 10 against in the space of five games which also saw two Carlisle, one Chesterfield and one Rochdale player (Ryan) sent off. Dale's 'A' team was amazed to find a TV crew and a host of pressmen at their game against Marine Reserves. Apparently the match referee had been 'booked' the previous week for swearing at a player! The first team injury crisis had, of course, had a knock-on effect on their other teams. The Reserves, with no professionals left, were routed 10-1 one week by an Everton 'A' side that contained not only seven first teamers but two full internationals! The unfortunate 'keeper on the receiving end was Raphael Torres, a former Bilbao player who had a stint at Rochdale while studying at Leeds University. Dale called upon former players like Jason Smart now playing in local football, while manager Sutton and 'A' team coach Jimmy Robson also turned out. At 54 he was more than three times as old as most of his teammates. Also included were two famous names in Greenhoff and Royle, Paul and Darren being the sons of former England internationals Brian and Joe.

Those supporters sporting car stickers reading *"Who needs Cantona when you've got Shaunie Reid"* were proved right when Reid settled the cup-tie with Blackpool four minutes from the end of extra time in the replay.

Unfortunately Dale went down 4-0 at Bolton in the second round after Jimmy Graham, who had never been dismissed before, was sent off for the second Saturday in succession. Ryan and Bowden also suffered two dismissals during the season. Against Colchester, for the first time ever in a Football League game, Dale had two penalties converted by different players, Mark Payne and Andy Flounders.

Christmas week was unusually profitable for Dale with a 5-1 victory over Lincoln inspired by Flounders' hat-trick (which included a 50 yard lob after the 'keeper had come out of his area to head clear) and a 2-0 success against Scunthorpe which saw Dale move into 5th spot at the close of the year. Unfortunately they were unable to carry this on, suffering dire defeats at bottom club Gillingham and at home to Hereford, only a couple of places higher, though they did win 4-0 at Darlington. Rochdale gave Halifax an own goal and a penalty, and had Kevin Rose struggling with a pulled hamstring for virtually the whole game, but came up trumps when former England schoolboy Steve Mulrain from Leeds, making his first full appearance, scored the winner. He had also scored when coming on as substitute the previous week. Tragically though, Mulrain badly broke his foot in a freak training accident a fortnight later and though he recovered to make one substitute appearance the following year he then quit professional football. On the other hand, Steve Doyle was finally able to make a comeback after a year out of action.

Two goals by Alan Reeves against Shrewsbury made Dale the top scorers in the division, even though the goals had dried up of late for Flounders and Whitehall (who had 25 goals between them half way through the season), and Sutton loaned Flounders to Rotherham, taking Don Page in exchange. Although both scored on their debuts, the moves never really worked out and both soon went 'home'. Another incoming player was Geordie Trevor Snowden, a £3000 signing from Seaham Red Star. Proclaimed the next "Gazza" by his new boss (and dubbed "Snazza" by the fans), he went on trial to Aston Villa almost as soon as he'd arrived. Although he figured in the squad, often as substitute, for the remainder of the season, he was never able to live up to this star billing and departed back to non-League football.

Dale were well beaten at Carlisle, then lost the home match against second placed Cardiff which was widely - if prematurely - seen as Dale's last chance to get in amongst the play-off places. Dale drew against Bury in sensational fashion when Rose went upfield for a last gasp corner and nearly scored himself, before Thackeray forced home his second goal in five minutes; coincidentally two of Thackeray's other goals (the full back netted eight altogether) came in remarkable circumstances against the same opponents.

Shaun Reid (left) and Richard Sharpe (right).

Before the Autoglass Trophy match, he and two other Yorkshire based players became stuck in traffic on the way to the ground and Thackeray phoned to say he was on the way but wouldn't make the kick-off. Put down as a substitute, he replaced YTS lad Tony Beever who had been holding the fort and proceeded to turn a one goal deficit into a 2-1 win. Probably the most popular goal, though, was Jonny Bowden's winner against long time leaders York. Not only Dale fans, but those of Cardiff and Wrexham - his former clubs - celebrated as it guaranteed the two Welsh clubs promotion. Bowden was also voted Match magazine's third division 'Matchman of the Month' for April. After some mixed results, three of the last four games ended in victories, Paul Butler's 89th minute winner in the last match ensuring another top half finish.

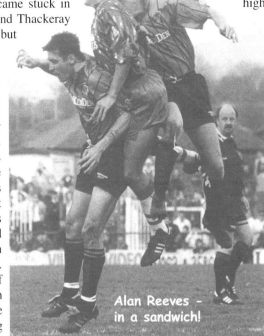

Alan Reeves - in a sandwich!

1993-94:

Four further experienced players were signed up in the summer of 1993; the ex-Everton and Sheffield Wednesday goalkeeper Martin Hodge, former Charlton winger Mark Stuart, Chesterfield centre forward Dave Lancaster and Cardiff defender Neil Matthews (who was injured even before the League season started). Hodge had to go off injured during the 1-1 draw at Darlington - ironically this was the first day on which substitute goalkeepers were permitted, although Dale didn't have one - but fortunately he recovered. Indeed he kept clean sheets in each of the next four games. The second leg Coca-Cola Cup-tie at York nearly saw him arrested, though, as police interviewed him for supposed indecent exposure when he pulled up his shirt to reveal his chest in response to York fans behind his goal calling him 'Sumo' (like the equally large Australian fast bowler, Merv Hughes). Hodge saved a penalty, Steve Doyle was sent off and Dave Sutton was reported to the FA for allegedly swearing at York fans. In the next round Dale lost 8-2 on aggregate to First Division Leicester.

A 1-0 win at Carlisle, where Hodge earned 10 out of 10 ratings in the press, saw Dale top the table, but they surprisingly lost to Wigan. Dale came back to win four League games in a row, blasting three goals in the last half hour to win 5-2 against Colchester (for the second season running) while all five against Chesterfield came in the first half hour. Dave Sutton was rewarded with the Third Division Manager of the Month award. The next game was against bogey side Doncaster Rovers and true to form (or otherwise) Dale lost 2-1. With new £30,000 signing from Bolton, Darren Oliver, in the side (as Doyle missed the team coach when his car broke down), Dale got a draw at Torquay.

But the top clash with Preston was settled by two highly dubious goals, from a Rochdale viewpoint. After several such reverses, Dale got back to winning ways where they had left off, beating Chesterfield again, this time in the cup. (With no real substitute goalkeeper, to comply with the rules Steve Mulrain sat on the bench with the gloves on for a bizarre last appearance at a senior game). On loan Paul Williams of Stockport netted to give Dale the points against Bury, but they went down at Scunthorpe in a match notable for Dale having a real substitute goalkeeper for the first time, non-contract player Neil Dunford.

In the second round of the cup Dale travelled to Burnley, and the 'battle of Turf Moor' began with Jimmy Graham stretchered off to hospital needing 47 stitches in a leg wound after a tackle by John Francis (which was not adjudged a foul by the referee). It ended with ten men playing nine, Jones and Thackeray (for retaliatory fouls on Francis) and Clarets' Monington having been sent off and several others booked. Three penalties were awarded (Whitehall scored one and missed one) and the unfortunate Jones (only on as substitute for Graham) also scored an own goal. More or less incidentally Burnley won 4-1 in between the mayhem. 16 year old Jamie Taylor was given a baptism of fire as Dale's second substitute. Thackeray's suspension was later quashed after the referee admitted he had got the wrong man when he showed Thackeray his second yellow card. After learning that the FA would not be taking action against Francis, Graham considered taking out a civil action, but eventually the matter went no further.

A dire goalless draw with next to bottom Darlington led to a bust up between the manager and some of his senior players. John Ryan was transferred to Bury a few days later and Andy Flounders was soon loaned to Carlisle (for a second time) while Sutton tried to find a buyer. Dale had earlier turned down several offers for Flounders which they thought too low, but in the end their most expensive buy headed off to non-League football, later appearing at Wembley for Brigg Town in 1996.

With both Jones and Butler suspended Dale borrowed Stockport's Alan Finley, and he enjoyed what must surely be the best loan spell ever, when Dale won, in his only game, 6-2 against Northampton. Remarkably this was the team's first six since the promotion season 25 years earlier. 'Bomber' Lancaster hit a hat-trick (another rare feat for Dale) and the other scorers were Whitehall, Stuart and young substitute Taylor.

Another four were netted against Torquay in their next home game, Lancaster taking his tally to 14 (all of them scored in two bursts of six games). A couple of weeks later though, manager Sutton placed Lancaster, along with the crowd's other favourites Whitehall and Reid, on the transfer list, in an effort to raise money to strengthen the squad.

Having lost only two of the last 11 games, Dale were right back in play-off contention. However, they blew what would turn out to be the crucial games of the season. First Carlisle, eight points adrift of Rochdale won 1-0, then Dale led Chester until a harsh penalty decision was compounded by too much of the Irish from Williams (now signed permanently) who was sent off for persistent dissent (while assistant manager Docherty was dismissed from the dugout). Williams was the sixth Rochdale player to walk during the season, veteran Steve Doyle having been dismissed twice. The following year Williams probably set a club record when he was booked 55 seconds after coming on as substitute.

Dale did get into the vital 7th place by beating Scarborough, with a late goal by Mark Stuart, but were crushed 5-1 by lowly Hereford and Stuart failed to repeat his rescue act when his penalty was saved in the return at Scarborough. With new boy Jason Peake - signed from Halifax in exchange for Alex Jones on transfer deadline day - in the side, Dale were denied victory against table-topping Wycombe by a late equaliser following the referee's decision to award a free kick against Hodge for handling a 'backpass' when a shot deflected off Reeves' thigh; the referee later admitted he had made a mistake. Dale won at Northampton when the two substitutes Taylor and Bowden conjured up a goal within a minute of coming on, but fell to an 89th minute strike by new leaders Shrewsbury. However, they beat fellow hopefuls Mansfield and Crewe and drew again with Wycombe. This match had twice been postponed at the last minute, the Dale team and their supporters getting to within a few miles of the ground on each occasion.

With two games to go they were in eighth spot, a point behind Chesterfield. Dale drafted in another signing, striker Kevin Formby, an ex-Royal Marine from Burscough, to play left back at Bury and he was the star of a hard fought 1-0 win which took them into the play-off places. However Carlisle had come from nowhere to beat both long time leaders Preston and certain champions Shrewsbury to go a point ahead of Rochdale. Like two years previously Dale's play-off hopes remained alive until the last 30 minutes of the campaign, when Carlisle settled their game. Rochdale themselves eventually went down 3-2 at home to Scunthorpe, centre forward Dave Lancaster netting the final goal of the season at the wrong end. Dale thus finished 9th with 60 points. Goalkeeper Martin Hodge and centre half Alan Reeves were selected for the PFA divisional team of the year and Reeves won the Dale 'Player of the Year' award for the third time in a row, as well as most of the other trophies at the club's awards night.

These included the EGP ("Exceedingly Good Pies") award sponsored by the editors of the new fanzine (successor to "The 92nd Club" of a few years earlier).

A talking point of the close season was the court case in which former Chelsea player Paul Elliot sued Welsh international Dean Saunders for causing the injury which ended his career. Dave Sutton was incensed, and demanded an apology, when Saunders was quoted as saying that players couldn't *"bottle out"* of challenges, otherwise they would *"end up playing for Rochdale"*. Sutton's own career, of course, had been ended by injuries received battling in the Dale's cause.

At the AGM the board were able to announce a significant profit of almost £20,000 in the year to May 1993. Much of the credit for this was down to Steve Walmsley's incredibly successful commercial department whose contribution had risen by a staggering £100,000. As usual when Dale had got their finances sorted out, though, outside influences took over again, this time in the shape of the new National Lottery, which Walmsley and others warned could sound the death knell for smaller sports clubs of all types. At least Walmsley could reflect on another job well done, when the Dale programme he edited was voted the best in Division 3. Moving up market, Executive Boxes were available for the first time at £3000 per season, and during the summer Spotland just missed out on hosting the World Cup Finals - the Lacrosse version, that is - when it was decided to hold all the games at Gigg Lane instead.

Jimmy Graham had been released at the end of the previous term and joined his old boss Terry Dolan at Second Division Hull, but the rest of the activity occurred right on the eve of the 1994-95 season. Indeed, Martin Hodge's £10,000 move to Plymouth came after the 'keeper played in the first two Lancashire Cup-ties. Also moving out were the long-serving but much injured Andy Milner to Chester on a free and top scorer Dave Lancaster surprisingly sold to non-League Halifax for a respectable fee of £7,500. Milner's direct replacement was Dale old boy Dave Thompson, who made the reverse move (but cost £6,000). The only other experienced newcomer was Derek Hall, for £10,000 from Hereford but, as it turned out, he rarely figured in the senior side.

1994-95:
Dale started the season as they couldn't possibly hope to continue by attracting 4,290 spectators to Spotland for their first Marsden Cup game and beating Manchester United 3-2. There was some disappointment that United 'only' selected a side of unknown up and coming youngsters - such as one David Beckham - but by the end of the year most of them would be regulars in United's championship winning side, and Gary Neville would end the season he started at Spotland by playing for England! Dale also recovered the Charity Rose Bowl, last played for in 1984, by beating Oldham 2-1.

They also had a friendly against a name from the past, walloping Accrington Stanley 7-0 with a Bowden hat-trick.

In their new white strip, with blue shorts, and wearing the logo of new sponsors Carcraft, a victory was secured at Bury when serious competition started, the game seeing the first (and last) direct battle of the Reid family, Shaun's more famous brother Peter turning out for the Shakers after losing his player-manager's job at Manchester City. Dale actually went top of the nascent table when they beat Chesterfield 4-1, providing excellent news for Radio 2 FM in Eire who had decided to 'adopt' the club.

Dale then sold defensive kingpin Alan Reeves - 'God' to the fans - to Wimbledon for £300,000. Reeves replaced John Scales who had moved to Liverpool for £2M and his debut coincided with the Dons first win of the season. The first post-Reeves game was won, but Barnet's Dougie Freedman helped himself to four goals in a 6-2 trouncing. Paul Williams grabbed two of Dale's four against Scarborough, and in the next match performed remarkably well in goal after a sickening head injury to young 'keeper Chris Clarke, who had been showing outstanding form in his first season in the League side. Williams had volunteered to go in goal for the suitably Irish reason that he used to play Gaelic football! (He also played one full reserve game in goal). 'Willo' had the dubious honour of holding one Northern Ireland cap from a game in which they had somehow contrived to draw with the Faroe Islands, and had a rather more elevated life style than most of his teammates, being the son-in-law of Stockport's multi-millionaire chairman. The match against Blackpool in the normally unremarkable Auto Windscreens Shield also saw the appearance of a new midfielder Alex Russell, son of the old Southport stalwart of the same name, a £4,000 buy from Burscough.

Reserve team 'keeper Neil Dunford, a 27 year old 'brickie', was called up for duty in the next game and sensationally earned the hero's laurels with a penalty save and a clean sheet as Dale beat Doncaster 2-0 and reclaimed a top four spot. However they lost to Fulham and Sutton brought in Matt Dickins on loan from Blackburn. Sadly Dickins would go down in Dale legend for all the wrong reasons. His debut was against bottom club Wigan who had lost nine of their 11 games (and had a new manager in Graham Barrow), but four goals flew - or rolled - past him in the first 37 minutes and he conceded 11 more in his other three Football League games. Chairman David Kilpatrick was later quoted as saying that Blackburn manager Kenny Dalgleish:

"Must have had a lot of good whisky" before paying out a quarter of a million for him. Dunford, incidentally, was next heard of playing centre forward for Milnrow in Sunday football.

Meantime Dave Sutton's attempts to sign new defenders, especially a protracted effort to tempt Huddersfield's Peter Jackson, had all come to naught - even Dale old boy Bill Williams, now back playing for Littleborough after nearly 10 years at Stockport, declined the offer of a League comeback after a run-out in the reserves. Following defeat in the cup at Walsall, the chairman admitted that Sutton's job could be under threat from 'supporter power' if things did not improve. Despite a pretty successful three years by Dale standards, Sutton had never been particularly popular with sections of the crowd, not least for his outspoken criticism of the fans on several occasions. He was particularly famous for his column in the programme which said *"just one word of encouragement is worth ten of criticism"*.

A centre half finally arrived in the shape of Carlisle's Peter Valentine, once a team-mate of Sutton's at Bolton, and he was followed by another on-loan goalkeeper, Oldham's Ian Gray. Valentine and Gray played their parts in a goalless draw with Colchester, but Dale then went down 1-0 at bottom club Hartlepool and Dave Sutton went down with them. His assistant Mick Docherty was appointed caretaker manager, and after making five team changes, he saw his side go through to the next round of the Auto Windscreens Shield when Andy Thackeray fired home a 'sudden death' penalty. Dale also claimed four points from the remaining two League games before Christmas, while the Board struggled to come up with the name of their new manager.

Besides Docherty, the interested parties were believed to have included the currently unemployed former managers John McGrath, Ian Atkins and Steve Wicks, as well as former Dale players Frank Lord and Bobby Downes, plus Sammy McIlroy, the manager of GM Vauxhall Conference leaders Macclesfield.

Christmas week was a disaster; three defeats (one in a 'lake' at Preston), one goal for, nine against, and Darren Oliver sent off in a rare first team appearance, for handling a goal bound shot (the third time in a year that referee Jeff Winter had sent a Rochdale player off). The New Year was more promising though, with a 2-0 victory over Torquay. One of the scorers was Richard Sharpe from Coco Expos of Orlando, Florida, whom Sutton had invited over for a trial after meeting him in the USA during the previous summer's World Cup.

25 years on - promotion heroes from 1969 at the reunion dinner in 1994 (Graham Smith, Dick Conner, Reg Jenkins, Dennis Butler and Joe Fletcher).

When Atkins and, eventually, McIlroy, turned down the manager's job, the Board handed the poison chalice to Mick Docherty. 'Doc junior' was thus able to add another club to the roster begun by his father, the famous (or in some quarters infamous) Tommy. The problems he would face were summed up by a snap poll taken for the fanzine; although 91 of 100 potential supporters interviewed were locals only 18 supported Rochdale compared to 41 followers of Manchester United. Just how many bosses had been unable to bring any tangible success had also been brought home a few weeks earlier when a grand 25th anniversary reunion dinner was held for the club's one and only promotion side.

John Deary

Although unpopular with some fans, who saw it as merely an extension of the Sutton regime, the players responded to the appointment with an against-the-odds victory against Second Division Stockport County in the Auto Windscreens Shield with only seven fully fit players - Shaun Reid playing with two broken ribs. They also remained unbeaten in the next four League games and won their AWS northern semi-final at Bury, who had been undefeated at home since Dale's opening day victory. With new signings Dean Martin from Scunthorpe and John Deary, a £25,000 buy from Burnley, adding experience to the midfield, Dale went on to stretch their excellent defensive run to just three goals against in nine games, and their overall run to only one defeat in 13 League games, but somehow moved up only from 15th place at the start of the year to 14th at the beginning of April.

Carlisle provided the opposition for the Northern Final of the Auto Windscreens Shield. The first leg in Cumbria saw diabolical conditions greet the players and supporters after their trip north. On winning the toss, Andy Thackeray elected to play against the gale force wind and driving rain in the first half, but his hopes of surviving the battering were literally blown away as Carlisle plundered three wind assisted goals before the break. Even so, when Whitehall pulled one back on the restart and Dale camped in the Carlisle penalty area the omens looked good. But the gods then deserted them in their (half) hour of need and the wind completely disappeared, the relieved home side breaking out to snatch what looked like a decisive fourth.

Nevertheless, with a place at Wembley at stake, Docherty and his men psyched themselves up for mission impossible in the second leg, and for a while it looked like they really might do it.

Two up in 22 minutes through Whitehall and Reid, a shot from Dave Thompson looked bound for the bottom corner before hitting a divot and going agonisingly wide. A relieved Carlisle finally settled the tie when veteran ex-Everton and Villa centre half Derek Mountfield scored from a corner.

The season subsequently petered out with Dale remaining stuck in 15th place. The worst was saved for last with Dale blasted 5-0 at Fulham, the debacle costing 16 year old YTS lad Phil Shore a promised League debut as substitute if things were going well. The durable Whitehall played in all 56 games and netted 10 League goals plus one in the League Cup, another in the Rose Bowl and six in the Auto Windscreens, but the player of the year was again a defender, Paul Butler.

Injury had forced Steve Doyle into retirement after 725 senior games in a 20 year career and he joined Dave Sutton at Chorley as player-coach. Jon Bowden also hung up his boots to join the backroom staff at Oldham, while Shaun Reid, with 240 Football League games for Dale behind him, the sixth highest tally ever, was sold to Bury for £25,000. The injury prone Neil Matthews also left (to play in China), but not before making his own bit of Rochdale history. When he was selected for the Northern Ireland 'B' side to play Scotland he became the first Rochdale player to win a senior international cap since his countrymen O'Connell and Halligan in 1919.

At a younger level, the club had started its own 'centre of excellence', run by their old centre half Keith Hicks, who was also the Football in the Community officer, and one of their first pupils won FA representative honours. Stephen Bywater was a fourth generation goalkeeper, following his father Dave, a one time Dale reserve and now coach at the centre, grandfather Les, the club's goalkeeper in the late 'forties, and Les' father before him.

Only one summer signing was made in 1995, the welcome addition of Ian Gray, whom Oldham had finally been persuaded to part with for £20,000. The chairman had vowed to resign if promotion was not achieved, but he was persuaded to change his mind by the rest of the board and by the support received from many fans. His rallying call to the players was typically forthright - go out and win the first five games and *"stuff it up the whingeing backsides"* of all those who had written them off as no-hopers.

1995-96:

Pre-season, Dale met Manchester United in a behind closed doors training match at the Cliff which they narrowly lost 3-2, but which gained international attention when it was queried whether Eric Cantona had breached his worldwide ban after the notorious incident with a spectator the previous season.

The serious business as far as Dale were concerned began with the visit of Cardiff City. Dale cruised into a two goal lead but eventually had a late Dave Thompson goal to thank for a point. Dale triumphed 2-1 in the Coca-Cola Cup first leg, but York reversed the scores at Bootham Crescent, Williams missing a great chance to settle the tie in the last minute of normal time, before York romped home with three extra time goals. Their reward, and Rochdale's loss, was the ultimate money-spinning tie against Manchester United (which York even won).

Meantime in the League, Dale looked like satisfying chairman Kilpatrick's exhortation, gaining a 4-0 victory against Hartlepool thanks to a hat-trick for Jamie Taylor in only his third start, and three excellent victories on their early season travels. The 1-0 win at Darlington saw Dale use three substitutes for the first time, while Exeter were demolished 4-2 by goals from Stuart, Deary, Whitehall (with a strike which won Granada TV's goal of the month) and Peake, to move them into the top four. The most remarkable result though came at Barnet, where Rochdale finally broke the jinx of 75 years and won a game in London at the 41st attempt. They did it in style, too, with Stuart (himself a rare Londoner in the Dale ranks) netting two of the four second half goals, the others again coming from Peake and Whitehall.

Rochdale won four of the next five games, in all competitions, too. In the Auto Windscreens they beat Darlington 5-2 thanks to a hat-trick, on his full debut, from recent signing Paul Moulden, the former Manchester City star whose father Tony had played for Rochdale in the 'sixties. Moulden junior had set up an amazing world record as a youngster when he scored 340 goals in one season for Bolton Lads Club. Second Division Rotherham were then despatched 5-3 in the FA Cup, Moulden and Peake netting a brace each. At this point Dale were the top scorers in the whole country with 48 goals in 21 games.

The Rotherham game was the zenith, however. Stuart had received a bad facial injury and was ruled out until after Christmas, and inexplicably without him the team managed only one goal in six League games.

They also lost Gray with a recurrence of hernia trouble. The one bright spot was in the FA Cup when John Deary scored twice to secure a replay at Darlington, which Dean Martin won with a flying header in extra time to earn a big pay day for the club after all, a trip to Liverpool in round 3.

Although manager Docherty was able to put out a fairly experienced team, the big day proved a disaster. A respectable 1-0 down up to the 42nd minute, changed when multi-million pound striker Stan Collymore struck twice to make it 3-0 at the break. Ian Rush came on as a second half substitute to score the goal he needed to set a new FA Cup scoring record and it finished 7-0. The one Dale man on the score sheet was Peter Valentine who put through his own goal. The scorer of the seventh was Jason McAteer, another multi-million pound man, who might have joined Rochdale as a youngster. After seeing him play for Marine Reserves against Dale's second string, coach Dave Grimbaldeston had asked him if he was interested in a trial at Spotland. Marine's boss objected to this approach, but took the hint and gave McAteer a first team chance, subsequently selling him to Bolton.

Andy Thackery and John Barnes with mascots and officials before the Liverpool match.

Rochdale continued to sink gradually down the table, their run extending to 13 games without a win, thanks to at least one classic case of snatching defeat from the jaws of victory. At Northampton, former Scunthorpe utility man, Ian Thompstone, came on as substitute in the 80th minute and scored with his first touch, but Dale still found time to let two in.

Against Lincoln, they finally managed to score more than once in a game for the first time in three months, but the fit again Stuart completed a bizarre 'hat-trick' by contriving to put the ball past on-loan Manchester United goalkeeper Kevin Pilkington, with no attacker within 20 yards of them, to make the final score 3-3.

The next man to try his luck in goal, Sheffield Wednesday's Lance Key, was the one to break the sequence (neither Clarke nor Pilkington played in a winning side), when his huge presence helped inspire a 2-1 win at champions-elect Preston, as well as victories over Torquay and Gillingham. The bemused Peake was credited with an own goal against Wigan, though, when his gentle tap back to the 'keeper was completely missed by Key, and then Whitehall missed not one but two penalties.

By Easter Valentine had been forced to retire through injury (and his projected promotion to coach for the following season had been vetoed by the board for lack of money), and Dale were missing nine other players. After a couple of valiant displays, despite having no recognised central defenders, the whole thing finally fell apart at home to Barnet who matched Dale's earlier 4-0 success at Underhill. Four youngsters had been pitched into the fray and one of them, trainee Neil Barlow, had the traumatic experience of giving away a goal after 16 seconds of his full debut, and being carried off five minutes later with a torn hamstring.

Dale scrambled five points from the last five games to finish 15th again. Steve Whitehall was everpresent for the third time in four years (and was top scorer with his best tally of 24), having now played 115 consecutive League and cup games. He passed the landmark of 200 League games for Rochdale near the end of the season, as, earlier, had Dave Thompson.

Paul Butler was again the player of the year, making it five years in a row between him and his former central defensive partner Alan Reeve. Another defender, Dave Bayliss, was young player of the year in his first season (despite one sending off and four separate suspensions). Even younger players were the first to appear in Dale colours at Wembley; Siddall Moor High School under-13s played a school representing Cambridge United before the Third Division Play-off Final.

Rumours of Mick Docherty's unhappiness at the prospect of running the side with only 16 or 17 players next season, and of Board Room displeasure at some of his signings (and the retained list) ended with Docherty's sacking a fortnight after the season ended (the break-up chronicled in Derek Alsop's 'fly-on-the-wall' account of the season, "Kicking in the Wind"). The Board immediately offered the manager's job to ex-Chester and Wigan boss Graham Barrow.

The two stars among the younger players, Jason Peake and Paul Butler, had already decide they wanted away and in the summer Butler moved to newly promoted neighbours Bury (whom he must have impressed in the season's two 1-1 draws as he scored both the Dale goals). Meanwhile, Peake surprisingly elected to join troubled Brighton who had just been relegated to the bottom division. The two deals eventually netted Rochdale around half a million pounds to guarantee survival for another season despite a slump in gates.

The new boss and his assistant Joe Hinnigan soon recruited some additional players, two of whom, Andy Farrell and Mark Leonard (back at Spotland for a second time) had played for him at Wigan. Along with midfielder Andy Gouck, the newcomers provided virtually a whole new defence, with right back Andy Fensome, who had won a Division 3 championship medal with Preston the previous term, central defender Keith Hill, also a promotion winner with Plymouth, and the rugged Alan Johnson, signed from Lincoln on the eve of the season.

1996-97:
Given the influx of foreign players into the English game, it was perhaps appropriate that Rochdale's first goal of 1996-97 was scored by trialist Mike Cecere, even if Dale's Italian did hail from Chester. Unfortunately, Swansea, under their 'Great Dane' Jan Molby, still won 2-1 even though their manager missed a penalty and got himself sent off. Dale did also give a trial to a genuine overseas player, Jose Carlos Aspin of Real Zaragoza.

Dale did not win any of their next five League games either, with their characteristic contrariness the only early success being a 2-1 Coca-Cola Cup victory over eventual Division 1 champions Barnsley. Equally perversely, they got their first three points of the season when reduced to nine men. Hill and Leonard were both sent off in the first half against Doncaster, but Dale came from behind to win 2-1 with goals from skipper Deary and substitute Gouck. They also won an equally stormy game against Orient, when the visitors were lucky to have only one man dismissed, and had their former West Ham star Alvin Martin reported to the FA by the police.

After Dale drew at Darlington, the Quakers' Robbie Painter made a quick change of sides, moving to Spotland on loan and subsequently signing permanently. An eight games undefeated run, including an easy win against bottom club Brighton which featured prominently on BBC Radio thanks to Rochdalian Liz Kershaw and her Brighton supporting co-presenter, took Dale to within three points of the play-off places, but they then lost to late goals at both Cardiff and Barnet. Dale for once comfortably negotiated a tricky cup-tie against top non-Leaguers Macclesfield and finally gained their first away win of the season at Torquay, thanks to new cult hero Alan Johnson. After he turned out with a particularly severe haircut, his manager commented: *"He even frightens me."*

Substitute Andy Thackeray scored in the FA Cup defeat by Notts County and with half a dozen players on the injured list, the former skipper regained his place in the side, playing in midfield (as later did his old full back partner Formby). After a poor run, Dale ended 1996 with a 1-0 win at Barrow's previous club, Wigan, and repeated that against Cardiff, but lost 3-0 to Brighton and had Bayliss sent off. In the next game Hill and Barnet's Devine both got red cards after a flare up and Scarborough also ended a man short.

After eight games without a win, Dale were looking over their shoulders at improving Brighton, and lack of goals cost both Whitehall and Painter their regular places, Alex Russell having to take much of the goalscoring responsibility. They weren't the only strugglers, though, as in the goalless draw with Hereford, their 6'-5" Finnish striker Kotilla got a newspaper rating of three and - as former Dale centre back Brian Taylor once said of one of his own perform- ances - *"they only start from 4"*. A year later the Finn had the last laugh by playing in the European Cup! Ian Gray, too, could have been playing on an inter- national stage, but for the Hereford game. He was selected for a Football League under-21s side to play the Italian Seria B under-21s, but had to pull out. He had also been the subject of a £200,000 bid from Bradford City.

Alex Russell

Fortunately Dale reawoke at this point, winning three in a row. Kevin Formby, whose failure to score in the three previous seasons had become a standing joke with his teammates, got the winner at Hartlepool. Further defeats followed, but Dale did win three of the last four, ruining Lincoln's play-off chances with a final day victory at Sincil Bank, to finish 14th, 11 short of the play-offs and 11 in front of relegated Hereford.

While the first team struggled, the Reserves had amazingly chalked up 13 straight wins and were not beaten until the final game of the season, walking away with the Pontins (Central) League Division 3 title. Another successful side was Rochdale Supporters Club, who were runners up in the Third Division Supporters League.

New hero Alan Johnson was undisputedly player of the season and the young player award went to Alex Russell, but several former stalwarts were on the way out, including Thackeray (who would have moved onto the coaching staff, but for financial constraints), Formby, Deary and Dave Thompson. 'Thommo' had totalled 322 appearances, 266 in the FL, placing him 4th in the all-time list. In addition Whitehall was known to want away, and before the next season got underway he had moved to Mansfield for £25,000. Whitehall, too, had reached the top 10 in appearances, with 298 in all, but it was his 95 goals which put him among all time Rochdale greats, behind only Reg Jenkins and Bert Whitehurst; he scored 25 at Mansfield the following term.

At the other end of their careers, four products of the School of Excellence signed up on the YTS scheme, including Stephen Bywater, who had already played for England under-16s and was on stand-by for an England Youth tour of Brazil, and Keith Hicks' son Graeme, while another 'scholar' David Walsh played for the North of England in his age group. Manag- er Graham Barrow had talks with a number of exper- ienced players during the summer of 1997, and duly signed Preston skipper Ian Bryson, former Oldham left back Andy Barlow, centre half John Pender from Wigan and ex-Barnet hot shot Mark Carter. Giving a trial to Cardiff full back Andy Scott cannot have made calling for the ball in defence any too easy, as Dale could now field an entire back division of Andys in Fensome, Barlow, Farrell, Scott and Gouck!

1997-98:
Alan Johnson badly damaged a knee in a practice match against Blackburn and before the season proper started Dale also lost the services of Pender and Bryson. On the day of the first pre-season game Ian Gray's agent informed Barrow that the out of contract goalkeeper had signed for Stockport (Dale eventually received a tribunal set fee of £200,000), so youth team 'keeper Bywater was called up at literally two hours' notice to face Blackpool and was the star in the 2-0 defeat. Gray had played in every match the previous term except one Lancashire Cup-tie when he was replaced by a trialist - his younger brother Kevin.

Barrow signed former 'keeper Lance Key in time for the first Football League game but the side still virtually picked itself (the manager decided not to risk Turkish centre back trialist Bilal Aksoy, formerly of Fenerbache). Dale lost at Notts County and also in the Coca-Cola Cup to Stoke, but Painter's third goal in successive games gave Rochdale the points against Mansfield. A visit to Orient, unpromising at the best of times, turned spectacularly worse after just 19 seconds when Hill got in the way of a shot and the referee not only gave a penalty but sent Hill off for deliberate handball. Near the end the referee repeated the process, giving another penalty and then sending off Leonard. By coincidence it had been Hill and Leonard who had walked in the Doncaster game the previous year, while the same referee also sent off two Hartlepool players at Orient.

Over 12,000 fans turned up to the first game at Stoke's new Britannia Stadium, but Dale refused to be overawed and came out with a draw on the night. Away League games were considerably less productive, but at home they won five out of six, defender Keith Hill twice netting vital goals and a real rarity, a Mark Stuart header, beating Hull. Barrow was still keen to strengthen the squad, though, and paid out £50,000 for Wigan striker Graham Lancashire, and later another £25,000 to secure Stockport 'keeper Neil Edwards.

Lancashire netted his first goal in a match against Bolton Wanderers to officially open the new WMG stand at the completely rebuilt Pearl Street End, and a few days later the new strike force of Lancashire and Painter (previously colleagues at Burnley) struck twice each as Dale, now with the veteran Bryson in midfield, steamrollered Darlington 5-0 to go 9th. Unfortunately this was as good as it got.

Gouck's strike earned the first away point of the season at Cambridge, but Lancashire was injured and Dale scored in only two of nine games, prompting unrest among the fans. The 3-0 win at Doncaster emphasised, though, just how far Rochdale had come over the previous ten years or so, and how relatively minor their current problems were; Rovers were 17 points behind at the bottom with no wins in 19 games, hardly any senior players and a virtually derelict stadium. When Dale returned to Belle Vue in the Auto Windscreens match, the crowd was 580, possibly the lowest at any competitive Dale game. Mind you, Dale's 1-0 defeat by Torquay was played in front of just 1729 fans in Spotland's million pound stands.

Dale had a successful spell at home, but then lost six times in a row, dropping them to 21st in the New Year. At Exeter, Dale followers who had baited the manager during the 3-0 defeat were involved in scuffles with other Dale fans as the support began to polarise into pro- and anti-Barrow factions. At a Supporters' Forum, chairman David Kilpatrick admitted that he did not know whether the under fire manager would be offered a new contract at the end of the season. In February Barrow asked for a clear the air meeting with the board and eventually in mid-March the board announced that he would be retained as manager for another season. . One man who had already gone was commercial manager Stephen Walmsley, who had taken over at Bury F.C. and Swinton R.L.F.C., and had been replaced by Richard Wild and Francis Collins. The latter - rather unusually, the former editor of the fanzine EGP, which was not averse to criticising the board - was later appointed the club's chief executive.

Meanwhile Dale had given the 16 year old Bywater his senior debut in the Auto Windscreens game at Carlisle, but he was let down by his more experienced colleagues in a 6-1 defeat. At the end of January he went on trial to West Ham and a few weeks later a permanent transfer was negotiated for the England under-17 goalkeeper, with Dale to receive £300,000 up front and up to £2M if he eventually became a regular full international; by the summer of 2001, he had got as far as making his debut for the England under-21s.

Bryson had been injured again and replaced by former Caernarvon Town player Gary Jones, signed from Swansea on the recommendation of Billy Ayres, who was helping with the coaching at Spotland. Next Johnson pulled up after only 30 minutes of his comeback in the reserves and to cap it, John Pender caught his studs in the turf when going for a challenge and suffered damage to his knee which terminated his career.

Dale eventually gained an away win - that at doomed Doncaster hardly counting - when Stuart capped a virtuoso performance at Hull with a trademark free kick, and three goals by Gouck (virtually doubling his career tally in four days) secured another six points. With Lancashire and Painter getting back on the score sheet after three month droughts, Dale produced an excellent run in, claiming 17 points from the last eight games and scoring four against both Scarborough and Doncaster. The home game against Rovers was judged by many the greatest mismatch between sides in the same division that they had ever seen. The season ended with a 2-1 win against Barnet (who made the play-offs anyway), thanks to Robbie Painter's 18th of the season. Dale actually gained more home wins (and conceded less home goals) than anyone except second placed Macclesfield, but the dire away form meant they finished 18th, 12 points behind Barnet. The final game also brought apparent proof of generations of football fans' opinions on officials' eye-sight when the referee sent off the Dale mascot Desmond - a 7 foot tall green dragon - because he couldn't tell him apart from the players!

It came as no surprise when Painter won the player of the year award, as well as a new goal of the season trophy, while Neil Edwards picked up awards from the Supporters Club plus his fellow players, and Andy Farrell received the award sponsored by Thwaites Brewers. Gouck and Fensome were the only regulars released but Alex Russell turned down new terms and signed for Cambridge.

Despite the moderate showing on the pitch, Rochdale was voted into third place in Total Football's survey of the best club to visit for a match. And the pies were still on form, too, Coleman's Football Food Guide ranking the fare at Spotland third in the whole League: *If such a thing as a Rochdale Tourist Board existed, its first function would be to erect signs reading 'You are now entering serious pie country'.*

The main summer signings for 1998 were full backs Paul Sparrow (Preston) and Dean Stokes (Port Vale), who had played for local side Milton when living in Rochdale, old boy Jason Peake back after two miserable years at Brighton and Bury, and Rotherham centre half Mark Monington. After a year's absence Dale also had the services of Alan Johnson, though he again spent much of his time on the treatment table.

1998-99:
Pre-season games saw Dale trounce Oldham 4-0 to reach the final of the Marsden Lancahire Cup for the first time, but they then lost to Wigan. They led Plymouth at half-time on the opening day but were unable to hang on and lost 2-1. One of the substitutes was David Gray, another product of the School of Excellence, who had scored five in a pre-season friendly. Rochdale also lost the next three, and the defensive style was criticised by fans already agitating for change by the second game of the season.

One of the 'Three Amigos' from Barrow's time at Wigan, Izzy Diaz, earned Dale their first win at Carlisle, and Mark Bailey's only senior goal beat Shrewsbury at Spotland. Even so, by the time Dale got their second home win at the end of September, they were down in 22nd place. From then until Christmas, though, they lost only twice in 14 games and rose as high as 13th. Sparrow, who had had a hard time at right back in the first few games of the season, reappeared at left back following injuries to Stokes and Barlow and scored twice in four games, while a new right back Mark Williams from Barrow, netted the only goal against Halifax. (Five of Dale's first six wins were by one goal to nil). Halifax's chairman, on securing promotion the previous May had commented *"The twin towers of Rochdale are looming now, and I never thought I would be so pleased to see them"*.

Dale had again lost Lancashire through injury and Leonard was forced to quit with persistent back problems, while Diaz decided to return to Spain. In the search for another striker, Dale first borrowed Peterborough's Miguel de Souza and then Preston's Michael Holt before signing the latter on permanent terms. They also acquired veteran Chesterfield striker Andy 'Bruno' Morris.

Dale had negotiated the first round of the FA Cup, the 37 year old Bryson running half the length of the field to settle the replay against Scarborough in the last minute. In round two they drew 0-0 with Rotherham despite Edwards getting stuck in a traffic jam and becoming Dale's first goalkeeper substitute when he came on to replace his deputy Lance Key (Key's only taste of action all season). In the replay, former Miller Mark Monington was sent off and his old side easily won 4-0. A stranger sending off came at Swansea, when Williams was given a second yellow card for a foul actually committed by Paul Carden. The mistaken identity was later sorted out and it was Carden who had to serve the suspension! The old year ended with an excellent victory at Hartlepool but only one of the first six League games of 1999 ended successfully. The visit of Hull City was chosen as a Sky TV live match and Dale put on an excellent show for the watching millions, winning 3-0 thanks to two headers from the relatively small Holt and a toe end from big 'Bruno'. A rare Bayliss goal won the game at Scunthorpe and at the end of February Dale still harboured play-off ambitions.

They had also battled through against the odds to the Northern semi-final of the AutoWindscreens Shield. Bad weather and the dire state of the Spotland pitch, exacerbated (according to the football contingent) by its use for Rugby League, led to a succession of postponements. (In fact, Spotland was used by the Dale, Hornets, Dale Reserves, Hornets' Academy side, Oldham RL and Bolton Wanderers Reserves!). The Football League eventually decreed that the 'home' games against both Stoke and Halifax would have to be played away. Morris and Holt shocked Second Division Stoke by netting a goal apiece in the first four minutes.

While at Halifax, Gary Jones equalised from the penalty spot with his first kick after coming on as substitute, before centre half Monington netted Dale's first ever 'golden goal' winner in extra time. Dreams of Wembley soon receded as Dale went out in the next round to Wigan and picked up only one point from four League games. Barrow bolstered the midfield with Jason Lydiate from Scarborough and Cardiff 'hard man' Gareth Stoker. One goal in six games was sufficient to earn six points, but not enough to keep the side in play-off contention.

Before Dale got too close to the bottom, an Andy Morris hat-trick saw off Chester, but they were unable to make any further headway and after another three defeats in a row, the Board finally gave up and sacked Graham Barrow and his assistant Joe Hinnigan. Barrow, who had often asked to be judged after three seasons, departed one match short. For the last game of the season youth coach David Hamilton and senior pro Ian Bryson were left in charge. They recalled Dean Stokes and Gary Jones after lengthy spells out of favour and their side gained a point at Brighton. Veteran Andy Barlow, playing on the wing, scored his first goal for the club with what turned out to be virtually his last touch as a Football League player.

Dale ended up 19th with only 54 points. Crowds had barely risen above 2000, except for the televised Hull game which attracted over 5000, and many fans felt that much of the ground made up over earlier seasons had been dissipated. The board released several of the older players, including Bryson, while Mark Stuart had, almost unnoticed, left for non-League Southport towards the end of the season. 'Stuey' had netted 47 goals in 244 games in all competitions. Even so, 16 players remained or were offered new contracts.

Soon to join Dale - Tony Ford

Despite his side only just missing the play-offs, Mansfield boss Steve Parkin had quit the following week due to the financial constraints at Field Mill, and he, plus his assistant Tony Ford, the longest serving player in the Football League, were quickly installed at Spotland. Following the diffusion of 'any three from five' substitutes from the Premier League and FA Cup to the Nationwide Football League, ever larger squads were required even by small clubs. However, apart from Ford, the only major signings on show in a pre-season tour of Scotland were Wayne Evans, a full back from Walsall, Chester midfielder Dave Flitcroft, and winger Graeme Atkinson from relegated Scarborough. Squad numbers also became compulsory, and Dale began with the numbers 1 to 20.

The opening day of the 1999-2000 campaign saw Dale become the first Football League visitors to Cheltenham Town, and the 40 year old Ford scored against the newboys in a 2-0 win. A goal from Clive Platt, on loan from Walsall, helped Dale towards a similar victory over Southend, and they went top of the table when they won 3-0 at York.

They slipped up at home a couple of times, but ran up further away wins at Chester, Rotherham - where Atkinson netted a last minute solo goal, after Monington had again been sent off against his former club - and Northampton, all without conceding a goal. This was by far the best start to a season - away from home - that the club had ever enjoyed. The club even managed some good publicity, with Neil Edwards, perhaps the shortest 'keeper in the League, having the best record. Platt, too, had been in tremendous form and Dale moved rapidly to make his transfer permanent for a new club record fee of £100,000.

However, on that day, the story the papers chose was that of the 'dust-up' between Dale mascot Desmond the Dragon and his Halifax counterpart Freddie the Fox!

A 1-0 defeat by leaders Barnet broke the sequence and Dale - with Lancashire out injured already - surprisingly then failed to score in any of the next six games. Indeed, they hadn't scored at Spotland since the first home game of the season, and were back down to 16th place before a cup replay against Burton Albion gave them the break they needed. Former fitness instructor Julian Dowe, who had played for Ayr United and Marbella in Spain, netted what turned out to be his only senior goal in the 3-0 win. Parkin had by now recruited the veteran striker Tony Ellis from Blackpool to partner Platt, and they both scored in the defeat of the boss's old club Mansfield.

After three fairly uninspiring draws - Ellis missing a penalty against Cheltenham - Rochdale then travelled to Brighton. A 2-0 lead was frittered away and Albion led 3-2 with ten minutes left, but then the lanky Platt popped up twice to seal a 4-3 win for the Dale. A seventh away win, at Carlisle, and a home victory over Shrewsbury put Dale right back in contention, but a vital match at Hartlepool went against them 3-2. Completely overturning their earlier form, Dale now won six out of seven at home in the League and also got through the first two rounds of the Auto Windscreens Shield, coming from two down to beat Macclesfield thanks to Monington's extra time golden goal, and winning a penalty-shoot out against Hull. Remarkably, the former match was the first time the Dale had won after trailing 2-0, for 30 years, but in the very next match the boot was on the other foot as Southend salvaged a point after Dale led 3-0 at half time.

The restored Lancashire's eighth goal in ten games helped Dale to another away win, at Halifax, but he was injured later in the game and, crucially, missed the next six, only one of which was won. The victory was at Carlisle in the Auto Windscreens, a match which saw Tony Ford - given an MBE in the New Year's Honours List - reach the phenomenal milestone of 1000 senior games (or even a few more, counting minor cup-ties), the first outfield player to do so. Richard Bott, Dale's new director with responsibility for publicity, and a journalist himself, had been hoping to interest Sky TV etc, but a Tuesday night game in the AWS was hardly prime material to work with.

Gary Jones - 'king ratter' according to player of the month sponsors Pomona - had become a fixture in the side since November and scored twice at Hull to scrape a point against 10 men. However, in the AWS Northern Final Dale were three down to Stoke within the first half hour and eventually lost 4-1 on aggregate. The Dale goal was scored by the previous season's top scorer Michael Holt. Remarkably neither he nor the other joint top marksman from the year before, Andy Morris, scored a single League goal.

Dale were also badly beaten by contenders Darlington and strugglers Leyton Orient, but three wins and three draws closed the gap again, the 4-2 success at Shrewsbury looking likely to put the Shrews down in the process. Having fought out a 3-3 draw at Peterborough, the team was unable to prevent the Posh winning at Spotland, but top scorer Ellis headed an injury time equaliser at Plymouth after Jones and Argyle's McGregor were sent off.

Though they had signed former Scotland under-21 left back Sean McAuley, Dale had recently been playing a wing back system, with Ford and Atkinson on the flanks, but both were ruled out by injury when new front runners Northampton visited Spotland, and Dale old boy Keith Welch had an easy time as his side won 3-0. Nevertheless, a rare goal by player of the year Wayne Evans eked out a 2-1 win at Macclesfield, Dale's tenth away victory of the campaign, to keep alive their outside chance of making the play-offs until the final day. Needing to win well and hope that Cheltenham, Hartlepool and Torquay lost, Dale could manage only a draw against Barnet, and it was Hartlepool - the only winners on the day - who claimed the last play-off place. Dale finished 10th with 68 points (their best yet), four behind them. Reversing the narrow defeat at Hartlepool back in January would have been sufficient to put the Dale in 7th position instead.

Rochdale scored more away goals than anyone in the Nationwide League, except Charlton and Barnsley in Division 1 and Preston in Division 2, but netted only 21 in 23 home games, less than anyone else in Division 3 apart from Chester, who went down, and Shrewsbury who made a last day escape. Acquisitions in the close season of 2000 included midfielders Michael Oliver from Darlington and Macclesfield's Paul Ware, former Welsh international winger Simon Davies, also from Macclesfield, and, after Dale returned from another pre-season Scottish tour, left back Lee Todd from Bradford City. On the way out, again, was Jason Peake who turned down Dale's terms to sign for Plymouth, while Graeme Atkinson was put out of action for the season by cruciate ligament damage.

2000-01:

Dale opened with a home draw against Darlington and then lost 2-1 at Brighton after Ellis and an Albion defender were sent off following a scuffle. The veteran striker atoned in the next game, a Worthington Cup-tie against First Division Blackburn Rovers, when he netted a last minute equaliser in what was billed as the battle of the Flitcrofts, Dale's Dave facing his brother Gary. In the second leg Rovers were awarded no less than three penalties and eventually won 6-1.

Tony Ellis gets his marching orders at Brighton.

Ellis had been suspended and on loan Gary Hamilton was not allowed to play against his own side, so 16 year old YTS striker David Walsh got a surprise run-out as substitute against their multi-million pound opponents.

Hamilton actually made an international appearance while with the club, as he played for Northern Ireland under-21s one night and Rochdale the next. Meantime Dale had obtained their first victories of the season, at home to Scunthorpe, and away at Halifax. Another youngster, winger Phil Hadland, came on as a substitute against Cardiff and grabbed the equaliser. As at the start of the previous term, Dale were in great form away from home, adding victories at Carlisle, York and Shrewsbury, Platt netting his 6th in eight games, and centre half Monington his third in successive games in the 4-0 demolition of the Shrews.

Dale were now second but with Lancashire injured again, Steve Parkin had been attempting to sign Southend's Martin Carruthers. However, a change in management at Roots Hall led to a recall for Carruthers and it was no surprise when he netted the only goal when the sides met. Nevertheless Dale dispatched fellow contenders Hartlepool and Cheltenham, defender Monington taking his tally to an amazing six in eight games, and played out a superb 2-2 draw with leaders Chesterfield. A sixth win in seven away games came at Exeter, Platt's last minute strike earning Rochdale's first win at St. James' Park since 1963. As in the previous year's AWS game, Dale came from two down to level the game with Macclesfield, the goals coming from the two substitutes, Paul Ware against his old club and the on-loan Christian Lee.

Mansfield ended Dale's run, and they also slipped up in both remaining cups (losing to a golden goal at non-League Doncaster in the AWS), but single strikes from Gary Jones accounted for both Blackpool and Hull. Just before the 'real' Millennium, on 1st January 2001 (most people having celebrated it a year too early), Tony Ford, at 41 years and 6 months, passed Jack Warner's record as Rochdale's oldest Football League player (justifying the younger supporters' chants of *"He's big, he's bad, he's older than my dad"*). A fluke by Wayne Evans defeated Darlington and despite a slip-up at home to Halifax, a superb 3-1 win over challengers Leyton Orient in a Sky TV live game kept Dale fourth with 47 points from 25 games. Unfortunately bad weather and the state of the Spotland pitch then conspired to cause several postponements; there were 10 before the end of the season.

Two goalless draws, at Cardiff - themselves on the back of a record-breaking winning sequence - and Scunthorpe, looked to be points well won, but in fact were the beginning of another goal drought, as had afflicted the side the year before. Struggling Torquay and York both beat the Dale 1-0 and, with Ford and Platt injured, Steve Parkin changed his defence to try to help out his attack, bringing in the potentially more constructive Simon Coleman in place of Keith Hill, to play in a back three. Coleman had been signed from Southend the previous summer but in an injury wrecked season had played only once. The experiment backfired disastrously as Shrewsbury, down in the bottom half, unbelievably inflicted Rochdale's worst ever home defeat, by seven goals to one.

Dale had conceded only eight in their previous 14 League games put together. In the aftermath they also went down badly at Southend, Flitcroft ending up in goal after Edwards was sent off for supposedly handling outside the area. After losing only four matches in 27 games, they had now lost four in a row. However, four draws steadied the ship, and it could have been so much better had Hartlepool and leaders Chesterfield not both snatched late equalisers. No blame was attached to YTS goalkeeper Matthew Gilks, though, who had a superb debut at Chesterfield in place of the suspended Edwards; the youngster also played part of the next match when Edwards went off injured.

After missing out on other possibles, Parkin had by now got the striker he wanted in Stoke's Paul Connor, who cost a new record £150,000. Connor scored in three successive games, but Dale still lost at Hull, who had come from nowhere into the play-off positions, despite being in receivership and having been unable to pay their players for a time. Lee Todd scored a dramatic last minute free-kick equaliser against champions-to-be Brighton, but even so Dale had now picked up only five points from 10 games and hadn't won for 12.

Just when it looked all over, Dale suddenly annihilated Carlisle 6-0, Connor grabbing that Dale rarity, a hat-trick. After a draw at Macclesfield when veteran ex-Dale reserve 'keeper Lee Martin saved Jones' penalty, Connor netted two more as Rochdale beat Exeter 3-1 at Easter. Though still only 10th, Dale had another six games to play at this point, compared to the three or four for their rivals. Unfortunately they blew the first one, losing 3-0 at Barnet (and not for the first time presenting a club with their last win before they disappeared out of the league). Rochdale then beat Lincoln 3-1 to reclaim a top eight spot. Chesterfield had been under investigation for numerous alleged illegalities involving payments to players and fake accounting, so although they still headed the table it was widely assumed that, having been found guilty on several counts, they would be docked sufficient points to prevent their promotion, in which case 8th place would be good enough to make the play-offs.

Regardless of that, the Dale would go a long way towards guaranteeing a place if they could get a result at Blackpool, their closest rivals. However, the Seasiders won 3-1 and Edwards was sent off again, for a professional foul. If Dale did make the play-offs, they would have to play them with the youngster Gilks in goal. Celebrating Steve Parkin's award as manager of the month, his side got back on course by beating Mansfield and dramaticaly, after being a goal down at the break, winning the final mid-week game against Plymouth (one of the numerous postponed matches fitted into the final weeks of the season).

Meantime the commission investigating Chesterfield had amazingly decided that they should be docked so few points that they wouldn't even drop out of the automatic promotion places, merely moving down from 2nd to 3rd.

Clive Platt, Dale's record signing.

The Football League, concerned at the apparent leniency, then asked the same panel to reconsider the punishment, but they refused to change their verdict, and with only two days of the season left, the League acquiesced. Dale now had to win their final game - or at least do as well as Blackpool - to stay ahead of their rivals and hang on to 7th place.

Just after half time on the last afternoon, Dale were still in pole position as Darlington pegged back an early Blackpool goal. However Blackpool soon retook the lead while Dale battled to break the deadlock at Plymouth. Twice Argyle defenders hacked the ball off the goal line, but the ball wouldn't run for Dale and the game ended scoreless. Dale were thus condemned to finish 8th, despite their best ever points tally of 70. To rub in Dale's disappointment, it was Blackpool who then went on to win the play-off final. Nevertheless, Rochdale could at least boast their best average gate for 30 years, at 3248.

The End! Gary Jones' shot is saved at Plymouth

Manager Parkin decided to release several of his older players, in particular centre backs Keith Hill and Mark Monington and strikers Tony Ellis and the injury prone Graham Lancashire, to give himself room for manoeuvre in the transfer market. The first signing of the summer was one of his own reserves, when the promising Matty Gilkes was put on a professional contract as Edwards' understudy. Another of the youngsters, striker Kevin Townson, was selected for the England under-17s squad for a match in Italy. A third, Phil Hadland, decided to move on though, and signed for Leyton Orient.

The main new signings, as expected, were for the centre of the defence - Wigan's Gareth Griffiths and Northampton's Richard Green, who had had a successful loan spell at Spotland. Macclesfield's former Republic of Ireland under-21 international midfielder Keiron Durkan and promising Chester youngster Matt Doughty also joined the Dale in July.

As the 2001-02 season approaches, it remains to be seen whether Steve Parkin can make it third time lucky or whether the millstone of the longest continuous spell in the bottom division will prove too heavy. Whichever it is, the hardy fans will be there to see it.

UP THE DALE!

ST. CLEMENTS PLAYING FIELDS
TO DENEHURST STADIUM

The ground on which Rochdale have played since their foundation has gone by a variety of names and the history of the ground actually predates that of Rochdale AFC.

In the beginning it was just St. Clements playing fields, and a pitch there, by the Church Inn, was used by Rochdale St. Clements rugby club in the 1890's, when they were fierce rivals of Rochdale Hornets. The secretary of St. Clements was Mr Harvey Rigg, a local businessman and late Victorian entrepreneur who also held the lease on the ground. When the breakaway Northern Union was formed Rigg persuaded St. Clements to stay with rugby union, leaving Hornets to go on to become the town's professional club. St. Clements' fortunes plummeted as a result, and they went bankrupt in 1897. Rigg found further tennants in the shape of, first, the original Rochdale football club and then Rochdale Town, but each of these folded soon after moving to Spotland from other homes. The ground was then used for local rugby competitions, but when Hornets started their own rival tournaments at the Athletic Grounds, Harvey Rigg decided to 'invent' his own tennants.

It thus came about that a keen rugby man was the prime mover in arranging the meeting in 1907 aimed at reforming a senior soccer side in the town, the present Rochdale AFC. The existence of the ground was therefore instrumental in the formation of the club, not the other - normal - way round!

The new club first played on the ground in August 1907, a practice game between the prospective Manchester League side and 'the rest', attracting 350 people who paid one old penny each to see it! The first serious game, a friendly against Oldham Athletic a couple of weeks later, was watched by about 2,000 people.

The following summer the pitch was brought up to the size required for the FA Cup. Improvements were also made to the ground to make room for more spectators, and the local derby with Heywood United in the Lancashire Combination attracted 5,000 of them. Although the ground was still little more than the original field, a game against Stockport County Reserves in 1910 raised the crowd figures to 7,000 and an FA Cup tie against Southern League Luton Town took the record to 9,933 the following year. In 1912, further ground improvements were made which raised the capacity to 15,000.

The club had become a limited company in 1910 and the company bought the ground outright for £1,700 in February 1914, enabling them to instigate more permanent ground developments. The ground at that time was, as now, bounded by Willbutts Lane (after which it soon came to be known) on one side, but the opposite side was still the remainder of the old playing field. Some of this was land used for the building of the old Main Stand which seated 700 people (and was for many years the smallest at any Football League ground). The rest subsequently disappeared under post-World War 1 housing developments.

Spotland, October 1925.
Record crowd for Bradford's visit.

Pearl Street packed for the FA Cup
visit of Notts County in 1949.

The Pearl Street End was a rather shallow banking, built up of compacted cinders and this was terraced for the first time with railway sleepers wedged in lengthwise to provide a footing. Like the Main stand, this structure was remarkably longlived. The Main Stand roof blew off in 1921, just after Rochdale joined the Football League, but, undaunted, the club added cover to the central part of the Pearl Street End in 1925 and the Willbutts Lane side was covered two years later. In the twenties, crowds of 10,000 were fairly common and the ground record for a League game was set in 1929 when Division 3 North leaders Bradford City, and their former Rochdale centre forward Bert Whitehurst, attracted 20,945 fans.

Although work on the terracing at the Sandy Lane End was carried out in 1937, by the Supporters Club, the next major change to the ground came in 1948. The pitch itself had always had a notorious slope, being 5 feet higher at the Pearl Street End than at Sandy Lane, which must have made viewing the game from the low terracing even more difficult. It was therefore decided to flatten it out, once and for all, prior to a cup-tie against Barrow. This was acheived by bulldozing the offending extra five feet off the top end and then putting the turf back on top. Unfortunately Barrow didn't fancy playing on a new laid lawn and the game had to be played at Oldham!

The excess earth, meanwhile, had been swept up into the south-east corner of the ground and became 'the hill', or Spion Kop, at the end of the Pearl Street terracing.

A year later crush barriers were put in place on the hill to provide extra capacity for the cup-tie against Notts County which attracted the largest ever crowd to Spotland of 24,231. Other cup-ties, in the fifties against Leeds and Chelsea were expected to attract gates of 30,000 - the official capacity was 32,000. Though these never actually materialised, no one then would have envisaged that the capacity would be officially restricted to not much more than a tenth of that figure 40 years later.

More modern concrete terracing was added around the ground over the years, this work continuing into the 1960s, carried out by volunteers from the Supporters Club.

However, the original wood and clinker survived under the Pearl Street cover until modern times. Cover, it should be said, was a relative term in the old Pearl Street End, as the high open ends seemed specially designed to funnel the wind and rain inside rather than keep them out!

In 1954 the main stand caught fire, requiring a partial rebuild, and the same year the first floodlights were installed, beating Old Trafford by 3 years! The poles for these lights, too, survived at the Pearl St. End, long after the lights themselves were replaced in 1971.

Main Stand, minus its roof: 1968

Cover at the Sandy Lane End was provided in 1961, again paid for by the Supporters Club and the 'Improvement Fund', while the roof of the main stand had to be replaced again when it collapsed under the weight of snow in 1966. In those days, (and for quite a long while later) it was possible to change ends at half time.

Pearl Street end in the mid-1970's.

Fans could therefore stand behind the goal the Dale were attacking for the whole match, though Pearl Street was considered the 'home' end.

The new floodlights were switched on by Sir Matt Busby in 1971, but little else was done to the ground until after the grim days of the late seventies when the club stared financial (and playing) disaster in the face more than once. In 1980 Spotland had been secretly sold to a company owned by the then chairman for £175,000. However, it wasn't the Dale but his other businesses which went bust and the incoming board were able to buy the ground back at a cut price from the Official Receivers in 1982.

The first 'modern' redevelopment then took place with the refurbishment of the Willbutts Lane side of the ground, which was renamed the F. S. Ratcliffe Stand. After the Bradford City fire and the Hillsborough disaster, more and more sections of old grounds like Spotland were closed by safety inspectors and the ground licensing authorities. One of the first to suffer was the antiquated Pearl St. End which was closed temporarily immediately after the Bradford fire in 1985.

Ground capacities were slashed as large parts of different grounds were cordoned off. Unfortunately, though, Dale rarely had crowds large enough for this to be a problem. From the immediate post war average of 7-8,000, crowds had slumped to 1,000 by the late seventies. What was left at the Pearl Street End had been given over to the (now segregated) away supporters and the Dale diehards moved to 'the Sandy'.

The Taylor Report on Hillsborough required lower division clubs to have at least half the ground with seated accomodation and instigated an unprecedented wave of development and modernisation around the country. While some clubs like Walsall and Northampton went for entirely new stadia, Rochdale, with a new financial stability engendered by Messrs Kilpatrick and Morris, decided to rebuild their old home. Rochdale Hornets had already started to groundshare with Dale in 1988-89 (at a rent of £11,000 a year), and in 1990 an official partnership with Hornets and Rochdale Council saw the ground transferred to the new Denehurst Park Stadium Company (though fans totally ignored the official change of name of the ground to Denehurst Stadium).

Money from the sale of the Hornets' old home at the Athletic Grounds and £400,000 grants from the Football Trust and others enabled the old main stand to be replaced in 1992 by a new £1.1m structure which was opened for the Boxing Day game against Scunthorpe. Another set of new floodlights were also turned on the same year.

The Sandy Lane End, which had suffered from both storm damage (in March 1992) and zealous safety officials, was soon refurbished too. Executive boxes first appeared at Spotland in 1994 and could be rented for £3000 per season.

The Main Stand in the 1970's

The new Stand gets underway during the Summer of 1992.

The new Main Stand at its opening on Boxing Day 1992

(Above) The WMG Stand at the Pearl Street end, under construction.

.... And after completion

By 1996 the Dale were well forward with plans for a brand new stand at the Pearl Street End, and though Hornets were somewhat less than keen, the football club eventually agreed with the council that they would underwrite any shortfall in its funding.

The actual work was completed much faster than these negotiations and the new £900,000 East, or WMG Stand (sponsored by financial director Graham Morris's company Wyatt, Morris and Golland), was formally opened by Nat Lofthouse before a friendly against Bolton Wanderers in October 1997.

With Hornets thinking bigger, too, and hoping for promotion to Rugby League's Premiership, plans were already afoot by April 1998 for the redevelopment of the fourth, Willbutts Lane, side of the ground with a 4000 seater stand completed during 2000-01. Sponsorship is, of course, the name of the game these days, and besides the WMG stand we now have, instead of the traditional names, the McDonald's Family Stand, the Thwaites Beer Stand and the Motorama Stand. The current official capacity is 10,200.

~ POST-WAR PROGRAMME PARADE ~
A selection of programme covers from
1947 - 2001

1946/7

OFFICIAL PROGRAMME, 2d.

Rochdale Association Football Club.

ROCHDALE
v.
SOUTHPORT

Saturday, December 7th, 1946
KICK-OFF 2.15 p.m.

Next Home Match: December 14th,
ROCHDALE V. HARTLEPOOLS UNITED
SECOND ROUND F.A. CUP

TIMES PRESS, 23 Baillie Street, Rochdale

1947/8

ROCHDALE FOOTBALL CLUB

Official
PROGRAMME

FOOTBALL LEAGUE — 3rd Division

ROCHDALE
versus
LINCOLN CITY
At WILLBUTTS' SPOTLAND
SATURDAY, FEB. 21st, 1948.
KICK-OFF — 3 p.m.
PRICE — TWOPENCE

Times Press, Baillie St., Rochdale.

1949/50

PROGRAMME 2d.

Rochdale Association Football Club Limited

ROCHDALE v.
CREWE ALEX.
SATURDAY, 23rd AUGUST Kick-off 3.0 p.m.

NEXT HOME MATCHES:
Tuesday, August 26th, K.O. 6.45 p.m. - Reserves v. Lancaster
Saturday, August 30th, K.O. 3.0 p.m. - Reserves v. Darwen

At your
service

JOHN JAMES SMITHIES Ltd.
Head Office: 16-18-20. OLDHAM ROAD, ROCHDALE
FOR YOUR REQUIREMENTS
DRAKE ST., Tel. 4164   OLDHAM RD., Tel. 4163
Builders Ironmongery   Iron and Steel
LIVSEY St., Tel. 4162   R.W. Pipe and
Mill Furnishing   Gutters
Engineers' Stores
Footballs
Sporting Ware
Trucks, Handcarts   Vale Locks
Ladders, Ropes   Tools

ALL CORRECT RESULTS
GREEN FINAL
★ The Popular Saturday
Night's Sports Paper

1951/2

OFFICIAL PROGRAMME

Rochdale Association Football Club Limited   Price 3d.

F.A. CUP—3rd Round

ROCHDALE v.
LEEDS UNITED
SATURDAY, JANUARY 12th
Kick-off 2.15 p.m.

ROCHDALE A.F.C.
Back row : WATSON, LYON, NICHOLLS, DOWNES, BUXTON, RADFORD,
Front row : ARTHUR, TOMLINSON, MIDDLEBROUGH, FOULDS, BETTS.

1957/8

ROCHDALE ASSOCIATION FOOTBALL CLUB LTD.

3D. OFFICIAL PROGRAMME **3**D.

Directors:
Chairman: F. S. RATCLIFFE, Esq.
Vice-Chairman: C. H. TATTERSALL, Esq.
G. BLACK, Esq., J. S. STONEY, Esq.
WALTER R. COMMINS.
Manager: H. CATTERICK.   Secretary: WALTER R. COMMINS.
Registered Office: WILLBUTTS, SPOTLAND, ROCHDALE. Tel. 49102.

ROCHDALE
v.
BRADFORD

Saturday, 19th April, 1958
Kick-Off 3.0 p.m.

NEXT HOME GAME

SATURDAY, 26th APRIL, 1958
Reserves v. PRESTON N. E. "A"

1962/3

ROCHDALE A·F·C

ROCHDALE v. MILLWALL
OFFICIAL PROGRAMME 6d.

1965/6

Rochdale
Association
Football Club

F.A. CUP — FIRST ROUND REPLAY
ROCHDALE
v.
FLEETWOOD
WEDNESDAY, 17th NOVEMBER, 1965
Kick-off 7.30 p.m.
OFFICIAL PROGRAMME **6d.**

ROCHDALE
ASSOCIATION
FOOTBALL
CLUB

FOOTBALL LEAGUE—Division 4

OFFICIAL PROGRAMME **6**D.

ROCHDALE
v
WORKINGTON
SATURDAY, 27th JANUARY

1967/8

ROCHDALE
ASSOCIATION
FOOTBALL CLUB

FOOTBALL LEAGUE
Division 4
ROCHDALE
v
SOUTHEND U.

Saturday
10th May
1969
Kick-off 3-0 p.m.

OFFICIAL PROGRAMME **1/-**

1968/9

OFFICIAL PROGRAMME OF ROCHDALE A.F.C.
Incorporating "FOOTBALL LEAGUE REVIEW"

1/-

VOICE
OF
SPOT-
LAND

Saturday, 29th November, 1969
Rochdale v. Fulham
League Division 3 — Kick-off 3-0 p.m.

1969/70

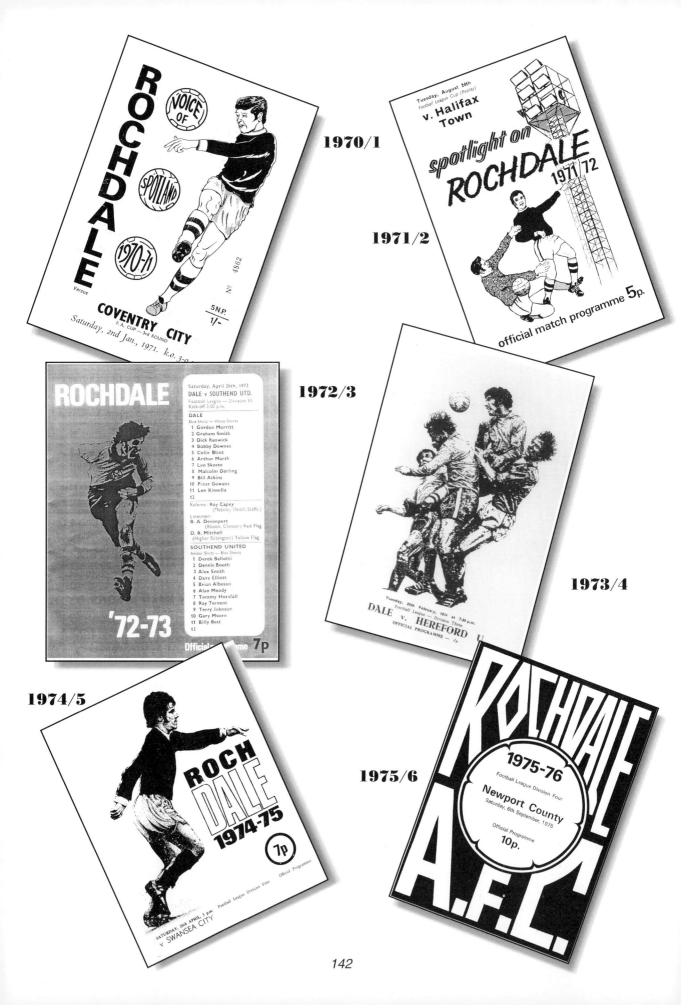

1970/1

1971/2

1972/3

1973/4

1974/5

1975/6

142

1976/7

1977/8

1978/9

1979/80

1980/1

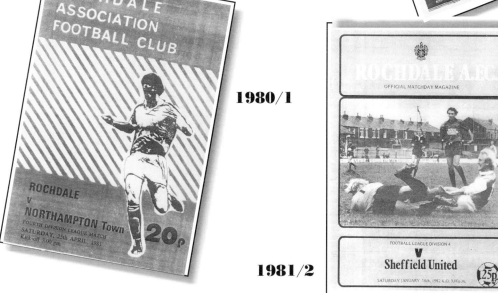

1981/2

1983/4

1984/5

1985/6

1986/7

1987/8

1988/9

1989/90

1990/1

1991/2

1992/3

1993/4

1994/5

1995/6

1997/8

1999/00

2000/01

THE MEN IN CHARGE 1907 - 2001

Rochdale have had a very large number of managers, secretary-managers, secretaries, caretaker managers and acting managers. The following provides biographies of all the men brave - or foolhardy - enough to take on the job.

Back in 1907, the modern concept of a football manager had not really been reached. **Herbert Hopkinson** was appointed the club's secretary at the first meeting and would also have been responsible for the playing side, assisted by the team's skipper Zach Holden (later their trainer). Hopkinson had been a goalkeeper with East Ward in the Rochdale and District League in the late 1890's and then served as their secretary from 1899 to 1902, before becoming secretary of the league itself.

In June 1909, the club appointed **Joe Blackett** as player-manager and secretary (though Harvey Rigg looked after the finances) and he led them to promotion from the second division of the Lancashire Combination and a Lancashire Junior Cup Final victory in his first season, plus the championship of the Lancashire Combination in his second and third. His last match for Rochdale was the drawn Manchester Senior Cup Final of 1912. He had started out as a reserve at Newcastle United, before joining Wolves (1897), Derby County (1900) and Middlesbrough (1901), and completed his tour of the major North East sides by joining Sunderland in 1904, though he never made their League side. He moved south to Luton in 1905 and then spent three years with Leicester Fosse before arriving at Rochdale. Initially in charge of all the playing affairs at the club, he later reverted to merely skippering the side. He moved on to Barrow in 1912, became Reading's trainer in 1913 and joined the Army Service Corps in 1915.

It is not clear at precisely which point Blackett ceased to have a managerial responsibility as well as playing, but he was replaced as secretary in 1910 by, in turn, Messrs **H. Morton, Harry Marshall** (previously assistant secretary at Rotherham) and **C. Wormwell** (one of the directors). They would have been assisted in some playing matters by trainer George Coe, who had previously held the same position at Bury and, in 1912-13, by player-reserve team coach Dan Cunliffe.

In August 1913, **Vince Hayes** was appointed player-manager. He had started as a player with Newton Heath Athletic and joined Newton Heath in February 1901, before they became Manchester United. Tried initially in various other positions, he played regularly for them as a left back but twice suffered broken legs which kept him out of action for long spells. He spent a season with Brentford before returning to United in 1908 and played in their Cup winning team of 1909, also gaining selection for the Football League representative side and the FA touring party to South Africa the following year. Later moving to Bradford, he was then appointed coach to the Norwegian national side for the Olympic games in Stockholm in 1912 and subsequently coached Wiener Sport Verein in Austria. He was also an official of the Players Union. He served Rochdale throughout World War I, taking them to the finals of both the Lancashire and Manchester Senior Cups in 1915. He also worked in Liverpool Docks (he was a boilermaker by trade) and from August 1916, Mr Wormwell reassumed the position of (honorary) secretary, while goalkeeper Billy Biggar became trainer to help look after the playing side. After Rochdale failed to gain admittance to the Football League in 1919 Hayes was appointed secretary-manager of Preston North End and from 1923 he was manager of future European giants Real Madrid.

Dale then had no manager as such from March 1919 until June 1920, though Mr Wormwell continued as secretary and the board of directors included two ex-professional players, George Ross of Bury and Rochdale (now landlord of the Star Inn) and Tommy Wilson (the proprietor of the Wellington Hotel), who no doubt added expertise to the team selection committee, especially after Wilson became chairman in October 1919 (see below).

In June 1920 **Billy Bradshaw** was given the position of player-manager. He had previously spent the best part of two decades with Blackburn Rovers, after starting out with his local side Padiham and then Accrington Stanley (Lancashire League champions in 1903). Primarily a left half and *"the recognised artist of the intermediate line"*, he played in Rovers' League Championship winning sides of 1912 and 1914. He appeared nearly 400 times for Rovers and scored from 36 consecutive penalties. He represented the Football League four times and won three full caps for England between 1910 and 1913. His stay at Rochdale was as brief as that at Blackburn had been long.

Bradshaw was released in September 1920 after just five games of the season as he had been unable to attend training sessions. Nevertheless, several former Blackburn colleagues whom he recruited for Rochdale did make an impact, including Jimmy Crabtree and Harry Dennison.

With Mr J. Lomax now installed as secretary, the chairman **Thomas Carter Wilson** became responsible for most of the playing matters. Wilson had had a long playing career, himself, figuring first in junior football with Ashton Town, Ashton North End (the 1896 Manchester Junior Cup winners) and Oldham County. He joined Swindon Town in 1897 and spent single seasons in turn at Blackburn Rovers, Swindon again, Millwall Athletic and Aston Villa, and two (1902 -1904) with Queens Park Rangers. A short but sturdy outside left, he then served Bolton Wanderers before moving to Leeds City in December 1906 and finally Manchester United in February 1908. He once represented England against Scotland in a match for Indian famine relief. Already a publican when he finished playing, he subsequently went into business in Chorley and became secretary-manager of the town's football team for four years. He moved to Rochdale in 1918, joined the board and was soon elected chairman. After Rochdale were elected to the Football League he had to forego his dual role as league rules of the time prevented ex-professional players from serving as club directors. Trainer George Vickers, the former Preston North End man appointed in July 1921, would have assisted the committee with team matters in the first league season. However, Wilson continued as official manager from July 1922 to February 1923. Mr Lomax, incidentally, remained as secretary until 1927.

The next appointee was **Jack Peart**, player-manager from February 1923 until the end of the 1923-24 season and then manager until July 1930. Peart, a centre forward, had started out with South Shields Adelaide in 1905 and moved successively to Treharris, then Second Division Sheffield United in 1907, Southern League Stoke in 1910 and then Newcastle United for £600 in 1912. He joined Notts County a year later, just too late to save them from relegation, but assisted them to promotion again the following term, when he also represented the Football League. He had earlier played against the FL XI for the Southern League. He guested primarily with Leeds United but also Barnsley (and once for Rochdale) during the Great War.

In November 1919 he joined Birmingham, but a couple of months later moved on to Derby County and became player-manager of Ebbw Vale later in 1920. He then transferred himself to Port Vale in 1922 and also served Norwich City before arriving at Willbutts Lane. During the mid-1920's Peart made Rochdale one of the top teams in the Northern section, but in 1930 he was tempted away to join Bradford City. Immediately winning promotion for the Bantams he took over at Fulham in 1935 and served them until his death in 1948, the side which he had built going on to claim promotion to Division 1 for the first time in the club's history.

Acting manager in the summer of 1930 was the club's senior professional **Harry Martin**. A tall rangy outside left, Martin had been a regular for Rochdale between 1925 and 1929, but more recently had been serving as player-trainer. (He made one last League appearance in 1930-31). Earlier in his career he had spent three seasons with Sutton Junction before joining Sunderland in January 1912. He played in their League championship winning side a year later and also in the Cup Final, having the misfortune to miss his side's best chance. He also won numerous international honours, playing for England both in a full international and a 1919 Victory international, as well as several times for the Football League. He moved on to Nottingham Forest in 1922 and was considered so vital to their battle against relegation that he was once carried back on to the field, having gone off injured, to convert a crucial penalty kick. After Rochdale he was trainer at York City and Mansfield Town, then becoming the Stags manager in December 1933. Sacked in 1935 he was trainer at Newport County and trainer and later coach at Swindon Town until the 1950's, playing as emergency goalkeeper in a wartime match when nearly 50.

Martin was overlooked for the permanent manager's job, though, as the board went instead for Billy - better known as **'Kiltie' - Cameron.** Cameron had played for Burnbank Athletic, Albion Rovers and Renton in the early years of the century and joined Second Division Glossop in 1904. He then had stints with Bolton Wanderers (1906) and Blackburn Rovers (from 1907), playing in their league championship winning side of 1912 before signing for Bury and then spending the last season before the war at Hull City. He became Bury manager in 1919 but was implicated, along with two directors, in a match fixing scandal when several Bury players were found guilty of throwing a match that Coventry City needed to win to avoid relegation. He was suspended for life by the Football League, but the sentence was commuted in 1929. His spell at Rochdale was disastrous, the side finishing next to bottom in 1931 and claiming an all time low 11 points the following season. He left the club at Christmas 1931.

Mr **Ernest Nixon** had been club secretary since taking over from Mr M. Menzies at the end of 1928 and was given the title of secretary-acting manager on the departure of Cameron. He presided over matters until April 1932 when **Herbert Hopkinson** took over the managerial side. Since resigning the secretary's post at Rochdale in 1909, Mr Hopkinson had become a well known Football League referee and refereed the Wales vs. Ireland international of 1927-28. He was also president of the Rochdale Sunday Schools League from 1927 until 1958. He was manager at the club he had helped to found, until January 1934, when, despite his relatively respectable first season, Rochdale had dropped back to the bottom spot again. Ernest Nixon thereupon resumed his role of secretary-acting manager until the next appointment was made.

July 1934 saw the arrival of an immensely experienced footballer in the shape of the England international **W. H. (Billy) Smith**. An outside left, Smith had joined Huddersfield from Hobson Wanderers way back in 1913 and was the first forward to play 500 League games for one club. He was also a remarkable goalscorer for a winger, netting well over a century. He played in the promotion side of 1920 and was a vital part of the three times League championship winning team of 1924-26. He also played in the FA Cup finals of 1922, 1928 and 1930, having missed the 1920 final through suspension after scoring the goal that won the semi-final. In 1922 he scored in the semi-final and in the Terriers' victory in the final itself. He represented the Football League three times between 1920 and 1928 and also won three full caps for England. In 1933-34, when Huddersfield had come close to reclaiming the title from Arsenal, Smith had still appeared quite regularly at the age of 38. Despite signing several former Huddersfield colleagues, and even playing a few games himself, the best he could do was to keep Rochdale (just) above the re-election zone, and he was sacked in November 1935.

Ernest Nixon took over yet again, this time with the title of caretaker manager, though in reality he was still essentially club secretary. Rochdale managed to reach 18th place in 1936-37 and had regained a certain amount of financial stability, but a supporters' protest group had been agitating for the appointment of a full time manager for some time. The decision was effectively made for the board just after the start of the following season when Nixon resigned, leaving them without a manager or secretary.

On 6 October 1937, they therefore appointed Glentoran manager **Sam Jennings** to the vacant position at Spotland. Jennings had had a long and well travelled career, guesting for Spurs and Notts County while serving in the Coldstream Guards during WWI. The legendary Major Frank Buckley signed him for Norwich City from Basford United in 1919, and he was sold to Middlesbrough for the substantial fee of £2500 a year later.

He also served Reading, West Ham United, Brighton, Nottingham Forest and Port Vale during the 1920's, winding up his League career with a short spells at Stockport and Burnley in 1931-32. He then became secretary and coach at Wisbech Town before departing for France as player-coach to Olympic de Marseilles. He was then briefly with Scarborough in 1934 before another stint coaching abroad, this time in Switzerland, before obtaining the Glentoran job in June 1936. Shortly after taking over at Rochdale he became ill with pleurisy, but nevertheless was given another year's contract in April 1938. However he was unable to carry out his duties after September of that year and eventually stepped down permanently in March 1939. Sadly he died at the age of only 45 in 1944.

Ted Goodier had been signed by Ernest Nixon in the summer of 1937 and became club captain under Sam Jennings. When Jennings became too ill to continue as manager in September 1938, the board promoted Goodier to player-manager. He signed a two year contract as manager in January 1939, the contract to take effect when Jennings' ended. Apart from three months in 1943 when he was tempted away to manage Birmingham, Goodier remained in charge at Spotland until 1952. He took them to their best placing since the days of Jack Peart in his first season and after the war fashioned a side which was able to finish as high as third in 1950, after winning the Lancashire Senior Cup (still then a prestigious competition) the year before. He also made a considerable profit for the club as a result of wheeler dealing in the transfer market. Rochdale had a poor season in 1951-52 and the following summer Goodier resigned. He then managed Wigan Athletic for a time, and though troubled with ill health returned to Football League management with Oldham Athletic in 1956, spending two seasons at Boundary Park. In his playing days, Goodier was a tough tackling wing half who had been on Bolton Wanderers groundstaff and played for Huddersfield Town and Lancaster Town before a stint at Oldham from 1925 to 1931. He had four seasons with QPR and one with Watford before returning north to Crewe and thence to Rochdale.

Rochdale quickly signed up Oldham Athletic coach **Jack Warner** to take over from Goodier. Warner had started out in Welsh junior football with Trelaw and Aberaman before signing for Swansea in January 1934. A steady wing half, he won his first Welsh cap while with the Swans and in 1938 was transferred to Manchester United.

He figured regularly for United during and immediately after the war, eventually moving on to be player-coach at Oldham in 1951. He prided himself on his fitness and selected himself for half of Rochdale's games in 1952-53, becoming their oldest player, aged 41 (a record later passed by Tony Ford). Rochdale finished only just above the re-election places and Warner left the club - and professional football - at the end of the season.

Next in the line was **Harry Catterick**, who was persuaded to move from Crewe Alexandra by Rochdale chairman Fred Ratcliffe. Though on Stockport County's books as a junior, he was playing for Cheadle Heath Nomads when signed by Everton in 1937. He was understudy to Tommy Lawton and, of course, lost many years to the war, so his appearances were limited, but he remained with Everton until being appointed player-manager of Crewe in December 1951. He then spent five seasons at Spotland, and with the help of some other former Evertonians like Jackie Grant and Eddie Wainwright made the Rochdale side one of the better footballing sides in the Northern Section. In his last year, his side finished 10th, to qualify for the new Third Division. The Dale board then allowed him to accept the offer of the manager's job at Sheffield Wednesday, and he was with them from August 1958 until resigning in April 1961, winning promotion in his first season and seeing his side finish runners-up to 'Spurs before he left. He then returned to Everton, where he earned the reputation as one of the greatest managers of that era. Everton - known as the 'school of science' - were League champions in 1963, FA Cup winners in 1966, finalists in 1968 and then champions again, with a new team, in 1970. He was promoted 'upstairs' to general manager in 1973, but spent a couple of years managing Preston North End before retiring in 1977.

Rochdale began the 1958-59 season without a manager, long serving secretary W. R. Commins being responsible for day to day administration, but in October **Jack Marshall** made the opposite move to Catterick, arriving from Sheffield Wednesday where he had been trainer-coach.. Marshall had played locally with Bacup Borough in the 'thirties, before signing for Burnley. He was forced to retire through injury soon after the war and in 1949 became coach at Bury. He took up a similar position at Stoke in 1951 and moved to Sheffield Wednesday three years later. While at Hillsborough he also acted as trainer to the England team.

When he arrived at Spotland, the Dale were already bottom of the table and he could not prevent their relegation. However he brought in a number of new players and introduced more modern tactics to the lower divisions, which enabled Rochdale to have a reasonably successful time the following season and earned 'Jolly Jack', as he was often known, a crack at managing First Division Blackburn Rovers. After six and a half years at Ewood Park he left in the wake of their relegation to Division 2 and returned to Sheffield Wednesday as assistant manager and later manager. He had a very brief stint as manager of Bury in 1969 and then spent the whole of the 1970's at Blackburn again, as their physiotherapist, before retiring.

When Jack Marshall left in September 1960, the club promoted one of the players whom Marshall had brought in, **Tony Collins**, to the manager's chair. Collins had been an amateur on Brentford's books just after the war but moved north to sign for Sheffield Wednesday in November 1947. He then began a tour of the third divisions which took in York City, Watford (twice), Norwich City, Torquay United and Crystal Palace, between 1949 and 1957. An outside left, he signed for Rochdale in the summer of 1959, but was actually on the injured list when made player-manager a year later. He did play in the second half of the season but then retired to concentrate on management. In 1961-62 he masterminded Rochdale amazing run to the League Cup Final, when they beat his old boss Jack Marshall's First Division side Blackburn Rovers in the semi-final. Dale came close to promotion in 1965, obtaining their best ever points tally in Division 4, but by 1967 they twice had to apply for re-election and early in the next campaign Collins resigned. He became chief scout at Leeds United under Don Revie and served under him on the England staff in the mid 'seventies. He had also been chief scout for Bristol City after leaving Spotland and became their assistant manager in 1976, serving as their caretaker manager (for all of 19 days), in 1980. After another short spell on Leeds' staff, he scouted for Manchester United through most of the 1980's and after a stint with Newcastle United finally became a scout for Millwall.

On Collins' departure, the Dale went for an experienced manager in **Bob Stokoe**. Stokoe had had a very long career with Newcastle United, whom he joined from Spen Juniors in 1947.

Although not a top star like, say, Jackie Milburn, he played around 300 games at centre half between 1950 and 1961 and won an FA Cup winners medal in 1955. In December 1961 he was appointed player-manager of Bury, continuing to play until 1964. Bury reached as high as 8th in Division 2 in 1963, but Stokoe resigned in 1965 and took over at Charlton Athletic. Two years later he was sacked but was immediately given the manager's job at Spotland. He kept them clear of re-election at the end of the '67-68 season and then acquired most of the players who would win promotion a year later. By then, though, Stokoe had left for Carlisle United in Division 2. In December 1970 he became manager of First Division Blackpool but was unable to keep them up, and in 1972 moved on again, to Sunderland. Becoming known as 'the messiah' by the Roker fans, he led Sunderland to one of the most improbable cup final wins of all time, when his Second Division side beat overwhelming favourites Leeds 1-0. He also got Sunderland promoted to Division 1 in 1976, but resigned his position after the Wearsiders made a dire start to the following campaign. A year later he became manager of Bury for a second time, then had a second spell at Blackpool (see below).

When Stokoe left, his assistant **Len Richley** stepped up to manage the Dale. Richley had already had a varied career but had not previously managed a League club. He had begun as an amateur playing for Sunderland's junior sides, then moved to Crystal Palace and to Tonbridge, as player-secretary. He finally made his Football League bow with Hartlepools, whom he joined in 1951, but in 1953, at the age of only 29, he was appointed player-manager of Holbeach United, later taking the same role at Kings Lynn who had several good cup runs, memorably knocking out Coventry City in 1961-62. He then became secretary at Bury under Bob Stokoe and acted as assistant manager from 1966. In March 1968 Stokoe recruited him as Rochdale's assistant manager and secretary (taking over the latter role from the very long serving Walter Commins). He then took up the managerial reins and guided the Dale to their one and only Football League promotion to date. Early in 1970, though, he had a disagreement with his board over club policy and resigned. The following summer he took over at Darlington, but after only one season left to become chief scout for Newcastle United, also serving as assistant manager for a time.

On Richley's departure, he was, in turn, replaced by his assistant **Dick Connor**. Another Geordie like Stokoe and Richley, Connor had been on Newcastle's books before joining South Shields in 1951 and then beginning his FL career with Grimsby Town. After seven seasons as a sturdy wing half, he moved to Southampton, and then to Tranmere Rovers for £3000 in 1961. He ended his playing career at Aldershot, becoming their assistant trainer in 1963, working his way up to trainer-coach. In December 1968, Len Richley recruited him in a similar capacity at Spotland and he soon took over as coach and assistant manager as the Richley - Connor double act propelled Rochdale to promotion and, for a while, the top of Division 3. Connor had just over three seasons in charge, but his contract was not renewed in the summer of 1973, even though Rochdale had just finished 13th in (the old) Division 3. He then became manager of Darlington for a year and, after a spell away from the game, working as an insurance man, he coached Grimsby Town from 1977. In 1981 he returned to Rochdale as coach and later assistant manager to Peter Madden.

A Scot, as the name would suggest, **Angus (Gus) McLean** became caretaker manager at Spotland in May and June 1973. He had been a tough centre half with Wolves, whom he joined from Hilton Main when he was only 14, when they finished in the top six in Division 1 three times in a row in the late 'forties. He then became player-manager of Aberystwyth Town in 1951 when he was still only 26. He later played for Bromsgrove Rovers but reappeared in the League as player-coach of Bury in 1953. He moved to Crewe a year later and in the mid-sixties joined the staff at Hartlepools United, taking over as manager when Brian Clough left in 1967. Hartlepools were promoted for the first time ever the following year, but were immediately relegated again, and McLean was sacked when they finished in the bottom four in 1970. He then became assistant manager and secretary at Spotland under Conner and remained as assistant after Walter Joyce took over. He was replaced in October 1975 and became assistant manager at Southport the following year.

Walter Joyce took over in June 1973, after a spell as youth team coach at Oldham Athletic, and brought a number of former Oldham juniors to Spotland over the next few years. His first season was a disaster as Dale won only twice all season and lost their Third Division status. Nevertheless, he survived for two more seasons before leaving 'by mutual consent' in 1976. As a player he had spent 10 years at Burnley, mostly in the reserves, before a £10,000 move to Blackburn Rovers in 1964. He then joined Oldham in 1967, graduating to their coaching staff two years later. He turned down the chance to coach the youth team at Manchester United to take the Rochdale job. After leaving Spotland he was coach and assistant manager at Bolton Wanderers until 1985 and had a similar position at Preston North End.

He was later Youth Development Officer at Preston and then at Bury. His son Warren was a player at Bolton and Preston, later figuring at Plymouth, Burnley and Hull, before following his father into management when he was appointed the Tigers' boss in 1998.

In May 1976 **Brian Green** became the first former Dale player to return to take over as manager (as opposed to being promoted from the ranks). He had first joined Rochdale from Haggate Lads in 1954 prior to his National Service (when he represented the Army). Primarily a centre forward, though he could play in most positions, he moved to Southport in 1959 and then, in quick succession, Bury, Colwyn Bay, Barrow, Runcorn, New Brighton, Altrincham, Exeter City, Chesterfield, Wisbech and Mossley. In 1964 he went to play for Australian club Sydney Prague, returning to the UK to play for Stalybridge Celtic and Ashton United, and manage Glossop before becoming coach at Barrow in 1968. Over the next few years he also coached Halifax Town and Southport, as well as having a spell in Kuwait. He won a coach of the year award while at Chester and then became coach to the Australian national side before returning to Spotland. He had a little over a year in charge and though Dale led Division 4 early in his first campaign, when he left to take a coaching job with Leeds, they were rooted at the foot of the League. Green was later Blackburn's assistant manager and held the same position at Stockport County before becoming a highly successful manager in Norway, especially with Brynn of Bergen, in the 1980's.

Another former player, **Mike Ferguson** was given the job of caretaker after Green's departure and then appointed manager. Ferguson had also had a long playing career, starting as a junior with Plymouth Argyle but returning to Lancashire to play for Accrington Stanley in 1960. When Stanley collapsed in March 1962, Blackburn Rovers bought his registration from the Football League for £1500 and six years later sold him to Aston Villa for £60,000. He later played for QPR and Cambridge United before arriving at Spotland in 1974. While with Rochdale he spent the summers with Los Angeles Aztecs in the NASL and towards the end of the 1975-76 season he went to Iceland to manage champions I. A. Akranes. He also coached Rossendale and had a brief playing comeback at Halifax before returning to Rochdale in September 1977, and taking the manager's job full time a month later.

He lasted only a year, with Dale bottom of the table throughout. He later managed in Sweden, was boss of Apoel Nicosia and had various coaching jobs in the Middle East. He became manager of Enfield in 1989.

When Ferguson was sacked in December 1978, former Dale coach **Peter Madden** was appointed caretaker manager, coach and trainer, and immediately signed several of the players who would lift Rochdale out of the bottom four. He had earlier been coach and then assistant manager at Spotland under Dick Connor and had followed him to Darlington, eventually succeeding Connor as the Quakers' boss in 1975. In his playing career he had been a powerful centre half with Rotherham United between 1955 and 1966, playing in the first ever Football League Cup Final. He also played briefly for Bradford Park Avenue before becoming player-manager of Skegness and moving from there to Spotland in 1970. He declined the chance to take on the manager's job permanently but stayed on as assistant (see below).

In January 1979, the board appointed **Doug Collins** as player-manager, even though he had not actually played for some time, being on Derby County's coaching staff. An apprentice with Rotherham (when Madden was club captain), he signed professional with Grimsby Town in 1963 but spent most of his career (1968 to 1976) with Burnley who bought him for £27,000. He later had short spells at Plymouth and Sunderland before playing in the NASL with Tulsa Roughnecks and then coaching at Derby in 1978. Although playing relatively little, Collins oversaw the amazing late season run when Dale won 7 games out of 8 to escape the clutches of the re-election zone. However, when this promise faded the following term, and Collins was sacked after just 10 months in charge. He subsequently managed in Australia.

After losing his job at Blackpool, Bob Stokoe had been scouting for Carlisle and had been a frequent visitor to Spotland. Within a couple of days of Collins' departure Stokoe was back in the hot seat at Rochdale, but had a disastrous time, Dale staying rooted to the foot of the table and scoring only one goal in a run of 15 games. He resigned at the end of the season and returned to Carlisle as their manager. He spent five seasons in charge, getting them back up to Division 2, before retiring, briefly, in 1985.

Carlisle struggled without him and he was soon reappointed, but was unable to save them from the drop and he left at the end of the season. Again joining Sunderland's staff, he was their caretaker manager from April to June 1987, later scouting for Chelsea.

This time **Peter Madden** agreed to step into the manager's shoes and, working on a shoestring budget, he amazingly resurrected the Dale as a force in Division 4, 15th in 1981 being their highest placing since they were relegated in 1974. It proved difficult to make any further progress, though, and Dale had slipped back to being re-election candidates when Madden was sacked in March 1983. He was later a publican and ran the successful Topham's side in Rochdale Sunday football.

Rochdale again went for a player-manager and recruited **Jimmy Greenhoff**. In a distinguished career starting at Leeds United in 1961, he had been the subject of several big money transfers, moving to Birmingham for £75,000 in 1968, Stoke for £100,000 a year later, and Manchester United for £120,000 in 1976. He won 4 England under-23 caps, represented England 'B' and the Football League, and won League Cup winners medals with both Leeds and Stoke. He also had one winners and one losers medal from FA Cup finals with Manchester United and Inter-Cities Fairs Cup Finals with Leeds. He played for Crewe Alexandra from December 1980 and also had a spell in the NASL with Toronto Blizzard, before becoming player-coach at Port Vale. On arrival at Spotland in March 1983, he signed his brother Brian (also of Leeds, Manchester United and England) as his assistant. Although they avoided the re-election places at the end of the season Rochdale were back in the bottom four the following season, and Greenhoff resigned exactly a year after taking charge. He subsequently coached at Port Vale again before leaving the professional game to run soccer schools.

When the Greenhoff brothers departed in March 1984, senior professional **Les Chapman**, already a veteran of around 600 League games, was given the caretaker manager's job until the end of the season. Though there were signs of improvement, Dale did not quite escape the bottom four and the board decided to bring in a new man at the end of the season. Chapman spent one more season at Spotland as player-assistant manager, then moved to Stockport County.

He soon became elevated to player-manager once more, in October 1985. He moved again the following year, becoming player-assistant manager (he continued playing until he was 39) and eventually manager at Preston North End. He was sacked early in the 1992-93 season and became youth team coach at Manchester City. Earlier in his career, Chapman had joined his home town club Oldham from High Barn in 1966 and was transferred to Huddersfield Town for £35,000 in 1969, returning to Oldham five years later. Originally a winger or midfielder he became a full back later in his career and spent the summer of 1978 playing for San Jose Earthquakes. In 1979 he joined Stockport and a year later switched to Bradford City for £10,000, moving to Rochdale in the summer of 1983.

In May 1984 **Vic Halom** moved from Northern Premier League champions Barrow to take over at Spotland. The son of a professional footballer from Hungary, Halom had signed professional for Charlton Athletic after his apprenticeship and made his League debut in 1966. From there he went to Orient, Fulham and Luton before joining Sunderland for £35,000 in 1973, in time to play in their famous FA Cup Final victory over Leeds. A powerful centre forward, he also helped them win the Second Division championship in 1976 but then joined Oldham for £25,000. He became player-coach at Rotherham in 1980 and also worked in Finland and Norway before taking over at Barrow for the 1983-84 season. He lasted two and a half seasons at Spotland, but a dearth of victories in the early part of the 1986-87 campaign led to his departure. He was later manager of Burton Albion and commercial manager at North Shields, and fought the 1992 General Election as the Liberal Democrat candidate for Sunderland North.

After one week, in which reserve team coach **Brian Taylor** (a former Dale stalwart at the end of a career which also took in Middlesbrough and Doncaster Rovers) took charge of the team for the FA Cup defeat by Wrexham, **Eddie Gray** moved in. Gray had spent 20 years with Leeds United, playing over 550 games between 1965 and 1985, and spending the last three of those as player manager. An old style winger, he had won 12 full caps for Scotland and had winners medals from the League Championship (1969 and 1974), the FA Cup (1972) and the League and Fairs Cups (both in 1968), as well as a string of runners-up medals.

After being sacked by Leeds he had been reserve team coach at Middlesbrough and then made a playing comeback with Whitby Town before joining Rochdale in December 1986. Rochdale managed to escape relegation to the Conference at the end of the season, but Gray's relatively expensive buys in the summer of 1987 were languishing

at the foot of the table until a financial crises, after the departure of chairman Tommy Cannon, forced him to use numerous youngsters instead. He left at the end of the season to take over at Hull, but lasted less than a year and then became manager at Whitby Town before returning to the back room staff at Leeds. His brother, Frank, was also a player for Leeds, as well as Forest and Sunderland, and similarly went into management in the lower divisions, with Darlington.

The next appointment certainly provided a new departure, as Dale went for South American style. **Danny Bergara** had played for Racing Club of Montevideo and as a youth international for his native Uruguay (his elder brother Mario played in the 1962 World Cup finals) before emigrating to Spain (with another brother, Nacho) when he was 20. A centre forward, he played for Real Mallorca

(Spanish second division champions in 1965), Seville and Tenerife between 1962 and 1973, but then came to England to coach at Luton Town under Harry Haslam. He followed Haslam to Sheffield United as assistant manager in 1978, and while at Bramhall Lane was also a coach to the England youth team. He spent some time coaching in Brunei and managed the amateur side Sheffield FC before getting a coaching job at Middlesbrough. He returned to Bramall Lane as coach in 1987 and moved to Rochdale in July 1988. After a promising start to the season, Dale dropped away after Christmas and when Stockport sacked their manager it was no surprise that Bergara, a friend of the Stockport chairman, moved to Edgeley Park. He subsequently took several of his Dale players to Stockport. Bergara had a long spell in charge, taking them to the Division 4 runners up spot in 1991 and several trips to Wembley in the Autoglass Trophy and in play-off finals, before leaving in 1995.

Next in line at Spotland, in March 1989, was **Terry Dolan**. It was Dolan's second time around at Rochdale, as he had finished his Football League career as a midfield man with them in the 1981-82 season. With Eccleshill United and Bradford City as an amateur, he turned professional with Bradford Park Avenue and played with them

until they were voted out of the League in 1970. He then joined Huddersfield Town, but they were then on a downward spiral from the First to the Fourth divisions, and Dolan returned to Bradford City for £10,000 in August 1976. He had five years as a regular before joining the Dale and then played and coached with Thackley and Harrogate Town. He returned to Bradford City again in 1985 working his way up from youth coach to manager by 1986-87. He almost steered City into Division 1 the following year, when they lost the play-off final to Middlesbrough, but was sacked in January 1989. At Spotland he managed Dale to their first top half finish for 20 years and a first ever trip to round five of the FA Cup in 1990. He was 'poached' by Hull City in February 1991 (Hull being ordered by the League to pay £40,000 compensation to the Dale), but despite a longish stint was unable to generate any success. In 1997 he became assistant manager at Huddersfield, and a couple of years later become boss of York City, dragging them away from the foot of Division 3.

Dave Sutton was signed by Danny Bergara in the close season of 1988, at the end of a career which had seem him figure at centre half with Plymouth Argyle, Reading (on loan) and most notably Huddersfield Town between 1973 and 1985, winning a Division 4 championship medal in 1980. He had also had three seasons at Bolton Wanderers before joining Dale, but had to retire through injury after 28 games for Rochdale. He then became the Dale's physio and was actually briefly in charge at Spotland between Bergara's departure and the arrival of Dolan. When Dolan and his assistants Jeff Lee and Bernard Ellison left for Hull, Sutton decided to stay and was handed the manager's job.

Dale finished the 1990-91 season comfortably enough and with Sutton's new signings Reeves, Flounders and Whitehall, to the fore they should have at least made the play-offs, but blew it in the last three weeks of the 1991-92 season. Dale again challenged the play-off places in the next two seasons, but following a slump in the early part of 1994-95, and with his position under review by the board, Sutton resigned. He subsequently took over as manager of Chorley.

Sutton's assistant **Mick Docherty** was left in charge - and somewhat in limbo - in December 1994 while the board attempted to coax first Ian Atkins and then Macclesfield's Sammy McIlroy into taking the job. When they finally declined, Docherty was given the job. With little money available, 'Doc junior' (his father Tommy was the famous manager of numerous clubs including Chelsea and Manchester United, as well as the Scottish national team) managed to steer Dale back towards the top of Division 3 in the first half of 1995-96, but a huge injury list slid them back down again. Docherty was known to be unhappy about having to plan for even more cuts the following season and in the summer the board decided to dispense with his services. Prior to his stint at Spotland, he had been an England youth international full back while with Burnley (Second Division champions in 1973) from 1967 to 1976, and then played for Sunderland before injury cut short his career in 1979. He was then taken on to the coaching staff at Sunderland and became their caretaker manager between April and June 1981, Sunderland winning at Liverpool on the final day to stay up. In 1983 Docherty became manager of Hartlepool, but they only won once in the first half of the season and was sacked. Coach at Wolves (where his father was manager) and Blackpool, he then returned to Burnley as assistant manager in 1989. He took up the same position at Hull in 1990 but was sacked in 1991 when Terry Dolan moved in and traded places with him, becoming Dave Sutton's assistant at Rochdale. After his time at Spotland he returned to Burnley again as coach in 1998.

Graham Barrow's name had been mentioned in the past as the sort of manager the Rochdale board should be trying to attract and in June 1996 they did so. Much of his playing career had been in non-League football, and he only joined Wigan (for £12,000) from Alt-rincham in 1981, when he was 27. Wigan were promoted a year later, and Barrow remained with them, as a tough tackling midfielder until he became Chester's player-coach in 1986.

He was promoted to assistant manager under Harry McNally (whom he had also served under at Altrincham and Wigan), continuing to play until he was nearly 40, and took over from McNally as manager in 1992. Chester were already at the bottom of the table and Barrow was unable to halt the slide into Division 3, but remarkably took the 66-1 no-hopers to promotion again the following year. However, a proposed takeover had fallen through and with virtually no players contracted for the following season, Barrow sensationally quit after Chester finished 2nd. His other old club, Wigan, were struggling at the bottom of Division 3, and in September 1994 he became manager at Springfield Park. He recruited a number of new players, including three Spaniards, but was replaced as manager in mid-season when they were in a challenging position for the play-offs. In his three years at Spotland, despite importing a number of players who had been with him at his previous clubs, Dale were never able to mount a serious promotion charge and he fell out of favour with the fans quite quickly. Sacked in April 1999 he became assistant manager at Notts County and subsequently managed Chester again - by now a non-League club - until the summer of 2001.

Youth team manager **David Hamilton** and senior pro **Ian Bryson** looked after the team for the final game of the 1998-99 season (though Bryson was then given a free transfer by the board).

Current incumbent **Steve Parkin** arrived in June 1999, along with his right hand man Tony Ford, the two of them previously having been in charge at Mansfield Town. Parkin started his playing career as an apprentice with Stoke City, turning professional with them in 1983. An England Schools and Youth international, he went on to play five games for England under-21's. A full back or midfield player, he was transferred to West Bromwich Albion for £190,000 in the summer of 1989 but suffered from a number of injuries and played relatively infrequently in three years at the Hawthorns. He joined his home town side Mansfield on a free transfer, and became club captain as they reached the Division 3 play-offs in 1995, but with injury curtailing his career he then joined their coaching staff. In October 1996, at the age of 30, he took over as their manager, soon signing up Tony Ford, a former clubmate at both Stoke and West Brom, as his player-coach. Bottom of the table early in the season, Mansfield finished in 11th place and just missed out on the play-offs by one place in 1999, despite not being able to sign any new players. He quit in the summer and joined Rochdale, and has taken them to within one win of the play-offs in each of his two seasons to date.

~ Statistical Section: ~

Who's Who sections (pages 157 - 177)

A full list is included for every player who has made a competitive match appearance for Rochdale since the club's formation: Pre-League 1907 - 1921 (including the First World War), Football League 1921 - 2001 (to end of 2000-01 season), Second World War 1939 - 1946.

The player's surname plus initials are shown, followed by the most commonly known first name. 'D.O.B.', Date of Birth, or year only, is given (where known), with Place of Birth (town or local area where known). 'First Season' and 'Last season' refers to the first (and last) seasons when competitive appearances where made for the club. No entry in the second column indicates a single season of appearance(s). The year indicates the first year of the season, e.g. 1974 refers to 1974-75. Previous and next clubs are shown where known. Appearances (including those as a used substitute) and Goals columns are split into League, FAC (F A Cup), FLC (Football League Cup and subsequent sponsors included names, plus other major cup competitions) and Other. See relevant section for exact definitions. Where a player has spent more than one period with the club, the appearances and goals have been consolidated, and a second line provides relevant additional details. For periods other than Football League seasons, similar - normally abbreviated - details apply. Further explanations are given under the relevant sections.

Seasonal Statistics (pages 178 - 301)

First column shows the (League) match number or cup round: Q = qualifying, R2 = second round, rep = replay, SF = semi-final, etc.
Second column shows the date of the match.
Third column shows the opponents, upper case (capitals) = 'home' game' and lower case = 'away' game.
Fourth column shows the final result, Rochdale's score first.
Fifth column shows the goalscorers. (og) indicates an own goal, with goalscorer's name, and (p) a goal scored from a penalty.
Sixth column shows the attendance. Official figures where known (Football League records from 1925-26) or (normally approximate) figures generally from newspaper reports.
Players grid: Shirt numbers worn are shown, with generally accepted positions for pre-War matches (when shirt numbering was not used), e.g. 1 = goalkeeper, 3 = left back, 8 = inside right, etc. Since the use of squad numbering the shirt numbers are not necessarily the actual number worn, but have been 'converted' to broadly follow the accepted positional convention. A number underlined indicates the player was substituted by player number 12, 14 or 15 (for convenience these numbers have been used, but do not necessarily relate to the actual shirt number used). Used substitutes only are shown.

Who's Who: Football League Players

Player			D.O.B	Place of Birth	First Season	Last Season	Previous Club	Next Club	League	FAC	FLC	Other	League	FAC	FLC	Oth.
Abbott	H	Harry	15/3/1895	Preston	1931		Lancaster Town	Wigan Athletic	32	1	0	1	0	0	0	0
Ainscow	A	Alan	15/07/53	Bolton	1989		Blackburn Rovers	Horwich RMI	20	1	3	2	0	0	0	1
Ainsworth	D	David	28/01/58	Bolton	1975		(App)	Mossley	2	0	0	0	0	0	0	0
Alford	CP	Carl	11/02/72	Manchester	1988		(YTS)	Burnley	4	0	0	0	0	0	0	0
Allatt	V	Vernon	28/05/59	Hednesford	1983		Halifax Town	Crewe Alexandra	40	3	3	3	8	1	0	1
Anders	J	Jimmy	08/03/28	St Helens	1953	1956	Bradford City	Bradford P.A.	123	6	0	6	28	2	0	3
Anders	JS	Jason	13/03/74	Rochdale	1990	1992	Crewe Alexandra	Dicken Green	17	1	2	1	1	0	0	0
Anderson	A	Alex	08/01/22	Glasgow	1947		Hearts	Dundalk	4	0	0	0	0	0	0	0
Anderson	E	Eddie	23/09/17	Glasgow	1947		Stirling Albion	Prescot Cables	1	0	0	0	0	0	0	0
Anderson	JL	Johnny	05/04/28	Glasgow	1959		Wrexham	Chester	28	4	0	1	5	1	0	0
Andrews	D	Derek	14/12/34	Bury	1955	1956	Army	Altrincham	22	2	0	1	4	0	0	1
Anstiss	HA	Harry	22/8/1899	Chiswick	1924	1925	Watford	Sheffield Wednesday	72	2	0	2	39	0	0	4
Appleyard	F	Fred	13/06/09	Rochdale	1928	1931	Norden St. James	Norden Congs.	6	1	0	1	0	0	0	0
Armitage	AM	Andy	17/10/68	Leeds	1988		Leeds United	Guiseley	36	2	3	4	0	0	0	0
Armstrong	W	Bill	03/07/12	Throckley	1931	1932	Throckley Welfare	Aston Villa	14	0	0	3	0	0	0	0
Arnold	SF	Steve	05/01/51	Crewe	1973		Liverpool	Weymouth	40	2	1	0	1	0	0	0
Arrowsmith	AW	Alf	11/12/42	Manchester	1970	1971	Bury	Macclesfield Town	46	2	1	6	14	3	0	4
Arthur	J	Jackie	14/12/17	Edenfield	1946	1953	Chester City	(to coach)	170	12	0	9	25	2	0	0
Ashurst	J	Jackie	12/10/54	Coatbridge	1992		Doncaster Rovers		1	0	1	0	0	0	0	0
Ashworth	JM	Joe	06/01/43	Huddersfield	1968	1971	Southend United	Chester City	133	8	8	12	3	1	0	1
Ashworth	N	Neil	16/01/68	Southend-on-Sea	1984	1985	(App)	Castleton Gabriels	1	0	1	1	0	0	0	0
Ashworth	PA	Phil	14/04/53	Burnley	1978		Southport	Portsmouth	11	0	2	0	0	0	1	0
Aspden	JR	Ray	06/02/38	Horwich	1955	1966	Bolton Wanderers	retired injured	297	9	20	20	2	0	0	0
Atkins	WM	Bill	09/05/39	Bingley	1972	1973	Halifax Town	Darlington	25	0	1	1	7	0	1	0
Atkinson	GW	Graeme	11/11/71	Hull	1997		Preston North End (loan)		46	3	7	0	5	1	0	0
					1999*			Scarborough								
Bailey	M	Mark	12/08/76	Stoke	1996	1998	Stoke City	Winsford United	67	1	8	0	1	0	0	0
Bailey	TW	Thomas		Ebbw Vale	1928		Merthyr Town	Buckley	1	0	0	0	0	0	0	0
Bain	D	David	05/08/00	Rutherglen	1932	1933	Halifax Town		52	2	1	3	5	0	0	0
Baird	TS	Tommy	07/06/11	Lugar	1937	1939+	St. Mirren		79	3	2	5	0	0	0	0
Baker	LH	Lawrie	18/11/1897	Sheffield	1929		Barnsley	Nelson	34	1	0	3	0	0	0	0
Baker	TW	Billy	17/08/05	Seaham Harbour	1935		Northampton Town	Horden Colliery Welfare	38	1	1	1	0	0	0	0
Ball	JA	Alan	23/09/24	Farnworth	1951		Oldham Athletic	Ashton United	5	0	0	0	1	0	0	0
Bannister	N	Neville	21/07/37	Brierfield	1965		Hartlepool United		19	0	1	3	2	0	0	0
Bannon	I	Ian	03/09/59	Bury	1976	1979	Clarence (Bury)	Oswestry	122	6	7	0	0	0	0	0
Barber	E	Eric	25/03/26	Stockport	1950	1951	Bolton Wanderers	Macclesfield Town	17	0	0	0	2	0	0	0
Barber	J	Jack	08/01/01	Salford	1927	1930	Halifax Town	Stockport County	142	5	0	11	4	0	0	0
Barkas	T	Tommy	27/03/12	South Shields	1946	1947	Halifax Town	Stockport County	44	3	0	4	17	1	0	1
Barks	W	Wilfred	1908	Chesterfield	1937		Dinnington Colliery		3	0	0	0	0	0	0	0
Barlow	A	Andy	24/11/65	Oldham	1997	1998	Blackpool	Ramsbottom United	67	2	3	0	1	0	0	0
Barlow	NK	Neil	24/03/78	Bury	1995		(YTS)		2	0	0	0	0	0	0	0
Barnes	CR	Ron	21/02/36	Bolton	1959	1960	Blackpool	Wrexham	91	6	4	4	7	1	2	0
Barnes	J	Joseph			^1921			New Church	3	0	0	0	0	0	0	0
Barratt	J	John	1916	Stafford	1938		Stafford Rangers		1	0	0	0	0	0	0	0
Barrott	W	Willie	06/10/08	Oldham	1933		Royton		1	0	0	0	0	0	0	0
Bartley	PJ	Philip	23/12/14	Bentley	1934		Norwich City	Mansfield Town	14	0	0	1	3	0	0	0
Barton	JW	Jack	1895	Southport	^1921		Pontypridd	Colwyn Bay	19	1	0	0	0	0	0	0
Bayliss	DA	David	08/06/76	Liverpool	1994	2000*	(App)		177	6	22	4	8	0	0	0
Beattie	J	James	24/08/10	Wishaw	1931		Shieldmuir Celtic	Glentoran	14	1	0	1	0	0	0	0
Beaumont	CP	Chris	05/12/65	Sheffield	1988		Denaby United	Stockport County	34	2	3	0	7	1	1	0
Bebbington	RK	Keith	04/08/43	Nantwich	1972	1973	Oldham Athletic	Winsford Athletic	60	4	3	5	6	0	0	0
Beel	GW	George	26/02/00	Bracebridge Heath	1932		Lincoln City	Tunbridge Wells Rangers	20	1	0	2	8	0	0	1
Beever	AM	Tony	18/09/74	Huddersfield	1992		Colne Valley HS		1	0	1	0	0	0	0	0
Bell	SG	Sydney			1932		Herrington Colliery		2	0	0	0	0	0	0	0
Bell	WG	Billy	16/06/53	Manchester	1974		Hyde United	Mossley	6	0	0	0	0	0	0	0
Bennett	TS	Tommy	1891	Walton	1921		Halifax Town		3	1	0	0	0	1	0	0
Benton	WH	Billy	05/12/1895	Walsall	1932	1933	Fleetwood	Rossendale	48	2	0	4	8	0	0	2
Bertram	W	Billy	31/12/1897	Brandon	1925	1930	Durham City	Accrington Stanley	198	8	0	10	72	2	0	3
Bettney	CJ	Chris	27/10/77	Chesterfield	1999		Chesterfield		24	1	5	0	0	0	0	0
Betts	E	Eric	27/07/25	Coventry	1951	1952	Nuneaton	Crewe Alexandra	52	4	0	0	8	2	0	0
Bimpson	JL	Louis	14/05/29	Rainford	1961	1962	Bournemouth	Wigan Athletic	54	1	8	7	16	0	4	1
Bimson	J	Jimmy	9/2/1899	Latham	1931		Skelmersdale		12	0	0	0	1	0	0	0
Birch	B	Brian	18/11/31	Salford	1960	1961	Oldham Athletic	Mossley	11	0	0	1	0	0	0	0
Birch	B (2)	Brian	09/04/38	Southport	1964	1965	Bolton Wanderers	Bangor City	61	5	2	4	6	0	0	0
Birch	JW	Walter	05/10/17	Ecclesfield	+1946	1952	Huddersfield Town	retired injured	243	14	0	12	10	2	0	1
Bissett	JT	Jimmy	19/6/1898	Lochee	1923		Southend United	Middlesbrough	42	2	0	2	3	0	0	0
Black	E	Edward			1931		Aberdeen	Gateshead	8	0	0	0	0	0	0	0
Black	N	Neville	19/06/31	Ashington	1953	1955	Exeter City	Ashington	62	1	0	4	13	0	0	1
Blackburn	W	William		Bury	1930		Black Lane Rovers		3	0	0	0	0	0	0	0
Blair	RV	Ronnie	26/09/49	Coleraine	1969	1971	Oldham Athletic	Oldham Athletic	74	4	7	14	3	1	0	0
					1982		Blackpool	Milton								
Blake	JB	Jimmy	05/05/66	Manchester	1983		(App)		2	0	0	0	0	0	0	0
Blant	C	Colin	07/10/46	Rawtenstall	1972	1973	Portsmouth	Darlington	51	1	3	2	0	0	0	0
Bliss	APD	Arnold	08/11/09	Woolstanton	1933		Stalybridge Celtic	Stafford Rangers	5	0	0	0	0	0	0	0
Blundell	CK	Chris	07/12/69	Billinge	1990		Oldham Athletic	Northwich Victoria	13	0	5	0	0	0	0	0
Bodell	N	Norman	29/01/38	Manchester	1958	1962		Crewe Alexandra	79	3	6	6	1	0	0	2
Bonnell	A	Arnold	23/03/21	Barnsley	1948		Barnsley	Shrewsbury Town	5	0	0	1	0	0	0	0
Boslem	W	Billy	11/01/58	Middleton	1975	1977	(App)	Buxton	44	4	2	0	1	0	0	0
Bowden	JL	Jon	21/01/63	Stockport	1991	1994	Wrexham	Oldham Athletic (coach)	106	8	8	5	17	1	0	1

Player			D.O.B	Place of Birth	First Season	Last Season	Previous Club	Next Club	Appearances				Goals			
									League	FAC	FLC	Other	League	FAC	FLC	Oth.
Bowie	JM	Jim	11/10/41	Howwood	1972		Oldham Athletic		3	0	0	2	0	0	0	0
Bowsher	SJ	Stan	3/10/1899	Newport	1932		Burnley	Newport County	10	0	0	1	0	0	0	0
Boxshall	D	Danny	02/04/20	Bradford	1952	1953	Bournemouth	Chelmsford City	11	0	0	1	3	0	0	0
Boyle	H	Harry	22/04/24	Glasgow	1950		Southport	Bangor City	175	9	0	6	0	0	0	0
					1952	1955	Bangor City	Altrincham								
Bracewell	K	Ken	05/10/36	Colne	1967		Toronto Falcons	Toronto Falcons	5	0	0	0	0	0	0	0
Bradbury	B	Barry	05/08/52	Rochdale	1972	1973	Matthew Moss	St. Gabriels	14	3	0	1	0	0	0	0
Bradbury	W	Bill	1883	Longton, Staffs	1922		Oldham Athletic	Burton Town	12	1	0	6	0	0	0	0
Braidwood	E	Ernie	14/4/1895	Heywood	1925	1928	Nelson	Gt. Harwood	87	2	0	3	1	0	0	0
Bramhall	J	John	20/11/56	Warrington	1986	1987	Bury	Halifax Town	86	2	14	5	13	0	1	0
Brears	P	Paul	25/09/54	Oldham	1973	1975	Oldham Athletic	New Mills	27	4	0	0	0	1	0	0
Brennan	M	Mike	17/05/52	Salford	1973	1974	Manchester City	Northwich Victoria	37	3	2	1	4	0	0	0
Brierley	H	Harry	02/08/14	Rochdale	1935	1936	Duckworths (R'dale)	Mossley	20	0	1	2	2	0	0	0
Brierley	J	John	09/09/04	Rochdale	1928		Manchester United	Witton Albion	14	0	0	1	7	0	0	0
Briggs	CE	Charlie	04/04/11	Newtown	1946	1947	Clyde	Chesterfield	12	0	0	1	0	0	0	0
Briggs	JC	Jack	1911	Lincoln	1938		Wisbech Town	Grantham	1	0	0	0	0	0	0	0
Brindle	JJ	Jack	12/07/17	Blackburn	+1945		Burnley	Chelsea	1	6	0	0	0	1	0	0
					1947		Chelsea	New Brighton								
Britton	J	Jimmy	27/05/20	Salford	1947	1948	Bradford P.A.	Rossendale	20	1	0	1	0	0	0	0
Brogden	L	Lee	18/10/49	Leeds	1971	1973	Rotherham United	Denver Dynamos	57	4	0	3	7	2	0	0
Broster	J	John	1889	Earlestown	^1921		QPR	Wigan Borough	9	0	0	2	0	0	0	0
					1922		Wigan Borough	Earlestown LMS								
Brown	AJ	Tony	17/09/58	Bradford	1989	1992	Scunthorpe United	retired injured	114	8	14	10	0	0	0	0
Brown	AR	Dick	14/02/11	Pegswood	1928	1929	Alnwick United	Sheffield Wednesday	40	1	0	6	10	0	0	2
Brown	C	Cyril	25/05/18	Ashington	1948	1950	Boston	Peterborough United	61	4	0	4	11	1	0	0
Brown	FW	Fred	1911	Birmingham	1931		Sunderland	Halifax Town	21	0	0	0	6	0	0	0
Brown	J	Jim	05/10/35	Manchester	1956	1960		Altrincham	52	3	3	2	4	1	0	0
Brown	J	John			1922				2	0	0	1	0	0	0	0
Brown	M	Malcolm	13/12/56	Salford	1988		Huddersfield Town	Stockport County	29	3	4	1	1	0	0	0
					1991		Stockport County	retired								
Brown	MA	Micky	08/02/68	Birmingham	1996		Preston NE (loan)	-	5	0	0	0	0	0	0	0
Brown	WJ	Bill	25/12/00	Dundee	1923	1927	Llanelly	Torquay United	178	9	0	8	0	0	0	0
Bruce	H	Harry			1930		Bankhead Albion	Bankhead Albion	2	0	0	1	0	0	0	0
Bryson	JIC	Ian	26/11/62	Kilmarnock	1997	1998	Preston North End	Bamber Bridge	54	5	3	0	1	2	0	0
Buchan	AR	Alistair	27/05/26	Aberdeen	1950	1953	Huntley		107	3	0	3	2	0	0	0
Buck	AR	Tony	18/08/44	Whitwell, Oxfordshire	1968	1972	Newport County	Northampton Town	84	6	3	10	29	2	0	2
Buckley	I	Ian	08/10/53	Oldham	1973		Oldham Athletic (loan)	-	6	0	0	0	0	0	0	0
Buckley	W	Walter	30/04/06	Eccleshall	1933	1935	Lincoln City	Runcorn	108	2	5	2	2	0	0	1
Buggie	LD	Lee	11/02/81	Bury	2000		Bury (loan)		2	0	0	0	0	0	0	0
Burgin	E	Ted	29/04/27	Sheffield	1960	1965	Leeds United	Glossop	207	10	17	12	0	0	0	0
Burke	M	Michael	28/06/04	Blythwood	1937		Southport	Burton Town	8	1	0	0	0	0	0	0
Burke	P	Peter	26/04/57	Rotherham	1980	1981	Halifax Town		68	3	2	1	2	1	0	0
Burns	H	Hugh 'Jock'	1894	Dumbarton	1921		Renton		15	0	0	0	0	0	0	0
Burns	W	Willie	10/12/69	Motherwell	1989	1990	Manchester City	East Fife	71	6	9	6	2	0	2	1
Burt	JHL	Jimmy	05/04/50	Harthill	1973		Northampton Town	Enderby Town	4	0	0	0	0	0	0	0
Bushby	A	Alan	15/01/32	Doncaster	1959	1960	Scunthorpe United	Goole Town	66	5	4	1	0	0	0	0
Butler	DA	Dennis	24/04/44	Macclesfield	1967	1972	Bolton Wanderers	retired injured	156	6	7	14	36	1	2	2
Butler	J	Jack			1933		Rossendale United	Darwen	5	0	1	1	0	0	0	0
Butler	PJ	Paul	02/11/72	Bradford	1990	1995	Bradford City	Bury	158	8	22	7	10	0	0	0
Butler	R	Reuben	10/10/1890	Stillington	1926		Crewe Alexandra	Accrington Stanley	5	0	0	2	0	0	0	2
Byrom	W	Bill	30/03/15	Blackburn	1946	1947	QPR	Stalybridge Celtic	30	3	0	0	0	0	0	0
Bywater	NL	Les	08/02/20	Lichfield	1947	1948	Luton Town	retired	34	2	0	3	0	0	0	0
Cairns	J	John	1902	Glasgow	1933		Crystal Palace	Toronto Scottish	5	0	0	0	0	0	0	0
Cairns	R	Ron	04/04/34	Chopwell	1959	1963	Blackburn Rovers	Southport	195	10	15	13	66	4	3	5
Calder	WC	Bill	28/09/34	Greenock	1966		Oxford United	Macclesfield Town	8	1	0	0	1	0	0	0
Calderbank	GR	Ray	08/02/36	Manchester	1953	1956	Hyde United	Nelson	1	0	0	1	0	0	0	0
Calloway	LJ	Laurie	17/06/45	Birmingham	1964	1967	Wolverhampton Wanderers	Blackburn Rovers	162	6	7	10	4	1	0	1
Cameron	H	Hugh			1921		Burnley		11	0	0	1	2	0	0	0
Campbell	JL	Joe	13/04/1894	Blackburn	1922	1926	Blackburn Rovers	Stalybridge Celtic	34	1	0	10	4	0	0	1
Carden	PA	Paul	29/03/79	Liverpool	1997	1999	Blackpool	Chester City	45	4	5	2	0	0	0	0
Carney	EF	Gene	1895	Bootle	1921		Pontypridd	New Brighton	10	0	0	1	6	0	0	0
Carney	S	Steve	22/09/57	Wallsend	1985		Darlington (loan)	-	4	0	1	0	0	0	0	0
Carr	A	Andrew	1909	Burradon	1936		Crewe Alexandra		32	1	1	2	0	0	0	0
Carr	ED	Everton	11/01/61	Antigua	1982		Halifax Town	Nuneaton Bor.	9	0	0	0	0	0	0	0
Carrick	MD	Dave	05/12/46	Evenwood	1973	1974	Preston North End	Droylsden	26	4	1	0	4	1	0	0
Carruthers	AN	Alex	12/05/15	Loganlea	1946		Falkirk	Rossendale United	13	3	0	1	4	2	0	0
Carter	MC	Mark	17/12/60	Liverpool	1947		Bury	Ashton United	11	0	2	0	2	0	0	0
Case	N	Norman	01/09/25	Prescot	1951		Yeovil Town	Cheltenham Town	2	0	0	0	0	0	0	0
Catlow	T	Thomas			1921		Mid-Rhondda		1	0	0	0	0	0	0	0
Caunce	L	Lewis	20/04/11	Earlestown	1932		Huddersfield Town	Wigan Athletic	18	1	0	2	0	0	0	0
Cavanagh	JL	John	04/08/61	Salford	1984		Bangor City		17	1	3	0	0	0	0	0
Cawthra	JR	Jack	15/08/04	Halifax	1924	1925	Leyland Motors		5	0	0	2	0	0	0	0
Cecere	MJ	Mike	04/01/68	Chester	1996		Exeter City		4	1	2	1	1	0	0	0
Chadwick	H	Harry		Rochdale	1933		Bagslate Meths.	Stalybridge Celtic	1	0	0	0	0	0	0	0
Chambers	PM	Phil	10/11/53	Barnsley	1985		Barnsley	Hartlepool United	10	0	2	0	0	0	0	0
Chapman	J	Josiah	12/10/..		1922			Rossendale United	5	0	0	0	0	0	0	0
Chapman	L	Les	27/09/48	Oldham	1983	1984	Bradford City	Stockport County	88	3	8	7	0	0	0	1
Chapman	VJ	Vinny	05/12/67	Newcastle	1989	1990	Huddersfield Town	retired injured	24	0	1	3	1	0	0	0
Charlton	F	Francis		Calderbrook	1930		Calderbrook St.James		3	0	0	1	0	0	0	0
Charlton	S	Stan	16/11/00	Little Hulton	1922		Oldham Athletic	Exeter City	38	1	0	6	0	0	0	0
Christie	AG	Alex	27/6/1896	Paisley	1924	1927	Norwich City	Exeter City	137	6	0	3	5	1	0	0
Churchill	T	Trevor	20/11/23	Barnsley	1948	1952	Leicester City	Swindon Town	110	1	0	4	0	0	0	0
Clark	H	Herbert			1921		Halifax Town		1	0	0	1	0	0	0	0
Clark	JW	Joe	15/2/1890	Willington Quay	1923		Southampton		16	0	0	3	1	0	0	0
Clarke	CJ	Chris	01/05/74	Barnsley	1994	1995	Bolton Wanderers	Chorley	30	1	5	4	0	0	0	0
Clarke	L	Len		Manchester	1934	1935	Macclesfield	Folkestone Town	29	1	3	0	17	0	2	0

Player			D.O.B	Place of Birth	First Season	Last Season	Previous Club	Next Club	Appearances					Goals			
									League	FAC	FLC	Other		League	FAC	FLC	Oth.
Clarke	PS	Paul	25/09/50	Chesterfield	1969	1971	Liverpool	Matlock Town	11	0	1	1		0	0	0	0
Clarke	TJ	Tim	19/09/68	Stourbridge	1992		Huddersfield Town (loan)	-	2	0	0	0		0	0	0	0
Clennell	J	Joe	19/2/1889	New Silksworth	1927		Bristol Rovers	Ebbw Vale	13	2	0	1		2	3	0	0
Cliff	E	Eddie	30/09/51	Liverpool	1979	1980	Tranmere Rovers		26	0	0	0		0	0	0	0
Clifton	W	William	1891	Preston	^1921		Preston NE		13	0	0	1		0	0	0	0
Clipson	R	Roy	18/04/09	Lincoln	1936		Goole Town		31	1	1	1		0	0	0	0
Cockcroft	VH	Vic	25/02/41	Birmingham	1967		Northampton Town	Kidderminster Harriers	42	1	0	1		0	0	0	0
Colbourne	N	Neil	25/08/56	Swinton	1979		Hyde United	Irlam Town	1	0	0	0		0	0	0	0
Cole	DA	David	28/09/62	Barnsley	1989	1990	Torquay United	Exeter City	84	7	9	5		7	0	0	0
Colleton	A	Tony	17/01/74	Manchester	1990		(YTS)		1	0	0	0		0	0	0	0
Collier	A	Austin	24/07/14	Dewsbury	1946	1947	Queen of the South	Halifax Town	6	0	0	0		0	0	0	0
Collinge	A	Arthur	20/07/1897	Rochdale	^1921		Rochdale Tradesmen	Rochdale Tradesmen	10	0	0	1		1	0	0	0
Collins	AN	Tony	19/03/26	Kensington	1959	1960	Crystal Palace	(to manager)	47	3	0	1		5	1	0	0
Collins	GF	Graham	05/02/47	Bury	1966			Witton Albion	7	0	1	0		0	0	0	0
Collins	JD	Doug	28/08/45	Newton, South Yorks	1978		Tulsa Roughnecks	(Australia)	8	0	0	0		0	0	0	0
Collins	JH	Jimmy	30/01/11	Bermondsey	1933		Tunbridge Wells	Stockport County	30	0	1	1		6	0	2	0
Coleman	S	Simon	13/03/68	Worksop	2000*		Southend United		5	0	0	0		0	0	0	0
Colvan	H	Hugh	24/09/25	Port Glasgow	1947		Hibernian		1	0	0	0		0	0	0	0
Comstive	PT	Paul	25/11/61	Southport	1982		Blackburn Rovers (loan)	-	9	0	1	0		2	0	0	0
Coneys	JJ	Jimmy	12/06/08	Rochdale	1933		Bolton Wanderers	Southport	2	0	0	0		0	0	0	0
					1933		Southport	Hurst									
Conning	TP	Peter	18/10/64	Liverpool	1986		Altrincham	Weymouth	39	2	6	3		1	0	2	0
Connor	JT	Jack	21/12/19	Todmorden	1948	1950	Ards	Bradford City	82	3	0	6		42	3	0	3
Connor	KH	Kevin	12/01/45	Radcliffe	1965	1966		Stoke City	23	1	0	3		1	0	0	0
Connor	P	Paul	21/01/79	Bishop Auckland	2000*			Stoke City	14	0	0	0		10	0	0	0
Conroy	SH	Steve	19/12/56	Chesterfield	1983	1984	Rotherham United	Rotherham United	49	3	5	7		0	0	0	0
Constantine	C	Clarence	1909	Bury	1931		Black Lane	Rossendale United	2	0	0	0		0	0	0	0
Cook	R	Reg		Scunthorpe	1934	1935	Huddersfield Town	retired injured	5	0	0	2		0	0	0	0
Cook	S	Stanley		Iron Acton	1936			Tunbridge Wells Rangers	1	0	1	2		0	0	0	0
Cooke	A	Albert	11/04/08	Royston	1928		Royston	Scunthorpe United	1	0	0	0		0	0	0	0
Cooke	J	Joe	15/02/55	Dominica	1984	1985	Bradford City	Wrexham	75	5	6	4		4	0	1	0
Cooper	G	George	01/10/32	Kingswinford	1958	1959	Crystal Palace	Stourbridge	32	0	0	1		9	0	0	0
Cooper	GS	Gary	15/02/55	Horwich	1973	1976	Horwich RMI	Southport	91	8	1	0		14	0	0	0
Cooper	T	Terry	11/03/50	Croesyceiliog	1981		Bradford City	retired	35	3	2	1		2	0	1	0
Copeland	SD	Simon	10/10/68	Sheffield	1988		Sheffield United	Gainsborough Trinity	28	2	4	4		0	0	0	0
Corcoran	T	Tommy	1907	Earlestown	1930		Bradford City	Guildford City	24	1	0	2		0	0	0	0
Cordell	JG	Graham	06/12/28	Walsall	1953	1954	Aston Villa	Brush Sports	15	1	0	3		0	0	0	0
Cornock	WB	Wally	01/01/21	Bondi, Australia	1947		Hereford United	(Australia)	1	0	0	0		0	0	0	0
Cornthwaite	CH	Christopher	13/07/17	Bury	1935	1936			6	0	0	0		0	0	0	0
Costello	P	Peter	31/10/69	Halifax	1990		Bradford City	Peterborough United	34	2	7	2		10	2	1	1
Coupe	JN	Joe	15/07/24	Carlisle	1951		Carlisle United	Workington	8	0	0	0		0	0	0	0
Cowan	D	David	30/11/10	West Carron	1930		Alva Albion R.	Stenhousemuir	24	1	0	1		2	1	0	0
Cowdrill	BJ	Barry	03/01/57	Birmingham	1991		Bolton Wanderers	Sutton Coldfield Town	15	0	0	0		1	0	0	0
Coyle	RP	Ronnie	19/08/61	Glasgow	1987		Middlesbrough	Raith Rovers	24	1	1	0		1	4	2	0
Crabtree	JJ	Jimmy	2/1895	Clitheroe	^1921	1922	Blackburn Rovers	Accrington Stanley	58	2	0	6		2	0	0	0
Craddock	CW	Claude'Joe'	02/08/02	Grimsby	1930		Sheppey United	Darlington	34	1	0	4		10	0	0	0
Crawford	PG	Graeme	07/08/47	Falkirk	1980	1982	York City	Northallerton	70	1	1	2		0	0	0	0
Crawshaw	CB	Cyril	02/03/16	Barton on Irwell	1936		Rossendale United	Fleetwood	2	0	0	0		0	0	0	0
Creamer	PA	Peter	20/09/53	Hartlepool	1978		Gateshead	(Australia)	20	0	0	0		0	0	0	0
Crerand	DB	Danny	05/05/69	Manchester	1987		Chapel Villa	Altrincham	3	0	0	0		0	0	0	0
Crompton	DG	David	06/03/45	Wigan	1966	1967		Rossendale United	17	0	0	0		0	0	0	0
Crompton	L	Len	26/03/02	Tottington	1929		Lancaster Town	Barnsley	11	0	0	1		0	0	0	0
Cross	D	David	08/12/50	Heywood	1969	1971	Heywood GS	Norwich City	59	5	6	5		20	1	2	3
Crossley	P	Paul	14/07/48	Rochdale	1965	1966	St. Clements	Preston North End	17	0	1	1		2	0	0	0
Crowe	FR	Frank	1893	Birmingham	1923		Chesterfield	Merthyr Town	18	2	0	3		5	0	0	0
Crowther	J	John	1911	Walsden	1931		Halifax Town	Bacup Borough	1	0	0	0		1	0	0	0
Crowther	K	Ken	17/12/24	Halifax	1950		Bradford P.A.	Nelson	2	0	0	0		0	0	0	0
Cuddy	P	Paul	21/02/59	Kendal	1977			Prestwich	1	0	0	0		0	0	0	0
Cunliffe	A	Arthur	05/02/09	Blackrod	+1945	1946	Hull City	(to coach)	23	9	0	2		5	3	0	0
Cunliffe	JG	Graham	16/06/36	Hindley	1964		Bolton Wanderers	retired	36	1	2	2		0	0	0	0
Cunliffe	JN	Jim	05/07/12	Blackrod	+1946		Everton	Everton	2	0	0	0		0	0	0	0
Dailey	J	Jim	08/09/27	Airdrie	1957	1958	Workington	Weymouth	53	2	0	2		25	0	0	0
Daniels	G	George	07/12/1888	Chorlton	1921	1922	Bury		35	2	0	1		1	0	0	0
Darling	MF	Malcolm	04/07/47	Arbroath	1971	1973	Norwich City	Bolton Wanderers	86	2	3	6		16	0	2	3
Daubney	R	Ray	07/12/46	Oldham	1966	1967		Stalybridge Celtic	12	0	0	3		2	0	0	0
Davies	SI	Simon	23/04/74	Winsford	2000		Macclesfield Town		12	1	3	0		1	0	0	0
Dawson	A	Adam	22/12/12	Craster	1937		Halifax Town	Southport	12	0	0	1		6	0	0	1
Dawson	J	Jason	09/02/71	Burslem	1989	1990	Port Vale	Stafford Rangers	55	6	6	2		7	1	0	0
Dean	AG	Andy	27/11/66	Salford	1983		Burnley	Salford	1	0	0	0		0	0	0	0
Dearden	KC	Kevin	08/03/70	Luton	1991		Tottenham Hotspur (loan)	-	2	0	0	0		0	0	0	0
Deary	JS	John	18/10/62	Ormskirk	1994	1996	Burnley	Southport	91	5	10	2		10	3	2	0
Dennison	H	Harry	4/11/1894	Bradford	^1921		Blackburn Rovers	Wigan Borough	33	1	0	1		17	1	0	0
Denton	RW	Roger	06/01/53	Stretford	1973		Bradford City (loan)	-	2	0	0	0		0	0	0	0
de Souza	MJ	Miguel	11/02/70	Newham	1998		Peterborough United (loan)	-	5	0	0	0		0	0	0	0
Devlin	J	Joe	12/03/31	Cleland	1956	1957	Accrington Stanley	Bradford P.A.	38	0	0	1		7	0	0	0
Diamond	B	Barry	20/02/60	Dumbarton	1984	1985	Barrow	Halifax Town	52	2	6	7		16	0	1	2
Diaz	I	Izzy	15/05/72	Valencia	1998		Wigan Athletic	(Spain)	14	3	1	0		2	0	0	0
Dickins	MJ	Matt	03/09/70	Sheffield	1994		Blackburn Rovers (loan)		4	0	1	0		0	0	0	0
Dobson	GF	George	7/11/10	Handsworth	1934		Southport	Rotherham United	15	1	2	1		5	0	0	0
Dolan	TP	Terry	11/06/50	Bradford	1981		Bradford City	Thackley	43	3	1	1		1	1	0	0
Douglas	TA	Tom	11/09/10	Whitletts, Ayr	1938		Witton Albion		8	0	0	2		0	0	0	1
Douglas	WJ	William			1934		Blackburn Rovers		1	0	0	0		0	0	0	0
Dow	DJ	David	10/06/47	Manchester	1966	1967	Avorton	Ellesmere Port	8	0	0	3		0	0	0	0
Dowe	JWL	Julian	09/09/75	Manchester	1999		Colne Dynamos	Morecambe	7	2	0	0		0	1	0	0

Player			D.O.B	Place of Birth	First Season	Last Season	Previous Club	Next Club	Appearances				Goals			
									League	FAC	FLC	Other	League	FAC	FLC	Oth.
Dowell	WA	Wayne	28/12/73	Durham	1996		Burnley	Doncaster Rovers	7	0	0	2	0	0	0	0
Downes	ER	Eric	25/08/26	Wigan	1950	1953	Chester	Horwich RMI	54	4	0	1	0	0	0	0
Downes	RD	Bobby	18/08/49	Bloxwich	1969	1973	Peterborough United	Watford	174	9	9	12	10	2	0	0
Doyle	M	Mike	25/11/46	Manchester	1983		Bolton Wanderers	retired	24	2	3	3	1	0	0	0
Doyle	SC	Steve	02/06/58	Neath	1990	1994	Hull City	Chorley	121	4	15	8	1	0	0	0
Doyle	T	Thomas	1916	Motherwell	1938		Celtic	Stockport County	29	1	1	3	0	0	0	0
Driver	R	Robert	1914	Summit	1935		Gravshock Lads		2	0	0	0	0	0	0	0
Drury	J	Jim	29/05/24	Cumnock	1951		Stirling Albion	Carlisle United	4	0	0	0	1	0	0	0
Dryburgh	TJD	Tom	23/04/23	Kirkcaldy	1948	1949	Aldershot	Leicester City	82	4	0	10	17	1	0	4
					1957		Oldham Athletic	King's Lynn								
Duff	JH	Joe	5/1913	Ashington	1935	1945+	Newcastle United	Cheltenham Town	132	10	2	12	26	1	1	2
Duffey	CP	Chris	08/01/52	Kirkby	1975		Shrewsbury Town (loan)	-	2	0	0	0	0	0	0	0
Duggan	AJ	Andy	19/09/67	Bradford	1987		Barnsley (loan)	-	4	1	0	0	0	0	1	0
					1990		Huddersfield Town									
Dunford	N	Neil	18/07/67	Rochdale	1994			Milnrow	2	1	0	0	0	0	0	0
Dungworth	JH	John	30/03/55	Rotherham	1976		Oldham Athletic (loan)	-	14	0	0	0	3	0	0	0
Duxbury	LE	Lee	07/10/69	Skipton	1989		Bradford City (loan)		10	1	0	0	0	0	0	0
Dwyer	PJ	Phil	28/10/53	Cardiff	1984		Cardiff City	South Wales Police	15	0	0	0	1	0	0	0
Earl	AT	Albert 'Sam'	10/02/15	Gateshead	+1947		Stockport County	New Brighton	4	2	0	0	1	0	0	0
Eastham	B	Brian	26/04/37	Bolton	1967		Toronto Blizzard	Sligo Rovers	13	0	1	2	0	0	0	0
Eastham	GR	George	13/09/14	Blackpool	1948		Swansea City	Lincoln City	2	1	0	2	0	0	0	0
Eastwood	J	Jimmy	12/04/15	Heywood	1937	+	Crewe Alexandra	Tunbridge Wells Rangers	28	2	1	1	0	0	0	0
Eaton	C	Cliff	15/10/10	Oldham	1934	1935	Portsmouth	Oldham Athletic	31	2	4	1	3	0	1	0
Edmonds	NA	Neil	18/10/68	Accrington	1988	1989	Oldham Athletic	Karlskrona	43	3	2	1	8	0	0	0
Edwards	NR	Neil	05/12/70	Aderdare	1997	2000	Stockport County		156	9	15	1	0	0	0	0
Edwards	SG	Steve	11/01/58	Birkenhead	1984		Crewe Alexandra	Tranmere Rovers	4	0	2	4	0	0	0	0
Edwards	WJ	Jack	06/07/29	Risca	1959	1960	Crystal Palace	Ashford	68	4	0	3	1	0	0	0
Elliott	SB	Steve	15/09/58	Haltwhistle	1989	1990	Bury	Guiseley	52	2	7	2	9	0	1	0
Elliott	SD	Sid	14/01/08	Sunderland	1935		Bradford City	FB Minter Sports	11	0	0	0	1	0	0	0
Ellis	AJ	Tony	20/10/64	Salford	1999	2000*	Stockport County		59	2	7	0	17	0	1	0
Ellison	JW	James	15/03/01	St. Helens	1928		Southampton	Connah's Quay	16	0	0	0	0	0	0	0
Emerson	A	Arthur	21/07/13	Bury	1935		Red Lumb		1	0	0	0	0	0	0	0
Emmerson	GAH	George	15/05/06	Bishop Auckland	1935	1936	QPR	Tunbridge Wells Rangers	66	2	1	2	12	0	0	0
English	TS	Tom	18/10/61	Cirencester	1984		Leicester City	Plymouth Argyle	3	0	0	0	1	0	0	0
Ennis	ME	Mark	06/01/62	Bradford	1983		Rochdale Joiners	Salford	1	0	0	0	0	0	0	0
Entwistle	RP	Bob	06/10/38	Bury	1958	1959	Macclesfield	Accrington Stanley	1	0	0	1	0	0	0	0
Esser	ED	David	20/06/57	Altrincham	1977	1981	Everton	Apoel Nicosia	180	10	9	1	24	2	1	0
Evans	DW	Wayne	28/08/71	Abermule	1999	2000*	Walsall		91	4	10	0	3	0	1	0
Evans	FJ	Fred	20/05/23	Petersfield	1953		Crystal Palace	Biggleswade Town	12	0	0	1	0	0	0	0
Everest	J	Jack	20/07/08	The Curragh	1930	1931	Stockport Co.	Blackpool	38	1	0	2	8	0	0	0
Farrell	A	Andy	07/10/65	Colchester	1996	1998	Wigan Athletic	Morecambe	118	6	11	4	0	0	0	0
Farrell	PJ	Peter	10/01/57	Liverpool	1982	1984	Port Vale	Crewe Alexandra	73	2	7	6	17	1	0	1
Farrer	P	Peter		St Helens	1921		Everton		12	0	0	0	0	0	0	0
Fawcett	DH	Des	1905	Middlesbrough	1936	1938	Mansfield Town	Wellington Town	93	3	2	5	0	0	0	0
Fearnley	HL	Harry	27/05/23	Morley	1955		Newport County	Winsford	1	0	0	0	0	0	0	0
Felgate	DW	David	04/03/60	Blaenau Ffestiniog	1978	1979	Bolton Wanderers (loan)	-	47	0	0	0	0	0	0	0
Fensome	AB	Andy	18/02/69	Northampton	1996	1997	Preston North End	Barrow	82	3	7	2	0	0	0	0
Ferguson	C	Charlie	22/04/30	Glasgow	1955	1958	Accrington Stanley	Oldham Athletic	150	6	0	5	3	0	0	1
Ferguson	MK	Mike	09/03/43	Burnley	1974	1975	Cambridge United	Halifax Town	69	10	3	0	5	1	0	0
Fergusson	WA	William	2/3/1897	Willenhall	1925		Reading	Rotherham United	21	3	0	2	19	2	0	0
Fielding	MA	Mike	03/12/65	Liverpool	1984		Barnsley (loan)	-	6	1	0	0	0	0	0	0
Fielding	PA	Paul	04/12/52	Rochdale	1972	1975	(App)	Southport	72	3	2	0	5	0	0	0
Finc	R	Bobby	13/2/59	Rochdale	1977		Milton	Tim Bobbin	1	0	0	0	0	0	0	0
Finley	AJ	Alan	10/12/67	Liverpool	1993		Stockport County (loan)	-	1	0	0	0	0	0	0	0
Finney	CW	Bill	05/09/31	Stoke-on-Trent	1958		Crewe Alexandra	Macclesfield Town	31	3	0	1	1	1	0	0
Firth	J	Joe	27/03/09	Glasshoughton	1938		York City		18	0	0	0	6	0	0	0
Fisher	FT	Fred	12/01/20	Wednesbury	1951		Grimsby Town	Boston United	1	0	0	1	0	0	0	0
Fitton	F	Fred	1911	High Crompton	1930		High Crompton St.Mary	Northwich Victoria	1	0	0	1	0	0	0	0
Fitton	F (2)	Fred	21/01/05	Bury	1933		Accrington Stanley	Nelson	13	1	0	1	6	0	0	0
Flannigan	T	Tommy	27/05/08	Edinburgh	1931		Darlington	Buxton	2	0	0	0	0	0	0	0
Fletcher	JM	Joe	25/09/46	Manchester	1966	1968	Manchester City	Grimsby Town	57	1	2	8	21	1	0	0
Flitcroft	DJ	Dave	14/01/74	Bolton	1999	2000*	Chester City		84	3	10	0	2	0	0	0
Flounders	AJ	Andy	13/12/63	Hull	1991	1993	Scunthorpe United	Halifax Town	85	6	13	9	31	1	1	3
Ford	T	Tony	14/05/59	Grimsby	1999	2000*	Mansfield Town		72	4	8	0	4	0	0	0
Formby	K	Kevin	22/07/71	Ormskirk	1993	1996	Burscough	Southport	67	5	15	5	1	0	0	0
Forster	GP	Geoff	03/08/54	Middlesbrough	1978		South Bank	Whitby Town	1	0	0	0	0	0	0	0
Forster	RH	Robert	03/11/09	Throckley	1931		Frickley Colliery		2	0	0	0	0	0	0	0
Foster	H	Harry			1921		Sudden Villa		2	0	0	0	0	0	0	0
Fothergill	AG	Ashley	03/10/69	Harrogate	1988		Middlesbrough	Whitby Town	9	0	1	0	0	0	0	0
Foulds	A	Bert	08/08/19	Salford	1950		Yeovil Town	Scarborough	61	4	0	2	24	0	0	0
					1951	1952	Scarborough	Crystal Palace								
Foweather	VJ	Vince		Oldham	1922		Oldham Athletic	Macclesfield Town	4	0	0	2	1	0	0	0
Frain	D	David	11/10/62	Sheffield	1988		Sheffield United	Stockport County	42	2	4	4	12	1	0	0
French	MJ	Micky	07/05/55	Eastbourne	1982		Aldershot	Lewes	36	1	3	3	11	0	0	1
Frost	D	Des	03/08/26	Congleton	1953	1954	Halifax Town	Crewe Alexandra	16	1	0	0	6	0	0	0
Gallacher	C	Con	25/04/22	Derry	1947		Hull City	Boston	6	0	0	0	1	0	0	0
Gamble	F	Frank	21/08/61	Liverpool	1984	1985	Barrow	Morecambe	46	2	6	3	9	0	1	0
Gardner	W	William	7/6/1893	Langley Moor	1932		Crewe Alexandra	retired	1	0	0	0	0	0	0	0
Garner	W	Willie	24/07/55	Stirling	1982		Celtic (loan)	-	4	0	1	0	0	0	0	0
Gastall	JWH	John	25/05/13	Oswaldtwistle	1938	+	Accrington Stanley	Bacup Borough	4	0	0	0	1	0	0	0
Gavin	MW	Mark	10/12/63	Baillieston	1987		Bolton Wanderers	Hearts	23	1	0	3	5	3	2	0
Gee	A	Arthur	1892	Earlestown	1922		Stalybridge Celtic	Ashton National	8	0	0	5	2	0	0	2
Gemmell	E	Eric	07/04/21	Manchester	1954	1955	Crewe Alexandra	Buxton	65	5	0	4	32	2	0	1
Gibson	PR	Paul	01/11/76	Sheffield	1999		Notts County (loan)		5	0	0	0	0	0	0	0
Gibson	SJ	Simon	10/12/64	Nottingham	1986		Preston North End	(Belgium)	5	1	3	2	0	0	0	0

Player			D.O.B	Place of Birth	First Season	Last Season	Previous Club	Next Club	Appearances					Goals			
									League	FAC	FLC	Other		League	FAC	FLC	Oth.
Gilfillan	R	Robert	14/03/26	Dunfermline	1951	1953	Cowdenbeath	Worcester City	62	1	0	2		11	0	0	0
Gilks	M	Matthew	04/06/82	Rochdale	2000*		(YTS)		3	0	0	0		0	0	0	0
Glover	BA	Bev	25/03/26	Manchester	1953	1958	Stockport County		169	9	0	9		1	0	0	0
Godfrey	AW	Tony	30/04/39	Newbury	1970	1971	Aldershot	Aldershot	71	3	4	5		0	0	0	0
Goodfellow	S	Syd	06/07/15	Woolstanton	1938		Glentoran	Chesterfield	41	1	1	5		2	0	0	2
Goodier	E	Ted	15/10/02	Farnworth	1937	1938	Crewe Alexandra	(to manager)	67	3	1	6		1	1	0	0
Goodison	CW	Wayne	23/09/64	Wakefield	1989	1990	Crewe Alexandra	Hyde United	79	5	9	5		4	1	2	0
Goodwin	D	Dave	15/10/54	Nantwich	1981		Bury	Crewe Alexandra	38	1	1	1		6	0	0	0
Gordon	JG	Jack	25/09/11	South Shields	1932	1933	Leeds United	Queen of the South	66	1	1	4		1	0	0	0
Gouck	AS	Andy	08/06/72	Blackpool	1996	1997	Blackpool	Southport	66	2	4	2		8	0	0	0
Gowans	PT	Peter	25/05/44	Dundee	1970	1973	Aldershot	Southport	144	5	6	15		21	0	1	1
Graham	A	Alex	26/08/12	Coatbridge	1937		West Ham United	Bradford	11	0	1	0		4	0	0	0
Graham	J	Jimmy	15/11/69	Glasgow	1989	1993	Bradford City	Hull City	137	12	23	10		1	0	1	0
Graham	JR	John	26/04/26	Leyland	1952		Wigan Athletic	Bradford City	10	0	0	0		1	0	0	0
Grant	D	Dave	02/06/60	Sheffield	1984	1986	Cardiff City	Macclesfield Town	97	6	10	5		2	0	0	0
Grant	JA	Jackie	08/09/24	High Spen	1956	1958	Everton	Southport	102	2	0	1		3	0	0	0
Grant	R	Reginald			1931				1	0	0	0		0	0	0	0
Gray	D	David	18/01/80	Rossendale	1998		(YTS)	Clitheroe	3	0	0	0		0	0	0	0
Gray	G	Gareth	24/02/70	Longridge	1991		Bolton Wanderers	Hyde United	6	2	5	0		0	0	0	0
Gray	IJ	Ian	25/02/75	Manchester	1994	1996	Oldham Athletic	Stockport County	78	5	11	3		0	0	0	0
Greaves	R	Roy	04/04/47	Farnworth	1982		Seattle Sounders	Bolton St.Thomas	21	1	0	0		0	0	0	0
Green	A	Adie	22/10/57	Leicester	1977		Leicester City (loan)	-	7	0	0	0		0	0	0	0
Green	BG	Brian	05/06/35	Droylsden	1954	1958	Haggate Lads	Southport	46	1	0	7		8	0	0	0
Green	L	Les	17/10/41	Atherstone	1967		Hartlepool United	Derby County	44	1	1	5		0	0	0	0
Green	RE	Richard	22/11/67	Wolverhampton	1999		Walsall (loan)	-	6	0	0	0		0	0	0	0
Greenhoff	B	Brian	28/04/53	Barnsley	1982	1983	Hong Kong	retired	16	1	1	0		0	0	0	0
Greenhoff	J	Jimmy	19/06/46	Barnsley	1982	1983	Port Vale	Port Vale (coach)	16	0	1	1		0	0	0	0
Gregory	A	Albert	1913	Manchester	1938		Manchester North End		9	0	0	1		0	0	0	0
Gregson	W	William	1908	Sunderland	1932		Herrington Colliery	Horden Colliery Welfare	1	0	0	2		0	0	0	0
Grierson	G	George	1905	Lesmahagow	1930		Preston North End	Ashton National	31	1	0	4		0	0	0	0
Griffiths	AA	Arthur	1908	Tonypandy	1938		Glentoran	Stoke City	14	0	0	3		5	0	0	0
Griffiths	IJ	Ian	17/04/60	Birkenhead	1983	1984	Tranmere Rovers	Port Vale	42	2	4	2		5	0	1	0
Grummett	J	Jim	11/07/45	Barnsley	1973	1974	Chester City	Boston United	33	0	1	0		2	0	0	0
Guy	G	George	1/11/1896	Bolton	1922		Bolton Wanderers	Aberaman Athletic	15	0	0	4		7	0	0	2
Guyan	GW	George	05/04/01	Aberdeen	1931		Swindon Town	Bath City	4	0	0	0		1	0	0	0
Haddington	RW	Ray	18/11/23	Scarborough	1952	1953	Bournemouth	Halifax Town	38	1	0	1		12	0	0	0
Hadland	PJ	Phil	20/10/80	Warrington	2000		Reading	Leyton Orient	32	1	2	0		2	0	0	0
Haines	JTW	Jack	24/04/20	Wickhamford	1953	1954	Bradford P.A.	Chester City	60	5	0	3		16	1	0	1
Haire	G	Garry	24/07/63	Sedgefield	1985		Darlington (loan)	-	3	0	0	0		0	0	0	0
Hales	H	Bert	21/11/08	Kettering	1935		Stockport County	Burton Town	38	1	1	1		4	0	0	0
Halkyard	C	Cecil	17/04/02	Rochdale	1924	1927	Accrington Stanley	Connah's Quay	15	0	0	6		0	0	0	0
Hall	DR	Derek	05/01/65	Ashton-under-Lyne	1994	1995	Hereford United	Hyde United	23	0	5	1		2	0	0	0
Hall	J	John		Heywood	1923	1929		Great Harwood	74	5	0	10		2	3	0	2
Hallard	W	Bill	28/08/13	St Helens	1946		Bradford P.A.	Accrington Stanley	17	3	0	2		2	0	0	0
Hallows	PCR	Paul	22/06/50	Chester	1974	1979	Bolton Wanderers	Oswestry Town	197	15	11	0		2	0	0	0
Halpin	JW	John	15/11/61	Broxburn	1991		Carlisle United	Gretna	31	3	5	4		1	1	0	1
Hamilton	G	Gary	06/10/80	Bambridge	2000		Blackburn Rovers (loan)		3	0	0	0		0	0	0	0
Hamilton	JS	Jimmy	16/08/06	New Cumnock	1931	1932	Ayr United	Wrexham	77	1	0	5		0	0	0	0
Hamilton	NR	Neville	19/04/60	Leicester	1981	1983	Mansfield Town	Wolverhampton W.	74	4	8	7		5	0	0	0
Hampton	PJ	Peter	12/09/54	Oldham	1987		Burnley	Carlisle United	19	1	0	3		1	4	2	0
Hamstead	GW	George	24/01/46	Rotherham	1976		Bury (loan)	-	4	0	0	0		0	0	0	0
Hancox	PA	Paul	22/07/70	Manchester	1987		(YTS)		2	0	0	0		0	0	0	0
Handley	B	Brian	21/06/36	Wakefield	1965		Bridgwater Town		3	0	0	0		0	0	0	0
Hanvey	K	Keith	18/01/52	Manchester	1973	1984	Swansea City	Grimsby Town	136	14	7	4		10	1	0	0
Hardman	JA	John	17/12/40	Bury	1960	1966	Bess's Boys	Witton Albion	40	2	2	7		2	0	0	0
Hardy	RM	Bob	1914	Hemsworth	1937		Dinnington Colliery		7	0	0	0		0	0	0	0
Hardy	JP	Jason	14/12/69	Manchester	1995		Bamber Bridge		7	0	0	0		0	0	0	0
Hargreaves	F	Frank	17/11/02	Ashton-under-Lyne	1930		Oldham Athletic	Bournemouth	9	0	0	1		3	0	0	1
Hargreaves	J	Joe	30/10/15	Accrington	+1945	1947	Rossendale United	Stalybridge Celtic	35	9	0	0		24	8	0	0
Hargreaves	T	Tom	29/10/17	Blackburn	1946		Blackburn Rovers	Nelson	7	0	0	0		0	0	0	0
Harker	CJ	Chris	29/06/37	Shiremoor	1968	1969	Grimsby Town	Stockton	92	3	2	5		0	0	0	0
Harley	LA	Les	26/09/46	Chester	1967		Blackpool (loan)	-	5	0	0	2		0	0	0	0
Harris	CS	Carl	03/11/56	Neath	1987	1988	Cardiff City	Exeter City	25	0	3	1		3	0	0	0
Hart	BP	Brian	14/07/59	Farnworth	1977	1979	Bolton Wanderers	Bangor City	78	6	2	0		0	2	0	0
Hasford	JW	Jason	01/04/71	Manchester	1989		Manchester City		1	0	0	1		0	0	0	0
Hawes	AR	Arthur	2/10/1895	Swanton Morley	1931		Wombwell	Goole Town	13	0	0	0		0	0	0	0
Haworth	G	Gary	25/04/59	Bury	1984		Radcliffe Bor.	Radcliffe Borough	1	0	0	1		0	0	0	0
Haworth	R	Richard			+1938		Manchester North End		9	0	0	4		1	0	0	0
Haworth	R	Roland	1914	Ramsbottom	+1937		Manchester North End		2	0	0	1		0	0	0	0
Hawson	A	Alex	23/10/23	Auchencairn	1948		Aberdeen	Burnley	1	0	0	0		0	0	0	0
Hayton	E	Eric	14/01/22	Carlisle	1951		Carlisle United	Workington	12	0	0	1		0	0	0	0
Hazzleton	J	Jim	29/09/30	Bolton	1951		Bury	Accrington Stanley	11	0	0	1		1	0	0	0
Heath	J	John	05/06/36	Heywood	1965		Wigan Athletic	Buxton	6	0	0	2		0	0	0	0
Heaton	PJ	Paul	24/01/61	Hyde	1983	1985	Oldham Athletic	(Finland)	89	5	8	6		9	1	0	0
Heaton	WH	Billy	26/08/18	Leeds	1950		Stalybridge Celtic	Witton Albion	5	1	0	0		0	0	0	0
Helliwell	D	Dave	28/03/48	Blackburn	1976		Workington	Morecambe	31	2	1	0		3	1	0	0
Hellyer	CD	Charles		Reading	1930		Tunbridge Wells	Bradford City	1	0	0	0		0	0	0	0
Henderson	WJ	William	13/11/18	Dumfries	1946		Queen of the South	Southport	17	3	0	2		0	0	0	0
Henshaw	G	Gary	18/02/65	Leeds	1989		Bolton Wan. (loan)	-	9	0	0	0		1	0	0	0
Hepton	S	Stan	03/12/32	Leeds	1960	1963	Bury	Southport	149	7	16	8		21	1	5	1
Herbert	JH	Joseph	23/1/1895	Kimbersworth	^1921		Swansea Town	Guildford United	16	1	0	0		4	0	0	0
Herring	PJ	Paul	01/07/73	Hyde	1990		(YTS)	Mossley	1	0	0	0		0	0	0	0
Heydon	C	Cecil	24/05/19	Birkenhead	1948		Doncaster Rovers		1	0	0	0		0	0	0	0
Heyes	G	George	16/11/37	Bolton	1958	1959		Leicester City	24	0	0	0		0	0	0	0
Hibberd	CM	Cyril	8/5/1895	Sheffield	1923		Chesterfield		2	0	0	1		0	0	0	0

Player			D.O.B	Place of Birth	First Season	Last Season	Previous Club	Next Club	Appearances League	FAC	FLC	Other	Goals League	FAC	FLC	Oth.
Hicks	G	Graham	17/02/81	Oldham	1998	1999*	(YTS)		1	1	0	0	0	0	0	0
Hicks	K	Keith	09/08/54	Oldham	1985	1986	Hereford United	Hyde United	32	4	2	6	1	0	0	0
Higgins	AM	Andy	12/02/60	Bolsover	1982	1983	King's Lynn	Chester City	33	2	2	3	6	0	0	2
Higgins	RJ	Bob	23/12/58	Bolsover	1980		Burnley	Morecambe	5	1	0	0	0	0	0	0
Hildersley	R	Ronnie	06/04/65	Kirkcaldy	1985		Chester City	Preston North End	16	0	0	0	0	0	0	0
Hilditch	MW	Mark	20/08/60	Royton	1977	1982	Shawside	Tranmere Rovers	213	12	14	3	42	3	1	1
					1990	1991	Wigan Athletic	Buxton								
Hill	JW	Jack	2/6/1895	Rochdale	^1921	1922	Brights (Rochdale)	Bacup Borough	43	2	0	5	11	0	0	0
Hill	JW	Jon	26/08/70	Wigan	1989	1990	Crewe Alexandra	Witton Albion	36	5	5	2	1	0	0	0
Hill	KJ	Keith	17/05/69	Bolton	1996	2000	Plymouth Argyle	Cheltenham Town	176	8	16	2	6	0	1	0
Hill	LG	Len	15/2/1899	Islington	1926		Southampton	Lincoln City	34	1	0	1	0	0	0	0
Hill	R	Roland	1911	Rochdale	1931		Greenbank	R'dale St. Mary's	2	1	0	0	0	0	0	0
Hill	T	Thomas			1932		Castleton		7	0	0	0	0	0	0	0
Hilley	C	Con	29/09/02	Glasgow	1931		Derry City	Coleraine	3	0	0	0	0	0	0	0
Hillhouse	JT	John	14/01/1898	Hurlford	1925	1926	Workington	Notts County	52	4	0	0	0	0	0	0
Hinchliffe	AG	Arthur	26/8/1897	Bolton	1921		Sheffield Wednesday	Doncaster Rovers	26	0	0	2	0	0	0	0
					1922		Birley Carr Institute					2				
Hindle	T	Tom	22/02/21	Keighley	1951		Halifax Town	Wigan Athletic	6	0	0	0	1	0	0	0
Hoad	SJ	Sid	27/12/1890	Eltham	^1921		Manchester City	Nelson	17	1	0	1	2	0	0	0
Hoadley	D	Dermot			1933		Birtley		2	0	0	1	0	0	0	0
Hobbs	EC	Ernest	30/04/10	Wellingborough	1938		Tunbridge Wells		6	0	0	1	0	0	0	0
Hodge	MJ	Martin	04/02/59	Southport	1993	1994	Hartlepool United	Plymouth Argyle	42	2	5	5	0	0	0	0
Hogan	C	Charlie	23/04/26	Bury	1952		Southport	Wigan Athletic	3	0	0	0	0	0	0	0
Hogg	T	Tommy	21/03/08	Brampton	1931		Bradford P.A.		10	0	0	0	1	0	0	0
Holden	JS	Stewart	21/04/42	Grange Moor	1966		Oldham Athletic	Wigan Athletic	21	0	0	0	0	0	0	0
Holden	SJ	Simon	09/03/68	Littleborough	1984		(App)	Wheatsheaf	49	1	1	2	4	1	2	0
					1986	1987	Wheatsheaf	Mossley								
Holmes	MA	Mick	09/09/65	Blackpool	1989	1990	Cambridge United	Torquay United	55	6	9	6	7	0	2	0
Holroyd	E	Eric	24/07/05	Rochdale	1927				1	0	0	0	0	0	0	0
Holt	MA	Michael	28/07/77	Barnoldswick	1998	1999	Preston North End	Accrington Stanley	38	2	7	0	7	0	2	0
Hood	RG	Ron	18/11/22	Cowdenbeath	1948		Aldershot	Shrewsbury Town	9	0	0	0	1	0	0	0
Hooker	E	Evan	1901	Chadderton	1929		Stockport County	Ashton National	25	0	0	0	0	0	0	0
Hooper	FW	Bill	14/11/1894	Darlington	1926		Darlington		20	1	0	2	1	0	0	0
Hope	H	Harry	1914	Newcastle	1933		Crawcrook Albion	Chopwell	2	0	0	0	0	0	0	0
Hope	P	Phil	24/4/1897	Kimblesworth	1929		Washington Colliery		13	0	0	3	1	0	0	0
Hopkins	AG	Arthur		Ebbw Vale	1924	1927	Ebbw Vale		36	5	0	8	0	0	0	0
Hornby	R	Ron	13/04/14	Rochdale	+1931		Rochdale St. Clements	Oldham Athletic	2	0	0	1	0	0	0	0
Horne	SF	Stan	17/12/44	Clanfield	1973	1974	Chester City	retired injured	48	4	1	0	5	0	0	0
Howard	AP	Andy	15/03/72	Southport	1992	1993	Fleetwood		20	1	3	1	3	0	0	0
Howarth	H	Harold	1912	Shaw	1938		Mossley		4	0	0	1	0	0	0	1
Howarth	W				1931				20	0	0	1	4	0	0	0
Howarth	J	Jack	27/02/45	Crook	1971	1972	Aldershot	Aldershot	40	1	2	3	12	0	0	1
Howe	HG	Harold	09/04/06	Hemel Hempstead	1934		Crystal Palace	Dartford	24	0	1	0	3	0	0	0
Howell	DG	Dean	28/11/80	Burton	2000		Crewe Alexandra (loan)		3	0	0	0	0	0	0	0
Howlett	CE	Charles	26/09/06	Auckland	1928		Durham City	Halifax Town	2	0	0	0	0	0	0	0
Howlett	HWA	Harry	23/06/10	Auckland	1928		Evenwood	Cockfield	1	0	0	0	0	0	0	0
Hoy	R	Bobby	10/01/50	Halifax	1977	1980	York City	Macclesfield Town	66	1	2	0	12	0	0	0
Hoyle	G	George	20/04/1896	Rochdale	1921		Sudden Villa		3	0	0	1	1	0	0	1
Hubbick	HE	Harry	12/11/10	Jarrow	1948	1950	Port Vale	Lancaster City	90	2	0	7	0	0	0	0
Hudson	CB	Carl	10/10/66	Bradford	1986		Bradford City	Thackley	15	2	3	0	1	0	1	0
Hudson	CJ	John	25/11/64	Middleton	1986		(Sweden)		19	0	0	0	1	0	0	0
Hughes	R	Bobby	5/8/1892	Pelaw	1924	1927	Brentford	Wigan Borough	127	5	0	2	48	2	0	0
Hughes	WA	Archie	02/02/19	Colwyn Bay	1950		Blackburn Rovers	Crystal Palace	9	0	0	1	0	0	0	0
Hughes	ZD	Zac	06/06/71	Bentley, Australia	1987	1988	Balderstone School	retired injured	2	0	4	0	0	0	0	0
Hulmes	GA	Gary	28/02/57	Manchester	1974	1975	Manchester City	Sligo	10	1	0	0	1	0	0	0
Humphreys	JS	John	18/07/64	Farnworth	1983		Oldham Athletic(loan)	-	6	0	0	0	0	0	0	0
Humpish	AE	Ted	03/04/02	Newcastle	1934		Stockport County	Ashton National	31	1	3	2	2	0	1	0
Hunt	MG	Mark	05/10/69	Farnworth	1986	1987	(App)		2	0	2	1	1	0	0	0
Hunt	SW	Wally	09/01/09	Doe Lea	1936	+1937	Torquay United	Stockport County	58	3	2	2	31	2	2	2
Huntley	E	Edward	1913	Dawdon	1935	1936	Easington Colliery	Newry Town	30	1	2	2	0	0	0	0
Hurst	C	Charlie	25/01/19	Denton	+1946		Oldham Athletic	Chelmsford City	4	0	0	0	1	0	0	0
Hurst	GJ	Graham	23/11/67	Oldham	1984		(App)	Mossley	1	0	0	0	0	0	0	0
Hussey	FM	Malcolm	11/09/33	Darfield	1958		Scunthorpe United		1	0	0	0	0	0	0	0
Hutchinson	JB	Barry	27/01/36	Sheffield	1967		Halifax Town		27	0	0	3	3	0	0	2
Hutchinson	R	Rob	09/05/55	Bolton	1974		Radcliffe Borough	Macclesfield Town	2	0	0	0	1	0	0	0
Huxley	FR	Frank	18/04/11	Chester	1935		Northern Nomads	Horden Colliery Welfare	1	0	0	- 0	0	0	0	0
Ives	A	Arthur	23/10/10	Lincoln	1934		Gainsborough Trinity	Worcester City	7	1	0	1	0	0	0	0
Jackson	H	Harry	12/05/34	Shaw	1955		Oldham Athletic	Stalybridge Celtic	1	0	0	0	0	0	0	0
Jackson	L	Len	10/05/23	Stockport	+1946	1947	Manchester City	Northwich Victoria	61	6	0	2	0	0	0	0
Jenkins	R	Reg	07/10/38	Millbrook	1964	1972	Torquay United	Millbrook	305	11	16	27	119	5	5	12
Jennings	HW	Bill	07/01/20	Norwich	1951		Ipswich Town	Crystal Palace	3	0	0	0	1	0	0	0
Johnson	AK	Alan	19/02/71	Wigan	1996	1998	Lincoln City	retired injured	62	3	5	2	4	1	0	0
Johnson	G	George	27/04/36	Manchester	1954			Buxton	1	0	0	0	0	0	0	0
Johnson	I	Ian	11/11/60	Oldham	1984	1986	Curzon Ashton	Altrincham	81	2	13	6	1	1	0	1
Johnson	MH	Matthew	26/07/10	South Shields	1935	1936	Brentford	Darwen	19	1	2	0	5	0	1	0
Johnson	SA	Steve	23/06/57	Liverpool	1983		Bury	Wigan Athletic	49	7	5	1	12	4	1	0
					1985		Bristol City (loan)	-								
					1989		Huskvana	Cork City								
Johnston	R	Ron	03/04/21	Glasgow	1947		Glasgow Perthshire	Exeter City	17	2	0	0	7	0	0	0
Jones	A	Alan	21/01/51	Grimethorpe	1980		Bradford City	Frickley Athletic	44	1	2	0	5	1	0	0
Jones	A	Alex	27/11/64	Blackburn	1991		Carlisle United	Motherwell	46	5	10	6	2	0	0	1
					1992	1993	Motherwell	Halifax Town								
Jones	A	Arthur			+1945	1946	Goslings		1	2	0	0	0	0	0	0
Jones	C	Christopher		Merthyr Tydfil	1928	1929	Gellifaelog Ams.		2	0	0	2	0	0	0	0
Jones	CMN	Chris	19/11/45	Altrincham	1978	1979	Doncaster Rovers	Le Havre	56	3	2	0	19	1	1	0

Player			D.O.B	Place of Birth	First Season	Last Season	Previous Club	Next Club	Appearances				Goals			
									League	FAC	FLC	Other	League	FAC	FLC	Oth.
Jones	GB	Benny	29/01/07	Newtown	1931		Swindon Town	Oldham Athletic	19	1	0	1	3	0	0	0
Jones	GR	Gary	03/06/77	Birkenhead	1997	2000*	Swansea City		120	7	11	2	17	0	2	0
Jones	GT	Gwyn	1912	Troedyrhiw	1934	+1936	Huddersfield Town	Stockport Co.	88	2	3	2	0	0	0	0
Jones	JA	Jimmy	03/08/27	Birkenhead	1955	1960	Accrington Stanley	retired	177	8	1	6	0	0	0	0
Jones	PB	Paul	13/05/53	Ellesmere Port	1988		Galway	Stockport Co.	14	0	0	0	2	0	0	0
Jones	R	Dicky	06/06/00	Ashton-in-Makerfield	1922		Oldham Athletic	Stockport Co.	32	1	0	7	0	0	0	0
Jones	RE	Rod	23/09/45	Ashton-under-Lyne	1971	1973	Burnley	Barrow	19	1	3	6	0	0	0	0
Jones	SC	Simon	16/05/45	Nettleham	1963	1966	Gainsborough Trinity	Bangor City	47	0	2	2	0	0	0	0
Jones	WS	Walter	09/01/25	Rochdale	1946		St. Chads (Rochdale)	Altrincham	2	0	0	0	2	0	0	0
Jordan	G	George	1904	Methil	1934		Newport County	Prescot Cables	17	1	2	1	0	0	0	0
Kapler	K	Konrad	25/02/25	Tychy, Poland	1949		Celtic	Morecambe	4	0	0	0	0	0	0	0
Kavanagh	EA	Eamonn	05/01/54	Manchester	1973		Manchester City	Bury	3	0	0	0	0	0	0	0
					1997	1998	Sheffield United	Northwich Victoria								
Keegan	GA	Ged	03/10/55	Little Horton	1984		Mansfield Town	Altrincham	2	0	1	4	0	0	0	0
Keeley	W	Walter	01/04/21	Manchester	1951		Accrington Stanley	Fleetwood	4	1	0	0	0	0	0	0
Keenan	GP	Gerry	25/07/54	Liverpool	1982		Port Vale	Ashton United	35	1	2	0	1	0	0	0
					1983		Ashton United	Rossendale United								
Keenan	WG	William	14/02/17	Musselburgh	1938	1939	West Calder		9	0	0	5	0	0	0	0
Kellett	A	Alfred	22/05/03	Preston	1926		Dick Kerr	Rossendale United	1	0	0	3	0	0	0	0
Kendall	A	Arnold	06/04/25	Halifax	1953	1956	Bradford City	Bradford P.A.	111	5	0	5	25	1	0	1
Kerry	DT	David	06/02/37	Derby	1963		Chesterfield	Kettering Town	12	0	2	1	4	0	1	0
Key	LW	Lance	13/05/68		1995		Sheffield Wed. (loan)		33	1	2	1	0	0	0	0
Kilner	AW	Andy	11/10/66	Bolton	1991		Stockport County (loan)	-	3	0	0	0	0	0	0	0
Kilsby	RHR	Reginald	23/08/10	Wollaston	1938	1939	Aldershot		23	1	1	7	6	0	0	1
Kinsella	L	Len	14/05/46	Alexandria	1971	1973	Carlisle United	retired	85	2	3	8	4	0	0	0
Kinsey	S	Steve	02/01/63	Manchester	1991		Tacoma (USA)		6	2	0	0	1	0	0	0
Kirkman	N	Norman	06/03/20	Bolton	+1946	1947	Burnley	Chesterfield	53	3	0	4	0	0	0	0
Kyle	K	Kevin	07/06/81	Stranraer	2000		Sunderland (loan)		6	0	0	0	0	0	0	0
Lacey	AJ	Tony	18/03/44	Leek	1975	1976	Port Vale	Stoke City (coach)	83	9	4	0	0	0	0	0
Lancashire	G	Graham	19/10/72	Blackpool	1997	2000	Wigan Athletic	Hednesford Town	83	1	10	2	23	0	2	3
Lancaster	D	Dave	08/09/61	Preston	1993		Chesterfield	Halifax Town	60	2	6	3	16	0	1	1
					1995	1996	Bury	Bamber Bridge								
Latham	A	Albert	1904	Hucknall	1930		Accrington Stanley	Hurst	8	0	0	1	1	0	0	0
Latimer	J	John	03/02/06	Hill o' Beath	1938		Queen of the South	Leith Athletic	1	0	0	0	0	0	0	0
Lawrence	C	Cyril	12/06/20	Salford	1946	1949	Blackpool	Wrexham	44	1	0	4	5	0	0	0
Lawrence	LO	Les	18/05/57	Wolverhampton	1984		Aldershot	Burnley	15	1	2	3	4	0	1	0
Lee	C	Chris	18/06/71	Batley	1990		Bradford City	Scarborough	26	2	7	3	2	0	1	1
Lee	C	Christian	08/10/76	Aylesbury	2000		Gillingham (loan)		5	0	0	0	1	0	0	0
Leech	VG	Vinny	06/12/40	Rochdale	1968	1970	Bury	retired injured	60	3	1	5	1	0	0	0
Lello	CF	Cyril	24/02/20	Ludlow	1956		Everton	Runcorn	11	0	0	0	0	0	0	0
Leonard	MA	Mark	27/09/62	St Helens	1991	1992	Bradford City	Preston North End	89	2	6	6	7	0	0	0
					1996	1998	Wigan Athletic	retired, injurded								
Lewins	GA	George	16/07/06	Walker on Tyne	1928		Reading	Manchester City	34	1	0	2	0	0	0	0
Lewis	DB	Bryn	16/05/13	Tonypandy	1938		Torquay United	Newry Town	1	0	0	0	0	0	0	0
Lewis	G	Gwyn	22/04/31	Bangor	1956		Everton	Chesterfield	27	1	0	0	11	0	0	0
Lewis	HH	Harry	1910	Merthyr Tydfil	1928	1930	Dowlais Utd.	Arsenal	62	1	0	6	16	0	0	1
Lindsay	T	Tom	11/03/03	Paisley	1929		Wigan Borough	Watford	7	0	0	0	1	0	0	0
Lister	AO	Alex "Sandy"	20/01/24	Glasgow	1952		Alloa Athletic		2	0	0	0	0	0	0	0
Lister	HF	Bert	04/10/39	Manchester	1964	1966	Oldham Athletic	Stockport County	56	3	4	2	16	2	1	1
Littler	O	Oswald	15/02/07	Billinge	1928		Northwich Victoria	Southampton	4	0	0	0	1	0	0	0
Livesey	J	Jack	08/03/24	Preston	+1947	1950	Doncaster Rovers	Southport	113	6	0	5	36	1	0	1
Lockett	PB	Phil	06/09/72	Stockport	1989	1990	(YTS)		3	0	0	0	0	0	0	0
Lockhart	C	Crichton 'Jock'	06/03/30	Perth	1957		Southend United	Gravesend & Northfleet	40	1	0	1	11	0	0	0
Lomas	A	Bert	14/10/24	Tyldesley	1950		Mossley	Chesterfield	9	3	0	0	0	0	0	0
Lomax	GW	Geoff	06/07/64	Droylsden	1987	1988	Carlisle United	Chorley	71	1	8	7	0	0	0	0
Longbottom	H	Harry			1933		Trinity Meths.		2	0	0	1	0	0	0	0
Longdon	CW	Charles	06/05/17	Mansfield	1947		Bournemouth	Bath City	2	0	0	0	0	0	0	0
Lord	F	Frank	13/03/36	Chadderton	1953	1960		Crewe Alexandra	122	3	3	3	54	0	2	0
Lowery	B	Bernard	1907	Kirkdale	1932		Liverpool	Chester City	1	0	0	0	0	0	0	0
Lucketti	CJ	Chris	28/09/71	Littleborough	1988		Whitworth Valley	Stockport County	1	0	0	2	0	0	0	0
Luke	NE	Noel	28/12/64	Birmingham	1992		Peterborough United		3	0	0	0	0	0	0	0
Lydiate	JL	Jason	29/10/71	Manchester	1998		Scarborough (loan)		14	0	0	0	1	0	0	0
Lynch	TJ	Tom "Paddy"	31/08/07	Tredegar	1929	1930	Rhymney	Colwyn Bay United	58	1	0	9	0	0	0	0
Lynn	J	Joe	31/01/25	Seaton Sluice	1951	1955	Exeter City		193	10	0	5	23	1	0	0
Lyons	AE	Eddie	20/05/20	Rochdale	+1953	1954	Crewe Alexandra	Dartford	19	3	0	2	1	0	0	0
Lyons	GW	George	01/05/35	Rochdale	1953	1956			29	0	0	1	4	0	0	0
Lyons	P	Paul	24/06/77	Leigh	1995		Manchester United		3	0	0	0	0	0	0	0
MacKenzie	DA	Don	30/01/42	Liverpool	1963	1964	Everton	New Brighton	41	0	0	2	7	0	0	0
Maguire	JS	Jim	03/02/32	Eaglesham	1956		Queen of the South		15	3	0	0	0	0	0	0
Makin	SH	Sammy	14/11/25	Radcliffe	+1945	1946	Moss Rovers	Droyslden	5	2	0	1	1	1	0	0
Malcolm	PA	Paul	11/12/64	Heworth	1984		Durham City	Shrewsbury Town	24	1	2	0	0	0	0	0
Mallalieu	H	Harry	28/8/1896	Rochdale	^1921		All Saints Oakenrod		3	0	0	0	0	0	0	0
Marcroft	EH	Ted	08/05/10	Rochdale	1936		Bacup Borough	Macclesfield Town	5	0	1	1	0	0	0	1
Marriott	S	Stan	21/07/29	Rochdale	1952		Rochdale YMCA	Rossendale United	6	0	0	0	2	0	0	0
Marsh	A	Arthur	04/05/47	Dudley	1971	1973	Bolton Wanderers	Darlington	90	3	2	6	0	1	0	0
Marshall	WH	Harry	16/02/05	Hucknall	1935	1937	Brierley Hill Alliance	Linfield	95	2	1	2	22	0	0	0
Martin	AF	Andrew	24/09/1896	Wigtown	1928		Halifax Town	Torquay United	32	1	0	1	1	0	0	0
Martin	DS	Dean	09/09/67	Halifax	1994	1996	Scunthorpe United	Lancaster City	53	4	4	4	0	1	0	1
Martin	H	Harry	5/12/1891	Selston	1925	1930	Nottingham Forest	York City (trainer)	93	7	0	7	18	3	0	1
Martin	HJ	Harold	15/03/55	Blackburn	1974		Bolton Wanderers	Mossley	13	0	0	0	0	0	0	0
Martin	JG	Jack	20/08/35	Dundee	1962	1963	Sheffield Wednesday	Alfreton Town	24	0	2	3	0	0	0	0
Martinez	E	Eugene "Eui"	06/07/57	Chelmsford	1980	1982	Bradford City	Newport County	116	5	6	3	16	0	1	0
Mason	FO	Frank	01/08/01	Solihull	1924	1926	Cardiff City	Merthyr Town	49	1	0	2	0	0	0	0
Mason	SJ	Stuart	02/06/48	Whitchurch	1976		Chester (loan)	-	2	0	0	0	0	0	0	0
Matthews	NP	Neil	03/12/67	Manchester	1993	1994	Cardiff City	(China)	19	1	7	5	0	0	0	0

Player			D.O.B	Place of Birth	First Season	Last Season	Previous Club	Next Club	Appearances				Goals			
									League	FAC	FLC	Other	League	FAC	FLC	Oth.
McAleer	J	Joe	08/03/10	Blythswood	1931	1932	Arbroath	Glenavon	35	1	0	3	8	0	0	2
McAllister	D	Don	26/05/53	Radcliffe	1984		Academia Setubal	Tampa Bay Rowdies	3	0	1	0	0	0	0	0
McAuley	S	Sean	23/06/72	Sheffield	1999	2000*	Scunthorpe United		14	0	1	0	0	0	0	0
McBain	GA	Gordon	04/09/34	Glasgow	1958		Kilmarnock		10	0	0	2	1	0	0	0
McClare	SP	Sean	21/01/78	Rotherham	1999		Barnsley (loan)		9	0	0	0	0	0	0	0
McClelland	JW	Johnny	11/08/30	Colchester	1955		Swindon Town	Clacton Town	24	0	0	1	5	0	0	0
McCluskie	JA	Jim	29/09/66	Rossendale	1983	1985	(App)	Mossley	18	0	1	1	0	0	0	0
McCormick	JM	Joe	15/07/16	Holywell	+1945	1947	Bolton Wanderers	Boston United	66	10	0	3	0	0	0	0
McCready	BT	Bernard	23/04/37	Dumbarton	1957	1958	Celtic	Oldham Athletic	29	2	0	3	0	0	0	0
McCulloch	WD	Billy	25/06/22	Edinburgh	1954	1957	Stockport County	retired	140	3	0	6	2	0	0	0
McDermott	JC	John	14/10/59	Manchester	1979			Wigan Athletic	8	0	0	0	1	0	0	0
McDowall	KF	Ken	06/05/38	Manchester	1960		Manchester United	Rhyl	6	0	1	1	0	0	0	0
McElhinney	GMA	Gerry	19/09/56	Derry	1982		Bolton Wanderers (loan)		20	0	0	0	1	0	0	0
McEwen	FK	Frank	15/02/48	Dublin	1966	1967	Manchester United	Drogheda	17	1	0	2	2	0	0	0
McGarry	AM	Arthur	1898	Burslem	1923	1924	Reading		42	2	0	6	1	0	0	0
McGeachie	G	George	26/10/16	Calder	1948	1950	Leyton Orient	Crystal Palace	90	5	0	6	6	0	0	0
McGeeney	PM	Paddy	31/10/66	Sheffield	1986		Sheffield United (loan)	-	3	0	0	0	0	0	0	0
McGhee	SW	(Dr) Wilson	02/05/1892	Maybole	1921		Glasgow University		2	0	0	0	0	0	0	0
McGlennon	T	Tom	20/10/33	Whitehaven	1957	1958	Blackpool	Burton Albion	61	4	0	4	2	0	0	0
McGuigan	J	Jimmy	01/03/34	Addiewell	1956	1958	Crewe Alexandra	Crewe Alexandra (coach)	70	4	0	3	2	0	0	0
McHale	R	Ray	12/08/50	Sheffield	1986		Swansea City	Scarborough	7	1	2	2	0	0	0	0
McInerney	ID	Ian	26/01/64	Liverpool	1990		Stockport County (loan)	-	4	0	0	0	1	0	0	0
McIntyre	JG	Joe	19/06/71	Manchester	1988			Port Vale	4	0	0	0	0	0	0	0
McKay	J	Joffre	21/01/37	Conan Bridge	1960	1961	Bury		9	2	3	2	0	0	0	0
McLaren	A	Andy	24/01/22	Larkhall	1955	1956	Southport	Fleetwood	44	1	0	1	12	0	0	0
McLaren	H	Hugh	13/01/01	Kilbirnie	1936	1937	Tranmere Rovers	Astley Bridge	64	1	0	1	1	0	0	0
McMahon	ID	Ian	07/10/64	Wells	1983	1985	Oldham Athletic	retired injured	91	4	9	6	8	0	0	0
McMurdo	AB	Alex	09/04/14	Cleland	1937		Queen of the South		2	0	0	0	0	0	0	0
McMurray	T	Thomas	24/07/11	Belfast	1937		Glenavon	Chelmsford City	23	2	0	0	1	0	0	0
McNichol	A	Alex	10/10/19	Baillieston	1950		Aldershot	Ramsgate	17	0	0	0	3	0	0	0
McQueen	ID	Ian	04/02/46	Manchester	1965	1966		Hyde United	16	0	0	2	4	0	0	0
McRorie	D	Danny	25/06/06	Glasgow	1933		Liverpool	Morton	5	0	0	0	0	0	0	0
Measham	I	Ian	14/12/64	Barnsley	1985		Huddersfield Town (loan)	-	12	0	0	0	0	0	0	0
Medd	GE	Gordon	17/08/25	Birmingham	1950		Walsall	York City	5	0	0	0	1	0	0	0
Mee	GW	George	12/04/00	Bulwell	1938		Accrington Stanley	Accrington Stanley	1	1	0	1	0	0	0	0
Melledew	ST	Steve	28/11/45	Rochdale	1966	1969	Whipp & Bourne	Everton	175	7	8	7	35	0	2	3
					1976	1977	Crewe Alexandra	Hillingdon Borough								
Melling	T	Terry	24/01/40	Haverton Hill	1968		Mansfield Town	Darlington	20	0	0	3	8	0	0	0
Mellish	SM	Stuart	19/11/69	Hyde	1987	1988	Blackpool	Altrincham	26	1	0	1	1	0	0	0
Middlebrough	A	Alan	04/12/25	Rochdale	1948	1951	Bradford City	retired	47	7	0	3	25	2	0	2
Milburn	S	Stan	22/10/26	Ashington	1958	1964	Leicester City	Spotland Meths.	238	13	18	6	26	1	0	0
Miles	U	Uriah	04/01/07	Newcastle-under-Lyme	1927	1928	Wrexham	Witton Albion	10	0	0	1	2	0	0	0
Millar	JMcV	Jock	31/12/06	Coatbridge	1937		New Brighton	Exeter City	26	1	0	0	8	0	0	0
Milligan	LC	Larry	20/04/58	Liverpool	1979		Aldershot	Barrow	9	0	0	0	0	0	0	0
Milligan	SJF	Steve	16/06/73	Hyde	1989		Ipswich Town	Castleton Gabriels	5	0	0	0	1	0	0	0
Mills	H	Harry	23/07/22	Bishop Auckland	1950		Tunbridge Wells	Halifax Town	1	0	0	0	0	0	0	0
Mills	J	John	09/04/00	Vale of Leven	1924		Fleetwood	Lancaster Town	16	1	0	1	3	0	0	1
Mills	N	Neil	27/10/63	Littleborough	1986		Tim Bobbin (R'dale)	Stockport County	10	2	2	3	0	1	1	0
Milne	M	Mike	17/08/59	Aberdeen	1978			Montrose	2	0	0	0	0	0	0	0
Milner	AJ	Andy	10/02/67	Kendal	1989	1993	Manchester City	Chester City	127	8	17	8	25	1	7	0
Milsom	J	Jack	02/05/08	Bedminster	1928	1929	Bristol Rovers	Bolton Wanderers	54	2	0	4	38	2	0	3
Mitchell	NN	Neil	07/11/74	Lytham	1995		Blackpool (loan)	-	4	0	0	0	0	0	0	0
Mitcheson	FJ	Frank	10/03/24	Stalybridge	1954	1955	Crewe Alexandra	Mossley	50	5	0	1	8	1	0	0
Mittell	JL	Jackie	28/02/06	Merthyr Tydfil	1927	1928	Penrhiwceiber	Wigan Borough	46	1	0	0	0	0	0	0
Molloy	G	Gerry	13/03/36	Rochdale	1955	1956			6	0	0	0	0	0	0	0
Monington	M	Mark	21/10/70	Bilsthorpe	1998	2000	Rotherham United	Boston United	95	8	8	1	12	1	3	0
Monks	A	Albert		Manchester	1927			Stalybridge Celtic	1	0	0	0	0	0	0	0
Moody	JH	Harry	12/3/1896	Rochdale	^1922	1927	Grimsby Town	retired injured	161	9	0	12	0	0	0	0
Moody	WA	William	22/2/1895	Rochdale	^1922		Cardiff City		1	0	0	0	0	0	0	0
Moore	A	Alan	07/03/27	Hebburn	1958		Swindon Town	Wisbech Town	11	0	0	1	2	0	0	1
Moore	AP	Tony	19/09/57	Wolverhampton	1984		Goole T	Belper Town	3	0	0	0	0	0	0	0
Moore	J	John	01/10/66	Consett	1987		Sunderland (loan)	-	10	0	0	0	2	0	0	0
Moore	RD	Ronnie	29/01/53	Liverpool	1985		Charlton Athletic	Tranmere Rovers	43	4	3	3	9	1	0	0
Moorhouse	A	Alan	12/10/25	Wardle	1946	1947	Blackburn Rovers	Bedford Town	17	0	0	0	3	0	0	0
Moran	E	Eddie	20/07/30	Cleland	1956	1958	Stockport County (loan)	Crewe Alexandra	43	1	0	0	13	0	0	0
Moremont	R	Ralph	24/09/24	Sheffield	1955			Chester	1	0	0	0	0	0	0	0
Morgan	SJ	Steve	28/12/70	Wrexham	1990	1991	Oldham Athletic	Stalybridge Celtic	23	0	0	2	3	0	0	0
Morgan	WA	Bill	26/09/26	Rotherham	1953	1954	Halifax Town		28	0	0	1	0	0	0	0
Morrin	AJ	Tony	31/07/46	Swinton	1977	1978	Stockport County (loan)	Bangor	30	1	3	0	0	0	0	0
Morris	AD	Andy	14/11/67	Sheffield	1998	1999	Chesterfield	Hucknall Town	32	0	5	0	7	0	1	0
Morris	W	Billy	01/04/31	Radcliffe	1952		Derby County		4	0	0	0	1	0	0	0
Morritt	GR	Gordon	08/02/42	Rotherham	1972		York City	Darlington	31	0	2	0	0	0	0	0
Mort	T	Tommy	1/12/1897	Kearsley	1921		Atrincham	Aston Villa	28	1	0	1	0	0	0	0
Morton	A	Albert	27/07/19	Newcastle	1953	1956	Sheffield Wednesday		89	4	0	1	0	0	0	0
Morton	GE	George	30/09/43	Liverpool	1962	1965	Everton	New Brighton	147	6	8	4	51	0	4	2
Moss	E	Ernie	19/10/49	Chesterfield	1987		Scarborough (loan)	-	10	0	0	0	2	0	0	0
Moss	J	Jackie	01/09/23	Blackrod	1946	1948	Bury	Leeds United	58	3	0	3	17	0	0	0
Mossman	DJ	David	27/07/64	Sheffield	1985		Sheffield Wednesday	Stockport County	8	0	2	0	0	0	0	0
Mottershead	BL	Brian	13/07/35	Rochdale	1953		Hamer YC		1	0	0	0	0	0	0	0
Moulden	PA	Paul	06/09/67	Farnworth	1995		Huddersfield Town	Bacup Borough	16	3	2	0	1	2	3	0
Moulden	A	Tony	28/08/42	Farnworth	1962	1966	Bury	Peterborough United	6	2	0	1	1	0	0	0
Mountford	RW	Bob	23/02/52	Stoke-on-Trent	1974	1977	Port Vale	Huddersfield Town	98	8	6	0	37	3	1	0
Mullen	J	Jimmy	16/03/47	Oxford	1976		Bury (loan)		8	0	0	0	0	0	0	0
Mullington	PT	Phil	25/09/56	Oldham	1975	1976	Oldham Athletic	Crewe Alexandra	75	5	4	0	6	1	0	0
					1978		Northwich Victoria	Carolyn Hill (H. Kong)								

Player			D.O.B	Place of Birth	First Season	Last Season	Previous Club	Next Club	Appearances League	FAC	FLC	Other	Goals League	FAC	FLC	Oth.
Mulrain	S	Steve	23/10/72	Lambeth	1992	1993	Leeds United	retired	8	0	1	0	2	0	0	0
Mulvaney	R	Dick	05/08/42	Sunderland	1974	1976	Oldham Athletic	Gateshead	73	9	1	0	4	0	0	0
Mulvoy	T	Terry	02/12/38	Manchester	1956				2	0	0	0	0	0	0	0
Murfin	C	Clarrie	02/04/09	Barnsley	1933		Scunthorpe United	Gainsbro' Trinity	26	0	1	1	7	0	0	0
Murphy	D	Danny	10/05/22	Burtonwood	1954	1956	Crewe Alexandra	Macclesfield Town	109	5	0	5	0	0	0	1
Murray	AF	Allan	31/05/07	Heywood	1927	1929	Heywood St.James	Great Harwood	12	0	0	1	1	0	0	0
Murray	DJ	David	1902	Wynberg, SA	1931		Swindon Town	(Jersey coach)	22	1	0	2	3	1	0	0
Murray	L	Leslie	29/09/28	Kinghorn	1952		Arbroath	Cowdenbeath	16	0	0	0	3	0	0	0
Murty	J	Joe	06/11/57	Glasgow	1974	1975	Oldham Athletic	Bury	21	1	0	0	2	0	0	0
Mycock	DC	David	18/09/69	Todmorden	1987	1988	Bolton Wanderers	Altrincham	22	1	2	0	0	0	0	0
Neary	J	John	14/12/15	Chorlton	1938	+1945	Manchester North End	Droylsden	1	2	0	0	0	0	0	0
Neville	DR	David	08/01/29	Birmingham	1955		Burton Albion	Crewe Alexandra	1	0	0	0	0	0	0	0
Newell	G	George	07/03/36	Rochdale	1957				1	0	0	1	0	0	0	0
Nicol	B	Benny	10/03/21	Glasgow	1949		Winsford United		5	0	0	2	1	0	0	0
Nicol	JM	James	24/11/09	Neilson	1934		Brechin City	Crewe Alexandra	27	0	0	2	11	0	0	0
Nicholls	GJ	George	13/12/1890	Hackney	1922		Ton Pentre	Leyton	17	0	0	4	0	0	0	0
Nicholls	JH	Jim	27/11/19	Coseley	1951	1952	Bradford P.A.		50	3	0	2	0	0	0	0
Nicholson	P	Peter	12/01/51	Cleator Moor	1982		Bolton Wanderers	Carlisle United	7	0	0	0	0	0	0	0
Nisbet	KH	Ken	09/06/07	Rosyth	1931		Sunderland	Gateshead	12	0	0	0	2	0	0	0
Norris	OP	Ollie	01/04/29	Derry	1960		Ashford Town	Ashford Town	2	0	0	1	1	0	0	0
Norton	DW	David	03/03/65	Cannock	1990		Notts County (loan)	-	9	0	2	0	0	0	0	0
Nuttall	H	Harry	9/11/1897	Bolton	1932		Bolton Wanderers	Nelson	35	1	0	1	0	0	0	0
Nuttall	J	Jimmy	07/04/00	Bolton	^1921	1923	Manchester United		59	0	0	5	0	0	0	0
O'Connor	MJ	Malcolm	25/04/65	Ashton-under-Lyne	1982	1983	Curzon Ashton	Curzon Ashton	16	1	1	1	3	0	0	1
O'Donnell	H	Hugh	15/02/13	Buckhaven	1946	1947	Blackpool	Halifax Town	40	2	0	2	14	1	0	1
O'Loughlin	N	Nigel	19/01/54	Rochdale	1976	1981	Shrewsbury Town	Ashton United	245	11	13	1	17	1	1	0
O'Shaughnessy	S	Steve	13/10/67	Wrexham	1988	1990	Bradford City	Exeter City	109	9	12	5	16	2	3	0
Oakes	J	John	16/01/21	Hamilton	1946		Queen of the South		1	0	0	0	0	0	0	0
Oates	RA	Bob	26/07/56	Leeds	1983		Scunthorpe United	Witton Albion	42	2	3	3	1	0	0	0
Oliver	BC	Brian	06/03/57	Liverpool	1975		Bury	Morecambe	3	1	0	0	0	0	0	0
Oliver	D	Darren	01/11/71	Liverpool	1993	1994	Bolton Wanderers	Altrincham	28	1	1	1	0	0	0	0
Oliver	EA	Ted	17/03/61	Manchester	1977	1979	(App)		22	0	1	0	1	0	0	0
Oliver	ED	Dougie	09/09/06	Ashington	1929	1930	Alnwick United	Guildford City	46	1	0	6	0	0	0	0
Oliver	M	Michael	02/08/75	Middlesbrough	2000*		Darlington		38	1	3	0	0	0	0	0
Owen	B	Bryn	25/04/39	Rochdale	1960	1961	Turf Hill	Mossley	6	0	0	5	0	0	0	0
Owen	GL	Griffith	1902	Liverpool	1926		Chester	Flint	3	0	0	1	0	0	0	0
Owen	LT	Terry	11/09/49	Liverpool	1977	1978	Cambridge United	Port Vale	83	2	2	0	21	2	0	0
Owens	JR	Reg		Wirral	1921		Pontypridd		14	0	0	1	7	0	0	0
Oxley	W	William	04/12/1899	Wallsend	1924		Walker Celtic	Manchester City	11	0	0	2	5	0	0	4
Page	DR	Don	18/01/64	Manchester	1992		Rotherham United (loan)	-	4	0	0	0	1	0	0	0
Painter	PR	Robbie	26/01/71	Wigan	1996	1998	Darlington	Halifax Town	112	7	9	2	30	0	1	0
Palin	LG	Leigh	12/09/65	Worcester	1991		Hull City (loan)	-	3	0	0	0	0	0	0	0
Parker	C	Carl	25/03/71	Burnley	1991	1992	Rossendale United	Morecambe	16	2	3	1	1	0	0	0
Parker	HD	Derrick	07/02/57	Wallsend	1987		Valkeakosken (Finland)	Northwich Victoria	7	0	1	0	1	1	1	0
Parkes	D	David	17/6/1892	Lye	1922	1927	Stoke City	Macclesfield Town	209	10	0	10	11	1	0	0
Parlane	DJ	Derek	05/05/53	Helensburgh	1986	1987	Racing Jet (Belgium)	Airdrie	42	1	4	2	10	3	1	0
Parr	SV	Steve	22/12/26	Bamber Bridge	1956	1957	Exeter City	Burscough	16	0	0	0	1	0	0	0
Parry	C	Colin	16/02/41	Stockport	1968	1971	Stockport County	Macclesfield Town	156	9	4	14	1	0	0	0
Parton	J	James	03/12/02	Barrow	1929		Barrow	Lancaster Town	7	0	0	1	0	0	0	0
Partridge	D	Don	22/10/25	Bolton	+1945	1955	Farnworth	Bolton Wanderers(Coach)	103	10	0	7	2	0	0	0
Payne	MRC	Mark	03/08/60	Cheltenham	1991	1992	Stockport County	Chorley	62	5	7	5	8	0	0	0
Peake	JW	Jason	29/09/71	Leicester	1993	1995	Halifax Town	Brighton & H.A.	176	12	20	7	17	3	1	3
					1998	1999	Bury	Plymouth Argyle								
Pearce	CL	Chris	07/08/61	Newport	1980	1982	Blackburn Rovers (loan)	-	41	1	6	2	0	0	0	0
Pearson	AV	Bert	6/9/1892	Hebburn	1923	1925	Llanelly	Stockport County	52	4	0	6	12	0	0	3
Pearson	DAJ	David	13/10/47	Shotton	1970		Southport	Morecambe	3	0	0	1	0	0	0	0
Pearson	DT	Dave	09/11/32	Dunfermline	1956	1957	Oldham Athletic	Crewe Alexandra	32	0	0	1	17	0	0	0
Peart	JG	Jack	3/10/1888	South Shields	^1922	1923	Norwich City	(to manager)	21	1	0	2	10	0	0	1
Pemberton	JM	John	18/11/64	Oldham	1984		Chadderton	Crewe Alexandra	1	0	0	0	0	0	0	0
Pender	JP	John	19/11/63	Luton	1997		Wigan Athletic	retired injured	14	1	2	0	0	0	0	0
Pennington	J	Jim	26/04/39	Golborne	1966		Oldham Athletic	Northwich Victoria	14	1	0	1	0	0	0	0
Peters	WT	William	10/10/06	Motherwell	1933		Bournemouth	Burton Town	1	0	0	0	0	0	0	0
Peyton	W	Warren	13/12/79	Manchester	1999			Morecambe	1	0	0	0	0	0	0	0
Phoenix	PP	Peter	31/12/36	Manchester	1962	1963	Oldham Athletic	Exeter City	36	2	1	0	4	1	0	0
Phoenix	RJ	Ron	30/06/29	Stretford	1960	1961	Manchester City	Altrincham	64	4	8	5	0	0	0	0
Pilkington	KW	Kevin	08/03/74	Hitchin	1995		Manchester United (loan)	-	6	0	0	0	0	0	0	0
Plane	E	Eddie		Whitworth	1927		Walsden	Walsden	2	0	0	1	0	0	0	0
					1931		Bacup Borough	Hallford Congs.								
Platt	CL	Clive	27/10/77	Wolverhampton	1999	2000*	Walsall		84	4	7	0	17	2	1	0
Platt	H	Harold	1910	Rochdale	1930	1931	Park Bridge St.James	Hartford Works	16	0	0	1	0	0	0	0
Plunkett	AETB	Adam	16/03/03	Blantyre	1930	1931	Loughborough Cor.	Stalybridge Celtic	18	0	0	0	0	0	0	0
Pollitt	J	Jack	29/03/37	Farnworth	1960		Accrington Stanley	Winsford United	6	2	0	0	1	1	0	0
Pomphrey	EA	Edric 'Syd'	31/05/16	Stretford	+1945		Notts County		9	4	0	0	0	0	0	0
Poole	MD	Mike	23/04/55	Morley	1973	1977	Coventry City	Portland Timbers	219	20	10	2	0	0	0	0
					1981		Portland Timbers					4				
Potter	H	Harry	20/05/23	Tyldesley	1952	1953	Shrewsbury Town	Rhyl	52	2	0	2	0	0	0	0
Powell	DM	Dai	19/01/35	Swansea	1958	1960	Blackpool	Rochdale Police	76	9	2	2	1	0	0	0
Powell	FM	Franny	17/06/77	Burnley	1995		Burnley	Southport	2	0	0	0	0	0	0	0
Power	G	George	10/05/04	Bolton	1928		Manchester City	Darwen	3	0	0	1	0	0	0	0
Prest	TW	Tommy	04/02/08	Darwen	+1938		Aldershot		21	1	0	0	6	0	0	0
Price	J	John	28/04/60	Nantwich	1977	1978	Middlewich Athletic	Macclesfield Town	12	1	0	0	0	0	0	0
Price	JR	James	01/02/78	Preston	1995		(YTS)	Chorley	3	0	0	0	0	0	0	0
Price	WB	Walter	14/02/21	Neston	1948		Tranmere Rovers		1	0	0	0	0	0	0	0
Priday	RH	Bob	29/03/25	Cape Town, SA	1953		Accrington Stanley		5	0	0	0	1	0	0	0
Priestley	PA	Phil	30/03/76	Wigan	1998	2000	Atherton LR	Bangor City	3	0	1	0	0	0	0	0

Player			D.O.B	Place of Birth	First Season	Last Season	Previous Club	Next Club	Appearances				Goals			
									League	FAC	FLC	Other	League	FAC	FLC	Oth
Prince	J	Jack	13/04/08	Crewe	1930		Port Vale	Wrexham	15	1	0	0	0	0	0	0
Proctor	JA	James	25/10/76	Doncaster	1995		Bradford City	Guiseley	3	0	0	0	0	0	0	0
Protheroe	S	Sid	16/12/10	Dowlais	1936	1937	Torquay United	Notts County	63	2	1	3	14	0	0	0
Prouse	WHO	Bill	23/03/00	Birmingham	1922	1923	Redditch Town	Fulham	51	1	0	3	18	0	0	1
Radcliffe	M	Mark	26/10/19	Hyde	1952		Witton Albion		1	1	0	0	0	0	0	0
Radcliffe	V	Vince	09/06/45	Manchester	1968		Peterborough United	King's Lynn	26	2	1	3	1	0	0	0
Radford	A	Alf	07/10/25	Rotherham	1951		Rotherham United	Swindon Town	27	3	0	1	0	0	0	0
Ratcliffe	JB	Barrie	21/09/41	Blackburn	1965		Scunthorpe United		12	3	2	2	1	0	0	1
Redfern	D	Dave	08/11/62	Sheffield	1984	1986	Sheffield Wednesday	Gainsborough Trinity	87	6	11	6	0	0	0	0
Redfern	L	Levi	18/02/05	Burton-on-Trent	1934		Bradford City	Sheffield United	25	1	1	2	3	0	0	0
Reed	AM	Adam	18/02/75	Bishop Auckland	1997		Blackburn Rovers (loan)		10	0	2	0	0	0	1	0
Rees	M	Mark	13/10/61	Smethwick	1986		Walsall (loan)	-	3	0	0	0	0	0	0	0
Reeve	FW	Fred	01/05/18	Clapton	1938		Tottenham Hotspur	Grimsby Town	27	1	1	5	3	0	0	0
Reeves	A	Alan	19/11/67	Birkenhead	1991	1994	Chester City	Wimbledon	121	6	17	11	9	0	1	1
Reid	DA	David	03/01/23	Glasgow	1947	1950	Glasgow Perthshire	Bradford	36	0	0	2	2	0	0	0
Reid	J	John	20/08/32	Newmains	1967		Torquay United	retired	39	1	1	3	3	0	0	0
Reid	S	Shaun	13/10/65	Huyton	1983	1988	Manchester City	York City	241	10	39	25	14	2	2	2
					1992	1994	York City	Bury								
Renwick	R	Dick	27/11/42	Gilsland	1972	1973	Stockport County		49	1	2	5	0	0	0	0
Reynolds	W	Wally	24/11/06	Ecclesall	1938	+1945	York City	Sheffield Wednesday	22	2	1	2	4	1	0	1
Richardson	BW	Brian	05/10/34	Sheffield	1966		Swindon Town		19	0	1	1	1	0	0	0
Richardson	JAS	Joe	17/03/42	Sheffield	1960	1964	Sheffield United	Tranmere Rovers	115	2	11	9	31	2	5	3
Ridge	R	Roy	21/10/34	Sheffield	1964	1965	Sheffield United	Worksop Town	85	3	5	4	0	0	0	0
Rigby	W	Will	1911	Atherton	1932	1933	Stockport County		46	1	1	3	5	1	0	0
Rigg	T	Tweedale	01/11/1896	Rochdale	^1924		Blackburn Rovers	Chester	2	0	0	0	0	0	0	0
Riley	HW	Hughie	12/06/47	Accrington	1967	1971		Crewe Alexandra	92	5	4	12	12	0	0	1
Rimmer	SA	Stuart	12/10/64	Liverpool	1994		Chester (loan)	-	3	0	0	0	0	0	0	0
Roberts	WE	Bill	22/10/18	Flint	+1946	1948			43	3	0	2	0	0	0	0
Roberts	WJ	Billy	09/04/63	Bradford	1988		Farsley Celtic	Farsley Celtic	1	0	0	0	0	0	0	0
Robinson	CA	Charlie	1906	Pegswood	1936	1937	Accrington Stanley	Blyth Spartans	18	0	1	0	0	0	0	0
Robinson	P	Peter	04/09/57	Ashington	1984		Blyth Spartans	Darlington	12	0	0	0	0	0	0	0
Robson	ER	Ed	21/8/1890	Hexham	1928		Grimsby Town		12	0	0	0	0	0	0	0
Robson	GA	Glenn	25/09/77	Sunderland	1996	1997	Murton	Harrogate Town	10	0	0	0	0	0	0	0
Robson	JC	Jack	24/03/06	Birtley	1933		Chester	Oldham Athletic	28	1	1	0	10	0	0	0
Robson	JW	Joe	26/10/1899	Ryhope	1925		Durham City	Lincoln City	4	0	0	1	0	0	0	0
Rodi	J	Joe	23/07/13	Glasgow	+1946		Boston United		9	0	0	0	3	0	0	0
Rose	K	Ken	18/08/30	Eckington	1953		Exeter City	Workington	11	0	0	0	0	0	0	0
Rose	KP	Kevin	23/11/60	Evesham	1990	1992	Bolton Wanderers	Kidderminster Harriers	71	4	6	2	0	0	0	0
Roseboom	E	Ted	24/11/1896	Glasgow	1924		Clapton Orient	Chesterfield	30	2	0	1	4	0	0	0
Ross	A	Alec		Aberdeen	1926			Dundee	1	0	0	0	1	0	0	0
Rothwell	R	Ron	10/07/20	Bury	1946	1951	Dunfermline	Rossendale United	48	2	0	4	1	0	0	0
Rowbotham	H	Harry	1911	Willington Quay	1936		Barrow	Tunbridge Wells Rangers	19	1	0	0	1	0	0	0
Rowe	RK	Robert	1911	Herrington	1932		Herrington Colliery	Jarrow	1	0	0	1	0	0	0	0
Royan	WOH	William	09/12/14	Kinloss	1938		Queen of the South	Glasgow Perthshire	5	0	0	2	1	0	0	0
Rudd	WT	Billy	13/12/41	Manchester	1967	1969	Grimsby Town	Bury	108	3	2	7	8	0	0	0
Rudman	H	Harold	04/11/24	Whitworth	1957		Burnley		21	1	0	1	2	0	0	0
Russell	A	Alex	17/03/73	Crosby	1994	1997	Burscough	Cambridge United	102	2	10	4	14	0	1	0
Russell	W	Billy	07/07/35	Hounslow	1966	1967	Bolton Wanderers	Scarborough	61	2	2	5	8	0	0	1
Ryan	DT	Darren	03/07/72	Oswestry	1994	1995	Stockport County	Chester City	32	4	9	5	2	0	0	0
Ryan	JB	John	18/02/62	Failsworth	1991	1993	Chesterfield	Bury	70	7	13	7	2	0	3	1
Ryder	DF	Derek	18/02/47	Leeds	1968	1971	Cardiff City	Southport	168	9	8	18	1	0	0	0
Ryder	F	Frank	07/03/09	Summerseats	1934		Torquay United	Ards	6	0	1	0	0	0	0	0
Sandham	W	William		Fleetwood	1922		Blackburn Rovers	Fleetwood	22	1	0	5	7	0	0	2
Sandiford	R	Bob	1900	Rochdale	^1921		Rochdale St.Peters	Bacup Borough	16	0	0	0	4	0	0	0
					1923	1924	Bacup Borough	York City								
Scaife	RH	Bobby	12/10/55	Northallerton	1977	1979	Hartlepool United	Whitby Town	98	4	4	0	9	2	0	0
Schofield	R	Robert	07/11/04	Rochdale	1926	1927		Newton Heath	17	0	0	2	6	0	0	0
Scott	AM	Andy	27/06/75	Manchester	1997		Cardiff City	Stalybridge Celtic	3	0	0	0	0	0	0	0
Scott	RW	Bob	22/02/53	Liverpool	1977	1978	Hartlepool United	Crewe Alexandra	71	2	5	0	3	0	0	0
Seal	J	Jimmy	09/12/50	Pontefract	1979	1980	Darlington	Gainsbro' Trinity	53	5	1	0	4	0	0	0
Searle	DP	Damon	26/10/71	Cardiff	1999		Carlisle United (loan)	-	14	0	0	0	0	0	0	0
Seasman	J	John	21/02/55	Liverpool	1984		Cardiff City (loan)	-	94	6	10	7	4	4	1	0
					1985	1987	Chesterfield	Northwich Victoria								
Seddon	DA	David	13/04/51	Rochdale	1973	1974	Stafford Rangers	Stafford Rangers	21	3	0	0	0	0	0	0
Seddon	IW	Ian	14/10/50	Prestbury	1977		Cambridge United	Wigan Athletic	31	0	3	0	3	0	0	0
Sharpe	R	Richard	14/01/67	Wokingham	1994		Coco Expos (USA)	Coco Expos (USA)	16	1	6	0	2	0	1	0
Sharples	H	Harry			1932		Macclesfield Town	Ashton National	2	0	0	0	0	0	0	0
Shaw	GP	Graham	07/06/67	Stoke-on-Trent	1994		Stoke City		22	3	3	2	0	0	1	0
Shaw	S	Steve	10/08/60	Manchester	1977		(App)	Buxton	6	1	0	0	0	0	0	0
Shearer	PA	Peter	04/02/67	Birmingham	1986		Birmingham City	Nuneaton Borough	1	0	1	0	0	0	2	0
Shehan	WJ	Joe		Rochdale	1921		Rochdale St.Johns	Rochdale Civil Service	1	0	0	0	0	0	0	0
Shelton	G	Gary	21/03/58	Nottingham	1993		Bristol City (loan)	-	3	0	0	0	0	0	0	0
Shepherd	T	Thomas			1932	1933	Castleton Baptists	Ashton National	4	0	0	1	0	0	0	0
Shonakan	JF	Joseph	29/11/13	Bolton	1932	1933	Bolton Wanderers	Wrexham	27	1	0	2	2	0	0	0
Shyne	C	Chris	10/12/50	Rochdale	1976	1978	Dyers Arms (R'dale)	Wigan Athletic	19	1	0	0	0	0	0	0
Sibley	TI	Tom	27/10/20	Porth	+1946	1947	Birmingham	Barry Town	23	2	0	1	3	0	0	0
Sievwright	GES	George	10/10/37	Broughty Ferry	1965		Tranmere Rovers	Macclesfield Town	32	3	2	4	1	1	0	0
Silverwood	E	Eric	25/07/06	Rochdale	1928		Rochdale St. Clements		2	0	0	0	0	0	0	0
Simmonds	RL	Lyndon	11/11/66	Pontypool	1986	1987	Leeds United	retired injured	65	1	2	3	22	4	3	0
Simpson	CWP	Charlie	11/07/54	Rochdale	1972		Sacred Heart (R'dale)	Rochdale Nomads	1	0	0	1	1	0	0	0
Skaife	S	Sam	10/12/09	Otley	1934	1936	Bradford P.A.		60	2	3	4	0	0	0	0
Skeete	LA	Leo	03/08/49	Liverpool	1972	1974	Ellesmere Port	Mossley	40	4	3	0	14	0	1	0
Skivington	MN	Mike	24/12/21	Glasgow	1947		Bury	Dundalk	1	0	0	0	0	0	0	0
Slack	A	Andy	09/06/59	Heywood	1977	1978	Bolton Wanderers	retired injured	15	0	2	0	0	0	0	0
Slicer	W	Walter			1933		Luton Town	Oswestry	4	0	0	0	0	0	0	0

Player			D.O.B	Place of Birth	First Season	Last Season	Previous Club	Next Club	Appearances				Goals			
									League	FAC	FLC	Other	League	FAC	FLC	Oth.
Small	C	Colin	09/11/70	Stockport	1989		Manchester City	Stalybridge Celtic	7	0	0	2	1	0	0	0
Smart	J	Jason	15/02/69	Rochdale	1985	1988	Milton	Crewe Alexandra	117	3	16	7	4	0	0	0
Smith	A	Albert	28/4/1887	Burnley	^1923	1924	Grimsby Town	(to coach)	13	0	0	3	0	0	0	1
Smith	C	Craig	02/08/76	Mansfield	1997		Derby County (loan)	-	3	0	1	0	0	0	0	0
Smith	GL	Graham	20/06/46	Pudsey	1966	1973	Leeds United	Stockport County	317	15	13	28	8	0	1	1
Smith	JR	John	2/4/1895	Pollokshaws	1933		Bury	Ashton National	25	1	0	2	8	0	0	1
Smith	MC	Mark	19/12/61	Sheffield	1988		Kettering Town	Huddersfield Town	27	2	4	3	7	0	0	1
Smith	TS	Tom		Higham	1933		Nelson	Luton Town	25	1	0	0	0	0	0	0
Smith	W	William		1912 Rochdale	1936		Halifax Town		4	0	1	0	1	0	0	0
Smith	WE	William	19/11/00	Sheffield	1925		Hartlepool United	Halifax Town	10	0	0	1	2	0	0	0
Smith	WH	Billy	23/5/1895	Tantobie	1934		Huddersfield Town	(to manager)	3	1	0	1	1	1	0	1
Smyth	HR	Bob	28/02/21	Manchester	1950		Halifax Town	Accrington Stanley	3	0	0	1	1	0	0	0
Sneddon	T	Tom	26/08/12	Livingston	1937	1946+	Queen of the South	(Czechoslovakia coach)	67	7	2	9	0	0	0	0
Sneyd	W	William			1921				4	0	0	0	0	0	0	0
Snookes	E	Eric	06/03/55	Smethwick	1978	1982	Southport	Bolton Wanderers	183	10	11	4	1	0	0	0
Snow	GEG	George	09/02/10	Newcastle	1932		Leeds United	Wrexham	41	1	0	4	12	0	0	3
Snowden	T	Trevor	04/10/73	Sunderland	1992	1993	Seaham Red Star	Northwich Victoria	14	0	0	2	0	0	0	0
Spargo	S	Steve	29/12/03	Burnley	1933		York City	Burton Town	4	0	0	0	0	0	0	0
Sparrow	P	Paul	24/03/75	Wandsworth	1998		Preston North End	Lancaster City	25	4	3	2	2	0	0	0
Spencer	L	Les	16/09/36	Manchester	1957	1959		Luton Town	74	7	0	5	17	2	0	1
Sperry	E	Edward	05/07/13	Warsop Vale	1937		Ollerton Colliery		3	0	0	0	0	0	0	0
Stafford	AG	Andy	28/10/60	Littleborough	1982		Stockport County	Mossley	1	0	0	2	1	0	0	0
Stanners	W	Walter	02/01/21	Cariden	1949				5	1	0	1	0	0	0	0
Stanton	B	Brian	07/02/56	Liverpool	1986	1987	Morecambe	Morecambe	49	0	1	3	4	3	1	0
Steele	E	Ernest	18/06/08	Middleton	+1931		Middleton	Oldham Athletic	19	1	0	2	3	0	0	0
Steen	AW	Alan	26/06/22	Crewe	1950	1951	Aldershot	Carlisle United	45	3	0	1	8	1	0	0
Stephenson	GR	Bob	19/11/42	Derby	1965	1966	Shrewsbury Town	Lockheed Leamington	51	1	2	0	16	0	1	0
Stephenson	J	John		Croxdale	1927		Durham City	Ashington	22	0	0	0	0	0	0	0
Stiles	JC	John	06/05/54	Manchester	1991		Doncaster Rovers (loan)	-	4	0	0	0	0	0	0	0
Stirling	E	Ed		Arbroath	1924		Dundee Hibernian		13	0	0	2	0	0	0	0
Stokes	DA	Dean	23/05/70	Birmingham	1998	1999	Port Vale		30	3	7	2	0	0	0	0
Stonehouse	B	Bernard	23/12/34	Manchester	1955	1956	Crewe Alexandra		19	0	0	2	1	0	0	1
Stonehouse	K	Kevin	20/09/59	Bishop Auckland	1989		Darlington	Bishop Auckland	14	1	4	3	2	1	0	1
Stoker	G	Gareth	22/02/73	Bishop Auckland	1998		Cardiff City	Scarborough	12	0	2	0	1	0	0	0
Storey	J	Jim	30/12/29	Rowlands Gill	1955	1956	Bournemouth	Darlington	24	1	0	3	1	0	0	0
Storf	DA	David	04/12/43	Sheffield	1963	1966	Sheffield Wednesday	Barrow	138	5	6	5	19	1	2	1
Stott	GRB	George	31/01/06	North Shields	1928	1930	Barnsley	Bradford City	109	2	0	11	30	0	0	4
Strong	L	Les	03/07/53	Streatham	1984		Crystal Palace		1	0	0	0	0	0	0	0
Stuart	MRN	Mark	15/12/66	Hammersmith	1993	1998	Huddersfield Town	Morecambe	202	10	20	12	41	1	3	2
Sullivan	LG	Les	8/1912	Croydon	1934		Lytham	Brentford	32	0	3	1	9	0	0	0
Summerscales	WC	Bill	04/01/49	Willesden	1975	1976	Port Vale	(Australia)	87	9	4	0	4	0	0	0
Sutcliffe	A	Arnold			1937		Breda Visada	Droylsden	2	0	0	0	0	0	0	0
Sutton	B	Brian	08/12/34	Rochdale	1952	1955	Norden YC	Rossendale United	13	0	0	0	0	0	0	0
Sutton	DW	Dave	21/01/57	Tarleton	1988		Bolton Wanderers	(to physio)	28	2	4	4	2	0	0	1
Swan	C	Carl	12/12/57	Sheffield	1982		Doncaster Rovers (loan)	-	3	1	0	0	0	0	0	0
Sweeney	A	Andy	15/10/51	Oldham	1975		Oldham Athletic	Mossley	17	1	2	0	0	0	0	0
Symonds	CRCH	Calvin	29/03/32	Bermuda	1955		Pembroke (Bermuda)	(West Indies)	1	0	0	0	0	0	0	0
Tapley	R	Reg	02/11/32	Nantwich	1956		Crewe Alexandra		1	0	0	1	0	0	0	0
Tapley	S	Steve	03/10/63	Camberwell	1984		Fulham (loan)	-	1	0	0	0	0	0	0	0
Tarbuck	AD	Alan	10/10/48	Liverpool	1976	1977	Shrewsbury Town	Bangor City	48	3	5	0	1	1	1	0
Taylor	AD	Alan	14/11/53	Hinckley	1973	1974	Morecambe	West Ham United	55	3	3	1	7	1	1	0
Taylor	B	Brian	29/06/42	Manchester	1963	1967		Altrincham	132	3	4	7	7	0	1	1
Taylor	B (2)	Brian	12/02/54	Hodthorpe	1978	1982	Doncaster Rovers	Whitworth Valley	154	7	6	1	10	0	0	0
Taylor	DJ	Danny	28/07/82	Oldham	1999		(YTS)		1	0	0	0	0	0	0	0
Taylor	F	Fred		Rotherham	1921		Maidstone United	Fletton United	19	0	0	1	0	0	0	0
Taylor	F (2)	Fred		1914 Heywood	1935		Heywood St. James		6	0	1	0	3	0	0	0
Taylor	JL	Jamie	11/01/77	Bury	1993	1996	Heywood St. James	Altrincham	36	1	4	2	4	0	1	0
Taylor	JL	John	25/06/49	Birmingham	1974		Chester (loan)	-	3	0	0	0	0	0	0	0
Taylor	S				1935				2	0	0	1	0	0	0	0
Taylor	SJ	Steve	18/10/55	Royton	1984	1986	Stockport County	Preston North End	101	4	10	6	46	5	5	0
					1988		Burnley	retired injured								
Tennant	D	Dave	13/06/45	Walsall	1970		Lincoln City	Corby Town	16	3	0	5	0	0	0	0
Thackeray	AJ	Andy	13/02/68	Huddersfield	1992	1996	Wrexham	Halifax Town	165	8	22	12	13	1	2	2
Thomas	GR	Geoff	05/08/64	Manchester	1982	1983	Ashe Labs	Crewe Alexandra	11	0	1	0	1	0	0	0
Thomas	WE	Billy	16/03/06	Chorlton	1934		Tranmere Rovers	Ashton National	6	0	1	1	1	0	0	0
Thompson	DS	David	27/05/62	Manchester	1981	1985	N. Withington	Notts County	266	13	30	13	24	0	0	3
					1994	1996	Chester	Southport								
Thompson	J	Jimmy	26/11/35	Chadderton	1960	1965	Exeter City	Bradford City	199	9	19	12	15	0	2	0
Thompson	ND	Nigel	01/03/67	Leeds	1987		Leeds United (loan)	-	5	0	0	0	0	0	0	0
Thompson	SC	Stuart	02/09/64	Littleborough	1982	1983	Blackburn Rovers	Chorley	31	1	0	0	8	0	0	0
Thomson	B	Bert	18/02/29	Glasgow	1958	1959	Yeovil Town	San Francisco Scots	55	2	0	2	1	0	0	0
Thompstone	IP	Ian	17/01/71	Bury	1995		Scunthorpe United	Scarborough	25	4	3	1	1	0	1	0
Thorpe	L	Levy	18/11/1889	Seaham Harbour	1924	1925	Lincoln City		31	2	0	1	0	0	0	0
Tippett	T	Tommy	13/07/04	Gateshead	1929	1930	Doncaster Rovers	Port Vale	70	2	0	7	47	0	0	6
Tobin	DJ	Don	01/11/55	Liverpool	1973	1975	Everton	Witton Albion	47	4	0	1	5	1	0	0
Todd	L	Lee	07/03/72	Hartlepool	2000*		Bradford City		40	1	2	0	3	0	0	0
Todd	TB	Tommy	01/06/26	Stonehouse, Lanarks	1956		Derby County		5	0	0	0	1	0	0	0
Tolson	W	Bill	29/03/31	Rochdale	1953	1954	Rochdale St. Albans	(Australia)	10	1	0	1	0	0	0	0
Tomlinson	F	Frank	23/10/25	Manchester	1951		Oldham Athletic	Chester City	20	2	0	0	2	2	0	0
Tompkinson	WV	Billy	18/6/1895	Stone	1923	1927	Aberdare Athletic	Stockport County	162	6	0	3	45	0	0	1
Tong	DJ	David	21/09/55	Blackpool	1985		Cardiff City	Bristol City	2	0	0	0	0	0	0	0
Torrance	GS	George	27/11/35	Glasgow	1957		Oldham Athletic	Albion Rovers	2	0	0	0	0	0	0	0
Towers	MA	Tony	13/04/52	Manchester	1984		Vancouver Whitecaps		2	0	0	0	3	0	0	0
Towner	AJ	Tony	02/05/55	Brighton	1985		Charlton Athletic	Cambridge United	5	3	0	0	0	0	0	0
Townsend	GE	George	29/07/57	Ashton-under-Lyne	1974	1975	Huddersfield Town	(Australia)	32	2	2	0	0	0	0	0

Player			D.O.B	Place of Birth	First Season	Last Season	Previous Club	Next Club	Appearances				Goals			
									League	FAC	FLC	Other	League	FAC	FLC	Oth.
Townson	K	Kevin	19/04/83	Liverpool	2000*		Everton		3	0	0	0	0	0	0	0
Trainer	J	Jack	14/07/52	Glasgow	1982		Waterford	Morecambe	7	0	2	3	0	0	0	0
Trippier	AW	Austin	30/08/09	Ramsbottom	1929	1930	Rochdale St.Clements	Oldham Athletic	12	0	0	1	1	0	0	0
Trotman	RW	Reg	8/1906	Bristol	1928		Bristol Rovers	Sheffield Wedensday	23	1	0	1	10	0	0	0
Tully	JA	Jim	1885	Newcastle	^1921	1922	Pontypridd		40	1	0	3	0	0	0	0
Turley	JW	John	26/01/39	Bebington	1964		Peterborough United	Cambridge United	22	1	1	2	5	0	0	1
Turnbull	GE	George			1930		Bankhead Albion	Darlington	10	0	0	1	2	0	0	0
Turner	AP	Andy	23/03/75	Woolwich	2000		Rotherham United (loan)	-	4	0	0	0	0	0	0	0
Twine	FW	Frank		Holborn	1931		Aldershot	Caernarvon United	10	0	0	0	0	0	0	0
Underwood	GR	George	06/09/25	Sheffield	1954		Scunthorpe United		19	0	0	0	0	0	0	0
Valentine	P	Peter	16/06/63	Huddersfield	1994	1995	Carlisle United	retired injured	50	4	3	2	2	0	0	0
Vause	PG	Peter	17/06/14	Chorley	1938	1939+	Darwen		20	0	1	4	13	0	0	0
Vizard	CJ	Colin	18/06/33	Newton-le-Willows	1957	1958	Everton		41	0	0	1	7	0	0	0
Wainman	WH	Harry	22/03/47	Hull	1972		Grimsby Town (loan)	-	9	0	0	1	0	0	0	0
Wainwright	EF	Eddie	22/06/24	Southport	1956	1958	Everton		100	5	0	2	27	3	0	0
Wakenshaw	RA	Rob	22/12/65	Seaton Deleval	1986		Carlisle United	Crewe Alexandra	29	2	6	0	5	2	2	0
Waldron	C	Colin	22/06/48	Bristol	1979		Atlanta Chiefs		19	3	0	0	1	0	0	0
Walkden	F	Frank	21/06/21	Aberdeen	+1946		Bolton Wanderers		1	0	0	0	0	0	0	0
Wall	G	George	20/2/1885	Boldon	1922		Hamilton Academical	Ashton National	30	1	0	7	1	0	0	0
Wallace	JC	John "Jock"	11/01/36	Glasgow	1957	1959	St. Roch's		7	0	0	1	0	0	0	0
Walling	DA	Dean	17/04/69	Leeds	1987	1989	Leeds United	Kitchener (Canada)	62	1	5	5	8	0	0	2
Walmsley	C	Clifford	25/11/10	Burnley	1933	1934	Reading	Stalybridge Celtic	59	2	2	3	0	0	0	0
Walters	J	Joe	04/1886	Stourbridge	1922		Millwall	Manchester North End	24	1	0	2	6	0	0	1
Wann	JD	Dennis	17/11/50	Blackpool	1979	1980	Darlington	Blackpool	66	5	4	0	7	0	0	0
Warburton	TC	Thomas	11/09/10	Bury	1930		Bury GSOB		2	0	0	0	0	0	0	0
Ward	F	Fred 'Yaffer'	30/1/1894	Lincoln	1926	1927	Lincoln City	Lincoln City	67	2	0	2	0	0	0	0
Ward	G	George			1930	1931	Macclesfield Town	Bury Co-op	33	0	0	2	0	0	0	0
Ward	P	Peter	15/10/64	Durham	1989	1990	Huddersfield Town	Stockport County	84	7	10	4	10	1	0	0
Ware	PD	Paul	07/11/70	Congleton	2000*		Macclesfield Town		30	1	3	0	2	0	0	0
Warner	J	Jack	21/09/11	Tonyrefail	1952		Oldham Athletic	retired	21	1	0	0	0	0	0	0
Warren	LA	Lee	28/02/69	Manchester	1987	1988	Leeds United	Hull City	31	1	0	4	1	0	2	0
Warriner	SW	Steve	18/12/58	Liverpool	1981	1982	Newport County	Tranmere Rovers	12	0	2	3	1	0	0	0
Wasilewski	Z	Adam	1925	Poland	1953				4	0	0	0	1	0	0	0
Watson	D	Don	27/08/32	Barnsley	1962	1963	Barnsley	Barrow	58	4	2	2	15	1	1	0
Watson	E	Edward	1899	Sunderland	1923		QPR		1	0	0	2	0	0	0	0
Watson	I	Ian	05/02/60	North Shields	1979		Sunderland (loan)	-	33	5	2	0	0	0	0	0
Watson	RH	Bert	26/08/00	Thelwall	1931		Southampton		17	1	0	1	8	0	0	0
Watson	TA	Tom	1904	South Shields	1928	1930	Consett	Guildford City	91	3	0	6	0	0	0	0
Watson	TL	Tom	10/1912	Shiney Row	1932		Accrington Stanley		7	0	0	2	6	0	0	0
Watson	W	Bill	29/05/16	South Hiendley	1948	1953	Chesterfield		200	7	0	7	0	0	0	0
Watson	WT	William	16/3/1899	Cambois	1932		Carlisle United	Accrington Stanley	39	1	0	4	12	0	0	1
Webster	W	Walter	03/06/06	Rochdale	1927	1928		Sheffield Wednesday	36	0	0	2	1	0	0	0
					1931		Oswestry	Guildford								
Webster	WG	Wally	22/5/1895	West Bromwich	1933		Torquay United	Stalybridge Celtic	38	1	1	2	0	0	0	0
Weir	A	Alan	01/09/59	South Shields	1979	1982	Sunderland	Hartlepool United	106	7	6	4	3	0	0	0
Welch	H	Bert		Pendleton	1931	1934	Whitworth Valley	Bangor City	57	0	2	3	0	0	0	0
Welch	KJ	Keith	03/10/68	Bolton	1986	1990	Bolton Wanderers	Bristol City	205	10	24	13	0	0	0	0
Weldon	A	Tony	12/11/00	Croy	1933		Dolphin	Dundalk	27	0	1	2	7	0	0	0
Wellings	B	Barry	10/06/58	Liverpool	1980	1982	York City	Tranmere Rovers	116	5	8	4	30	1	3	1
Wells	WD	David	16/12/40	Eccleston	1963		Blackburn Rovers		8	1	0	1	0	0	0	0
West	T	Tom	08/12/16	Salford	1946		Oldham Athletic	Nelson	4	0	0	2	2	0	0	0
Wheatley	B	Barry	21/02/38	Sandbach	1966		Crewe Alexandra	Witton Albion	13	1	1	2	4	0	0	0
Wheelhouse	B	Ben	23/09/02	Rothwell	1932	1933	Halifax Town	Denaby United	66	2	0	5	2	0	0	0
Whelan	AM	Tony	20/11/52	Salford	1974	1976	Manchester City	Fort Lauderdale	124	14	5	0	20	1	0	0
Whellans	R	Robbie	14/02/69	Harrogate	1989		Bradford City	Harrogate Town	11	0	1	2	1	0	0	0
Whiston	D	Don	04/04/30	Chesterton	1958		Crewe Alexandra		14	0	0	3	0	0	0	0
Whitaker	C	Colin	14/06/32	Leeds	1961	1962	QPR	Oldham Athletic	54	2	11	5	11	0	1	2
White	EW	Winston	26/10/58	Leicester	1986		Bury (loan)	-	4	0	0	0	0	0	0	0
White	G	George			1931		Hull City		1	0	0	0	0	0	0	0
Whitehall	SC	Steve	08/12/66	Bromborough	1991	1996	Southport	Mansfield Town	238	15	29	16	75	3	14	3
Whitehead	NJ	Norman	22/04/48	Liverpool	1968	1971	Southport	Rotherham United	156	9	8	18	11	1	1	1
Whitehouse	JE	Jim	19/09/24	West Bromwich	1950	1951	Walsall	Carlisle United	46	2	0	2	13	2	0	0
Whitehurst	AJ	Bert	22/6/1898	Fenton	1923	1927	Stoke City	Liverpool.	169	8	0	10	117	7	0	4
Whitelaw	J	John		Falkirk	1931		London (Canada)		1	0	0	0	0	0	0	0
Whiteside	E	Ernest	01/02/1889	Lytham	1921		Halifax Town		3	0	0	0	0	0	0	0
Whitington	C	Craig	03/09/70	Brighton	1994		Huddersfield Town (loan)	-	1	0	0	0	0	0	0	0
Whitworth	H	Harry	01/12/20	Radcliffe	+1951	1952	Bury	Southport	70	2	0	2	9	0	0	0
Whyke	P	Peter	07/07/39	Barnsley	1961		Barnsley	Scarborough	5	1	1	3	0	0	0	0
Whyte	C	Charlie	1911	Bridgemill	1934		Arbroath	Oldham Athletic	9	0	0	1	1	0	0	0
Wiggins	JA	Joe	01/04/90	Wembley	1935		Gillingham	Oldham Athletic	27	0	0	1	14	0	0	1
Wilkinson	ES	Ernie	13/02/47	Chesterfield	1967		Exeter City (loan)	-	9	0	0	0	0	0	0	0
Williams	DP	David	18/09/68	Liverpool	1991		Burnley (loan)	-	6	0	1	1	0	0	0	0
Williams	I	Idris		Merthyr	1929	1931	Tredomen	Rossendale United	83	1	0	10	5	0	0	0
Williams	I (2)	Idris		Treharris	1937		Halifax Town	Rossendale United	4	0	0	0	0	0	0	0
Williams	MT	Mark	10/11/78	Liverpool	1998		Barrow	Rotherham United	14	4	0	0	1	0	0	0
Williams	PA	Paul	08/09/63	Sheffield	1993	1995	Stockport County	Altrincham	37	1	5	5	7	0	0	3
Williams	RS	Ralph	21/10/05	Aberdare	1932		Southport	Merthyr Town	8	0	0	1	1	0	0	0
Williams	WHJ	Bert	24/09/25	Manchester	1949		Bury	Aldershot	8	0	0	1	3	0	0	0
Williams	WR	Bill	07/10/60	Rochdale	1981	1984	Ashe Labs	Stockport County	95	4	8	6	2	0	0	0
Williamson	R	Bob	06/12/33	Edinburgh	1966	1967	Leeds United	Chorley	36	1	1	1	0	0	0	0
Williamson	TW	Tim	07/04/00	Pollokshaws	1932		Southport	Alloa Athletic	7	1	0	0	2	0	0	0
Willis	RS	Bobby	31/01/01	Tynemouth	1923	1925	Dundee	Halifax Town	64	3	0	7	1	0	0	0
Wilson	F	Frank		Motherwell	1937		Glentoran		7	0	1	0	6	0	0	0
Wilson	SA	Scott	25/10/80	Radcliffe	1999		(YTS)	Radcliffe Borough	1	0	0	0	0	0	0	0
Windridge	DH	Dave	07/12/61	Atherstone	1988		Bury	Colne Dynamos	5	0	0	0	0	0	0	0

Player			D.O.B	Place of Birth	First Season	Last Season	Previous Club	Next Club	Appearances				Goals			
									League	FAC	FLC	Other	League	FAC	FLC	Oth.
Winspear	J	Jack	24/12/46	Leeds	1967		Cardiff City		16	0	0	2	3	0	0	0
Winton	GD	Doug 'Jock'	06/10/29	Perth	1961	1963	Aston Villa		119	6	14	7	0	0	0	0
Withington	RS	Dick	08/04/21	South Shields	1947		Blackpool	Chesterfield	32	3	0	0	6	0	0	1
Wolstencroft	A	Albert			1921			Northwich Victoria	1	0	0	1	0	0	0	0
Wood	E	Eric	13/03/20	Bolton	+1945	1946		Bolton Wanderers	148	12	0	12	15	1	0	0
Wood	P	Paul	20/03/70	Saddleworth	1988		Sheffield United (loan)	-	5	0	2	0	0	0	0	0
Wood	WC	William			1927			Newcastle United	1	0	0	0	0	0	0	0
Woods	?				1930				1	0	0	0	0	0	0	0
Woods	MA	Micky	09/03/62	Halifax	1986		Guiseley	Colne Dynamos	6	1	3	1	3	0	0	0
Woods	W	Billy	12/03/26	Farnworth	+1945		Moss Grove	Bradford P.A.	28	5	0	3	2	6	0	0
					1948	1949	Bradford	Barrow								
Worrall	A	Arthur			1932		Sandbach Ramblers	Buxton Town	1	0	0	0	0	0	0	0
Worthy	A	Albert	01/11/05	Pilsley	1934	1936	Southend United	GainsboroughTrinity	99	2	2	1	1	0	1	0
Wragg	D	Doug	12/09/34	Nottingham	1961	1963	Mansfield Town	Chesterfield	103	4	12	9	15	0	0	2
Wyness	GD	George	11/08/07	Monkswearmouth	1934	1935	Chester	Notts County	70	1	1	2	0	0	0	0
Wynn	J	Jimmy	04/09/11	Wallsend	1936	+1939	Rotherham United (loan)	Scunthorpe United	86	3	1	7	64	1	0	2
Yarwood	JW	Jack	1891	Stockport	^1921		Merthyr Town		11	1	0	2	0	0	0	0
Young	AF	Alan	26/10/55	Kirkcaldy	1986	1987	Notts County	Shepshed C'house (manager)	28	0	4	1	2	0	1	0
Young	AW	Archie	10/12/06	Twechar	1938		Gillingham		1	0	0	0	0	0	0	0
Young	NJ	Neil	17/02/44	Manchester	1974		Preston North End	Macclesfield Town	13	3	1	0	4	1	0	0

Played in Cup ties or other games only

Player			D.O.B	Place of Birth	First Season	Last Season	Previous Club	Next Club	Appearances				Goals			
Anchor	R	Roy		Salford	1959				0	0	0	1	0	0	0	0
Barber	K	Kevin	1936		1957		Bolton Wanderers		0	0	0	1	0	0	0	0
Bishop	GA	George	1901	Tredegar	1925		Ebbw Vale	Merthyr Town	0	0	0	1	0	0	0	0
Bywater	SM	Stephen	07/06/81	Manchester	1997		Fletcher Moss	West Ham United	0	0	1	0	0	0	0	0
Cheetham	J	Jimmy	1928	Rochdale	1948			Bury	0	0	0	1	0	0	0	0
Chesters	A	Arthur	1912	Salford	+1945		Exeter City		0	6	0	0	0	0	0	0
Clegg	H				1928				0	0	0	1	0	0	0	0
Cutler					1966				0	0	0	1	0	0	0	0
Doyle	J	Jamie	01/10/61	Glasgow	1987		Motherwell	Partick Thistle	0	0	0	3	0	0	0	0
Duckworth	R	Dick	06/06/06	Harpurhey	1926		Carlisle United	Oldham Athletic	0	0	0	2	0	0	0	1
Dutton	T	Tommy	11/11/06	Southport	1939	+		Mansfield Town	0	0	0	2	0	0	0	0
Fairclough	D	David	05/01/57	Liverpool	1986		Oldham Athletic	Beveran (Belgium)	0	0	0	1	0	0	0	1
Ferguson	A	Alex		Monifieth	1939		Hearts		0	0	0	2	0	0	0	0
Gray	K	Kevin	05/04/78	Manchester	1996		Stockport County		0	0	0	1	0	0	0	0
Halfpenny	D	David	1901	Swansea	1928			Workington	0	0	0	1	0	0	0	0
Hardman	B	Brian			1964	1966			0	0	0	2	0	0	0	0
Heywood	W				1927		Royton Ams.		0	0	0	1	0	0	0	0
Hughes	PA	Phil	19/11/64	Belfast	1991		Wigan Athletic	Telford United	0	0	0	3	0	0	0	0
Hunt	D	Dave	1954	Swinton	1972				0	0	0	3	0	0	0	0
Jones	T	Tom	1923		1948		Derby County		0	0	0	1	0	0	0	0
Kennedy	J			Rothmines	1938		Scarborough		0	0	0	1	0	0	0	1
Knowles	HE	Harold	1914	Rotherham	1938		Rotherham United		0	0	1	0	0	0	1	0
Lancaster	A				1926			Newcastle Ams.	0	0	0	2	0	0	0	0
Lee	S	Steve			1968				0	0	0	1	0	0	0	0
Lillywhite	G	George			1930		Sedgeley Park		0	0	0	1	0	0	0	0
Milne	C	Charlie	1885	Manchester	^1922		Tranmere Rovers		0	0	0	1	0	0	0	0
Oddie	R				1928				0	0	0	1	0	0	0	0
Pearce	J	Jim		Chirk	1939	+1945	Bristol City	Cardiff City	0	4	0	4	0	0	0	0
Pickard	OA	Owen	18/11/69	Barnstaple	1994		Hereford United	Dorchester Town	0	0	0	1	0	0	0	0
Pollard	H	Henry		Liverpool	1939		Exeter City		0	0	0	2	0	0	0	0
Quinn	C	Charles	11/03/01	Kilmarnock	1925		Peterborough	Queen of the South	0	0	0	1	0	0	0	0
Rhodes	RA	Richard	18/02/08	Wolverhampton	1939		Swansea Town		0	0	0	4	0	0	0	0
Roberts	H	Henry			1938			Rotherham United	0	1	0	0	0	0	0	0
Robertson	P	Peter	02/08	Dundee	1939			Arbroath	0	0	0	4	0	0	0	0
Sanders	JCA	Jim	15/10/32	Marlborough	1960		Crystal Palace	Cheltenham Town	0	0	0	1	0	0	0	0
Thompson	CD	Chris	24/01/60	Walsall	1991		Walsall	Fleetwood	0	0	0	2	0	0	0	0
Walsh	D	David	12/07/83	Rochdale	2000*		(YTS)		0	0	1	0	0	0	0	0
Wilkinson	SJ	Steve	01/09/68	Lincoln	1988		Leicester City (loan)	-	0	0	0	3	0	0	0	0

^ Also played in pre-FL seasons (see separate table)
+ Also appeared in WWII (see separate table)
* Still with Rochdale as of August 2001
FLC = FL Cup + Division 3N Cup + AM Cup
Other = Lancashire Cup, Manchester Cup, Rose Bowl, Northern Floodlit Cup, expunged League games, FL Jubilee games
FAC appearances include 1945-46 season

Pre-League Who's Who

Player			First Season	Last Season	Previous Club	Next Club	Appearances			Goals		
							League	FAC	Other	League	FAC	Oth.
Allan	J	Jack	1913		Leeds City	Coventry City	26	0	4	17	0	2
Alston	E		1907		Lincoln City		17	0	2	0	0	0
Anderson	H		1919		Altrincham		2	0	0	0	0	0
Anderson	WS		1914	1916			20	0	3	1	0	2
Annesley	F		1917				1	0	0	0	0	0
Ashworth	C	Clifford	1918				1	0	0	0	0	0
Aspey	H		1907				1	0	0	0	0	0
Aspinall	W		1907		Rossendale United		25	0	3	7	0	2
Baines	F	Fred	1918		Leeds City	Rotherham County	41	5	3	0	0	0
			1920		Rothenham County	Accrington Stanley						
Barker	FJ	Frank	1909		Darlington	Colne	24	0	4	13	0	3
Ball	M	Martin	1907	1909	Morris Green	Walkden Central	59	1	7	0	0	0
Bamford	T	Tom	1920		Burnley		2	0	0	0	0	0
Bamford	W	Billy	1912	1920			8	0	2	0	0	0
Baker			1911				1	0	0	0	0	0
Barlow	R		1907	1908	Bolton		42	0	6	17	0	2
Barnes	J	Joseph	1920*			New Church	7	0	3	0	0	0
Barnes	H		1908	1909	Accrington Stanley	Great Harwood	18	2	0	6	2	0
Barnett	A	Albert	1915		Cardiff City	(quest)	3	0	0	0	0	0
Barton	JW	Jack	1912	1918*	Southport Park Villa	Blackburn Rovers	108	7	11	0	0	0
Bellis	R		1918		(army)		8	0	0	2	0	0
Berry	T		1917		Mersey Athletic		7	0	0	0	0	0
			1919		Altrincham							
Best	G		1918		Altrincham		4	0	0	1	0	0
Biggar	W	Billy	1910	1916	Watford	Leyland Motors	183	23	27	0	0	0
Birnie	EI	Ted	1912		Mulheim	Leyton	28	4	5	1	2	0
Blackett	J	Joe	1909	1911	Leicester Fosse	Barrow	87	10	14	4	1	1
Bowden	1		1908		Bury		0	1	0	0	0	0
Bracey	FC	Fred	1909	1911	Bradford P.A.		39	1	8	22	0	3
Bradshaw	W	Bill	1920		Blackburn Rovers		5	0	0	0	0	0
Braithwaite	F		1919		Coppull		1	0	0	0	0	0
Brannick	J	James	1915		St. Mirren		17	0	0	4	0	0
Brindle	R		1919		Stalybridge Celtic		3	0	0	0	0	0
Broome	TA	Tom	1911	1913	Salford United	Preston North End	53	6	7	5	0	2
			1918		Preston North End	(quest)						
Broster	J	John	1916		QPR	(quest)	39	4	4	2	0	0
			1920*		QPR	Wigan Borough						
Brown	A		1918	1919	Woodhouses		4	0	0	0	0	0
Brown	W(1)	William	1914	1915	Brighton & H.A.	Hobson Wanderers	38	5	8	21	1	9
Brown	W(2)	Billy	1915		Exeter City		1	0	0	0	0	0
Buckley	D		1918				4	0	0	0	0	0
Buckley	W		1907	1910	Newbold		7	1	2	0	0	3
Bunting	W	Wilfred	1917	1918	Manchester United	Southport Vulcan	27	0	0	2	0	0
Burroughs	J		1907				1	0	0	0	0	0
Bussy			1920		Syke UMO		1	0	0	0	0	0
Butler	JH	Joe	1915		Lincoln City	Stockport County	3	0	0	0	0	0
Butterworth	H	(ir)	1919				2	0	0	0	0	0
Butterworth		(cf)	1919				1	0	0	1	0	0
Butterworth	JE	(wh)	1916		Oldham Athletic	(quest)	3	0	0	0	0	0
Butterworth	J	(rh/or)	1918				2	0	0	0	0	0
Butterworth	RH	(gk)	1917	1918	Denton		7	0	0	0	0	0
Byrom	T	Thomas	1920		Blackburn Rovers	Oldham Athletic	18	4	0	9	1	0
Caldwell	A	Alfred	1914	1916	Oldham Athletic	Oldham Athletic	42	0	2	0	0	0
Cam	JC		1919				2	0	0	0	0	0
Campey	A	Arthur	1911		Leeds City	Knaresborough	0	0	1	0	0	0
Capper	A	Alf	1917		Sheffiield Wednesday	(quest)	1	0	0	0	0	0
Carruthers	WG		1917				1	0	0	0	0	0
Carthy	J		1909		Stalybridge Rovers		9	0	1	3	0	1
Causer	AH	Arthur	1915	1916	Glossop	Preston North End	40	0	0	0	0	0
Chadwick	F		1918		Patricroft		1	0	0	0	0	0
Challinor	H		1919		Bristol City		1	1	1	0	0	0
Challinor	S	Sam	1915		Everton	(quest)	5	0	0	0	0	0
Chamberlain	WT		1913		Manchester United	Merthyr Town	16	1	1	0	0	0
Chick	WJ	William	1911	1912	Norwich City	Barrow	63	8	13	12	3	0
Clark	DH		1913				2	0	1	1	0	0
Clark	E		1907	1908			3	0	0	0	0	0
Clegg	C		1913				0	0	1	0	0	0
Clifton	W	William	1920*		Preston North End		20	3	3	4	1	1
Clouston	H		1912		Newton Heath	Newton Heath	4	0	0	1	0	0
Clutton			1920		Kidsgrove		1	0	0	0	0	0
Coates	HJ		1913		Bradford City		2	0	0	0	0	0
Collinge	A	Arthur	1920*		Rochdale Tradesmen	Rochdale Tradesmen	13	0	5	2	0	4
Connor	E	Edward	1920		Exeter City		28	4	3	1	1	0
Cooper	J		1919		Newcastle United		11	0	0	4	0	0
Cooper	W	William	1910		Castleford	Lincoln City	31	9	2	1	0	0
Costelli	J		1911		Altrincham	Glossop	1	0	0	0	0	0
Crabtree	J		1912				8	0	1	0	0	0
Crabtree	JJ	Jimmy	1920*		Blackburn Rovers	Accrington Stanley	30	5	4	0	0	0
Craven	R		1907		Oswaldtwistle		19	0	1	6	0	0
Crawshaw	RL	Dick	1918		Stockport County	(quest)	1	0	0	0	0	0
Crompton	J		1920		Farnworth		0	0	1	0	0	0
Crossan	D	Danny	1910	1918	Bradford P.A.	Deceased	135	7	11	1	0	0
Cuffe	JA	John	1915		Glossop	(quest)	5	0	0	0	0	0
Cunliffe	ED	Dan	1912		Heywood		11	2	0	2	0	0
Curtis	F	Fred	1916		Wolverhampton Wanderers	(quest)	1	0	0	0	0	0
Cuthbertson	R	Robert	1908		Tottington		2	0	0	0	0	0

170

Player			First Season	Last Season	Previous Club	Next Club	Appearances			Goals		
							FAC	FLC	Other	FAC	FLC	Oth.
Cutts	EH	Ernest	1910		Handsworth & Tretton	Rotherham Town	5	0	0	1	0	0
Daniels	H		1919		Bolton W.E.	Aberaman Athletic	25	3	1	2	1	0
Davenport	T		1918		Norden		3	0	0	0	0	0
Davidson	W		1907				1	0	0	0	0	0
Davie	J		1919	1920	Perth		29	2	1	0	0	0
Davies	SC	Stan	1918		Royal Welch Fus.	Preston North End	6	0	0	2	0	0
Davies	W		1912				4	0	0	1	0	0
Dannison	H	Hary	1920*		Blackburn Rovers	Wigan Borough	29	5	4	22	1	4
Derbyshire	R		1907				1	0	1	0	0	0
Dixon			1919				1	1	0	0	0	0
Donaghy	C	Charles	1908		Chelsea	(USA)	12	0	0	4	0	0
Donald			1918				1	0	0	0	0	0
Doxford	JH		1920		Leeds City		0	0	1	0	0	0
Duckworth	TH		1917	1918	Stalybridge		6	0	0	0	0	0
Earnshaw	S		1907		St. Clements		2	0	0	0	0	0
Eccles	A		1919		Smallbridge		9	0	0	2	0	0
Farnworth			1919				1	0	0	0	0	0
Fielding	N		1916				1	0	0	0	0	0
Flaherty	J		1917		Walkden Central	Oldham Athletic	4	0	0	7	0	0
Fleetwood	T	Tommy	1908	1910	Hindley Central	Everton	88	12	8	36	4	4
Fletcher	H		1914		Little Lever		1	0	0	0	0	0
Freeborough	J	Jimmy	1909	1911	Bradford P.A.	Denton	65	7	8	7	0	0
Frith	RW	Billy	1916		Luton Town	South Shields	3	0	0	0	0	0
Galvin	P	Patrick	1908	1909	Glossop	Eccles Borough	65	1	6	15	0	0
Gledhill	TA		1907				1	0	0	0	0	0
Goodwin	EW	Ernest	1917	1918	Leeds City	Leeds City	39	0	0	11	0	0
Goodwin	J		1913	1912	Jarrow		11	2	4	0	0	0
Greenhalgh	F		1909	1910	Salford United		14	4	2	0	0	0
Greenhalgh	W		1919		Bury		4	0	0	0	0	0
Gregson	A	Alf	1910	1912	Bury Unitarians	Grimsby Town	74	6	11	35	4	6
Grierson	RT	Rob	1910		Bradford P.A.	Hartlepool	55	9	6	19	4	1
			1913		Swansea							
Gutteridge	G	George	1918		Everton	Clock Face	1	0	0	0	0	0
Hales	W		1919		Walkden Central		1	0	0	0	0	0
Hall	JE	John	1909		Brighton & H.A.	South Shields	34	3	5	8	2	1
Hall			1911		Eccles Borough		3	0	1	0	0	0
Hall			1918		Leeds City	(guest)	1	0	0	0	0	0
Hallas	JE		1917		Oldham Athletic		3	0	0	0	0	0
Halligan	W	Bill	1916	1918	Manchester United	Preston North End	94	0	0	68	0	0
Hampson	T	Tom	1918		Leeds City	Walker Celtic	1	0	0	0	0	0
Hampson	W	Bill	1908		Bury	Norwich City	22	0	0	1	0	0
Harding	A		1917		Woodhouses		1	0	0	0	0	0
Hardman	J	Joe	1907	1908			17	1	6	4	0	4
Hardman	JW	Billy	1907				9	0	5	0	0	0
Hardy	P	Percy	1912		Hebden Bridge		2	0	0	0	0	0
Harrison	G		1909		Exeter City	Manchester City	6	0	0	4	0	0
Harrison	J		1916		Heywood		3	0	0	0	0	0
Hartley	PW	Percy	1910		Exeter City		6	2	0	0	0	0
Hartley	W		1916				1	0	0	0	0	0
Hawksworth	E	Ernest	1913	1918	Sudden Villa	Blackburn Rovers	66	4	4	21	2	2
Hawkyard	E		1907		Oakenrod	Bolton Wanderers	7	0	0	0	0	0
Hayes	JV	Vince	1913	1918	Wiener SV	Preston (man)	38	0	2	1	0	0
Haynes			1914		Heywood United		4	0	0	0	0	0
Heap	F	Fred	1913	1918	(school)	Bury	37	0	0	13	0	0
Heap	R	Bob	1909	1908	Failsworth	Cheltenham Coll.	17	0	0	8	0	0
Hebden	JT	Jack	1916		Castleford	Castleford	7	0	0	0	0	0
Henderson	JT	Jimmy	1910	1913	Clapton Orient	South Liverpool	154	19	20	3	2	0
			1919	1916	South Liverpool	Rochdale Pioneers						
Hennifer	L	Levi	1908		Oldham Athletic		1	0	0	0	0	0
Hepworth	W		1907		St. Mary's		1	0	0	0	0	0
Herbert	JH	Joseph		1920*	Swansea	Guildford	8	0	0	4	0	0
Herring	F	Frank	1919		Woodhouses		2	0	0	0	0	0
Hesmondhalgh	T	Tom	1919		Horwich	Exeter City	25	0	1	12	0	0
Hibbert	W	Billy	1918		Newcastle United	(guest)	1	0	0	0	0	0
Higgins	J		1919		Castleton		2	0	0	0	0	0
Hill	JW	Jack	1919	1920*	Brights	Bacup Borough	12	0	6	0	0	0
Hoad	SJ	Sid		1920*	Manchester City	Nelson	22	1	1	3	0	0
Holden	Z	Zach	1907	1910	Haslingden	(to trainer)	52	1	6	1	0	0
Holt	B		1914		Bacup Borough		1	0	0	0	0	0
Holt	H		1915		Exeter City		5	0	0	1	0	0
Horridge	GB	George	1919		Bury		7	3	0	2	0	0
Howarth			1911				1	0	0	0	0	0
Howarth			1917		Liverpool		1	0	0	0	0	0
Hoyle	J	James	1907		Shuttleworth		3	0	0	0	0	0
Hunt			1917				1	0	0	0	0	0
Hurst	BH	Bould	1919		Nelson		21	4	2	0	0	0
Hurst	G		1918		Bolton Wanderers		2	0	0	0	0	0
Jackson	J	(rh)	1918		Newton Heath		7	0	0	1	0	0
Jackson		(lb)	1918		Manchester GS		1	0	0	0	0	0
Jackson	S		1907				1	0	0	0	0	0
Jephcott	PG		1919		Carlisle United		1	0	0	0	0	0
Johnson	A	(ir)	1917		Bury		4	0	0	1	0	0
Johnson		(lb)	1918				2	0	0	0	0	0
Jones	A		1917	1918	Bolton Wanderers		12	0	0	0	0	0
Jones	JH		1910	1909	Pendlebury	Heywood United	10	1	0	7	0	0
Joy	G	George	1907	1908	Failsworth		26	0	6	1	0	0
Kay	G	George	1915		Distillery	West Ham United	27	0	0	3	0	0
Kay	JL		1913	1914		(army)	56	5	8	1	0	0
Kay	PJ		1917				4	0	0	0	0	0

Player			First Season	Last Season	Previous Club	Next Club	Appearances			Goals		
							League	FAC	Other	League	FAC	Oth.
Kay	T	Tom	1916	1918	Bolton Wanderers	Stoke City	63	0	0	0	0	0
Kehoe	W		1916		Accrington Stanley	Burnley	5	0	0	1	0	0
Kelly	P	(cf)	1918				3	0	0	1	0	0
Kelly		(rh)	1918				1	0	0	0	0	0
Kelly	W		1908		Bury		0	1	0	0	0	0
Kelly	WB	William	1914		Blyth Spartans		35	5	8	12	4	3
Kenyon	J	Jimmy	1910		Bradford P.A.	Millwall	33	7	1	17	2	0
			1915		Stockport County	(guest)						
Kenyon	L	Lawrence	1911		Bury Tradesmen		1	0	0	0	0	0
Kenyon	L		1919		Tottenham Hotspur		4	0	0	0	0	0
Kershaw	A		1907				1	0	0	0	0	0
Kingsley	M	Matt	1907		QPR	Barrow	21	0	5	0	0	0
Kirkpatrick	G		1918		Atherton		1	0	0	0	0	0
Lawton	R		1908				4	0	0	0	0	0
Lee	A		1917		Hurst		2	0	0	0	0	0
Lee	C		1915		Clapton Orient		3	0	0	0	0	0
Lee	JC		1919		Exeter City		1	0	0	0	0	0
Leigh	T	Thomas 'Ginger'	1912		Croydon Common	South Liverpool	7	0	1	0	0	0
Lennox	P		1917				2	0	0	0	0	0
Lilley	R	Bob	1914	1918	Little Lever Lads	Horwich RMI	15	2	5	0	0	0
Lingard	AE		1919		Bury		24	4	1	5	0	0
Litherland	J		1916	1917			6	0	0	0	0	0
Lloyd	S	Sam	1917		Rochdale Hornets (RL)		1	0	0	0	0	0
Lomax	J		1907	1908	Radcliffe		5	0	0	0	0	0
Lovett	W	William	1911	1912	Hindley Central	Exeter City	31	2	5	11	0	4
Lowe	E		1920		QPR		19	5	2	9	2	0
Lunn	L	Lawrence	1920		Royston Ams	Oldham Athletic	1	0	0	0	0	0
Makin	T	Tom	1919		Crewe Alexandra		3	0	0	0	0	0
Malkin	W		1919		Port Vale		7	0	0	0	0	0
Mallalieu	H	Harry	1919	1920*	All Saints (Oakenrod)		36	2	5	7	2	0
Manning	JT	John	1910		Bradford P.A.	Lincoln City	25	8	1	5	0	0
Mansfield	E	Eversley	1910		Northern Nomads		2	0	0	0	0	0
Marcroft			1910				1	0	0	0	0	0
Marshall	J	Jack	1913		St. Pauls (Southport)	Shelbourne	9	0	0	0	0	0
Martin	WH		1911		Bristol Rovers		1	0	0	0	0	0
Matthews			1909		Atherton		3	0	0	0	0	0
McCallum			1918				1	0	0	0	0	0
McCormack			1908				4	0	0	0	0	0
McDonald	T	Tom	1920		Tranmere Rovers		4	0	2	0	0	0
McDonald	W		1917		Liverpool		8	0	0	0	0	0
McKenzie	J	James	1911		Cardiff City		1	0	0	0	0	0
McKinley	D		1912		Aberdare		8	1	1	4	0	0
McOwen	J		1918		(army)		6	0	0	0	0	0
McShea	A	Andrew	1909		Clyde		3	0	0	0	0	0
McWilliam	H	Harry	1908		Oldham Athletic		3	0	0	0	0	0
Meadowcroft	J		1907	1908	Whitworth	Glossop	30	1	4	2	1	0
Meehan	J	John	1919		Manchester City	Manchester United	23	3	2	1	0	0
Meehan	T	Tom	1916		Walkden Central	Manchester United	19	0	0	5	0	0
			1917		Manchester United	(guest)						
Meynell	WT	Thomas	1911		Clapton Orient	Goole Town	30	1	7	2	0	2
Millership	H	Harry	1916	1918	Blackpool	Leeds City	31	0	0	0	0	0
Mills	A		1907		Bolton		2	0	0	0	0	0
Mills	JB		1907		Bolton Wanderers		3	0	0	0	0	0
Mills	JT	James	1919		All Saints (Rochdale)	Bolton Wanderers	19	1	1	7	0	0
Mills			1909		Tonge		1	0	0	0	0	0
Milne	C	Charlie	1913		Huddersfield Town	Halifax Town	90	10	9	7	2	1
			1914	1919*	Halifax Town	Pontypridd						
Mitchell	C	Charles	1908	1909	Bradford City		17	1	0	4	0	0
Mitton	J	John	1917		Burnley	Bury	3	0	0	1	0	0
Moody	JH	Harry	1918*		(RAF)	Mid Rhondda	3	0	0	0	0	0
Moody	WA	William	1918*		(army)	Mid Rhondda	5	0	1	0	0	0
Moon	HC	Harry	1910	1911	Llanhilleth	Southend	1	0	0	1	0	0
Morgan	H	Harker	1907		Nelson	Nelson	103	5	14	2	0	0
			1908	1913	Nelson							
Morris	J	James	1912	1913			7	0	2	0	0	0
Mulrooney	F		1908		(Jersey)		17	0	0	2	0	0
Musgrave	JH		1907		Bury		1	0	0	0	0	0
Naylor	J		1907		Heywood		1	0	0	0	0	0
Neave	R	Robert	1914	1915	Chesterfield		38	5	8	8	1	0
Newman	A		1919				1	0	0	0	0	0
Nuttall	J	Jimmy	1918		Bolton Wanderers	Manchester United	72	9	7	2	0	0
			1919	1920*	Manchester United							
Nuttall	T		1920		Leyland	Leyland	1	0	0	0	0	0
O'Connell	P	Pat	1916	1918	Manchester United	Dumbarton	85	0	0	9	0	0
Oliver	WH		1919				1	0	0	0	0	0
Openshaw	W	William	1908	1909	Salford United	Macclesfield	69	4	6	7	1	0
Page	J	John	1911	1912	South Liverpool	Everton	17	3	2	0	0	0
			1916		Everton	(guest)						
Page	T	Tom	1911	1912	Liverpool	Everton	67	7	8	45	5	4
			1915	1917	St. Mirren	(guest)						
Page	W	Willie	1919		South Liverpool	Cardiff City	1	0	0	0	0	0
Parkinson	H		1908		Accrington Stanley		3	0	1	0	0	0
Parry	TA		1919		(army)	Rochdale Tradesmen	7	0	0	3	0	0
Peake	R	Bob	1911		Cardiff City		2	0	3	1	0	2
Pearson	F	Frank	1908		Luton Town	Eccles Borough	11	0	0	6	0	0
Peart	JG	Jack	1918*		Notts County	(guest)	1	0	0	0	0	0
Perks	R		1917		(army)		1	0	0	0	0	0
Petty	E		1907	1909	Newbold		14	1	0	0	0	0
Pickup	P		1914	1919			8	0	0	0	0	0

Player			First Season	Last Season	Previous Club	Next Club	Appearances			Goals		
							league	FAC	Other	League	FAC	Oth.
Plant	H		1908		Eccles Borough		21	1	1	0	1	1
Plumley	W		1913	1919			8	0	0	0	0	0
Poles	A		1916				1	0	0	0	0	0
Poles	J		1917				1	0	0	0	0	0
Rawlings	A	Archie	1914	1917	Northampton	Dundee	102	4	7	13	0	0
Reeves			1910			Bacup	2	0	0	0	0	0
Reynolds	G		1918		Altrincham		1	0	0	0	0	0
Reynolds	J	Jack	1911		New Brompton	Switzerland (coach)	28	1	8	7	0	0
Riddell	N	Norman	1910		Morpeth Town	Clapton Orient	15	7	2	0	0	0
Rigg	T	Tweedale	1914	1918*		Blackburn Rovers	45	0	1	1	0	0
Riley	J		1917		Shawclough		1	0	0	0	0	0
Roberts	JW		1917		Woodhouses		5	0	0	2	0	0
Roberts	WR		1916		Manchester United	(quest)	2	0	0	0	0	0
Robinson	J		1909		Macclesfield		2	1	1	0	0	0
Roscoe	P		1916				1	0	0	0	0	0
Ross	D	Davie	1919		Dundee		2	0	0	0	0	0
Ross	G	George	1907		Bury		5	0	2	1	0	0
Sandiford	R	Bob	1920*		Rochdale St. Peters	Bacup Borough	7	0	5	1	0	3
Semple	W	Billy	1918		Southport	(quest)	1	0	0	0	0	0
Sheldon	FJ		1917	1919	Everton		9	0	0	4	0	0
Smethurst	J		1907				1	0	0	0	0	0
Smith	A	Albert	1910	1918*	Bradford P.A.	Grimsby Town	304	22	28	79	3	12
Smith	H		1918		Woodhouses		2	0	0	0	0	0
Smith	J		1918				1	0	0	0	0	0
Smith	R		1916				1	0	0	0	0	0
Smith	T		1919		Sunderland		2	0	0	0	0	0
Smith	W	Wally	1915		Birmingham	(quest)	1	0	0	1	0	0
Sommersqill	R		1917				3	0	0	0	0	0
Southworth	T		1914	1915			8	0	0	1	0	0
Spink	TW	Tommy	1912	1913	Fulham	Grimsby Town	71	8	10	4	0	1
Spoor	G	George	1913		Moor Park Villa		1	0	0	0	0	0
Spriggs	F	Frank	1911		Merthyr Town		3	0	4	2	0	2
Spruce	S	Sam	1918		New Moss Coll.	Bury	28	0	0	0	0	0
Stamford	J	James	1911		Manchester United	Glossop	2	0	0	1	0	0
Stansfield	E		1908				2	0	0	0	0	0
Stansfield			1920		Heywood United		1	0	0	0	0	0
Stocks			1917				1	0	0	0	0	0
Stott	F	(cf)	1919				1	0	0	0	0	0
Stott	J	(qk)	1919				10	0	0	0	0	0
Stott	J	(cf)	1918				1	0	0	1	0	0
Swann	JW		1914	1915	Northern Nomads	Manchester United	8	0	0	0	0	0
Swift	H		1915		Third Lanark		11	0	0	3	0	0
Tansey	E		1920		St. Johns		2	0	0	0	0	0
Tattersall	J	(cf/ch)	1913	1914	Barrowfield		6	0	0	1	0	0
Tattersall		(lh)	1917				1	0	0	0	0	0
Tattersall		(lh)	1919				3	0	0	0	0	0
Tattum	B	Bernard	1911	1912	Hindley Central	Macclesfield	5	0	1	0	0	0
Taylor	J		1908	1909	Salford United	Haslingden	72	4	6	0	0	1
Taylor	J	(lb)	1913				1	0	0	0	0	0
Taylor	J	(lb)	1918	1920	RAMC		11	0	1	0	0	0
Taylor	W			1919	Littleborough		4	0	1	0	0	0
Thomas	R	Bob	1916	1918	Tranmere Rovers	Luton Town	55	0	0	29	0	0
Thomason	E	Edward		1910	Nottingham Forest	Nelson	34	6	2	1	0	0
			1912		Nelson	Hurst						
			1912		Hurst							
Thornley	B	Bert	1920		Chester		2	0	0	0	0	0
Thornley	T	Thomas	1908		Pendlebury		13	1	1	2	0	1
Thorpe	H		1920				7	0	0	0	0	0
Thorpe	J	Joseph	1909		Darwen		9	0	0	0	0	0
Tierney	H	Herbert	1916	1919	Goole Town	Aberaman Athletic	49	4	1	2	0	0
Tolley	J		1907		Lydgate		20	0	4	11	0	2
Towers			1914				1	0	0	0	0	0
Tully	J	Jim	1912	1919*	West Stanley	Pontypridd	204	17	18	18	4	2
Turnbull	A	Alex 'Sandy'	1915		Manchester United	(quest)	1	0	0	0	0	0
Turnbull	WW		1912		Greenock Morton	York City	5	0	2	0	0	0
Turner	L		1920		All Saints (Rochdale)		4	1	1	0	0	0
Turner			1919		Heywood United		5	0	0	0	0	0
Turner	EF	Eli	1916	1918	Stoke	(quest)	3	0	0	0	0	0
Tyler	HE	Herbert	1916		Manchester City	(quest)	1	0	0	0	0	0
Walkden	L		1916				1	0	0	0	0	0
Walker	A		1913	1920	Bury		88	5	4	27	2	0
Walmesley	J		1908		Tottington		2	0	0	0	0	0
Walters	CE		1916				3	0	0	0	0	0
Ward	W		1920		Padiham	Rossendale	10	0	1	1	0	0
Watson	R	Bob	1913		Stalybridge Celtic		18	1	2	4	0	1
Wemyss	WA		1916		Glossop		2	0	0	0	0	0
West	J		1917	1918	Woodhouses		4	0	0	0	0	0
Wilcock	J		1908		Walkden Central		2	0	0	0	0	0
Wilkinson	H	Harry	1908		Oswaldtwistle Rovers		2	0	0	0	0	0
Wilkinson			1919				1	0	0	0	0	0
Wilson	J	Joe	1920		Millwall	Fleetwood	19	5	0	1	0	0
Wilson	T	Tom	1920				2	0	1	0	0	1
Wolfe			1919				2	0	0	0	0	0
Wood	F		1919		Burscough Rangers	Wigan Borough	30	3	1	0	0	0
Worth	A	Albert	1909		Stockport County	Grimsby Town	38	3	6	19	1	5
Wright	W		1909		Southport Central		1	0	0	0	0	0
Wynn	CE		1907				6	0	0	1	0	0
Yarwood	JW	Jack	1915	1918	Merthyr Town	Merthyr Town	89	5	4	1	0	0
			1920*		Merthyr Town							

World War 1 League Appearances Summary

Seasons total for: 1916/17 - 1918/19: Wartime League, 1919/20: Central League

(all appearances are included in pre-League Who's Who)

Player	1916/17 Apps	Goals	1917/18 Apps	Goals	1918/19 Apps	Goals	1919/20 Apps	Goals
Anderson H.							2	
Anderson W.S.	3							
Annesley F.			1					
Ashworth C.					1			
Baines F.					10			
Bamford W.							2	
Barton J.W.	4				6			
Bellis R.					7	2	1	
Berry F.							6	
Berry T.			1					
Best G.					4	1		
Biggar W.	10							
Brindle R.							3	
Broome T.A.					1			
Broster J.	2							
Brown A.					2		2	
Buckley D.					4			
Bunting W.			18		9	2		
Butterworth							1	1
Butterworth H.					2			
Butterworth J.					2			
Butterworth J.E.	3							
Butterworth R.H.			5		2			
Caldwell A	9							
Cam J.C.					2			
Capper A.			1					
Carruthers W.G.			1					
Causer A.H.	20							
Chadwick F.					1			
Challinor H.							1	
Cooper J.							11	4
Crawshaw R.L.					1			
Crossan D.	13	1	21		8			
Curtis F.	1							
Daniels H.							25	2
Davenport T.					3			
Davie J.							6	
Davies S.C.					6	2		
Dixon							1	
Donald					1			
Duckworth T.H.			3		3			
Eccles A.							9	2
Farnworth							1	
Fielding F.	1							
Flaherty J.			4	7				
Frith R.W.	3							
Goodwin E.W.			11	3	28	8		
Greenhalgh W.							4	
Gutteridge G.					1			
Hales W.							1	
Hall					1			
Hallas J.			3					
Halligan W.	34	18	33	36	27	14		
Hampson T.					1			
Harding A.			1					
Harrison J.	3							
Hartley W.	1							
Hawksworth E.					9	4		
Hayes J.V.	2		27		2			
Heap F.					13	3		
Hebden J.T.	7							
Henderson J.T.	13		18		10		1	
Herring F.							2	
Hesmondhalgh T.							25	12
Hibbert W.					1			
Higgins J.							2	
Hill J.W.							1	
Horridge G.B.							7	2
Howarth			1					
Hunt			1					
Hurst B.							21	
Hurst G.					2			
Jackson			1					
Jackson J.					7	1		
Jephcott P.G.							1	
Johnson					2			
Johnson A			4	1				
Jones A.			11		1			
Kay P.J.			4					
Kay T.	6		28		29			
Kehoe W.	5	1						
Kelly			1					
Kelly P.			3	1				
Kenyon L.							4	
Kirkpatrick G.			1					
Lee A.			2					
Lee J.C.							1	
Lennox P.			2					
Lilley R.			1					
Lingard A.E.							24	5
Litherland J.	1		5					
Lloyd S.			1					
Makin T.							3	
Malkin W.							7	
Mallalieu H.							17	4
McCallum			1					
McDonald W.			8					
McOwen J.					6			
Meehan J.							23	1
Meehan T.	18	5	1					
Millership H.	23		5		3			
Mills J.T.							19	7
Milne C.			1				35	4
Mitton J.			3	1				
Moody J.H.					3			
Moody W.A.					5			
Newman A.							1	
Nuttall J.					8		30	2
O'Connell P.	17		33	6	35	3		
Oliver W.H.							1	
Page J.	4							
Page T.	5	2	19	12				
Page W.							1	
Parry T.A.							7	3
Peart J.G.			1	1				
Perks R.			1					
Pickup P.							5	
Plumley W.							3	
Poles A.	1							
Poles J.			1					
Rawlings A.	35	3	5					
Reynolds G.					1			
Rigg T.	11	1	26		7			
Roberts J.W.			5	2				
Roberts W.R.	2							
Roscoe P.	1							
Ross D.							2	
Semple W.					1			
Sheldon F.J.			7	4			2	
Smith A.	27	3	34	8	35	9		
Smith H.					2			
Smith J.					1			
Smith R.	1							
Smith T.							2	
Somersgill R.			3					
Spruce S.					28			
Stocks			1					
Stott F.							1	
Stott J.							10	
Stott J.					1	1		
Tattersall			1				3	
Taylor J.					1		5	
Taylor W.							4	
Thomas R.	26	14	10	6	19	9		
Thomason E.					3			
Tierney H.	24				2		23	2
Tully J.	23	1	19	2	1		30	
Turner							5	
Turner E.F.	2				1			
Tyler H.E.	1							
Walkden L.	1							
Walker A.	26	12	6	2	1		21	7
Walters C.E.	3							
Wemyss W.A.	2							
West J.					4			
Wilkinson							1	
Wolfe							2	
Wood E.							30	
Yarwood J.W.	2				14			

World War 2 Who's Who

Player			First Season	Last Season	Previous Club	Next Club	Apps.	Goals
Acton	H	Harold	1944				2	1
Ainsworth	A	Alf	1939	1944	New Brighton	Guest	16	3
Ainsworth	W	Walter	1944		Plymouth Argyle	Guest	6	3
Ancell	RFD	Bob	1941		Newcastle Utd	Guest	1	1
Anderson	A	Alfie	1939		Third Lanark	Guest	10	1
Ashbridge	K	Kenneth	1945		Halifax Town	Guest	3	
Atkinson	K	Kenneth	1944				2	
Bailey	A	Arthur	1944		Oldham Athletic	Guest	1	
Baird	TS	Tommy	*1939		St Mirren		1	
Banner	JE	John	1943	1944			2	
Barker	J	Jeffrey	1941	1942	Aston Villa	Guest	3	
Bartholomew	R	Roly	1941	1942	Grimsby Town	Guest	11	6
Bate	J		1944		Aston Villa	Guest	1	
Bawn	S	Sam	1945				1	
Bebb	D	David	1942				5	1
Bellis	A	Alf	1940	1941	Port Vale	Guest	9	2
Birch	JW	Wally	1945*		Huddersfield Town	Retired	11	
Blood	JF	John	1942		Exeter City	Guest	3	
Boulter	LM	Les	1941		Brentford	Guest	1	
Bradford	L	Lewis	1942	1943	Preston NE	Guest	72	
Bradley	J	John	1944		Southampton	Guest	1	
Bradshaw	J	Jack	1944				2	
Breakwell	T	Thomas	1942	1943	Wrexham	Guest	20	
Breedon	J	Jack	1945		Manchester Utd	Guest	4	
Brindle	J	Jack	1945*		Burnley	Chelsea	18	9
Brinton	JV	Jack	1944		Derby County	Guest	2	1
Brown			1942				2	
Burdett	T	Tommy	1939		Bury	Guest	2	2
Burnikell	WF	Bill	1942		Aldershot		1	
Byrne			1942				1	
Byrom	W	Bill	1939	1945*	QPR	Guest	85	
Carey	WJ	William	1939	1940	Aston Villa	Guest	22	
Carrick	R	Roy	1943				1	
Carter	DFA	Don	1939		Bury	Guest	3	1
Chadwick	C	Cliff	1939		Middlesbrough	Guest	1	
Chambers	J	James	1944		Worcester City		1	
Chaney	A	Alfred	1944				1	
Chester	TH	Tom	1939		Notts County	Guest	5	
Chesters	A	Arthur	1941	1945*	Crystal Palace		69	
Chew	J	John	1940		Luton Town	Guest	1	
Clarke			1940				1	
Clive			1945				1	
Cload	H	Harry	1942				8	4
Cochrane	D	David	1944		Leeds United	Guest	2	1
Cochrane	T	Thomas	1944		Bradford P A	Guest	4	1
Cole	GD	Doug	1944		Chester	Guest	2	
Collinge	A	Albert	1942				1	
Colquhoun	DM	Duncan	1939	1942	Bradford City	Guest	41	7
Connor	J	John	1940		Bolton Wanderers	Guest	17	
Connor	S		1943			Guest	1	
Constantine	J	Jimmy	1944	1945	Ashton National	Manchester City	14	
Cornwell	E	Ellis	1942	1944	Chorley	Accrington Stanley	33	
Cunliffe	A	Arthur	1944	1945*	Hull City	Retired	32	5
Cunliffe	JN	Jim	1940	1944*	Everton	Guest	90	47
Curran	F	Frank	1942		Bristol City	Guest	1	
Cutting	SW	Stan	1941	1942	Exeter City	Guest	13	1
Davenport	A	Andrew	1941				5	
Davies	AM	Alex	1941		Sheffield Wednesday	Guest	1	
Davies	RG	Bob	1943	1944	Nottingham Forest	Guest	2	
Delaney	R	Robert	1941				1	
Dobson	J	Jack	1945		Norden		5	
Dooley	TE	Tommy	1941	1943	Accrington Stanley	Guest	21	1
Duff	J	Joe	*1939	1945*	Newcastle Utd	Cheltenham Town	186	35
Duffy	R	Robert	1942		Celtic	Guest	13	1
Dutton	T	Tommy	*1939	1941	Mansfield Town		37	6
Earl	AT	Sam	1939*		Hartlepools United	Guest	1	
Eastwood	E	Eric	1940		Manchester City	Guest	3	
Eastwood	J	Jimmy	*1939	1944	Tunbridge Wells		68	3
Ellis	J	Jack	1939		Clapton Orient	Guest	2	
Farrow	GH	George	1940		Blackpool	Guest	1	
Fenton	M	Micky	1940		Middlesbrough	Guest	1	
Fielding	WJ	Bill	1943		Cardiff City	Guest	12	
Folds	W	William	1942		Leicester City		1	
Foxton	JD	Jack	1944		Bolton Wanderers	Guest	1	
France	F	Frank	1941	1942			2	
Gallimore	L	Len	1942		Watford	Guest	6	
Gallon	JW	John	1943	1944	Swansea Town	Guest	23	5
Garfoot	CA	Arthur	1942		Stockport County		1	
Gastall	JWH	John	*1944		Accrington Stanley		2	
Gee	H	Harry	1942	1943	Birmingham	Guest	44	19
Gemmell	J	Jim	1944		Bury	Guest	3	
Goodall	EI	Edward	1942		Bolton Wanderers	Guest	3	
Gorman	W	Willie	1941		Brentford	Guest	8	
Graham	W	Billy	1940		Norwich City	Guest	2	
Griffiths	A	Albert	1944				1	

Player			First Season	Last Season	Previous Club	Next Club	Apps.	Goals
Griffiths	R	Robert	1945				1	
Grimsditch	SW	Walker	1944		Bolton Wanderers	Guest	7	
Haigh	G	George	1943	1945	Hurst		61	3
Hall	HHC		1944		Bolton Wanderers	Guest	2	
Hall	J	Jack	1939	1941	Tottenham Hotspur		38	
Halton	RL	Reg	1939		Bury	Guest	1	
Hamilton	W		1945		St Bernards		2	
Hanna	S		1941		Halifax Town	Guest	1	
Hanson	AJ	Alf	1944	1945	Chelsea	Guest	19	11
Hargreaves	J	Joe	1945*		Rossendale Utd	Stalybridge Celtic	24	19
Harker	J	Jack	1942	1945	Bolton Wanderers		40	38
Harker	W	Willie	1939	1940	Stockport County		12	1
Harrison	J	James	1940	1944		Chorley	22	5
Haworth	R	Richard	*1939	1941	Manchester NE		4	1
Haworth	R	Roland	*1940		Manchester NE		1	
Hesketh			1944		Preston NE	Guest	1	
Heyes	K	Kenneth	1940				1	
Higham	J	Jack	1944	1945			2	
Hornby	R	Ron	*1942		Burnley	Guest	1	
Horrabin	W	Walter	1940	1942			20	10
Horton	J		1941		QPR	Guest	8	
Horton	L	Les	1940	1943	Tylderley United	Oldham Athletic	15	
Howshall	T	Tommy	1945		Southport	Guest	1	
Hughes	A		1940			Guest	1	
Hughes	AL		1944		Bolton Wanderers	Guest	1	
Hunt	GS	George	1940		Bolton Wanderers	Guest	5	
Hunt	SW	Wally	*1939	1944	Southport	Guest	26	14
Hurst	C	Charlie	1945*		Oldham Athletic	Guest	5	
Isherwood	D		1940				1	
Jackson	L	Len	1945*		Manchester City		5	
John	WR	Roy	1941		Swansea Town		6	
Johnson	JC	Jack	1940		Accrington Stanley	Guest	1	
Jones	A	Arthur	1945*		Goslings		13	3
Jones	A		1942				1	1
Jones	D	David	1941				9	7
Jones	DLG	David	1942				15	3
Jones	DOE	Ossie	1941		Crewe Alexandra	Monsarto	1	
Jones	GT	Gwyn	*1939	1945	Walsall	Guest	8	
Jones	J		1941				2	
Jones	J		1943	1944	Torquay United	Guest	16	2
Jones	JT	John	1945		Northampton Town	Guest	2	
Jones	T	Tom	1940	1944	Oldham Athletic	Guest	59	1
Jones	VA	Verdum	1941	1942	Derby County	Guest	13	5
Joseph	AE	Arthur	1943				1	
Keddie	J		1945		Hamilton Accademical	Guest	1	
Keen	ERL	Ike	1940		Hereford United		19	
Kennan	W	William	*1944		West Calder		1	
Kershaw	V	Vincent					5	1
Kindred	J		1945			Guest	1	1
Kirk	J	John	1945			Peterborough	6	
Kirkman	N	Norman	1940	1941*	Burnley	Guest	6	
Lievesley	L	Les	1943		Crystal Palace	Guest	1	
Livesay	J	Jack	1945*		Preston NE	Guest	1	1
Livingstone	A	Archie	1939		Bury	Guest	2	2
Lowe	H		1944		Swindon Town		5	
Lunn	G	George			Aston Villa	Guest	1	
Lyons	AE	Eddy	1944*		Bury	Guest	5	
Macauley	J		1943	1944		Guest	2	
MacFadyen	W	Willie	1941		Clapton Orient	Guest	2	
Makin	S	Sammy	1944	1945*	Moss Rovers	Droylsden	31	7
Malam	A	Albert	1944		Doncaster Rovers	Guest	2	
Mangham	W		1941	1944	Bolton Wanderers	Guest	3	
Manning	J		1942		Huddersfield Town	Guest	1	
Marsh	FK	Frank	1942		Chester	Guest	1	
Maudsley	R	Richard	1943		Millwall		4	
McCormick	JM	Joe	1945*		Bolton Wanderers	Boston United	30	1
McGaitie			1943		Blackpool	Guest	1	
McGowan	J		1939		Bury	Guest	1	
Meek	J	Joe	1945		Swansea Town	Guest	4	1
Middleton	J	John	1941		Stockport County		1	
Miller	N		1942				1	
Miller	W	Willie	1943		Bradford City	Guest	7	
Milligan	E	Edward	1943		Aston Villa		3	1
Molloy	P	Peter	1945		Bradford City	Guest	5	
Morris	E	Ernest	1943	1944			20	10
Mountford	RC	Reg	1940		Huddersfield Town		4	
Muir	M	Matthew	1944				15	
Muir	R	Robert	1945				1	
Murphy	G	George	1942	1943	Bradford City	Guest	6	3
Mycock	A	Albert	1944		Manchester Utd	Guest	2	
Neary	J	John	*1939	1945*	Manchester NE	Droylsden	63	1
Neilson	R		1945		Manchester City	Guest	3	
Nevin	GW	George	1939		Lincoln City		1	
Nuttall	H	Harry	1945				1	
O'Mahoney	M	Michael	1943				3	
Olive	F		1944	1945		Guest	4	

Player			First Season	Last Season	Previous Club	Next Club	Apps.	Goals
Olsen	TB	Tommy	1939		Bury	Guest	13	1
Palfreyman	H	Herbert	1942		Aldershot		3	
Partridge	D	Don	1945*		Farnworth		15	
Patton	SA	Samuel	1941				3	
Pearce	J	Jim	*1939	1945*	Bristol City	Cardiff City	35	1
Pickstock	SA		1944		Wolves	Guest	1	1
Pitt	C	Cliff	1941		Macclesfield Town	Bangor City	7	
Pomphrey	EA	Syd	1945*		Notts County		31	
Prest	TW	Tommy	*1939		Aldershot		5	1
Rawlings	JSD	Syd	1939	1940	Millwall	Guest	22	6
Redwood	DJ	Doug	1939		Walsall		7	3
Reeday	M	Maurice	1940		Leicester City	Guest	1	
Reid	J	John	1944	1945			13	7
Revell	H	Harry	1944				1	
Reynolds	W	Wally	*1939	1944*	York City		19	3
Richardson	A	Arthur	1939		Chesterfield		15	15
Richardson	N	Norman	1945		New Brighton	Guest	1	
Richmond	G	Gilbert	1941	1942	Burnley	Guest	14	
Richmond	N	Norman	1942				1	
Roberts	SA	Sid	1944		Chester	Trial	2	1
Roberts	WE	Bill	1945*				5	
Robinson	JJ	Jack	1940		Manchester City	Guest	1	
Robinson	A	Alick	1939		Burnley	Guest	3	
Robson	EA	Ernest	1939	1941	Aldershot		12	
Rodi	J	Joe	1945*		Grimsby Town		7	5
Rothwell	B		1940				1	
Rudd	W	Bill (snr)	1943				2	
Schofield			1942				1	
Seddon	H	Harry	1940	1944	Stockport County		8	1
Shadwell	J		1939		Exeter City	Guest	1	
Shaw			1942				1	
Shields	J		1941		Celtic	Guest	3	
Sibley	TI	Tommy	1943*		Birmingham	Guest	3	3
Sidebottom	W	Wally	1940		Bolton Wanderers	Guest	17	11
Smith	F	Fred	1941				11	1
Smith	J	Jack	1941				1	
Smith	T		1945		Stoke City		1	
Smith	TM	Tommy	1942		Preston NE	Guest	2	
Smith	TS	Tommy	*1939	1940	Burnley	Guest	23	
Sneddon	TS	Tommy	*1939	1945	Queen of the South	Czechoslovakia	61	
Steele	EA	Ernest	*1939		Crystal Palace	Guest	3	
Strachan	D		1944		Preston NE	Guest	6	
Strong	JG	Jim	1942		Walsall	Guest	28	
Sutherland	HR	Harry	1940		Leeds United	Guest	1	
Sweeney	FT		1942		Everton		1	
Swinburne	TA	Tommy	1941		Newcastle Utd	Guest	5	
Taylor	F	Fred	1945				2	1
Taylor	J	James	1944		Manchester City	Guest	1	
Taylor	J		1939				7	
Taylor	JT	Joe	1940		Oldham Athletic	Guest	2	
Taylor	P	Percy	1940	1944			40	9
Thompson			1942				1	
Thorpe	JA	James	1941	1942			6	
Thorpe	W		1944		Blackpool	Guest	1	
Toseland	EA	Ernie	1945		Sheffield Wednesday		4	2
Toser	EW	Ernie	1941		Millwall	Guest	1	
Treanor	J	Jim	1941	1944	Hull City	Guest	44	1
Turner	LA	Leslie	1940		New Brighton	Guest	4	
Vause	PG	Perter	*1939	1940	Darwen		10	2
Walkden	F	Francis	1940*		Bolton Wanderers		1	
Walmsley	J		1945		Preston NE	Guest	1	
Walsh	W	Bill	1941		Millwall	Guest	3	
Walton	G	George	1942		Walsall	Guest	5	
Warburton	A	Arthur	1939	1943	QPR	Guest	30	
Webb			1942				1	
Webster	R	Dick	1941		Sheffield Utd	Guest	7	1
Whalley			1942				1	
Wharton	JE	John	1943		Preston NE	Guest	3	1
Whittaker	F		1944		Arsenal	Guest	7	
Whittaker	W	William	1941		Kingstonian		2	
Whittle	W	William	1944	1945			5	
Whitworth	H	Harry	1941*		Bury	Guest	1	
Wildsmith	T	Tommy	1942	1943	Frickley Colliery		21	
Wilson	CM	Charles	1944		Stockport County	Guest	1	
Windle	C	Charles	1943		Exeter	Guest	1	
Wood	E	Eric	1942	1945*	Bolton Wanderers		92	39
Wood	J		1940	1941	Charlton Athletic	Guest	5	1
Wood	R		1941				2	
Woods	W	Billy	1944		Bolton Wanderers	Guest	2	
			1945*		Moss Grove	Bradford	13	1
Wotherspoon	J	James	1944				1	
Wright	F	Frank	1941		Crystal Palace	Guest	1	
Wynn	J	Jimmy	*1939	1940	Rotherham Utd	Scunthorpe	21	5
Yates	R	Robert	1945				1	
Young	J	James	1944				2	1

Note: All wartime games 1939-46, except Football League games from abandoned 1939-40 season and FA Cup ties for 1945-46 season (these are included in main table)   * before or after seasons played, indicates also played pre- or post-war.

1907-08 Manchester League

#	Date		Opponent	Score	Scorers	Att	Hawkyard E	Alston E	Ball M	Earnshaw S	Morgan H	Holden Z	Wynn C	Naylor J	Mills A	Hepworth W	Craven R	Musgrave JH	Barlow R	Mills JB	Aspinall W	Tolley J	Meadowcroft C	Kingsley M	Joy G	Hogle J	Hardman JW	Hardman J	Ross G	Derbyshire R	Clarke E	Petty E	Buckley W	Lomas J
1	Sep	7	TONGE	2-2	Craven, Wynn	2000	1	2	3	4	5	6	7	8	9	10	11																	
2		14	Buxton	0-3		550	1	2	3	4	5	6	7			10	11	8	9															
3		21	RAMSBOTTOM	3-1	Tolley, Morgan, OG	2500	1	4	3		5	6	7				11		9	2	8	10												
4		28	Salford U.	1-6	Barlow		1	4	3		5	6					11		9	2	8	10	7											
5	Oct	5	HOLEY HILL	2-2	Barlow, Craven	1000		2	3		5	6					11		9		8	10	7	1										
6		12	Altrincham	1-4	Craven(pen)	2000		2	3		5	4					11		9		8	10	7	1										
7		26	Denton	1-9	Barlow				3		5						11		9	2	10	8	7	1										
8	Nov	2	SALFORD U.	4-1	Tolley(3), Barlow	2000		2	3		5	4					11		9		10	8	7	1	6									
9		9	Newton Heath	2-1	Meadowcroft(2)			2	3		5	4					11		9		10	8	7	1	6									
10		16	STRETFORD	7-1	Barlow(3), Joy, Tolley(2), Craven			2	3		5	4					11		9		10	8	7	1	6									
11		23	Berry's	1-2	Craven			2	3		5	4					11		9		10	8	7	1	6									
12	Dec	7	Macclesfield	0-2		3500		2	3		5	4					11		9		10	8	7	1	6									
13		14	NORTHWICH VICTORIA	4-2	Tolley(3), Barlow	1500			3		5	4					11		9		10	8	7	1	6	2								
14		21	Hooley Hill	3-3	Craven, Aspinall, Barlow				3		5	4					11		9		10	8	7	1	6	2								
15		26	Sale Holmfield	1-4	Aspinall			1	3		5	4					11		9		10	8	7		6	2								
16		28	DENTON	1-1	Barlow	2000			3		5	4					11		9		10	8	7	1	6					2				
17	Jan	1	Ramsbottom	0-2					6		5	4					10		9		8	7	1	2	3		11							
18		4	Stretford	1-1	Aspinall			1	6		5	4					10		9		8	7		2	3		11							
19		25	ALTRINCHAM	2-2	Aspinall, Tolley	2000			6		5	4					10		9		8	7	1	2	3		11							
20	Feb	1	Tonge	1-1	Barlow(pen)				6		5	4					10		9		8	7	1	2	3		11							
21		8	Witton A.	3-0	Aspinall(2), J.Hardman			8	6		5								9		10	7	1	2	3		11	4						
22		22	BUXTON	3-0	Ross, Morgan, Aspinall				6		5	4							9		10	7	1	2	3		11		8					
23		29	MACCCLESFIELD	1-0	J.Hardman				6		5	4							9		10	7	1	2	3		11		8					
24	Mar	21	ECCLES BOROUGH	2-4	Tolley, Barlow	2000		4			5		7						9		8		1		2		11	6			3				
25		28	BERRY'S	0-4		2000		4											9		10	7	1		2		11	6	8		3				
26	Apr	11	Northwich Victoria	0-3		3000					5						10				8	7	1		3		11				9	2	4	6
27		15	Eccles Borough	0-0		1500	1				5						10		9			7			3		11				8	2	6	4
28		17	SALE HOLMFIELD	2-1	J.Hardman(2)	1000			6		5						10		9			7	1		3		11					2		4
29		18	Witton A.	0-1			1	8	6				7				10		9								11					2	3	4
30		25	NEWTON HEATH	1-0	Barlow	950	1		6		5		7				10		9								11					2	3	4
			Apps.				7	17	26	2	24	25	6	1	2	1	19	1	26	3	25	20	24	21	23	3	9	14	5	1	3	5	4	5
			Goals								2	1					6		13		7	11	2		1			9	1					

Played in one game: A.Kershaw (4 in 5), T.A.Gledhill (6 in 6), J.Smethurst (4 in 7), W.Davidson (6 in 7), J.Riley (10 in 24), S.Jackson (5 in 25), H.Aspey (8 in 28), J.Burroughs (8 in 30),

One own goal

Manchester Junior Cup

	Date		Opponent	Score	Scorers	Att	Alston E	Ball M	Earnshaw S	Morgan H	Holden Z	Craven R	Barlow R	Aspinall W	Tolley J	Meadowcroft C	Kingsley M	Joy G	Hardman JW	Hardman J
	Jan	11	SALFORD U.	1-1	J.Hardman	2000	4	6		5			9	10	8	7	1	2	3	11
		18	SALFORD U.	4-0	Tolley(2), Aspinall(2)	1500	4	6		5		11	9	10	8	7	1	2	3	
	Feb	15	DENTON	4-0	J.Hardman(3), Barlow	2500		6		5	4		9	8	7	1	2	3	11	10
SF	Mar	7	New Mills*	1-1	Barlow	2000		6		5	4		9	10	7	1	2	3	11	8
SFr		14	New Mills+	0-1		2000		6		5	4		9	10	7	1	2	3	11	8

* Played at Berry's F.C.   + Played at Salford United

Friendlies

	Date		Opponent	Score	Scorers	Att	Alston E	Ball M	Earnshaw S	Morgan H	Holden Z	Naylor J	Mills A	Hepworth W	Craven R	Barlow R	Mills JB	Aspinall W	Tolley J	Meadowcroft C	Kingsley M	Joy G	Hardman JW	Hardman J	Clarke E	Petty E	Lomas J
	Sep	3	OLDHAM A.	1-4	Craven(pen)	2000	2	3	4	5	6	10	8	11	9												
	Oct	19	Accrington S.	2-3	Barlow(2)	1200	3			5				11		9	2	10	8	7	1						
	Apr	4	BASFORD U.	4-0	Barlow, Meadowcroft, J.Hardman, Lomas					5						9		8	7	1		3	11	6	10	2	4

Played v Oldham: Hewitt (1), W.Pendlebury (7)
v Accrington S.: J.Smethurst (4), W.Davidson (6)

		P	W	D	L	F	A	Pts
1	Denton	30	21	5	4	108	48	47
2	Northwich Victoria	30	15	10	5	75	53	40
3	Eccles Borough	30	16	7	7	59	44	39
4	Macclesfield	30	16	5	9	63	39	37
5	Tonge	30	14	8	8	67	46	36
6	Altrincham	30	13	6	11	63	53	32
7	Witton Albion	30	12	8	10	52	54	32
8	Sale Holmfield	30	14	3	13	70	53	31
9	Ramsbottom	30	10	8	12	61	68	28
10	ROCHDALE	30	10	8	12	49	63	28
11	Buxton	29	9	7	13	34	52	25
12	Hooley Hill	30	8	9	13	56	59	25
13	Berry's	29	9	5	15	46	65	23
14	Salford United	30	9	5	16	49	68	23
15	Stretford	30	5	10	15	43	75	20
16	Newton Heath	30	3	6	21	33	88	12

1908-09 Lancashire Comb. Div. 2

#	Date		Opponent	Score	Scorers	Att	Taylor J.	Joy G.	Openshaw W	Holden Z	Galvin P	Ball M	Parkinson H	Plant H	Mitchell C	Barlow R	Hardman J	Thornley T	Meadowcroft C	Petty E	Pearson F	Donaghy C	Morgan H	Fleetwood T	Buckley W	Hampron W	Lawton R	Heap R	Wilkinson H	McWilliams H	Mulrooney F	McCormack C	Cuthbertron R	Barnes H
1	Sep	1	EARLESTOWN	1-0	Barlow	2000	1	2	3	4	5	6	7	8	9	10	11																	
2		5	BACUP	0-3		3000	1	2	3	4	5	6	7	8	9	10	11																	
3		26	Manchester C. Res.	1-9	Pearson	4000	1		3	4	5	6		10				8	7	2	9	11												
4	Oct	3	TURTON	1-0	Pearson	1000	1	4	3	5	8	6		10					7	2	9	11												
5		10	STOCKPORT CO. RES.	2-1	Pearson, Galvin	2700	1		3	4	8	6		10						2	9	11	5	7											
6		13	HASLINGDEN	3-2	Galvin(2), Donaghy	3000	1		3	4	8	6		10						2	9	11	5	7											
7		17	Chorley	1-3	Pearson	3000	1		3	4	8	6		10						2	9	11	5	7											
8		24	Heywood U.	0-0		5000	1		3	4		6						10	7	2		11	5	8											
9		31	ASHTON T.	3-1	Openshaw(pen),Thornley,Galvin	3000	1		3	4	9	6						10	7	2		11	5	8											
10	Nov	7	Barrow	1-0	Donaghy	1500	1		3	4	9	6						10		2		11	5	8											
11		14	Pendlebury	2-2	Openshaw(2,1pen)	1000	1		3	4	9	6						10		2		11	5	8											
12		21	BRYNN CENTRAL	7-0	Donaghy(2,1p),Fleetwood(2),Galvin(3)	2500	1		3	4	9	6		7				10				11	5	8	2										
13		28	ST. HELENS T.	4-1	Fleetwood,Thornley,Galvin(2)	3000	1		3	4	9	6		7				10				11	5	8		2									
14	Dec	5	PENDLEBURY	1-3	OG	4000			3	4	9	6		7				10				11	5	8		2	1								
15		19	St. Helens T.	0-0		1000	1		3	4		6	11	7				9					5	8		2		10							
16		25	Hyde	1-3	Openshaw	5000	1		3	4	9	6		7				10					5	8		2									
17		26	HEYWOOD U.	1-0	Fleetwood	5500	1		3	4	9	6		7		11	10						5	8		2									
18	Jan	1	Ashton T.	0-2		1000	1		3	4	9	6		7				10			8		5			2			11						
19		2	Earlestown	1-2	Pearson	1000	1		3	4	10	6		7							9		5	8		2			11						
20		16	Turton	1-5	Holden	150	1		3	7	9	6		11	10								5	8		2				4					
21		23	HYDE	0-1		2500	1		3	4		6		11	10			9					5	8		2									
22	Feb	6	ECCLES BOROUGH	2-0	Mitchell, Pearson	3000	1		3	4		6			10					7	9		5			2		8			11				
23		13	Glossop Res.	0-3		550	1		3	4	9	6			10					7			5			2		8			11				
24		20	MANCHESTER C. RES.	0-3		4000	1		3	4		6			10							9			2			8			11	5	7		
25		27	Oswardtwistle	1-0	Mulrooney		1		3		2				10							9				6		8			11	5	7		
26	Mar	6	Eccles Borough	0-2		5000	1		3		2			7	10	9									4			8			11	5			6
27		17	Haslingden	2-4	Mitchell, Openshaw(pen)	1000	1		3			6		7	10	8									5		2				11				9
28		20	GLOSSOP RES.	0-1		2000			3		5			7	10	8										2	1				11	6			9
29		27	Great Harwood	2-1	Heap, Barnes	800			3		4	6			10	8									5		2	1	7		11				9
30		30	OSWALDTWISTLE	9-0	Barnes(4),Barlow,Mulrooney,Heap(3)	700			3		4	6			10	8									5		2	1	7		11				9
31	Apr	3	Clitheroe Central	1-1	Mitchell		1		3						10	7					4		5			2		8		6	11			9
32		5	Stockport Co. Res.	1-3	Heap		1		3		10					7					6	5	2			8			4	11			9
33		9	Bacup	1-2	Barlow		1		3					6	10	7						5			2		8			11				9
34		10	CLITHEROE CENTRAL	2-1	Barnes, Heap	1500	1		3		5	6			10	7						4			2		8			11				9
35		12	LANCASTER T.	4-1	Galvin,Barlow,Fleetwood,Heap	1500	1		3	4	5	6				7								10		2		8			11				9
36		17	CHORLEY	3-2	Hampson, Heap, Mitchell	2000	1		3		5	6			10	7						4			2		8			11				9
37		20	BARROW	0-1		1000	1		3		5	6			10	7						4			2		8			11				9
38		28	Lancaster T.	0-0		500	1		3	4	5	6				7								10		2		8			11				9
			Apps.				34	3	38	26	30	32	3	21	17	16	3	13	6	9	11	12	23	27	3	22	4	16	2	3	17	4	2	13
			Goals						5	1	10			4	4		2				6	4		5	1		8			2			6

Played: L.Hennifer (7 in 21), J.Walmesley (4 in 27 & 28)
Played: J.Wilcock (7 in 10 & 11), E.Stansfield (4 in 25 & 33)
Match 16: One man short.

One own goal

Abandoned

Jan	9	OSWALDTWISTLE	0-0			1		3		10	6		7				11			9		5	8		2				4				

FA. Cup

PQ	Sep	19	ACCRINGTON S.	3-5	Plant,Meadowcroft,Openshaw	2000	1		3	4	5	6		10				11	8	7														

Played: W.Kelly (2), J.Bowden (9)

Lancashire Junior Cup

Sep	12	HINDLEY CENTRAL	2-3	Plant, Thornley	2500	1	2	3	4	5	6	7	8				10	11	9														

Friendlies

Dec	12	MANCHESTER C. RES.	3-1	Openshaw, Petty, Thornley		1		3	4	9	6		7		8		10		11			5			2									
Jan	30	PRESTON N.E.	1-1	Morgan		1		3		4	6		7	10					9		5			2		8								
Mar	13	STOCKPORT CO. RES.	4-3	Galvin(3), Barnes	1000	1		3		8	6		7	10								4		2						11	5	9		

Played: J.Worrall (11 v Preston)

		P	W	D	L	F	A	Pts
1	Manchester City Res.	38	24	8	6	132	49	56
2	Chorley	38	25	2	11	125	56	52
3	St. Helens Town	38	23	6	9	98	53	52
4	Hyde	38	23	5	10	91	58	51
5	Stockport County Res.	38	21	8	9	101	47	50
6	Eccles Borough	38	22	6	10	86	48	50
7	Haslingden	38	19	7	12	102	79	45
8	Lancaster Town	38	17	6	15	71	66	40
9	Barrow	38	18	4	16	80	85	40
10	ROCHDALE	38	16	5	17	59	63	37
11	Glossop Reserves	38	15	5	18	77	69	35
12	Earlestown	38	16	3	19	67	90	35
13	Heywood United	38	14	6	18	78	99	34
14	Bacup	38	13	6	19	60	86	32
15	Clitheroe Central	38	12	8	18	73	89	32
16	Ashton Town	38	10	12	16	56	70	32
17	Turton	38	14	3	21	96	93	31
18	Pendlebury	38	9	6	23	54	111	24
19	Oswaldtwistle	38	8	3	27	45	135	19
20	Great Harwood*	38	6	1	31	55	148	13

* Great Harwood took over the fixtures of Brynn Central who disbanded

1909-10 Lancashire Comb. Div. 2

#	Date		Opponent	Score	Scorers	Att.	Tay J	Bla J	Ope W	Gal P	Gre F	Fre J	Hal JE	Fle T	McS A	Jon JH	Wor A	Mor H	Wri W	Hea R	Bar H	Rob J	Mit C	Buc W	Pet E	Bra FC	Ball M	Bak FJ	Mat	Mil	Tho J	Hol Z	Car J	Har G
1	Sep	4	BACUP	2-1	Jones, Worth	5000	1	2	3	4	5	6	7	8	9	10	11																	
2		7	Earlestown	1-2	Galvin	500	1	2	3	8	5	6	7	4	9	10	11																	
3		11	CLITHEROE CENTRAL	1-1	Jones	4000	1		3	9	5	6	7			10	11	4	6	8		9												
4		14	Glossop Res.	1-1	Worth	400	1				5	6	7		8	10	11	4			9													
5		25	HEYWOOD U.	1-1	Bracey	6000	1	2	3		5	6	7	8			11	4			9					10								
6	Oct	16	Pendlebury	3-0	Fleetwood, Bracey(2)		1	2				6	7	8			11	4				3				10	5	9						
7		23	ASHTON T.	0-0			1	2		5		6	7	8			11	4				3				10								
8		30	BLACKPOOL RES.	1-0	Baker	4000	1	2	3	5		6	7	8			11	4								10		9						
9	Nov	2	EARLESTOWN	2-0	Worth, Baker		1	2	3	5		6	7	8			11	4								10		9						
10		6	Heywood U.	1-3	Freeborough	8500	1	2	3	5		6	7	8			11	4								10		9						
11		13	LANCASTER T.	6-0	Worth, Fleetwood, Baker(3), Hall	3000	1	2	3	5		6	7	8			11	4								10		9						
12		17	Atherton	4-0	Blackett(pen), Baker(3)		1	2	3	5		6	7	8			11	4								10		9						
13	Dec	4	PENDLEBURY	11-0	Bracey(4),Hall(2),Fleetwood,Worth(2),Jones,Freeborough	2500	1	2		5		6	7	8		10	11	4								9			3					
14		11	Blackpool Res.	2-1	Bracey, Fleetwood	2000	1	2	3	5		6	7	8			11	4								10		9						
15		18	BARROW	5-1	Blackett(pen),Worth(2),Jones,Galvin	2500	1	2	3	5		6	7			8	11	4								10		9						
16		25	Stockport Co. Res.	1-3	Hall	7000	1	9	3	5		6	7	8			11	4								10			2					
17		27	ATHERTON	2-0	Fleetwood, Jones	5500	1		3	5		6	7	8		10	11	4								9			2					
18	Jan	3	Ashton T.	4-4	Bracey, Blackett, Jones, Worth	1200	1	2	3	5		6		8		10	11	4								7				9				
19		15	Lancaster T.	1-2	Worth		1		3	5		6	7	8		10	11	4										9			2			
20		22	TURTON	2-0	Worth, Fleetwood	1500	1		3	5			7	8			11									10					6	4	9	
21	Feb	8	GREAT HARWOOD	4-0	Hall, Fleetwood(3)	1000	1	2	3	5		6	7	8			11											9				4	10	
22		22	DARWEN	3-0	Galvin, Openshaw(pen), Fleetwood		1		3	5	6	2	7	8			11	4								10							9	
23		26	ROSSENDALE U.	2-1	Carthy, Hall		1		3	5			7	8			11	4										9			2		10	
24	Mar	5	Barrow	1-1	Fleetwood		1	2	3	5		6		8			11	4										9			7		10	
25		8	HASLINGDEN	3-0	Galvin, Carthy, Openshaw (pen)	2000	1	2	3	5		6	7	8			11	4										9					10	
26		12	WALKDEN CENTRAL	8-0	Galvin,Hall,Worth,Fleetwood,Baker(3),Carthy	2500	1	2	3	5		6	7	8			11	4										9					10	
27		16	Eccles Borough	0-2		500	1	2	3	5		6	7	8			11	4										9					10	
28		19	GLOSSOP RES.	1-1	Bracey		1	2	3	5		6	7	8			11	4								10								9
29		25	Bacup		Harrison		1	2		5		6	7	8			11	4								10					3			9
30		28	STOCKPORT CO. RES.	4-1	Bracey(2), Worth(2)	7000	1	2		5		3	7	8			11	4								10		9			6			
31	Apr	6	Haslingden	2-0	Harrison(2)	2500	1		3	5		2		8			11	4								10		7			6			9
32		9	Rossendale U.	1-3	Harrison	2500	1		3	5		2		8			11	4								10		7			6			9
33		12	Turton	0-2			1		3	5		2	7	8			11	6								10		4					9	
34		16	ECCLES BOROUGH	1-0	Hall(pen)	2500	1		3	5		2	7	8			11	6								10		9						4
35		19	Great Harwood	2-1	Baker, Worth		1		3	5	6	2	7	8			11	4										9						
36		26	Clitheroe Central	5-0	Worth(4), Jones	300	1	2		5	6	3	7	8		10	11	4										9						
37		27	Walkden Central	1-1	Baker		1	2		5	6	3	7	8			11	4								10		9						
38		30	Darwen	2-0	Fleetwood, Freeborough(pen)		1			5			7	8			11	4								10								9
			Apps.				38	28	31	35	9	37	34	35	3	10	38	34	1	1	2	2				26	1	24	3	1	9	1	9	6
			Goals					3	2	5		3	8	13		7	19									12		13					3	4

Abandoned

						Tay	Bla	Ope		Gal		Hal	Fle			Wor	Mor								Bra		Bak						
Nov	27	Haslingden	1-3	Blackett		1	2	3	5			6	7	8		11	4								10		9						

FA. Cup

PQ	Sep	18	RAMSBOTTOM	1-1	Barnes	2500	1		3		5	6	7	8			11	4			9	2	10											
PQr		21	RAMSBOTTOM	4-0	Hall(2), Fleetwood, Barnes	500	1		3		5	6	7	8			11	4			9			2	10										
Q1	Oct	2	Haslingden	1-3	Worth	3000	1	2	3		5	6	7	8	9		11	4								10								

* At Burnden Park.

Lancashire Junior Cup

R1	Oct	9	PADIHAM	10-2	Buckley(2),Fleetwood(2),Hall,Bracey,Worth(2),Taylor(pen)		1	2					5	7	8		11	4				3		9		10	6							
R2	Nov	20	Darwen	3-3	Bracey, Baker, Worth	1000		2	3	5		1	6	7	8		11	4								10		9						
R3		29	DARWEN	1-0	Buckley	1500	1	2	3	5			6	7	8		11	4				9				10								
QF	Jan	8	ROSSENDALE U.	4-0	Fleetwood(2),Blackett(p),Baker	2000	1	2	3	5	7	6		8			11	4								10		9						
SF	Feb	19	EARLESTOWN	1-0	Carthy	2500	1		3	5			6	7	8		11	4										9				6	10	
F	Mar	25	Eccles Borough *	3-2	Worth(2),Baker		1	2	3	5			6	7	8		11	4								10		9						

* At Burnden Park.

Friendlies

Jan	1	BLACKPOOL RES.	2-1	Mills, Carthy	1500			2	5	7						11										6			3	9		4	10	
Feb	12	MONMOUTHSHIRE	5-0	Carthy(3), Baker, Fleetwood	2000	1	2	3	5		6		8			11	4								7		9					10	
Apr	2	HURST	3-0	Harrison, Fleetwood, Galvin	800	1		3	5	4	2		8			11									10		7				6		9
	23	NORTHERN NOMADS	5-0	Baker(2), Bracey, Worth(2)	1000	1		3	5	6	2			8		11									10		9						

Played v Blackpool: Turner(1), White (8). v. Northern Nomads: Miller(4), A.Walker(7), Wilding sub. in goal

		P	W	D	L	F	A	Pts
1	Glossop Res.	38	29	5	4	120	35	63
2	Stockport County Res.	38	28	4	6	133	41	60
3	Blackpool Res.	38	27	5	6	118	31	59
4	ROCHDALE	38	23	8	7	92	33	54
5	Haslingden	38	25	3	10	113	45	53
6	Rossendale United	38	21	4	13	105	69	46
7	Atherton	38	20	5	13	78	60	45
8	Earlestown	38	18	7	13	80	71	43
9	Heywood United	38	16	6	16	72	76	38
10	Eccles Borough	38	17	4	17	61	52	38
11	Darwen	38	15	6	17	71	68	36
12	Great Harwood	38	14	6	18	74	77	34
13	Ashton Town	38	13	7	18	67	84	33
14	Lancaster Town	38	13	6	19	71	88	32
15	Barrow	38	12	8	18	60	78	32
16	Bacup	38	11	1	26	63	111	23
17	Walken Central	38	10	3	25	65	128	23
18	Clitheroe Central	38	9	4	25	52	101	22
19	Turton	38	7	7	24	45	126	21
20	Denton*	38	1	3	34	23	189	5

* Denton replaced Pendlebury.

1910-11 Lancashire Comb. Div. 1

Division 1

No	Date	Opponent	Score	Scorers	Att
1	Sep 3	COLNE	3-0	Bracey(2), Fleetwood	5000
2	5	Chorley	0-4		3000
3	10	Bury Res.	0-1		6000
4	19	Blackburn R. Res.	5-1	Henderson,Smith,Fleetwood(2),Manning	2000
5	24	CHORLEY	2-1	Manning,Freeborough(pen)	5000
6	Oct 8	OLDHAM A. RES.	3-1	Fleetwood, Kenyon(2)	4000
7	22	ACCRINGTON S.	4-2	Smith, Grierson(3)	7000
8	29	Nelson	3-2	Grierson, Kenyon(2)	5000
9	Nov 12	BURY RES.	5-0	Smith(3), Kenyon, Fleetwood	4000
10	15	BOLTON W. RES.	4-0	Fleetwood(2), Manning, Smith	2000
11	Dec 10	Manchester U,. Res.	2-0	Kenyon(2)	1500
12	17	Southport Central	2-2	OG, Grierson	1000
13	24	Preston N.E. Res.	1-0	Freeborough	3000
14	26	LIVERPOOL RES.	2-1	Fleetwood, Manning	6500
15	27	Volron W. Res.	2-2	Smith(pen), Grierson	3000
16	31	St. Helens Rec.	1-3	Smith(pen)	1000
17	Jan 2	ST. HELENS REC.	4-1	Fleetwood(3), Kenyon	3500
18	7	MANCHESTER U. RES.	4-1	Smith, Grierson,Blackett,Kenyon	6000
19	14	Glossop Res.	3-1	Kenyon(2), Fleetwood	
20	21	EVERTON RES.	1-1	Cutts	9500
21	28	Accrington S.	1-0	Smith	4000
22	Feb 4	NELSON	2-1	Fleetwood, Smith	5000
23	11	Blckpool Res.	2-3	Fleetwood(2)	2500
24	18	BLACKPOOL RES.	2-0	Kenyon, Fleetwood	3500
25	25	STOCKPORT CO. RES.	1-0	Freeborough	3000
26	Mar 4	MANCHESTER C. RES.	3-1	Freeborough(p),Grierson,Fleetwood	3000
27	11	Oldham A. Res.	3-1	Fleetwood, Grierson, Kenyon	10000
28	18	Colne	1-3	Gregson	3000
29	21	BURNLEY RES.	4-1	Grierson, Kenyon(2), Smith	1000
30	25	Burnley Res.	0-0		3000
31	Apr 1	SOUTHPORT CENTRAL	1-0	Moon	7000
32	3	Stockport Co. Res.	1-1	Kenyon	1000
33	8	GLOSSOP RES.	4-0	Bracey, Smith(3)	4000
34	14	Liverpool Res.	2-2	Manning, Gregson	16000
35	15	PRESTON N.E. RES.	2-0	Grierson(2)	5500
36	17	Everton Res.	0-1		6000
37	22	BLACKBURN R. RES.	4-3	Bracey(3), Henderson	4000
38	29	Manchester C. Res.	3-4	Smith, Kenyon, Cooper	2000

Division 1 — appearances (shirt numbers)

Player columns: Reeves · Blackett J · Riddell N · Cooper W · Thomason E · Freeborough J · Manning JT · Fleetwood T · Grierson RT · Bracey FC · Smith A · Hartley PW · Biggar W · Henderson JT · Morgan H · Kenyon J · Greenhalgh F · Crossan D · Cutts EH · Gregson A · Moon HC · Mansfield E · Marcroft · Kennedy D · Jones JH

No	Ree	Bla	Rid	Coo	Tho	Fre	Man	Fle	Gri	Bra	Smi	Har	Big	Hen	Mor	Ken	Gre	Cro	Cut	Gre	Moo	Man	Mar	Ken	Jon
1	1	2	3	4	5	6	7	8	9	10	11														
2	1	2			5	3	7	8	9	10	11	6													
3		2		4	5	3	7	8	9	10	11			1		6									
4		2		4	5	3	7	8	10		11		6	1		9									
5		2		4	5	3	7	8	10		11		6	1		9									
6		2		4	5	3	7	8	10		11		1	6		9									
7		2	3	4	5		7	8	10		11		1	6		9									
8		2	3		5	4	7	8	10		11		1	6		9									
9		2	3	4			7	8	10		11		1	6		9	5								
10		2	3	4			7	8	10		11		1	6		9	5								
11		2		4		5	7	8	10		11		1	6		9		3							
12			3	4		5	7	8	10		11		1	6		9		2							
13		2		4		5	7	8	10		11		1	6		9		3							
14		2		4	5	3	7	8	10		11	9	1	6											
15		2		4	3	7	5	6	9		8	11	10	1	4										
16		2	3	4	5	6	7	8			10		11	1		9									
17		2	3	4		5	7	8	10		11	6	1			9									
18		2	3	4		6	7	8	10		11		1			9		3							
19		2	5	4		7		8	10		11		1	6		9		3							
20		2		4	5	6		8	10		11		1			9		3	7						
21		2		4	5	6		8	10		11		1			9		3	7						
22		2	5	4		6		8	10		11		1			9		3	7						
23		2		4		5		8	10		11		1			9		3	7						
24		2	3		5			8			11		1	6		9	6	3		7	10				
25			2		5	7		8			11		1	6		9	4	3		10					
26				5	2		9	10			11		1	6	4	7		3		8					
27		2		5			9	10			11		1	6	4	7		3		8					
28		2			5	9		10			11		1	6	4	7		3		8					
29		2		4	5	7		10			11		1	6		9		3		8					
30		2		4	5	7		10			11		1	6		9		3		8					
31		2		4	5						11		1	6		7		3		8	9	10			
32		2		4	5	6	7				11		1			9		3		8		10			
33		2	5			6	7			10	11		1	4		9		3		8					
34		2		4	5		7		10		11		1	6		9		3		8					
35		2		4	5		7		10		11		1	6		9		3		8					
36		2		4	5		7		10		11		1	6		9		3		8					
37		2		4	5	6	7		10	11	11		1	9				3		8				10	
38		2		4	5		7				11		1	6		9		3		8					
Apps.	2	35	15	31	27	28	25	26	31	5	38	6	36	28	3	30	5	23	5	15	1	2	1		
Goals		1		1		4	5	18	12	6	16			2		17			1	2	1				

FA. Cup

Rd	Date	Opponent	Score	Scorers	Att
PQ	Sep 17	EARLESTOWN	2-1	Grierson, Fleetwood	2500
Q1	Oct 1	ST. HELENS T.	2-1	Grierson, Henderson	2000
Q2	15	Heywood U.	4-3	Fleetwood,Grierson,Smith(pen),Kenyon	8000
Q3	Nov 5	ST. HELENS REC.	1-0	Grierson	4000
Q4	19	STOCKPORT CO.	0-0		6941
Q4r	21	Stockport Co.	0-0		1500
Q42r	28	Stockport Co.*	1-0	Blackett	2276
Q5	Dec 3	LUTON TOWN	1-1	Fleetwood	9933
Q5r	7	Luton Town	2-3	Kenyon, Smith(pen)	4000

* Played at Oldham.

FA Cup — appearances

Rd	Bla	Rid	Coo	Tho	Fre	Man	Fle	Gri	Smi	Big	Hen	Mor	Ken	Gre
PQ	2		4	5	3	7	8	10	11	6	1		9	
Q1	2	7	5	3			8	10	11	6	1	9	4	
Q2	2	3	4	5		7	8	10	11	1	6		9	
Q3	2	3	4	5		7	8	10	11	1	6		9	
Q4	2	3	4			7	8	10	11	1	6		9	5
Q4r	2	3	4	5		7	8	10	11	1	6		9	
Q42r	2	3	4	5		7	8	10	11	1	6		9	
Q5	2	3	4	5		7	8	10	11	1	6		9	
Q5r	2	3	4		5	7	8	10	11	1	6		9	

Lancashire Senior Cup

Rd	Date	Opponent	Score	Scorers	Att	Bla	Rid	Coo	Tho	Man	Fle	Gri	Bra	Smi	Big	Hen	Ken
R1	Sep 26	COLNE	2-0	Smith (2)	1000	2	3	4	5	7	8	10	9	11	1	6	
R2	Oct 10	Burnley	0-1		1500	2	3	4	5	7	8	10		11	1	6	9

Friendlies

Date	Opponent	Score	Scorers	Att	Ree	Rid	Tho	Man	Fle	Gri	Bra	Smi	Hen	Ken	Ken(D)	Jon
Sep 1	HEYWOOD U.	4-0	Bracey(2),Fleetwood(2)	2000	1	3	2	7	8	10	11	6	4	5	9	
Nov 26	NORTHERN NOMADS	1-0	Kennedy	500			5	7	8	11	6	1	2	4	9	10

League Table

		P	W	D	L	F	A	Pts
1	ROCHDALE	38	25	6	7	87	45	56
2	Everton Res.	38	21	7	10	81	35	49
3	Bolton Wand. Res.	38	19	10	9	72	59	48
4	Liverpool Res.	38	19	8	11	76	59	46
5	Blackburn Rovers Res.	38	17	7	14	66	63	41
6	Colne	38	17	5	16	67	56	39
7	Nelson	38	15	8	15	64	63	38
8	Accrington Stanley	38	15	8	15	82	78	38
9	Chorley	38	11	15	12	55	60	37
10	Manchester United Res.	38	15	7	16	75	69	37
11	Southport Central	38	11	15	12	53	61	37
12	Preston N.E. Res.	38	14	9	15	43	55	37
13	St. Helens Recreation	38	14	9	15	43	55	37
14	Blackpool Res.	38	14	8	16	52	62	36
15	Bury Res.	38	15	6	17	61	67	36
16	Burnley Res.	38	15	5	18	62	69	35
17	Glossop City	38	13	8	17	49	62	34
18	Manchester City Res.	38	11	9	18	49	76	31
19	Stockport County Res.	38	7	12	19	42	78	26
20	Oldham Athletic Res.	38	9	7	22	42	73	25

Chorley v Liverpool abandoned after 25 mins. Result (0-1) stood.

1910-11 Season
Back: Irlam, Wood, East, Wormwell, Barlow, Chantry, Kenworthy, Tweedale, Heap (Directors)
Middle: Schofield (Asst.Trainer), Riddell, Grierson, Freeborough, Blackett, Biggar, Kenyon, Morgan, Coe (Trainer)
Front: Cooper, Manning, Thomasson, Gregson, Henderson, Bracey, Crossan, Smith

1911-12 Season
Back: Morgan,Chick, Blackett, Biggar, Crossan, Meynell, Henderson, Page
Front: Reynolds, Gregson, Spriggs, Peake, Smith

1911-12 Lancashire Comb. Div. 1

League Match Results

No	Date		Opponent	Score	Scorers	Att
1	Sep	2	DENTON	5-0	Spriggs(2),Smith,Chick,Peake	4000
2		23	Accrington Stanley	1-0	Smith	2000
3	Oct	7	Hyde	1-5	Gregson	2000
4		14	ACCRINGTON S.	3-1	T.Page, Gregson, Reynolds	3000
5		21	Heywood U.	1-1	Smith	4000
6		28	Eccles Borough	2-1	Lovett, Gregson	4000
7	Nov	4	ST. HELENS T.	3-1	Gregson(2), Lovett	3000
8		11	St. Helens T.	3-0	Lovett, Gregson(2)	4000
9		25	Haslingden	1-2	Gregson	2500
10	Dec	2	CHORLEY	2-0	Gregson, Lovett	2500
11		9	Bacup	7-1	Meynell,Gregson,T.Page(4),Smith	1500
12		16	BARROW	5-0	Reynolds,T.Page,Smith,Lovett,Gregson	3000
13		23	Walkden Central	3-0	Lovett,T.Page(2)	300
14		25	ST. HELENS REC.	2-0	Lovett, OG	5000
15		26	Chester	1-3	Stamford	6000
16		30	Denton	0-3		2500
17	Jan	1	CHESTER	3-0	Smith, Reynolds, Lovett	6000
18		16	Colne	1-0	Chick	2000
19		20	ROSSENDALE U.	3-0	Smith, Gregson, Broome	1500
20		27	COLNE	3-0	Smith, T.Page, Gregson	2000
21	Feb	3	Rossendale U.	2-1	T.Page, Reynolds	1000
22		10	HYDE	2-0	Chick, T.Page	5000
23		24	HEYWOOD U.	2-2	Gregson(2)	4000
24	Mar	2	ECCLES BOROUGH	4-0	Meynell,Gregson,Smith,Bracey	2000
25		23	Nelson	3-0	Bracey, Reynolds, Henderson	2000
26		30	HASLINGDEN	3-0	Gregson, Reynolds(2)	2000
27	Apr	5	St. Helens Rec.	1-1	Bracey, Reynolds, Henderson	2000
28		6	Chorley	0-0		2000
29		8	NELSON	3-0	Lovett, Bracey, Broome	2000
30		13	BACUP	9-0	T.Page(4),Lovett(2),OG,Gregson(2)	2000
31		20	Barrow	0-1		4500
32		27	WALKDEN CENTRAL	3-1	Gregson(2), Smith	1000

League Appearances (shirt numbers)

No	Biggar W	Blackett J	Crosson D	Chick WI	Meynell WT	Henderson JT	Reynolds J	Gregson W	Spriggs F	Peake R	Smith A	Morgan H	Page T	Broome TA	McKenzie J	Bracey FC	Lovett W	Kenyon L	Hall	Stamford J	Costelli T	Martin WH	Howarth	Page J	Tattum B	Barker
1	1	2	3	4	5	6	7	8	9	10	11															
2	1	2	3	4	5	6	7	8	9	10	11															
3	1	2		4		6	7	8	9		11	5	3				10									
4	1	2		4	5	6	7	8			11	3	9				10									
5	1	2		4	5	6	7	8			11	3	9				10									
6	1	2		4	5	6	7	8			11	3	9				10									
7	1	2		4	5	6		8			11	3	9				10	7								
8	1		3	4	5	6		8			11	2	9				10									
9	1	2	3	4	5	6	7	8			11						9		10							
10	1	2	3	4	5	6	7	8			11						9		10							
11	1	2	3	4	5		7	8			11	6	9				10									
12	1	2		4	5	6	7	8			11	3	9				10									
13	1	2		4	5	6		8			11	3	9				10		7							
14	1	2		4	5	6	7	8			11	3					10			9						
15	1	2		4	5	6	7	8			11	3					10			9						
16	1	2		4		6	7	8			11	9	5				10				3					
17	1	2		4	5	3	7	8			11	9	6				10									
18	1	2		4	5	6		8			11	9					10				7					
19	1	2	3	4	5	6	7	8			11		9	10												
20	1		3	4	5	6	7	8			11	2	9	10												
21	1		3	4	5		7	8			11	2	9	6			10									
22	1		3	4	5						11	2	9	6			10						7			
23	1		3	4	5		7	8			11		9	6			10							2		
24	1		3	4	5		7	8			11		9			6	10							2		
25	1	2	3	4	5	9	7	8								6	10								11	
26	1	2		4	5	6	7	8						3		9	10								11	
27	1	2	3	4	5	6	7	8								9	10								11	
28	1	2	3	4	5	6	7	8								9	10								11	
29	1	2	3	4	5	9	7	8								6	10								11	
30	1	2	3	4	5		7	8			11	9	6				10									
31	1		3	4	5		7	8						6		9	10							2	11	
32	1		3	4	5		7	8			11			6			10							2		9
Apps	32	24	20	31	30	26	28	32	3	2	26	14	17	14	1	8	25	1	3	2	1	1	1	4	5	1
Goals				3	2	1	7	21	2	1	10		15	2		4	11			1						

One own goal

Abandoned

Date		Opponent	Score	Att	Lineup (shirt numbers)
Jan	6	Colne	0-1	1000	Biggar 1, Blackett 2, Chick 4, Meynell 5, Henderson 6, Gregson 8, Smith 11, Morgan 3, Page T 9, Lovett 10, Costelli 7

Lancashire Comb. Divisional Play-off

Date		Opponent	Score	Scorers	Att	Lineup
Sep	13	Haslingden	2-0	Smith, Meynell	500	Biggar 1, Blackett 2, Chick 4, Meynell 5, Henderson 6, Reynolds 7, Spriggs 9, Smith 11, Bracey 8, Campey A 3, Moon HC 10

FA. Cup

Round	Date		Opponent	Score	Att	Lineup
Q4	Nov	18	Barrow	0-1	7000	Biggar 1, Crosson 3, Chick 4, Meynell 5, Henderson 6, Reynolds 7, Gregson 8, Smith 11, Morgan 2, Page T 9, Lovett 10

Lancashire Senior Cup

Round	Date		Opponent	Score	Scorers	Att	Lineup
R1	Sep	19	BARROW	1-2	Spriggs	600	Biggar 1, Crosson 3, Chick 4, Meynell 5, Henderson 6, Reynolds 7, Gregson 8, Spriggs 9, Peake 10, Smith 11, Morgan 2

Manchester Senior Cup

Round	Date		Opponent	Score	Scorers	Att	Lineup
	Sep	12	Denton	4-2	Maynell, Peake(2), Spriggs		Biggar 1, Blackett 2, Chick 4, Meynell 5, Henderson 6, Reynolds 7, Spriggs 8, Peake 10, Smith 11, Morgan 3, Page T 9
		26	NORTHERN NOMADS	3-0	Gregson(3)	1000	Biggar 1, Blackett 2, Crosson 3, Chick 4, Henderson 6, Reynolds 7, Gregson 8, Spriggs 9, Peake 10, Smith 11, Morgan 5
	Oct	9	STOCKPORT CO.	5-0	Lovett(2), Smith(2), T.Page	1500	Biggar 1, Blackett 2, Chick 4, Meynell 5, Henderson 6, Reynolds 7, Gregson 8, Smith 11, Morgan 3, Page T 9, Lovett 10
SF	Nov	27	Manchester C.	2-0	Smith, Lovett	1500	Biggar 1, Blackett 2, Crosson 3, Chick 4, Meynell 5, Henderson 6, Reynolds 7, Gregson 8, Smith 11, Lovett 10, Kenyon 9
F	Mar	27	Manchester U.*	0-0		3000	Biggar 1, Blackett 2, Crosson 3, Chick 4, Meynell 5, Henderson 6, Reynolds 7, Gregson 8, Lovett 10, Kenyon 9, Tattum 11
Fr	Apr	30	Manchester U.+	1-1	Gregson		Biggar 1, Blackett 2, Crosson 3, Chick 4, Meynell 5, Henderson 6, Reynolds 7, Gregson 8, Smith 11, Page T 9, Lovett 10

* Played at Manchester City. + Played at Oldham.

Friendlies

Date		Opponent	Score	Scorers	Att	Lineup
Sep	16	BLACKPOOL RES.	4-0	Smith, Peake, Spriggs, Reynolds	2000	Biggar 1, Blackett 2, Chick 4, Meynell 5, Henderson 6, Reynolds 7, Spriggs 9, Peake 10, Smith 11, Bracey 8
	30	EVERTON RES.	2-0	Gregson(2)	1500	Biggar 1, Blackett 2, Chick 4, Henderson 6, Reynolds 7, Gregson 8, Spriggs 9, Smith 11, Broome 5, McKenzie 3, Moon HC 10
Jan	13	STOKE	3-1	T.Page(2), Broome	1000	Biggar 1, Blackett 2, Crosson 3, Chick 4, Meynell 5, Henderson 6, Gregson 8, Smith 11, Morgan 9, Page T 10, Lovett 7
Feb	17	PRESTON N.E. RES.	3-1	Gregson, Lovett	500	Biggar 1, Crosson 3, Chick 4, Meynell 5, Gregson 8, Bracey 9, Lovett 6, Martin WH 11, Howarth 10, Page J 7, Tattum 2
Mar	16	Hartlepool	2-1	Gregson, Reynolds	2000	Biggar 1, Blackett 2, Crosson 3, Chick 4, Meynell 5, Henderson 6, Reynolds 7, Gregson 8, Smith 11, Lovett 10

Played: Fisher (3 v Blackpool Res.), Hardwick (9 v Hartlepool)

League Table

		P	W	D	L	F	A	Pts
1	ROCHDALE	32	23	4	5	82	24	50
2	St. Helens Recreation	32	19	6	7	69	49	44
3	Hyde	32	17	5	10	69	41	39
4	Barrow	32	15	9	8	66	48	39
5	Colne	32	16	6	10	59	43	38
6	Chester	32	15	7	10	74	50	37
7	Chorley	32	14	7	11	50	43	35
8	Rossendale United	32	12	9	11	58	48	33
9	Eccles Borough	32	13	6	13	52	50	32
10	Accrington Stanley	32	12	6	14	71	68	30
11	Haslingden	32	11	8	13	54	53	30
12	Heywood United	32	11	5	16	40	68	27
13	Nelson	32	9	7	16	58	66	25
14	Denton	32	11	3	18	52	78	25
15	St. Helens Town	32	8	8	16	45	60	24
16	Walken Central	32	6	7	19	37	74	19
17	Bacup	32	6	5	21	41	114	17

1912-13 Central League

Player columns: Biggar W, Leigh T, Crossan D, Chick WJ, Birnie EL, Henderson JT, Spink TW, Gregson A, Page T, Tully J, Smith A, Page J, Lovett W, McKinley D, Broome TA, Thomason E, Turnbull WW, Morris J, Morgan H, Cunliffe D, Clouston H, Goodwin J, Davies W, Barton JW, Hardy P, Crabtree J, Bamford W

#	Date	Opponent	Result	Scorers	Att.
1	Sep 2	PRESTON N.E. RES.	2-0	Tully, Gregson	3500
2	Sep 7	Bradford C. Res.	1-2	Gregson	3000
3	Sep 14	EVERTON RES.	3-0	T.Page(2), Tully	6000
4	Sep 21	Bury Res.	1-0	McKinley	3000
5	Sep 24	BARNSLEY RES.	4-0	Tully(2), Gregson(2)	1500
6	Sep 28	Glossop Res.	0-2		4000
7	Oct 1	BOLTON W. RES.	3-0	Gregson, T.Page, Chick	1000
8	Oct 5	Blackpool Res.	1-1	T.Page	2500
9	Oct 19	Crewe A.	2-6	Gregson, Smith	3000
10	Oct 26	BURNLEY RES.	0-6		2000
11	Nov 6	Bolton W. Res.	0-0		
12	Nov 9	STALYBRIDGE CELTIC	3-1	Chick(pen), McKinley, T.Page	6000
13	Nov 23	Stockport Co. Res.	2-2	T.Page, Spink	3000
14	Dec 7	MANCHESTER U. RES.	2-0	Tully, Gregson	4000
15	Dec 25	BRADFORD C. RES.	1-1	Chick(pen)	7000
16	Dec 26	Southport Central	4-0	T.Page(2), Chick, Tully	5000
17	Dec 28	BLACKPOOL RES.	4-1	Tully, Chick(2), T.Page	5000
18	Jan 1	Liverpool Res.	1-7	Clouston	3000
19	Jan 4	Everton Res.	2-3	McKinley, Tully	1500
20	Jan 18	BURY RES.	2-0	T.Page(2)	1000
21	Jan 22	Manchester U. Res.	0-4		1000
22	Jan 25	STOCKPORT CO. RES.	1-0	Spink	1500
23	Feb 1	OLDHAM A. RES.	0-1		3000
24	Feb 4	MANCHESTER C. RES.	1-0	McKinley	500
25	Feb 8	Oldham A. Res.	1-1	Chick	6000
26	Feb 15	Manchester C. Res.	2-1	T.Page, Smith	6000
27	Feb 22	Preston N.E. Res.	1-2	Tully	4000
28	Mar 1	GLOSSOP RES.	5-1	Gregson, Chick(pen), Spink, Smith, Tully	2000
29	Mar 6	Barnsley Res.	3-1	Smith, Gregson(2)	1500
30	Mar 15	Stalybridge Celtic	1-1	Tully(pen)	4000
31	Mar 21	BLACKBURN R. RES.	0-0		5000
32	Mar 22	SOUTHPORT CENTRAL	8-0	Cunliffe(2), Gregson(3), Chick, Smith, Birnie	3000
33	Mar 24	LIVERPOOL RES.	0-0		4000
34	Apr 5	CREWE A.	2-2	T.Page, Thomason	2000
35	Apr 12	Burslem P.V.	0-1		3000
36	Apr 15	BURNLEY RES.	2-2	Tully, Davies	1000
37	Apr 24	Blackburn R. Res.	0-2		500
38	Apr 26	BURSLEM P.V.	2-0	T.Page(2)	1500

Apps: 32, 7, 16, 32, 28, 31, 37, 27, 25, 34, 33, 9, 6, 8, 23, 4, 5, 6, 5, 11, 4, 9, 4, 8, 2, 8, 4

Goals: 9, 1, 3, 13, 15, 12, 5, 4, 1, 2, 1, 1

FA. Cup

	Date	Opponent	Result	Scorers	Att.
Q1	Oct 12	Macclesfield	5-3	Smith, Tully(2), Birnie, Gregson	
Q2	Nov 2	NEWTON HEATH	5-0	Henderson, Birnie, Tully, Chick(p), T.Page	2000
Q3	Nov 16	STALYBRIDGE C.	2-1	Gregson(2)	3000
Q4	Nov 30	ACCRINGTON S.	6-1	Tully, Chick(pen), T.Page(4)	5000
Q5	Dec 14	DARLINGTON	1-1	Gregson	7045
Q5r	Dec 18	Darlington	1-0	Chick(pen)	7018
R1	Jan 11	SWINDON T.	0-2		8801

Lancashire Senior Cup

	Date	Opponent	Result	Scorers	Att.
R1	Sep 23	ACCRINGTON S.	2-1	T.Page, Lovett, Smith	400
R2	Oct 7	Barrow	1-2	Gregson	3000

Manchester Senior Cup

Date	Opponent	Result	Scorers	Att.
Sep 17	Manchester U.*	0-5		1000
Feb 25	MANCHESTER C.	2-1	Tully, T.Page	1515
Mar 12	Bolton W.	1-1	Gregson	
Apr 1	BOLTON W.	1-2	T.Page	3000

* Replay of 1911-12 final, at Bury.

Friendlies

Date	Opponent	Result	Scorers	Att.
Dec 21	HEYWOOD U.	3-2	Turnbull, Davies, OG	2000

Played: J.C. Jackson (2), C.Robinson(7)

		P	W	D	L	F	A	Pts
1	Manchester United Res.	38	22	11	5	79	30	55
2	Bradford City Res.	38	22	6	10	96	50	50
3	Burnley Res.	38	22	4	12	87	46	48
4	Burslem Port Vale	38	19	7	12	55	38	45
5	Stalybridge Celtic	38	16	13	9	65	48	45
6	Oldham Athletic Res.	38	18	9	11	58	50	45
7	ROCHDALE	38	17	10	11	67	51	44
8	Barnsley Res.	38	19	6	13	57	49	44
9	Liverpool Res.	38	18	7	13	56	45	43
10	Everton Res.	38	18	5	15	80	68	41
11	Blackburn Rovers Res.	38	14	10	14	68	62	38
12	Manchester City Res.	38	12	12	14	46	54	36
13	Southport Central	38	13	6	19	45	75	32
14	Crewe Alexandra	38	13	5	20	64	68	31
15	Bolton Wanderers Res.	38	9	13	16	43	50	31
16	Blackpool Res.	38	9	12	17	41	63	30
17	Stockport County Res.	38	11	7	20	43	75	29
18	Preston N.E. Res.	38	9	8	21	47	77	26
19	Bury Res.	38	8	8	22	46	95	24
20	Glossop Res.	38	7	9	22	40	89	23

1913-14 Central League

#		Date	Opponent	Score	Scorers	Att.	Biggar W.	Barton J.W.	Crossan D.	Milne C.	Broome T.A.	Henderson J.T.	Spink T.W.	Watson R.	Allan J.	Grierson R.T.	Smith A.	Tully J.	Kay J.L.	Goodwin J.	Bamford W.	Coates H.J.	Clark D.H.	Hawksworth E.	Chamberlain W.	Morris J.	Hayes J.V.	Marshall J.	Tattersall J.	Spoor G.	Walker A.	Plumley W.	Taylor J.	Heap T.
1	Sep	2	BURY RES.	7-0	Allan (5), Smith, Watson	4000	1	2	3	4	5	6	7	8	9	10	11																	
2		3	Manchester C. Res.	0-1		10000	1	2	3	4	5	6	7	8	9	10	11																	
3		6	HUDDERSFIELD T. RES.	2-0	Watson, Smith		1	2	3	4	5	6	7	8	9	10	11																	
4		13	Bradford C. Res.	0-0			1	2	3	4	5	6	7	8		9	11	10																
5		20	PORT VALE	0-1		5000	1	2	3	4	5		7	8		10	11	9	6															
6	Oct	1	Huddersfield T. Res.	2-1	Grierson, Allan		1	2		4	5	3	7	8	9	10	11	6																
7		4	EVERTON RES.	0-1		4000	1	2		4	5	6	7	8	9	10	11			3														
8		11	Blackpool Res.	2-2	Allan, Grierson	3000	1	2		4	5	3	7		9	8	11	6	10															
9		18	BURNLEY RES.	4-0	Allan(2), Broome(2,1pen)	3000	1	2		4	5	3	7	10	9	8	11	6																
10		25	Port Vale	1-2	Allan	9000	1	2		4	5	3	7		9	8	11	6	10															
11	Nov	1	Blackburn R. Res.	0-0		3500	1	2		4	5	3	7	8	9		11	6	10															
12		8	Preston N.E. Res.	2-1	Hawksworth(2)	3000	1	2		4	5	3	7		9		11					6	8	10										
13		15	OLDHAM A. RES.	1-2	Allan	2000	1			4	5	2	7		9		11	8				6		10	3									
14		22	BLACKBURN R. RES.	5-4	Clark, Broome, Smith(3)			2		4	5		7		9		11	6					8	10	3									
15	Dec	6	Manchester U. Res.	0-2		3500	1	2		4	5		7		9		11	6						10	3									
16		20	BLACKPOOL RES.	1-0	Hawksworth	2000		2			5	6	7			4	11	9						10		1	3	8						
17		25	Bolton W. Res.	1-2	Allan	4000	1	2			5	6	7		9	4	11		10					8			3							
18		26	Southport Central	2-1	Grierson, Milne		1	2		6	5		7		9	4	11		10					8			3							
19		27	CREWE A.	2-0	Allan, Smith(pen)	1500	1				5	3	7	8	9	4	11		10				6		2									
20	Jan	1	STALYBRIDGE CELTIC	0-1		3500	1	2			5	3	7		9	4	11		10				6				8							
21		3	Liverpool Res.	3-2	Grierson, Smith, Allan	4000	1	2			5	3	7		9	4	11		10				6				8							
22		10	MANCHESTER C. RES.	4-1	OG, Hawksworth, Grierson, Tully	4000	1	2			5		4	7		10	11	9	6								3							
23		17	Crewe A.	1-1	Smith	4000	1	2			5		7		9	10	11	4	6								3							
24		24	BRADFORD C. RES.	1-1	Allan	2000	1	2			5		7		9	10	11	4	6								3							
25		31	Bury Res.	2-1	Smith, Grierson	2500	1	2			5		7			9	11	4	6					10			3			8				
26	Feb	7	Everton Res.	2-4	Spink, Milne	2500	1	2			5		7			9	11	4	6					10			3			8				
27		14	STOCKPORT CO. RES.	2-4	Grierson, Hawksworth	2000	1	2			5		7		4	9	11	6						10			3			8				
28	Mar	2	Burnley Res.	0-4			1	2			5		7	8		9	11	6						10			3							
29		7	Stockport Co. Res.	1-3	Smith(pen)	2800	1	2					7			9	11	4	6					10			3			8	5			
30		14	PRESTON N.E. RES.	1-1	Smith	1500	1	2		4			3	7			11	9	6					10						8	5			
31		21	Oldham A. Res.	1-0	Tattersall	3000	1	2			5		3	7	10		11	4	6											8	9			
32		28	MANCHESTER U. RES.	0-1		1500	1			5			3	7			11	4	6					10	2					8	9			
33	Apr	4	BARNSLEY RES.	0-2		1500	1			5			6	7	8		11	4	10						2						9	3		
34		10	Stalybridge Celtic	1-1	Allan	6000	1	2		5			3		10	9	11	7	6											8				
35		11	Southport Central	4-1	Tully, Walker, Smith(2,1pen)	3000	1	2	3	5			4		10	9	11	7	6											8				
36		13	BOLTON W. RES.	2-0	Watson, Allan	2000	1		3	5			4		10	9	11	7	6		2									8				
37		14	Barnsley Res.	1-1	Smith	3000	1	2					4		10	9	11	7	6		5							3		8				
38		28	LIVERPOOL RES.	2-2	Smith(pen), Watson	1000		2		5			7	10			11	4	6											8		1	3	9
			Apps.				36	33	7	36	15	27	34	18	26	24	38	33	23	2	2	2	19	16	1	1	9	5	1	5	1	1	1	1
			Goals							2	3		1	4	17	7	15	2					1	5							1	1		

FA. Cup

	Date	Opponent	Score	Scorers	Att.	Biggar W.	Barton J.W.	Crossan D.	Milne C.	Broome T.A.	Henderson J.T.	Spink T.W.	Watson R.	Allan J.	Grierson R.T.	Smith A.	Tully J.	Kay J.L.	Goodwin J.	Bamford W.	Coates H.J.	Clark D.H.	Hawksworth E.	Chamberlain W.
Q4	Nov 29	Barrow	0-3		7000	1	2		4	5	6	7		9		11	8						10	3

Lancashire Senior Cup

	Date	Opponent	Score	Scorers	Att.	Biggar W.	Barton J.W.	Crossan D.	Milne C.	Broome T.A.	Henderson J.T.	Spink T.W.	Watson R.	Allan J.	Grierson R.T.	Smith A.	Tully J.	Kay J.L.	Goodwin J.	Bamford W.	Coates H.J.	Clark D.H.	Hawksworth E.	Chamberlain W.
R1	Sep 23	Nelson	3-1	Smith, Broome, Spink	1000	1	2		4	5	6	7	8	9	10	11			3					
R2	Oct 6	BARROW	2-0	Watson, Milne		1	2		4	5	6	7	8	9	10	11				3				
R3	Oct 20	BOLTON W.	3-2	Allan(2), Grierson	1200	1	2		4	5	3	7		9	8	11	6							
SF	Nov 10	Blackpool*	1-4	Broome(pen)	2000	1			4	5	3	7		9		11	6				8		10	2

* Played at Blackburn. Played: C.Clegg (10 v Bolton W.).

Manchester Senior Cup

Date	Opponent	Score		Barton J.W.		Broome T.A.	Henderson J.T.	Spink T.W.		Allan J.	Grierson R.T.	Smith A.	Tully J.	Kay J.L.					Hawksworth E.	Chamberlain W.	Morris J.	Hayes J.V.	Marshall J.
Feb 11	Manchester U.	0-5		2		5		6	7		9	11	4	10						3	1	8		

Friendlies

Date	Opponent	Score	Scorers	Att.	Biggar W.	Barton J.W.		Milne C.	Broome T.A.	Henderson J.T.	Spink T.W.	Watson R.	Allan J.	Grierson R.T.	Smith A.	Tully J.	Kay J.L.		Bamford W.		Clark D.H.	Hawksworth E.	Chamberlain W.				Spoor G.	Walker A.
Sep 27	Chesterfield	2-5	Allan, Watson		1				5		6	7	8	9	10	11			3							2	
Dec 13	ASTON VILLA RES.	1-1	Hawksworth	1000		2					6	7		4		11	10				8	3	1				9

Played: J.Broad(4 v Chesterfield), W.Bird (5 v Aston Villa)

		P	W	D	L	F	A	Pts
1	Everton Res.	38	20	9	9	83	57	49
2	Crewe Alexandra	38	20	8	10	57	49	48
3	Stalybridge Celtic	38	20	7	11	72	43	47
4	Port Vale	38	17	11	10	78	62	45
5	Blackburn Rovers Res.	38	18	7	13	93	72	43
6	Manchester United Res.	38	19	4	15	49	43	42
7	Liverpool Res.	38	17	8	13	57	54	42
8	Bradford City Res.	38	18	4	16	68	56	40
9	Manchester City Res.	38	16	8	14	57	51	40
10	ROCHDALE	38	15	9	14	60	51	39
11	Burnley Res.	38	16	6	16	57	72	38
12	Blackpool Res.	38	13	11	14	48	52	37
13	Oldham Athletic Res.	38	14	8	16	51	49	36
14	Huddersfield Town Res.	38	11	11	16	46	49	33
15	Bury Res.	38	14	5	19	58	86	33
16	Preston N.E. Res.	38	11	9	18	62	81	31
17	Barnsley Res.	38	12	6	20	46	62	30
18	Southport Central	38	10	10	18	43	58	30
19	Stockport County Res.	38	11	7	20	44	71	29
20	Bolton Wanderers Res.	38	10	8	20	48	59	28

1914-15 Central League

#	Date	Match	Score	Scorers	Att
1	Sep 1	LIVERPOOL RES.	4-1	Brown, Rawlings, Kelly(2)	2000
2	8	Southport Central	0-1		
3	12	HUDDERSFIELD T. RES.	3-0	Brown, Smith(pen), Rawlings	1000
4	19	Stalybridge Celtic	0-0		
5	26	STALYBRIDGE CELTIC	1-1	Anderson	3000
6	Oct 3	Huddersfield T. Res.	0-0		1000
7	10	BURNLEY RES.	1-1	Brown	3000
8	17	Blackpool Res.	3-3	Brown(2), Neave	1000
9	24	MANCHESTER C. RES.	0-1		
10	31	BLACKBURN R. RES.	5-1	Kelly(2), Brown(2), Tully	1200
11	Nov 7	Liverpool Res.	1-5	Neave	
12	14	Bury Res.	3-1	Smith, Brown, Hawksworth	
13	28	Crewe A.	0-1		
14	Dec 12	Burnley Res.	1-4	Hawksworth	4000
15	25	STOCKPORT CO. RES.	1-1	Brown	1000
16	26	BARNSLEY RES.	6-1	OG,Brown(3),Smith(pen),Rawlings	1500
17	Jan 1	BOLTON W. RES.	1-1	Smith	1000
18	2	Manchester U. Res.	0-4		
19	16	Port Vale	1-2	Kelly	
20	23	Crewe A.	6-1	Kelly, Brown(3), Hawksworth	
21	Feb 6	BRADFORD C. RES.	2-3	Kay, Smith	1000
22	16	PRESTON N.E. RES.	0-1		500
23	20	Blackburn R. Res.	2-1	Haynes, Rawlings	
24	24	Manchester C. Res.	1-1	Brown	4000
25	27	OLDHAM A. RES.	0-1		1400
26	Mar 6	BURY RES.	1-1	Brown	1000
27	13	Preston N.E. Res.	1-0	Kelly	
28	20	PORT VALE	1-2	Brown	1200
29	24	Bolton W. Res.	2-2	Kelly(2)	3000
30	27	Barnsley Res.	1-2	Kelly	1000
31	31	Bradford C. Res.	0-0		
32	Apr 3	BLACKPOOL RES.	7-1	Milne,Neave(4),Brown,Kelly	
33	5	Stockport Co. Res.	0-1		3000
34	10	Everton Res.	2-1	Hayes, Smith	
35	13	SOUTHPORT CENTRAL	1-0	Hawksworth	500
36	17	Oldham A. Res.	3-1	Brown(2), Southworth	2000
37	24	MANCHESTER U. RES.	0-0		1000
38	27	EVERTON RES.	2-2	Neave, Kelly	1000

Apps: 27 28 14 37 37 33 35 35 36 15 37 6 18 4 13 6 1 11 1 1 4 4 1 6 6 1 1
Goals: 1 7 1 4 12 21 1 6 1 5 1 1 1

Players: Biggar W., Barton J.W., Lilley R., Tully J., Neave R.A., Kay J.L., Rawlings A.J., Kelly W.B., Brown W., Anderson W.S., Smith A., Walker A., Milne C., Plumley W., Hawksworth E., Hayes J.V., Pickup P., Crossan D., Tattersall J., Towers, Haynes, Southworth T., Holt B., Caldwell A., Swann J.W., Rigg T., Fletcher H.

Abandoned

Date	Match	Score
Feb 13	Bradford C. Res.	0-0

FA. Cup

Rd	Date	Match	Score	Scorers	Att
Q4	Nov 21	STALYBRIDGE CELTIC	3-2	Kelly(3)	4000
Q5	Dec 5	HARTLEPOOL	2-0	Brown, Neave	2000
Q6	19	WATFORD	2-0	Kelly, Hawksworth	
R1	Jan 9	GILLINGHAM	2-0	Walker, Hawksworth	6000
R2	30	Oldham A.	0-3		18668

Lancashire Senior Cup

Rd	Date	Match	Score	Scorers	Att
R1	Sep 23	Fleetwood	3-2	Brown(2), Anderson	1000
R2	Oct 5	NELSON	3-2	Anderson, Brown, Tully	1000
R3	20	SOUTH LIVERPOOL	2-0	Kelly, Smith	1000
SF	Nov 9	Oldham A. *	2-0	Brown(2)	1500
F	Dec 7	Burnley +	1-4	Smith	2000

* Played at Bury   + Played at Hyde Road

Manchester Senior Cup

Rd	Date	Match	Score	Scorers	Att
R2	Mar 16	OLDHAM A.	2-0	Brown, Smith	
SF	Aor 19	Hurst	5-2	Hawksworth, Brown(3), Smith	
F	May 1	Stockport Co. *	3-4	Kelly(2), Hawksworth	6000

* Played at Hyde Road. a.e.t.

		P	W	D	L	F	A	Ps
1	Huddersfield Town Res.	38	27	6	5	90	39	59
2	Manchester City Res.	38	26	8	4	76	50	56
3	Port Vale	38	25	10	3	84	42	53
4	Burnley Res.	38	21	12	5	80	41	47
5	Stockport County Res.	38	18	12	8	66	57	44
6	Liverpool Res.	38	18	13	7	64	47	43
7	Bradford City Res.	38	18	13	7	66	55	43
8	Manchester Utd. Res.	38	14	14	10	59	47	38
9	ROCHDALE	38	12	13	13	63	50	37
10	Bolton Wanderers Res.	38	16	17	5	70	76	37
11	Bury Res.	38	13	16	9	59	66	35
12	Everton Res.	38	14	18	6	71	77	34
13	Preston N.E. Res.	38	11	16	11	49	56	33
14	Barnsley Res.	38	13	18	7	48	70	33
15	Crewe Alexandra	38	14	19	5	54	85	33
16	Oldham Athletic Res.	38	12	18	8	50	52	32
17	Blackburn Rovers Res.	38	14	20	4	71	87	32
18	Stalybridge Celtic	38	9	20	9	42	77	27
19	Southport Central	38	10	22	6	42	68	18
20	Blackpool Res.	38	7	4	27	35	95	18

No	Date	Opponent	Score	Scorers	Att	Swann J.W.	Barton J.W.	Caldwell A.	Anderson W.S.	Lee C.	Yarwood J.W.	Rawlings A.J.	Southworth T.	Walker A.	Hawksworth E.	Smith A.	Biggar W.	Tully J.	Swift H.	Neave R.A.	Kay G.	Kenyon J.	Brannick J.	Cuffe J.A.	Holt H.	Butler J.H.	Heap F.	Causer A.H.	Crossan D.	Challinor S.	Page T.	Barnett A.	Smith W.
1	Sep 4	Burnley	1-6	A.Smith	3000	1	2	3	4	5	6	7	8	9	10	11																	
2	11	SOUTHPORT CENTRAL	1-0	Neave			2	3	9			7		8	10	11	1	4	5	6													
3	18	Preston N.E.	2-1	Walker, A.Smith	1600		2	3			6	9		7	10	11	1	8	5		4												
4	25	OLDHAM A.	0-0		4000		2	3			6	7	9	8	10	11	1		5		4												
5	Oct 2	Stockport Co.	0-2		2500		2	3			6	7		8	10	11	1	9	5		4												
6	9	EVERTON	1-2	A.Smith	5000		2				6		8	7	10	11	1	4			5	9											
7	16	Liverpool	2-2	A.Smith, Kay	12000		2	3			6	7			10	11	1		5		4	9	8										
8	23	BOLTON W.	2-4	A.Smith(pen), Hawksworth	4000		2	3	9		6	7			10	11	1	4			5		8										
9	30	Bury	1-3	Hawksworth	4000		2	3			6	7		9	11	10	1	10	5		4		8										
10	Nov 6	MANCHESTER C.	0-2		4000		2				6			9	11	10	1	4			5	3	8	7									
11	13	Manchester U.	0-2		4000		2				6		9		10	11	1	4	5			3	8	7									
12	20	Stoke	1-1	Brannick			2	3			6				10	11	1		5		4	7	8	3									
13	27	BLACKPOOL	2-3	A.Smith(pen), Holt	4000		2				6			9	10	11	1				5		8	7	3								
14	Dec 4	BURNLEY	1-0	Heap	2000		2	3			6				10	11	1	4	5			7	8				7						
15	11	Southport Central	2-2	Hawksworth, Heap	1000	1	2	3			6	7			10	11			5		4		8				9						
16	18	PRESTON N.E.	2-4	Brannick(2)	1000		2	3	4	6		7				11			5				8				9	1					
17	25	Oldham A.	3-2	Walker, Heap, Brannick	4062		2	3			6	1		7	10	11			5				8				9						
18	Jan 1	STOCKPORT CO.	0-1		1500		2				6	7			10	11			5		4		8				9	1	3				
19	8	Everton	2-3	A.Smith, Heap	6000		2		6			4	7		10	11			5				8				9	1	3				
20	15	LIVERPOOL	3-1	Hawksworth(2), Heap	3000			3			6	7			10	11			5		6		8				9	1	3	4			
21	22	Bolton W.	0-3		3000		2				6	7			10	11					4		8				9	1	3	5			
22	29	BURY	2-1	Rawlings, Walker	4000		2		6			5	7	8		11					4		10				9	1	3				
23	Feb 5	Manchester C.	1-4	Heap	8000		2		6			5	7	10		11			4				8				9	1	3				
24	12	MANCHESTER U.	2-2	Swift(2)	3000		2				6	7	8		10	11		10	5								9	1	3	4			
25	19	Stoke	3-1	Page, Swift, Hawksworth	3000		2				6	7		9		11			5				8				9	1	3	4	10		
26	26	Blackpool	0-4		4000			2			6	7		9		11			5								10	1	3	4		8	
27	Mar 4	LEEDS C.	0-1		3000						6	7	8			11			5		4		3				9	1	2			10	
28	11	Bradford C.	0-5		500						6	7	8			11			5		4		3				9	1	2			10	
29	18	Bradford C.	4-3	Rawlings, Walker, Heap, W.Smith(p)	3000			3			6	7	8			11			5		4						9	1					10
30	25	Barnsley	1-0	Heap	2000			3			6	7	8	10		11			5		4						9	1	2				
31	Apr 1	Huddersfield T.	1-2	Hawksworth	4000			3			6	7	8	10		11			5		4						9	1	2				
32	8	Leeds C.	1-3	Walker	2000		2	3			6	7	8	10		11			5		4						9	1					
33	15	BRADFORD C.	3-0	Rawlings(2), Kay	3000		2				6	7	8	10		11			5		4						9	1	3				
34	21	HUDDERSFIELD T.	1-1	Kay	3000		2				6	7	8	10		11			5		4						9	1	3				
35	22	Bradford C.	2-5	Heap, Rawlings	3000		2				6	7	8	10		11			5		4						9	1	3				
36	29	BARNSLEY	2-1	Heap, Rawlings	2800		2	3			6	7	8	10		11			5		4						9	1					
		Apps.				2	29	27	2	3	34	27	4	23	25	36	10	27	11	1	27	3	17	5	5	3	23	20	16	5	1	3	1
		Goals										6		5	7	7		3	3	1	3		4		1		10			1		1

* Subsidiary tournament - Midland Section - Northern Division
Played: W.Brown(#1) (10 in 16/9 in 28), A.Turnbull (10 in 10)
W.Brown (#2)(3 in 6), P.Pickup (2 in 29/6 in 36)

	Principal Tournament	P	W	D	L	F	A	Pts
1	Manchester City	26	16	3	7	61	35	35
2	Burnley	26	14	5	7	71	43	33
3	Blackpool	26	14	3	9	54	41	31
4	Everton	25	15	0	10	59	42	30
5	Oldham Athletic	25	13	3	9	52	44	29
6	Liverpool	26	11	7	8	48	42	29
7	Stockport County	26	13	3	10	47	43	29
8	Stoke City	26	10	7	9	43	46	27
9	Southport Central	26	9	6	11	41	41	24
10	Bury	26	10	3	13	46	52	23
11	Manchester United	26	7	8	11	41	51	22
12	Bolton Wanderers	26	9	3	14	48	65	21
13	ROCHDALE	26	7	5	14	34	56	19
14	Preston N.E.	26	4	2	20	23	67	10

Oldham v Everton not played.

	Subsidiary Tournament	P	W	D	L	F	A	Pts
1	Leeds City	10	7	1	2	21	13	15
2	Bradford	10	6	0	4	27	17	12
3	Huddersfield Town	10	4	3	3	19	15	11
4	Bradford City	10	4	1	5	18	20	9
5	ROCHDALE	10	4	1	5	15	21	9
6	Barnsley	10	2	0	8	13	27	4

Back:
Walker, Yarwood, Lee, Barton, Causer, Heap, Hawksworth, Hayes(Sec.).

Front:
Rawlings, Caldwell, Brannick, Kay, Brown, Smith.

1916-17 Football League Lancashire Section

#	Date	Opponent	Score	Scorers	Att	1	2	3	4	5	6	7	8	9	10	11
						Causer	Anderson	Caldwell	Tully	Rigg	Tierney	Rawlings	Walker	Curtis	Halligan	Kehoe
1	Sep 2	Stockport Co.	0-3			Causer	Anderson	Caldwell	Tully	Rigg	Tierney	Rawlings	Walker	Curtis	Halligan	Kehoe
2	9	BURY	2-0	T.Page, OG	2000	"	Barton	Crossan	J.Page	"	"	"	"	T.Page	"	"
3	16	Stoke	1-1	Kehoe	6000	"	Weymess	Caldwell	"	Walters	"	"	Rigg	"	Turner	"
4	23	SOUTHPORT CENTRAL	1-1	Halligan	2000	"	J.Page	Crossan	Henderson	"	"	"	T.Page	Halligan	Thomas	"
5	30	Blackburn R.	1-6	Thomas	5000	"	Weymess	"	Walker	Tierney	Caldwell	"	"	Halligan	Thomas	"
6	Oct 7	MANCHESTER C.	2-2	T.Page(pen), Halligan	2000	"	Tyler	"	Tierney	Rigg	"	"	"	Halligan	Thomas	Walker
7	14	Everton	0-3		11000	"	Barton	"	J.Page	"	Tierney	"	Thomas	"	A.Smith	Roscoe
8	21	BLACKPOOL	4-1	Thomas(3), Halligan	2000	"	"	"	Tully	Frith	"	"	Walker	Thomas	Halligan	A.Smith
9	28	BOLTON W.	0-6		1000	"	Crossan	Caldwell	"	"	"	"	"	"	"	"
10	Nov 4	Port Vale	1-1	Tully		"	Anderson	"	Tierney	"	Walters	"	"	"	"	Tully
11	11	OLDHAM A.	4-1	Thomas, Halligan(2), Smith	3000	"	"	Henderson	Tully	Tierney	Caldwell	"	"	"	"	A.Smith
12	18	Preston N.E.	2-1	Halligan, Rawlings		"	Caldwell	Butterworth	"	Tully	"	"	"	"	"	"
13	25	BURNLEY	1-2	Halligan	1000	"	Millership	Caldwell	Tully	"	Butterworth	Walker	Rawlings	"	"	"
14	Dec 2	Manchester U.	1-1	Thomas	3000	"	"	Crossan	"	"	Yarwood	Rawlings	R.Smith	"	"	"
15	9	LIVERPOOL	3-2	Rawlings, Walker(2)	4000	"	Tierney	"	"	O'Connell	"	"	Walker	"	"	"
16	16	STOCKPORT CO.	4-0	Thomas(2), Halligan(2)	1000	Biggar	Millership	"	Tierney	"	Henderson	"	"	"	"	"
17	23	Bury	2-1	Smith, Crossan(pen)	1000	Causer	"	"	Tully	"	Tierney	"	"	"	"	"
18	30	STOKE	0-1		3000	Biggar	"	Hayes	Henderson	"	"	Walker	Tully	"	"	"
19	Jan 6	Southport Central	0-3		2000	"	"	Harrison	Tierney	"	Henderson	Rawlings	Meehan	"	"	"
20	13	BLACKBURN R.	3-0	Thomas(2), Meehan	2000	Causer	"	Crossan	Tully	"	Tierney	"	"	"	"	"
21	20	Manchester C.	1-2	Thomas	7000	"	"	"	"	"	"	"	"	"	"	"
22	27	EVERTON	2-1	Halligan, Meehan	2000	"	"	Henderson	"	"	"	"	"	"	"	"
23	Feb 3	Blackpool	2-0	Thomas, Halligan		"	"	"	Walker	"	"	"	"	"	"	"
24	10	Bolton W.	3-1	Walker(3)	1500	Biggar	"	Hayes	Litherland	"	Harrison	"	"	Walker	"	"
25	17	PORT VALE	1-3	Thomas	1000	"	"	Barton	Tully	"	Walker	"	"	Thomas	"	"
26	24	Oldham A.	0-1		3500	"	"	Hebden	"	"	"	"	"	"	"	"
27	Mar 3	PRESTON N.E.	1-2	Rawlings	2000	"	"	Hartley	Rigg	"	Butterworth	"	"	"	"	Walker
28	10	Burnley	3-4	Walker, Thomas, Halligan		"	"	Fielding	Poles	Rigg	Harrison	"	"	"	"	"
29	17	MANCHESTER U.	2-0	Meehan, Halligan	2000	"	"	Roberts	Tully	O'Connell	Broster	"	"	"	"	A.Smith
30	24	Liverpool	0-4			"	"	"	Rigg	"	"	"	"	"	"	"
31*	21	Bolton W.	1-0	Smith		Kay	"	Hebden	Henderson	Rawlings	Tully	Walkden	"	Walker	"	"
32*	Apr 6	Bury	2-0	Walker, Meehan	3000	"	"	"	Tully	O'Connell	Henderson	Rawlings	"	"	"	"
33*	7	OLDHAM A.	2-2	Halligan(2)	3000	"	"	"	"	Rigg	"	"	"	"	"	"
34*	9	Bury	3-2	Halligan(2), Rigg	2000	"	"	"	"	"	"	"	"	"	"	"
35*	14	BOLTON W.	5-1	Walker(4), Meehan	2000	"	"	"	"	"	"	"	"	"	"	"
36*	21	Oldham A.	2-1	Walker, Halligan		"	"	"	"	O'Connell	Tierney	"	"	"	"	"

* Subsidiary tournament

Friendlies

Date	Opponent	Score	Scorers	Att	1	2	3	4	5	6	7	8	9	10	11
Dec 25	OLDHAM A.	6-2	Halligan(2),Tully(3),O'Connell	1000	Biggar	Millership	Crossan	Tierney	O'Connell	Harrison	Henderson	Rigg	Tully	Halligan	A.Smith

	Principal Tournament	P	W	D	L	F	A	Pts
1	Liverpool	30	19	8	3	62	26	46
2	Stockport County	30	18	7	5	61	31	43
3	Stoke City	30	16	7	7	64	36	39
4	Manchester City	30	14	9	7	49	29	37
5	Everton	30	15	7	8	62	41	37
6	Burnley	30	15	4	11	73	56	34
7	Manchester United	30	13	6	11	48	54	33
8	Rochdale	30	12	5	13	47	54	29
9	Southport Central	30	10	8	12	40	43	28
10	Bolton Wanderers	30	9	6	15	59	65	24
11	Blackburn Rovers	30	10	4	16	52	66	24
12	Preston N.E.	30	8	7	15	47	65	23
13	Bury	30	7	8	15	40	63	22
14	Oldham Athletic	30	8	6	16	36	65	22
15	Port Vale	30	7	7	16	50	60	21
16	Blackpool	30	6	7	17	44	80	19

	Subsidiary Tournament	P	W	D	L	F	A	Pts
1	Rochdale	6	5	1	0	15	6	11
2	Everton	6	4	1	1	16	5	9
3	Burnley	6	4	1	1	14	9	9
4	Manchester United	6	4	0	2	15	9	8
5	Stockport County	6	2	3	1	6	10	7
6	Stoke City	6	3	0	3	11	6	6
7	Preston N.E.	6	2	2	2	8	7	6
8	Bolton Wanderers	6	3	0	3	12	12	6
9	Liverpool	6	2	1	3	13	10	5
10	Oldham Athletic	6	2	1	3	9	8	5
11	Blackpool	6	2	1	3	10	12	5
12	Port Vale	6	2	1	3	9	12	5
13	Manchester City	6	2	1	3	3	11	5
14	Blackburn Rovers	6	2	0	4	11	15	4
15	Southport Central	6	1	1	4	5	15	3

1917-18 Football League Lancashire Section

#	Date	Opponent	Res	Scorers	Att	1	2	3	4	5	6	7	8	9	10	11
1	Sep 1	BURNLEY	9-0	O'Connell,Flaherty(4),Halligan(4)	2000	T.Kay	Henderson	Crossan	Tully	O'Connell	Litherland	Rawlings	Walker	Flaherty	Halligan	Smith
2	8	Burnley	2-2	Flaherty, O'Connell	1200	"	Hayes	"	"	"	"	"	"	"	"	"
3	15	MANCHESTER U.	3-0	Halligan(2), Tully	3000	"	"	"	"	"	Henderson	"	"	Rigg	"	"
4	22	Manchester U.	1-1	Milligan	3000	"	"	"	Rigg	"	"	"	Litherland	Walker	"	"
5	29	SOUTHPORT CENTRAL	6-0	Walker,Halligan(2),Smith,Flaherty(2)	3000	"	"	"	"	"	"	Hunt	Walker	Flaherty	"	"
6	Oct 6	Southport Central	2-2	Walker, Halligan	1000	"	"	"	"	"	Tattersall	Somersgill	Henderson	Walker	"	"
7	13	STOCKPORT CO.	0-1		3000	"	"	"	"	"	Henderson	"	Tully	Annesley	"	"
8	20	Stockport Co.	0-2		2000	"	"	"	"	"	"	Capper	Howarth	Halligan	Perks	"
9	27	Oldham A.	1-2	Smith	1500	"	"	"	Bunting	"	Rigg	Somersgill	Johnson	Carruthers	Halligan	"
10	Nov 3	OLDHAM A.	1-0	Halligan(pen)	2000	"	"	"	"	"	"	Harding	"	Mitton	"	"
11	10	Bury	1-2	Halligan	2000	"	"	"	"	"	"	Jones	"	"	"	"
12	17	BURY	7-5	Mitton, Halligan(5), Smith	1500	Lee	"	"	"	Rigg	Tully	"	O'Connell	"	"	"
13	Dec 1	STOKE	0-0		15000	T.Kay	Millership	"	"	O'Connell	Rigg	"	Tully	T.Page	"	"
14	8	Liverpool	1-5	Page	12000	Lee	"	Hallas	"	"	"	"	"	"	"	"
15	15	LIVERPOOL	1-0	Page	4500	T.Kay	"	Crossan	"	Rigg	Tully	"	O'Connell	"	"	"
16	22	Blackpool	3-1	Sheldon(2), O'Connell	3000	R.Butterworth	"	Hayes	"	"	"	Sheldon	T.Page	Roberts	O'Connell	"
17	29	BLACKPOOL	6-3	Smith(2),OG,Johnson,Halligan,Sheldon	1000	T.Kay	"	"	Rigg	O'Connell	"	Johnson	T.Page	Halligan	"	"
18	Jan 5	Manchester C.	1-1	Page		"	Hayes	Henderson	"	"	"	Rawlings	Sheldon	"	"	"
19	12	MANCHESTER C.	1-4	Halligan	3000	"	Rigg	"	Bunting	"	"	Lloyd	"	"	"	"
20	19	BLACKBURN R.	6-0	Halligan(4), Page(2)	1500	"	Hayes	Hallas	Rigg	"	Milne	Jones	Tully	"	"	"
21	26	Blackburn R.	3-1	Halligan(3)		"	"	McDonald	Henderson	"	Rigg	"	Bunting	"	"	"
22	Feb 2	EVERTON	2-2	Sheldon, O'Connell	4000	"	McDonald	Hayes	"	"	"	"	Sheldon	Thomas	Flaherty	"
23	9	Everton	2-2	Thomas, Halligan		"	"	"	Rigg	"	Tully	Sheldon	Thomas	T.Page	Halligan	"
24	16	Port Vale	1-1	Page		Berry	"	"	"	"	Henderson	"	"	"	"	"
25	23	PORT VALE	2-0	Thomas, Page	2000	T.Kay	"	"	"	"	Tully	Goodwin	"	"	"	"
26	Mar 2	Bolton W.	1-1	Page	3000	"	"	"	"	"	Poles	"	"	"	"	Jones
27	9	BOLTON W.	5-2	Halligan(4), Goodwin	4000	"	"	"	"	"	Tully	"	"	"	"	Smith
28	16	Preston N.E.	4-3	Page(2), Halligan(2)		"	"	"	Tully	Rigg	Henderson	"	"	"	"	"
29	23	PRESTON N.E.	4-3	Smith,Thomas,Tully,Halligan	3000	"	Crossan	"	"	O'Connell	"	"	Bunting	Thomas	"	"
30*	29	OLDHAM A.	2-3	Thomas, Halligan	4000	"	Litherland	Hallas	Bunting	"	J.Kay	"	T.Page	"	"	"
31*	30	BURY	2-1	Thomas(2)	3000	"	Hayes	Crossan	"	"	"	Jones	"	"	"	Goodwin
32*	Apr 1	Oldham A.	0-1		4000	"	Henderson	"	"	"	"	"	Halligan	Stocks	Litherland	Smith
33*	6	Bury	4-1	Roberts(2), Page, O'Connell		R.Butterworth	Hayes	"	"	"	"	Goodwin	T.Page	Roberts	Halligan	"
34*	13	Bolton	1-2	Page		"	Henderson	"	"	Lennox	Duckworth	"	Roberts	T.Page	"	"
35*	20	BOLTON	4-0	Smith(2), Goodwin, Halligan		"	Hayes	"	"	"	Henderson	"	"	Duckworth	"	"
36#	27	Stoke	2-1	Goodwin, O'Connell	10000	"	Henderson	"	"	O'Connell	Duckworth	"	Meehan	Roberts	Tully	"

* Subsidiary Tournament.   # Principal Tournament.

Friendlies

Date	Opponent	Res	Scorers	Att	1	2	3	4	5	6	7	8	9	10	11
May 4	BURY	1-1	O'Connell	1500	R.Butterworth	West	Crossan	Bunting	O'Connell	Duckworth	Marshall	Halligan	Meehan	Henderson	Smith

Principal Tournament		P	W	D	L	F	A	Pts
1	Stoke City	30	22	4	4	109	27	48
2	Liverpool	30	21	6	3	101	26	48
3	Everton	30	19	6	5	92	36	44
4	ROCHDALE	30	15	9	6	78	47	39
5	Manchester City	30	15	8	7	57	28	38
6	Stockport County	30	17	3	10	59	32	37
7	Bolton Wanderers	30	13	4	13	68	70	30
8	Manchester United	30	11	8	11	45	49	30
9	Oldham Athletic	30	11	6	13	50	59	28
10	Preston North End	30	12	3	15	38	53	27
11	Port Vale	30	9	8	13	47	58	26
12	Blackpool	30	9	6	15	38	67	24
13	Southport Central	30	8	6	16	33	69	22
14	Bury	30	8	5	17	46	64	21
15	Burnley	30	4	5	21	29	100	13
16	Blackburn Rovers	30	2	1	27	22	127	5

Subsidiary Tournament		P	W	D	L	F	A	Pts
1	Liverpool	6	5	0	1	24	7	10
2	Everton	6	5	0	1	19	7	10
3	Manchester City	6	4	1	1	11	4	9
4	Preston North End	6	4	1	1	10	8	9
5	Blackpool	6	4	0	2	18	9	8
6	Bolton Wanderers	6	3	1	2	11	9	7
7	Oldham Athletic	6	3	1	2	9	9	7
8	Manchester United	6	3	1	2	6	7	7
9	Stoke City	6	2	2	2	10	5	6
10	ROCHDALE	6	3	0	3	13	8	6
11	Burnley	6	2	1	3	10	11	5
12	Bury	6	1	2	3	8	15	4
13	Stockport County	6	2	0	4	6	13	4
14	Port Vale	6	1	0	5	4	15	2
15	Blackburn Rovers	6	1	0	5	3	13	2
16	Southport Central	6	0	0	6	1	23	0

1918-19 Football League Lancashire Section

#	Date	Opponent	Score	Scorers	Att	1	2	3	4	5	6	7	8	9	10	11
1	Sep 7	Liverpool	0-4		15000	T.Kay	Gutteridge	Millership	Duckworth	O'Connell	Bunting	Goodwin	Thomason	Thomas	Halligan	A.Smith
2	14	LIVERPOOL	1-2	Thomas	1000	"	Hayes	Henderson	Bunting	"	Tully	"	"	"	"	"
3	21	Burnley	4-2	Bellis(2), Smith(2)		R.Butterworth	Henderson	Buckley	"	"	Duckworth	"	Bellis	"	"	"
4	28	BURNLEY	2-1	Halligan(2,1pen)	2000	T.Kay	"	Crossan	Buckley	"	"	"	Thomason	"	"	"
5	Oct 5	Stockport County	2-2	Thomas, Halligan	1500	"	"	"	Bunting	"	Buckley	"	Thomas	Bellis	"	"
6	12	STOCKPORT COUNTY	4-1	Halligan(3,1pen), Thomas	3000	"	Millership	"	"	"	Spruce	"	"	"	"	"
7	19	Southport Vulcan	3-3	Bunting, Goodwin, Thomas	1500	"	Hayes	"	"	Spruce	Buckley	"	"	"	O'Connell	"
8	26	SOUTHPORT VULCAN	5-2	Best, O'Connell,Smith,Thomas,Kelly	3000	"	Henderson	"	"	O'Connell	Spruce	"	"	P.Kelly	Best	"
9	Nov 2	MANCHESTER U.	1-3	Bunting	3000	"	"	"	"	"	"	"	"	Walker	Bellis	"
10	9	Manchester U.	1-0	Jackson	6000	"	"	"	"	"	"	"	J.Jackson	P.Kelly	Best	"
11	16	STOKE	3-2	Smith(2), Halligan	4500	"	"	"	J.Jackson	"	"	"	Best	"	Halligan	"
12	23	Stoke	1-1	Thomas	5000	"	"	Johnson	"	"	Turner	"	Thomas	Bellis	"	"
13	30	BURY	0-2		3000	"	"	"	"	"	Spruce	Donald	"	"	"	"
14	Dec 7	Bury	1-2	Halligan	4000	"	West	Tierney	"	"	"	Goodwin	"	J.Smith	"	"
15	14	BLACKPOOL	1-0	Smith	3000	"	"	McOwen	"	"	"	"	"	Best	"	"
16	21	Blackpool	1-5	Goodwin	3000	West	Barton	"	"	"	"	"	"	Halligan	Hawksworth	"
17	28	Oldham A.	1-0	Hawksworth	4000	T.Kay	"	"	Spruce	"	Halligan	"	"	Heap	"	"
18	Jan 11	Manchester C.	1-1	Smith	15000	"	"	"	"	"	"	"	"	Reynolds	Crawshaw	"
19	18	MANCHESTER C.	4-5	Thomas(2), O'Connell, Smith	6000	"	West	"	"	"	Tierney	"	"	Hibbert	Halligan	"
20	25	Port Vale	0-2		3000	"	Davenport	"	"	"	Rigg	Davies	W.Moody	Hawksworth	"	"
21	Feb 1	PORT VALE	2-0	Goodwin, Hawksworth	3000	"	"	Taylor	"	"	"	Goodwin	Halligan	Heap	Hawksworth	"
22	8	Bolton W.	2-3	Goodwin(2)	7000	"	"	Baines	"	"	"	"	"	"	"	"
23	15	BOLTON W.	2-2	Halligan, Hawksworth	6000	"	Chadwick	Jackson	Rigg	"	Yarwood	Spruce	"	"	"	"
24	22	PRESTON N.E.	1-2	Halligan	5000	"	Yarwood	Baines	Spruce	"	Rigg	Jones	"	"	"	"
25	Mar 1	Preston N.E.	1-2	Heap	5000	"	"	Lilley	"	Rigg	Yarwood	Davies	Ashworth	"	"	"
26	8	BLACKBURN R.	3-1	Halligan, Heap, Hawksworth	4500	"	Barton	"	Spruce	"	Rigg	Yarwood	Halligan	"	"	"
27	15	Blackburn R.	2-4	O'Connell, Thomas	12000	"	Nuttall	"	"	"	Yarwood	J.Butterworth	Thomas	"	Halligan	"
28	22	Everton	1-3	Heap	15000	"	Barton	Nuttall	Kelly	Spruce	"	Goodwin	"	"	Davies	Semple
29	29	EVERTON	1-3	Goodwin	7000	"	"	Baines	Spruce	O'Connell	"	"	Halligan	"	"	A.Smith
30*	Apr 5	Bury	3-0	Davies(2), Halligan	6000	"	Nuttall	"	"	"	"	"	Davies	"	Halligan	"
31*	12	BURY	0-2		3000	"	"	"	"	"	"	"	"	"	"	"
32*	18	OLDHAM A.	0-2		6000	Hampson	Millership	"	"	"	Broome	"	W.Moody	"	Yarwood	"
33*	19	Bolton W.	1-2	Goodwin	5000	H.Moody	Nuttall	"	"	"	Yarwood	"	"	H.Smith	Brown	"
34*	21	Oldham A.	0-5		10000	R.Butterworth	"	McCallum	J.Butterworth	"	"	"	"	"	"	"
35*	26	Bolton W.	1-2	Peart	7000	H.Moody	"	Hurst	Spruce	"	Hall	Kirkpatrick	Peart	Halligan	Yarwood	"
36	29	OLDHAM A.	5-0	Goodwin,Halligan(2),Smith,Stott	1000	"	"	"	"	"	Yarwood	Goodwin	W.Moody	Stott	Halligan	"

* Subsidiary Tournament (and Lancashire Cup Qualifying tournament)

	Principal Tournament	P	W	D	L	F	A	Pts
1	Everton	30	27	2	1	108	26	56
2	Stoke City	30	20	3	7	84	36	43
3	Liverpool	30	19	4	7	82	33	42
4	Bolton Wanderers	30	15	6	9	58	58	36
5	Manchester City	30	15	3	12	57	36	33
6	Southport Vulcan	30	15	3	12	49	53	33
7	Preston North End	30	12	6	12	41	51	30
8	Stockport County	30	11	7	12	48	52	29
9	Manchester United	30	11	5	14	51	50	27
10	ROCHDALE	30	11	5	14	56	61	27
11	Blackpool	30	10	5	15	45	61	25
12	Port Vale	30	10	4	16	39	77	24
13	Burnley	30	10	3	17	54	76	23
14	Bury	30	7	6	17	27	58	20
15	Oldham Athletic	30	7	4	19	39	62	18
16	Blackburn Rovers	30	5	4	21	35	83	14

	Lancashire Section - Subsidiary Tournament - Section B							
1	Oldham Athletic	6	5	0	1	17	4	10
2	Bolton Wanderers	6	5	0	1	16	9	10
3	ROCHDALE	6	1	0	5	5	13	2

1919-20 Central League

		Opponent	Score	Scorers	Att	1	2	3	4	5	6	7	8	9	10	11
1	Aug 30	STALYBRIDGE CELTIC	2-1	Eccles, Cooper	1000	Berry	Anderson	Higgins	Herring	Cooper	Tierney	Brindle	Eccles	Bellis	Jephcott	Lingard
2	Sep 2	CREWE A.	1-4	Cooper(pen)	1000	"	"	"	"	"	"	"	"	Brown	Newman	"
3	6	Southport	2-2	Eccles, Cooper	1500	"	Pickup	Wood	Milne	"	Greenhalgh	"	"	Tully	Ross	"
4	10	Crewe A.	0-2			"	"	"	Tully	Milne	"	Parry	"	Cooper	"	"
5	13	Blackpool Res.	0-3		3000	J.Stott	"	"	Greenhalgh	Cooper	Milne	"	"	Tully	Brown	"
6	20	BLACKPOOL RES.	2-1	Lingard, Milne	1000	Berry	"	J.Taylor	Milne	"	Greenhalgh	Kenyon	H.Butterworth	Eccles	Hales	"
7	27	Bolton W. Res.	1-7	Daniels		Sheldon	"	Wood	"	"	Tierney	"	"	Smith	Daniels	"
8	Oct 4	EVERTON RES.	2-0	Lingard, Walker	800	Berry	J.Taylor	"	"	"	"	Sheldon	Walker	"	"	"
9	11	Huddersfield T. Res.	0-3			J.Stott	"	"	"	"	"	Parry	Daniels	Walker	Eccles	"
10	18	OLDHAM A. RES.	1-3	Tierney	1500	"	Nuttall	"	"	"	"	Page	Walker	Oliver	Daniels	"
11	25	Manchester U. Res.	2-2	Cooper, Daniels		"	"	"	Meehan	Milne	"	Kenyon	Cooper	Makin	"	"
12	Nov 1	MANCHESTER U. RES.	3-2	Parry(2), Walker		"	"	"	"	"	"	Walker	Parry	"	"	"
13	8	Stalybridge Celtic	0-2		3000	Hurst	"	"	"	"	"	Lee	Walker	"	Tully	Daniels
14	15	BOLTON W. RES.	6-0	Walker(4), Lingard, Meehan		"	"	"	Tully	"	"	Challinor	Meehan	Walker	Lingard	"
15	Dec 13	Manchester C. Res.	1-4	Horridge	5000	"	"	"	"	"	"	Meehan	Horridge	"	Daniels	Lingard
16	25	Oldham A. Res.	2-4	Hesmondhalgh, Lingard		"	Tierney	Dixon	"	"	Tattersall	"	"	Hesmondhalgh	Lingard	Daniels
17	26	BURY RES.	4-4	Hesmondhalgh(2),Horridge,Milne		"	Nuttall	Wood	"	"	Tierney	"	"	"	Daniels	Lingard
18	27	Everton Res.	1-1	Tierney		"	"	Tully	Nuttall	Meehan	Wilkinson	Tattersall	Turner	Mills	"	Tierney
19	Jan 3	BRADFORD C. RES.	0-0			Plumley	Nuttall	Henderson	"	Milne	Tully	Mills	Walker	"	Mallalieu	Tierney
20	17	BLACKBURN R. RES.	0-1			Hurst	"	Wood	Tully	"	Tierney	"	Horridge	"	"	Lingard
21	24	Nelson	0-1			Horridge	"	"	"	"	"	Parry	Walker	"	"	"
22	31	ASTON VILLA RES.	0-1			Plumley	"	"	"	Horridge	"	Malkin	Mills	"	"	"
23	Feb 7	NELSON	3-0	Nuttall(en),Mills,Hermondhalgh		"	"	"	"	"	Tattersall	"	"	"	"	"
24	14	Tranmere R.	0-3		4500	Hurst	"	"	Meehan	Milne	Tierney	"	"	"	Walker	"
25	17	STOCKPORT CO. RES.	3-1	Hesmondhalgh(2), Lingard		"	"	J.Taylor	"	"	"	"	"	"	Daniels	"
26	21	PORT VALE RES.	3-3	Mills(2), Hesmondhalgh		"	J.Taylor	Bamford	"	"	Tully	"	"	"	Lingard	Daniels
27	28	LIVERPOOL RES.	1-0	Milne		"	Wood	Nuttall	Tully	"	Meehan	Wolfe	"	"	Mallalieu	"
28	Mar 4	Blackburn R. Res.	0-0			"	"	"	"	"	Tierney	Cam	"	"	Wolfe	"
29	6	BURNLEY RES.	1-1	Butterworth		"	"	"	"	"	"	Hesmondhalgh	Butterworth	Mallalieu	"	"
30	13	Burnley Res.	2-2	Mallalieu, Hesmondhalgh	3000	J.Stott	"	"	"	Davie	Milne	W.Taylor	Mills	Hesmondhalgh	"	"
31	18	Preston N.E. Res.	1-2	Mallalieu		Hurst	"	"	Meehan	"	W.Taylor	Hill	"	"	"	"
32	25	MANCHESTER C. RES.	2-0	Mills(2)		"	"	"	Tully	"	Meehan	Walker	"	W.Taylor	"	"
33	27	SOUTHPORT	1-0	Hesmondhalgh		"	"	"	"	Milne	"	"	"	Mallalieu	"	"
34	Apr 2	HUDDERSFIELD T. RES	3-4	Nuttall(pen), Walker, Mallalieu	1500	"	"	"	"	"	"	Kenyon	"	Walker	"	W.Taylor
35	3	TRANMERE R.	1-3	Mills		"	Tully	"	Eccles	"	"	Walker	"	Hesmondhalgh	"	Daniels
36	5	Stockport Co. Res.	2-0	Hesmondhalgh, Mills		"	Wood	"	Tully	"	"	"	"	"	"	"
37	6	Bury Res.	1-6	Mallalieu		"	"	"	"	"	"	"	"	"	"	"
38	10	PORT VALE RES.	1-5	Milne		J.Stott	Tully	"	Walker	"	Tierney	Parry	"	"	Malkin	Turner
39	14	Bradford C. Res.	2-1	OG, Parry		"	Wood	"	Tully	"	Davie	"	Walker	"	Mallalieu	"
40	17	PRESTON N.E. RES.	0-2			"	Tully	"	Meehan	"	"	Farnworth	"	F.Stott	"	"
41	24	Aston Villa Res.	1-6	Hesmondhalgh	14000	Hurst	Wood	"	Tully	"	Meehan	Walker	Malkin	Hesmondhalgh	Daniels	"
42	May 1	Liverpool Res.	1-1	Hesmondhalgh	4000	J.Stott	Bamford	Tully	Meehan	"	Davie	"	Eccles	"	Mallalieu	Daniels

F.A. Cup

		Opponent	Score	Scorers	Att	1	2	3	4	5	6	7	8	9	10	11
4Q	Nov 22	MONKS HALL	1-0	Daniels	1000	Hurst	Nuttall	Wood	Tully	Milne	Tierney	Challinor	Meehan	Walker	Lingard	Daniels
5Q	Dec 6	STALYBRIDGE CELTIC	1-0	Milne	2000	"	"	"	"	"	"	Walker	"	Horridge	"	"
6Q	20	South Liverpool	2-1	Milne, Walker	6000	"	"	Henderson	"	"	"	Meehan	Horridge	Walker	Daniels	Lingard
1	Jan 10	Arsenal	2-4	Mallalieu(2)	27000	"	"	Wood	"	"	"	Mills	"	"	Mallalieu	"

Lancashire Junior Cup

		Opponent	Score	Scorers		1	2	3	4	5	6	7	8	9	10	11
	Nov 29	Skelmersdale	0-1			Hurst	Nuttall	Bamford	Tully	Milne	Tierney	Challinor	Meehan	Walker	Lingard	Daniels

Manchester Cup

		Opponent	Score		Att	1	2	3	4	5	6	7	8	9	10	11
	Mar 30	MOSSLEY	0-1		1000	Hurst	Wood	Nuttall	Tully	Milne	Meehan	Walker	Mills	Hesmondhalgh	Mallalieu	W.Taylor

		P	W	D	L	F	A	Pts
1	Blackpool Res.	42	28	2	12	94	51	58
2	Aston Villa Res.	42	26	4	12	104	57	56
3	Crewe Alexandra	42	23	8	11	85	56	54
4	Tranmere Rovers	42	23	5	14	103	60	51
5	Preston N.E. Res.	42	21	9	12	104	65	51
6	Stalybridge Celtic	42	21	9	12	72	55	51
7	Manchester United Res.	42	21	5	16	86	79	47
8	Everton Res.	42	19	8	15	83	66	46
9	Blackburn Rovers Res.	42	18	6	18	79	82	42
10	Liverpool Res.	42	15	11	16	65	63	41
11	Bradford City Res.	42	17	7	18	78	77	41
12	Huddersfield Town Res.	42	16	8	18	69	73	40
13	Nelson	42	16	8	18	63	71	40
14	Port Vale Res.	42	16	7	19	67	69	39
15	Manchester City Res.	42	17	5	20	65	77	39
16	Southport	42	15	6	21	71	76	36
17	Oldham Athletic Res.	42	15	6	21	67	92	36
18	Burnley Res.	42	15	5	22	66	71	35
19	ROCHDALE	42	12	10	20	58	88	34
20	Bolton Wanderers Res.	42	13	8	21	61	106	34
21	Bury Res.	42	11	10	21	53	83	32
22	Stockport County Res.	42	8	5	29	43	123	21

1920-21 Central League

Central League

No	Date	Opponents	Result	Scorers	Att	Thorpe H.	Yarwood J.W.	Bamford W.	Broster J.	Davie J.	Bradshaw W.	Clifton W.	Byrom T.	Braithwaite F.	Mallalieu H.	Connor E.	Baines F.	Dennison H.	Ward W.	MacDonald	Taylor J.	Hill J.	Crabtree J.J.	Bamford T.	Hoade S.	Nuttall J.	Wilson J.	Lowe E.	Wilson T.	Turner L.	Tansey E.	Herbert J.H.	Collinge A.	Sandiford R.	Barnes J.
1	Aug 28	NELSON	1-3	Byrom	5000	1	2	3	4	5	6	7	8	9	10	11																			
2	Sep 4	Nelson	2-1	Dennison, Clifton		1	2		4	5	6	7	8			11	3	9	10																
3	7	STALYBRIDGE CELTIC	4-1	Byrom(2,1pen), Dennison(2)	4000	1	2		4	5	6	7	8			11	3	9	10																
4	11	BURNLEY RES.	0-1		4500	1	2		4	5	6	7	8			11	3	9	10																
5	18	Burnley Res.	4-3	Dennison, Byrom, Clifton, Ward			6		4	5		7	8			11	3	9	10	1	2														
6	20	Stalybridge Celtic	0-3				6		4	5			8			11	3	9	10	1	2	7												
7	25	SOUTHPORT	3-0	Dennison(2), Hoade	5000			3	4	5	6	7				11		9	10				1	2	8										
8	Oct 2	Southport	0-5				6		4	5		7	8		10	11		9					1	2		3								
9	9	Bradford C. Res.	3-0	Byrom(pen), Lowe, Dennison	4000		6		4			7	8			11	3	10					1			2	5	9							
10	16	BRADFORD C. RES.	2-3	Byrom(pen), Dennison			6		4			7	8			11	3	10					1			2	5	9							
11	23	Bolton W. Res.	2-1	Clifton, Byrom	10000		6		4			7	9			11	3	10					1		8	2	5								
12	26	BOLTON W. RES.	1-2	Hoade	4500		6		4			7	9			11	3	10					1		8	2	5								
13	Nov 6	Tranmere R.	1-6	Byrom	8000				4	6		7	10			11	3	9					1		8	2	5								
14	13	TRANMERE R.	3-1	Connor, Lowe(2)	3000		6		4				8			11	3	9					1		7	2	5	10							
15	17	Huddersfield T. Res.	3-1	Lowe(2), Hoade	500		6		4			7	9			11	3						1		8	2	5	10							
16	23	Blackpool Res.	1-2	Byrom					4		6		8			11	3	9					1		7	2	5	10							
17	Dec 11	EVERTON RES.	3-1	Dennison(2), Lowe	4000		6		4				8			11	3	9					1			2	5	10	7						
18	25	OLDHAM A. RES.	0-2		5000		6		4	7			8		10	11	3	9					1			2	5								
19	27	Oldham A. Res.	0-0		4000		6		4	5			8			11	3	9					1			2		10	7						
20	Jan 1	Blackburn R. Res.	2-2	Lowe, Broster			6		4	8						11	3	9					1		7	2	5	10							
21	15	PRESTON N.E. RES.	2-1	Broster, Wilson	3000		6		4						8	11							1		7	3	5			10					
22	18	HUDDERSFIELD T. RES.	0-3		1500		6		4	2							8			1					7	3	5	10		11					
23	22	Preston N.E. Res.	0-3		4000		6		4	8		7				11	3	9					1			2	5	10							
24	29	Crewe A.	0-3		6000	11			4	6			8		10		3	9					1		7	2	5								
25	Feb 5	CREWE A.	5-1	Lowe(2),Mallalieu,Dennison(2)	4000		6		4							11	3	9					1		8	2	5	10				7			
26	8	MANCHESTER C. RES.	1-1	Mallalieu	4000		6		4							11	3	9					1		8	2	5	10				7			
27	22	BLACKPOOL RES.	1-1	Herbert	4000		3		4	5						11		9					1		7	2		6				8	10		
28	26	BURY RES.	2-1	Mallalieu, Herbert	3000		6		4	5						11		9			3		1		7	2						8	10		
29	Mar 5	Bury Res.	2-1	Herbert, Yarwood			6		4	5		7				11	3						1		8	2		10				9			
30	8	BLACKBURN R. RES.	0-3		2500		6		4	5						11	3						1		8	2		9	7			10			
31	12	STOCKPORT CO. RES.	3-1	Clifton, Collinge, Dennison			5		4			7			8	11	3	9					1			2							10		
32	19	Stockport Co. Res.	0-0				5		4						8	11	3	9			6		1		7	2						10		
33	26	Manchester U. Res.	2-1	Dennison(2)	6000		5		4							11	3	9			6		1		7	2							10	8	
34	28	Manchester C. Res.	0-2				5		4							11	3	9			6		1		7	2						10	8	
35	Apr 2	MANCHESTER U. RES.	3-1	Dennison(3)	6000		5		4			7				11	3	9					1			2							10	8	5
36	11	Aston Villa Res.	0-5		4000		6		4			7					3									2		10		11			8		5
37	16	ASTON VILLA RES.	1-0	Sandiford	5000		3		4			7				11		9			6		1			2							10	8	5
38	20	Everton Res.	0-1		4000		3			6		7			8						4		1			2		9		11			10	8	5
39	23	Liverpool Res.	2-0	Collinge, Dennison			5		6							11	3	9			1				7	2							10	8	
40	30	LIVERPOOL RES.	3-0	Dennison(3)	4000	1	3		4							11		9			6					2						7	10	8	5
41	May 2	Port Vale Res.	0-5												4	3		9						2						7	5	6	10	8		2
42	7	PORT VALE RES.	1-2	Herbert	2000	1			6			7				11							4		8	2	5					9	10		

Played: T.Nuttall (2 in 21), Thornley (9 in 21 & 22), Lund (1 in 36), Clutton (9 in 36), Stansfield (1 in 41), Bussey (11 in 41)

Apps. Thorpe H. 6, Yarwood J.W. 39, Bamford W. 1, Broster J. 37, Davie J. 22, Bradshaw W. 5, Clifton W. 20, Byrom T. 18, Braithwaite F. 1, Mallalieu H. 19, Connor E. 28, Baines F. 31, Dennison H. 29, Ward W. 10, MacDonald 4, Taylor J. 5, Hill J. 11, Crabtree J.J. 30, Bamford T. 2, Hoade S. 22, Nuttall J. 34, Wilson J. 19, Lowe E. 18, Wilson T. 2, Turner L. 4, Tansey E. 2, Herbert J.H. 8, Collinge A. 13, Sandiford R. 7, Barnes J. 7

Goals Yarwood 1, Broster 2, Clifton 4, Byrom 9, Mallalieu 3, Connor 1, Dennison 22, Ward 1, Hoade 3, Wilson J. 1, Lowe 9, Herbert 4, Collinge 2, Sandiford 1

FA. Cup

Rd	Date	Opponents	Result	Scorers	Att
Q4	Nov 20	FLEETWOOD	1-0	Connor	3000
Q5	Dec 4	TRANMERE R.	1-0	Dennison	3000
Q6	18	Coventry C.	1-1	Lowe	18000
Q6r	21	COVENTRY C.	2-1	Lowe, Byrom(pen)	9000
R1	Jan 8	Plymouth A.	0-2		24287

Manchester Senior Cup

	Date	Opponents	Result	Scorers	Att
	Mar 21	Oldham A.	4-4	Collinge(2), Sandiford(2)	
	Apr 5	OLDHAM A.	4-3	Dennison(3), Sandiford	2500
	18	Ashton National	1-1	Collinge	3000
	25	ASHTON NATIONAL	3-0	Collinge, Dennison, Clifton	4000
SF	May 5	Manchester U.	0-2		1000

Lancashire Junior Cup

Date	Opponents	Result	Scorers	Att
Sep 16	Eccles U.	1-3	T.Wilson	5000

Played: J.H.Doxford (2), A.Walker (3), J.Crompton (9)

Friendlies

Date	Opponents	Result	Scorers
Feb 12	Darlington	3-3	Dennison(2), Collinge
19	Oldham A.	5-5	Hoade, Dennison(2), Herbert(2)

Played: E.Fuller(2), Bussey(11) v Oldham

Final Table

		P	W	D	L	F	A	Pts
1	Manchester United Res.	42	26	5	11	102	57	57
2	Crewe Alexandra	42	23	7	12	92	57	53
3	Bolton Wanderers Res.	42	22	8	12	71	58	52
4	Aston Villa Res.	42	22	7	13	101	52	51
5	Preston N.E. Res.	42	21	8	13	76	55	50
6	Oldham Athletic Res.	42	21	8	13	56	54	50
7	Tranmere Rovers	42	21	7	14	87	63	49
8	Everton Res.	42	21	6	15	85	74	48
9	Burnley Res.	42	18	7	17	84	73	43
10	ROCHDALE	42	19	5	18	63	73	43
11	Manchester City Res.	42	12	18	12	62	57	42
12	Blackburn Rovers Res.	42	14	14	14	73	69	42
13	Stalybridge Celtic	42	16	9	17	73	74	41
14	Huddersfield Town Res.	42	17	7	18	55	58	41
15	Liverpool Res.	42	16	8	18	72	65	40
16	Blackpool Res.	42	15	9	18	59	62	39
17	Nelson	42	14	9	19	71	70	37
18	Southport	42	13	6	23	68	98	32
19	Bradfrod City Res.	42	12	7	23	49	89	31
20	Port Vale	42	10	11	21	40	73	31
21	Stockport County Res.	42	10	10	22	45	117	30
22	Bury Res.	42	5	12	25	46	82	22

1921/22 20th in Division 3(N)

#	Date		Opponent	Score	Scorers	Att
1	Aug	27	ACCRINGTON STANLEY	6-3	Owens 3, Dennison 2, Carney(p)	7000
2	Sep	3	Accrington Stanley	0-4		11000
3		10	HALIFAX TOWN	3-3	Hill, Dennison, Carney (p)	8000
4		17	Halifax Town	1-1	Collinge	10000
5		24	SOUTHPORT	0-1		6000
6	Oct	1	Southport	1-2	Sandiford	6000
7		8	TRANMERE ROVERS	2-1	Herbert 2	5000
8		15	Tranmere Rovers	0-7		6000
9		22	STOCKPORT COUNTY	0-1		3000
10		29	Stockport County	0-3		10000
11	Nov	5	STALYBRIDGE CELTIC	2-1	Hoad 2 (1p)	5000
12		12	Stalybridge Celtic	0-1		6000
13		19	GRIMSBY TOWN	0-2		5000
14		26	Grimsby Town	0-3		8000
15	Dec	10	Wigan Borough	2-3	Dennison 2 (1p)	5000
16		24	WALSALL	7-0	Owens 3, Dennison 2 (2p), Dani…	5000
17		26	Crewe Alexandra	0-2		
18		27	CREWE ALEXANDRA	2-0	Dennison 2	
19		31	Hartlepools United	3-5	Sandiford, Owens, Herbert	7000
20	Jan	14	HARTLEPOOLS UNITED	0-1		
21		21	Darlington	1-2	Herbert	2000
22		28	DARLINGTON	0-2		4000
23	Feb	4	LINCOLN CITY	0-2		
24		11	Lincoln City	2-1	Dennison, Greaves (og)	
25		18	Ashington	3-7	Dennison 2, Carney	3000
26		25	ASHINGTON	2-1	Dennison, Hoyle	3000
27	Mar	4	BARROW	0-1		3000
28		11	Barrow	0-1		5250
29		18	DURHAM CITY	1-0	Dennison	4000
30		25	Durham City	2-0	Hill 2	1500
31	Apr	1	WREXHAM	3-0	Hill 2, Carney	4000
32		8	Wrexham	1-1	Hill	3000
33		14	WIGAN BOROUGH	4-2	Carney 2, Dennison, Hill	3000
34		15	NELSON	2-2	Dennison 2	3000
35		18	Walsall	0-4		5000
36		22	Nelson	1-4	Hill	
37		29	CHESTERFIELD	0-1		3000
38	May	6	Chesterfield	1-2	Cameron	6000

Played in games 6 and 7: SW McGhee (11). In game 9: T Catlow (4).
Played in games 27 and 28: H Foster (7).
Played in 4 games, 35 to 38: AG Hinchliffe (5)

Player appearances

#	Crabtree JI	Nuttall J	Shehan WJ	Hill JW	Farrer P	Yarwood JW	Hoad SJ	Sandiford R	Dennison H	Owens JR	Carney EF	Collinge A	Mort T	Barnes J	Clark H	Broster J	Wolstencroft A	Whiteside E	Mallalieu H	Sneyd W	Tully J	Herbert JH	Barton JW	Taylor Fred	Clifton W	Burns H	Bennett TS	Daniels G	Cameron H	Hoyle G
1	1	2	3	4	5	6	7	8	9	10	11																			
2	1	2		4		6	7	8	9	10	11		3	5																
3	1	2	6		5		7		9		11	10	3		4		8													
4	1	2		4			7	8	9			10	3	5					6	11										
5	1	2		4			7	8	9			10	3	5					6	11										
6		2		4				8	9			10	3					5			1	6	7							
7	1	2		6	5		7	8	9				3									4	10							
8	1			4	5		7	8		10			3							11		6	9	2						
9	1	2		10				8			11		3									6	9		5	7				
10	1	2						8	9		11	10	3									6			5	7	4			
11	1	2				6	7	8			11		3									4	10		5	9				
12	1	2		4			7	8			11		3									6	10		5	9				
13	1	2					7				10		3									6	8		5		4	9	11	
14	1			4			7	8		10			3									6	2		5			9	11	
15	1			6					10	8												4	2	7	5			9	11	
16	1	2					7		9	8			3									6			5		4	11	10	
17	1	3		10			7		9	8			6									2	4		5				11	
18	1	3					7		9	8			6									2	4		5			11	10	
19	1	5						8	9				3									6	7	2	4			11	10	
20		2			5		7	10	9	8			3								1		4		6			11		
21		2			5			8	9				3								1	6	10		4	7		11		
22		2			5			8	9				3									6	10		4	7		11		
23	1	2		4				8	9				3									6			5	7		11	10	
24	1	3						8	9				5									6	7	2	4			11	10	
25	1	3						8	9				5									6	7	2	4			11	10	
26	1	2			5			8			10		3									6	7		4			11		9
27	1	2		6	5			8			10		3												4			11		9
28	1			8	5								3									6		2	4			11	10	9
29	1			8					10				3									6	2	4	7	5		11		9
30	1			8	4			9	10				3									6	2		7	5		11		
31	1			8	4			9	10				3									6	2		7	5		11		
32	1			8	4			9	10				3									6	2		7	5		11		
33	1	3		8	4			9	10													6	2		7	5		11		
34	1	3		8	4				9	10												6	2		7	5		11		
35	1	3		8	4				10													6	7	2				11		
36	1	3		8	4				9		10											6		2	7			11		
37	1	3		8	4				10													6	7	2				11		9
38		3		8	4				10		6										1	7	2					11		9
Apps	34	30	1	25	12	11	17	12	33	14	10	10	28	3	1	1	1	3	3	4	31	16	19	19	13	15	3	26	11	3
Goals				8			2	2	17	7	6	1										4					1		2	1

One own goal

F.A. Cup

	Date		Opponent	Score	Scorers		Crabtree			Hill		Yarwood	Hoad			Owens											Herbert	Barton	Taylor			Bennett	Daniels	Cameron	Hoyle
Q5	Dec	3	Nelson	2-3	Dennison, Bennett		1			6		5	7			10		3								4	8	2			9	11		

Lancashire Senior Cup

	Date		Opponent	Score	Att
R1	Sep	14	Stockport County	0-2	2000

Line-up: 1 2 6 5 7 9 11 10 3 4 8

Manchester Cup

	Date		Opponent	Score	Scorers	Att
	Feb	28	Bolton Wanderers	1-2	Hoyle	3000

Line-up: 1 2 6 5 8 3 4 7 11 10 9

Division 3 (N) Final Table

		P	W	D	L	F	A	W	D	L	F	A	Pts
1	Stockport County	38	13	5	1	36	10	11	3	5	24	11	56
2	Darlington	38	15	2	2	52	7	7	4	8	29	30	50
3	Grimsby Town	38	15	4	0	54	15	6	4	9	18	32	50
4	Hartlepools United	38	10	6	3	33	11	7	2	10	19	28	42
5	Accrington Stanley	38	15	1	3	50	15	4	2	13	23	42	41
6	Crewe Alexandra	38	13	1	5	39	21	5	4	10	21	35	41
7	Stalybridge Celtic	38	14	3	2	42	15	4	2	13	20	48	41
8	Walsall	38	15	2	2	52	17	3	1	15	14	48	39
9	Southport	38	11	6	2	39	12	3	4	12	16	32	38
10	Ashington	38	13	2	4	42	22	4	2	13	17	44	38
11	Durham City	38	14	0	5	43	20	3	3	13	25	47	37
12	Wrexham	38	12	4	3	40	17	2	5	12	11	39	37
13	Chesterfield	38	12	2	5	33	15	4	1	14	15	52	35
14	Lincoln City	38	11	2	6	32	20	3	4	12	16	39	34
15	Barrow	38	11	2	6	29	18	3	3	13	13	36	33
16	Nelson	38	7	6	6	27	23	6	1	12	21	43	33
17	Wigan Borough	38	9	4	6	32	28	2	5	12	14	44	31
18	Tranmere Rovers	38	7	5	7	41	25	2	6	11	10	36	29
19	Halifax Town	38	9	4	4	36	37	1	5	13	19	48	29
20	ROCHDALE	38	9	2	8	34	24	2	2	15	18	53	26

1922/23 12th in Division 3(N)

#	Date		Opponent	Score	Scorers	Att	Crabtree JJ	Bradbury W	Charlton S	Tully J	Parkes D	Jones R	Nicholls GJ	Sandham W	Guy G	Gee A	Wall G	Campbell JL	Hill JW	Foweather V	Broster J	Nuttall J	Moody WA	Walters J	Moody JH	Daniels G	Hinchliffe AG	Prowse WH	Brown, John	Chapman J	Peart JG	Milne C
1	Aug	26	Crewe Alexandra	1-0	Guy	5000	1	2	3	4	5	6	7	8	9	10	11															
2	Sep	2	CREWE ALEXANDRA	1-1	Guy	8000	1	2	3	4	5	6	7	8	9	10	11															
3		9	Lincoln City	1-0	Gee	5000	1	2	3	4	5	6		8	9	10	11	7														
4		16	LINCOLN CITY	1-1	Sandham	10000	1	2	3	4	5	6		8	9	10	11	7														
5		23	WREXHAM	5-0	Guy 4, Gee	5000	1	2	3		5	6		8	9	10	11	7	4													
6		30	Wrexham	1-3	Wall	6000	1	2	3		5	6			9	10	11	7	4	8												
7	Oct	7	DARLINGTON	2-2	Parkes 2	8000	1	2	3		5	6				10	11	7	9	8	4											
8		14	Walsall	0-0		7000	1		3		5	6			9	10	11	7	4	8		2										
9		21	Grimsby Town	1-1	Sandham	8000	1		3	4	5	6		8	9		11	7				2	10									
10		28	GRIMSBY TOWN	0-1		9000	1	4	3		5	6		8	9		11	7				2	10									
11	Nov	4	Hartlepools United	2-0	Crabtree 2	4000	10	2	3		5	6		9			11	7	4			8	1									
12		11	HARTLEPOOLS UNITED	4-0	Walters 2, Sandham 2	6000	1	2	3		5	6		9			11	7	4			8	10									
13		25	Nelson	2-1	Hill, Walters	6000	1		3		5	6		8			11	7	9			2	10	4								
14	Dec	4	TRANMERE ROVERS	0-0		3000	1		3		5	6		8			11	7	9			2	10	4								
15		23	SOUTHPORT	3-2	Prowse 2, Tootle (og)	3000	1		3		5	6	7		9		11					2	10	4	8							
16		25	Southport	1-0	Hill		1		3		5	6	7		9		11		10			2		4	8							
17		26	Chesterfield	0-4		6000	1		3		5	6			9		11	7				2	10	4	8							
18		30	ASHINGTON	2-0	Guy, Campbell	3000	1		3		5	6			8	9		7				2	10	11	4							
19	Jan	2	Darlington	1-1	Sandham	3000			3		5	6	7	8								2	10	1	11	4	9					
20		6	Ashington	0-2		4000			3		5	6	7					11				2	10	1		4	8					
21		13	NELSON	0-3		6000	1		3		5	6		8			11	7	9			2	10		4							
22		20	BARROW	3-1	Walters 2, Parkes	4000	1		3	6	5	9	7	8								2	10		11	4						
23		27	Barrow	1-4		3000	1		3		5	6		8			11	7				2	10		4		9					
24	Feb	3	Accrington Stanley	1-2	Sandham	6000	1		3	6	5	9	7	8								2	10		11	4						
25		10	ACCRINGTON STANLEY	1-1	Foweather	4000		2	3		5	6		8					7	9			10	1	11	4						
26		24	WALSALL	0-2		4000	1	2	3	8	5	6	7	9			11						10			4						
27	Mar	3	Halifax Town	0-1		8000			3			6	7		9		11					2	10	1		4	8	5				
28		10	HALIFAX TOWN	0-1		6000			3		5	6	7				11					2	10	1		4	8		9			
29		17	BRADFORD PARK AVE.	0-3		5000			3		6	5			7	8	11					2	10	1		4			9			
30		24	Bradford Park Avenue	0-3		8000			3			6					11	7	10			2	8	1		4		5	9			
31		30	CHESTERFIELD	0-2					3		5			9				7	8			2		1	11	4		10	6		
32	Apr	2	Stalybridge Celtic	0-0			1		3		5	6		7					8		4	2			11	6	10			9	
33		3	STALYBRIDGE CELTIC	2-0	Hill, Prowse				3		5	6	7						8		4	2			1	11	10			9	
34		7	Tranmere Rovers	0-2		7000			3		5	6	7				11		8		4	2			1		10			9	
35		14	DURHAM CITY	2-0	Peart 2	3000			3		5		7				11		8		4	2		10	1		6			9	
36		21	Durham City	1-1	Peart				3		5						11	7	8		4	2		10	1		6			9	
37		28	WIGAN BOROUGH	3-2	Walters, Prowse, Peart	4000			3		5						11	7	8		4	2		10	1		6	8		9	
38	May	5	Wigan Borough	0-6		6000			3			6	7	8			11		9		4	2		10	1				5		
					Apps		24	12	38	9	35	32	17	22	15	8	30	21	18	4	8	27	1	24	15	9	22	11	2	5	9	
					Goals		2				3			7	7	2	1	1	3	1				6				4			4	

One own goal

F.A. Cup

	Date		Opponent	Score	Scorers	Att	Crabtree JJ	Bradbury W	Charlton S	Tully J	Parkes D	Jones R	Nicholls GJ	Sandham W	Guy G	Gee A	Wall G	Campbell JL	Hill JW	Foweather V	Broster J	Nuttall J	Moody WA	Walters J	Moody JH
Q4	Nov	18	NELSON	0-1		10000	1	2	3		5	6		9			11	7	4					8	10

Lancashire Senior Cup

	Date		Opponent	Score	Scorers	Att	Crabtree JJ	Bradbury W	Charlton S	Tully J	Parkes D	Jones R	Nicholls GJ	Sandham W	Guy G	Gee A	Wall G	Campbell JL	Hill JW	Foweather V	Broster J	Nuttall J	Moody WA	Walters J	Milne C
PR	Aug	30	Accrington	2-1	Guy, Gee	7000	1	2	3	4		6	7	8	9	10	11								5
PR	Sep	12	MANCHESTER U.	1-0	Sandham	5000	1	2	3	4	5	6		8	9	10	11	7							
PR	Oct	2	Stockport Co.	2-2	Campbell, Gee	5000	1	2	3		5	6			10	11	7	9	8	4					
PRr		10	STOCKPORT CO.	0-0		3000		2	3		5	6		9	10	11	7	4	8			1			
PRr2		18	Stockport Co.*	1-4	Guy	3000	1		3		5	6	7	8	9	10	11		4				2		

* Played at Hyde Road

Manchester Cup

	Date		Opponent	Score	Scorers	Att	Bradbury W	Charlton S	Tully J	Parkes D	Jones R	Nicholls GJ	Sandham W	Wall G	Nuttall J	Moody WA	Walters J	Prowse WH	Peart JG
	Feb	13	Oldham A.	1-1	Walters	2000	2	3		5	6	7	8	11		10	1	4	9
		20	OLDHAM A.	1-3	Sandham		2		8	5	6	7	9	11	3	10	1	4	

		P	W	D	L	F	A	W	D	L	F	A	Pts
1	Nelson	38	15	2	2	37	10	9	1	9	24	31	51
2	Bradford Park Ave.	38	14	4	1	51	15	5	5	9	16	23	47
3	Walsall	38	13	4	2	32	14	6	4	9	19	30	46
4	Chesterfield	38	13	5	1	49	18	6	2	11	19	34	45
5	Wigan Borough	38	14	3	2	45	14	4	5	10	19	28	44
6	Crewe Alexandra	38	13	3	3	32	9	4	6	9	16	29	43
7	Halifax Town	38	11	4	4	29	14	6	3	10	24	32	41
8	Accrington Stanley	38	14	2	3	40	21	3	5	11	19	44	41
9	Darlington	38	13	3	3	43	14	2	7	10	16	32	40
10	Wrexham	38	13	5	1	29	12	1	5	13	9	36	38
11	Stalybridge Celtic	38	13	2	4	32	18	2	4	13	10	29	36
12	ROCHDALE	38	8	5	6	29	22	5	5	9	13	31	36
13	Lincoln City	38	9	7	3	21	11	4	3	12	18	44	36
14	Grimsby Town	38	10	3	6	35	18	4	2	13	20	34	33
15	Hartlepools United	38	10	6	3	34	14	0	6	13	14	40	32
16	Tranmere Rovers	38	11	4	4	41	21	1	4	14	8	38	32
17	Southport	38	11	3	5	21	12	1	4	14	11	34	31
18	Barrow	38	11	2	6	31	17	2	2	15	19	43	30
19	Ashington	38	10	3	6	34	33	1	5	13	17	44	30
20	Durham City	38	7	9	3	31	19	2	1	16	12	40	28

1923/24 2nd in Division 3(N)

#	Date	Opponent	Score	Scorers	Att	Moody JH	Bissett JT	Brown WJ	Willis RS	Parkes D	Crowe FR	Tompkinson WV	Prouse WHO	Whitehurst AJ	Pearson AV	Clark JW	Campbell JL	Peart JG	McGarry AM	Nuttall J	Smith A	Watson E	Hall J	Sandiford R	Hibberd CM
1	Aug 25	DURHAM CITY	2-0	Tompkinson, Prouse	6000	1	2	3	4	5	6	7	8	9	10	11									
2	27	Wigan Borough	0-3		15000	1	2	3	4	5	6	7	8	9	10	11									
3	Sep 1	Durham City	0-0		4000	1	2	3	4	5	6	11	8		10			7	9						
4	3	WIGAN BOROUGH	1-0	Prouse	8000	1	2	3	4	5	10	11	8					7	9	6					
5	8	Bradford Park Avenue	2-4	Whitehurst 2	8000	1	2	3	4	5	10	11	8	9				7		6					
6	15	BRADFORD PARK AVE.	3-0	Crowe 2, Peart	7000	1	2	3	4	5	10	7	8			11		9	6						
7	22	Chesterfield	1-1	Prouse	9700	1	2	3	4	5	10	7	8			11		9	6						
8	29	CHESTERFIELD	3-0	Crowe 2, Whitehurst	8000	1	2	3	4	5	10	7	8	9		11			6						
9	Oct 6	Rotherham County	0-0		8000	1	2	3	4	5	10	7	8	9		11			6						
10	13	ROTHERHAM COUNTY	1-0	Whitehurst	8000	1	2	3	4	5	10	7	8	9		11			6						
11	20	Wrexham	1-1	Peart	4700	1	2		4	5			8	10	11		7	9	6		3				
12	27	WREXHAM	0-0		7000	1	2	3	4	5		7	8		10	11		9	6						
13	Nov 3	Doncaster Rovers	0-0		7000	1	2	3	4	5	10	7	8	9		11			6						
14	10	DONCASTER ROVERS	2-0	Prouse, Bissett (p)	6500	1	2	3	4	5	10	7	8	9		11			6						
15	24	Darlington	2-2	Peart, Tompkinson	5800	1	2	3	4	5	10	7	8			11		9	6						
16	Dec 8	Southport	1-0	Pearson	5000	1	2	3	4	5		7	8	9	10				6		11				
17	15	BARROW	3-1	Whitehurst 2, Pearson	5000	1	2	3	4	5		7	8	9	10				6		11				
18	22	Barrow	2-1	Peart, Prouse	2000	1	2	3		5		7	8		10			9	6		11	4			
19	25	Lincoln City	2-0	Peart, Pearson	7000	1	2	3	4	5		7	8		10			9	6		11				
20	26	LINCOLN CITY	1-0	Whitehurst	8000	1	2	3	4	5		7	8	9	10				6		11				
21	29	CREWE ALEXANDRA	1-0	Willis	5000	1	2	3	4	5		7	8	9	10				6		11				
22	Jan 5	Crewe Alexandra	2-0	Prouse, Parkes	6000	1	2	3	4	5		7	8	9	10				6		11				
23	8	SOUTHPORT	2-2	Whitehurst 2 (1p)	2000	1	2	3	4	5		11	8	9	10		7		6						
24	12	HARTLEPOOLS UNITED	1-0	Prouse	4000	1	2	3	4	5		7	8	9		11			6				10		
25	19	ASHINGTON	1-0	Bissett (p)	6000	1	2	3	4	5		7	8	9	10				6		11				
26	26	Ashington	0-1		5500	1	2	3	4	5	10	7	8	9		11			6						
27	Feb 2	WALSALL	1-0	Pearson	5000	1	2	3	4	5		7	8	9	10	11			6						
28	9	Walsall	1-0	Tompkinson	5000	1	2	3	4	5		7	8	9		11			6					10	
29	16	WOLVERHAMPTON W.	0-0		16161	1	2	3	4	5		7	8	9	10	11			6						
30	Mar 1	NEW BRIGHTON	6-2	Pearson, Whitehurst 3, Prouse, Tompkinson	3000	1	2	3	4	5		7	8	9	10	11			6						
31	8	New Brighton	1-1	Peart	7000	1	2	3	4	5		7	8	10	11			9	6						
32	15	Grimsby Town	0-1		7000	1	2	3	4	5		7	8	10	11			9	6						
33	22	GRIMSBY TOWN	4-2	McGarry, Whitehurst, Clarke, Sandiford	5000	1	2	3	4	5		7	8	9		11			6					10	
34	26	Wolverhampton Wan.	0-0		12000	1	2	3	4	5		7	8	9	10	11			6						
35	29	Halifax Town	1-0	Prouse	4000	1	2	3	4	5		7	8	9	10	11			6						
36	Apr 5	HALIFAX TOWN	3-0	Prouse, Whitehurst, Pearson	6000	1	2	3	4	5		7	8	9	10	11			6						
37	12	Hartlepools United	2-1	Prouse, Bissett (p)	5000	1	2		4	5			8	9	10	11	7		6		3				
38	18	DARLINGTON	0-0		6000	1	2	3	4	5		7	8	9	10	11			6						
39	22	TRANMERE ROVERS	1-0	Crowe	5000		2	3	4	5	10		8	9	11				6		7				1
40	26	Accrington Stanley	1-0	Pearson	6000	1	2	3	4	5	10		8	9	11				6		7				
41	28	Tranmere Rovers	1-2		8000		2	3	4	5		7	8	9					6		11				1
42	May 3	ACCRINGTON STANLEY	4-1	Tompkinson 2, Prouse 2	5000	1	2	3	4	5		7	8	9	11				6					10	
		Apps				40	42	40	39	42	18	38	40	35	34	16	6	12	39	2	12	1	1	3	2
		Goals					3		1	1	5	6	14	14	7	1		6	1					1	

Abandoned

Date	Opponent	Score	Scorers	Att	Moody JH	Bissett JT	Brown WJ	Willis RS	Parkes D	Crowe FR	Tompkinson WV	Prouse WHO	Whitehurst AJ	Pearson AV	Clark JW	Campbell JL	Peart JG	McGarry AM	Nuttall J	Smith A	Watson E	Hall J	Sandiford R	Hibberd CM
Apr 10	Tranmere R.	2-2	Prouse, Whitehurst	6000	1	2	3	4	5		7	8	9	10	11			6						

F.A. Cup

	Date	Opponent	Score	Scorers	Att	Moody JH	Bissett JT	Brown WJ	Willis RS	Parkes D	Crowe FR	Tompkinson WV	Prouse WHO	Whitehurst AJ	Pearson AV	Clark JW	Campbell JL	Peart JG	McGarry AM	Nuttall J	Smith A	Watson E	Hall J	Sandiford R	Hibberd CM
Q4	Nov 17	SKELMERSDALE	4-0	Hall 3, Whitehurst	2000	1	2	3	4	5		7	8	9		11			6				10		
Q5	Dec 1	Accrington Stanley	0-1		7000	1	2	3	4	5	10	7	8			11		9	6						

Q4 played at home by arrangement

Lancashire Cup

	Date	Opponent	Score	Scorers	Att	Moody JH	Bissett JT	Brown WJ	Willis RS	Parkes D	Crowe FR	Tompkinson WV	Prouse WHO	Whitehurst AJ	Pearson AV	Clark JW	Campbell JL	Peart JG	McGarry AM	Nuttall J	Smith A	Watson E	Hall J	Sandiford R	Hibberd CM
R1	Sep 12	Wigan B.	0-0		6000	1	2	3	4	5			8	10			7	9	6			11			
R1r	Oct 2	WIGAN B.	1-0	Peart		1	2	3	4	5			8	7	10	11		9	6						
R2	16	OLDHAM A.	1-5	Prouse		1		3	4	5		7	8	9	10	11			6			2			

Manchester Cup

	Date	Opponent	Score	Scorers	Moody JH	Bissett JT	Brown WJ	Willis RS	Parkes D	Crowe FR	Tompkinson WV	Prouse WHO	Whitehurst AJ	Pearson AV	Clark JW	Campbell JL	Peart JG	McGarry AM	Nuttall J	Smith A	Watson E	Hall J	Sandiford R	Hibberd CM
R2	Mar 4	Bury	1-8	Smith				4	5			8	7			11		6	3	9	2		10	1

		P	W	D	L	F	A	W	D	L	F	A	Pts
1	Wolverhampton Wan.	42	18	3	0	51	10	6	12	3	25	17	63
2	ROCHDALE	42	17	4	0	40	8	8	8	5	20	18	62
3	Chesterfield	42	16	4	1	54	15	6	6	9	16	24	54
4	Rotherham County	42	16	3	2	46	13	7	3	11	24	30	52
5	Bradford Park Ave.	42	17	3	1	50	12	4	7	10	19	31	52
6	Darlington	42	16	5	0	51	19	4	3	14	19	34	48
7	Southport	42	13	7	1	30	10	3	7	11	14	32	46
8	Ashington	42	14	4	3	41	21	4	4	13	18	40	44
9	Doncaster Rovers	42	13	4	4	41	17	2	8	11	18	36	42
10	Wigan Borough	42	12	5	4	39	15	2	9	10	16	38	42
11	Grimsby Town	42	11	9	1	30	7	3	4	14	19	40	41
12	Tranmere Rovers	42	11	5	5	32	21	2	10	9	19	39	41
13	Accrington Stanley	42	12	5	4	35	21	4	3	14	13	40	40
14	Halifax Town	42	11	4	6	26	17	4	6	11	16	42	40
15	Durham City	42	12	5	4	40	23	3	4	14	19	37	39
16	Wrexham	42	8	11	2	24	12	2	7	12	13	32	38
17	Walsall	42	10	5	6	31	20	4	3	14	13	39	36
18	New Brighton	42	9	9	3	28	10	2	4	15	12	43	35
19	Lincoln City	42	8	8	5	29	22	2	4	15	19	37	32
20	Crewe Alexandra	42	6	7	8	20	24	1	6	14	12	34	27
21	Hartlepools United	42	5	7	9	22	24	2	4	15	11	46	25
22	Barrow	42	7	7	7	25	24	1	2	18	10	56	25

1923-24 Season (players plus officials named only)
Back: Unknown reserves
3rd Row: Bissett, Willis, McGarry, Moody, (Watson?), Brown, far right -Peart (Manager)
2nd Row: Tompkinson, Prouse, Whitehurst, Clark, Crowe
Front: [slightly behind] Smith (Trainer), Campbell, Parkes, Pearson, [corner] Henderson (Trainer)

1925-26 Season
Back: Brown, Christie, Moody, Willis, Hopkins
Front: Tompkinson, Anstiss, Fergusson, Parkes (Captain), Smith, Hughes

1924/25 6th in Division 3(N)

#	Date		Opponent	Score	Scorers	Att	Moody JH	Hopkins AG	Brown WJ	Willis RS	Parkes D	Thorpe L	Tompkinson WV	Anstiss HA	Whitehurst AJ	Roseboom E	Pearson AV	Stirling E	Oxley W	Hughes R	Christie AG	Mills J	Mason F	Smith A	Rigg T	McGarry AM	Campbell IL	Hall J	Sandiford R	Cawthra JR	Halkyard C
1	Aug	30	Hartlepools United	1-1	Tompkinson	6000	1	2	3	4	5	6	7	8	9	10	11														
2	Sep	6	WIGAN BOROUGH	3-2	Anstiss 2, Roseboom	11000	1	2	3	4	5	6	7	8	9	10	11														
3		13	DARLINGTON	2-1	Anstiss 2	6000	1	2	3	4	5	6	7	8	9	10	11														
4		17	New Brighton	0-5		6000	1	2	3	4	5	6	7	8	9	10	11														
5		20	Bradford Park Avenue	0-0		12000	1		3	4	5	6	7	8		10		2	9	11											
6		27	WREXHAM	3-1	Tompkinson 2, Oxley	10000	1		3	4	5	6	7	8		10		2	9	11											
7	Oct	4	Rotherham County	3-1	Hughes 2, Anstiss	7000	1		3	4	5	6	7	8	9	10		2		11											
8		11	CHESTERFIELD	2-1	Whitehurst, Roseboom	6000	1		3	4	5	6	7	8	9	10	11	2													
9		18	Accrington Stanley	2-2	Hughes, Christie	7500	1		3		5	6	7	8	9	10		2		11	4										
10		25	Walsall	2-0	Anstiss 2	7000	1		3		5	6	7		9	10		2		11	4	8									
11	Nov	1	TRANMERE ROVERS	2-1	Hughes, Roseboom	6000	1		3		5	6	7		9	10		2		11	4	8									
12		8	Lincoln City	2-1	Tompkinson 2	8000	1		3		5	6	7		9	10		2		11	4	8									
13		15	Grimsby Town	1-1	Anstiss	8000	1		3		5	6	7		9	10		2		11	4	8									
14		22	Nelson	0-1		5000	1		3		5	6	7		9	10	11	2			4	8									
15	Dec	6	Southport	0-0		7000	1		3		5	6	7		9	10					4	8	2		11						
16		20	Durham City	2-3	Hughes, Roseboom	2000	1		3		5	6	7	8		10		2	9	11	4									
17		25	CREWE ALEXANDRA	5-0	Hughes 2, Mills, Tompkinson, Anstiss	10000	1		3		5	6	7		9	10				11	4	8	2								
18		26	Crewe Alexandra	0-2		6000	1		3		5	6	7		9	10				11	4	8	2								
19		27	HARTLEPOOLS UNITED	3-1	Mills, Anstiss 2	5000	1		3		5	6	7		9	10				11	4	8	2		2						
20	Jan	2	Ashington	3-4	Parkes, Anstiss, Mills	4000	1		3		5	6	7		9	10				11	4	8	2								
21		3	Wigan Borough	3-2	Tompkinson, Hughes, Anstiss	6000	1		3		5	6	7		9	10				11	4	8	2								
22		10	DURHAM CITY	3-0	Whitehurst, Anstiss 2	8000	1		3		5	6	7		9	10				11	4	8	2								
23		17	Darlington	0-2		8000	1		3		5	6	7		9	10				11	4		2								
24		24	BRADFORD PARK AVE.	2-2	Whitehurst 2	8000	1			4	5	6	7	9	8	10				11			2		3						
25		31	Wrexham	0-1		3000	1		3	4	5	6	7	9	8	10				11			2								
26	Feb	7	ROTHERHAM COUNTY	4-1	Pearson 2, Oxley, Tompkinson	5000	1		3	4	5			7	8	10	11	9					2				6				
27		14	Chesterfield	0-2		6000	1		3	4	5				9	10	11		7			8	2				6				
28		21	ACCRINGTON STANLEY	0-1		6000	1		3	4	5				9	10				11	6	8	2			7					
29		24	DONCASTER ROVERS	5-2	Anstiss 2, Oxley 2, Campbell	1000	1		3	4	5			8		10			9	11	6		2			7					
30		28	WALSALL	3-0	Hughes, Anstiss, Campbell	3000	1		3	4	5			8		10			9	11	6		2			7					
31	Mar	7	Tranmere Rovers	1-3	Oxley	6000	1				5	6		8		10		3	9	11	4		2			7					
32		14	LINCOLN CITY	3-0	Tompkinson, Hughes, Anstiss	3000	1		3	4	5		7	8					9	11	6		2					10			
33		21	Barrow	0-1		3700	1		3	4	5		7	8		10			9	11	6		2								
34		28	NELSON	0-1		8000	1		3	4	5		7	8		10			9	11	6		2								
35	Apr	4	ASHINGTON	0-0		4000	1		3	4	5		7	8	9					11	6		2					10			
36		10	HALIFAX TOWN	3-1	Whitehurst, Anstiss 2	3000	1		3		5	6	7		9	10				11	4	8	2								
37		11	SOUTHPORT	1-0	Anstiss	4000	1		3		5	6	7		9	10				11	4	8	2								
38		13	Halifax Town	1-3	Sandiford	6000	1		3		5	6	7		9	10				11	4		2						8		
39		14	NEW BRIGHTON	2-0	Campbell, Hughes	3500					5	6		8		10		3	9	11	4		2			7				1	
40		18	Doncaster Rovers	1-2	Whitehurst	3000	1		3		5		7	8	9		11				4		2			6		10			
41		28	BARROW	5-1	Whitehurst 3, Anstiss, Pearson	3000	1		3	4	5		7	8	9		10	3		11			2								6
42	May	1	GRIMSBY TOWN	2-0	Tompkinson 2	3000	1	2	3	4	5		7	8	9					11	6										
					Apps		41	5	39	21	41	30	36	42	22	30	11	13	11	33	29	16	25	1	2	3	5	3	1	1	1
					Goals						1		11	23	9	4	3		5	11	1	3					3		1		

F.A. Cup

	Date		Opponent	Score	Scorers	Att	Moody JH		Brown WJ	Willis RS	Parkes D	Thorpe L	Tompkinson WV	Anstiss HA	Whitehurst AJ	Roseboom E	Pearson AV		Oxley W	Hughes R	Christie AG	Mills J	Mason F
Q5	Nov	29	Halifax Town	1-0	Christie (p)	12000	1		3	2	5	6	7	9		10	11				4	8	
Q6	Dec	13	Norwich City	0-1		10000	1		3		5	6	7	9		10	8			11	4		2

Lancashire Cup

	Date		Opponent	Score	Scorers	Att	Moody JH	Hopkins AG		Willis RS	Parkes D	Thorpe L	Tompkinson WV	Anstiss HA		Roseboom E		Stirling E	Oxley W	Hughes R
R1	Sep	2	Southport	3-5	Tompkinson, Anstiss, Oxley	5000	1	2		4	5	6	7	8		10		3	9	11

Manchester Cup

	Date		Opponent	Score	Scorers	Att
R1	Feb	3	MANCHESTER UNIV.	10-C	Anstiss(3), Pearson(3), Oxley(3), Whitehurst	
R2	Mar	7	ASHTON NATIONAL	1-3	Mills	1500

			Brown WJ	Willis RS						Roseboom E	Pearson AV	Stirling E	Oxley W	Hughes R		Mills J		Smith A		McGarry AM	Campbell IL	Hall J	Sandiford R	Cawthra JR	Halkyard C
R1			2	6				8	10		11	3	9		4			5		7		1			
R2		3	2	4					9		11				8				7	6		10	1		5

Division 3 (N) final table

		P	W	D	L	F	A	W	D	L	F	A	Pts
1	Darlington	42	16	4	1	50	14	8	6	7	28	19	58
2	Nelson	42	18	2	1	58	14	5	5	11	21	36	53
3	New Brighton	42	17	3	1	56	16	6	4	11	19	34	53
4	Southport	42	17	2	2	41	7	5	5	11	18	30	51
5	Bradford Park Ave.	42	15	5	1	59	13	4	7	10	25	29	50
6	ROCHDALE	42	17	2	2	53	16	4	5	12	22	37	49
7	Chesterfield	42	14	3	4	42	15	3	8	10	18	29	45
8	Lincoln City	42	13	4	4	39	19	5	4	12	14	39	44
9	Halifax Town	42	11	5	5	36	22	5	6	10	20	30	43
10	Ashington	42	13	4	4	41	24	3	6	12	27	52	42
11	Wigan Borough	42	10	7	4	39	16	5	4	12	23	49	41
12	Grimsby Town	42	10	6	5	38	21	5	3	13	22	39	39
13	Durham City	42	11	6	4	38	17	2	7	12	12	51	39
14	Barrow	42	14	4	3	39	22	2	3	16	12	52	39
15	Crewe Alexandra	42	11	7	3	35	24	2	6	13	18	54	39
16	Wrexham	42	11	5	5	37	21	4	3	14	16	40	38
17	Accrington Stanley	42	12	5	4	43	23	3	3	15	17	49	38
18	Doncaster Rovers	42	12	5	4	36	17	2	5	14	18	48	38
19	Walsall	42	10	6	5	27	16	3	5	13	17	37	37
20	Hartlepools United	42	9	8	4	28	21	3	3	15	17	42	35
21	Tranmere Rovers	42	11	3	7	40	29	3	1	17	19	49	32
22	Rotherham County	42	6	5	10	27	31	1	2	18	15	57	21

197

1925/26 3rd in Division 3(N)

Player columns (in order): Moody JH, Hopkins AG, Brown WI, Willis RS, Parkes D, Christie AG, Tompkinson WV, Anstiss HA, Fergusson WA, Smith WE, Hughes R, Robson IW, Whitehurst AJ, Pearson AV, Hillhouse J, Martin H, Campbell JL, Bertram W, Cawthra JR, Thorpe L, Mason F, Halkyard C, Braidwood E, Quinn C, Bishop GA

#	Date	Opponent	Score	Scorers	Att	Moo	Hop	Bro	Wil	Par	Chr	Tom	Ans	Fer	Smi	Hug	Rob	Whi	Pea	Hil	Mar	Cam	Ber	Caw	Tho	Mas	Hal	Bra	Qui	Bis
1	Aug 29	HARTLEPOOLS UNITED	6-0	Tompkinson 2, Fergusson 2, Hughes, Anstiss	9321	1	2	3	4	5	6	7	8	9	10	11														
2	Sep 1	Halifax Town	1-1	Hughes (p)	7362	1	2	3	4	5	6	7	8	9	10	11														
3	5	Wigan Borough	2-2	Fergusson 2	7590	1	2	3	4		6	7	8	9	10	11	5													
4	8	ROTHERHAM UNITED	2-2	Tompkinson, Hughes	5643	1	2	3	4		6	7	8	9	10	11	5													
5	12	Tranmere Rovers	5-3	Hughes 2, Parkes, Anstiss, Whitehurst	9136	1	2	3		5	6	7	8			11	4	9	10											
6	15	HALIFAX TOWN	2-1	Anstiss 2	6528	1	2	3		5	6	7	8			11	4	9	10											
7	19	WALSALL	2-0	Tompkinson, Hughes	3484	1	2	3		5	6	7	8			11		9	10	4										
8	26	Chesterfield	2-1	Pearson, Dennis (oq)	5073	1	2	3		5	6		8			7		9	10	4	11									
9	Oct 3	BRADFORD PARK AVE.	2-0	Pearson, Tompkinson	16295	1	2	3		5	6	7		9		11			10	4			8							
10	10	Grimsby Town	0-3		11602	1	2	3		5	6			9		7			10	4	11		8							
11	17	ASHINGTON	1-3	Anstiss	4089	1	2	3		5	6			9		7			10	4	11		8							
12	24	Barrow	3-1	Tompkinson, Fergusson, Tubb (oq)	2534	1	2	3		5	6	7		9	10	11				4			8							
13	31	CREWE ALEXANDRA	2-0	Fergusson, Smith	3936	1	2	3		5	6		7	9	10	11				4			8							
14	Nov 2	Rotherham United	4-0	Fergusson, Hughes, Bertram 2	5363	1	2	3		5	6		7	9	10	11				4			8							
15	7	New Brighton	0-3		2142	1	2	3		5	6		7	9	10	11				4			8							
16	14	WREXHAM	1-2	Fergusson	6032	1	2	3		5	6		7	9	10	11				4			8							
17	21	Doncaster Rovers	2-2	Fergusson, Hughes	4831		2	3			6		10	9		7				4	11		8				1	5		
18	Dec 5	Lincoln City	2-0	Fergusson, Hughes	5153	1	2	3		5	6			9		7		10		4	11		8							
19	19	Coventry City	2-2	Fergusson, Whitehurst	11110	1		3		5	6			9		7		10		4	11		8	2						
20	26	DURHAM CITY	5-0	Fergusson 2, Christie, Whitehurst, Bertram	5222	1		3		5	6			9		7		10		4	11		8	2						
21	Jan 1	Durham City	2-0	Whitehurst, Hughes	2681	1		3		5	6			9		7		10		4	11		8	2						
22	2	Hartlepools United	2-4	Whitehurst, Smith	6057	1		3		5	6				10			9		4	11	7	8		2					
23	16	WIGAN BOROUGH	2-1	Hughes, Fergusson	4365	1		3		5	6			9		7		10		4	11		8			2				
24	23	TRANMERE ROVERS	3-2	Fergusson, Bertram, Whitehurst	4074	1		3		5	6			9		7		10		4	11		8			2				
25	25	SOUTHPORT	3-1	Hughes, Fergusson, Bertram	2624	1		3		5	6			9		7		10		4	11		8			2				
26	30	Walsall	5-1	Fergusson 2, Whitehurst, Hughes, Martin	2361	1		3		5	6			9		7		10		4	11		8			2				
27	Feb 6	CHESTERFIELD	2-4	Saxby (oq), Martin	8342	1		3		5	6			9		7		10		4	11		8			2				
28	13	Bradford Park Avenue	1-3	Hughes	24893	1		3		5	6			9		7		10			11		8			2		4		
29	20	GRIMSBY TOWN	5-2	Whitehurst 2, Anstiss, Bertram, Hughes	7544	1		3		5	6		10			7		9		4	11		8			2				
30	27	Ashington	1-0	Whitehurst	4270	1		3		5	6		10			7		9		4	11		8			2				
31	Mar 6	BARROW	2-1	Whitehurst, Bertram	5524	1		3		5	6		10			7		9		4	11		8			2				
32	13	Crewe Alexandra	2-3	Whitehurst, Anstiss	6034	1		3		5	6		10			7		9		4	11		8			2				
33	20	NEW BRIGHTON	2-1	Anstiss, Martin (p)	6794	1	2	3			6		7			10		9		4	11		8					5		
34	23	NELSON	2-0	Anstiss, Whitehurst	2981	1	2	3			6	7	10					9		4	11		8					5		
35	27	Wrexham	0-1		6855	1	2	3			6	7	10					9		4	11		8					5		
36	Apr 2	Accrington Stanley	3-1	Anstiss, Christie, Tompkinson	5264	1		3			6	7	10					9		4	11		8			2		5		
37	3	DONCASTER ROVERS	4-1	Christie, Bertram 3	6792	1		3			6		10					9		4	11		8			2		5		
38	5	ACCRINGTON STANLEY	3-2	Anstiss 2, Martin	7890	1		3		5	6	7	10					9			11		8			2		4		
39	10	Southport	7-1	Anstiss 3, Whitehurst 3, Bertram	4699	1		3		5	6	7	10					9			11		8			2		4		
40	17	LINCOLN CITY	0-1		6797	1		3		5	6		10					9			11		8			2		4		
41	24	Nelson	3-1	Anstiss, Fergusson, Hughes	6215	1		3		5	6	7	10	9			11	8								2		4		
42	May 1	COVENTRY CITY	4-1	Whitehurst 2, Christie, Tompkinson	2352	1		3		5	6	9	10				7	8			11					2		4		
		Apps				38	21	42	4	34	42	16	30	21	10	36	4	29	7	31	28	1	31	4	1	21	1	10		
		Goals									1	4	8	16	19	2		16	18	2		4		11						

Three own goals

F.A. Cup

	Date	Opponent	Score	Scorers	Att	Moo	Hop	Bro	Wil	Par	Chr	Tom	Ans	Fer	Smi	Hug	Rob	Whi	Pea	Hil	Mar	Cam	Ber	Caw	Tho	Mas	Hal	Bra	Qui	Bis
R1	Dec 1	WEST STANLEY	4-0	Hughes 2, Martin (p), Fergusson	1661	1	2	3		5	6			9		7		10		4	11		8							
R2	12	Chilton Colliery	1-1	Fergusson	5000	1	2	3		5	6			9		7		10		4	11		8							
rep	17	CHILTON COLLIERY	1-2	Parkes		1	2	3		5	6			9		7		10		4	11		8							
*	Nov 28	WEST STANLEY	1-1	Hughes	5000	1	2	3			6		10	9		7				4	11		8		5					

* Abandoned

Lancashire Cup

	Date	Opponent	Score	Scorers	Att	Moo	Hop	Bro	Wil	Par	Chr	Tom	Ans	Fer	Smi	Hug	Rob	Whi	Pea	Hil	Mar	Cam	Ber	Caw	Tho	Mas	Hal	Bra	Qui	Bis
R1	Oct 6	Nelson	1-3	Bertram	2500	1	2	3			6			9			5			10	4		11	7	8					

Manchester Cup

	Date	Opponent	Score	Scorers	Att	Moo	Hop	Bro	Wil	Par	Chr	Tom	Ans	Fer	Smi	Hug	Rob	Whi	Pea	Hil	Mar	Cam	Ber	Caw	Tho	Mas	Hal	Bra	Qui	Bis
	Feb 16	Ashton National	0-1			1	2						9	8			10			4	11	7					6		3	5

		P	W	D	L	F	A	W	D	L	F	A	Pts
1	Grimsby Town	42	20	1	0	61	8	6	8	7	30	32	61
2	Bradford Park Ave.	42	18	2	1	65	10	8	6	7	36	33	60
3	ROCHDALE	42	16	1	4	55	25	11	4	6	49	33	59
4	Chesterfield	42	18	2	1	70	19	7	3	11	30	35	55
5	Halifax Town	42	12	5	4	34	19	5	6	10	19	31	45
6	Hartlepools United	42	15	5	1	59	23	3	3	15	23	50	44
7	Tranmere Rovers	42	15	2	4	45	27	4	4	13	28	56	44
8	Nelson	42	12	8	1	67	29	4	3	14	22	42	43
9	Ashington	42	11	6	4	44	23	5	5	11	26	39	43
10	Doncaster Rovers	42	11	7	3	52	25	5	4	12	28	47	43
11	Crewe Alexandra	42	14	3	4	43	23	3	6	12	20	38	43
12	New Brighton	42	13	4	4	51	29	4	4	13	18	38	42
13	Durham City	42	14	5	2	45	19	4	1	16	18	51	42
14	Rotherham United	42	13	3	5	44	28	4	4	13	25	64	41
15	Lincoln City	42	14	2	5	42	28	3	3	15	24	54	39
16	Coventry City	42	13	6	2	47	19	3	0	18	26	63	38
17	Wigan Borough	42	12	5	4	53	22	1	6	14	15	52	37
18	Accrington Stanley	42	14	0	7	49	34	3	3	15	32	71	37
19	Wrexham	42	9	6	6	39	31	2	4	15	24	61	32
20	Southport	42	9	6	6	37	34	2	4	15	25	58	32
21	Walsall	42	9	4	8	40	34	1	2	18	18	73	26
22	Barrow	42	4	2	15	28	49	3	2	16	22	49	18

1926/27 2nd in Division 3(N)

No	Date	Opponent	Score	Scorers	Att	Hill LG	Mason F	Brown WJ	Braidwood E	Parkes D	Christie AG	Tompkinson WV	Bertram W	Butler R	Whitehurst AJ	Martin H	Hopkins AG	Ross A	Hillhouse J	Hooper FW	Owen GL	Halkyard C	Ward F	Hughes R	Campbell JL	Schofield R	Kellett A	Moody JH	Hall J	Lancaster	Duckworth R
1	Aug 28	Accrington Stanley	1-0	Martin	7335	1	2	3	4	5	6	7	8	9	10	11															
2	31	CREWE ALEXANDRA	3-1	Bertram, Parkes, Martin	7440	1	2	3	4	5	6	7	8	9	10	11															
3	Sep 4	DURHAM CITY	1-3	Ross	7947	1		3	4	5	6	7			8	10	11	2	9												
4	6	Crewe Alexandra	0-4		5282	1		2	5	3	6	7				10	11			4	8	9									
5	11	Tranmere Rovers	1-0	Whitehurst	9810	1		2	4	5	6	7			10	11					8	9	3								
6	13	Barrow	3-2	Parkes, Martin, Whitehurst	4001	1		2	4	5	6	7			10	11					8	9	3								
7	18	WREXHAM	3-1	Hughes, Hooper, Whitehurst	7564	1		2	4	5	6	7			10	11				8			3	9							
8	25	SOUTHPORT	1-0	Tompkinson	4308	1		2	4	5	6	7			10	11				8			3	9							
9	Oct 2	Stockport County	0-3		10161	1		2	4	5	6	7			10	11				8			3	9							
10	9	HARTLEPOOLS UNITED	3-0	Martin, Tompkinson, Whitehurst	2596	1		2	4	5	6	7	8		9	11			10				3								
11	16	Ashington	2-2	Whitehurst 2	2282	1		2	4	5	6	7	8		9	11			10				3								
12	23	NEW BRIGHTON	1-1	Whitehurst	6751	1		2	4	5	6	7	8		9	11			10				3								
13	30	Wigan Borough	3-0	Hughes, Bertram, Whitehurst	3486	1		2	4	5	6		8		9	11			10				3	7							
14	Nov 6	DONCASTER ROVERS	7-2	Whitehurst 3, Hughes, Martin 3	3654	1		2	4	5	6		8		9	11			10				3	7							
15	13	Stoke City	1-3	Bertram	11213	1		2	4	5	6		8		9	11			10				3	7							
16	20	ROTHERHAM UNITED	2-1	Whitehurst, Braidwood	4795	1		2	4	5	6		8		9	11			10				3	7							
17	Dec 4	WALSALL	4-4	Whitehurst, Tompkinson, Martin 2	5009	1		2	4	5	6	7	8		9	11							3	10							
18	11	Rotherham United	1-1	Whitehurst	3296	1		2	4	5	6		8	10	9	11							3	7							
19	18	CHESTERFIELD	8-1	Schofield 2, Whitehurst 5, Martin	5768	1		2	4	6	5		8		9	11							3	7		10					
20	25	LINCOLN CITY	7-3	Schofield 2, Whitehurst 3, Hughes 2	8921	1		2	4	6	5		8		9	11							3	7		10					
21	27	Lincoln City	3-2	Whitehurst 2, Schofield	7812	1		2	4	6	5				9	11				8			3	7		10					
22	Jan 1	Halifax Town	0-1		10846	1		2	4	6	5	7	8		9								3	11		10					
23	8	Bradford Park Avenue	1-5	Tompkinson	7423	1		2	4	6	5	7	8		9								3	11		10					
24	15	ACCRINGTON STANLEY	2-1	Bertram, Parkes (p)	2992	1		2	4	6	5	7	8		9								3	11		10					
25	22	Durham City	3-1	Whitehurst 3	1886	1		2	4	6	5	7	8		9								3	11		10					
26	29	TRANMERE ROVERS	3-1	Hughes 2, Tompkinson	5020	1		2	4	6		7	8		9								3	11		10	5				
27	Feb 5	Wrexham	2-2	Schofield, Whitehurst	3717	1		2	4	5	6	7	8		9								3	11		10					
28	12	Southport	1-1		3409	1		2	4	5	6		8	11	9								3		7	10					
29	19	STOCKPORT COUNTY	2-0	Bertram, Tompkinson	10239	1		2	4	6	5	7	8		9								3	11		10					
30	26	Hartlepools United	2-3	Hughes, Whitehurst	4000	1		2	4	6	5	7	8		9								3	11		10					
31	Mar 5	ASHINGTON	5-0	Hughes 2, Whitehurst 3	2482	1		2	4	5		7	8		9					10		6	3	11							
32	12	New Brighton	2-1	Bertram, Whitehurst	4442	1		2	4	5		7	8		9					10		6	3	11							
33	19	WIGAN BOROUGH	4-1	Whitehurst, Bertram 2, Tompkinson	6434	1		2	4	5		7	8		9					10		6	3	11							
34	26	Doncaster Rovers	2-3	Hughes, Bertram	5779	1		2	4	5		7	8		9					10		6	3	11							
35	Apr 2	STOKE CITY	4-0	Bertram, Whitehurst, Hughes 2	12727			2	4	5	6	7	8		9					10			3	11				1			
36	5	Nelson	1-3	Tompkinson	5871			2	4	5	6	7	8		9					10			3	11				1			
37	16	BRADFORD PARK AVE.	3-0	Whitehurst 2, Hughes	8871			2	4	5	6	7	8		9					10			3	11				1			
38	18	HALIFAX TOWN	2-0	Tompkinson, Bertram	8501			2	4	5	6	7	8		9					10			3	11				1			
39	19	BARROW	5-1	Hughes 2, Bertram, Whitehurst 2	3910			2	4	5	6	7	8		9				10				3	11				1			
40	23	Walsall	1-4	Hughes	2421			2	4	5	6	7	8		9				10				3	11				1			
41	30	NELSON	2-1	Whitehurst 2	3871		2		4	5	6	7	8		9			3						11				1	10		
42	May 7	Chesterfield	3-2	Whitehurst, Hall	4307			2	4	5	6	7	8		9								3	11				1	10		
		Apps				34	3	41	40	28	33	34	35	5	42	21	2	1	21	20	3	6	35	32	1	14	1	8	2		
		Goals							1	3		9	13		44	10		1		1				16		6			1		

F.A. Cup

Rd	Date	Opponent	Score	Scorers	Att	Hill LG	Mason F	Brown WJ	Braidwood E	Parkes D	Christie AG	Tompkinson WV	Bertram W	Butler R	Whitehurst AJ	Martin H	Hopkins AG	Ross A	Hillhouse J	Hooper FW	Owen GL	Halkyard C	Ward F	Hughes R	Campbell JL	Schofield R	Kellett A	Moody JH	Hall J	Lancaster	Duckworth R
R1	Nov 27	Accrington Stanley	3-4	Whitehurst 2, Bertram	7000	1		2	4	5	6		8		9	11				10			3	7							

Lancashire Cup

Rd	Date	Opponent	Score	Scorers	Att	Hill LG	Mason F	Brown WJ	Braidwood E	Parkes D	Christie AG	Tompkinson WV	Bertram W	Butler R	Whitehurst AJ	Martin H	Hopkins AG	Ross A	Hillhouse J	Hooper FW	Owen GL	Halkyard C	Ward F	Hughes R	Campbell JL	Schofield R	Kellett A	Moody JH	Hall J	Lancaster	Duckworth R
R2	Sep 28	Burnley	0-1			1		2	4	5					9	10				8	6	3	11	7							

Manchester Cup

Rd	Date	Opponent	Score	Scorers	Att	Hill LG	Mason F	Brown WJ	Braidwood E	Parkes D	Christie AG	Tompkinson WV	Bertram W	Butler R	Whitehurst AJ	Martin H	Hopkins AG	Ross A	Hillhouse J	Hooper FW	Owen GL	Halkyard C	Ward F	Hughes R	Campbell JL	Schofield R	Kellett A	Moody JH	Hall J	Lancaster	Duckworth R
R2	Feb 15	MOSSLEY	5-0	Butler(2), Hall(2), Duckworth			2							9		3				10		6		7		5	1	11	4		8
R3	Mar 1	Manchester N.E.	1-2	Whitehurst			2							9		3				8		6		11	10	5	1		4		7

Back: Henderson (Trainer), Roberts (Asst. Sec.) Hooper, Parkes, Braidwood, Christie, Brown, Martin, Hill, Lancaster, Moody, Kellett, Hillhouse, Ross, Peart (Manager)
Front: Campbell(Asst.Train.), Hopkins, Tompkinson, Halkyard, Bertram, Whitehurst, Owen, Hughes

#		Date	Opponent	Score	Scorers	Att	Moody JH	Brown WJ	Ward F	Braidwood E	Parkes D	Christie AG	Tompkinson WV	Bertram W	Whitehurst AJ	Barber J	Hughes R	Martin H	Hall J	Clennell J	Hopkins AD	Halkyard C	Stephenson J	Plane E	Wood WC	Schofield R	Mittell JL	Murray AF	Miles U	Webster W	Holroyd E	Monks A	Heywood	Kellett A
1	Aug	27	Barrow	3-1	Bertram, Barber, Whitehurst	7783	1	2	3	4	5	6	7	8	9	10	11																	
2		30	STOCKPORT COUNTY	2-1	Bertram, Hughes	10253	1	2	3	4	5	6	7	8	9	10	11																	
3	Sep	3	NELSON	1-0	Whitehurst	9869	1	2	3	4	5	6	7	8	9	10	11																	
4		10	Wigan Borough	2-1	Bertram, Whitehurst	5275	1	2	3	4	5	6	7	8	9	10		11																
5		17	Rotherham United	1-3	Whitehurst	4911	1	2	3	4	5	6	7	8	9			11	10															
6		24	SOUTHPORT	5-1	Whitehurst, Parkes, Bertram (2), Tompkinson	6264	1	2	3	4	5	6	7	8	9			11	10															
7	Oct	1	Durham City	2-3	Tompkinson, Gurkin (og)	2354	1	2	3	4	5	6	7	8	9			11	10															
8		8	WREXHAM	3-0	Tompkinson 2, Whitehurst	7493	1	2	3	4	5	6	7	8	9			11	10															
9		15	Chesterfield	3-1	Hughes, Whitehurst 2	5439	1	2	3	4	5	6	7	8	9			11	10															
10		22	LINCOLN CITY	0-3		5229	1	2	3	4	5	6	7	8		9		11	10															
11		29	Hartlepools United	2-0	Parkes, Hughes	4086	1	2	3	4	5	6	7	8	9		11			10														
12	Nov	12	New Brighton	1-2	Bertram	4409	1	2	3	4	5		7	8	9		11			10														
13		19	BRADFORD CITY	3-3	Russell (og), Tompkinson, Whitehurst	5952	1			3	4	5	7	8	9		6		10	11			2											
14	Dec	3	CREWE ALEXANDRA	4-0	Whitehurst 2, Tompkinson, Martin	3991	1			3	4	5	7		9		6	8	10	11			2											
15		17	DARLINGTON	4-1	Whitehurst 2, Tompkinson, Hughes	3912	1			3		5	7	8	9	4	6		10	11			2											
16		24	Doncaster Rovers	2-5	Whitehurst, Bertram	5291	1				5	3	7	8	9	4	6		10	11			2											
17		27	Bradford Park Avenue	1-4	Bertram	21762	1				5		7	8	9	4	6		10	11			2	3										
18		31	BARROW	3-0	Tompkinson 2, Clennell	3973	1				5		7	8	9	4	6		10	11			2	3										
19	Jan	2	Stockport County	1-5	Tompkinson	10571	1				5		7	8	9	4	6		10	11			2	3										
20		3	BRADFORD PARK AVE.	0-4		5481			3		5		7	8	9	4	6		10	11			2	1										
21		7	Nelson	3-6	Whitehurst 2, Clennell	2539					5		7	8	9	4	6		10	11			2	1		3								
22		14	Ashington	1-5	Whitehurst	1223			3		5	4	7	8	9		6		10	11			2			1								
23		21	WIGAN BOROUGH	3-0	Bertram, Whitehurst 2	3626			3		5	4	7	8	9		6		10	11			2			1								
24	Feb	4	Southport	1-3	Tompkinson	2731			3		5	4	7	8	9		6		10	11			2			1								
25		11	DURHAM CITY	1-0	Bertram	1458			3		5	4	7	8	9		6		10	11			2			1								
26		18	Wrexham	1-2	Whitehurst	4157			3		5	4	7	10	9		11	8			6		2					1						
27		25	CHESTERFIELD	5-1	Whitehurst 4, Bertram	2602			3		5	4	7	8	9		11	10			6		2					1						
28		28	ROTHERHAM UNITED	2-1	Whitehurst, Hall	1885			3	4	5		7	8	9		11	10			6		2					1						
29	Mar	3	Lincoln City	1-3	Whitehurst	5760			3	4	5			8	9		11	10			6		2				7						
30		10	HARTLEPOOLS UNITED	0-1		2582			3		5	4		8	9		11	10			6		2				7			1				
31		17	Accrington Stanley	0-1		3885			3		5			8	9	10	11			4	6		2				7			1				
32		24	NEW BRIGHTON	0-0		2404			3	4	5		7	8	9		6						2				1		10					
33		31	Bradford City	2-2	Miles, Hughes	10565			3	4	5		7		8		6						2				1		9	10				
34	Apr	6	Tranmere Rovers	0-3		10053			3	4	5		7	8	9		6						2				1		10					
35		7	ASHINGTON	2-2	Bertram, Whitehurst	3309			3	5		4	7	8	10	6							2				1		9					
36		9	TRANMERE ROVERS	1-2	Whitehurst	3069			3		5	4	7	8	9			6					2				1		10					
37		10	Halifax Town	1-1	Whitehurst	3595			3		4	10	8	9	5		11	6					2				1			7				
38		14	Crewe Alexandra	1-1	Miles	2887			3		4	10	8	9			11	6					2				1	5		7				
39		21	HALIFAX TOWN	2-2	Murray, Whitehurst	2099				4	7	8	9	5	11		6						2				1	3		10				
40		28	Darlington	0-1		2708		2		4	7	8	9	5	11		6						3				1			10				
41	May	1	ACCRINGTON STANLEY	3-2	Whitehurst 2, Bertram	1443		2		4		8	9	5	7		6						3				1			10	11			
42		5	DONCASTER ROVERS	1-0	Webster	1768		2		4	7	8	9	5			11	6					3				1		10			1		
			Apps				19	16	32	27	29	33	38	40	41	29	26	16	20	13	8	7	22	2	1	3	19	5	7	7	1	1		
			Goals								2		11	13	32	1	5	1	1	2								1	2	1				

Two own goals

Abandoned

	Date	Opponent	Score	Scorers	Att	Moody JH	Brown WJ	Ward F	Braidwood E	Parkes D	Christie AG	Tompkinson WV	Bertram W	Whitehurst AJ	Barber J	Hughes R	Martin H	Hall J	Clennell J
	Nov 5	ACCRINGTON STANLEY	1-1	Tompkinson	3000	1	2	3	4	5		7	8	9	6	11			10

F.A. Cup

	Date	Opponent	Score	Scorers	Att	Moody JH	Brown WJ	Ward F	Braidwood E	Parkes D	Christie AG	Tompkinson WV	Bertram W	Whitehurst AJ	Barber J	Hughes R	Martin H	Hall J	Clennell J	Stephenson J	Plane E
R1	Nov 26	CROOK TOWN	8-2	Whitehurst 4, Clennell 3, Martin	4139	1		3	4	5		7		9	6		11	10	8	2	
R2	Dec 10	Darlington	1-2	Bertram	7571	1	3		4	5		7	8	9	6		11	10		2	

Lancashire Cup

	Date	Opponent	Score	Scorers	Att	Moody JH	Brown WJ	Braidwood E	Parkes D	Christie AG	Tompkinson WV	Bertram W	Whitehurst AJ	Barber J	Martin H	Schofield R
R2	Oct 12	Manchester U.	2-4	Whitehurst (2)		1	2	4	5	6	7	8	9	10	11	3

Manchester Cup

	Date	Opponent	Score	Scorers	Att	Ward F	Parkes D	Hughes R	Hall J	Clennell J	Stephenson J	Mittell JL	Miles U	Webster W	Heywood	Kellett A
R2	Jan 10	Mossley	0-4			3	5	11	8	2	4	10	7	9	1	6

		P	W	D	L	F	A	W	D	L	F	A	Pts
1	Bradford Park Ave.	42	18	2	1	68	22	9	7	5	33	23	63
2	Lincoln City	42	15	4	2	53	20	9	3	9	38	44	55
3	Stockport County	42	16	5	0	62	14	7	3	11	27	37	54
4	Doncaster Rovers	42	15	4	2	59	18	8	3	10	21	26	53
5	Tranmere Rovers	42	14	6	1	68	28	8	3	10	37	44	53
6	Bradford City	42	15	4	2	59	19	3	8	10	26	41	48
7	Darlington	42	15	1	5	63	28	6	4	11	26	46	47
8	Southport	42	15	2	4	55	24	5	3	13	24	46	45
9	Accrington Stanley	42	14	4	3	49	22	4	4	13	27	45	44
10	New Brighton	42	10	7	4	45	22	4	7	10	27	40	42
11	Wrexham	42	15	1	5	48	19	3	5	13	16	48	42
12	Halifax Town	42	11	7	3	47	24	2	8	11	26	47	41
13	ROCHDALE	42	13	4	4	45	24	4	3	14	29	53	41
14	Rotherham United	42	11	6	4	39	19	3	5	13	26	50	39
15	Hartlepools United	42	10	3	8	41	35	6	3	12	28	46	38
16	Chesterfield	42	10	4	7	46	29	3	6	12	25	49	36
17	Crewe Alexandra	42	10	6	5	51	28	2	4	15	26	58	34
18	Ashington	42	10	5	6	54	36	1	6	14	23	67	33
19	Barrow	42	10	8	3	41	24	0	3	18	13	78	31
20	Wigan Borough	42	8	8	3	30	32	2	5	14	26	65	30
21	Durham City	42	10	5	6	37	30	1	2	18	16	70	29
22	Nelson	42	8	4	9	50	49	2	2	17	26	87	26

1928/29 17th in Division 3(N)

No	Month	Date	Opponent	Score	Scorers	Att	Mittell JL	Ellison IW	Lewins GA	Braidwood E	Barber J	Hall J	Miles U	Bertram W	Littler O	Webster W	Martin AF	Trotman RW	Milsom J	Brierley J	Stott GRB	Bailey TW	Watson TA	Power G	Martin H	Howlett CE	Howlett H	Silverwood E	Murray AF	Lewis HH	Robson ER	Appleyard F	Brown AR	Cooke A	Jones C	Halfpenny
1	Aug	25	DONCASTER ROVERS	1-3	Bertram	4275	1	2	3	4	5	6	7	8	9	10	11																			
2		27	Barrow	3-3	Trotman, Brierley, Milsom	7660	1	2	3	4	5	6	7				11	8	9	10															
3	Sep	1	Ashington	1-2	A Martin	3244	1	2	3	4	5	6					11	8	9	10	7														
4		4	BARROW	4-2	Trotman, Brierley, Stott, Milsom	3668	1	2	3	4	5	6					11	8	9	10	7														
5		8	SOUTH SHIELDS	1-2	Stott	6913	1	3	2		5	6					11	8	9	10	7	4													
6		15	Nelson	0-3		6715	1	3	2		5	6	4				11	8	9	10	7														
7		22	DARLINGTON	5-0	Trotman 2, Stott, Milsom 2	4990	1	3	2		5	6	4	8			11	10	9		7														
8		29	Southport	1-1	Milsom	4861	1	3	2		5	6	4	8			11	10	9		7														
9	Oct	6	WIGAN BOROUGH	0-0		5227	1		2	4	5	6		8	9		11	10			7		3													
10		13	NEW BRIGHTON	4-2	Milsom 2, Trotman, H Martin	5096		2		4	5	6		8				10	9		7		3	1	11											
11		20	Crewe Alexandra	1-1	Bertram	3493	1	2		4	5	6		8				10	9		7		3		11											
12		27	TRANMERE ROVERS	5-1	Bertram 2, Trotman(2), Milsom	4691	1	2		4	5	6		8				10	9		7		3		11											
13	Nov	3	Stockport County	0-4		11661	1	2		4	5	6		8				10	9		7		3		11											
14		10	HALIFAX TOWN	2-2	Barber, Milsom	2038	1	2		4	5	6		8			11	10	9		7		3													
15		17	Lincoln City	0-2		5586	1	2		4	5	6		8			11	10	9		7		3													
16	Dec	1	Accrington Stanley	2-2	Bertram, Milsom	4711	1	2			5	4		8			6	9	10		7		3		11											
17		8	HARTLEPOOLS UNITED	7-4	Stott, Brierley 4, Bertram, H Martin	3017	1	2			5	6		8				9	10		7		3		11	4										
18		15	Carlisle United	2-4	Stott, Barber	5838	1	2			5	6		8				9	10		7		3		11	4										
19		22	ROTHERHAM UNITED	2-1	Bertram 2	2120	1	2			5	4		8			6	9	10		7		3		11											
20		25	WREXHAM	4-4	Milsom 2, Trotman, Bertram	7608	1	2		4	5	6		8			11	10	9		7		3													
21		26	Wrexham	0-3		10877		2		4	6		7	8			5	10	9				3	1	11											
22		29	Doncaster Rovers	2-4	Brierley, Littler	4191	1	2		4	6	6		8	7	5	4	9	10	11			3													
23	Jan	5	ASHINGTON	5-0	Milsom 3, Bertram, H Martin	2464	1	2		4	6	6		8			5	10	9		7		3		11											
24		12	CARLISLE UNITED	4-0	Milsom 2, Trotman, Bertram	5115	1	2		4	6	6		8			5	10	9		7		3		11											
25		19	South Shields	2-5	Milsom, Stott	3900	1	2		4	6	6		8			5	10	9		7		3		11											
26		26	NELSON	2-1	Milsom, Bertram	4902	1	2		4	6	6		8			5	10	9		7		3		11											
27	Feb	2	Darlington	3-5	Bertram 2, Stott	2452	1	2		4	6	6		8			5	10	9		7		3		11											
28		9	SOUTHPORT	1-1	Trotman	3369	1	2		4	6	6		8			5	10	9		7		3		11											
29		16	Wigan Borough	1-4	Robb (og)	3940		2		5							6	9	10		7		3	1	11				8	4						
30		23	New Brighton	1-6	Milsom	2946	1	2		5							6	9	10		7		3		11				8	4						
31	Mar	2	CREWE ALEXANDRA	2-1	Lewis, Milsom	3356		2		5	4						6	9	8	7			3		11					10	1					
32		9	Tranmere Rovers	1-5	Milsom	4055		2		5	4			8		10		9			7		3		11						1		6			
33		16	STOCKPORT COUNTY	1-3	Milsom	11281		2		4	5	8					6	9			7		3		11					10	1					
34		23	Halifax Town	1-1	Milsom	3787		2		5	4			8			6	9			7		3		11					10	1					
35		29	Chesterfield	1-2	Milsom	4730		2		5	4			8			6	9	10		7		3		11						1					
36		30	LINCOLN CITY	0-2		4848		2		5	4	8					6	9			7		3							10	1		11			
37	Apr	1	CHESTERFIELD	2-1	Lewis 2	3329		2		5	4	8					6	9			7		3		11					10	1					
38		6	Bradford City	0-0		22669		2		5	4	8					6	9			7		3		11					10	1					
39		13	ACCRINGTON STANLEY	2-1	Bertram 2	2894		2		5	4	8					6	9			7		3							10	1					
40		20	Hartlepools United	2-0	Lewis, Bertram	1835		2		5	4	8					6	9			7		3							10	1					
41		30	BRADFORD CITY	1-3	Bertram	20945		2		5	4	8					6	9			7		3		11					10	1					
42	May	4	Rotherham United	0-5		2899		2		4							6	9			7		3		11						1			5	8	
			Apps				27	16	34	10	36	40	3	31	4	15	32	23	40	14	39	1	34	3	27	2	1	2	2	10	12	1	1	1	1	1
			Goals								2			18	1		1	10	25	7	7				3					4						

One own goal

F.A. Cup

	Date	Opponent	Score	Scorers	Att	Mittell	Ellison			Barber	Hall		Bertram			MartinAF	Trotman	Milsom		Stott		Watson		Martin H										
R1	Nov 24	Chesterfield	2-3	H Martin, Milsom	5214	1	2			5	6		8				10	9		7		3		11												

Note: FA Cup R1 — Mittell 1, Ellison 2, Braidwood 4, Barber 5, Hall 6, Stott 7, Bertram 8, Milsom 9, Trotman 10, Martin H 11, Watson 3.

Lancashire Cup

	Date	Opponent	Score	Scorers	Att
R1	Sep 17	Barrow	1-2	H.Martin	2758

Lancashire Cup R1 lineup — Power 1, Watson 2, Lewins 3, Hall 4, Halfpenny 5, Barber 6, Stott 7, Trotman 8, Milsom 9, Webster 10, Martin H 11.

Manchester Cup

	Date	Opponent	Score	Scorers	Att
R2	Feb 27	Manchester C.	2-3	Milsom(2)	5214

Oddie at No.1, Clegg at No.3

Manchester Cup R2 lineup — Oddie 1, Ellison 2, Clegg 3, Hall 4, Barber 5, Webster 6, Stott 7, Bertram 8, Milsom 9, Robson 10, Martin H 11.

Division 3 (N) — Final Table

		P	W	D	L	F	A	W	D	L	F	A	Pts
1	Bradford City	42	17	2	2	82	18	10	7	4	46	25	63
2	Stockport County	42	19	2	0	77	23	9	4	8	34	35	62
3	Wrexham	42	17	2	2	59	25	4	8	9	32	44	52
4	Wigan Borough	42	16	4	1	55	16	5	5	11	27	33	51
5	Doncaster Rovers	42	14	3	4	39	20	6	7	8	37	46	50
6	Lincoln City	42	15	3	3	58	18	6	3	12	33	49	48
7	Tranmere Rovers	42	15	3	3	55	21	7	0	14	24	56	47
8	Carlisle United	42	15	3	3	61	27	4	5	12	25	50	46
9	Crewe Alexandra	42	11	6	4	47	23	7	2	12	33	45	44
10	South Shields	42	13	5	3	57	24	5	3	13	26	50	44
11	Chesterfield	42	13	2	6	46	28	5	3	13	25	49	41
12	Southport	42	13	5	3	52	27	3	3	15	23	58	40
13	Halifax Town	42	11	7	3	42	24	2	6	13	21	38	39
14	New Brighton	42	11	3	7	40	28	4	6	11	24	43	39
15	Nelson	42	14	1	6	48	28	3	4	14	29	62	39
16	Rotherham United	42	12	5	4	44	23	3	4	14	16	54	39
17	ROCHDALE	42	12	4	5	55	34	1	6	14	24	62	36
18	Accrington Stanley	42	11	5	5	42	22	2	3	16	26	60	34
19	Darlington	42	12	6	3	47	26	1	1	19	17	62	33
20	Barrow	42	7	6	8	42	37	3	2	16	22	56	28
21	Hartlepools United	42	9	4	8	35	38	1	2	18	24	74	26
22	Ashington	42	6	5	10	31	52	2	2	17	14	63	23

#	Date	Opponent	Score	Scorers	Att	Crompton L	Hope P	Watson TA	Parton J	Hooker E	Barber J	Stott GRB	Bertram W	Milsom J	Lewis HH	Lindsay T	Hall J	Baker LH	Jones C	Tippett T	Brown AR	Murray AF	Lynch TJ	Oliver ED	Williams I	Trippear AW	Martin H
1	Aug 31	Lincoln City	0-0		6415	1	2	3	4	5	6	7	8	9	10	11											
2	Sep 3	CHESTERFIELD	2-1	Hope, Barber	5878	1	2	3	4	5	6	7	8	9	10	11	11										
3	7	TRANMERE ROVERS	2-1	Milsom, Bertram	4403	1	2	3			6	7	8	9			11	4	5	10							
4	14	Halifax Town	3-2	Tippett, Stott, Wheelhouse (oq)	4982	1	2	3		5		7	8		10			4	6	9	11						
5	17	DARLINGTON	4-1	Brown, Bertram, Tippett 2	5614	1	2	3		5		7	8		10			4	6	9	11						
6	21	ROTHERHAM UNITED	1-2	Milsom	4700	1	2	3		5		7	8		10			4	6	9	11						
7	28	Wrexham	0-8		5445	1	2	3			6	7	8	9				4	5	10	11						
8	Oct 5	South Shields	2-2	Bertram, Stott	3876	1		3	2	6	5	7	8	9	10			4			11						
9	12	ACCRINGTON STANLEY	4-0	Milsom 2, Brown 2	5362	1		3		6	5	7	8	9	10			4			11	2					
10	19	BARROW	6-1	Milsom 2, Bertram 4	4151			3		6	5	7	8	9	10			4			11	2	1				
11	26	Port Vale	3-3	Milsom 2, Brown	8902			3		6	5	7	8	9	10			4			11	2	1				
12	Nov 2	NEW BRIGHTON	5-0	Bertram, Milsom 2, Lewis 2	3136		2				5	7	8	9	10		6	4			11		1	3			
13	9	Stockport County	2-4	Milsom 2	12903		2				5	7	8	9	10		6	4			11		1	3			
14	23	Crewe Alexandra	1-6	Milsom	4011			3		6	5	7	8	9	10			4			11	2	1				
15	Dec 14	WIGAN BOROUGH	2-1	Tippett, Bertram	1826		2			6	5	7	8			10		4		9	11		1	3			
16	21	Wigan Borough	1-3	Tippett	2518		2			6	5	7	8			10		4		9	11		1	3			
17	25	DONCASTER ROVERS	2-4	Tippett, Bertram	2996	1	2			6	5	7	8			10		4		9	11			3			
18	26	Doncaster Rovers	1-3	Tippett	7799	1	2			6	5	7	8			10		4		9	11			3			
19	Jan 1	Chesterfield	0-2		5293		2				6	7	8			10		5		9	11		1	3	4		
20	4	Tranmere Rovers	2-2	Tippett, Brown	3273		2				6		8			10		5		9	11		1	3	4	7	
21	11	SOUTHPORT	2-2	Tippett 2	2101		2				6		8			10		5		9	11		1	3	4	7	
22	14	Nelson	0-1		1359		2	3	10		5	7	8				6	4		9	11		1				
23	18	HALIFAX TOWN	0-3		2759		2	3		6	5		8			10		4		9	11		1				7
24	25	Rotherham United	4-0	Tippett 2, Stott, Bertram	5915		2			6	5	7	8			10		4		9	11		1	3			
25	Feb 1	WREXHAM	5-4	Stott 3, Tippett, Lewis	2637		2		8	6	5	7			10			4		9	11		1	3			
26	8	SOUTH SHIELDS	2-0	Tippett, Stott	3176		2			6	5	7	8			10		4		9	11		1	3			
27	15	Accrington Stanley	2-6	Bertram 2	4361		2			6	5	7	8			10		4		9	11		1	3			
28	22	Barrow	0-2		3216		2			6	5	7	8			10		4		9	11		1	3			
29	Mar 1	PORT VALE	0-0		7177		2			6	5	7	8			10		4		9	11		1	3			
30	8	New Brighton	0-2		4160					6	5	7	8			10		4		9	11	2	1	3			
31	15	STOCKPORT COUNTY	3-1	Williams, Tippett 2	4516		2			6	5	7	8			10				9	11		1	3	4		
32	22	York City	0-6		4720		2			6	5	7	8			10				9	11		1	3	4		
33	29	CREWE ALEXANDRA	3-1	Tippett 2, Stott	2370		2			6	5	7	8			10				9	11		1	3	4		
34	Apr 5	Southport	3-2	Lewis 2, Stott	2703		2			6	5	7	8			10				9	11		1	3	4		
35	8	LINCOLN CITY	3-4	Tippett 3	1046		2			6	5	7	8			10				9	11		1	3	4		
36	12	NELSON	4-1	Brown 2, Bertram, Stott	2621		2	3	9	6	5	7	8			10					11		1		4		
37	18	HARTLEPOOLS UNITED	1-1	Stott	2441		2				5	7	8			10		6		9	11		1	3	4		
38	19	Carlisle United	0-2		2987		2		9		5	7	8			10		6			11		1	3	4		
39	21	Hartlepools United	8-2	Brown 2, Tippett 6	3655		2	3			5	7	8			10		6		9	11		1		4		
40	22	Darlington	0-3		3013		2				5	7	8			10		6		9	11		1	3	4		
41	29	CARLISLE UNITED	2-0	Stott 2	1758		2				5	7	8			10		6		9	11		1	3	4		
42	May 3	YORK CITY	4-2	Lewis, Tippett 2, Brown	1564		2				5	7	8			10		6		9	11		1	3	4		
		Apps				11	13	39	7	25	42	39	41	14	32	7	8	34	1	30	39	5	31	26	15	3	
		Goals					1				1	13	14	13	6					29	10				1		

One own goal

Abandoned

Date	Opponent	Score	Scorers	Crompton L	Hope P	Watson TA	Parton J	Hooker E	Barber J	Stott GRB	Bertram W	Milsom J	Lewis HH	Lindsay T	Hall J	Baker LH	Jones C	Tippett T	Brown AR	Murray AF	Lynch TJ	Oliver ED	Williams I	Trippear AW	Martin H
Dec 28	LINCOLN CITY	1-1			2				6	7	8			10		5		9	11		1	3	4		

F.A. Cup

Rd	Date	Opponent	Score	Scorers	Att	Crompton L	Hope P	Watson TA	Parton J	Hooker E	Barber J	Stott GRB	Bertram W	Milsom J	Lewis HH	Lindsay T	Hall J	Baker LH	Jones C	Tippett T	Brown AR	Murray AF	Lynch TJ	Oliver ED	Williams I	Trippear AW	Martin H
R1	Nov 30	Accrington Stanley	1-3	Milsom	5500		2				5	7	8	9			6	4		10	11		1	3			

Lancashire Cup

Rd	Date	Opponent	Score	Scorers	Crompton L	Hope P	Watson TA	Parton J	Hooker E	Barber J	Stott GRB	Bertram W	Milsom J	Lewis HH	Lindsay T	Hall J	Baker LH	Jones C	Tippett T	Brown AR	Murray AF	Lynch TJ	Oliver ED	Williams I	Trippear AW	Martin H
R1	Sep 9	Nelson	4-3	Milsom, Tippett, Bertram, Stott		2	3		6	5	7	8		10			4		9	11		1				
R2	Oct 16	Manchester U.	0-5		1		3			5	7	8	9	10		6	4			11	2					

Manchester Cup

Rd	Date	Opponent	Score	Scorers	Att	Crompton L	Hope P	Watson TA	Parton J	Hooker E	Barber J	Stott GRB	Bertram W	Milsom J	Lewis HH	Lindsay T	Hall J	Baker LH	Jones C	Tippett T	Brown AR	Murray AF	Lynch TJ	Oliver ED	Williams I	Trippear AW	Martin H
R3	Mar 4	Aston National	6-1	Tippett(2), Brown(2), Lewis, Stott	3300		2				5	7				10	6	8		9	11		1	3	4		
SF	Apr 1	WIGAN B.	3-3	Tippett(2), Stott	3000		2				5	7	8			10		6		9	11		1	3	4		
SFr	9	Wigan B.	0-0				2				5	7	8			10		6		9			1	3	4		11
SF2r	30	WIGAN B.	1-2	Tippett			2					7	8			10		5	6	9	11		1	3	4		

		P	W	D	L	F	A	W	D	L	F	A	Pts
1	Port Vale	42	17	2	2	64	18	13	5	3	39	19	67
2	Stockport County	42	15	3	3	67	20	13	4	4	39	24	63
3	Darlington	42	14	2	5	71	29	8	4	9	37	44	50
4	Chesterfield	42	18	1	2	53	15	4	5	12	23	41	50
5	Lincoln City	42	12	8	1	54	23	5	6	10	29	38	48
6	York City	42	11	7	3	43	20	4	9	8	34	44	46
7	South Shields	42	11	6	4	49	32	7	4	10	28	42	46
8	Hartlepools United	42	14	4	4	50	24	4	7	10	31	50	45
9	Southport	42	11	5	5	49	31	4	8	9	32	43	43
10	ROCHDALE	42	14	3	4	57	30	4	4	13	32	61	43
11	Crewe Alexandra	42	12	5	4	55	28	5	3	13	27	43	42
12	Tranmere Rovers	42	12	4	5	57	35	4	5	12	26	51	41
13	New Brighton	42	13	4	4	48	22	3	4	14	21	57	40
14	Doncaster Rovers	42	13	5	3	39	22	2	4	15	23	47	39
15	Carlisle United	42	13	4	4	63	34	3	3	15	27	67	39
16	Accrington Stanley	42	11	4	6	55	30	3	5	13	29	51	37
17	Wrexham	42	10	5	6	42	28	3	3	15	25	60	34
18	Wigan Borough	42	12	4	5	44	26	1	3	17	16	62	33
19	Nelson	42	9	4	8	31	25	4	3	14	20	55	33
20	Rotherham United	42	9	4	8	46	40	2	4	15	21	73	30
21	Halifax Town	42	7	7	7	27	26	3	1	17	17	53	28
22	Barrow	42	9	4	8	31	28	2	1	18	10	70	27

1930/31 21st in Division 3(N)

#	Date		Opponent	Score	Scorers	Att	Prince J	Watson TA	Oliver ED	Williams I	Barber J	Grierson G	Stott GRB	Bertram W	Tippett T	Lewis HH	Hargreaves F	Corcoran T	Latham A	Everest J	Hellyer CD	Craddock CW	Fitton F	Cowan D	Appleyard F	Blackburn W	Platt H	Turnbull G	Ward G	Warburton TC	Lynch TJ	Bruce H	Plunkett AETB	Trippier AW	Charlton F	Martin H
1	Aug	30	NELSON	5-4	Hargreaves,Tippett 2, Stott,Dixon(og)	4822	1	2	3	4	5	6	7	8	9	10	11																			
2	Sep	1	CHESTERFIELD	2-3	Stott, Everest	4384	1		3		5	6	7	8		10	11	2	4	9																
3		6	Crewe Alexandra	1-3	Latham	3635	1	2	3			6	7		9	10	8		4	5	11															
4		8	Barrow	0-0		6873	1	2	3			6	7		9	10	11		4	5																
5		13	WREXHAM	4-3	Bertram, Craddock, Stott, Tippett	5073	1	2	3			6	7	8	9	11			4	5		10														
6		15	BARROW	4-2	Stott 2, Tippett 2	3957	1	2	3			6	7	8	9	11			4	5		10														
7		20	Tranmere Rovers	3-7	Hargreaves 2, Lewis	5700	1	2	3			6	7	8	9	10	11		4	5																
8		27	CARLISLE UNITED	1-3	Bertram	3165	1		3		4	6	2	7	8	9	10	11		5																
9	Oct	4	York City	0-3		4308	1		3		4	6	2	7	8	11				5		10	9													
10		11	ROTHERHAM UNITED	6-1	Everest,Lewis,Craddock(2),Tippett,Bertram	3480	1		3		4	6	2	7	8	11	10			5		9														
11		18	WIGAN BOROUGH	0-4		6975	1		3		4	6	2	7	8	9				5		10		11												
12		25	Darlington	1-1	Craddock	3234	1		3	4		6	2	7	8	9				5		10		11												
13	Nov	1	LINCOLN CITY	4-2	Tippett, Stott 2, Craddock	4307	1		3		4	6	2	7	8	11	10			5		9														
14		8	Hull City	1-3	Stott	7719	1		3		4	6	2	7	8	11	10			5		9														
15		15	DONCASTER ROVERS	3-5	Lewis 3	2985	1			3	4	5	2	7	8		10					9		11	6											
16		22	Gateshead	2-0	Lewis, Tippett	1129			3		5	4		8	7		10	2				9		11	6					1						
17	Dec	6	New Brighton	1-2	Williams	2369			3	7	5	2		8	9	10		6				4		11						1						
18		20	Hartlepools United	0-4		3083			3		4	6	7	8	9	10								11	2	5				1						
19		25	Southport	0-4		6157			3	4			7	8	11	10		6				9			2	5				1						
20		26	SOUTHPORT	0-4		1934			3	4			7	8	11	10						6			2	5	9			1						
21		27	Nelson	0-0		2774			3	4	5		7		8			2						10				9	6	1	11					
22	Jan	1	Accrington Stanley	3-2	Craddock 2, Tippett	3724			3	4	5		7		8			2				9		10						1						
23		3	CREWE ALEXANDRA	1-0	Stott	2326			3	4	5		7		8			2				10		11						1						
24		10	STOCKPORT COUNTY	1-0	Tippett	2553			3	4	5		7		11			2				8		10				9	6	1						
25		17	Wrexham	1-1	Stott	4405			3	4	5	6	7		11			2				8		10				9		1						
26		24	TRANMERE ROVERS	1-3	Turnbull	3694			3	4	5		7		11			2				8		10				9	6	1						
27		31	Carlisle United	1-7	Turnbull	2224	3			4	5	6	7		11			2				8		10				9		1						
28	Feb	7	YORK CITY	2-2	Craddock 2	2577				4		6			7			2				8		9						1		3				
29		14	Rotherham United	3-1	Cowan, Tippett, Craddock	5047				4	5	6	7			9	10	3				8		11						1	2					
30		16	HALIFAX TOWN	2-3	Tippett 2	1118				4	5	2	7			9	10	3				8		11						1						
31		21	Wigan Borough	0-3		3364				4	5	2	7			9		3				8					10	6		1						
32	Mar	7	Lincoln City	0-5		6040				4	5	6			9		10	2				8		11			7			1			3			
33		14	HULL CITY	1-0	Goldsmith (og)	3465				4	5			7	9		11	2				8		10				6		1			3			
34		21	Doncaster Rovers	0-4		2997				4	5	6			11			2				9		10						1			3	7	8	
35		28	GATESHEAD	0-1		1555				4	5	6			9			2				8		10						1			3	7		11
36	Apr	3	ACCRINGTON STANLEY	1-6	Williams	3024				4	5	6			11		9	2				8		10						1			3	7		
37		4	Stockport County	2-2	Cowan, Tippett	5046		3		4	5	6			9			2				8		10						1	11		1			
38		6	Chesterfield	1-4	Tippett	5089		3		4	5				9			2				8		10				6		1				7	11	
39		11	NEW BRIGHTON	2-0	Tippett, Trippier	1855		3		4	5	6			9			2				8		10						1				7	11	
40		18	Halifax Town	0-1		2875		3		4	10	6			9			2				8							11	1				7		
41		21	DARLINGTON	1-2	Tippett	1573		3		7	5	4			10			2		9		8							6	1					11	
42		25	HARTLEPOOLS UNITED	1-2	Tippett	1586				7	4				9			2		5		8		10					6	1			3		11	
			Apps				15	18	20	34	35	31	31	20	40	20	9	24	8	16	1	34	1	24	3	3	10	11	2	27	2	6	9	3	1	
			Goals							2			10	3	18	6	3		1	2		10		2				2						1		

Played in one game: Woods (28,5)

Two own goals

F.A. Cup

	Date		Opponent	Score	Scorers	Att	P		O		Ba	Gr	St	Be	Ti	Le	Ha	Co				Cr		Cw	Ap
R1	Nov	29	DONCASTER ROVERS	1-2	Cowan	5526	1		3		5	4		8	7	10		2				9		11	6

Lancashire Cup

	Date		Opponent	Score	Scorers	Att			O	Wi	Ba	Gr	St	Be	Ti	Le		Co		Ev		Cr		Cw		Bl					Ly
R2	Sep	30	BURY	2-1	Stott, Bertram	1700			3		4	6	2	7	8	9				5		10		11							1
R3	Nov	11	MANCHESTER U.	0-1		1950			3		4	5	2	7	8	11	10					9				6					1

Manchester Cup

	Date		Opponent	Score	Scorers	Att	Wi	Gr	St	Ti	Ha	Co	La		Cr			Tu		Wa	Ly			Tp	Ch
R3	Mar	4	Manchester C.	1-0	Hargreaves	2300	4	6	7		10	3	5		8			9		1	2				
SF	Apr	15	Manchester U.	0-2			3	4/5/6		9		2			8		10			1				7	11

Lillywhite No.11 in R3

		P	W	D	L	F	A	W	D	L	F	A	Pts
1	Chesterfield	42	19	1	1	66	22	7	5	9	36	35	58
2	Lincoln City	42	16	3	2	60	19	9	4	8	42	40	57
3	Wrexham	42	16	4	1	61	25	5	8	8	33	37	54
4	Tranmere Rovers	42	16	3	2	73	26	8	3	10	38	48	54
5	Southport	42	15	3	3	52	19	7	6	8	36	37	53
6	Hull City	42	12	7	2	64	20	8	3	10	35	35	50
7	Stockport County	42	15	5	1	54	19	5	4	12	23	42	49
8	Carlisle United	42	13	4	4	68	32	7	1	13	30	49	45
9	Gateshead	42	14	4	3	46	22	2	9	10	25	51	45
10	Wigan Borough	42	14	4	3	48	25	5	1	15	28	61	43
11	Darlington	42	9	6	6	44	30	7	4	10	27	29	42
12	York City	42	15	3	3	59	30	3	3	15	26	52	42
13	Accrington Stanley	42	14	2	5	51	31	1	7	13	33	77	39
14	Rotherham United	42	9	6	6	50	34	4	6	11	31	49	38
15	Doncaster Rovers	42	9	8	4	40	18	4	3	14	25	47	37
16	Barrow	42	13	4	4	45	23	2	3	16	23	66	37
17	Halifax Town	42	11	6	4	30	16	2	3	16	25	73	35
18	Crewe Alexandra	42	13	2	6	52	35	1	4	16	14	58	34
19	New Brighton	42	12	4	5	36	25	1	3	17	13	51	33
20	Hartlepools United	42	10	2	9	47	37	2	4	15	20	49	30
21	ROCHDALE	42	9	1	11	42	50	3	5	13	20	57	30
22	Nelson	42	6	7	8	28	40	0	0	21	15	73	19

1931/32 21st in Division 3(N)

League – Division 3(N)

#		Date	Opponent	Score	Scorers	Att
1	Aug	29	ACCRINGTON STANLEY	2-2	Jones, Guyan	6974
2		31	Rotherham United	0-5		6431
3	Sep	5	Wrexham	0-4		7390
4		7	Stockport County	1-3	Watson	3941
5		12	CARLISLE UNITED	4-3	Everest, Steele, Watson 2	4383
6		15	STOCKPORT COUNTY	1-0	Williams	4384
7		19	Crewe Alexandra	0-1		6358
8		26	DARLINGTON	1-1	McAleer	3703
9	Oct	3	DONCASTER ROVERS	3-1	Watson 2, McAleer	4614
10		10	Southport	1-3	Steele	5442
11		17	Halifax Town	2-3	Everest, Murray	4082
12		24	WALSALL	0-1		2845
13		31	Gateshead	1-3	Jones	7227
14	Nov	7	NEW BRIGHTON	3-2	Everest 2, Jones	1888
15		14	Barrow	1-4	Watson	2542
16		21	HULL CITY	3-6	Nisbet, Watson 2	4593
17	Dec	5	CHESTER	0-3		3199
18		12	Hartlepools United	0-3		3085
19		25	Tranmere Rovers	1-9	Murray	5719
20		26	TRANMERE ROVERS	3-6	Brown, Murray, Everest	3933
21	Jan	2	Accrington Stanley	0-3		1824
22		9	Lincoln City	0-3		6737
23		16	WREXHAM	2-4	Everest, Steele	1743
24		23	Carlisle United	0-4		3812
25		30	CREWE ALEXANDRA	2-3	Howarth, Brown	1978
26	Feb	6	Darlington	1-3	Nisbet	2764
27		13	Doncaster Rovers	0-2		2856
28		20	SOUTHPORT	0-1		2894
29		27	HALIFAX TOWN	1-4	Crowther	3154
30	Mar	5	Walsall	1-2	Brown	2601
31		12	GATESHEAD	0-3		2526
32		19	New Brighton	1-1	Brown	2362
33		25	York City	2-5	McAleer, Howarth	5285
34		26	BARROW	0-6		2189
35		28	YORK CITY	3-5	McAleer, Brown 2	1387
36	Apr	2	Hull City	1-4	Hogg	3611
37		9	LINCOLN CITY	3-5	Williams, McAleer 2	1938
38		16	Chester	2-7	McAleer, Howarth	4658
39		23	HARTLEPOOLS UNITED	1-3	Bimson	1379
40	May	7	ROTHERHAM UNITED	1-4	Howarth	1724

Appearances (shirt numbers) — best reading

Columns: Abbott H, Beattie J, Plunkett AETB, Armstrong W, Everest J, Ward G, Steele E, Murray DJ, Guyan G, Jones GB, Hilley C, Hamilton JS, Williams I, Forster RH, Platt H, Watson RH, McAleer J, Black E, Appleyard F, Brown FW, Nisbet KH, Hill R, Welch H, Howarth H, Webster W, Twine FW, Bimson J, Hawes AR, Hogg T, Hornby R

#	Ab	Be	Pl	Ar	Ev	Wa	St	Mu	Gu	Jo	Hi	Ha	Wi	Fo	Pa	Wt	Mc	Bl	Ap	Br	Ni	HR	We	Ho	Web	Tw	Bi	Haw	Hog	Hor
1	1	2	3	4	5	6	7	8	9	10	11																			
2	1		3		5	6	7	8	9	10		2	4	11																
3	1		3		5	6	7	8	9	10			11	4																
4	1				5		7	8	9	10	6	2				4	11													
5	1		3		9	6	7	5		10		2	8			4	11													
6	1		3		9	6	7	5		10		2	8			4	11													
7	1		3		5	6	7	9		10		2	8			4	11													
8	1		3			6	7	8				2	4			5	11	9												
9	1		3			6	7	4				2	8			5	11	9												
10	1		3		4	6	7	8		10		2				5	11	9												
11	1		3		4	6	7	8	9			2	10			5	11													
12	1		3		4	6	7			10		2	8			5	11													
13	1		3		9	6	7	8		10		2	4			5	11													
14	1		3		9	6	7	8		10		2	4			5	11													
15	1		3		9	6	7					2	4			8	11	5	10											
16	1		3		9	6	7					2	4			5	11			8	10									
17	1		3		5	4						2	7				11	9		8	10		6							
18	1		3		5							2	7				11	9		8				6						
19			3		9	6		5				2	4				11			8	10		1	7						
20			3		5					10		2	4		6		11			9	7		1	8						
21	1		3		9		5				11	2	4		6					8	10		7							
22	1		3				6	5				2	4		5					8	10		7							
23	1		3		9	6		8			11	2	4		5						10		7							
24	1				9	6				10		2	4				11	5		8			7							
25	1		3									2	4				11	5	6	8			7	9						
26	1		3			6				10		2	4				11	5		8			7	9						
27	1		3				8					2	4				11	5						10	6					
28	1		3					8				2	4				11	5					7		2	6	10			9
29	1		3					8				2	4					5					7		2	6	10			11
30	1			5								2	4				11			8			7	9		6	10	3		
31	1			5								2	4				11			9				8		6	10	3	7	
32	1		3									2	4				9			8				11	5	6	10		7	
33	1		3									2	4				9			8				11	5	6	10		7	
34	1											2	4				9			8				11	3	5	6	10	7	
35						6						2	4				11			8			1	7	3	5	10		9	
36												2	4				9			8			1	7	6	3	11	5	10	
37												2	4				9			8			1	11	5	3	6	10	7	
38												2	4				9			8			1	11	5	3	6	10	7	
39					7							2	4				9			8			1	11	5	3	6	10	9	
40					5							2	4				9			8			1	11	6	3		10	7	
Apps	32	14	12	4	22	22	19	22	4	19	3	39	34	2	13	17	20	8	2	21	12	2	8	20	14	10	12	13	10	2
Goals					6		3	3	1	3			2			8	7			6	2			4			1		1	

Played in one game: R Grant (game 12, at 9), J Whitelaw (18,10),
G White (27,9), J Crowther (29,9 - 1 goal).
Played in games 4 and 24: C Constantine (3).
Played in games 8 and 9: T Flannigan (10).

F.A. Cup

R	Date	Opponent	Score	Scorers	Att	Ab	Pl	Ev	St	Mu	Jo	Ha	Wi	Mc	Bl	Ap
R1	Nov 28	Scunthorpe United	1-2	Murray	5000	1	3	5	7	8	10	2	4	11	9	6

Lancashire Cup

R	Date	Opponent	Score	Scorers	Att	Ab	Pl	Ar	Ev	Wa	St	Jo	Ha	Wi	Wt	Mc
R2	Sep 22	ACCRINGTON STANLEY	0-1	Murray		1	3	4	5	6	7	10	2	8	9	11

Manchester Cup

R	Date	Opponent	Score	Scorers	Att
R3	Feb 24	Manchester City	0-6		

Players: Steele 6, Murray 7, Jones 9, Hamilton 3, Williams 2, Platt 10, Watson 4, Howarth 8, Webster 5, Hornby 11.
Played at No.1 E. Plane

Final Division 3(N) table

		P	W	D	L	F	A	W	D	L	F	A	Pts
1	Lincoln City	40	16	2	2	65	13	10	3	7	41	34	57
2	Gateshead	40	15	3	2	59	20	10	4	6	35	28	57
3	Chester	40	16	2	2	54	22	5	6	9	24	38	50
4	Tranmere Rovers	40	15	4	1	76	23	4	7	9	31	35	49
5	Barrow	40	16	1	3	59	23	8	0	12	27	36	49
6	Crewe Alexandra	40	15	3	2	64	24	6	3	11	31	42	48
7	Southport	40	14	5	1	44	15	4	5	11	14	38	46
8	Hull City	40	14	1	5	52	21	6	4	10	30	32	45
9	York City	40	14	3	3	49	24	4	4	12	27	57	43
10	Wrexham	40	14	2	4	42	25	4	5	11	22	44	43
11	Darlington	40	12	1	7	41	27	5	3	12	25	42	38
12	Stockport County	40	12	3	5	31	15	1	8	11	24	38	37
13	Hartlepools United	40	10	4	6	47	37	6	1	13	31	63	37
14	Accrington Stanley	40	14	4	2	56	20	1	2	17	19	60	36
15	Doncaster Rovers	40	12	3	5	38	27	4	1	15	21	53	36
16	Walsall	40	12	3	5	42	30	4	0	16	15	55	35
17	Halifax Town	40	11	6	3	36	18	2	2	16	25	69	34
18	Carlisle United	40	9	7	4	40	23	2	4	14	24	56	33
19	Rotherham United	40	10	3	7	41	23	4	1	15	22	49	32
20	New Brighton	40	8	5	7	25	23	0	3	17	13	53	24
21	ROCHDALE	40	4	2	14	33	63	0	1	19	15	72	11

1932/33 18th in Division 3(N)

#		Date	Opposition	Score	Scorers	Att	Caunce L	Hamilton JS	Wheelhouse B	Gordon JG	Nuttall H	Benton WH	Bell SG	Watson TL	Rowe RK	Snow GEG	Watson WT	Rigby W	Hill T	Armstrong W	Lowery B	Gardiner W	Beel GW	McAleer J	Bain D	Shonakan J	Williamson TW	Gregson W	Welch H	Sharples H	Worrall A	Williams RS	Bowsher SJ	Shepherd
1	Aug	27	CARLISLE UNITED	0-1		4898	1	2	3	4	5	6	7	8	9	10	11																	
2		29	Barrow	1-1	TL Watson	4786	1	2	3	4	5	6		8	9	10	11	7																
3	Sep	3	York City	6-2	TL Watson 4, Snow 2	4363	1	2	3	4	5	6		9		10	11	7	8															
4		6	BARROW	0-0		4441	1	2	3	4		6		9		10	11	7	8	5														
5		10	CREWE ALEXANDRA	1-4	WT Watson	6475	1	2	3	5		6				10	11	7	8		4	9												
6		17	Doncaster Rovers	0-1		4094	1	2	3	4	5	6		9		10	11	7					8											
7		24	Southport	0-2		5928	1	2	3	4	5	6				10	11	7					8	9										
8	Oct	1	MANSFIELD TOWN	2-1	Bain 2	5945	1	2	3	4	5	6				10	11	7					8		9									
9		8	Rotherham United	0-2		2555	1	2	3	4	5	6				10	11	7					8		9									
10		15	ACCRINGTON STANLEY	2-0	WT Watson, Beel	7041	1	2	3	4	5	6				10	11						9			7	8							
11		22	DARLINGTON	1-1	Beel	5822	1	2	3	4	5	6				10	11						9			7	8							
12		29	Stockport County	3-2	Bain, Beel 2	4292	1	2	3	4	5	6				10	11						8	9	7									
13	Nov	5	GATESHEAD	1-0	Bain	8650	1	2	3	4	5	6				10	11						8	9	7									
14		12	Walsall	1-2	Beel	5068	1	2	3	4	5	6				10	11						8	9	7									
15		19	WREXHAM	3-1	WT Watson, Williamson 2	7897	1	2	3	4	5	6				10	11						8			7	9							
16	Dec	3	HALIFAX TOWN	1-0	Benton (p)	3608	1		3	4	5	6				10	11						8			7	9	2						
17		10	Mansfield Town	1-4	WT Watson	4441	1	2	3	4	5	6				10	11						8			7	9							
18		17	BARNSLEY	2-3	WT Watson, Snow	4071	1	2	3	4	5	6		9		10	11						8			7								
19		24	Hull City	1-1	WT Watson	10881		2	3		4	6					11		10	5			8	9		7			1					
20		26	New Brighton	3-0	WT Watson, Benton (p), Shonakan	3738		2	3		4	6				8	11		10	5				9		7			1					
21		27	NEW BRIGHTON	1-0	McAleer	6055		2	3		4	6				8	11		10	5				9		7			1					
22		31	Carlisle United	2-2	WT Watson 2	4093		2	3		4	6				10	11			5			8	9		7			1					
23	Jan	2	Hartlepools United	0-3		3359		2	3		4	6				10	11			5			8	9		7			1					
24		7	YORK CITY	1-4	Beel	3968		2		8	4	6				10				5			9		3	7	11		1					
25		18	Tranmere Rovers	1-3	Beel	1719		2	3		4	6				8			10	5			9	11		7			1					
26		21	Crewe Alexandra	1-3	TL Watson	3287			2		4	6		9		10				5			8	11	3	7			1					
27		28	DONCASTER ROVERS	2-3	Snow, Shonakan	2390				4	6	3				10	11			5			9			7	8		1	2				
28	Feb	4	SOUTHPORT	1-3	WT Watson	3349			3	4	5	6				8	11						10			7			1	2	9			
29		18	ROTHERHAM UNITED	2-2	Snow, Beel	1932		2	3	4	5	10				6	11						8	9		7			1					
30	Mar	4	Darlington	1-5	WT Watson	2533		2	3	4	5	10				6	11						9	8	7				1					
31		11	STOCKPORT COUNTY	0-2		4151		2	3	4	5	8				6	11								10	7			1			9		
32		18	Gateshead	0-3		2797		2			4	6				10	11	7							3	8			1			9	5	
33		25	WALSALL	1-1	Benton	2979		2	3	4		8				10	11								6	7			1			9	5	
34	Apr	1	Wrexham	1-4	Snow	5505		2	3		4	6				10	11					7	8			1					9	5	
35		8	TRANMERE ROVERS	0-3		3007		2	3		4	6				10	11						8	7			1			9	5			
36		14	Chester	0-2		9870		2	3	4		8				10	11						9	6	7			1				5		
37		15	Halifax Town	0-2		4032		2	3	4		8				10	11						9	6	7			1				5		
38		17	CHESTER	2-0	Snow, Bennet (og)	3742		2	3	4		8				9	11	7					6			1				10	5			
39		22	HARTLEPOOLS UNITED	6-2	Snow 2, Rigby 2, Benton, Williams	3249		2	3	4		8				10	11	7					6			1				9	5			
40		29	Barnsley	1-3	Snow	1931		2	3	5	4	8				10	11	7					6			1				9				
41	May	3	Accrington Stanley	3-0	WT Watson, Bain, Rigby	1013		2	3	4	6	8				10	11	7					9			1						5		
42		6	HULL CITY	3-2	Benton, Snow 2	4387		2	3	4	6	8				10	11	7					9			1						5		
					Apps		18	38	39	32	35	42	2	7	1	41	39	14	7	10	1	1	20	15	20	27	7	1	24	2	1	8	10	
					Goals							5		6		12	12	3					8	1	5	2	2					1		

One own goal

F.A. Cup

		Date	Opposition	Score		Att	Caunce L		Wheelhouse B	Gordon JG	Nuttall H	Benton WH				Snow GEG	Watson WT						Beel GW	McAleer J	Bain D	Shonakan J								
R1	Nov	26	STOCKPORT COUNTY	0-2		9592	1		3	2	5	6				10	11						8		4	7	9							

Lancashire Cup

		Date	Opposition	Score	Scorers	Att	Caunce L	Hamilton JS	Wheelhouse B	Gordon JG	Nuttall H	Benton WH				Snow GEG	Watson WT	Rigby W			Lowery B		Beel GW										
R1	Sep	19	ACCRINGTON ST.	2-2	Snow, W.T. Watson	1300	1	2	3	4	5	6			9	10	11	7					8											
R1r	Oct	5	Accrington St.	2-4	Snow, Beel	1300	1	2	3	4		6			7	9	11				5		8											

Manchester Cup

		Date	Opposition	Score	Scorers	Att		Hamilton JS		Gordon JG		Benton WH				Snow GEG	Watson WT		Hill T				Beel GW	McAleer J		Shonakan J			Welch H	Sharples H	Worrall A	Williams RS		Shepherd
R3	Feb	7	OLDHAM A.	5-3	Snow, McAleer(2), Benton(2)			2		4		8				10	11		5				9			7			3	1				6
SF	Apr	10	Manchester C.	0-4		750		2				8				6	10						11	4		7			3	1		9	5	

Final League Table — Division 3 (North)

		P	W	D	L	F	A	W	D	L	F	A	Pts
1	Hull City	42	18	3	0	69	14	8	4	9	31	31	59
2	Wrexham	42	18	2	1	75	15	6	7	8	31	36	57
3	Stockport County	42	16	2	3	69	30	5	10	6	30	28	54
4	Chester	42	15	4	2	57	25	7	4	10	37	41	52
5	Walsall	42	16	4	1	53	15	3	6	12	22	43	48
6	Doncaster Rovers	42	13	8	0	52	26	4	6	11	25	53	48
7	Gateshead	42	12	5	4	45	25	7	4	10	33	42	47
8	Barnsley	42	14	3	4	60	31	5	5	11	32	49	46
9	Barrow	42	12	3	6	41	24	6	4	11	19	36	43
10	Crewe Alexandra	42	16	3	2	57	16	4	0	17	23	68	43
11	Tranmere Rovers	42	11	4	6	49	31	6	4	11	21	35	42
12	Southport	42	15	3	3	54	20	2	4	15	16	47	41
13	Accrington Stanley	42	12	4	5	55	29	3	6	12	23	47	40
14	Hartlepools United	42	15	3	3	56	29	1	4	16	31	87	39
15	Halifax Town	42	12	4	5	39	23	3	4	14	32	67	38
16	Mansfield Town	42	13	4	4	57	22	1	3	17	27	78	35
17	Rotherham United	42	14	3	4	42	21	0	3	18	18	63	34
18	ROCHDALE	42	9	4	8	32	33	4	3	14	26	47	33
19	Carlisle United	42	8	7	6	34	25	5	0	16	17	50	33
20	York City	42	10	4	7	51	38	3	2	16	21	54	32
21	New Brighton	42	8	6	7	42	36	3	4	14	21	52	32
22	Darlington	42	9	6	6	42	32	1	2	18	24	77	28

Results

#		Date	Opponent	Score	Scorers	Att
1	Aug	26	DARLINGTON	1-0	JR Smith	4633
2		30	Hartlepools United	1-2	JR Smith	4580
3	Sep	2	Gateshead	1-2	JR Smith	4226
4		5	HARTLEPOOLS UNITED	3-0	Rigby, Weldon, Murfin	4766
5		9	ACCRINGTON STANLEY	0-1		7437
6		16	Chesterfield	0-3		9969
7		23	CREWE ALEXANDRA	2-0	Weldon, Collins	5621
8		30	TRANMERE ROVERS	1-0	Weldon	5229
9	Oct	7	Barnsley	1-4	Murfin	8970
10		14	MANSFIELD TOWN	2-2	Murfin, JR Smith	5334
11		21	New Brighton	2-0	Murfin, JR Smith	4450
12		28	ROTHERHAM UNITED	0-2		4322
13	Nov	4	Walsall	0-2		5567
14		18	Chester	1-7	Fitton	4477
15	Dec	2	Barrow	3-5	Collins, Robson, Benton	3736
16		9	BARNSLEY	3-1	Fitton, Robson, Benton	2641
17		16	Stockport County	1-4	Robson	3790
18		23	HALIFAX TOWN	1-2	Benton	3258
19		25	Southport	0-3		4956
20		26	SOUTHPORT	3-3	Fitton 2, Gordon	3944
21		30	Darlington	1-1	Collins	3770
22	Jan	6	GATESHEAD	2-0	Collins, Wheelhouse	3220
23		13	DONCASTER ROVERS	0-2		3186
24		20	Accrington Stanley	3-1	Collins, Rigby, Weldon	2851
25		27	CHESTERFIELD	0-1		4151
26	Feb	3	Crewe Alexandra	1-4	Robson	2766
27		6	CARLISLE UNITED	0-1		1261
28		10	Tranmere Rovers	0-4		3612
29		20	YORK CITY	3-6	Robson 3	800
30		24	Mansfield Town	0-5		4502
31	Mar	3	NEW BRIGHTON	1-1	Fitton	2534
32		10	Rotherham United	0-4		2227
33		17	WALSALL	3-3	Weldon 3	2108
34		24	York City	1-6	Murfin	3382
35		30	WREXHAM	1-2	Buckley	3052
36		31	CHESTER	6-0	JR Smith, Wheelhouse, Fitton, Robson	2942
37	Apr	2	Wrexham	1-4	Robson	5061
38		7	Doncaster Rovers	0-5		4873
39		14	BARROW	1-2	Robson	2298
40		21	Carlisle United	0-3		2762
41		28	STOCKPORT COUNTY	1-1	Murfin	7544
42	May	5	Halifax Town	2-4	Murfin, Collins	3434

Appearances and goals

Players (columns): Welch H, Webster WG, Wheelhouse B, Gordon JG, Bain D, Buckley W, Rigby W, Cairns J, Smith JR, Weldon A, Murfin C, Butler J, Hope H, Chadwick H, Barrott W, Spargo S, Collins JH, Hoadley D, McRonie D, Walmsley C, Peters WT, Slicer W, Fitton F(2), Robson JC, Benton WH, Smith TS, Shepherd T, Coneys JI, Bliss APD, Longbottom H

#	Wel	Web	Whe	Gor	Bai	Buc	Rig	Cai	SmJR	Weld	Mur	But	Hop	Cha	Bar	Spa	Col	Hoa	McR	Walm	Pet	Sli	Fit	Rob	Ben	SmTS	She	Con	Bli	Lon
1	1	2	3	4	5	6	7	8	9	10	11																			
2	1	2	3	4	5	6	7	8	9	10	11																			
3	1	2		4	3	6	7	8	9	10	11	5																		
4	1	2		4	3	6	7		9	10	11	5	8																	
5	1	2		4	3	6	7	8	9		11	5		10																
6	1	2		4	3	6	7	8	9	10																				
7	1	2		4	3	6	7		9	10						5	8		11											
8	1	2		4	3	6	7		9	10						5	8		11											
9	1	2		4	3	6	7		9	10						5	8													
10	1	2	3	4		6			9	10	11					5	8	7												
11		2	3	4	5	6			9	10	11						8	7			1									
12		2	3			6			9	10	11						8	7			1	4								
13		2	3			4				10	11						9		5	8	1									
14	1	2	3			4											10				1		5	9	11	8				
15			2		4	3	6					7					10						9	11	8	5				
16			2			4	6					10	7					1					9	11	8	5				
17		2	3	4	6							10	7					1					9	11	8	5				
18		2	3			4	6					10	7					1					9	11	8	5				
19		2	3			4	6	7				10						1					9	11	8	5				
20		2		4	3			7				10					8	1					9	11		5	6			
21		2		4	3			8				10	7				9	1						11		5	6			
22		2	7	4	3	6		8				10					9	1						11		5				
23		2		4	3	6		8				10	7				9	1						11		5				
24		2		4	3	6		8				10	7				9	1						11		5				
25		2	7	4	3	6		8				10					9	1						11		5				
26		2	7	4	3	6						10					9	1						11		5	8			
27		2	3	4	7	6	8					10						1					9	11		5				
28			2	4	3	6	8					10	7				9	1						11		5				
29			2	4	6		8					10	7				9	1				3		11		5				
30			2	4	9		8					10	7	5				1				3		11		6				
31		2		5			8					10	7					1				3	9	11			6			4
32		2		5			7	8					9					1					10	11	3	6				4
33		2	3		4		6	7	8	10								1					9	11	6				5	
34		2	3			4	6	7		10	11							1					9	11			8	5		
35		2	3	4		6	8			10	7							1						11					5	
36		2	3	4		6	7		8								10						9	11			5			
37		2		4	3	6	7		8								10						9	11			5			
38		2	3	4		6				8	10	7						9						11			5			
39		2	3	4		6	8				10	7						9						11			5			
40		2	3	4		6	8				10	7						9						11			5			
41		2		4		6	8				10	7						9						11			5		3	
42		2		4		6	8				10	7						9						11			5		3	

	Wel	Web	Whe	Gor	Bai	Buc	Rig	Cai	SmJR	Weld	Mur	But	Hop	Cha	Bar	Spa	Col	Hoa	McR	Walm	Pet	Sli	Fit	Rob	Ben	SmTS	She	Con	Bli	Lon
Apps	11	38	27	34	32	34	32	5	25	27	26	5	2	1	1	4	30		5	31	1	4	13	28	6	25	4	2	5	2
Goals			2	1		1	2		8	7	7						6						6	10	3					

Abandoned

	Date	Opponent	Score	Scorers																													
	Nov 11	YORK C.	1-2	Robson		2		4	6				10			5				8	7	1			3	9	11						

F.A. Cup

	Date	Opponent	Score	Scorers	Att	Web	Whe		Bai	Buc	Rig		SmJR									Hoa					Fit	Rob	Ben	SmTS
R1	Nov 25	Sutton Town	1-2	Rigby	4946	2	3		5	6	7		9									1					10	11	8	4

Third Division North Cup

	Date	Opponent	Score	Scorers
R1	Jan 22	STOCKPORT COUNTY	2-4	Collins 2

Teams: Webster 2, Gordon 4, Bain 3, Buckley 6, Cairns 8, Weldon 10, Hoadley 7, McRonie 5, Collins 9, Peters 1, Robson 11

Lancashire Cup

	Date	Opponent	Score	Scorers	Att
R1	Sep 26	BURY	1-2	J.R.Smith	2500

Teams: Welch 1, Webster 2, Wheelhouse 3, Gordon 4, Bain 5, Buckley 6, Rigby 7, Smith JR 9, Weldon 10, Collins 8, Hoadley 11

Manchester Cup

	Date	Opponent	Score
R3	Feb 28	Manchester U.	0-9

Teams: Webster 2, Wheelhouse 3, Buckley 6, Rigby 7, Cairns 8, Weldon 10, Murfin 11, Butler 4, Walmsley 1, Fitton 9, Longbottom 5

Final League Table — Division 3 (North)

		P	W	D	L	F	A	W	D	L	F	A	Pts
1	Barnsley	42	18	3	0	64	18	9	5	7	54	43	62
2	Chesterfield	42	18	1	2	56	17	9	6	6	30	26	61
3	Stockport County	42	18	3	0	84	23	6	8	7	31	29	59
4	Walsall	42	18	2	1	66	18	5	5	11	31	42	53
5	Doncaster Rovers	42	17	1	3	58	24	5	8	8	25	37	53
6	Wrexham	42	14	1	6	68	35	9	4	8	34	38	51
7	Tranmere Rovers	42	16	2	3	57	21	4	5	12	27	42	47
8	Barrow	42	12	5	4	78	45	7	4	10	38	49	47
9	Halifax Town	42	15	2	4	57	30	5	2	14	23	61	44
10	Chester	42	11	6	4	59	26	6	0	15	30	60	40
11	Hartlepools United	42	14	3	4	54	24	2	4	15	35	69	39
12	York City	42	11	5	5	44	28	4	3	14	27	46	38
13	Carlisle United	42	11	6	4	43	23	4	2	15	23	58	38
14	Crewe Alexandra	42	12	3	6	54	38	3	3	15	27	59	36
15	New Brighton	42	13	3	5	41	25	1	5	15	21	62	36
16	Darlington	42	11	4	6	47	35	2	5	14	23	66	35
17	Mansfield Town	42	9	7	5	49	29	2	5	14	32	59	34
18	Southport	42	6	11	4	35	29	2	6	13	28	61	33
19	Gateshead	42	10	3	8	46	40	2	6	13	30	70	33
20	Accrington Stanley	42	10	6	5	44	38	3	1	17	21	63	33
21	Rotherham United	42	5	7	9	31	35	5	1	15	22	56	28
22	ROCHDALE	42	7	5	9	34	30	2	1	18	19	73	24

1934/35   20th in Division 3(N)

#	Date		Opponent	Result	Scorers	Att	Walmsley C	Worthy A	Ives A	Wyness GD	Jordan G	Buckley W	Ryder F	Humpish AE	Bartley PI	Douglas WI	Howe HG	Whyte C	Cook R	Nicol JM	Redfern L	Smith WH	Thomas WE	Sullivan LG	Dobson GF	Jones GT	Eaton C	Clarke L	Welch H	Skaife S
1	Aug	25	Lincoln City	0-3		6765	1	2	3	4	5	6	7	8	9	10	11													
2		28	BARROW	0-1		4396	1	2	3	4	5	6		8	10	9	11	7												
3	Sep	1	TRANMERE ROVERS	1-1	Whyte	6582	1	2		4	5	6		8	10	9	11	7	3											
4		3	Barrow	1-1	Bartley	5556	1	2		4	5	6	10	8	9		11	7	3											
5		8	Wrexham	0-2		6588	1	2		4	5	6		8	9		11	7	3	3	10									
6		15	HALIFAX TOWN	2-4	Nicol, Thomas	7830	1	2		4	5	9		8				7	3	10			6	11						
7		22	Rotherham United	0-4		3807	1	2		5		6	8	4	9				7	3	10			11						
8		29	WALSALL	1-0	Sullivan	2511	1	2	3		5	6		4					7		10	8		9	11					
9	Oct	6	Chesterfield	0-2		4413	1	2	3		5	6		4					7		10	8		9	11					
10		13	MANSFIELD TOWN	1-0	Sullivan (p)	3684	1	2	3		5	6		4	9				7		10	8			11					
11		20	ACCRINGTON STANLEY	2-2	Nicol, Redfern	5263	1	2	3		5	6		4	9						10	8			11	7				
12		27	Gateshead	0-2		3197	1	2		4	5	6	7		9						10	8			11	6				
13	Nov	3	STOCKPORT COUNTY	0-5		5045	1	2		4	5	3			9		11				10	8			7	6				
14		10	Crewe Alexandra	1-4	Clarke	3620	1	2			5	3					11				10	4	7			6	8	9		
15		17	HARTLEPOOLS UNITED	3-2	Nicol 2, Dobson	3782		2		5		3									10	6	11		7		8	9	1	4
16	Dec	1	SOUTHPORT	2-2	Clarke, Smith	2869				5	2		8							6	11			7	3	10	9	1	4	
17		15	NEW BRIGHTON	3-1	Clarke 3	3095				5	2		8							6			11	7	3	10	9	1	4	
18		22	York City	1-0	Eaton	3003				5	2		8							6			11	7	3	10	9	1	4	
19		25	DARLINGTON	1-3	Sullivan	5466				5	2		8							6			11	7	3	10	9	1	4	
20		26	Darlington	2-2	Sullivan, Clarke	6943		2		5										10	6		11	7	3	8	9	1	4	
21		29	LINCOLN CITY	2-0	Nicol 2	4531				5		2					7			10	6		11		3	8	9	1	4	
22	Jan	5	Tranmere Rovers	1-4	Clarke	6816				5		2		8			7				6		11		3	10	9	1	4	
23		12	Doncaster Rovers	0-1		5895				5		2		8			7				6		11		3	10	9	1	4	
24		19	WREXHAM	3-3	Humpsih, Howe, Sullivan (p)	4702				5		2		8			7			10	6		11		3		9	1	4	
25		26	Halifax Town	1-1	Clarke	7133		2		5				8			7				6		11		3	10	9	1	4	
26	Feb	2	ROTHERHAM UNITED	1-3	Humpish	4212		2		5				8			7				6		11		3	10	9	1	4	
27		9	Walsall	0-0		6954		2		5				8			7				6		11		3	10	9	1	4	
28		16	CHESTERFIELD	0-2		2033		2	3	5							7			10	6		11	8			9	1	4	
29		23	Mansfield Town	0-1		4788	1	2		5		6			9		8						11	7	3	10			4	
30	Mar	2	Accrington Stanley	5-2	Nicol 2, Sullivan 2, Clarke	2019	1	2		5		6					7			10	8		11		3		9		4	
31		9	GATESHEAD	6-1	Howe 2, Nichol, Redfern, Sullivan, Clarke	3562	1	2		5		6					7			10	8		11		3		9		4	
32		16	Stockport County	1-3	Nicol	7735	1	2		5		3	6				7			10	8		11				9		4	
33		23	CREWE ALEXANDRA	3-0	Sullivan, Clarke 2	1889	1	2		5		6		8			7			10			11		3		9		4	
34		30	Hartlepools United	0-0		2955	1	2		5		6		8			7			10			11		3		9		4	
35	Apr	3	Chester	0-1		3004	1	2		5		6		8			7			10			11		3	9			4	
36		6	DONCASTER ROVERS	0-1		7154	1	2		5		6		8			7			10			11		3		9		4	
37		13	Southport	1-2	Clarke	2315	1	2		5		6		8			7			10			11		3		9		4	
38		19	Carlisle United	0-0		4417	1			5		6		8			7						2	11		3	10	9		4
39		20	CHESTER	3-3	Bartley 2, Dobson	6933	1			5		6		8	9					10			2	11	7	3			4	
40		22	CARLISLE UNITED	3-1	Nicol, Dobson 2	5711	1			5		6		8	9					10			2	11	7	3			4	
41		27	New Brighton	0-1		1875		2		5		6		8	9								11	7	3			4	
42	May	4	YORK CITY	2-0	Redfern, Dobson	5212	1	2		5		6									8		11	7	3	10	9		4
			Apps				28	31	7	33	17	37	6	31	14	1	24	9	5	27	25	3	6	32	15	28	17	24	14	28
			Goals											2	3		3	1		11	3	1	1	9	5		1	13		

F.A. Cup

	Date		Opponent	Result	Scorers	Att					Jordan	Buckley		Humpish						Nicol	Redfern			Sullivan	Dobson	Jones	Eaton			Skaife
R1	Nov	24	Wrexham	1-4	Smith	5500	1				5	2		8						6	11			7	3	10	9			4

Third Division North Cup

	Date		Opponent	Result	Scorers	Att
R1	Dec	8	Carlisle United	1-1	Eaton	2000
rep	Jan	8	CARLISLE UNITED	3-0	Humpish, Clarke 2	1500
R3	Mar	25	Stockport County	0-3		1500

Bye in R2

Lancashire Cup

	Date		Opponent	Result	Scorers	Att
R1	Sep	11	OLDHAM A.	2-3	Buckley, Smith	4000

Manchester Cup

	Date		Opponent	Result	Scorers	Att
R1	Feb	19	Bury	0-3		4000

		P	W	D	L	F	A	W	D	L	F	A	Pts
1	Doncaster Rovers	42	16	0	5	53	21	10	5	6	34	23	57
2	Halifax Town	42	17	2	2	50	24	8	3	10	26	43	55
3	Chester	42	14	4	3	62	27	6	10	5	29	31	54
4	Lincoln City	42	14	3	4	55	21	8	4	9	32	37	51
5	Darlington	42	15	5	1	50	15	6	4	11	30	44	51
6	Tranmere Rovers	42	15	4	2	53	20	5	7	9	21	35	51
7	Stockport County	42	15	2	4	57	22	7	1	13	33	50	47
8	Mansfield Town	42	16	3	2	55	25	3	6	12	20	37	47
9	Rotherham United	42	14	4	3	56	21	5	3	13	30	52	45
10	Chesterfield	42	13	4	4	46	21	4	6	11	25	31	44
11	Wrexham	42	12	5	4	47	25	4	6	11	29	44	43
12	Hartlepools United	42	12	4	5	52	34	5	3	13	28	44	41
13	Crewe Alexandra	42	12	6	3	41	25	2	5	14	25	61	39
14	Walsall	42	11	7	3	51	18	2	3	16	30	54	36
15	York City	42	12	5	4	50	20	3	1	17	26	62	36
16	New Brighton	42	9	6	6	32	25	5	2	14	27	51	36
17	Barrow	42	11	5	5	37	31	2	4	15	21	56	35
18	Accrington Stanley	42	11	5	5	44	36	1	5	15	19	53	34
19	Gateshead	42	12	4	5	36	28	1	4	16	22	68	34
20	ROCHDALE	42	9	5	7	39	35	2	6	13	14	36	33
21	Southport	42	6	6	9	27	36	4	6	11	28	49	32
22	Carlisle United	42	7	6	8	34	36	1	1	19	17	66	23

1934-35 Season
Back: Mulrooney (Asst. Train.), Wyness, Walmsley, Jordan, Skaife, Buckley
Front: Smith*, Eaton*, Redfern*, Clarke, Humpish, Dobson* (* believe correct)

1935-36 Season
Far Back: Eaton, Jones, Baker, Huntley
Back: Wyness, Sutcliffe, Clarke, Skaife, Cook, Wiggins, Worthy
Front: Johnson, Buckley, Duff, Hales, Emmerson

1935/36 20th in Division 3(N)

No	Date	Opponent	Res	Scorers	Att	Baker TW	Worthy A	Jones GT	Huntley E	Wyness GD	Buckley W	Emmerson GAH	Duff JH	Wiggins IA	Marshall WH	Hales H	Taylor F	Johnson MH	Elliott SD	Skaife S	Taylor S	Brierley H	Eaton C	Emerson A	Huxley FR	Driver R	Clarke L	Cornthwaite CH	Cook R
1	Aug 31	CREWE ALEXANDRA	2-1	Marshall, Hales	9036	1	2	3	4	5	6	7	8	9	10	11													
2	Sep 2	Stockport County	0-4		11919	1	2	3	4	5	6	7	8	9	10	11													
3	7	Accrington Stanley	4-2	Marshall, Johnson 2, F Taylor	4212	1	2	3	4	5	6		8		10	11	7	9											
4	10	STOCKPORT COUNTY	1-1	F Taylor	10238	1	2	3	4	5	6		8		10	11	7	9											
5	14	SOUTHPORT	2-1	F Taylor, Marshall	5605	1	2	3	4	5	6		8		10	11	7	9											
6	21	Chester	2-5	Buckley, Marshall	6914	1	2	3	4	5	6		8		10	11	7		9										
7	28	LINCOLN CITY	0-0		7052	1	2	3	4		5			9	10	11	7					6	8						
8	Oct 5	Halifax Town	0-2		7396	1	2	3				7			10	11		9				6	8						
9	12	York City	1-2	Marshall	4487	1	2	3	4	5		7			10	11						6	8	9					
10	19	OLDHAM ATHLETIC	2-6	Worthy, Duff	4985	1	2		4	5		7	8		10	11			9			6			3				
11	26	Wrexham	1-0	Duff	4063	1	2	3		5		7	8		10	11		9		4		6							
12	Nov 2	ROTHERHAM UNITED	1-1	Marshall	5786	1	2	3		5		7	8		10	11		9		4		6							
13	9	Mansfield Town	0-3		4762		2	3		5		7	8		10	11		9		4		6				1			
14	16	HARTLEPOOLS UNITED	0-1		4878	1	2	3		5		7		9	10	11		8		4		6							
15	23	Carlisle United	3-4	Eaton, Hales 2	6029			3			6	5	7			2	8	11	9	4			10					1	
16	Dec 7	Tranmere Rovers	2-5	Wiggins 2	5657	1	2	3		5	6			9		11	7	8		4			10						
17	14	GATESHEAD	5-0	Wiggins 2, Clarke 3	2966	1	2	3		5		7		9		11				4		6	10				8		
18	21	Darlington	0-4		3422	1	2	3		5		7		9		11				4		6	10				8		
19	25	BARROW	1-1	Wiggins	5031	1	2	3		5	6			9		11				4			10				8		
20	26	Barrow	2-6	Wiggins, G Emmerson	4383	1	2			5	3	7	6	9		11		8		4									
21	28	Crewe Alexandra	1-3	Elliot	4856	1	2		4	5	3	7	6	9		11		10	8										
22	Jan 1	Chesterfield	2-2	Johnson 2	11138	1	2	3	4	5	6	7	8			11		9				10							
23	4	ACCRINGTON STANLEY	2-2	Duff, Johnson (p)	4822	1	2	3	4	5	6	7				11		9				10							
24	18	Southport	1-1	Wiggins	2475	1	2	3	4	5	6	7		9		11			8			10							
25	25	CHESTER	1-1	Eaton	4420	1	2	3	4	5	6	7		9		11							10				8		
26	Feb 1	Lincoln City	1-5	Clarke	4835	1	2	3	4	5	6	7		9		11							10				8		
27	8	HALIFAX TOWN	2-0	Duff, Williams (og)	4309	1	2	3	4	5	6	7	8	9	10	11													
28	15	YORK CITY	2-3	Wiggins 2	4670	1	2	3	4	5	6	7	8	9	10	11													
29	22	Oldham Athletic	3-3	Duff 2, Marshall	6051	1	2	3	4	5	6	7	8	9	10	11													
30	29	MANSFIELD TOWN	3-1	Duff 2, Wiggins	2227	1	2	3	4	5	6	7	8	9	10	11													
31	Mar 7	Rotherham United	0-6		2957	1	2		4	5	3	7	8	9	6	11		10											
32	14	WREXHAM	2-1	Wiggins 2	3307	1	2	3	4	5	6	7	8	9	10	11													
33	21	Hartlepools United	0-1		4110	1	2	3	4	5	6	7	8	9	10	11													
34	28	CARLISLE UNITED	0-0		3722		2	3	4	5	6	7	8	9	10	11												1	
35	31	WALSALL	6-4	Duff 2, Wiggins 2, Marshall, G Emmerson	1942		2			5	6	7	8	9	10	11				4								1	
36	Apr 4	Walsall	0-1		3396	1	2	3		5	6		8	9	10	11	7			4									
37	10	New Brighton	0-2		3299	1	2	3		5	6	7	8	9	10	11				4									
38	11	TRANMERE ROVERS	0-0		5760	1	2	3		5	6	7	8		10	11		9		4									
39	13	NEW BRIGHTON	1-0	Hales	4124	1	2	3		5	6	7	8		10	11		9		4									
40	18	Gateshead	0-1		1996	1	2	3		5	6	7	8	9	10	11				4									
41	25	DARLINGTON	1-1	Marshall	2927	1	2	3		5	6	7	8	9	10	11				4									
42	May 2	CHESTERFIELD	1-1	G Emmerson	3551	1	2	3		5	6	7	8	9	10	11				4									
		Apps				38	41	38	24	37	37	35	31	27	31	38	6	15	11	16	2	10	14	1	1	2	5	2	
		Goals					1				1	3	10	14	9	4	3	5	1				2				4		

One own goal

F.A. Cup

Rd	Date	Opponent	Res	Scorers	Att	Baker TW	Worthy A	Jones GT	Huntley E	Wyness GD	Buckley W	Emmerson GAH	Duff JH	Wiggins IA	Marshall WH	Hales H	Taylor F	Johnson MH	Elliott SD	Skaife S	Taylor S	Brierley H	Eaton C
R1	Nov 30	Halifax Town	0-4		7431	1	2	3	6	5		7	8			11		9		4		10	

Third Division North Cup

Rd	Date	Opponent	Res	Scorers	Att	Baker TW	Worthy A	Jones GT	Huntley E	Wyness GD	Buckley W	Emmerson GAH	Duff JH	Wiggins IA	Marshall WH	Hales H	Taylor F	Johnson MH	Elliott SD	Skaife S	Taylor S	Brierley H	Eaton C
R1	Oct 1	Oldham Athletic	3-6	Worthy, Duff, Johnson	967	1	2	3	4		5		8			11	7	9				6	10

Lancashire Cup

Rd	Date	Opponent	Res	Scorers	Att	Baker TW	Jones GT	Emmerson GAH	Duff JH	Wiggins IA	Hales H	Skaife S	Taylor S	Brierley H	Eaton C	Cook R
R1	Sep 23	New Brighton	1-3	Wiggins		1	3	7	8	9	11	4	5	6	10	2

		P	W	D	L	F	A	W	D	L	F	A	Pts
1	Chesterfield	42	15	3	3	60	14	9	9	3	32	25	60
2	Chester	42	14	5	2	69	18	8	6	7	31	27	55
3	Tranmere Rovers	42	17	2	2	75	28	5	9	7	18	30	55
4	Lincoln City	42	18	1	2	64	14	4	8	9	27	37	53
5	Stockport County	42	15	5	1	45	18	5	6	10	20	31	48
6	Crewe Alexandra	42	14	4	3	55	31	5	5	11	25	45	47
7	Oldham Athletic	42	13	5	3	60	25	5	4	12	26	48	45
8	Hartlepools United	42	13	6	2	41	18	2	6	13	16	43	42
9	Accrington Stanley	42	12	5	4	43	24	5	3	13	20	48	42
10	Walsall	42	15	2	4	58	13	1	7	13	21	46	41
11	Rotherham United	42	14	3	4	52	13	2	6	13	17	53	41
12	Darlington	42	16	3	2	60	26	1	3	17	14	53	40
13	Carlisle United	42	15	3	3	44	19	1	7	13	12	43	40
14	Gateshead	42	11	10	0	37	18	2	4	15	19	58	40
15	Barrow	42	9	9	3	33	16	4	3	14	25	49	38
16	York City	42	10	8	3	41	28	3	4	14	21	67	38
17	Halifax Town	42	12	3	6	34	22	3	4	14	23	39	37
18	Wrexham	42	12	3	6	39	18	3	4	14	27	57	37
19	Mansfield Town	42	12	3	5	55	25	1	4	16	25	66	33
20	ROCHDALE	42	8	10	3	35	26	2	3	16	23	62	33
21	Southport	42	9	8	4	31	26	2	1	18	17	64	31
22	New Brighton	42	8	5	8	29	33	1	1	19	14	69	24

1936/37 18th in Division 3(N)

#	Date	Opponents	Score / Scorers	Att	Fawcett DH	Worthy A	Jones GT	Robinson CA	Carr A	Skaife S	Emmerson GAH	Duff JH	Hunt SW	Marshall WH	Protheroe S	Huntley E	Clipson R	Johnson MH	Brierley H	Cook S	Marcroft EH	Smith W	Wynn J	McLaren H	Comthwaite CH	Rowbotham H	Crawshaw CB
1	Aug 29	Crewe Alexandra	2-2 Hunt 2	4754	1	2	3	4	5	6	7	8	9	10	11												
2	31	MANSFIELD TOWN	1-3 Hunt	5297	1	2	3	4	5	6	7	8	9	10	11												
3	Sep 5	CHESTER	0-1	5806	1	2	3		5	6	7	8	9	10	11	4											
4	9	Mansfield Town	2-6 Duff, Marshall	7404	1	2	3		5	6	7	8	9	10	11	4											
5	12	Stockport County	0-3	6722	1		3		5	6	7	8	9	10		4	2	11									
6	15	SOUTHPORT	2-1 Hunt, Emmerson	3256	1	2	3		5	6	7	8	9	10		4		11									
7	19	Barrow	0-3	3435	1	2	3		5	6	7	8	9			4			10								
8	26	YORK CITY	3-0 Protheroe, Hunt 2 (1p)	4598	1		3		5	4		8	9	10	11		2		6		7						
9	Oct 3	Carlisle United	0-1	6916	1		3		5	4		8	9	10	11		2		6		7						
10	10	HARTLEPOOLS UNITED	1-1 Marshall	5171	1		3		5	4		8	9	10			2	11	6		7						
11	17	WREXHAM	0-6	2380	1	2			5	4		8	9	10			3	11	6		7						
12	24	Darlington	1-4 Hunt	4796	1				5	6		8	9		11	4	3			2	7			10			
13	31	GATESHEAD	0-2	3991	1		3			4	7	6	9	10	11		2						8	5			
14	Nov 7	Hull City	1-1 Marshall	6963		2				4	7	6	9	10	11		3							5	1	8	
15	14	NEW BRIGHTON	4-0 Protheroe, Hunt 3	3356		2				4	7	6	9	10	11		3							5	1	8	
16	21	Lincoln City	3-5 Hunt 2, Marshall	4595		2			5		7	6	9	10	11		3							4	1	8	
17	Dec 5	Oldham Athletic	0-3	4872	1	2				4		6	9	10	11		3							5		8	7
18	12	PORT VALE	0-0	2218	1		3		5			6	9		11		2							4		8	7
19	19	Rotherham United	1-1 Protheroe	4043	1		3		5			6	9		11		2						7	4		8	
20	25	TRANMERE ROVERS	2-1 Hunt (p), Wynn	6558	1		3		5			6	9		11		2						7	4		8	
21	26	CREWE ALEXANDRA	2-0 Rowbotham, Protheroe	5099			3		5		7	6	9	10	11		2							4	1	8	
22	Jan 1	Southport	1-1 Emmerson	6579	1	2			5		7	6	9		10		3		11					4		8	
23	2	Chester	2-2 Emmerson, Hunt	4514	1	2			5		7	6	9		10		3		11					4		8	
24	9	STOCKPORT COUNTY	2-2 Emmerson, Brierley	10034	1	2			5		7	6	9		10		3		11					4		8	
25	16	Tranmere Rovers	3-4 Wynn 2, Hunt	5748	1	2			5		7	6	9		11		3						10	4		8	
26	23	BARROW	3-1 Wynn, Hunt, Brierley	2606	1	2			5		7	6	9				3		11				10	4		8	
27	Feb 6	CARLISLE UNITED	3-0 Wynn, Hunt, Emmerson	4428	1	2	3		5		7	6	9		11								10	4		8	
28	10	York City	1-4 Wynn	2292	1	2	3		5		7	6	9		11								10	4		8	
29	13	Hartlepools United	1-4 Wynn	4180	1		3		5		7	6	9			2							10	4		8	
30	20	Wrexham	1-0 Wynn	2844	1		3		5			6	9	10	11		2						8	4			
31	27	DARLINGTON	4-0 Wynn, Hunt, Emmerson, Protheroe	3179	1		3		5		7	6	9	10	11		2						8	4			
32	Mar 6	Gateshead	1-3 Wynn	1726	1		3		5		7	6	9		11		2						8	4			
33	13	HULL CITY	4-0 Wynn, Hunt, Emmerson, Marshall	3952	1		3				7	6	9	10	11		2				5		8	4			
34	20	New Brighton	1-5 Bullock (og)	2929	1	2					7	6	9	10	11		3				5		8	4			
35	26	HALIFAX TOWN	3-5 Wynn, Hunt, Marshall	5000	1	2					7	6	9	10	11		3						8	4			
36	27	LINCOLN CITY	2-3 Wynn, Marshall	6630	1	2		5	3			6	9	10	11								7	4		8	
37	29	Halifax Town	2-3 Wynn, Smith	5898	1	2		5	3			6		10	11							9	7	4		8	
38	Apr 3	Accrington Stanley	1-3 Wynn	4096	1	2		5	3		7	6							11			9	8	4			10
39	10	OLDHAM ATHLETIC	3-0 Emmerson 2, Protheroe	7422	1	2		5			7	6	9	10	11		3						8	4			
40	17	Port Vale	1-1 Hunt	2148	1		3		5		7	6	9	10	11		2						8	4			
41	24	ROTHERHAM UNITED	1-0 Hunt	4243	1		3		5		7	6	9	10	11		2						8	4			
42	27	ACCRINGTON STANLEY	4-1 Hunt 2, Wynn, Protheroe	2820	1		3		5		7	6	9	10	11		2						8	4			
			Apps		38	27	22	9	32	16	31	42	40	34	33	6	31	4	10	1	5	4	22	30	4	19	2
			Goals								9	1	24	7	7				2			1	16			1	

One own goal

F.A. Cup

Rnd	Date	Opponents	Score / Scorers	Att	Fawcett DH	Worthy A	Jones GT	Robinson CA	Carr A	Skaife S	Emmerson GAH	Duff JH	Hunt SW	Marshall WH	Protheroe S	Huntley E	Clipson R	Johnson MH	Brierley H	Cook S	Marcroft EH	Smith W	Wynn J	McLaren H	Comthwaite CH	Rowbotham H	Crawshaw CB
R1	Nov 28	Crewe Alexandra	1-5 Hunt	5000	1	2			5		7	6	9	10	11		3							4		8	

Third Division North Cup

Rnd	Date	Opponents	Score	Att	Fawcett DH	Worthy A	Jones GT	Robinson CA	Carr A	Skaife S	Emmerson GAH	Duff JH	Hunt SW	Marshall WH	Protheroe S	Huntley E	Clipson R	Johnson MH	Brierley H	Cook S	Marcroft EH	Smith W	Wynn J	McLaren H	Comthwaite CH	Rowbotham H	Crawshaw CB
R1	Oct 13	Southport	0-3	1620	1				5	6	7		9			4	3	10		2	11	8					

Lancashire Cup

Rnd	Date	Opponents	Score / Scorers	Att	Fawcett DH	Worthy A	Jones GT	Robinson CA	Carr A	Skaife S	Emmerson GAH	Duff JH	Hunt SW	Marshall WH	Protheroe S	Huntley E	Clipson R	Johnson MH	Brierley H	Cook S	Marcroft EH	Smith W	Wynn J	McLaren H	Comthwaite CH	Rowbotham H	Crawshaw CB
R1	Sep 23	Accrington Stanley	3-2 Duff, Marcroft, Hunt		1		3		5	6		8	9		11	4				10	2	7					
R2	Oct 20	BLACKBURN ROVERS	1-3 Hunt	1000	1				5	6	7	8	9	10	11	4	3			2							

League table — Division 3 (North)

		P	W	D	L	F	A	W	D	L	F	A	Pts
1	Stockport County	42	17	3	1	59	18	6	11	4	25	21	60
2	Lincoln City	42	18	1	2	65	20	7	6	8	38	37	57
3	Chester	42	15	5	1	68	21	7	4	10	19	36	53
4	Oldham Athletic	42	13	7	1	49	25	7	4	10	28	34	51
5	Hull City	42	13	6	2	39	22	4	6	11	29	47	46
6	Hartlepools United	42	16	1	4	53	21	3	6	12	22	48	45
7	Halifax Town	42	12	4	5	40	20	6	5	10	28	43	45
8	Wrexham	42	12	3	6	41	21	4	9	8	30	36	44
9	Mansfield Town	42	13	1	7	64	35	5	7	9	27	41	44
10	Carlisle United	42	13	6	2	42	19	5	2	14	23	49	44
11	Port Vale	42	12	6	3	39	23	5	4	12	19	41	44
12	York City	42	13	3	5	54	27	3	8	10	25	43	43
13	Accrington Stanley	42	14	2	5	51	26	2	7	12	25	43	41
14	Southport	42	10	8	3	39	28	2	5	14	34	59	37
15	New Brighton	42	10	8	3	36	16	3	3	15	19	54	37
16	Barrow	42	11	5	5	42	25	2	5	14	28	61	36
17	Rotherham United	42	11	7	3	52	28	3	0	18	26	63	35
18	ROCHDALE	42	12	3	6	44	27	1	6	14	25	59	35
19	Tranmere Rovers	42	10	8	3	52	30	2	1	18	19	58	33
20	Crewe Alexandra	42	6	8	7	31	31	4	4	13	24	52	32
21	Gateshead	42	9	8	4	40	31	2	2	17	23	67	32
22	Darlington	42	6	8	7	42	46	2	6	13	24	50	30

1937/38 17th in Division 3(N)

#	Date	Opponent	Score	Scorers	Att	Fawcett DH	Baird TS	Sneddon T	McLaren H	Robinson CA	Duff JH	McMurdo AB	Burke M	Hunt SW	Marshall WH	Protheroe S	Sperry E	Graham A	Goodier E	Wilson F	Eastwood J	Wynn J	Millar JMcV	McMurray T	Haworth Roland	Hardy R	Barks W	Williams I(2)	Sutcliffe A	Dawson A
1	Aug 28	YORK CITY	0-0		8448	1	2	3	4	5	6	7	8	9	10	11														
2	30	Tranmere Rovers	2-3	Hamilton (og), Marshall	8508	1	2		4	5	6	7		9	10	11	3	8												
3	Sep 4	Bradford City	1-3	Protheroe	5997	1	2		4	5		7		9	10	11	3	8	6											
4	7	TRANMERE ROVERS	0-0		4480	1	2	3	4	5		7		9	10	11		8	6											
5	11	SOUTHPORT	3-2	Hunt 2, Marshall	5915	1	2	3	4	5				9	10	11		8	6	7										
6	13	Halifax Town	3-2	Protheroe 2, Wilson	2409	1	2	3	4	5				9	10	11		8	6	7										
7	18	Doncaster Rovers	0-5		10647	1	2	3	4	5				9	10	11		8	6	7										
8	25	CREWE ALEXANDRA	1-4	Hunt	5632	1	2	3		5				9	10	11		8	6	7	4									
9	Oct 2	ROTHERHAM UNITED	2-0	Graham, Wynn	5019	1	2	3		6				9		11		10	5	7	4	8								
10	9	Chester	1-4	Hunt	5913	1	2	3		5	6			9		11		10		7	4	8								
11	16	Barrow	1-0	Graham	4332	1	2	3		6				9		11		10	5	7	4	8								
12	23	WREXHAM	6-1	Graham 2, Wynn 2, Hunt, Protheroe	4193	1	2	3		6				9		7		10	5		4	8		11						
13	30	Hartlepools United	3-3	Marshall 2, Wynn	5087	1	2	3		6				9	10	7			5		4	8		11						
14	Nov 6	LINCOLN CITY	0-1		9074	1	2	3		6				9	10	7			5		4	8		11						
15	13	Hull City	1-4	Wynn	8848	1	2				6			9	10	7	3		5		4	8		11						
16	20	NEW BRIGHTON	2-1	Wynn, Hunt	5295	1	2	3			6			9	10	11			5		4	8		7						
17	Dec 4	OLDHAM ATHLETIC	1-1	Hunt (p)	4460	1	2	3						9					5		4		11	7	6		8	10		
18	11	Darlington	4-2	Wynn 2, Millar 2	1378	1	2												5		4	9	11	7	6		8	10	3	
19	18	PORT VALE	1-1	Wynn	3560	1	2				6				10				5		4	9	11	7			8		3	
20	25	ACCRINGTON STANLEY	0-1		9146	1	2	3			6					11			5		4	9		7		8		10		
21	27	Accrington Stanley	1-0	Wynn	4700	1	2	3			6				10	11			5		4	8	9	7						
22	Jan 1	York City	5-0	Wynn 3, Millar, Marshall	5971	1	2	3			6				10	11			5		4	8	9	7						
23	8	Gateshead	1-3	Protheroe	9504	1	2	3			6				10	11			5		4	8	9	7						
24	15	BRADFORD CITY	2-0	Protheroe, Wynn	3234	1	2	3			6				10	11			5		4	8	9	7						
25	22	Southport	0-2		3282	1	2				6				10	11			5		4	8	9	7					3	
26	29	DONCASTER ROVERS	4-5	Millar 2, Marshall, Wynn	5069	1	2				6				10	11			5		4	8	9	7					3	
27	Feb 5	Crewe Alexandra	1-5	McLaren	3393	1	2		3		6				10	11			5		4	8	9	7						
28	12	Rotherham United	0-1		9282	1	2	3			6				10				5		4	8	11						7	9
29	19	CHESTER	4-0	Wynn (p), Dawson, Millar, Done (og)	5728	1	2	3			6				10				5		4	8	11	7						9
30	26	BARROW	3-3	McMurray, Dawson 2	6243	1	2	3			6				10				5		4	8	11	7						9
31	Mar 5	Wrexham	1-2	Tunney (og)	3620	1	2	3			6					10			5		4	8	11	7						9
32	12	HARTLEPOOLS UNITED	2-2	Dawson, Protheroe	5615	1	2	3			6				10	7			5		4	8	11							9
33	19	Lincoln City	0-2		6836	1	2	3	4		6								5			8	11	7				10		9
34	26	HULL CITY	0-0		5761	1	2	3			6		8		10	11			5		4		9	7						
35	Apr 2	New Brighton	0-2		3419	1	2	3			6		8		10				5		4		11	7						
36	9	GATESHEAD	2-2	Wynn, Millar	5240	1	2	3	4		6		8		10				5			9	11	7						
37	15	CARLISLE UNITED	3-1	Wynn 2 (1p), Millar	4648	1	2	3	4		6		8		10				5			9	11	7						
38	16	Oldham Athletic	2-4	Duff, Eaves (og)	17106	1	2	3	4		6				10	11			5			8		7						9
39	18	Carlisle United	1-0	Dawson	5609	1	2	3	4		6				10				5			9	11	7						9
40	23	DARLINGTON	1-1	Dawson	4028	1	2	3	4		6				10				5				11	7						9
41	30	Port Vale	1-4	Wynn (p)	2992	1	2	3	4		6					11			5			9						10		
42	May 7	HALIFAX TOWN	1-1	Craig (og)	2065	1	2	3	4		6				10	11			5			8							7	9
					Apps	42	42	34	34	9	18	2	8	18	30	30	3	11	39	7	28	28	26	23	2	7	3	4	2	12
					Goals				1		1			7	6	7		4		1		20	8	1						6

Five own goals

F.A. Cup

	Date	Opponent	Score	Scorers	Att																								
R1	Nov 27	LINCOLN CITY	1-1	Hunt	11500	1	2	3			6			9	10	11			5		4	8		7						
rep	Dec 1	Lincoln City	0-2		6474	1	2	3			6		10	9					5		4	8	11	7						

Third Division North Cup

	Date	Opponent	Score	Scorers	Att																								
R1	Sep 21	OLDHAM ATHLETIC	2-3	Hunt 2	1000	1	2	3		5				9	10	11		8	6	7	4									

Lancashire Cup

	Date	Opponent	Score	Scorers																									
R1	Apr 18	Blackburn Rovers	1-4	Dawson		1	2	3	4		6				10	11			5			8		7						9

		P	W	D	L	F	A	W	D	L	F	A	Pts
1	Tranmere Rovers	42	15	4	2	57	21	8	6	7	24	20	56
2	Doncaster Rovers	42	15	4	2	48	16	6	8	7	26	33	54
3	Hull City	42	11	8	2	51	19	9	5	7	29	24	53
4	Oldham Athletic	42	16	4	1	48	18	3	9	9	19	28	51
5	Gateshead	42	15	5	1	53	20	5	6	10	31	39	51
6	Rotherham United	42	13	6	2	45	21	7	4	10	23	35	50
7	Lincoln City	42	14	3	4	48	17	5	5	11	18	33	46
8	Crewe Alexandra	42	14	3	4	47	17	4	6	11	24	36	45
9	Chester	42	13	4	4	54	31	3	8	10	23	41	44
10	Wrexham	42	14	4	3	37	15	2	7	12	21	48	43
11	York City	42	11	4	6	40	25	5	6	10	30	43	42
12	Carlisle United	42	11	5	5	35	19	4	4	13	22	48	39
13	New Brighton	42	12	5	4	43	18	3	3	15	17	43	38
14	Bradford City	42	11	6	3	46	21	2	4	15	20	48	38
15	Port Vale	42	11	8	2	45	27	1	6	14	20	46	38
16	Southport	42	8	8	5	30	26	4	6	11	23	56	38
17	ROCHDALE	42	7	10	4	38	27	6	1	14	29	51	37
18	Halifax Town	42	9	7	5	24	19	3	5	13	20	47	36
19	Darlington	42	10	4	7	37	31	1	6	14	17	48	32
20	Hartlepools United	42	10	8	3	36	20	0	4	17	17	60	32
21	Barrow	42	9	6	6	28	20	2	4	15	13	51	32
22	Accrington Stanley	42	9	2	10	31	32	2	5	14	14	43	29

1938/39 15th in Division 3(N)

#		Date	Opponent	Score	Scorers	Att	Fawcett DH	Baird TS	Sneddon T	Duff JH	Goodier E	Reeve FW	Howarth H(2)	Douglas TA	Hawarth, Richard	Goodfellow S	Griffiths AA	Keenan WG	Royan W	Young AW	Wynn J	Barrett J	Gregory A	Hobbs EC	Doyle T	Kilsby RH	Prest TW	Mee GW	Latimer J	Reynolds W	Vause PG	Firth J	Briggs JC	Lewis DB	Gastall JWH	Neary J
1	Aug	27	Rotherham United	1-7	Griffiths	7438	1	2	3	4	5	6	7	8	9	10	11																			
2		30	CARLISLE UNITED	2-3	Griffiths, Howarth	5217	1		3			5	6	7	8	10	4	11	2	9																
3	Sep	3	OLDHAM ATHLETIC	1-2	Royan	7357	1	2	3	6	5		7			10	11		9	4	8															
4		6	DONCASTER ROVERS	1-1	Goodfellow	4469	1	2	3	6	5			8	7	10	11		9			4														
5		10	YORK CITY	2-2	Goodfellow, Griffiths	5494	1	2	3	6	5			8	7	10	11		9			4														
6		12	Doncaster Rovers	0-5		5530	1	2	3	6				8	7	10	11		9			4	5													
7		17	Wrexham	0-1		3565	1		3	6	5		7	8	9	10	11	2				4														
8		24	GATESHEAD	5-2	Duff,Griffiths,Wynn,Reeve,Conroy(og)	6393		2	3	8	5	6				4	11				9					1	7	10								
9	Oct	1	Hartlepools United	2-4	Wynn 2	4446		2	3	8	5	6			11	4					9					1	7	10								
10		8	DARLINGTON	6-1	Wynn 3, Reeve, Duff, Griffiths	5232		2	3	8	5	6				4	11				9					1	7	10								
11		15	Halifax Town	1-2	Kilsby	5626		2	3	8	5	6				4	11				9					1	7	10								
12		22	NEW BRIGHTON	2-0	Duff, Prest	7292		2		8	5	6				4	11	3			9					1		10	7							
13		29	Barrow	1-3	Goodier	6533		2		8	5	6				4	11	3			9					1	7	10								
14	Nov	5	CHESTER	5-2	Kilsby 2, Wynn 2 (2p), Duff	6732		2		8	5	6				4		3			9					1	7	10	11							
15		12	Bradford City	0-3		6615		2		6	5				8	4	11	3			9					1	7	10								
16		19	HULL CITY	3-3	Wynn 2, Reynolds, Prest	6690			3	5						4	11	2			9	6				1	8	10		7						
17	Dec	3	STOCKPORT COUNTY	0-1		6293			3	5	6			8		4		2			9					1	11	10		7						
18		10	Accrington Stanley	5-0	Kilsby 2, Prest, Duff, Wynn (p)	3836		2	3	8	5	6				4					9					1	11	10		7						
19		17	BARNSLEY	2-1	Wynn, Prest	5466		2	3	8	5	6				4					9					1	11	10		7						
20		24	ROTHERHAM UNITED	0-1		5811		2	3	8	5	6				4					9					1	11	10		7						
21		26	Southport	1-4	Vause	6606		2	3	8	5	6				4					9					1		10		7	11					
22		27	SOUTHPORT	5-0	Duff 2, Wynn, Prest, Reynolds	6293		2	3	8						4					9			5	1		10		7	11					
23		31	Oldham Athletic	2-1	Wynn, Reeve	11644		2	3	8		6				5					9					1		10		7	11	4				
24	Jan	11	Lincoln City	2-2	Duff 2	1847		2	3	10	5					4					9	6				1				7	11	8				
25		14	York City	7-0	Vause 3, Firth 2, Wynn (p), Duff	3826		2	3	10	5					4					9	6				1				7	11	8				
26		21	WREXHAM	0-0		7250		2	3	10	5					4					9	6				1				7	11	8				
27		28	Gateshead	2-2	Vause, Wynn	2846		2	3	10		6				4					9			5	1		10		7	11	8					
28	Feb	4	HARTLEPOOLS UNITED	3-4	Wynn 2 (1p), Duff	5557		2	3	8		6				4					9			5	1		10		7	11						
29		11	Darlington	2-1	Firth 2	3011		2	3	10						4					9	6		5	1				7	11	8				
30		18	HALIFAX TOWN	4-5	Wynn 3 (1p), Vause	6521		2	3	10						4					9	6		5	1				7	11	8				
31		25	New Brighton	1-3	Wynn	3296		2		3	5	6				4					9					1		10		7	11	8				
32	Mar	4	BARROW	2-2	Reynolds, Vause	4734		2		3		6				5					9					1	4	10		7	11	8				
33		11	Chester	0-0		4375		2		3		6				5					9					1	4			7		8	10	11		
34		18	BRADFORD CITY	1-1	Prest	5651		2		3		6			11	5					9					1	4	10		7		8				
35		25	Hull City	3-3	Duff, Wynn, Vause	3975		2		3		6				5					9					1	4			7	11	8				
36	Apr	1	LINCOLN CITY	4-0	Wynn 2, Vause, Kilsby	4314	1		3	10		6				5		2			9						4				11	8			7	
37		7	Crewe Alexandra	1-4	Firth	6678		2	3	10		6				5					9					1	4			7	11	8				
38		8	Stockport County	2-1	Wynn, Vause	6485		2	3	10	5	6				4					9						7				11	8				
39		10	CREWE ALEXANDRA	5-0	Wynn, Vause 2, Firth, Gastall	7786	1	2	3	10	5					4					9						6				11	8			7	
40		15	ACCRINGTON STANLEY	4-1	Duff 2, Vause, Wynn	3981	1	2	3	8					10	4					9						6				11				7	5
41		22	Barnsley	0-2		8403	1	2	3	10	5					4					9						6				11	8			7	
42		29	Carlisle United	1-5	Reynolds	2800	1	2	3	10	5	6				9											4			7	11	8				
			Apps				13	37	31	41	28	27	4	8	9	41	14	9	5	1	36	1		9	6	29	23	21	1	1	22	20	18	1	1	4	1
			Goals							14	1	3				1	2	5		1	28						6	6			4	13	6			1	

One own goal

F.A. Cup

	Date	Opponent	Score	Scorers	Att																											
R1	Nov 26	Halifax Town	3-7	Wynn, Duff, Goodier	10000		2		8	5	6				4					9					1	7	10	11							

Played at no. 3: H Roberts

Third Division North Cup

	Date	Opponent	Score	Scorers	Att																											
R1	Jan 2	Accrington Stanley	1-2	Knowles	1600		2	3	10		6				5					9					1	4			7	11						

Played at no. 8: Knowles

Lancashire Cup

	Date	Opponent	Score	Scorers	Att																											
R1	Sep 21	Oldham A.	0-0			1			3	5	6		7	8	11	2		9				10	4												
R1r	Oct 11	OLDHAM A.*	2-2	Duff, Wynn			2	3	8	5	6				10	4	11			9					1	7									
R1r2	18	OLDHAM A.*	1-2	Kilsby			2	3	8	5	6				10	4				9					1	7		11							

* after extra time

Football Lge Jubilee

	Date	Opponent	Score	Scorers																												
	Aug 20	Halifax T.	1-4	Kennedy				3		5	6		10		4		2	9		8					1	7									
	Aug 23	HALIFAX T.	5-1	Goodfellow (2p),Haworth,Douglas,Reeve		1	2	3	4	5	6	7	8	9	10	11																			

Kennedy at No.11 in first match

		P	W	D	L	F	A	W	D	L	A	Pts
1	Barnsley	42	18	2	1	60	12	12	5	4	22	67
2	Doncaster Rovers	42	12	5	4	47	21	9	9	3	26	56
3	Bradford City	42	16	2	3	59	21	6	6	9	35	52
4	Southport	42	14	5	2	47	16	6	5	10	38	50
5	Oldham Athletic	42	16	1	4	51	21	6	4	11	38	49
6	Chester	42	12	5	4	54	31	8	4	9	39	49
7	Hull City	42	13	5	3	57	25	5	5	11	49	46
8	Crewe Alexandra	42	12	5	4	54	23	7	1	13	47	44
9	Stockport County	42	13	6	2	57	24	4	3	14	53	43
10	Gateshead	42	11	6	4	45	24	3	8	10	43	42
11	Rotherham United	42	12	4	5	45	21	5	4	12	43	42
12	Halifax Town	42	9	10	2	33	22	4	6	11	32	42
13	Barrow	42	11	5	5	46	22	5	4	12	43	41
14	Wrexham	42	15	2	4	46	28	2	5	14	51	41
15	ROCHDALE	42	10	5	6	58	29	5	4	12	53	39
16	New Brighton	42	11	2	8	46	32	4	7	10	41	39
17	Lincoln City	42	9	6	6	40	33	3	3	15	59	33
18	Darlington	42	12	2	7	43	30	1	5	15	62	33
19	Carlisle United	42	10	5	6	44	33	3	2	16	78	33
20	York City	42	8	5	8	37	34	4	3	14	58	32
21	Hartlepools United	42	10	4	7	36	33	2	3	16	61	31
22	Accrington Stanley	42	6	5	10	30	39	1	1	19	64	20

1937-38 Season
Back: Mulrooney (Trainer), Sneddon, McLaren, Robinson, Baird, Goodier, Fawcett, Sperry, Duff
Middle: Wilson (Dir.), Burke, Graham, Hunt, Curwood, Marshall, Wynn, Nixon (Sec.)
Front: McMurdo, Protheroe

1939-40 Season
Back: Foulds (Dir.), Baird, Vause, Robertson, Dewhurst (Dir.), Robson, Dutton, Hall (Dir.), Sneddon, Muir
Wynn, Pollard, Ferguson, Grundy, Flowers, Bottomley
Middle: Harker, Richardson, Reynolds, Duff, Goodier (Manager), Prest, Haworth
Kilsby, Redwood, Mulrooney (Trainer)
Front: Nevin, Keenan, Neary, Pearce, Howarth

1939-40 Season

Division 3 North - Abandoned

#	Date	Opponent	Result	Scorers	Att	1	2	3	4	5	6	7	8	9	10	11
1	Aug 26	Doncaster Rovers	0-2		10564	Robertson	Keenan	Sneddon	Rhodes	Pearce	Kilsby	Ferguson	Duff	Wynn	Dutton	Vause
2	29	WREXHAM	1-0	Wynn	6300	"	"	"	"	"	"	Reynolds	Pollard	"	Deff	"
3	Sep 2	YORK CITY	1-0	Reynolds	6288	"	"	"	"	"	"	"	"	"	"	"

Regional League - North West Division

#	Date	Opponent	Result	Scorers	Att	1	2	3	4	5	6	7	8	9	10	11
4	Oct 21	BARROW	1-3	Harker	2300	Ellis	Duff	Jones	Eastwood	Neary	Harker	Steele	Prest	Wynn	Dutton	Olsen
5	28	Southport	2-3	Dutton, Duff	2000	"	Baird	Nevin	"	"	Warburton	"	Duff	"	"	"
6	Nov 11	ACCRINGTON STANLEY	5-1	Dutton(2), Hunt(2), Wynn	3098	Carey	Chester	Duff	"	Pearce	"	Anderson	Wynn	Hunt	"	"
7	18	Bolton Wanderers	0-4		2200	"	"	"	"	"	"	"	"	"	"	"
8	25	PRESTON N.E.	1-1	Richardson	3291	"	"	"	"	"	"	"	"	Richardson	"	"
9	Dec 2	Burnley	1-3	Wynn	1181	"	"	Smith	"	"	"	"	Duff	Wynn	"	"
10	9	CARLISLE UNITED	3-1	Wynn, Richardson(2)	1756	"	Smith	Duff	"	"	"	"	"	Wynn	Richardson	"	"
11	23	Oldham Athletic	3-0	Richardson(3)	1579	"	"	"	"	Harker	"	"	"	"	"	"
12	Jan 6	Bury	1-3	Richardson	4437	"	"	"	"	Pearce	Harker	"	"	"	"	Vause
13	20	BLACKBURN ROVERS	1-5	Anderson	1629	Robson	Chester	"	"	"	Shadwell	"	"	"	"	Olsen
14	Feb 10	Barrow	1-1		2229	"	Taylor	"	"	"	Harker	Chadwick	Prest	"	Olsen	Anderson
15	24	SOUTHPORT	1-2	Richardson	1300	Carey	"	"	"	"	"	Anderson	"	"	Dutton	Vause
16	Mar 9	Accrington Stanley	1-4	Ainsworth	950	Hall	"	Sneddon	"	"	Warburton	Steele	Ainsworth	"	Duff	"
17	16	BOLTON WANDERERS	2-2	Vause, Wynn	2405	"	"	"	"	"	"	Colquhoun	Duff	Wynn	Ainsworth	"
18	23	Preston N.E.	0-5		5000	"	"	Duff	"	Harker	"	Earl	Ainsworth	"	Olsen	Dutton
19	30	BURNLEY	1-1	Ainsworth	2500	"	"	Byrom	"	Pearce	"	Rawlings	Duff	"	Ainsworth	Olsen
20	Apr 6	Carlisle United	2-1	Olsen, Duff		"	Sneddon	"	"	"	"	"	"	Richardson	Olsen	Redwood
21	24	Blackpool	2-7	Rawlings, Richardson	2500	"	"	"	"	"	"	"	"	"	Prest	Colquhoun
22	May 18	Bury	2-3	Richardson, Duff	1305	Carey	Taylor	"	"	Harker	"	Colquhoun	Wynn	"	Duff	Haworth
23	25	OLDHAM ATHLETIC	3-1	Richardson, Carter, Livingstone	2003	"	Robinson	"	"	"	"	"	Livingstone	"	"	Carter
24	28	BLACKPOOL	3-3	Richardson(2), Livingstone	1850	"	"	"	"	McGowan	"	Burdett	"	"	"	"
25	Jun 3	Blackburn Rovers	2-4	Burdett(2)	353	"	"	"	"	Halton	"	Colquhoun	Duff	"	Burdett	"

Jubilee Fund

#	Date	Opponent	Result	1	2	3	4	5	6	7	8	9	10	11
26	Aug 19	HALIFAX TOWN	3-1	Robertson	Baird	Sneddon	Rhodes	Pearce	Kilsby	Ferguson	Duff	Wynn	Dutton	Vause

War League Cup

#	Date	Opponent	Result	Scorers	Att	1	2	3	4	5	6	7	8	9	10	11
27	Apr 13	ACCRINGTON STANLEY	3-0	Pearce, Duff, Redwood	2500	Carey	Sneddon	Byrom	Eastwood	Pearce	Warburton	Reynolds	Duff	Wynn	Dutton	Redwood
28	20	BURY	1-0	Prest	7531	"	"	"	"	"	"	Colquhoun	"	**	Prest	"
29	27	Bury	1-1	Duff	6885	"	"	"	"	"	"	"	"	"	Dutton	"
30	May 7	Everton	1-5	Redwood	8335	"	"	"	"	"	"	"	"	"	"	"
31	11	EVERTON	4-2	Colquhoun, Duff(2), Richardson	6601	"	"	"	"	Harker	"	"	Wynn	Richardson	Duff	Haworth

Lancashire Cup

#	Date	Opponent	Result	1	2	3	4	5	6	7	8	9	10	11
32	Nov 4	Blackburn Rovers	1-2	Carey	Baird	Duff	Eastwood	Pearce	Warburton	Andesron	Wynn	Hunt	Dutton	Olsen

(n.b. probable line-up)

	P	W	D	L	F	A	Pts.
Bury	22	16	4	2	64	30	34
Preston N.E.	22	15	5	2	63	27	32
Blackpool	22	13	3	6	75	36	32
Bolton W.	22	13	5	4	55	30	30
Oldham A.	22	11	9	2	55	61	24
Burnley	22	9	8	5	48	43	23
Barrow	22	8	10	4	54	57	20
Blackburn R.	22	7	11	4	37	40	18
ROCHDALE	22	5	12	5	38	58	15
Southport	22	5	13	4	34	62	14
Carlisle United	22	4	14	4	38	68	12
Accrington S	22	2	14	6	31	78	10

1940/41 Season (North League)

	P	W	L	D	F	A	G/Ave
Preston N.E.	29	18	4	7	81	37	2.189
Chesterfield	35	20	9	6	76	40	1.900
Manchester City	35	18	7	10	104	55	1.890
Barnsley	30	18	8	4	86	49	1.775
Everton	34	19	8	7	85	51	1.666
Blackpool	20	13	4	3	56	34	1.646
Halifax Town	30	10	7	13	64	51	1.254
Manchester Utd.	35	14	13	8	80	65	1.249
Lincoln City	27	13	7	7	65	53	1.226
Newcastle United	23	12	11	0	49	41	1.195
Huddersfield Town	33	11	16	6	69	58	1.189
Middlesbrough	27	16	10	1	84	71	1.183
New Brighton	26	15	10	1	97	82	1.182
Burnley	35	17	11	7	62	53	1.169
Leeds United	30	13	9	8	62	54	1.148
Liverpool	37	15	16	6	91	82	1.102
Wrexham	29	15	9	5	78	71	1.098
Chester	35	14	15	6	94	89	1.056
Doncaster Rovers	32	15	10	7	77	74	1.040
Oldham Athletic	37	17	16	4	78	77	1.012
Grimsby Town	27	12	13	2	60	63	.952
Bradford PA	31	9	15	7	64	74	.864
Rotherham Utd.	29	12	12	5	48	57	.842
Blackburn Rovers	32	9	13	10	49	60	.816
Bury	38	10	19	9	80	100	.800
Bolton Wands.	16	6	8	2	31	40	.775
Tranmere Rovers	25	6	13	6	44	60	.733
Sheffield Utd.	25	6	13	6	44	60	.733
Bradford City	29	8	18	3	72	99	.727
ROCHDALE	32	12	15	5	64	92	.695
Southport	28	7	19	2	61	88	.693
York City	25	7	14	4	49	71	.690
Hull City	23	8	12	3	44	67	.656
Sheffield Wed.	30	9	15	6	50	78	.641
Stockport County	29	9	15	5	54	93	.580
Crewe Alex.	24	2	19	3	32	84	.380

(Final positions determined on goal average)

> Note: During the War-time seasons, leagues were formed on a general countrywide regional basis. Fixtures were then played against others on a more local basis, i.e. each club did not play every other on a 'home' and 'away' format within their league (e.g. Rochdale never played the likes of Middlesbrough or Bristol City). Consequently the final league tables were on a composite basis. In addition, some matches were 'double-headers' for other competitions - as indicated on the detailed statistics pages

1941/42 Season (North League 1st Championship)

	P	W	L	D	F	A	Pts
Blackpool	18	14	3	1	75	19	29
Lincoln City	18	13	4	1	54	28	29
Preston N.E.	18	13	4	1	58	18	27
Manchester Utd.	18	10	2	6	79	27	26
Stoke City	18	12	4	2	85	51	26
Everton	18	13	4	2	56	36	26
Blackburn Rovers	18	10	2	6	40	24	26
Liverpool	18	10	3	5	66	44	26
Gateshead	18	11	3	4	39	35	26
Sunderland	18	9	5	4	50	30	22
Huddersfield Town	18	10	7	1	48	33	21
Doncaster Rovers	18	8	5	5	45	53	21
Bradford P.A.	18	7	5	6	41	31	20
Grimsby Town	18	7	5	6	39	31	20
Barnsley	18	7	5	6	38	39	20
Newcastle Utd.	18	7	6	5	33	37	19
Sheffield Wed.	18	7	7	4	48	54	19
Manchester City	18	8	7	3	58	38	18
Sheffield Utd.	18	6	6	6	36	40	18
Burnley	18	6	6	6	29	41	17
Halifax Town	18	6	8	4	30	49	16
Oldham Athletic	18	6	8	4	28	52	16
ROCHDALE	18	6	8	4	27	31	15
Chesterfield	18	6	8	5	27	31	15
Chester	18	6	9	3	45	53	15
Middlesbrough	18	6	9	3	44	56	15

Top 25 clubs only shown (of 38 total)

(2nd Championship)

	P	W	L	D	F	A	Pts
ROCHDALE	13	5	8	0	23	39	10

Only those clubs playing 18 matches or more qualified for the Championship, of which there were 22 (varied between 18 and 23 matches), Rochdale were one of 29 who played less than the minimum (varied between 8 and 17).

League Cup Qualifying Competition

	P	W	L	D	F	A	Pts
Bournemouth & B.	8	4	3	1	22	11	21	6
Swansea Town	8	1	3	4	9	21	6
Halifax Town	9	3	6	0	13	29	6
ROCHDALE	10	2	6	2	15	30	6
Luton Town	10	2	6	2	12	30	6
Tranmere Rovers	10	2	6	2	12	30	6
Stockport County	10	1	5	2	10	27	4
Mansfield Town	7	1	5	1	12	38	5
Walsall	10	2	8	0	9	29	4
Sheffield Wed.	8	1	6	1	8	25	3

1942/43 Season (North League 1st Championship)

	P	W	L	D	F	A	Pts
Tranmere Rovers	18	5	10	3	36	63	13
Wolverhampton W.	18	5	11	2	28	41	12
Crewe Alexandra	18	4	10	4	43	64	12
Middlesbrough	18	4	10	4	30	50	12
ROCHDALE	18	5	11	2	43	67	11
Wrexham	18	3	11	4	28	45	10
Leeds United	18	3	11	4	28	45	10
Oldham Athletic	18	4	12	2	30	63	10
Bradford City	18	3	12	3	31	52	9
Bolton Wanderers	18	3	11	3	23	41	9
Doncaster Rovers	17	3	11	3	23	41	9
Mansfield Town	18	2	12	4	25	65	8

Bottom 12 only shown (of 48 total)

(2nd Championship)

	P	W	L	D	F	A	Pts
Liverpool	20	15	1	4	64	32	32
Lovell's	20	11	4	5	63	32	27
Manchester C	19	11	4	4	43	24	27
Aston Villa	20	13	6	1	44	30	27
Sheffield W	20	9	3	8	43	26	26
Manchester U	19	11	5	3	52	26	25
York	18	11	5	2	52	26	25
Huddersfield	19	11	5	3	48	28	25
Coventry	20	11	6	3	42	34	24
Stoke	20	10	6	4	42	34	24
WBA	20	11	7	2	49	40	24
Notts Co	20	9	6	5	40	37	23
Blackpool	19	8	4	7	49	31	23
Newcastle	19	10	6	3	62	42	23
Chesterfield	18	8	5	5	55	38	21
Blackburn	19	8	5	6	41	33	22
Bristol C	19	8	7	4	35	30	20

Top 28 clubs shown only (of 54 total)

League North Cup Qualifying Competition

	P	W	L	D	F	A	Pts
Manchester C	10	7	1	2	30	15	16
ROCHDALE	10	7	1	2	31	16	16
Liverpool	10	6	1	3	32	10	15
Lovell's Ath.	10	6	2	2	32	10	15
Chesterfield	10	7	2	1	31	14	14
Huddersfield T.	9	7	2	0	31	14	14
Sheffield Wed.	10	5	3	2	20	16	14
Coventry City	10	7	3	0	16	14	14
Stoke City	10	6	3	1	24	16	13
York City	10	5	4	1	33	17	13
Manchester U.	10	5	4	1	27	15	13
Newcastle Utd.	10	4	5	1	37	21	13

Only top 28 qualified. 19 clubs did not qualify, bottom 12, only, shown. Final positions based on average points from games played

1943/44 Season North League 1st Championship

	P	W	L	D	F	A	Pts
Blackpool	18	12	2	4	56	20	28
Manchester U	18	13	3	2	56	30	28
Liverpool	18	13	4	1	72	26	27
Doncaster R.	18	11	2	5	45	26	27
Bradford PA	18	11	3	4	65	28	26
Huddersfield T.	18	12	4	2	48	25	26
Northampton T.	18	10	3	5	43	25	25
Aston Villa	18	11	4	3	43	27	25
Sunderland	18	10	5	3	46	31	23
Hartlepool	18	10	5	3	44	31	23
Everton	18	9	5	4	60	34	22
Blackburn R.	18	10	6	2	47	32	22
ROCHDALE	18	8	6	4	43	41	22
Sheffield U.	18	8	5	5	30	26	21
Lincoln City	18	8	8	2	51	40	20
Birmingham	18	9	7	2	38	31	20
Manchester C	18	9	7	2	38	35	20
Mansfield T.	18	8	8	6	32	33	20
Derby County	18	8	8	6	43	45	20
Chester	18	7	8	6	40	43	20

Top 20 clubs only shown (of 50 total)

North League 2nd Championship

	P	W	L	D	F	A	Pts
Bath	21	16	2	3	78	26	34
Wrexham	21	15	2	4	62	29	34
Liverpool	21	14	5	2	71	38	30
Birmingham	20	12	3	5	47	19	29
Rotherham	21	12	4	5	54	30	29
Aston Villa	21	13	5	3	50	34	29
Blackpool	20	12	5	3	53	27	29
Cardiff	21	13	7	1	53	28	27
Manchester U	21	10	7	4	55	38	27
Bradford PA	20	11	5	4	50	30	26
Newcastle	21	11	8	2	48	35	24
Everton	21	10	8	3	42	35	24
Stoke	21	12	8	1	73	39	25
Leicester	21	10	6	5	66	45	25
Darlington	21	11	8	2	50	32	24
Nottingham F	20	9	5	6	32	26	24
Sheffield U	21	11	8	2	53	35	24
Coventry	21	10	7	4	48	37	24
Manchester C	21	10	8	3	42	35	24
Lovell's	21	10	8	2	48	30	22
Gateshead	21	9	8	4	45	53	22
Doncaster Rovers	17	9	8	0	42	36	18
Derby County	20	8	8	5	29	28	21
ROCHDALE	20	8	7	5	40	36	21

Top 24 clubs only shown (of 50 total)

North Cup Qualifying Competition

	P	W	L	D	F	A	Pts
Bristol City	10	4	1	1	17	16	12
Darlington	10	4	3	3	28	14	11
Oldham Ath	10	4	3	3	24	14	11
ROCHDALE	10	5	4	1	21	14	11
Derby County	10	5	4	1	20	16	11
Aston Villa	10	5	4	1	20	16	11
Hartlepools Utd.	10	5	4	1	25	25	11
Gateshead	10	4	4	3	27	28	11
GRIMSBY TOWN	10	5	4	1	18	17	11
Leeds United	10	5	5	0	19	16	10
York City	10	5	5	0	22	19	10
Burnley	10	4	5	2	22	19	10

Top 20 clubs not shown (21st - 32nd shown only). Top 32 qualified (of 56 total)

1940-41 Season

North Regional League

#	Date	Opponent	Score	Scorers	Att	1	2	3	4	5	6	7	8	9	10	11
1	Aug 31	MANCHESTER UNITED	1-3	Cunliffe	2827	Carey	E.Eastwood	Duff	Warburton	Neary	Connor	Rawlings	Cunliffe	G.Hunt	Graham	Sidebottom
2	Sep 7	BURNLEY	1-2	Sidebottom	2100	"	"	Byrom	"	"	"	"	Duff	"	"	"
3	14	Crewe Alexandra	1-1	Duff	1000	"	"	Connor	J.Eastwood	Taylor	Warburton	Vause	"	"	Dutton	"
4	21	Stockport County	0-4		2500	"	Smith	"	"	"	"	"	"	"	"	"
5	28	Bury	3-7	Vause, Cunliffe, Dutton	2365	"	Duff	"	"	Smith	"	"	Cunliffe	S.W.Hunt	"	"
6	Oct 5	PRESTON N.E.	2-1	Dutton, Sidebottom	1999	Hall	Sneddon	"	"	Harker	"	"	"	"	"	"
7	12	BLACKBURN ROVERS	1-1	Dutton	2246	"	Smith	"	"	"	"	"	"	"	"	"
8	19	Blackburn Rovers	0-2		1200	"	Mountford	"	"	"	Smith	Sutherland	Duff	G.Hunt	"	"
9	26	Southport	3-2	Cunliffe(2), Kershaw	1500	"	"	"	"	Neary	Dutton	Kershaw	Cunliffe	S.W.Hunt	Sidebottom	Vause
10	Nov 2	BRADFORD P.A.	1-1	Sidebottom	803	"	Sneddon	"	"	Jones	"	"	"	S.W.Hunt	"	Bellis
11	9	Preston N.E.	0-5		300	"	"	"	"	"	Keen	"	Duff	"	"	Dutton
12	16	STOCKPORT COUNTY	5-3	Sidebottom(2),Rawlings,Hunt,Cunliffe	2130	"	Mountford	"	"	"	"	Rawlings	Cunliffe	"	"	Bellis
13	23	Burnley	1-0	Hunt	1500	"	"	"	"	"	"	"	"	Fenton	S.W.Hunt	Sidebottom
14	30	SOUTHPORT	10-0	Sidebottom(5),Rawlings(2),Hunt(2),Bellis	1002	"	Smith	"	"	"	Dutton	"	"	S.W.Hunt	Sidebottom	Bellis
15	Dec 7	Bradford P.A.	4-2	Rawlings, Duff, Hunt, Stephen(og)	850	"	"	"	"	"	Keen	"	Duff	"	"	"
16	14	Manchester United	4-3	Sidebottom, Hunt(2), Cunliffe	1000	"	"	"	"	"	"	"	Cunliffe	"	"	Dutton
17	21	CREWE ALEXANDRA	1-0	Duff	1300	"	"	"	"	"	Duff	"	"	"	"	"
18	25	OLDHAM ATHLETIC	2-3	Hunt, Rawlings	2806	"	Sneddon	Duff	"	"	Keen	Kershaw	Rawlings	"	Dutton	Bellis
19	28	BURY	0-3		1700	"	"	"	"	"	"	Rawlings	Isherwood	"	"	"
20+	Jan 4	Manchester City+	1-9	Hunt	2000	"	J.Eastwood	"	Robinson	Rothwell	"	P.Taylor	Rawlings	Harrison	S.W.Hunt	Seddon
21+	11	MANCHESTER CITY+	1-6	Wood	1588	"	Johnson	Smith	J.Eastwood	Jones	"	Kershaw	Ainsworth	Wood	Duff	"
22	15	CREWE ALEXANDRA	5-0	Duff(2), Hunt, Ainsworth, Seddon	523	"	Smith	Reeday	"	"	Dutton	Rawlings	"	S.W.Hunt	"	"
23	Mar 8	Crewe Alexandra	5-2	Horrabin(4), Eastwood	500	"	"	"	Duff	Keen	Turner	"	P.Taylor	J.Eastwood	Harrobin	Hughes
24	15	BRADFORD CITY	2-1	P.Taylor, Horrabin	1380	"	"	"	"	J.Eastwood	"	Keen	"	Rawlings	"	Ainsworth
25	22	Huddersfield Town	0-11		386	Heys	"	"	"	"	"	"	"	"	"	Dutton
26	29	LEEDS UNITED	2-3	Horrabiin, Duff	784	Hall	"	Kirkman	"	Jones	Dutton	"	"	"	Duff	"
27	Apr 5	Stockport County	1-1	Horrabin	820	"	"	"	"	"	Duff	"	Horton	"	Rawlings	Dutton
28	12	STOCKPORT COUNTY	3-1	P.Taylor, Jones, Horrabin	1438	"	Duff	"	"	"	Keen	"	"	"	"	"
29	14	OLDHAM ATHLETIC	0-4		1733	"	"	"	"	"	"	"	"	"	"	Walkden
30	19	BOLTON WANDERERS	1-3	P.Taylor	726	"	"	"	"	Farrow	"	"	"	"	"	Haworth
31	26	Bradford City	3-3	Haworth(Richard), Duff, Harrison	500	"	Smith	Wood	Clarke	Turner	"	"	"	"	Duff	"
32	May 10	Oldham Athletic	0-5		1189	"	"	Duff	Keen	Jones	Dutton	"	"	Wood	Chew	Colquhoun

League War Cup

#	Date	Opponent	Score	Scorers	Att	1	2	3	4	5	6	7	8	9	10	11
33	Feb 15	Newcastle United	2-1	P.Taylor, Bellis	3000	Hall	Smith	Sneddon	J.Eastwood	Neary	Keen	P.Taylor	Duff	Wynn	S.W.Hunt	Bellis
34	22	NEWCASTLE UNITED	1-3	Wynn	3000	"	Sneddon	Smith	"	Jones	"	"	"	"	"	"

+ Games 20 and 21 also counted as the first round of the Lancashire Cup

1941-42 Season

Football League - Northern Section

#	Date	Opponent	Score	Scorers	Att	1	2	3	4	5	6	7	8	9	10	11
1	Aug 30	OLDHAM ATHLETIC	3-2	Duff(2), Colquhoun	2445	Hall	Gorman	Byrom	Treanor	Davenport	Webster	Taylor	Cunliffe	Horrabin	Duff	Colquhoun
2	Sep 6	Oldham Athletic	0-3		3000	"	"	J.Wood	"	"	Dutton	"	L.Horton	"	"	"
3	13	Burnley	1-3	Duff	2000	"	"	Sneddon	"	"	Webster	"	"	J.Wood	"	"
4	20	BURNLEY	1-1	Cunliffe	1995	Swinburne	"	"	"	"	"	Colquhoun	Cunliffe	Davies	"	Bellis
5	27	Halifax Town	2-4	Webster, Duff	3500	J.Smith	"	"	"	"	"	Hanna	"	Horrabin	"	Colquhoun
6	Oct 4	HALIFAX TOWN	2-2	D.Jones, Wright	2014	Swinburne	"	"	"	Whitaker	"	Taylor	"	Wright	D.Jones	"
7	11	PRESTON N.E.	1-5	Colquhoun	2894	Hall	"	"	"	"	"	"	"	"	Boulter	"
8	18	Preston N.E.	0-6		3000	Swinburne	Sneddon	Duff	"	Neary	Toser	Colquhoun	"	"	Ainsworth	Haworth
9	25	Southport	1-4	D.Jones	1500	"	Gorman	Sneddon	"	"	Webster	Taylor	"	D.Jones	"	Colquhoun
10	Nov 1	SOUTHPORT	4-2	D.Jones, Cunliffe(2), V.Jones	975	"	J.Horton	"	Dooley	"	Treanor	Colquhoun	D.Jones	Cunliffe	V.Jones	F.Smith
11	8	BURY	1-0	V.Jones	1700	Robson	"	"	"	"	"	"	V.Jones	"	Duff	"
12	15	Bury	3-2	V.Jones, Dooley, Hunt	1474	"	Duff	"	"	"	"	Hunt	Cunliffe	V.Jones	R.Wood	Whitworth
13	22	Bolton Wanderers	3-3	Cunliffe(3)	2200	"	"	"	Barker	"	"	Taylor	"	"	"	F.Smith
14	29	BOLTON WANDERERS	1-0	Cunliffe	1500	"	J.Horton	"	Dooley	"	"	"	"	"	Duff	"
15	Dec 6	BLACKBURN ROVERS	2-2	Taylor, Duff	488	"	"	"	"	"	"	"	Duff	"	Shields	"
16	13	Blackburn Rovers	2-8	V.Jones(2)	1299	"	Duff	"	"	"	"	Colquhoun	Cunliffe	"	"	Middleton
17	20	BLACKPOOL	0-5		1500	"	"	"	"	"	"	Taylor	V.Jones	Horrabin	"	Colquhoun
18	25	Blackpool	1-0	Cunliffe	11500	"	J.Horton	"	"	"	"	"	Cunliffe	"	Duff	F.Smith
19*	27	OLDHAM ATHLETIC	1-0	Colquhoun	2317	"	"	"	"	"	"	Colquhoun	"	V.Jones	"	"
20*	Jan 3	Oldham Athletic	2-3	Cunliffe, Horrabin	1000	Pitt	Eastwood	"	"	"	"	"	"	Horrabin	"	"
21*	10	LEEDS UNITED	2-0	F.Smith, Taylor	2107	"	Mangham	"	"	"	Duff	Taylor	"	"	D.Jones	"
22*	17	Leeds United	0-5		3000	"	"	Duff	Colquhoun	Cunliffe	Treanor	"	L.Horton	"	V.Jones	"
23*	Feb 14	Manchester City	0-5		4000	Robson	J.Horton	Paton	Delaney	Neary	"	Colquhoun	McFadyen	Walsh	Duff	"
24*	21	Southport	1-2	Duff	1000	John	"	Byrom	Paton	Treanor	Dooley	Taylor	Cunliffe	"	"	McFadyen
25*	Mar 14	LIVERPOOL	2-8	Treanor, Ancell	2373	"	Paton	Ancell	Dooley	Neary	Treanor	"	"	"	"	Bartholomew
26*	21	MANCHESTER CITY	3-1	Cutting, Cunliffe(2)	2323	Chesters	Sneddon	Richmond	"	"	Treanor	Cutting	Colquhoun	"	Duff	V.Jones
27*	28	Liverpool	2-5	Bartholomew(2)	5000	"	"	"	"	Cutting	"	Duff	"	Thorpe	D.Jones	"
28+	Apr 11	Bury	3-4	Cunliffe, Colquhoun, D.Jones	1648	Pitt	Eastwood	Kirkman	Dooley	"	Cutting	France	"	"	"	Colquhoun
29+	18	BURY	4-1	D.Jones(2), Duff, Bartholomew	2010	"	"	Richmond	Cutting	"	Duff	Colquhoun	"	"	"	Bartholomew
30+	25	BLACKPOOL	2-0	Colquhoun, Bartholomew	2736	"	Byrom	"	"	"	"	"	O.Jones	Wood	"	"
31+	May 2	Blackpool	1-5	D.Jones	6000	"	"	"	"	"	"	L.Horton	"	"	"	"

* Games 19 to 27 were in the League War Cup Qualifying Competiiton (The second game against Southport was not played)
+ Games 28 to 31 were in the Lancashire Cup
Both sets of games also contributed to the Second League Competition

1942-43 Season

#	Date	Opponent	Score	Scorers	Att	1	2	3	4	5	6	7	8	9	10	11
1	Aug 29	Southport	1-1	Bartholomew	1200	Strong	Bradford	G.Richmond	Walton	Smith	Cutting	Colquhoun	Cunliffe	V.Jones	Miller	Bartholomew
2	Sep 5	SOUTHPORT	2-3	Colquhoun, Bartholomew	800	Goodall	Duff	"	Cutting	Bradford	Walton	"	"	"	Curran	"
3	12	HALIFAX TOWN	1-3	A.Jones	1744	"	Gallimore	"	Garfoot	"	Duff	A.Jones	Brown	Horton	Manning	"
4	19	Halifax Town	0-3		3000	Folds	"	"	Cutting	"	"	Colquhoun	N.Richmond	"	D.Jones	Bebb
5	26	OLDHAM ATHLETIC	3-1	Cunliffe(2), Bebb	1441	Strong	"	Barker	"	"	"	Bebb	Cunliffe	V.Jones	"	Bartholomew
6	Oct 3	Oldham Athletic	0-1		2464	"	"	Bradford	"	Smith	"	France	"	"	"	Bebb
7	10	BLACKBURN ROVERS	1-5	Cunliffe	1325	Goodall	Baker	G.Richmond	Walton	Bradford	"	Colquhoun	"	Thorpe	Whalley	"
8	17	Blackburn Rovers	0-6		850	Strong	Gallimore	"	Bradford	Neary	Walton	"	"	Hunt	Wood	D.Jones
9	24	BLACKPOOL	3-4	Cunliffe, D.Jones, Wood	1800	"	"	"	Walton	Bradford	Duff	"	"	"	"	D.Jones
10	31	Blackpool	0-5		8000	"	Sneddon	"	Cutting	"	"	Thompson	"	"	"	Bartholomew
11	Nov 7	Burnley	0-5		2018	"	"	"	"	"	Duffy	Gee	"	"	Duff	Bebb
12	14	BURNLEY	2-1	Harker, Gee	903	"	Bradford	Sneddon	Dooley	T.Jones	Duff	"	"	Harker	Wood	Hornby
13	21	STOCKPORT COUNTY	3-1	Cunliffe, Duffy, Cload	1355	"	"	"	"	"	Duffy	Colquhoun	"	Duff	"	Cload
14	28	Stockport County	2-3	Wood(2)	1500	"	"	"	"	"	"	Gee	"	Harker	"	"
15	Dec 5	Bolton Wanderers	4-4	Cload(2), Harker(2)	1500	"	"	Byrom	Breakwell	"	"	"	"	"	"	"
16	12	BOLTON WANDERERS	3-1	Cunliffe(2), Harker	1432	"	"	Sneddon	"	Treanor	"	"	"	"	"	"
17	19	BURY	6-3	Gee,Eastwood,Cunliffe,Harker(2),Wood	717	"	"	Byrom	Eastwood	Wildsmith	Breakwell	"	"	"	"	Brown
18	25	Bury	3-4	Cload, Wood(2)	2880	"	"	"	Duff	"	Duffy	Eastwood	Wood	Shaw	D.Jones	Cload
19*	26	OLDHAM ATHLETIC	4-3	Cunliffe(2), Eastwood, Wood	4582	"	"	"	Breakwell	T.Jones	"	Gee	Cunliffe	Eastwood	Wood	D.Jones
20*	Jan 2	Oldham Athletic	3-2	Gee, Cunliffe, Wood	1496	"	"	Sneddon	"	Wildsmith	"	"	Harker	"	"	"
21*	9	BLACKBURN ROVERS	4-0	Cunliffe, Wood, D.Jones, Harker	1737	"	"	"	Neary	Duffy	"	"	"	"	"	"
22*	16	Blackburn Rovers	2-2	Harker, Cunliffe	2000	"	"	"	"	Duffy	Murphy	"	"	"	"	Colquhoun
23*	23	Stockport County	4-3	Gee, Harker(2)	2000	"	"	Murphy	"	"	Gee	"	"	"	"	D.Jones
24*	30	STOCKPORT COUNTY	6-0	Wood, Harker(2), Cunliffe(3)	2601	"	"	Sweeney	"	Wildsmith	"	"	"	"	"	Cload
25*	Feb 6	BURY	3-2	Gee(2), D.Jones	4234	"	"	Sneddon	"	T.Jones	"	"	"	"	"	D.Jones
26*	13	Bury	0-1		4863	"	"	Wildsmith	"	"	Murphy	"	"	"	"	Cload
27*	20	BURNLEY	4-2	Murphy(3), Wood	3916	"	"	"	"	Neary	T.Jones	"	"	Murphy	"	D.Jones
28*	27	Burnley	1-1	Gee	2399	"	"	Byrom	"	T.Jones	Schofield	"	"	Horrabin	"	Cload
29*	Mar 6	BLACKBURN ROVERS	1-2	Harker	7296	"	"	Blood	"	Neary	Murphy	"	"	Harker	"	D.Jones
30*	13	Blackburn Rovers	1-3	Wood	7865	"	"	"	"	T.Jones	Treanor	"	"	Wood	D.Jones	"
31+	20	OLDHAM ATHLETIC	1-0	Cunliffe	2722	"	"	"	"	Wildsmith	Burnikell	"	"	Horrabin	Wood	Byrne
32+	27	Oldham Athletic	1-3	Cunliffe	2300	Chesters	"	Bryrom	Cornwell	Duff	Palfreyman	Taylor	"	"	"	D.Jones
33#	Apr 3	BURNLEY	4-0	Cunliffe, Gee, Duff(2)	1783	Strong	"	"	Breakwell	Neary	T.Jones	Gee	"	Duff	"	Palfreyman
34#	10	Burnley	0-2		1500	Chesters	"	"	Duff	T.Jones	Webb	Collinge	"	Horton	"	"

Matches 19 to 34 were the Second League Competition
Matches 19 to 30 were also in the League War Cup, matches 31 and 32 in the Lancashire Cup

1943-44 Season

Football League North

#	Date	Opponent	Score	Scorers	Att	1	2	3	4	5	6	7	8	9	10	11
1	Aug 28	Blackpool	1-6	Harker	8000	Fielding	Bradford	Byrom	Dooley	T.Jones	Duff	McGaitie	Cunliffe	Harker	Wood	Rudd
2	Sep 4	BLACKPOOL	2-6	Cunliffe, Harker	4330	"	"	Wildsmith	"	Neary	Murphy	Gee	"	"	"	Duff
3	11	SOUTHPORT	6-1	Harker(5), Wood	2032	"	"	Byrom	Eastwood	Wildsmith	Treanor	"	Duff	"	"	Maudsley
4	18	Southport	4-4	Harker(4)	2700	"	"	"	Dooley	Neary	Eastwood	Duff	Cunliffe	"	"	Horton
5	25	Oldham Athletic	0-2		2570	"	"	"	Breakwell	"	Haigh	Taylor	"	Duff	"	Horton
6	Oct 2	OLDHAM ATHLETIC	2-1	Harker, Wood	2023	"	"	"	Duff	Wildsmith	"	"	"	Harker	"	Maudsley
7	9	Halifax Town	2-2	Harker, Duff	3160	"	"	"	"	"	Breakwell	"	"	"	"	
8	16	HALIFAX TOWN	4-3	Mulligan, Gee, Cunliffe(2)	2343	"	"	"	"	"	Haigh	Gee	"	"	Mulligan	Miller
9	23	Blackburn Rovers	1-6	Cunliffe	3822	Chesters	"	"	Mulligan	"	"	"	"	"	Wood	
10	30	BLACKBURN ROVERS	2-1	Wood, Cunliffe	3161	"	"	"	Breakwell	"	"	"	"	"	"	
11	Nov 6	BURNLEY	3-1	Wood, Harker, Gee	3214	"	"	"	Duff	"	"	"	"	"	"	
12	13	Burnley	0-2		2200	"	"	"	"	"	"	"	"	"	"	
13	20	Stockport County	3-1	Cunliffe(2), Redwood	1800	"	"	"	"	T.Jones	"	"	Horton	Cunliffe	"	Redwood
14	27	STOCKPORT COUNTY	2-0	Harker(2)	1122	"	"	"	"	"	"	"	Cunliffe	Harker	"	
15	Dec 4	BRADFORD CITY	2-1	Harker(2)	2290	"	"	"	"	"	"	"	"	"	"	Miller
16	11	Bradford City	0-3		2500	"	"	"	Treanor	"	"	Taylor	"	Wood	Joseph	Duff
17	18	Bury	4-1	Harrison,Harker, Gee, Wood	2134	"	"	"	Duff	"	"	Gee	"	Harker	Wood	Harrison
18	25	BURY	5-0	Gee,Cunliffe,Wood,Harrison,Harker	3103	"	"	"	"	"	"	"	"	Harker	Wood	Harrison
19*	27	BOLTON WANDERERS	5-0	Harker(4), Cunliffe		"	"	"	"	"	"	"	Mulligan	"	"	
20*	Jan 1	Bolton Wanderers	2-2	Gee, Harrison	6786	"	"	"	"	"	"	"	"	"	"	
21*	8	Blackburn Rovers	1-3	Wood	4530	Fielding	"	Wildsmith	"	"	"	Taylor	Windle	Carrick	"	"
22*	15	BLACKBURN ROVERS	4-0	Wood(2), Gee, Harrison	4055	"	"	Byrom	"	"	"	Gee	Cunliffe	Harker	"	"
23*	22	Burnley	2-2	Gee(2)	1825	"	"	"	"	"	"	"	Wood	"	Morris	"
24*	29	BURNLEY	3-1	Morris(2), Taylor	5000	"	"	"	"	"	"	Taylor	"	"	"	"
25*	Feb 5	SOUTHPORT	0-0		4330	Chesters	"	"	"	"	"	Gee	"	"	"	Taylor
26*	12	Southport	4-2	Gee(2), Harrison, Harker	3500	"	"	"	"	"	"	"	Cunliffe	"	Wood	Harrison
27*	19	Blackpool	0-2		8000	"	"	"	"	"	"	"	"	Wood	Miller	
28*	26	BLACKPOOL	0-2		9911	"	"	"	Wildsmith	"	"	"	Cornwall	Morris	Wood	
29*	Mar 4	Burnley	3-3	Gee, Wood, Sibley	6166	"	"	"	Lievesley	T.Jones	"	"	Duff	"	"	Sibley
30*	11	BURNLEY	2-1	Duff, Sibley	7023	"	"	"	Wildsmith	"	"	"	"	"	"	
31*	18	Blackpool	0-8		25000	"	"	"	Treanor	"	"	"	"	Cornwall	"	Rudd
32*	25	BLACKPOOL	2-1	Duff(2)	8706	"	"	"	"	"	Duff	O'Mahoney	Wood	Morris	Harrison
33+	Apr 1	OLDHAM ATHLETIC	4-0	Wood, Duff, Haigh(2)	4188	"	"	"	Duff	Wildsmith	"	Gee	Wood	Harrison	"	Wharton
34+	8	Oldham Athletic	2-0	Wood, Whaton	7620	"	"	"	Duff	Wildsmith	"	Gee	Wood	Harrison	"	Wharton
35+	10	STOCKPORT COUNTY	1-4	Wood	5700	"	"	"	Cornwall	Haigh	Duff	O'Mahoney	Wood	"	Harrison
36+	15	Stockport County	2-3	Sibley, Wood	3000	"	"	"	Duff	Davies	Haigh	Taylor	Banner	Harrison	Wood	Sibley
37#	22	Tranmere Rovers	0-1		1500	"	"	"	Warburton	Wildsmith	"	Connor	Wood	"	Wharton	J.Jones
38#	29	TRANMERE ROVERS	4-1	Morris(2), Wood, Taylor	1690	"	"	"	Duff	Macauley	"	Taylor	Gallon	Wood	Morris	Wharton

* Matches 19 to 38 in the League Second Competition, matches 19 to 32 also in the League Cup (North), matches 33 to 36 in the Lancashire Cup
NB. Match 30 was 1-1 at full time. This score counted in the League. Rochdale won the Cup tie 2-1 after extra time.
Match 14 was abandoned after 74 minutes, but the result stood.

1944-45 Season

Football League North

	Date	Opponent	Score	Scorers	Att	1	2	3	4	5	6	7	8	9	10	11
1	Aug 26	BLACKPOOL	3-7	W.Ainsworth, Morris(2)	7071	Chesters	Manghan	Byrom	Treanor	T.Jones	Haigh	Duff	W.Ainsworth	Morris	Gallon	A.Cunliffe
2	Sep 2	Blackpool	0-3		4000	"	Duff	"	Macauley	"	"	Taylor	"	Griffiths	"	J.Jones
3	9	Blackburn Rovers	0-3		3000	"	Cornwall	"	Treanor	Neary	Bradshaw	J.Jones	"	Duff	Bradley	Atkinson
4	16	BLACKBURN ROVERS	2-0	W.Ainsworth, Acton	2850	"	"	"	Duff	T.Jones	Treanor	Gastall	"	Acton	A,Ainsworth	"
5	23	Burnley	2-2	Duff, W.Ainsworth	4213	"	"	"	"	"	Muir	"	"	Chaney	"	Harrison
6	30	BURNLEY	3-1	Gallon, D Cochrane, Duff	3612	Grimsditch	"	"	Treanor	"	"	Duff	Gallon	D.Cochrane	"	"
7	Oct 7	BOLTON WANDERERS	2-2	Gallon, P.Taylor	4100	"	"	"	Duff	Neary	Haigh	Taylor	"	"	"	"
8	14	Bolton Wanderers	0-0		4000	"	"	"	"	"	Treanor	J.Jones	"	Acton	Morris	"
9	21	Accrington Stanley	2-1	Morris (2)	3449	"	"	Cole	W.Ainsworth	T.Jones	Duff	Reynolds	"	Morris	Strachan	J.Jones
10	28	ACCRINGTON STANLEY	3-0	Morris(2), Roach (og)	2135	Chesters	"	Lowe	Duff	Neary	Haigh	"	"	"	T.Cochrane	A.Cunliffe
11	Nov 4	PRESTON N.E.	5-2	Gallon,Reynolds,T Cochrane,Wood(2)	3100	"	"	Duff	W.Ainsworth	"	"	"	"	"	"	Wood
12	11	Preston N.E.	1-2	J.Jones	2700	"	"	Byrom	Duff	T.Jones	"	"	"	"	Wood	J.Jones
13	18	Southport	2-2	Hunt, J.Jones	3000	"	"	"	"	Neary	"	"	"	Hunt	"	"
14	25	SOUTHPORT	1-1	Roberts	3326	"	"	"	"	"	"	"	"	Reid	Roberts	"
15	Dec 2	OLDHAM ATHLETIC	2-3	Reid(2)	2621	"	"	Duff	Eastwood	T.Jones	"	"	"	"	"	"
16	9	Oldham Athletic	2-0	Reid, Reynolds	5658	"	"	Byrom	Muir	Neary	"	"	Duff	"	Strachan	Makin
17	16	Halifax Town	2-4	Pickstock, Makin	1800	"	"	"	J.Jones	Duff	"	"	Pickstock	"	"	"
18	23	HALIFAX TOWN	3-0	Reynolds, Reid, Young	4760	"	"	"	Muir	Neary	"	"	Duff	"	Gallon	Young
19*	25	Accrington Stanley	1-0	Gallon	5800	"	"	"	"	"	"	"	"	"	"	"
20*	30	ACCRINGTON STANLEY	1-1	Haigh	4063	"	"	"	Duff	"	"	"	Reid	Constantine	"	Makin
21*	Jan 13	Blackburn Rovers	2-3	Gallon, Constantine	3017	"	"	"	"	"	"	"	Gallon	"	Reid	"
22*	20	PRESTON N.E.	1-1	Reid	1934	"	"	"	Muir	"	Duff	"	Reid	"	Gallon	J.Jones
23*	27	Preston N.E.	1-1	Reid	1755	"	"	Lowe	Duff	"	Treanor	"	Gallon	Reid	Strachan	"
24*	Feb 3	Burnley	0-2		5657	"	"	"	Treanor	"	Haigh	Gallon	J.Cunliffe	"	Duff	"
25*	10	BURNLEY	0-4		4607	Grimsditch	"	Duff	Muir	"	"	Reynolds	"	Harker	Strachan	Revell
26*	17	BLACKPOOL	3-6	OG, Hanson(2)	2554	Hall	"	"	Wilson	Chambers	Foxton	"	A.Ainsworth	Constantine	T.Cochrane	Hanson
27*	24	Blackpool	0-4		7000	"	"	Lowe	Duff	Neary	Cole	Reid	Gallon	"	Strachan	J.Jones
28*	Mar 3	BLACKBURN ROVERS	0-8		2887	Hesketh	"	"	"	"	Muir	Reynolds	"	"	T.Cochrane	"
29+	10	BLACKBURN ROVERS	0-1		2670	Chesters	"	Lyons	Whittaker	"	Haigh	Duff	"	Weatherspoon	Malam	Seddon
30+	17	Blackburn Rovers	0-4		3000	"	Muir	"	Davies	"	Whittaker	A.Ainsworth	Duff	Constantine	"	J.Jones
31#	#	Tranmere Rovers	1-0	Brinton	2376	"	"	"	Duff	"	Haigh	Hughes	Banner	"	Bailey	Brinton
32#	31	TRANMERE ROVERS	4-1	Duff, Constantine(2), Makin	2379	Grimsditch	Cornwall	Muir	Whittaker	"	"	Duff	Eastwood	"	Morris	Makin
33#	Apr 2	Chester	0-3		3000	"	Muir	Lyons	"	"	"	"	Harker	"	"	"
34#	7	Stockport County	0-3		3042	Thorpe	Keenan	"	"	"	Muir	Makin	Duff	"	Bate	A.Cunliffe
35#	14	STOCKPORT COUNTY	0-2		1671	Chesters	Cornwall	Muir	Duff	Gemmell	Haigh	"	J.Jones	Constantine	Wood	Thorpe
36#	21	OLDHAM ATHLETIC	1-2	Wood	1776	"	Muir	G.Jones	"	"	"	"	J.Cunliffe	Mycock	"	Hanson
37#	28	Oldham Athletic	0-2		1297	"	Duff	"	Whittaker	"	Bradshaw	"	Mycock	Harker	Woods	"
38#	May 5	CHESTER	2-1	Hanson(2)	708	Olive	"	"	"	Pearce	Haigh	"	Higham	Whittle	Morris	"

Matches 19 to 38 in the Second Championship
Matches 19 to 28 also in the League Cup (North), matches 29 and 30 in the Lancashire Cup

North League 1st Championship

	P	W	L	D	F	A	Pts
Huddersfield T.	18	14	1	3	50	22	31
Derby County	18	14	3	1	54	19	29
Sunderland	18	12	2	4	52	25	28
Aston Villa	18	12	3	3	54	19	27
Everton	18	12	4	2	58	25	26
Wrexham	18	11	4	3	40	18	25
Doncaster R.	18	12	6	0	48	27	24
Bradford PA	18	10	4	4	45	31	24
Bolton Wands.	18	9	3	6	34	22	24
Manchester C.	18	9	5	4	53	31	22
Stoke City	18	9	5	4	37	25	22
Birmingham	18	8	4	6	30	21	22
Barnsley	18	10	6	2	42	32	22
Rotherham U.	18	9	5	4	31	25	22
WBA	18	9	5	4	36	30	22
Liverpool	18	9	6	3	41	30	21
Grimsby Town	18	9	6	3	37	29	21
Halifax Town	18	8	5	5	30	29	21
Chester	18	9	6	3	45	45	21
Blackpool	18	9	7	2	53	38	20
Burnley	18	8	6	4	39	27	20
Leeds Utd.	18	9	7	2	53	42	20
Sheffield W.	18	9	7	2	34	30	20
Chesterfield	18	8	7	3	30	19	19
Darlington	18	9	8	1	52	45	19
Wolves	18	7	6	5	31	27	19
ROCHDALE	18	7	6	5	35	33	19
Crewe Alex.	18	9	8	1	43	41	19
Blackburn R.	18	7	7	4	30	29	18
Manchester U.	18	8	8	2	40	40	18

(Top 30 clubs shown only)

North League 2nd Championship

	P	W	L	D	F	A	Pts
Hartlepools U.	21	8	10	3	34	54	19
Coventry City	21	6	9	6	36	53	18
Nottingham F.	17	5	5	7	23	25	17
Tranmere R.	23	8	14	1	40	56	17
Halifax Town	18	6	7	5	22	35	17
Lincoln City	17	6	7	4	42	51	16
Manchester C.	19	7	10	2	32	43	16
Northampton T.	14	6	5	3	23	30	15
Oldham A.	21	7	13	1	39	56	15
Stockport C.	19	7	12	0	31	50	14
Middlesbrough	24	6	16	2	40	73	14
Walsall	18	5	10	3	24	33	13
Swansea T.	20	6	13	1	42	63	13
Port Vale	21	5	14	2	27	60	12
Mansfield T.	12	5	6	1	22	38	11
Hull City	18	5	12	1	30	54	11
ROCHDALE	20	4	13	3	17	49	11
Southport	22	3	16	3	33	82	9

North Cup Qualifying Competition

	P	W	L	D	F	A	Pts
Sunderland	10	4	5	1	24	22	9
Grimsby Town	10	3	4	3	20	19	9
Mansfield T.	10	4	5	1	18	34	9
Preston N.E.	10	4	4	2	14	16	8
Lincoln City	10	3	5	2	21	33	8
York City	10	3	6	1	25	29	7
Middlesbrough	10	3	6	1	23	30	7
Walsall	10	3	6	1	13	21	7
Southport	10	3	6	1	19	40	7
Port Vale	10	3	6	1	13	30	7
Bath City	10	3	7	0	28	34	6
Swansea Town	10	3	7	0	27	33	6
Hull City	10	2	7	1	15	25	5
Tranmere R.	10	2	7	1	15	28	5
ROCHDALE	10	1	6	3	9	30	5
Oldham Ath.	10	2	8	0	19	28	4
Sheffield W.	10	1	7	2	14	29	4
Stockport C.	10	2	8	0	14	35	4
Coventry City	10	1	8	1	16	35	3
Aberaman	10	1	8	1	17	46	3
Chester	10	1	8	1	14	39	3
Notts. County	10	1	9	0	12	33	2

(Bottom 22 clubs shown only.
Top 32 of 60 only, qualified)

1945-46 Season

Division 3 North : West

No	Date	Opponent	Score & Scorers	Att	1	2	3	4	5	6	7	8	9	10	11
1	Aug 25	Wrexham	1-4 Reid	6000	Olive	Pomphrey	Muir	McCormick	Neary	Haigh	A.Jones	Meek	Reid	Wood	Hanson
2	Sep 1	WREXHAM	3-1 Constantine, Meek, Hanson	3289	"	"	Lunn	"	"	Molloy	"	"	Constantine	"	"
3	8	OLDHAM ATHLETIC	4-2 Constantine(3), Hanson	4097	Chesters	"	G.Jones	Molloy	"	Haigh	"	Woods	"	"	"
4	15	Oldham Athletic	1-2 Taylor	6278	Breedon	"	Griffiths	McCormick	"	Molloy	"	Meek	"	Woods	Taylor
5	22	Stockport County	0-7	4993	Chesters	"	G.Jones	Molloy	"	Haigh	"	"	Harker	"	Hanson
6	29	STOCKPORT COUNTY	4-2 Livesay, Hanson(2), A.Jones	3724	Breedon	Clive	Pomphrey	McCormick	Pearce	Partridge	"	Brindle	Livesley	Wood	"
7	Oct 6	Southport	2-1 Hargreaves(2)	3500	Chesters	Pomphrey	Duff	"	"	"	"	"	Hargreaves	Hanson	Cunliffe
8	13	SOUTHPORT	5-0 Hargreaves(2), Hanson(3)	4804	Breedon	"	"	Higham	"	"	"	"	"	"	"
9	20	CHESTER	3-1 Hargreaves(2), Brindle	6693	"	"	Sneddon	Duff	"	"	"	"	"	"	"
10	27	Chester	3-3 Brindle(2), A.Jones	4123	Chesters	"	Duff	McCormick	"	"	"	"	"	"	"
11	Nov 3	BARROW	3-0 Cunliffe, Hargreaves, A.Jones	4133	"	"	"	"	"	"	"	"	"	Wood	"
12	10	Barrow	1-2 Brindle	4387	"	"	"	"	"	"	"	"	Hanson	Woods	"
13	Dec 1	Crewe Alexandra	4-1 Brindle(2), Makin(2)	3500	"	Jackson	Pomphrey	"	"	"	Makin	"	Hargreaves	Wood	"
14	22	Tranmere Rovers	2-3 Duff, Hargreaves	3000	"	Pomphrey	Sneddon	"	"	Duff	Wood	"	"	Hanson	"
15	25	ACCRINGTON	2-0 Brindle(2)	7614	"	"	"	Duff	"	Partridge	Makin	"	"	"	"
16	26	Accrington	2-4 Duff(2)	8043	"	"	"	"	"	"	"	"	"	Wood	"
17	29	CREWE ALEXANDRA	3-2 Hargreaves, Duff, Toseland	6849	"	Jackson	Pomphrey	"	"	"	Toseland	"	"	"	"
18*	Jan 12	SOUTHPORT	1-3 Toseland	4377	"	"	Duff	McCormick	Neary	Keddie	"	"	"	"	"
19*	19	Chester	0-2	1500	Kirk	Duff	G.Jones	"	Neilson	Partridge	"	Woods	"	Hanson	"
20*	26	CHESTER	6-1 Walters (og), Wood(3), Woods, Makin	2500	"	Sneddon	"	Duff	"	McCormick	Makin	Brindle	Wood	Woods	"
21*	Feb 2	STOCKPORT COUNTY	2-3 Wood, Burrows (og)	3416	"	Jackson	Sneddon	"	"	"	"	"	"	"	"
22*	9	Stockport County	2-2 Cunliffe, Makin	6500	"	Sneddon	Duff	McCormick	Pearce	Hamilton	"	Hargreaves	"	"	"
23*	16	CREWE ALEXANDRA	2-2 Wood(2)	3816	"	"	"	"	"	Partridge	"	Brindle	"	"	"
24*	23	Crewe Alexandra	1-3 Hargreaves	3880	Ashbridge	"	"	Richardson	"	McCormick	"	Wood	"	Brindle	"
25*	Mar 2	WREXHAM	1-2 Hargreaves	3775	"	Pomphrey	Sneddon	McCormick	"	Hamilton	"	Duff	"	Woods	"
26*	9	Wrexham	1-2 Hargreaves	6800	"	Jackson	Pomphrey	"	Birch	Hurst	"	Wood	Hargreaves	"	"
27*	16	Southport	2-0 Hargreaves, Cunliffe	3500	J.Jones	Sneddon	"	Hurst	"	Dobson	"	"	"	McCormick	"
28+	23	BARROW	2-1 Makin, Wood	2100	"	"	"	"	"	"	"	"	"	"	"
29+	30	Barrow	2-1 Rodi, Hargreaves	4014	Walmsley	"	"	McCormick	"	"	"	"	"	Rodi	"
30+	Apr 6	LINCOLN CITY	2-3 Rodi, Hargreaves	4128	Yates	Pomphrey	Byrom	Hurst	"	McCormick	"	"	"	"	"
31+	13	Lincoln City	2-1 Rodi, McCormick	4942	Chesters	Byrom	Pomphrey	"	"	Dobson	"	McCormick	Wood	"	"
32	19	TRANMERE ROVERS	0-0	3243	Roberts	"	"	Whittle	"	"	Baum	Smith	Hargreaves	Wood	Makin
33+	20	OLDHAM ATHLETIC	3-1 Cunliffe, Hargreaves, Wood	4200	"	"	"	"	"	McCormick	Makin	Wood	"	Rodi	Cunliffe
34+	22	Oldham Athletic	4-0 Hargreaves(2), Cunliffe, Rodi	5800	"	Sneddon	"	"	"	"	"	"	"	"	"
35+	27	Southport	0-2	1200	"	"	"	"	"	"	"	"	"	Nuttall	"
36+	May 4	SOUTHPORT	2-1 Rodi, Wood	3191	"	Byrom	"	Partridge	"	Howshall	Kindred	McCormick	Wood	"	"

* Matches 18 to 27 in Division 3 North West Cup
+ Matches 28 to 31 and 33 to 36 in Division 3 Second Championship

F.A. Cup

Rd	Date	Opponent	Score & Scorers	Att	1	2	3	4	5	6	7	8	9	10	11
R1	Nov 17	Stockport County	2-1 Brindle, Woods	6000	Chesters	Pomphrey	Sneddon	Duff	Pearce	Partridge	A.Jones	Brindle	Hargreaves	Woods	A.Cunliffe
R1	24	STOCKPORT COUNTY	1-1 Hargreaves(2)	6158	"	"	"	"	"	"	"	"	"	"	"
R2	Dec 8	Tranmere Rovers	1-3 Wood	7000	"	"	Duff	McCormick	"	"	Makin	"	"	Wood	"
R2	15	TRANMERE ROVERS	3-0 Hargreaves(2), Makin	6500	"	"	Sneddon	"	"	"	"	"	"	"	"
R3	Jan 5	Bury	3-3 Cunliffe, Hargreaves, Reynolds	13248	"	Duff	"	"	Neary	"	Reynolds	"	"	"	"
R3	8	BURY	2-4 Hargreaves(2)	8712	"	"	"	"	"	"	"	"	"	"	"

Lancashire Senior Cup

Rd	Date	Opponent	Score & Scorers	1	2	3	4	5	6	7	8	9	10	11
R1	Sep 5	Manchester United	1-5 Constantine	Olive	Pomphrey	Duff	McCormick	Haigh	Molloy	A.Jones	Wood	Constantine	Hanson	Taylor
R1	Jan 1	MANCHESTER UNITED	2-0 Brindle, Hargreaves	Kirk	Jackson	Pomphrey	"	Neary	Partridge	Toseland	Brindle	Hargreaves	"	Makin

Division Three North: West — First Half Season

	P	W	L	D	F	A	Pts
Accrington S.	18	10	4	4	37	19	24
ROCHDALE	18	10	6	2	43	35	22
Crewe Alex.	18	9	6	3	43	31	21
Chester	18	8	5	5	44	38	21
Wrexham	18	8	6	4	30	25	20
Tranmere R.	18	9	7	2	33	31	20
Stockport C.	18	6	9	3	38	38	15
Oldham Ath.	18	5	8	5	29	32	15
Barrow	18	4	10	4	21	44	12
Southport	18	3	11	4	22	47	10

Division Three North: West Cup

	P	W	L	D	F	A	Pts
Stockport C.	10	7	2	1	26	15	15
Southport	10	6	2	2	20	13	14
Accrington S.	10	6	3	1	24	17	13
Oldham Ath.	10	4	2	4	18	15	12
Crewe Alex.	10	3	3	4	23	27	10
Wrexham	10	4	5	1	21	20	9
Chester	10	4	5	1	26	25	9
Tranmere R.	10	4	5	1	17	25	9
ROCHDALE	10	2	6	2	18	20	6
Barrow	10	1	8	1	13	29	3

(Only top 8 qualified)

1946/47 6th in Division 3(N)

Player columns (left to right): Roberts WE, Pomphrey EA, Byrom W, Hallard W, Birch IW, McCormick JM, Makin SH, Wood E, Hargreaves J, Rodi J, Cunliffe A, Sneddon T, Hurst C, West T, Hargreaves T, Barkas T, Partridge D, Henderson WJ, Kirkman N, Cunliffe IN, Jackson L, Woods W, Carruthers AN, Jones W, Moorhouse A, Moss J, Sibley TI, O'Donnell H, Briggs CE, Arthur J

#		Date	Opponent	Score	Scorers	Att
1	Aug	31	Doncaster Rovers	1-2	A Cunliffe	8279
2	Sep	3	WREXHAM	0-1		5515
3		7	YORK CITY	0-1		8315
4		9	Oldham Athletic	2-3	Wood, J Hargreaves	11470
5		14	NEW BRIGHTON	2-2	Makin, Hurst	5612
6		17	OLDHAM ATHLETIC	1-3	Barkas	8097
7		21	Halifax Town	0-3		4119
8		25	Wrexham	2-2	J Hargreaves, A Cunliffe	7775
9		28	CARLISLE UNITED	6-0	J Hargreaves 3, Rodi, A Cunliffe, Barkas	7414
10	Oct	5	Accrington Stanley	3-2	Rodi 2, Barkas	4865
11		12	BARROW	1-1	A Cunliffe	7327
12		19	Tranmere Rovers	3-2	Carruthers 2, Barkas	7553
13		26	DARLINGTON	3-0	J Hargreaves, Barkas, Woods	6493
14	Nov	2	Hull City	1-0	Hallard	22616
15		9	GATESHEAD	2-3	J Hargreaves 2	8031
16		16	Hartlepool United	3-0	Wood 2, Barkas	7323
17		23	CREWE ALEXANDRA	1-1	Birch	6449
18	Dec	7	SOUTHPORT	0-0		4467
19		21	CHESTER CITY	2-1	Hallard, Barkas	7738
20		25	STOCKPORT COUNTY	1-4	J Hargreaves	7153
21		26	Stockport County	2-5	W Jones 2	14408
22		28	DONCASTER ROVERS	2-3	J Hargreaves, Wood	13555
23	Jan	4	York City	3-2	J Hargreaves 2, Carruthers	5363
24		18	New Brighton	2-1	J Hargreaves 2	5380
25		22	Lincoln City	3-2	A Cunliffe, Barkas, J Hargreaves	3249
26		25	HALIFAX TOWN	1-0	Carruthers	7504
27	Feb	1	Carlisle United	3-1	West 2, Moorhouse	9140
28	Mar	1	Darlington	1-4	Moorhouse	4931
29		8	HULL CITY	5-2	J Hargreaves, Barkas 2, Moss 2	6565
30		22	HARTLEPOOL UNITED	1-0	Barkas	7504
31		29	Crewe Alexandra	2-2	Sibley, O'Donnell	3247
32	Apr	4	BRADFORD CITY	0-1		10539
33		5	LINCOLN CITY	2-0	Sibley, O'Donnell	6634
34		7	Bradford City	1-0	Barkas	10267
35		12	Southport	2-0	Moss 2	4949
36		19	ROTHERHAM UNITED	1-1	O'Donnell	11908
37		26	Chester City	0-1		4278
38	May	10	Barrow	2-2	J Hargreaves 2	5322
39		17	Gateshead	2-2	J Hargreaves 2	4314
40		24	ACCRINGTON STANLEY	5-1	Moss, J Hargreaves, Barkas 3	6758
41		31	TRANMERE ROVERS	3-0	J Hargreaves 2, Barkas	5529
42	Jun	7	Rotherham United	3-3	O'Donnell 2, Barkas	10375

Played in one game: F Walkden (18, at 11), Arthur Jones (21,7), R Rothwell (25,2), J Oakes (28,7), C Lawrence (37,9).
In three games 40 to 42: A Collier (at 6).

Apps: 21, 9, 9, 17, 35, 35, 5, 31, 30, 9, 23, 2, 4, 4, 7, 36, 6, 17, 36, 2, 27, 15, 13, 2, 10, 17, 10, 14, 4, 4

Gls: 2, 1, 1, 4, 23, 3, 5, 1, 2, 17, 1, 4, 2, 2, 5, 2, 5

F.A. Cup

	Date	Opponent	Score	Scorers	Att
R1	Nov 30	BISHOP AUCKLAND	6-1	*See below	8319
R2	Dec 14	HARTLEPOOLS UTD.	6-1	Woods 3, A Cunliffe, Carruthers 2	6500
R3	Jan 11	Charlton Athletic	1-3	Woods	23271

Scorers in R1: J Hargreaves 2, A Cunliffe, Birch, Barkas, Woods

Lancs Cup

Date	Opponent	Score	Att
Oct 15	Chester	0-2	3000
22	CHESTER	0-1	2456

		P	W	D	L	F	A	W	D	L	F	A	Pts
1	Doncaster Rovers	42	15	5	1	67	16	18	1	2	56	24	72
2	Rotherham United	42	20	1	0	81	19	9	5	7	33	34	64
3	Chester	42	17	2	2	53	13	8	4	9	42	38	56
4	Stockport County	42	17	0	4	50	19	7	2	12	28	34	50
5	Bradford City	42	12	5	4	40	20	8	5	8	22	27	50
6	ROCHDALE	42	9	5	7	39	25	10	5	6	41	39	48
7	Wrexham	42	13	5	3	43	21	4	7	10	22	30	46
8	Crewe Alexandra	42	12	4	5	39	26	5	5	11	31	48	43
9	Barrow	42	10	2	9	28	24	7	5	9	26	38	41
10	Tranmere Rovers	42	11	5	5	43	33	6	2	13	23	44	41
11	Hull City	42	9	5	7	25	19	7	3	11	24	34	40
12	Lincoln City	42	12	3	6	52	32	5	2	14	34	55	39
13	Hartlepools United	42	10	5	6	36	26	5	4	12	28	47	39
14	Gateshead	42	10	3	8	39	33	6	3	12	23	39	38
15	York City	42	6	4	11	35	42	8	5	8	32	39	37
16	Carlisle United	42	10	5	6	45	38	4	4	13	25	55	37
17	Darlington	42	12	4	5	48	26	3	2	16	20	54	36
18	New Brighton	42	11	3	7	37	30	3	5	13	20	47	36
19	Oldham Athletic	42	6	5	10	29	31	6	3	12	26	49	32
20	Accrington Stanley	42	8	3	10	37	38	6	1	14	19	54	32
21	Southport	42	6	5	10	35	41	1	6	14	18	44	25
22	Halifax Town	42	6	3	12	28	36	2	3	16	15	56	22

1947/48 12th in Division 3(N)

League matches

#	Date	Opponent	Score	Scorers	Att
1	Aug 23	BARROW	2-2	Arthur, Hargreaves	9210
2	28	Hull City	0-0		25525
3	30	Wrexham	1-5	Wood	9926
4	Sep 2	HULL CITY	1-0	Moss	9027
5	6	HALIFAX TOWN	2-1	Moss, Withington	10868
6	9	ACCRINGTON STANLEY	1-3	Birch (p)	8551
7	13	Oldham Athletic	1-1	Withington	15310
8	20	New Brighton	0-0		7135
9	27	SOUTHPORT	2-1	Moss, Arthur	8213
10	Oct 4	Lincoln City	0-3		12246
11	11	YORK CITY	3-0	O'Donnell 2, Sibley	8743
12	18	Mansfield Town	1-1	O'Donnell	12268
13	25	CHESTER	2-2	Arthur, Withington	9582
14	Nov 1	Crewe Alexandra	1-2	O'Donnell	8552
15	8	CARLISLE UNITED	2-1	O'Donnell, Withington	8777
16	15	Rotherham United	1-4	Earl	13141
17	22	HARTLEPOOLS UNITED	0-2		4502
18	Dec 6	DARLINGTON	2-1	Davison (og), Johnston	7475
19	25	Bradford City	0-4		13983
20	27	BRADFORD CITY	2-0	Johnston, O'Donnell	6145
21	Jan 1	Accrington Stanley	2-1	Wood, O'Donnell	5785
22	3	WREXHAM	2-1	Johnston, Moss	9687
23	10	Gateshead	0-5		3857
24	17	Halifax Town	3-2	Johnston 2, O'Donnell	7310
25	24	Tranmere Rovers	1-4	Johnston	4880
26	31	OLDHAM ATHLETIC	2-0	Withington, Wood	12987
27	Feb 7	NEW BRIGHTON	1-0	Lawrence	4496
28	14	Southport	2-2	Withington, Arthur	7708
29	28	York City	0-0		7311
30	Mar 6	MANSFIELD TOWN	1-2	O'Donnell	9990
31	13	Chester	1-2	Arthur	6427
32	20	CREWE ALEXANDRA	1-2	Gallacher	7092
33	26	STOCKPORT COUNTY	1-2	Lawrence	7183
34	27	Carlisle United	0-5		10912
35	29	Stockport County	0-4		11002
36	Apr 3	ROTHERHAM UNITED	1-0	Arthur	7314
37	6	LINCOLN CITY	1-1	Wood	8467
38	10	Hartlepools United	1-4	Moorhouse	7907
39	13	Barrow	1-0	Wood	5188
40	17	GATESHEAD	2-1	Livesey, Reid	7031
41	24	Darlington	0-0		4614
42	May 1	TRANMERE ROVERS	1-1	Johnston	5269

Played in one game: JJ Brindle (19, 8), H Colvan (30, 8), E Anderson (34,3), MN Skivington (34,5).

Appearances and goals

	Briggs CE	Jackson L	Kirkman N	Wood E	Birch JW	Collier A	Arthur J	Barkas T	Hargreaves J	Moss J	O'Donnell H	Lawrence C	McCormick JM	Withington R	Roberts WE	Sibley TI	Moorhouse A	Byrom W	Earl AT	Cornock	Bywater NL	Johnston R	Britton J	Longdon CW	Rothwell R	Partridge D	Anderson A	Gallacher C	Reid DA	Livesey J
Apps	8	34	17	34	41	3	24	8	5	20	26	24	31	32	17	13	7	21	4	1	12	17	18	2	9	13	4	6	4	3
Goals				5	1		6		1	4	9	2		6		1	1		1			7						1	1	1

One own goal

Appearance grid (shirt numbers)

#	Briggs	Jackson	Kirkman	Wood	Birch	Collier	Arthur	Barkas	Hargreaves	Moss	O'Donnell	Lawrence	McCormick	Withington	Roberts	Sibley	Moorhouse	Byrom	Earl	Cornock	Bywater	Johnston	Britton	Longdon	Rothwell	Partridge	Anderson	Gallacher	Reid	Livesey
1	1	2	3	4	5	6	7	8	9	10	11																			
2	1	2	3	4	5	6	7	8		10	11	9																		
3	1	2	3	4	5	6	7	8		10	11	9																		
4	1	2	3	4	5		7			10	11	9	6	8																
5	1	2	3	4	5		7	8		10	11		6	9																
6	1	2	3	4	5		7	8		10	11		6	9																
7		2	3	6	5				9	10			4	8	1	7	11													
8		2	3	6	5			10	9		11		4	8	1	7														
9		2	3	6	5		7	8		10	9		4		1	11														
10		2	3	6	5		7	8		10	9		4		1	11														
11		2	3	6	5		7			10	9		4	8	1	11														
12		2	3	6	5		7			10	9		4	8	1	11														
13		2	3	6	5		7			10	9		4	8	1	11														
14		2	3	6	5		7			10	9		4	8	1	11														
15	1		3	6	5		7				9		4	8		11		2	10											
16	1		3	6	5		7				9		4	8		11		2	10											
17		2	3	4	5		7		9		11		6	8					10	1										
18		2		6	5		7						4	8			11	3	10		1	9								
19					5		7						4						10		11	2	1	9	3	6				
20					5						10	11	7		8			3			1	9	6			2	4			
21		2		9	5						10	11	7		8			3			1		6				4			
22		2			5						10	11	7		8			3			1	9	6							
23		2			5						10	11	7		8			3			1	9	6				4			
24		2			5						10	11	7	4	8			3			1	9	6							
25		2			5						10	11	7	4	8			3			1	9	6							
26		2		10	5							11	7	4	8			3			1	9	6							
27		2		10	5							11	7	4	8			3			1	9	6							
28		2		10	5							11	7	4	8			3			1	9	6			2				
29		2		10	5							11	7	4	8			3			1	9	6							
30		2		10	5							11	7	4				3			1	9	6							
31				9	5		8					11	7	10				2				6			3	4	1			
32		2			5		11					7	4	8				3			1	9	6					10		
33		2		9	5		11					7		8				3			1		6			4		10		
34				4			10							8	7	11					9	6			2	1				
35				6	5							7		10	11			1	9		2		4		8					
36		2			5		7		9			4		8				11	3		1					6		10		
37		2		9	5							7	4	8				11	3		1					6		10		
38				9	5							7	4	8			11	2			1					3	6		10	
39		2		9	5							7	4	8	1											3	6		10	
40		2		9	5							7	4	8	1											3	6		10	11
41		2		8	5							7			1								9	4		3	6		10	11
42		2		10	5							7			1							9	4			3	6	8		11

F. A. Cup

Rd	Date	Opponent	Score	Scorers	Att
R1	Nov 29	York City	1-0	Birch (p)	9830
R2	Dec 13	GILLINGHAM	1-1	O'Donnell	11110
rep	20	Gillingham	0-3		17078

Round 2 a.e.t.

Rd	Jackson	Wood	Birch	Arthur	Barkas	Hargreaves	O'Donnell	McCormick	Withington	Roberts	Sibley	Byrom	Earl	Johnston
R1	2	4	5	7			9	6	8	1	11	3	10	
R2	2	6	5	7	10	11		4	8	1		3		9
rep	2	6	5	7				4	8	1	11	3	10	9

Lancashire Cup

Date	Opponent	Score	Scorers	Att
Sep 23	PRESTON N.E.	3-0	Barkas, O'Donnell, Withington	5000
Oct 28	Southport	0-1		3000

Date	Briggs	Jackson	Kirkman	Wood	Birch	Arthur	Barkas	Moss	O'Donnell	McCormick	Withington	Roberts	Sibley	Anderson
Sep 23		2	3	6	5		8	10	9	4	7	1	11	
Oct 28	1	2	3	6		7	10	11	9	4	8			5

Division 3 (North) final table

		P	W	D	L	F	A	W	D	L	F	A	Pts
1	Lincoln City	42	14	3	4	47	18	12	5	4	34	22	60
2	Rotherham United	42	15	4	2	56	18	10	5	6	39	31	59
3	Wrexham	42	14	3	4	49	23	7	5	9	25	31	50
4	Gateshead	42	11	5	5	48	28	8	6	7	27	29	49
5	Hull City	42	12	5	4	38	21	6	6	9	21	27	47
6	Accrington Stanley	42	13	1	7	36	24	7	5	9	26	35	46
7	Barrow	42	9	4	8	24	19	7	9	5	25	21	45
8	Mansfield Town	42	11	4	6	37	24	6	7	8	20	27	45
9	Carlisle United	42	10	4	7	50	35	8	3	10	38	42	43
10	Crewe Alexandra	42	12	4	5	41	24	6	3	12	20	39	43
11	Oldham Athletic	42	6	10	5	25	25	8	3	10	38	39	41
12	ROCHDALE	42	12	4	5	32	23	3	7	11	16	49	41
13	York City	42	8	7	6	38	25	5	7	9	27	35	40
14	Bradford City	42	10	4	7	38	27	5	6	10	27	39	40
15	Southport	42	10	4	7	34	27	4	7	10	26	36	39
16	Darlington	42	7	8	6	30	31	6	5	10	24	39	39
17	Stockport County	42	9	6	6	42	28	4	6	11	21	39	38
18	Tranmere Rovers	42	10	1	10	30	28	6	3	12	24	44	36
19	Hartlepools United	42	10	6	5	34	23	4	2	15	17	50	36
20	Chester	42	11	6	4	44	25	2	3	16	20	42	35
21	Halifax Town	42	4	10	7	25	27	3	3	15	18	49	27
22	New Brighton	42	5	6	10	20	28	3	3	15	18	53	25

1948/49 7th in Division 3(N)

#	Date		Opponent	Score	Scorers	Att	Roberts WE	Watson W	Bonnell A	Heydon C	Price WB	Partridge D	Lawrence C	Eastham GR	Livesey J	Brown C	Dryburgh TJD	Birch JW	Reid DA	Arthur J	Moss J	Wood E	Bywater NL	Rothwell R	Middlebrough A	Britton J	Hood R	Hawson A	McGeachie G	Connor JT	Churchill T	Woods W	Hubbick H	Jones T	Cheetham J
1	Aug	21	Hartlepools United	1-6	Brown	10383	1	2	3	4	5	6	7	8	9	10	11																		
2		24	GATESHEAD	3-0	Wood, Livesey, Arthur	9955	1	2	3			4				11	10	5	6	7	8	9													
3		28	DARLINGTON	3-4	Brown 2, Wood	12326	1	2	3			4				11	10	5	6	7	8	9													
4		30	Gateshead	1-2	Livesey	7410		2				4				11	10	5	6	7	8	9	1	3											
5	Sep	4	Oldham Athletic	1-0	Wood	18065		2				4	7	10			11	5	6		8	9	1	3											
6		7	CARLISLE UNITED	1-0	Moss	8343		2				4	7			10	11	5	6		8	9	1	3											
7		11	New Brighton	2-1	Livesey, Moss	8385		2				4				10	11	5	6	7	8	9	1	3											
8		18	Carlisle United	1-1	Birch (p)	12539		2				4				10	11	5	6	7	8	9	1	3											
9		18	CHESTER	3-1	Arthur, Dryburgh, Moss	11965		2				4				10	11	5	6	7	8	9	1	3											
10		25	Southport	1-3	Livesey	9643		2				4				10	11	5	6	7	8	9	1	3											
11	Oct	2	CREWE ALEXANDRA	3-0	Wood, Dryburgh, Reid	10836		2				4				10	11	5	6	7	8	9	1	3											
12		9	ACCRINGTON STANLEY	4-1	Wood, Dryburgh, Moss 2	11151		2				4				10	11	5	6	7	8	9	1	3											
13		16	Rotherham United	1-3	Birch (p)	16750		2				4				10	11	5	6	7	8	9	1	3											
14		23	HULL CITY	1-1	Birch (p)	14967		2				4				10	11	5	6	7	8	9	1	3											
15		30	Doncaster Rovers	0-1		18860		2				4					11	5	6	7	8	10	1	3	9										
16	Nov	6	BRADFORD CITY	1-1	Moss	8707		2				4				10	11	5		7	8	9	1	3		6									
17		13	Halifax Town	1-2	Wood	7743			3			4					11	5		7	8	9	1	2		6	10								
18		20	WREXHAM	2-1	Moss, Middlebrough	7760			3			4					11	5		7	8	10	1	2	9	6									
19	Dec	18	HARTLEPOOLS UNITED	0-1		5803		2				6				10	11	5		7	8	9	1	3				4							
20		25	Stockport County	2-2	Moss, Dryburgh	10641			3			6					11	5		7	8	10	1	2					4	9					
21		27	STOCKPORT COUNTY	2-0	Dryburgh, Birch (p)	10510		2				6	7				11	5			8	10	1	3					4	9					
22	Jan	1	Darlington	1-6	Middlebrough	9887		2				6	7				11	5			8	10	1	3	9				4						
23		15	OLDHAM ATHLETIC	1-2	Birch (p)	8252		2				6					11	5		7	8								4	9	1	10			
24		22	NEW BRIGHTON	1-1	Connor	5867		2				6					11	5		7	8								4	9	1	10	3		
25		29	Barrow	1-0	Livesey	7321		2				4	7		8		11	5		6										9	1	10	3		
26	Feb	5	Chester	1-2	Livesey	5570		2				4	7		8		11	5		6										9	1	10	3		
27		12	Tranmere Rovers	0-0		7246		2				4			8		11	5		6									7	9	1	10	3		
28		19	SOUTHPORT	1-0	Connor	4322		2				4			8		11	5		7										9	1	10	3		
29		26	Crewe Alexandra	2-1	Connor 2	6062	1	2				4			8		11	5		7										9		10	3		
30	Mar	12	ROTHERHAM UNITED	2-0	Arthur, Connor	9840		2				4			8		11	5		7										9	1	10	3		
31		19	Hull City	1-1	Hood	36509		2				4			8		11	5		7							10			9	1		3		
32		26	DONCASTER ROVERS	0-2		8637	1	2				4			8		11	5		7										9		10	3		
33	Apr	2	Bradford City	0-1		10314		2				4	7		8	10	11	5											6	9	1		3		
34		4	MANSFIELD TOWN	1-0	Connor	3362		2						10	8		11	5		7									4	9	1	6	3		
35		9	HALIFAX TOWN	1-0	Connor	6885		2						10	8		11	5		7									4	9	1	6	3		
36		15	York City	1-1	Livesey	12438		2						10	8		11	5		7									4	9	1	6			
37		16	Wrexham	0-2		8494		2							8		11	5		7									4	9	1	6	3		
38		18	YORK CITY	2-0	Connor, Birch (p)	7758		2					7		8		11	5											4	9	1	6	3		
39		23	BARROW	3-0	Livesey, Lawrence, Connor	7757		2					7		8		11	5											4	9	1	6	3		
40		27	Accrington Stanley	0-0		5446		2					7		8		11	5											4	9	1	6	3		
41		30	Mansfield Town	0-2		9885		2					7		8		11	5											4	9	1	6	3		
42	May	7	TRANMERE ROVERS	2-1	Dryburgh, Connor	5923		2					7		8		11	5		6									4	9	1		3		
					Apps		5	40	5	1	1	33	12	2	32	9	39	41	14	28	21	34	22	20	4	2	9	1	21	22	15	10	19		
					Goals								1		8	3	6	6	1	3	8	6					2		1	10					

F.A. Cup

	Date		Opponent	Score	Scorers	Att	Watson W	Partridge D	Lawrence C	Eastham GR	Brown C	Dryburgh TJD	Birch JW	Arthur J	Moss J	Wood E	Bywater NL	Rothwell R	Middlebrough A	Britton J	Hood R
R1	Nov	27	BARROW	1-1	Middlebrough	12077		4		10		11	5	7	8		1	6	9	2	3
rep	Dec	4	Barrow	0-2		9570	2	4	7	8		11	5			10	1	6	9		3

First tie a.e.t. Played at Oldham.

Lancashire Cup

	Date		Opponent	Score	Scorers	Att	Roberts WE	Watson W	Bonnell A	Partridge D	Lawrence C	Eastham GR	Livesey J	Dryburgh TJD	Birch JW	Reid DA	Arthur J	Moss J	Wood E	Bywater NL	Rothwell R	Middlebrough A	Britton J	McGeachie G	Connor JT	Churchill T	Woods W	Hubbick H	Jones T	Cheetham J
	Oct	26	Bury	2-1	Dryburgh(2)	3300	1	2		4				11	5	6	7	8	10		3	9							6	10
	Nov	9	EVERTON	1-1	Birch(pen)	2372			3	4		8		11	5		7			1	2		9							
		16	Everton	1-0	Middlebrough	5103				4		8		11	5		7		10	1	2	9	3							
SF	May	3	Manchester C.	2-0	Lievsey, Connor	3812		2			7		8	11	5		6							4	9	1	10	3		
F		10	Blackpool	1-0	Connor	13174		2			7		8	11	5		6			1				4	9		10	3		

Final played at Oldham

League Table

		P	W	D	L	F	A	W	D	L	F	A	Pts
1	Hull City	42	17	1	3	65	14	10	10	1	28	14	65
2	Rotherham United	42	16	4	1	47	17	12	2	7	43	29	62
3	Doncaster Rovers	42	10	8	3	26	12	10	2	9	27	28	50
4	Darlington	42	10	3	8	42	36	10	3	8	41	38	46
5	Gateshead	42	10	6	5	41	28	6	7	8	28	30	45
6	Oldham Athletic	42	12	4	5	49	28	6	5	10	26	39	45
7	ROCHDALE	42	14	3	4	37	16	4	6	11	18	37	45
8	Stockport County	42	13	5	3	44	16	3	6	12	17	40	43
9	Wrexham	42	12	6	3	35	22	5	3	13	21	40	43
10	Mansfield Town	42	13	6	2	39	15	1	8	12	13	33	42
11	Tranmere Rovers	42	8	9	4	23	19	5	6	10	23	38	41
12	Crewe Alexandra	42	13	4	4	31	18	3	5	13	21	56	41
13	Barrow	42	10	8	3	27	13	4	4	13	14	35	40
14	York City	42	11	3	7	49	28	4	6	11	25	46	39
15	Carlisle United	42	12	7	2	46	32	2	4	15	14	45	39
16	Hartlepools United	42	10	5	6	34	25	4	5	12	11	33	38
17	New Brighton	42	10	4	7	25	19	4	4	13	21	39	36
18	Chester	42	10	7	4	36	19	1	6	14	21	37	35
19	Halifax Town	42	8	4	9	26	27	4	7	10	19	35	35
20	Accrington Stanley	42	11	4	6	39	23	1	6	14	16	41	34
21	Southport	42	6	5	10	24	29	5	4	12	21	35	31
22	Bradford City	42	7	6	8	29	31	3	3	15	19	46	29

1949/50 3rd in Division 3(N)

#	Date	Opponent	Score	Scorers	Att	Churchill T	Watson W	Hubbick H	McGeachie G	Birch JW	Wood E	Lawrence C	Livesey J	Connor JT	Williams WHJ	Dryburgh TJD	Woods W	Nicol B	Kapler K	Arthur J	Middlebrough A	Rothwell R	Brown C	Stanners W	Partridge D	Reid DA
1	Aug 20	GATESHEAD	1-3	Connor	6837	1	2	3	4	5	6	7	8	9	10	11										
2	25	Doncaster Rovers	0-0		21567	1	2	3	6	5	4	7	8	9		11	10									
3	27	Hartlepools United	2-1	Lawrence 2	10519	1	2	3	6	5	4	7	8	9				10	11							
4	30	DONCASTER ROVERS	0-1		11271	1	2	3	6	5	4	9	8					10	11	7						
5	Sep 3	DARLINGTON	2-0	Woods, Connor	8120	1	2	3	6	5	4	7	8	9			10		11							
6	5	CHESTER	0-1		7543	1	2	3	6	5	4	7	8	9			10		11							
7	10	New Brighton	4-0	Livesey, Williams, Dryburgh, Middlebrough	5986	1	2	3	6	5	4		10		8	11				7	9					
8	14	Chester	2-0	Dryburgh, Middlebrough	5165	1	2	3	6	5	4		10		8	11				7	9					
9	17	HALIFAX TOWN	1-0	Dryburgh	8755	1	2	3	6	5	4		10		8	11				7	9					
10	24	Oldham Athletic	0-0		23716	1	2	3	6	5	4		10		8	11				7	9					
11	Oct 1	Bradford City	1-2	Arthur	12707	1	2	3	6	5	4		10	9	8	11				7						
12	8	YORK CITY	3-1	Connor, Livesey 2	8049	1		3	6	5	4		8	9		11				7		2	10			
13	15	Tranmere Rovers	0-1		10820	1		3	6	5	4		8	9		11				7		2	10			
14	22	CREWE ALEXANDRA	2-1	Connor 2	9790	1	2	3	6	5	4		8	9		11				7			10			
15	29	Barrow	1-0	Arthur	5105	1	2	3	6	5	4		8	9		11				7			10			
16	Nov 5	LINCOLN CITY	2-0	Connor, Dryburgh	8867	1	2	3	6	5	4		8	9		11				7			10			
17	12	Rotherham United	3-4	Connor 2, Dryburgh	9113	1	2	3	6	5	4		8	9		11				7			10			
18	19	CARLISLE UNITED	1-0	Brown	7323		2	3	6	5	4		8	9		11				7			10	1		
19	Dec 3	ACCRINGTON STANLEY	2-0	Dryburgh, McGeachie	5349	1	2	3	6	5	4		8	9		11				7			10			
20	17	Gateshead	3-1	Livesey 3	3997		2	3	6	5	4		8	9		11				7			10	1		
21	24	HARTLEPOOLS UNITED	4-0	Dryburgh 2, Connor, Livesey	7439		2	3	6	5	4		8	9		11				7			10	1		
22	26	SOUTHPORT	2-0	Livesey, Connor	13406		2	3	6	5	4		8	9		11				7			10	1		
23	27	Southport	2-3	Brown, Dryburgh	14766		2	3	6	5	4		8	9		11				7			10	1		
24	31	Darlington	1-1	Livesey	8196	1	2	3	6	5	4		8	9		11				7			10			
25	Jan 14	NEW BRIGHTON	4-0	Birch (p), Livesey, McGeachie, Brown	9300	1	2	3	6	5	4		8	9		11				7			10			
26	21	Halifax Town	2-3	Connor 2	10398	1	2	3	6	5	4	7	8	9		11							10			
27	28	Mansfield Town	1-1	Nicol	11492	1	2	3	6		4		8	9		11		7					10		5	
28	Feb 4	OLDHAM ATHLETIC	1-0	Connor	14516	1	2	3	6	5	4		8	9		11		7					10		5	
29	11	Wrexham	0-3		5638	1	2	3	6	5	4		8	9		11				7			10			
30	18	BRADFORD CITY	2-2	Williams 2	8980	1	2	3		5	4			9	8	11				7			10		6	
31	25	Carlisle United	0-2		9525	1	2	3		5	4		10	7	8	11					9				6	
32	Mar 4	MANSFIELD TOWN	7-1	Livesey 3, Middlebrough 2, Dryburgh, Arthur	6336	1	2	3		5	4		8			11				7	9		10		6	
33	11	Crewe Alexandra	1-0	Brown	11781	1	2	3			4		8			11				7	9		10		5	6
34	18	BARROW	2-1	Livesey, Arthur	8391	1	2	3			4		8			11				7	9		10		5	6
35	25	Lincoln City	0-2		11009	1	2	3			4		8	9		11				7			10		5	6
36	Apr 1	ROTHERHAM UNITED	1-0	Connor	7653	1	2	3		5	4		8	9		11				7			10			6
37	7	Stockport County	1-1	Glover (og)	14751	1	2	3		5	4		8	9		11				7			10			6
38	8	York City	2-2	Livesey 2	6102	1	2	3		5	4		8	9		11				7			10			6
39	10	STOCKPORT COUNTY	1-1	Arthur	6711	1	2	3		5	4		8	9		11				7			10			6
40	15	TRANMERE ROVERS	3-0	Connor, Brown, Dryburgh	7773	1	2	3	6	5	4		8	9		11				7			10			6
41	22	Accrington Stanley	0-1		7302	1	2	3	6	5	4			9		11		8		7			10			
42	29	WREXHAM	1-1	Connor	3397	1		3		5	4		8	9		11				7		2	10			6
		Apps				37	39	42	31	37	41	7	40	34	8	38	3	5	4	33	8	3	30	5	8	9
		Goals							2	1		2	16	16	3	11	1	1		5	4		5			

One own goal

F.A. Cup

	Date	Opponent	Score	Scorers	Att	Churchill T	Watson W	Hubbick H	McGeachie G	Birch JW	Wood E	Lawrence C	Livesey J	Connor JT	Williams WHJ	Dryburgh TJD	Woods W	Nicol B	Kapler K	Arthur J	Middlebrough A	Rothwell R	Brown C	Stanners W	Partridge D	Reid DA
R1	Nov 26	Rhyl	3-0	Connor 2, Dryburgh	7852		2	3	6	5	4		8	9		11				7			10	1		
R2	Dec 10	NOTTS COUNTY	1-2	Brown	24231	1	2	3	6	5	4		8	9		11				7			10			

One own goal

Lancashire Cup

	Date	Opponent	Score	Scorers	Att	Churchill T	Watson W	Hubbick H	McGeachie G	Birch JW	Wood E	Lawrence C	Livesey J	Connor JT	Williams WHJ	Dryburgh TJD	Woods W	Nicol B	Kapler K	Arthur J	Middlebrough A	Rothwell R	Brown C	Stanners W	Partridge D	Reid DA
	Oct 25	BLACKPOOL	0-0		1413	1	2	3	6	5	4			9		11		8		7			10			
	Nov 9	Blackpool	1-0	Dryburgh	2500		2	3	6	5	4	7	8	9		11							10	1		
	Feb 8	Bolton Wanderers	1-0	Dryburgh	3339	1	2	3	6		4		8	9		11				7			10	5		
SF	Apr 18	BURNLEY	1-2	Connor	7878	1	2	3		5	4			9	8	11				7			10			6

		P	W	D	L	F	A	W	D	L	F	A	Pts
1	Doncaster Rovers	42	9	9	3	30	15	10	8	3	36	23	55
2	Gateshead	42	13	5	3	51	23	10	2	9	36	31	53
3	ROCHDALE	42	15	3	3	42	13	6	6	9	26	28	51
4	Lincoln City	42	14	5	2	35	9	7	4	10	25	30	51
5	Tranmere Rovers	42	15	3	3	35	21	4	8	9	16	27	49
6	Rotherham United	42	10	6	5	46	28	9	4	8	34	31	48
7	Crewe Alexandra	42	10	6	5	38	27	7	8	6	30	28	48
8	Mansfield Town	42	12	4	5	37	20	6	8	7	29	34	48
9	Carlisle United	42	12	6	3	39	20	4	9	8	29	31	47
10	Stockport County	42	14	2	5	33	21	5	5	11	22	31	45
11	Oldham Athletic	42	10	4	7	32	31	6	7	8	26	32	43
12	Chester	42	12	3	6	47	33	5	3	13	23	46	40
13	Accrington Stanley	42	12	5	4	41	21	4	2	15	16	41	39
14	New Brighton	42	10	5	6	27	25	4	5	12	18	38	38
15	Barrow	42	9	6	6	27	20	5	3	13	20	33	37
16	Southport	42	7	10	4	29	26	5	3	13	22	45	37
17	Darlington	42	9	8	4	35	27	2	5	14	21	42	35
18	Hartlepools United	42	10	3	8	37	35	4	2	15	15	44	33
19	Bradford City	42	11	1	9	38	32	1	7	13	23	44	32
20	Wrexham	42	8	7	6	24	17	2	5	14	15	37	32
21	Halifax Town	42	9	5	7	35	31	3	3	15	23	54	32
22	York City	42	6	7	8	29	33	3	6	12	23	37	31

1950/51 11th in Division 3(N)

					Churchill T	Watson W	Hubbick H	McGeachie G	Birch JW	Reid DA	Arthur J	Livesey J	Connor JT	Brown C	Steen AW	Lomas A	Whitehouse JE	Medd GE	Hughes WA	Wood E	Partridge D	Foulds A	Smyth HR	Middlebrough A	Boyle H	Rothwell R	Heaton WH	Crowther K	McNichol A	Buchan AR	Downer ER	Barber E	Mills H
1	Aug	19	Darlington	2-0 Arthur, Connor	10530	1	2	3	4	5	6	7	8	9	10	11																		
2		21	Bradford Park Avenue	1-0 Arthur	19058	1	2	3	4	5	6	7	8	9	10	11																		
3		26	STOCKPORT COUNTY	1-1 Livesey	13075	1	2	3	4	5	6	7	8	9	10	11																		
4		29	BRADFORD PARK AVE.	1-2 Livesey	10743		2	3	4	5	6	7	8	9	10	11	1																		
5	Sep	2	Halifax Town	1-1 Connor	10219		2	3	4	5	6	7	10	9				1	8	11															
6		5	SHREWSBURY TOWN	5-0 Medd, Connor 3, Livesey	8863		2	3	4	5	6	7	10	9				1	8	11															
7		9	HARTLEPOOLS UNITED	3-1 Connor 2, Whitehouse	9146		2	3	4	5	6	7	10	9				1	8	11															
8		11	Shrewsbury Town	2-0 Connor 2	8017		2	3	4	5	6	7	10	9	11				8		1															
9		16	Gateshead	1-4 Whitehouse	13607		2	3	4	5	6	7	10	9			11		8		1															
10		23	CREWE ALEXANDRA	1-1 McGeachie	8576		2	3	6	5		7	10	9			11		8		1	4														
11		30	New Brighton	5-1 Steen, Livesey, McGeachie 2(2p), Brown	4852		2	3	6	5		7	8	9	10	11			8		1	4														
12	Oct	7	YORK CITY	0-1	8123		2	3	6			7	8	9			11			1	4	5	10												
13		14	Barrow	3-4 Whitehouse, Middlebrough, Brown	5645		2	3	5			7	11		10				8		1	4			6	9										
14		21	ACCRINGTON STANLEY	3-1 Connor, Birch (p), Smyth	8027		2	3	4	5		7	11	9	10				8		1				6												
15		28	Carlisle United	0-4	13295		2		4	5		7	11	9	10				8		1				6		3									
16	Nov	4	TRANMERE ROVERS	2-3 Arthur, Livesey	7886		2	3	6	5		7	11	9	10				8		1	4															
17		11	Southport	1-1 Brown	6374			3	6	5		7			10			1	8			4				9			2	11						
18		18	ROTHERHAM UNITED	0-2	7986			3	6	5		7	8		10			1	9			4							2	11						
19	Dec	2	SCUNTHORPE UNITED	2-0 Middlebrough 2	5213			4	5			7	8		6	11	1	10				2			9	3										
20		23	Stockport County	2-2 Whitehouse, Middlebrough	10152		2		4	5		7			6	11	1	8							9	3			10							
21		25	Lincoln City	2-4 Arthur, Middlebrough	9873			4	5			7			6	11	1	8	10			2			9	3										
22	Jan	13	Hartlepools United	0-0	7585	1	2		5			7	8	9	6	11				4						3			10							
23		16	CHESTER	2-3 Steen, Whitehouse	1435	1	2		5			7	10	9	6	11		8								3				4							
24		20	GATESHEAD	2-0 Livesey (p), Middlebrough	5612	1	2		5				8		6	11		7				4				9	3				10						
25		27	Chester	3-1 Livesey 2, Whitehouse	4534	1	2		5				8	9	6	11		7									3				10						
26	Feb	3	Crewe Alexandra	1-3 Livesey (p)	6941	1	2		4	5			8	9	6	11		7									3				10						
27		10	OLDHAM ATHLETIC	0-1	14238	1	2		5				8		6	11		7								9	3				4	10					
28		17	NEW BRIGHTON	1-0 Middlebrough	3689	1	2	3	4	5		7	8			11										9						10	6				
29		24	York City	2-2 Livesey (p), Steen	7664	1	2	3	4	5		7	8			11										9						10	6				
30	Mar	3	BARROW	1-0 Middlebrough	5509	1	2	3	4	5		7	8			11										9						10	6				
31		10	Accrington Stanley	2-1 Whitehouse, Connor	4281	1	2		4	5		7		9		11		8									3						10	6				
32		17	CARLISLE UNITED	4-1 Steen, Connor 2, McNichol	6190	1	2		4	5		7		9		11		8									3						10	6				
33		24	Tranmere Rovers	1-2 McNichol	8328	1	2		4	5		7		9		11		8									3						10	6				
34		26	BRADFORD CITY	4-0 Connor 2, McNichol, Steen	4233	1	2		4	5		7		9		11		8									3						10	6				
35		27	Bradford City	1-2 Connor	16164	1	2		4				8	9		11							7				3						10	6	5		
36		31	SOUTHPORT	1-1 Whitehouse	3781	1	2		4	5		7		9		11		8									3						10	6			
37	Apr	7	Rotherham United	0-3	14202	1	2		4	5			11	9		7		8									3						10	6			
38		10	HALIFAX TOWN	0-0	3342	1	2	3	4	5			11			7		8								9						10	6			
39		14	MANSFIELD TOWN	0-0	4000	1	2	3	4	5		7	8			11		10								9							6			
40		16	Mansfield Town	0-1	11384	1	2	3	4	5		7	8		10	11						9											6			
41		17	LINCOLN CITY	3-0 Foulds, McGeachie, Livesey	3533	1	2	3	4	5		7	10			11		8				9											6			
42		21	Scunthorpe United	0-3	9229	1	2	3		5		7	10			11						8											6	4	9	
43		24	Oldham Athletic	0-2	13503	1	2	3		5			8			11					4					9						10	6	4	7	
44		28	WREXHAM	2-0 Barber, Middlebrough	3288	1	2	3		5			11					8								9						10	6	4	7	
45	May	2	Wrexham	1-3 Whitehouse	3633	1	2	3		5			11					8						10		9							6	4	7	
46		5	DARLINGTON	0-0	3448	1	2	3	4	5			10																11				6		7	9
				Apps		28	42	29	38	43	9	35	38	26	22	32	9	32	5	9	8	5	6	3	15	17	2	5	2	17	19	4	5	1
				Goals					4	1		4	11	16	3	5		9	1				1	1	9					3			1	

F.A. Cup

						Churchill T	Watson W	Hubbick H	McGeachie G	Birch JW	Reid DA	Arthur J	Livesey J	Connor JT	Brown C	Steen AW	Lomas A	Whitehouse JE	Medd GE	Hughes WA	Wood E	Partridge D	Foulds A	Smyth HR	Middlebrough A	Boyle H	Rothwell R	Heaton WH	Crowther K	McNichol A
R1	Nov	25	WILLINGTON	3-1 Whitehouse 2 (1p), Middlebrough	7657				4	5		7	8		6	11	1	10				2			9	3				
R2	Dec	9	Ashington	2-1 Livesey, Steen	13191		2		4	5		7	8		6	11	1								9	3			10	
R3	Jan	9	CHELSEA	2-3 Connor, Arthur	17817		2		6	5		7	10	9		11	1	8			4					3				

Lancashire Cup

						Hubbick H	McGeachie G	Arthur J	Livesey J	Whitehouse JE	Medd GE	Wood E	Partridge D	Foulds A	Smyth HR	Rothwell R
	Oct	11	Accrington Stanley	1-2 Middlesbrough	2000	3	4	7	11	8	1	5	10	6	9	2

		P	W	D	L	F	A	W	D	L	F	A	Pts
1	Rotherham United	46	16	3	4	55	16	15	6	2	48	25	71
2	Mansfield Town	46	17	6	0	54	19	9	6	8	24	29	64
3	Carlisle United	46	18	4	1	44	17	7	8	8	35	33	62
4	Tranmere Rovers	46	15	5	3	51	26	9	6	8	32	36	59
5	Lincoln City	46	18	1	4	62	23	7	7	9	27	35	58
6	Bradford Park Ave	46	15	3	5	46	23	8	5	10	44	49	54
7	Bradford City	46	13	4	6	55	30	8	6	9	35	33	52
8	Gateshead	46	17	1	5	60	21	4	7	12	24	41	50
9	Crewe Alexandra	46	11	5	7	38	26	8	5	10	23	34	48
10	Stockport County	46	15	3	5	45	26	5	5	13	18	37	48
11	ROCHDALE	46	11	6	6	38	18	6	5	12	31	44	45
12	Scunthorpe United	46	10	12	1	32	9	3	6	14	26	48	44
13	Chester	46	11	6	6	42	30	6	3	14	20	34	43
14	Wrexham	46	12	6	5	37	28	3	6	14	18	43	42
15	Oldham Athletic	46	10	5	8	47	36	6	3	14	26	37	40
16	Hartlepools United	46	14	5	4	55	26	2	2	19	9	40	39
17	York City	46	7	12	4	37	24	5	3	15	29	53	39
18	Darlington	46	10	8	5	35	29	3	5	15	24	48	39
19	Barrow	46	12	3	8	38	27	4	3	16	13	49	38
20	Shrewsbury Town	46	11	3	9	28	30	4	4	15	15	44	37
21	Southport	46	9	4	10	29	25	4	13	27	47		36
22	Halifax Town	46	11	6	6	36	24	0	6	17	14	45	34
23	Accrington Stanley	46	10	4	9	28	29	1	6	16	14	72	32
24	New Brighton	46	7	6	10	22	32	4	2	17	18	58	30

224

1949-50 Season
Back: Watson, Wood, Birch, Stanners, Hubbick, McGeachie
Front: Arthur, Livesey, Connor, Brown, Dryburgh

1951-52 Season
Back: Watson, Lynn, Nicholls, Downes, Buchan, Radford
Front: Arthur, Tomlinson, Middleborough, Foulds, Betts

No	Date	Opponent	Score	Scorers	Att	Churchill T	Watson W	Fisher FT	Whitworth H	Birch JW	Buchan AR	Barber E	Whitehouse JE	Jennings HW	Lynn J	Steen AW	Radford A	Hazzleton J	Drury J	Hayton E	Arthur J	Middlebrough A	Nicholls JH	Downes ER	Rothwell R	Gilfillan R	Coupe JN	Betts E	Keeley W	Foulds A	Tomlinson F	Ball JA	Case N	Hindle T	Partridge D
1	Aug 18	CARLISLE UNITED	0-4		6026	1	2	3	4	5	6	7	8	9	10	11																			
2	22	Darlington	1-2	Jennings	5962	1	2		4	5	6	7	8	9			11	3	10																
3	25	Stockport County	0-1		9544	1	2		4	5	6	7	8	9	10			3					11												
4	28	DARLINGTON	6-2	*See below	4727	1	2			5	6		8				11	3	10	4	7	9													
5	Sep 1	WORKINGTON	2-0	Middlebrough, Whitehouse	5701	1	2			5	6		8				11	3	10	4	7	9													
6	4	MANSFIELD TOWN	1-0	Arthur (p)	6046		2			5	6		8				11	3	10	4	7	9	1												
7	8	Barrow	0-4		7326	1	2			5	6	11	8					3	10		7	9				4									
8	15	GRIMSBY TOWN	0-0		6181		2				6		8				11			4	7	9	1	5	3										
9	17	Mansfield Town	1-1	Whitehouse	10413		2		4		6		8				11			10	7		1	5	3	9									
10	22	Wrexham	0-2		7359		2		4		6		8	9			11			10	7		1	5	3										
11	29	CHESTERFIELD	2-0	Whitehouse, Barber	6496	1	2		10	5	6	9	8				11			4	7				3											
12	Oct 6	HARTLEPOOLS UNITED	3-0	Whitworth, Hazzleton, Steen	5574	1	2		7	5	6	9	8			11		10		4							3									
13	13	Bradford City	0-3		13505		2		9	5	6		8			7		10		4			1				3	11								
14	20	York City	0-2		4994	1	2		9	5	6		8			7				4			1				3	11			10					
15	27	Chester	0-4		4628		2		8	5	6										7	9	1		4		3	11			10					
16	Nov 3	LINCOLN CITY	0-1		2457	1	2		7		6	9				4							5				3	11			10	8				
17	10	Scunthorpe United	1-3	Betts	8374				9		6	7				4	8	3										11	10							
18	17	TRANMERE ROVERS	3-2	Tomlinson, Middlebrough 2	4158		2				6					4		3	10		7	9	1	5				11			8					
19	Dec 1	CREWE ALEXANDRA	1-0	Foulds	4278		2		4		6						3				7	9	1	5				11		10	8					
20	8	Gateshead	0-1		6055		2		4						6		3				7	9	1	5				11		10	8					
21	22	STOCKPORT COUNTY	0-0		5857		2				6				4		3				7	9	1	5				11		10	8					
22	25	Oldham Athletic	1-1	Betts	23001		2		9		6				4		3				7		1	5				11		10	8					
23	26	OLDHAM ATHLETIC	2-2	Tomlinson, Foulds	12430		2		9		6				4		3				7		1	5				11		10	8					
24	29	Workington	1-1	Middlebrough	6244		2				6				4		3				7	9	1	5				11		10	8					
25	Jan 5	BARROW	4-1	Foulds 2, Middlebrough 2	5451				2		6				4		3				7	9	1	5				11		10	8					
26	15	ACCRINGTON STANLEY	3-1	Betts, Middlebrough, Foulds	1792				2		6				4		3				7	9	1	5				11		10	8					
27	19	Grimsby Town	0-4		12780		2				6				4		3				7	9	1	5				11		10	8					
28	26	WREXHAM	1-5	Buchan	4244		2		7		6				4		3					9	1	5				11		10	8					
29	Feb 9	Chesterfield	1-5	Ball	9055	1	2		9	5	6	7			4												3	11			8	10				
30	16	Hartlepools United	1-1	Betts	8403		2				4				6						7		1	5				3	11		8	10	9			
31	23	HALIFAX TOWN	0-2		5703		2		10		4				6						7		1	5				3	11		8		9			
32	Mar 1	BRADFORD CITY	1-1	Foulds	4274		2			5					4						7	9	1		3	6		11			10	8				
33	6	Carlisle United	1-1	Hindle	3978				2	5	6				4								1		3	7				8	9	10		11	
34	8	York City	1-1	Foulds	8136				2	5	6	9			4								1		3				8	7	10		11	
35	15	CHESTER	0-5		4561				2	5	6				4								1		3	7				9	8	10		11	
36	22	Lincoln City	0-2		13646	1	3		2			9			6						10			5				11			8			7		4
37	29	SCUNTHORPE UNITED	1-2	Whitworth	1226		3		2						6						10	7	9	1	5				8					11		4
38	Apr 2	Accrington Stanley	0-0		4081		2		7		6				10		3	9					1	5				11			8					4
39	5	Tranmere Rovers	3-4	Gilfillan, Drury, Lynn (p)	3400		2		7		6				8		3	9	11				1	5		10										4
40	12	SOUTHPORT	1-0	Foulds	3916	1	2		7	5					8		3		11					6		10				9						4
41	14	BRADFORD PARK AVE.	1-1	Partridge	5540	1	2			5		7			8		3		11					6		10				9						4
42	15	Bradford Park Avenue	1-1	Arthur (p)	10235	1				5							3				7	9		6	2	10		11		8					4
43	19	Crewe Alexandra	0-1		4055	1				5							3				7	9		6	2	10				8				11	4
44	22	Southport	2-1	Foulds 2	2872	1				5	6				8		3								2	10		11		9	7				4
45	26	GATESHEAD	0-3		3174	1			7	5	6				8		3							9	2	10		11							4
46	28	Halifax Town	0-1		5635	1			2		6				9		3									5		10		11	8	7			4
		Apps				19	35	1	31	23	38	12	14	3	31	13	27	11	4	12	25	20	27	29	13	12	8	26	4	23	20	5	2	6	11
		Goals					2			1	1	4	1	1	3		1	1			2	10				1		4		10	2	1		1	1	1

Scorers in game 4: Middlebrough 3, Whitehouse, Steen 2

F.A. Cup

No	Date	Opponent	Score	Scorers	Att	Churchill T	Watson W	Fisher FT	Whitworth H	Birch JW	Buchan AR	Barber E	Whitehouse JE	Jennings HW	Lynn J	Steen AW	Radford A	Hazzleton J	Drury J	Hayton E	Arthur J	Middlebrough A	Nicholls JH	Downes ER	Rothwell R	Gilfillan R	Coupe JN	Betts E	Keeley W	Foulds A	Tomlinson F
R1	Nov 24	Ilkeston Town	2-0	Betts 2 (1p)	9000		2				6					4	3				7	9	1	5				11		10	8
R2	Dec 15	Gillingham	3-0	Tomlinson 2, Arthur	15686		2				6					4	3				7	9	1	5				11		10	8
R3	Jan 12	LEEDS UNITED	0-2		21526				2		6					4	3				7	9	1	5				11		10	8

Lancashire Cup

Date	Opponent	Score	Scorers	Att	Fisher FT	Whitworth H	Birch JW	Buchan AR	Whitehouse JE	Radford A	Hazzleton J	Drury J	Hayton E	Arthur J	Nicholls JH
Oct 11	Preston N.E.	0-1	Betts 2 (1p)		2 9	5	6		8	11	3	10	4	7	1

1952/53 22nd in Division 3(N)

#		Date	Opponent	Score	Scorers	Att	Churchill T	Potter H	Boyle H	Warner J	Birch JW	Buchan AR	Arthur J	Lister AO	Foulds A	Gilfillan R	Betts E	Whitworth H	Lynn J	Nicholls JH	Murray L	Sutton B	Hogan C	Downes ER	Haddington RW	Watson W	Radcliffe M	Morris W	Marriott S	Partridge D	Graham JR	Boxshall D
1	Aug	23	CREWE ALEXANDRA	0-1		7000	1	2	3	4	5	6	7	8	9	10	11															
2		25	Bradford Park Avenue	1-2	Whitworth	12060	1	2	3	4	5	6			9	10	11	7	8													
3		30	Port Vale	2-5	Foulds, Gilfillan	15448	1	2	3	4	5	6			9	10	11	7	8													
4	Sep	2	BRADFORD PARK AVE.	1-0	Foulds	6647		2	3	4	5	6			9	10	11	7	8	1												
5		6	CHESTER	3-1	Betts, Gilfillan, Lynn	6557		2	3	4	5	6			9	10	11	7	8	1												
6		9	Southport	0-1		5175		2	3	4	5	6			9	10	11	7	8	1												
7		13	Scunthorpe United	1-5	Foulds	7381	1	2	3		5	6			9	10	11	7	4		8											
8		16	SOUTHPORT	0-0		5330		2	3		5	6			9	10	11	7	4		8	1										
9		20	STOCKPORT COUNTY	2-2	Lynn, Gilfillan	8623		2	3		5	6			9	10		7	4		8	1	11									
10		23	WORKINGTON	2-0	Murray, Betts	5075		2	3		5	6			9	10	11	7	4		8	1										
11		27	Bradford City	3-0	Foulds 3	10898		2	3		5	6			9	10	11	7	4		8	1										
12		30	GATESHEAD	2-3	Gilfillan 2	4848		2	3		5	6			9	10	11	7	4		8	1										
13	Oct	4	Oldham Athletic	0-1		23026		2	3		5	6			9	10	11	7	4	1	8										
14		11	WREXHAM	4-1	Arthur 2 (1p), Whitworth, Murray	8016		2	3		5	6	11		9	10		7	4	1	8										
15		18	Barrow	1-2	Gilfillan	5789		2	3		5	6	11		9	10		7	4	1	8										
16		25	GRIMSBY TOWN	0-2		12291		2	3		5	6	11		9	10		7	4	1	8										
17	Nov	1	York City	0-2		9430		2			5	6			9		11		4		8	1	7		10	3						
18		8	TRANMERE ROVERS	3-0	Gilfillan, Foulds, Betts	6101		2	3		5	6			9	8	11	7	4	1					10							
19		15	Chesterfield	0-1		6752			3		5	6			9	8	11	7	4	1					10	2						
20		29	Accrington Stanley	1-2	Gilfillan	4060		2	3		5	6			9	7	11		4						10		1	8				
21	Dec	6	Chester	0-3		3324		2	3		5	6				8	11	7	4	1					10				9			
22		13	Mansfield Town	1-2	Marriott	6211	1	2	3		5	6				8	11	7	4						10				9			
23		20	Crewe Alexandra	2-4	Haddington, Whitworth	4454	1	2	3			6				8	11	7	4						10				9		5	
24		26	Darlington	2-3	Lynn (p), Marriott	6406	1	2	3		5	6				8	11	7	4						10				9			
25		27	DARLINGTON	3-1	Haddington 3	6461		2	3		5	6			9	8	11	7	4	1					10							
26	Jan	1	Gateshead	1-3	Foulds	3729			3		5	6			9	8	11	7	4	1					10	2						
27		3	PORT VALE	1-1	Lynn (p)	6899			3		5	6			9	8	11	7	4	1					10	2						
28		10	Carlisle United	0-5		7282			3			6				8	11	7	4	1					10	2				9	5	
29		24	SCUNTHORPE UNITED	2-2	Betts, Lynn (p)	5050			3		5	6				8	11	7	4	1					10	2				9		
30		31	CARLISLE UNITED	1-2	Haddington	3447	1		3			6			9	8	11	7	4						10	2					5	
31	Feb	7	Stockport County	0-2		5689	1		3		5	6			9	8	11	7	4						10	2						
32		21	OLDHAM ATHLETIC	3-1	Buchan, Whitworth, Foulds	15502			3			6	7		10	8		9	4	1						2				11	5	
33		28	Wrexham	0-3		7879			3			6	7		10	8		9	4	1						2				11	5	
34	Mar	7	BARROW	6-2	Whitworth 3, Foulds, Morris, Graham	5239			3			6			10	8		9	4	1						2		7	11		5	
35		14	Grimsby Town	2-3	Foulds 2	10578	1		3			6			10	8		9	4							2		7	11		5	
36		21	YORK CITY	0-3		6373	1		3			6			10	8		9	4							2		7	11		5	
37		24	BRADFORD CITY	2-1	Foulds, Haddington	2140			3			6	7		10			9	4	1					8	2			11		5	
38		28	Tranmere Rovers	0-1		4276			3			6	7		10			9	4	1					8	2			11		5	
39	Apr	3	Hartlepools United	1-2	Boxshall	8777			3			6	7			10	11		4	1					8	2					5	9
40		4	CHESTERFIELD	0-2		4803		2	3		5	6	7			10	11		4	1					8							9
41		6	HARTLEPOOLS UNITED	3-1	Murray 2, Arthur (p), Boxshall	3378		2	3			6	7			10			4	1	11				8						5	9
42		11	Workington	2-1	Haddington, Arthur (p)	3193		2	3			6	7			10			4	1	11				8						5	9
43		14	HALIFAX TOWN	1-1	Gilfillan	3429		2	3			6	7			10			4	1	11				8						5	9
44		18	ACCRINGTON STANLEY	1-0	Haddington	4706		2	3			6	7			10			4	1					8					11	5	9
45		25	Halifax Town	1-3	Boxshall	4826		2	3			6	7			10			4	1					8					11	5	9
46		29	MANSFIELD TOWN	1-0	Gilfillan	4282		2	3			6	7			10			4	1					8					11	5	9
				Apps			11	31	45	21	23	40	15	2	32	41	26	39	40	23	16	11	3	4	25	22	1	4	6	7	10	8
				Goals								1	4		13	10	4	7	5		3				8			1	2		1	3

F.A. Cup

	Date	Opponent	Score	Scorers	Att			Boyle H		Birch JW	Buchan AR			Foulds A	Gilfillan R	Betts E	Whitworth H	Lynn J	Nicholls JH					Haddington RW							
R1	Nov 22	Bradford Park Avenue	1-2	Lynn (p)	13525		2	3		5	6			9	8	11	7	4	1					10							

Lancashire Cup

	Date	Opponent	Score	Att		Potter H	Boyle H			Buchan AR			Foulds A	Gilfillan R	Betts E	Whitworth H	Lynn J	Nicholls JH		Sutton B		Downes ER	Haddington RW							
	Oct 14	BLACKPOOL	0-1	2205		2	3			6			9	10	11	7	4			1		5	8							

		P	W	D	L	F	A	W	D	L	F	A	Pts
1	Oldham Athletic	46	15	4	4	48	21	7	11	5	29	24	59
2	Port Vale	46	13	9	1	41	10	7	9	7	26	25	58
3	Wrexham	46	18	3	2	59	24	6	5	12	27	42	56
4	York City	46	14	5	4	35	16	6	8	9	25	29	53
5	Grimsby Town	46	15	5	3	47	19	6	5	12	28	40	52
6	Southport	46	16	4	3	42	18	4	7	12	21	42	51
7	Bradford Park Ave.	46	10	8	5	37	23	9	4	10	38	38	50
8	Gateshead	46	13	6	4	51	24	4	9	10	25	36	49
9	Carlisle United	46	13	7	3	57	24	5	6	12	25	44	49
10	Crewe Alexandra	46	13	5	5	46	28	7	3	13	24	40	48
11	Stockport County	46	13	8	2	61	26	4	5	14	21	43	47
12	Tranmere Rovers	46	16	4	3	45	16	5	1	17	20	47	47
13	Chesterfield	46	13	6	4	40	23	5	5	13	25	40	47
14	Halifax Town	46	13	5	5	47	31	3	10	10	21	37	47
15	Scunthorpe United	46	10	6	7	38	21	6	8	9	24	35	46
16	Bradford City	46	14	7	2	54	29	0	11	12	21	51	46
17	Hartlepools United	46	14	6	3	39	16	2	8	13	18	45	46
18	Mansfield Town	46	11	9	3	34	25	5	5	13	21	37	46
19	Barrow	46	15	6	2	48	20	1	6	16	18	51	44
20	Chester	46	10	7	6	39	27	1	8	14	25	58	37
21	Darlington	46	13	4	6	33	27	1	2	20	25	69	34
22	ROCHDALE	46	12	5	6	41	27	2	0	21	21	56	32
23	Workington	46	9	5	9	40	33	2	5	16	15	58	32
24	Accrington Stanley	46	7	9	7	25	29	1	2	20	14	60	27

1952-53 Season
Back: Humpish (Trainer), Watson, Birch, Sutton, Buchan, Boyle
Front: Whitworth, Gilfillan, Haddington, Lynn, Foulds, Betts

1953-54 Season
Back: Pridav, Lynn, Downes, Morton, Potter, Boyle
Front: Arthur, Morgan, Anders, Haddington, Rose

1953/54 — 19th in Division 3(N)

No	Date	Opponent	Score	Scorers	Att	Cordell IG	Potter H	Boyle H	Lynn J	Downes ER	Buchan AR	Rose K	Gilfillan R	Evans FJ	Black N	Anders J	Morton A	Haddington RW	Wasilewski A	Priday RH	Morgan WA	Arthur J	Partridge D	Boxshall D	Kendall A	Mottershead BL	Watson W	Haines JTW	Lord F	Tolson W	Frost D	Lyons E	Lyons GW	Glover BA	Calderbank
1	Aug 22	Carlisle United	0-7		8378	1	2	3	4	5	6	7	8	9	10	11																			
2	25	TRANMERE ROVERS	0-1		5689		2	3	4	5	6	7	8	9		11	1	10																	
3	29	ACCRINGTON STANLEY	1-0	Haddington	8375		2	3	4	5	6	7	8			11	1	10	9																
4	Sep 1	Tranmere Rovers	1-5	Priday	6100		2	3	4	5	6	7		8		11	1	10		9															
5	5	Grimsby Town	2-3	Haddington, Anders	12305		2	3	4	5				9		8	1	10			11	6	7												
6	8	HALIFAX TOWN	0-1		6105		2	3	4	5				9		8	1	10			11	6	7												
7	12	STOCKPORT COUNTY	0-0		7634		2	3	6	5				9	8	11	1	10					7		4										
8	14	Halifax Town	1-1	Haddington	6186		2	3	6	5				9	8		1	10			11		7		4										
9	19	Southport	1-1	Wasilewski	5748		2	3	4	5				8			1	10	9		11		7		6										
10	22	CHESTERFIELD	0-1		3070		2	3	6	5				8		11	1	10	9				4		7										
11	26	Wrexham	0-2		12602		2	3	6	5						11	1	10	9				4		7	8									
12	28	Chesterfield	1-2	Kendall	8308		2	3	6					9	10	11	1	8					4		7		5								
13	Oct 3	MANSFIELD TOWN	1-0	Haddington	7483		2	3	6					9		11	1	8					4		7		5		10						
14	10	SCUNTHORPE UNITED	1-1	Haines	7873		2	3	6					9		11	1	8					4		7		5		10						
15	17	Workington	1-0	Kendall	7070		2	3	6						10	11	1						4	9	7		5	8							
16	24	GATESHEAD	0-1		6308		2	3	6	5					10	11	1						4	9	7			8							
17	31	Hartlepools United	0-6		6763		2	3	6	5					10	11	1						4		7			8	9						
18	Nov 7	DARLINGTON	3-0	Haines 2, Frost	2601		2	3	6	5						11	1						4		7			8		10	9				
19	14	Barnsley	1-2	Frost	8146		2	3	6	5	4					11	1								7			8		10	9				
20	28	Port Vale	0-6		16841			3	6	5	4				10	2	11	1							7			8			9				
21	Dec 5	CREWE ALEXANDRA	4-1	Haines 3, Frost	4451			3	6					2	10	11	1						4		7		5	8			9				
22	12	Chester	0-2		3578			3	6					2	10	11	1						4		7		5	8			9				
23	19	CARLISLE UNITED	2-1	Kendall, Haines	4654		2	3	6						10	11	1						4		7		5	8			9				
24	25	BRADFORD CITY	3-2	Black 2, Anders	5693			3	6					2	10	11	1						4		7		5	8			9				
25	26	Bradford City	0-4		10366				5	6			8	2	10	11	1						4							9	3	7			
26	CHESTER		4-0	Lord 2, Anders, Kendall	7226		3		6					2	10	11	1						4		7		5	8	9						
27	Jan 9	YORK CITY	1-2	Haines	5575		3		6					2	10	11	1						4		7		5	8	9						
28	16	GRIMSBY TOWN	4-1	Lord 2, Haines, Lynn	4936				6					2	10	11	1						4		7		5	8	9			3			
29	23	Stockport County	2-1	Kendall, Anders	6651				6					2	10	11	1						4		7		5	8	9			3			
30	30	York City	2-1	Kendall, Lynn (p)	5650			2	6						10	11	1						4		7		5	8	9			3			
31	Feb 6	SOUTHPORT	2-0	Black, Kendall	6549			2	6						10	11	1						4		7		5	8	9			3			
32	13	WREXHAM	6-2	Lord 3, Kendall 2, Haines	5078			2	6						10	11	1						4		7		5	8	9			3			
33	20	Mansfield Town	0-2		8234			2	6						10	11	1						4	5	7			8			9	3			
34	27	Scunthorpe United	1-1	Arthur	7260			2	6					10		11	1						4	7	5				9	8		3			
35	Mar 6	WORKINGTON	4-2	E Lyons, G Lyons, Lynn, Anders	4683			2	6							11	1						4				5	8	9	10		3	7		
36	13	Gateshead	1-2	Lord	4847				6							11	1						4	5		7	2	8	9	10		3			
37	20	HARTLEPOOLS UNITED	2-2	Black, Haines	6583			2	6						10	11	1						4		7			8	9			3		5	
38	27	Darlington	0-0		3978	1		3	6						10	11						4	2		7			8	9					5	
39	Apr 3	BARNSLEY	1-1	Lord	5785	1		3	6						10	11						4			7	2		8	9					5	
40	7	Accrington Stanley	0-1		5124	1		3	6						10	11						4			7	2		8	9					5	
41	10	Bradford Park Avenue	2-2	Black, Anders	7099	1		3	6						10	11						4			7	2		8	9					5	
42	16	BARROW	1-0	Kendall	5865	1		3	6						10	11						4			7	2		8	9					5	
43	17	PORT VALE	0-0		14749	1		3	6						10	11						4			7	2		8	9					5	
44	19	Barrow	2-4	Partridge, Lord	4306	1		2	6						10	11						4						9	8			3	7	5	
45	24	Crewe Alexandra	1-2	Anders	2965		2	3	6							11	1						4		7			8	9	10		3		5	
46	27	BRADFORD PARK AVE.	0-1		3818		2	3	6							11	1						4		7			8	9					5	10
			Apps			8	21	42	43	17	10	11	9	12	26	44	38	13	4	5	26	6	18	3	32	1	22	31	21	7	9	13	3	10	1
			Goals						4						5	7		4	1	1		1	1		10			11	10		2	1	1		

F.A. Cup

Rd	Date	Opponent	Score	Att																														
R1	Nov 21	Grimsby Town	0-2	8536		2	3	6	5						11	1						4		7			8		10	9				

Lancashire Cup

Date	Opponent	Score	Att																												
Oct 20	SOUTHPORT	0-2	862	1	2	3		5	6		4	7	10	11					9							8							

		P	W	D	L	F	A	W	D	L	F	A	Pts
1	Port Vale	46	16	7	0	48	5	10	10	3	26	16	69
2	Barnsley	46	16	3	4	54	24	8	7	8	23	33	58
3	Scunthorpe United	46	14	7	2	49	24	7	8	8	28	32	57
4	Gateshead	46	15	4	4	49	22	6	9	8	25	33	55
5	Bradford City	46	15	6	2	40	14	7	3	13	20	41	53
6	Chesterfield	46	13	6	4	41	19	6	8	9	35	45	52
7	Mansfield Town	46	15	5	3	59	22	5	6	12	29	45	51
8	Wrexham	46	16	4	3	59	19	5	5	13	22	49	51
9	Bradford Park Ave.	46	13	6	4	57	31	5	8	10	20	37	50
10	Stockport County	46	14	6	3	57	20	4	5	14	20	47	47
11	Southport	46	12	5	6	41	26	5	7	11	22	34	46
12	Barrow	46	12	7	4	46	26	4	5	14	26	45	44
13	Carlisle United	46	10	8	5	53	27	4	7	12	30	44	43
14	Tranmere Rovers	46	11	4	8	40	34	7	3	13	19	36	43
15	Accrington Stanley	46	12	7	4	41	22	4	3	16	25	52	42
16	Crewe Alexandra	46	9	8	6	30	26	5	5	13	19	41	41
17	Grimsby Town	46	14	5	4	31	15	2	4	17	20	62	41
18	Hartlepools United	46	10	8	5	40	21	3	6	14	19	44	40
19	ROCHDALE	46	12	5	6	40	20	3	5	15	19	57	40
20	Workington	46	10	9	4	36	22	3	5	15	23	58	40
21	Darlington	46	11	3	9	31	27	1	11	11	19	44	38
22	York City	46	8	7	8	39	32	4	6	13	25	54	37
23	Halifax Town	46	9	6	8	26	21	3	4	16	18	52	34
24	Chester	46	10	7	6	39	22	1	3	19	9	45	32

1954/55 12th in Division 3(N)

No	Date	Opponent	Score	Scorers	Att	Morton A	McCulloch WD	Lyons E	Morgan WA	Glover BA	Lynn J	Kendall A	Haines JTW	Lord F	Mitcheson FJ	Anders J	Underwood G	Boyle H	Murphy D	Frost D	Black N	Tolson W	Green BG	Gemmell E	Cordell JG	Partridge D	Lyons GW	Johnson G
1	Aug 21	GRIMSBY TOWN	0-3		6915	1				5	6	7	8	9	10	11												
2	25	BRADFORD CITY	1-2	Kendall	5901	1				5	4	7	8		10	11	2	3	6	9								
3	28	Bradford Park Avenue	1-1	Frost	10819	1		8		5	4	7				11	2	3	6	9				10				
4	Sep 1	Bradford City	0-1		11604	1			8	5	4	7				11	2	3	6	9				10				
5	4	Oldham Athletic	0-0		11484	1		8		5	4	7				11	2	3	6	9				10				
6	8	CREWE ALEXANDRA	1-1	Anders	4154	1		8		5	4	7				11	2	3	6	9				10				
7	11	TRANMERE ROVERS	2-0	Kendall, Green	4313	1				5	4	7			10	11	2	3	6				8	9				
8	15	Crewe Alexandra	2-2	Haines 2	4022	1				5	4	7	8		10	11	2	3	6				9					
9	18	Stockport County	4-1	Frost 2, Black, Lynn	9923	1				5	4	7			10	11	2	3	6	8	9							
10	22	DARLINGTON	2-2	Anders, Frost	4099	1				5	4	7	8		10	11	2	3	6	9								
11	25	HARTLEPOOLS UNITED	2-1	Gemmell, Haines	6222	1				5	4	7	8		10	11	2	3	6					9				
12	29	Darlington	2-2	Gemmell 2	9598	1				5	4	7	8		10	11	2	3	6					9				
13	Oct 2	Gateshead	1-0	Haines	8010					5	4	7	10		8	11	2	3	6					9	1			
14	9	BARNSLEY	3-0	Lynn (p), Anders, Kendall	11552					5	4	7	10		8	11	2	3	6					9	1			
15	16	Scunthorpe United	2-2	Mitcheson, Anders	10331					5	4	7	10		8	11	2	3	6					9	1			
16	23	WREXHAM	2-1	Anders 2	5902					5	4	7	10		8	11	2	3	6					9	1			
17	30	Accrington Stanley	4-5	Anders, Gemmell 2, Lynn (p)	12626		3			5	4	7	10		8	11		2	6					9	1			
18	Nov 6	MANSFIELD TOWN	2-0	Lynn (p), Kendall	6527					5	4	7	10		8	11	2	3	6					9	1			
19	13	Workington	0-1		5653		3			5	4	7	10		8	11		2	6					9	1			
20	27	Southport	0-1		3365	1	3				4	7	8			11		2	6		9			10		5		
21	Dec 4	YORK CITY	1-1	Anders	4051	1	3			5	4	7	10		8	11		2	6					9				
22	18	Grimsby Town	1-1	Glover	7853	1				5	4	7	8			11	2	3	6					9			10	
23	25	Carlisle United	2-7	Anders, Gemmell	6556	1				5	4	7		10		11	2	3	6					9			8	
24	27	CARLISLE UNITED	1-2	Gemmell	8274	1				5	4	7		10	8	11	2	3	6					9				
25	Jan 1	BRADFORD PARK AVE.	3-2	Haines, Hindle (og), Gemmell	6976	1	2			5	4	7	10		8	11		3	6					9				
26	22	Tranmere Rovers	1-3	Gemmell	4644	1	2			5	4	7	10		8	11		3	6					9				
27	29	CHESTERFIELD	0-0		5171	1	2			5	4	7	10		8	11		3	6					9				
28	Feb 5	STOCKPORT COUNTY	1-1	Kendall	9026	1	2			5	4	7	10		8	11		3	6					9				
29	12	Hartlepools United	1-3	Black	6611	1	2			5	4	7		9		11		3	6		10			8				
30	19	GATESHEAD	4-0	Kendall, G Lyons, Gemmell 2	4823	1	2			5	4	7	8					3	6		10			9			11	
31	Mar 5	SCUNTHORPE UNITED	2-0	Kendall, Lynn (p)	6078	1	2			5	4	7	8		10	11		3	6					9				
32	12	Wrexham	0-0		7048	1	2			5	4	7	8		10	11		3	6					9				
33	16	Halifax Town	2-1	Gemmell, Kendall	2836	1	2			5	4	7	8		10	11		3	6					9				
34	19	ACCRINGTON STANLEY	0-0		11654	1	2			5	4	7	8		10	11		3	6					9				
35	26	Mansfield Town	2-3	Gemmell, Mitcheson	2561	1	2			5	4	7	8		10	11		3	6					9				
36	Apr 2	WORKINGTON	2-1	Lynn 2 (2p)	5229	1	2			5	4		8		10	11		3	6					9			7	
37	8	Chester	2-1	Gemmell, Lynn (p)	7293	1	2			5	4	7	8		10	11		3	6					9				
38	9	Barrow	2-4	Gemmell, G Lyons	5047	1	2	10		5		7		4	8			3	6					9			11	
39	11	CHESTER	2-0	Kendall, Anders	6466	1	2			5	4	7	10				8	3	6					9			11	
40	16	SOUTHPORT	0-0		5567	1	2			5	4	7		9	8	11		3	6					10				
41	20	OLDHAM ATHLETIC	2-1	Gemmell 2	6181	1	2			5	4	7			8	11		3	6					9				
42	23	York City	0-2		9981	1	2			5	4	7			8	11		3	6		9			10				
43	27	BARROW	4-1	Mitcheson 2, Black, Gemmell	2726	1	2			5	4	7			8			3	6		9			10			11	
44	30	HALIFAX TOWN	2-2	Kendall, Mitcheson	4850	1	2			5	4	7			8			3	6		9			10			11	
45	May 2	Chesterfield	1-3	Gemmell	5622	1	2			5	4	7			8	11		3	6		9			10				
46	3	Barnsley	0-2		11682	1	2			5	4	7			8	11		3	6		9			10				
		Apps				39	24	6	2	45	45	45	29	4	33	41	19	45	45	7	18	3	2	36	7	1	9	1
		Goals								1	8	10	5		5	10				4	3		1	19			2	

One own goal

F.A. Cup

Rd	Date	Opponent	Score	Scorers	Att	Morton A	McCulloch WD	Lyons E	Morgan WA	Glover BA	Lynn J	Kendall A	Haines JTW	Lord F	Mitcheson FJ	Anders J	Underwood G	Boyle H	Murphy D	Frost D	Black N	Tolson W	Green BG	Gemmell E	Cordell JG	Partridge D	Lyons GW	Johnson G
R1	Nov 20	Tranmere Rovers	3-3	Mitcheson, Anders, Gemmell	8927			3		5	4	7	10		8	11		2	6					9	1			
rep	23	TRANMERE ROVERS	1-0	Gemmell	5652	1		3		5	4	7	10		8	11		2	6					9				
R2	Dec 11	HINCKLEY ATHLETIC	2-1	Kendall, Anders	8586	1		3		5	4	7	10		8	11		2	6					9				
R3	Jan 8	CHARLTON ATHLETIC	1-3	Haines	16938	1	2			5	4	7	10		8	11		3	6					9				

Lancashire Cup

Date	Opponent	Score	Scorers	Att	Morton A	McCulloch WD	Lyons E	Morgan WA	Glover BA	Lynn J	Kendall A	Haines JTW	Lord F	Mitcheson FJ	Anders J	Underwood G	Boyle H	Murphy D	Frost D	Black N	Tolson W	Green BG	Gemmell E	Cordell JG	Partridge D	Lyons GW	Johnson G
Oct 6	BLACKBURN ROVERS	4-1	Gemmel, Haines, Murphy, Anders	4300		4	3		5		7	10		8	11		2	6					9	1			
Feb 16	BURNLEY	2-1	Black, Kendall	2186		2	3		5	4	7	8	9					6		11			10	1			
Mar 28	OLDHAM ATHLETIC	0-1		5510	1	2		6	5	4	7	8				10		3					9			11	

		P	W	D	L	F	A	W	D	L	F	A	Pts
1	Barnsley	46	18	3	2	51	17	12	2	9	35	29	65
2	Accrington Stanley	46	18	2	3	65	32	7	9	7	31	35	61
3	Scunthorpe United	46	14	6	3	45	18	9	6	8	36	35	58
4	York City	46	13	5	5	43	27	11	5	7	49	36	58
5	Hartlepools United	46	16	3	4	39	20	9	2	12	25	29	55
6	Chesterfield	46	17	1	5	54	33	7	5	11	27	37	54
7	Gateshead	46	11	7	5	38	26	9	5	9	27	43	52
8	Workington	46	11	7	5	39	23	7	7	9	29	32	50
9	Stockport County	46	13	4	6	50	27	5	8	10	34	43	48
10	Oldham Athletic	46	14	5	4	47	22	5	5	13	27	46	48
11	Southport	46	10	9	4	28	18	6	7	10	19	26	48
12	ROCHDALE	46	13	7	3	39	20	4	7	12	30	46	48
13	Mansfield Town	46	14	4	5	40	28	4	5	14	25	43	45
14	Halifax Town	46	9	9	5	41	27	6	4	13	22	40	43
15	Darlington	46	10	7	6	41	28	4	7	12	21	45	42
16	Bradford Park Ave.	46	11	7	5	29	21	4	4	15	27	49	41
17	Barrow	46	12	4	7	39	34	5	2	16	31	55	40
18	Wrexham	46	9	6	8	40	35	4	6	13	25	42	38
19	Tranmere Rovers	46	9	6	8	37	30	4	5	14	18	40	37
20	Carlisle United	46	12	1	10	53	39	3	5	15	25	50	36
21	Bradford City	46	9	5	9	30	26	5	5	14	17	29	36
22	Crewe Alexandra	46	8	10	5	45	35	2	4	17	23	56	34
23	Grimsby Town	46	10	4	9	28	32	3	4	16	19	46	34
24	Chester	46	10	3	10	23	25	2	6	15	21	52	33

1955/56 12th in Division 3(N)

#		Date	Opponent	Score	Scorers	Att	Morton A	Storey J	Boyle H	Lynn J	McCulloch WD	Murphy D	Kendall A	Mitcheson FJ	Gemmell E	McClelland JW	Anders J	Black N	Neville DR	Fearnley HL	Partridge D	Sutton B	Green BG	Andrews D	Aspden JR	Jones JA	Morement R	Symonds CRCH	Ferguson C	Lord F	Glover BA	Stonehouse B	McLaren A	Jackson H	Lyons GW	Molloy G
1	Aug	20	Grimsby Town	1-1	McClelland	11694	1	2	3	4	5	6	7	8	9	10	11																			
2		24	Accrington Stanley	0-3		12016	1	2	3	4	5	6	7	8	9	10	11																			
3		27	Bradford Park Ave.	4-2	Mitcheson, Gemmell, Kendall, Black	4648	1		3	4	5	6	7	8	9	10	11						11													
4		29	ACCRINGTON STANLEY	1-1	Kendall	8086	1		3	4	5	6	7	8	9	10	11		2																	
5	Sep	3	OLDHAM ATHLETIC	4-4	Lynn, Mitcheson, Kendall, Black	10824			3	4	2	6	7	8	9	10		11				1	5													
6		5	BARROW	5-1	Black, Andrews, McClelland, Gemmell, McCulloch	4618			3	5	2	6	7		9	8		11						1	4	10										
7		10	Chesterfield	2-7	Gemmell, McClelland	9381			3	4	2	6	7		9	8		11						1		10	5									
8		15	Barrow	0-2		5157			3	5	2	6	7			8		11								10		1	4	9						
9		17	TRANMERE ROVERS	1-3	Anders	5518			3	4	2	6	7	8	9	10	11											1		5						
10		21	CHESTER	4-2	Gemmell 2, Lynn 2 (2p)	2936			3	4	2	6	7	8	9	10	11											1		5						
11		24	Southport	0-2		3949			3	4	2	6	7	8	9	10	11											1		5						
12		28	Darlington	0-2		5222			3	4	2	6	7	8	9	10		11										1		5						
13	Oct	1	GATESHEAD	1-1	Andrews	5358				4	2	3	7		9		11	10						8				1		5	6					
14		8	York City	2-1	Gemmell 2	9742				4	3	6	7	10	9	8		11										1		2	5					
15		15	SCUNTHORPE UNITED	3-2	Gemmell 2, Kendall	6110				4	3	6	7	10	9	8		11										1		2	5					
16		22	Crewe Alexandra	0-0		4922				4	3	6	7	8	9	10	11											1		2	5					
17		29	HARTLEPOOLS UNITED	1-4	Gemmell	4388				6	3	10	7		9		11							4	8			1		2	5					
18	Nov	5	Stockport County	0-0		9337				4	3	6			8	9	10	11						7				1		2	5					
19		12	MANSFIELD TOWN	1-1	Mitcheson	4660				4	3	6		8	9	10	11							7				1		2	5					
20		26	HALIFAX TOWN	2-1	McClelland, Black	4354				4	3	6				9	11	10										1		2	5	7	8			
21	Dec	3	Bradford City	2-2	Whyte (og), McLaren	10072				4	3	6			10	9		7	11									1		2	5		8			
22		17	GRIMSBY TOWN	2-0	Gemmell, Anders	4547				4	3	6	7		10	9	11											1		2	5		8			
23		24	Bradford Park Avenue	3-3	Gemmell 2, Anders	7743				4	3	6	7		9		11								10			1		2	5		8			
24		26	CARLISLE UNITED	5-2	McLaren 2, Anders, Kendall, Lynn (p)	4698	1			4	3	6	7	10	9		11													2	5		8			
25		27	Carlisle United	2-1	Jackson, Anders	4429	1			4	3	6	7				11								10						5			8	9	
26		31	Oldham Athletic	2-2	Anders, McLaren	10179	1		3	4	2	6	7		9		11								10						5		8			
27	Jan	7	Wrexham	0-0		6679	1			4	3	6	7		9		11								10						2		5	8		
28		21	Tranmere Rovers	1-2	Andrews	4732	1			4	3	6	7				11						9	10						2		5	8			
29		28	DERBY COUNTY	0-5		7466				4	3	6	7		9		11								10	1					2		5	8		
30	Feb	4	SOUTHPORT	1-3	Lynn (p)	2845				4	3	6	7		9		11								10	1					2		5	8		
31		11	Gateshead	1-4	Black	1932			3	4	2	6	7		9	11	10							8		1					5					
32		18	YORK CITY	3-1	Anders 2, Storey	3923		9	3	4	2	6	7			8	10									1					5	11				
33	Mar	3	CREWE ALEXANDRA	1-0	Anders	4260		9	3	4	2	6	7			8	10									1					5	11				
34		10	Hartlepools United	0-1		8150	2	3			4	6			7	8	10					9				1					5		11			
35		17	WREXHAM	1-0	Anders	4285	2	3			4	6			9	7	10									1					5		11	8		
36		22	Scunthorpe United	2-1	Andrews, Anders (p)	4865	2	3			4	6			9		7							10		1					5		11	8		
37		24	Mansfield Town	0-6		8563	2	3			4	6	11		9		7							10		1					5			8		
38		30	WORKINGTON	1-0	Stonehouse	4057				2	4	6				9	11	10								3	1				5		7	8		
39		31	STOCKPORT COUNTY	0-0		4643	2		3		4	6				11	10									1				5		9	7	8		
40	Apr	2	Workington	1-0	Lord	5548	2		3	4		6														10			1	5		9	11	8	7	
41		7	Halifax Town	1-1	McCulloch	3212	2		3		4	6					11									10			1	5		9	7	8		
42		14	BRADFORD CITY	3-1	Lord, McLaren, McClelland	3879	2		3		4	6				10	11												1	5		9	7	8		
43		18	CHESTERFIELD	1-5	Lord	2518	2		3		4	6				10	11												1	5		9	7	8		
44		21	Derby County	0-2		13077	2				4	3			9											10			1	5			11	8	7	6
45		24	DARLINGTON	1-0	Lord	2542	2				4	3														10			1	9	5		11	8	7	6
46		28	Chester	0-0		4213	2				5	3											4	10		1				9			11	8	7	6
			Apps				9	18	26	34	45	46	30	17	29	24	34	18	1	1	1	2	5	22	2	34	1	1	33	8	19	15	23	1	4	3
			Goals					1		5	2		5	3	13	5	11	5						4						4		1	5	1		

One own goal

F.A. Cup

| R1 | Nov | 19 | YORK CITY | 0-1 | | 8992 | | | 4 | 3 | 6 | | | 8 | 9 | | 11 | 10 | | | | | | | | 7 | | 1 | | 2 | 5 | | | | | |

Lancashire Cup

	Oct	24	BOLTON WANDERERS	1-1	Andrews	3070			6	3	10	7		9			11							4	8			1		2	5					
	Feb	15	Bolton Wanderers	2-0	Stonehouse, Anders	1432	9	3			2	6	7			8	10							4		1					5	11				
	Mar	7	BLACKBURN ROVERS	1-2	Anders	2733	2	3	4	5	6				7	8	10						9			1						11				

Back: McLelland, Murphy, McCulloch, Morton, Storey, Boyle
Front: Kendall, Mitcheson, Lynn, Gemmell, Black

		P	W	D	L	F	A	W	D	L	F	A	Pts
1	Grimsby Town	46	20	1	2	54	10	11	5	7	22	19	68
2	Derby County	46	18	4	1	67	23	10	3	10	43	32	63
3	Accrington Stanley	46	17	4	2	61	19	8	5	10	31	38	59
4	Hartlepools United	46	18	2	3	47	15	8	3	12	34	45	57
5	Southport	46	12	9	2	39	18	11	2	10	27	35	57
6	Chesterfield	46	18	1	4	61	21	7	3	13	33	45	54
7	Stockport County	46	16	4	3	65	22	5	5	13	25	39	51
8	Bradford City	46	16	5	2	57	25	5	2	13	33	45	49
9	Scunthorpe United	46	12	4	7	40	26	8	4	11	35	37	48
10	Workington	46	13	4	6	47	20	6	5	12	28	43	47
11	York City	46	12	4	7	44	24	7	5	11	41	48	47
12	ROCHDALE	46	13	5	5	46	39	4	8	11	20	45	47
13	Gateshead	46	15	4	4	56	32	2	7	14	21	52	45
14	Wrexham	46	11	5	7	37	28	5	5	13	29	45	42
15	Darlington	46	11	6	6	41	28	5	3	15	19	45	41
16	Tranmere Rovers	46	11	4	8	33	25	5	5	13	26	59	41
17	Chester	46	10	6	7	41	35	5	5	11	47	49	40
18	Mansfield Town	46	13	6	4	59	21	1	5	17	25	60	39
19	Halifax Town	46	10	6	7	40	27	4	5	14	26	49	39
20	Oldham Athletic	46	7	12	4	48	36	3	6	14	28	50	38
21	Carlisle United	46	11	3	9	45	36	4	5	14	17	49	38
22	Barrow	46	11	6	6	44	25	1	3	19	17	58	33
23	Bradford Park Ave.	46	13	4	6	47	38	0	3	20	14	84	33
24	Crewe Alexandra	46	9	4	10	32	35	0	6	17	18	70	28

231

1956/57 13th in Division 3(N)

#	Date		Opponent	Score	Scorers	Att.	Jones JA	Ferguson C	McCulloch WD	Grant JA	Glover BA	McGuigan J	Kendall A	Wainwright EF	Todd TB	Lewis G	Anders J	Murphy D	Lyons GW	Lord F	Stonehouse B	McLaren A	Morton A	Devlin J	Storey J	Green BG	Tapley R	Lello CF	Parr SV	Molloy G	Moran E	Pearson DT	Mulvoy T	Brown J	Andrews D	Calderbank R
1	Aug	18	BARROW	1-0	Lewis	3546	1	2	3	4	5	6	7	8	9	10	11																			
2		20	Mansfield Town	3-2	Lewis 2, Todd	13441	1	2	3	4	5	6	7	8	9	10	11																			
3		25	Hull City	0-2		13089	1	2	3		5	6	7	8	9	10	11	4																		
4		29	MANSFIELD TOWN	0-0		7360	1	2	3	4	5	6	7	8	9	10				11																
5	Sep	1	WORKINGTON	0-0		7414	1	2	3	4	5	6		8		10	11		7	9																
6		8	Halifax Town	1-2	Lord	8137	1	2	3	4	5	6		8		10			7	9	11															
7		12	DARLINGTON	3-0	Wainwright 2, McLaren	3188	1	2	3	4	5	6		8					7	9		11	10													
8		15	OLDHAM ATHLETIC	0-2		10353		2	3	4	5	6			9	8			7			11	10	1												
9		19	Derby County	0-3		19405	1	2	3	4	5	6				8		11	7	9		10														
10		22	SCUNTHORPE UNITED	3-0	Devlin, McLaren, Wainwright	6320	1	2	3	4	5	6				8			7	9		10		11												
11		26	DERBY COUNTY	3-1	McLaren, Lewis 2	4835	1	2	3	4	5	6				8			7	9		10		11												
12		29	Crewe Alexandra	6-1	Lewis 2, Lord, Devlin, Wainwright 2 (1p)	5947	1	2	3	4	5	6				8			7	9		10		11												
13	Oct	6	Southport	1-0	Lewis	5501	1	2	3	4	5	6				8			7	9		10		11												
14		13	CHESTERFIELD	1-0	Lewis	9011	1	2	3	4	5	6				8			7	9		10		11												
15		20	Tranmere Rovers	2-2	Lord, Lewis	6540	1	2	3	4	5	6				8			7	9		10		11												
16		27	HARTLEPOOLS UNITED	1-0	Wainwright	12237	1	2	3	4	5	6				8			7	9		10		11												
17	Nov	3	Bradford City	1-1	Wainwright	15887	1	2	3	4	5	6				8			7	9		10					11									
18		10	STOCKPORT COUNTY	2-2	Lord, Lewis	10394	1	2	3	4	5	6				8			7	9						11			10							
19		24	ACCRINGTON STANLEY	0-2		11071	1	5	3	4		6				9			11	7	8					2			10							
20	Dec	1	Chester	2-2	McLaren, McGuigan	5492	1	5	3	4		11				8			7	9		10				2			6							
21		15	Barrow	0-2		3718	1	2	5	4		6				8			7	11		10							3							
22		25	Wrexham	1-4	McLaren	5105	1	2	5	4		11				8			7							9		6	3							
23		26	WREXHAM	0-2		4375	1	2	5	4			7	8										10	11	9		6	3							
24		29	Workington	0-5		6144	1	2	5	4				8					7	11						9		6	3							
25	Jan	1	Darlington	3-4	McLaren, Wainwright 2	4461		5	2	4				8					7			10	1		3	9		6		11						
26		5	Gateshead	1-2	Lyons	1430		5	2	4				8		9			7			10	1		3			6		11						
27		12	HALIFAX TOWN	1-1	Lord	5527		5	2	4				8					7	9		10			3			6		11						
28		19	Oldham Athletic	1-0	Devlin	9006	1	5	2	4				8				6	7	9		10		11					3							
29		26	GATESHEAD	0-0		4561	1	5	2	4				8		9		6	7			10		11					3							
30	Feb	2	Scunthorpe United	0-1		6080	1	5	2	4				8		9		6	7										3		10					
31		9	CREWE ALEXANDRA	1-1	Lord	3829	1	5	2	4				8				6	7	9									3		10					
32		16	SOUTHPORT	6-1	Lord 3, Devlin 2, Green	3988	1	2	3	4	5			8				6		9				11		7					10					
33		23	Chesterfield	2-2	Lord, Moran	4200	1	2	3	4	5			8				6		9				11		7					10					
34	Mar	2	TRANMERE ROVERS	1-0	Grant	5499	1	2	3	4	5			8				6		9				11		7					10					
35		5	HULL CITY	4-3	McLaren, Lord 3	4296	1	2	3	4	5							6		9		8		11		7					10					
36		9	Hartlepools United	0-0		9339	1	2	3	4	5							6		9		8		11		7					10					
37		16	BRADFORD CITY	4-1	Wainwright(p), Moran, Pearson, Lord	7399	1	2	3	4	5		7					6		9				11							10	8				
38		23	Stockport County	1-3	Moran	15652	1	2	3	4	5		7					6		9				11							10	8				
39		30	CARLISLE UNITED	2-1	Devlin, Ferguson	5521	1	2	3	4	5							6		9				11							10	8				
40	Apr	6	Accrington Stanley	1-2	Parr	9527	1		3	4	5							6		8				11	2	7			9		10					
41		13	CHESTER	2-1	Pearson 2	4501	1		3	4	5							6		9				11		7			2		10	8				
42		20	York City	0-4		7203	1		3	4	5		7					6		9				11					2		10	8				
43		22	BRADFORD PARK AVE.	2-1	Lord, Moran	5007	1		3	4	5	6				8								11					2		10		7			
44		23	Bradford Park Avenue	0-0		6280	1		3	4	5					8		6						11		9			2		10		7			
45		27	YORK CITY	1-0	Pearson	4215	1		3	4	5	6				8								11					2		9	10	7			
46		30	Carlisle United	1-2	Bond (og)	3999	1		3	4	5	6				8								11					2		10	9	7			
				Apps			43	39	46	45	33	26	4	38	5	27	4	18	13	33	4	21	3	27	6	14	1	11	15	3	14	7	2	4		
				Goals				1		1		1		10	1	11			1	15		7		6		1			1		4	4				

One own goal

F.A. Cup

	Date		Opponent	Score	Att.	Jones JA	Ferguson C	McCulloch WD	Grant JA	McGuigan J	Wainwright EF	Lewis G	Lord F	Morton A	Green BG	Brown J
R1	Nov	17	Scunthorpe United	0-1	8655	1	5	3	4	6	8	9	7	10	2	11

Lancashire Cup

	Date		Opponent	Score	Att.	Jones JA	Ferguson C	Grant JA	Glover BA	McGuigan J	Lord F	McLaren A	Devlin J	Green BG	Lello CF	Calderbank R
	Oct	30	CHESTER	0-3	2086	1	2	4	5	6	8	7	3	9	11	10

		P	W	D	L	F	A	W	D	L	F	A	Pts
1	Derby County	46	18	3	2	69	18	8	8	7	42	35	63
2	Hartlepools United	46	18	4	1	56	21	7	5	11	34	42	59
3	Accrington Stanley	46	15	4	4	54	22	10	4	9	41	42	58
4	Workington	46	16	4	3	60	25	8	6	9	33	38	58
5	Stockport County	46	16	3	4	51	26	7	5	11	40	49	54
6	Chesterfield	46	15	5	1	60	22	5	4	14	36	57	53
7	York City	46	14	4	5	43	21	7	6	10	32	40	52
8	Hull City	46	14	6	3	45	24	7	4	12	39	45	52
9	Bradford City	46	14	3	6	47	31	8	5	10	31	37	52
10	Barrow	46	16	2	5	51	22	5	7	11	25	40	51
11	Halifax Town	46	16	2	5	40	24	5	5	13	25	46	49
12	Wrexham	46	12	7	4	63	33	7	3	13	34	41	48
13	ROCHDALE	46	14	6	3	38	19	4	6	13	27	46	48
14	Scunthorpe United	46	9	5	9	44	36	6	10	7	27	33	45
15	Carlisle United	46	9	5	9	44	36	7	4	12	32	49	45
16	Mansfield Town	46	13	3	7	58	38	4	7	12	33	52	44
17	Gateshead	46	9	6	8	42	40	8	4	11	30	50	44
18	Darlington	46	11	5	7	47	36	6	3	14	35	59	42
19	Oldham Athletic	46	9	7	7	35	31	3	8	12	31	43	39
20	Bradford Park Ave.	46	11	2	10	41	40	5	1	17	25	53	35
21	Chester	46	8	7	8	40	35	2	6	15	15	49	33
22	Southport	46	8	8	7	31	34	3	4	16	21	60	32
23	Tranmere Rovers	46	5	9	9	33	38	2	4	17	18	53	27
24	Crewe Alexandra	46	5	7	11	31	46	1	2	20	12	64	21

1957/58 — 10th in Division 3(N)

#		Date	Opponent	Score	Scorers	Att	Jones JA	Ferguson C	Rudman H	Grant JA	Glover BA	McGlennon T	Lockhart C	Wainwright EF	Pearson DT	Moran E	Devlin J	McCready BT	Green BG	Vizard CI	Torrance GS	McCulloch WD	McGuigan J	Dailey J	Parr SV	Dryburgh TJD	Newall G	Brown J	Spencer L	Wallace JC	Barber K
1	Aug	24	Mansfield Town	4-2	Lockhart 2, Moran, Pearson	9925	1	2	3	4	5	6	7	8	9	10	11														
2		28	ACCRINGTON STANLEY	3-0	McGlennon, Devlin, Wainwright (p)	12030		2	3	4	5	6	7	8	9	10	11	1													
3		31	WORKINGTON	1-0	Pearson	10388		2	3	4	5	6	7	8	9	10	11	1													
4	Sep	2	Accrington Stanley	2-3	Vizard, Pearson	15454		2	3	4	5	6	7		9		11	1				8	10								
5		7	Bradford City	0-1		13223		2	3	4	5	6	7	8	9		11	1					10								
6		11	DARLINGTON	5-4	Wainwright 2(1p), Moran, Rudman,	4037		2	3	4	5	6	7	8	9	10	11	1													
7		14	HULL CITY	2-1	Lockhart, Vizard	7612		2	3	4	5	6	7	8		10	11	1	9												
8		18	Darlington	2-4	Wainwright, Grant	3599		2	3	4	5	6	7	8		10	11	1	9												
9		21	Stockport County	3-0	Wainwright, Green, Lockhart	12480		2		4	5	6	7	8		10			9	11	1	3									
10		25	SCUNTHORPE UNITED	1-4	Bushby (og)	5278		2		4	5	6	7		8	10		1	9	11		3									
11		28	HALIFAX TOWN	5-1	Pearson 4, Moran	5309		2		4	5	11	7		9	10		1		8		3	6								
12	Oct	3	Scunthorpe United	0-2		11636		2		4	5		7		9	10		1		8	11	3	6								
13		5	BURY	1-1	Moran	18728		2	3	4	5		7	8	9	10	11	1					6								
14		12	Barrow	1-2	Vizard	5668		5	2	4			7	8	9		11	1		10		3	6								
15		19	CHESTERFIELD	3-4	Lockhart 2, McGuigan	6441		5	2	4			7	8		10	11	1				3	6	9							
16		26	Tranmere Rovers	1-3	Pearson	10425	1	5	2	4			7	8	10					11			6	9	3						
17	Nov	2	HARTLEPOOLS UNITED	7-0	Dailey 5, Lockhart, Moran	5508	1	2	3	4	5		7	8		10				11			6	9							
18		9	Bradford Park Avenue	2-2	Green, Wainwright	8965	1	2	3	4	5		7	8					9				6						11		
19		23	Southport	2-0	Green, Dailey	2880	1	2	3	4			7	8		10							6	9					11	5	
20		30	YORK CITY	2-1	Dailey 2 (1p)	6297	1	2	3	4			7	8		10					5		6	9					11		
21	Dec	14	OLDHAM ATHLETIC	1-3	Dailey	6684	1	2	3	4			7	8		10							6	9					11		
22		21	MANSFIELD TOWN	3-0	Dailey, Vizard, Pearson	4371	1	2		4	5		7		8	10				11		3	6	9							
23		25	WREXHAM	2-0	Moran, Pearson	3342	1	2		4	5		7		8	10				11		3	6	9							
24		26	Wrexham	0-2		9204	1	2		4	5	3		8		10			7				6	9					11		
25		28	Workington	2-1	Vizard, Dailey (p)	8932	1	2		4	5		7	8		10				11		3	6	9							
26	Jan	4	CREWE ALEXANDRA	3-0	Moran, Lockhart, Wainwright	4784	1	2		4	5		7	8	9	10				11		3	6								
27		11	BRADFORD CITY	0-2		7277	1	2		4	5		7	8		10				11		3	6	9							
28		18	Hull City	1-2	Dailey	8991	1	2		4	5	11		8		10						3	6	9					7		
29	Feb	1	STOCKPORT COUNTY	3-0	Dailey 3	7804	1	2		4	5		7	8		10				11		3	6	9							
30		15	Bury	1-4	Lockhart	12308	1	2		4	5		7	8		10				11		3	6	9							
31		22	SOUTHPORT	2-0	Lockhart, Pearson	3734	1	2		4	5		7	8	10					11		3	6	9							
32	Mar	1	Chesterfield	2-2	Pearson, Wainwright	8533	1	2		4	5		7	8	10					11		3	6	9							
33		8	TRANMERE ROVERS	2-0	Vizard, Dailey	4018	1	2		4	5		7	8	10					11		3	6	9							
34		11	CARLISLE UNITED	1-0	Dailey	4079	1	2		4	5		7	8	10					11		3	6	9							
35		15	Hartlepools United	3-1	Lockhart, Dailey, Moran	5862	1	2		4	5	6	7	8		10				11		3		9							
36		22	BARROW	1-1	Grant	5082	1	2		4	5			8	7	10				11		3	6	9							
37		29	Carlisle United	0-1		3991	1	2		4	5		7		10	8				11		3	6	9							
38	Apr	4	GATESHEAD	0-0		5106	1	2		4	5		7	8	10					11		3	6	9							
39		5	CHESTER	1-1	Moran	3273	1	2		4	5	11	7			8						3	6	9						10	
40		7	Gateshead	2-3	Wainwright, Dailey	5110	1	2		4	5	6	7	8								3		10						11	9
41		12	York City	0-1		5123	1	2		4	5	11		8	7								6	9						10	3
42		16	Chester	0-2		3449	1	2	4	7	5	11		8									6	9						10	3
43		19	BRADFORD PARK AVE.	1-2	Ferguson (p)	4912	1	2		4	5	11	7	8								3	6	9						10	
44		21	Crewe Alexandra	0-0		3000	1	2	4		5	11	7	8					9			3	6							10	
45		26	Oldham Athletic	0-0		10919	1	2	3	4	5		7	8		10							6	9						11	
46		29	Halifax Town	1-4	Pearson	7419	1	2	3	4	5		7	8	10								6	9							
				Apps			32	46	21	45	41	21	40	38	25	27	11	12	14	25	2	25	34	29	1	5	1	1	7	3	
				Goals				1	2	2		1	11	9	13	9	1		3	6			1	19							

One own goal

F.A. Cup

R1	Nov 16 DARLINGTON	0-2		8395	1	2	3	4	5	11	7	8		10							6	9							

Lancashire Cup

Dec 2 MANCHESTER CITY	0-2		1795		2	3			6	7		9			1		8	10						11	5			4

		P	W	D	L	F	A	W	D	L	F	A	Pts
1	Scunthorpe United	46	16	5	2	46	19	13	3	7	42	31	66
2	Accrington Stanley	46	16	4	3	53	28	9	5	9	30	33	59
3	Bradford City	46	13	7	3	42	19	8	8	7	31	30	57
4	Bury	46	17	4	2	61	18	6	6	11	33	44	56
5	Hull City	46	15	6	2	49	20	4	9	10	29	47	53
6	Mansfield Town	46	16	3	4	68	42	6	5	12	32	50	52
7	Halifax Town	46	15	5	3	52	20	5	6	12	31	49	51
8	Chesterfield	46	12	8	3	39	28	6	7	10	32	41	51
9	Stockport County	46	15	4	4	54	28	3	7	13	20	39	47
10	ROCHDALE	46	14	4	5	50	25	5	4	14	29	42	46
11	Tranmere Rovers	46	12	6	5	51	32	6	4	13	31	44	46
12	Wrexham	46	13	8	2	39	18	4	4	15	22	45	46
13	York City	46	11	8	4	40	26	6	4	13	28	50	46
14	Gateshead	46	12	5	6	41	27	3	10	10	27	49	45
15	Oldham Athletic	46	11	7	5	44	32	3	10	10	28	52	45
16	Carlisle United	46	13	3	7	56	35	6	3	14	24	43	44
17	Hartlepools United	46	11	6	6	45	26	5	6	12	28	50	44
18	Barrow	46	9	7	7	36	32	4	8	11	30	42	41
19	Workington	46	11	6	6	46	33	3	7	13	26	48	41
20	Darlington	46	15	3	5	53	25	2	4	17	25	64	41
21	Chester	46	7	10	6	38	26	6	3	14	35	55	39
22	Bradford Park Ave.	46	8	6	9	41	41	5	5	13	27	54	37
23	Southport	46	8	3	12	29	40	3	3	17	23	48	28
24	Crewe Alexandra	46	6	5	12	29	41	2	2	19	18	52	23

1958/59 24th in Division 3

League Matches

#		Date	Opponent	Score	Scorers	Att
1	Aug	23	Stockport County	0-1		12171
2		25	PLYMOUTH ARGYLE	0-2		8442
3		30	READING	1-0	Dailey (p)	6629
4	Sep	4	Plymouth Argyle	1-2	Spencer	26961
5		6	Colchester United	1-2	Dailey (p)	8141
6		10	SWINDON TOWN	1-1	Wainwright	6617
7		13	BOURNEMOUTH	2-1	Dailey, Spencer	6361
8		17	Swindon Town	1-2	Green	9558
9		20	Norwich City	1-2	Spencer	16422
10		23	TRANMERE ROVERS	1-4	Green	3854
11		27	SOUTHEND UNITED	1-1	Spencer	5719
12		29	Tranmere Rovers	1-2	McBain	16878
13	Oct	4	Bury	1-6	Dailey	11865
14		7	QUEEN'S PARK RANGERS	2-2	Green, Lord	4276
15		11	NOTTS COUNTY	1-2	Ferguson (p)	5306
16		18	Chesterfield	0-0		8253
17		25	NEWPORT COUNTY	1-1	Wainwright	4998
18	Nov	1	Halifax Town	1-2	Spencer	7129
19		8	ACCRINGTON STANLEY	1-0	Wainwright	6286
20		22	HULL CITY	0-1		5562
21		29	Bradford City	1-7	Spencer	6223
22	Dec	13	Brentford	1-2	Moore	9432
23		20	STOCKPORT COUNTY	0-2		4056
24		26	DONCASTER ROVERS	1-0	Wainwright	4075
25		27	Doncaster Rovers	1-1	Vizard	7237
26	Jan	3	Reading	0-3		11240
27		24	WREXHAM	3-1	Wainwright 2, Moore	5200
28		31	Bournemouth	0-0		9945
29	Feb	2	Southampton	1-6	Wainwright	7199
30		7	NORWICH CITY	1-2	Dailey	4608
31		14	Southend United	1-3	Lord	8766
32		21	BURY	1-0	Dailey	4241
33		28	Notts County	1-1	Wainwright (p)	6394
34	Mar	7	CHESTERFIELD	0-0		3340
35		14	Newport County	0-1		4469
36		16	COLCHESTER UNITED	0-1		3510
37		21	HALIFAX TOWN	1-0	Spencer	3544
38		27	MANSFIELD TOWN	2-2	McGlennon, Finney	3537
39		28	Accrington Stanley	2-4	Spencer, Powell	4412
40		30	Mansfield Town	0-0		5863
41	Apr	4	SOUTHAMPTON	1-0	Cooper	3948
42		11	Hull City	1-2	Cooper	13377
43		18	BRADFORD CITY	0-3		4330
44		20	Queen's Park Rangers	0-3		7280
45		25	Wrexham	0-1		5244
46		27	BRENTFORD	0-0		2191

Appearances and Goals

	Jones JA	Ferguson C	Whiston D	Grant JA	Glover BA	McGuigan J	McBain GA	Wainwright EF	Dailey J	Moran E	Maguire JS	Spencer L	McCready CJ	McGlennon T	Vizard CJ	Powell DM	Finney CW	Thomson B	Green BG	Heyes G	Wallace IC	Lord F	Brown J	Aspden JR	Moore A	Milburn S	Cooper G	Bodell N	Entwhistle RP	Hussey RM
Apps	25	32	14	12	21	10	10	24	24	2	15	35	17	40	16	24	31	24	11	4	4	11	17	24	11	20	15	11	1	1
Goals		1					1	8	6			8		1	1	1	1		3			2			2		2			

F.A. Cup

		Date	Opponent	Score	Scorers	Att
R1	Nov	15	Hartlepools United	1-1	Wainwright	7164
rep		19	HARTLEPOOLS UNITED	3-3	Finney, Wainwright, Spencer	8763
rep2		27	Hartlepools United	1-2	Wainwright	6126

Both replays a.e.t. Replay 2 at Old Trafford

Lancashire Cup

	Date	Opponent	Score	Scorers	Att
Oct	13	Preston N.E.	1-1	Ferguson (p)	
	27	PRESTON N.E.	1-0	Spencer	1540
Dec	8	Manchester United	1-3	Moore	7644

Division 3 Final Table

		P	W	D	L	F	A	W	D	L	F	A	Pts
1	Plymouth Argyle	46	14	7	2	55	27	9	9	5	34	32	62
2	Hull City	46	19	3	1	65	21	7	6	10	25	34	61
3	Brentford	46	15	5	3	49	22	6	10	7	27	27	57
4	Norwich City	46	13	6	4	51	29	9	7	7	38	33	57
5	Colchester United	46	15	2	6	46	31	6	8	9	25	36	52
6	Reading	46	16	4	3	51	21	5	4	14	27	42	50
7	Tranmere Rovers	46	15	3	5	53	22	6	5	12	29	45	50
8	Southend United	46	14	6	3	52	26	7	2	14	33	54	50
9	Halifax Town	46	14	5	4	48	25	7	3	13	32	52	50
10	Bury	46	12	9	2	51	24	5	5	13	18	34	48
11	Bradford City	46	13	4	6	47	25	5	7	11	37	51	47
12	Bournemouth	46	12	9	2	40	18	5	3	15	29	51	46
13	Queen's Park Rgs.	46	14	6	3	49	28	5	2	16	25	49	46
14	Southampton	46	12	7	4	57	33	5	4	14	31	47	45
15	Swindon Town	46	13	4	6	39	25	3	9	11	20	32	45
16	Chesterfield	46	12	5	6	40	26	5	5	13	27	38	44
17	Newport County	46	15	2	6	43	24	2	7	14	26	44	43
18	Wrexham	46	12	6	5	40	30	2	8	13	23	47	42
19	Accrington Stanley	46	10	8	5	42	31	5	4	14	29	56	42
20	Mansfield Town	46	11	5	7	38	42	3	8	12	35	56	41
21	Stockport County	46	9	7	7	33	23	4	3	16	32	55	36
22	Doncaster Rovers	46	13	2	8	40	32	1	3	19	10	58	33
23	Notts County	46	8	9	3	39	39	3	4	16	22	57	29
24	ROCHDALE	46	8	7	8	21	26	0	5	18	16	53	28

1959/60 — 12th in Division 4

#	Date	Opponent	Res	Scorers	Att	Jones JA	Milburn S	Powell DM	Bodell N	Aspden JR	Bushby A	Barnes CR	Cairns R	Lord F	Anderson IL	Collins AN	Thomson B	Edwards WI	Cooper G	Spencer L	Brown J	Heyes G	Wallace J	Anchor R	Entwistle RP
1	Aug 22	Southport	2-2	Milburn (p), Lord	5168	1	2	3	4	5	6	7	8	9	10	11									
2	27	GILLINGHAM	1-0	Cairns	6382	1	2	3	9	5	6	7	8		10	11	4								
3	29	MILLWALL	0-1		6474	1	2	3	9	5	6	7	8		10	11	4								
4	Sep 3	Gillingham	0-2		5649	1		3	4	5	6	7	8			11		2	9	10					
5	5	Torquay United	1-1	Spencer	7369	1	5	3			6	7	8			11	4	2	9	10					
6	8	DARLINGTON	2-0	Spencer, Cooper	5135	1	5	3			6	7	8			11	4	2	9	10					
7	12	NORTHAMPTON T	2-2	Milburn (p), Thompson	5686	1	5	3			6	7	8			11	4	2	9	10					
8	16	Darlington	0-0		4951	1	5	3			6	7	8			11	4	2	9	10					
9	19	Doncaster Rovers	1-2	Cairns	5066	1	5	3			6	7	8	9		11	4	2		10					
10	22	BARROW	4-1	Milburn 3 (1p), Collins	5117	1	9	3		5	6	7	8		10	11	4	2							
11	26	WORKINGTON	1-1	Milburn	5671	1	9	3		5	6	7	8		10	11	4	2							
12	28	Barrow	0-3		5368	1	9	3		5	6	7	8		10	11	4	2							
13	Oct 3	CARLISLE UNITED	3-0	Milburn (p), Cairns, Barnes	4897	1	5	3			6	7	8		9	11	4	2	10						
14	5	Gateshead	2-1	Cooper, Milburn (p)	5804	1	5	3			6	7	8		9	11	4	2	10						
15	10	Walsall	2-4	Cooper, Milburn (p)	8552	1	5	3			6	7	8		9	11	4	2	10						
16	13	GATESHEAD	2-0	Cooper, Anderson	4770	1	5	3			6	7	8		9	11	4	2	10						
17	17	HARTLEPOOLS UNITED	2-0	Milburn (p), Anderson	4856	1	5	3			6	7	8		9	11	4	2	10						
18	24	Crewe Alexandra	3-1	Anderson, Cooper 2	7617	1	5	3			6	7	8		9	11	4	2	10						
19	31	CHESTER	0-0		5643	1	5	3			6	7	8		9	11	4	2	10						
20	Nov 7	Crystal Palace	0-4		14906	1	5	3			6	7	8		9	11	4	2	10						
21	21	Stockport County	1-2	Spencer	7629	1	5	3	6			7	10		9		4	2		8	11				
22	28	EXETER CITY	3-0	Cairns, Spencer, Collins	4856	1	5	3	4		6	7	10		9	11		2		8					
23	Dec 12	OLDHAM ATHLETIC	2-0	Cairns 2	5317	1	5	3	4		6	7	10		9	11		2		8					
24	19	SOUTHPORT	1-0	Cairns	2508	1	5	3	4		6	7	10		9	11		2		8					
25	26	Notts County	1-2	Cooper	14582	1	2		4	5	6	7	9					3	10	8	11				
26	28	NOTTS COUNTY	1-4	Brown	4044	1	2		4	5	6	7	10	9				3		8	11				
27	Jan 2	Millwall	0-2		9862		5		4		6	7	10		9			2	3	8	11		1		
28	9	Aldershot	0-0		3537		5		4		6	7	10		9			2	3	8	11		1		
29	16	TORQUAY UNITED	4-2	Milburn 2, Anderson, Barnes	3422		9		4	5	6	11			10			2	3	8		7	1		
30	23	Northampton Town	1-3	Milburn	5355		9		4	5	6	11			10			2	3	8		7	1		
31	Feb 6	DONCASTER ROVERS	2-0	Milburn, Edwards	3740		9	3	4	5	6	11	8		10			2				7	1		
32	13	Workington	0-2		2486		9	3	4	5	6	11	8		10			2				7	1		
33	27	WALSALL	0-2		4468		2	3	4	5	6	11	8		10					9		7	1		
34	Mar 5	Hartlepools United	1-0	Anderson	3286		2	3		5	6	7	10		9	11		4		8			1		
35	12	CREWE ALEXANDRA	4-2	Spencer, Collins, Milburn (p), Barnes	3826		2	3		5	6	7	10		9	11		4		8			1		
36	15	BRADFORD PARK AVE.	0-1		3814		2	3	4	5	6	11	10	8	9							7	1		
37	19	Chester	1-2	Lord	3965			4	3	5	6	11		9	10			2		8		7	1		
38	26	CRYSTAL PALACE	4-0	Lord 2, Spencer, Cairns	2562			3	4	5	6	7	10	9		11		2		8			1		
39	29	Carlisle United	1-1	Cairns	2258			3	4	5	6	7	10	9		11		2		8			1		
40	Apr 2	Bradford Park Avenue	0-0		5955			3	4	5	6	7	10	9		11		2		8			1		
41	9	STOCKPORT COUNTY	3-0	Spencer, Lord, Barnes	3422		2		4	5	6	7	10	9		11		3		8			1		
42	16	Exeter City	1-4	Barnes	6419		2		4	5	6	7	10	9		11		3		8			1		
43	18	ALDERSHOT	2-0	Cairns, Barnes	4301		2			5	6	7	10	9		11	4	3		8			1		
44	23	WATFORD	3-3	Spencer, Lord, Collins	4371		2			5	6	7	10	9		11	4	3		8			1		
45	26	Watford	1-2	Spencer	17774		2	3		5	6	11	10	9			4			8		7	1		
46	30	Oldham Athletic	0-1		5199		2	3		5	6	11	10	9			4			8		7	1		
				Apps		26	41	35	23	27	45	46	43	14	28	34	31	38	17	32	6	20			
				Goals			15					6	10	6	5	4	1	1	7	9	1				

F.A. Cup

Rnd	Date	Opponent	Res	Scorers	Att	Jones JA	Milburn S	Powell DM	Bodell N	Aspden JR	Bushby A	Barnes CR	Cairns R	Lord F	Anderson IL	Collins AN	Thomson B	Edwards WI	Cooper G	Spencer L	Brown J	Heyes G	Wallace J	Anchor R	Entwistle RP
R1	Nov 14	CARLISLE UNITED	2-2	Cairns, Collins	5811	1	5	3			6	7	10		9	11	4	2		8					
rep	17	Carlisle United	3-1	Brown, Cairns, Barnes	10000	1	5	3	6			7	10		9		4	2		8	11				
R2	Dec 5	BRADFORD CITY	1-1	Spencer	11828	1	5	3	4		6	7	10		9	11		2		8					
rep	9	Bradford City	1-2	Anderson	16435	1	5	3	4		6	7	10		9	11		2		8					

R1 replay a.e.t.

Lancashire Cup

Date	Opponent	Res	Scorers	Jones JA	Milburn S	Powell DM	Bodell N	Aspden JR	Bushby A	Barnes CR	Cairns R	Lord F	Anderson IL	Collins AN	Thomson B	Edwards WI	Cooper G	Spencer L	Brown J	Heyes G	Wallace J	Anchor R	Entwistle RP
Oct 28	Accrington Stanley	1-0	Bodell					6	5	7		9	10	11	4	2		8				1	3
Feb 9	Preston N.E.	1-2	Bodell	1		3	4	5	6	11	8					10	7					2	9

		P	W	D	L	F	A	W	D	L	F	A	Pts
1	Walsall	46	14	5	4	57	33	14	4	5	45	27	65
2	Notts County	46	19	1	3	66	27	7	7	9	41	42	60
3	Torquay United	46	17	3	3	56	27	9	5	9	28	31	60
4	Watford	46	17	2	4	62	28	7	7	9	30	39	57
5	Millwall	46	12	8	3	54	28	6	9	8	30	33	53
6	Northampton Town	46	13	6	4	50	22	9	3	11	35	41	53
7	Gillingham	46	17	4	2	47	21	4	6	13	27	48	52
8	Crystal Palace	46	12	6	5	61	27	7	6	10	23	37	50
9	Exeter City	46	13	7	3	50	30	6	4	13	30	40	49
10	Stockport County	46	15	6	2	35	10	4	5	14	23	44	49
11	Bradford Park Ave.	46	12	10	1	48	25	5	5	13	22	43	49
12	ROCHDALE	46	15	4	4	46	19	3	6	14	19	41	46
13	Aldershot	46	14	5	4	50	22	4	4	15	27	52	45
14	Crewe Alexandra	46	14	3	6	51	31	4	6	13	28	57	45
15	Darlington	46	11	6	6	40	30	6	3	14	23	43	43
16	Workington	46	10	8	5	41	20	4	6	13	27	40	42
17	Doncaster Rovers	46	13	3	7	40	23	3	7	13	29	53	42
18	Barrow	46	11	8	4	52	29	4	3	16	25	58	41
19	Carlisle United	46	9	6	8	28	28	6	5	12	23	38	41
20	Chester	46	10	8	5	37	26	4	4	15	22	51	40
21	Southport	46	9	7	7	30	32	1	7	15	18	60	34
22	Gateshead	46	12	3	8	37	27	0	6	17	21	59	33
23	Oldham Athletic	46	5	7	11	20	30	3	5	15	21	53	28
24	Hartlepools United	46	9	2	12	40	41	1	5	17	19	68	27

1960/61 17th in Division 4

No	Mon	Day	Opponent	Score	Scorers	Att	Jones JA	Milburn S	Powell DM	Phoenix RJ	Aspden JR	Bushby A	Barnes CR	Hepton S	Lord F	Cairns R	Brown J	Bodell N	Edwards WI	McKay J	Pollitt J	McDowell KF	Owen B	Hardman JA	Richardson JAS	Collins AN	Burgin E	Norris OP	Thompson J	Birch B	Sanders JCF
1	Aug	20	Stockport County	0-1		6617	1	2	3	4	5	6	7	8	9	10	11														
2		22	Mansfield Town	2-0	Brown, Lord	8130	1	2	3	4	5	6	7	8	9	10	11														
3		27	EXETER CITY	3-1	Hepton, Lord 2	3099	1	2	3	4	5	6	7	8	9	10	11														
4		30	MANSFIELD TOWN	1-2	Lord	5547	1	2	3	4	5	6	7	8	9	10	11														
5	Sep	3	Peterborough United	3-4	Lord 2, Cairns	14285	1	2	3	8	5	6	7		9	10	11	4													
6		6	Carlisle United	2-1	Lord, Cairns	5262	1	2		8	5	6	7		9	10	11	4	3												
7		10	SOUTHPORT	0-1		4654	1	2		8	5	6		7	9	10	11	4	3												
8		13	CARLISLE UNITED	2-1	Lord 2	4023	1	2			5	6	7	8	9	10	11	4	3												
9		17	Darlington	0-1		4641	1	2			5	6	7	8	9	10	11	4	3												
10		20	OLDHAM ATHLETIC	3-0	Ferguson (og), Cairns, Lord	7353	1	2		6	5		7	8	9	10	11	4	3												
11		24	CRYSTAL PALACE	2-2	Hepton 2	4819	1	2		6	5		7	8	9	10	11	4	3												
12		27	Oldham Athletic	2-0	Brown, Lord	6477	1	2		6	5		7	8	9	10	11	4	3												
13	Oct	1	Doncaster Rovers	2-3	Cairns 2	3798	1	2	3		6	5		7	8	9	10	11	4												
14		3	HARTLEPOOLS UNITED	4-0	Lord 3, Brown	3852	1	2	3	4	5	6	7	8	9	10	11														
15		8	CHESTER	2-0	Lord, Hepton	3826	1	2	3	4	5	6	7	8	9	10	11														
16		15	Crewe Alexandra	0-3		7256	1	2	3	4	5	6	7	8	9	10	11														
17		22	YORK CITY	0-0		4889		2		4	5	6	7	8	9	10	11		3	1											
18		29	Accrington Stanley	0-2		4243		2		4	5	6	7	8	9	10	11		3	1											
19	Nov	12	Barrow	0-1		3801		2	3	4	5	6	7	8		10				1	9	11									
20		19	GILLINGHAM	2-0	Cairns 2	3044		2	3	4	5	6	7	8		10				1		11									
21	Dec	3	NORTHAMPTON T	1-1	Lord	2173		2	3	4	5	6	7	8		10				1		11									
22		10	Aldershot	0-3		4930		2	3	4	5		7	8	9	10				1		11	6								
23		26	WREXHAM	2-1	Milburn (p), Cairns	3305	1	2		4	5		7	8	9	10		6	3						11						
24		27	Wrexham	0-2		6754		2			5		7	4	9	10	11	6	3	1						8					
25		31	Exeter City	0-1		4365		2		4	5		7	8		10		6	3	1	9				11						
26	Jan	7	Bradford Park Avenue	1-2	Cairns	7375		2		4	5		7	8	9	10	11	6	3	1											
27		21	Southport	1-0	Hepton	3135		2		4	5		7	8	9	10		6	3							11	1				
28		28	MILLWALL	4-0	Hepton, Collins, Lord, Cairns	2840		2		4	5		7	8	9	10		6	3							11	1				
29	Feb	4	DARLINGTON	1-0	Hepton	3171		2		4	5		7	8	9	10		6	3							11	1				
30		11	Crystal Palace	1-4	Cairns	17655		2		4	5	6	7	8		10			3							11	1	9			
31		18	DONCASTER ROVERS	2-1	Norris, Cairns	3173		5	3	4		6	7	8				2								11	1	9			
32		25	Chester	1-3	Pollitt	3877		2		4	5	6	7	8		10	11		3		9						1				
33	Mar	4	CREWE ALEXANDRA	3-0	Hepton, Cairns 2	4035		2		4	5		7	8		10		6	3		9					11	1				
34		11	York City	0-2		5477		2		4	5		7	8		10	11	6	3		9						1				
35		18	ACCRINGTON STANLEY	3-2	Cairns 2, Hepton	4067		2			5		7	9		10		4	3							11	1			6	8
36		25	Millwall	1-4	Milburn (p)	7126		2			5		7	9	8			4	3			11					1			6	10
37		31	Workington	0-3		2871		2		4	5		7			10	11	8	3		9						1			6	
38	Apr	1	BARROW	0-0		2785				4	5		7	9	8			2	3							11	1			6	10
39		3	WORKINGTON	2-0	Cairns, Hepton	3086			3	4	5		7	8	9			2								11	1			6	10
40		8	Gillingham	0-0		4807			3	4	5		11	8	9			2					7				1			6	10
41		10	STOCKPORT COUNTY	1-1	Hepton	3215			3	4	5		7	8	9			2								11	1			6	10
42		15	BRADFORD PARK AVE.	2-3	Hepton, Thompson (p)	5342			3		5	6	7	8	9		11									2	1		4		10
43		18	PETERBOROUGH UTD.	2-2	Cairns 2	5424				4	5		11	7	9	8			3							2	1			6	10
44		22	Northampton Town	1-5	Cairns	9535				4	5		11	7	9	8			3							2	1			6	10
45		24	Hartlepools United	0-2		3771					5		7	4	9	10			3							2	8	11	1	6	
46		29	ALDERSHOT	1-1	Barnes	2648					5		7	4	9				3						11	2		8		6	10
				Apps			17	37	17	41	43	21	45	43	31	45	24	24	30	9	6	6	1	5	4	13	20	2	12	10	
				Goals				2						1	12	17	20	3								1		1	1		

One own goal

Abandoned Game

	Mon	Day	Opponent	Score	Scorers	Att	Jones JA	Milburn S	Powell DM	Phoenix RJ	Aspden JR	Bushby A	Barnes CR	Hepton S	Lord F	Cairns R	Brown J	Bodell N	Edwards WI	McKay J	Pollitt J	McDowell KF	Owen B	Hardman JA	Richardson JAS	Collins AN	Burgin E	Norris OP	Thompson J	Birch B	Sanders JCF
	Jan	14	PETERBOROUGH UTD.	1-0	Hepton	5424		2		4	5		7	8	9	10		6	3							11	1				

		P	W	D	L	F	A	W	D	L	F	A	Pts
1	Peterborough Utd.	46	18	3	2	85	30	10	7	6	49	35	66
2	Crystal Palace	46	16	4	3	64	28	13	2	8	46	41	64
3	Northampton Town	46	16	4	3	53	25	9	6	8	37	37	60
4	Bradford Park Ave.	46	16	5	2	49	22	10	3	10	35	52	60
5	York City	46	17	3	3	50	14	4	6	13	30	46	51
6	Millwall	46	13	3	7	56	33	8	5	10	41	53	50
7	Darlington	46	11	7	5	41	24	7	6	10	37	46	49
8	Workington	46	14	3	6	38	28	7	4	12	36	48	49
9	Crewe Alexandra	46	11	4	8	40	29	9	5	9	21	38	49
10	Aldershot	46	16	4	3	55	19	2	5	16	24	50	45
11	Doncaster Rovers	46	15	0	8	52	33	4	7	12	24	45	45
12	Oldham Athletic	46	13	4	6	57	38	6	3	14	22	50	45
13	Stockport County	46	14	4	5	31	21	4	5	14	26	45	45
14	Southport	46	12	6	5	47	27	7	0	16	22	40	44
15	Gillingham	46	9	7	7	45	34	6	6	11	19	32	43
16	Wrexham	46	12	4	7	38	22	5	4	14	24	34	42
17	ROCHDALE	46	13	7	3	43	19	4	1	18	17	47	42
18	Accrington Stanley	46	12	4	7	44	32	4	4	15	30	56	40
19	Carlisle United	46	10	7	6	43	37	3	6	14	18	42	39
20	Mansfield Town	46	10	3	10	39	34	6	3	14	32	44	38
21	Exeter City	46	12	3	8	39	32	2	7	14	27	62	38
22	Barrow	46	11	5	7	33	28	3	5	15	19	51	37
23	Hartlepools United	46	10	4	9	46	40	2	4	17	25	63	32
24	Chester	46	9	7	7	38	35	2	2	19	23	69	31

(1960/61 season continued)

F.A. Cup

						Jones JA	Milburn S	Powell DM	Phoenix RJ	Aspden IR	Bushby A	Barnes CR	Hepton S	Lord F	Cairns R	Brown J	Bodell N	Edwards WJ	McKay J	Pollitt J	McDowell KF	Owen B	Hardman JA	Richardson JAS	Collins AN	Burgin E	Norris OP	Thompson J	Birch B	Sanders JCF
R1	Nov 5	Crewe Alexandra	1-1	Pollitt	8923		2	3	4	5	6	7	8	9	10					1	11									
rep	8	CREWE ALEXANDRA	1-2	Cairns	7148		2	3	4	5	6	7	8	9	10					1	11									

F.L. Cup

						Jones JA	Milburn S	Powell DM	Phoenix RJ	Aspden IR	Bushby A	Barnes CR	Hepton S	Lord F	Cairns R	Brown J	Bodell N	Edwards WJ	McKay J	Pollitt J	McDowell KF	Owen B	Hardman JA	Richardson JAS	Collins AN	Burgin E	Norris OP	Thompson J	Birch B	Sanders JCF
R1	Oct 10	SCUNTHORPE UNITED	1-1	Lord	4274	1	2	3	4	5	6	7	8	9	10	11														
rep	20	Scunthorpe United	1-0	Hepton	5727		2		4	5	6	7	8	9	10	11	3		1											
R2	25	SOUTHEND UNITED	5-2	Hepton, Lord, Cairns, Barnes 2	3591		2		4	5	6	7	8	9	10	11	3		1											
R3	Nov 21	Blackburn Rovers	1-2	Richardson	6316		2	3	4	5	6	7	9		10				1		11			8						

Lancashire Cup

						Jones JA	Milburn S	Powell DM	Phoenix RJ	Aspden IR	Bushby A	Barnes CR	Hepton S	Lord F	Cairns R	Brown J	Bodell N	Edwards WJ	McKay J	Pollitt J	McDowell KF	Owen B	Hardman JA	Richardson JAS	Collins AN	Burgin E	Norris OP	Thompson J	Birch B	Sanders JCF
	Nov 14	Manchester City	1-0	Hepton	2500				5		7	8		9			3		1		11	2	4	10						6
	Feb 21	Burnley	0-3		4416				4	5		7		10	11		3				2	6	8		1	9				

1959-60 Season
Back: Milburn, Powell, Jones, Bushby, Aspden, Thomson
Front: Barnes, Cairns, Bodell, Anderson, Collins

1961/62 — 12th in Division 4

#	Date		Opponent	Score	Scorers	Att	Burgin E	Milburn S	Winton GD	Phoenix RJ	Aspden JR	Thompson J	Wragg D	Hepton S	Bimpson JL	Cairns R	Whitaker C	Bodell N	Richardson JAS	Owen B	Hardman JA	Birch B	Whyke P	Mackay J
1	Aug	19	HARTLEPOOLS UNITED	3-1	Cairns, Whittaker, Milburn (p)	2400	1	2	3	4	5	6	7	8	9	10	11							
2		23	MILLWALL	4-1	Bimpson, Cairns, Wragg, Milburn (p)	3346	1	2	3	4	5	6	7	8	9	10	11							
3		26	Crewe Alexandra	1-2	Cairns	6731	1	2	3	4	5	6	7	8	9	10	11							
4		28	Millwall	1-1	Cairns	11672	1	2	3	4	5	6	7	8	9	10	11							
5	Sep	2	EXETER CITY	3-0	Whittaker 2, Milburn (p)	5062	1	2	3	4	5	6	7	8	9	10	11							
6		6	GILLINGHAM	3-1	Cairns 2, Hepton	5239	1	2	3	4	5	6	7	8	9	10	11							
7		9	Wrexham	0-3		11982	1	2	3	4	5	6	7	8	9	10	11							
8		16	DONCASTER ROVERS	2-3	Hepton, Bimpson	5138	1	2	3	4	5	6	7	8	9	10	11							
9		18	Darlington	0-2		7908	1	2	3		5	6	7	4	9	10	11	8						
10		23	Workington	1-2	Wragg	3659	1	2	3		5	6	7	4	9	10	11	8						
11		30	YORK CITY	3-1	Hepton, Bimpson 2	4201	1		3	4	5	6	7	8	9	10	11			2				
12	Oct	11	CHESTERFIELD	1-1	Cairns	4827	1		3	4	5		7	8	9	10	11	6		2				
13		14	Oldham Athletic	2-2	Cairns, Bimpson	17029	1		3	4	5		7	8	9	10	11			2	6			
14		18	DARLINGTON	1-3	Wragg	3702	1	2	3	4	5	6	7	8	9	10	11							
15		21	STOCKPORT COUNTY	3-3	Hepton, Cairns, Bimpson	4413	1	2	3		5	6	7	8	9	10	11					4		
16		28	Aldershot	0-3		7420	1	2	3	4	5	6	7	8	9	10	11							
17	Nov	11	Carlisle United	2-2	Hepton, Hardman	5263	1	2	3	4		6	7	8		9	11				10			5
18		18	COLCHESTER UNITED	0-1		4618	1	2	3	4		6	7	8	9	10	11							5
19	Dec	2	TRANMERE ROVERS	1-0	Cairns	2872	1	2	3			6		8	9	10	11		4				7	5
20		9	Southport	0-3		4712	1	2	3			6		8	9	10	11		4				7	5
21		16	Hartlepools United	1-3	Richardson	2387	1	2	3			6		8	9	10	11		4				7	5
22		26	Mansfield Town	1-0	Richardson	6357	1	2	3		5	6	7	8	9	10	11		4					
23	Jan	13	Exeter City	3-1	Richardson 2, Cairns	4003	1	2	3		5	6	7	8	9	10	11		4					
24		20	WREXHAM	2-1	K Barnes (og), Hepton	4208	1	2	3		5	6	7	8	9	10	11		4					
25		27	Chester	3-2	Wragg 2, Richardson	4082	1	2	3		5	6	7	8	9	10	11		4					
26		31	BRADFORD CITY	4-1	Thompson, Richardson, Cairns, Hepton	1998	1	2	3		5	6	7	8	9	10	11		4					
27	Feb	3	Doncaster Rovers	2-1	Bodell, Whittaker	4032	1	2	3		5	6	7	8	9	10	11		4					
28		10	WORKINGTON	1-3	Hepton	4016	1	2	3		5	6	7	8	9	10	11		4					
29		17	York City	1-2	Richardson	5168	1	2	3		5	6	7	8	9	10	11		4					
30	Mar	3	OLDHAM ATHLETIC	3-1	Bimpson, Cairns, Wragg	9213	1	2	3		5	6	7		9	8	11	10	4					
31		9	Stockport County	2-5	Whittaker, Wragg	4248	1	2	3		5	6	7		9	8	11	10	4					
32		13	CREWE ALEXANDRA	3-0	Wragg, Bimpson, Thompson	3809	1	2	3				7		9	10	11	8						
33		17	ALDERSHOT	1-0	Cairns	3627	1	2	3				7		9	10	11	8						
34		23	Bradford City	0-1		6652	1	2	3	4		6	7		9	10	11	8			5			
35		31	CARLISLE UNITED	1-1	Whittaker	2453	1		3	4	5	6	7		9	10	11	8		2				
36	Apr	7	Colchester United	1-1	Richardson	4616	1	2	3		5	6	7		9	10	11	8	4					
37		11	MANSFIELD TOWN	3-2	Richardson, Bimpson, Aspden	3045	1	2	3		5	6	7		9	10	11	8	4					
38		14	CHESTER	3-2	Bimpson, Whittaker, Cairns	3061	1	2	3		5	6	7		9	10	11	8	4					
39		16	Chesterfield	0-1		2932	1	2	3		5	6	7		9	10	11	8	4					
40		20	Barrow	1-0	Wragg	6732	1	2	3		5	6	7	10	9		11	8	4					
41		21	Tranmere Rovers	0-2		3720	1	2	3	4	5	6	7	8	9	10	11							
42		23	BARROW	0-2		4008	1			4	5	6	7	8	9	10	11		3	2				
43		28	SOUTHPORT	2-0	English (og), Bimpson	1940	1	2	3	8	5	6			9	10	11	4					7	
44	May	3	Gillingham	2-4	Milburn, Whittaker	2964	1	2	3	8	5	6			9	10	11	4					7	
			Apps				44	42	40	23	38	42	39	35	33	44	44	18	23	5	8	1	5	
			Goals					4			1	2	9	8	11	15	8	1	9		1			

Two own goals

Expunged Games

		Opponent	Score	Scorers	Att	Burgin E	Milburn S	Winton GD	Phoenix RJ	Aspden JR	Thompson J	Wragg D	Hepton S	Bimpson JL	Cairns R	Whitaker C	Bodell N	Richardson JAS
Oct	7	ACCRINGTON STANLEY	1-0	Whittaker	5364	1	2	3	4	5	6	7	8	9	10	11		
Feb	24	Accrington Stanley	2-0	Bimpson, Cairns	2650	1	2	3		5	6	7		9	8	11	10	4

		P	W	D	L	F	A	W	D	L	F	A	Pts
1	Millwall	44	16	3	3	47	18	7	7	8	40	44	56
2	Colchester United	44	17	4	1	78	24	6	5	11	26	47	55
3	Wrexham	44	12	6	4	56	23	10	3	9	40	33	53
4	Carlisle United	44	15	3	4	35	22	7	5	10	29	41	52
5	Bradford City	44	14	5	3	58	32	7	4	11	36	54	51
6	York City	44	17	2	3	62	19	3	8	11	22	34	50
7	Aldershot	44	16	4	2	56	20	6	1	15	25	40	49
8	Workington	44	12	6	4	40	23	7	5	10	29	47	49
9	Barrow	44	12	7	3	49	20	5	7	10	25	38	48
10	Crewe Alexandra	44	16	3	3	53	24	4	3	15	26	46	46
11	Oldham Athletic	44	12	7	3	47	26	5	5	12	30	44	46
12	ROCHDALE	44	14	3	5	47	28	5	4	13	24	43	45
13	Darlington	44	13	5	4	37	24	5	4	13	24	49	45
14	Mansfield Town	44	14	3	5	51	19	5	3	14	26	47	44
15	Tranmere Rovers	44	15	2	5	53	37	5	2	15	17	44	44
16	Stockport County	44	13	3	6	42	27	4	6	12	28	42	43
17	Southport	44	13	5	4	36	25	4	4	14	25	46	43
18	Exeter City	44	11	5	6	43	32	2	6	14	19	45	37
19	Chesterfield	44	11	3	8	43	38	3	6	13	27	49	37
20	Gillingham	44	10	6	6	48	30	3	5	14	25	64	37
21	Doncaster Rovers	44	8	5	9	34	29	3	2	17	26	56	29
22	Hartlepools United	44	6	5	11	27	35	6		14	25	66	27
23	Chester	44	5	9	8	36	37	2	3	17	18	59	26

F.A. Cup

	Date	Opponent	Score	Scorers	Att	Burgin E	Milburn S	Winton GD	Phoenix RJ	Aspden JR	Thompson J	Wragg D	Hepton S	Bimpson JL	Cairns R	Whitaker C	Bodell N	Richardson JAS	Owen B	Hardman JA	Birch B	Whyke P	Mackay J
R1	Nov 4	HALIFAX TOWN	2-0	Milburn (p), Hepton	6838	1	2	3	4	5	6	7	8		9	11				10			
R2	25	WREXHAM	1-2	Cairns	8741	1	2	3	4		6	7		9	8	10					5	11	

F.L. Cup

	Date	Opponent	Score	Scorers	Att	Burgin E	Milburn S	Winton GD	Phoenix RJ	Aspden JR	Thompson J	Wragg D	Hepton S	Bimpson JL	Cairns R	Whitaker C	Bodell N	Richardson JAS	Owen B	Hardman JA	Birch B	Whyke P	Mackay J
R1	Sep 13	Southampton	0-0		7783	1	2	3		5	6	7	8	9	10	11	4						
rep	27	SOUTHAMPTON	2-1	Bimpson 2	5449	1	2	3	4	5	6	7	8	9	10	11							
R2	Oct 4	DONCASTER ROVERS	4-0	Bimpson 2, Hepton, Cairns	5476	1	2	3	4	5	6	7	8	9	10	11							
R3	Nov 14	CHARLTON ATHLETIC	1-0	Whittaker	5298	1	2	3	4		6	7	8	9	10	11					5		
R4	Feb 7	YORK CITY	2-1	Hepton, Thompson	7312	1	2	3		5	6	7	8		9	11	4	10					
SF1	Mar 19	BLACKBURN ROVERS	3-1	Richardson 2, Cairns	9828	1	2	3	4	5	6	7		9	8	11		10					
SF2	Apr 4	Blackburn Rovers	1-2	Hepton	11700	1	2	3		5	6	7	4	9	10	11		8					
F1	Apr 26	NORWICH CITY	0-3		11123	1	2	3		5	6	7	8	9	10	11	4						
F2	May 1	Norwich City	0-1		19709	1	2	3		5	6			9	10	11	4	8				7	

Lancashire Cup

Date	Opponent	Score	Scorers	Att	Burgin E	Milburn S	Winton GD	Phoenix RJ	Aspden JR	Thompson J	Wragg D	Hepton S	Bimpson JL	Cairns R	Whitaker C	Bodell N	Richardson JAS	Owen B	Hardman JA	Birch B	Whyke P	Mackay J
Oct 25	EVERTON	1-0	Cairns	1971	1		3		5		7	4	9	10			8		2	6	11	
Apr 17	Liverpool	0-0		2600				4	5	6	7			10		3	8	2	9		11	1
May 7	LIVERPOOL	1-3	Cairns	1799	1		3	8	5	6			9	10	11	4			2		7	

Rose Bowl

Date	Opponent	Score	Scorers	Att	Burgin E	Milburn S	Winton GD	Phoenix RJ	Aspden JR	Thompson J	Wragg D	Hepton S	Bimpson JL	Cairns R	Whitaker C	Bodell N	Richardson JAS	Owen B	Hardman JA	Birch B	Whyke P	Mackay J
Aug 12	Oldham Athletic	2-1	Wragg(2)	9525	1		3	4	5	6	7	10	9	8	11			2				

1961-62 Season
Back: Milburn (Captain), Hepton, Aspden, Burgin, Thompson, Winton
Front: Wragg, Richardson, Bimpson, Cairns, Whitaker

1962-63 Season
Back: Milburn, Hepton, Martin, Burgin, Watson, Winton   Front: Wragg, Thompson, Hardman, Cairns, Whitaker

No	Date	Opponent	Score	Scorers	Att	Burgin E	Milburn S	Winton GD	Hepton S	Aspden JR	Thompson J	Wragg D	Watson D	Bimpson JL	Cairns R	Whitaker C	Martin IG	Hardman JA	Richardson JAS	Bodell N	Morton GE	Phoenix PP	Moulden A
1	Aug 18	Mansfield Town	0-1		6121	1	2	3	4	5	6	7	8	9	10	11							
2	25	WORKINGTON	3-2	Whittaker 2, Cairns	2850	1	2	3	4	5	6	7	8	9	10	11							
3	27	Stockport County	0-1		6389	1	5	3	4		6	7	8	9	10	11	2						
4	Sep 1	Exeter City	2-0	Hardman, Cairns	4320	1	5	3	4		6	7			10	11	2	9					
5	8	CHESTERFIELD	3-2	Watson 2, Cairns	3649	1	5	3	4		6	7	9		10	11	2		8				
6	12	Gillingham	1-2	Richardson	5851	1	5	3	4		6	7	9		10	11	2		8				
7	15	OLDHAM ATHLETIC	1-1	Watson	12125	1	2	3	4		6	7	9		10	11			8				
8	22	Brentford	0-1		10753	1	2	3	4	5	6	7		9	10	11			8				
9	29	YORK CITY	1-0	Bimpson	3030	1	2	3		5	6	7		9	10	11			4		8		
10	Oct 2	BARROW	6-0	Bimpson 2, Whittaker, Wragg, Morton 2	3244	1	2	3		5	6	7		9	10	11			4		8		
11	6	Hartlepools United	0-4		3850	1	2	3		5	6	7		9	10				8		4		11
12	13	DARLINGTON	1-1	Cairns	3131	1	2	3	4	5	6	7		9	10				8		11		
13	16	STOCKPORT COUNTY	1-0	Thompson (p)	3797	1	2	3	4	5	6	11	9	7							8		10
14	20	Southport	1-1	Milburn	4231	1	2	3	4	5	6	11	9	7							8		10
15	23	DONCASTER ROVERS	3-1	Morton 2, Aspden	3534	1	2	3	4	5	6	7	9								8	11	10
16	27	ALDERSHOT	1-1	Morton	2905	1	2	3	4	5	6	7	9								8	11	10
17	30	Doncaster Rovers	2-2	Moulden, Watson	9764	1	2	3	4	5	6	7	9								8	11	10
18	Nov 10	OXFORD UNITED	2-1	Cairns, Morton	2351	1	2	3	4	5	6	7	9		10						8	11	
19	17	Bradford City	2-1	Watson, Morton	4396	1	2	3	4	5		7	9		10				6		8	11	
20	Dec 1	Torquay United	1-2	Watson	4155	1	2	3	4	5	10	7	9	8					6			11	
21	15	MANSFIELD TOWN	3-1	Phoenix 2, Morton	2375	1	2	3	4	5	6	7	9		10						8	11	
22	22	Workington	0-1		2173	1	2	3	4	5	6	7	9		10						8	11	
23	29	CREWE ALEXANDRA	2-0	Phoenix, Watson	3596	1	2	3		5	6	7	9		10				4		8	11	
24	Feb 2	Oldham Athletic	1-5	Cairns	14839	1	2	3	4	5	6	7	9		10						8	11	
25	Mar 5	GILLINGHAM	1-1	Watson	2442	1	2	3	4	5	6	7	9		10						8	11	
26	9	SOUTHPORT	1-0	Bimpson	2327	1	2	3	4	5	6	7	8	9	10							11	
27	12	HARTLEPOOLS UNITED	2-1	Cairns, Milburn (p)	2857	1	2	3	4	5	6	7	9		10				8			11	
28	16	Aldershot	0-2		4693	1	2	3	4	5	6	7	9		10				8			11	
29	20	BRENTFORD	3-5	Milburn (p), Morton 2	5680	1	2	3	4	5	6	7			9				10		8	11	
30	23	NEWPORT COUNTY	3-3	Richardson 2, Morton	2829	1	2		4	5	6	7			9		3		10		8	11	
31	27	Crewe Alexandra	2-1	Phoenix, Richardson	6073	1	2		4	5	6	7			9		3		10		8	11	
32	30	Tranmere Rovers	2-3	Hepton, Cairns	8819	1	2		4	5	6	7			9		3		10		8	11	
33	Apr 6	BRADFORD CITY	2-1	Richardson, Thompson	2710	1	2		4	5	6	7			9		3		10		8	11	
34	8	Darlington	0-3		3129	1		3	4	5	6	7			9		2		10		8	11	
35	13	Oxford United	0-0		6085	1	2		4	5	6	7			9		3		10		8	11	
36	15	Chester	0-1		4979	1	2	3	4	5	6	7			9				10		8	11	
37	16	CHESTER	0-0		2926	1		3		5	6	7	4	9	10		2				8	11	
38	20	TORQUAY UNITED	3-0	Cairns, Wragg 2	1785	1		3		5	6	7	4	9	10		2				8	11	
39	22	Barrow	1-1	Cairns	3928	1		3		5	6	7	4	9	10		2				11	8	
40	27	Lincoln City	0-3		2281	1		3		6	5	7	4	9	10		2				8	11	
41	May 4	York City	0-1		4442	1		3		6	5	7	4	9	10		2				11	8	
42	7	LINCOLN CITY	1-0	Morton	2101	1	2	3		5	6	7	4		9				10		8	11	
43	11	EXETER CITY	3-0	Morton, Cairns 2	1403	1	2	3		5	6	7	4		9				10		8	11	
44	17	Chesterfield	3-1	Cairns 2, Richardson	4412	1	2	3		6	5	7	4		9				10		8	11	
45	20	Newport County	1-1	Morton	2387	1	2	3		6	5	7	4		9				10		8	11	
46	23	TRANMERE ROVERS	2-0	Wragg, Cairns	2385	1	2	3		6	5	7	4		9				10		8	11	
		Apps				46	40	41	35	42	40	42	33	21	40	10	16	6	24	3	30	32	5
		Goals					3		1	1	2	4	8	5	14	3		1	6		14	4	1

F.A. Cup

	Date	Opponent	Score	Scorers	Att	Burgin E	Milburn S	Winton GD	Hepton S	Aspden JR	Thompson J	Wragg D	Watson D	Bimpson JL	Cairns R	Whitaker C	Martin IG	Hardman JA	Richardson JAS	Bodell N	Morton GE	Phoenix PP	Moulden A
R1	Nov 3	York City	0-0		4663	1	2	3	4	5	6	7	9								8	11	10
rep	6	YORK CITY	1-2	Phoenix	6225	1	2	3	4	5	6	7	9								8	11	10

F.L. Cup

	Date	Opponent	Score	Scorers	Att	Burgin E	Milburn S	Winton GD	Hepton S	Aspden JR	Thompson J	Wragg D	Watson D	Bimpson JL	Cairns R	Whitaker C	Martin IG	Hardman JA	Richardson JAS	Bodell N	Morton GE	Phoenix PP	Moulden A
R1	Sep 5	Southport	0-0		3555	1	5	3	4		6	7	8		10	11	2	9					
rep	18	SOUTHPORT	1-2	Watson	3431	1	2	3	10	5	6	7	9			11			4		8		

Replay a.e.t.

Lancashire Cup

	Date	Opponent	Score	Scorers	Att	Burgin E	Milburn S	Winton GD	Hepton S	Aspden JR	Thompson J	Wragg D	Watson D	Bimpson JL	Cairns R	Whitaker C	Martin IG	Hardman JA	Richardson JAS	Bodell N	Morton GE	Phoenix PP	Moulden A
	Sep 26	Blackpool	0-3			1		3	4	5	6	7		9	10		2				8	11	

Rose Bowl

	Date	Opponent	Score	Scorers	Att	Burgin E	Milburn S	Winton GD	Hepton S	Aspden JR	Thompson J	Wragg D	Watson D	Bimpson JL	Cairns R	Whitaker C	Martin IG	Hardman JA	Richardson JAS	Bodell N	Morton GE	Phoenix PP	Moulden A
	Aug 11	OLDHAM A.	2-3	Whitaker, Cairns	6146	1	2	3	8		6	7	S	9	10	11	S	5			S		4

S - indicates second-half subs. for players underlined.

		P	W	D	L	F	A	W	D	L	F	A	Pts
1	Brentford	46	18	2	3	59	31	9	6	8	39	33	62
2	Oldham Athletic	46	18	4	1	65	23	6	7	10	30	37	59
3	Crewe Alexandra	46	15	4	4	50	21	9	7	7	36	37	59
4	Mansfield Town	46	16	4	3	61	20	8	5	10	47	49	57
5	Gillingham	46	17	3	3	49	23	5	10	8	22	26	57
6	Torquay United	46	14	8	1	45	20	6	8	9	30	36	56
7	ROCHDALE	46	16	6	1	48	21	4	5	14	19	38	51
8	Tranmere Rovers	46	15	3	5	57	25	5	7	11	24	42	50
9	Barrow	46	14	7	2	52	26	5	5	13	30	54	50
10	Workington	46	13	4	6	42	20	4	9	10	34	48	47
11	Aldershot	46	9	9	5	42	32	6	8	9	31	37	47
12	Darlington	46	13	3	7	44	33	6	3	14	28	54	44
13	Southport	46	11	9	3	47	35	4	5	14	25	71	44
14	York City	46	12	6	5	42	25	4	5	14	25	37	43
15	Chesterfield	46	7	10	6	43	29	6	6	11	27	35	42
16	Doncaster Rovers	46	9	10	4	36	26	5	4	14	28	51	42
17	Exeter City	46	9	6	8	27	32	7	4	12	30	45	42
18	Oxford United	46	10	10	3	44	27	3	5	15	26	44	41
19	Stockport County	46	9	7	7	34	29	6	4	13	22	41	41
20	Newport County	46	11	6	6	44	29	3	5	15	32	61	39
21	Chester	46	11	5	7	31	23	4	4	15	20	43	39
22	Lincoln City	46	11	1	11	48	46	2	8	13	20	43	35
23	Bradford City	46	8	5	10	37	40	3	5	15	27	65	32
24	Hartlepools United	46	5	7	11	33	39	2	4	17	23	65	25

1963/64 20th in Division 4

#		Date	Opponent	Result	Scorers	Att	Burgin E	Milburn S	Winton GD	Hepton S	Aspden JR	Thompson J	Wragg D	Morton GE	Cairns R	Richardson JAS	Storf DA	Phoenix PP	Kerry DT	Watson D	Wells WD	Jones SC	Martin IG	Taylor B	MacKenzie DA	Hardman JA
1	Aug	24	York City	3-0	Cairns, Richardson, Morton	5446	1	2	3	4	5	6	7	8	9	10	11									
2		28	BRIGHTON & HOVE ALB	1-1	Thompson	5662	1	2	3	4	5	6	7	8	9	10	11									
3		31	BARROW	1-3	Richardson	4216	1	2	3	4	5	6	7	8	9	10	11									
4	Sep	7	Torquay United	0-1		4787	1	2	3	4	5	6		8	9	10	11	7								
5		10	Brighton & Hove Albion	1-3	Kerry	7181	1	2	3	4	5	6		10		8	11	7	9							
6		14	Oxford United	1-1	Kerry	6761	1	2	3	9	5	6		10			11	7	8	4						
7		21	WORKINGTON	5-0	Richardson 2, Storf, Morton, Kerry	3366	1	2	3	4	5	6	7	10		8	11		9							
8		28	Newport County	1-1	Thompson	4878	1	2	3	4	5	6	7	8		10	11		9							
9	Oct	2	Chester	0-2		5220	1	2	3	4	5	6	7	10		8	11		9							
10		5	STOCKPORT COUNTY	1-0	Richardson	3995	1	2	3	4	5	6		10	9	8	11	7								
11		12	TRANMERE ROVERS	1-1	Kerry	3731	1	2	3	4	5	6		10	9	8	11		7							
12		16	CHESTERFIELD	0-1		2698	1	2	3	6	5		7	10		8	11			9	4					
13		19	Darlington	2-3	Storf, Morton	3439	1	2			4	5		10	7	8	11			9		3				
14		23	Bradford Park Avenue	2-2	Richardson, Morton	5484	1	5	3	4		6		10	7	8	11			9		2				
15		26	Hartlepools United	2-0	Morton, Storf	2764	1	5	3			6		10	7	8	11			9	4	2				
16		30	BRADFORD PARK AVE.	0-0		2490	1	5	3	4		6		10	7	8	11			9		2				
17	Nov	2	Exeter City	1-0	Richardson	6249	1	5	3	4		6		10	7	8	11			9		2				
18		9	SOUTHPORT	4-0	Watson, Cairns 2, Richardson	2690	1	5	3	4		6		10	7	8	11			9		2				
19		23	LINCOLN CITY	2-2	Richardson, Cairns	2407	1	5	3	4		6		10	7	8	11			9		2				
20		30	Bradford City	0-2		4595	1	5	3	4		6		10	7	8	11			9		2				
21	Dec	14	YORK CITY	2-0	McKenzie, Watson	2203	1	2	3	4	5	6		8		10	11			9					7	
22		20	Barrow	2-1	Arrowsmith (og), Richardson	1978	1	2	3	4	5	6		8		10	11			9					7	
23		28	HALIFAX TOWN	4-1	McKenzie, Watson 2, Morton	3678	1	2	3	4	5	6		8		10	11			9					7	
24	Jan	4	Gillingham	0-0		8099	1	2	3	4	5	6		8		10	11			9					7	
25		11	TORQUAY UNITED	1-2	Storf	3080	1	2	3	4	5	6		8		10	11			9					7	
26		18	OXFORD UNITED	0-0		2436	1	2	3	4	5	6		8	10		11			9					7	
27	Feb	1	Workington	0-3		2832	1	2	3	4	5	6		8		10	11			9					7	
28		8	NEWPORT COUNTY	0-1		2444	1	2	3	9	5	6	7	8	10		11									4
29		15	Stockport County	0-1		3487	1	2	3		5	6	7	8	9	10	11									4
30		21	Tranmere Rovers	1-2	McKenzie	6560	1	2	3		5	6	7				11			8				9	10	4
31		25	ALDERSHOT	2-2	Wragg, Watson	2329	1	2	3		5	6	7				11			8				9		4
32		29	DARLINGTON	2-1	McKenzie, Thompson	2355	1	2	3		5	6	7	8			11			9				4	10	
33	Mar	4	CHESTER	1-0	Wragg	2322	1	2	3		5	6	7	8			11			9				4	10	
34		7	Hartlepools United	1-1	Milburn	2836	1	2	3		5	6	7	8			11			9				4	10	
35		11	Halifax Town	2-3	Watson, Morton	3911	1	2	3		5	6	7	8			11			9				4	10	
36		14	EXETER CITY	1-3	Morton	2113	1	2			5	6	7	8		9	11						3	4	10	
37		20	Southport	1-2	Thompson	2206	1	2			9	5	6	7	8	10	11						3	4		
38		24	Doncaster Rovers	0-2		5160		2			9	5	6	7	8	10	11					1	3	4		
39		28	CARLISLE UNITED	1-1	Morton	2736		2			9	5	6	7	8	10	11					1	3	4		
40		31	DONCASTER ROVERS	2-2	Richardson, Martin	2181		2			9	5	6		8	10	11					1	3	4	7	
41	Apr	4	Lincoln City	0-2		3643					9	5	6		10	8	11					1	3	4	7	2
42		6	Chesterfield	1-1	Cairns	4277			3	2	5	6	7	10	9		11			8			1	4		
43		11	BRADFORD CITY	1-2	Watson	4824		2	3			5	6	7		9	11			8			1	4	10	
44		18	Aldershot	1-1	Cairns	3742	1	2			3	5	6		7	9	10			11				8	4	
45		21	Carlisle United	0-1		11556	1	2	3	4	5	6	7			10			11	7	9			8		
46		25	GILLINGHAM	2-1	McKenzie, Cairns (p)	2737	1	2	3	4	5	6	7		9					10				8	11	
				Apps			40	44	38	36	39	45	22	40	23	33	45	4	12	25	8	6	8	15	18	5
				Goals				1				4	2	9	7	11	4		4	7			1		5	

One own goal

F.A. Cup

	Date	Opponent	Result	Scorers	Att	Burgin E	Milburn S	Winton GD	Hepton S	Aspden JR	Thompson J	Wragg D	Morton GE	Cairns R	Richardson JAS	Storf DA	Phoenix PP	Kerry DT	Watson D	Wells WD	Jones SC
R1	Nov 18	CHORLEY	2-1	Watson, Richardson	5381	1	5	3	4		6		10	7	8	11			9		2
R2	Dec 7	Barnsley	1-3	Richardson	9431	1	2	3	4	5	6		8	7	10	11			9		

F.L. Cup

	Date	Opponent	Result	Scorers	Att	Burgin E	Milburn S	Winton GD	Hepton S	Aspden JR	Thompson J	Wragg D	Morton GE	Cairns R	Richardson JAS	Storf DA	Phoenix PP	Kerry DT	Watson D
R1	Sep 4	CHESTER	1-1	Morton	2919	1	2	3	4	5	6		8	9	10	11	7		
rep	18	Chester	5-2	Thompson, Morton 2, Kerry, Storf	5083	1	2	3	4	5	6	7	8		10	11		9	
R2	25	Halifax Town	2-4	Richardson, Morton	4774	1	2	3	4	5	6	7	8		10	11		9	

Lancashire Cup

Date	Opponent	Result		Att	Hepton S	Thompson J	Wragg D	Morton GE	Watson D	Wells WD	Jones SC	Martin IG	Taylor B	MacKenzie DA	Hardman JA
Nov 27	Chester	0-1		2096	4	6	7	10	8	9	3	1	2	5	11

Rose Bowl

Date	Opponent	Result	Scorers	Att	Burgin E	Milburn S	Winton GD	Hepton S	Aspden JR	Thompson J	Wragg D	Morton GE	Cairns R	Richardson JAS	Storf DA
Aug 17	Oldham Athletic	5-3	Morton(2), Richardson(2), Cairns	8697	1	2	3	4	5	6	7	8	9	10	11

		P	W	D	L	F	A	W	D	L	F	A	Pts
1	Gillingham	46	16	7	0	37	10	7	7	9	22	20	60
2	Carlisle United	46	17	3	3	70	20	8	7	8	43	38	60
3	Workington	46	15	6	2	46	19	9	5	9	30	33	59
4	Exeter City	46	12	9	2	39	14	8	9	6	23	23	58
5	Bradford City	46	15	3	5	45	24	10	3	10	31	38	56
6	Torquay United	46	16	6	1	60	20	4	5	14	20	34	51
7	Tranmere Rovers	46	12	4	7	46	30	8	7	8	39	43	51
8	Brighton & Hove A.	46	13	3	7	45	22	6	9	8	26	30	50
9	Aldershot	46	15	3	5	58	28	4	7	12	25	50	48
10	Halifax Town	46	14	4	5	47	28	3	10	10	30	49	48
11	Lincoln City	46	15	2	6	49	31	4	7	12	18	44	47
12	Chester	46	17	3	3	47	18	2	5	16	18	42	46
13	Bradford Park Ave.	46	13	5	5	50	34	5	4	14	25	47	45
14	Doncaster Rovers	46	11	8	4	46	23	4	4	15	24	52	42
15	Newport County	46	12	3	8	35	24	5	5	13	29	49	42
16	Chesterfield	46	8	9	6	29	27	7	3	13	28	44	42
17	Stockport County	46	12	7	4	32	19	3	5	15	18	49	42
18	Oxford United	46	10	7	6	37	27	4	6	13	22	36	41
19	Darlington	46	8	9	6	40	37	6	3	14	26	56	40
20	ROCHDALE	46	9	8	6	36	24	3	10	13	20	35	39
21	Southport	46	12	6	5	42	29	3	3	17	21	59	39
22	York City	46	9	3	11	29	26	5	4	14	23	40	35
23	Hartlepools United	46	8	7	8	30	36	4	2	17	24	57	33
24	Barrow	46	4	10	9	30	36	2	8	13	21	57	30

1964/65 6th in Division 4

#	Date		Opponent	Score	Scorers	Att.	Burgin E	Ridge R	Calloway LJ	Cunliffe IG	Aspden JR	Thompson J	Richardson JAS	Morton GE	Turley JW	Jenkins R	Storf DA	Taylor B	Birch B(2)	MacKenzie DA	Milburn S	Hardman IA	Lister HF	Hardman B
1	Aug	22	York City	1-2	Richardson	4348	1	2	3	4	5	6	7	8	9	10	11							
2		26	STOCKPORT COUNTY	4-0	Jenkins 2, Morton 2	4458	1	2	3	4	5	6	7	8	9	10	11							
3		29	LINCOLN CITY	2-0	Morton, Richardson	4306	1	2	3	4	5	6	7	8	9	10	11							
4	Sep	5	Brighton & Hove Albion	0-3		14023	1	2	3	4	5	6	7	8	9	10	11							
5		7	TORQUAY UNITED	1-0	Morton	4641	1	2	3	4	5		10	8		9	11	6	7					
6		12	OXFORD UNITED	3-3	Jenkins, Beavon (og), Morton	4473	1	2	3	4	5	6	10	8		9	11		7					
7		16	Torquay United	1-2	Turley	5238	1	2	3		5	6	7	8	9	10	11	4						
8		19	Barrow	2-2	Morton, Jenkins	3159	1	2	3	4	5	6	7	8	9	10	11							
9		26	HARTLEPOOLS UNITED	3-0	Jenkins 2, Morton	3736	1	2	3	4	5	6	7	8	9	10	11							
10		30	BRADFORD CITY	3-1	Turley, Jenkins, Storf	4623	1	2	3	4	5	6	7	8	9	10	11							
11	Oct	3	Wrexham	3-2	Jenkins, Turley 2	7184	1	2	3	4	5	6	7	8	9	10	11							
12		7	Bradford City	2-0	Jenkins 2	3395	1	2	3	4	5	6	7	8	9	10	11							
13		10	DARLINGTON	1-1	Morton	5007	1	2	3	4	5	6	7	8	9	10	11							
14		14	CHESTER	2-1	Morton, Jenkins	4845	1	2	3	4	5	6		8	9	10		7				11		
15		17	Crewe Alexandra	1-1	Jenkins	3619	1	2	3	4	5	6	7	8	9	10						11		
16		24	NEWPORT COUNTY	2-0	Storf (p), Birch	4283	1	2	3	4	5	6		8	9	10	11		7					
17		26	Southport	0-1		3642	1	2	3	4	5	6		8	9	10	11		7					
18		31	Halifax Town	2-1	McKenzie, Jenkins	4089	1		3	4	5	6		8		9			7	11	2			
19	Nov	7	NOTTS COUNTY	1-1	Jenkins	4804	1	3		4	5	6		8		9			7	11	2			
20		21	DONCASTER ROVERS	2-1	Storf (p), Jenkins	4752	1		3	4	5	6	7			10	11		8		2		9	
21		28	Aldershot	2-1	Thompson, Jenkins	5412	1		3	4	5	6				10	11	8	7		2		9	
22	Dec	12	YORK CITY	1-2	Turley	3051	1		3	4	5	6	8		9	10	11		7		2			
23		18	Lincoln City	1-1	Jenkins	3177	1		3	4	5	6		8	9	10			7	11	2			
24		26	Tranmere Rovers	1-4	Morton	13497	1		3	4	5	6		8	9	10			7	11	2			
25		28	TRANMERE ROVERS	0-1		5008	1	2	3	4	5	6	7	8	9	10				11				
26	Jan	9	BRADFORD PARK AVE.	4-3	Jenkins 2, Thompson, McCalman (og)	4377	1	2	3	4	5	6	7			10		8		11	9			
27		16	Oxford United	2-2	Taylor, Richardson	8681	1	2	3	4	5	6	7			10		8		11	9			
28		23	BARROW	3-0	Milburn, Richardson, Taylor	3812	1	2	3		5	6	7			10		8		11	9	4		
29		30	Chesterfield	1-1	Jenkins	5091	1	2	3		5	6	7			10				11		4	9	
30	Feb	6	Hartlepools United	1-1	Birch	5049	1	3	8		5	6				10			7	11	2	4	9	
31		13	WREXHAM	2-1	Thompson, Lister	3728	1	2	3		5	6		8		10			7	11		4	9	
32		15	Stockport County	2-1	Morton, Thompson	8645	1	2	3		5	6	7	8		10			4	11			9	
33		20	Darlington	0-2		2606	1	2	3		5	6	7	8		10			4	11			9	
34		27	CREWE ALEXANDRA	1-0	Jenkins	4442	1	2	3	4	5	6		8		10			7	11			9	
35	Mar	10	Chester	1-0	Jenkins	8550	1	2	3	4	5	6		8		10			7	11			9	
36		13	HALIFAX TOWN	3-0	McKenzie, Morton, Lister	4829	1	2	3	4	5	6		8		10			7	11			9	
37		20	Notts County	0-0		3219	1	2	3	4	5	6		8		10			7	11			9	
38		22	BRIGHTON & HOVE ALB	2-2	Thompson (p), Morton	7005	1	2	3	4	5	6		8		10			7	11			9	
39		26	CHESTERFIELD	1-2	Morton	6383	1	2	3	4	5	6		8		10			7	11			9	
40		29	Newport County	3-2	Birch, Jenkins, Lister	2761	1	2	3	4	5	6		8	7	10			11				9	
41	Apr	3	Doncaster Rovers	2-2	Jenkins, Birch	7842	1	2	3	4	5	6		8		10			11		5		9	
42		10	ALDERSHOT	3-1	Jenkins, Morton 2	4139	1	2	3	4	5	6	11	8		10			7				9	
43		16	Millwall	0-0		15389	1	2	3	4	5	6	9	8		10			7	11				
44		17	Bradford Park Avenue	0-0		10636	1	2	3		5	6	11	8		10		4	7		9			
45		21	MILLWALL	0-2		8031	1	2	3		5	6		8		10		4	11		9		7	
46		24	SOUTHPORT	2-0	Richardson, Morton	2882	1	2	3		5	6	7	8		10		4		11				
					Apps		46	40	45	36	45	45	31	35	22	46	18	11	27	23	14	6	16	
					Goals							5	5	17	5	25	3	2	4	2	1		3	

Two own goals

Abandoned

Date		Opponent	Score		Att.																		
Dec	5	TRANMERE ROVERS	0-1		5008	1		3	4	5	6		8	9	10	11		7		2			

F.A. Cup

	Date		Opponent	Score		Att.																		
R1	Nov	14	Workington	0-2		5376	1		3	4	5	6			9	10	11		7		2	8		

F.L. Cup

	Date		Opponent	Score	Scorers	Att.																		
R1	Sep	2	Stockport County	3-1	Turley, Richardson, Storf	3450	1	2	3	4	5	6	7	8	9	10	11							
R2		23	Rotherham United	0-2		8934	1	2	3	4	5	6	7	8		10	11			9				

Lancashire Cup

Date		Opponent	Score	Scorers	Att.																		
Nov	3	Bury	1-2	Richardson	2608	1		3		4	5	6		8		10		7	2	9			11

Rose Bowl

Date		Opponent	Score	Scorers	Att.																		
Aug	14	OLDHAM ATHLETIC	1-2	Turley	5160	1	2	3	4	5	6	7	8	9	10				11				

	Team	P	W	D	L	F	A	W	D	L	F	A	Pts
1	Brighton & Hove A.	46	18	5	0	68	20	8	6	9	34	37	63
2	Millwall	46	13	10	0	45	15	10	6	7	33	30	62
3	York City	46	20	1	2	63	21	8	5	10	28	35	62
4	Oxford United	46	18	4	1	54	13	5	11	7	33	31	61
5	Tranmere Rovers	46	20	2	1	72	20	7	4	12	27	36	60
6	ROCHDALE	46	15	4	4	46	22	7	10	6	28	31	58
7	Bradford Park Ave.	46	14	8	1	52	22	6	9	8	34	40	57
8	Chester	46	19	1	3	75	26	6	5	12	44	55	56
9	Doncaster Rovers	46	13	6	4	46	25	7	5	11	38	47	51
10	Crewe Alexandra	46	11	8	4	55	34	7	5	11	35	47	49
11	Torquay United	46	11	5	7	41	33	10	2	11	29	37	49
12	Chesterfield	46	13	5	5	36	22	7	3	13	22	48	48
13	Notts County	46	12	7	4	43	23	3	7	13	18	50	44
14	Wrexham	46	12	5	6	59	37	5	4	14	25	55	43
15	Hartlepools United	46	11	10	2	44	28	4	3	16	17	57	43
16	Newport County	46	14	5	4	54	26	3	3	17	31	55	42
17	Darlington	46	14	2	7	52	30	4	4	15	32	57	42
18	Aldershot	46	14	3	6	46	25	1	4	18	18	59	37
19	Bradford City	46	9	2	12	37	36	3	6	14	33	52	32
20	Southport	46	9	5	9	35	45	3	7	13	23	44	32
21	Barrow	46	9	4	10	30	38	3	2	18	29	67	30
22	Lincoln City	46	8	4	11	35	33	3	2	18	23	66	28
23	Halifax Town	46	8	4	10	41	37	2	3	19	17	66	28
24	Stockport County	46	8	4	11	30	34	2	3	18	14	53	27

1965/66 — 21st in Division 4

#		Date	Opponent	Res	Scorers	Att	Jones SC	Ridge R	Calloway LJ	Birch B(2)	Aspden JR	Thompson J	Bannister N	Morton GE	Stephenson GR	Jenkins R	Storf DA	Lister HF	Ratcliffe JB	Hardman JA	Sievwright GE	Taylor B	Burgin E	McQueen ID	Heath J	Connor KH	Handley B	Crossley P
1	Aug	21	ALDERSHOT	1-0	Storf	3955	1	2	3	4	5	6	7	8	9	10	11											
2		24	Bradford Park Avenue	2-1	Stephenson, Bannister	5486	1	2	3	4	5	6	7	8	9	10	11											
3		28	Newport County	1-1	Thompson	3673	1	2	3	4	5	6	7	8	9	10	11											
4	Sep	4	TORQUAY UNITED	2-3	Lister, Jenkins	3720	1	2	3	4		6	12	8	7		10	9	11	5								
5		11	Chesterfield	1-4	Morton	4887	1	2	3	4		6		8	7		10	9	11			5						
6		14	BRADFORD PARK AVE.	2-3	Jenkins, Morton	4806	1	2	3		5	6	7	8			10	9	11			4						
7		18	Colchester United	0-2		4919	1	2	3	11	5	6	7	8			10	9				4						
8		24	LUTON TOWN	1-2	Morton	3692		2	3	7	5	6	11	8			10	9				4	12	1				
9	Oct	2	Barrow	2-0	Morton, Jenkins	4763		2	3	4	5	6		8		10	11	9	7					1				
10		5	SOUTHPORT	3-0	Lister, Morton, Storf	4188		2	3	4	5	6		8		10	11	9	7					1				
11		8	BRADFORD CITY	5-1	Lister 2, Morton 2, Ratcliffe	4027		2	3	4	5	6		8		10	11	9	7					1				
12		16	Crewe Alexandra	1-3	Lister	4019		2	3	4	5	6		8		10	11	9	7					1				
13		22	PORT VALE	1-0	Morton	4195		2	3		5	6		8		10	11	9	7			4		1				
14		29	Halifax Town	1-4	Stephenson	2786		2	3		5	6		8	9	10	11		7			4		1				
15	Nov	5	CHESTER	3-0	Jenkins 3	3122		2	3	4	5		7	12	8	10		9	11			6		1				
16		20	LINCOLN CITY	0-1		2547		2	3	4	5		7	8		10		9	11			6		1				
17		22	Southport	0-4		2326		2	3	4		6		8		10		7	11			9	5	1				
18	Dec	10	Tranmere Rovers	2-6	Birch, Lister	6463		2	3	4	5		11	8		10		7				6		1	9			
19		18	CREWE ALEXANDRA	2-1	Taylor, Jenkins	1486	1	2	3		5		11	8	7	10					4	6			9			
20		27	WREXHAM	6-0	Jenkins 2, Morton, Bannister, McQueen, Stephenson	4187	1	2	3		5		11	8	7	10					4	6			9			
21	Jan	1	Bradford City	1-2	McQueen	4807	1	2	3		5		11	8	7	10					4	6			9			
22		8	NOTTS COUNTY	0-2		2677	1	2	3		5		7	8		10	11				4	6			9			
23		15	Port Vale	1-2	Taylor	4262	1	2	3		5		11	8	7	10					4	6			9			
24		29	Aldershot	3-2	Calloway, Taylor 2	2967	1	3	9	4	5			8		10	11	7				2	6					
25	Feb	5	NEWPORT COUNTY	2-1	Storf, Morton	2167	1	3	9	4	5			8	10		11	7				2	6					
26		12	DONCASTER ROVERS	0-1		2542	1	3	9	4	5			8	10		11	7				2	6					
27		19	Torquay United	0-4		5504	1	3	9	4	5			8	10		11	7				2	6					
28		26	CHESTERFIELD	1-1	Jenkins	2292		3	7	5				8	10	11					4	6			1	2	9	
29		28	Darlington	1-3	Stephenson	8633		3		4			7	8	10		11					6	5		1	2	9	
30	Mar	4	Doncaster Rovers	0-2		12255		3	2	4			7	8	10							6	5		1			
31		8	Barnsley	0-5		3426		3	2	4	5		7	8	10							9	6		1			
32		11	COLCHESTER UNITED	0-1		1780		3		4			8	10	9	7					6	5			1	2		
33		19	Luton Town	1-4	Storf	7381		3	2	4			7	10		11	9					6	5	8	1	12		
34		25	BARROW	4-0	Jenkins, Lister, Stephenson 2	1743	1	2	3	4	5		7	8	10	11	9					6						
35		30	Wrexham	2-2	Jenkins, Lister	5390	1	2	3	4	5		7	8	10	11	9				12	6						
36	Apr	2	Chester	2-1	Stephenson 2	6361	1	2	3		5		11	8	7	10					4	6						
37		9	STOCKPORT COUNTY	4-0	Lister, Calloway, Stephenson, Storf	3281	1	2	3		5		7	8	10	11	9				4	6						
38		11	BARNSLEY	2-1	Jenkins (p), Lister	3316	1	2	3		5		7	8	10	11	9				4	6						
39		16	Lincoln City	0-2		2884	1	2	3	4			7	8	10	11					6	5		9				
40		19	HALIFAX TOWN	0-1		2186	1	2	3	9	5		7	8	10	11					4	6						
41		22	DARLINGTON	1-2	Morton	2427	1	2	3	4	5		7	8	10	11	9					6						
42		26	HARTLEPOOLS UNITED	3-1	Stephenson 2, Lister	1964	1	2	3		5		7	8	10	11	9				6	4						
43		29	Stockport County	1-3	Sievwright	5503	1	2	3		5	12	7	8	10	11	9				6	4						
44	May	6	TRANMERE ROVERS	3-5	King (oq), Stephenson, Birch	2085	1	2	3	4				8	10	9	11					6	5					7
45		16	Hartlepools United	0-0		5779	1	2	3	4	5			8			10	11				6		9				7
46		21	Notts County	3-3	McQueen, Storf, Stephenson	3488	1	2	3	4	5			8		10	11				6			9			12	7
					Apps		29	45	44	34	37	15	19	42	34	39	32	29	12	1	32	32	11	9	6	5	3	3
					Goals				2	2		1	2	11	13	13	6	11		1	1	1	4	3				

One own goal

F.A. Cup

		Date	Opponent	Res	Scorers	Att	Jones SC	Ridge R	Calloway LJ	Birch B	Aspden JR	Thompson J	Bannister N	Morton GE	Stephenson GR	Jenkins R	Storf DA	Lister HF	Ratcliffe JB	Hardman JA	Sievwright GE	Taylor B	Burgin E	McQueen ID
R1	Nov	13	Fleetwood	2-2	Lister, Sievwright	6150		2	3	4	5		7	8		10		9	11			6		1
rep		17	FLEETWOOD	5-0	Jenkins 3, Calloway, Lister	5084		2	3	4	5	9		8		10		7	11			6		1
R2	Dec	8	ALTRINCHAM	1-3	Jenkins	8367		2	3	8		6				10	11	9	7			4	5	1

F.L. Cup

		Date	Opponent	Res	Scorers	Att	Jones SC	Ridge R	Calloway LJ	Birch B	Aspden JR	Thompson J	Bannister N	Morton GE	Stephenson GR	Jenkins R	Storf DA	Lister HF	Ratcliffe JB	Hardman JA	Sievwright GE	Taylor B	Burgin E	McQueen ID
R1	Sep	1	Barrow	1-1	Stephenson	4814	1	2	3	4	5	6		8	7	10		9	11					
rep		8	BARROW	3-1	Lister, Jenkins 2	2090	1	2	3			6		8	7	10		9	11			4	5	
R2		22	Southampton	0-3		12188		2	3	11	5	6	7	8		10		9				4		1

Lancashire Cup

		Date	Opponent	Res	Scorers	Att	Jones SC	Ridge R	Calloway LJ	Birch B	Aspden JR	Thompson J	Bannister N	Morton GE	Stephenson GR	Jenkins R	Storf DA	Lister HF	Ratcliffe JB	Hardman JA	Sievwright GE	Taylor B	Burgin E	McQueen ID	Heath J	Connor KH	Handley B
R1	Nov	2	MANCHESTER CITY	1-0	Ratcliffe	1115		2	3	4	5		7	8	10	9			11			6		1			
R2	Feb	23	Chester	3-1	Taylor, Jenkins, Lister	2104			3	7	5			8	10	11	9				4	6				1	2
SF	Apr	14	Burnley	0-2		1338			3	4	5		7	8		11		10				6			9	1	2

Division Four Final Table

		P	W	D	L	F	A	W	D	L	F	A	Pts
1	Doncaster Rovers	46	15	6	2	49	21	9	5	9	36	33	59
2	Darlington	46	16	3	4	41	17	9	6	8	31	36	59
3	Torquay United	46	17	2	4	43	20	7	8	8	29	29	58
4	Colchester United	46	13	7	3	45	21	10	3	10	25	26	56
5	Tranmere Rovers	46	15	1	7	56	32	9	7	7	37	34	56
6	Luton Town	46	19	2	2	65	27	5	6	12	25	43	56
7	Chester	46	15	5	3	52	27	5	7	11	27	43	52
8	Notts County	46	9	8	6	32	25	10	4	9	29	28	50
9	Newport County	46	14	6	3	46	24	4	6	13	29	51	48
10	Southport	46	15	6	2	47	20	3	6	14	21	49	48
11	Bradford Park Ave.	46	14	2	7	59	31	7	3	13	43	61	47
12	Barrow	46	8	3	8	48	31	4	7	12	24	45	47
13	Stockport County	46	12	4	7	42	29	6	2	15	29	41	42
14	Crewe Alexandra	46	12	4	7	42	23	4	5	14	19	40	41
15	Halifax Town	46	11	6	6	46	31	4	5	14	21	44	41
16	Barnsley	46	11	6	6	43	24	4	4	15	31	54	40
17	Aldershot	46	12	6	5	47	27	3	4	16	28	57	40
18	Hartlepools United	46	13	4	6	44	22	4	4	16	19	53	40
19	Port Vale	46	12	7	4	38	18	3	2	18	10	41	39
20	Chesterfield	46	8	9	6	37	35	5	4	14	25	43	39
21	ROCHDALE	46	12	1	10	46	27	4	4	15	25	60	37
22	Lincoln City	46	9	7	7	37	29	4	4	15	20	53	37
23	Bradford City	46	10	5	8	37	34	2	8	13	26	60	37
24	Wrexham	46	10	4	9	43	43	3	5	15	29	61	35

Rose Bowl

	Jones SC	Ridge R	Calloway LJ	Birch B(2)	Aspden JR	Thompson J	Bannister N	Morton GE	Stephenson GR	Jenkins R	Storf DA	Lister HF	Ratcliffe JB	Hardman JA	Sievwright GE	Taylor B	Burgin E	McQueen ID	Heath J	Connor KH	Handley B	Crossley P
Aug 11 Oldham Athletic 1-1 Stephenson 6723	1	2			5	6	7		8	10	11	9		2	12	4						

1964-65 Season (Above)
Back: Birch, Ridge, Burgin, Jones, Cunliffe, Storf
Middle: Collins (Manager), Calloway, Thompson
(Captain), Taylor, Hardman, Jenkins,
Turley, Emptage (Trainer)
Front: Milburn, Morton, Richardson,
Aspen, McKenzie

1965-66 Season (Left)
Back: Calloway, Jones, Burgin, Ridge
3rd Row: Jenkins, Taylor, Birch, Storf
2nd Row: Morton, Aspden, Thompson, Hardman
Front: Lister, Ratcliffe, Bannister, Sievwright

1966/67 — 21st in Division 4

Results

No	Date		Opponent	Score	Scorers	Att
1	Aug	20	Crewe Alexandra	1-2	Wheatley	3069
2		27	BARROW	1-3	Lister	2752
3	Sep	2	York City	1-1	Wheatley	5046
4		6	LUTON TOWN	3-0	Wheatley, Russell, Crossley	2472
5		10	LINCOLN CITY	1-0	Russell	2905
6		17	Chesterfield	0-0		5003
7		24	STOCKPORT COUNTY	1-0	Storf	5756
8		29	Luton Town	1-3	Crossley	6435
9	Oct	1	Aldershot	0-4		4273
10		8	BARNSLEY	1-1	Richardson	2784
11		15	Newport County	2-2	Wheatley, Stephenson	4650
12		19	Chester	2-3	Stephenson, Storf	4316
13		22	BRENTFORD	1-3	Russell	2632
14		29	Halifax Town	1-1	McQueen	2771
15	Nov	5	HARTLEPOOLS UNITED	3-2	Russell 2, Calder	2005
16		12	Exeter City	0-0		3625
17		19	BRADFORD CITY	0-1		3108
18	Dec	3	SOUTHEND UNITED	1-2	Lister	1733
19		10	Wrexham	2-4	Russell, Storf	6904
20		17	CREWE ALEXANDRA	0-1		1432
21		27	Notts County	0-2		4810
22		31	Barrow	0-2		6871
23	Jan	14	Lincoln City	2-0	Storf, Jenkins	3983
24		21	CHESTERFIELD	2-1	Jenkins 2	2255
25		27	NOTTS COUNTY	1-1	Jenkins	2358
26	Feb	3	Stockport County	2-2	Daubrey, Stephenson	9908
27		11	ALDERSHOT	2-1	Jenkins 2 (1p)	2494
28		18	Bradford Park Avenue	3-0	Storf, Jenkins (p), McEwan	4823
29		25	Barnsley	1-3	Daubrey	7585
30	Mar	1	CHESTER	0-1		2140
31		4	NEWPORT COUNTY	2-0	Russell, Jenkins	2039
32		11	BRADFORD PARK AVE.	1-0	Jenkins	2143
33		18	Brentford	0-4		6610
34		25	TRANMERE ROVERS	1-2	Connor	2478
35		27	Port Vale	1-2	Taylor	2254
36		28	Port Vale	0-5		3004
37	Apr	1	Hartlepools United	1-2	Jenkins	5952
38		8	EXETER CITY	1-0	Calloway	1294
39		10	SOUTHPORT	1-1	Smith	2644
40		15	Bradford City	1-4	Fletcher	4119
41		22	HALIFAX TOWN	3-0	Fletcher 2, Melledew	2416
42		24	Southport	2-1	Jenkins (p), Storf	5469
43		29	Southend United	0-0		8236
44	May	2	YORK CITY	2-2	Jenkins 2 (1p)	2017
45		6	WREXHAM	1-3	Fletcher	2066
46		12	Tranmere Rovers	1-3	Jenkins (p)	12123

Appearances and Goals

Player	Apps	Goals
Williamson R	34	
Smith GL	46	1
Calloway LJ	46	1
Richardson B	19	1
Taylor B	44	1
Collins GF	7	
Crossley P	14	2
Russell W	34	7
McQueen ID	7	1
Wheatley B	13	4
Storf DA	43	6
Lister HF	11	2
Hardman JA	9	
Moulden A	1	
Pennington J	14	
Stephenson GR	17	3
Connor KH	18	1
Calder WC	8	1
Jenkins R	30	14
Melledew ST	23	1
Daubrey R	11	2
Fletcher JM	9	4
McEwen FK	10	1
Holden JS	21	
Jones SC	12	
Crompton DG	9	
Dow DJ	1	
Cutler		
Hardman B		
Riley HW		
Aspden JR		

F.A. Cup

	Date		Opponent	Score	Scorer	Att
R1	Nov	26	BARROW	1-3	Storf	3784

Team: Williamson 1, Smith 5, Calloway 3, Taylor 4, Russell 6, McQueen 8, Storf 11, Stephenson 7, Connor 2, Calder 9, Jenkins 10

F.L. Cup

	Date		Opponent	Score	Scorer	Att
R1	Aug	23	Bury	0-2		3724

Team: Williamson 1, Smith 2, Calloway 3, Richardson 4, Taylor 5, Collins 6, Crossley 7, Russell 8, Wheatley 10, Storf 11, Lister 9

Lancashire Cup

Date		Opponent	Score	Scorer	Att
Dec	6	BURY	1-2	Calloway (p)	709

Rose Bowl

Date		Opponent	Score	Scorer	Att
Aug	13	OLDHAM ATHLETIC	1-2	Storf	3807

Division 4 — Final Table

		P	W	D	L	F	A	W	D	L	F	A	Pts
1	Stockport County	46	16	5	2	41	18	10	7	6	28	24	64
2	Southport	46	19	2	2	47	15	4	11	8	22	27	59
3	Barrow	46	12	8	3	35	18	12	3	8	41	36	59
4	Tranmere Rovers	46	14	6	3	42	20	8	8	7	24	23	58
5	Crewe Alexandra	46	14	5	4	42	26	7	7	9	28	29	54
6	Southend United	46	15	5	3	44	12	7	4	12	26	37	53
7	Wrexham	46	11	12	0	46	20	5	8	10	30	42	52
8	Hartlepools United	46	15	3	5	44	29	7	4	12	22	35	51
9	Brentford	46	13	7	3	36	19	5	6	12	22	37	49
10	Aldershot	46	14	4	5	48	19	4	8	11	24	38	48
11	Bradford City	46	13	4	6	48	31	6	6	11	26	31	48
12	Halifax Town	46	10	11	2	37	27	5	3	15	22	41	44
13	Port Vale	46	9	7	7	33	27	5	8	10	22	31	43
14	Exeter City	46	11	6	6	30	24	3	9	11	20	36	43
15	Chesterfield	46	13	6	4	33	16	4	2	17	27	47	42
16	Barnsley	46	8	7	8	30	28	5	8	10	30	36	41
17	Luton Town	46	15	5	3	47	23	1	4	18	12	50	41
18	Newport County	46	9	9	5	35	23	3	7	13	21	40	40
19	Chester	46	10	4	9	35	23	5	5	11	30	46	40
20	Notts County	46	10	7	6	31	25	3	4	16	22	47	37
21	ROCHDALE	46	10	4	9	30	27	3	7	13	23	48	37
22	York City	46	11	5	7	45	31	1	6	16	20	48	35
23	Bradford Park Ave.	46	7	6	10	30	34	4	7	12	22	45	35
24	Lincoln City	46	7	8	8	39	39	2	5	16	19	43	31

246

1967/68 19th in Division 4

No	Date		Opponent	Score	Scorers	Att	Green L	Melledew ST	Calloway LJ	Reid J	Smith GL	Eastham B	Winspear J	Russell W	Fletcher JM	Jenkins R	Riley HW	Taylor B	Cockroft VH	Hutchinson JB	Crompton DG	McEwen FK	Daubney R	Williamson R	Dow DJ	Harley LA	Butler DA	Rudd WT	Bracewell K	Wilkinson ES
1	Aug	19	Newport County	1-1	Calloway	4858	1	2	3	4	5	6	7	8	9	10	11													
2		26	YORK CITY	3-2	Riley 2, Fletcher	2536	1		3	8		6	7	4	9	10	11	5	2											
3	Sep	2	LINCOLN CITY	1-2	Melledew	2467	1	12	3	4	5			8	7	10	11	6	2	9										
4		4	Hartlepools United	1-1	Fletcher	8361	1	4	3	8	5			7	9	10	11	6	2											
5		9	Brentford	0-4		5646	1	4	3	8	5		7	6	9	10	11		2		12									
6		16	BRADFORD PARK AVE.	1-1	Fletcher	2579	1		3	11	5	6		7	9	10			4	2	8									
7		23	Doncaster Rovers	0-2		6530	1		3	10	5	6		7	9	11			4	2	8									
8		25	HARTLEPOOLS UNITED	1-1	Winspear	2041	1		3	11	5	6	7	10	9	12			4	2	8									
9		30	LUTON TOWN	2-2	Winspear, Jenkins	1884	1	12	3	8	5	6	7		9	10	11		4	2										
10	Oct	3	Barnsley	1-1	Fletcher	4663	1	8		10	5	3	7		9		11		4	2			6							
11		7	Bradford City	0-0		5174	1		3	8	5		7	10	9		11	6	2			12								
12		14	CREWE ALEXANDRA	1-1	Winspear	2397	1	4	3	10	5		7		9			6	2			11	8							
13		21	Notts County	0-2		5832	1	4	3	10	5		7		9			6	2			11	8							
14		23	BARNSLEY	1-0	Fletcher	3368	1	4	3	11	5	6	7		9	10			2	8										
15		28	PORT VALE	3-1	Hutchinson, Reid, Jenkins (p)	2566	1	4	3	11	5		7	10	9			6	2	8										
16	Nov	4	Chester	1-0	Melledew	4068	1	4	3	11	5		7		9	10		6	2	8										
17		11	CHESTERFIELD	1-4	Jenkins	2391	1	4		11	5	3	7		9	10		6	2	8										
18		18	Exeter City	1-3	Jenkins	4072	1	4	3	11		6			9	10			6	2	9				7					
19		25	DARLINGTON	1-0	Jenkins	1692	1	4		3	5				11			7	6	2	8				9					
20	Dec	2	Aldershot	1-2	Fletcher	4687	1	4	3	11	5				9	10			6	2					7					
21		16	NEWPORT COUNTY	4-3	Reid 2, Fletcher, Melledew	1662	1		4	3	11	6		7	8	9	5		2	10						1				
22		23	York City	1-4	Russell	3329	1		8	3	11		6	12	7	9	5		2	10						1				
23		26	Wrexham	0-2		9767	1			3				6	8	9	5	7	4	2	10	11								
24		30	WREXHAM	3-0	Showell (og), Jenkins (p), Hutchinson	1799	1			3				7	9	5	4	2	10	11	8									
25	Jan	6	Lincoln City	2-3	Peden (og), McEwan	5480	1	12	3		6				7	9	5	4	2	10	11	8								
26		20	Bradford Park Avenue	0-0		3334	1	4	3		6				8	9	5		2	10			7							
27		27	WORKINGTON	1-3	Fletcher	1606	1	4		3	6			7	11	9	5	12	8	2							7			
28	Feb	3	DONCASTER ROVERS	2-0	Melledew, Fletcher	1728	1	8		3	6				10	9	5		4	2	11						7			
29		10	Luton Town	1-4	Fletcher	10040	1	8	12	3	6				10	9	5		4	2	11						7			
30		17	SOUTHEND UNITED	0-1		2370	1	4	3	8	5				9	10	12		2							6	7	11		
31		24	EXETER CITY	2-2	Melledew, Rudd	2159	1	2	3		6				9	10			4						5	7	11	8		
32	Mar	2	Crewe Alexandra	1-2	Fletcher	4570	1	2	3		6				9	10			4						5	7	11	8		
33		9	Halifax Town	0-2		4933	1	7	3	12	2				9	10			4						6		11	8	5	
34		16	Notts County	0-0		1895	1	2			6				7	10			3	9							11	8	5	4
35		18	BRENTFORD	1-1	Melledew	1725	1	2		6	4				7	10			3	9							11	8	5	
36		23	Port Vale	1-1	Butler	3151	1	2		10	6				7	9			3								11	8	5	4
37		30	CHESTER	1-1	Fletcher	2212	1	2		10	6				7	9			3								11	8	5	4
38	Apr	6	Chesterfield	2-0	Fletcher, Kettlebrough (og)	7159	1	2		10	6				7	5			3	9							11	8		4
39		13	BRADFORD CITY	3-2	Fletcher 2, Hutchinson	4625	1	2		10	6				7	5			3	9							11	8		4
40		15	SWANSEA TOWN	1-2	Jenkins (p)	3076	1	2		10	6			7		5	12		3	9							11	8		4
41		16	Swansea Town	0-1		4978	1			10	2			7		5	11	6	3	9								8		4
42		20	Darlington	0-2		3241	1			8	2				12			5	7	4	3	9					11	10	6	
43		27	ALDERSHOT	0-2		2001	1	10			12							5	7	6	3	9					11	8	4	
44		29	HALIFAX TOWN	2-1	Melledew, Riley	1929	1	8		3					9			5	7	4	2				6		11	10		
45	May	4	Workington	1-0	Butler	1405	1	8		3					9			5	7	4	2				6		11	10		
46		10	Southend United	1-3	Riley	5744	1	9		3	4						8	7	5	11					2		10			
					Apps		44	38	27	39	42	13	16	27	38	42	20	30	42	27	8	7	1	2	7	5	15	16	5	9
					Goals			7	1	3			3	1	15	7	4			3		1					2	1		

Three own goals

F.A. Cup

	Date		Opponent	Score	Scorers	Att																								
R1	Dec	9	Tranmere Rovers	1-5	Fletcher	4500	1	4	3	11	5			8	9	10		6	2						7					

F.L. Cup

	Date		Opponent	Score	Att												
R1	Aug	23	BURY	0-1	4848	1	2	3	8	5	6	7	9	10	11	4

Lancashire Cup

Date		Opponent	Score	Scorers	Att
Oct	31	MANCHESTER UNITED	1-1	Mutchinson	1981
Nov	22	Manchester United*	0-1		
Jan	15	Manchester United	0-7		5267

* Abandoned

Northern Floodlit Cup

Date		Opponent	Score	Scorers	Att
Feb	13	Wigan Athletic	2-3	Russell, Hutchinson	654
	26	WIGAN ATHLETIC	1-1	Melledew	1146

Rose Bowl

Date		Opponent	Score	Scorers	Att
Aug	12	OLDHAM ATHLETIC	1-1	Lawson (og)	2548

		P	W	D	L	F	A	W	D	L	F	A	Pts
1	Luton Town	46	19	3	1	55	16	8	9	6	32	28	66
2	Barnsley	46	17	6	0	43	14	7	7	9	25	32	61
3	Hartlepools United	46	15	7	1	34	12	10	3	10	26	34	60
4	Crewe Alexandra	46	13	10	0	44	18	7	8	8	30	31	58
5	Bradford City	46	14	5	4	41	22	9	6	8	31	29	57
6	Southend United	46	12	8	3	45	21	8	6	9	32	37	54
7	Chesterfield	46	15	4	4	47	20	6	7	10	24	30	53
8	Wrexham	46	17	3	3	47	12	3	10	10	25	41	53
9	Aldershot	46	10	11	2	36	19	8	6	9	34	36	53
10	Doncaster Rovers	46	12	8	3	36	16	6	7	10	30	40	51
11	Halifax Town	46	10	6	7	34	24	5	10	8	18	25	46
12	Newport County	46	11	7	5	32	22	5	6	12	26	41	45
13	Lincoln City	46	11	3	9	41	31	6	6	11	30	37	43
14	Brentford	46	13	4	6	41	24	5	3	15	20	40	43
15	Swansea Town	46	11	8	4	38	25	5	2	16	25	52	42
16	Darlington	46	6	11	6	31	27	6	6	11	16	26	41
17	Notts County	46	10	7	6	27	27	5	4	14	26	52	41
18	Port Vale	46	10	5	8	41	31	2	10	11	20	41	39
19	ROCHDALE	46	9	8	6	35	32	3	6	14	16	40	38
20	Exeter City	46	9	7	7	30	30	2	9	12	15	35	38
21	York City	46	9	6	8	44	30	2	8	13	21	38	36
22	Chester	46	6	6	11	35	38	3	8	12	22	40	32
23	Workington	46	8	8	7	35	29	2	3	18	19	58	31
24	Bradford Park Ave.	46	3	7	13	18	35	1	8	14	12	47	23

1968/69 3rd in Division 4: Promoted

No		Date	Opponent	Res	Scorers	Att	Harker CJ	Radcliffe V	Ryder DF	Leech VG	Parry C	Ashworth JM	Whitehead NJ	Fletcher JM	Jenkins R	Rudd WT	Butler DA	Riley HW	Melledew ST	Smith GL	Melling T	Buck AR	Lee
1	Aug	10	SCUNTHORPE UNITED	3-2	Jenkins 2 (2p), Butler	3253	1	2	3	4	5	6	7	8	9	10	11						
2		17	Colchester United	0-0		3969	1	2	3	4	5	6	7	12	9	10	11		8				
3		24	EXETER CITY	1-1	Melledew	3225	1	2	3	4	5	6	7		9	10	11		8				
4		26	Brentford	1-1	Melledew	9149	1	2	3	4	5	6	7		9	10	11		8	12			
5		31	Port Vale	1-1	Melledew	4591	1	2	3	4	5	10	7		9	11	12		8	6			
6	Sep	7	PETERBOROUGH UTD.	1-1	Melledew	4030	1	2	3	4	5	6	7	12	9	10	11		8				
7		14	Chesterfield	1-1	Melledew	5903	1	2	3	4	5	6	12	7	9	10	11		8				
8		17	Doncaster Rovers	0-2		12183	1	2	3	4	5	6			9	10	11	7	8				
9		21	BRADFORD CITY	6-0	Fletcher 2, Melledew 2, Rudd, Butler	4136	1	2	3	4	5	6		7		10	11		8	9			
10		28	York City	0-0		3509	1	2	3	4	5	6		7		10	11		8	9			
11	Oct	5	WORKINGTON	0-0		4535	1	2	3	4	5	6	7		12	10	11		8	9			
12		7	BRENTFORD	0-0		5181	1	2	3	4	5	6	7			10	11		8	9			
13		12	Darlington	0-0		7113	1		3	4	5	6	7		9	10	11			2	8		
14		19	SWANSEA TOWN	0-1		4771	1	2	3	4	5	6	7		12	10	11		8	9			
15		26	Southend United	3-1	Butler 2, Melledew	9486	1	2	3	4	5		7			10	11		8	6	9		
16	Nov	2	BRADFORD PARK AVE.	6-0	Rudd 2 (1p), Butler, Melledew, Melling, Radcliffe	2795	1	2	3	4	5		7			10	11		8	6	9		
17		4	NEWPORT COUNTY	0-1		4223	1	2	3		5	6	7		12	10	11		8	4	9		
18		9	Aldershot	0-0		5185	1	2	3	4	5		7		9	10	11		8	6			
19		23	Wrexham	2-3	Melling 2	5663	1	2	3	4	5		7			10	11		8		9		
20		30	NOTTS COUNTY	0-0		2673	1	2	3		5	6	7	8		10	11		12	4	9		
21	Dec	7	Grimsby Town	0-2		2714	1	2	3		5	6	7		9	11	12		8	4	10		
22		21	Swansea Town	0-3		5703	1	2	3		5	6	7		10	8	11				9		
23		26	Workington	2-1	Jenkins 2	2921	1		3	4	5	6	7		10	8	11			2	9		
24	Jan	4	GRIMSBY TOWN	6-1	Jenkins 3 (1p), Melling, Rudd, Whitehead	2038	1		3	4	5	6	7		10	8	11			2	9		
25		11	Bradford Park Avenue	4-1	Melling 3, Whitehead	5453	1		3	4	5	6	7		10	8	11			2	9		
26		18	ALDERSHOT	3-0	Butler 2, Melling	3305	1		3	4	5	6	7			8	11		10	2	9		
27	Feb	1	Lincoln City	0-0		8621	1		3	4	5	6	7		10	8	11		12	2	9		
28		10	Newport County	1-1	Butler	2607	1	6	3	4	5		7		10	8	11			2	9		
29		24	DARLINGTON	2-0	Jenkins 2	3815	1		3	4	5	6	7		10	8	11			2	9		
30	Mar	1	Scunthorpe United	0-0		3102	1	5	3	4		6	7			8	11			2	10	9	
31		8	COLCHESTER UNITED	4-0	Butler 2, Jenkins, Buck	4988	1		3	4	5	6	7		10	8	11			2		9	
32		10	LINCOLN CITY	2-1	Buck, Butler	5803	1		3	4	5	6	7		10	8	11			2		9	
33		15	Exeter City	2-2	Buck 2	4061	1		3	4	5	6	7		10	8	11			2		9	
34		22	PORT VALE	1-0	Butler	4860	1		3	4	5	6	7		10	8	11			2		9	
35		29	Peterborough United	1-0	Buck	4107	1		3	4	5	6	7		10	8	11		12	2		9	
36	Apr	5	YORK CITY	2-1	Buck, Smith	6886	1		3	4	5	6	7		10	8	11			2		9	
37		7	DONCASTER ROVERS	0-0		12647	1		3	4	5	6	7		10	8	11			2		9	
38		8	Chester	1-2	Melledew	3820	1		3	4	5	6	7		10	8	11		12	2		9	
39		12	Bradford City	1-1	Ashworth	9449	1		3	4	5	6	7		10	8	11		12	2		9	
40		14	CHESTER	4-1	Butler 2, Buck, Melledew	4884	1		3	4	5	6	7			8	11		10	2		9	
41		19	CHESTERFIELD	0-0		7600	1		3	4	5	6	7		12	8	11		10	2		9	
42		23	WREXHAM	2-1	Buck, Butler (p)	6635	1	6	3	4	5		7			8	11		10	2		9	
43		28	Notts County	1-1	Jenkins	3678	1	6	3	4	5		7		12	8	11		10	2		9	
44		30	HALIFAX TOWN	1-0	Butler	12806	1	6	3	4	5		7		10	8	11		9	2			
45	May	8	Halifax Town	0-1		17186	1		3	4	5	6	7		10	8	11		9	2		12	
46		10	SOUTHEND UNITED	3-0	Mellewdew, Jenkins 2 (1p)	9095	1		3	4	5	6	7		10	8	11		9	2		12	
						Apps	46	26	46	43	45	39	42	10	33	46	46	1	31	33	20	17	
						Goals		1				1	2	2	13	4	16		12	1	8	8	

F.A. Cup

	Date	Opponent	Res		Att	Harker CJ	Radcliffe V	Ryder DF	Leech VG	Parry C	Ashworth JM	Whitehead NJ	Fletcher JM	Jenkins R	Rudd WT	Butler DA	Riley HW	Melledew ST	Smith GL	Melling T	Buck AR	Lee
R1	Nov 16	Barnsley	0-0		11414	1	2	3	4	5	6	7			10	11		8	9			
rep	18	BARNSLEY	0-1		7340	1	2	3	4	5	6	7		12	10	11		8	9			

F.L. Cup

	Date	Opponent	Res		Att	Harker CJ	Radcliffe V	Ryder DF	Leech VG	Parry C	Ashworth JM	Whitehead NJ	Fletcher JM	Jenkins R	Rudd WT	Butler DA	Riley HW	Melledew ST	Smith GL	Melling T	Buck AR	Lee
R1	Aug 14	Workington	1-2	Melledew	2558	1	2	3	4	5	6	7	8	9	10	11		12				

		P	W	D	L	F	A	W	D	L	F	A	Pts
1	Doncaster Rovers	46	13	8	2	42	16	8	9	6	23	22	59
2	Halifax Town	46	15	5	3	36	18	5	12	6	17	19	57
3	ROCHDALE	46	14	7	2	47	11	4	13	6	21	24	56
4	Bradford City	46	11	10	2	36	18	7	10	6	29	28	56
5	Darlington	46	11	6	6	40	26	6	12	5	22	19	52
6	Colchester United	46	12	8	3	31	17	8	4	11	26	36	52
7	Southend United	46	15	3	5	51	21	4	10	9	27	40	51
8	Lincoln City	46	13	6	4	38	19	4	11	8	16	33	51
9	Wrexham	46	13	7	3	41	22	5	7	11	20	30	50
10	Swansea Town	46	11	8	4	35	20	8	3	12	23	34	49
11	Brentford	46	12	7	4	40	24	6	5	12	24	41	48
12	Workington	46	8	11	4	24	17	7	6	10	16	26	47
13	Port Vale	46	12	8	3	33	15	4	6	13	13	31	46
14	Chester	46	12	4	7	43	24	4	9	10	33	42	45
15	Aldershot	46	13	3	7	42	23	6	4	13	24	43	45
16	Scunthorpe United	46	10	5	8	28	22	8	3	12	33	38	44
17	Exeter City	46	11	8	4	45	24	5	3	15	21	41	43
18	Peterborough Utd.	46	8	9	6	32	23	5	7	11	28	34	42
19	Notts County	46	10	8	5	33	22	2	10	11	15	35	42
20	Chesterfield	46	7	7	9	24	22	6	8	9	19	28	41
21	York City	46	12	8	3	36	25	2	3	18	17	50	39
22	Newport County	46	9	9	5	31	26	2	5	16	18	48	36
23	Grimsby Town	46	5	7	11	25	31	4	8	11	22	38	33
24	Bradford Park Ave.	46	5	8	10	19	34	0	2	21	13	72	20

Lancashire Cup

					Harker CJ	Radcliffe V	Ryder DF	Leech VG	Parry C	Ashworth JM	Whitehead NJ	Fletcher JM	Jenkins R	Rudd WT	Butler DA	Riley HW	Melledew ST	Smith GL	Melling T	Buck AR	Lee
Oct	22	Oldham Athletic	1-1	Melledew		1	2	3	<u>4</u>			7		5	10	11	12	8	6	9		
	28	OLDHAM ATHLETIC	2-2	Melledew, Hunter (og)	1977	1	2	3	4	5		7		12	10	11		<u>8</u>	6	9		
Nov	25	OLDHAM ATHLETIC	0-1		2458	1	2	3	4	5	6	7	8		10	11				9		

Rose Bowl

					Harker CJ	Radcliffe V	Ryder DF	Leech VG	Parry C	Ashworth JM	Whitehead NJ	Fletcher JM	Jenkins R	Rudd WT	Butler DA	Riley HW	Melledew ST	Smith GL	Melling T	Buck AR	Lee
Aug	2	Oldham Athletic	1-2	Smith		1		3	4	5	6	7	8	9	10	11			12			2

1968-69 Season
Back: Jenkins, Tyrie, Ashworth, Smith, Harker, Parry
Middle: Melledew, Whitehead, Fletcher, Rudd, Leech, Radcliffe
Front: Butler, Ryder, Riley (Inset) Buck

1969/70 9th in Division 3

#		Date	Opponent	Score	Scorers	Att	Harker CJ	Smith GL	Ryder DF	Downes RD	Parry C	Ashworth JM	Whitehead NJ	Rudd WT	Buck AR	Jenkins R	Butler DA	Cross D	Melledew ST	Riley HW	Leech VG	Clarke PS	Blair RV	Tennant D
1	Aug	9	ORIENT	0-3		7114	1	2	3	4	5	6	7	8	9	10	11	12						
2		16	Stockport County	1-0	Jenkins	5338	1	2	3	4	5	6	7	8		10	11		9					
3		23	BURY	3-3	Melledew, Jenkins 2	9752	1	2	3	4	5	6	7	8		10	11		9					
4		27	Brighton & Hove Albion	0-2		13904	1	2	3	4	5	6	7	8	12	10	11		9					
5		30	Walsall	4-1	Jenkins 2 (1p), Butler, Melledew	6666	1	2	3	4	5	6	7	8		10	11		9					
6	Sep	6	BARROW	1-0	Melledew	6562	1	2	3	4	5	6	7	8		10	11		9					
7		13	Gillingham	2-2	Buck 2	4364	1	2	3	4	5	6	7	8	9	10	11							
8		15	ROTHERHAM UNITED	4-2	Downes 2, Buck, Jenkins (p)	6749	1	2	3	4	5	6	7	8	9	10	11							
9		20	BRADFORD CITY	1-2	Jenkins	9203	1	2	3	4	5	6	7	8	9	10	11			12				
10		27	Bristol Rovers	3-3	Buck 3	8673	1	2	3		5	6	7	8	9	10	11				4			
11		29	Bournemouth	3-0	Leech, Jenkins 2 (2p)	4775	1	2	3		5	6	7	8	9	10	11				4			
12	Oct	4	SHREWSBURY TOWN	3-0	Buck, Rudd, Wood (og)	6492	1	2	3	12	5	6	7	8	9	10	11				4			
13		6	STOCKPORT COUNTY	2-0	Jenkins, Butler	7889	1	2	3	12	5	6	7	8	9	10	11				4			
14		11	Plymouth Argyle	3-2	Butler 2, Jenkins	9458	1	2	3		5	6	7	8	9	10	11				4			
15		18	TRANMERE ROVERS	4-0	Butler 2, Buck, Jenkins	7892	1	2	3		5	6	7	8	9	10	11				4			
16		25	Southport	3-0	Jenkins, Buck, Dunleavy (og)	5834	1	2	3		5	6	7	8	9	10	11				4			
17	Nov	1	READING	3-2	Butler, Buck, Ryder	7977	1	2	3		5	6	7	8	9	10	11				4			
18		3	Mansfield Town	2-1	Jenkins (p), Butler	4588	1	2	3		5	6	7	8	9	10	11				4			
19		8	Halifax Town	1-3	Buck	7570	1	2	3		5	6	7	8	9	10	11				4			
20		22	Luton Town	0-2		15876	1	2	3		5	6	7	8	9	10	11				4			
21		24	MANSFIELD TOWN	2-1	Buck, Rudd	6833	1	2	3		5	6	7	8	9	10	11				4			
22	Dec	6	Bury	1-2	Buck	9849	1	2	3		5	6	7	8	9	10	11			12	4			
23		13	GILLINGHAM	0-0		5439	1	2	3	4	5	6	7	8	9	10	11			12				
24		20	Barrow	0-2		2128	1	2	3	4	5	6	7	8	9	10	11							
25	Jan	17	BRISTOL ROVERS	0-0		5701	1	2	3	4	5	6	7	8	9	10	11							
26		23	Doncaster Rovers	1-3	Jenkins	6237	1	2	3	4	5	6	7	8	9	10	11			12				
27		26	BOURNEMOUTH	0-1		5286	1	2	3		5	6	7	8	9	10	11	12		4				
28		31	Shrewsbury Town	0-1		4091	1	2	3		5	6	7	8	9	10	11			4				
29	Feb	4	Bradford City	3-0	Riley, Buck 2	10236	1	2	3		5	6	7	8	9	10	11			4				
30		7	PLYMOUTH ARGYLE	2-1	Riley, Cross	4833	1	2	3		5	6	7	8	9	10	11	12		4				
31		21	SOUTHPORT	1-1	Ashworth	4312	1	2	3		5	6	7	8		11	10			4				
32		28	Reading	0-1		14307	1	2	3	12	5	6	7	8	9		11	10		4				
33	Mar	3	Barnsley	0-1		9548	1	2	3	10	5		7	8			11	9		4		6		
34		9	TORQUAY UNITED	1-1	Butler	3604	1	2	3	10	5	6	7	8			11	9		4				
35		14	Fulham	0-2		6708	1	2	3	10	5	6	7	8			11	9		4			12	
36		16	Doncaster Rovers	2-0	Riley, Cross	4496	1	2	3	10	5		7	8			11	9		4		6		
37		21	BARNSLEY	1-1	Cross	4887	1	2	3	11	5	6	7	8		10		9		4				
38		27	Tranmere Rovers	0-0		7192	1	2	3	11	5	6	7	8		10		9		4				
39		28	Torquay United	0-3		5280	1	2	3	12	5	6	7	8		10	11	9		4				
40		30	HALIFAX TOWN	5-0	Jenkins 3, Whitehead, Riley	5346	1	2	3	10	5	6	7	8		9	11	12		4				
41	Apr	4	BRIGHTON & HOVE ALB	2-1	Butler, Jenkins	4762	1	2	3	10	5	6	7	8		9	11			4				
42		9	WALSALL	1-2	Rudd	4404	1	2	3	11	5	6		8		9	7	12		4			10	
43		11	Orient	2-2	Downes 2	13260	1	2	3	11	5	6		8		9	7	12		4			10	
44		14	Rotherham United	1-3	Blair	6382	1	2	3	11	5	6		8		9	7			4			10	
45		18	FULHAM	0-1		5077	1	2	3	11	5	6	12	8		9	7			4			10	
46		25	LUTON TOWN	1-2	Jenkins	5886	1	2	3	11	5	6		8		10	7	9		4			12	
					Apps		46	46	46	30	46	44	42	46	28	40	44	16	5	24	13	3	5	
					Goals			1	4		1	1	3	15	20	10	3	3	4	1		1	

Two own goals

Abandoned

		Date	Opponent	Score	Scorers	Att	Harker CJ	Smith GL	Ryder DF	Downes RD	Parry C	Ashworth JM	Whitehead NJ	Rudd WT	Buck AR	Jenkins R	Butler DA	Cross D	Melledew ST	Riley HW	Leech VG
Nov		29	FULHAM	2-2	Buck, Riley	6861	1	2	3		5	6	7	8	9	10	11			12	4
Jan		10	Bradford City	0-1			1	2	3	4	5	6	7	8	9	10	11				

		P	W	D	L	F	A	W	D	L	F	A	Pts
1	Orient	46	16	5	2	43	15	9	7	7	24	21	62
2	Luton Town	46	13	8	2	46	15	10	6	7	31	28	60
3	Bristol Rovers	46	15	5	3	51	26	5	11	7	29	33	56
4	Fulham	46	12	9	2	43	26	8	6	9	38	29	55
5	Brighton & Hove A.	46	16	4	3	37	16	7	5	11	20	27	55
6	Mansfield Town	46	14	4	5	46	22	7	7	9	24	27	53
7	Barnsley	46	14	6	3	43	24	5	9	9	25	35	53
8	Reading	46	16	3	4	52	29	5	8	10	35	48	53
9	ROCHDALE	46	11	6	6	39	24	7	4	12	30	36	46
10	Bradford City	46	11	6	6	37	22	6	6	11	20	28	46
11	Doncaster Rovers	46	13	4	6	31	19	4	8	11	21	35	46
12	Walsall	46	11	4	8	33	31	6	8	9	21	36	46
13	Torquay United	46	9	9	5	36	22	5	8	10	26	37	45
14	Rotherham United	46	10	8	5	36	19	5	6	12	26	35	44
15	Shrewsbury Town	46	10	12	1	35	17	3	6	14	27	46	44
16	Tranmere Rovers	46	10	8	5	38	29	4	8	11	18	43	44
17	Plymouth Argyle	46	10	7	6	32	23	6	4	13	24	41	43
18	Halifax Town	46	10	9	4	31	25	4	6	13	16	38	43
19	Bury	46	13	4	6	47	29	2	7	14	28	51	41
20	Gillingham	46	7	6	10	28	33	6	7	10	24	31	39
21	Bournemouth	46	8	9	6	28	27	4	6	13	20	44	39
22	Southport	46	11	5	7	31	22	3	5	15	17	44	38
23	Barrow	46	7	9	7	28	27	1	5	17	18	54	30
24	Stockport County	46	4	7	12	17	30	2	4	17	10	41	23

(season 1969/70 continued)

F.A. Cup

					Harker CJ	Smith GL	Ryder DF	Downes RD	Parry C	Ashworth JM	Whitehead NJ	Rudd WT	Buck AR	Jenkins R	Butler DA	Cross D	Melledew ST	Riley HW	Leech VG	Clarke PS	Blair RV	Tennant D
R1	Nov 15 Workington	1-2 Whitehead		2570	1	2	3	12	5	6	7	8	9	10	11				4			

F.L. Cup

					Harker CJ	Smith GL	Ryder DF	Downes RD	Parry C	Ashworth JM	Whitehead NJ	Rudd WT	Buck AR	Jenkins R	Butler DA	Cross D	Melledew ST	Riley HW	Leech VG	Clarke PS	Blair RV	Tennant D
R1	Aug 13 Bolton Wanderers	3-6 Butler 2, Jenkins		10057	1	2	3		5	6	7	8	9	10	11	4						

Lancashire Cup

			Harker CJ	Smith GL	Ryder DF	Downes RD	Parry C	Ashworth JM	Whitehead NJ	Rudd WT	Buck AR	Jenkins R	Butler DA	Cross D	Melledew ST	Riley HW	Leech VG	Clarke PS	Blair RV	Tennant D
	Sep 24 Burnley	0-2		2	3		5	6	7	8	9	10	11				4			1

Rose Bowl

			Harker CJ	Smith GL	Ryder DF	Downes RD	Parry C	Ashworth JM	Whitehead NJ	Rudd WT	Buck AR	Jenkins R	Butler DA	Cross D	Melledew ST	Riley HW	Leech VG	Clarke PS	Blair RV	Tennant D
	Jul 26 OLDHAM ATHLETIC	5-1 Jenkins(3), Butler, Buck	1	2	3	12	5	6	7	8	9	10	11				4			

1969-70 Season
Back: Buck, Clarke, Cross, Tennant, Harker, Ashworth, Parry, Jenkins, Connor (Manager)
Middle: Rudd, Melledew, Smith, Riley, Leech, Ryder, Downes, Whitehead
Front: Ashworth, Butler, Mandzuk

1970/71 16th in Division 3

#		Date	Opponent	Score	Scorers	Att.	Godfrey AW	Smith GL	Ryder DF	Riley HW	Parry C	Ashworth IM	Whitehead NJ	Arrowsmith AW	Jenkins R	Gowans PT	Butler DA	Cross D	Clarke PS	Blair RV	Downes RD	Tennant D	Pearson DAI	Buck AR	Leech VG
1	Aug	15	BRISTOL ROVERS	1-1	Butler	4628	1	2	3	4	5	6	7	8	9	10	11								
2		22	Port Vale	1-4	Jenkins (p)	6196	1	2	3	4		6	7		9	10	11	8	5	12					
3		29	BRADFORD CITY	0-0		5600	1	2	3	4		6	7		9	10	11	8	5						
4		31	DONCASTER ROVERS	1-0	Robertson (og)	3551	1	2	3	4		6	7		9		11	8	5	10					
5	Sep	4	Torquay United	0-3		6165	1	2	3	4		6	7	12	9		11	8	5	10					
6		12	FULHAM	1-2	Gowans	4429	1	2	3	4		6	7	12	9		11	8	5	10					
7		19	Rotherham United	1-5	Butler	6928	1	2	3	4		6		8	9		11	7	12	5		10			
8		26	READING	1-2	Jenkins	3840		2	3	4		6	7		9		11	8	5			10	1		
9	Oct	3	Mansfield Town	2-3	Butler, Jenkins	7038		2	3	4		6	7	12	9		11	8				5	10	1	
10		10	ASTON VILLA	1-1	Jenkins	7537		2	3	4	5	6	7	9	8			11			10	1			
11		17	Bristol Rovers	2-2	Jenkins, Sheppard (og)	11794		2	3	4	5	6	7	9	8			11			10	1			
12		21	Brighton & Hove Albion	1-1	Arrowsmith	7551		2	3	4	5	6	7	9	8			11			10	1			
13		24	BARNSLEY	1-0	Arrowsmith	5462		2	3	4	5	6	7	9	8			11			10	1			
14		31	Walsall	3-0	Arrowsmith, Butler, Gowans	4667		2	3	4	5	6	7	9		8	11				10	1			
15	Nov	2	PLYMOUTH ARGYLE	1-1	Whitehead	5033		2	3	4	5	6	7	9		8	11	12			10	1			
16		7	WREXHAM	4-1	Smith, Gowans, Riley, Arrowsmith	4591		2	3	4	5	6	7	9		8	11				12	10	1		
17		10	GILLINGHAM	0-1		3291		2	3	4	5	6	7	9		8	11				12	10	1		
18		14	Preston North End	1-3	Whitehead	13451				4	5		7		9		11			8	6	3	10	1	2
19		28	Swansea City	2-4	Cross, Whitehead	7178				4	5		7		9		10	11	8		6	3	1	2	
20	Dec	5	SHREWSBURY TOWN	1-2	Jenkins	3217		2		3	4	5	6	7	9	12	10	11			8		1		
21		19	PORT VALE	0-3		3619	1			3	4	5	6	7				11	9	8	10	1		2	12
22		26	Halifax Town	4-1	Butler 3, Cross	5584		2		3	4	5	6	7				11	9	8	10	1			
23	Jan	9	Plymouth Argyle	2-2	Whitehead, Buck	6140		2		3	4	5	6	7				11	9		10	1		8	12
24		16	BRIGHTON & HOVE ALB	3-3	Riley 3	4938		2		3	4	5	6	7			12	11	9		10	1		8	
25		30	SWANSEA CITY	0-0		3220	1			3	4	5	6	7	8		10	11	9	2				12	
26	Feb	6	Shrewsbury Town	2-0	Cross 2	3759	1			3	11	5	6	7	9		10		8	2	12				4
27		10	Chesterfield	1-1	Arrowsmith	10466	1			3	11	5	6	7	9		10		8	2					4
28		13	CHESTERFIELD	2-0	Gowans, Arrowsmith	3750	1			3	11	5	6	7	9		10		8	2					4
29		20	Gillingham	0-0		3979	1			3	4	5	6	7	9		11		8	2	10				
30		22	BURY	2-0	Arrowsmith 2	9088	1			3	4	5	6	7	9		11		8	2	10				
31		27	WALSALL	2-0	Jenkins, Arrowsmith	4369	1			3		5	6	7	9		11		8	2	10				
32	Mar	6	Barnsley	2-2	Arrowsmith, Gowans	4872	1			3	4	5	6	7	9	10	11		8	2	12				
33		8	TRANMERE ROVERS	0-0		4498	1			3	4	5	6	7	9	8	11		12	2	10				
34		13	PRESTON NORTH END	1-2	Cross	10345	1			3		5	6	7	9	12	4	11	8	2	10				
35		16	Bury	2-0	Blair, Arrowsmith	8047	1			3	4	5	6	7	9	10			8	2	11				
36		20	Wrexham	1-3	Jenkins	4152	1			3	4	5	6	7	9	10			8	2	11				
37		27	TORQUAY UNITED	2-0	Jenkins, Cross	3704	1			3	4		6	7				9	8	5	10				
38	Apr	3	Bradford City	0-3		4536	1	2	3	4	5		7	12	8		11	9		6	10				
39		7	Fulham	0-2		10054	1	2	3	4		6	7		8	10	11	9		5					
40		10	HALIFAX TOWN	0-3		5756	1	2	3	4			7		8	10	11	9		6					
41		12	MANSFIELD TOWN	1-1	Arrowsmith	3898	1	2	3	4	5		7	9	10		12			6	11			8	
42		17	Aston Villa	0-1		18406	1	2	3	12	5		7	9	10		11			6	4			8	
43		19	Tranmere Rovers	2-0	Jenkins 2	3357	1	2	3	4	5		7		10			11	9	6	8				
44		24	ROTHERHAM UNITED	4-3	Cross, Jenkins 2 (1p), Mielczarek (og)	3561	1	2	3	4	5		7		10			11	9	6	8				
45		27	Doncaster Rovers	2-1	Butler, Cross	2884	1	2	3			5	6	7			10	12	11	9	4	8			
46	May	1	Reading	1-1	Cross	5746	1					6	7			10	4	11	9	5	8			12	
			Apps				30	31	44	42	35	38	45	31	30	33	30	33	3	36	37	16	3	7	4
			Goals					1		4			4	12	13	5	8	9		1				1	

Three own goals

F.A. Cup

#		Date	Opponent	Score	Scorers	Att.	Godfrey AW	Smith GL	Ryder DF	Riley HW	Parry C	Ashworth IM	Whitehead NJ	Arrowsmith AW	Jenkins R	Gowans PT	Butler DA	Cross D	Clarke PS	Blair RV	Downes RD	Tennant D	Pearson DAI	Buck AR	Leech VG
R1	Nov	21	OLDHAM ATHLETIC	2-0	Arrowsmith 2	13879		2	3	4	5	6	7	9		11				12	8	10	1		
R2	Dec	12	Darlington	2-0	Downes, Blair	5595	1	2	3	4	5	6	7		9					8	11	10			
R3	Jan	11	COVENTRY CITY	2-1	Cross, Butler	13011		2	3	4	5	6	7				11	9		10	1			8	
R4		23	COLCHESTER UNITED	3-3	Ashworth, Buck 2	12321		2	3	4	5	6	7				11	9		10	1			8	
rep		25	Colchester United	0-5		11205	1	2	3	4	5	6	7				11	9		12	10			8	

F.L. Cup

#		Date	Opponent	Score	Scorers	Att.	Godfrey AW	Smith GL	Ryder DF	Riley HW	Parry C	Ashworth IM	Whitehead NJ	Arrowsmith AW	Jenkins R	Gowans PT	Butler DA	Cross D	Clarke PS	Blair RV	Downes RD	Tennant D	Pearson DAI	Buck AR	Leech VG
R1	Aug	19	SOUTHPORT	1-0	Jenkins	4057	1	2	3	4	5	6	7	8	9	10	11	12							
R2	Sep	9	Crystal Palace	3-3	Whitehead, Gowans, Jenkins	16265	1	2	3	4		6	7		9	11		8	5	10					
rep		14	CRYSTAL PALACE	1-3	Smith	8911	1	2	3	4		6	7		9	11		8	5	10					

		P	W	D	L	F	A	W	D	L	F	A	Pts
1	Preston North End	46	15	8	0	42	16	7	9	7	21	23	61
2	Fulham	46	15	6	2	39	12	9	6	8	29	29	60
3	Halifax Town	46	16	2	5	46	22	6	10	7	28	33	56
4	Aston Villa	46	13	7	3	27	13	6	8	9	27	33	53
5	Chesterfield	46	13	8	2	45	12	4	9	10	21	26	51
6	Bristol Rovers	46	11	5	7	38	24	8	8	7	31	26	51
7	Mansfield Town	46	13	7	3	44	28	5	8	10	20	34	51
8	Rotherham United	46	12	10	1	38	19	5	6	12	26	41	50
9	Wrexham	46	12	8	3	43	25	6	5	12	29	40	49
10	Torquay United	46	12	6	5	37	26	7	5	11	17	31	49
11	Swansea City	46	11	5	7	41	25	4	11	8	18	31	46
12	Barnsley	46	12	6	5	30	19	5	5	13	19	33	45
13	Shrewsbury Town	46	11	6	6	37	28	5	7	11	21	34	45
14	Brighton & Hove A.	46	8	10	5	28	20	6	6	11	22	27	44
15	Plymouth Argyle	46	6	12	5	39	33	6	7	10	24	30	43
16	ROCHDALE	46	8	8	7	29	26	6	7	10	32	42	43
17	Port Vale	46	11	6	6	29	18	4	6	13	23	41	42
18	Tranmere Rovers	46	8	11	4	27	18	2	11	10	18	37	42
19	Bradford City	46	7	6	10	23	25	6	8	9	26	37	40
20	Walsall	46	10	1	12	30	27	4	10	9	21	30	39
21	Reading	46	10	7	6	32	33	4	4	15	16	52	39
22	Bury	46	7	9	7	30	23	5	4	14	22	37	37
23	Doncaster Rovers	46	8	5	10	28	27	5	4	14	17	39	35
24	Gillingham	46	6	9	8	22	29	4	4	15	20	38	33

(1970/71 season continued)

Lancashire Cup

				Score	Scorers	Att	Godfrey AW	Smith GL	Ryder DF	Riley HW	Parry C	Ashworth JM	Whitehead NJ	Arrowsmith AW	Jenkins R	Gowans PT	Butler DA	Cross D	Clarke PS	Blair RV	Downes RD	Tennant D	Pearson DAJ	Buck AR	Leech VG
1R	Sep	16	Burnley	1-1	Butler (p)			2	3	4		6	7	8	9		11	12		5	10	1			
1Rr		23	BURNLEY	1-0	Jenkins	1802		2	3	4		6	7		9	10	11	8		5		1			
2	Oct	13	Blackburn Rovers	2-0	Arrowsmith(2)		1	2	3	12	5	6	7	9	8	10	11			4					
3	Feb	15	EVERTON	3-1	Jenkins(2), Filey	1111			3	4	5	6	7		8		11			2	10	1		9	
SF	Mar	4	Chorley	0-0					3	4	5	6	7		10					2	11	1		9	
SFr		29	CHORLEY	2-1	Jenkins, Whitehead	1410	1	6	3	4	5		7	9	8	11					10		2		
F	May	3	OLDHAM ATHLETIC	3-2	Cross(2), Ashworth	7003	1	2	3			6	7		10	4	11	9		5	8				

Rose Bowl

			Score	Scorers	Att	Godfrey AW	Smith GL	Ryder DF	Riley HW	Parry C	Ashworth JM	Whitehead NJ	Arrowsmith AW	Jenkins R	Gowans PT	Butler DA	Cross D	Clarke PS	Blair RV	Downes RD	Tennant D	Pearson DAJ	Buck AR	Leech VG
	Aug	8	Oldham Athletic	2-1	Arrowsmith, Cross	5078	1	2	3	4	5	6	7		9	10	8	11	12	14					

1970-71 Season
Back: Smith, Jenkins, Parry, Tennant, Godfrey, Clarke, Cross, Ashworth (Captain)
Middle: Whitehead, Butler, Buck, Downes, Leech, Riley
Front: Ryder, Gowans, Manzduk, Blair, Arrowsmith

1971/72 18th in Division 3

League matches

#		Date	Opponent	Score	Scorers	Att.
1	Aug	14	Notts County	0-4		10879
2		21	MANSFIELD TOWN	2-1	Cross, Jenkins	3554
3		28	Aston Villa	0-2		24280
4	Sep	3	TRANMERE ROVERS	2-1	Ashworth, Cross (p)	3691
5		11	Bournemouth	1-4	Cross	8856
6		13	Torquay United	1-1	Cross	8885
7		18	OLDHAM ATHLETIC	1-1	Gowans	10926
8		25	Barnsley	3-3	Jenkins 2, Cross	5805
9		27	PLYMOUTH ARGYLE	3-2	Kinsella, Cross, Davey (og)	4519
10	Oct	2	TORQUAY UNITED	5-0	Cross 2(1p), Arrowsmith, Gowans, Whitehead	4551
11		9	Blackburn Rovers	0-3		8492
12		16	NOTTS COUNTY	1-1	Darling	4848
13		19	Halifax Town	2-2	Kinsella 2	3288
14		23	BRISTOL ROVERS	3-1	Whitehead, Downes, Buck	4753
15		30	Swansea City	0-1		7743
16	Nov	6	CHESTERFIELD	0-2		4818
17		13	Wrexham	3-1	Whitehead, Buck 2	7749
18		26	Walsall	0-3		3575
19	Dec	4	ROTHERHAM UNITED	2-1	Jenkins, Gowans	3384
20		17	Tranmere Rovers	0-2		2800
21		27	BRADFORD CITY	0-1		4722
22	Jan	1	Oldham Athletic	2-3	Gowans 2	8885
23		8	ASTON VILLA	1-0	Whitehead (p)	5874
24		22	Plymouth Argyle	1-4	Darling	9187
25		29	HALIFAX TOWN	3-2	Parry, Howarth 2	3124
26	Feb	5	SHREWSBURY TOWN	0-0		3502
27		12	Bristol Rovers	2-5	Darling 2	7344
28		19	SWANSEA CITY	1-1	Arrowsmith	3097
29		26	Chesterfield	0-2		6599
30	Mar	4	WREXHAM	1-0	Davis (og)	2643
31		11	BLACKBURN ROVERS	2-1	Howarth, Gowans	6542
32		13	Port Vale	3-2	Howarth 2, Gowans	3157
33		18	Mansfield Town	1-3	Darling	5121
34		20	York City	0-2		4539
35		25	BOURNEMOUTH	1-1	Howarth	4437
36	Apr	1	Bradford City	1-1	Brogden	4889
37		3	BARNSLEY	0-2		3848
38		8	Shrewsbury Town	1-2	Blair	2539
39		12	Bolton Wanderers	1-2	Howarth	6057
40		15	WALSALL	0-0		3027
41		17	YORK CITY	1-2	Buck	2776
42		22	Rotherham United	1-5	Gowans	4569
43		24	BOLTON WANDERERS	1-2	Howarth, Darling	4826
44		29	BRIGHTON & HOVE ALB	1-2	Jenkins (p)	4283
45	May	3	Brighton & Hove Albion	1-1	Gowans	34644
46		12	Port Vale	1-1	Jenkins (p)	2475

Appearances / Goals

	Jones RE	Blair RV	Ryder DF	Smith GL	Parry C	Ashworth JM	Buck AR	Jenkins R	Cross D	Downes RD	Butler DA	Gowans PT	Whitehead NJ	Clarke PS	Godfrey AW	Riley HW	Kinsella L	Arrowsmith AW	Darling M	Marsh A	Howarth J	Brogden L
Apps	5	30	32	44	30	12	27	20	10	36	18	38	27	5	41	5	35	15	34	28	21	16
Goals		1			1	1	4	6	8	1		9	4				3	2	6		8	1

Two own goals

F.A. Cup

	Date	Opponent	Score	Scorers	Att.
R1	Nov 20	BARNSLEY	1-3	Arrowsmith	5185

R1 line-up numbers: Smith 4, Ryder 3, Parry 2, ... Ashworth 5, Buck 9, Jenkins 10, Gowans 12, Whitehead 7, Godfrey 1, Kinsella 6, Arrowsmith 8, Darling 11

F.L. Cup

	Date	Opponent	Score	Scorers	Att.
R1	Aug 18	Halifax Town	1-1	Rhodes (og)	5195
rep	24	HALIFAX TOWN	2-2	Cross 2	6016
rep2	31	Halifax Town	0-2		5718

First replay a.e.t.

Division 3 final table

	Team	P	W	D	L	F	A	W	D	L	F	A	Pts
1	Aston Villa	46	20	1	2	45	10	12	5	6	40	22	70
2	Brighton & Hove A.	46	15	5	3	39	18	12	6	5	43	29	65
3	Bournemouth	46	16	6	1	43	13	7	10	6	30	24	62
4	Notts County	46	16	3	4	42	19	9	9	5	32	25	62
5	Rotherham United	46	12	8	3	46	25	8	7	8	23	27	55
6	Bristol Rovers	46	12	4	7	54	26	4	10	9	21	30	54
7	Bolton Wanderers	46	11	8	4	25	13	6	8	9	26	28	50
8	Plymouth Argyle	46	13	6	4	43	26	7	4	12	31	38	50
9	Walsall	46	12	8	3	38	16	3	10	10	24	41	48
10	Blackburn Rovers	46	14	4	5	39	22	5	5	13	15	35	47
11	Oldham Athletic	46	11	4	8	37	35	6	7	10	22	28	45
12	Shrewsbury Town	46	13	5	5	50	29	4	5	14	23	36	44
13	Chesterfield	46	10	5	8	25	23	8	3	12	32	34	44
14	Swansea City	46	10	6	7	27	21	7	4	12	19	38	44
15	Port Vale	46	10	10	3	27	21	3	5	15	16	38	41
16	Wrexham	46	10	5	8	33	26	6	3	14	26	37	40
17	Halifax Town	46	11	6	6	31	22	2	6	15	17	39	38
18	ROCHDALE	46	11	7	5	35	26	1	6	16	22	57	37
19	York City	46	8	8	7	32	22	4	4	15	25	44	36
20	Tranmere Rovers	46	9	7	7	34	30	1	9	13	16	41	36
21	Mansfield Town	46	5	12	6	19	26	3	8	12	22	37	36
22	Barnsley	46	6	6	10	7	23	30	3	8	12	9	34	36
23	Torquay United	46	8	6	9	31	31	2	6	15	10	38	32
24	Bradford City	46	6	6	8	9	27	32	5	2	16	18	45	32

Lancashire Cup

			Jones RE	Blair RV	Ryder DF	Smith GL	Parry C	Ashworth JM	Buck AR	Jenkins R	Cross D	Downes RD	Butler DA	Gowans PT	Whitehead NJ	Clarke PS	Godfrey AW	Riley HW	Kinsella L	Arrowsmith AW	Darling M	Marsh A	Howarth J	Brogden L
Oct 13 BLACKPOOL	3-0	Gowans, Buck, Arrowsmith		1	6	3	2	5		9				4	7					10	8	11		
Dec 6 MANCHESTER UNITED	1-1	Jenkins	3764	1	4	3	2	5		9	8			11	10	7				6				
22 Manchester United	1-4	Jenkins		1	4	3	2	5		9	10			11	8	7				6	12			

Rose Bowl

			Jones RE	Blair RV	Ryder DF	Smith GL	Parry C	Ashworth JM	Buck AR	Jenkins R	Cross D	Downes RD	Butler DA	Gowans PT	Whitehead NJ	Clarke PS	Godfrey AW	Riley HW	Kinsella L	Arrowsmith AW	Darling M	Marsh A	Howarth J	Brogden L
Jul 31 Oldham Athletic	0-4		4946	13	8	3	2	5	6	10	11	9			12		7		1	4					

1971-72 Season
Back: Madden (Coach), Jenkins, Cross, Clarke, Jones, Godfrey, Ashworth (Captain), Parry, Blair, Connor (Manager)
Middle: Whitehead, Gowans, Downes, Buck, Butler, Riley, Ryder, Smith
Front: Arrowsmith, Simpson, Williams, Mandzuk

1972/73 13th in Division 3

Football League Division 3

#	Date	Opponent	Score	Scorers	Att	Morritt GR	Smith GL	Downes RD	Gowans PT	Blant C	Kinsella L	Butler DA	Darling M	Howarth J	Jenkins R	Bebbington RK	Marsh A	Brogden L	Buck AR	Renwick R	Bradbury B	Wainman WH	Bowie JM	Jones RE	Fielding PA	Atkins WM	Simpson CWP	Skeete LA
1	Aug 12	PORT VALE	0-0		2661	1	2	3	4	5	6	7	8	9	10	11												
2	19	Blackburn Rovers	1-1	Howarth	6172	1	2	3	4	5	6	7	8	9	10	11												
3	26	CHARLTON ATHLETIC	0-2		2584	1	2	3	4	5	6		8	9	10	11	7		12									
4	28	Southend United	2-1	Jenkins, Howarth	8862	1	2	8	4	5	6		7	9	10	11				3								
5	Sep 2	Swansea City	3-2	Jenkins, Howarth, Gowans	2457	1	2	7	4	5	6		8	9	10	11				3								
6	9	TRANMERE ROVERS	1-1	Jenkins	2326	1	2		4	5	6	7	8	9	10	11				3								
7	16	Notts County	2-2	Brogden, Gowans	7991	1	2		10	5	6		8	9		11	4	7		3								
8	19	Scunthorpe United	2-1	Darling 2	3710	1	2		10	5	6		8	9		11	4	7		3								
9	23	WREXHAM	1-0	Brogden	3412	1	2		10	5	6		8	9		11	4	7		3								
10	25	WALSALL	2-1	Brogden, Bebbington	4749	1	2		10	5	6		8	9		11	4	7		3								
11	30	Grimsby Town	0-1		12131	1	2		10	5	6		8	9		11	4	7	12	3								
12	Oct 7	WATFORD	1-0	Franks (og)	3871		2		10	5	6		8	9	12	11	4	7		3	1							
13	9	HALIFAX TOWN	0-0		5425		2		10	5	6		8	9	12	11	4	7		3	1							
14	14	Shrewsbury Town	2-3	Darling, Jenkins (p)	2502		2			4	5	6	8	9	10	11		7		3	1							
15	21	BOLTON WANDERERS	2-2	Gowans, Jenkins	7168		2			4	5	6	8	9	10	11		7		3								
16	24	Bournemouth	2-4	Bebbington, Gowans	11741		2			4	5	6	8	9	10	11		7		3		1	12					
17	28	Brentford	0-1		9201		2			4	5	6	8	9	12	11		7		3		1	10					
18	Nov 4	Walsall	2-0	Howarth, Jenkins	5682		2			7	5	6	8	9	10	11	4			3		1						
19	11	SCUNTHORPE UNITED	0-2		2551		2			7	5	6	8	9	10	11	4			3		1	12					
20	25	CHESTERFIELD	1-2	Buck	1982		2				5	4	8			11	10	7	9	3	6	1			12			
21	Dec 2	Rotherham United	0-0		4590		2		8	5	6		10			11	3	7	9		4			1				
22	9	BRISTOL ROVERS	0-0		1792		2	12	8	5	6		10			11	3	7	9		4			1				
23	23	OLDHAM ATHLETIC	0-0		6702		2	4	10		6		8			11	5	7		3				1		9		
24	26	Wrexham	3-3	Atkins 2, Darling	3958		2	4	10		6		8			11	5	7		3				1		9		
25	30	BLACKBURN ROVERS	0-1		5116		2	4	10	5			8			11	4	7		3				1		9		
26	Jan 6	Charlton Athletic	0-1		5048		2	10		5	6		8			11	4	7		3				1		9		
27	29	BOURNEMOUTH	1-0	Darling	3575	1	2	4	7	5			8				10	11	6	3						9		
28	Feb 3	Halifax Town	0-0		2422	1	2	4	7	5			8				10	11	6	3						9		
29	6	Tranmere Rovers	1-0	Atkins	8329	1	2	4	7	5	11		8				10		6	3						9		
30	10	NOTTS COUNTY	4-1	Jenkins 2, Downes, Brindley (og)	3092	1	2	4	7	5	11		8				10		6	3						9		
31	24	PLYMOUTH ARGYLE	0-6		2622	1	2	4	7	5	11		8				6	12		3						9		
32	Mar 2	Watford	0-0		5338	1	2	4	7	5	11		8				10		6	3						9		
33	6	Bristol Rovers	0-0		11767	1	2	4	7	5	11		8				10		6	3						9		
34	10	SHREWSBURY TOWN	1-1	Darling	2195	1	2	4	7	5	11		8				10	6	12	3						9		
35	12	SWANSEA CITY	1-1	Darling	2037	1	2			10	5	6	8				9	11	4	7	3							
36	17	Bolton Wanderers	1-2	Atkins	18154	1	2		7	10	5	6	8					12	4	11	3					9		
37	19	YORK CITY	1-0	Bebbington	2100	1	2	8	10	5	6					9	11	4	7	3							
38	24	BRENTFORD	0-1		1747			10	4	5	6			9		11	2	7		3	12							
39	31	Chesterfield	1-2	Simpson	3576	1	2	12	10			6	8				11	5		3	7					9	4	
40	Apr 7	ROTHERHAM UNITED	0-1		1588	1	2	4	10		6		8				11	5	7	3						9		
41	9	Port Vale	0-0		6413	1	2	4	7	5	10		8					6	11	3						9		
42	14	York City	2-1	Gowans, Atkins	2387	1	2	4	10	5	11		8					6	7	3						9		
43	20	Oldham Athletic	0-0		9289	1	2	4	10	5	11		8					6	7	3						9		
44	23	GRIMSBY TOWN	3-2	Wiggington (og), Atkins, Skeete	1911	1	2	4	10	5	11		8					6		3						9		7
45	28	SOUTHEND UNITED	3-2	Darling, Skeete, Atkins	2081	1	2	4	10	5	11		8				12	6		3						9		7
46	May 1	Plymouth Argyle	2-3	Gowans, Skeete	9917	1	2	4	10	5	11		8				12	6		3						9		7
		Apps				31	45	29	44	42	43	3	45	19	25	37	37	28	5	41	5	9	3	6	1	21	1	3
		Goals					1		6				8	4	8	3		3	1							7	1	3

Three own goals

F.A. Cup

	Date	Opponent	Score	Scorers	Att	Smith	Gowans	Blant	Kinsella	Darling	Howarth	Jenkins	Bebbington	Marsh	Buck	Renwick	Bradbury
R1	Nov 18	BANGOR CITY	1-2	Jenkins (p)	3181	2	4	5	6	8	9	10	11	7	12	3	1

F.L. Cup

	Date	Opponent	Score	Scorers	Att	Morritt	Smith	Downes	Gowans	Blant	Kinsella	Butler	Darling	Howarth	Jenkins	Bebbington	Marsh	Renwick
R1	Aug 16	Blackburn Rovers	1-0	Darling	6292	1	2	3	4	5	6	7	8	9	10	11		
R2	Sep 6	Manchester City	0-4		17222	1	2	7	4	5	6		8	9	10	11	12	3

Lancashire Cup

	Date	Opponent	Score	Scorers	Att	Smith	Downes	Gowans	Blant	Kinsella	Darling	Howarth	Jenkins	Bebbington	Marsh	Brogden	Buck	Renwick	Bradbury	Wainman	Bowie	Atkins	Skeete	Hunt	Poole
2	Oct 16	MANCHESTER CITY	1-1	Smith	1521	2	7			6	10	9		11	5	12	8	3	1	4					
2r	Nov 8	Manchester City	4-2	Howarth, Darling, Jenkins(2)		2		4		6	12	9	10	11	5			3		7	1		8		
3	Dec 13	BURY	0-0			2	4	7		6	10			11		5			3				8	9	1
3r	Jan 13	Bury	1-5	Darling		2	4	10	5		8			11	6	7		3				9		12	1

Rose Bowl

	Date	Opponent	Score	Scorers	Att	Smith	Gowans	Downes	Blant	Kinsella	Butler	Darling	Howarth	Jenkins	Bebbington	Marsh	Buck	Renwick	Bradbury
	Jul 28	OLDHAM ATHLETIC	1-2	Darling	2973	2	4	12	5	11	7	14	9	10	15	6	8	3	1

Back: Smith, Blair, Jenkins, Blant, Jones, Howarth, Bradbury, Marsh, Renwick
Middle: Madden (Train.), Darling, Butler, Buck, Gowans, Downes, Kinsella, Connor (Man.)
Front: Brogden, Williams, Fielding, Simpson

		P	W	D	L	F	A	W	D	L	F	A	Pts
1	Bolton Wanderers	46	18	4	1	44	9	7	7	9	29	30	61
2	Notts County	46	17	4	2	40	12	6	7	10	27	35	57
3	Blackburn Rovers	46	12	8	3	34	16	8	7	8	23	31	55
4	Oldham Athletic	46	12	7	4	40	18	7	9	7	32	36	54
5	Bristol Rovers	46	17	4	2	55	20	3	9	11	22	36	53
6	Port Vale	46	15	6	2	41	21	6	5	12	15	48	53
7	Bournemouth	46	14	6	3	44	16	3	10	10	22	28	50
8	Plymouth Argyle	46	14	3	6	43	26	6	7	10	31	40	50
9	Grimsby Town	46	16	2	5	45	18	4	6	13	22	43	48
10	Tranmere Rovers	46	12	8	3	38	17	3	8	12	18	35	46
11	Charlton Athletic	46	12	7	4	40	24	5	4	14	23	43	45
12	Wrexham	46	11	9	3	39	23	3	8	12	16	31	45
13	ROCHDALE	46	8	8	7	22	26	6	9	8	26	28	45
14	Southend United	46	13	6	4	40	14	4	4	15	21	40	44
15	Shrewsbury Town	46	10	10	3	31	21	5	4	14	15	33	44
16	Chesterfield	46	13	6	4	37	22	4	5	14	20	39	43
17	Walsall	46	14	3	6	37	26	4	4	15	19	40	43
18	York City	46	8	10	5	24	14	5	5	13	18	32	41
19	Watford	46	11	8	4	32	23	1	9	13	11	25	41
20	Halifax Town	46	9	8	6	29	23	4	7	12	14	30	41
21	Rotherham United	46	12	4	7	34	27	5	3	15	17	38	41
22	Brentford	46	12	5	6	33	18	2	8	18	15	51	41
23	Swansea City	46	11	5	7	37	29	3	4	16	14	44	37
24	Scunthorpe United	46	8	7	8	18	25	2	3	18	15	47	30

1973/74 24th in Division 3: Relegated

Player columns (left to right): Jones RE, Smith GL, Hanvey K, Arnold SF, Marsh A, Kinsella L, Taylor AD, Brears P, Atkins WM, Darling M, Downes RD, Skeete LA, Gowans PT, Fielding PA, Blant C, Renwick R, Poole MD, Burt JHL, Bebbington RK, Brennan M, Brogden L, Bradbury B, Kavanagh EA, Cooper GS, Horne SF, Grummett J, Buckley I, Seddon DA, Carrick MD, Tobin DJ

#		Date	Opponent	Score	Scorers	Att.
1	Aug	25	BRIGHTON & HOVE ALB	1-1	Darling	2665
2	Sep	1	Walsall	0-0		5211
3		8	TRANMERE ROVERS	0-1		2749
4		11	Plymouth Argyle	0-5		7066
5		15	Shrewsbury Town	0-2		2516
6		17	BOURNEMOUTH	3-3	Skeete, Kinsella, Hanvey	2108
7		22	SOUTHPORT	2-2	Darling, Skeete	2380
8		29	Southend United	2-1	Arnold, Taylor (p)	5039
9	Oct	3	Bournemouth	0-2		8836
10		6	HUDDERSFIELD T	1-1	Skeete	3220
11		13	Oldham Athletic	1-3	Brennan	7846
12		20	Charlton Athletic	0-3		5038
13		22	PLYMOUTH ARGYLE	1-3	Downes	1437
14		27	GRIMSBY TOWN	1-1	Skeete	1549
15	Nov	3	Port Vale	1-3	Skeete	3223
16		10	WATFORD	1-3	Brogden	1459
17		17	Wrexham	0-3		3793
18	Dec	8	BLACKBURN ROVERS	1-2	Brogden	3660
19		22	SOUTHEND UNITED	1-1	Brogden	1073
20		26	Chesterfield	0-1		5775
21		29	Tranmere Rovers	1-1	Downes (p)	2766
22	Jan	1	WALSALL	0-1		2117
23		5	York City	1-2	Horne	3923
24		12	SHREWSBURY TOWN	3-2	Grummett, Downes, Skeete	957
25		20	Brighton & Hove Albion	1-2	Skeete	18900
26		26	Grimsby Town	1-5	Gowans	5548
27	Feb	3	YORK CITY	1-3	Horne	2205
28		5	CAMBRIDGE UNITED	0-2		588
29		16	OLDHAM ATHLETIC	1-3	Bebbington	5923
30		23	Huddersfield Town	0-5		5679
31		26	HEREFORD UNITED	1-1	Brennan	1195
32	Mar	2	CHESTERFIELD	1-2	Brennan	1566
33		5	Bristol Rovers	1-1	Bebbington	11188
34		10	Southport	0-0		1708
35		13	Aldershot	0-4		1742
36		16	CHARLTON ATHLETIC	1-1	Grummett	850
37		23	Watford	0-4		5616
38		25	Bristol Rovers	0-1		1499
39		30	PORT VALE	1-1	Horne	982
40	Apr	3	Hereford United	1-2	Hanvey	6659
41		6	Cambridge United	3-3	Carrick 2, Downes (p)	2704
42		13	WREXHAM	0-0		1119
43		15	ALDERSHOT	2-2	Skeete, Bebbington	885
44		20	Blackburn Rovers	1-3	Carrick	4517
45		22	Halifax Town	0-1		1431
46		27	HALIFAX TOWN	1-1	Skeete	1320

Played in games 29, 30: RW Denton (at 3).

Apps: Jones 8, Smith 30, Hanvey 39, Arnold 40, Marsh 25, Kinsella 7, Taylor 36, Brears 1, Atkins 4, Darling 7, Downes 42, Skeete 27, Gowans 29, Fielding 14, Blant 9, Renwick 8, Poole 38, Burt 4, Bebbington 23, Brennan 27, Brogden 13, Bradbury 9, Kavanagh 3, Cooper 6, Horne 27, Grummett 19, Buckley 6, Seddon 8, Carrick 10, Tobin 9

Goals: Hanvey 2, Arnold 1, Kinsella 1, Taylor 1, Darling 2, Downes 4, Skeete 9, Gowans 1, Bebbington 3, Brennan 3, Brogden 3, Horne 3, Grummett 2, Carrick 3

F.A. Cup

		Date	Opponent	Score	Scorers	Att.
R1	Nov	24	SOUTH SHIELDS	2-0	Marsh, Brogden	1554
R2	Dec	15	Grantham	1-1	Brogden	3224
rep		18	GRANTHAM	3-5	Taylor, Hanvey, Downes	1266

Replay a.e.t.

F.L. Cup

		Date	Opponent	Score	Scorers	Att.
R1	Aug	29	HARTLEPOOL UNITED	5-3	*See below	1856
R2	Oct	10	BOLTON WANDERERS	0-4		7241

Scorers in R1: Embleton (og), Atkins, Darling, Taylor, Skeete

Lancashire Cup

	Date	Opponent	Score
	Oct 15	Bolton Wanderers	0-4

(Last season of old competition)

		P	W	D	L	F	A	W	D	L	F	A	Pts
1	Oldham Athletic	46	13	6	4	50	23	12	6	5	33	24	62
2	Bristol Rovers	46	15	6	2	37	15	7	11	5	28	18	61
3	York City	46	13	8	2	37	15	8	11	4	30	23	61
4	Wrexham	46	15	6	2	44	15	7	6	10	19	28	56
5	Chesterfield	46	14	6	3	31	16	7	8	8	24	26	56
6	Grimsby Town	46	14	6	3	48	21	4	9	10	19	29	51
7	Watford	46	12	6	5	34	21	7	6	10	30	35	50
8	Aldershot	46	13	6	4	47	22	6	5	12	18	30	49
9	Halifax Town	46	9	11	3	23	15	5	10	8	25	36	49
10	Huddersfield Town	46	14	5	4	37	16	3	8	12	19	39	47
11	Bournemouth	46	11	5	7	25	23	5	10	8	29	35	47
12	Southend United	46	10	7	6	40	30	6	7	10	22	32	46
13	Blackburn Rovers	46	13	4	6	38	21	5	6	12	24	43	46
14	Charlton Athletic	46	13	5	5	43	29	6	3	14	23	44	46
15	Walsall	46	11	7	5	37	19	5	6	12	20	29	45
16	Tranmere Rovers	46	10	8	5	31	15	5	7	11	19	29	45
17	Plymouth Argyle	46	13	6	4	37	17	4	4	15	22	37	44
18	Hereford United	46	10	5	8	31	25	4	10	9	22	32	43
19	Brighton & Hove A.	46	10	3	10	31	31	6	8	9	21	27	43
20	Port Vale	46	12	6	5	37	23	2	8	13	15	35	42
21	Cambridge United	46	11	7	5	36	27	2	2	19	12	54	35
22	Shrewsbury Town	46	7	7	9	24	24	3	4	16	17	38	31
23	Southport	46	4	14	5	19	20	2	2	19	16	62	28
24	ROCHDALE	46	1	12	10	24	38	1	5	17	14	56	21

1973-74 Season
Back: Smith, Blant, Renwick, Kinsella, Poole, Morritt, Jones, Arnold, Marsh, Skeete, Atkins
Middle: Gowans, Bebbington, Brogden, Bradbury, Downes, Darling, Taylor, Cooper, Hanvey
Front: Moran, Fielding, Tobin, Phillips

1974-75 Season
Back: Joyce (Manager), Townsend, Cooper, Skeete, Hanvey, Brennan, Oliver, Whelan, Young, Fielding, Worthington, Butler (Coach), Campbell (Trainer)
Front: Moran, Waring, Hallows, Seddon, Carrick, Ferguson (Captain), Taylor, Tobin, Martin, Phillips, Murty, Ainsworth

			Result	Scorers	Att	Poole MD	Hallows PCR	Whelan AM	Horne SF	Grummett J	Ferguson MK	Taylor AD	Carrick MD	Skeete LA	Brennan M	Young NJ	Martin HJ	Fielding PA	Cooper GS	Tobin DJ	Hanvey K	Brears P	Seddon DA	Taylor, John L	Hulmes G	Mulvaney R	Townsend GE	Hutchinson R	Mountford RW	Murty J	Bell WG
1	Aug	17 Shrewsbury Town	1-1	Young	3513	1	2	3	4	5	6	7	8	9	10	11																
2		24 TORQUAY UNITED	1-1	Taylor	1271	1	2	3	4	5	6	7	8	12	9	11			7	10												
3		30 Mansfield Town	0-2		3779	1	2	3	4	5	6	8		9		11		10	7	12												
4	Sep	7 BARNSLEY	3-1	Taylor, Horne, Skeete	1376	1	2	3	4	5	6	8	7	9		11					10											
5		13 Doncaster Rovers	1-4	Carrick	1928	1	2	3	4	5	6	8	7	9		11					10											
6		16 Darlington	2-1	Taylor 2	2345	1	2	3	4	5	7	8	11	9							12	10	6								
7		21 WORKINGTON	2-0	Ferguson 2 (1p)	1385	1	2	3	4	5	7	8	11								9	10	6								
8		23 BRENTFORD	0-0		1587	1	2	3	4	5	7	8	11			12					9	10	6								
9		28 Lincoln City	0-3		2461	1	2	3	4	5	7	8	11			12					9	10	6								
10		30 READING	0-2		1684	1	2	3	4	5	7	8	11		9	10						6	12								
11	Oct	4 Stockport County	3-2	Brennan, Whelan, Crowther (og)	2354	1	2	11	4	5	7	8			10			6		9				3								
12		12 ROTHERHAM UNITED	1-2	Young	1684	1	2	11	4	5	7	8			10	12	6			9				3								
13		18 Swansea City	3-3	Skeete, Taylor, Hulmes	2767		2	11	4	5	7	8		10			6			9				3	1	12						
14		21 NORTHAMPTON T	2-2	Cooper, Horne	1379		2	11	4		7	8		10			6			9				3	1		5					
15		26 NEWPORT COUNTY	2-4	Ferguson (p), Taylor	1208		2	11	4	3	7	8		10		12	6			9					1		5					
16	Nov	2 Chester	0-4		3291	1	2	11	4		7	8		10			6			9				3			5					
17		5 Northampton Town	1-0	Whelan	5695	1	2	9	4		7	8	11								6	10	3				5					
18		9 CAMBRIDGE UNITED	0-0		1116	1	2	9	4		7	8	11								6	10	3				5					
19		16 Scunthorpe United	2-2	Taylor, Whelan	1787	1	2	9	4		7	8	11								6	10	3				5					
20		30 EXETER CITY	1-1	Mulvaney	1033	1	2	9	4		7		8			11					6	10	3			12	5					
21	Dec	7 Crewe Alexandra	1-0	Young	1803	1	2	9	4		3		8			11					6	10	12			7	5					
22		21 Hartlepool	0-5		1991	1	2	9			7		11		8			4			6	10				12	5	3				
23		26 DONCASTER ROVERS	2-0	Fielding, Hutchinson	1077	1	2	9			7			12				4		11	6	10					5	3	8			
24		28 Bradford City	0-1		3250	1	2	9			7							4	12	11	6	10					5	3	8			
25	Jan	4 DARLINGTON	2-0	Mountford 2	1217	1	2	9			7							4		11	6	10					5	3		8		
26		11 CREWE ALEXANDRA	3-0	Ferguson, Whelan, Fielding	1749	1	2	9			7							4		11	6	10					5	3		8		
27		18 Exeter City	1-2	Fielding	3560	1	2	9			7							4		11	6	10					5	3		8		
28	Feb	1 Cambridge United	1-1	Mountford	3118	1	2	9			7							4	12	11	6	10					5	3		8		
29		8 CHESTER	0-1		2273	1	2	9			7							4		11	6	10					5	3		8	12	
30		14 Southport	0-1		1569	1	2	9			7					5		4		11	6	10					3			8	12	
31		17 BRADFORD CITY	1-1	Mountford	2004	1	2	9			7					5		4		11	6	10					3			8		
32		22 SCUNTHORPE UNITED	4-2	Whelan, Mountford 2, Hallows	1430	1	2	9			7					5		4		11	6						3			8	10	
33	Mar	1 MANSFIELD TOWN	0-1		2317	1	2	9			7							4		11	6	10					5	3		8		
34		8 Brentford	0-3		4460	1	2	9			7	10						4		11	6						5	3		8		12
35		11 SOUTHPORT	3-3	Mountford 2, Mulvaney	1191	1	2	9			7							4		11	6	10					5	3		8		
36		15 Lincoln City	1-1	Whelan	1517	1	2	9			7				3	4				11	6	10					5			8	12	
37		17 SHREWSBURY TOWN	0-0		1427	1	2	9			7				11	12	4	8			6						5	3			10	
38		22 Barnsley	3-5	Cooper 2, Young	3594	1	2	9			7				11		4	8			6						5	3			10	
39		29 HARTLEPOOL	3-0	Fielding, Hanvey, Whelan	1297	1	2	9			7				11		4	8			6						5	3			10	
40		31 Workington	1-2	Mulvaney	1870	1	2	9			7				12		4	11			6						5	3		8	10	
41	Apr	5 Newport County	2-3	Mountford, Whelan	1801	1	2	9								12	4	7		11	6						5	3		8	10	
42		9 Reading	1-2	Hanvey	3861	1	2	9			7						4			11	6	10					5	3		8		
43		12 STOCKPORT COUNTY	3-0	Whelan 2, Cooper	1880	1	2	9			7						4	8	11	6	10						5	3				
44		19 Rotherham United	1-3	Cooper	7536	1	2	9									4	8	11	6	10	12				5	3			7		
45		23 Torquay United	0-3		2718	1	2	9									4	8	11	6	10	12				5	3			7		
46		26 SWANSEA CITY	1-0	Mountford	1548	1	2	9								11		4		10	6	7	3				5			8		
		Apps				43	46	46	21	14	42	19	16	10	10	13	13	27	22	26	35	24	13	3	4	30	23	2	16	6	6
		Goals					1	10	2		5	6	1	2	1	4		4	5		2				1	3		1	10		

One own goal

			Result	Scorers	Att	Poole MD	Hallows PCR	Whelan AM	Horne SF	Ferguson MK	Carrick MD	Skeete LA	Brennan M	Hanvey K	Brears P	Seddon DA	Mulvaney R
R1	Nov	23 MARINE	0-0		2041	1	2	9	4	7	11	8	12	6	10	3	5
rep		27 Marine	2-1	Carrick, Young	2540	1	2	9	4	7	8		11	6	10	3	5
R2	Dec	14 TRANMERE ROVERS	1-1	Brears	2221	1	2	9	4	7	8		11	6	10	3	5
rep		16 Tranmere Rovers	0-1		3244	1	2	3	4		8	9	11	6	10	12	5

R1 replay a.e.t.

			Result	Att	Poole MD	Hallows PCR	Whelan AM	Horne SF	Grummett J	Ferguson MK	Taylor AD	Carrick MD	Skeete LA	Brennan M	Young NJ	Martin HJ	Cooper GS
R1	Aug	20 Preston North End	0-1	7780	1	2	3	4	5	6	7	8	9	10	11		12

		P	W	D	L	F	A	W	D	L	F	A	Pts
1	Mansfield Town	46	17	6	0	55	15	11	6	6	35	25	68
2	Shrewsbury Town	46	16	3	4	46	18	10	7	6	34	25	62
3	Rotherham United	46	13	7	3	40	19	9	8	6	31	22	59
4	Chester	46	17	5	1	48	9	6	6	11	16	29	57
5	Lincoln City	46	14	8	1	47	14	7	7	9	32	34	57
6	Cambridge United	46	15	5	3	43	16	5	9	9	19	28	54
7	Reading	46	13	6	4	38	20	8	4	11	25	27	52
8	Brentford	46	15	6	2	38	14	3	7	13	15	31	49
9	Exeter City	46	14	3	6	33	24	5	8	10	27	39	49
10	Bradford City	46	10	5	8	32	21	7	8	8	24	30	47
11	Southport	46	13	7	3	36	19	2	10	11	20	37	47
12	Newport County	46	13	5	5	43	30	6	4	13	25	45	47
13	Hartlepool	46	13	6	4	40	24	3	5	15	12	38	43
14	Torquay United	46	10	7	6	30	25	4	7	12	16	36	42
15	Barnsley	46	10	7	6	34	24	5	4	14	28	41	41
16	Northampton Town	46	12	6	5	43	22	3	5	15	24	51	41
17	Doncaster Rovers	46	10	9	4	41	29	4	3	16	24	50	40
18	Crewe Alexandra	46	9	9	5	22	16	2	9	12	12	31	40
19	ROCHDALE	46	9	9	5	35	22	4	4	15	24	53	39
20	Stockport County	46	10	8	5	26	27	2	6	15	17	43	38
21	Darlington	46	11	4	8	38	27	2	6	15	16	40	36
22	Swansea City	46	9	4	10	25	31	6	2	15	21	42	36
23	Workington	46	7	5	11	23	29	3	6	14	13	37	31
24	Scunthorpe United	46	7	8	8	27	29	0	7	16	14	49	29

1975/76   15th in Division 4

#	Date		Opponents	Score	Scorers	Att	Poole MD	Hallows PCR	Townsend GE	Mulvaney R	Summerscales WC	Hanvey K	Fielding PA	Mountford RW	Whelan AM	Lacey AJ	Sweeney A	Cooper GS	Ferguson MK	Murty J	Tobin DJ	Hulmes G	Duffey CP	Oliver BC	Mullington PT	Boslem W	Brears P	Ainsworth D
1	Aug	16	Reading	0-2		4717	1	2	3	4	5	6	7	8	9	10	11	12										
2		23	SWANSEA CITY	2-1	Mountford 2	1169	1	2	3		5	6		8	10	4	11	9	7	12								
3		30	Huddersfield Town	0-0		4185	1	2	3		5	6		8	10		11	9	7									
4	Sep	6	NEWPORT COUNTY	4-3	Cooper 2, Mountford 2	1119	1	2	3	4	5	6		8	10		11	9	7									
5		13	Torquay United	0-1		1852	1	2		4	5	6	12	8	10	3	11	9	7									
6		20	BRADFORD CITY	0-0		2004	1	2		4	5	6		8	10	3	11	9	7									
7		24	Crewe Alexandra	0-0		4294	1	2		4	5	6		8	10	3	11	9	7									
8		26	Stockport County	1-0	Mountford	3436	1	2		4	5	6	12	8	10	3	11	9	7									
9	Oct	4	EXETER CITY	0-1		1234	1	2		4	5	6	12	8	10	3	11	9	7									
10		11	Scunthorpe United	3-1	Mountford 2, Whelan	2671	1	2			5	6	4	8	10	3		9	7	12	11							
11		18	WATFORD	2-1	Summerscales, Tobin	1528	1	2			5	6	4	8	10	3		9	7		11							
12		22	Bournemouth	1-2	Tobin	4395				2	5		4	8	10	3		9	7		11							
13		25	Southport	1-0	Tobin	1447	1	2			5		4	8	10	3		9	7		11							
14	Nov	1	TRANMERE ROVERS	4-1	Tobin, Whelan, Mountford 2	2047	1	2			5	6	4	8	10	3		9	7		11							
15		3	NORTHAMPTON T	0-2		2995	1	2			5	6	4	8	10	3		9	7		11	12						
16		8	Lincoln City	0-2		7063	1	2			5	6	4	8	10	3	12	9	7									
17		14	CAMBRIDGE UNITED	1-1	Mulvaney	1562	1	2			5	6		8	10	3		11	9	7	12	4						
18		29	WORKINGTON	1-1	Tobin	1361	1	2	3		5			8	10	6		4	7		11			9				
19	Dec	6	Brentford	0-3		4853	1	2	12		5			8	10			4	7		11			9				
20		20	HARTLEPOOL	1-1	Murty	1156	1	2		4	5	6			10	3		9	7	11			8					
21		26	Barnsley	1-2	Mountford	3486	1	2			6	5		8	9	3		4		7	10	12			11			
22		27	DARLINGTON	1-0	Murty	1659	1	2	3		6	5		8	9			4		7					11			
23	Jan	17	Bradford City	0-3		3059	1	2		4	5	6	10	8	9	3					7				11			
24		20	Doncaster Rovers	2-1	Hanvey, Fielding	3586	1	2		4	5	6	10	8	9	3		12			7				11			
25		24	TORQUAY UNITED	2-2	Hanvey, Whelan	1448	1	2			5	6	10	8	9	3		12			7				11			
26	Feb	7	Northampton Town	1-1	Whelan	5393	1	2		4	5	6	10	8	9	3					7				11			
27		10	BOURNEMOUTH	2-2	Whelan, Mountford	1392	1	2		4	5	6	10	8	9	3					7				11			
28		14	LINCOLN CITY	0-0		2439	1	2		4	5	6		8	9	3			10	7					11			
29		21	Cambridge United	0-0		2048		2		4	5	6		8	9	3			7	10		12		1	11			
30		28	SOUTHPORT	2-0	Mountford, Summerscales	1261		2		4	5	6		8	9	3	11		10	7						6		
31	Mar	1	HUDDERSFIELD T	0-0		3791	1	2		4	5	6		8	9	3			10	7						11		
32		6	Tranmere Rovers	1-0	Mullington	3354	1	2		4	5	6		8	9	3			10	7						11		
33		9	Exeter City	0-1		3102	1	2		4	5	6		8	9	3			10	7				12		11		
34		12	SCUNTHORPE UNITED	1-1	Cooper	1430	1	2		4	5	6		8	9	3			10	7						11		
35		16	Watford	0-3		3886	1	2		4	5	6		8	9	3			10	7						11		12
36		20	Workington	0-1		941	1	2			5			8	9	3			10	7			11			6	4	
37		22	CREWE ALEXANDRA	0-1		1128	1	2			5			8	9	3		12	10	7			11			6	4	
38		27	BRENTFORD	1-2	Boslem	894		2	3	4	5	6		8					10	7				1	11	12	9	
39		31	Hartlepool	0-3		1561		2	3	4	5		7	8	9									1	11	6		
40	Apr	3	READING	0-0		913	1	2		4	5		7	8		3			10						11	6	9	
41		5	STOCKPORT COUNTY	2-3	Mountford, Whelan (p)	1287	1	2		4	5		7	8	9	3			10				6		11			
42		10	Newport County	1-1	Mullington	1331	1	2		4	5	6	7		9	3			10						11	8		
43		16	DONCASTER ROVERS	1-0	Mountford	1462	1	2		4	5	6	12	8	9	3			7						11		10	
44		17	BARNSLEY	0-0		1386	1	2		4	5	6	7	8	9	3			10						11			12
45		20	Darlington	0-4		1957	1	2		4	5	6		8	9	3			7						11		10	
46		23	Swansea City	1-1	Cooper	1664	1	2		4	5	6	7	8		3		12	10						11			
					Apps		43	45	9	38	43	28	30	44	44	41	17	41	27	15	12	6	2	3	26	9	2	2
					Goals					1	2	2	1	14	6			4		2	5				2	1		

F.A. Cup

	Date		Opponents	Score	Scorers	Att	Poole MD	Hallows PCR	Townsend GE	Mulvaney R	Summerscales WC	Hanvey K	Fielding PA	Mountford RW	Whelan AM	Lacey AJ	Sweeney A	Cooper GS	Ferguson MK	Murty J	Tobin DJ	Hulmes G	Duffey CP	Oliver BC	Mullington PT	Boslem W	Brears P	Ainsworth D
R1	Nov	22	Workington	1-1	Ferguson	1190	1	2			4	5	6	8	10	3		9	7		11							
rep		26	WORKINGTON	2-1	Mountford, Whelan	2354	1	2			5	6	4	8	10	3		9	7		11							
R2	Dec	13	Gateshead	1-1	Albeson (og)	4600		2	3		5			8	9			11	4	7	10			1				
rep		15	GATESHEAD	3-1	Mountford, Morrison (og), Tobin	2607	1	2	3		5	6		8	10	4		9	7		11							
R3	Jan	3	Norwich City	1-1	Mullington	14187	1	2			4	5	6	8	10	3		9	7						11			
rep		6	NORWICH CITY	0-0		8284	1	2			4	5	6	8	10	3		9	7	12					11			
rep2		13	Norwich City	1-2	Mountford	18868	1	2			4	5	6	10	8	9	3		7						11			

Round 1 replay and Round 3 replay a.e.t.

F.L. Cup

	Date		Opponents	Score	Scorers	Att	Poole MD	Hallows PCR	Townsend GE	Mulvaney R	Summerscales WC	Hanvey K	Fielding PA	Mountford RW	Whelan AM	Lacey AJ	Sweeney A	Cooper GS	Ferguson MK	Murty J
R1/1	Aug	18	Bury	0-2		4561	1	2	3		5	6	4	8	9	10	11		7	
R1/2		26	BURY	0-2		3725	1	2	3	12	5	6		8	10	4	11	9	7	

		P	W	D	L	F	A	W	D	L	F	A	Pts
1	Lincoln City	46	21	2	0	71	15	11	8	4	40	24	74
2	Northampton Town	46	18	5	0	62	20	11	5	7	25	20	68
3	Reading	46	19	3	1	42	9	5	9	9	28	42	60
4	Tranmere Rovers	46	18	3	2	61	16	6	7	10	28	39	58
5	Huddersfield Town	46	11	6	6	28	17	10	8	5	28	24	56
6	Bournemouth	46	15	5	3	39	16	5	7	11	18	32	52
7	Exeter City	46	13	7	3	37	17	5	7	11	19	30	50
8	Watford	46	16	4	3	38	18	6	2	15	24	44	50
9	Torquay United	46	12	6	5	31	24	6	8	9	24	39	50
10	Doncaster Rovers	46	10	6	7	42	31	9	5	9	33	38	49
11	Swansea City	46	14	8	1	51	21	2	7	14	15	36	47
12	Barnsley	46	8	8	3	34	16	2	8	13	18	32	44
13	Cambridge United	46	7	10	6	36	28	7	5	11	22	34	43
14	Hartlepool	46	10	6	7	37	29	6	4	13	25	49	42
15	ROCHDALE	46	7	11	5	27	23	5	7	11	13	31	42
16	Crewe Alexandra	46	10	7	6	36	21	3	8	12	22	36	41
17	Bradford City	46	9	7	7	35	26	3	10	10	28	39	41
18	Brentford	46	12	7	4	37	18	2	6	15	19	42	41
19	Scunthorpe United	46	11	3	9	31	24	3	7	13	19	35	38
20	Darlington	46	11	7	5	30	14	3	3	17	18	43	38
21	Stockport County	46	8	7	8	23	23	5	5	13	20	53	38
22	Newport County	46	8	7	8	35	33	5	2	16	22	57	35
23	Southport	46	6	6	11	27	31	2	4	17	14	46	26
24	Workington	46	5	4	14	19	43	2	3	18	11	44	21

1975-76 Season

Back:Joyce(Manager),Townsend,Cooper,Mountford,Whelan,Oliver,Poole,Summerscales,Hanvey,Mulvaney,Horne,Campbell(Coach)

Front: Hallows, Ainsworth, Fielding, Tobin, Murty, Lacey, Hulmes, Sweeney

1976-77 Season

Back: Green (Manager), Helliwell, Hanvey, Summerscales, Poole, Laisby, Bannon, Mulvaney, O'Loughlin, Campbell (Trainer)

Front: Hallows, Mullington, Mountford, Melledew (Captain), Cooper, Lacey, Tarbuck

1976/77 18th in Division 4

Two own goals

#	Date	Opponent	Score	Scorers	Att	Poole MD	Hallows PCR	Lacey AJ	Hanvey K	Summerscales WC	O'Loughlin N	Helliwell D	Melledew ST	Whelan AM	Mullington PT	Tarbuck AD	Boslem W	Mountford RW	Mulvaney R	Cooper GS	Bannon I	Mason SJ	Hamstead GW	Dungworth JH	Mullen J	Shyne C
1	Aug 21	Scunthorpe United	1-0	Mountford	3536	1	2	3		5	6		7	9	10	11		8								
2	23	CAMBRIDGE UNITED	2-2	Hanvey (p), Mullington	1716	1	2	3	4	5	6	12	7	9	10	11		8								
3	28	COLCHESTER UNITED	1-0	Hanvey	1440	1	2	3	4	5	6	7	8	9	10	11			12							
4	Sep 4	Halifax Town	0-0		2003	1	2	3	6	5	10	7	8	9	12	11			4							
5	11	Exeter City	1-2	Hanvey (p)	2829	1	2	3	4	5	6		7	9	10	11		12		8						
6	18	WATFORD	3-1	O'Loughlin, Mullington, Melledew	1760	1	2	3	6	5	10		7	9	8	11			4							
7	25	Crewe Alexandra	1-1	Hanvey	2454	1	2	3	6	5	10		7	9	8	11			4							
8	Oct 2	BOURNEMOUTH	0-0		1807	1	2	3	6	5	10		7	9	8	11			4							
9	9	Workington	2-0	Mullington, Mountford	1423	1	2	3	4	5	6		7	9	10	11		8								
10	16	SOUTHEND UNITED	0-0		2302	1	2	3	4	5	6	12	7	9	10	11		8								
11	23	Hartlepool	0-2		1492	1	2	3	4	5	6	12	7	9	10	11		8								
12	27	Aldershot	2-0	Whelan, O'Loughlin	4654	1	2	3	4	5	6		7	9	10	11		8								
13	30	DONCASTER ROVERS	1-0	Mountford	2436	1	2	3	4	5	6		7	9	10	11		8								
14	Nov 1	DARLINGTON	2-2	Tarbuck, Summerscales	2577	1	2	3	4	5	6	12	7	9	10	11		8								
15	6	Southport	1-1	Whelan	1729	1	2	3		5	6	12	7	9	10	11	4			8						
16	13	NEWPORT COUNTY	0-0		2482	1	2	3		5	6	12	7	9	10	11	4			8						
17	26	Huddersfield Town	1-2	Cooper	5240	1	2	3		5	6	8	7	9		11	4			12						
18	Dec 27	BRADFORD CITY	0-1		2942	1	2	3		5			7	9		11		8		10	4	6				
19	29	Stockport County	1-0	Mountford	3842	1	2	3		5			7	9		11		8		10	4	6				
20	Jan 8	SWANSEA CITY	1-0	Cooper	1436	1	2	3		5	12		7	9	6	11		8		10	4					
21	11	Doncaster Rovers	0-2		3008	1	2	3		5	12		7	9	6	11		8		10	4					
22	15	Cambridge United	0-0		3607	1	2	3	6	5	10	12	7	9	8	11			4							
23	22	SCUNTHORPE UNITED	5-0	Peacock (og), Melledew, O'Loughlin, Cooper	1640	1	2	3	6	5	10	11	7	9	8			12	4							
24	25	BARNSLEY	2-3	Mullington, Mountford	2474	1	2		6	5	10		7	3	8		9		4	12				11		
25	29	Torquay United	0-2		2453	1	2		4	5	6	10	7	3	8		9							11		
26	Feb 5	Colchester United	0-1		4943	1	2		6	5	3	12	7	11	8		9		4					10		
27	12	HALIFAX TOWN	4-1	Summerscales, Mountford, Helliwell, Cooper	2255	1	2			5	3	10	7	11		6	9		8	4				12		
28	19	EXETER CITY	1-2	Whelan (p)	1523	1	2	3		5	6	10	7	11	12		9		8	4						
29	22	Brentford	2-3	Melledew, Helliwell	3307	1	2	3		5	6	10	7	11	12		9		8	4						
30	26	Watford	1-3	Melledew	6331	1	2	3		5	6	10	7	11		4	9		8							
31	Mar 1	SOUTHPORT	3-0	Whelan, Melledew 2	1153	1	2	3		5	6		7	11	10	4	9		8							
32	5	CREWE ALEXANDRA	0-1		1609	1	2	3		5	6	12	7	11	10		9		8	4						
33	12	Bournemouth	1-1	Dungworth	3400	1	2	3		5	6		7	10			9			4				8	11	
34	19	WORKINGTON	0-3		1737	1	2	3		5	6	12	7	10			9			4				8	11	
35	25	Southend United	0-3		5677	1	2	3		5	6	10	7		12		4	9						8	11	
36	Apr 2	HARTLEPOOL	0-1		858	1	2	3		5	6	10	7		12		4	9						8	11	
37	6	Bradford City	0-3		5263	1	2	3		5	6	10	7		11		4	9	12					8		
38	9	STOCKPORT COUNTY	1-1	Mountford	1489	1	2	3		5	6	10		11		7	9	12	4					8		
39	12	Darlington	2-0	O'Loughlin, Dungworth	2586	1	2	3		5	6	10		11		7	9		4					8		
40	16	ALDERSHOT	2-1	Earles (og), Helliwell	1038	1	2	3			6	10	7		11		5	9		4				8		
41	23	Newport County	0-3		2206	1	2	3			6	10	7		11		5	9		4				8	12	
42	26	TORQUAY UNITED	0-1		852	1	2	3			6	12	7		10			9		4				8	11	
43	30	HUDDERSFIELD T	2-2	Mountford 2	1626	1	2	3		5	6	7			11			9	10	4				8		
44	May 3	Swansea City	2-3	Mountford 2	10689	1	2	3		5	6	7	12		11			9	10	4				8		
45	7	Barnsley	0-2		2531		2	3		5	6	7	9		11				10	4				8	12	1
46	14	BRENTFORD	2-3	Dungworth, Mullen	977		2	3		5	6	7	9		12				10	4				8	11	1
				Apps		44	46	42	19	44	44	31	43	34	40	22	13	34	5	22	23	2	4	14	8	2
				Goals					4	2	3	3	6	4	4	1		12		5				3	1	

F.A. Cup

	Date	Opponent	Score	Scorers	Att	Poole	Hallows	Lacey	Hanvey	Summerscales	O'Loughlin	Helliwell	Melledew	Whelan	Mullington	Tarbuck	Boslem	Mountford	Mulvaney	Cooper
R1	Nov 20	NORTHWICH VICTORIA	1-1	Helliwell	3641	1	2	3		5	6	8	7	9	10	11			4	12
rep	22	Northwich Victoria	0-0		4273	1	2	3		5	6	8	7	9	10	11			4	
rep2	29	Northwich Victoria	1-2	Tarbuck	4909	1	2	3		5	6		7	9		11		8	4	10

Replay a.e.t. Replay 2 at Maine Road.

F.L. Cup

	Date	Opponent	Score	Scorers	Att	Poole	Hallows	Lacey	Hanvey	Summerscales	O'Loughlin	Helliwell	Melledew	Whelan	Mullington	Tarbuck	Boslem	Mountford
R1/1	Aug 14	BLACKBURN ROVERS	0-1		3547	1	2	3	4	5	6	7	8	9	10	11		
R1/2	18	Blackburn Rovers	1-4	Melledew	5232	1	2	3	4	5	6		7	9	10	11		8

		P	W	D	L	F	A	W	D	L	F	A	Pts
1	Cambridge United	46	16	5	2	57	18	10	8	5	30	22	65
2	Exeter City	46	17	5	1	40	13	8	7	8	30	33	62
3	Colchester United	46	19	2	2	51	14	6	7	10	26	29	59
4	Bradford City	46	16	7	0	51	18	7	6	10	27	33	59
5	Swansea City	46	18	3	2	60	30	7	5	11	32	38	58
6	Barnsley	46	16	5	2	45	18	7	4	12	17	21	55
7	Watford	46	15	7	1	46	13	3	8	12	21	37	51
8	Doncaster Rovers	46	16	2	5	47	25	5	7	11	24	40	51
9	Huddersfield Town	46	15	5	3	36	15	4	7	12	24	34	50
10	Southend United	46	11	9	3	35	19	4	10	9	17	26	49
11	Darlington	46	13	5	5	37	25	5	8	10	22	39	49
12	Crewe Alexandra	46	16	6	1	36	15	3	5	15	11	45	49
13	Bournemouth	46	13	8	2	39	13	2	10	11	15	31	48
14	Stockport County	46	10	10	3	29	19	3	9	11	24	38	45
15	Brentford	46	14	3	6	48	27	4	4	15	29	49	43
16	Torquay United	46	12	5	6	33	22	5	4	14	26	45	43
17	Aldershot	46	10	8	5	29	19	6	3	14	20	40	43
18	ROCHDALE	46	8	7	8	32	25	5	5	13	18	34	38
19	Newport County	46	11	6	6	33	21	3	4	16	9	37	38
20	Scunthorpe United	46	11	6	6	32	24	2	5	16	17	49	37
21	Halifax Town	46	11	6	6	36	18	0	8	15	11	40	36
22	Hartlepool	46	8	9	6	30	20	2	3	18	17	53	32
23	Southport	46	3	12	8	17	28	0	7	16	16	49	25
24	Workington	46	3	7	13	23	42	1	4	18	18	60	19

1977/78 24th in Division 4

#	Date	Opponent	Score	Scorers	Att	Poole MD	Hallows PCR	O'Loughlin N	Morrin AJ	Scott RW	Bannon I	Melledew ST	Seddon IW	Mountford RW	Esser ED	Tarbuck AD	Boslem W	Oliver EA	Cuddy P	Owen LT	Shyne C	Scaife RH	Shaw S	Green A	Hoy R	Hart BP	Slack A	Hilditch MW	Price J	Finc R
1	Aug 20	Barnsley	0-4		3901	1	3	9	10	5	6	7	8			11	4	2	12											
2	27	DARLINGTON	2-0	Seddon, Mountford	1295	1	2	3		5	6	7	8	9	10	11	4													
3	Sep 3	Grimsby Town	1-2	Seddon	2731	1	2	3		5	6	7	8	9	10	11														
4	10	Swansea City	0-3		4750	1	2	3	4	5	6	7	8	9	10	11				12										
5	13	BRENTFORD	1-2	Owen	1164	1	2	3	4	5	6	7	8		10	11				9										
6	17	NEWPORT COUNTY	0-1		1114	1	2	3	4	5	6	12	8	9	10	11				7										
7	24	Aldershot	0-2		3633	1	2	3	4	5	6	9	8		10	11				7										
8	27	Hartlepool United	0-1		3389	1	2	3	4	5	6	9	8		10	11	12			7										
9	Oct 1	WATFORD	2-3	Pritchett (og), Melledew	1278	1	2	3		5	6	9	8		10	11	4	12		7										
10	4	HALIFAX TOWN	3-1	Owen, Melledew 2	1201		2	4		5	6	9	8		10	11		3		7	1									
11	7	Stockport County	0-2		4927		2	3		5	6	9	8		10	11		12		7	1	4								
12	11	Northampton Town	1-3	Melledew	2965	1	2	3		5		9	8		10	11	6			7		4								
13	15	DONCASTER ROVERS	3-1	Owen, Melledew, Esser	1963	1	2	3		5		9	8		10	11	6			7		4								
14	17	HUDDERSFIELD T	0-0		2489	1	2	3		5	6	9	8		10	11				7		4								
15	21	York City	2-2	Melledew, Scaife	1669	1	2	3		5	6	9	8		10	11				7		4								
16	29	NORTHAMPTON T	1-1	O'Loughlin (p)	1198	1	2	3		5	6	9	8		10	11				7		4								
17	Nov 5	Crewe Alexandra	1-2	Seddon	2378	1	2	3	12		6	9	8		10	11	5			7		4								
18	12	BOURNEMOUTH	1-1	Owen	962	1	2	3	8	5	6				10	11	12			7		4								
19	19	Scunthorpe United	0-1		2204	1		3	8	5	6				10		2			7		4		11						
20	Dec 3	SOUTHEND UNITED	1-2	Scaife	902	1		3		4	5	6	9		10		2			7		4		11						
21	10	Torquay United	0-3		2144	1		10	4	5	6	9			12		2			7				8		11	3			
22	17	Halifax Town	1-3	Scott	1918	1	2	10	4	5		9				6				7				8		3	11			
23	26	WIMBLEDON	3-0	Scaife 2, O'Loughlin	1283	1	2	10	4		6	9			11		5			7				8		3				
24	28	Reading	3-4	Owen 2, Esser	5066	1	2	10	4	5	12	9			11		6			7				8		3				
25	31	Southport	1-3	Esser	1908	1	2			4		6			10		5	3		7		8	11	9						
26	Jan 2	CREWE ALEXANDRA	0-2		1441	1			4		6	9			10		5	2		7		8	11	3						
27	7	Huddersfield Town	1-3	Scaife	5486				4		6	9			10		5	2		7		8	3	11				1		
28	14	BARNSLEY	1-1	Owen	2668		3		4	5	6	9			10		2			7		8		11				1		
29	24	Darlington	0-1		1578			3	4	5	6	9			10		2	12		7		8		11				1		
30	Feb 11	Newport County	0-3		4288			3	4	5	6	9			10		2			7		8		11				1		
31	25	Watford	0-1		10139		2	3	4	5	6	9	12		10					7		8		11				1		
32	27	SWANSEA CITY	2-1	Hoy, Melledew	1057		2	3	4	5	6	9	7		10							8		11				1		
33	Mar 4	STOCKPORT COUNTY	2-1	Owen, O'Loughlin (p)	2278		2	3	4	5	6		7		10					9		8		11				1		
34	6	Brentford	0-4		7215		2	3	4		6	9	7		10					12		8		11				1		
35	10	Doncaster Rovers	1-1	Owen	2755		2	3	4	5	6	9	7		10					11		8						1		
36	18	YORK CITY	1-2	O'Loughlin (p)	1046		2	3	4	5	6	9	7		10					11		8						1		
37	20	GRIMSBY TOWN	1-3	Scaife	787			3	4	5	6	9	7		10	2				11		8						1		
38	27	Wimbledon	1-5	Esser	2737		2	11	4	5	6		7		10			3		12		8	9					1		
39	Apr 1	SOUTHPORT	2-1	Esser 2	966		2	11		5	6		4		10	7				9		8			3			1		
40	4	HARTLEPOOL UNITED	0-1		972		2	11		5	6		4		10	7				9		8			3			1		
41	8	Bournemouth	0-1		2549		2	11		5	6		4		10	7				9	1	8			3					
42	15	SCUNTHORPE UNITED	1-1	Hallows	857		2	11		5	6		4		10	7				9	1	8			3		12			
43	21	Southend United	1-3	Esser	11565		2	11		5	6		4		10	7				9	1	8			3					
44	24	READING	1-0	Hilditch	734		2	11		5	6		4			7				9	1	8			3		10			
45	29	TORQUAY UNITED	1-3	O'Loughlin (p)	742		2	11		5	6					7	4	8		9	1				3		10		12	
46	May 1	ALDERSHOT	0-0		923	2	11			5	6					7	4	8		9	1				3				10	12
		Apps				24	37	43	29	40	43	35	31	4	41	26	22	12	1	42	8	34	6	7	9	8	14	3	2	1
		Goals					1	5		1		6	3	1	7					10		6					1			

One own goal

F.A. Cup

	Date	Opponent	Score	Scorers	Att	Poole MD		O'Loughlin N	Morrin AJ	Scott RW	Bannon I		Seddon IW		Esser ED		Boslem W			Owen LT		Scaife RH		Green A	Hoy R					
R1	Nov 26	Scarborough	2-4	Owen 2	4798	1		3	8	5	6		9		10		2			7				4	11					

F.L. Cup

	Date	Opponent	Score	Scorers	Att	Poole MD	Hallows PCR	O'Loughlin N	Morrin AJ	Scott RW	Bannon I	Melledew ST	Seddon IW	Mountford RW	Esser ED	Tarbuck AD	Boslem W	Oliver EA
R1/1	Aug 13	HALIFAX TOWN	1-1	Tarbuck	1512	1	2	3	4	5	6	7	8	9	10	11	12	
R1/2	16	Halifax Town	2-1	Mountford, Esser	1784	1	2	3	4	5	6	7	8	9	10	11		
R2	31	LEEDS UNITED	0-3		8664	1		3	4	5	6	7	8	9	10	11	12	2

		P	W	D	L	F	A	W	D	L	F	A	Pts
1	Watford	46	18	4	1	44	14	12	7	4	41	24	71
2	Southend United	46	15	5	3	46	18	10	5	8	20	21	60
3	Swansea City	46	16	5	2	54	17	7	5	11	33	30	56
4	Brentford	46	15	6	2	50	17	6	8	9	36	37	56
5	Aldershot	46	15	8	0	45	16	4	8	11	22	31	54
6	Grimsby Town	46	14	6	3	30	15	7	5	11	27	36	53
7	Barnsley	46	15	4	4	44	20	3	10	10	17	29	50
8	Reading	46	12	7	4	33	23	6	7	10	22	29	50
9	Torquay United	46	12	6	5	43	25	4	9	10	14	31	47
10	Northampton Town	46	9	8	6	32	30	8	5	10	31	38	47
11	Huddersfield Town	46	13	5	5	41	21	2	10	11	22	34	45
12	Doncaster Rovers	46	11	8	4	37	26	3	9	11	15	39	45
13	Wimbledon	46	8	11	4	39	26	6	5	12	27	41	44
14	Scunthorpe United	46	12	6	5	31	14	2	10	11	19	41	44
15	Crewe Alexandra	46	11	8	4	34	25	4	6	13	16	44	44
16	Newport County	46	14	6	3	43	22	2	5	16	22	51	43
17	Bournemouth	46	12	6	5	28	20	2	9	12	13	31	43
18	Stockport County	46	14	4	5	41	19	2	6	15	15	37	42
19	Darlington	46	10	8	5	31	22	4	5	14	21	37	41
20	Halifax Town	46	7	10	6	28	23	3	11	9	24	39	41
21	Hartlepool United	46	12	4	7	34	29	3	3	17	17	55	37
22	York City	46	8	7	8	27	31	4	5	14	23	38	36
23	Southport	46	5	13	5	30	32	1	6	16	22	44	31
24	ROCHDALE	46	8	6	9	29	28	0	2	21	14	57	24

1977-78 Season
Back: Green (Manager), Boslem, Scott, Shyne, Mountford, Bannon, O'Loughlin, Campbell (Trainer)
Front: Esser, Seddon, Melledew, Hallows, Tarbuck
Sitting: Shaw, Oliver

1978-79 Season
Back: Ashworth, Shyne, Hart, Slack, Bannon
Middle: Ferguson (Man.), Suthurst (Dir.), Stanley, Snookes, Scaife, Scott, Price, Shaw, Stoney (Dir.), Robson (Trainer)
Front: Morrin, Esser, O'Loughlin, Ratcliffe (Chair.), Hallows, Oliver, Owen

1978/79 20th in Division 4

#		Date	Opponent	Score	Scorers	Att	Slack A	Hallows PCR	Snookes E	Hart BP	Scott RW	Bannon I	Owen LT	Scaife RH	Ashworth P	Mullington PT	O'Loughlin N	Esser ED	Shyne C	Hoy R	Hilditch MW	Price J	Oliver EA	Morrin AJ	Felgate DW	Forster GP	Creamer PA	Taylor B(2)	Jones CMN	Collins JD	Milne M
1	Aug	19	YORK CITY	1-2	Scaife	1241	1	2	3	4	5	6	7	8	9	10	11	12													
2		23	Reading	0-2		4481		2	3	4	5		7	6	9	10	11	12		1	8										
3		26	ALDERSHOT	1-1	Owen	976		2	3	4	5		7	6	9	10	11			1	8										
4	Sep	2	Port Vale	1-1	Owen	3222		2	3	4	5		7	6	9	10	11			1	8										
5		9	PORTSMOUTH	0-2		1479		2	3	4	5		7	6	9	12	11	10		1	8										
6		13	Wigan Athletic	0-3		5736		2		4	5		7	6	12		11	3		1	8	9	10								
7		16	Bournemouth	1-3	Owen	2674		2		4		5	7	6			11	3		1	8	9	10								
8		23	HEREFORD UNITED	0-2		1068		2		4	5		7	6	12	11	3	10		1	8	9									
9		25	WIMBLEDON	0-0		1263		2		4	5		7	6	9	11	3	10		1	8										
10		30	Grimsby Town	0-4		3929		2	3	4	5				6	9	11	10		1	8		7								
11	Oct	7	HALIFAX TOWN	1-1	Hoy	1579		2	3	4	5		7	6		10	11	9		8	12				1						
12		14	Torquay United	1-1	Scaife	2818		2	3	4	5		7	6			11	10		9	8				1						
13		17	Newport County	0-0		3472		2	3	4	5		7	6			11	10		12	9	8			1						
14		21	DARLINGTON	2-1	Owen, Esser	1272		2	3	4	5		7	6			11	10		8	9				1						
15		28	Hartlepool United	1-5	Esser	3084		2	3	4	5		7	6			11	9		8	12	10			1						
16	Nov	4	CREWE ALEXANDRA	2-1	Hoy 2 (1p)	1352		2	3	4	5		7	6	9			10		8	12	11			1						
17		11	PORT VALE	0-1		1882			3	4	5		7	6	9		2	10		8	11	12			1						
18		18	Aldershot	0-1		3043			3	4	5	12	7	6			2	10		8	9	11			1						
19	Dec	2	Doncaster Rovers	0-1		2248				4	5	2	7	6			3	10		8	9	11			1						
20		9	Barnsley	0-3		3136				4	5	2	7	6			3	10		8	9	11			1		12				
21		26	Bradford City	0-1		4940				6	5	12	8	4			10	11		7					1			2	3	9	
22		30	Scunthorpe United	4-0	Owen, Hoy 2, Jones	2714				6	5	12	8	4			10	11		7					1			2	3	9	
23	Jan	13	Portsmouth	1-1		11596			6		5	12	8	4			10	11		7					1			2	3	9	
24	Feb	3	Wimbledon	2-3	Jones, Hoy	3064			6		5	12	8	4			10	11		7					1			2	3	9	
25	Mar	3	Darlington	2-0	Jones, Esser	1495			6		5		8	4			10	11		7					1			2	3	9	12
26		10	HARTLEPOOL UNITED	1-1	Hoy (p)	1931			6		5		8	4			10	11		7					1			2	3	9	
27		13	GRIMSBY TOWN	2-5	Jones, Snookes	2345			6		5		8	4			10	11		7					1			2	3	9	12
28		19	WIGAN ATHLETIC	0-2		3627				6	5			4			10	11	1	7	12				1			2	3	9	8
29		21	Hereford United	2-2	Jones 2	2351		3	2				11	4			10			7					1		6	5	9	8
30		24	READING	1-0	Hoy	1567		3	2				11	4			10	12		7					1		6	5	9	8
31		27	York City	1-2	Owen	2295		3	2				11	4			10	8		7					1		6	5	9	
32		31	Northampton Town	0-1		1653		3	2			5	11	4			10	8		7	12				1			6	9	
33	Apr	3	BOURNEMOUTH	2-1	Jones, Scott	1136		3	2		5		11	8			10	7							1		4	6	9	
34		7	DONCASTER ROVERS	2-0	Owen 2	1606		3	2	5			11	8			10	7		12					1		4	6	9	
35		11	HUDDERSFIELD T	0-2		2020		3	2	5			11				10	8		12	7				1		4	6	9	
36		14	BRADFORD CITY	1-0	Scott	2262		3	2	5			11				10			7	9				1		4	6		8	12
37		16	Stockport County	0-3		2863			2	5			11				10	12		7	9				1		4	6		8	3
38		17	Huddersfield Town	0-1		3346			2			5	11				10	8		7	9	3			1		4	6		
39		21	SCUNTHORPE UNITED	1-0	Taylor	1224		3				5	11				4	8		7	9				1		2	6		10
40		23	NEWPORT COUNTY	1-0	Esser	1457		3	2			5	11				10	8		7	9	4			1			6		
41		28	Barnsley	3-0	Owen 2, Hoy	12051		3	2			5	11				10	8		7		4			1			6	9	
42	May	1	STOCKPORT COUNTY	2-0	Esser, Hoy	2117		3	2			5	11				10	8		7		4			1			6	9	
43		5	NORTHAMPTON T	4-1	Oliver, Jones 2, O'Loughlin	1751		3	2			5					10	8		7	11		4		1			6	9	
44		7	Halifax Town	1-2	Hilditch	2150		3	2			5	11				10	8		7	12		4		1			6	9	
45		9	TORQUAY UNITED	1-0	Hilditch	2359	7	3	2			5					10	8			11		4		1			12	6	9	
46		18	Crewe Alexandra	2-1	Jones, Hilditch	2031		3	2			5					10	8		7	11		4		1			12	6	9	
			Apps				1	18	35	39	31	20	41	34	11	9	45	40	10	41	27	10	8	1	35	1	20	26	21	8	2
			Goals						1		2		11	2			1	5		10	3		1					1	10		

F.A. Cup

		Date	Opponent	Score		Att			Snookes	Hart	Scott		Owen	Scaife			O'Loughlin	Esser		Hoy	Hilditch	Price									
R1	Nov	25	DROYLSDEN	0-1		3252			3	4	5		7	6			2	10		1	8	9	11								

F.L. Cup

		Date	Opponent	Score	Scorers	Att	Slack	Hallows	Snookes	Hart	Scott	Bannon	Owen	Scaife	Ashworth	Mullington	O'Loughlin	Esser
R1/1	Aug	12	Crewe Alexandra	0-1		1914	1	2	3	4	5	6	7	8	9	10	11	12
R1/2		14	CREWE ALEXANDRA	2-4	O'Loughlin, Ashworth	1344	1	2	3	4	5	6	7	8	9	10	11	12

		P	W	D	L	F	A	W	D	L	F	A	Pts
1	Reading	46	19	3	1	49	8	7	10	6	27	27	65
2	Grimsby Town	46	15	5	3	51	23	11	4	8	31	26	61
3	Wimbledon	46	18	3	2	50	20	7	8	8	28	26	61
4	Barnsley	46	15	5	3	47	23	9	8	6	26	19	61
5	Aldershot	46	16	5	2	38	14	4	12	7	25	33	57
6	Wigan Athletic	46	14	5	4	40	24	7	8	8	23	24	55
7	Portsmouth	46	13	7	3	35	12	7	5	11	27	36	52
8	Newport County	46	12	5	6	39	28	9	5	9	27	27	52
9	Huddersfield Town	46	13	8	2	32	15	5	3	15	25	38	47
10	York City	46	11	6	6	33	24	7	5	11	18	31	47
11	Torquay United	46	14	4	5	38	24	5	4	14	20	41	46
12	Scunthorpe United	46	12	3	8	33	30	5	8	10	21	30	45
13	Hartlepool United	46	7	12	4	35	28	6	6	11	22	38	44
14	Hereford United	46	12	8	3	35	18	3	5	15	18	35	43
15	Bradford City	46	11	5	7	38	26	6	4	13	24	42	43
16	Port Vale	46	8	10	5	29	28	6	4	13	28	42	42
17	Stockport County	46	11	5	7	33	21	3	7	13	25	39	40
18	Bournemouth	46	11	6	6	34	19	3	5	15	13	29	39
19	Northampton Town	46	12	4	7	40	30	3	5	15	24	46	39
20	ROCHDALE	46	11	4	8	25	26	4	5	14	22	38	39
21	Darlington	46	8	8	7	25	21	3	7	13	24	45	37
22	Doncaster Rovers	46	8	8	7	25	22	5	3	15	25	51	37
23	Halifax Town	46	7	5	11	24	32	2	3	18	15	40	26
24	Crewe Alexandra	46	3	7	13	24	41	3	7	13	19	49	26

1979/80 24th in Division 4

#	Date	Opponent	Res	Scorers	Att	Watson I	Hallows PCR	Snookes E	Weir A	Bannon I	Taylor B(2)	Hoy R	Wann JD	Hilditch MW	O'Loughlin N	Jones CMN	Scaife RH	Esser ED	Hart BP	Oliver EA	Cliff E	McDermott IC	Milligan LC	Waldron C	Seal J	Felgate DW	Colbourn N
1	Aug 18	BOURNEMOUTH	0-2		2310	1	2	3	4	5	6	7		9	10	11	8	12									
2	20	Stockport County	1-1	Esser	3554	1	2	3	4	5	6			9	10	11	8	7									
3	24	HARTLEPOOL UNITED	1-0	Jones	2180	1	2	3	4	5	6			9	10	11	8	7									
4	31	Darlington	1-3	Weir (p)	1655	1		3	2	5	6	12	8	9	10	11	4	7									
5	Sep 8	WALSALL	1-1	Weir	2174	1		3	4	5	6	7	8	9	10		12	11	2								
6	15	Torquay United	0-3		2551	1		3	4	5	6	7	8	9	10		12	11	2								
7	18	Halifax Town	0-1		2390	1		3	4	5	6		10	9		12	8	11	2	7							
8	22	PORTSMOUTH	1-2	Weir	2423	1		3	4	5	6	7	8	9		11	10	12			7						
9	29	Port Vale	1-5	Esser	2835	1			3	5	6	7	11	9		10	4	8			2	12					
10	Oct 2	HALIFAX TOWN	2-2	Scaife, Hoy (p)	2351	1			4	5	6	7		9		11	10	8	2		3						
11	6	York City	2-3	McDermott, Jones	2462	1		3	4	5	6			9		11	10	8	12		2	7					
12	9	STOCKPORT COUNTY	0-1		2300	1			4		5	7		9	6	11	8	10	3		2	12					
13	12	PETERBOROUGH UTD.	0-0		1692	1			4	5	6	7	8	9	10	12					2	11	3				
14	20	Crewe Alexandra	1-2	Wann	2129	1			4		6		8	9	10	12		7			2	11	3	5			
15	24	Wigan Athletic	1-1	Jones	5036	1			4		6		8	9		10		7			2	11	3	5			
16	26	NORTHAMPTON T	3-2	Jones 3	1468	1			4		6		8	9		10		7			2	11	3	5			
17	Nov 3	Bournemouth	0-4		3188	1		3	4		6	12	8	11		10		7			2				5	9	
18	6	WIGAN ATHLETIC	0-2		2929	1		3	4		6	11	8	12		10		7			2				5	9	
19	17	Hereford United	1-1	Marshall (og)	2767	1	2	3	6	5		11	8	10	4			7	12							9	
20	30	Scunthorpe United	0-2		1887	1	2	3	4	6			8	10	11			7	5			12				9	
21	Dec 4	ALDERSHOT	2-1	Hilditch, Taylor	1230	1		3		6	4		8	11	10	12		7	2						5	9	
22	21	Huddersfield Town	1-5	Seal	4550	1		3	10	6	4		8	11		12		7	2						5	9	
23	29	Hartlepool United	1-1	Seal	3151	1		3		2	6		8	11	4		10	7							5	9	
24	Jan 1	Bradford City	2-1	Esser, Seal	5433	1		3	12	2	6		8	11	4		10	7							5	9	
25	11	DARLINGTON	2-2	Hilditch, Taylor	1693	1		3		2	6		8	11	4		10	7							5	9	
26	25	Tranmere Rovers	1-5	Esser (p)	1890	1		3		2	6		8	11	4		10	7	12						5	9	
27	Feb 9	Portsmouth	0-3		12207	1			3	4	6			11	8	10		7	2						5	9	
28	12	DONCASTER ROVERS	3-2	Jones 2, Taylor	1512	1			3	4	6			11	8	9		7	2						5	10	
29	15	Port Vale	0-2		1784	1			3	4	6			11	8	9	12	7	2						5	10	
30	19	Walsall	0-2		6007	1			3		6			11	8	9	4	7	2						5	10	
31	23	Peterborough United	0-2		3796	1			3	12	6			11	8	9	4	7	2						5	10	
32	Mar 1	CREWE ALEXANDRA	0-0		1807	1			3	12	6			11	8	9	4	7			2				5	10	
33	8	Northampton Town	0-0		2370	1		3			6		11	9	8		4	7			2				5	10	
34	11	LINCOLN CITY	1-1	Esser	1108	1		3			6			11	8	9	4	7	12		2				5	10	1
35	14	YORK CITY	0-2		1142	1		3			6		10	11	8	9	4	7	5		2					12	1
36	22	Aldershot	0-3		2798			3	10	12				9	8		4	7	5		2		6			11	1
37	Apr 1	HUDDERSFIELD T	0-2		4979			3	6	5				9	8	10	4	7	2							11	1
38	5	Lincoln City	0-0		3635			3	6	5				11	8	9	4	7	2							10	1
39	7	BRADFORD CITY	0-1		3201			3	6	5				11	8	9	10	7	4		2					12	1
40	12	Newport County	0-1		8127			3	6	5				11	8	9	4	7	2					12		10	1
41	15	TORQUAY UNITED	0-0		958			3	6	5			11		8	9	4	7	2							10	1
42	18	SCUNTHORPE UNITED	0-1		993			3	6	12	5		11	9	8		4	7	2							10	1
43	26	Doncaster Rovers	0-2		2493			3	4	5			7	11	8	9			2			12		6		10	1
44	29	NEWPORT COUNTY	2-0	Seal, O'Loughlin	1671				4	5			11	9	8	7			2		3			6		10	1
45	May 2	TRANMERE ROVERS	2-0	Hilditch, Jones	1082				4	5	12		11	9	8	7			2		3			6		10	1
46	6	HEREFORD UNITED	0-2		1318				6	5	4		11	9	8				2	7	3					10	1
		Apps				33	5	30	39	36	36	12	27	44	36	35	30	39	31	2	21	8	9	19	30	12	1
		Goals							3		3	1	1	3	1	9	1	5				1			4		

One own goal

F.A. Cup

	Date	Opponent	Res	Scorers	Att	Watson I	Hallows PCR	Snookes E	Weir A	Bannon I	Taylor B(2)	Hoy R	Wann JD	Hilditch MW	O'Loughlin N	Jones CMN	Scaife RH	Esser ED	Hart BP	Oliver EA	Cliff E	Seal J
R1	Nov 24	SCUNTHORPE UNITED	2-1	Hart, Jones	1985	1	2	3		6			8	10	4	11			7	5		9
R2	Dec 15	Tranmere Rovers	2-2	Hilditch 2	2529	1		3	10	4	6		8	11					7	2		5 9
rep	18	TRANMERE ROVERS	2-1	Hilditch, Hart	2707	1		3	10	4	6		8	11					7	2		5 9
R3	Jan 8	BURY	1-1	O'Loughlin	10739	1		3		2	6		8	11	4	12	10		7			5 9
rep	21	Bury	2-3	Scaife 2	8082	1		3	6	5			8	11	4	12	10	7	2			9

F.L. Cup

	Date	Opponent	Res	Scorers	Att	Watson I	Hallows PCR	Snookes E	Weir A	Bannon I	Taylor B(2)	Hoy R	Wann JD	Hilditch MW	O'Loughlin N	Jones CMN	Scaife RH
R1/1	Aug 11	Blackpool	1-1	Jones	5342	1	2	3	4	5	6	7	8	9	10	11	12
R1/2	14	BLACKPOOL	0-1		4500	1	2	3	4	5	6	7	8	9	10	11	12

		P	W	D	L	F	A	W	D	L	F	A	Pts
1	Huddersfield Town	46	16	5	2	61	18	11	7	5	40	30	66
2	Walsall	46	12	9	2	43	23	11	9	3	32	24	64
3	Newport County	46	16	5	2	47	22	11	2	10	36	28	61
4	Portsmouth	46	15	5	3	62	23	9	7	7	29	26	60
5	Bradford City	46	14	6	3	44	14	10	6	7	33	36	60
6	Wigan Athletic	46	13	5	5	42	26	8	8	7	34	35	55
7	Lincoln City	46	14	8	1	43	12	4	9	10	21	30	53
8	Peterborough Utd.	46	14	3	6	39	22	7	7	9	19	25	52
9	Torquay United	46	13	7	3	47	25	2	10	11	23	44	47
10	Aldershot	46	10	7	6	35	23	6	6	11	27	30	45
11	Bournemouth	46	8	9	6	32	25	5	9	9	20	26	44
12	Doncaster Rovers	46	11	6	6	37	27	4	8	11	25	36	44
13	Northampton Town	46	14	5	4	33	16	2	7	14	18	50	44
14	Scunthorpe United	46	11	9	3	37	23	3	6	14	21	52	43
15	Tranmere Rovers	46	10	4	9	32	24	4	9	10	18	32	41
16	Stockport County	46	9	7	7	30	31	5	5	13	18	41	40
17	York City	46	9	6	8	35	34	5	5	13	30	48	39
18	Halifax Town	46	11	9	3	29	20	2	4	17	17	52	39
19	Hartlepool United	46	10	7	6	36	28	4	3	16	23	36	38
20	Port Vale	46	8	6	9	34	24	4	6	13	22	46	36
21	Hereford United	46	8	7	8	22	21	3	7	13	16	31	36
22	Darlington	46	7	11	5	33	26	2	6	15	17	48	35
23	Crewe Alexandra	46	10	6	7	25	27	1	7	15	10	41	35
24	ROCHDALE	46	6	7	10	20	28	1	6	16	13	51	27

1979-80 Season
Back: Bannon, Ashworth, Lambert, Hilditch, Slack, Hart, Scaife
Middle: Collins (Manager), Wright, Wann, O'Loughlin, Snookes, Hallows, Jones, Corless (Trainer), Madden (Asst. Manaer)
Front: Esser, Hoy, Taylor, Weir, Oliver

1980-81 Season
Back: Probert, Snookes, Senior, Hilditch, Burke
Middle: Hoy, O'Loughlin, Seal, Wann, Cliff, Weir, Taylor, Madden (Manager)
Front: Oliver, Esser, Wellings, Jones, Martinez, Sitting: Lambert, Stanley

1980/81 15th in Division 4

#		Date	Opponent	Score	Scorers	Att	Pearce CL	Jones, Alan	Snookes E	Esser ED	Weir A	Taylor B(2)	Wann JD	O'Loughlin N	Hilditch MW	Wellings B	Martinez E	Burke P	Seal J	Cliff E	Hoy R	Crawford PG	Higgins RJ
1	Aug	16	Stockport County	2-2	Hilditch, Esser	2739	1	2	3	4		6	7	8	9	10	11			5			
2		19	SCUNTHORPE UNITED	4-0	Hilditch 2, Burke, Taylor	2427	1	2	3	4		6	7	8	9	10	11	5					
3		23	HARTLEPOOL UNITED	1-1	Hilditch	5230	1	2	3	4		6	7	8	9	10	11	5					
4		29	Tranmere Rovers	1-3	Esser	1828	1	2		4	5	6	7	8	9	10	11				3		
5	Sep	6	TORQUAY UNITED	2-1	Martinez, Wann	1777	1	2	3	4		6	7	8	9	10	11	5					
6		13	Peterborough United	2-2	Wellings, Hilditch	3906		2	3	4		6	7	8	9	10	11	5				1	
7		17	Hereford United	0-3		2475		2	3	4		6	7	8	9	10	11	5				1	
8		20	BRADFORD CITY	0-2		3221		2	3	4		6	7	8	9	10	11	5		12		1	
9		27	Bournemouth	1-2	Hilditch	2557		2	3	4		6	7	8	9	10	11	5				1	
10		30	HEREFORD UNITED	0-0		2328		2	3	4		6	7	8	9	10	11	5	12			1	
11	Oct	4	WIGAN ATHLETIC	3-0	Wann 2, Hilditch	3479		2	3	4		6	7	8	9	10	11	5				1	
12		8	Lincoln City	0-3		3641		2	3	4	12	6	7	8	9	10	11	5				1	
13		11	Aldershot	0-0		3017		2	3	4	12	6	7	8	9	10	11	5				1	
14		18	BURY	2-1	Hilditch, Wellings	4306		2	3	4		6		8	9	10	11	5			7	1	
15		21	WIMBLEDON	2-0	O'Loughlin, Wellings	2391		2	3	4		6		8	9	10	11	5		12	7	1	
16		25	Crewe Alexandra	0-1		3291		2		4	3	6	12	8	9	10	11	5			7	1	
17		28	Darlington	4-4	Taylor, Esser, Jones, Wellings	1579		2	3	4	3	6		8	9	10	11	5				1	
18	Nov	1	MANSFIELD TOWN	1-4	O'Loughlin	2636		2	3	4		6	7	8	9	10	11	5	12			1	
19		4	LINCOLN CITY	1-0	Hilditch	2257	7		3		2	6		8	9	10	11	5	4			1	
20		8	Port Vale	1-1	Esser	2774	7		3	12	2	6		8	9	10	11	5	4			1	
21		11	Scunthorpe United	1-1	Wellings	2030	7		3	12	2			8	9	10	11	5	4			1	6
22		29	Doncaster Rovers	2-1	Wellings, Lister (og)	2502			3	4	2	6		8	9	10	11	5	7			1	12
23	Dec	6	SOUTHEND UNITED	0-2		2214	12		3	4	2			8	9	10	11	5	7			1	6
24		12	Stockport County	2-1	Martinez, Wellings	1901			3	4	2		7	8	9	10	11	5				1	6
25		20	Northampton Town	2-3	Wellings 2	1705	12		3	4	2		7	8	9	10	11	5				1	6
26		26	HALIFAX TOWN	1-1	Wellings (p)	2628	12		3	4	2	6	7	8	9	10	11	5				1	
27		27	York City	2-1	Wellings, Martinez	2828		2	3			6	7	8	9	10	11	5	4			1	
28	Jan	3	CREWE ALEXANDRA	2-0	Jones 2	2540		2	3		12	6	7	8	9	10	11	5	4			1	
29		17	DONCASTER ROVERS	2-2	Taylor, Wellings (p)	3021		2	3			6	7	8	9	10	11	5	4			1	
30		24	TRANMERE ROVERS	3-1	Wann, Seal, Wellings	2731		2	3		12	6	7	8	9	10	11	5	4			1	
31		31	Hartlepool United	2-2	Taylor, Esser	3867		2	3	4		6	7	8		10	11	5	9			1	
32	Feb	7	PETERBOROUGH UTD.	2-3	Wann, Burke	2865		2	3	4		6	7		9	10	11	5	8			1	
33		14	Torquay United	0-2		1628		2	3	4	8	6	7		9	10	11	5	12			1	
34		21	BOURNEMOUTH	0-0		1846		2	3	4		6	7	8	9	10	11	5				1	
35	Mar	7	Wigan Athletic	1-0	Taylor	6029		2		4		6	7	8		10	11	5	9	3		1	
36		8	Bradford City	1-2	Esser	2926		2		4		6	7	8	9	10		5	11	3		1	
37		14	ALDERSHOT	0-2		1834		2	3	4	12	6	7	8	9	10		5	11			1	
38		21	Bury	1-3	Hilditch	3931	12		3		4	6	7	8	9	10	11	5		2		1	
39		28	DARLINGTON	0-0		1656		2	3	4	5	6	7	8	9	10	11					1	
40	Apr	4	Mansfield Town	2-2	Hilditch, Wellings	2597		2	3	4	5	6	7	8	9	10	11		12			1	
41		12	PORT VALE	2-1	Esser, Martinez	2590		2	3	4		6	7	8	9	10	11	5	12			1	
42		18	YORK CITY	3-2	Taylor, Hilditch, Jones	1651		2	3		12	6	7	8	9	10	11	5	4			1	
43		20	Halifax Town	0-2		2278		2	3		6		7	8	9	10	11	5	4			1	
44		28	Wimbledon	1-4	Wann	3884		2	3		4	6	7	8	9	10	11					1	
45	May	1	Southend United	1-1	Jones	10857		2	3		4	6	7	8	9	10	11	5				1	
46		3	NORTHAMPTON T	0-1		1474		2	3	4		6	7	8	9	10	11			12		1	
			Apps				5	44	41	36	25	41	39	44	44	46	44	41	23	5	4	41	5
			Goals					5		7		6	6	2	12	14	4	2	1				

One own goal

F.A. Cup

| R1 | Nov | 22 | Mansfield Town | 1-3 | Jones (p) | 3280 | 7 | | 3 | 4 | 2 | 6 | | 8 | 9 | 10 | 11 | | | | | 1 | 5 |

F.L. Cup

| R1/1 | Aug | 9 | Carlisle United | 0-2 | | 2257 | 1 | 2 | 3 | 4 | 5 | 6 | 7 | 8 | 9 | 10 | 11 | | | | | | |
| R1/2 | | 12 | CARLISLE UNITED | 1-1 | Martinez | 1806 | 1 | 2 | 3 | 4 | 6 | | 7 | 8 | 9 | 10 | 11 | 5 | 12 | | | | |

		P	W	D	L	F	A	W	D	L	F	A	Pts
1	Southend United	46	19	4	0	47	6	11	3	9	32	25	67
2	Lincoln City	46	15	7	1	44	11	10	8	5	22	14	65
3	Doncaster Rovers	46	15	4	4	36	20	7	8	8	23	29	56
4	Wimbledon	46	15	4	4	42	17	8	5	10	22	29	55
5	Peterborough Utd.	46	11	8	4	37	21	6	10	7	31	33	52
6	Aldershot	46	12	9	2	28	11	6	5	12	15	30	50
7	Mansfield Town	46	13	5	5	36	15	7	4	12	22	29	49
8	Darlington	46	13	6	4	43	23	6	5	12	22	36	49
9	Hartlepool United	46	14	3	6	42	22	6	6	11	22	39	49
10	Northampton Town	46	11	7	5	42	26	7	6	10	23	41	49
11	Wigan Athletic	46	13	4	6	29	16	5	7	11	22	39	47
12	Bury	46	10	8	5	38	21	7	3	13	32	41	45
13	Bournemouth	46	9	8	6	30	21	7	5	11	17	27	45
14	Bradford City	46	9	9	5	30	24	5	7	11	23	36	44
15	ROCHDALE	46	11	6	6	33	25	3	9	11	27	45	43
16	Scunthorpe United	46	8	12	3	40	31	3	8	12	20	38	42
17	Torquay United	46	13	2	8	38	26	5	3	15	17	37	41
18	Crewe Alexandra	46	10	7	6	28	20	3	7	13	20	41	40
19	Port Vale	46	10	8	5	40	23	2	7	14	17	47	39
20	Stockport County	46	10	5	8	29	25	6	2	15	15	32	39
21	Tranmere Rovers	46	12	5	6	41	24	1	5	17	18	49	36
22	Hereford United	46	8	8	7	29	20	3	5	15	9	42	35
23	Halifax Town	46	9	3	11	28	32	2	9	12	16	39	34
24	York City	46	10	2	11	31	23	2	7	14	16	43	33

1981/82   21st in Division 4

No		Date	Opponent	Score	Scorers	Att	Crawford PG	Weir A	Snookes E	Dolan TP	Taylor B(2)	Cooper T	Hamilton NR	O'Loughlin N	Esser ED	Wellings B	Martinez E	Hilditch MW	Poole MD	Burke P	Goodwin D	Warriner SW	Williams WR	Thompson DS
1	Aug	29	Bury	0-3		3925	1	2	3	4	5	6	7	8	9	10	11	12						
2	Sep	5	HARTLEPOOL UNITED	2-1	Martinez, Goodwin	1481			3	4	5	6		8	9	10	11	7	1	2	12			
3		12	Peterborough United	1-5	Wellings (p)	3768			3	4	5	6		8	9	10	11	7	1	2	12			
4		19	PORT VALE	1-2	O'Loughlin	1824		2	3			6	11	4	8	10		7			5	9		
5		22	BLACKPOOL	0-0		2763		2	3			6		4	8	10		7	9	1	5	11		
6		26	Bournemouth	0-1		5146		2	3	12		6		4	8	10		7	9	1	5	11		
7		30	Bradford City	0-2		5388		2	3	7		6		4	8	10		9		1	5	11		
8	Oct	4	ALDERSHOT	0-0		1821			3	4		6	2	8	7	10	11	9	1	5	12			
9		11	COLCHESTER UNITED	1-2	Wellings	1366			3	4		6	2	7	8	10	11	9	1	5	12			
10		17	Halifax Town	0-0		2140			3	4		6	2	8		10	11	9	1	5	7			
11		21	Crewe Alexandra	2-1	Goodwin, Wellings	1827			3	4		6	2	8		10	11	9	1	5	7			
12		24	STOCKPORT COUNTY	4-1	Martinez 2, Hilditch, Goodwin	1778	12		3	4		6	2	8		10	11	9	1	5	7			
13		31	Darlington	0-2		1454			3	4		6	2	8		10	11	9	1	5	7			
14	Nov	3	TRANMERE ROVERS	0-0		1663			3	4		6	2	8		10	11	9	1	5	7			
15		8	TORQUAY UNITED	1-0	Goodwin	1790	12		3	4		6	2	8		10	11	9	1	5	7			
16		14	Mansfield Town	3-4	Hilditch 2, Wellings (p)	2300			3	4		6	2	8		10	11	9	1	5	7			
17		28	WIGAN ATHLETIC	1-1	Hilditch	2765		2	3	4		6		8		10	11	9	1	5	7			
18	Dec	5	Hereford United	0-0		2312			3	4		6		8	7	10		9	1	5	11			
19	Jan	13	HALIFAX TOWN	0-1		1122			3	4		6	2	8	12	10		9	1	5	7			
20		16	SHEFFIELD UNITED	0-1		3966		2	3	4		6	5	7	8	10	11	9	1					
21		23	BURY	1-1	Martinez	3583		2	3	4		6	5	8		10	11	9	1		7			
22		30	Port Vale	1-1	Martinez	3835		2	3	4		6		8		10	11	9	1	5	7			
23	Feb	6	PETERBOROUGH UTD.	1-1	Hamilton	1241		2	3	4		6		8		10	11	9	1	5	7	12		
24		10	Blackpool	1-1	Hilditch	3294		2	3	4	5	6		8		10	11	9	1		7			
25		14	Aldershot	2-2	Cooper, Hilditch	2079		2	3	4		6	5	8		10	11	9	1		7			
26		20	BOURNEMOUTH	0-1		1295		2	3	4		6	5	8		10	11	9	1		7			
27		26	Colchester United	2-3	O'Loughlin, Hilditch	2760		2	3	4		6	5	8	11	10		9	1		7			
28	Mar	2	Northampton Town	1-2	O'Loughlin	1916		2	3	4		6	5	8	7	10	12	9	1		11			
29		9	CREWE ALEXANDRA	1-0	Goodwin	1060	1	2	3	4		6	7	8	12	10	11				5	9		
30		12	Stockport County	4-0	Martinez, Hilditch 2, Wellings	2079	1	2	3	4		6		8	12	10		9			5	7		
31		16	Tranmere Rovers	0-2		1141	1	2	3	4		6		8	7	10	11	9			5			
32		20	DARLINGTON	3-2	O'Loughlin, Wellings (p), Hilditch	1252	1	2	3	4		6		8	7	10	11	9			5	12		
33		27	Torquay United	1-2	Hilditch	1468	1	2	3	4		6	5	8		10		9			7			
34		31	Hartlepool United	1-1	Wellings (p)	1259	1	2	3	4		6		8		10	11	9			5	7	12	
35	Apr	3	MANSFIELD TOWN	1-1	Hilditch	1276	1	2	3	4		6	7	8		10	11	9					8	
36		6	HULL CITY	0-1		1738	1	2	3	4		6		8	12	10	11	9			5	7		
37		10	Scunthorpe United	0-1		1742	1	2	3	4	5	6	7	8		10	11				9			
38		12	YORK CITY	2-0	Martinez, Wellings (p)	1421	1	6	3	4	5		7	2	12	10	11				9		8	
39		17	HEREFORD UNITED	0-1		1342	1	6	3	4	5		7	2	8	10	11	12			9			
40		20	SCUNTHORPE UNITED	1-1	Wellings (p)	1129	1	6	3	4	5		7	8		12	11	9			10		2	
41		24	Wigan Athletic	1-1	Martinez	6153	1	6	3	4	5		7	8		10	11	9					2	
42		27	York City	2-1	Hilditch 2	2089	1	6	3	4	5		7	8		10	11	9					2	
43	May	1	BRADFORD CITY	1-1	Dolan (p)	3080	1		3	4	5	6		8		10	11	9				2	8	
44		4	Sheffield United	1-3	Wellings	21140	1		3	4	5	6		8		10	11	9			7	2		
45		8	Hull City	1-2	Cooper	3411	1		3	4	5	6	7	8		10	11				9	2		12
46		15	NORTHAMPTON T	5-3	Martinez, Wellings, Warriner, O'Loughlin, Goodwin	1056	1	6	3		5			4	8	10	11				9	2	12	7
					Apps		19	34	44	43	37	35	21	33	24	46	43	40	27	27	38	8	6	2
					Goals					1		2	1	5		11	9	14			6	1		

F.A. Cup

	Date	Opponent	Score	Scorers	Att	Crawford PG	Weir A	Snookes E	Dolan TP	Taylor B(2)	Cooper T	Hamilton NR	O'Loughlin N	Esser ED	Wellings B	Martinez E	Hilditch MW	Poole MD	Burke P	Goodwin D
R1	Nov 21	HULL CITY	2-2	Dolan, Esser	2722			3	4		6	2	8	12	10	11	9	1	5	7
rep	24	Hull City	2-2	Burke, Esser	4063		2	3	8		6	4	7		10	11	9	1	5	
rep2	30	Hull City	0-1		3628			3	4		6	2	8	7	10	11	9	1	5	

Both replays a.e.t. Second replay at Elland Road, Leeds.

F.L. Cup (Milk Cup)

	Date	Opponent	Score	Scorers	Att	Crawford PG	Weir A	Snookes E	Dolan TP	Taylor B(2)	Cooper T	Hamilton NR	O'Loughlin N	Esser ED	Wellings B	Martinez E	Hilditch MW	Poole MD	Burke P
R1/1	Sep 1	Huddersfield Town	1-3	Cooper	6713			3	4	5	2		8	9	10	7	11	1	6
R1/2	15	HUDDERSFIELD TOWN	2-4	Wellings, Hilditch	3775	1	2	3		5	6	12	4	8	10	7	9		11

Rose Bowl

	Date	Opponent	Score	Scorers	Att	Crawford PG	Weir A	Snookes E	Dolan TP	Taylor B(2)	Cooper T	Hamilton NR	O'Loughlin N	Esser ED	Wellings B	Martinez E	Hilditch MW	Poole MD	Burke P	Goodwin D
	Aug 24	OLDHAM ATHLETIC	1-0	Hilditch	2462	1	2	3	4	5	6	12	8	9	10	7	14	13	15	11

		P	W	D	L	F	A	W	D	L	F	A	Pts
1	Sheffield United	46	15	8	0	53	15	12	7	4	41	26	96
2	Bradford City	46	14	7	2	52	23	12	6	5	36	22	91
3	Wigan Athletic	46	17	5	1	47	18	9	8	6	33	28	91
4	Bournemouth	46	12	10	1	37	15	11	9	3	25	15	88
5	Peterborough Utd.	46	16	3	4	46	22	8	7	8	25	35	82
6	Colchester United	46	12	6	5	47	23	8	6	9	35	34	72
7	Port Vale	46	9	12	2	26	17	9	4	10	30	32	70
8	Hull City	46	14	3	6	36	23	5	9	9	34	38	69
9	Bury	46	13	7	3	53	26	4	10	9	27	33	68
10	Hereford United	46	10	9	4	36	25	6	10	7	28	33	67
11	Tranmere Rovers	46	9	7	7	27	25	7	9	7	24	31	60
12	Blackpool	46	11	5	7	40	26	4	8	11	26	34	58
13	Darlington	46	10	5	8	36	28	5	8	10	25	34	58
14	Hartlepool United	46	9	8	6	39	34	4	8	11	34	50	55
15	Torquay United	46	9	8	6	30	25	5	5	13	17	34	55
16	Aldershot	46	8	7	8	34	29	5	8	10	23	39	54
17	York City	46	9	5	9	45	37	5	3	15	24	54	50
18	Stockport County	46	10	5	8	34	28	2	8	13	14	39	49
19	Halifax Town	46	6	11	6	28	30	3	11	9	23	42	49
20	Mansfield Town	46	8	6	9	39	39	5	4	14	24	42	47
21	ROCHDALE	46	7	9	7	26	22	3	7	13	24	40	46
22	Northampton Town	46	9	5	9	32	27	2	4	17	25	57	42
23	Scunthorpe United	46	7	9	7	26	35	2	6	15	17	44	42
24	Crewe Alexandra	46	3	6	14	19	32	3	3	17	10	52	27

1981-82 Season
Back: Dolan, Hilditch, Crawford, Taylor (Captain), Poole, Snookes, Cooper
Middle: Madden (Man.), O'Loughlin, Weir, Wellings, Goodwin, Burke, Connor (Asst. Man.)
Front: Warriner, Lambert, Hamilton, Esser, Martinez

1982-83 Season
Back: D.Thompson, Pearce, Hilditch
Middle: Blair, French, Trainer, Stafford, S.Thompson, Snookes, Williams, P.Madden (Manager)
Front: D.Madden, Wellings, Warriner, Hamilton, Martinez, Farrell, Weir, Boden

1982/83 20th in Division 4

#	Mon	Date	Opponent	Score	Scorers	Att	Pea	War	Sno	Bla	Tra	Wei	TDS	Ham	Fre	Wel	Far	Mar	Wil	Hil	Sta	Kee	Com	Gar	Tay	Tho	Swa	Gre	McE	Nic	TSC	GrJ	GrB	Car	Hig	Cra
1	Aug	28	Darlington	0-3		1672	1		3	4	5	6	7	8	9	10	11	12																		
2	Sep	4	CHESTER	0-1		1490	1		3	2	5	6	12	8	9	10	7			4	11															
3		7	HARTLEPOOL UNITED	2-0	Stafford, Wellings	987	1	2	3	4	5		7		12	10	8			6	9	11														
4		10	Colchester United	1-4	Wellings (p)	2638	1	2	3		5	6	12	8	9	10	7			4	11															
5		18	SWINDON TOWN	1-1	Hilditch	1407	1	2			5		7	8	9	10	4	12	6	11				3												
6		25	Mansfield Town	1-2	Comstive	2002	1				5		7	8		10	4		6	11			9	2	3												
7		27	Stockport County	2-2	Hamilton, Wellings	1873	1				5		7	8		10	4		6	11			9	2	3												
8	Oct	2	BURY	0-0		3236	1		3				7	8		10	4		6	9				2	11	5											
9		8	Crewe Alexandra	1-1	French	2168	1		3				7	8	9	10	4		6	11				2													
10		16	BLACKPOOL	3-1	Hilditch, Wellings (p), Comstive	2001	1		3				7		9	10	4		6	11				2	8	5											
11		19	Wimbledon	0-3		2294	1		3				7		9	10	4	12	6	11				2	8		5										
12		23	HALIFAX TOWN	2-2	Hilditch, D Thompson	1733	1		3				7		9	10	4	12	6	11				2	8	5											
13		30	Hereford United	0-1		2402	1		3		5		7	8	9	10			4	6	11			2					12								
14	Nov	2	NORTHAMPTON T	2-0	Keenan, Hamilton	1019	1		3				7	8	9	10			4	6	11			2							5						
15		6	PORT VALE	3-3	French, Wellings 2	2220	1		3				7		9	10	4			6	11			2							5	8					
16		13	Peterborough United	0-1		2245	1		3				7		9	10	4	12	6	11				2							5	8					
17		27	Torquay United	2-3	Hamilton, Hilditch	2522	1		3				4	12	7	10	8		11				2								5	6				
18	Dec	4	BRISTOL CITY	1-0	Farrell	1307	1		3				12	11	7	10	8			9				2							4	5	6				
19		11	WIMBLEDON	0-2		1096	1	11					7			10	4			6	9			2							8	5	3	12			
20		18	ALDERSHOT	3-1	D Thompson, Martinez, French(p)	888	1		3				7		9		4		11	6	10			2							8	5					
21		27	Scunthorpe United	1-1	French (p)	4989	1		3				7		9		4		11	6	10			2							8	5					
22		28	YORK CITY	1-0	Farrell	2127	1		3				7		9	12	4		11	6	10			2							8	5					
23	Jan	1	Hull City	1-2	D Thompson	9059	1		3				7		9	10	4		11	6	2										8	5					
24		3	TRANMERE ROVERS	4-2	Mooney(og), Hilditch, McElhinney, Martinez	1758	1		3				7		9	12	4		11	6	10							2			8	5	2				
25		8	Chester	2-5	French, Zelem (oq)	1729	1		3		4	7		9	12	8		11	6									2			5	2					
26		15	DARLINGTON	1-1		1233	1		3				7		9	4				11	6								2			8	5	2				
27		22	Swindon Town	1-4	Hilditch	5442	1		3				7		9	12	4		11	6	10							2			8	5	2				
28	Feb	5	MANSFIELD TOWN	2-2	D Thompson, Farrell	1031	1		3				7		9		4		11	6	10			2							8	5					
29		12	Bury	0-0		4376	1		3				7		9		4			10		2	11					6			8	5					
30		26	Blackpool	0-1		2373	1		3				7		9		4		12	10		2	11					6			8	5					
31	Mar	4	Halifax Town	0-0		2128	1		3				7		9				2	10			11					6			4	5	8				
32		12	HEREFORD UNITED	4-1	French 3, S Thompson	2000	1		3				7		9		4	11		12								6		2	5		8	10			
33		15	CREWE ALEXANDRA	2-0	S Thompson, Farrell	2497	1		3				7		9		4	11										6		2	5		8	10			
34		19	Port Vale	0-4		5129	1		3			11	7				9											6		2	5		12	10	8		
35		26	PETERBOROUGH UTD.	1-1	Higgins	1560	1						7				4	11					2					6			5		8	10		3	9
36	Apr	2	York City	0-1		3357	1						7				4	11	8				2					6				12	9	10		3	5
37		4	SCUNTHORPE UNITED	0-1		2056							7				4	11	6				2							5		8	10		3	9	1
38		9	Bristol City	0-0		4780							7		9				6	11			2										10	8	3	5	1
39		16	STOCKPORT COUNTY	1-0	French (p)	1829							7		9				6	11			2										10	8	3	5	1
40		19	Northampton Town	1-1	French	1728							7	8	9		4		6	11													10	2	3	5	1
41		23	Aldershot	4-6	Farrell 2, Hilditch, D Thompson	1651							7	8	9		4		5	11			6								12		10	2	3		1
42		26	COLCHESTER UNITED	2-1	Higgins, French	1270							7		9		4	11					3					6					8	10	2	5	1
43		30	TORQUAY UNITED	2-2	Farrell, S Thompson	1359							7		9		4	11	12				3					6					8	10	2	5	1
44	May	7	Hartlepool United	0-3		1015			3				7		9		4	11	6	10								12					8		2	5	1
45		14	HULL CITY	1-3	Martinez	2730							7		9		4	11	6	10		2											8		3	5	1
46		16	Tranmere Rovers	0-0		1985			3				7		9		4	11	12	10		2				6			8						5	1
			Apps				36	4	33	3	7	8	46	14	36	24	43	29	37	39	1	30	9	4	14	1	3	21	20	7	12	12	7	9	11	10
			Goals										5	3	11	5	9	3		7	1	1	2						1			3				2	

Played in one game: MJ O'Connor (37 at 12)

Two own goals

F.A. Cup

		Date	Opponent	Score	Scorers	Att	Pea	War	Sno	Bla	Tra	Wei	TDS	Ham	Fre	Wel	Far	Mar	Wil	Hil	Sta	Kee	Com	Gar	Tay	Tho	Swa	Gre	McE
R1	Nov	20	Altrincham	1-2	Wellings (p)	3053	1		3			6	7	12	9	10			4			11		2			5	8	

F.L. Cup (Milk Cup)

		Date	Opponent	Score	Scorers	Att	Pea	War	Sno	Bla	Tra	Wei	TDS	Ham	Fre	Wel	Far	Mar	Wil	Hil	Sta	Kee	Com	Gar	Tay
R1/1	Aug	30	Port Vale	0-1		2565	1		3	2	5	6		8	9	10	7			4	11				
R1/2	Sep	14	PORT VALE	2-0	Wellings 2 (1p)	1536	1	2		3	5		7	8	9	10	4	12		6	11				
R2/1	Oct	5	BRADFORD CITY	0-1		2196	1		3				7	8		10	4			6	9			2	11	5
R2/2		27	Bradford City	0-4		3206	1	4	3				7	12	9	10			8	6	11			2	

Lancashire Cup

	Date	Opponent	Score	Scorers	Att	Pea	War	Sno	Bla	Tra	Wei	TDS	Ham	Fre	Wel	Far	Mar	Wil	Hil	Sta	Cra
	Aug 14	Bury	1-2	French			2	3	4	5	6	7	8	9	10		12	14	11		1
	17	BURNLEY	0-0		2591	1	2	3	4	5	6	7	8	9	10		12		11		
	21	Oldham Athletic+	2-2	D.Thompson, Wellings		1	2	3	4	5	6	7	8	9	10	11					

+ Also Rose Bowl

		P	W	D	L	F	A	W	D	L	F	A	Pts
1	Wimbledon	46	17	4	2	57	23	12	7	4	39	22	98
2	Hull City	46	14	8	1	48	14	11	7	5	27	20	90
3	Port Vale	46	15	4	4	37	16	11	6	6	30	18	88
4	Scunthorpe United	46	13	7	3	41	17	10	7	6	30	25	83
5	Bury	46	15	4	4	43	20	8	8	7	31	26	81
6	Colchester United	46	17	5	1	51	19	7	4	12	24	36	81
7	York City	46	18	4	1	59	19	4	9	10	29	39	79
8	Swindon Town	46	14	3	6	45	27	5	8	10	16	27	68
9	Peterborough Utd.	46	13	6	4	38	23	4	7	12	20	29	64
10	Mansfield Town	46	11	6	6	32	26	5	7	11	29	44	61
11	Halifax Town	46	9	8	6	31	23	7	4	12	28	43	60
12	Torquay United	46	12	3	8	38	30	5	4	14	18	35	58
13	Chester	46	8	6	9	28	24	7	5	11	27	36	56
14	Bristol City	46	10	8	5	32	25	3	9	11	27	45	56
15	Northampton Town	46	10	8	5	43	29	4	4	15	22	46	54
16	Stockport County	46	11	8	4	41	31	3	4	16	19	48	54
17	Darlington	46	8	5	10	27	30	5	8	10	34	41	52
18	Aldershot	46	11	5	7	40	35	1	10	12	21	47	51
19	Tranmere Rovers	46	8	8	7	30	29	5	3	15	19	42	50
20	ROCHDALE	46	11	6	4	38	25	0	8	15	17	48	49
21	Blackpool	46	10	8	5	32	23	4	4	16	23	51	49
22	Hartlepool United	46	11	5	7	30	24	2	4	17	16	52	48
23	Crewe Alexandra	46	9	5	9	35	32	2	3	18	18	39	41
24	Hereford United	46	8	6	9	19	23	3	2	18	23	56	41

Final League Tables: 1983/84 - 1988/89

1983/84 season: Div. 4		P	W	D	L	F	A	W	D	L	F	A	F	A	Pts
1	York City	46	18	4	1	58	16	13	4	6	38	23	96	39	101
2	Doncaster Rovers	46	15	6	2	46	22	9	7	7	36	32	82	54	85
3	Reading	46	17	6	0	51	14	5	10	8	33	42	84	56	82
4	Bristol City	46	18	3	2	51	17	6	7	10	19	27	70	44	82
5	Aldershot	46	14	6	3	49	29	8	3	12	27	40	76	69	75
6	Blackpool	46	15	4	4	47	19	6	5	12	23	33	70	52	72
7	Peterborough Utd.	46	15	5	3	52	16	3	9	11	20	32	72	48	68
8	Colchester United	46	14	7	2	45	14	3	9	11	24	39	69	53	67
9	Torquay United	46	13	7	3	32	18	5	6	12	27	46	59	64	67
10	Tranmere Rovers	46	11	5	7	33	26	6	10	7	20	27	53	53	66
11	Hereford United	46	11	6	6	31	21	5	9	9	23	32	54	53	63
12	Stockport County	46	12	5	6	34	25	5	6	12	26	39	60	64	62
13	Chesterfield	46	10	11	2	34	24	5	4	14	25	37	59	61	60
14	Darlington	46	13	4	6	31	19	4	4	15	18	31	49	50	59
15	Bury	46	9	7	7	34	32	6	7	10	27	32	61	64	59
16	Crewe Alexandra	46	10	8	5	35	27	6	3	14	21	40	56	67	59
17	Swindon Town	46	11	7	5	34	23	4	6	13	24	33	58	56	58
18	Northampton Town	46	10	8	5	32	32	3	6	14	21	46	53	78	53
19	Mansfield Town	46	9	7	7	44	27	4	6	13	22	43	66	70	52
20	Wrexham	46	7	6	10	34	33	4	9	10	25	41	59	74	48
21	Halifax Town	46	11	6	6	36	25	1	6	16	19	64	55	89	48
22	ROCHDALE	46	8	9	6	35	31	3	4	16	17	49	52	80	46
23	Hartlepool United	46	7	8	8	31	28	3	2	18	16	57	47	85	40
24	Chester City	46	7	5	11	23	35	0	8	15	22	47	45	82	34

1984/85 season: Div. 4		P	W	D	L	F	A	W	D	L	F	A	F	A	Pts
1	Chesterfield	46	16	6	1	40	13	10	7	6	24	22	64	35	91
2	Blackpool	46	15	7	1	42	15	9	7	7	31	24	73	39	86
3	Darlington	46	16	4	3	41	22	8	9	6	25	27	66	49	85
4	Bury	46	15	6	2	46	20	9	6	8	30	30	76	50	84
5	Hereford United	46	16	2	5	38	21	6	9	8	27	26	65	47	77
6	Tranmere Rovers	46	17	1	5	50	21	7	2	14	33	45	83	66	75
7	Colchester United	46	13	7	3	49	29	7	7	9	38	36	87	65	74
8	Swindon Town	46	16	4	3	42	21	5	5	13	20	37	62	58	72
9	Scunthorpe United	46	14	6	3	61	33	5	8	10	22	29	83	62	71
10	Crewe Alexandra	46	10	7	6	32	28	8	5	10	33	41	65	69	66
11	Peterborough Utd.	46	11	7	5	29	21	5	7	11	25	32	54	53	62
12	Port Vale	46	11	8	4	39	24	3	10	10	22	35	61	59	60
13	Aldershot	46	11	6	6	33	20	6	2	15	23	43	56	63	59
14	Mansfield Town	46	10	8	5	25	15	3	10	10	16	23	41	38	57
15	Wrexham	46	10	6	7	39	27	5	3	15	28	43	67	70	54
16	Chester City	46	11	3	9	35	30	4	6	13	25	42	60	72	54
17	ROCHDALE	46	8	7	8	33	30	5	7	11	22	39	55	69	53
18	Exeter City	46	9	7	7	30	27	4	7	12	27	52	57	79	53
19	Hartlepool United	46	10	6	7	34	29	4	4	15	20	38	54	67	52
20	Southend United	46	8	8	7	30	34	5	3	15	28	49	58	83	50
21	Halifax Town	46	9	3	11	26	32	6	2	15	16	37	42	69	50
22	Stockport County	46	11	5	7	40	26	2	3	18	18	53	58	79	47
23	Northampton Town	46	10	1	12	32	32	4	4	15	21	42	53	74	47
24	Torquay United	46	5	11	7	18	24	4	3	16	20	39	38	63	41

1985/86 season: Div. 4		P	W	D	L	F	A	W	D	L	F	A	F	A	Pts
1	Swindon Town	46	20	2	1	52	19	12	4	7	30	24	82	43	102
2	Chester City	46	15	5	3	44	16	8	10	5	39	34	83	50	84
3	Mansfield Town	46	13	8	2	43	17	10	4	9	31	30	74	47	81
4	Port Vale	46	13	9	1	42	11	8	7	8	25	26	67	37	79
5	Orient	46	11	6	6	39	21	9	6	8	40	43	79	64	72
6	Colchester United	46	12	6	5	51	22	7	7	9	37	41	88	63	70
7	Hartlepool United	46	15	6	2	41	20	5	4	14	27	47	68	67	70
8	Northampton Town	46	9	7	7	44	29	9	3	11	35	29	79	58	64
9	Southend United	46	13	4	6	43	27	5	6	12	26	40	69	67	64
10	Hereford United	46	15	6	2	55	30	3	4	16	19	43	74	73	64
11	Stockport County	46	9	9	5	35	28	8	4	11	28	43	63	71	64
12	Crewe Alexandra	46	10	6	7	35	26	8	3	12	19	35	54	61	63
13	Wrexham	46	11	5	7	34	24	6	4	13	34	56	68	80	60
14	Burnley	46	11	3	9	35	30	5	8	10	25	35	60	65	59
15	Scunthorpe United	46	11	7	5	33	23	4	7	12	17	32	50	55	59
16	Aldershot	46	12	5	6	45	25	5	2	16	21	49	66	74	58
17	Peterborough Utd.	46	9	11	3	31	19	4	6	13	21	45	52	64	56
18	ROCHDALE	46	12	7	4	41	29	2	6	15	16	48	57	77	55
19	Tranmere Rovers	46	9	1	13	46	41	6	8	9	28	32	74	73	54
20	Halifax Town	46	10	8	5	35	27	4	4	15	25	44	60	71	54
21	Exeter City	46	10	4	9	26	25	3	11	9	21	34	47	59	54
22	Cambridge United	46	12	2	9	45	38	3	7	13	20	42	65	80	54
23	Preston North End	46	7	4	12	32	41	4	6	13	22	48	54	89	43
24	Torquay United	46	8	5	10	29	32	1	5	17	14	56	43	88	37

1986/87 season: Div. 4		P	W	D	L	F	A	W	D	L	F	A	F	A	Pts
1	Northampton Town	46	20	2	1	56	20	10	7	6	47	33	103	53	99
2	Preston North End	46	16	4	3	36	18	10	8	5	36	29	72	47	90
3	Southend United	46	14	4	5	43	27	11	1	11	25	28	68	55	80
4	Wolverhampton W.	46	12	3	8	36	24	12	4	7	33	26	69	50	79
5	Colchester United	46	15	3	5	41	20	6	4	13	23	36	64	56	70
6	Aldershot	46	13	5	5	40	22	7	5	11	24	35	64	57	70
7	Orient	46	15	2	6	40	25	5	7	11	24	36	64	61	69
8	Scunthorpe United	46	15	3	5	52	27	3	9	11	21	30	73	57	66
9	Wrexham	46	8	13	2	38	24	7	7	9	32	27	70	51	65
10	Peterborough Utd.	46	10	7	6	29	21	7	7	9	28	29	57	50	65
11	Cambridge United	46	12	6	5	37	23	5	5	13	23	39	60	62	62
12	Swansea City	46	13	3	7	31	21	4	8	11	25	40	56	61	62
13	Cardiff City	46	6	12	5	24	18	9	4	10	24	32	48	50	61
14	Exeter City	46	11	10	2	37	17	0	13	10	16	32	53	49	56
15	Halifax Town	46	10	5	8	32	32	5	5	13	27	42	59	74	55
16	Hereford United	46	10	6	7	33	23	4	5	14	27	38	60	61	53
17	Crewe Alexandra	46	8	9	6	38	35	5	5	13	32	37	70	72	53
18	Hartlepool United	46	6	11	6	24	30	5	7	11	20	35	44	65	51
19	Stockport County	46	9	6	8	25	27	4	6	13	15	42	40	69	51
20	Tranmere Rovers	46	6	10	7	32	37	5	7	11	22	35	54	72	50
21	ROCHDALE	46	8	8	7	31	30	3	9	11	23	43	54	73	50
22	Burnley	46	9	7	7	31	35	3	6	14	22	39	53	74	49
23	Torquay United	46	8	8	7	28	29	2	10	11	28	43	56	72	48
24	Lincoln City	46	8	7	8	30	27	4	5	14	15	38	45	65	48

1987/88 season: Div. 4		P	W	D	L	F	A	W	D	L	F	A	F	A	Pts
1	Wolverhampton W.	46	15	3	5	47	19	12	6	5	35	24	82	43	90
2	Cardiff City	46	15	6	2	39	14	9	7	7	27	27	66	41	85
3	Bolton Wanderers	46	15	6	2	42	12	7	6	10	24	30	66	42	78
4	Scunthorpe United	46	14	5	4	42	20	6	12	5	34	31	76	51	77
5	Torquay United	46	10	7	6	34	16	11	7	5	32	25	66	41	77
6	Swansea City	46	9	7	7	35	28	11	3	9	27	28	62	56	70
7	Peterborough Utd.	46	10	5	8	28	26	10	5	8	24	27	52	53	70
8	Leyton Orient	46	13	4	6	55	27	6	8	9	30	36	85	63	69
9	Colchester United	46	10	5	8	23	22	9	5	9	24	29	47	51	67
10	Burnley	46	12	5	6	31	22	8	2	13	26	40	57	62	67
11	Wrexham	46	13	3	7	46	26	7	3	13	23	32	69	58	66
12	Scarborough	46	12	8	3	38	19	5	6	12	18	29	56	48	65
13	Darlington	46	13	6	4	39	25	5	5	13	32	44	71	69	65
14	Tranmere Rovers	46	14	2	7	43	20	5	7	11	18	33	61	53	64
15	Cambridge United	46	10	6	7	32	24	6	7	10	18	28	50	52	61
16	Hartlepool United	46	9	7	7	25	25	6	7	10	25	32	50	57	59
17	Crewe Alexandra	46	7	11	5	25	19	6	8	9	32	34	57	53	58
18	Halifax Town	46	11	7	5	37	25	3	7	13	17	34	54	59	55
19	Hereford United	46	8	7	8	25	27	6	5	12	16	32	41	59	54
20	Stockport County	46	7	7	9	26	26	5	8	10	18	32	44	58	51
21	ROCHDALE	46	5	9	9	28	34	6	6	11	19	42	47	76	48
22	Exeter City	46	8	6	9	33	29	3	7	13	20	39	53	68	46
23	Carlisle United	46	9	5	9	38	33	3	3	17	19	53	57	86	44
24	Newport County	46	4	5	14	19	36	2	2	19	16	69	35	105	25

1988/89 season: Div. 4		P	W	D	L	F	A	W	D	L	F	A	F	A	Pts
1	Rotherham United	46	13	6	4	44	18	9	10	4	32	17	76	35	82
2	Tranmere Rovers	46	15	6	2	34	13	6	11	6	28	30	62	43	80
3	Crewe Alexandra	46	13	7	3	42	24	8	8	7	25	24	67	48	78
4	Scunthorpe United	46	11	9	3	40	22	10	5	8	37	35	77	57	77
5	Scarborough	46	12	7	4	33	23	9	7	7	34	29	67	52	77
6	Leyton Orient	46	16	2	5	61	19	5	10	8	25	31	86	50	75
7	Wrexham	46	12	7	4	44	28	7	7	9	33	35	77	63	71
8	Cambridge United	46	13	7	3	45	25	5	7	11	26	37	71	62	68
9	Grimsby Town	46	11	9	3	33	18	6	6	11	32	41	65	59	66
10	Lincoln City	46	12	6	5	39	26	6	4	13	25	34	64	60	64
11	York City	46	10	8	5	43	27	7	5	11	19	36	62	63	64
12	Carlisle United	46	9	6	8	26	25	6	9	8	27	27	53	52	60
13	Exeter City	46	14	4	5	46	23	4	2	17	19	45	65	68	60
14	Torquay United	46	15	2	6	32	23	2	6	15	13	37	45	60	59
15	Hereford United	46	11	8	4	40	27	3	8	12	26	45	66	72	58
16	Burnley	46	12	6	5	35	20	2	7	14	17	41	52	61	55
17	Peterborough Utd.	46	10	3	10	29	32	4	9	10	23	42	52	74	54
18	ROCHDALE	46	10	10	3	32	26	3	4	16	24	56	56	82	53
19	Hartlepool United	46	10	6	7	33	33	4	4	15	17	45	50	78	52
20	Stockport County	46	8	10	5	31	20	2	11	10	23	32	54	52	51
21	Halifax Town	46	10	7	6	42	27	3	4	16	27	48	69	75	50
22	Colchester United	46	8	7	8	35	30	4	7	12	25	48	60	78	50
23	Doncaster Rovers	46	9	6	8	32	32	4	4	15	17	46	49	78	49
24	Darlington	46	3	12	8	28	38	5	6	12	25	38	53	76	42

1983/84 22nd in Division 4

			Score	Scorers	Att	Conroy SH	Oates RA	Chapman L	Farrell PJ	Williams WR	Doyle M	Thompson DS	Hamilton NR	Higgins AM	O'Connor MJ	Griffiths IJ	Allatt V	Greenhoff J	Johnson SA	Thompson SC	Thomas GR	Keenan GP	Greenhoff B	McMahon ID	Reid S	Ennis ME	Blake JB	Heaton PJ	Humphreys JS	McCluskie JA	Dean AG
1	Aug	27	CREWE ALEXANDRA	1-0	Farrell (p)	1732	1	2	3	4		6	7	8	5			10	11	9												
2	Sep	3	York City	0-2		2772	1	2	3	4	6		7	8	5			10	11	9												
3		6	Wrexham	1-5	Johnson	1684	1	2	3	4	6		7	8	5			10	11	9												
4		10	READING	4-1	Farrell, Allatt 2, Johnson	1276	1	2	3	4		6	7	8	5		11	10		9												
5		17	Colchester United	0-4		1955	1	2	3	4		6	7	8	5		11	10		9												
6		24	Northampton T	1-1	Johnson	1402	1	2	3	4	5	6	7	8			11	10		9	12											
7		27	HARTLEPOOL UNITED	2-0	Farrell 2	1380	1	2	3	4	5	6	7	8			11	10		9												
8	Oct	1	Swindon Town	1-2	Johnson	2808	1	6	3	4	2			8	5		11	10		9	7											
9		8	Blackpool	2-0	Farrell, S Thompson	3216	1	5	3	4	2	6	7		8		11	10		9	12											
10		15	CHESTERFIELD	2-4	Allatt, Scrimgeour (og)	1781	1	5	3	4	2	6	7	8	12		11	10		9												
11		18	PETERBOROUGH UTD.	2-1	Higgins, Doyle	1299	1	5	3	4	2	6	7	8	9		11	10														
12		22	Darlington	0-1		1307	1	5	3		2	6	7	8	12		4	10		9		11										
13		29	CHESTER CITY	1-1	Hamilton	1496	1	5	3	4		6	7	8	9		11	10		12		2										
14	Nov	1	Mansfield Town	0-3		2536	1	5	3	4		6	7	8	9		11	10		12		2										
15		5	STOCKPORT COUNTY	2-2	Farrell (p), Oates	1682	1	5	3	4		6	7	8		10	11			9		2										
16		12	Tranmere Rovers	2-2	Farrell (p), Johnson	2457	1	5	3	4	7	6		8		10	11			9		2										
17		26	Aldershot	1-2	Johnson	1686	1	5	3	4	7	6	12	8			11	10		9		2										
18	Dec	3	HEREFORD UNITED	3-3	O'Connor, Higgins, Farrell	1261	1		3	4	2	6	7	8	5	10			11	9				12								
19		17	BRISTOL CITY	0-1		1501	1		3	4	5	6	11	8	7		12	10		9				2								
20		26	Bury	1-3	Johnson	4097	1		3	4	5	6	7	8	11		12	10		9				2								
21		27	HALIFAX TOWN	1-1	Higgins	1870	1	2	3		6		7	4	5	8	11	10		9	12											
22		31	Torquay United	2-4	S Thompson, Williams	1801	1	2	3	4	6		7	8	5	12	11	10		9												
23	Jan	2	DONCASTER ROVERS	3-3	D Thompson, S Thompson 2	2001	1	2	3				7	8	5	10	11	9		4												
24		14	Crewe Alexandra	1-0	Thomas	2640	1	6	3				7				11	4		9	8		2	5	10							
25		28	Reading	0-0		4162	1	6	3				7				11	4		12	9	8	2	5	10							
26	Feb	4	SWINDON TOWN	3-3	Griffiths, D Thompson, Allatt (p)	1297	1	6	3				7				11	4		12	9	8		5	10	2						
27		11	Northampton Town	1-1	S Thompson	2022	1	6	3				7		5		11	4		9	8			2	10							
28		14	MANSFIELD TOWN	0-0		1095	1	6	3				7	12	5		11	4		9	8		2	10								
29		18	Chester City	0-1		1383	1	6	12				7	8	5			4		9	11		2	3	10							
30		25	DARLINGTON	2-0	Higgins, Allatt	995	1	6	3	4			7	8	9		11	10					2	5								
31	Mar	3	Peterborough United	0-2		2835	1	6	3			2	7	8			11	10		9	4			5								
32		5	Stockport County	1-2	McMahon	2115	1		3	4	6		7	8			11	9			10			5			2					
33		10	TRANMERE ROVERS	2-3	Griffiths, D Thompson	1263	1	6	3	4			7	8		12	11	9			10			5			2					
34		13	Bristol City	1-1	O'Connor	7101	1	2	3		6		7	8		9	11	10						5	4							
35		17	BLACKPOOL	1-0	Griffiths	3147	1	2	3	12	6		7	8		9	11	10						5	4							
36		24	Chesterfield	0-3		2955	1	6	3	7				8		9	11			12				5	4			2	10			
37		27	YORK CITY	0-2		1786	1	2	3		6		7	8		9	11	10						5	4				12			
38		31	Hartlepool United	2-1	Griffiths, O'Connor	1245	1	2	3		6			8		9	11	10						5	4				7			
39	Apr	7	WREXHAM	1-2	Allatt	1228	1	2	3		6			8		9	11	10						5	4			12	7			
40		14	Hereford United	1-2	Allatt	2796	1	2	3		6	5	7	8		9	11	10							4							
41		17	COLCHESTER UNITED	0-0		809	1	5	4			6	7	8			11	10		9				3	2							
42		21	BURY	0-2		2203	1	5	4			6	9				11	10						3	2			8	7	12		
43		23	Halifax Town	0-5		1422	1	5	4			6		8			11	10		9				3	2			12		7		
44		28	ALDERSHOT	3-1	Allatt, D Thompson, Griffiths	853	1	2	3			6	7	8			11	10						5	4					9		
45	May	5	Doncaster Rovers	0-3		3396	1	2			4	6	7	8			11							5						10	9	3
46		7	TORQUAY UNITED	1-0	Williams	943	1	2	3			8	6	7			12	11						5	4					10	9	
					Apps	46	42	45	25	27	24	40	39	22	15	41	40	4	19	19	10	5	9	21	17	1	2	5	6	5	1
					Goals		1		8	2	1	4	1	4	3	5	8		7	5	1		1								

One own goal

F.A. Cup

R1	Nov	19	CREWE ALEXANDRA	1-0	Farrell	2465	1	5	3	4	2	6	7	8			11	10		9												
R2	Dec	13	York City	2-0	Johnson 2	5203	1		3	4	5	6	11	8	7			10		9				2								
R3	Jan	7	TELFORD UNITED	1-4	Allatt	4889	1	12	3		6		7	8	5	10	11	9			4			2								

F.L. Cup

| R1/1 | Aug | 30 | STOCKPORT COUNTY | 0-3 | | 1839 | 1 | 2 | 3 | 4 | | 6 | 7 | 8 | 5 | | 12 | 10 | 11 | 9 | | | | | | | | | | | | |
| R1/2 | Sep | 12 | Stockport County | 2-2 | Griffiths, Johnson | 2167 | 1 | 2 | 3 | 4 | | 6 | 7 | 8 | 5 | | 11 | 10 | | 9 | | | | | | | | | | | | |

Associate Members' Cup

| R1 | Feb | 22 | PRESTON NORTH END | 0-3 | | 1300 | 1 | 6 | 3 | 10 | | 4 | 7 | 8 | | 12 | 11 | 9 | | | 14 | | | 2 | 5 | | | | | | | |

Lancashire Cup

	Aug	13	BOLTON WANDERERS	3-3	O'Connor,Chapman,D Thompson	1550	1	2	3	4	5	6	7	8	9	10	11	12														
		16	Bury	2-2	Allatt, Higgins		1	2	3	4	5	6	7	8	9			10	11													
		20	WIGAN ATHLETIC	2-3	Higgins, Farrell(p)		1	2	3	4	5	6	7	8	9		11	10		12												

1983-84 Season
Back: Greenhoff (Play/Man), D.Thompson, S.Thompson, Conroy, Williams, Oates, Johnson, Allatt, Doyle
Front: O'Connor, Hamilton, Farrell, Griffiths, Chapman, Higgins

1984-85 Season
Back: Thompson, Edwards, McMahon, Lawrence, Conroy, Hanvey, Cooke, McCluskie
Front: Heaton, Keegan, Diamond, Griffiths, Chapman, Reid

1984/85 — 17th in Division 4

Player columns (left → right): Conroy SH, Edwards SG, Chapman L, Farrell PJ, Cooke J, Hanvey K, Thompson DS, Keegan GA, Lawrence LO, Diamond B, Heaton PJ, Reid S, McMahon ID, Williams WR, Haworth G, Griffiths JI, Malcolm PA, Cavanagh JL, English TS, Fielding MA, Moore AP, Seasman J, Johnson I, Taylor SJ, Gamble F, McAllister D, Redfern D, Grant D, Dwyer PJ, Robinson P

League (Division 4)

#	Date	Opponent	Score	Scorers	Att.	Con	Edw	Cha	Far	Coo	Han	Tho	Kee	Law	Dia	Hea	Rei	McM	Wil	Haw	Gri	Mal	Cav	Eng	Fie	Moo	Sea	Joh	Tay	Gam	McA	Red	Gra	Dwy	Rob
1	Aug 25	HEREFORD UNITED	0-1		1396	1	2	3		5	6	7	8	9	10	11		4	12																
2	Sep 1	Mansfield Town	1-5	McMahon	2627	1		3	12	5	6	7	8	9	10			4	2		11														
3	8	WREXHAM	0-2		1162	1	2	3		5	6	7			10	11	12	8	4	9															
4	15	Hartlepool United	2-0	English. Lawrence	1574			3	10	5	6	7		9		11		4				1	2	8											
5	18	Northampton Town	0-0		1653			3	10	5	6	7		9		11		4				1	2	8											
6	22	TORQUAY UNITED	0-0		1006			3	10	5	6			9	7	11		4				1	2	8											
7	29	Tranmere Rovers	1-3	Heaton	1452			3	10	5	6			9	11	7	4	12	8			1	2												
8	Oct 2	ALDERSHOT	1-2	Lawrence	960		2	10		5	6	7		9	11	8		4	12			1													
9	5	Stockport County	1-1	Lawrence	2681		3	8		5	6	7		9	11			4	10			1	2												
10	13	PORT VALE	1-2	Cooke	1722			8		5	6	7		9	11	12		4	10			1	2												
11	20	PETERBOROUGH UTD.	2-1	Diamond 2	1063			8		5	6	7		9	10	11		3	2			1			4	12									
12	23	Darlington	0-1		3344			8		5	6	7		9	10	11		3	2			1			4	12									
13	27	Crewe Alexandra	1-3	Lawrence	2406			8		5		7			10	11	12	3	6			1			4	2									
14	Nov 3	SWINDON TOWN	0-1		1082			4			6	7		9	8	11	2	5				1					3		10						
15	6	BURY	1-1	Diamond (p)	3380			4			6	7		9	8	11		5				1	2				3		10						
16	10	Exeter City	1-1	Thompson	2323			4			6	7		9	8	11						1	2				3		10						
17	24	COLCHESTER UNITED	1-1	Cooke	1028			3		5		7			8	11		4				1	2						10		6	9			
18	Dec 11	Chester City	1-0	Heaton	1209			3		5		7			8	11		4		6		1	2						10			9			
19	15	SOUTHEND UNITED	2-2	Diamond, Taylor	1040			3		5		7			8	11		4		6		1	2						10			9			
20	21	CHESTERFIELD	3-1	Diamond, McMahon, Taylor	1177			3		5		7			8	11		4		6		1	2						10			9			
21	26	Blackpool	0-3		5641			3		5		7			8	11		4		6		1	2						10			9	12		
22	Jan 1	HALIFAX TOWN	2-0	Gamble, Taylor	1671			3		5		7			8	2	10	4	6			1							9	11					
23	Feb 2	TRANMERE ROVERS	2-1	Heaton, Taylor	1249			3		5		7			11	10		4	6			1	12						9	8	2				
24	9	Torquay United	0-1		1186			3		5		7			8	2	10	4	6			1							9	11					
25	16	NORTHAMPTON T	3-0	Diamond 2, Thompson	1228			3		5		7			8	2	10	4	6			1							9	11					
26	23	Swindon Town	1-2	Reid	2938			3				7			8	2	10	4	6			1	12						9	11	5				
27	26	Scunthorpe United	2-4	Taylor 2	1694			3		5		7			8	2	10	4				1							9	11	6				
28	Mar 2	CREWE ALEXANDRA	1-3	Diamond	1483			3		5					8	10				6								2	9			7	1		
29	5	DARLINGTON	1-2	Taylor	1341			10		5					8	2		4		6			12				3		9	7			1		
30	9	Peterborough United	1-1	Diamond	2475			10		5		7			8	2		4		6							3		9	11			1		
31	16	Port Vale	1-3	Gamble	2788			10		5		7			8	2		4		6							3		9	11			1		
32	29	Bury	2-2	Diamond, Gamble	4559			10		5		7			8	2		4											9	11		1	3	6	
33	Apr 3	Hereford United	2-1	Heaton, Larkin (og)	3426			10		5		7			8	2		4											9	11		1	3	6	12
34	6	BLACKPOOL	1-1	Taylor	3555			10		5		7			8	2		4											9	11		1	3	6	12
35	8	Halifax Town	2-0	Gamble, McMahon	1706			10		5		7			8	2		4											9	11		1	3	6	12
36	13	EXETER CITY	2-0	Diamond, McMahon	1181			10		5		7			8	11		4											9			1	3	6	2
37	19	Colchester United	1-1	Diamond (p)	1858			10		5		7			8	11		4											9			1	3	6	2
38	23	Wrexham	0-2		1335			10		5					8	7		4										12	9	11		1	3	6	2
39	27	CHESTER CITY	1-2	Taylor	1358			10				7			8	2		4										12	9	11		1	3	6	5
40	30	HARTLEPOOL UNITED	4-3	Brownlie (og), Gamble, Heaton, Taylor	910			10				7			8	2		4										12	9	11		1	3	6	5
41	May 3	Southend United	2-0	Dwyer, Taylor	1761			10		5		7			8	11		4											9			1	3	6	2
42	6	SCUNTHORPE UNITED	3-3	Diamond 2 (2p), Taylor	1482			10		5		7			8	11		4											9			1	3	6	2
43	8	STOCKPORT COUNTY	0-0		1399			10		5		7			8	11		4											9	12		1	3	6	2
44	11	Chesterfield	0-0		7006					5		7			8	11	10												9			1	3	6	2
45	14	MANSFIELD TOWN	2-1	Diamond (p), Cooke	1098					5		7			8	2	10	4											9	11		1	3	6	
46	17	Aldershot	0-5		1572					5		7			8	2	10	4									3		9	11		1		6	
		Apps				3	4	43	5	41	15	40	2	15	43	41	21	38	25	1	1	24	17	3	6	3	8	8	30	21	3	19	14	15	12
		Goals								3		2		4	15	5	1	4												12	5				1	

Played in 1 game: JM Pemberton (8, at 3), L.Strong (10 at 3). S Tapley (28, at 7), N Ashworth, (46, at 7), GJ Hurst (46, at 12). Played in 28 at 12 and 29 at 11: MA Towers.

Two own goals

F.A. Cup

Rnd	Date	Opponent	Score	Scorers	Att.	Con	Edw	Cha	Far	Coo	Han	Tho	Kee	Law	Dia	Hea	Rei	McM	Wil	Haw	Gri	Mal	Cav	Eng	Fie	Moo	Sea	Joh	Tay	Gam
R1	Nov 17	DONCASTER ROVERS	1-2	Heaton	2319						8	6	7		9	10	11		5			1	2		3		4			

F.L. Cup (Milk Cup)

Rnd	Date	Opponent	Score	Scorers	Att.	Con	Edw	Cha	Far	Coo	Han	Tho	Kee	Law	Dia	Hea	Rei	McM	Wil	Haw	Gri
R1/1	Aug 27	Stockport County	1-3	Lawrence	2274	1	2	3		5	6	7	10	9	11			4	8		
R1/2	Sep 4	STOCKPORT COUNTY	1-2	Diamond (p)	1211	1	2	3	4	5		7		9	10	12		8	6		11

A.M.Cup (Freight Rover Trophy)

Rnd	Date	Opponent	Score	Scorers	Att.	Cha	Coo	Tho	Dia	Hea	McM	Wil	Haw	Mal	Cav	Sea	Joh	Tay	Gam	McA	Red	Gra
R1/1	Feb 5	PRESTON NORTH END	2-2	Taylor, Gamble	1093	3	5	7	11	10	4	6		1	2			9	8			
R1/2	19	Preston North End	1-0	Taylor	1853	3		7	8	2	10	4	6	1	12			9	11	5		
R2	Mar 12	BOLTON WANDERERS	0-1		2650		10	5	7		8	3	4		2		6	9	11			1

Lancashire Cup

Date	Opponent	Score	Scorers	Att.	Con	Edw	Cha	Far	Coo	Han	Tho	Kee	Law	Dia	Hea	Rei	McM	Wil	Haw
Aug 11	Wigan Athletic	1-3	Diamond	1217	1	2	3	4	5	6	7	8	9	10	11	12	14		
14	BURNLEY	1-0	Diamond	1344	1	2	3		5	6	7	8	9	10	11	4	12	14	
18	Blackpool	0-1		1363	1	2	3			6	7	8	9	11	4	10	5	12	

Played in 1 game: S.Holden (Aug 18 at 14)

Rose Bowl

Date	Opponent	Score	Scorers	Att.	Con	Edw	Cha	Far	Coo	Han	Tho	Kee	Law	Dia	Hea
Aug 8	OLDHAM ATHLETIC	0-0		1490	1	2	3	4	5	6	7	8	9	10	11

1985/86 18th in Division 4

#	Date	Opponent	Score	Scorers	Att	Redfern D	Heaton PJ	Johnson I	Reid S	Cooke J	Hicks K	Diamond B	Taylor SJ	Moore RD	McMahon ID	Gamble F	McCluskie JA	Grant D	Seasman J	Chambers PM	Hildersley R	Tong DJ	Haire G	Thompson DS	Towner AJ	Johnson SA	Mossman DJ	Carney S	Smart I	Measham I	Ashworth N
1	Aug 17	ALDERSHOT	2-0	Taylor, Diamond (p)	1069	1	11	2	4	5	6	7	8	9	10			3		12											
2	24	Torquay United	2-1	Compton (og), Moore	1305	1	2	6		5		7	8	9	4	11		3	10												
3	26	STOCKPORT COUNTY	4-1	Heaton, Seasman, Taylor, Moore (p)	2053	1	7	2		5			8	9	4	11		10	6	3											
4	31	Port Vale	1-1	Taylor	3043	1	7	2		5			8	9	4	11		10	6	3											
5	Sep 7	PETERBOROUGH UTD.	2-1	Gamble 2	2600	1	7	2		5			8	9	4	11		10	6	3											
6	13	Hartlepool United	0-2		2148	1	7	2		5		12	8	9	4	11		10	6	3											
7	21	Burnley	0-1		4241	1	2			5			7	8	9	4		3	10		12										
8	28	NORTHAMPTON T	3-2	Heaton, Moore, Grant	1954	1	7	2		5			8	9	4	11		10	6	3	12										
9	Oct 1	Orient	0-5		2650	1	7	2		5			8	9	4	11		10	6	3	12										
10	5	Swindon Town	0-4		3299	1	7	2		5			8	9	4	11	12	10	6	3										
11	12	CREWE ALEXANDRA	1-0	Taylor	1776	1	7	2		5	6		8	9	4	11	12	3	10												
12	19	PRESTON NORTH END	1-1	Taylor	2527	1	2	3		5	6		8			11	9		10					7	12						
13	23	Hereford United	2-2	Taylor 2	2761	1	2	3			5	9	8		4	11			6					7	12						
14	26	Tranmere Rovers	0-2		1552	1	2	3			5		8	9	4	11			6	10				7	12						
15	Nov 2	WREXHAM	3-2	Taylor 2 (2p), Gamble	1600	1	2			5	6	12	8	9	4	11		3	10					7							
16	5	EXETER CITY	1-1	Taylor (p)	1243	1	2			5	6	7	8	9	4	11		3	10												
17	8	Colchester United	1-0	McMahon	2624	1	2			5	6	7	8	9	4	11		3	10												
18	23	SCUNTHORPE UNITED	1-0	Taylor	1586	1	2			5	6	7	8	9	4	11		3	10						12						
19	30	Mansfield Town	2-3	Taylor, Hicks	2593	1	2	12		5	6		8	9	4	11		3	10						7						
20	Dec 21	TORQUAY UNITED	5-0	Taylor 2, Moore 2, Thompson	1685	1	2			5	6		8	9	4			3	10					7	11	12					
21	26	Halifax Town	1-1	Taylor	2253	1	2			5	6		8	9	4			3	10					7	11	12					
22	28	Stockport County	0-3		4005	1	2			5	6		8	9	4			3	10					7	11	12					
23	Jan 1	CAMBRIDGE UNITED	2-1	Moore, Cooke	2049	1	2	12		5	6		8	9	4			3	10					7	11						
24	11	PORT VALE	3-3	Seasman, Gamble, Taylor (p)	2445	1	2	4			6		8	5		11		3	10					7	9						
25	18	Aldershot	1-2	S Johnson	1375	1	2	4			6		8	5		12		3	10					7	9	11					
26	25	HARTLEPOOL UNITED	0-2		2301	1	2	10			6		8	9	4	12		3						7		11	5				
27	Feb 4	HEREFORD UNITED	1-1	Moore	1081	1	2				6		8	9	4			3						7		11	5				
28	8	Preston North End	1-1	Taylor (p)	3268	1	4	2	10		6		8	9	7			3								11	5				
29	15	Chester City	1-1	Taylor	3259	1		2	10		6		8	9	4	7		3								11	5				
30	Mar 1	Northampton Town	0-1		2146	1	7	2		5	6		8	9	4			3	10		12					11					
31	8	SWINDON TOWN	1-2	Moore	1989	1	10	2		5	6		8	9	4			3						7		11					
32	11	Wrexham	0-2		1378	1	10	2		5	6		8	9	4	11		3			12			7							
33	15	Crewe Alexandra	2-4	McMahon, Booth (og)	1683	1	10	2		5	6		8	9	4			3			12			7		11					
34	18	BURNLEY	1-0	Taylor (p)	2406	1		2		5			8	9	4		11	3	10					7				6			
35	22	TRANMERE ROVERS	1-1	McMahon (p)	1558	1	8	2		5				9	4		11	3	10					7						6	
36	28	Cambridge United	0-1		1992	1	4	2		5			8	9			11	3	10					7						6	
37	31	HALIFAX TOWN	1-0	Moore	1931	1	4	2		5			8	9			11	3	10					7						6	
38	Apr 4	Exeter City	0-2		1713	1	4	2		5			8	9			11	3	10					7						6	
39	12	COLCHESTER UNITED	3-3	Taylor 2 (1p), Baker (og)	1182	1	7	2		5	6		8				11	3	10					9						4	
40	18	Scunthorpe United	1-3	Heaton	1406	1	4	3		5	6		8			11				10				7						2	
41	21	SOUTHEND UNITED	2-1	Taylor, Thompson	936	1	2	3		5	6		8	9						10	11			7							
42	26	MANSFIELD TOWN	1-1	Taylor	1936	1	2	3		5	6		8	9			12			10	11			7							
43	29	CHESTER CITY	1-2	Taylor (p)	1963	1	2	3		5	12		8	9			6			10	11			7							
44	May 2	Southend United	0-5		1411	1	2	12	11		6		8	5			9	3		10				7							
45	5	ORIENT	1-4	Taylor	1299	1	2	12	10		6		8	9	4			3			11			7							
46	7	Peterborough United	1-1	Heaton	1592	1	2	3	10		6		8	9						5	11			7							
		Apps				46	43	39	8	34	31	9	45	43	32	25	13	41	30	10	16	2	3	27	5	6	8	4	1	12	
		Gls					4			1	1	1	25	9	3	4			1	2				2		1					

Three own goals

F.A. Cup

Rnd	Date	Opponent	Score	Scorers	Att	Redfern D	Heaton PJ	Johnson I	Reid S	Cooke J	Hicks K	Diamond B	Taylor SJ	Moore RD	McMahon ID	Gamble F	McCluskie JA	Grant D	Seasman J	Chambers PM	Hildersley R	Tong DJ	Haire G	Thompson DS	Towner AJ	Johnson SA
R1	Nov 16	DARLINGTON	2-1	Taylor 2	2153	1	2			5	6	7	8	9	4	11		3	10							
R2	Dec 7	Scunthorpe United	2-2	Taylor 2	2868	1	2			5	6		8	9	4	11		3	10					12	7	
rep	10	SCUNTHORPE UNITED	2-1	Taylor, Moore	5066	1	2			5	6		8	9	4			3	10					7	11	
R3	Jan 9	Manchester United	0-2		40223	1	2			5	6		8	9	4			3	10					7	12	11

F.L. Cup (Milk Cup)

Rnd	Date	Opponent	Score	Scorers	Att	Redfern D	Heaton PJ	Johnson I	Reid S	Cooke J	Hicks K	Diamond B	Taylor SJ	Moore RD	McMahon ID	Gamble F	McCluskie JA	Grant D	Seasman J	Chambers PM	...	Ashworth N
R1/1	Aug 20	Wrexham	0-4		1751	1	2	6	4	5		7	8	9	10			3	11			12
R1/2	Sep 3	WREXHAM	2-1	Taylor, Cooke	1251	1	7	2		5		12	8	9	4	11		10	6	3		

A.M. Cup (Freight Rover Trophy)

Rnd	Date	Opponent	Score	Scorers	Att	Redfern D	Heaton PJ	Johnson I	Reid S	Cooke J	Hicks K	Taylor SJ	Moore RD	McMahon ID	McCluskie JA	Grant D	Seasman J	Chambers PM	Thompson DS	Towner AJ	Johnson SA	Mossman DJ	Carney S
R1	Jan 20	CHESTER CITY	1-0	Butler (og)	1164	1	2	3			6	8	9	4	12	14	5	10		7	11		
R1	28	Wigan Athletic	0-6		2106	1	2	10	8		6			4	12	3				7	9	11	5

Lancashire Cup

Date	Opponent	Score	Att	Redfern D	Heaton PJ	Johnson I	Reid S	Cooke J	Hicks K	Diamond B	Taylor SJ	Moore RD	McMahon ID	Gamble F	McCluskie JA	Grant D	Seasman J	...	Ashworth N
Aug 3	Bolton Wanderers	0-2		1	2	3	4	5	6	7	8	9	10	11					
6	BURNLEY	0-7	1099	1		6	4	5		7	8	9	10	12	11	3			2
10	BURY	0-1	1005	1	2	3	4	5		7	8	9	12	11		6	10		

276

1985-86 Season
Back: Wanless (Physio), Halom (Manager), Hicks, S.Johnson, I.Johnson, Redfern, Moore,
McCluskie, Seasman, Gamble, Kenyon (Sec.)
Front: McMahon, Heaton, Cooke, Taylor, Thompson, Grant

1986-87 Season
Back: Jones (Trainer), Hicks, Grant, Hudson, Johnson, Welsh, Redfern, Gibson, Shearer, Bramhall,
Young, B.Taylor (Res. Team Coach)
Middle/Front: Chadwick, Reid, Mills, S.Taylor, Hurst, Conning, Seasman, McKenna, Front: Hallam, Hunt, Smart, Mycock

1986/87 — 21st in Division 4

#	Date		Opponent	Score	Scorers	Att	Redfern D	Johnson I	Grant D	Gibson SJ	Bramhall J	Hicks K	Mills N	Taylor SJ	Conning TP	Reid S	Seasman J	Hudson CB	McHale R	Woods MA	Smart I	Shearer PA	Young AF	Wakenshaw RA	Rees M	White EW	McGeeney P	Holden SJ	Stanton B	Parlane DJ	Welch KJ	Hudson CJ	Simmonds RL	Hurt MG	Fairclough D
1	Aug	23	CREWE ALEXANDRA	1-1	Young	2004	1	2	3		5	6	12	8	11	10			7				4	9											
2		30	Cardiff City	0-0		3546	1	2	3	6	5		10	8	11	12			7				4	9											
3	Sep	6	NORTHAMPTON T	1-2	Taylor	1606	1	2	3	6	5		10	8	11			12	7				4	9											
4		12	Stockport County	1-1	Taylor	2192	1	2	3		5			8	11	12		6	7				4	9	10										
5		16	Orient	0-3		2100	1	2	3		5			8	11	12		6	7				4	9	10										
6		20	COLCHESTER UNITED	1-0	Taylor	1276	1	2	3		5			8		7	11	6					4	9	10										
7		26	Southend United	3-5	Reid, Seasman, Taylor	2225	1	2			5			8	3	7	11	6	12				4	9	10										
8	Oct	4	EXETER CITY	0-0		1307	1	2	3		5			8		7	11	6					4	9	10										
9		11	Peterborough United	1-1	Taylor (p)	2289	1	2	3		5			8		7	11	6					4	9	10										
10		18	Lincoln City	1-1	CB Hudson	1357	1	2	3		5		12	8		7	11	6					4	9	10										
11		21	HEREFORD UNITED	2-0	Young, Wakenshaw	1088	1	2	3		5		12	8		7	11	6					4	9	10										
12	Nov	1	Swansea City	0-1		5612	1	2	3		5			9		7	11	6			12	4			10	8									
13		4	Wolverhampton Wan.	0-0		3949	1	2	3		5			9		7	11	6				4			10	8									
14		8	HARTLEPOOL UNITED	0-2		1467	1	2	3		5				11	7		6				4		9	10	12	8								
15		22	Aldershot	1-2	Wakenshaw	1921	1	2	3	12	5		9		10	7		6	8			4		11											
16		29	TORQUAY UNITED	3-3	Bramhall 2, Grant	1251	1	2	3	12	5			9		7		6				4		11	10	8									
17	Dec	13	SCUNTHORPE UNITED	1-1	Woods	1244	1	2			5		10		11	7	12	9	6			8			3	4									
18		20	Cambridge United	0-3		1838	1	2	3	6	5		12		11	10		9				8			4	7									
19		26	TRANMERE ROVERS	0-1		1452	1	2	3		5				11	10		6				9	8		4	7									
20		27	Halifax Town	1-3	Woods	1667	1	2	3		5		12		11	10			8	6		9			4	7									
21	Jan	1	Burnley	3-0	Stanton, Woods, Parlane	4217	1	2	3		5				11	10			8	6					4	7	9								
22		24	Northampton Town	0-5		5484	1	2	3		5				11	10			9	6					4	7	8								
23	Feb	7	ORIENT	0-0		1419					5				2	10	4		6			9	11					12	7	8	1	3			
24		13	Colchester United	0-2		2020			3		5				2	10	4		6				8					12	7	9	1	11			
25		21	SOUTHEND UNITED	1-2	Bramhall	1262			3		5		12		2	10	4		6				7						9	1	11	8			
26		24	ALDERSHOT	3-1	CJ Hudson, Smart, Stanton	1092			3		5				10	2			6								4	7	9	1	11	8			
27		28	Wrexham	2-2	Stanton, Bramhall	1901			3		5				10	2			6		12					4	7	9	1	11	8			
28	Mar	10	CARDIFF CITY	0-0		1386			3		5				10	2			6		12	7					4		9	1	11	8			
29		14	LINCOLN CITY	1-1	Parlane	1490			3		5				10		2		6			7					4		9	1	11	8			
30		18	Hereford United	1-0	Parlane	1890			3		5				10		2		6		12	7					4		9	1	11	8			
31		21	PETERBOROUGH UTD.	3-2	Simmonds 2, Bramhall	2170			3		5				10		6				12	7					4	2	9	1	11	8			
32		25	WREXHAM	3-3	Parlane 2, Simmonds	1852			3		5				10		2		6		12						4	7	9	1	11	8			
33		28	Exeter City	1-1	Simmonds	1977			3		5				10	7			6								4	2	9	1	11	8			
34		31	Crewe Alexandra	1-5	Holden	1504			3		5				10	7			6		12						4	2	9	1	11	8			
35	Apr	4	Hartlepool United	1-1	Bramhall	1168		2	3		5				10	7			6		9						4			1	11	8			
36		7	PRESTON NORTH END	0-2		4986		2	3		5				10	7			6		12						4	9		1	11	8			
37		11	WOLVERHAMPTON W.	0-3		3812		2			5				7	10			6		11					12	4	9	1	3	8			
38		14	Preston North End	4-2	Johnson, Simmonds, Wakenshaw 2	10212		2	3		5				7	4			6		10	12						9	1	11	8			
39		18	BURNLEY	0-2		5739		2	3		5				7	4			6			10				12		9	1	11	8			
40		20	Tranmere Rovers	1-1	Simmonds (p)	2168		2	3		5				7	10					6	12	11				4		9	1		8			
41		25	CAMBRIDGE UNITED	2-0	Simmonds (p), Parlane	1698		2	3		5				7	10	6					11					4		9	1		8			
42		29	SWANSEA CITY	2-0	Conning, Simmonds (p)	2052		2	3		5				7	10	6					12	11				4		9	1		8			
43	May	2	Torquay United	1-2	Bramhall	3020		2	3		5				7	10	6					9	11				4			1	12	8			
44		4	HALIFAX TOWN	5-3	Simmonds (p), Bramhall 2, Wakenshaw, Holden	2990		2	3		5				7	10	6					11					4		9	1		8			
45		6	STOCKPORT COUNTY	2-1	Parlane, Simmonds	4840		2	3		5				7	10	6					11					4		9	1		8			
46		9	Scunthorpe United	0-2		2347		2	3		5				7	10	6					9					4			1	11	8		12
					Apps		22	34	42	5	46	1	10	9	40	41	24	15	7	6	38	1	28	29	3	4	3	24	17	23	24	19	22	1	
					Gls			1	1		9			5	1	1	1			3	1		2	5				2	3	7		1	10		

F.A. Cup

Rd	Date		Opponent	Score	Scorers	Att	Redfern D	Johnson I	Grant D	Gibson SJ	Bramhall J	Hicks K	Mills N	Taylor SJ	Conning TP	Reid S	Seasman J	Hudson CB	McHale R	Woods MA	Smart I	Shearer PA	Young AF	Wakenshaw RA	Rees M	White EW	McGeeney P	Holden SJ	Stanton B	Parlane DJ	Welch KJ	Hudson CJ	Simmonds RL	Hurt MG	Fairclough D
R1	Nov	15	Nuneaton Borough	3-0	Wakenshaw, Mills, Johnson	3586	1	2	3		5		9		11	7		6	8			4		10											
R2	Dec	6	WREXHAM	1-4	Wakenshaw	2822	1	2	3	9	5		10		11	7		6	14		4			8				12							

F.L. Cup (Littlewoods Challenge Cup)

Rd	Date		Opponent	Score	Scorers	Att	Redfern D	Johnson I	Grant D	Gibson SJ	Bramhall J	Hicks K	Mills N	Taylor SJ	Conning TP	Reid S	Seasman J	Hudson CB	McHale R	Woods MA	Smart I	Shearer PA	Young AF	Wakenshaw RA	Rees M	White EW	McGeeney P	Holden SJ	Stanton B	Parlane DJ	Welch KJ	Hudson CJ	Simmonds RL	Hurt MG	Fairclough D
R1/1	Aug	26	BURNLEY	1-1	Taylor	1937	1	2	3	6	5		11	8		10			7				4	9											
R1/2	Sep	2	Burnley	3-1	Shearer 2, Mills	2605	1	2	3	6	5		10	8	11			7				4	9												
R2/1		23	Watford	1-1	Conning	9670	1	2	3		5			8	9	7	11	6				4		10											
R2/2	Oct	7	WATFORD	1-2	Taylor (p)	5449	1	2	3		5			8		7	11	6				4	9	10											

A.M. Cup (Freight Rover Trophy)

Rd	Date		Opponent	Score	Scorers	Att	Redfern D	Johnson I	Grant D	Gibson SJ	Bramhall J	Hicks K	Mills N	Taylor SJ	Conning TP	Reid S	Seasman J	Hudson CB	McHale R	Woods MA	Smart I	Shearer PA	Young AF	Wakenshaw RA	Rees M	White EW	McGeeney P	Holden SJ	Stanton B	Parlane DJ	Welch KJ	Hudson CJ	Simmonds RL	Hurt MG	Fairclough D
PR	Dec	2	Darlington	2-2	Conning, CB Hudson	766	1	2	3	9	5				8	7		6			10	4					11								
PR	Jan	6	YORK CITY	1-1	Wakenshaw	783	1	2			5				3	10	12			9	6			11					4	7	8				
R1		27	CHESTERFIELD	3-0	Bramhall, Young, Wakenshaw	890	2		3		5				12	10	4			14	6		9	11						7	8	1			
QF	Feb	10	MIDDLESBROUGH	0-0		2615	2		3		5				12	10	4				6		9	11						7	8	1			

QF lost on penalties 3-4 a.e.t

Lancashire Cup

Date		Opponent	Score	Scorers	Att	Redfern D	Johnson I	Grant D	Gibson SJ	Bramhall J	Hicks K	Mills N	Taylor SJ	Conning TP	Reid S	Seasman J	Hudson CB	McHale R	Woods MA	Smart I	Shearer PA	Young AF	Wakenshaw RA	Rees M	White EW	McGeeney P	Holden SJ	Stanton B	Parlane DJ	Welch KJ	Hudson CJ	Simmonds RL	Hurt MG	Fairclough D
Aug	9	Blackburn Rovers	1-1	Fairclough	1577	1	2	3	4	5	6	7	8	10	11	12																		9
	12	BURY	1-2	Johnson	1722	1	2	3	4	5	6	7	8	10	11	9	12																	
	16	Blackpool	0-0		1175	1	2	3		5	6	7	8	14	11	9		10	12	4														

1987/88 21st in Division 4

#		Date	Opponent	Score	Scorers	Att	Welch KJ	Lomax GW	Hampton PJ	Reid S	Bramhall J	Seasman J	Stanton B	Simmonds RL	Gavin MW	Smart J	Holden SJ	Parlane DJ	Hunt MG	Walling DA	Thompson ND	Coyle RP	Hughes ZD	Parker HD	Mycock DC	Warren LA	Duggan AJ	Mellish SM	Moore J	Harris CS	Hancox PA	Moss E	Crerand DB	Young AF	Doyle J
1	Aug	15	Hereford United	0-0		2652	1	2	3	4	5	6	12	8	11			9			7	10													
2		22	PETERBOROUGH UTD.	1-1	Parlane	1770	1	2	3	4	5	7		8	11		6	9				10													
3		28	Halifax Town	2-1	Simmonds 2 (1p)	2275	1	2	3	4	5	7		8	11		6	9				10													
4		31	CREWE ALEXANDRA	2-2	Gavin, Stanton	2346	1	2	3	4	5	7	12	8	11		6	9				10													
5	Sep	5	Scunthorpe United	0-1		1959	1	2	3	4	5	7		8	11		6	9		12	14	10													
6		12	STOCKPORT COUNTY	0-1		2124	1	2		4	5	7		8	11		6	12	9			3		10												
7		15	Torquay United	0-5		1965	1	2	3	4	5	7		8	11		6	9		14	12	10													
8		19	Exeter City	1-1	Hunt	2628	1	2	3	4		7	12	8	11		6		9			10	5												
9		26	BURNLEY	2-1	Bramhall, Parlane	4655	1	2	3	4	5	7	12	8	11		6	9				10													
10		29	Wolverhampton Wan.	0-2		5533	1		3	4	5	2	7	8			6	12	9	14	11	10													
11	Oct	3	CARLISLE UNITED	1-2	Smart	1940	1	2	3	4	5	7	12	8	11		6	9				10													
12		9	Tranmere Rovers	1-6	Bramhall	2303	1	2	3	4	5	7	12	8			6	9				10			11										
13		17	DARLINGTON	1-3	Parker	1471	1	2	3			7			11	4	12	9				10	6	8											
14		20	Leyton Orient	0-8		2995	1	2	3		5			8	11	6	12	9				10	7	4											
15		24	BOLTON WANDERERS	2-2	Bramhall, Parlane	4294	1	2	3	4	5	7		8			6	9				10		11											
16		31	Cardiff City	0-1		3046	1	2	3	4	5			8			6	9				10		11		7									
17	Nov	3	COLCHESTER UNITED	1-4	Simmonds	1399	1	2	3	4	5			8			6	9				10		11		7									
18		7	SWANSEA CITY	2-3	Simmonds, Gavin	1253	1		3	4		2		8	11	6		9				10	12			7	5								
19		21	Cambridge United	2-1	Simmonds, Hampton	2104	1	6	3	4		2		8	11			9				10				7	5								
20		28	SCARBOROUGH	1-1	Coyle	1838	1	6	3	4		2		8	11			9				10				7	5								
21	Dec	12	Wrexham	3-2	Gavin, Bramhall, Simmonds	1409	1	6			5	4		8	11	2	7			9						3			10						
22		19	NEWPORT COUNTY	3-0	Walling, Gavin 2	1491	1	6			5	4		8	11	2	7			9						3			10						
23		26	Burnley	0-4		7013	1	6			5	4		8	11	2	7			9		12				3			10						
24		28	HARTLEPOOL UNITED	0-2		1851	1	6		4	5	2	12	8	11					9	7					3			10						
25	Jan	1	Halifax Town	0-0		2050	1	6		4	5	2		8	11		12			9	7					3			10						
26		2	Stockport County	1-1	Gavin	2441	1	6		4	5		2	8	11					9	7					3			10						
27		9	Peterborough United	1-1	Moore	3230	1	6		4	5		3	8	11	2	7												10	9					
28		16	EXETER CITY	0-0		1431	1	6		4	5		3	8	11	2	12												10	9	7				
29		26	Torquay United	1-1	Smart	1281	1	6		4	5		3	8		2	11												10	9	7				
30		29	Crewe Alexandra	1-0	Simmonds	2107	1	6		4	5		3	8		2	7												10	9	11				
31	Feb	6	SCUNTHORPE UNITED	2-1	Russell (og), Mooney (og)	1455	1	6		4	5		3	8		2	7												10	9	11				
32		13	Hartlepool United	1-1	Simmonds (p)	2120	1	6		4	5		3	8		2	7												10	9	11				
33		20	HEREFORD UNITED	3-1	Moore, Simmonds, Holden	1568	1	6		4	5		3	8		2	7								12	10				9	11				
34		27	Carlisle United	0-2		1983	1	6					2	8		5	7			11						3	10			4	9		12		
35	Mar	1	WOLVERHAMPTON W.	0-1		2805	1	6					2	8		5	7			11						3	10			4	9		12		
36		5	Darlington	1-2	Seasman	1773	1	6			5	7	3	8		2	11										10			4	9				
37		12	TRANMERE ROVERS	0-0		1622	1	6			5	7	3	8		2	11										10			4			9		
38		26	Bolton Wanderers	0-0		4875	1	6			5	2	3	8			7								12	10			4		11	9		
39		29	CARDIFF CITY	2-2	Harris, Simmonds (p)	1435	1	6			5	7	3	8		2										10			4		11	9		
40	Apr	2	Swansea City	3-0	Simmonds 2, Moss	5367	1	6			5	7	3	8		2										10			4		11	9		
41		4	CAMBRIDGE UNITED	2-1	Smart, Holden	1596	1	6			5	7	3	8		2	12									10			4		11	9		
42		8	Colchester United	0-1		1864	1	6			5	7	3	8		2	12									10			4		11	9		
43		23	LEYTON ORIENT	1-3	Moss	1390	1	6			5	7	3	8		2	12									10			4		11	9		
44		30	Scarborough	1-2	Harris	1852	1	6			5	2	3	8			12									10			4		11	9	7		
45	May	2	WREXHAM	1-2	Warren	1539	1	6			5	2	3	8			4									10					11	9	7		
46		7	Newport County	1-0	Walling	2560	1	6			5	2	3	8						12						10					11	9	7		
			Apps				46	44	19	28	40	32	32	43	23	36	25	19	1	12	5	24	2	7	11	31	3	12	10	15	2	10	3		
			Gls					1		4	1	1		12	5	3	2	3		1		2		1		1			1	1		2			

Two own goals

F.A. Cup

		Date	Opponent	Score		Att	Welch		Hampton	Reid		Seasman		Simmonds	Gavin		Holden	Parlane		Walling		Coyle			Mycock	Warren	Duggan								
R1	Nov	14	WREXHAM	0-2		1831	1		3	4		2		8	11		6	9		12		10			7	5									

F.L. Cup (Littlewoods Challenge Cup)

		Date	Opponent	Score	Scorers	Att	Welch	Lomax	Hampton	Reid	Bramhall	Seasman	Stanton	Simmonds	Gavin	Smart	Holden	Parlane		Walling		Coyle		Parker											
R1/1	Aug	18	TRANMERE ROVERS	3-1	Reid, Coyle, Parlane	1598	1	2	3	4	5	7	12	8	11		6	9				10													
R1/2		25	Tranmere Rovers	0-1		2314	1	2	3	4	5	7		8	11		6	9		14		10													
R2/1	Sep	22	WIMBLEDON	1-1	Simmonds (p)	2801	1	2	3	4	5	7	12	8	11		6					9		10											
R2/2	Oct	6	Wimbledon	1-2	Parker	2605	1	2	3		5	7	12	8			6	4		9		10		11											

A.M. Cup (Sherpa Van Trophy)

		Date	Opponent	Score	Scorers	Att	Welch	Lomax	Hampton	Reid	Bramhall	Seasman	Stanton	Simmonds	Gavin	Smart	Holden	Parlane	Hunt			Coyle		Parker	Mycock	Warren	Duggan								
PR	Oct	13	TRANMERE ROVERS	0-0		920	1		3	4	5		2	8			7					12		10	6	9	11								
PR	Nov	24	Burnley	2-3	Seasman, Simmons (p)	2677	1	6	3	4		2		8	11			9				10				7	5								
R1	Jan	19	Preston North End	1-3	Simmons	2983	1	3		4	5			8	11	2	12			9			6			10				7					

Lancashire Cup

		Date	Opponent	Score			Welch	Lomax	Hampton	Reid	Bramhall	Seasman	Stanton	Simmonds	Gavin	Smart	Holden			Walling	Thompson	Coyle											Young	Doyle
	Aug	1	Preston North End	0-1			1	2	3	4	5	6	7	8	11																			9	10
		5	Bury	0-2			1	2	3	4	5	7		8	11	6			9	12															10
		8	Wigan Athletic	0-4			1	2	3	4		6		8	11	5	7	9																		10

279

1987-88 Season
Back: Seasman, Walling, Welch, Bramhall, Redfern, Coyle, Smart
Front: Stanton, Simmonds, Hampton, Gavin, Reid, Holden, Lomax

1988-89 Season
Back: Walling, Armitage, Mellish, Smith, Smart, Welch, O'Shaughnessy, Copeland, Mycock, Beaumont, Jones (Trainer)
Middle: Harris, Simmonds, Lomax, Bergara (Manager), Sutton, Reid, Frain
Front: Lucketti, Worsley, Hancox, Buckley, Appleby, Hughes, Hedderman, Allen

1988/89   18th in Division 4

League (Division 4)

No		Date	Opponent	Score	Scorers	Att	Welch KJ	Copeland SD	Armitage AM	Lomax GW	Sutton DW	Smart J	Reid S	Smith MC	Walling DA	Frain D	O'Shaughnessy S	Mycock DC	Harris CS	Mellish SM	Beaumont CP	Edmonds NA	Wood P	Fothergill AG	Windridge DH	Alford CP	Roberts WJ	Brown M	Taylor SJ	McIntyre IG	Jones PB	Lucketti CJ	Hughes ZD	Warren L	Wilkinson S
1	Aug	27	Burnley	1-2	Frain	7511	1	2	3	4	5	6	8	9	12	11	10					7													
2	Sep	3	ROTHERHAM UNITED	0-2		2107	1	2	3	4	5	14	6	8	12	11	10		7			9													
3		10	Scarborough	3-3	Harris, Sutton, O'Shaughnessy	2456	1	2	3		5	4	6	8	9	11	10		7																
4		17	EXETER CITY	2-1	Smith, Frain	1375	1	2			5	4	6	8	12	11	10	3	7			9													
5		20	DONCASTER ROVERS	2-0	Edmonds, Frain (p)	1645	1	2		6	5	4		8	9	11	10	3				7													
6		24	Grimsby Town	3-1	Smith 2, Mellish	2939	1	2		6	5	4	12	8	9	11	10	3		14		7													
7	Oct	1	CREWE ALEXANDRA	2-1	Edmonds, Smith	2227	1	2	3		5	4	6	8	9	11	10					7													
8		4	Hartlepool United	1-0	Toman (og)	2363	1	2	3		5	4	6	8	9	11	10					7													
9		8	STOCKPORT COUNTY	1-1	Reid	3021	1	2	3		5	4	6	8	9	11	10	12				7													
10		14	Halifax Town	1-4	Smith	2553	1	2	3		5	4	6	8	9	11	10			14	12	7													
11		22	SCUNTHORPE UNITED	1-0	Edmonds	2250	1	3	2		5	4	6	8		11	10		7			9													
12		26	Hereford United	4-4	Frain 2, Beaumont, Sutton	2071	1		2		5	4	6	8	14	11	10		7		9	3													
13		29	DARLINGTON	2-2	Edmonds 2	2462	1	3	2		5	4	6	8		11	10		7		9														
14	Nov	4	Tranmere Rovers	0-2		3740	1	2	3		5	4	6	8	12	11			7			9													
15		8	Torquay United	0-1		1931	1	2	3		5	4	6	8	9	11	12		10			7													
16		12	WREXHAM	3-3	Reid, Beaumont, Frain	2280	1	2	14	3	5	4	6	8	12	11	10		7		9														
17		26	YORK CITY	2-0	Smith, Beaumont	1886	1	2	4	3	5		6	8		11	10		7		9	12													
18	Dec	3	Peterborough United	0-1		3272	1	2	12		5		6	8		11	4	3			9	10	7												
19		16	COLCHESTER UNITED	1-1	O'Shaughnessy	1261	1	6	3	2	5		4	8	12	11	7				9	10													
20		26	Carlisle United	0-1		10013	1	2	3		5		6	8	12	11	4		7		9	10													
21		30	Cambridge United	0-2		2319	1	2	3	6	5		2	8	9	11	4	12	7			10													
22	Jan	2	LEYTON ORIENT	0-3		2036	1	12	3	2	5			8	9	11	4	6	7	14		10													
23		7	LINCOLN CITY	2-2	Smith, Walling	1515	1	2	3	6	5	4		8	9	11			7			10													
24		14	Rotherham United	1-3	Frain	4530	1	2	3		5	4		8	9	11	6		7		12	10													
25		21	BURNLEY	2-1	Frain (p), Beaumont	5812	1	2	3		5	4		8		11	6		7		9	10													
26		28	Exeter City	1-5	Beaumont	2428	1	2	3	14	5	4		8		11	6		7		9	10	12												
27	Feb	4	Doncaster Rovers	1-1	Beaumont	1868	1	2	3	6	5	4		8		11	12		7		9	10													
28		11	GRIMSBY TOWN	0-2		1621	1	2	3		5	4		8		11	12	6	7	14	9	10													
29		17	Stockport County	0-3		2848	1	2		5		4		8		11	6	3	7		9	10	12												
30		28	HEREFORD UNITED	2-2	O'Shaughnessy, Taylor	1060	1	6		11		4					5	3	7		9							4	8	10					
31	Mar	4	Scunthorpe United	0-4		4098	1	2	3	5		4			12		6		7		9	10						8	11						
32		11	TRANMERE ROVERS	3-1	Beaumont, O'Shaughnessy 2	2168	1	12	3		4				9	11	6		7		10	2						8	14	5					
33		11	Darlington	2-1	Taylor, Wlaing	1876	1		3		4				9	11	6		7		10	2						8		5					
34		18	SCARBOROUGH	2-1	Jones 2	1636	1		3		4				9	11	6		7		10	2						8		5					
35		25	Leyton Orient	0-3		4591	1		3		4				9	11	6		7		10	2						8		5					
36		27	CARLISLE UNITED	0-0		2145	1		3		4				9	11	6		7		10							2	8	12	5				
37		31	Colchester United	0-3		3631	1		3	6	4				9	11			7		10							2	8		5				
38	Apr	5	Lincoln City	1-4	Edmonds	2033	1		3	6	4				11	12	8		7		10							2	9		5				
39		8	CAMBRIDGE UNITED	2-1	Frain, Edmonds	1314	1		3	6					11	4	8		7		10							2	9		5				
40		14	Crewe Alexandra	1-3	Frain	4144	1		3	10	4				12	11	6		8		7							2	9		5				
41		22	HARTLEPOOL UNITED	0-0		1406	1		3	10	4				9	6	8		7	11	14							2	12		5				
42		25	HALIFAX TOWN	1-1	Frain	1378	1	6	3		4				10	11	8	12	7	14	2								9		5				
43		29	York City	3-3	Walling, Edmonds, O'Shaugh'ss	1920	1	6			4				10	11	8	3	7	12	2								9		5				
44	May	1	TORQUAY UNITED	2-1	Taylor, Frain (p)	1239	1		3		4				10	11	8	6	7	12	2								9		5				
45		6	PETERBOROUGH UTD.	0-0		1430	1		3		4				10	11	8	6	7									12	2	9		5				
46		13	Wrexham	1-2	Taylor	3125	1		3		4				10	11	8	6	7									12	2	9		5				
				Apps			46	28	36	27	27	42	18	27	34	42	41	11	10	14	34	39	5	9	5	4	1	11	17	4	14	1			
				Goals							2		2	7	3	12	6		1	1	7	8							4		2				

One own goal

F.A. Cup

		Date	Opponent	Score	Scorers	Att	Welch	Copeland	Armitage	Lomax	Sutton	Smart	Reid	Smith	Walling	Frain	O'Shaughnessy	Mycock	Beaumont	Edmonds	Wood
R1	Nov	19	Huddersfield Town	1-1	Edmonds	6178	1	2	3	4	5		6	8		11	7		10	9	
rep		28	HUDDERSFIELD TOWN	3-4	Beaumont, Reid (p), Frain	5645	1	2	4		5		6	8		11	7	3	12	10	9

F.L. Cup (Littlewoods Challenge Cup)

		Date	Opponent	Score	Scorers	Att	Welch	Copeland	Armitage	Lomax	Sutton	Smart	Reid	Smith	Walling	Frain	O'Shaughnessy	Harris	Mellish	Warren L
R1/1	Aug	30	BURNLEY	3-3	O'Shaugh'ssy, Reid (p), Beaum	3669	1	2	3	4	5	6	8	9		11	10	7	12	
R1/2	Sep	6	Burnley	1-2	O'Shaughnessy	6673	1	2	3		5	12	6	8	9	11	10	7		4

A.M. Cup (Sherpa Van Trophy)

		Date	Opponent	Score	Att	Welch	Copeland	Armitage	Sutton	Smart	Reid	Smith	Frain	O'Shaughnessy	Mycock	Beaumont	Edmonds	Wood	Mellish	Lomax	Warren L
PR	Dec	6	Blackpool	0-2	1228	1	2	3	5	4	6	8	11	9		10	7	12			
PR		13	WIGAN ATHLETIC	0-2	1134	1	6	12	5		4	8	11	7	3	9	10	14		2	4

Lancashire Cup

	Date	Opponent	Score	Scorers	Att	Welch	Copeland	Armitage	Lomax	Sutton	Smart	Reid	Smith	Walling	Frain	O'Shaughnessy	Mycock	Warren L	Wilkinson S
Aug	6	WIGAN ATHLETIC	1-0	Walling	886	1	2	3	4	5	6	7	8	9	11	10		10	
	9	BURY	1-0	Walling	1129	1	2	3	4	5	6	7		9	11	12	10	10	8
	13	Bolton Wanderers*	1-1	Reid	2423	1	2	3	4	5	6	7	12	9	11	10		10	8

* lost 5-4 on penalites

Rose Bowl

	Date	Opponent	Score	Scorers	Att	Welch	Copeland	Armitage	Lomax	Sutton	Smart	Reid	Smith	Walling	Frain	O'Shaughnessy	Mycock	Harris	Mellish	Warren L	Wilkinson S
Aug	20	Oldham Athletic	2-5	Sutton, Smith	2663	1	2	3	4	5	6	7	8	9	11	12		14	16	10	15

1989/90 12th in Division 4

	Date	Opponent	Score	Scorers	Att	Welch KJ	Goodison CW	Chapman VJ	Cole DA	Ward P	Small C	Holmes MA	Whellans R	Burns W	Stonehouse K	Hill JW (2)	Edmonds NA	Hasford JW	Dawson J	Ainscow A	Walling DA	Brown AJ	O'Shaughnessy S	Elliott SB	Johnson SA	Graham J	Milner AJ	Duxbury LE	Henshaw G	Milligan SJF	Lockett PB	Hughes ZD	Lucketti CJ
1	Aug 19	BURNLEY	2-1	Walling, Harris (og)	5420	1	2	3	5	6		8		10	11					7	9	4											
2	26	Scunthorpe United	1-0	Cole	2808	1	2		5	6		8		10	11	3				7	9	4											
3	Sep 2	WREXHAM	0-3		2331	1	2		5	6		8	14	10	11	3	12			7	9	4											
4	9	York City	0-1		2250	1	2	3	5	6		8	9	10	11					7		4	12										
5	16	COLCHESTER UNITED	2-2	Whellans, Walling	1466	1	2		5			8	9	12	11	3				7	10	4	6										
6	23	Torquay United	0-1		1809	1	2		5		14	8	9	12	11	3				7	10	4	6										
7	26	HARTLEPOOL UNITED	0-0		1511	1	2	3	5		14	8	9	6		7	11	12			10	4											
8	30	Chesterfield	1-2	Stonehouse (p)	3047	1	2		5	6	9	8	14	7	11	3				12	10	4											
9	Oct 7	Grimsby Town	2-1	Elliott, Jobling (og)	3996	1	2		5	6		8		10	11	3				7	12	4		9									
10	14	PETERBOROUGH UTD.	1-2	Elliott	1767	1	2		5	12		8		6	11	3				7	10	4		9									
11	17	EXETER CITY	1-0	Holmes	1337	1	2		5	6		8	11	10		3				7	12	4		9									
12	21	Halifax Town	0-1		1864	1	2		5	6		8		10		3	14			7	12	4		9	11								
13	28	SCARBOROUGH	1-0	Johnson	1402	1	2		5	6		12		10	11	3				7			4	9	8								
14	31	Gillingham	0-1		3127	1	2		5	6		12		10	11	3				7	14		4	9	8								
15	Nov 4	Hereford United	3-1	Johnson, Elliott 2	2235	1	2			6		7		10		3						5	4	9	8	11							
16	11	DONCASTER ROVERS	1-3	Goodison (p)	1716	1	2		12	6		7		10		3					14	5	4	9	8	11							
17	25	CARLISLE UNITED	1-2	O'Shaughnessy	1920	1	2		5	6					9	3	7					4	10	12	8	11							
18	Dec 2	Cambridge United	3-0	O'Shaughnessy, Elliott, Dawson	2289	1	2		5	6		7		3					12			4	10	9	8	11							
19	16	LINCOLN CITY	1-0	Stonehouse (p)	1216	1	2		5			7		3	6				9			4	10		8	11							
20	26	Stockport County	1-2	Goodison (p)	4216	1	2		5	6		7	12	3		14			9			4	10		8	11							
21	30	Aldershot	1-1	Ward	2055	1	2		5	6		7		3					9			4	10	12	8	11							
22	Jan 1	SOUTHEND UNITED	0-1		1521	1	2		5	6		7		3	12				9				4	10	8	11							
23	13	SCUNTHORPE UNITED	3-0	Burns, O'Shaughnessy 2	1781	1	2		5	6		7		3					9			4	10		8	11							
24	20	Burnley	1-0	Ward	8174	1	2		5	6		7	12	3					9			4	10			11	8						
25	Feb 3	TORQUAY UNITED	0-0		1909	1	2		5	6		7				3			9			4			12	11	8	10					
26	6	YORK CITY	0-1		1821	1	2		5	6		7		3		11			9			4	10		12		8	14					
27	10	Colchester United	2-1	Cole, Johnson	2744	1	2		5	6				3		11			9			4	10		8			7					
28	13	Wrexham	1-1	Cole	1552	1	2	11	5	6				3					9			4	10		8		12	7					
29	24	Carlisle United	1-0	Walling	4904	1	2		5	6		7		3					9			4	10		8			11					
30	Mar 3	MAIDSTONE UNITED	3-2	Cole, Holmes, Johnson	2085	1	2		5	6		7		3					9			4	10		8			11					
31	6	CHESTERFIELD	1-0	Ward	2810	1	2		5	6		7		3					9			4	10		8			11					
32	10	Hartlepool United	1-2	O'Shaughnessy	2771	1	2		5	6		7	12	3		14					9	4	10		8			11					
33	17	GRIMSBY TOWN	0-1		3059	1	2		5	6		7	12	3		14			8			4	10		9			11					
34	21	Peterborough United	1-0	Ward	3445	1	2		5	6		7		3		10			9			4					12	11	8				
35	24	Exeter City	0-5		4701	1	2		5			7		3		6			10		12	4			9		11		8				
36	27	CAMBRIDGE UNITED	2-0	Milner, O'Shaughnessy	1669	1	2		5			7		3		6			9			4	10		12		11		8				
37	31	HALIFAX TOWN	0-2		2499	1	2		5	9		7		3		6						4	10	14	12		11		8				
38	Apr 4	Maidstone United	0-2		1507	1	2		5	6	8	12		3					9	7	14	4	11	10									
39	7	Scarborough	1-2	Cole	1799	1	2		5	6	8	12		3					14	7		4	10	9			11						
40	10	GILLINGHAM	1-0	Ward	1334	1			5	6	8			3					10	2		4		9			7			11			
41	14	Southend United	2-3	Small, Goodison (p)	2584	1	2		5	6	8			3					10	11		4		9			7		12				
42	16	STOCKPORT COUNTY	1-1	Goodison (p)	3194	1	2		5	6				3					10	11		4		9			7		8				
43	21	Lincoln City	2-1	Milligan, Elliott	2470	1	2			6				3					10	11		4		9			7		8	5			
44	24	ALDERSHOT	2-0	Henshaw, Dawson	1419	1	2			6		14		3					10	11		4	12	9			7		8	5			
45	28	Doncaster Rovers	0-4		2191	1	2		5	6		12		3					10			4	14	9			7		8	11			
46	May 5	HEREFORD UNITED	5-2	O'Shaughnessy 2 (1p), Milner 3	1429	1	2		12	6		11		5					8			4	10	9			7			3	14		
					Apps	46	45	4	43	40	7	39	11	44	14	25	4	1	27	20	16	43	30	22	24	11	16	10	9	5	1		
					Goals		4		5	5	1	2	1	1	2				2		3		8	6	4		4		1	1			

Two own goals

F.A. Cup

	Date	Opponent	Score	Scorers	Att	Welch KJ	Goodison CW	Chapman VJ	Cole DA	Ward P	Small C	Holmes MA	Whellans R	Burns W	Stonehouse K	Hill JW (2)	Edmonds NA	Hasford JW	Dawson J	Ainscow A	Walling DA	Brown AJ	O'Shaughnessy S	Elliott SB	Johnson SA	Graham J	Milner AJ	Duxbury LE	Henshaw G	Milligan SJF	Lockett PB	Hughes ZD	Lucketti CJ
R1	Nov 17	Marine	1-0	Stonehouse	3525	1	2		5	6					9	3	7			12		4	10		8	11							
R2	Dec 9	LINCOLN CITY	3-0	Ward, Johnson, O'Shaughnesssy	2369	1	2		5	6		7		3					9			4	10		8	11							
R3	Jan 6	WHITLEY BAY	1-0	Johnson	5781	1	2		5	6		7		3		12			9			4	10		8	11							
R4	27	NORTHAMPTON T	3-0	O'Shaugh'ssy,Dawson,Goodison(	9048	1	2		5	6		7		3					9			4	10			11	8						
R5	Feb 17	Crystal Palace	0-1		17044	1	2		5	6		7		3		14			9			4	10		12		11	8					

R1 played at Anfield

F.L. Cup (Littlewoods Challenge Cup)

	Date	Opponent	Score	Scorers	Att	Welch KJ	Goodison CW	Chapman VJ	Cole DA	Ward P	Small C	Holmes MA	Whellans R	Burns W	Stonehouse K	Hill JW (2)	Edmonds NA	Hasford JW	Dawson J	Ainscow A	Walling DA	Brown AJ	O'Shaughnessy S	Elliott SB	Johnson SA	Graham J	Milner AJ	Duxbury LE	Henshaw G	Milligan SJF	Lockett PB	Hughes ZD	Lucketti CJ
R1/1	Aug 22	BOLTON WANDERERS	2-1	Holmes, Goodison	3464	1	2		5	6		8		10	11	3				7	9	4											
R1/2	28	Bolton Wanderers	1-5	Burns	4637	1	2		5	6		8	12	10	11	3				7	9	4											

A.M. Cup (Leyland DAF Cup)

	Date	Opponent	Score	Scorers	Att	Welch KJ	Goodison CW	Chapman VJ	Cole DA	Ward P	Small C	Holmes MA	Whellans R	Burns W	Stonehouse K	Hill JW (2)	Edmonds NA	Hasford JW	Dawson J	Ainscow A	Walling DA	Brown AJ	O'Shaughnessy S	Elliott SB	Johnson SA	Graham J	Milner AJ	Duxbury LE	Henshaw G	Milligan SJF	Lockett PB	Hughes ZD	Lucketti CJ
PR	Nov 28	Chester City	0-0		1222	1	2		5	6		7				3						4	10	9	8	11							
PR	Dec 12	TRANMERE ROVERS	0-1		1078	1	2			6		7		3	12				9			4	10	5	8	11							
rep	20	CHESTER CITY	1-2	Holmes	787	1	2		5			7		3	6	12			9	14	8		10			11						4	

Lancashire Cup

Date	Opponent	Score	Scorers	Att	Welch KJ	Goodison CW	Chapman VJ	Cole DA	Ward P	Small C	Holmes MA	Whellans R	Burns W	Stonehouse K	Hill JW (2)	Edmonds NA	Hasford JW	Dawson J	Ainscow A	Walling DA	Brown AJ	O'Shaughnessy S	Elliott SB	Johnson SA	Graham J	Milner AJ	Duxbury LE	Henshaw G	Milligan SJF	Lockett PB	Hughes ZD	Lucketti CJ
Aug 5	BLACKPOOL	0-0		1085	1	2	3	5	6	7	8	9	10	11	12	14																4
8	BURY	1-3	Burn	1382	1	2	3	5	6	7	8	9	10	11			14		12													4
12	Preston North End	2-1	Stonehouse, Ainslow		1	2	3	5	6		8		10	11				14	7	9	4	12										

Final League Tables 1989/90 - 1994/95

1989/90 season: Div. 4

		P	W	D	L	F	A	W	D	L	F	A	F	A	Pts
1	Exeter City	46	20	3	0	50	14	8	2	13	33	34	83	48	89
2	Grimsby Town	46	14	4	5	41	20	8	9	6	29	27	70	47	79
3	Southend United	46	15	3	5	35	14	7	6	10	26	34	61	48	75
4	Stockport County	46	13	6	4	45	27	8	5	10	23	35	68	62	74
5	Maidstone United	46	14	4	5	49	21	8	3	12	28	40	77	61	73
6	Cambridge United	46	14	3	6	45	30	7	7	9	31	36	76	66	73
7	Chesterfield	46	12	9	2	41	19	7	5	11	22	31	63	50	71
8	Carlisle United	46	15	4	4	38	20	6	4	13	23	40	61	60	71
9	Peterborough Utd.	46	10	8	5	35	23	7	9	7	24	23	59	46	68
10	Lincoln City	46	11	6	6	30	27	7	8	8	18	21	48	48	68
11	Scunthorpe United	46	9	9	5	42	25	8	6	9	27	29	69	54	66
12	ROCHDALE	46	11	4	8	28	23	9	2	12	24	32	52	55	66
13	York City	46	10	5	8	29	24	6	11	6	26	29	55	53	64
14	Gillingham	46	9	8	6	28	21	8	3	12	18	27	46	48	62
15	Torquay United	46	12	2	9	33	29	3	10	10	20	37	53	66	57
16	Burnley	46	6	10	7	19	18	8	4	11	26	37	45	55	56
17	Hereford United	46	7	4	12	31	32	8	6	9	25	30	56	62	55
18	Scarborough	46	10	5	8	35	28	5	5	13	25	45	60	73	55
19	Hartlepool United	46	12	4	7	45	33	3	6	14	21	55	66	88	55
20	Doncaster Rovers	46	7	7	9	29	29	7	2	14	24	31	53	60	51
21	Wrexham	46	8	8	7	28	28	5	4	14	23	39	51	67	51
22	Aldershot	46	8	7	8	28	26	4	7	12	21	43	49	69	50
23	Halifax Town	46	5	9	9	31	29	7	4	12	26	36	57	65	49
24	Colchester United	46	9	3	11	26	25	2	7	14	22	50	48	75	43

1990/91 season: Div. 4

		P	W	D	L	F	A	W	D	L	F	A	F	A	Pts
1	Darlington	46	13	8	2	36	14	9	9	5	32	24	68	38	83
2	Stockport County	46	16	6	1	54	19	7	7	9	30	28	84	47	82
3	Hartlepool United	46	15	5	3	35	15	9	5	9	32	33	67	48	82
4	Peterborough Utd.	46	13	9	1	38	15	8	8	7	29	30	67	45	80
5	Blackpool	46	17	3	3	55	17	6	7	10	23	30	78	47	79
6	Burnley	46	17	5	1	46	16	6	5	12	24	35	70	51	79
7	Torquay United	46	14	7	2	37	13	4	11	8	27	34	64	47	72
8	Scunthorpe United	46	17	4	2	51	20	3	7	13	20	42	71	62	71
9	Scarborough	46	13	5	5	36	21	6	7	10	23	35	59	56	69
10	Northampton Town	46	14	5	4	34	21	4	8	11	23	37	57	58	67
11	Doncaster Rovers	46	12	5	6	36	22	5	9	9	20	24	56	46	65
12	ROCHDALE	46	10	9	4	29	22	5	8	10	21	31	50	53	62
13	Cardiff City	46	10	6	7	26	23	5	9	9	17	31	43	54	60
14	Lincoln City	46	10	7	6	32	27	4	0	9	18	34	50	61	59
15	Gillingham	46	9	9	5	35	27	3	9	11	22	33	57	60	54
16	Walsall	46	7	12	4	25	17	5	5	13	23	34	48	51	53
17	Hereford United	46	9	10	4	32	19	4	4	15	21	39	53	58	53
18	Chesterfield	46	8	12	3	33	26	5	2	16	14	36	47	62	53
19	Maidstone United	46	9	5	9	42	34	4	7	12	24	37	66	71	51
20	Carlisle United	46	12	3	8	30	30	1	6	16	17	59	47	89	48
21	York City	46	8	6	9	21	23	3	7	13	24	34	45	57	46
22	Halifax Town	46	9	6	8	34	29	3	4	16	25	50	59	79	46
23	Aldershot	46	8	7	8	38	43	2	4	17	23	58	61	101	41
24	Wrexham	46	8	7	8	33	34	2	3	18	15	40	48	74	40

1991/92 season: Div. 4

		P	W	D	L	F	A	W	D	L	F	A	F	A	Pts
1	Burnley	42	14	4	3	42	16	11	4	6	37	27	79	43	83
2	Rotherham United	42	12	6	3	38	16	10	5	6	32	21	70	37	77
3	Mansfield Town	42	13	4	4	43	26	10	4	7	32	27	75	53	77
4	Blackpool	42	17	3	1	48	13	5	7	9	23	32	71	45	76
5	Scunthorpe United	42	14	5	2	39	18	7	4	10	25	41	64	59	72
6	Crewe Alexandra	42	12	6	3	33	20	8	4	9	33	31	66	51	70
7	Barnet	42	16	1	4	48	23	5	5	11	33	38	81	61	69
8	ROCHDALE	42	12	6	3	34	22	6	7	8	23	31	57	53	67
9	Cardiff City	42	13	3	5	42	26	4	12	5	24	27	66	53	66
10	Lincoln City	42	9	5	7	21	24	8	6	7	29	20	50	44	62
11	Gillingham	42	12	5	4	41	19	3	7	11	22	34	63	53	57
12	Scarborough	42	12	5	4	39	28	3	7	11	25	40	64	68	57
13	Chesterfield	42	6	7	8	26	28	8	4	9	23	33	49	61	53
14	Wrexham	42	11	4	6	31	26	3	5	13	21	47	52	73	51
15	Walsall	42	5	10	6	28	26	7	3	11	20	32	48	58	49
16	Northampton Town	42	5	9	7	25	23	6	4	11	21	34	46	57	46
17	Hereford United	42	9	4	8	31	24	3	4	14	13	33	44	57	44
18	Maidstone United	42	6	9	6	24	22	2	9	10	21	34	45	56	42
19	York City	42	6	9	6	26	23	2	7	12	16	35	42	58	40
20	Halifax Town	42	7	5	9	23	35	3	3	15	11	40	34	75	38
21	Doncaster Rovers	42	6	2	13	21	35	3	6	12	19	30	40	65	35
22	Carlisle United	42	5	9	7	24	27	2	4	15	17	40	41	67	34

1992/93 season: Div. 3 (Division re-numbering - formerly Div.4)

		P	W	D	L	F	A	W	D	L	F	A	F	A	Pts
1	Cardiff City	42	13	7	1	42	20	12	1	8	35	27	77	47	83
2	Wrexham	42	14	3	4	48	26	9	8	4	27	26	75	52	80
3	Barnet	42	16	4	1	45	19	7	6	8	21	29	66	48	79
4	York City	42	13	6	2	41	15	8	6	7	31	30	72	45	75
5	Walsall	42	11	6	4	42	31	11	1	9	34	30	76	61	73
6	Crewe Alexandra	42	13	3	5	47	23	8	4	9	28	33	75	56	70
7	Bury	42	10	7	4	36	19	8	2	11	27	36	63	55	63
8	Lincoln City	42	10	6	5	31	20	8	3	10	26	33	57	53	63
9	Shrewsbury Town	42	11	3	7	36	30	6	8	7	21	22	57	52	62
10	Colchester United	42	13	3	5	38	26	5	2	14	29	50	67	76	59
11	ROCHDALE	42	10	3	8	38	29	6	7	8	32	41	70	70	58
12	Chesterfield	42	11	3	7	32	28	4	8	9	27	35	59	63	56
13	Scarborough	42	7	7	7	32	30	8	2	11	34	41	66	71	54
14	Scunthorpe United	42	8	7	6	38	25	6	5	10	19	29	57	54	54
15	Darlington	42	5	6	10	23	31	7	8	6	25	22	48	53	50
16	Doncaster Rovers	42	6	5	10	22	28	5	9	7	20	29	42	57	47
17	Hereford United	42	7	9	5	31	27	3	6	12	16	33	47	60	45
18	Carlisle United	42	7	5	9	29	27	4	6	11	22	38	51	65	44
19	Torquay United	42	6	4	11	18	26	6	3	12	27	41	45	67	43
20	Northampton Town	42	6	5	10	19	28	5	3	13	29	46	48	74	41
21	Gillingham	42	9	4	8	32	28	0	9	12	16	36	48	64	40
22	Halifax Town	42	3	5	13	20	35	6	4	11	25	33	45	68	36

1993/94 season: Div. 3

		P	W	D	L	F	A	W	D	L	F	A	F	A	Pts
1	Shrewsbury Town	42	10	8	3	28	17	12	5	4	35	22	63	39	79
2	Chester City	42	13	5	3	35	18	8	6	7	34	28	69	46	74
3	Crewe Alexandra	42	12	4	5	45	30	9	6	6	35	31	80	61	73
4	Wycombe Wanderers	42	11	6	4	34	21	8	7	6	33	32	67	53	70
5	Preston North End	42	13	5	3	46	23	5	8	8	33	37	79	60	67
6	Torquay United	42	8	10	3	30	24	9	6	6	34	32	64	56	67
7	Carlisle United	42	10	4	7	35	23	8	6	7	22	19	57	42	64
8	Chesterfield	42	8	8	5	32	22	8	6	7	23	26	55	48	62
9	ROCHDALE	42	10	5	6	38	22	6	7	8	25	29	63	51	60
10	Walsall	42	7	5	9	28	26	10	4	7	20	27	48	53	60
11	Scunthorpe United	42	9	7	5	40	26	6	7	8	24	30	64	56	59
12	Mansfield Town	42	9	3	9	28	30	6	7	8	25	32	53	62	55
13	Bury	42	9	6	6	33	22	5	5	11	22	34	55	56	53
14	Scarborough	42	8	4	9	29	28	7	4	10	26	33	55	61	53
15	Doncaster Rovers	42	8	6	7	24	26	6	4	11	20	31	44	57	52
16	Gillingham	42	8	8	5	27	23	4	7	10	17	28	44	51	51
17	Colchester United	42	8	4	9	31	33	5	6	10	25	38	56	71	49
18	Lincoln City	42	7	4	10	26	29	5	7	9	26	34	52	63	47
19	Wigan Athletic	42	6	7	8	33	33	5	5	11	18	37	51	70	45
20	Hereford United	42	6	4	11	34	33	6	2	13	26	46	60	79	42
21	Darlington	42	7	5	9	24	28	3	6	12	18	36	42	64	41
22	Northampton Town	42	6	7	8	25	23	3	4	14	19	43	44	66	38

1994/95 season: Div. 3

		P	W	D	L	F	A	W	D	L	F	A	F	A	Pts
1	Carlisle United	42	14	5	2	34	14	13	5	3	33	17	67	31	91
2	Walsall	42	15	3	3	42	18	9	8	4	33	22	75	40	83
3	Chesterfield	42	11	7	3	26	10	12	5	4	36	27	62	37	81
4	Bury	42	13	7	1	39	13	10	4	7	34	23	73	36	80
5	Preston North End	42	13	3	5	37	17	6	7	8	21	24	58	41	67
6	Mansfield Town	42	10	5	6	45	27	8	6	7	39	32	84	59	65
7	Scunthorpe United	42	12	2	7	40	30	6	6	9	28	33	68	63	62
8	Fulham	42	11	5	5	39	22	5	9	7	21	32	60	54	62
9	Doncaster Rovers	42	9	5	7	28	20	8	5	8	30	23	58	43	61
10	Colchester United	42	8	5	8	29	30	8	5	8	27	34	56	64	58
11	Barnet	42	8	7	6	37	27	7	4	10	19	36	56	63	56
12	Lincoln City	42	10	7	4	34	22	5	4	12	20	33	54	55	56
13	Torquay United	42	10	8	3	35	25	4	5	12	19	32	54	57	55
14	Wigan Athletic	42	7	6	8	28	30	7	4	10	25	30	53	60	52
15	ROCHDALE	42	8	6	7	25	23	4	8	9	19	44	44	67	50
16	Hereford United	42	9	6	6	22	19	3	7	11	23	43	45	62	49
17	Northampton Town	42	8	5	8	25	29	2	9	10	20	38	45	67	44
18	Hartlepool United	42	9	5	7	33	32	2	5	14	10	37	43	69	43
19	Gillingham	42	8	7	6	31	25	2	4	15	15	39	46	64	41
20	Darlington	42	7	5	9	25	24	4	3	14	18	33	43	57	41
21	Scarborough	42	4	7	10	26	31	4	3	14	23	39	49	70	34
22	Exeter City	42	5	5	11	25	36	3	5	13	11	34	36	70	34

1989-90 Season
Back: Sutton (Physio), Hill, Edmonds, Walling, O'Shaughnessy, Brown, Welch, Cramer, Cole, Hughes,
Stonehouse, Taylor, Burns, Ellison (Youth Dev. Officer)
Middle: Small, Hasford, Holmes, Goodison, Dolan (Manager), Ainscow, Lee (Asst. Manager), Whellans, Dawson, Ward, Chapman
Front: Jones, Lucketti, Hedderman, Buckley, Smith, Lockett, Barrow, Milligan, Herring, Alford

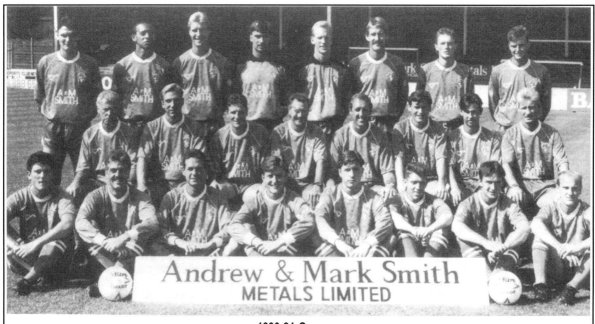

1990-91 Season
Back: Burns, Johnson, Cole, Welch, Gray, Brown, Milner, O'Shaughnessy
Middle: Ellison (Youth Dev. Officer), Goodison, Holmes, J.Lee (Asst. Manager), Dolan (Manager), Ward, Dawson, Sutton (Physio)
Front: Hill, Hilditch, Elliott, Costello, Hughes, Chapman, C.Lee, Graham

1990/91 12th in Division 4

#	Date		Opponent	Score	Scorers	Att	Welch KJ	Goodison CW	Graham J	Brown AJ	Cole DA	Burns W	Milner AJ	Lee C	Elliott SB	Holmes MA	Dawson J	Hill JW (2)	Butler PJ	Chapman VI	O'Shaughnessy S	Hilditch MW	Costello P	Ward P	Blundell CK	Norton DW	Doyle SC	Lockett PB	McInerney ID	Rose KP	Anders JS	Morgan SJ	Colleton A	Duggan AJ	Herring PJ	Gray G
1	Aug	25	ALDERSHOT	4-0	Hilditch, Holmes, Ward 2	1619	1		3	4			2	7	8	12	11					5	9	10	6											
2	Sep	1	Blackpool	0-0		3357	1	4	3		14		2	7	8	12	11					5	9	10	6											
3		8	STOCKPORT COUNTY	1-0	Elliott	2825	1	2	3			5	4	7	8	6	11	14		12			9	10												
4		15	DONCASTER ROVERS	0-3		2607	1	2	3		12			7	8	11	14					5	9	10	6	4										
5		18	Hartlepool United	2-2	McPhail (og), Costello	5725	1	2	3	4	5				8	9	11	12				6		7	10											
6		22	SCARBOROUGH	1-1	Holmes	1715	1	2	3		5	4			8	9	11	12				6		7	10											
7		29	WALSALL	3-2	Elliott, Holmes (p), Costello	1930	1		3				2	7	8	9	11	14		12		5		10	6	4										
8	Oct	2	Cardiff City	1-0	Milner	3391	1		3		2			7	8	9	11	12				5		10	6	4										
9		6	Gillingham	2-2	Milner, Holmes (p)	3340	1		3		2			7	8	9	11	14				5		10	6	4										
10		13	CHESTERFIELD	3-0	Costello 2, Ward	2492	1		3		2			7	8	9	11	14	12			5		10	6	4										
11		20	TORQUAY UNITED	0-0		3385	1		3		5			7	8	9	11						12	10	6	4	2									
12		24	Lincoln City	2-1	Holmes (p), Dawson	1974	1				5				8	9	11	12			3	7		10	6	4	2									
13		27	Burnley	0-1		7969	1				5				8	9	11	12			3	7		10	6	4	2									
14	Nov	3	DARLINGTON	1-1	O'Shaughnessy	2881	1	12	3		5			7	8	9	11	14			4			10	6	2										
15		10	Scunthorpe United	1-2	Elliott	3070	1		3	7	5				8	9	11	12			4			10	6	2										
16		24	CARLISLE UNITED	0-1		1733	1		3		5			7	8	9		12			4			10	6		2	11								
17	Dec	1	Northampton Town	2-3	Milner, Lee	3809	1		3			5		7	8		14				12	9		10	6	4	2	11								
18		15	WREXHAM	2-0	Costello, Graham	1510	1		3		6	5		7	8						4			10	9		2	11								
19		21	Halifax Town	0-2		1831	1		3		6	12		5	7	8				14	4			10	9		2	11								
20		29	MAIDSTONE UNITED	3-2	Burns (p), Milner, Lee	1778	1	4			5	2		7	8	9				10	3				6			11								
21	Jan	2	Peterborough United	1-1	Cole	3687	1	4		12	5	2		7	8	9				10	3	14		6				11								
22		12	BLACKPOOL	2-1	Costello, Dawson	2661	1	2	3	4	5			7	8	9				10		12		6				11								
23		19	Aldershot	2-2	Dawson 2	1856	1	2	3	4	5				8	9				10	12	7		6				11								
24		25	Doncaster Rovers	0-1		3433	1	2			4	5			8	12				10	3	6		7	9			11								
25		30	Hereford United	0-2		1925	1	2			4	5			12	9					3	6		10	11					8	7					
26	Feb	6	Scarborough	0-0		955	1	2			4	5				9				7	3	6		12	10					8		11				
27		16	Carlisle United	1-1	McInearny	2505		2			4	5		14				9	12		3	6		10	11					8	7	1				
28		23	SCUNTHORPE UNITED	2-1	Costello 2	1832		2			5	4						9			3	6		10	11					8	7	1		12		
29	Mar	2	NORTHAMPTON T	1-1	Costello	1890		2			5	4		14				9	12		3	6		10	11					8	7	1				
30		9	Wrexham	1-2	Dawson	1323	1	2	12		5	4	7					9			3	6		10	11					8			14			
31		12	CARDIFF CITY	0-0		1569	1	2			14	5	4	7				9			3	6		10	11					8	12					
32		16	Walsall	1-0	Costello	2890	1	2			6		4	12	9			14			3	5	10	7	11					8						
33		19	Chesterfield	1-1	O'Shaughnessy	3048	1	2			6	12	4	14	9			10			3	5		7	11					8						
34		23	GILLINGHAM	1-3	Ward	1654	1	2	12		6	9	4	10							3	5	14	7	11					8						
35		26	Stockport County	0-3		3697	1	2	7		4	5			12			14			3	6	10	9	11					8						
36		30	York City	2-0	Morgan 2	2120	1	2	3		6	12		10				14			5		9		11					8		7		4		
37	Apr	1	HALIFAX TOWN	1-1	Hilditch	2040	1	2	3	6	4	12	10								5	9		11					8		7					
38		6	Maidstone United	1-0	Milner	1340	1	2	3	4	6	5	12				14			7		10	11					8			9					
39		13	PETERBOROUGH UTD.	0-3		2382	1	2	3	4	6	5	7				11					8				10		12	9					14		
40		16	YORK CITY	2-1	Cole, Hill	1331	1	2	3	4	6	5	7				12				10		11	14	8				9							
41		20	Torquay United	1-3	Morgan	3049	1	2	3	4	6	5	7				12				10		11	14	8				9							
42		23	HARTLEPOOL UNITED	0-0		1686	1	2		4		5	7	9				11	3			6	12	8					10							
43		27	LINCOLN CITY	0-0		1481	1	2		4	12	5	7	9				11	3	14		6		8					10							
44		30	HEREFORD UNITED	2-1	Chapman, Ward	1166	1	2		4	12	5	7	10					3			6		11					9							
45	May	4	BURNLEY	0-0		7344	1	2		4	12	5	7	10				14	3			6		11					9							
46		11	Darlington	0-2		9160	1	2		4	12	5	7	10		14			3			6		11					9							
			Apps				43	34	28	26	41	27	35	26	30	16	28	11	2	20	38	14	34	44	13	9	31	2	4	3	2	11	1	1	1	
			Goals					1			2	1	5	2	3	5	5	1			1	2	2	10	5						1			3			

One own goal

F.A. Cup

	Date		Opponent	Score	Scorers	Att	Welch KJ	Goodison CW	Graham J	Brown AJ	Cole DA	Burns W	Milner AJ	Lee C	Elliott SB	Holmes MA	Dawson J	Hill JW	Butler PJ	Chapman VI	O'Shaughnessy S	Hilditch MW	Costello P	Ward P	Blundell CK
R1	Nov	17	SCUNTHORPE UNITED	1-1	Costello	3259	1		3		5	2		8	9	11	7				4		10	6	
rep		20	Scunthorpe United	1-2	Costello	3761	1		3		5	2	12	8	9	11	7				4	14	10	6	

Replay a.e.t.

F.L. Cup (Rumbelows League Cup)

	Date		Opponent	Score	Scorers	Att	Welch KJ	Goodison CW	Graham J	Brown AJ	Cole DA	Burns W	Milner AJ	Lee C	Elliott SB	Holmes MA	Dawson J	Hill JW	Butler PJ	Chapman VI	O'Shaughnessy S	Hilditch MW	Costello P	Ward P	Blundell CK
R1/1	Aug	28	SCARBOROUGH	4-0	Lee, O'Shaugh'ssy, Milner, Cos	1448	1	12	3	4		2	7	8		11					5	9	10	6	
R1/2	Sep	5	Scarborough	3-3	Elliott, Goodison (p), Milner	968	1	2	3		5	4	7	8	6	11					9	10			
R2/1		25	SOUTHAMPTON	0-5		3885	1		3		5	2	7	8	9	12	14				6	11	10	4	
R2/2	Oct	10	Southampton	0-3		6754	1		3		2			8	9	11	7	12			5	10	6	4	

A.M. Cup (Leyland DAF Cup)

	Date		Opponent	Score	Scorers	Att	Welch KJ	Goodison CW	Graham J	Brown AJ	Cole DA	Burns W	Milner AJ	Lee C	Elliott SB	Holmes MA	Dawson J	Hill JW	Butler PJ	Chapman VI	O'Shaughnessy S	Hilditch MW	Costello P	Ward P	Blundell CK	Norton DW	Doyle SC	Lockett PB	McInerney ID	Gray G
PR	Nov	27	Preston North End	1-3	Milner	1951	1		3			5	7	8	9		14					12	10	6	4	2		11		
PR	Dec	18	CARLISLE UNITED	1-0	Burns (p)	718		12	3		6	5	7	8							4		10	9	11	2				1
R1	Jan	22	Wigan Athletic	0-2		1200	1	2			4	5			8	14				10	3	6		7	9	12		11		

Lancashire Cup

	Date		Opponent	Score	Scorers	Att	Welch KJ	Goodison CW	Graham J	Brown AJ	Cole DA	Burns W	Milner AJ	Lee C	Elliott SB	Holmes MA	Dawson J	Hill JW	O'Shaughnessy S	Hilditch MW	Costello P	Ward P	Blundell CK
	Aug	11	Preston North End	1-1	Lee		1	2	3	4	5	6	7	8	9	10	11	12					
		14	Bury	1-1	Costello		1	2	3	4	12	6	7	8		11				5	9	10	
		18	BLACKBURN ROVERS	0-2		1483	1		3	4		2	7	8	12	11				5	9	10	6

1991/92 8th in Division 4

No	Date	Opponent	Score	Scorers	Att	Ryan JB	Brown AJ	Reeves A	Jones Alex	Payne MRC	Doyle SC	Flounders AJ	Milner AJ	Halpin JW	Whitehall SC	Morgan SJ	Graham J	Butler PI	Hilditch MW	Dearden KC	Gray G	Brown M	Williams DP	Bowden IL	Palin LG	Kinsey S	Rose KP	Kilner AW	Cowdrill BJ	Parker C	Stiles JC	Leonard MA	Hughes PA
1	Aug 17	YORK CITY	1-1	Tuthill (og)	2247	3	4	5	6		8	9	10	11	2	12	7	14			1												
2	31	LINCOLN CITY	1-0	Flounders (p)	2086	3	4	5	6	12	8	9	10	11	2	14	7			1													
3	Sep 3	Walsall	3-1	Flounders 2 (1p), Milner	3111	3	4	5	6	11	8	9	10		12	2	7						1										
4	7	Cardiff City	2-1	Ryan, Reeves	4029	3	4	5	6	11	8	9	12		10	2	7						1										
5	14	NORTHAMPTON T	1-0	Milner	2631	3	4	5	6	11		9	8		10	2	12	7					1										
6	17	ROTHERHAM UNITED	1-1	Whitehall	4033	3	4	5	6	11		9	8	10	2		7		12				1										
7	21	Burnley	1-0	Milner	8633	3	4	5	6	11		9	8	12	2		7						1	10									
8	28	DONCASTER ROVERS	1-1	Bowden	2653	3	4	5	6	12	8	9	11		2		7		14				1	10									
9	Oct 12	MANSFIELD TOWN	0-2		3871		4	5	6	10	8	9	12	3	11		7				1	2	14										
10	19	Maidstone United	1-1	M Brown	1016		4	5	6		8	9	12	11	10		3	14			1	2	7										
11	26	HALIFAX TOWN	1-0	Flounders	2323	3	4	5			8	9		6	14		7				1	2	12		10	11							
12	Nov 2	CHESTERFIELD	3-3	Flounders, Halpin, Kinsey	1852	3	4	5			8	9		6	14		7				1	2	12		10	11							
13	5	Scunthorpe United	2-6	Bowden 2	2331	3	4	5	12		8	9		6			7				1	2	14		10	11							
14	9	Hereford United	1-1	Judge (og)	2942	7	4	5	6			9	12	11	10		3				1	2	8										
15	23	BARNET	1-0	Bowden	3033		4	5	6	7	8	9	14	11			3					2		10			1	12					
16	30	Scarborough	2-3	Flounders, Milner	1643		4	5	6		8	9	7	11			3	5				2		10			1						
17	Dec 14	BLACKPOOL	4-2	Flounders, Milner, Whitehall 2	2892	7	4				6	9	8	11	12		3	5				2		10			1	14					
18	26	York City	1-0	Flounders	2788	7	4				6	8	9	11	12		3	5				2		10			1						
19	28	Lincoln City	3-0	Whitehall, Milner, Flounders	2916	7	4				6	5	9	8	11		3	12				2					1						
20	Jan 1	WALSALL	1-1	Flounders (p)	3001	7					6		9	8	11	10	3	5	14			2					1	12					
21	11	Carlisle United	0-0		2494		4				6	7	9	8	11	12	3	5				2		10			1						
22	18	CREWE ALEXANDRA	1-0	Flounders	2965		4				6	7	9	8	11	12	3	5				2		10			1						
23	Feb 8	Halifax Town	1-1	Flounders	2213		4				6	7	9	8	12		3	5				2		10			1	11					
24	11	SCARBOROUGH	2-2	Flounders (p), Reeves	2069		4	14			6	7	9	8	12		3	5				2		10			1	11					
25	15	Blackpool	0-3		4632		4				6	8	9		11	12								10			1	7	3				
26	22	CARLISLE UNITED	3-1	Milner, Bowden, Whitehall	1691	12	4	2			6	8	9	7	14	11		5						10			1		3				
27	29	Wrexham	1-2	Whitehall	3458	12	4	2			6	8	9	7	14	11		5						10			1		3				
28	Mar 3	Crewe Alexandra	1-1	Flounders	3870	11	4	5			6	8	9	7				2						10			1		3				
29	7	GILLINGHAM	2-1	Flounders, Milner	1941	11	4	5			6	8	9	7			12	14						10			1		3				
30	10	SCUNTHORPE UNITED	2-0	Milner, Lister (og)	2036	11	4	5			6	8	9	7			12	14						10			1		3				
31	14	Chesterfield	1-0	Whitehall	3231	11	4	5				8	9		6	7	12							10			1		3				
32	17	Gillingham	0-0		2322	11	4	5				8	9		6	7	14	12	2								1		3	10			
33	21	HEREFORD UNITED	3-1	Payne, Whitehall, Flounders (p)	2122		4	5				8	9	6	12	7	10	11	2								1		3	14			
34	28	Barnet	0-3		3099			5		6		9			12	11		2						10			1		3	4	7	8	
35	31	Northampton Town	2-2	Cowdrill, Bowden	2010	11	4	2			6		9					5						10			1		3			7	8
36	Apr 4	CARDIFF CITY	2-0	Reeves, Milner	2651	11	4	2			6		9	7				5						10			1		3			12	8
37	7	MAIDSTONE UNITED	1-2	Flounders	2248	11	4	5			6		9	7			12	2						10			1		3				8
38	11	Rotherham United	0-2		5112	11					5		9	8			12	2						10			1		3			14	7
39	20	Doncaster Rovers	0-2		2255	7	4	5			6		9	8	11	14		12						10			1		3				2
40	22	WREXHAM	2-1	Parker, Leonard	1944	7	4	5			6		9	8				14	3	2				12			1			11			10
41	May 2	Mansfield Town	1-2	Patne	5671	7	4	5			6		9	8				14	3	2				12			1			11			10
42	5	BURNLEY	1-3	Ryan	8175	7	4	5			6		9	8				12	3								1			11			10
		Apps				32	40	34	13	34	27	42	33	31	34	12	31	25	2	2	6	18	6	31	3	6	28	3	15	6	4	9
		Goals				2		3		2		17	10	1	8							1		6		1			1	1	1		1

Three own goals

Expunged

	Date	Opponent	Score	Scorers	Att	Ryan JB	Brown AJ	Reeves A	Jones Alex	Payne MRC	Doyle SC	Flounders AJ	Milner AJ	Halpin JW	Whitehall SC	Morgan SJ	Graham J	Butler PI				Brown M	Williams DP
	Oct 4	Aldershot	1-1	Halpin	2443	3	4	5	6	14	8	9	12	11	10		7					2	1

F.A. Cup

	Date	Opponent	Score	Scorers	Att	Ryan JB	Brown AJ	Reeves A	Jones Alex	Payne MRC	Doyle SC	Flounders AJ	Milner AJ	Halpin JW	Whitehall SC	Morgan SJ	Graham J	Butler PI			Gray G	Brown M	Williams DP	Bowden IL	Palin LG
R1	Nov 16	Gretna	0-0		2037	7	4	5	6			9	14	11	10		3				1	2	8	12	
rep	27	GRETNA	3-1	Bowden, Milner, Flounders	4300		4		5	6	8	9	7	11	14		12				1	2	10	3	
R2	Dec 7	HUDDERSFIELD T	1-2	Halpin	5776	7	4			6	5	9	8	11	14		3	12				2	10	1	

F.L. Cup (Rumbelows League Cup)

	Date	Opponent	Score	Scorers	Att	Ryan JB	Brown AJ	Reeves A	Jones Alex	Payne MRC	Doyle SC	Flounders AJ	Milner AJ	Halpin JW	Whitehall SC	Morgan SJ	Graham J	Butler PI	Hilditch MW		Gray G	Brown M	Williams DP
R1/1	Aug 20	CARLISLE UNITED	5-1	Milner 2, Ryan, Whitehall 2	1650	3	4	5	6		8	9	10	11	2		7				1		
R1/2	27	Carlisle United	1-1	Ryan	1572	3	4	5	6		8	9	12	11	2		7				1	10	
R2/1	Sep 25	Coventry City	0-4		5982	3	4	5	6	2	8	9	10	11	12		7	14			1		
R2/2	Oct 8	COVENTRY CITY	1-0	Milner	2288	3	4	5	6	14	8	9	10		12		7	11			1	2	

A.M. Cup (Autoglass Trophy)

	Date	Opponent	Score	Scorers	Att	Ryan JB	Brown AJ	Reeves A	Jones Alex	Payne MRC	Doyle SC	Flounders AJ	Milner AJ	Halpin JW	Whitehall SC	Morgan SJ	Graham J	Butler PI	Hilditch MW		Gray G	Brown M	Williams DP	Bowden IL
PR	Oct 22	PRESTON NORTH END	1-1	Whitehall	1255		4	5	6		8	9	11	3	10				12		1	2	7	
PR	Dec 10	Bolton Wanderers	1-4	Milner	1507	7	4			6		9	8	11			3	5				2	10	1

Lancashire Cup

	Date	Opponent	Score	Scorers	Att	Ryan JB	Brown AJ	Reeves A	Jones Alex	Payne MRC	Doyle SC	Flounders AJ	Milner AJ	Halpin JW	Whitehall SC	Morgan SJ	Graham J																Hughes PA
	Aug 5	Bolton Wanderers	1-0	Payne		3	4	5	6	7	8	9	10	11	12																		1
	7	WIGAN ATHLETIC	2-3	Whitehall, Reeves	953	3	4	5	6	7	8	9	10	11	12	14																	1
	10	BLACKPOOL	2-1	Ryan, Flounders (p)	950	3	4	5	6		8	9	10	11	2	12	7																1

1991-92 Season
Back: Docherty (Asst. Man.), Graham, Herring, Hughes, Milner, Halpin, Robson (Yth Dev. Off.)
Middle: Ryan, Whitehall, Butler, Gray, Reeves, Brown, Chapman
Front: Lockett, Morgan, Sutton (Manager), Doyle (Captain), Flounders

1992-93 Season
Back: Stock (Physio), Milner, Bowden, Reeves, Rose, Butler, Brown, Ryan, Robson (Yth Team Man.)
Middle: Thackeray, Payne, Flounders, Docherty (Asst. Man.), Sutton (Man.), Whitehall, Graham, Reid
Front: Anders, Howard, Parker

1992/93 11th in Division 3 *

Divisions re-numbered - formerly Division 4

#		Date	Opponent	Score	Scorers	Att	Rose KP	Thackeray AJ	Graham J	Reid S	Brown AJ	Bowden JL	Ryan JB	Payne MRC	Flounders AJ	Whitehall SC	Parker C	Howard AP	Anders JS	Milner AJ	Reeves A	Ashurst J	Jones Alex	Butler PJ	Beever AM	Mulrain S	Doyle SC	Clarke TJ	Snowden T	Page DR	Luke NE	Leonard MA
1	Aug	15	HALIFAX TOWN	2-3	Flounders, Milner	2497	1	2	3	4	5	6	7	8	9	10				11	12											
2		22	Wrexham	1-3	Whitehall	2661	1	2	3	8	4	11	7	6	9	14				12	5	10										
3		29	SCARBOROUGH	3-0	Whitehall 2, Thackeray	1585	1	2	3	8	4	6	7		9	14	12			11	5											
4	Sep	5	Shrewsbury Town	2-1	Milner, Whitehall	2547	1	2	3	4			9	7	8	10		12		11	5		6									
5		15	GILLINGHAM	1-1	Payne (p)	1879	1	2	3	4			9	7	8	10				11	5		6									
6		19	DARLINGTON	3-1	Whitehall, Reeves, Bowden	1854	1	2	3	4			9	7	8	12	10			11	5		6									
7		26	Hereford United	1-1	Jones	1834	1	2	3	4			7		8	9	10			14	12	11	5	6								
8	Oct	3	Cardiff City	1-1	Payne (p)	6486	1	2	3	4			9	7	8	10				14	12	11	5	6								
9		10	CARLISLE UNITED	2-2	Whitehall 2	2543	1	2	3	4	12		7	8	9	10				14	11	5		6								
10		17	York City	0-3		4161	1	2	3	4	6	12	7	8	9	10				14	11	5										
11		24	WALSALL	4-3	Whitehall, Milner, Payne, Flounders	1834	1	2	3	4			7		8	9	10			11	5		6									
12		31	Chesterfield	3-2	Bowden 2, Anders	3094	1	2	3	4			7		8	9	10		12	11	5		6									
13	Nov	3	Torquay United	2-0	Whitehall, Reid	2064	1	2	3	4			7	6	8	9	10	12		14	11	5										
14		7	CREWE ALEXANDRA	0-1		3058	1	2	3	4			7	6	8	9	10			12	11	5										
15		21	Colchester United	4-4	Payne (p), Milner, Flounders 2 (1p)	3172	1	2	3	4			7	6	8	9	10	12		14	11	5										
16		28	DONCASTER ROVERS	1-1	Flounders (p)	2094	1	2	3	4			7	6	8	9	10	11		14	5					12						
17	Dec	12	Barnet	0-2		2778	1	2		4			10	7	8	9	11		3		5		6			12						
18		19	LINCOLN CITY	5-1	Flounders 3, Whitehall, Howard	1793	1	2		4			7	3	8	9	11	12	14	10	5		6									
19		26	SCUNTHORPE UNITED	2-0	Whitehall, Flounders	3043	1	2		4			7	3	8	9	11		12	10	5		6									
20	Jan	2	Doncaster Rovers	1-1	Payne	2559	1	2	12	4			7	3	8	9	11			10	5		6									
21		8	Gillingham	2-4	Thackeray, Payne (p)	3050	1	2	11	4			7	3	8	9	10	14	12		5		6									
22		16	HEREFORD UNITED	1-3	Reid	1751	1	2		4			11	7	8	9	10	3	12		5		6									
23		23	Darlington	4-0	Flounders 2, Whitehall 2	1710	1	2	11	4				7	8	9	10	3			5		6			12						
24		30	WREXHAM	1-2	Mulrain	4500	1	2	11	4				7	8	9	10	3			5		6	14		12						
25	Feb	6	Halifax Town	3-2	Butler, Reid (p), Mulrain	1906	1		3	4			9	7		10					5		6	2		11	8					
26		13	SHREWSBURY TOWN	2-0	Reeves 2	2446		2	3	4			12	7	9	10					5		6			8	11	1	14			
27		20	Scarborough	1-1	Page	1765		2	3	4			12	7		10					5		6			8	11	1	14	9		
28		27	Carlisle United	0-3		3021	1	2	3	4			8	7		10					5		6			11			12	9		
29	Mar	6	CARDIFF CITY	1-2	Bowden	2831	1	2	3	4			7		8	10			14		5		6			11			12	9		
30		9	NORTHAMPTON T	0-3		1446	1	2	3	4			9			10		7			5		6			8			11	12		
31		12	Crewe Alexandra	1-1	Thackeray	3515	1	2	3	4			7			10			12		5		6	9		8			11			
32		16	Bury	2-2	Thackeray 2	3315	1	2	3	4			7			10			8		5		6	9					11			
33		20	TORQUAY UNITED	1-0	Saunders (og)	1594	1	2	3	4			7		9	10					5		6	8					11			
34		27	COLCHESTER UNITED	5-2	Jones,Howard,Thackeray,Whitehall,Bowden.	1783	1	2	3				12		9	10	7	14			5		6	4					11		8	
35	Apr	2	Northampton Town	0-1		3037	1	2	3	4				12	9	10	7	14			5		6	8					11			
36		6	BARNET	0-1		1661	1	2	3	4					9	10	12				5		8						11	7	6	
37		10	Scunthorpe United	1-5	Reid	2926	1	2	3	4					9	10	14				5		6	8					11	7	12	
38		13	BURY	1-2	Flounders	2905	1	2	3	4			8		12	9	10				5		6						11	7		
39		17	Lincoln City	2-1	Bowden 2	2922	1	2	3				8		4	9	10	14			5		6	12					11	7		
40		24	YORK CITY	1-0	Bowden	3920	1	2	3	4			8	12	9	10					5		14	6					11	7		
41	May	1	Walsall	1-3	Flounders	4118	1	2	3	4			8		9	10	12				5		6						11	7		
42		8	CHESTERFIELD	2-1	Flounders, Butler	1544	1	2	3	4			8		9	10	7				5	6							11	12		
			Apps				40	41	38	40	5	35	26	28	32	42	10	15	15	18	41	1	29	16	1	6	18	2	13	4	3	
			Goals					6		4		8		6	14	14		2	1	4	3		2	2		2				1		

One own goal

Abandoned

		Date	Opponent	Score		Att	Rose	Thac	Grah	Reid		Bowd	Ryan	Payn	Floun	Whit	Park	Howa		Miln	Reev		Jone									
	Jan	19	SCUNTHORPE UNITED	0-0		1046	1	2	12	4			11	7	8	9	10	3	14		5		6									

F.A. Cup

		Date	Opponent	Score	Scorers	Att	Rose	Thac	Grah	Reid		Bowd	Ryan	Payn	Floun	Whit	Park	Howa	Ande	Miln	Reev		Jone									
R1	Nov	14	Blackpool	1-1	Whitehall	4069	1	2	3	4			7	6	8	9	10	12		11	5											
rep		25	BLACKPOOL	1-0	Reid	3408	1	2	3	4			7	6	8	9	10	14	12	11	5											
R2	Dec	5	Bolton Wanderers	0-4		6876	1	2	3	4			10	7	8	9	11		12		5		6									

R1 replay a.e.t.

F.L. Cup (Coca Cola Cup)

		Date	Opponent	Score	Scorers	Att	Rose	Thac	Grah	Reid	Brwn	Bowd	Ryan	Payn	Floun	Whit	Park	Howa		Miln	Reev		Jone									
R1/1	Aug	18	Crewe Alexandra	1-4	Reeves	2558	1	2	3	8	4	11	7	6	9					10	5											
R1/2		25	CREWE ALEXANDRA	1-2	Ryan	1302	1	2	3	4	12		7	8	9	14		10		11	5	6										

A.M. Cup (Autoglass Trophy)

		Date	Opponent	Score	Scorers	Att	Rose	Thac	Grah	Reid		Bowd	Ryan	Payn	Floun	Whit	Park	Howa	Ande	Miln	Reev		Jone	Butl	Beev							
R1	Dec	1	BOLTON WANDERERS	0-0		1348	1	2	3	4			10	7	12	9	11	8		14	5		6									
R1	Jan	12	Bury	2-1	Thackeray 2	1215	1	12		4			9	7	8		10	2	11		5		6	3								
R2	Feb	2	SCUNTHORPE UTD.	1-2	Graham	1312	1		3				7		9	10	2	11	12		5		6	14	8	4						

Lancashire Cup

		Date	Opponent	Score		Att																										Leon
	Jul	29	Bury+	0-1			1	2	3	4	5	6	7	8	9	11	12	14	15													10
	Aug	1	Bolton Wanderers	0-0			1	2	3	4	5	6	7	8	9	12				11												10

+ at Radcliffe Borough

288

1993/94 — 9th in Division 3

#	Date	Opponent	Score	Scorers	Att	Hodge MJ	Matthews NP	Graham J	Reid S	Reeves A	Butler PJ	Ryan JB	Doyle SC	Lancaster D	Whitehall SC	Stuart MRN	Thackeray AJ	Jones, Alex	Bowden IL	Flounders AJ	Snowden T	Taylor IL	Milner AJ	Mulrain S	Oliver D	Howard AP	Williams PA	Finley AJ	Shelton G	Peake IW	Formby K
1	Aug 14	Darlington	1-1	Thackeray	2327	1		3	4	5	6		8		11	10	7	2	12	9											
2	21	GILLINGHAM	3-0	Butler, Whitehall, Stuart	2092	1		3	4	5	6		8		11	10	7	2		9			12								
3	28	Carlisle United	1-0	Reeves	5438	1		3	4	5	6		8		11	10	7	2	14	9			12								
4	31	WIGAN ATHLETIC	1-2	Whitehall	2628	1		3	4	5	6		8		11	10	7	2	14	9			12								
5	Sep 4	CHESTER CITY	2-0	Whitehall, Doyle	3063	1		3	4	5	6	12	8		11	10	7	2		9											
6	11	Colchester United	5-2	Lancaster 2, Butler, Reeves, Whitehall	2776	1		3	4	5	6	12			11	10	7	2	8	9			14								
7	18	HEREFORD UNITED	2-0	Lancaster 2	2645	1		3	4	5	6	11		8	9	10	7	2					14	12							
8	25	CHESTERFIELD	5-1	Reid, Whitehall 2, Lancaster, Stuart	2481	1		3	4	5	6	11		8	9	10	7	2		14			12								
9	Oct 2	Doncaster Rovers	1-2	Lancaster	3101	1		3	4	5	6	11		8	9	10	7	2		12			14								
10	9	Torquay United	1-1	Stuart	3874	1		3	4	5	6	11			9	10	7	2	14				12			8					
11	16	WALSALL	0-0		2923	1		3	4	5	6	11		8	9	10	7	2					12								
12	23	Preston North End	1-2	Stuart	8491	1	14		4	5	6	11		8	9	10	7	2					12	3							
13	30	LINCOLN CITY	0-1		2551	1		8	3	4	5	6		12	9	10	7	2					11	14							
14	Nov 2	MANSFIELD TOWN	1-1	Howard	2042	1	2		4	5	6			8	9	10	7	12					11	3		14					
15	6	Crewe Alexandra	1-2	Williams	4049	1	2			5	6			8	9	10	7		4					14		3	12	11			
16	20	BURY	2-1	Bowden, Williams	3758	1		12		5	6	11		8	9		7	2	4							3	10				
17	27	Scunthorpe United	1-2	Stuart	3106	1		9		5	6	11		8	14		7	12	2	4						3	10				
18	Dec 11	Gillingham	2-1	Lancaster 2	2493	1	2		4	5	6	7		9	10	11			8			14	12		3						
19	18	DARLINGTON	0-0		2205	1			4	5		7		9	10	11	2		6			8	12		3						
20	Jan 1	NORTHAMPTON T	6-2	Lancaster 3, Whitehall, Stuart, Taylor	2453	1			4	5				8	9	10	11	2				12	7		3						
21	4	Wigan Athletic	0-0		1912	1			4	5	6			8	9	10	11	2				12	7		3						
22	15	Walsall	0-1		4437	1			4	5	6			8	9	10	11	2	14			12	7		3						
23	22	TORQUAY UNITED	4-1	Thackeray, Lancaster 2, Whitehall	2319	1			4	5	6			8	9	14	11	2		12		10	7		3						
24	29	Lincoln City	1-1	Milner	2703	1		3	4	5	6			9	10	11	2					8	7				12				
25	Feb 5	PRESTON NORTH END	2-1	Stuart, Whitehall	4317	1		3	4	5	6			9	10	11	2		6			8	7				12				
26	12	Shrewsbury Town	1-1	Whitehall	4882	1		3	4	5				9	14	11	2		6	12			7				10		8		
27	19	CARLISLE UNITED	0-1		2926	1		3	4	5	6			14	10	11	2					12					9		8		
28	26	Chester City	1-3	Milner	3475	1		3	4	5	6				10	11	2					12	7			14	9		8		
29	Mar 1	SCARBOROUGH	2-1	Reid, Stuart	1827	1	2	3	4	5	6		8	12		10	7						11	14		9					
30	5	COLCHESTER UNITED	1-1	Stuart	2202	1		3	4	5	6		8	9	10	7	2		12				11			14					
31	12	Hereford United	1-5	Whitehall	1964	1		3	4	5	6		8	9	10	7		2	11							12					
32	19	Chesterfield	1-1	Whitehall	3282	1		3	4	5	6		8	9	11	7	2		10							12					
33	26	DONCASTER ROVERS	0-1		2165	1			4	5	6		8		10	7	2		14						3	9				11	12
34	Apr 2	Scarborough	1-2	Thackeray	1448	1			4	5	6		8	9		12	2					14	7		3	10				11	
35	4	WYCOMBE WANDERERS	2-2	Whitehall, Bowden	2575	1		3	4	5	6		8	9	10	7	2		12				14							11	
36	9	Northampton Town	2-1	Stuart, Bowden	3330	1		3	4	5	6		8	9	10	7	2		12				14							11	
37	12	SHREWSBURY TOWN	2-1	Reid	2402	1		3	4	5	6		8	9	10	7	2		12				14							11	
38	16	Mansfield Town	1-0	Thackeray	2362	1		3	4	5	6		8	9	10	7	2		12											11	14
39	19	Wycombe Wanderers	1-1	Stuart	5266	1		3	4		6		8	9	10	7	2		5											11	12
40	23	CREWE ALEXANDRA	2-1	Stuart, Whitehall	3096	1		3	4	5	6		8	9	10	7	2		12				14							11	
41	30	Bury	1-0	Stuart	3272	1			4	5	6		8	9	10	7		2												11	3
42	May 7	SCUNTHORPE UNITED	2-3	Reeves, Lancaster	3118	1			4	5	6		8	9		10	7	2	12								14			11	3
		Apps				42	6	29	39	41	38	12	34	40	39	42	37	4	29	11	1	10	25	2	19	5	11	1	3	10	5
		Goals							3	3	2		1	14	14	13	4		3				1	2		1	2				

F.A. Cup

R	Date	Opponent	Score	Scorers	Att	Hodge MJ	Graham J	Reid S	Reeves A	Butler PJ	Ryan JB	Doyle SC	Whitehall SC	Stuart MRN	Thackeray AJ	Jones, Alex	Bowden IL	Flounders AJ	Oliver D	Milner AJ
R1	Nov 13	Chesterfield	1-0	Stuart (p)	3457	1			5	6	11	8	9	10	7	2	4		3	
R2	Dec 4	Burnley	1-4	Whitehall (p)	11388	1	3	8	5	6	11		9	10	7	2	12	4		14

F.L. Cup (Coca Cola Cup)

R	Date	Opponent	Score	Scorers	Att	Hodge MJ	Graham J	Reid S	Reeves A	Butler PJ	Ryan JB	Doyle SC	Lancaster D	Whitehall SC	Stuart MRN	Thackeray AJ	Jones, Alex	Bowden IL	Flounders AJ	Milner AJ	Oliver D
R1/1	Aug 17	YORK CITY	2-0	Stuart, Flounders (p)	1952	1	3	4	5	6		8		11	10	7	2	14	9	12	
R1/2	24	York City	0-0		2835	1	3	4	5	6		8		11	10	7	2		9	12	
R2/1	Sep 21	LEICESTER CITY	1-6	Carey (og)	4499	1	3	4	5	6	11	8		9	10	7	2			12	
R2/2	Oct 6	Leicester City	1-2	Lancaster	7612	1	12	4	5	6	11		8	9		7	2	3	14	10	

A.M. Cup (Autoglass Trophy)

R	Date	Opponent	Score	Scorers	Att	Hodge MJ	Graham J	Reid S	Reeves A	Butler PJ	Ryan JB	Doyle SC	Whitehall SC	Thackeray AJ	Bowden IL	Flounders AJ	Taylor IL	Oliver D
R2	Nov 30	Stockport County	0-4		2484	1	10	14	5	6	11	8	9	7	12	2	4	3

Lancashire Cup

Date	Opponent	Score	Scorers	Hodge MJ	Matthews NP	Graham J	Reid S	Reeves A	Butler PJ	Ryan JB	Doyle SC	Lancaster D	Whitehall SC	Stuart MRN	Thackeray AJ	Milner AJ	Mulrain S
Jul 23	BOLTON WANDERERS	3-4	Thackeray, Flounders, Seagraves (og)	1	2	3	4	5	6	7	8	9	10	11	12	14	
26	Blackpool	1-2	Bowders	1		3	4	5	6		8		12	11	7	9	14
31	BURNLEY	4-1	Stuart, Lancaster, Flounders, Jones	1		3	4	5	6			8	11	10	7	9	12

289

1993-94 Season
Back: Jones, Bowden, Butler, Reeves, Hodge, Lancaster, Milner, Whitehall
Middle: Docherty (Man.), Dawson (Physio), Anders, Stuart, Mulrain, Ryan, Beever, Doyle,
Jones, (Yth Team Coach) Robson, (Yth & Res. Team Man.)
Front: Snowdon, Flounders, Reid, Sutton (Manager), Howard, Thackeray, Graham

1994-95 Season
Back: Walmsley (Comm. Man.), Sharpe, Matthews, Hall, Butler, Valentine, Clarke, Peake, Bowden, Stuart,
Thompson, Deary, Robson (Yth Team Man.)
Front: Taylor, Ryan, Reid, Thackeray, Docherty (Manager), Whitehall, Formby, Russell, Oliver

Player columns (left→right): Clarke CJ · Thackeray AJ · Formby K · Reid S · Reeves A · Matthews NP · Thompson DS · Peake IW · Bowden IL · Whitehall SC · Stuart MRN · Ryan DT · Williams PA · Doyle SC · Butler PJ · Hall DR · Rimmer SA · Dunford N · Russell A · Dickens MJ · Taylor IL · Sharpe R · Oliver D · Gray I · Valentine P · Whitington C · Martin DS · Deary JS · Shaw GP · Bayliss DA

League — Division 3

#	Date	Opponent	Score	Scorers	Att	Cl	Th	Fo	Re	Rv	Ma	Th	Pe	Bo	Wh	St	Ry	Wi	Do	Bu	Ha	Ri	Du	Ru	Di	Ta	Sh	Ol	Gr	Va	Wt	Mt	De	Sw	By
1	Aug 13	Bury	1-0	Thompson	3230	1	2	3	4	5	6	7	8	9	10	11	12																		
2	20	CHESTERFIELD	4-1	Reid, Thompson, Thackeray, Whitehall.	2122	1	2	3	4	5	6	7	8		10	11	14	9		12															
3	27	Gillingham	1-1	Hall	3009	1	2	3	4	5		7	12		10	11		9		6	8														
4	30	LINCOLN CITY	1-0	Whitehall	1974	1	2	3	4	5		7	12		10	11		9	14	6	8														
5	Sep 3	HEREFORD UNITED	1-3	Williams	2258	1	2	3	4	5		7	8		10			9	12	6				11											
6	10	Northampton Town	2-1	Reid, Thompson	2887	1	2	3	4		5	7	8		12			9	10	6				11											
7	13	Barnet	2-6	Reid (p), Williams	1688	1	2	3	4		5	7	8		10		14	11	6		12			9											
8	17	BURY	0-3		3748	1	2	3	4		5	7			10	11		9		6	8														
9	24	Scarborough	4-2	Williams 2, Whitehall, Butler	1201	1	2	3	4		5	7	12		10	11		9		6	8					14										
10	Oct 1	DONCASTER ROVERS	2-0	Peake, Williams	2445		2	3	12			7	8		10	11	14	9	5	6			1						4							
11	8	FULHAM	1-2	Whitehall	2573		2	3	4				12	8	10	11		9	5	6			1						14							
12	15	Wigan Athletic	0-4		2007		2	3	4				7	8	10	11	14	9	5	6			1			12										
13	22	Torquay United	1-4	Thackeray	2547		2	3	4				7		10		11	9	5	6	8						1	14	12							
14	29	MANSFIELD TOWN	3-3	Butler, Whitehall 2	1968		2		4		5	7	8		10	11				6							1	12	9	3						
15	Nov 5	Carlisle United	1-4	Stuart	6000		2	3	4		5		12	8		10	9	11		6							1		14	7						
16	19	COLCHESTER UNITED	0-0		1903		2	3	4		5				10	11			9	7	6						12		1	8						
17	26	Hartlepool United	0-1		1387		2		4		5		7		10	11			12	6							14	3	1	8	9					
18	Dec 10	Chesterfield	2-2	Russell, Whitehall (p)	2457		2					7	8	9	10		11	12		6	14					4		3	1	5						
19	17	GILLINGHAM	2-1	Stuart, Valentine	1665		2					7	8	9	10	4	11			6	12						14	3	1	5						
20	26	Preston North End	0-3		10491		2	3				7	8	9	10	4	11			6						12		14	1	5						
21	27	WALSALL	0-2		2438		2					7	8	9	10	11				6						14	12	3	1	5						
22	31	Scunthorpe United	1-4	Butler	2653		2		4			7	8	12	10	11	14			6							9	3	1	5						
23	Jan 7	TORQUAY UNITED	2-0	Sharpe, Thompson	1636		2		4			7	8	9	10					6							11	3	1	5						
24	14	Exeter City	0-0		2316		2	3	4	14		7	8		10	12				6							11		1	5			9			
25	21	CARLISLE UNITED	1-1	Peake	3289		2	3	4			7	8		10	11				6							12		1	5			9			
26	Feb 4	HARTLEPOOL UNITED	1-0	Deary	1848	1	2	3	4			7	8		10	11				6							12		1	5			14	9		
27	11	Colchester United	0-0		3080	1	2	3	4			7	8		10	12				6							11		1	5			14	9		
28	18	EXETER CITY	0-1		1945	1	2	3	4	14		7	8		10	11				6						12				5			9			
29	25	Doncaster Rovers	1-0	Sharpe	2246	1	2	3	4	12		7	8		10					6			14				11			5			9			
30	Mar 7	Mansfield Town	1-1	Whitehall	2931	1	2	3	4			7	8		10	14	12			6							11			5			9			
31	11	NORTHAMPTON T	0-0		1894	1	2	3	4			7	8		10	12	14			6							11			5			9			
32	18	Lincoln City	2-2	Thompson, Valentine	2939	1	2	3				7	8		10	12	14			6							9			5			4	11		
33	21	DARLINGTON	2-0	Thompson, Whitehall	1471	1	2					7	3		10	9	8			6							12			5			4	11		
34	25	Hereford United	0-0		1998	1	2					7	3		10		11			6							12			5			4	8	9	
35	Apr 1	BARNET	2-2	MacDonald (og), Thackeray	1834	1	2					7	3		12		11			6										5			4	8	9	6
36	8	SCUNTHORPE UNITED	1-2	Ryan	1720	1	2					7	3	12	10		11			6							14			5			4	8	9	
37	15	Walsall	0-0		3766	1	2					7	3	12	10		11			6										5			4	8		
38	17	PRESTON NORTH END	0-1		4012	1	2	12				7	3		10		9	11		6										5			4	8		
39	22	Darlington	0-4		1886	1	2	3				7	4	14	10	9	11			6										5			12	8		
40	25	SCARBOROUGH	1-1	Ryan	1170	1	2					7	3		10		9	11		6							12			5			4	8		
41	29	WIGAN ATHLETIC	1-0	Whitehall (p)	1949	1	2					7	3		10		9	11		6							12			5			4	8		
42	May 6	Fulham	0-5		4342	1		2				7	3		10		9	12		6							11			5			4	8		
				Apps		24	41	28	28	5	13	40	39	11	42	31	24	14	11	39	9	3	2	7	4	9	16	9	12	27	1	15	17	4	1
				Goals			3		3			6	2		10	2	2	5		3	1			1			2			2			1			

One own goal

F.A. Cup

	Date	Opponent	Score		Att	Cl	Th	Fo	Re	Rv	Ma	Th	Pe	Bo	Wh	St	Ry	Wi	Do	Bu	Ha	Ri	Du	Ru	Di	Ta	Sh	Ol	Gr
R1	Nov 12	Walsall	0-3		3619		2	3	4		5			8	10	11	12	9	7	6			1			14			

F.L. Cup (Coca Cola Cup)

	Date	Opponent	Score	Scorers	Att	Cl	Th	Fo	Re	Rv	Ma	Th	Pe	Bo	Wh	St	Ry	Wi	Do	Bu	Ha
R1/1	Aug 16	MANSFIELD TOWN	1-2	Whitehall	1746	1	2	3	4	5	6	7	8	9	10	11	14			12	
R1/2	23	Mansfield Town	0-1		2234	1	2	3	4	5		7			10	12	11	9		6	8

A.M. Cup (Auto Windscreens Shield)

	Date	Opponent	Score	Scorers	Att	Cl	Th	Fo	Re	Rv	Ma	Th	Pe	Bo	Wh	St	Ry	Wi	Do	Bu	Ha	Ri	Du	Ru	Di	Ta	Sh	Ol	Gr	Va	Wt	Mt
R1	Sep 27	Blackpool	2-1	Stuart, Burke (og)	1817	1	2	3			5		7	8	10	11	12	9		6				4								
R1	Oct 18	WIGAN ATHLETIC	1-0	Taylor	1004		2	3	4				7		10			9	5	6	8				1				12	11		
R2	Nov 28	DARLINGTON	2-2	Whitehall 2	1069		2	3	4		5		7		10	12	11			8	6								14	9		1
QFN	Jan 11	STOCKPORT COUNTY	2-1	Whitehall 2	2154		2	3	4		5		7	8	10	11				6	12					14				9		1
SFN	Feb 7	Bury	2-1	Sharpe, Reid	3341		2	3	4		5		7	8	10	14				6							12			9		1	11
FN1	28	Carlisle United	1-4	Whitehall (p)	8647	1	2	3	4		5		7	8	10	14				6	12									11		9
FN2	Mar 14	CARLISLE UNITED	2-1	Whitehall, Reid	4082	1	2	3	4		5		7	8	10	14	12			6										9		11

R2 won 4-3 on penalties a.e.t.

Lancashire Cup

	Date	Opponent	Score	Scorers	Att	Cl	Th	Fo	Re	Rv	Ma	Th	Pe	Bo	Wh	St	Ry	Wi	Do	Bu	Ha	Ri							Gr	Va	Wt	Mt
	Jul 23	MANCHESTER UNITED	3-2	Stuart(p), Williams, Reid	4290	1	2	3	4	5	14			11		10	7	12	9	8	6											
	26	BURY	2-0	Peake, Williams	1370	13	2	3	4	5	6		8	14	10	7	11	9												12			
	30	BURNLEY	0-2		2024	1	2		4	5	6			9	10	7	12			8										11	14	3	

MJ Hodge 13 v Man. Utd, 11 v Bury

Rose Bowl

	Opponent	Score	Scorers	Cl	Th	Fo	Re	Rv	Ma	Th	Pe	Bo	Wh	St	Ry	Wi	Do	Bu	Ha	Ri	Du	Ru	Di	Ta	Sh	Ol	Gr	Va
	OLDHAM ATHLETIC	2-1	Whitehall, Williams	1	2	3	4	5	6	7	8		10	11	14	9								17	12			16

O.Pickard at 15

Final League Tables 1995/96 - 2000/01

1995/96 season: Div. 3

		P	W	D	L	F	A	W	D	L	F	A	F	A	Pts
1	Preston North End	46	11	8	4	44	22	12	9	2	34	16	78	38	86
2	Gillingham	46	16	6	1	33	6	6	11	6	16	14	49	20	83
3	Bury	46	11	6	6	33	21	11	7	5	33	27	66	48	79
4	Plymouth Argyle	46	14	5	4	41	20	8	7	8	27	29	68	49	78
5	Darlington	46	10	6	7	30	21	10	12	1	30	21	60	42	78
6	Hereford United	46	13	5	5	40	22	7	9	7	25	25	65	47	74
7	Colchester United	46	13	7	3	37	22	5	11	7	24	29	61	51	72
8	Chester City	46	11	9	3	45	22	7	7	9	27	31	72	53	70
9	Barnet	46	13	6	4	40	19	5	10	8	25	26	65	45	70
10	Wigan Athletic	46	15	3	5	36	21	5	7	11	26	35	62	56	70
11	Northampton Town	46	9	10	4	32	22	9	3	11	19	22	51	44	67
12	Scunthorpe United	46	8	8	7	36	30	7	7	9	31	31	67	61	60
13	Doncaster Rovers	46	11	6	6	25	19	5	5	13	24	41	49	60	59
14	Exeter City	46	9	9	5	25	22	4	9	10	21	31	46	53	57
15	ROCHDALE	46	7	8	8	32	33	7	5	11	25	28	57	61	55
16	Cambridge United	46	8	8	7	34	30	6	4	13	27	41	61	71	54
17	Fulham	46	10	9	4	39	26	2	8	13	18	37	57	63	53
18	Lincoln City	46	8	7	8	32	26	5	7	11	25	47	57	73	53
19	Mansfield Town	46	6	10	7	25	29	5	10	8	29	35	54	64	53
20	Hartlepool United	46	8	9	6	30	24	4	4	15	17	43	47	67	49
21	Leyton Orient	46	11	4	8	29	22	1	7	15	15	41	44	63	47
22	Cardiff City	46	8	6	9	24	22	3	6	14	17	42	41	64	45
23	Scarborough	46	5	11	7	22	28	3	5	15	17	41	39	69	40
24	Torquay United	46	4	9	10	17	36	1	5	17	13	48	30	84	29

1996/97 season: Div. 3

		P	W	D	L	F	A	W	D	L	F	A	F	A	Pts
1	Wigan Athletic	46	17	3	3	53	21	9	6	8	31	30	84	51	87
2	Fulham	46	13	5	5	41	20	12	7	4	31	18	72	38	87
3	Carlisle United	46	16	3	4	41	21	8	9	6	26	23	67	44	84
4	Northampton Town	46	14	4	5	43	17	6	8	9	24	27	67	44	72
5	Swansea City	46	13	5	5	37	20	8	3	12	25	38	62	58	71
6	Chester City	46	11	8	4	30	16	7	8	8	25	27	55	43	70
7	Cardiff City	46	11	4	8	30	23	9	5	9	26	31	56	54	69
8	Colchester United	46	11	9	3	36	23	6	8	9	26	28	62	51	68
9	Lincoln City	46	10	8	5	35	25	8	4	11	35	44	70	69	66
10	Cambridge United	46	11	5	7	30	27	7	6	10	23	32	53	59	65
11	Mansfield Town	46	9	8	6	21	17	7	8	8	26	28	47	45	64
12	Scarborough	46	9	9	5	36	31	7	6	10	29	37	65	68	63
13	Scunthorpe United	46	11	3	9	36	33	7	6	10	23	29	59	62	63
14	ROCHDALE	46	10	6	7	34	24	4	10	9	24	34	58	58	58
15	Barnet46		9	9	5	32	23	5	7	11	14	28	46	51	58
16	Leyton Orient	46	11	6	6	28	20	4	6	13	22	38	50	58	57
17	Hull City	46	9	8	6	29	26	4	10	9	15	24	44	50	57
18	Darlington	46	11	5	7	37	28	3	5	15	27	50	64	78	52
19	Doncaster Rovers	46	9	7	7	29	23	5	3	15	23	43	52	66	52
20	Hartlepool United	46	8	6	9	33	32	6	3	14	20	34	53	66	51
21	Torquay United	46	9	4	10	24	24	4	7	12	22	38	46	62	50
22	Exeter City	46	6	9	8	25	30	6	3	14	23	43	48	73	48
23	Brighton & Hove A.	46	12	6	5	41	27	1	4	18	12	43	53	70	47
24	Hereford United	46	6	8	9	26	25	5	6	12	24	40	50	65	47

1997/98 season: Div. 3 *(* 3 points deducted)*

		P	W	D	L	F	A	W	D	L	F	A	F	A	Pts
1	Notts County	46	14	7	2	41	20	15	5	3	41	23	82	43	99
2	Macclesfield Town	46	19	4	0	40	11	4	9	10	23	33	63	44	82
3	Lincoln City	46	11	7	5	32	24	9	8	6	28	27	60	51	75
4	Colchester United	46	14	5	4	41	24	7	6	10	31	36	72	60	74
5	Torquay United	46	14	4	5	39	22	7	7	9	29	37	68	59	74
6	Scarborough	46	14	6	3	44	23	5	9	9	23	35	67	58	72
7	Barnet	46	10	8	5	35	22	9	5	9	26	29	61	51	70
8	Scunthorpe United	46	11	7	5	30	24	8	5	10	26	28	56	52	69
9	Rotherham United	46	10	9	4	41	30	6	10	7	26	31	67	61	67
10	Peterborough Utd.	46	13	6	4	37	16	5	7	11	26	35	63	51	67
11	Leyton Orient	46	14	5	4	40	20	5	7	11	22	27	62	47	66*
12	Mansfield Town	46	11	9	3	42	26	5	8	10	22	29	64	55	65
13	Shrewsbury Town	46	12	3	8	35	28	4	10	9	26	34	61	62	61
14	Chester City	46	12	7	4	34	15	5	3	15	26	46	60	61	61
15	Exeter City	46	10	8	5	39	25	5	7	11	29	38	68	63	60
16	Cambridge United	46	11	8	4	39	27	3	10	10	24	30	63	57	60
17	Hartlepool United	46	10	12	1	40	22	2	11	10	21	31	61	53	59
18	ROCHDALE	46	15	3	5	43	15	2	4	17	13	40	56	55	58
19	Darlington	46	13	6	4	43	28	1	6	16	13	44	56	72	54
20	Swansea City	46	8	8	7	24	16	5	3	15	25	46	49	62	50
21	Cardiff City	46	5	13	5	27	22	4	10	9	21	30	48	52	50
22	Hull City	46	10	6	7	36	32	1	2	20	20	51	56	83	41
23	Brighton & Hove A.	46	3	10	10	21	34	3	7	13	17	32	38	66	35
24	Doncaster Rovers	46	3	3	17	14	48	1	5	17	16	65	30	113	20

1998/99 season: Div. 3

		P	W	D	L	F	A	W	D	L	F	A	F	A	Pts
1	Brentford	46	16	5	2	45	18	10	2	11	34	38	79	56	85
2	Cambridge United	46	13	6	4	41	21	10	6	7	37	27	78	48	81
3	Cardiff City	46	13	7	3	35	17	9	7	7	25	22	60	57	80
4	Scunthorpe Utd.	46	14	3	6	42	28	8	5	10	27	30	69	58	74
5	Rotherham Utd.	46	11	8	4	41	26	9	5	9	38	35	79	61	73
6	Leyton orient	46	12	6	5	40	30	7	9	7	28	29	68	59	72
7	Swansea City	46	11	9	3	33	19	8	5	10	23	29	56	48	71
8	Mansfield Town	46	15	2	6	38	18	4	8	11	22	40	60	58	67
9	Peterborough Utd.	46	11	4	8	41	29	7	8	8	31	27	72	60	66
10	Halifax Town	46	10	8	5	33	25	7	7	9	25	31	58	56	66
11	Darlington	46	10	6	7	41	24	8	5	10	28	34	69	58	65
12	Exeter City	46	13	5	5	32	18	4	7	12	15	32	47	50	63
13	Plymouth Argyle	46	11	6	6	32	19	6	4	13	26	35	58	54	61
14	Chester City	46	6	12	5	28	30	7	6	10	29	36	57	66	57
15	Shrewsbury Town	46	11	6	6	36	29	3	8	12	16	34	52	63	56
16	Barnet	46	10	5	8	30	31	4	8	11	24	40	54	71	55
17	Brighton & H.A.	46	8	3	12	25	35	8	4	11	24	31	49	66	55
18	Southend United	46	8	6	9	24	21	6	6	11	28	37	52	58	54
19	ROCHDALE	46	9	8	6	22	21	4	7	12	20	34	42	55	54
20	Torquay United	46	9	9	5	29	20	3	8	12	18	38	47	58	53
21	Hull City	46	8	5	10	25	28	6	6	11	19	34	44	62	53
22	Hartlepool United	46	8	7	8	33	27	5	5	13	19	38	52	65	51
23	Carlisle United	46	8	8	7	25	21	3	8	12	18	32	43	53	49
24	Scarborough	46	8	3	12	30	39	6	3	14	20	38	50	77	48

1999/00 season: Div. 3

		P	W	D	L	F	A	W	D	L	F	A	F	A	Pts
1	Swansea City	46	15	6	2	32	11	9	7	7	19	19	51	30	85
2	Rotherham United	46	13	5	5	43	17	11	7	5	29	19	72	36	84
3	Northampton Town	46	16	2	5	36	18	9	5	9	27	27	63	45	82
4	Darlington	46	13	9	1	43	15	8	7	8	23	21	66	36	79
5	Peterborough United	46	14	4	5	39	30	8	8	7	24	24	63	54	78
6	Barnet	46	12	6	5	36	24	9	6	8	23	29	59	53	75
7	Hartlepool United	46	16	1	6	32	17	5	8	10	28	32	60	49	72
8	Cheltenham Town	46	13	4	6	28	17	7	6	10	22	25	50	42	70
9	Torquay United	46	12	6	5	35	20	7	6	10	27	32	62	52	69
10	ROCHDALE	46	8	7	8	21	25	10	7	6	36	29	57	54	68
11	Brighton & H.A.	46	10	7	6	38	25	7	9	7	26	21	64	46	67
12	Plymouth Argyle	46	12	10	1	38	18	4	8	11	17	33	55	51	66
13	Macclesfield Town	46	9	7	7	36	30	9	4	10	30	31	66	61	65
14	Hull City	46	7	8	8	26	23	8	6	9	17	20	43	43	59
15	Lincoln City	46	11	6	6	38	23	4	8	11	29	46	67	69	59
16	Southend United	46	11	5	7	37	31	4	6	13	16	30	53	61	56
17	Mansfield Town	46	9	6	8	33	26	7	2	14	17	39	50	65	56
18	Halifax Town	46	7	5	11	22	24	8	4	11	22	34	44	58	54
19	Leyton Orient	46	7	7	9	22	22	6	6	11	25	30	47	52	52
20	York City	46	7	10	6	21	21	5	6	12	18	32	39	53	52
21	Exeter City	46	8	6	9	27	30	3	5	15	19	42	46	72	44
22	Shrewsbury Town	46	5	6	12	20	27	4	7	12	20	40	40	67	40
23	Carlisle United	46	6	8	9	23	27	3	4	16	19	48	42	75	39
24	Chester City	46	5	5	13	20	36	5	4	14	24	43	44	79	39

2000/01 season: Div. 3 *(* 9 points deducted)*

		P	W	D	L	F	A	W	D	L	F	A	F	A	Pts
1	Brighton & H.A.	46	19	2	2	52	14	19	6	8	21	21	73	35	92
2	Cardiff City	46	16	7	0	56	20	7	6	10	39	38	95	58	82
3	Chesterfield	46	16	5	2	46	14	9	9	5	33	28	79	42	80*
4	Hartlepool United	46	12	8	3	40	23	9	6	8	31	31	71	54	77
5	Leyton Orient	46	13	7	3	31	18	7	8	8	28	33	59	51	75
6	Hull City	46	12	7	4	27	18	7	10	6	20	21	47	39	74
7	Blackpool	46	14	4	5	50	26	8	2	13	24	32	74	58	72
8	ROCHDALE	46	11	8	4	36	25	7	9	7	23	23	59	48	71
9	Cheltenham Town	46	12	5	6	37	27	6	9	8	22	25	59	52	68
10	Scunthorpe United	46	13	7	3	42	16	5	4	14	20	36	62	52	65
11	Southend United	46	10	8	5	29	23	5	10	8	26	30	55	53	63
12	Plymouth Argyle	46	13	5	5	33	17	2	8	13	21	44	54	61	58
13	Mansfield Town	46	12	7	4	40	26	3	6	14	24	46	64	72	58
14	Macclesfield Town	46	10	5	8	23	21	4	9	10	28	41	51	62	56
15	Shrewsbury Town	46	12	5	6	30	26	3	5	15	19	39	49	65	55
16	Kidderminster Harriers	46	10	6	7	29	27	3	8	12	18	34	47	61	53
17	York City	46	9	6	8	23	26	4	7	12	19	37	42	63	52
18	Lincoln City	46	9	9	5	36	28	3	6	14	22	38	58	66	51
19	Exeter City	46	8	9	6	22	20	4	5	14	18	38	40	58	50
20	Darlington	46	10	6	7	28	23	2	7	14	16	33	44	56	49
21	Torquay United	46	8	9	6	30	29	4	4	15	22	48	52	77	49
22	Carlisle United	46	8	8	7	26	26	3	7	13	16	39	42	65	48
23	Halifax Town	46	7	6	10	33	32	5	5	13	21	36	54	68	47
24	Barnet	46	9	8	6	44	29	3	1	19	23	52	67	81	45

1995-96 15th in Division 3

#	Date	Opponent	Score	Scorers	Att	Gray I	Russell A	Formby K	Thompstone I	Valentine P	Butler P	Thompson D	Martin D	Shaw G	Whitehall SC	Peake J	Williams P	Ryan D	Bayliss D	Hall D	Deary J	Taylor J	Moulden P	Hardy J	Stuart MN	Thackeray A	Mitchell N	Clarke C	Price J	Pilkington K	Lancaster D	Key L	Procter J	Powell F	Barlow N	Lyons F
1	Aug 12	CARDIFF CITY	3-3	Whitehall(2,1p), Thompson	2321	1	2	3	4	5	6	7	8		9	10	11	12	14																	
2	19	Darlington	1-0	Whitehall(p)	2139	1	2	3	4	5	6	7			9	10	11	15	14	8	12															
3	26	HARTLEPOOL UNITED	4-0	Taylor(3), Thompson	1794	1	2	3			6	7	8		10	11	12		5		4	9	14													
4	29	Torquay United	0-1		2139	1	2	3	14		6	7	8		10	11			12	5		4	9	15												
5	Sep 2	NORTHAMPTON TOWN	1-2	Butler	2193	1	2				6	7	8		10	11				5		4	9	12	3	14										
6	9	Lincoln City	2-1	Whitehall(p), Stuart	2408	1	2	3			6	7	8	12	10	11	14			5		4			9											
7	12	Fulham	1-1	Deary	3848	1					6		8	7	10	11	9			5		4		12	3		2									
8	16	MANSFIELD TOWN	1-1	Stuart	2173	1	15		14		6	7	8	9	10	11				5		4		3	12	2										
9	23	Doncaster Rovers	3-0	Whitehall(p), Schofield, Stuart(og)	2217	1	15		14		6	7	8	12	10	11				5	3	4			9	2										
10	30	EXETER CITY	4-2	Stuart, Deary, Whitehall, Peake	2052	1					6	7	12	8	10	11	14			5		4			9	2										
11	Oct 7	Gillingham	0-1		7785	1	15	3			6	7	8	12	10	11				5		4			9	2										
12	14	COLCHESTER UNITED	1-1	Stuart	2193	1		3	12		6	7		8	10	11				5		4	14		9	2										
13	21	Barnet	4-0	Peake, Stuart(2), Whitehall	2039	1		3		5	6	7	8		10	11						4			9	2										
14	28	CAMBRIDGE UNITED	3-1	Moulden, Whitehall(2)	2344	1		3		5	6	7			10	11						4	8		9	2										
15	31	CHESTER CITY	1-3	Peake	3018	1		3	14	5	6	7			12	10	11					4	8		9	2										
16	Nov 4	Scunthorpe United	3-1	Stuart, Whitehall(2)	3003	1		3	8	5	6	7	4		12	10	11								9	2										
17	18	HEREFORD UNITED	0-0		2619	1		3	11	5	6	7	4		12	10	14	9					8			2										
18	25	Plymouth Argyle	0-2		6558	1		3	2		6	7	4	9	10	11		5	12	8			14													
19	Dec 9	DONCASTER ROVERS	1-0	Whitehall(p)	2168	1		3	2	5	6			12	8	10	11	14	9			4							7							
20	16	Exeter City	0-2		3152		2	3		5		7	8	12	10	11	15	9	6				14					4	1							
21	22	Leyton Orient	0-2		5399		2	3		5	6	7	8		10	11	14	4					9					12	1							
22	Jan 2	Wigan Athletic	0-2		2624		2	3		5	6	7	8		10	11	12		14						15	9	1									
23	13	Darlington	1-2	Whitehall(p)	1945					14	5	6	7	4	12	10	11			8	15	9	3		2		1									
24	20	Cardiff City	0-1		2230		2		3	5		7	8	12	10	11			6	14		4	15		9			1								
25	23	Scarborough	1-1	Peake	1400	1	2			5		7	4	8	10	11			6						9					3						
26	Feb 3	Hartlepool United	1-1	Whitehall	1927		2		12	5	6	7	8		10	11			15		4	14			9					3	1					
27	10	SCARBOROUGH	0-2		1662		2		14	5	6	7	12		10	11					4	8			9					3	1					
28	13	BURY	1-1	Butler	3048		2		9		6	7	8		10	3			5		4				11						1					
29	17	FULHAM	1-1	Stuart	1923		2		9	12	6	7	8		10	3			5		4	14	15		11						1					
30	20	Northampton Town	1-2	Thompston	3090		2		12	5		7	8		10	3			6		4				11								1	9		
31	27	LINCOLN CITY	3-3	Whitehall(p), Stuart(2)	1253		2		14	5		7	8		10	3			6		4				11	12							1	9		
32	Mar 2	Preston North End	2-1	Whitehall, Stuart	9698					5	6	7	8		10	3					4				11	2							9	1		
33	9	LEYTON ORIENT	1-0	Lancaster	1934		14		12	5	6	7	8		10	3	15				4				11	2							9	1		
34	12	PRESTON NORTH END	0-3		5497		14		12	5	6	7	8		10	3	15				4				11	2							9	1		
35	16	Bury	1-1	Butler	3473		9		5		6	7			10	3			12	4	8				11	2							1			
36	19	TORQUAY UNITED	3-0	Deary, Whitehall(p), Thompson	1206		8			6	7			10	3				5		4	12			11	2							9	1		
37	23	WIGAN ATHLETIC	0-2		2870		8			6	7	12		10	3				5		4				11	2							9	1		
38	30	GILLINGHAM	2-0	Stuart, Thompson	2098				5	6	7	8		10	3			12	14	4				11	2							9	1		
39	Apr 2	Colchester United	0-1		3021					7	5			10	9			6	4	8	12	3		11	2							1	15	14	
40	6	Cambridge United	1-2	Lancaster	2186					7	4			10	3			6		5	12			11	2					9	1	8	14	15	
41	8	BARNET	0-4		1492					7	4			10	8			6		12	15			11	2					9	1	14		5	3
42	13	Chester City	2-1	Whitehall(2)	2158					6	7	8		10	3			5	9	4				11	2						1				
43	16	Mansfield Town	2-2	Hall, Whitehall	1814					6	7	8		10	3			5	9	4	12			11	2					14	1				
44	20	SCUNTHORPE UNITED	1-1	Deary	1654				12	6	7			10	3			5	8	4				11	2					9	1				14
45	27	PLYMOUTH ARGYLE	0-1		2355				12	6	7			10	3			5	8	4				11	2					9	1				
46	May 4	Hereford United	0-2		5880				5	6				10	3				8	4	7		12	11	2					9	1				14
		Apps				20	25	18	25	23	38	43	37	18	46	46	12	7	28	14	36	16	16	7	34	29	4	6	3	6	14	14	3	2	2	3
		Goals						1			3	4			20	4				1	4	3	1		13							2				

One own goal

FA. Cup

R	Date	Opponent	Score	Scorers	Att	Gray I	Russell A	Formby K	Thompstone I	Valentine P	Butler P	Thompson D	Martin D	Shaw G	Whitehall SC	Peake J	Williams P	Ryan D	Bayliss D	Hall D	Deary J	Taylor J	Moulden P	Hardy J	Stuart MN	Thackeray A	Mitchell N	Clarke C	Price J
R1	Nov 11	ROTHERHAM UNITED	5-3	Moulden(2), Whitehall(p), Peake(2)	3817	1		3	15	5	6	7	4	12	10	11							14			8		9	2
R2	Dec 2	DARLINGTON	2-2	Deary(2)	3732	1		3	2	5	6	7	8	12	10	11		14			4		9						
R2r	12	Darlington	1-0	Martin	4131	1	12	3	2	5		7	8		10	11		9	6	4									
R3	Jan 6	Liverpool	0-7		28126			3	15	5	6	7	8	12	10	11		14			4		9			2		1	

F.L.Cup (Coca-Cola Cup)

R	Date	Opponent	Score	Scorers	Att	Gray I	Russell A	Formby K	Thompstone I	Valentine P	Butler P	Thompson D	Martin D	Shaw G	Whitehall SC	Peake J	Williams P	Ryan D	Bayliss D	Hall D	Deary J	Taylor J
R1	Aug 15	YORK CITY	2-1	Shaw, Thompstone	1390	1	2	3	4	5	6	7		9	10	11			8			
R1	22	York City	1-5*	Tuthill (og)	2130	1	2	3		5	6	7	14		10	11	9	12	8		4	

* a.e.t.

A.M. Cup (Auto Windscreens Shield)

R	Date	Opponent	Score	Scorers	Att	Gray I	Russell A	Formby K	Thompstone I	Valentine P	Butler P	Thompson D	Martin D	Shaw G	Whitehall SC	Peake J	Williams P	Ryan D	Bayliss D	Hall D	Deary J	Taylor J	Moulden P	Hardy J	Stuart MN	Thackeray A	Mitchell N
R1	Sep 26	Lincoln City	3-4	Whitehall, Peake, Deary	1238	1		3			6	7	8		10	11	12			5		4			9	2	
R1	Oct 24	DARLINGTON	5-2	Whitehall, Gregan (og), Moulden(3)	1055	1		3	15	5	6	7	14	12	10	11				4			8		9	2	
R2	Nov 28	Chesterfield	1-2	Whitehall	2344	1		3	2		6	7	4	11	10			12	5	8		9					

Lancashire Cup

Date	Opponent	Score	Scorers	Att	Gray I	Russell A	Formby K	Thompstone I	Valentine P	Butler P	Thompson D	Martin D	Shaw G	Whitehall SC	Peake J	Williams P	Ryan D	Bayliss D	Hall D	Deary J	Taylor J	Moulden P	Hardy J	Stuart MN	Thackeray A
Jul 22	Preston North End	2-2	Martin, Thompson		1		3		5	6	7	8	9	10	11	12		15		4				14	2
29	BLACKPOOL	0-1		1265	1		3	2	5	6	7	8	10		11	9	14	12		4					

293

1995-96 Season
Back: Whitehall, Stuart, Butler, Williams, Thompstone, Valentine, Bayliss
3rd Row: Bywater (School of Excellence), Robson (Yth Team & Res. Coach), Shaw, Ryan, Gray, Clarke, Martin,
Deary, Docherty (Manager), Hicks (School of Excellence)
2nd Row: Dawson (Physio), Hall, Peake, Thompson, Formby, Russell, Taylor, Thackeray, Jones ('A' Team Coach)
Front: Stanley, Sweetenham, Adams, Ogden, Shore, Matthews, Taylor, Barlow

1996-97 Season
Back: Stuart, Leonard, Cecere, I.Gray, Lancaster, K.Gray, Bayliss, Farrell
Middle: Robson (Yth Team Man.) Russell, Formby, Martin, Whitehall, Thompson, Deary, Gouck,
Thackeray, Bywater (Centre of Excellence Coach)
Front: Hicks (Centre of Excellence Dir.), Fensome, Taylor, Price, Barrow (Manager), Dowell, Hill, Barlow,
Lyons, Hinnighan (1st Team Coach/Physo)

1996-97 14th in Division 3

No	Date	Opponent	Score	Scorers	Att	Gray I	Fensome A	Formby K	Johnson A	Hill K	Farrell A	Russell A	Deary J	Leonard M	Whitehall SC	Stuart MN	Cecere M	Martin D	Thompson D	Bayliss D	Lancaster D	Gouck A	Brown M	Painter PR	Bailey M	Thackeray A	Dowell W	Robson G	Taylor I	Gray K
1	Aug 17	Swansea City	1-2	Cecere	4272	1	2	3	4	5	6	7	8	9	10	11	12		14	15										
2	24	COLCHESTER UNITED	0-0		1816	1	2	3	4	5	6	7	8	9	10	11	12		14	15										
3	27	FULHAM	1-2	Whitehall	1689	1	2	3	4	5	6	7	8	9	10	11	12		14											
4	31	Mansfield Town	0-0		1861	1	2		4	5	6	11	8	9	10	12			7	3	14									
5	Sep 7	Hull City	1-1	Deary	3451	1	2		4	5	6	7	8	9	10	11			12	3		14								
6	10	CHESTER CITY	0-1		1774	1	2		4	5	6	12	8	9	10	14			7	3	15	11								
7	14	DONCASTER ROVERS	2-1	Deary(p), Gouck	1811	1	2		4	5	6	10	8	9		11			12	3		14	7							
8	21	Hereford United	0-3		2135	1	2		4	5	6	10	8	9	14	11			12	3			7							
9	28	LEYTON ORIENT	1-0	Whitehall(p)	1994	1	2		4		6		8		10	11			12	3	9	6	7							
10	Oct 5	Darlington	1-1	Stuart	3071	1	2		4	5	6	10	8		9	11				3	14	12	7							
11	12	CARLISLE UNITED	2-2	Painter, Thompson	3320	1	2		4	5	6		8	9		11			14	3		12	7	10						
12	15	LINCOLN CITY	2-0	Whitehall, Painter	1411	1	2		4	5		7			9	10	11			3		6		8						
13	19	Cambridge United	2-2	Stuart, Painter	3163	1	2		4	5	12	7			9	10	11			3		6		8						
14	26	Scunthorpe United	2-2	Stuart, Whitehall	2628	1	2		4	5		7			9	10	11			3		6		8						
15	29	BRIGHTON & H.A.	3-0	Whitehall(2), Painter	1913	1	2		4	5	12	7			9	10	11			3		6		8						
16	Nov 2	EXETER CITY	2-0	Johnson, Hill	2134	1	2		4	5	3	7			9	10	11		12			6		8						
17	5	Cardiff City	1-2	Whitehall	2834	1	2		4	5	3	7			9	10	11		12			6		8						
18	9	Barnet	2-3	Pardew (og), Deary	2405	1	2		4	5	3	7	12	9	10	11						6		8						
19	23	Northampton Town	2-2	Farrell(2)	3836	1	2		4	5	3			8	9	10	11			12	14	6		7						
20	30	SCUNTHORPE UNITED	1-2	Painter	1969	1	2		4	5	6	14	8	9	10			12	7	3				11						
21	Dec 3	Torquay United	1-0	Johnson	1087	1	2		4	5	6		8		10	9			12	3				11	7					
22	14	HARTLEPOOL UNITED	1-3	Whitehall	1618	1	2		4	5			8		10	9			12	3				11	7	6	14			
23	21	Wigan Athletic	1-0	Whitehall(p)	3311	1			4	5			8	9	10					2				11	7	6	3			
24	Jan 14	Chester City	0-0		1679	1			4	5			8	9	10		12			2				11	7	6	3			
25	18	CARDIFF CITY	1-0	Leonard	1704	1			4	5			8	9	10	12			14	2				11	7	6	3			
26	25	Brighton & Hove Albion	0-3		4468	1			4	5	12	14	8	9		11			15	2				10	7	6	3			
27	Feb 1	BARNET	1-1	Russell	1623	1	2		4	5	6	12	8	9	10				7	3	14	15		11						
28	4	SCARBOROUGH	3-3	Painter, Hill, Russell	1166	1	2		4	5	6	7	8	9	12				14	3				10	11					
29	8	Exeter City	0-0		2849	1	2		4	5	6	7	8		10									9	11	3				
30	11	Leyton Orient	1-2	Painter	2406	1	2	12	4	5	6	7	8		10				15			14		9	11	3				
31	15	NORTHAMPTON TOWN	1-1	Deary	1988	1	2	12	4	5		7	8	9	14				15	3		6		10	11					
32	18	HEREFORD UNITED	0-0		1074	1	2	11	4	5		10	8	9	12				7			6				3				
33	22	Scarborough	2-2	Russell, Sutherland (og)	2384	1		11	4	5	2	10	8	9	12				7			6			14	3				
34	25	HULL CITY	1-2	Russell	1349	1	12	11	4	5	2	7	8	9	10							6	14			3		15		
35	Mar 1	TORQUAY UNITED	2-1	Leonard, Gouck	1469	1	2	12	4	5	3	7	8	9	12	11						6								
36	8	WIGAN ATHLETIC	3-1	Deary, Johnson, Russell	3254	1	2	10	4	5	3	7	8	9	12	11						6								
37	15	Hartlepool United	2-1	Russell, Formby	1448	1	2	10	4	5	3	7	8	9		11						6								
38	21	Colchester United	0-1		3211	1	2	10	4	5	3	7	8	9		11						6			12		14			
39	25	Doncaster Rovers	0-3		2201	1	2	12	4	5	3	7	8	9		11						6			12		14			
40	29	SWANSEA CITY	2-3	Russell(2)	1884	1	2	12	4	5	3	7	8	9								6			14	10				
41	31	Fulham	1-1	Gouck	7866	1	2	11	4	5	3	7	8	9								6			12	10				
42	Apr 5	MANSFIELD TOWN	0-1		1620	1	2	12	4	5	3	7	8	9								6			11	10			14	
43	12	DARLINGTON	2-0	Leonard, Johnson	1638	1	2		4	5	6	7	8	9								12			10	3				
44	26	CAMBRIDGE UNITED	3-0	Stuart(2), Russell	1810	1			4	5	6	10	8	9		11			7							2	3			
45	29	Carlisle United	2-3	Leonard, Stuart	4882	1	12		4	5	6	10	8	9	14	11			7							2	3			
46	May 3	Lincoln City	2-0	Hill, Stuart	6495	1	2		4	5	6		8	9		11			7							10	3			
		Apps				46	40	16	46	43	40	39	38	39	35	31	4	1	28	24	6	28	5	27	15	17	7	3	1	
		Goals						1	4	3	2	9	5	4	9	7	1		1			3		7						

Two own goals

F.A. Cup

	Date	Opponent	Score	Scorers	Att	Gray I	Fensome A	Formby K	Johnson A	Hill K	Farrell A	Russell A	Deary J	Leonard M	Whitehall SC	Stuart MN	Cecere M	Martin D	Thompson D	Bayliss D	Lancaster D	Gouck A	Brown M	Painter PR	Bailey M	Thackeray A	Dowell W	Robson G	Taylor I	Gray K
R1	Nov 16	Macclesfield Town	2-0	Deary, Johnson	3134	1	2		4	5	3		7	9	10	11						6		8						
R2	Dec 6	Notts County	1-3	Thackeray	3584	1	2		4	5	6		8	10		9			12	3				11	7	14				

F.L. Cup (Coca-Cola Cup)

	Date	Opponent	Score	Scorers	Att	Gray I	Fensome A	Formby K	Johnson A	Hill K	Farrell A	Russell A	Deary J	Leonard M	Whitehall SC	Stuart MN	Cecere M	Martin D	Thompson D	Bayliss D	Lancaster D	Gouck A	Brown M	Painter PR	Bailey M	Thackeray A	Dowell W	Robson G	Taylor I	Gray K
R1	Aug 20	BARNSLEY	2-1	Deary, Whitehall	2426	1	2	3	4	5	6	7	8	9	10	11	14		12											
R1	Sep 3	Barnsley	0-2		5638	1	2		4	5	6	7	8	9		11			12	3	10					14				

A.M. Cup (Auto Windscreens Shield)

	Date	Opponent	Score	Scorers	Att	Gray I	Fensome A	Formby K	Johnson A	Hill K	Farrell A	Russell A	Deary J	Leonard M	Whitehall SC	Stuart MN	Cecere M	Martin D	Thompson D	Bayliss D	Lancaster D	Gouck A	Brown M	Painter PR	Bailey M	Thackeray A	Dowell W	Robson G	Taylor I	Gray K
R1	Dec 10	Carlisle United	0-2		3622	1	2		4	5		6	8		10	9			12	3				11	7	14				

Lancashire Cup

	Date	Opponent	Score	Scorers	Att	Gray I	Fensome A	Formby K	Johnson A	Hill K	Farrell A	Russell A	Deary J	Leonard M	Whitehall SC	Stuart MN	Cecere M	Martin D	Thompson D	Bayliss D	Lancaster D	Gouck A	Brown M	Painter PR	Bailey M	Thackeray A	Dowell W	Robson G	Taylor I	Gray K
	Jul 30	Blackpool	1-1	Thackeray		1	2			5	4			10	11	7	9	6				8				12	3			
	Aug 3	Morecombe	1-2	Whitehall			2			5	4	14		9	11	7	10		12	15	6					8	3			1

1997-98 18th in Division 3

#	Date	Opponent	Res	Scorers	Att	Key L	Fensome A	Barlow A	Hill K	Farrell A	Gouck A	Bailey M	Painter PR	Leonard M	Russell A	Stuart MN	Carter M	Bayliss D	Scott A	Smith C	Bryson I	Lancashire G	Edwards N	Robson G	Pender J	Reed A	Atkinson G	Jones G	Carden P	Bywater S
1	Aug 9	Notts County	1-2	Painter	4173	1	2	3	4	5	6	7	8	9	10	11	12	14	15											
2	16	MANSFIELD TOWN	2-0	Russell, Painter	2133	1	2	3	4	5	6	12	8	9	7	11	10													
3	23	Leyton Orient	0-2		3463	1	2	3	4	5	6	14	8	9	7	11	10			12										
4	30	PETERBOROUGH UNITED	1-2	Painter	2104	1	2	3	4	5	6	12	8	9	7	11	14			10										
5	Sep 2	MACCLESFIELD TOWN	2-0	Carter, Hill	2197	1	2	3	4	5	6	7	8	9		11	12	10												
6	9	Shrewsbury Town	0-1		2410	1	2	3		5	6	7	8		10	11	9	4		12										
7	13	Cardiff City	1-2	Carter(p)	4306	1	2	3	4		6	7	8	9	11	12	10	5												
8	20	HULL CITY	2-1	Hill, Stuart	2085	1	2	3	4		6	7	8	9	11	12	10	5												
9	27	Brighton & Hove Albion	1-2	Bayliss	1544	1	2	3	4		6	7	8	9	11	12	10	5												
10	Oct 4	SCUNTHORPE UNITED	2-0	Russel, Painter(p)	2087	1	2		4	5		7	8	9	11	12		3			6	10								
11	11	DARLINGTON	5-0	Painter(2,1p),Lancashire(2),Russell	2134	1	2	12	4	5		7	8	9	11			3			6	10								
12	18	Cambridge United	1-1	Gouck	2703	1	2	3	4	5	6	7	8	9	11	12	15	14				10								
13	21	Barnet	1-3	Leonard	1310	1	2	3	4	5	6	7	8	9	11	12		14				10								
14	25	ROTHERHAM UNITED	0-1		2267	1	2	3	4	5	6	7	8	9	11	12	14					10								
15	Nov 1	chester City	0-4		2431	1	2	3	4	5	6		8	9	10	11					7									
16	4	LINCOLN CITY	0-0		1537		2	3	4	5	6	12	8	9	10	11					7		1							
17	8	COLCHESTER UNITED	2-1	Stuart, Painter(p)	1702		2	3	4	5	6		8	9	10	11					7		1							
18	18	Hartlepool United	0-2		1666		2	3	4	7	6	12	8	9		11					10		1	5						
19	22	DONCASTER ROVERS	3-0	Stuart(2), Lancashire	1503			3	4			7	8	9		11		2			6	10	1	12	5					
20	29	TORQUAY UNITED	0-1		1729			3	4		12	7	8	9		11		2			6	10	1	14	5					
21	Dec 6	Scarborough	0-1		1705		2				6	7	8	9		12		3			11	10	1	14	5	4				
22	13	SWANSEA CITY	3-0	Painter(2), Leonard	1482		2			10	6	7	8	9		14		3			12		1	15	5	4		11		
23	23	Exeter City	0-3		3378			3		10	6		8	9	12	14					7		1		5	4		11		
24	26	SHREWSBURY TOWN	3-1	Lancashire, Painter, Bryson	2247		2	3		10	6	7	8	9		12					14	12	1		5	4		11		
25	28	Macclesfield Town	0-1		2666	1	2	3		5	6		8	9		12					7	10				4		11		
26	Jan 3	Mansfield Town	0-3		2303	1	2			3	6	12	8	9		14			15		7	10			5	4		11		
27	10	NOTTS COUNTY	1-2	Farrell	2387			3		10	6	7	8	9				2			12		1	14	5	4		14		
28	17	Peterborough United	1-3	Farrell	5676			3	12	10		7	8		9	11		2			14		1		5	4			6	
29	24	LEYTON ORIENT	0-2		1774		2				6	12	8		10	11			3		9		1	14	5	4			7	
30	31	CARDIFF CITY	0-0		1445		2	3	4		6					11	12				9		1		5	10			7	
31	Feb 7	Hull City	2-0	Russell, Stuart	4031	1	2	3	4	9	6	7	8		10	11					12		1		5					
32	14	Scunthorpe United	0-2		2284		2	3	4	9	6	7	8		10	11	12						1		5					
33	21	BRIGHTON & H.A.	2-0	Jones, Gouck	1865		2		4	9	6		8	5	10	11		3			12		1					7		
34	24	CAMBRIDGE UNITED	2-0	Gouck(2)	1192		2		4	9	6		8	5	10	11		3					1					7		
35	28	Darlington	0-1		2181		2	12	4	9	6		8	5	10	11		3			14		1					7		
36	Mar 3	Colchester United	0-0		2112		2	12	4	9	6		8	5	10	11		3					1					7		
37	7	CHESTER CITY	1-1	Lancashire	1955		2	3	4	10	6		8	5		11						9	1					7		
38	14	Lincoln City	0-2		2992	1	2	3	4		6	7	8	5	14	11	12		15									9	10	
39	21	HARTLEPOOL UNITED	2-0	Painter(p), Farrell	1395	1	2	3	4	6		7	8	5	12	11						9							10	
40	28	DONCASTER ROVERS	4-1	Painter,Stuart,Farrell,Lancashire	1858		2	3	4	10	6		8	5		12		14				9	1					7		
41	Apr 9	Torquay United	0-0		2796		2	3	4	10	6		8	12		11		5				9	1					7		14
42	11	SCARBOROUGH	4-0	Painter(2), Lancashire, Farrell	1795		2	3	4	10	6	12	8			11		5				9	1					7		14
43	18	Swansea City	0-3		2854		2	3	4	10	6		8			11		5				9	1					7		12
44	18	EXETER CITY	3-0	Lancashire(2), Bayliss	1850		2	3	4	10	6		8			11		5				9	1					7		12
45	25	Rotherham United	2-2	Jones, Painter(p)	3463		2	3	4	10	6	12	8			11		5	14				1					7		9
46	May 2	BARNET	2-1	Gouck, Painter	2102		2	3	4		6	12	8			11		5				9	1		14			7		10
				Apps.		19	42	38	37	40	38	33	45	33	31	45	11	29	3	3	15	27	27	7	14	10	6	17	7	
				Goals						2	4	5		17	2	4	7	2	2		1	9								

F.A. Cup

| R1 | Nov 15 | WREXHAM | 0-2 | | 3956 | | 2 | 3 | 4 | 5 | 6 | | 8 | 9 | 10 | 11 | | | | | 7 | | 1 | 12 | | | | | | |

F.l. Cup (Coca-Cola Cup)

| R1 | Aug 12 | STOKE CITY | 1-3 | Painter | 2509 | 1 | 2 | 3 | 4 | 5 | 6 | 7 | 8 | 9 | | 11 | 10 | | | | | | | | | | | | | |
| R1 | 27 | Stoke City | 1-1 | Russell | 12768 | 1 | 2 | | 4 | 5 | 6 | 7 | 8 | 9 | 10 | 11 | 14 | 3 | | 12 | | | | | | | | | | |

A.M. Cup (Auto Windscreens Shield)

| R1 | Dec 9 | Doncaster Rovers | 1-0 | Reed | 580 | | 2 | | | 10 | 6 | 7 | 8 | 9 | | 12 | | 3 | | | 11 | | 1 | | 5 | 4 | | | | |
| R2 | Jan 6 | Carlisle United | 1-6 | Stuart | 2350 | | 2 | | | | 6 | 12 | 7 | 8 | | 14 | 11 | 3 | | | 10 | 9 | | | 5 | 4 | | | | 1 |

Lancashire Cup

Not competed.

1997-98 Season
Back: Irwin, Bryson, Painter, Farrell, Stuart, Russell, G.Robson, Taylor
Middle: Hicks (Centre of Excel. Dir.), J.Robson (Yth Team Coach), Pender, Leonard, S.Bywater, Gray, Hill,
Bayliss, D.Bywater (Centre of Excel.), Hinnigan (Coach/Physio)
Front: Fensome, Barlow, Bailey, Barrow (Manager), Gouch, Whitehall, Carter

1998-99 Season
Back: Hicks (Centre of Excel.), T.Jones ('A' Team Coach), Hamilton (Yth Team Coach), Hill, Robson, Leonard,
Edwards, Key, Monington, Gray, Johnson, Bywater (Centre of Excel.), Hinnigan (1st Team Coach/Physio)
Middle: G.Jones, Bryson, Stokes, Painter, Barrow (Manager), Lancashire, Bayliss, Stuart, Sparrow
Front: Edghill, Bailey, Barlow, Peake, Carden, Farrell

1998-99 19th in Division 3

#		Date	Opponent	Score	Scorers	Att	Edwards N	Sparrow P	Stokes D	Hill K	Bayliss D	Johnson I	Farrell A	Lancashire G	Leonard M	Peake J	Stuart MN	Gray D	Bailey M	Jones G	Diaz I	Painter PR	Bryson I	Monington M	Williams M	Barlow A	de Souza M	Holt M	Carden P	Morris A	Priestley P	Lydiate J	Stoker G	Hicks G	Key L
1	Aug	8	Plymouth Argyle	1-2	Lancashire(p)	5547	1	2	3	4	5	6	7	8	9	10	11	12		14	15														
2		15	TORQUAY UNITED	0-2		1713	1					6	8		9	10	15	11		11		7	12	14											
3		22	Carlisle United	1-0	Diaz	3627	1	2	3	4	5	6	10		12	15	11			9		7	8	14											
4		29	DARLINGTON	0-0		1953	1		3	4	2		6			11		9				7	8	10	5										
5		31	Brentford	1-2	Diaz	4873	1	12	3	4	2		6			11	15	9	14	7	8		10	5											
6	Sep	5	SHREWSBURY TOWN	1-0	Bailey	1660	1		3	4	2		6			9	12	7	8	10	5														
7		8	Hull City	1-2	Hill	3433	1	12	3	4	2		6			11	14	9		7	8	10	5												
8		12	SCUNTHORPE	2-2	Painter(p), Monington	1929	1	2	3	4			6			11		9		7	8	10	5												
9		19	Cardiff City	1-2	Painter	4643	1	2	3	4		12	6	14	15	11		9		7	8	10	5												
10		26	LEYTON ORIENT	2-1	Lancashire, Painter	1742	1			4		15	12	9	14	11		6		7	8	10	5	2	3										
11	Oct	3	Southend United	1-1	Lancashire	3686	1			4			12	9	14	11		6	7	8	10	5	2	3											
12		11	HALIFAX TOWN	1-0	Williams	3628	1			4	5		9	12	11			6	7	8	10		2	3											
13		17	Peterborough	0-2		4536	1			4		12	9		11			14	6	7	8	10	5	2	3										
14		20	Rotherham United	2-2	Sparrow, Monington	3105	1	3		4		6	9	12	11	14			7	8	10	5	2												
15		31	Barnet	1-0	Painter	1413	1	3		4		6			11			12	7	8	10	5	2		9										
16	Nov	7	MANSFIELD TOWN	1-0	Peake	2142	1	3		4	12	6			11			14	7	8	10	5	2		9										
17		10	EXETER CITY	1-1	Sparrow	1639	1	3		4	6			11	12			7	8	10	5	2		9											
18		17	SCARBOROUGH	0-1		1536	1	3		4		6			11	7		12	8	10	5	2		9	15										
19		21	Chester City	1-1	Holt	2495	1	3		4		6			11		2		14	8	10	5		9	12	7									
20	Dec	12	Swansea City	1-1	Peake	4010	1			4		6			11		12	14	8	10	5	2	3	9	7										
21		19	BRIGHTON & H.A.	2-1	Painter, Monington	2153	1	2		4		6			11				8	10	5	3	9	7											
22		26	CARLISLE UNITED	1-1	Peake	2900	1	2		4	6	7			11				8	10	5	3		9											
23		28	Hartlepool	1-0	Holt	2218	1	2		4	6				11				8	10	5	3	12	7	9										
24	Jan	2	Darlington	0-3		2807	1	2		4	6	5			11	15			8	10	12	3	14	7	9										
25		9	PLYMOUTH ARGYLE	1-1	Holt	1922		2		4	6	5			12		5		8	10	14	3	11	7	9	1									
26		16	Torquay United	1-2	Morris	2205	1	2		4	6	5			12		14		8	10	15	3	11	7	9										
27		23	BRENTFORD	2-0	Holt, Painter	2113	1	3			5	6	4		12	15	14		8	10	2		11	7	9										
28		30	HARTLEPOOL	0-1		1943	1	3		15	6	4			10	12			2	8	5		14	11	7	9									
29	Feb	6	Shrewsbury Town	2-3	Peake, Morris	2561	1	3		4	12	6			10	14			2	8	5		11	7	9										
30		12	HULL CITY	3-0	Holt(2), Morris	5374	1			6	7				10				8	5	3	11	2	9											
31		20	Scunthorpe	1-0	Bayliss	3749	1	12		5	7				10		14		8	3	11	2	9	6	4										
32		27	CARDIFF CITY	1-1	Peake	2431	1	2		4	6	14			10			15	12	5	3	11	7	9	8										
33	Mar	6	Leyton Orient	0-3		4927	1			4	6	14			10	12			8	5	3	2	9	7	11										
34		13	Mansfield Town	1-3	Lydiate	2555	1				6	12			10		2		14	5	3	11	7	9	4	8									
35		20	BARNET	0-0		1502	1			7	6				10		2		14	5	3	11	12	9	4	8									
36		26	Scarborough	0-1		2206	1			4	6				10		12		14	8	5	3	11	2	9	7									
37		30	SOUTHEND UNITED	1-0	Morris	1344	1			4	6				10				8	12	5	3	2	9	11	7									
38	Apr	3	PETERBOROUGH	0-3		1696	1		15	4	6				10			11	8	14	5	3	12	2	9	7									
39		5	Halifax Town	0-0		2759	1			4	6				10				8	12	5	3	2	9	11	7									
40		10	ROTHERHAM UNITED	0-0		2516	1			4	6				10				8	12	5	3	14	2	9	11	7								
41		13	Cambridge United	1-1	Stoker	4690	1		4	3	6				10				11	5	12	2	9	8	7										
42		17	CHESTER CITY	3-1	Morris(3)	1712	1		4	3	2				10		14		11	5	12	8	7	9	6										
43		24	Exeter City	1-2	Holt	2543	1		4	3	2				10		11		5	12	14	7	9	6	8										
44		27	CAMBRIDGE UNITED	0-2		1408	1		4		2				10		8		11	5	3	7	9	6											
45	May	1	SWANSEA CITY	0-3		1654	1		4		2				10			12	8	5	3	11	7	9	6										
46		8	Brighton & Hove Albion	1-1	Barlow	4646	1	12	3	4					10			6		7	5	11	8	9	14	2									
			Apps.				45	25	11	33	25	16	38	11	8	38	19	3	19	20	14	40	39	37	14	29	5	24	25	25	1	14	12	1
			Goals					2			1	1				3			5			1	2	6		3	1	1	7	7		1	1	

F.A. Cup

		Date	Opponent	Score	Scorers	Att	Edwards N	Sparrow P	Stokes D	Hill K	Bayliss D	Johnson I	Farrell A	Lancashire G	Leonard M	Peake J	Stuart MN	Gray D	Bailey M	Jones G	Diaz I	Painter PR	Bryson I	Monington M	Williams M	Barlow A	de Souza M	Holt M	Carden P	Morris A	Priestley P	Lydiate J	Stoker G	Hicks G	Key L
R1	Nov	13	Scarborough	1-1	Bryson	1860	1	3		4			6			11	9			7	12	8	10	5	2										
R1r		24	SCARBOROUGH	2-0	Monington, Bryson	1850	1	3		4	12		15			10	11		14	7	8	6	5	2					9							
R2	Dec	5	ROTHERHAM UNITED	0-0		3346	13	3		4		6				11	9			12	8	10	5	2					7							1
R2r		15	Rotherham United	0-4		3424	1	3		4		6				11	9		14	15	8	10	5	2	12				7							

F.L. Cup (Worthington Cup)

		Date	Opponent	Score	Scorers	Att	Edwards N	Sparrow P	Stokes D	Hill K	Bayliss D	Johnson I	Farrell A	Lancashire G	Leonard M	Peake J	Stuart MN	Gray D	Bailey M	Jones G	Diaz I	Painter PR	Bryson I	Monington M	Williams M
R1	Aug	11	Wigan Athletic	0-1		2252	1	2	3	4	5	6	8	14	9	10		12	7				11		
R1		18	WIGAN ATHLETIC	0-1		1697	1		3	4	2	5	6	9		11		10	7	8					

A.M. Cup (Auto Windscreens Shield)

		Date	Opponent	Score	Scorers	Att	Edwards N	Sparrow P	Stokes D	Hill K	Bayliss D	Johnson I	Farrell A	Lancashire G	Leonard M	Peake J	Stuart MN	Gray D	Bailey M	Jones G	Diaz I	Painter PR	Bryson I	Monington M	Williams M	Barlow A	de Souza M	Holt M	Carden P	Morris A	Priestley P	Lydiate J	Stoker G
R2	Feb	2	STOKE CITY*	2-1	Morris, Holt	7361	1	12		4	14		6			10			2	8		5		3				7	9	11			
NQF		23	HALIFAX TOWN#	2-1†	Jones(p), Monington	2327	1	2	3	4		6			10				12	14	5							8	9	11	7		
NSF	Mar	8	WIGAN ATHLETIC	0-2		2484	1			4		6	14		10				2	12	5			3				7	9	11	8		

*played at Stoke, # played at Halifax († won on extra time golden goal)

Lancashire Cup

		Date	Opponent	Score	Scorers	Att	Edwards N	Sparrow P	Stokes D	Hill K	Bayliss D	Johnson I	Farrell A	Lancashire G	Leonard M	Peake J	Stuart MN	Gray D	Bailey M	Jones G	Diaz I	Painter PR	Morris A	Key L
SF	Jul	21	OLDHAM ATHLETIC+	4-0	Lancashire(2), Peake(2)	902		2	3		4	5	6	9	14	10	11	15		7		8	12	1
F		28	Wigan Athletic	1-3	Lancashire		1	2	3			6	4	8	9	10	11			7		12	14	

+ Also Charity Rose Bowl

1999-2000 10th in Division 3

#	Date		Opponent	Score	Scorers	Att	Edwards N	Evans W	Stokes D	Peake J	Bayliss D	Hill K	Flitcroft D	Ford T	Morris A	Lancashire G	Atkinson G	Holt M	Platt CL	Jones G	Carden P	Monington M	Searle D	Dowe J	Green R	Ellis A	Bettney C	Peyton W	Priestley P	Gibson P	McAuley S	McClare S	Wilson S	Taylor D	Hicks G
1	Aug	7	Cheltenham Town	2-0	Atkinson, Ford	5189	1	2	3	4	5	6	7	8	9	10	11	14	12																
2		14	SOUTHEND UNITED	2-0	Platt, Peake	2253	1	2	3	4	5	6	7	8		10	11	9	12																
3		21	York City	3-0	Lancashire, Platt, Atkinson	3034	1	2	3	4	5	6	7	8	14	10	11	9	15	12															
4		28	EXETER CITY	0-2		3113	1	2	3	4	5	6		8	14	10	11	9	7	12															
5		30	chester City	2-0	Atkinson, Platt	2644	1	2	3	4	5	6	7	8		10	11	9	14	12															
6	Sep	3	HALIFAX TOWN	0-1		4208	1	2	3	4	5	6	7	8	12	10	11		9			14	15												
7		11	DARLINGTON	0-0		3253	1	2	3	4		6	7	10			11	8	9	14	12	5													
8		18	Rotherham United	1-0	Atkinson	3568	1	2	3	4		6	7	10			11	8	9	12	5	14	15												
9		25	SWANSEA CITY	0-0		2975	1	2		4			7				11	8	9	10	5	3	12	6											
10	Oct	2	Northampton Town	1-0	Platt	4860	1	2		4		6	7	10			11	8	9	12	3	14	5												
11		9	Barnet	0-0		2765	1	2		4		6	7	10			11	8	9	12	3	14	5												
12		16	PLYMOUTH ARGYLE	0-0		3105	1	2		4		6	7				11	8	9	12	10	3	14	5											
13		19	MACCLESFIELD TOWN	0-1		2397	1	2		4		6	7				11	8	9	12	10	14	3	15	5										
14		22	Swansea City	0-1		4843	1	2		4		6	7				11	12	9	8	14	3	10	5											
15	Nov	2	HULL CITY	0-2		2365	1	2	3	4		6	7	8		14	15	9	12		5	11			10											
16		6	Torquay United	0-1		2351	1	2		12		6	7	8			11	9	4		5	3			10	14										
17		14	MANSFIELD TOWN	2-1	Platt, Ellis	2709	1	2		4	6		14	8			11	9	7		5	3			10	12										
18		23	Leyton Orient	0-0		2990	1	2		4	6		12	8		14	11	9	7		5	3			10	15										
19		27	Lincoln City	1-1	Jones	3424	1	2		4	6			8		12	14	9	7		5	3			10	11										
20	Dec	4	CHELTENHAM TOWN	0-0		2245	1	2		4	5	6		12	8		14	9	7			3			10	11										
21		10	Brighton & Hove Albion	4-3	Bayliss, Atkinson, Platt(2)	5049	1	2		4	5	6	7	15		12	11	9	8			3			10	14										
22		26	Carlisle United	2-1	Ellis, Flitcroft	3812	1	2	3	4	5	6	7			12	11	9	8						10											
23		28	SHREWSBURY TOWN	2-1	Lancashire, Peake	2924	1	2	3	4	5	6	7	12		10	11		8						9	14										
24	Jan	3	Hartlepool	2-3	Westwood (og), Ellis	4498	1	2	3	4	5	6	7	12		10	11		8						9	14										
25		8	BRIGHTON & H.A.	1-0	Lancashire	2596	1	2	3	4		6	7			10	12	14	8		5				9	11										
26		15	Southend United	3-3	Jones, Lancashire(2)	3190	1	2	3	4		6	7			10	12	14	8		5				9	11										
27		22	YORK CITY	2-1	Lancashire, Ellis	2580	1	2	3		6		10	11		14	8	15	5						9	7	4									
28		29	Exeter City	0-2		2525	1	2		4	6		7	3		10	11		12	8	5				9			13								
29	Feb	5	CHESTER CITY	2-1	Lancashire, Bayliss	3093		2	3	4	6		7	12		10			14	8	5				9	11			1							
30		12	Halifax Town	2-0	Lancashire, Peake	3504		2	12	4		6	7	14		10			15	8	5				9	11			1	3						
31		19	LINCOLN CITY	1-1	Bayliss	3166		2		4	5	6	7	12	14				10	11	9				10	11			1	3						
32		26	ROTHERHAM UNITED	0-1		4131		2			5	6	7	4	14			12	9	8					10	11			1	3						
33	Mar	4	Darlington	1-4	Ellis	5333		2		4	5	6	7	8	14			11	9	12					10				1	3						
34		11	Hull City	2-2	Jones(2,1p)	4219		2	3	12	5	6	7	4			11		9	8	10				10	14	1		15							
35		18	LEYTON ORIENT	1-4	Ellis	2472	1	2		4		6	7			12	14	8	9		5				9	11			3							
36		25	CARLISLE UNITED	3-2	Monington(2), Ellis	2417	1	2		12	6	14	7	3		10	11	15	8		5	9			9					4						
37		28	Mansfield Town	0-0		2257	1	2		12	14	6	7	3		10	11		8		5	9			9					4						
38	Apr	1	Peterborough	3-3	Ford, Ellis, Peake	5587	1	2		4	5		7	3		10	11		12	8					9					6						
39		5	TORQUAY UNITED	1-1	Jones	1529	1	2		4	5	6	7	3		10	11		12	8					9	14							15			
40		8	HARTLEPOOL	2-0	Platt, Peake	2332	1	2		4	5	6	7	3		10	11	12	9	8						14					15					
41		15	Shrewsbury Town	4-2	Platt, Peake, Jones(p), Ellis	4158	1	2		4		6	7	3		10	11		9	8	5				12					14						
42		18	PETERBOROUGH	1-2	Jones(pen)	2816	1	2		4		6	7	3		12	11		9	8	5				10					15	14					
43		22	Plymouth Argyle	1-2	Ellis	6205	1	2		4		6	7	11		12			9	8	5				10	14				3	15					
44		24	NORTHAMPTON TOWN	0-3		2891	1	2		4	6		7			12			9	8	5				10	14				3	11					
45		29	Macclesfield Town	2-1	Flitcroft, Evans	2202	1	2		12	14	6	7			10			15	8	5				9	11				3	4					
46	May	6	BARNET	1-1	Ellis	2347	1	2	3		5	6	7					12	9						10	11					8	4	15	14	
			Apps				40	46	19	43	29	38	43	34	7	29	40	41	41	39	13	24	14	7	6	31	24	1	2	5	13	9	1	1	
			Goals							6	3		2	2		8	5		8	7		2													

One own goal

F.A. Cup

	Date		Opponent	Score	Scorers	Att	Edwards N	Evans W	Stokes D	Peake J	Bayliss D	Hill K	Flitcroft D	Ford T	Morris A	Lancashire G	Atkinson G	Holt M	Platt CL	Jones G	Carden P	Monington M	Searle D	Dowe J	Green R	Ellis A	Hicks G
R1	Oct	30	Burton Albion	0-0		3103	1	2	3	4			7	8		11	14	9	12		5		10				6
R1r	Nov	9	BURTON ALBION	3-0	Platt, Peake, Dowe	2633	1	2	3	4	6		14	10		11	8	9	7	15	5		12				
R2		20	Wrexham	1-2	Atkinson	3408	1	2	3	4	6		14	8		11		9	7		5			10	12		

F.L. Cup (Worthington Cup)

	Date		Opponent	Score	Scorers	Att	Edwards N	Evans W	Stokes D	Peake J	Bayliss D	Hill K	Flitcroft D	Ford T	Morris A	Lancashire G	Atkinson G	Holt M	Platt CL	Jones G	Monington M
R1	Aug	10	CHESTERFIELD	1-2	Lancashire	1910	1	2	3	4	5	6	7	8	9	10	11	12			14
R1		24	Chesterfield	1-2	Evans	2067	1	2	3	4	5	6	7	9	12	10	11	8			

A.M. Cup (Auto Windscreens Shield)

	Date		Opponent	Score	Scorers	Att	Edwards N	Evans W	Stokes D	Peake J	Bayliss D	Hill K	Flitcroft D	Ford T	Morris A	Lancashire G	Atkinson G	Holt M	Platt CL	Jones G	Carden P	Monington M	Ellis A	McAuley S
R2	Jan	11	MACCLESFIELD	3-1*	Monington(2), Lancashire	1112	1	2	3	4		6	7			12	11	9	14		5		10	8
NQF		25	HULL CITY	0-0+		1745	1	2			3	6	7	12		10	11	9	14	15	5		14	8
NSF	Mar	7	Carlisle United	1-0	Hill	1792		2	3		5	6	7	4			11	9	8				10	12
NF		14	STOKE CITY	1-3	Holt	4241	1	2		4		6	7	3		14	12	9	8		5		10	11
NF		22	Stoke City	0-1		16896	1	2		4	6		7	3		10	11	14	8		5		9	12

* won on extra time golden goal
+ a.e.t. won 5-4 on penalties

Lancashire Cup

Not competed

1999-2000 Season
Back: G.Jones, Bayliss, Morris, Lenagh, Flitcroft, G.Hicks
Middle: K.Hicks (Centre of Excel. Dir.), Peake, Evans, Edwards, Monington, Hill, Priestley, Carden, Holt, Thorpe (Physio)
Front: Hamilton (Yth Team Coach), Lancashire, Stoker, Ford (Asst. Man.), Atkinson, Parkin (Manager),
Stokes, Wilson, T.Jones (Youth Coach)

2000-01 Season
Back: K.Hicks (Centre of Excel.), Monington, Byliss, Platt, Priestley, Flitcroft, McAuley, T.Jones (Youth Coach)
Middle: Thorpe (Physio), Ellis, G.Jones, Oliver, Edwards, Lancashire, Evans, Hamilton (Yth Dev. Off.)
Front: Townson, G.Hicks, Coleman, Ford OBE (Asst. Man.), Parkin (Manager), Atkinson, Hill, Ware

2000-01 8th in Division 3

#	Date	Opponent	Res	Scorers	Att	Edwards N	Evans W	Todd L	Ford T	Bayliss D	Hill K	Flitcroft D	Ware P	Ellis A	Platt C	Davies S	Oliver M	Hadland P	Hamilton G	Lancashire G	Jones G	Monington M	Coleman S	Buggie L	Lee C	Kyle K	McAuley S	Howell D	Townson K	Connor P	Gilks M	Turner A	Walsh D
1	Aug 12	DARLINGTON	1-1	Davies(pen)	3255	1	2	3	4	5	6	7	8	9	10	11	12	14	15														
2	19	Brighton & Hove Albion	1-2	Ford	6076	1	2	3	4	5	6	7	8	9	10	11	12	15			14												
3	26	SCUNTHORPE UNITED	3-2	Ellis, Platt, Ware	2561	1	2	3	4	5	6	7	12	9	10	14	11				8												
4	28	Halifax Town	2-1	Platt, Jones	2783	1	2	3	4	5	6	7	12	9	10		11		14		8												
5	Sep 2	CARDIFF CITY	1-1	Hadland	2844	1	2	3	4	5	6	7	12		10	11	9	15	14		8												
6	9	Carlisle United	2-1	Platt, Todd	3906	1	2	3		5	6	7	8		10	14	9	11			4	12											
7	12	YORK CITY	2-0	Platt, Monington	2215	1	2	3			6	7	8	9	10		12	11			4	5											
8	16	TORQUAY UNITED	2-1	Monington, Ellis	2871	1	2	3			6	7	8	9	10						11	5	4										
9	23	Shrewsbury Town	4-0	Ellis, Platt, Monington, Bayliss	3427	1	2	3	14		6	7	8	9	10		12	11			4	5		15									
10	30	SOUTHEND UNITED	0-1		3264	1	2	3	15		6	7	8	9	10		12	11			4	5		14									
11	Oct 6	Kidderminster Harriers	0-0		3094	1	2	3	4		6	7	8	9	10		12				11	5											
12	14	HARTLEPOOL UNITED	2-1	Ford, Jones(pen)	2813	1	2	3	4		6	7	8	9	10		12				11	5											
13	17	CHESTERFIELD	2-2	Jones(pen), Monington	5008	1	2	3	4		6	7		9	10		12	11			8	5											
14	21	Cheltenham Town	2-0	Monington(2)	4033	1	2	3	4		6	7	14	9	10		15	11			8	5			12								
15	24	MACCLESFIELD TOWN	2-1	Lee, Ware	3608	1	2	3	4		6	7	14	9	10		15	11			8	5			12								
16	28	Exeter City	1-0	Platt	2606	1	2	3	4		6		8		10		11	12			7	5			9								
17	Nov 4	BARNET	0-0		3657	1	2	3	4		6		8	12	10			11			7	5			9								
18	11	Mansfield Town	0-1		2453	1	2	3	4		6		8	9	10		11	12			7	5			14								
19	Dec 2	BLACKPOOL	1-0	Jones	4186	1	2	3	4		6		8	9	10		11	12		14	7	5											
20	16	Lincoln City	1-1	Ellis	2320	1	2	3	4		6	12	8	9	10		11				7	5											
21	23	Leyton Orient	1-1	Jones(pen)	4398	1	2	3	4		6		8	12	10		11	9		14	7	5											
22	26	HULL CITY	1-0	Jones	4327	1	2	3	4		6	7	14	9	10		11	12			8	5											
23	Jan 6	Darlington	2-1	Ellis, Evans	3481	1	2	3	4		6	7		9	10		11	12			8	5											
24	13	HALIFAX TOWN	0-1		4123	1	2	3	4		6	7		9	10		11	14		12	8	5											
25	28	LEYTON ORIENT	3-1	Ellis, Jones, Hadland	3676	1	2	3	4		6	7		9	10		12	14		11	8	5					15						
26	Feb 2	Cardiff City	0-0		11912	1	2	3	4	5	6	7		9	10		12				8	11											
27	13	Scunthorpe United	0-0		2821	1	2	3	4		6	7		12	10		14	11			8		15			9							
28	17	Torquay United	0-1		2195	1	2	3	4		6	7		9	10		11	12			8					14							
29	20	YORK CITY	0-1		2807	1	2	3			6	7		9	10		14	11			8		15			12							
30	24	SHREWSBURY TOWN	1-7	Lancashire	2647	1	2	3			6	15	7	14	9		12			10	8	5	4			11							
31	Mar 3	Southend United	0-3		3681		2			5	6	7	12		9					4	10	8				3		14	15				
32	6	Hartlepool United	1-1	Lancashire	3492	1	2	3		5	6	7								4	10	8						11	9				
33	10	KIDDERMINSTER H.	0-0		2552	1	2	3	11		6	7					12			4	10	8			5			9	14	15			
34	17	Chesterfield	1-1	Connor	4338		2	3	11		6	7					12			4	10	8			5					9	1		
35	23	CHELTENHAM TOWN	1-1	Connor	2713	1	2	3			6	7		14						4	10	8			5					9	3	12	
36	27	Hull City	2-3	Bayliss, Connor	7365		2	3		5	6	7	8				12		14	4	10									9	1	11	
37	Apr 3	BRIGHTON & H.A.	1-1	Todd	2444	1	2	3	4		6	7			10		12	15		14	8	5								9		11	
38	10	CARLISLE UNITED	6-0	Jones, Todd, Connor(3), Evans	2892	1	2	3	4		6	7	15		10		11			14	8	5								9			
39	14	Macclesfield Town	0-0		2255	1	2	3	4		6	7			10		11				8	5								9			
40	16	EXETER CITY	3-0	Connor(2), Bayliss	2773	1	2	3	4		6	7	12		10		11			15	8	5								9			
41	21	Barnet	0-3		2381	1	2		4		6	15	7	11	10		3			14	8	5								9			12
42	23	LINCOLN CITY	3-1	Platt, Connor, Monington	2592	1	2		4	6	3	7			10		11	12			8	5								9			
43	26	Blackpool	1-3	Lancashire	5470	1	2		4	6	3	7	15		10		11			14	8	5								9			
44	28	Mansfield Town	1-0	Platt	3114	1	2		4	6	3	7			10		11	12			8	5								9			
45	May 1	PLYMOUTH ARGYLE	2-1	Elliott(og), Connor	4027	1	2		4	6	3	7	12		10		11			14	8	5								9			
46	5	Plymouth Argyle	0-0		5125	1	2		4	6	3	7	15		10		11	12			8	5								9			
		Apps.				44	45	40	38	41	25	41	30	28	43	12	38	32	3	16	44	34	5	2	5	6	1	3	3	14	3	4	
		Goals					2	3	2	3			2	6	8		2			3	8	7			1					10			

F.A. Cup

Rd	Date	Opponent	Res	Scorers	Att	Edwards N	Evans W	Todd L	Ford T	Bayliss D	Hill K	Flitcroft D	Ware P	Ellis A	Platt C	Davies S	Oliver M	Hadland P	Hamilton G	Lancashire G	Jones G	Monington M	Coleman S	Buggie L	Lee C	Kyle K	McAuley S	Howell D	Townson K	Connor P	Gilks M	Turner A	Walsh D
R1	Nov 18	Cambridge United	1-2	Platt	3142	1	2	3	4		6		8	14	10		12	9		11	15	7			5								

Worthington Cup

Rd	Date	Opponent	Res	Scorers	Att	Edwards N	Evans W	Todd L	Ford T	Bayliss D	Hill K	Flitcroft D	Ware P	Ellis A	Platt C	Davies S	Oliver M	Hadland P	Hamilton G	Lancashire G	Jones G	Monington M	Coleman S	Buggie L	Lee C	Kyle K	McAuley S	Howell D	Townson K	Connor P	Gilks M	Turner A	Walsh D
R1	Aug 22	BLACKBURN ROVERS	1-1	Ellis	4873	1	2	3	4	5	6	7	8	9	10	14	11				12												
R1	Sep 5	Blackburn Rovers	1-6	Platt	12977	1	2	3	4	5	6	15	8		10	11	9	12			7												14

L.D.V. Trophy

Date	Opponent	Res	Scorers	Att	Edwards N	Evans W	Todd L	Ford T	Bayliss D	Hill K	Flitcroft D	Ware P	Ellis A	Platt C	Davies S	Oliver M	Hadland P	Hamilton G	Lancashire G	Jones G	Monington M	Coleman S	Buggie L	Lee C	Kyle K	McAuley S	Howell D	Townson K	Connor P	Gilks M	Turner A	Walsh D
Dec 5	Doncaster Rovers	2-3*	Jones(pen), Campbell (og)	1453	1	2				6			15	8	9	10	12		11	4				14	7	5			3			

* lost to extra time 'golden goal'

Ian Bailey, Rochdale
Jean Phillipps
Rhodri Phillipps
Jonathan Simon McGaw, Rochdale
John Newton, Healey, Rochdale
John Gugas, Drighlington, Bradford
Christopher Rodgers, Rochdale
Bill Midgley, Rochdale
Trevor Clarke, Northampton
David Harness, Scholes, Cleckheaton
David James, Oxford
David J Gartside, Rochdale
Francis Finnigan, Salford
Wayne Skeffington, Mossley, Lancs
Jeremy Alderson, Leigh, Lancashire
Derek W Lomax, Hawkshaw
Phil Barton, Bishops Stortford
Matthew Phillip Russell, Sudden
Edward Brewis, Syke, Rochdale
Richard Brewis, Syke, Rochdale
David Schofield, Middleton
Peter Taylor, Chesterfield
Richard Wild, Newhey
The Smith-Markl Family, Rochdale
Darroll N Wike, Blackburn
Alexander Earnshaw, Newbold, Rochdale
Mark Wilbraham, Littleborough
Neil Faragher, Watersheddings, Oldham
John Bryan Meyrick, Littleborough
P B Ridehaugh, Rochdale
J R Ridehaugh, Belgium
John Clarke, Littleborough
Nick Johnson, Rochdale
Janet Beecheno, London
David Messom, Bamford
Steve Beaumont, Norden, Rochdale
David Sibbert, Oxfordshire
David Mobberley, Bromsgrove, Worcs
Derek Lord, Whitworth
Andrew Irving, Farnborough, Hampshire
Alan Holt, Rochdale
Keith Buckley, Whitworth
Francis Collins, Rochdale
Darren Kay, Milnrow, Rochdale
David Rodgerson, Rochdale
Paul Moss, Rochdale
Jack Sunderland, Facit
Chris, Jake & Nick Tattersall
David Forbes, Liversedge, West Yorkshire
Steve Ashworth, Spotland, Rochdale

Dale Wilkinson, Milnrow, Rochdale
Richard Brooks, Wardle, Rochdale
Dave Dutton, Heywood, Lancashire
Brian Moss, College Bank
Lilian Stoney, Rochdale
Andy Bell, Hurstead, Wardle
Nigel MacDonald, Red Lumb
Barry Inston
Ian Barker, Rochdale
Mavis Shellard, Wardle
Rodney Sunderland, Littleborough
John Dunn, United/Rochdale
Keith O'Loughlin, Lancashire
Tony Shaw, East Coker, Somerset
Julian Hoyle, Garstang, Lancashire
Mike Rowley, Littleborough, Rochdale
Paul Leedham, Rochdale
Keith Maguire, Littleborough
Lee Atkin, Shaw
Mr Brendan Schofield
Ian Bailey
Chris Brierley, Blackpool
Stephen Howarth, Coventry
Wilf Willman, Rochdale
The Dowber Family, Accrington
Alan Fearn, Bentmeadows, Rochdale
Thomas Slater, Syke, Rochdale
Rory McNicholas, Charlotte, USA
Richard Ward, Nunney
Peter Ward, Rochdale
Peter G Redford, Littleborough
The Webster Family, Norden, Rochdale
Stephen Peacock, Ince, Wigan
Charles Peacock, Bamford, Rochdale
Jack Clough, Pontefract
Emma Perry, Beverley
John Clough, Hull
Clive & Jennifer Piggott, Littleborough
Stephen & Tom Buckley
Stephen Thorpe, Cirencester, Gloucestershire
Adam Taylor, Chrystal Palace
David Martin
Chris Johnson, Rochdale
Mike Johnson, Barnet
Mark Cryer, Heywood
Stan Bartram, Shaw
Mr Michael S Butcher, Walsden
Geoffrey Wolfenden
Mike Bewsher, Ingatestone
Peter & Jack Frankland, Shaw

Subscribers ~

Lee Johnson, Rochdale
Brent Risby, Rochdale
Leonard Risby, Rochdale
Mark Harris, Balderstone
Roger Crofts, Norden, Rochdale
Andrew Crofts, Pokhara, Nepal
Geoff Ferguson, Rochdale
James O'Neill, Shawclough
Alan Wild, Harbone, Birmingham
Michael Przyszlak Rodgers, Rochdale
Kevin Finan, Rochdale
David Whitfield, Littleborough
Christine Anthony Jordan Hassett
Glenn Mills, Shawclough
Geoff Poole, Milnrow
John Collins, Syke, Rochdale
Stuart Clarke, Worthing
Barry Warburton, Droylsden, Manchester
Ian Nigel Parker, Castleton
The Woolfenden Family, Birmingham
Chris Tokariuk, Whitworth
Ian Jacques, Portsmouth
Terry Moore, Bristol
Lewis C Woodall, Bamford
Dave Windross
Chas Sumner, Kelsall, Cheshire
M.J. Cripps, Sussex
David Keats, Thornton Heath
Richard Wells
Mark Tyler, Billericay Town F.C.
George Mason
Peter Cogle, Aberdeen
David E. Griffiths, Llandudno
Derek Hyde
George Painter, Castle Cary
Phil Hollow, Plymouth Argyle
Moira & Fredeick Furness
Gordon Macey, Q.P.R. Historian
Paul Johnson, Birmingham City
Steve Emms, Evesham
John Treleven
Colin Cresswell
David, Frank, Olive Lewis
Graham Spackman
L.A. Zammit
Fred Lee, Plymouth Argyle
B.H. Standish
Alan Davies
Allan Grieve, Tillicoultry, Scotland
James Jordan

Jonny Stokkeland, Kvinesdal, Norway
Tony Lacey 75-76
David J. Godfrey
A.N. Other
Mr. G.E. Lunn, Tyldesley
Mr. J. Holbrook, Bristol
Richard Owen (Portsmouth FC Historian)
Robin Isherwood
Andrew Wood
David Jowett, Keighley
Michael John Griffin
Philip Harry Whitehead
B. Watson, Doncaster Rovers F.C.
J. Ringrose
Richard Stocken, Cheshire
Dave Parine, Warlingham
David Lumb
R.Brackley, Oundle, Peterborough
J.R. Orton
Richard Shore
Keith and Kieron Coburn
Rob Grillo, Keighley, Yorkshire
Roger Wash
Bob Lilliman
Gareth A. Evans
Dave McPherson, Colchester
Geoffrey Wright
Reg Rothwell from Jill
Terry Surridge
John & James Davies
David J. Yates, Leeds
Chris Marsh, Chesterfield
W.D. Phillips
Robert M. Smith, Stevenage
Christer Svensson, Ödeshög, Sweden
Phil Martin, Tarporley, Cheshire
Stephen Kieran Byrne
Peter Miles, Southend, Essex
Mick McKonkey, Luton
Olav Ramstad, Oslo, Norway
S. Metcalfe
David and Matthew Fleckney
Harry and Nigel Spencer
John Rawnsley
Richard Lane, Norwell, Notts.
Mark McIntyre, Bradford P.A.
Michael Grayson
Trond T Isaksen, Norway
Geoff Allman
Arran and Nicholas Matthews

~ Yore Publications ~

Established in 1991 by Dave Twydell, Yore Publications have become the leading publishers of Football League club histories. Nearly thirty have been produced, and although many are now out of print, some clubs for which copies are still available include - Scarborough, Wycombe Wanderers, Lincoln City, Notts County, Barnsley, Bury and Scunthorpe United. Each history is a large page quality hardback with dustjacket and contains a well illustrated written history, full statistics and line-ups for at least all Football League seasons are included, with many named team groups.

A number of Football League Who's Who books (biography and statistics of every League player) have also been produced, including Chesterfield, Reading, Portsmouth, and Hull City.

Non-League football is another feature of our publications, especially the 'Gone But Not Forgotten' series (published twice yearly), each of which contains around six (written and illustrated) abbreviated histories of defunct clubs and/or former grounds (also Videos available).

Compilation histories of former Football League and Scottish League clubs (plus a video), and Un-usual titles (e.g. 'The Little Red Book of Chinese Football') are also included in our stocks. The most recent in this category is 'Denied F.C. - The Football League Election Struggles', the stories behind the non-Leaguers hoping to gain election, the struggles of those to remain within, including the full seasonal voting figures (from 1888), etc.

Two or three free Newsletters are posted each year. For your first copy, please send a S.A.E. to:
Yore Publications (Ref R/W),
12 The Furrows, Harefield, Middx. UB9 6AT.
Or visit our web sites:
www.yorepublications.sageweb.co.uk   or   www.yore.demon.co.uk/index.html